PHOENIX ASSURANCE
AND THE DEVELOPMENT OF BRITISH INSURANCE

VOLUME II

The Era of the Insurance Giants, 1870–1984

This is the second of two volumes covering the business history of one of the United Kingdom's oldest and largest insurance offices, based upon probably the best archive in the business. This volume covers the period from 1870 to the absorption of the Phoenix by Sun Alliance (now Royal & Sun Alliance) in 1984.

The Phoenix papers are used to analyse the triumphs and trials, not only of a single insurance venture, but of an entire financial sector in a notably turbulent century. Insurance is concerned with the way people drive, the way they retire, or buy their homes, or invest, or educate their children, or go to war. It follows that a major insurance history also throws light on many aspects of modern British social history. As the great composite offices expanded to offer fire, accident, marine and life insurance across a single 'counter', so they caught within their dealings an increasingly representative slice of British commercial and social life.

CLIVE TREBILCOCK is a Fellow and Director of Studies in History and Senior Tutor at Pembroke College, Cambridge. He has published widely on business history, defence and industrial studies, the history of technology, and comparative industrialisation. His publications include *The Vickers Brothers: Armament and Enterprise, 1854–1914* (1977), *The Industrialisation of the Continental Powers, 1789–1914* (1981), and *Phoenix Assurance and the British Insurance Industry*, vol. I (1985).

PHOENIX ASSURANCE
AND THE DEVELOPMENT OF BRITISH INSURANCE

VOLUME II

The Era of the Insurance Giants, 1870–1984

CLIVE TREBILCOCK

Phoenix Assurance is a member of the Royal & Sun Alliance Insurance Group

PUBLISHED BY THE PRESS SYNDICATE OF THE UNIVERSITY OF CAMBRIDGE
The Pitt Building, Trumpington Street, Cambridge CB2 1RP, United Kingdom

CAMBRIDGE UNIVERSITY PRESS
The Edinburgh Building, Cambridge CB2 2RU, UK http://www.cup.cam.ac.uk
40 West 20th Street, New York, NY 10011-4211, USA http://www.cup.org
10 Stamford Road, Oakleigh, Melbourne 3166, Australia

First published 1998

Printed in the United Kingdom at the University Press, Cambridge

Typeset in Plantin 10/12pt. [VN]

A catalogue record for this book is available from the British Library

ISBN 0 521 25415 9 hardback

CONTENTS

ILLUSTRATIONS

COLOUR PLATES
(between pages 296 and 297)

PLATES

FIGURES

TABLES

PREFACE

The Phoenix was one of the greatest companies in British insurance history. It endured for just over two centuries and for the whole of that time operated within the league of the 'First Eleven' offices. For most of the present century, it batted around the middle of the order, but, in earlier times, it had occupied more elevated positions still. As one of the founding offices of the insurance business, its archives cover an unusually extended span, but they are also of an unusual richness in quality. The combination makes the Phoenix papers a prime source for the history of insurance.

I was briefed to write something more than the history of a single company. And I trust that a major archive has allowed me to do this. Insurance offers a window on society. In this volume, the window opens upon a modern Britain in which people experience the retreat of killer diseases, die for their country, learn to drive, live longer, buy their own houses, 'invent'[1] retirement and cope with the many travails of the Welfare State and postwar affluence. But insurance is involved not only in the everyday lives of the people but in the great affairs of the nation, as it creates an empire (and gains markets), goes to war, experiences economic recession, goes to war again, is blitzed, decolonises (and loses markets), invents nationalisation, discovers 'Europe', rejects nationalisation and attempts to manage an economy in post-industrial maturity. Insurance was deeply involved in the experiences of the people – and generated products addressed to many of them – and deeply affected by the affairs of the nation. Its history offers important perspectives at both levels; there is much more here than the history of a single business.

And, from the vantage point of that business, there is the vital perspective which looks towards the competition: the deeds of a company are

[1] The term is taken from L. Hannah, *Inventing Retirement* (Cambridge, 1986).

only interesting when matched against the deeds of its rivals. So the methodology of this volume, like that of its predecessor, is widely comparative: the story is that of the Phoenix *and* the British insurance industry.

The result of considering the aggregate as well as the individual is twofold: the history of the Phoenix is also the history of the advance of the UK's formidable financial services sector; and the history of the Phoenix is also the history of the rise of the multi-divisional, multinational corporation, and everything that this involves for business organisation.[2]

There is a danger that business history, however widely drawn, will turn out to be merely the commercial equivalent of high politics or 'the view from the bridge'.[3] But, as one great business historian has argued, it can be more than that, not just the view from the bridge, but the view of those on the bridge.[4] This history attempts that perspective but also adds others; there is quite a lot of comment from the engine room. Policy, and the men who make it, may dominate the story: the strongest account comes from the boardroom and the chief executive's office. Up to a point, this has to be true; not least because there would be little interest in the story otherwise. But I have tried to offer a corrective for the major part of this volume's timespan, at least until 1945. There is scope within the business record for a kind of 'local' or 'social' history. So I have tried to construct not only a sociology of the Board but also a portrayal of staff life in the office, with its illnesses, hours, conventions, pay troubles, and interruption by war service. As 'ordinary people' have taken an honourable place in the work of many kinds of historian, so they should in that of the business historian.

It has not been possible to extend the full range of this treatment beyond 1945. My brief from the start was to write a detailed history of the period 1782–1945 and an outline history of the post-1945 period. I had complete access to the entire paper record for the earlier long period, but the analysis for the years 1945–84 is based on extensive oral evidence, reinforced by the public paper record, and selective access to the private record. The result is in fact much more substantial than might have been feared. Witnesses were generous with their time, and with their own records of key periods and issues. I encountered the classic problem with oral evidence: that witnesses diverged, with wholly good grace, in their recollections of the same events and decisions. Much hard work was

[2] See A. D. Chandler, *The Visible Hand* (Cambridge, Mass., 1977).

[3] D. Wainwright, *The Times*, 13 February 1978, reviewing T. C. Barker, *The Glassmakers: Pilkingtons, the Rise of an International Company, 1826–1976* (London, 1977).

[4] D. C. Coleman, *Courtaulds: A History*, Vol. III (Oxford, 1980), p. vi.

required to reconcile different versions with one another, and the papers to hand; but this was done, and the interpretation offered here has the concurrence of all the main actors. I owe them much for their flexibility and their willingness to explain. Whether the result is, historically, any 'worse' than history derived entirely from the paper record, where the participants cannot protest, is a moot point.

But it is certainly different from history derived from the paper record. For the period before 1945, I have read all that there is to read, and come to my own judgements. For the period after 1945, I listened to the men who managed Phoenix in the 1970s and 1980s and acted as arbiter between their accounts of the postwar years. The result is agreed between the historian and the witnesses as the most plausible reconstruction that can be attained at this date. But the participants are presenting their own account; the historian moderates rather than judges.

This method of investigating the recent past necessarily has limitations. There are obvious problems in writing about individuals who are still alive. Staff records are, equally obviously, a sensitive area; and without them it is not possible to write the 'local history' of the office. So I decided on an even-handed approach: in the final chapter, there is no sociology of the Board and no social history of the clerks. This chapter is very much 'the view from the bridge'; it is executive history drawn from those who were steering the ship. Its value lies in the integrity of their accounts and the number of significant events occurring at sea.

In an enterprise as large as the Phoenix history, it is inevitable that I should have incurred debts to a great number of people. The final chapter would not have been possible without the generosity, objectivity and good sense of Phoenix's final generation of managers whose names appear in it. In recent times, I have been particularly grateful for advice from Ron Bishop, Ken Wilkinson and Ralph Petty, and my understanding of the period 1964–84 was hugely assisted by Bill Harris. I was conspicuously well served by the research assistants who helped launch volume II, Dr Robin Pearson, Dr Mary Short, Ray Tye and Pam Judd, although the latter part of the operation was a solitary affair. It is noteworthy that two of the researchers who assisted with the two volumes of this history, Richard Davenport-Hines and Robin Pearson, have gone on to become significant historians in their own right. That is both a matter of satisfaction and an indirect measure of their value to the project. Ray Tye, of course, was a Phoenix institution, less a researcher of history than the stuff of it.

To the three Phoenix and Sun Alliance managers who had the unenviable task of finding the itinerant historian the essentials of office life in

King William Street and Bartholomew Lane I owe a special debt. Kevin Croker, the late Ian Smith and Brian Sole were unstinting with their time, guidance and hospitality. While no doubt wondering why on earth they should have been saddled with this responsibility, they discharged it with endless patience, and were utterly invaluable.

Much of the pictorial material in this volume, including advertising material of an astonishing variety and richness, comes from Phoenix's own records. But for permission to reproduce some items, we are indebted to the following: Getty Images (Plates 1.3, 1.4, 3.3, 3.4, 6.1, 6.2, 6.4, 6.5, 6.6. 8,8. 8.11, 8.12, 10.1, 10.2, 10.3, 10.4, 11.1, 11.4, 11.5, 11.6, 11.7, 11.9, 11.10, 11.11, 12.2, 12.3, 12.10); Times Newspapers (Plate 1.8); the Imperial War Museum (Plate 11.8); Barclays (Figures 8.1, 8.2, 8.3); and Ian Joy Photographic (Colour Section 6)

In many ways, the greatest debt in the Phoenix history is to its old competitor, Sun Alliance, which ended the competition by taking over Phoenix in 1984. A book that began as a celebration of two centuries of business life thus ended as a work of commemoration of a major force in British insurance history. It has been the appreciation at Sun Alliance of the Phoenix's place in the history of the entire industry which has kept the project alive and allowed it to be completed. This has been a long and intricate process, and has required patience from all concerned. I am especially grateful to three successive chief executives of Sun Alliance, Geoffrey Bowler, Sir Roger Neville and Roger Taylor, for the interest they have taken in the story of one of their longest-lived and most distinguished rivals. It is rare – though not unprecedented – for the history of one company to be supported by another. The Phoenix deserves its memorial; but Sun Alliance deserves all credit for acknowledging this.

Plate 1.1 The nesting habits of the Phoenix (Punch Cartoon by George Morrow, 17 January 1934)

CHAPTER 1

PHOENIX IN THE HOME MARKET, 1870–1914

1. THE BIRD IN ITS SECOND CENTURY

The 'Arabian bird', the phoenix of legend, is supposed to live a thousand years, then build itself a funeral pyre, burst into melodious song, and, while fanning the flames with its wings, voluntarily cremate itself. This, of course, is merely a prelude to its better known, though more difficult, knack of reconstituting itself from the consequential ashes. Nor is the timespan between phoenix cycles undisputed, some authorities avoiding the compelling symmetry of the millennium for periods both shorter and longer. Tacitus, indeed, with a startlingly low bid of 250 years and alarming prescience, came within a half-century of the life of the insurance Phoenix.

By January 1882 the Phoenix Assurance Company had lived 100 years, completing in the New Year, the first of its two centenaries. The celebrations lived up neither to the derring-do of its mythical namesake nor to the splendour of the second centenary in 1982, the festivities for which gathered Phoenix representatives, colleagues and clients from all corners of the globe. Rather, the Board contented themselves with the publication of a two-page circular, issued to the press and the public on 17 January 1882. This document was the spiritual ancestor of this two-volume history. It averaged a page per century; here the rate of exchange is closer to a book per century.

Encouragingly, the pamphleteers of 1882 related a few flaming incidents of earlier decades from which the Phoenix had escaped with feathers uncarbonised and totted up the £13 million that the company had disbursed to singed clients in the process. But, for all their brevity and directness, they made some proud boasts. Phoenix, they claimed, had 'steadily grown stronger as it had grown older' – although, of course, by the Tacitus estimate, it was scarcely middle-aged, and, by full Arabian standards a mere stripling – and had 'reached a point of prosperity rarely, if ever, achieved by any competitor'.[1] Some great names, not least the Sun, Royal Exchange or Royal might have quarrelled with aspects of this, but the Phoenix was permitted a centenarian's indulgence on its birthday. At least fifteen newspapers ran columns which borrowed fairly slavishly from the circular, adding a little, usually very little, journalistic comment here and there.[2] The centenary circular proved effectively cheap publicity.

But it also gave some useful clues to the thinking of the current management. There were some comments on the blended virtues of endurance and adaptability:

> The majority of ventures, originated a hundred years ago, ceased to exist before England acquired its present position as the first commercial country in the world, and many of those which still exist, do so in a manner more suited to the days of their birth than to those in which they now find themselves.

However, the Board was aware that at some points in its recent past, particularly in the mid-century decades, the Phoenix itself might not have resisted the taint of conservatism, and they sported their defence on this point.[3] They argued that the Phoenix had never chased the maximum business but rather the sensible business, which sometimes meant, 'having had to stand aside . . . and thus, for the moment, appear less enterprising, knowing that the competition in which they were asked to take part . . . must eventually result in disaster'.[4]

Several of the points raised here – the problem of commercial longevity, the constraint of old practices, the proper attitude to competition – were major issues of the day in the more general sphere of the British economy. For this second volume of the Phoenix history opens, in the early 1870s, just a decade before the centenary, at a difficult juncture in the history of the UK economy, and indeed of the world economy.

The period between 1840 and 1870 had seen a major surge of industrialisation in several key economies; in particular, the 'take-off' phase of development for France, the USA and the German states may be located within this period.[5] The launch of these economies into the manufacturing era was based primarily upon railway construction, the expansion of the capital goods industries, such as iron, steel and engineering, and the

[1] Centenary Circular, 17 January 1882.
[2] *Morning Post*, 20 January 1882,and *Morning Advertiser*, 21 January 1882, did rather better.
[3] See vol. I, pp. 687–704. [4] Centenary Circular.
[5] See Clive Trebilcock, *The Industrialisation of the Continental Powers* (London, 1981).

financial innovation of investment banking. Britain, the industrial pioneer from the eighteenth century, and an earlier developer, nevertheless enjoyed the railway expansion, agricultural adaptation and phenomenal growth in overseas trade of the 'mid-Victorian Boom'. Phoenix growth may not have proved dramatic in this period, but there had been plenty afoot in the larger economic world.

By contrast, the years from 1873 to 1896 saw the first 'Great Depression' in the new international manufacturing economy. This was a period of falling prices and profits, and of slowing rates of growth, rather than of absolute reductions in national output or income levels, and the experience was unevenly shared between economies. Germany and the USA underwent relatively brief doldrums and recovered early and fast; but Britain came under more pressure. There is enormous debate as to the reasons – poor training, bad management, scarce resources, out-moded institutions amongst others – but there is agreement that Britain's retardation was more protracted and that it was connected with largely unavoidable losses to the new competitive pressures in world trade. Of course, a monopoly in the export of manufactures could not be maintained indefinitely, and the rise of American and German industry in particular necessitated a contraction in Britain's share of global commerce. However, questions remain as to whether the contraction need have been as large as it was, and over the small measure of structural adjustment displayed by the UK economy 1870–1914, in the face of this challenge.[6]

After the mid-1890s the world economy moved into upswing once more. The USA, Germany, and, after 1900 and to a lesser extent, France, grew strongly on a new technological base made up of chemicals, electrical engineering, bicycle manufacture and automobile construction. New economies such as Italy, Japan, Russia and the Scandinavian countries moved into the 'take-off' phase. Britain too experienced a recovery in the period 1896–1914. There was a 'home boom' in the 1890s which saw heavy activity in house construction, suburban railway building, brewing and bicycles. Export activity also revived strongly in the 1900s, reaching a peak in 1913. However, Britain was riding the world upswing, rather than participating in it. New technologies made less impact on industrial structure here than in competing economies. The exports offered to expanding world demand in the 1910s differed little from those offered to

[6] There is a massive literature of controversy. The most recent items, which deal most closely with the issue of structural rigidity, are W. P. Kennedy, *Industrial Structure, Capital Markets and the Origins of British Decline* (Cambridge, 1987) and W. Lazonick and E. Elbaum, *The Decline of the British Economy* (Oxford, 1986).

less enthusiastic consumers in the 1870s. The economy hardly altered in underlying composition; it merely tagged along with the upswing in world demand. The one exception is the great expansion in the 'invisibles' sector of the UK economy, the huge advance in its capacity to offer services to the world – in the form of capital, shipping and, of course, insurance.

It was suitable that the Phoenix Centenary Circular, issued by a venture almost precisely as old as Britain's industrial primacy, should have mused upon the problems of energising long-established institutions, growing older healthily and resisting competition effectively.

2. PHOENIX REVIVAL AT HOME, 1870–1914

The Great Depression, industrial insurances and the launch of the branch system

As argued earlier, the tempo of Phoenix enterprise was not closely synchronised with that of the British economy in the second half of the nineteenth century. When the economy was enjoying its mid-century buoyancy, Phoenix was in no mood to participate. When the economy slowed down after 1870, Phoenix became minded to try harder. In the event, it tried hardest abroad; and it was the revival of its great exporting role which did most to re-invigorate the performance of the whole company. But here too there was a certain lack of rhythm. It was not the London offices but the newer ventures of Liverpool which spearheaded the great drive in the British exportation of insurance invisibles in the last third of the century. Phoenix, like many of the older offices, joined the drive only after it was well under way (see Chapter 2).

Nevertheless, Phoenix recovered its purpose in this overseas resurgence and also it revived at home. Gross home fire premiums in money terms grew by 85.7% between 1871/2 and 1911. Although this was dwarfed by the increases in foreign fire premiums – 637.8% for the same period – it was scarcely trivial. The second great burst of Phoenix foreign adventuring put domestic business in its place – all UK business provided 49.8% of total premium income in 1871/2 but only 19.9% by 1911 – yet it did not swamp it. One-fifth of the Phoenix's world fire premiums in 1911 still amounted to around £400,000.

Phoenix's progress to that point kept only roughly in step with that of the UK economy as a whole. The office's home business did quite nicely through most of the 1870s, which was a poor decade for UK performance generally. It hit an exceedingly rough patch in 1879–82, but then regained balance in the later 1880s, again scarcely an auspicious period for the nation's economic life. Growth in home premium receipts slowed once more in the early 1890s, but recovered strongly between 1896 and 1905, which was a period of economic upswing for the national economy (compare Table 1.1 for these points, and much of the following analysis).

The classic industry-related insurances which had been the underwriting speciality of the early Phoenix rebuilt well in the early 1870s, rising to a peak in 1876–7. Premium income from cotton mills rose by 50% over these years, and from all industrial risks by 24%; income from all merchandise risks remained roughly stable at high values. The 'sundries' category of business, used in the Annual Analysis of Business to cover mainly domestic housing policies, grew strongly throughout the twenty-year period 1871/2 – 1890/1, by some 46%. The majority of the 1870s was perceived as a period of good business for the Phoenix.

In particular, the span of years 1876–8 saw large transfers to reserves, exceptional payments to shareholders,[7] and even bonuses of 10% 'on their salaries . . . presented to the whole of the establishment', and paid after review of the business transacted in 1875, 1876 and 1877.[8] These were true bonuses financed by good profits and thus unlike the grace and favour subvention of 1872, when the Board had decided that 'in consideration of the present exceptionally high prices of the necessaries of life, a Bonus of 10% be given to all servants of the Company whose salaries do not exceed £300 a year, but with a distinct intimation that the gift will not form any precedent for the future'.[9]

The expansion of business which paid for this also required increases in the size of the office staff. Seven additional junior clerks were taken on in 1870,[10] while the growth in agency business by £16,000 between 1872 and 1874 convinced the Trustees that they needed another clerk to handle it,[11] and increases in foreign income and yet more home agency business produced the same conclusion in 1875 and again in 1877.[12]

At this point, home and foreign fire premiums were advancing neck and neck; each expanded by about 20% between 1871/2 and 1879/80. So

[7] The usual half-yearly dividend of £3 per share was supplemented for the second half-years of 1875–6, 1876–7 and 1877–8 by bonuses per share of 10 guineas, £12 and 10 guineas respectively. The Phoenix share of this era, until the capital reorganisation of 1895, was a £400 share of which £40 was deemed to be paid up. Phoenix Directors' Minutes, W22, pp. 100, 196, 294, 12 April 1876, 11 April 1877, 3 April 1878.

[8] *Ibid.*, W22, p. 79, 5 January 1876; W22, p. 188, 21 January 1877; W22, p. 268, 21 January 1878.

[9] *Ibid.*, V21, p. 237, 6 November 1872. This came at the price peak, immediately prior to the long slide in prices which began in 1873.

[10] *Ibid.*, V21, p. 39, 28 September 1870.

[11] Phoenix Trustees' Minutes, 13 August 1874.

[12] *Ibid.*, 22 April 1875, 24 January 1877.

Table 1.1.(a) *Total gross fire premiums by category of business and total foreign fire premium (£), 1871/2–1915; annual averages*

	Cotton Mills	All Mills	Sugar Houses	All Industrial	Marine	Merchandise, Etc.	Craft, Trade	Mansions	Farming Insurances	Sundries	Public Meeting Places	Commercial and Retail	Transport	All Home	All Foreign
1871/2–75/6	14,167	29,445	3,116	35,492	476	30,571	8,018	7,349	12,209	147,351	–	–	–	235,382	250,249
1876/7–80/1	12,803	27,333	1,313	31,022	389	29,283	8,504	10,030	12,602	168,548	–	–	–	254,410	271,647
1881/2–85/6	11,849	25,508	1,043	28,988	281	29,012	8,831	11,718	12,566	187,574	–	–	–	273,434	499,204
1886/7–90/1	13,346	33,684	778	37,985	487	31,680	11,095	12,679	12,493	208,847	–	–	–	320,072	593,347
1891/2–95[a]	13,838	32,971	660	57,921	256	32,913	15,822	13,527	12,297	174,572	19,395	–	–	329,326	745,349
1896–1900	14,584	–	–	89,110	229	42,327	32,785	15,810	21,836	78,835	28,388	52,131	1,273	362,905	826,044
1901–05	13,926	–	–	97,020	250	46,167	38,738	17,666	23,354	122,024	28,568	56,313	1,523	451,717	1,481,429
1906–10	11,134	–	–	90,662	185	49,436	37,268	16,778	23,302	131,359	24,557	52,882	1,712	434,030	1,494,331
1911–15	9,258	–	–	81,500	202	45,693	15,914	15,914	22,860	–	19,807	36,511	2,206	–	–

Note: [a] 4.75 years

Table 1.1.(b) *Total fire premiums by category of business in % share and total foreign fire premium (with loss ratio for each category), 1871/2–1915 (selected years)*

	Cotton Mills	All Mills	Sugar Houses	All Industrial	Marine	Merchandise, Etc.	Craft, Trade	Mansions	Farming Insurances	Sundries	Public Meeting Places	Commercial and Retail	Transport	All Home	All Foreign
1871/2–75/6	2.9 (86.2)	6.1 (83.3)	0.8 (88.3)	7.3 (78.9)	0.09 (73.0)	6.3 (32.8)	1.7 (58.0)	1.5 (61.1)	2.5 (58.9)	30.3 (55.5)	–	–	–	48.5 (58.1)	51.5 (66.1)
1876/7–80/1	2.5 (75.4)	5.2 (65.5)	0.3 (52.8)	6.0 (69.1)	0.07 (47.0)	5.6 (38.4)	1.6 (78.9)	1.9 (61.2)	2.4 (56.8)	32.1 (37.6)	–	–	–	48.5 (51.0)	51.5 (54.0)
1881/2–85/6	1.5 (81.1)	3.3 (74.9)	0.1 (1.5)	3.8 (72.2)	0.03 (45.7)	4.0 (80.3)	1.2 (91.1)	1.5 (30.9)	1.6 (61.2)	24.6 (55.7)	–	–	–	35.7 (60.0)	64.2 (62.9)
1886/7–90/1	1.5 (55.4)	3.7 (63.7)	0.1 (201.5)	4.2 (59.9)	0.05 (165.8)	4.2 (91.8)	1.2 (63.6)	1.4 (12.4)	1.4 (49.4)	23.0 (48.9)	–	–	–	35.1 (53.8)	64.9 (64.2)
1896–1900	1.2 (90.0)	–	–	7.5 (71.0)	0.02 (51.3)	3.6 (70.2)	2.8 (76.5)	1.3 (28.4)	1.8 (73.2)	6.6 (33.7)	2.4 (22.9)	4.4 (53.5)	0.1 (91.6)	30.5 (59.0)	69.5 (65.4)
1901–5	0.7 (78.6)	–	–	5.1 (69.0)	0.01 (15.9)	2.4 (53.5)	2.0 (61.4)	0.9 (47.7)	1.2 (54.2)	6.4 (41.3)	1.5 (14.2)	2.9 (70.2)	0.1 (13.7)	22.6 (54.6)	77.4 (57.9)
1906–10	0.6 (74.6)	–	–	4.7 (56.9)	0.01 (63.0)	2.6 (37.8)	1.9 (52.0)	0.9 (30.4)	1.2 (51.2)	6.8 (31.8)	1.3 (24.5)	2.7 (64.1)	0.1 (13.8)	22.5 (43.9)	77.5 (63.4)
1911–15	a (104.9)	–	–	a (85.2)	a (81.8)	a (37.5)	a (52.7)	a (112.2)	a (58.7)	a	a (36.8)	a (57.6)	a (74.6)	a	a

Note: [a] no data after 1911.
Source: Phoenix Annual Analysis of Business of All Departments.

it was as much improvement at home as improvement abroad which underlay the Phoenix's advance down to the late 1870s; it was only after 1880, though immediately after, that foreign fire premiums, and particularly US fire premiums, broke decisively free. However, the pattern of development in Phoenix's home market during the 1870s suggests that the Great Depression did not exert an immediate effect on the insurance trade.

On the other hand, it is entirely clear that it exerted effect enough; for the insurers the downturn was simply lagged or delayed. The recession in UK manufacturing hit the insurers in the late 1870s. Between the single years 1876/7 and 1880/1 Phoenix premiums derived from cotton mills fell by 50% and the income from all industrial categories of risk by 38% (note: Table 1.1 displays five year *averages* for premiums). The same pattern is evident in the share of total Phoenix underwriting committed to industrial business. This stood at 7.5% of worldwide premiums in 1871/2 and held up at 6.7% until 1877/8; but, by 1881/2, the share was down to 3.9% and reached its nadir for the period 1870–1910 at 3.6% in four separate years within the decade 1881/2–1890/1 (compare the five-year results given in Table 1.1). It did not break 7% again until 1896, traditionally the cyclical turning point at which the first Great Depression came to an end.

Within the general run of industrial business, textile mills had caused trouble as early as 1868 when 'the very unsatisfactory results of the company's business in cotton and woollen mills' led the Trustees to rule that 'all such risks, whether at present on the books or proposed hereafter, should be expressly inspected' and to appoint a Mr Hawley as surveyor of mill risks from December 1868.[13] But industrial business then improved in the 1870s, although loss rates remained high, around 70% in many years. True difficulty came in the later 1870s as an upsurge in competition among insurers was superimposed upon falling levels of premium drawn from industrial clients. Phoenix's newly appointed inspector of agencies, Musgrave Heaphy, himself brought in as a defensive measure in March 1877, reported over a year later that industrial business was 'assailled, as well as other departments, by the action of the Mutual Offices'.[14] Heaphy planned to have Phoenix 'combine with the Northern offices' in order to see off the mutuals.

However, Heaphy was encountering trouble with the big industrial

[13] Phoenix Trustees' Minutes, 9 December 1868, 22 December 1869.

[14] Heaphy was appointed to this post 21 March 1877; he had previously been inspector and surveyor of mills from October 1874; Phoenix Directors' Minutes W22, p. 187. His report is in Trustees' Minutes, 22 August 1878. This was the same Musgrave Heaphy, who, as an electrical engineer, wrote Phoenix's insurance rules for electrical installations, and, in so doing, created the industrial standard.

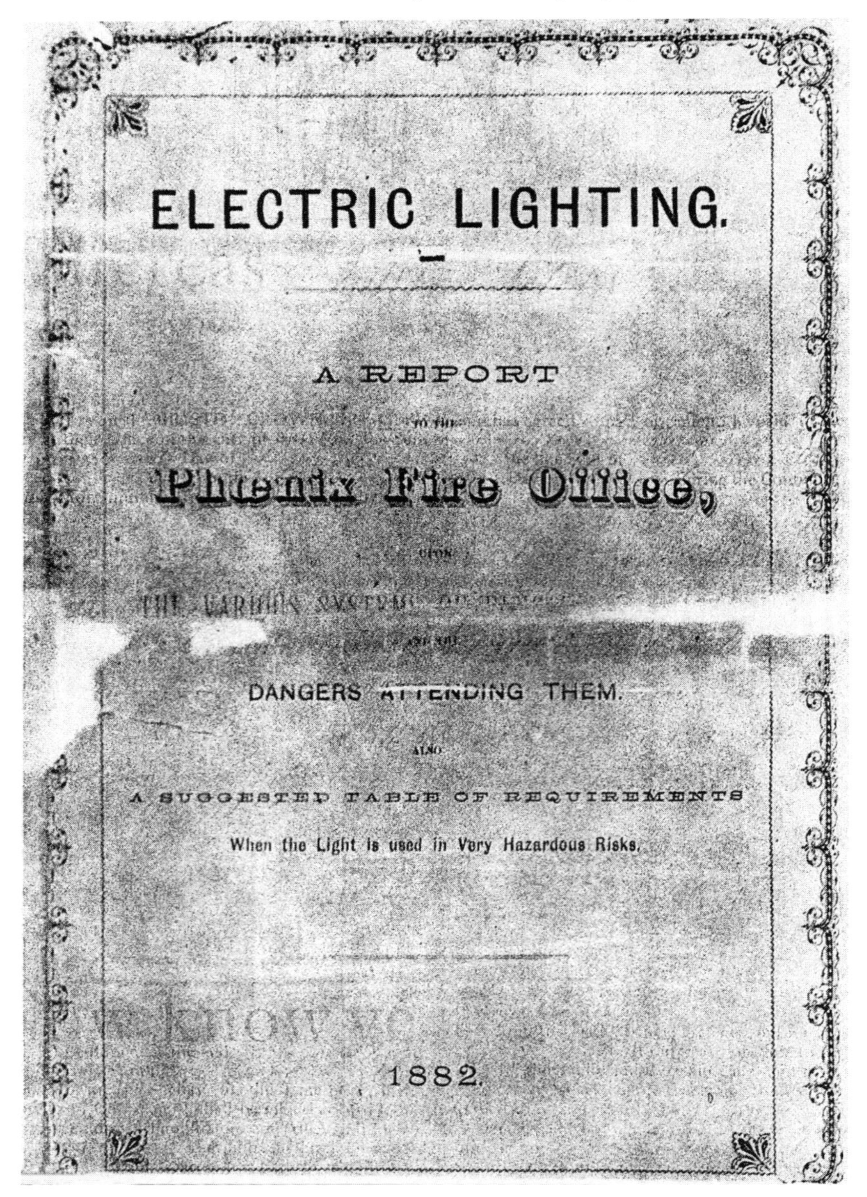

ELECTRIC LIGHTING.

A REPORT

TO THE

Phœnix Fire Office,

UPON

THE VARIOUS SYSTEMS [illegible]

AND THE

DANGERS ATTENDING THEM.

ALSO

A SUGGESTED TABLE OF REQUIREMENTS

When the Light is used in Very Hazardous Risks.

1882.

Plate 1.2 The Electricity Rules of Musgrave Heaphy.

agencies. Liverpool had managed a net profit of £11,804 between 1866 and 1878, but by the later year the cotton trade was so poor that Phoenix had to reduce the rent charged to their agent, a cotton broker.[15] In the context of reduced trade, a row broke out within the agency partnership of Tate and Land in Manchester. Land complained that Tate took two-thirds of the commission but did little of the work. The Trustees sent Heaphy to investigate, heard his comments, terminated the joint agency, and arranged for Land to continue alone.[16] But they were not pleased with the state of their industrial operations.

Matters were soon to deteriorate further. The 'Northern offices', which had started out as allies against the mutuals, developed into villains of another competitive piece. By 1879, Phoenix was experiencing a progressive decrease in the business reported by its main country agencies. Glasgow was yielding 'but a small percentage profit'[17], while the state of trade in Manchester was so depressed that the company was unable even to let space in its new office building, 'due to the present numerous suites of offices standing empty'.[18] Even a new General Agency for Ireland, created for David Drimonie of Dublin, after his meeting with the Trustees in January 1876, 'to select and appoint agents in Ireland, principally, bankers, solicitors and land agents' was in trouble by 1879. Despite his grandiose title of 'Secretary for Ireland', and his 20% commission, Drimonie was having to cut out all insurances on 'farming stock, ships, drapers, toy shops, bacon-curers, oil merchants and wood risks of all kinds', in an effort to make Irish business 'at last profitable'.[19]

After wondering in 1878 whether they needed to increase agents' commissions in order to give their sales force more edge against the competition,[20] Phoenix were under no illusion by the next year. In Manchester, Land argued that he must have the freedom, and the bank-roll, to appoint sub-agents if he was to compete successfully, and that meant a 15% commission rate in place of the 10% to which Phoenix had adhered previously. In June 1879, Phoenix conceded 15% commission to

[15] *Ibid.*, 16 May 1878.

[16] *Ibid.*, 25 December 1878. Alfred Tate was the grandson of that William Tate who had first assumed the Manchester agency in 1785. Thomas Land, by far Alfred's senior in insurance matters, had joined Alfred's father in the agency in 1852 and had suffered Alfred himself from 1872. Thomas Land soldiered on alone from 1878, and served with distinction as Phoenix's first manager in Manchester, 1880–1902. He was succeeded by his son John, who held this office from 1902 until 1931. If the Tate and Land agencies are rolled together, therefore, they compose a single relationship which endured with Phoenix for a remarkable 146 years. See also G. Hurren, *Phoenix Renascent* (privately printed, London, 1973), pp. 170–1.

[17] Phoenix Trustees' Minutes, 20 March 1879. [18] *Ibid.*, 5 June 1879.

[19] *Ibid.*, 24 February, 9 March 1876, 2 October 1879. [20] *Ibid.*, 18 July 1878.

main agents on new cotton insurances and 20% on new ordinary insurances.[21]

In the course of the next year, the Minute Books clarify the nature of the competitive problem. The most affected areas were Manchester, Hull, Preston, Ashton and Blackburn. The latter reported premiums down by 75% due to 'the withdrawal of cotton mill insurances',[22] while Preston lamented 'severe competition'.[23] The nub of the issue was that the 'Northern offices' had been appointing their industrial policy-holders as agents, and thus allowing their clients the full 10% commission usually due to agents. This, of course, was tantamount to a full 10% discount on the cost of an industrial policy.

Phoenix's response was a series of organisational innovations. A further inspector of agencies was brought in from October 1880, to ginger up local operations for both Phoenix and Pelican.[24] But more important was the introduction of the local secretary system. This converted important agents, or, sometimes, delegated Phoenix employees, into local secretaries on a 10% commission, but with the power to appoint their own sub-agents, on a further individual 10% .The most troubled mill towns were given this treatment in April 1880.[25] In 1881 it was extended to Glasgow, where the Scottish offices were doing for their patch what the northern provincials had already done to the mill towns, as well as to Nottingham, and, in 1882, to Birmingham, Bristol and Edinburgh.[26] In Yorkshire, where the whole county yielded a mere £4,000 in premiums in 1880, Edward Bagshaw was appointed surveyor and inspector of agents.[27] This title was used again for the appointment of Thomas Milne at Newcastle – 'where business is at present very limited' in January 1882.[28] The terminology was slightly different, but their main task was the same as that of the local secretaries: to pre-empt heavy provincial competition in the industrial regions.

In fact, however, a far more crucial issue underlay these tactics. And it is significant that it was associated with the industrial business which had provided Phoenix's earliest stock in trade. The issue was the transition from the traditional agency system of selling insurance to the branch system of insurance promotion. In the agency system, of course, the company selects individuals from other professions well-placed to recommend insurance; they may be solicitors, brokers, shopkeepers, or many others. But, however convenient and effective this system may have been,

[21] *Ibid.*, 5 June 1879. [22] *Ibid.*, 24 June 1880. [23] *Ibid.*, 14 October 1880.
[24] *Ibid.*, 21 October 1880. [25] *Ibid.*, 15 April 1880.
[26] *Ibid.*, 10 March, 2 June 1881, 21 January, 4 May, 26 October 1882.
[27] *Ibid.*, 10 November 1881. [28] *Ibid.*, 5 January 1882.

the snag was that the prime allegiance of the agent was always to his original calling. In the branch system, a full-time insurance manager exercises supervision over a team of agents but also controls an office of clerks who give continuous attention to the administration of the business. The result should be a more whole-hearted commitment and a closer attention to the course of the business. It was natural that such a response should be evoked in a period of heightened competition, when trade was more difficult to secure. The first full Phoenix branches were created at Manchester and Hull in 1880.

But the first use of the term 'branch' in the modern sense to occur in the Phoenix archive is probably the reference to a financial transaction on behalf of the Leeds agency in August 1882, when the Trustees minuted that they had authorised the payment of 'the current expenses of the Yorkshire Branch'.[29] Certainly, too, the organisational implications of the local secretary system were acted upon quickly: by early 1883, the secretaries already had their chief clerks. Indeed, Bagshaw at Leeds already wanted a salary increase for his, and Phoenix had quickly to define the pay scales for all staff in the local branches.[30] Generally, the reforms proved to be worth their cost.

The first year of branch operation went well at Leeds, Newcastle and Birmingham. Premium receipts from Birmingham indeed advanced by around 20%, from £9,791 in 1881 to £12,001 in 1882.[31] And, in spring 1885, the energetic Bagshaw was awarded a salary increase 'on the ground of the progress of the business under his charge and of its profitable character'.[32] This was comment very different from the complaints about the Yorkshire trade in 1880.

However, there were still trouble spots. In Liverpool, the home of the really successful insurance innovators and exporters of the late nineteenth century such as the Royal and the Liverpool & London & Globe, local competition had a particularly sharp edge.[33] Indeed, a good deal of the difficulties created in the industrial markets by the 'Northern offices' emanated from Liverpool, and dealing in the city itself was particularly hard going for a London office of the Phoenix's type. The company had suffered a marked diminution of business, and the Trustees were con-

[29] *Ibid.*, 24 August 1882. [30] *Ibid.*, 7 February 1883.
[31] *Ibid.*, 12 April 1883. [32] *Ibid.*, 30 April 1885.
[33] See C. Trebilcock, 'The City, Entrepreneurship and Insurance: Two Pioneers in Invisible Exports: the Phoenix Fire Office and the Royal of Liverpool, 1800–90' in N. McKendrick and B. Outhwaite (eds.), *Business Life and Public Policy: Essays in Honour of D. C. Coleman* (Cambridge, 1986), pp. 137–72, for more extensive treatment of the comparisons and contrasts between Phoenix and the newer ventures of Liverpool and the transatlantic insurance trade.

cerned. In September 1885, they recommended the current remedy: that the agency of Hilton and Walthew be paid off and the company's Liverpool operation converted into a branch under W. A. Harris, Phoenix's second inspector of agencies. Harris had been confirmed in post in 1881, after a good first six months when he had succeeded 'in the selection of a number of influential men of business for appointment as Agents in Towns and places where the office was not hitherto sufficiently represented'.[34] Now, the Trustees decided to make Harris local secretary and surveyor for Liverpool and District, with his own staff of clerks, and 5% of the Liverpool profits. Moreover, in order to increase Phoenix's presence, where the Liverpool offices had all too much commercial muscle-power in evidence, the company's directors were to be encouraged to make occasional attendance at Liverpool. They were to be paid a 10 guinea fee for every appearance. In 1885, two of them, John Baxendale and Walter Bird, agreed to travel north.[35]

Liverpool was a special problem, but the creation of the Phoenix branch there was already an established response. Liverpool in 1885 rounded off the first batch of Phoenix branch initiatives. By the mid-1880s, the main branch locations were Manchester and Hull (1880); Leeds, Birmingham, Bristol, Newcastle (1881); Edinburgh and Glasgow (1885); and Liverpool (1885). All were effectively business-getting systems; for many years yet the preparation of policies, renewals, loss adjustments and settlements would be handled in London. And the Phoenix branch structure of 1885 was not significantly enlarged until 1896, when the advance of business in Wales and the West Country provoked the creation of further offices in Cardiff and Plymouth.

In comparison with the reactions of similar offices, this looks like quite quick work. The Sun created its first branches slightly after the Phoenix, with establishments at Glasgow and Edinburgh in 1881, and by 1885 had a total of five outside London. The Royal Exchange created its first provincial offices, at Birmingham, Bristol and Manchester in 1881, but waited until 1886 to create its first full branch (Manchester); by 1889 it had a half-dozen more.[36] Similarly, the REA had appointed its first inspector of agencies in 1881, while Phoenix by that time had two of them, and had installed the first some four years previously.[37] Interestingly, the two other eighteenth-century veterans gave their reasons as an increase in

[34] Phoenix Directors' Minutes, X23, p. 142, 29 June 1881.

[35] *Ibid.*, Y24, p. 137, 7 October 1885; Trustees' Minutes, 17 and 24 September, 15 October 1885.

[36] Hereafter the Royal Exchange Assurance is known by its long-term acronym REA.

[37] P. G. M. Dickson, *The Sun Insurance Office, 1710–1960* (London, 1960), p. 136; B. E. Supple, *The Royal Exchange Assurance 1720–1970* (Cambridge, 1970), pp. 288–9.

the effectiveness of marketing or relief of administrative strain on head office; but the problem of meeting competitive pressures in industrial markets, which appears to be the main pre-occupation in the Phoenix minutes, does not appear among their arguments.

The move towards a more deliberate method of selling was associated with a revival of Phoenix's fortunes in the 1880s. Recovery in premium earnings for cotton mills, all mills and all industrial business began in the early 1880s and continued during the decade, though all these sectors also demonstrated some frailty towards its end. All industrial business showed an increase of 59.3% between 1881/2 and 1888/9, but of 53.1% between 1881/2 and 1890/1. All merchandise premiums showed a similar pattern with increases of 52.0% and 39.1% over the same timespan. Sundries, that is, mostly domestic housing insurances, grew year on year from 1881/2 to 1889/90, but then fell sharply. However, it is worth bearing in mind that all foreign premiums advanced by 88.6% over the decade.

Certainly, Phoenix began to behave again like a more prosperous company. The manifestations of this showed on the home front and clearly not all the causes were foreign. The bonuses to shareholders, which had reached £12 per share, on top of the usual dividend of £3, in the half year ending March 1879, had slipped to £7 10s by March 1881 and to £3 by March 1883 and stayed at that level into 1886. In autumn 1883 a bare £5,000 had been added to the Reserve Fund. However, by March 1887 the shareholders' bonus had edged up again to a healthy £6 and maintained this level right through to March 1894. Similarly, in October 1886 £40,000 was transferred to the Reserve, the largest such augmentation of substance since the early 1870s, and this was followed by a further £30,000 in October 1888, carrying the total fund to £800,000.[38] The directors were particularly pleased with the results of 1886, and voted a 10% bonus upon the salaries of all staff, both at Phoenix House, and in all the branches, in celebration of this.

They celebrated in other ways too. In June 1885, they took themselves off to dinner at the Ship Hotel, Greenwich, courtesy of the London Steamboat Co.'s packet from Speaker's Stairs, and they bought themselves a Turkish carpet for the boardroom (£72, less 15% discount). The boardroom was also repainted and varnished. The foreign and other working departments got, if not Turkish carpet, at least new linoleum throughout. And even the Phoenix messengers were spruced up, as the Board 'revived the old custom of having Phoenix badges on their coats

[38] This was thought sufficient to entitle the Reserve Fund to a 3.5% accrual of interest every quarter from this point on. Trustees' Minutes, 11 and 18 October 1888.

(on the left heart [sic])'.[39] Leaving aside the question of just how much heart the average Phoenix messenger possessed, the historian can only express satisfaction that the improvement of business fortunes produced such obviously uplifting effects. We might also wonder, however, what Phoenix House looked like when business was bad. Perhaps the most concrete proof that it continued well was provided by a further most significant change to the building in 1887: running hot water was installed in the directors' lavatory.[40] Perhaps more ominously, the £20 per year previously spent on 'office beer' was, from early 1887, given instead to the 'Lunch Committee', 'who are to be responsible for providing suitable refreshments for the clerks at moderate charges'.[41] One can only hope that the clerks profited by this reform and that the word 'suitable' contained no prohibitionist intent.

Renewal on the docksides

Some of Phoenix's first work in the eighteenth and early nineteenth century had been done on the docks and wharves of the Port of London. The 'merchandise' sector of trade was second only to the industrial among the company's longest established activities. However, the commitment of most insurers to this kind of underwriting had been badly shaken by the great docklands inferno at Tooley Street in 1861,[42] and the last three decades of the nineteenth century formed a period, at least for the London offices, of readjustment and rethinking in respect to the insurances offered on warehouses, wharves and cargoes unladen or awaiting embarkation.

Concomitant with its revived energy in the pursuit of industrial business, Phoenix also took an enterprising line after 1870 in its handling of merchandise business. In February 1869, the Phoenix Board considered the restrictions imposed on London mercantile business in the wake of the Tooley Street disaster. They found 'great structural improvements to the wharves, generally tending to limit the extension of fires'. Where the subdivision of wharves were 'numerous and satisfactory, as at Cotton's', they decided to double the maximum of insurances accepted.[43] Reviewing the whole London mercantile market in 1877, they were surprised by the small proportion of insurable property which actually was insured. Upon the recommendation of the Trustees, the Board decided to rescind the restrictions they had earlier imposed upon insurances on public

39 *Ibid.*, 21 May, 4 and 18 June 1885.

40 *Ibid.*, 10 January 1887.

41 *Ibid.*, 6 January 1887.

42 See vol. I, pp. 424ff.

43 *Ibid.*, p. 353, 24 February 1869.

wharves and insurances of a single sum split between several wharves.

This Phoenix tendency towards the liberalisation of the mercantile market continued throughout the 1870s and 1880s. Even in Tooley Street itself, limits on warehouses were relaxed from £75,000 to £100,000, and on granaries at Bermondsey wharf from £15,000 to £20,000, each of these in October 1879.[44] On the Liverpool waterfront also, limits were advanced by similar proportions around this time.[45] Back in London, the construction of large new warehouses in the Whitechapel and Millwall Docks during 1880 encouraged Phoenix to double its total ceiling for the area to £480,000.[46]

Such faith was not misplaced, at least not at Phoenix House. By 1884, some offices wished to increase rates on warehouse insurances 'owing to the unfavourable experience of most of the offices'. Phoenix was not opposed to the increase, but the Board observed rather smugly that their company did not share the adverse experience.[47]

Broadly, they were correct in their optimism. Mercantile insurances made up around 5% of Phoenix's worldwide premiums in the 1870s and around 4% during the 1880s, but of home premiums alone they still accounted for 11–12% in the final years of the century. Loss ratios on these useful shares of trade were indeed comparatively benign. For the decade 1871/2–1880/1 the loss outcome was a satisfactory annual average of 37.7% and for the longer period 1871/2–1886/7, a still reassuring 48.6%. Although the later 1880s witnessed higher rates of damage – pushing the annual average for the decade 1881/2–1890/1 up to 87.6% and the trading outcome well into the red – the period 1901–1905 saw a return to annual loss averages of 53.5% and to moderate profit.

The insurance of new technology, new construction and old wealth

Within the categories of home insurance defined by Table 1.1 Phoenix agreed to cover a number of individual risks, which, being more or less complex, technical, bizarre, exotic or innovative, provide a fairly apt summary of late-nineteenth century economic and social patterns. These risks, of course, are the outstanding ones, simply because the values are large enough to deserve a separate note of record in the Directors' or Trustees' Minutes. But, even if exceptional in value, they impart a certain flavour of the time which does not seem atypical.

Thus, Phoenix was involved in the arrangements for that particular symbol and icon of mid-Victorian architectural bravura, the Alexandra

[44] Trustees' Minutes, 16 October 1879. [45] *Ibid.*, 29 May 1879.
[46] *Ibid.*, 8 and 29 April 1880. [47] *Ibid.*, 23 October 1884.

Plate 1.3 Alexandra Palace, *c.* 1900.

Palace. Built on Muswell Hill, and incorporating the 1862 exhibition site of the Palace of Industries, this was north London's competitor to Paxton's Crystal Palace, which had been the display case for the 1851 Great Exhibition and was re-erected at Sydenham in 1854. Alexandra Palace was completed in 1873 and then anticipated its great predecessor by sixty-three years: it burned down immediately; Crystal Palace burned down in 1936. Rebuilt by J. Johnson, in 1873 and 1874, the second attempt at Alexandra Palace opened in 1875. Its style was more relaxed than that of the Crystal Palace, running to waxworks and a canoeing lake. The neo-Renaissance stone and brick frontage still stands and the central hall may well be 'the most impressive of all nineteenth-century engineering spaces'.[48]

In April 1873 Phoenix had taken £10,000 of the initial cover and £20,000 on the works of art that were moved in for display, but then developed reservations and would take no more.[49] In 1874, the major offices agreed to divide the palace into seven sections, and Phoenix,

[48] R. Dixon and S. Muthesius, *Victorian Architecture* (London, 1988), p. 88.
[49] Directors' Minutes, V21, p. 287, 21 May 1873.

understandably wary, would have no truck with the theatre section – another comment on where the Victorians could, or could not, be trusted – and placed a limit of £5,000 on the other six sections. But then, in April 1874, Phoenix agreed to take a 1/10th share, on all seven sections, and in the whole of the £160,000 worth of cover that was being sought. But then apparently, the other offices developed their own reservations and agreed to limit total cover to only £80,000. Rather stalwartly, having decided to commit itself to a particular number, Phoenix stuck with it, and so ended up with a 20% stake in this impressive, costly and recently flammable piece of Victoriana.[50]

Co-insurance, a standard and essential practice, particularly on large industrial risks ever since the eighteenth century, was still clearly a working imperative here.[51] The sharing of risk between the offices, either by this means or by reinsurance, was also pronounced in two very different large-scale examples of Phoenix's underwriting. One was akin in type to Alexandra Palace. Liverpool Street Station too was an extravaganza in iron and glass, a construction of a new age and posing new problems. Engineered by Edward Wilson of the Great Eastern Railway, Liverpool Street ranked alongside Manchester Central as the most important station construction of the 1870s.[52] The western side dates from 1874/5, while the eastern was opened twenty years later, in 1894. In autumn 1874, Phoenix was offered £90,000 on the station and £40,000 on the roof. The office was interested in stations, not least for their potential in publicity value, and the directors accepted the whole sum, but, with a caution perhaps not justified by events, they retained only £10,000 of the total, arranging to share the rest with the usual circle of leading London companies.[53]

The second case was that of the Bridgewater pictures. The trustees of the late duke, the fifth and the grandson of the great canal-building nobleman of the classic Industrial Revolution period, were seeking to insure the art collection at Bridgewater House, no doubt itself part of the surplus from the earlier transport ventures, for some £179,000 in early 1881. Phoenix in 1879 had already raised its limits on mansion houses from £10,000 to £15,000 in the countryside and – because large houses were nearer to good fire-fighting facilities in the capital – from £15,000 to £20,000 in London.[54] By 1881, the company held £10,000 worth of cover on Bridgewater House, so accepted a £39,000 share of the pictures and

[50] Trustees' Minutes, 23 April 1874. [51] See vol. 1, pp. 367ff.
[52] Dixon and Muthesius, *Victorian Architecture*, p. 106
[53] Trustees' Minutes, 10 September 1874.
[54] Directors' Minutes, W22, p. 389, 9 July 1879.

Plate 1.4 The approach to Liverpool Street Station, around 1900.

left the rest to their colleagues.[55] The counterpoint here between the urban-metropolitan wealth behind Liverpool Street and the landed-magnate wealth behind the Bridgewater collection is agreeable; but the insurers' reflex of communal protection was the same.

So it was with other works of art. Even Bridgewater's pictures were outshone by the crown jewels of the Queen of Spain. They spent a while at Christie, Manson and Woods in 1874. At this time, they were valued at £300,000, but Phoenix took only £30,000 for itself. In contrast, when offered £30,000 on the building of the Westminster Aquarium in 1875, Phoenix accepted the whole of it; perhaps the presence, or prospect, of so much water calmed underwriting nerves.[56] Oddly enough – or perhaps only oddly at first glance – warships also seem to have exercised a sedative effect upon the insurers. The second glance reveals that this was because warships were now ironclads. As early as 1873, Phoenix accepted the enormous sum of £200,000 on a metal-hulled frigate building for the new Imperial German Navy on the Isle of Dogs – indeed, in the light of that navy's subsequent activities, there is some irony in the fact that one of its first truly modern vessels was constructed in a British yard – and forbore

[55] Trustees' Minutes, 24 March, 14 April 1881.
[56] *Ibid.*, 17 June 1875.

to reinsure any of it. Similarly, in 1882, Phoenix took several tranches in the 5,700 ton 'steel armour-clad turret ship' *Riachuelo*, building for the Brazilian government at Samuda Brothers yard at Millwall, making a total of £222,000 by June 1883.[57] This represented about 60% of the vessel's cost at launch in 1883.[58] Here at least was one area where advancing technology reduced the fire hazard: the new generation of warships mostly generated fire only when they chose to, whereas earlier walls of oak were prone to less directed ignition.

In other sectors, particularly in regard to public buildings, such as hospitals, workhouses, churches and town halls, increasing competition brought reduced rates. In 1879, Phoenix was forced down to 3s 8d per £100 on all public buildings, with the single exception of the much-distrusted theatres. It is again a true echo of the values, interests and activities of late nineteenth-century Britain that the insurance companies should find themselves in competition for the business generated by the classic municipal and charitable defences against the rigours of Victorian city life. As the institutions of social relief and local government multiplied, so, particularly in a period of increasingly difficult trade, the insurers were anxious to tap a stream of demand more lively than many.

In much the same mood as they cut rates in this pursuit, they also broadened the range of insurable risk. Again in 1879, damage by lightning without fire was recognised as a class of fire insurance. Phoenix accepted the hazard, added 6d per £100 to the annual rate but circulated to the churchwardens of the kingdom that the office would insure only churches fitted with lightning conductors.[59]

Upon the church steeple, market pressure, technological progress, and municipal propriety came to a very Victorian conjunction.

The British home boom of the 1890s and the foreign adventures of the Phoenix

After the Baring Crisis of 1890, in which the greatest merchant bank in the City was almost brought down by financial upsets in Latin America, the patterns of British investment were disturbed.[60] Associated tremors across the foreign markets drove a considerable amount of frightened money swiftly back to Britain. Here, the capital markets were so arranged

[57] Directors' Minutes, X23, p. 258, 12 July 1882; Trustees' Minutes, 19 October 1882, 14 June 1883. [58] *Brassey's Naval Annual*, 1886.

[59] Trustees' Minutes, 21 August, 13 November 1879.

[60] This, of course, was the *first* Baring Crisis. The second, in Singapore, just over a century later, did sink the bank.

that not many of these repatriated funds found their way into the sectors, where, according to the requirements of long-term growth, they most needed to go: the high-risk new technologies such as chemicals and electrical engineering which hungered for venture capital. On the other hand, the traditional bolt-hole for money in flight – government securities, and especially consols – were currently offering poor yields. Consequently, much of this investment worked its way towards another traditional safe haven: real estate, in this case, house construction and suburban development. In the 1890s, the industries to benefit were building, commuter railways, brewing and bicycles.[61]

Confidence in foreign investment returned from the mid-1900s. And, by that time, the world manufacturing upswing of the period 1896–1914 was well launched. Expanding opportunities overseas, combined with fading memories of the City's problems in the early 1890s, pulled British foreign investment into a renewed, and record, surge in the years 1905–14. This massive revival of foreign lending transferred great quantities of purchasing power to Britain's debtors overseas – mainly, at this time, the less wealthy primary producing economies – and some of this was used to purchase British manufactures. The domestic industries which benefited from the demand generated in this way were the traditional ones: cotton, coal, metals, shipbuilding and engineering. Unfortunately, neither this investment upswing, nor predecessors of the same type, did much to modify the structural rigidity and attachment to old industries from which Britain suffered in the decades before the First World War.[62]

Nevertheless, in these years, there was some advance in the home demand for the products of the new industrial sector – such as motor cars and cycles (though less than in Continental economies like the German and French) – and a great deal of advance in consumer retailing of branded goods and household articles.

These currents in the larger economy show up in Phoenix's pattern of trade for the decade and a half before the Great War. The five-year averages for all industrial business dip sharply in the first half of the 1880s, then recover in the second half. But a real break in trend is evident in the 1890s and 1900s, with levels two and three times higher than in the previous twenty years (see Table 1.1). Clearly, also, some technological shift is present within the aggregates for industrial insurances. Rather

[61] E. Sigsworth and J. Blackman, 'The Home Boom of the 1890s', *Yorkshire Bulletin of Economic and Social Research*, 17 (1965), pp. 75–97. The new suburbs needed commuter railways and public houses; the bicycles formed the connection between home, station and pub.

[62] Kennedy, *Industrial Structure*.

fittingly, the last reference to Phoenix's oldest technology of all occurs between 1891 and 1895, as the last premiums for sugar houses are entered. But more significant is the pattern for the traditional cotton mill sector: as premium receipts from the broad range of industry soared, revenue from Britain's most venerable staple trade, and the Phoenix's industrial favourite from the early nineteenth century, the manufacture upon which the company had developed its reputation as a specialist industrial insurer, at length slipped away. The implication is obviously that the Phoenix was taking an increasing amount of its industrial business from the heavier and newer sectors.

Merchandise receipts, dealing with goods in store or transit, had been notably stable from 1871 to 1895. But they too improved by 28.6% between the quinquennium 1891/2–1895 and 1896–1900 and by 50.2% between 1891/2–1895 and 1906–10 (see Table 1.1). Here, Phoenix's turnover was tracking the UK's revival in the export trade. Similarly, the appearance in Table 1.1 of substantial numbers on the commercial and retail account from the mid-1890s mirrored the major expansion in high-street selling which characterised the final decades of the nineteenth century in Britain. Ventures like Marks & Spencer, Sainsbury, Home and Colonial, and Lipton were growing rapidly in this era, and the advance of such businesses and their lesser colleagues created a significant opportunity for the insurers.[63] Indeed, Phoenix, by the 1910s, was weaving not only insurance but also investment connections around such opportunities: thus, in 1912, the company consented to providing a series of loans for drapery firms recommended by Debenhams Ltd, in return for a block of guaranteed retail insurances.[64]

Superficially, the performance of the 'sundries' category in Table 1.1 from 1896 looks odd, given that there is a building boom in progress and that this set of accounts contained Phoenix's domestic house insurances. But the apparent decline of this sector is a paper effect only: it is produced by the isolation from the 'sundries' column of the receipts from meeting places, commercial and retail properties and transport insurances. If these are re-aggregated, the enlarged 'sundries' results for 1901–5 and 1906–10 match or surpass the peak result for the five-year period 1886/7–1890/1. It is probable, therefore, that the effects of suburban growth are also safely captured in the Phoenix's income returns. Even farming insurances perk up as they should, as rising prices from the mid-1890s provide a little relief from the extended period of agricultural doldrums which had persisted from the early 1870s.

[63] P. Mathias, *The Retailing Revolution* (London, 1967).
[64] Directors' Minutes, E30, p. 162, 10 July 1912.

The Phoenix, in the years on either side of 1900, behaves like a creature resident within the UK home economy. The nation was undergoing a recovery phase and the Phoenix was a sufficiently large organisation to feel these beneficial pressures. Yet, if beneficial, these pressures were also becoming increasingly marginal for the company. Until the early 1880s, the home and foreign premium flows of the Phoenix were roughly on a footing in terms of value. By the early 1900s, the foreign premium flow was nearly 3.5 times the domestic one, despite the considerable advance of the latter. Though it still responded to the promptings of the national market place, the Phoenix was becoming less and less a home bird and more and more a cosmopolitan one. Its renewed wanderlust is described in Chapters 2, 3 and 4.

3. FIRST STEPS IN ADVERTISING

The revival of Phoenix's home trade was associated with a definite, if not entirely consistent, stiffening of the company's will to market insurance. Advertising received quite close attention and a budget of over £2,000 even in the early 1870s. In 1873, the total came to £2,300 and included £480 paid to W. H. Smith for exhibiting Phoenix posters on their newspaper stands at railway stations and £426 for the printing of Phoenix Almanacs. However, possibly as a result of the buoyant insurance conditions of the mid-1870s, the company fell prone in 1875 to one of the periodic bouts of disillusion with self-promotion that are scattered throughout its second century. Its advertisements in the *Standard* and the *Daily News* were cut from three to two exposures per week, in *The Times* from four to two, while the quarterly advertisements in the *Telegraph*, the *Pall Mall Gazette*, the *Standard* and the *Daily News* were reduced from three to one per year and that in the *Despatch* cancelled altogether. Perhaps more seriously, the contract with W. H. Smith was allowed to lapse at the end of the year.[65]

This proved a serious miscalculation. The reduction in advertising activity came just before the lagged impact of the Great Depression hit the Phoenix. The combined effect made a marked dent in premium income. In July 1879, the trustees observed that, since abandoning its railway placards in 1876, the Phoenix had suffered a fall in home premiums of £6,000 p.a., or just over 2%,[66] and they saw a connection between these two facts. They decided to re-stiffen the Phoenix's com-

[65] Trustees' Minutes, 4 March 1875, 25 November 1875.

[66] The Annual Analysis of Business gives £256,649 for total UK gross fire premiums in 1876–7 and £250,465 in 1878–9.

mitment to publicity: W. H. Smith was to be asked for a greatly enlarged number of poster sites (2,000), with the placards also to be increased in size. Phoenix would take a five-year contract and was prepared to spend £1,500 on it.[67] This was the prelude to a major campaign aimed largely at railway travellers.

Employing tactics similar to the W. H. Smith scheme, Phoenix arranged to erect posters on 130 stations belonging to the North Eastern Railway and on 300 stations of the Scottish railways. Moreover, Phoenix firemarks were to be displayed on the stations of the South Eastern Railway Company, which were insured by the Phoenix. Early in 1881, Phoenix also accepted a proposal from Smith's to extend the original station displays: for a further payment of £500 p.a., Phoenix received an additional 4,000 posters at stations where previously it had lacked any presence.

Then, after having covered the stations, Phoenix caught the train: in 1880, the office hung posters in 660 carriages of the Metropolitan Railway,[68] and in 1881, through the Mirror Advertising Company – probably the Phoenix's first involvement with a specialised advertising agency – arranged for more to be displayed in 100 first-class carriages of the London, Brighton and South Coast Railway.[69]

The company also showed good awareness of the publicity value of its first centenary in 1882. It is noticeable that the flurry of activity in railway advertising was concentrated in 1880 and 1881, and, at the same time, that an additional 1,000 poster sites were taken in 'corn markets and other public buildings'. More precisely angled was the printing of 25,000 special almanacs for 1882 and the production, for a total cost of £131, of 10,000 coloured centenary posters.[70]

The importance of favourable comment in the newspaper columns was clearly grasped. But the issue was handled with a directness which would find few parallels in present-day relations between the press and the insurers. The Phoenix Board wrote their own article about their centenary and then paid the editor of the *Morning Post* £100 to print it; finally, they had 50,000 copies run off for use as handbills. This proved a shrewd move since almost all subsequent newspaper comment was derived from

[67] Trustees' Minutes, 3 July 1879.

[68] Julian Barnes wrote in *Metroland* (London, 1980), pp. 33–4, 'As the Metropolitan Railway had pushed westward in the 1880s, a thin corridor of land was opened up with no geographical or ideological unity: you lived there because it was an area easy to get out of. The name Metroland – adopted during the First World War both by estate agents and the railway itself – gave the string of rural suburbs a spurious integrity'.

[69] Trustees' Minutes, 2 and 16 September, 28 October 1880, 20 January 1881.

[70] *Ibid.*, 20 January 1881, 21 April 1881.

Plate 1.5 Early advertising by gift: the calendar for 1897.

the piece in the *Morning Post*; effectively, the many press notices of the Phoenix's 100th birthday were self-generated.[71]

Even the new organisational structure could be put to work in a promotional way. It was traditional, of course, to embellish discreetly the Head Offices of the great insurance companies, so that the public remarked and remembered their presence and purpose. Nevertheless, in 1882 it was thought appropriate to embellish Phoenix House a little further: accordingly, five Phoenix emblems in bronze were acquired for its main entrance and staircase. But now, of course, the presence of dedicated branch offices in the provinces gave additional opportunities for such ceremonious display. So, in 1882 the main Phoenix branch and general agency offices each received their own Phoenix emblem, but in stalwart stone rather than the metropolitan gleam of bronze.[72]

This early concern with image appears to have proved durable. In 1884, after the directors had expressed concern that neither Brentwood nor Brighton – through both of which some of their members had recently passed – displayed sufficient evidence of Phoenix presence, Agency Inspector Harris was instructed to see that the company received sufficient exposure in such sensitive localities.[73] And, when Harris made his own personal contribution to the publicising of insurance, by writing his *Insurance Cyclopaedia*, Phoenix chipped in to assist with publication costs, guaranteeing the purchase of fifty copies.[74] Nor was Harris the only Phoenix employee to supply free publicity of a constructively technical kind. Musgrave Heaphy wrote the standard treatise on insurance and electric lighting, and was also rewarded by the Board for this contribution both to underwriting standards in general and to the réclame of the Phoenix in particular.[75]

4. FIGHTING THE FLAMES: THE OFFICES AND THE BRIGADES

Just before this volume opens, disaster had enforced the most extensive rearrangement of fire-fighting services of the nineteenth century. The huge conflagration at Tooley Street in June 1861 exposed the inadequacy of the privately maintained facilities – represented in London by the Fire Engine Establishment, and financed directly by the insurance offices – for combating large urban fires. That dockland inferno had been sufficient to trigger an inquiry by a House of Commons Committee in 1862 and it duly recommended that fire-fighting, under the conditions of rapid expansion

[71] *Ibid.*, 12 and 26 January 1882. [72] *Ibid.*, 27 April, 14 September 1882.
[73] *Ibid.*, 16 October 1884. [74] *Ibid.*, 25 November 1886.
[75] *Ibid.*, 13 April 1882. They gave him 50 guineas for 'his valuable report on electric lighting'.

in the city, should be a public rather than private obligation. The committee emphasised that there was no other large city in Europe or America where fire protection was not supplied by the public authorities and funded from the public purse. They argued that a new brigade should be formed under the direction of the Metropolitan Police.

The insurers themselves were of a mind with the parliamentarians; they were clear that the pace of mid-century urban expansion had taken the job of fire-fighting beyond their resources. Immediately after the fire in Tooley Street the offices abdicated sole responsibility for the safety of London and informed the government that they intended to disband the Establishment and surrender its engine-houses, pumps and equipment to whatever authority the government chose to select for the job.[76]

Moved by the *laissez-faire* spirits of the day, the government was not anxious to assume a new public function, and took its time in choosing. Eventually, in 1865, it passed the Metropolitan Fire Brigade Act which, in 1866, transferred the Establishment's manpower and facilities to the control of the Metropolitan Board of Works. Phoenix for one would have preferred that the supervision of fire-fighting should have gone to a more powerful agency of central government, but had to be content with the contemporary leaning towards governmental minimalism.[77] Nevertheless, the companies saved money. The responsibility for the upkeep and renewal of £30,000 worth of fire-fighting apparatus passed with the free gift from the companies to the Board. And, in place of an outlay of £25,000 per year, the offices were now to help out the Board by a subscription of £35 per year for every £1 million of cover they provided in London.

Spared the major part of the burden of fire-fighting in the metropolis, the offices switched resources towards fire salvage, a field more clearly related to private gain than to public service. In 1866 they formed the London Salvage Corps to provide an expert means of limiting fire damage and retrieving value from the flames.[78] In 1899 the London County Council took over the control of fire-fighting from the Metropolitan Board of Works, but, in other respects, these two authorities, the Brigade and the Corps, continued to provide London's main defences against fire into modern times.

Outside London, arrangements for fire-fighting remained in many

[76] See Dickson, *The Sun Insurance Office*, pp. 129–31; Supple, *Royal Exchange Assurance*, p. 216; also vol. I, p. 133.

[77] Vol. I, pp. 140–1.

[78] London's was actually the second Salvage Corps; the first had been formed in Liverpool in 1842.

towns 'casual and irregular'[79] until 1900 and later. However, the larger cities, such as Manchester, Glasgow and Liverpool mostly followed London's lead. The big insurers often helped them along – the Sun, for instance, permitted annual grants to local brigades from around mid-century, although these were drawn upon less and less towards the end of the century. Like Phoenix, and the other older offices, the Sun maintained engines in the provinces until the 1880s but was able increasingly to withdraw as a greater number of local authorities followed the metropolitan pattern and brought the fire services under their own control.[80]

Very early in the span of this volume, Phoenix completed a small transaction which was highly symbolic of the changes affecting the organisation of fire-fighting. In 1816, the Danish Church in Wellclose Square had granted the company a 99-year lease, at a nominal rent of a guinea a year, upon the site of the Phoenix Engine House in this stronghold of sugar refining. Between then and the mid-century, local needs and local industries altered, and by the 1860s the Phoenix engine and stabling had fallen into disrepair. On the other hand, a different local need was perceived by the parson of St Mary's Whitechapel, who wanted the site for an elementary school. Recognising the virtue of the argument, Phoenix in 1872 assigned the lease without charge, for as long as the building was employed as a school.[81] The retreat of the fire offices from fire-fighting and the advance of the church in education aptly captures some of the turbulence in the debate over public versus private obligation which was a feature of the late-century decades. The transformation of the engine-house into a schoolroom symbolised the tug-of-war between public and private impulses in different areas of social provision.[82]

Similarly, the Phoenix Board's interest in fire-fighting in the period after the Metropolitan Fire Brigade Act inclined towards the area in which the companies could maintain a legitimate interest in private profit, the London Salvage Corps. One of its first preoccupations was with the prevention of fraudulent fires – which, of course, illegitimately reduced the level of private profit. In January 1871, the large offices were cooperating to appoint a detective to the Salvage Corps, so that London fires might be properly investigated, also to compose for the Corps a register of persons known to be connected with fire insurance fraud, and to pursue joint prosecutions for fraud or arson in the name of the Corps.[83]

79 Dickson, *The Sun Insurance Office*, pp. 129–31. 80 *Ibid.*

81 The site was still employed as a school a century later.

82 Directors' Minutes, V21, p. 186, 10 April 1872.

83 Trustees' Minutes, 19 January 1871. However, legal representation was still to be selected by the company attacked.

In the next year, the Salvage Corps needed new premises for its main station. These were found in Watling Street, and a committee of the five largest contributing offices, including Phoenix, was formed to raise the £15,000 needed to acquire them. In the event, Phoenix took a lead role in the undertaking, lending the Salvage Corps nearly a third of the total, £4,500 at 6% interest.[84] In 1903, Phoenix was still contributing to necessary extensions at Watling Street, providing one-seventh of about £30,000 required for improvements to the building.[85]

In the provinces, matters were less resolved; a motley array of systems for combating fire persisted, and Phoenix was involved in a fair cross-section of them. In Manchester by 1872, the fire brigade was under the control of the City Corporation and Phoenix needed to contribute a fairly modest £100 per year as its share of the offices' support of the municipal effort.[86] By contrast, later in the same year, Phoenix was meeting the bill for repairs to its own fire engine at Cheltenham, and for kitting out the firemen with the appropriate livery and equipment – which, undoubtedly, they needed, for they had received no refurbishment since 1858.[87] But, on yet a third hand, matters were differently disposed in Glasgow; by 1878, this city possessed its own salvage corps, then five years old; it was modelled on the London system, with the various offices making *pro rata* contributions to its upkeep. On this occasion, Phoenix paid about one-twentieth of the cost of the Glasgow Corps' freehold premises in Albion Street, at a total outlay of £966.[88] Exactly the same requirement came up in Liverpool in 1879, and Phoenix dutifully paid its one-thirteenth share in housing this pioneer of the Salvage Corps.[89] All of these organisations were to have useful lives of well over a century.

Yet, if the offices were willing to collaborate in the joint-funding of profit-related salvage operations, they were not willing to be inveigled back into any major responsibility for the public service of fire-fighting. While Phoenix had put a little investment into Cheltenham, it was less disposed to take on the burden of Gloucester. There, an old engine – 'inherited from the Protector', so it must have been very old[90] – needed replacement. Preferring to avoid the cost of that, Phoenix neatly side-stepped the obligation: it presented the veteran pump as a free gift to the city.[91] Rather more seriously, the fire offices rebelled in unison in 1884 when the Metropolitan Board of Works apparently sought to turn the

[84] *Ibid.*, 9 May, 24 October 1872. [85] *Ibid.*, 18 May, 15 June 1904.
[86] *Ibid.*, 12 September 1872. [87] *Ibid.*, 31 October 1872.
[88] *Ibid.*, 31 October 1878. [89] *Ibid.*, 12 June 1879.
[90] Phoenix absorbed the Protector in 1837. See vol. I, pp. 499–506.
[91] Trustees' Minutes, 20 March 1879.

clock back by promoting a Bill to increase the contributions paid to the London Fire Brigade by the insurers. The chairman of the Atlas, Sir William Baynes, was sufficiently exercised to propose a joint delegation to the Home Secretary.[92]

When the feathers stopped flying, however, this was perceived as a trimming of balance; the principle of local government control of the fire brigades was established and it spread as inexorably from the capital to the provinces in the final third of the century as the provision of police services had spread from Peel's London to the cities and towns of Britain in its middle third.

5. THE DIRECTION OF THE PHOENIX, 1870–1914

A spate of heavy mortality between 1866 and 1872 removed no fewer than eight directors who were with us at the close of volume I. Among these were not only stalwarts from the Pelican such as William Cotton and Dr Gordon and long-standing family connections such as E. H. Hawkins II and Matthew Whiting II (who served from 1819 to 1871) but also some of the more anonymous names from the mid-century like J. T. Oxley and W. J. Lancaster and such lesser lights from the City as H. H. Toulmin and Travers Buxton.

However, Phoenix did not take the opportunity to make any striking replacements. There was another Oxley back on the Board within five years, and, alongside him, in the shape of Major Rohde Hawkins, a director who carried not one but two traditional Phoenix names. The same was true of John Coope Davis who served 1866–81, ending as Trustee. Among the clutch of appointments at the inception of this volume perhaps only two stand out. One, John Clutton, was 'the best known and most highly respected surveyor of the nineteenth century'[93] and the founding president of the Institution of Chartered Surveyors; he sat on the Board from autumn 1867 until March 1896, again joining a distinguished company tradition. The other was the late nineteenth-century's perfect banker, Sir John Lubbock MP, a man repelled by 'the controversial or aggressive' but 'unshaken by rumours of the unforeseen'[94] (however, in later years, he was sufficiently ruffled by the unforeseen event at San Francisco in 1906).[95] By 1870, Lubbock was senior partner in Robarts, Lubbock & Co., 'one of the oldest, most

[92] Directors' Minutes, X23, p. 435, 2 April 1884.
[93] F. M. L. Thompson in *The Dictionary of Business Biography*, vol. I, ed. D. J. Jeremy (London, 1984), pp. 701–3.
[94] See vol. I, pp. 681–2. [95] See below, pp. 279–82.

extensive and prosperous banking institutions in the City',[96] MP for Maidstone, and many things besides.

These two men, though both of high ability and achieving eminence, could scarcely have been more different. Lubbock was the scholar-banker, the author of thirty books, beginning with *Prehistoric Times* in 1865, and proceeding to range over the fields of anthropology, geology, zoology, entomology, botany, politics, education and, rather far down the list, banking. He was a quite extraordinarily path-breaking scientist in several fields: the first to detect the evolutionary interaction between insects and flowers, the first to employ the maze for testing the learning behaviour of animals, and the first to distinguish between the Palaeolithic and Neolithic cultures, the names of which we owe to him. Together with T. H. Huxley, Lubbock had been the principal supporter of his friend and neighbour Charles Darwin in the controversy which had followed the publication of the *Origin of Species* of 1860. In return, Darwin valued the opinion of Huxley and Lubbock over 'that of any other man in England'.

That opinion also drew up, for a lecture at a Working Men's College, a list of One Hundred Best Books, which, when published, proved a best-selling guide to self-education for some two decades. Lubbock's list included Marcus Aurelius, Epictetus, Spinoza and Confucius and is a telling guide, not only to his own interests but also to his vision of the working man.

Certainly, John Clutton would have read few of Lubbock's suggestions. He had attended only the local grammar school at Cuckfield, Sussex, and testified late in life that 'I have a hundred times felt my inferiority when mixing with educated men'.[97] Destined to be a solicitor, he was instead brought into his father's surveying office, in order to help rescue a failing business, at the age of seventeen. He had no training and learned the business the practical way. But he arrived at the right time, at the start of the railway boom, and he was quick to spot the opportunity. First, he acted for local landowners in negotiating a path for the London and Brighton Railway and then, from the other side, was the chief force in acquiring land for the South East and Eastern County Railways. By the 1840s he was a major expert in, and arbitrator of, railway cases, but, also in the 1840s, he took Messrs Cluttons, in a major diversification, into the role of Surveyor and Agent to the Church Commissioners for the southern counties. Between 1845 and 1860 John Clutton carried out the first

[96] The original venture, Lubbock, Forster & Co. was founded in 1772.
[97] J. C. Rogers, 'Memoir of John Clutton', *Transactions of the Surveyors' Institution*, 29, 1896–7.

systematic description of Church property for 200 years. By 1847 he was adviser to the Royal Forests and by 1851 Crown Receiver for all royal estates in the Midlands and south. This self-made professional was attractive to Phoenix for his vast range of contacts amidst really large institutional property-holders, and no doubt also for his railway expertise. But virtually all that he shared with Lubbock was the fact that both had terminated formal education at the age of fifteen. However, as a place to terminate it, Lubbock's Eton – as Clutton was painfully aware – had some advantages over Clutton's Cuckfield.

This diffidence perhaps explains why Clutton left little overt trace in Phoenix's dealings during his thirty years on the Board: very likely, he was more important in supplying connections than in forming policy. By contrast, Lubbock left many traces. Although he sat on the Phoenix Board from 1866 until 1913, he was probably at the height of his influence in financial matters between 1880 and 1900. Indeed, he withdrew from daily attendance at his own bank in 1882 in order to concentrate on the wider issues. He was chairman of the Council of Foreign Bondholders from 1890, its president 1900–13; and chairman of the Central Association of Bankers in 1897 and chairman of the Committee of London Clearing Banks, 1898–1913. In addition, he had held the presidency of the London Chamber of Commerce, 1888–93. In the House, where he sat, very suitably, as MP for London University from 1880,[98] he dealt with 'all sorts of small, and in many cases vexatious, pieces of parliamentary business, for the proper conduct of which the bankers were concerned'.[99] The 'banking busy bee' of volume I had earned by 1900 a different title: 'the father of banking in the City'.[100]

In politics he was, again consistently with a temperament which preferred detail to passion, determinedly non-partisan. He remained friends with Gladstone after they differed over Home Rule, and throughout the period up to his removal to the House of Lords in 1900, stayed aloof from party politics.[101] The legislation which he introduced continued to indicate a kindly nature,[102] a concern for the practical small scale, and the width of his own intellectual interests. His most famous piece of law-making, the Bank Holiday Act, came right at the start of the period of this volume, in 1871; and he remained with this area of interest. He was

98 And was its vice-chancellor, 1872–80. From 1870 to 1880 he sat as MP for Maidstone.

99 *The Times*, 29 May 1913.

100 He also somehow found time to be a member of the L.C.C. 1889–92, its vice-chairman 1889–90, its chairman 1890–2 and alderman, 1892–8.

101 He became, loosely, a commonsensical Liberal Unionist.

102 Which reputedly extended to making pets of his experimental insects and mourning the passing of a favourite queen ant. *The World and his Wife*, May 1905.

Plate 1.6 The Plumage Bill: Lord Avebury as St Francis.

genuinely concerned with the plight of shop assistants and improved it with piecemeal private members' bills in 1880, 1890, 1904 and 1908. This was kindly practicality. The rest is summed up by the Wild Birds Protection Act of 1880, the Open Spaces Act of 1890, and, above all, the Ancient Monuments Acts of 1882 and 1901. When the time came, there was deep antiquarian significance even in his choice of lordly title: Lord Avebury.[103]

Lubbock possessed a warm personality but a somewhat cool and narrow intellect. His interests could scarcely have been wider and he possessed scientific vision, but it operated within a defined ambit and followed from minute observation. Also, he was too many things: banker, scientist, scholar, politician, popular author, public servant. It was a

[103] See P. Eynon-Smart in *The Dictionary of Business Biography*, vol. III, ed. D. J. Jeremy (London, 1985), pp. 873–5.

combination which generated affection and a reputation for business sagacity, but it did not guarantee business vision. *The Times*' obituary in 1913 put a finger on this problem when its author wrote that Avebury 'was of great service to the business world . . . *in ordinary times*'.[104] This shrewd and lucid conservative was a major – if perhaps not wholly enlivening – influence upon the Phoenix for the best part of fifty years. Lubbock was a man of huge probity and energy, disciplined caution and remarkable concern for detail; of his intellectual power there can be no question; of his intellectual perspective there could be much more.

But among the Phoenix Board of 1880, Lubbock stands on a lonely eminence. Apart from O. E. Coope, there is no one to touch him for cleverness or commercial eminence, and everyone senior to him is either of advanced age or of minor stature. And, at the junior end of the Board, among the recent appointments, there are still too many question marks of anonymity. Clutton remains an exception, but not a vociferous one.

The expansionism of Phoenix policy in the period 1870–90 – which was definite but measured in the home market, more dramatic in the foreign – is consistent with this array of personalities.

Certainly, the Board of 1880 represents something of a low point in the professionalism or prestige of the Phoenix directors. That of 1870 had at least combined the force of original 'sugar' names like Whiting and Goodhart with the repute of eminent men of business or finance like Octavius Coope or Kirkman Hodgson. Goodhart was still there in 1880, but Coope was in his last twilight; Clutton had brought solidity rather than incisiveness and only Lubbock projected any brighter – if intellectually chilly – radiance. By 1890, in contrast, though the anonymous question marks continued to lurk, a new double emphasis is evident among the new names on the Board: more of them have either substantial aristocratic connection like Folkestone or Ponsonby or clear professional/commercial attribution like Baxendale of Pickford's or Walter Bird, merchant; and sometimes, like Portman, they have both (see Table 1.2). Certainly, the decorative glitter of title and connection was to strengthen in the period 1890–1914.

Continuing doubts about the internal musculature of the Board have particular importance in a period when no modern executive core of management had yet emerged and the small staff of senior company 'servants' which preceded it was indifferently manned.[105]

There was no assistant director or secretary before 1900 to compare

104 *The Times*, 29 May 1913 (my emphasis). The San Francisco disaster (see below, pp. 266–82) was for Phoenix, of course, a most extra-ordinary time.

105 See vol. 1, pp. 675ff for similar doubts about the Boards of the 1850s and 1860s.

Table 1.2. *The Phoenix Board 1870–1910 (listed by seniority)*

1870 Name	1870 Connection	1880 Name	1880 Connection	1890 Name	1890 Connection	1900 Name	1900 Connection	1910 Name	1910 Connection
M. Whiting	Family	O. E. Coope	Brewing/Family	G. A. Fuller	Finance	C. E. Goodhart	Family	Lord Avebury	Finance/Pelican
O. E. Coope	Brewing/Family	G. A. Fuller	Finance	C. E. Goodhart	Family	W. J. Thompson	?	Hon E. Portman	Law/Land
K. D. Hodgson MP	Finance/Family	C. E. Goodhart	Family	W. J. Thompson	?	Lord Avebury	Finance/Pelican	J. Baxendale	Commerce
G. A. Fuller	Finance	W. J. Thompson	?	Hon. J. Byng	City/Land	Hon. E. Portman	Law/Land	B. Bovill	Land
B. Shaw	?	Hon. J. Byng	City/Land	Sir J. Lubbock MP	Finance/Pelican	J. Baxendale	Commerce	W. Bird	Commerce
Dr J. Gordon	Pelican	Sir J. Lubbock	Finance/Pelican	J. Clutton	Surveying	B. Bovill	Land	Hon E. Ponsonby	Family/Pelican/Land
C. E. Goodhart	Family	J. C. Davis	Family	C. T. Lucas	Land?	W. Bird	Commerce	R. K. Hodgson	Finance/Family/Pelican
W. J. Thompson	?	J. Clutton	Surveying	D. R. Smith	?	Hon E. Ponsonby	Family/Pelican/Land	Sir A. Lucas	Family
H. H. Toulmin	City/Land	J. S. Oxley	Family	Hon E. Portman MP	Law/Land	R. K. Hodgson	Finance/Family/Pelican	R. Clutton	Surveying
T. Buxton	City/Land	C. T. Lucas	Land?	C. Magnay	?	A. C. Lucas	Family	F. Lescher	?
Hon J. Byng	City/Land	D. R. Smith	?	J. Baxendale	Commerce	R. Clutton	Surveying	Adm. Lucas	Navy
O. H. Ince	Family	C. Rivaz	?	B. Bovill	Land	F. Lescher	?	Hon Stuart Pleydell-Bouverie	Family/Land/Industry
Sir J. Lubbock	Finance/Pelican	Maj. Rohde Hawkins	Service/Family	W. Bird	Commerce	Adm. Lucas	Navy	T. D. Murray	?
J. C. Davis	Family			Hon. E. Ponsonby	Family/Pelican/Land	G. Gadsden	Law	G. T. T. Treherne	Law
J. Clutton	Surveying			Rt Hon. Viscount Folkstone MP	Land	Hon Stuart Pleydell-Bouverie	Family/Land/Industry	Rt Hon Viscount Dillon	Scholar/Pelican
								Lord George Hamilton	Politics/Pelican
								A. T. Hawes	Law/Pelican
								J. Sorley	Pelican
								J. Tryon	Law/Pelican
								Lord Winterstoke	Industry/Pelican
								Sir W. Anson	Scholar/Law Life
								J. S. Beale	Law Life
								W. R. Malcolm	Finance/Law Life
								F. Fladgate	Law/Industry/Law Life

with Stonestreet, Jenkin Jones or Richter, and the position of the managerial 'core' was not redefined for new times until the appointment of H. B. Guernsey as manager of the Phoenix in 1902.[106] The playwright-insurer George Lovell had already completed fifty years of service with the Phoenix by January 1870 and had been secretary for almost twenty.[107] The great foreign investigator from the 1840s, J. J. Broomfield, did come to assist Lovell as joint secretary from 1873[108] – the Board apparently perceiving the need for a managerial shot in the arm – and he took over completely in 1878, after Lovell's sudden illness and swift death.[109]

Undoubtedly, the re-emergence of the Phoenix as a powerful direct overseas insurer in the 1880s owed much to Broomfield's inclinations and skills. The break in the trend of foreign premiums – they more than doubled during his brief tenure, 1878–84 – exactly synchronises with his time as secretary. But, having set the pattern, and put much of his energies into the foreign sector, Broomfield himself attained his half-century with the Phoenix in 1884. Sensible in this as in all things, he then resigned, being rewarded by the Board with the largely meaningless title of Honorary Director.[110] Given the pattern of the premium returns 1870–90, it is clear that Broomfield wrenched the tiller, and that the Board permitted him to do so, but he did not remain long at the helm.[111] He was succeeded by the brothers MacDonald (William Chambers and Francis Bienfait), who had both served for nearly forty years by the time they achieved the joint secretaryship. F. B. MacDonald had been assistant secretary to Broomfield from 1878, but at a third of his master's salary, and W. C. MacDonald had been appointed accountant at the same time, at a half of the same figure.[112]

In Phoenix anecdote and folklore the MacDonalds were cheerful Dickensian figures, but they have left little more substantial trace. Broomfield took foreign earnings briskly to a two-thirds share of all premiums by 1884 and that is where the overseas share remained at the end of the MacDonald era in 1901. These were the last of the old-style secretaries of the Phoenix, very much servants of the Board and single (or, in their case, double) functionaries with little between them and their small teams of clerks.

[106] Phoenix Directors' Minutes, 27, p. 72, 29 January 1902.

[107] The Board marked his half-century with a present of £500. *Ibid.*, U, p. 441, 19 January 1870. At this time, the salary of a junior clerk was £60 p.a. See vol. I for more on these long-serving worthies.

[108] Salary of £1,500 p.a. against the £2,000 paid to Lovell.

[109] Directors' Minutes, W22, p. 310, 22 May 1878.

[110] *Ibid.*, X23, p. 442, 30 April 1884.

[111] He died late in 1892, after nearly a decade of retirement. *Ibid.*, Z25, p. 353, 4 January 1893.

[112] Directors' Minutes, W22, p. 310, 22 May 1878.

Under these circumstances, the management of the office until the turn of the century remained in the transitional state detected in volume I.[113] The executive was still undeveloped: it was restricted to a very few individuals of inadequate status vis-à-vis the Board and had not yet specialised, multiplied and divisionalised in the modern style. For its part, the Board no longer contained many individuals with direct industrial or insurance experience but had not yet acquired many of the widely experienced 'outsiders' from the City, business or public life whose function it is to be guided by, and themselves inform, a professional executive cadre. Day-to-day control of the office, therefore, really did revolve around the Committees of Directors who met regularly, usually twice a week, in different combinations of individuals, to form policy in specific areas of business. Much then turned on the quality of these people.

The appointments of the 1870s – J. S. Oxley (1871–81), whose main claim to fame seems to have been in fathering a general – W. M. Whitbread (1871–6), C. Rivaz (1877–84), C. T. Lucas (1872–95) – apparently a moderate Horsham landowner – Major Rohde Hawkins (1879–84) and Dudley R. Smith had made no enormous stir in the world and continued in the same mode at the Phoenix. From 1881, however, there is a clear change in style, and we might again suspect the hand of Broomfield, perhaps guiding Coope. The recruitment of J. Baxendale of Pickford's in 1882 (–1915) and the specific invitation to Walter Bird (–1921), a merchant with knowledge of the American trade, is consistent with Broomfield's expansionist commercial and overseas strategy. So, too, perhaps was the appointment of Bristow Bovill (1882–1944), a classic 'working director' and deputy chairman of great endurance (1908–20). Almost all the others had aristocratic connections: the Hon. Edwin Portman (1881–1921); the Hon. Edwin Ponsonby (1885–1939); Viscount Folkestone (1887–1900). The list of directors for 1890 contained no fewer than three 'Honourables', one baronet, one viscount and three MPs.

In terms of personality, this was a very mixed bunch indeed. Bird, of Montague Lodge, Datchet, had no qualifying shares of his own, and had the necessary quota loaned to him by J. S. Oxley; he passed on the dividends meticulously to the true owner. His advice on foreign markets was listened to, and he had a lifelong devotion to 'the dear old Phoenix'.[114] Bristow Bovill, too, was a committed Phoenix hand. He became a director at the age of twenty-eight, and remained one for sixty-two years. He served as trustee 1897–1908, then as deputy chairman for twelve years;

[113] See vol. I, pp. 702–4.

[114] W. Bird to Sir Gerald Ryan, 19 October 1920. 'I have lived, and loved the Phoenix nearly all my life, and I will die there.' In fact, he died at home, of 'creeping palsy' in July 1921.

and, in addition, Phoenix used him as a representative on the London Board of Union Marine, after that Liverpool company was absorbed in 1911, and on the Board of Norwich Union Fire, while that office was under Phoenix suzerainty, 1920–5.[115] A keen sportsman, shot and fisherman, and a great rider to hounds in his younger days, Bovill had some other interests as a JP and as a director of a few railway companies; but his real passions seem to have been his estate at Bury House, Basingstoke, and his attendance at the Phoenix.[116] This was assiduous; he was effectively a professional director 'who each week took a personal interest in the examination of all Fire Losses and matters affecting the Fire Department'.[117] From 1908, he was on the Fire, Life and Accident, and Finance Committees and can rarely have been out of the place during the working week.

The aristocrats had more varied commitments. The Hon. Edwin Portman was the younger son of the 1st Viscount Portman, and brother of the 2nd Viscount Oxford; by the standards of the time, he took energetically to being a younger son and became a barrister, as well as, perhaps more characteristically, holding North Dorset for the Liberals, 1885–9. Portman also amassed a serious personal holding in Phoenix, with 1,360 of the £10 shares. The Hon. Edwin Ponsonby was the youngest son of the 2nd Lord de Mauley, and, after Eton, had a more conventional career as a county dignitary, ranging from the Woodstock Petty Sessions to the duties of Deputy Lieutenant. His link with Phoenix was the rather enterprising marriage into brewery money, through Emily Dora, the daughter of Octavius Coope. Much later, Ponsonby himself wrote that Octavius had 'got me elected on the "Phoenix" to look after the Family interests'.[118] The last, and the most elevated, of the aristocratic appointments of the 1880s was that of the Rt Hon. Viscount Folkestone MP (1887–1900). Folkestone was the junior title of the Bouverie family, Earls of Radnor, this Bouverie succeeding to the senior title, as the 6th Earl in 1900.

It is easy to imagine that Sir John Lubbock would have had little difficulty settling into this company, and perhaps less in directing it to a view. At first attempt, it is more difficult to imagine how the erudite humanitarian might have dealt with J. Baxendale. This sportsman had swum his way through Harrow and rowed his way through Pembroke, Oxford. He acquired some gloss as a JP and Deputy Lieutenant, and a

[115] See below, pp. 427–42, 469–85.
[116] His railway interests were mostly somewhat later, or somewhat minor: the Dominican Atlantic (1908), the Midland & South Western Junction (1918), and the Plymouth and Dartmoor.
[117] *The Bird*, August 1944.
[118] Ponsonby to Chairman Walters, 20 July 1939.

good deal more by marrying – in a reversal of the Ponsonby match – Frances Scott, sole heiress of the last Earl Egremont. But he remained a hearty to the soles of his riding boots. He was master of the Hursley Hounds, 1892–1902 and confided to *Who's Who* that his recreations were 'all field sports'. More surprisingly, he reminded his biographers that he had won the Swimming Prize at Harrow and appeared many times for his college eight; indeed, eight of these times are cited. Part of Baxendale's heart had clearly never left the Isis. We could speculate that Lubbock's first response might have been to suggest some improving books. But then, at the second attempt, one remembers that Sir John could do anything, and that one newspaper article of the 1900s shows him, well into his seventies, bashing a golf ball quite competently around the course near his Farnborough home.[119] A quick round would probably have set him square with Baxendale.

While these appointments were ending an era, its termination was emphasised in a sadder way. In November 1886, Octavius Edward Coope, the last of the really powerful descendants of the founding fathers, died. Appropriately, the Minute Books display more emotion than usual, regretting the passing of 'a lamented friend . . . justly regarded as the Father of the Society'.[120] The well-known portrait was given to the Board by his widow the next year.[121]

During the 1890s, there was no great activity in further changing the nature of the Board. Some relatively small players passed away: the veteran but minor financier G. A. Fuller at length retired in September 1891; C. T. Lucas died in December 1895, the Hon. James Byng in May 1897, and Dudley Smith in September 1897. This Lucas was replaced by a rather more eminent nephew, A. C. (later Sir Arthur) Lucas in March 1896. More seriously, the death of John Clutton in March 1896 brought the immediate appointment of his second son, Ralph (1896–1912), the hardest working of four and the one to whom John Clutton had entrusted the surveying business. The speed of response was measure of the value placed by Phoenix on the Clutton connection. Bovill and Ponsonby gained seniority and became Trustees, both in 1897. But the most important additions of the decade were those of R. K. Hodgson in 1894 (–1924) and Admiral C. D. Lucas in 1897 (–1914).[122]

119 *Daily Chronicle*, 30 April 1909.

120 Phoenix Directors' Minutes, Y24, p. 236, 1 December 1886.

121 *Ibid.*, p. 305, 10 August 1887. See vol. I, p. 364 for the portrait.

122 A further minor one, in an older style, was the appointment, also in 1897, at the third attempt, of Joseph Lescher, DL, JP, High Sheriff of Essex in 1885, Papal Count, Baron of France, Count of the Holy Roman Empire, and, beyond the age of 75, enthusiastic huntsman with the Essex Union.

Plate 1.7 Lord Avebury at golf, 1909.

Robert Kirkman Hodgson, of Barings, carried this long-standing connection into the new century. He was the son of K. D. Hodgson MP, governor of the Bank of England and Phoenix director until 1879, but he had financial standing in his own right. Educated at Eton and Trinity, Cambridge, he later went on to acquire a third connection of interest to Phoenix by marrying Lady Honora Janet, younger daughter of the 9th Earl of Cork.[123] The Ponsonby, Baxendale and Hodgson marriages are

[123] They had three sons and a daughter, born into an age cohort sadly representative of an era and a class. Two of the sons were killed in action in the First World War, within a week of one another, both at Ypres in March 1915. From 1916, R. K. Hodgson frequently found it impossible to attend the Board.

The first V.C. In June, 1854, off Bomarsund, Charles Lucas, a mate in the Hecla, seized a fused and burning shell that had fallen on deck and threw it overboard. He was immediately promoted lieutenant and subsequently awarded the V.C. He became a rear-admiral.

Plate 1.8 Rear-Admiral Lucas VC in 1854.

characteristic of the City – Land alliances which were forming at this time.[124]

Rear-Admiral Charles Davis Lucas was characteristic of very little. He won the first of all VCs in 1854, while serving at the siege of Bomarsund during the Crimean War, by throwing a live Russian shell overboard from the deck of HMS *Hecla*. It is unclear whether this showed great bravery or great commonsense; but it seems worth the medal either way. There is a legend that he rose from the ranks,[125] but actually he seems to have begun conventionally as a cadet and midshipman (his rank on the *Hecla*), and to have stemmed from an Irish county family, the Lucases of Drummargole, Co. Armagh, and Clontibret, Co. Monaghan. Lucas served in the Mediterranean, then on HMS *Fox* throughout the Burmese War of 1852–3; he took part in the storming and capture of Rangoon, Dalla, Pegu, Prome and Meaday, and assumed command of a gunboat on the Irrawaddy in the final stages. He then moved to the Baltic during the war against Russia, and, after winning the VC enjoyed a quieter time, on various stations, for the remainder of his naval career. He made commander in 1862, captain in 1869 and rear-admiral in 1885.[126] His marriage was also into an eminent naval family: the match in 1879 was with Frances Hall, only daughter of Admiral Sir William Hall, FRS, the first seaman to take an ironclad warship around the Cape. Not to be outdone, Lady Hall was daughter of Admiral Lord Torrington. This was the 6th Lord Torrington; the 1st had been Admiral Byng. The Byng connection was important to Admiral Lucas and it was he in 1911 who presented to the Phoenix Board a portrait of their erstwhile colleague, the Hon. James Byng, himself a frustrated seadog.[127]

Fittingly, it fell to Admiral Lucas to announce to the Board, as its chairman in 1901, the death of the monarch whose medal he bore. He lamented 'the national sorrow that has befallen us in the loss of our beloved queen, conspicuous throughout her reign for wisdom and goodness'[128] and the Board received the news 'standing in solemn silence'. Hardly more than a year earlier Victoria had elevated Sir John Lubbock to the peerage as Lord Avebury.

The end of the Victorian era brought also a new age for the Phoenix Board: the period 1901–14 introduced some decisive changes. These were

124 See Y. Cassis 'Bankers in English Society in the Late Nineteenth Century', *Economic History Review*, 38 (1985), pp. 210–29.
125 See K. Chesney, *A Crimean War Reader* (London, 1975).
126 The *Courier*, 14 August 1914.
127 Phoenix Directors' Minutes, 29, p. 385, 29 March 1911. Byng had wanted to follow the family tradition but had been prevented by illness. See vol. 1, p. 683.
128 *Ibid.*, 26, p. 458, 23 January 1901.

the result partly of necessary adaptation to changing conditions (witness the creation of a genuine chief executive position by Guernsey's appointment in 1902); partly of the development within the Phoenix of a distinctively active managerial style (due largely to the arrival of G. H. Ryan as Guernsey's successor in 1908); and partly of the selection for the Phoenix of a growth strategy which involved the building of a composite insurance office, bringing in new companies by acquisition, and thus forcing managerial specialisation and adding new faces and talents to the main Board.[129]

Three of the four appointments which came early in the new century, between 1900 and 1904, were important.[130] They came about as the result of the successive deaths of Lord Radnor, and of the long-serving Charles Emanuel Goodhart and W. J. Thompson.[131] The Radnor connection was clearly too good to lose, and when the new earl wrote to Lord Avebury 'to express the great satisfaction it would be to himself if the Board thought proper to elect his brother . . . to the vacant seat', the Hon. Stuart Pleydell-Bouverie was promptly appointed.[132] This Bouverie had a further value: in another match between aristocracy and plutocracy, he had married a daughter of Albert Vickers, one of the third-generation industrialists who had established Vickers, Son and Maxim Ltd as an armoury of global importance.[133] After Harrow, the independently minded Bouverie had undergone an apprenticeship as a railway engineer, and actually worked at Vickers as assistant to the superintendent of ordnance at the turn of the century.[134] To achieve such landed and industrial connection at a stroke was rare. It was clearly prized by Phoenix, for, when Bouverie's brother, the Earl, requested a loan of £90,000 in 1912,

129 One of the talents absorbed by acquisition was to have huge influence over the Phoenix for the best part of thirty years. This was Gerald Ryan who arrived with the Pelican merger of 1908. Ryan had been actuary of the British Empire and had moved to Pelican when Phoenix's sister company absorbed the British Empire in 1903. See below, pp. 308–17 and passim.

130 The fourth was of T. D. Murray (1903–11), elected 30 September 1903 (Phoenix Directors' Minutes, 27, p. 212).

131 Also of the minor figure, the solicitor G. Gadsden, who served briefly 1898–1902.

132 Phoenix Directors' Minutes, 26, p. 447, 14 November 1900.

133 Thus, curiously, Pleydell-Bouverie constituted not only a link between Phoenix and the Radnors but also between this work of the present author and an earlier one. See C. Trebilcock, *The Vickers Brothers; Armament and Enterprise 1854–1914* (London, 1977). Pleydell-Bouverie, despite being 37 years of age in 1914, had a distinguished war, ending as Colonel the Hon. Stuart Pleydell-Bouverie, DSO, the medal being won at Ypres, where the sons of his colleague Hodgson had died. He was also a prominent freemason, and, judging by his occasional reports on his travels to Ryan, a director who developed a genuine insurance expertise.

134 He was also a director of several Vickers' subsidiaries, including the Electric & Ordnance Accessories Co. Ltd, and the Wolseley Motor Co.

against property and ground rents in Folkestone and Chancery Lane, the proposal was swiftly satisfied 'on account of the value of the fire connection'.[135] It was, of course, the property-owning aspect of landed wealth which appealed to a fire company; but then, equally, industrialists also controlled large blocks of buildings requiring insurance.

The second appointment brought a considerable reinforcement of the financial element on the Board. The directors had sought this strengthening by inviting Edgar Lubbock, younger brother of Lord Avebury and a senior figure both within Robarts, Lubbock and Co., and within the City generally, to join their number. Avebury reported in November 1902 that Edgar was 'very gratified' by the invitation.[136] By 1907 Edgar Lubbock was deputy governor of the Bank of England, and anticipating a term as governor. He was granted leave by the Phoenix Board to absent himself from the main Wednesday meeting since the India Committee of the Bank met at the same time; he would do his committee work on two other days of the week.[137] The exception was obviously worthwhile in order to keep the ear and the advice of the governor of the Bank. Unfortunately, however, Edgar deprived them of both by dying suddenly later in 1907.[138]

More durable, but equally indicative of an intention on the part of the Board, was the appointment in 1904 (–1923) of the Welshman, George Gilbert Treherne Treherne.[139] Educated at Eton and Balliol, Treherne had rowed for Oxford in 1859; so he outstroked Baxendale. He was also an amateur archaeologist of some note (the first president of the Carmarthenshire Archaeological Society); so he would have been congenial to Avebury. However, Phoenix had sought him out for neither of these reasons. There is some evidence that both Phoenix and Pelican were looking around the turn of the century, perhaps under Ryan's influence, for bright solicitors. Phoenix had tried once in 1898 with George Gadsden, but he had lasted only a few years; Treherne was the other partner in Gadsden and Treherne. He was a cheerful, lively man who attracted affection easily, but he had a quick mind and he was to combine well with the lawyers who came across to the Phoenix Board on the absorption of Pelican in 1908. It was Treherne's motion which kept the Phoenix in the American Pacific Coast trade after the San Francisco earthquake of 1906 almost convinced the faint-hearted (including Avebury) to run for home.[140]

[135] Phoenix Directors' Minutes, 30, pp. 112, 120, 17 and 24 April 1912.
[136] *Ibid.*, 27, p. 150, 12 November 1902.
[137] Trustees' Minutes, 22 May 1907.
[138] Directors' Minutes, 28, p. 104, 11 September 1907.
[139] *Ibid.*, 27, p. 257, 27 April 1904. [140] See below, pp. 280–2.

Plate 1.9 Gerald Ryan in 1911.

Undoubtedly, the main impact upon the Phoenix Board in the period 1870–1914 was delivered by the new arrivals who joined it as a result of corporate acquisition. The first step in this process was the sisterly merger in 1908 between the Phoenix and its venerable partner the Pelican Life Office. The preconditions for this accord between relatives were the Pelican's healthy revival[141] during the 1890s and the recruitment to it in 1902 from the British Empire Life of the brilliant actuary, Gerald Ryan. Ryan was an outstanding corporate strategist who had seen the prospect of building a fully composite insurance company around the core of the Phoenix and Pelican offices. It was this logic which lay behind the absorption of Pelican by Phoenix in 1908, and the subsequent rapid acquisitions in the life and marine markets: Law Life in 1910 and Union Marine in 1911.[142]

If George Griffin Stonestreet was the 'first founder' of the Phoenix, the title of 'second founder' must go to Ryan. Changes in corporate structure of the kind envisaged by Ryan clearly require separate analysis, and this is provided in Chapter 5. However, the incorporation of new companies also brought the entry of new personalities. With these acquisitions came sudden waves of new manpower washing on to the Board. Thus, upon the accommodation with Pelican on 1 January 1908, the Phoenix Board

[141] See vol. I, pp. 614–15. [142] See below, pp. 331–40, 343–57.

increased in number from fifteen to twenty-one and, upon the merger with Law Life in 1910, to 25, the maximum permitted under the company's articles.[143]

The detachment drafted in from Pelican was considerable, both in numbers and in potency. True to Ryan's interest in legal capacity, it included one judge and two solicitors, as well as a fellow actuary, but there was also another antiquarian peer, a retired politician of considerable stature and an industrialist of outstanding wealth and achievement.

The judge, the Hon. Judge Bompas, KC had been originally a director of the British Empire, then of Pelican; he was advanced in years, died in 1909 and exerted little influence on the Phoenix.[144] The same was not true of the solicitors. Alexander Travers Hawes JP of Baker, Baker and Hawes had been with Pelican since 1901 and remained with Phoenix until his death in 1924. He added to his Phoenix seat, directorships in Brunner Mond, the Castner-Kellner Alkali Company and the Holborn Viaduct Land Co. These were significant companies and Hawes was a man of substance. Probably, however, his legal colleague, John Tryon of Saltwell, Tryon and Saltwell had more direct impact on the company. Tryon was a man of cheerful disposition but sharp mind. He became director of the British Empire in 1902, as result of a personal invitation from Ryan, and he stayed with Phoenix the rest of his long life, dying in 1941. He remained lucid into his ninety-second year, but he was at the height of his powers in the 1900s and 1910s. He, too, added directorships to his Phoenix place, but not such distinguished ones as Hawes: Tryon's were in the Earl of Dudley's Baggeridge Colliery and the Metropolitan Industrial Dwellings Co., both for the period 1918–25. Tryon brought a freshness of vision to problems, cutting through complexities with an uncluttered good sense.

The actuary in the detachment was James Sorley, who had been general manager of the Pelican from September 1895 to July 1903. Sorley had presided over the revived Pelican of the 1890s,[145] and was rewarded, unusually, with a Board seat when Ryan took over the chief executive role in 1903. He served as Phoenix director 1908–24. The antiquarian was the Rt Hon. Viscount Dillon (1908–32).[146] The actuary was an understandable choice for director of an insurance company, but this antiquarian was a very odd one. Dillon was an Irish landowner with huge estates in Roscommon and a scholar-collector of great eminence and fiery temper.

[143] Average Board attendance, in the half-year before the Phoenix–Pelican accord was eleven directors; in the half-year after, the figure was sixteen.

[144] Phoenix Directors' Minutes, 28, p. 406, 10 March 1909. [145] See vol. 1, pp. 611–15.

[146] Harry Dillon-Lee, 17th Viscount, succeeded to the title 1892.

Plate 1.10 Ditchley Hall.

In 1899, Dillon sold 90,000 acres of Mayo and Roscommon – which maintained 4,000 tenants to whom he had been a humane landlord – to the Congested Districts Board, in order to concentrate his attention upon his great house in Oxfordshire, at Ditchley Park. More accurately, it was to concentrate upon his great passion, which was in the Tower of London, and easily reached by train from Ditchley. A dozen years of military service in the Rifle Brigade (1862–74) had left Dillon with an abiding interest in uniforms and, by extension, the history of arms and armour and of medieval costume. On these subjects he became a world authority. He was curator of the Tower of London Armouries 1892–1913, a founding Fellow of the British Academy from 1902 and received an Honorary DCL from Oxford in 1913.[147] The antiquarian theme was so pronounced in Dillon's interest that Lady Dillon even laid out the gardens at Ditchley in armorial shapes and heraldic colours.

Where Avebury was a part-time scholar, if a prolific one, Dillon was a professional. He became an expert on armour by dismantling the pieces in the Tower and wearing them; he wrote on tournaments, military equipment and the soldier's life in periodicals ranging from *Archaeologica* to the *Boy's Own Paper*, and he answered every proper inquiry to the Tower in his own longhand. He was also a formidable eccentric, insisting on travelling third class (but reserving his seat with a distinctive walking stick, left on the train), spurning lunch for tea and biscuits in the local Aerated Bread Company shop and covering the distance from Padding-

[147] He was also president of the Royal Archaeological Institute 1892–8; president of the Society of Antiquaries,1897–1904; chairman of the Trustees of the National Portrait Gallery, 1894–1928; Trustee of the British Museum, 1905–32; and Trustee of the Wallace Collection, 1918–31.

Plate 1.11 Lord Dillon.

ton to the Tower and back on foot.[148] But all this in its way is of a piece. The peculiarity is that such a man should also be a director of a major City institution. Of course, by 1910 the Phoenix Board contained a distinctive minority of scholars – Avebury, Treherne, Dillon and the constitutional lawyer, Sir William Anson[149] – and there was almost a mafia of antiquarians. Perhaps the Phoenix Board relished their analytical skills. Or it may be that Ryan liked them: he listed among his own pastimes, antiquities and clocks and was as keen an archaeologist as he was golfer. Certainly, Dillon was clever, thorough, lion-hearted and did not suffer fools at all.

Nevertheless, perhaps in all respects other than this, he sat particularly oddly with another Pelican peer brought across in 1908 – the Rt Hon.

[148] 'Viscount Dillon, 1844–1932', *Proceedings of the British Academy*, 18 (1932).
[149] See below, pp. 51–3.

Lord Winterstoke (1908–11). Where Dillon was the idiosyncratic magnate-democrat, Winterstoke was one of the late nineteenth-century's most successful capitalist entrepreneurs. For Winterstoke was W. H. Wills of the Bristol tobacco dynasty and he was perhaps the most powerful influence on its fortunes.[150] Educated at Mill Hill and University College, London, William Wills was prevented by illness from becoming a lawyer, and instead joined the family firm in 1846. A third-generation product of this Congregationalist family of tobacco merchants, W. H. Wills took over direct management of the business 1865–80, and, then, as chairman, maintained a pervasive influence on policy until his death in 1911. He established the Wills brand name during the period of consumer expansion in the 1870s and introduced the first Wills cigarette, which was hand-made, in 1871. When his nephews took over management after 1880, he pressed them to gain exclusive control of the Bonsack cigarette-making machine in 1883, and must take part of the credit for the introduction of the mass-produced 'Woodbine', penny-a-packet, cigarette in 1888. The resulting impact upon the cigarette trade made personal, family and commercial fortunes; and William's own annual income went up from a fairly serious £50,000 in 1894 to a very serious £200,000 in 1901.

In that year, it became necessary to protect such wealth, and the British market, from an attempted invasion by the American Tobacco Company. Wills led thirteen British firms in a counter-offensive which took the form of the Imperial Tobacco Company. Of its £12 million total capital, the Wills share was £7 million, and W. H. Wills was its chairman 1901–11. Unlike Dillon, Lord Winterstoke rather enjoyed luxury, and lived in some style at Combe Lodge, Blagdon, and on his much-prized motor yacht, *Sabrina*.[151]

Outranking even these unusual men in stature, however, was the last of the Pelican directors who chose to convert to Phoenix, the Rt Hon. Lord George Hamilton, statesman (1908–25). Lord George, Harrovian and third son of the Duke of Abercorn,[152] entered the Commons as Tory MP for the County of Middlesex in 1868 at the age of twenty-three, and then

[150] William Henry Wills, Lord Winterstoke of Blagdon (1830–1911), baronet 1892, peer 1905. Liberal MP for Coventry 1880–95; then for Bristol East, 1895–1900. Estate at January 1911, £2,548,210.

[151] See B. W. Alford in the *Dictionary of Business Biography*, vol. v, ed. D. J. Jeremy (London, 1986), pp. 842–5.

[152] This was the 10th Earl and 1st Duke, twice viceroy of Ireland and a major figure in Victorian high society. He was married to the daughter of Earl Russell, and the pair made 'the handsomest and most distinguished couple of their time' *The Times*, obituary, 23 September 1927.

Plate 1.12 'Spy's' view of Lord George Hamilton in 1879.

continued to represent the Ealing Division of Middlesex until 1906. A favourite of Disraeli, and one of the Young Turks promoted by him, Lord George made an early reputation for fierce parliamentary attacks upon Gladstone, and was tipped as a possible future leader of the Conservative Party.

This promise was never fully made good. Nevertheless, Hamilton's political career was that of a distinguished second string. Disraeli made him Under-Secretary of State for India in 1874, and he thus graduated to the Treasury Bench at the age of twenty-nine. The Prime Minister's first offer had been the under-secretaryship for Foreign Affairs but Lord George had owned up to being 'doubtful of his French'; he accepted the India job on the assurance that 'there would be no necessity of speaking either Hindustani or Persian'.[153] Later in 1885 he became a reforming First Lord of the Admiralty in the Salisbury government and in 1889 introduced the Naval Defence Act, the first and decisive step in modern-

[153] *Ibid.*

ising the Royal Navy for the arms race of the pre-1914 era, and the first definition of the 'two-power standard'.[154] His final government post, in the Salisbury and Balfour administrations, was that of Secretary of State for India, 1895–1903,[155] although he also chaired the very important Royal Commission upon the Poor Law and Unemployment of 1905–9. For thirty years no Tory government was formed in which Hamilton did not occupy a prominent position. Throughout much of his time as a cabinet minister, Hamilton was also a director of the Pelican (1885-1908), and, after his withdrawal from politics, he became its deputy chairman in 1907.

Once Pelican was subsumed in Phoenix in 1908, Hamilton became the chairman of the new composite, and remained so until 1920. He had not been the first choice. That had fallen upon Sir John Gorst, his superior as chairman of the Pelican. But Gorst, a Tory MP for all but seven years of the four decades 1866–1906, and the brilliant organiser of the party in the period 1868–80,[156] was seventy-three years old by 1908 and had had his fill of public and business life.[157] So Pelican's second most senior Tory took the chairmanship of the revamped Phoenix, with the trusty Bristow Bovill as his deputy. Phoenix was by no means Hamilton's only commercial interest. He also held directorships in banking institutions (the Chartered Bank of India; the Bank of Australia), and in property companies (the American Freehold Land Co.; the Union Surplus Lands Co.), and in many of the London railways (the Metropolitan, the Underground Electric, the Great Northern, Piccadilly and Brompton, the Central London, and the Whitechapel and Bow). By 1912, he was chairman also of the Metropolitan District Railway and of the London Underground Electric Railway.[158]

All this boardroom activity seems to have been a matter as much of

[154] This was the crucial doctrine by which the Royal Navy was required to be equal in strength to the combined fleets of the next two most powerful maritime nations.

[155] He resigned, along with the Chancellor of the Exchequer, Ritchie, over Joseph Chamberlain's campaign for Tariff Reform and the threat that it represented to Free Trade views like his own. However, the Prime Minister, Balfour, told neither of the Free Traders that he already had the resignation of Colonial Secretary Chamberlain in his pocket. His stint at the India Office, through a difficult period of drought and famine, also established a record for duration.

[156] Gorst was also a member of Lord Randolph Churchill's 'Fourth Party' of 1880–5, and Solicitor-General, 1885–6.

[157] Three other Pelican directors also declined the translation: Messrs Phillips, Young and Pleydell-Bouverie. The last was the Hon. Seymour Pleydell-Bouverie, cousin of Stuart, who had been a Pelican director since 1887. He was in poor health from pneumonia in 1907 and retired on that ground; nevertheless he survived until 1927.

[158] His brother, Lord Claud Hamilton, was chairman of the Great Eastern Railway Company.

necessity as of choice. While in office, Hamilton had 'suddenly lost the larger part of my private fortune by the failure of a bank' and resolved that 'whenever I was released from official work, I would make strenuous efforts to rehabilitate my financial position'.[159] To tide him over, he was voted in 1900 a pension in regard to his twenty years' service as a cabinet minister.[160] This attracted much criticism, which in turn drew from Hamilton in 1914, the statement about 'rehabilitation' which provides the clue to his financial strategy. Generally, his strenuous efforts were appreciated by the boards which he graced.

Hamilton was a man of charm and wit, a polished speaker with a winning voice, the accomplishments which had so impressed Disraeli. As an administrator he was composed and thorough, wholly conscientious but sound rather than brilliant. His civilised mildness of manner in the end kept him in the second rank. His obituarist in *The Times* wrote, 'his own political imagination was not to be inflamed, and he had neither the will, nor the power to inflame the imagination of others'.[161] This judgement was delivered in the political sphere, but it could easily be extended to others. Hamilton was a smooth chairman but no great leader of men.

In chairing the Phoenix down to 1914, he had to cope with one last major influx of directors from outside.[162] These were the four recruits brought in by the Phoenix takeover of Law Life in 1910. The newcomers were J. S. Beale (1910–12), W. R. Malcolm (1910–23), F. (later Sir Francis) Fladgate (1910–37), and Sir William Anson (1910–14). Three of these appointments were interesting. Malcolm was a classical scholar who had a successful career in the Civil Service before becoming a director and senior partner in Coutts and Co. (also holding directorships in two utility companies, Westgate Gas and Westgate Water); he had been a director of Law Life since 1875.[163] Fladgate, who was another solicitor by training, had even more powerful interests in public utilities, but in his case in the

159 Cited by the *Liverpool Courier*, 21 March 1923.

160 He gave this up in 1923, after it had paid him £44,206 over the period since 1900. At this time there was in the Commons a vociferous socialist campaign against capitalist excess.

161 *The Times*, 23 September 1927.

162 Also, in 1908, the reorganised Phoenix created a West End Board to handle the fire and accident business generated through the company's Charing Cross office. Its membership was heavily hyphenated: Maj. the Hon. Charles Strathavon-Heathcote-Drummond-Wiloughby, the Hon. Michael H. Hicks-Beach and George Cornwallis-West. Phoenix Directors' Minutes 28, p. 262, 8 July 1908. Bernard Johnson of Cluttons was added to this Board in 1912 after the departure, through death, of Ralph Clutton from the main Board in July 1912. His removal brought a further individual influx to the main Board as Helenus Robertson was brought in from Union Marine to replace him. But Robertson was the only borrowing from Union Marine before the First World War.

163 He also left a substantial estate of £273,390 net in 1928.

Plate 1.13 Hamilton in 1907, safe from the cartoonist's pen.

field of electricity generation; he had been a director of Law Life since 1888. However, he was also an early director of the Charing Cross, West End and City Electricity Supply Co., at a particularly sensitive point in the development of the generating industry. Electrification of suburban tramway and railway services between 1904 and 1910 produced important additions to demand, which previously had been restricted almost entirely to lighting needs, and thus solved the problem of under-utilised plant from which the industry suffered in its early stages. Fladgate was one of the pioneers of the electricity industry in this period. When nine London generating companies joined forces in 1920 to form the London Power Co., Fladgate became its first chairman and was a major force in the construction by this company of the Battersea Power Station.[164]

The final addition to the Board to come through corporate acquisition in the pre-1914 era had eminence of quite a different kind. This was Sir William Reynell Anson, don, constitutional lawyer, and politician. Anson was MP for Oxford University 1899–1905 and, as parliamentary secretary

[164] He was knighted for public services in the King's Birthday Honours List of June 1932.

Plate 1.14 Sir Francis Fladgate.

to the Board of Education 1902–5, saw in the Balfour Act which, at long last, launched the provision of state secondary education in Britain.[165] However, Anson was also an outstanding scholar, the leading constitutionalist of his day and an innovating teacher of English law at Oxford; he was Warden of All Soul's from 1881 and instrumental in its late nineteenth-century regeneration. Like his Board colleague, Avebury, Anson too had been a vice-chancellor of a university, in his case, Oxford, in 1898. There cannot have been many boards of directors in 1910 with two former heads of universities among their number. Though 'precise and orderly in habits of mind, he was completely free from pedantry . . . a man of learning but also a man of affairs'.[166] He was also a man of strong views but was good at expressing them courteously. He must have made good company for Avebury and Dillon.

The Phoenix Board which resulted around 1910 was very different

[165] Anson's predecessor at the Education Department, who drafted the Bill in 1901, was Gorst. See p. 50 above.

[166] *Dictionary of National Biography*, Twentieth Century (Oxford, 1927), 1919–21, pp. 8–10.

from that of 1880. At the earlier date Lubbock was the only member of clear eminence and Byng the only one with aristocratic connection. By 1910, Avebury, Admiral Lucas, Dillon, Hamilton, Winterstoke, Anson and Fladgate were all leaders in their various and very different fields, and some ten directors, nearly half the Board, could boast title or aristocratic links. There were other significant coteries also within the Board of 1910. No fewer than eight members had professional training in the law, surveying or actuarial science while three more were bankers. There was also the odd bond of scholarly interest which linked Avebury, Dillon, Treherne, Malcolm and Anson. Certainly, the Phoenix of the antebellum years was not short of brain power among its directors – some of them, quite literally, were among the shining intellects of their day. The range of ability too is impressive, from industry and commerce, through finance and the law, to the armed services and academe. There could not have been many circumstances that the Phoenix could encounter which one or other of these directors did not know something about.

To a certain degree, the newcomers were all Ryan's men. For the process which ended with his appointment as general manager of the Phoenix in January 1908 had been a protracted exercise in company acquisition, in which he had looked as carefully at the men to be acquired as at the assets.[167] And this remained true of his approach on both sides of 1908. However, some were more Ryan's men than others. Dillon had been with him at the British Empire since the 1890s; Hawes had joined Pelican in 1901, when it was already firmly in Ryan's sights; Tryon was invited by Ryan to join the British Empire in 1902, just before the merger with Pelican; and Sorley was a close actuarial colleague who had been Ryan's opposite number at Pelican during the negotiations of the mid-1900s. All told, some eleven members of the Board of 1910 had connections with the life assurance business, through British Empire or Pelican, before they had come to the Phoenix.

None of these connections guaranteed unanimity, however; and perhaps this was just as well. A test case was the major disaster of the San Francisco earthquake and fire of 1906. Of course, this occurred before the big Board reshuffle of 1908, but it did put pressure upon the new-style Phoenix directors with their professional and aristocratic connections. Moreover, the repercussions of San Francisco, and the policy choices they posed, endured long beyond 1908. The effect of the changes was clearly to provide voices able and willing to challenge the long-sustained authority of Avebury. Always 'repelled by the controversial or aggressive',

[167] See below, pp. 299–329.

Avebury in old age was given to still more emphatic outbreaks of prudence. Even before San Francisco, in the poor trading conditions of the early 1900s, Avebury wished to reduce the Phoenix dividend by 5 shillings; but, in 1905, his fellow Trustees took against him and he was outvoted.[168] After the earthquake, Avebury argued strongly that Phoenix should evacuate the Pacific Slope and 'felt strongly' that the dividend should be slashed by 10 shillings. Again, the elder statesman was outvoted: the Board would reduce the dividend by 5 shillings only and they would not come out of the earthquake zone.[169]

Neither aristocratic nor even family connection held: the Hon. Edwin Portman and Avebury's brother, Edgar Lubbock, were united in opposing 'the hasty action' of withdrawal. In a placatory move, Bovill and the newly established executive officials, with whom the long-practised 'working director' seemed naturally to side, agreed that the Phoenix might retire from the transatlantic danger area, but only if agreement on a satisfactory 'earthquake clause' was not forthcoming among the British offices. Then the solicitor G. G. T. Treherne, a director of only three years' standing, proposed the amendment which stopped Avebury and defined the line against withdrawal.[170]

The interaction of personalities among old and new types of director was already crucial to the policy balance of the Phoenix by the early 1900s. The advent of the strong cohort from Pelican in 1908 did not much change this. Avebury remained in a minority on the American issue and the inability of the conservatives to propose an alternative to the large transatlantic trade ensured that, for better or worse, Phoenix stayed where it was. It is highly characteristic of Avebury that he may have been right to be prudent about America but lacked the commercial vision to create a replacement strategy capable of attracting directors less conservative than himself. This makes it especially peculiar that the one ally whom he did attract from among the Pelican men was the great entrepreneur Lord Winterstoke. In autumn 1908, the two noble lords dissented from the communal Board decision to maintain the business activity of the new composite company in all foreign markets, which effectively meant all the USA. However, it does not seem that Winterstoke was any more able than Avebury to propose an effective alternative to a heavy stake in the American market. And thus the remainder of the enlarged Board remained unconvinced.[171]

[168] Trustees' Minutes, 22 February 1905.
[169] Phoenix Directors' Minutes, 28, pp. 51–2, 13 March 1907.
[170] *Ibid.*, p. 72, 29 May 1907. For a detailed discussion of these events, see below, pp. 280–2.
[171] *Ibid.*, pp. 313–14, 7 October 1908.

One reflection of the eminence of this group of men was the care they took to have pictures made of themselves and some of their forebears in the immediate pre-war years. Not without presumption, and in early 1909, shortly after his arrival, Winterstoke began the game by presenting an engraving (not the original) of a portrait (of himself) to the Company ('to hang in the Boardroom').[172] Next, they heard in May 1910 that a 1782 portrait of John Coope I was to be auctioned at Christie's. Avebury directed that Phoenix should bid for it – but, cautious as ever, stipulated that they should not go above £100. Fortunately, the company secured it for 32 guineas (and it is reproduced on p. 24 of volume I). Then Admiral Lucas presented the portrait – fittingly, for this unpretentious individual, it was of someone else – of the Hon. James Byng to the Board. This seemed to remind them that Avebury had sat on the Pelican Board for fifty-two years and on the Phoenix one for forty-five years. Stung by the embarrassing lack of roundness in these numbers into the realisation that they should have acted earlier, the directors decided, on the same day, to commission a painting of the current Father of the Society.[173] Sir Hubert von Herkorner CVO painted it; and it was received by the Board 'with unqualified satisfaction', and at a cost of £630, rather more than the £100 set upon the head of John Coope, at the end of June 1911. It is indeed very distinguished.[174] Thereupon, Sir Arthur Lucas presented a portrait of his uncle, C. T. Lucas, director 1872–95. The Board may have been reminded by the contrast in quality in the two pictures – though this is unlikely – that Herkoner, perhaps the outstanding portraitist of his day, had, around 1895, also painted the Board's other vice-chancellor: the portrait of Sir William Anson was hung in the Hall of All Soul's.

Such pictorial activity perhaps presaged the end of lives. Certainly, the history of the Phoenix Board in the era 1870–1914 ended as it began, with an outbreak of mortality. Winterstoke died at the start of 1911 then, in a rush, Ralph Clutton in July 1912, Avebury in May 1913,[175] Anson in June 1914 and Admiral Lucas, perhaps having had enough of wars, on 7 August 1914. In addition, Bristow Bovill was taken seriously ill in April 1914 and Baxendale was absent from Board meetings from May to November through illness.

The only replacements of these losses came late in the period. Both

[172] *Ibid.*, 28, p. 397, 24 February 1909.

[173] *Ibid.*, 29, p. 385, 29 March 1911.

[174] *Ibid.*, p. 463, 26 July 1911; it is reproduced in vol. I, p. 680. The bargain portrait of John Coope I is in *ibid.*, p. 24.

[175] In his memory, Phoenix helped endow a scholarship at London University, and his bank marked his passing by amalgamating with Coutts & Co. *Ibid.*, 30, p. 427, 26 November 1913; *Ibid.*, 31, p. 78; 22 July 1914.

Plate 1.15 Sir Joseph White Todd.

were eminent. Sir Helenus Robertson, chairman of Union Marine and a Liverpool shipowner of weight, joined the Phoenix Board in 1912. And Sir Joseph White Todd, who had begun as a merchant banker in Havana in the 1870s and was by the 1910s chairman of the Central Argentine Railway Co., followed in the next year. He was sought out by Ryan for his considerable knowledge of Latin America in general and of the region's railways in particular, and was invited to join the Board as replacement for Avebury late in 1913 (–1926).[176] Ryan was definitely in quest of influence in Argentina and looked at three other contenders at least before settling on White Todd. Lord George Hamilton found him 'a fine specimen of a successful merchant, quick, intelligent, with great confidence in himself (and) . . . also an exceptionally good linguist'.[177]

[176] He was also a director of the Buenos Aires Western Railway and a member of the International Sugar Committee. He had made one fortune as a merchant banker in Havana by 1885, when he was 41 years of age.

[177] Hamilton to Ryan, 30 October 1913. One remembers, however, Lord George's diffidence about accepting his first government post at the Foreign Office for lack of French.

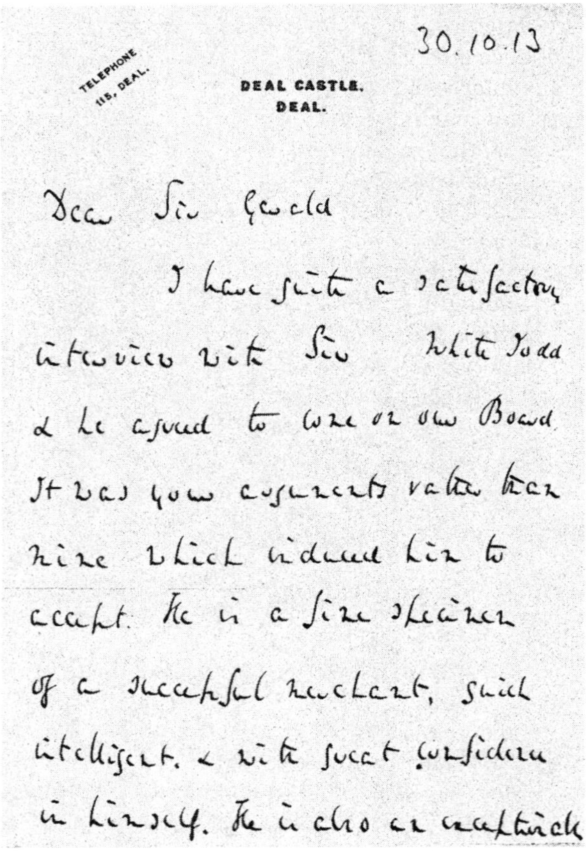

30.10.13

TELEPHONE 115, DEAL.

DEAL CASTLE.
DEAL.

Plate 1.16 Hamilton appraises White Todd.

These were strong appointments, well in the new tradition, but they came at the end of an era, and really belonged to the next.

On the face of it, all of these directors, and all of the Phoenix Boards before 1914, were non-executive. Guernsey and Ryan attended Board meetings but were not directors. Lord George Hamilton was the first permanent chairman of the Phoenix – previously the position had rotated among senior directors – but he was not a full-time executive, however involved he was in company affairs. On the other hand, Deputy Chairman Bristow Bovill (referred to at the time as a 'working director') was rarely absent from the office. And the Phoenix's committee system –

which long pre-dated 1908, but was reorganised into an array of fire, life, accident and finance groups at that time – brought selected directors into the office on a regular weekly cycle. This ensured that the directors who attended could not avoid being closely aware of the current detail of business. Certainly, they appear immune from one contemporary criticism that non-executive directors 'do not get sufficient daily contact with the business to learn it'.[178] Directors, usually the more energetic members of the Board, who participated in committee systems like that maintained by the Phoenix were properly neither executive nor non-executive. There was a group, including Hamilton and Bovill, within the Phoenix of the 1900s which is perhaps best described as semi-executive. Whether he had the title or not, however, Ryan clearly represented the shape of things to come: he was a very substantial precursor of modern executive power.

6. THE SHAPE OF THE COMPANY: FROM DEED OF SETTLEMENT TO LIMITED LIABILITY

The historic Phoenix was not a limited company but an extended partnership operating under a Deed of Settlement.[179] The third edition of the Deed was dated 1836 and declared that the company should continue from the 1st January of that year for 100 years. This document defined the rights and responsibilities of the shareholders and made provision for the investment of the company's funds, for extending its powers and for the general management of its affairs.

Among the many aspects of company life that the Deed did not provide for were the limitation of shareholder liability and the disclosure of financial information. In a world becoming increasingly complex, dangerous and curious, these omissions alone were likely to assure that the 1836 Deed did not fulfil its centenarian ambitions. The directors in 1802 had congratulated themselves that the Phoenix had been 'born free', that it had escaped the trammels of the Royal Charter and secured its liberty by choosing the Deed of Settlement as its constitutional vehicle. By the late century, however, this freedom was beginning to look a little peculiar, for, over a period of 113 years, it had permitted the Phoenix to avoid the publication of any accounts of revenue or expenditure, capital or reserves. The only piece of detail about itself that the company had vouchsafed to

178 Eldridge Johnson of the Victor Talking Machine Co. to A. C. Clark of the Gramophone Co., 23 February 1916, quoted in S. P. Martland, 'A Business History of the Gramophone Co., 1897–1918' (unpubl. Ph.D. thesis, University of Cambridge, 1992).

179 See vol. I, pp. 69–72, 73–7, 122.

the public (or to its proprietors, in any more than a general sense) was the total amount paid out in losses since the foundation of 1782. Until the 1890s, the strength and capacity of the Phoenix might be guessed at, but it could not be known. Although the Phoenix did business like a large public company, it was technically little more than a wealthy private partnership. Availing itself of the secrecy which this status commanded, it remained very tight-lipped, even with its partners, about the facts of its business life.

By the 1870s, there were those among the shareholders who were beginning to get uneasy on this score. Non-disclosure was, of course, linked with unlimited liability, since, if shareholders were not told enough about the strength of the company, they could fear the worst about the weakness for which they might be liable. Late in 1872, shareholder pressure was sufficient for the Trustees to request the company solicitor to prepare for Counsel's attention 'a proposition on limiting the personal liabilities of the Shareholders.'[180] The issue then came up at every meeting of the Trustees between 1 January and 12 February 1873, six sessions in all, and it subsided again only when Counsel advised against tampering with the Deed. Probably also, Counsel allayed the Trustees' concern 'as to the extent to which Resolutions of the Proprietors can modify the constitution of the Company'.[181] Here it seems as if the Board and Trustees successfully fought off an exercise in shareholder power aimed at knowing more and risking less. The defeated proprietors can scarcely have been reassured by an amendment to the Deed in 1875 which halved the number of general meetings of the company from four to two per year.[182]

But another attempt, in 1880, involving a famous Phoenix name and a large block of shares, emphasised that the shareholders' concern was an enduring one. The Hodgson brothers, John and William, of Gilston Park, relatives of Phoenix directors K. D. Hodgson and R. K. Hodgson, and substantial proprietors in their own right, were not easily shrugged off. They succeeded in achieving an audience with Octavius Coope in which they suggested again that the Phoenix 'should be registered under the Limited Liability Act'. In the event, however, Counsel's opinion of 1872 saved the Board once more: they wrote to John, enclosing the learned argument. Hodgson went quiet.[183]

However, the rebels were actually more in tune with the times than was the Board. By the 1890s some of the directors and Trustees were them-

[180] Trustees' Minutes, 28 November, 5 December 1872. [181] *Ibid.*, 1 January 1873.
[182] Directors' Minutes, W22, p. 49, 29 September 1875.
[183] *Ibid.*, X23, p. 64, 29 September 1880.

selves beginning to realise this, and when Sir John Lubbock joined their number in 1894, policy began to shift. It is likely that Lubbock was more concerned with two issues – 'inconvenient legislation' currently before Parliament which might prejudice 'dealing with the Company's investments, in the event of the death of one of the Trustees', and the modernisation of the capital structure of the Phoenix – rather than with the fears preoccupying the shareholders.[184] But any major attempt to tidy the constitution was likely to affect these matters as well. Lubbock virtually admitted as much when he told the Board that he wanted, 'at the first convenient opportunity to move for a committee to consider the desireableness of altering the Company's Deed of Settlement *so as to bring it in accord with modern legislation*'.[185] Moreover, the committee was intended to study the desirability of securing an Act of Parliament, 'authorizing the alteration of the Company's Deed of Settlement *in various particulars affecting its capital and liability*'.[186]

Lubbock duly obtained his committee – consisting of himself, Bovill, Byng, Lucas, Ponsonby, Portman and Dudley Smith – and it produced a draft bill 'for an Act annulling the Deed of Settlement, making new laws, the extension and definition of the objects of the Company, the regulation and increase of capital, the substitution of new for existing capital and sub-division of capital . . . the liability of members.'[187] An Extraordinary General Meeting of Proprietors unanimously approved this formula on 6 February 1895, and by October the legislation was in place.[188]

Almost immediately, Lubbock used it to propose a subdivision of the Phoenix capital: in place of the old, unwieldy shares of £400 apiece with £40 paid, he suggested a more modern system of £50 shares with £5 paid. There would be 53,766 of these new shares instead of 6,722 of the old type. The effect of this was to change the dividend pattern from one where a £3 payment was made twice a year, with a bonus of 30 shillings for the first half-year and a bonus of £6 for the second half-year, a pattern of dividend and bonus which had been stable for the last decade, to one paying a much simpler yield of 35 shillings on the £5 share, split into one half-year payment of 12 shillings and another of 23 shillings. This level of yield lasted into the next century (see Table 1.3) Indeed, a pattern of distribution similar to this remained in force until Helenus Robertson, using an extension of Lubbock's logic, proposed a further division of shares in 1913.[189]

Shareholders can only have been gratified by the returns displayed in

[184] *Ibid.*, Z25, p. 469, 16 May 1894. [185] *Ibid.*, p. 457, 2 May 1894. My emphasis.
[186] *Ibid.*, p. 466, 9 May 1894. My emphasis. [187] *Ibid.*, 26, p. 41, 12 December 1894.
[188] *Ibid.*, pp. 67, 123, 13 March, 9 October 1895. [189] See below Section 10.

Table 1.3. *Phoenix shares, dividends and bonuses, 1870–1900*

Year	Payment date	Dividend	Bonus	Total % annual yield
1870/1–1873/4	Sept.	£3		22.50 on £40
	April	£3	£3	paid
1874/5	Sept.	£4 10s		30.00 on £40
	April	£3	£4 10s	paid
1875/6	Sept.	£3	£1 10s	45.00 on £40
	April	£3	£10 10s	paid
1876/7	Sept.	£3	£1 10s	48.75 on £40
	April	£3	£12	paid
1877/8	Sept.	£3		41.25 on £40
	April	£3	£10 10s	paid
1878/9	Sept.	£3	£3	52.50 on £40
	April	£3	£12	paid
1879/80	Sept.	£3	£1 10s	45.00 on £40
	April	£3	£10 10s	paid
1880/1–1881/2	Sept.	£3	£1 10s	37.50 on £40
	April	£3	£7 10s	paid
1882/3–1884/5	Sept.	£3	£1 10s	26.25 on £40
	April	£3	£3	paid
1885/6	Sept.	£3	£1 10s	30.00 on £40
	April	£3	£4 10s	paid
1886/7–1894/5	Sept.	£3	£1 10s	33.75 on £40
	April	£3	£6	paid
1895/6	Sept.	£3	£1 10s	34.25 on £5
	April	£1. 3s		paid
1896/7–1899/1900	Sept.	£0 12s		35.00 on £5
	April	£1 3s		paid

Table 1.3 overleaf, but until 1895 they had to guess at what had produced them. Lubbock may have been most interested in sorting out the Phoenix capital structure - and here the banker's expertise was instrumental in achieving a modern system - but the outcome of the Act which achieved this was also to reveal much more about the variables that generated Phoenix profits. Probably, the Phoenix shareholders had possessed no means of knowing that the company's total assets had amounted to £656,679 in 1850, grown to £1,021,425 by 1878 and reached £1,173,083

by 1884. Under the provisions of the 1895 Act, however, they had to be told that the reorganised paid-up capital was £268,880; that the General Reserve was set at £573,790; and that the Insurance Funds (standing security against unexpired risks and outstanding claims) stood at £605,000. Total assets were thus *publicly* established at £1,447,670 in 1895. However, the new Phoenix Act improved disclosure; it still did not supply limited liability.

According to George Hurren's *Phoenix Renascent*, this unveiling was greeted with 'general delight at the position of strength disclosed'.[190] In fact, of course, it is difficult to imagine the citizenry dancing in the streets at the news, though it is easy to sense the relief of the shareholders; and perhaps to detect a ripple of polite applause from informed parties in the City. The gain in knowledge and security from the disclosure of Phoenix's operating fundamentals must surely have outweighed any sentimental loss as the 1813 Act and the 1836 Deed ceased to be the constitutional keystones of the Phoenix and the 1895 Act took over this structural role.

Nevertheless, it remained true that the shareholders still lacked the protection of limited liability. No doubt, they had been reassured that the risks from which they needed protection were scarcely pressing, given the amplitude of the reserves that were now displayed to them. And, in any case, they did not have to wait much longer. In November 1901, Phoenix at last surrendered its final eighteenth-century characteristic and became incorporated under the Companies Acts as a venture with limited liability.

7. THE FUNDS OF THE PHOENIX: HOME AND FOREIGN INVESTMENT, 1870–1914

The half-century before 1914 was one of great activity in the investment affairs of the nation and great complexity in the investment affairs of insurance offices. For one thing, the most dependable long-term performers in the insurance portfolios – British government consols, loans to local authorities and mortgages on landed property – all underwent marked reductions in yields between 1870 and the end of the century. Consols were depressed between 1881 and 1888, and, after Chancellor Goschen's conversion of that year, worsened further to stand at a lowly 2.5% by 1896–8. Loans to local authorities, from which Phoenix, like many other offices, had drawn 5% and more in their heyday, sported a

[190] Hurren, *Phoenix Renascent*, p. 104.

median yield of under 3% by 1897. At the same time, the depression of agriculture, intensifying from about 1884, dragged down the price of land; this in turn sliced 25% off the value of rents in the century's last quarter and blasted much of the gilt off the mortgage market.[191]

On the other hand, the enormous expansion of the UK's overseas investment, in the golden age of Britain's role as an international creditor, opened new, if distant, vistas to the big institutional investors of the City. Deflected from tried and trusted remedies at home, they were forced in the quest for yield, to canvass prospects from which, in the past, they would have flinched as unsuitable to the high security and sober mood of their calling. Foreign railway bonds, overseas mortgages, loans to municipalities in far-off lands increasingly entered their books in the 1880s and 1890s, and then created major revisions in them in the 1900s and 1910s. There was a clear parallelism between the national investment patterns of the world's largest creditor economy and the investment patterns of the big insurance offices. By 1914, the UK boasted a total investment aggregate of about £12,000 million, of which a remarkable £4,000 million was placed overseas. Total insurance funds, concentrated in over 100 institutions, were pressing up to the £500 million mark, and thus represented about 5% of UK total investment. Perhaps as much as 30–40% of insurance investment was also foreign investment by the time of the First World War.[192]

These new linkages cut many ways. If the more adventurous among City investors still regarded insurance investment in the 1910s as a 'laughing stock' for its conservatism,[193] it was undoubtedly true that the enforced purchase of foreign assets had made institutional investment strategies far less conservative than they had been. In this respect, foreign governments had added their own measure of force to the pressures exerted by low UK yields. They increasingly insisted – and the US government insisted most stringently – that foreign insurers should maintain 'guarantees' or deposits of investments *within* their export markets, as proof of their ability to meet claims, and often that they hold these sureties in the assets of the host countries.[194] This official requirement for security pushed British insurers willy-nilly into a global diversification of their portfolios. However, such far-flung connections also meant that any major hiatus in the international investment markets – such as the Baring

[191] There is a particularly expert summary of these trends in Supple, *Royal Exchange Assurance*, pp. 330–48.

[192] *Ibid.*, p. 346.

[193] See Roger Ryan, 'Insurance Investment before 1914', paper presented to the History Forum of the Chartered Insurance Institute, 25 April 1988.

[194] See Chapter 2.

Crisis, which commenced with the repudiation of an Argentinian government loan in 1890, and almost felled Britain's largest merchant bank – would be transmitted back into the accounts of those responsible for the fire policies and life cover of the British middle classes.

Nevertheless, the pattern of yields on insurance investments between 1860 and 1900 left few other options. The average yield hovered around 4.5% in the early 1870s but soon began to slide, reaching 4.2% around 1885, then collapsing to 4.0% by 1890, and further still to 3.76% by 1900. Worse, this was the yield on *accumulated* investment, first purchased years back; that on new investment would have been about 0.5% below these levels.[195]

Such lean returns made the insurance offices very choosy as to which investment prospects they accepted, very unfriendly to the early repayment of loans contracted at higher rates, and very anxious to find investments offering higher rewards.

The offices also acted in the late nineteenth century under the influence of the investment conventions defined by the great actuary, A. H. Bailey.[196] His controlling view was that, in order to effectively guarantee the security of policies, the offices should not hold securities, the value of which fluctuated widely. This advice pointed a way towards mortgages and local loans, and, later, as yields continued to fall, Bailey conceded entry to the menu for debentures, preference shares and bonds. If these same categories of investment could be found abroad, so much the better, because yields were higher there. British government securities, by contrast, were frowned upon because, being mostly undated before 1914, their capital value did vary widely with the currents in the money markets. The performance of home gilts in the twenty years before 1914 was to prove the truth of this warning.

For the Phoenix this balance of forces produced an investment response which split into two distinct phases: a period of selectivity and concentration upon return between 1870 and 1900 and a period of growing interest in volume and diversification between 1900 and 1914. The first was associated with an inclination towards home investment, the second with a growing tilt towards overseas investment. And of course this pattern fits that of the international business cycle which saw a strong upswing from around the middle 1890s.

[195] That is, the marginal yield. See Supple, *Royal Exchange Assurance*, p. 334.

[196] A. H. Bailey, 'On the Principles on which the Funds of Life Assurance Societies should be Invested', *Assurance Magazine*, 10 (1861).

Phoenix investment patterns 1870–1900

Under the circumstances of the Great Depression of 1873–96, conventional mortgage business was particularly unappealing. Phoenix certainly swung hard away from it; the contraction in the share of the company's portfolio given to this line was the strongest downward trend in the Phoenix funds, particularly in the 1880s (see Table 1.4). Between 1875 and 1880 the Trustees accepted some £1.4 million in mortgages, between 1881 and 1895 only just over £127,000. Especially marked was the avoidance of the classic aristocratic mortgages on big estates and these were being refused even in the mid-1870s: thus Phoenix declined £125,000 on the Grosvenor estates in 1872 and £45,000 on Col. Palmer's Nazing Park in 1873, as well as £14,000 on Cudworth Hall, near Banbury in 1875.[197]

The business that was accepted on broad acres and great houses did not fare well, nor increase the appetite for more. In the early 1870s, Phoenix participated in a famous mortgage for Lord Southampton, and by December 1872, held £67,500 of a total £200,000 first charge on his property. A dozen years later, the office was approached by Henry Beauclerk, now in straitened circumstances and soliciting aid on the grounds that he had been instrumental in introducing the Southampton business to Phoenix. The tactic misfired, for poor Beauclerk had fallen not only upon hard times but also upon poor information. Phoenix, with some tartness, set him straight: 'A large portion of the Southampton estate having been sold, and the insurance withdrawn from this office, together with the severe loss of nearly £20,000 sustained by the burning of his lordship's mansion at Whittlebury...' composed a list of falling rentals, lost business and fire damage which failed to excite the Board's charity.[198]

In 1887, Lord Granville's loan proved less damaging but quite sufficiently irritating. This noble lord could repay; but that, in 1887, was the trouble. Granville wanted to extinguish the outstanding balance of £30,000 on his mansion in Carlton House Terrace; Phoenix did not want him to do so because at this time, they could not reinvest the proceeds at more than a paltry 3.5%. The Trustees demanded compensation for the 1% on capital which they would lose over the coming two

[197] But Phoenix also declined many other things at similar times, among them £50,000 at the tempting price of 5% on a Darlington stone quarry in 1872, £40,000 on a Glasgow office project, and £50,000 on the borough rates of Batley and Dewsbury, both in 1873, and £20,000 on a cotton mill at Ashton in 1875. Trustees' Minutes, 20 June, 4 July 1872; *ibid.*, 17 July, 14 August, 16 October 1873; 14 January, 22 July 1875.

[198] *Ibid.*, 22 May 1884.

years or provision of alternative securities for their purchase at 4.5% yield. The state of the market was sufficient for it to be worth Granville's while to offer 0.5% compensation; and both parties settled for this.[199]

Even when a conventional aristocratic mortgage was accepted, as one was at the late date of 1890, no doubt because it offered the untypically high rate of 4.5%, the transaction ran into trouble. In March 1890, Lord Grimston secured a £10,000 loan on his mansion and estate at St Albans;[200] but, by March 1893, after much pressing, he had succeeded in getting the rate reduced to 3.75%. Only a promise to direct all his insurance business Phoenix's way eased the office's retreat in an increasingly soggy market.[201]

But of course not all mortgage business was of such a traditional type. Even before 1870, Phoenix, along with other offices, had accepted mortgages as a way of extending credit to industrial concerns, harbour schemes, warehouse interests and housing developments, and these and many other similar projects continued to appear in the mortgage lists after 1870. The heading 'mortgages and title deeds' is not as stuffy as may be sometimes assumed; plenty of enterprise could be concealed behind this unpromising exterior.

The Phoenix Trustees composed the investment committee of the late nineteenth-century Phoenix and they considered, and rejected, many proposals of this type in the 1870s, before investment activity sank to low levels in the 1880s and 1890s. Clearly not everything which Phoenix acquired by way of new investment was recorded by the Trustees: the rebuilding of mortgages in the first half of the 1890s for instance provokes only silence from their Minutes. But they did record the great majority of investment decisions, and, for the most part, there is a reassuring tally between their entries in the Minutes and the behaviour of the numbers in the Ledgers. The profile of acceptances and rejections by the Trustees, therefore, should provide a fair guide to the company's investment stance (see Table 1.4).

The pattern which emerges from the acceptance of new investments is quite strong. There are two surges of marked activity, in 1875–81 and 1889–91, but conspicuously low levels of acquisitions for the portfolio in the periods 1883–8 and 1892–5. In the phases of strong acquisition, there is quite a marked tendency towards house, property and mortgages, but also a definite tendency towards industrial and commercial assets (each category scored more than 50% of acquisitions by value in four of the ten high-spending years). The 49.5% share of mortgages in the overall total of

[199] *Ibid.*, 2 June 1887. [200] Directors' Minutes, Z 25, p. 85, 5 March 1890.
[201] Trustees' Minutes, 9 March 1893.

Table 1.4. *New investments accepted by the Trustees: % by type of all acceptances, 1875–95*

	Local authority loans on rates, etc.	House, property and mortages	Railways	Docks & canals	Warehouses	Industrial & commercial	Total £
1875	–	100.0	–	–	–	–	135,000
1876	42.7	38.4	–	–	–	18.8	265,500
1877	29.6	63.0	–	6.7	0.7	–	1,485,000
1878	16.6	54.7	–	–	–	28.8	302,100
1879	–	69.1	–	–	–	29.5	71,200
1880	–	–	–	–	100.0	–	12,000
1881	4.0	8.7	–	10.2	–	78.9	250,800
1882	–	33.0	–	–	–	67.0	45,000
1883	–	100.0	–	–	–	–	11,000
1884	–	–	–	–	–	–	0
1885	–	–	–	100.0	–	–	15,000
1886	–	–	100.0	–	–	–	25,000
1887	–	–	100.0	–	–	–	40,000
1888	–	–	100.0	–	–	–	35,000
1889	83.0[a]	–	17.0	–	–	–	48,000
1890	–	41.0	–	–	–	59.0	135,000
1891	–	16.7	–	–	–	83.3	115,000
1892	–	100.0	–	–	–	–	5,000
1893	–	–	–	–	–	100.0	4,000
1894	100.0[b]	–	–	–	–	–	30,000
1895	100.0[b]	–	–	–	–	–	30,000
1875/95	23.3	49.5	3.5	1.7	0.7	18.5	3,059,600

Notes: [a] = Colonial government bonds, [b] = UK consols.
Source: Trustees' Minutes.

over £3 million in acceptances is very heavily due to the activity *before* 1881.

However, it pays to examine the composition of these categories more closely. The heavy property concentration of 1875 actually ranged from a development of freehold houses in the Tottenham Court Road to the Irish estates of Sir Richard Wallace.[202] In 1876, there were three classic local authority loans to Burslem and Ryde Councils and to Bromley Cemetery, while the commercial element was represented wholly by shops and offices in Liverpool and Newcastle. In the very active year of 1877, six local authorities won favour but the property element was both pronounced and varied, with £60,000 going on the Imperial Buildings, Holborn Viaduct, £20,000 in the purchase of mortgage debentures in the

[202] *Ibid.*, 22 July 1875, 2 September 1875.

Land Securities Co. and £213,000 in a genuine development project, as loans against debentures for the intended reconstruction of Victoria Street, Westminster. In this busiest investment year of the sample, the prospects most likely to be accepted were property or local government projects and those most likely to be turned down – despite a £100,000 success for the Mersey Docks and Harbour Board – were harbour and transport proposals (one canal, two harbours, two docks) and industrial and commercial ventures (one distillery, one hop and malt exchange).

Indeed the contents of the 'industrial and commercial' category at this time were almost invariably commercial *rather* than industrial; there is in fact no genuine manufacturing venture among the high scores for the 'industrial and commercial' column. Thus in 1878 this element was represented by a loan to the Greenwich Coal Wharf and £35,000 to Cubitts for the building of a new hotel in Covent Garden; in 1879 it was made up of office buildings; and these featured again in 1881, together with quayside construction in Newcastle and the Athenaeum Club in Leeds, although this year did also see £15,000 committed to the debentures of the Millwall Dock Co. In 1868, the Trustees had also fluttered with the debentures of the Imperial Gas Co., and had renewed this interest in 1872; but they followed through no further.[203]

The Coliseum office block in Leeds provided the 'industrial and commercial' component for 1882, while the double high score in 1890 and 1891 was provided by two sequential loans to the London Commercial Sale Rooms in Mincing Lane which together came to £170,000.[204] Until the turn of the century, however, it seems that Phoenix shared the suspicion of industrial investment – even at the debenture or preference stock level – which affected the whole of the late nineteenth-century capital market and the City of London in particular. This neglect of investment in manufacturing in the world's first industrial economy is a paradox that has often been remarked upon, and it would have been surprising had Phoenix managed to step outside it. However, this leaves the main indicator of enterprise in investment to be supplied from another direction. It relies, in the event quite convincingly, upon the wide variety of activity which was displayed in the 'house, property and mortgage' category.

[203] *Ibid.*, 4 July 1872.

[204] There was a wrangle in 1896 when the Sale Rooms paid off the mortgage without giving the requisite six months' notice. Phoenix counsel opined that the company was entitled to the lost interest and the conflict was resolved with a 100 guinea settlement. But with returns so much the centre of attention, Phoenix was alerted to insist on six months' notice from the Dover Harbour Board, which also repaid in 1896. *Ibid.*, 30 April, 27 May and 10 September 1896.

Enterprise was shown also in the increased commitment to railways in the very lean years of the later 1880s. Phoenix had held railway debentures for some decades – although the company had been much slower than the Pelican in accumulating them – but between 1886 and 1889 it produced its most energetic burst of purchasing since the beginning of the railway era.[205] This lifted the face value of its rail assets by some eight times and nearly £170,000 between 1885 and 1889. The purchases were cast over a range of British companies, from the Metropolitan in 1886, through the London and Southwestern and the Great Northern in 1887 to the Lancashire and Yorkshire and the London and Northwestern in 1888, and were mostly in 3.5% and 4% debentures, with some 4% preference stock.[206]

It is noticeable that the renewed interest in railway securities came at a time when almost nothing else was stirring in the field of Phoenix's investment activity. Clearly, the Trustees were looking for a way out of the malaise that was afflicting their more usual areas of concentration. The same pattern is evident with regard to foreign investment. Phoenix already held, from the 1870s, substantial amounts of US and Canadian government stock, but these had been acquired as part of the compulsory insurance guarantees that were particularly stressed by the North American authorities. The purchase of colonial government stock – from the Cape and from Victoria and South Australia in 1878, and from New South Wales, Queensland, Tasmania and New Zealand in 1889, another year in which little else moved but a small amount of railway investment – represented the first *willed* diversifications of the portfolio towards major foreign opportunities. This opened a path that was to become much more heavily trodden in the 1900s, especially in relation to American railway stock.[207]

But, of course, the pattern of what the Trustees rejected, and when, could be as significant as the pattern of their acceptances (see Table 1.5). The first striking feature is that the years of heavy acceptances were also the years of heavy rejections: of the ten years of active investment in the period 1875–95, seven were also years of heavy repudiation of investment prospects. In particular, the years 1876–8 stand out. On the other hand, the years of very suppressed investment activity, in the middle 1880s and

[205] See vol. I, pp. 661–2.

[206] Directors' Minutes, Y24 p. 307, 24 August 1887; *ibid.*, p. 390, 18 July 1888.

[207] Although plenty of the later foreign acquisitions were also the product less of investors' sensitivity than of governments' demands for guarantees. See below pp. 75, 81–2, 203, 246–7, *passim*. However, there were almost no deposit requirements in Australia before 1900, so most of Phoenix's colonial purchases of the 1870s and 1880s were indeed free investment choices.

Table 1.5. *New investments rejected by the Trustees: % by type of all rejections, 1875–95*

	Local authority loans on rates, etc	House, property and mortages	Railways	Docks & canals	Warehouses	Industrial & commercial	Total £
1875	–	10.4	–	–	–	89.6	134,000
1876	10.7	78.6	–	10.3	–	0.3	1,000,000
1877	8.5	37.4	–	30.3	–	18.8	1,964,000
1878	37.7	32.6	–	5.4	–	24.4	1,533,750
1879	11.3	63.3	–	10.4	5.2	10.0	381,550
1880	–	100.0	–	–	–	–	13,000
1881	–	100.0	–	–	–	–	61,000
1882	–	47.0	22.0	–	–	31.0	225,000
1883	–	100.0	–	–	–	–	42,250
1884	–	100.0	–	–	–	–	75,000
1885	–	50.0	–	–	–	50.0	70,000
1886	–	100.0	–	–	–	–	31,500
1887	–	–	–	–	–	–	?
1888	–	–	–	–	–	–	?
1889	–	–	–	–	–	–	?
1890	4.9[a]	24.4	–	9.8	–	58.5	205,000
1891	–	–	–	–	–	–	?
1892	–	100.0	–	–	–	–	1,000
1893	–	100.0	–	–	–	–	73,000
1894	100.0	–	–	–	–	–	25,000
1895	–	100.0	–	–	–	–	10,000

Note: [a] = City of Rome bonds.
Source: Trustees' Minutes.

early 1890s, also witnessed low or zero levels of rejection. This suggests that little was coming forward to be either accepted or rejected, or that the Trustees had let it be known that they had little interest in contemplating any standard type of investment in these times.

In other types of year, where there was much investment, the sectors of heaviest rejection – house, property, mortgages and commercial ventures – were also the sectors of heaviest acceptances. The unifying feature is the yield. In years of low acceptances and low rejections, few or no yields offered proved attractive. In years of high acceptances and high rejections, it was the yield offered, rather than the sector of investment, which determined the outcome.

Thus, in 1874 over £500,000 was rejected amidst concerns about levels of reward; and almost all of the £1 million worth of investments which was repudiated in 1876 was turned down because of unsatisfactory rates of return. In that year, virtually everything that was offered at 4–4.25% was declined while virtually everything offered at 4.25–4.5 % was accepted. In 1877, rejection was standard at 4.25%, acceptance usual at around

4.5%. Also, a prospect could cross the dividing line between acceptance and rejection by revising the rate of return offered. Accordingly, a £57,000 loan of 1876 sought on security of the borough rates of Ryde, on the Isle of Wight, first of all failed at 4.0%, then succeeded at 4.5%. By 1891, however, the increasing pressure on yields was shown by the fact that most rejections were falling in the 3.5–4.0% band, while most new investments had to reach 4.0% before the Trustees would smile upon them.

Yields apart, two other distinct prejudices emerge from the Trustees' records over this twenty-five year period. First, the absence of industrial ventures from the Investment Committee's acceptance files was not mirrored by similar omissions from their rejection files. They began the period by turning down a cotton mill and a colliery in 1875 and kept up their resolve with William Holland's distillery, rejected for £50,000 in 1877, and Sidgwick's Brewery of Romford, turned down in 1885 for £35,000. No issue of temperance seems to have been involved in the latter two cases, since not even 'a freehold hydropathic establishment at Ilkley' in 1879 could whet the Trustees' interest or even their curiosity.

The second prejudice rather dents Phoenix's image as a precocious property-developer. For it transpires that the Trustees did not like committing funds to *unfinished* buildings. A huge amount of capital was lavished on freehold property, shops and offices – £800,000 of £1.4 million accepted in 1877, £170,000 of £302,100 accepted in 1878, £130,000 of £250,000 accepted in 1881 – but Phoenix preferred the bricks and mortar to be in place. In 1883, the Trustees turned down £22,500 on the Victoria Street development, despite its promised 5% yield, because the buildings concerned were in the course of construction, while in the lean year of 1884 they walked away from £40,000 worth of property ripe for development in Plymouth, Exeter and Bristol 'since they were not favourable to the principle of making advances for the development of intending purchases'.[208]

Clearly, the Phoenix acceptance strategy, though not without touches of enterprise, was a very rigorous one. Its main achievement, however, seems to have been the securing of above-average yields for new investment. True, Phoenix did accept reductions of yield for favoured clients: in 1888 a long-running loan to the Kent Waterworks was scaled down to 3.5%, and, in the same year, the Dover Harbour Board's 4.5%, running since 1873, was revised to 4%, but the Harbour Board had given Phoenix all their insurance.[209] Broadly, Phoenix held its rates well. When, around

[208] Trustees' Minutes, 30 October 1884. [209] *Ibid.*, 27 November 1873, 12 April 1888.

Table 1.6. *Phoenix fire fund: main categories of investment, 1883–1914 (%)*

	UK govt	US govt	Other govt	UK railway	Foreign railway	UK industrial/ commercial	Mortgages	Total £
1883	22.6	25.3	1.0	2.4	1.2	–	47.2	1.02
1885	33.1	26.3	1.7	2.1	1.3	1.3	34.1	1.15
1890	33.2	23.5	6.4	10.5	2.8	–	23.2	1.31
1895	30.0	21.4	7.6	–	7.8	–	34.3	1.29
1900	18.2	22.7	15.2	2.6	14.3	1.0	26.8	1.39
1905	16.1	16.3	11.4	–	19.4	5.4	25.6	1.78
1910	2.5	4.5	27.2	2.0	27.3	7.2	23.3	1.96
1914	–	4.4	31.6	1.3	21.5	8.7	25.4	1.94

Note: Almost all railway and industrial–commercial investments are debentures or preferences shares. Mortgages here subsume land and property holdings.
Source: Phoenix Assurance Annual Accounts.

1880, the average yield on all new UK insurance investments was between 3.5 and 4.0%, Phoenix was still achieving 4.5% and even the odd 5% on its fresh acquisitions. Even a decade later, when the average marginal yield on new investments was hovering around 3.5%, Phoenix was rejecting anything below 4%, and still obtaining the occasional 5% – as it did on property in Oxford in 1890.

However, in the thirty years before the Great War, pressure on rates led to marked changes in the overall shape of the fire portfolio (see Table 1.6).The total size of the Phoenix fire funds almost doubled between 1883 and 1914, but the shifts in their distribution between investment types were equally dramatic. Mortgages and property had reacted to poor values of agricultural land in the 1880s by settling to around one-quarter of the total portfolio by 1890, and, apart from a brief rally between 1892 and 1895, stabilised around this share for the rest of the period. The temporary swing back towards property in the early 1890s again echoed themes within the national economy.

After the Baring Crisis of 1890, much British investment overseas was frightened homewards and there was a concerted rush to find domestic outlets for it. Low-yielding consols provided no answer, and the financial structure which might have linked such funds with domestic industrial prospects was still lacking.[210] Property had more obvious attractions to offer. The building cycle was due for an upswing in the 1890s, and the ageing of the housing stock combined with the influx of capital to provide a remarkable surge in house construction. This was the core of the 'Home

[210] See, for example, Kennedy, *Industrial Structure*.

Boom of the 1890s', and one of the greatest of the periodic expansions of the Victorian suburbs.[211] The mortgage-property bulge in the Phoenix accounts of the early 1890s represents the company's share in this national phenomenon.

But mortgages and property were almost stable compared with developments in other sectors. In the period of short investment pickings in the 1880s, UK gilts had conquered nearly one-third of the portfolio, but by 1905 this share had been halved, and by 1910, it was a mere 2.5%. The share of the US government also contracted sharply, from around 1900, as the authorities' requirements for insurance guarantees could be met from a decreasing proportion of the total portfolio and an increasing variety of American assets. It is clear that, in the later 1890s and 1900s new investment forces were beginning to stir.

Phoenix investment patterns 1900–14

The marked change in investment patterns from the turn of the century owed its shape to four main influences. These were: the intensified pressure from foreign governments for the deposit in overseas markets of insurance guarantees; the greater willingness of the Phoenix to invest in higher risk stocks, such as preference and even a few ordinary shares, which at long last allowed greater access to genuine UK industrials; the revival of aristocratic loans, but of a type associated with life interests and policies rather than the traditional mortgages on big estates; and, above all, a major redirection of the portfolio towards US railway stock, mostly bonds but including also a little preference stock. These areas were the major gainers by the outflows of funds from UK and US government securities. Certainly, the sentiment was more positive than that of the years of the Great Depression, however mythical that may or may not have been. It is also noteworthy that the new strategy was embarked upon well before the Phoenix achieved full composite status by the fusion and mergers of the period 1908–14,[212] and well before the managerial control of Gerald Ryan. This suggests that the Phoenix investors were reacting

[211] Sigsworth and Blackman, 'The Home Boom of the 1890s'. Other post-Baring effects were odder. Phoenix holdings in empire and foreign government stock, the type most implicated in the Argentinian crisis, were increased but *domestic* railway debentures were sold off. However, these may have been regarded as the riskiest (though scarcely very risky) part of the company's UK investments, and thus a suitable source of supply for the £100,000 or so that was to be switched into the expanding construction sector. Certainly, the movements of the UK railway and UK mortgage holdings 1890–3 were strongly inversely related (see Table 1.6).

[212] See below, Chapter 5.

more to world investment opportunities than to changes in the company's structure or leadership.[213]

The rise of foreign governments, coming from virtually nothing to over one-sixth of the entire portfolio by 1910, represented one of the major overseas opportunities opened for Phoenix by the global investment expansion of the pre-war years (see Table 1.6). But, in these years, the opportunity was not one which the insurance exporter needed to detect or choose freely; if he was an active exporter, sovereign states queued up to impose it on him. Between 1896 and 1905, the peak period for this sort of international surveillance by the financial authorities, no fewer than eleven new governments demanded insurance deposits, with a nominal value of over £112,000, from the Phoenix.[214] Meanwhile, one more familiar insurance protectionist, the Canadian government and its provinces, made almost yearly increases to demands totalling some £84,000, some of which could be met in UK or other Imperial assets. Indeed, in 1909, when Canada demanded a further $150,000, Phoenix met the requirement with an appropriate value of Western Australia 3.5% inscribed stock.[215]

Undoubtedly, by 1914, the deposits required by foreign governments made up the great majority of the Phoenix's holdings in US, Canadian and other overseas government stock, and a slightly less dominant portion of empire government stock. Naturally, these investments earned interest and they could be switched between stocks to achieve better interest returns. But they could not be switched out of the country concerned without the loss of the right to transact business there. Also, the national governments could force increases in deposits at times very unfavourable for the purchase of investments. Thus, early in 1909, the increase of insurance business required Phoenix to purchase $160,000 of US securities and $150,000 of Canadian securities at prices far above par.[216] On the other hand, forced entry to investment purchases in central government stock could spark an insurer's interest in other prospects in the same market. In this vein, in 1913, Phoenix bought heavily into municipal stock in the cities of Christiania, Port Arthur (Ontario), Victoria (British Columbia), Winnipeg, Regina and Moose Jaw. The result was a mixed bag of compulsions and choices, good spread and high prices, old hat and new openings.

[213] However, it is not possible to measure how much influence Ryan was exerting from outside the walls in the early 1900s.

[214] These included: Peru in 1897, Bulgaria and Argentina in 1898, Japan and the Transvaal in 1903, and Chile in 1905.

[215] Trustees' Minutes, 5 May 1909.

[216] Directors' Minutes, 28, pp. 403–4, 6 March 1909.

In comparison, there was nothing forced about the Phoenix's approach to British industrial and commercial prospects in the 1900s, and it remained cautious. But it did develop. British railway interests never bettered 1–3% of the total Phoenix portfolio after 1900; they had a tendency to slide and they were almost wholly debentures. And the acceptance of manufacturing prospects came slowly enough: in 1898 Phoenix was still turning down a £10,000 interest in the Southover Brewery in Sussex, even at the debenture level, and, on the last day of the century no brewery, nor indeed industrial, stock was listed among the company's assets.[217]

From 1900, however, Phoenix became significantly more interested in British breweries, often with an eye to exploiting both the insurance and the investment potential. The company took £2,500 in the debentures of Locke and Smith, brewers of Great Berkhamstead, in November 1901; the venture had insured with Phoenix for many years, and the company needed the investment 'in order to preserve the insurance of this old connection'.[218] In 1903, £20,000 of debentures in the Isleworth Brewery were taken up on condition that all the fire cover was transferred to Phoenix.[219] Similar considerations attended a long-running relationship with Whitbread shares. The brewery was a large insurer with Phoenix, and the office went in and out of its shares, a purchase of £1,300 in debentures in 1906 being an early example.[220] By the end of 1903, Phoenix had interests in five breweries, the largest being in Isleworth, and the total summing to £37,500, all in debenture stock.[221] These brewery interests represented almost the entire commitment to industrial stock at this juncture, at 2.4% of the investment portfolio.[222]

By 1914, Phoenix still had interests in five breweries, including one of nearly £7,000 in Ohllson's Cape Breweries, acquired in 1905, but these had been joined by seven other manufacturing or high-technology utility ventures, making up a total commitment to the industrial sector of £70,377.[223] At this point, such a sum represented 3.6% of the total Phoenix fire portfolio.[224] Within the United Kingdom, the breweries had

[217] Trustees' Minutes, 19 January 1898. [218] *Ibid.*, 14 November 1911.

[219] *Ibid.*, 28 January 1903. Within months, the Trustees in more commercial, or perhaps thespian, vein took £10,000 of the new 4.5% debentures in the Wyndham Theatre group, then worth about £0.25 million, and controlling the Criterian, the New Theatre and the Wyndham itself.

[220] Directors' Minutes, 27, pp. 392, 396, 3 and 17 January 1906.

[221] They were Charrington, Ind Coope, Whitbread, Locke & Smith, and Isleworth.

[222] The exception was a £5,000 stake in the debentures of the Imperial Tobacco Co.

[223] These were two American telephone companies: AT&T and the New York Telephone Co. The AT&T holding was acquired late in 1905. Trustees' Minutes, 22 November 1905.

[224] The figure in Table 1.6 rolls together industrial and commercial holdings.

been joined by Associated Portland Cement, the Anglo-Brazilian Meat Co. and Brush Electrical Engineering, while Imperial Tobacco maintained its hold from a decade or so previously. However, the interest in the Isleworth brewery, at nearly £19,000, was by far the largest of the industrial connections.

It is striking that all these holdings were in debenture or preference stock. Indeed, in 1914, the only ordinary stock held by the Phoenix was some £11,000 in the London and Southwest Rail Co. and the office's commitment even to preference stock, at £23,284, represented barely 1% of the total portfolio. If the increase in attention to the industrial sector suggests a slightly increased taste for adventure, it was expressed nevertheless in a highly conservative selection of stock.

On the other hand, the office's industrial holdings had been more widely scattered than is suggested by the asset list for 1914 alone. In 1908 debenture and bond holdings were reported in the Castner-Kellner Alkali Co. and in Western Union Telegraph.[225] And in 1912, a year of heavy buying and selling, an interest was taken in the P & O Steam Navigation Co., only for £35,000 of stock in three different shipping companies to be sold off in the next few months. At much the same time, £25,000 was taken up in the debentures or bonds of the General Electric Co. and the Sao Paulo Electricity Co., a preoccupation with electrification which suggests the influence perhaps of Fladgate. Also in 1912, over £36,000 went to Milford Docks against specified mortgages in order 'to meet capital expenditure'.[226] One year later, a parcel of armament and metal equities were briefly held and sold: over £13,000 worth of ordinary shares in Armstrong Whitworth, Guest, Keen and Nettlefold and Vickers were disposed of in March 1913.[227] At least the sale of defence-related shares in such a year puts a comfortable distance between Phoenix and the 'merchants of death' interpretation of early twentieth-century capitalism. Ironically, however, Phoenix probably sold them on swiftly because they were ordinary shares. However, it is interesting that at least three of these categories of shares were linked with Phoenix Directors (Hawes, Fladgate, Bouverie).[228]

As the company's interest in modern technology was cautiously expanded, a very traditional investment appeared to undergo a revival. This was the aristocratic loan. Phoenix, of course, had moved away from a traditional attachment to mortgages against aristocratic estates as land prices had fallen in the last decades of the nineteenth century, and Pelican

[225] Directors' Minutes, 28, p. 300, 23 September 1908.
[226] *Ibid.*, 30, p. 206, 2 October 1912. [227] *Ibid.*, p. 288, 5 March 1913.
[228] See above, Section 5.

had sharply reduced its commitment in this sector as early as the 1860s.[229] But by 1909, the new composite Phoenix was listing loans of £26,000 to Lord Wilton, £20,000 to Baroness von Eckardstein, £103,000 to Lord Kenmare, as well as further large engagements to Earl de la Warr, Lady du Cane and Lord Haldon. By 1911 these names had been joined in the Phoenix books by Lord Francis Hope, Lord Dudley, Sir Horace Rumbold and Lord Walsingham. Some of these transactions were of a familiar kind based on broad acres. In 1911, for instance, a loan on the security of the Egglestone Estate, Barnard Castle, was approved, 'subject to the mansion and moor' being satisfactorily let.[230]

But when, in July 1911, Lord Francis Hope was seeking an enormous loan of £200,000 at 4.5%, he offered as security, not land but a life interest and assurance policies; and, when, later in the year, Lord Dudley sought an additional £50,000 on top of the £62,000 already extended, he too produced a life interest and life policies as his guarantees.[231] The first proposal was considered sufficiently out of the normal to require vetting by a special committee of Lord George Hamilton, Bristow Bovill and two other directors; but the second was taken almost as a formality. The Committee decided that Phoenix needed safeguards with respect to Lord Hope, requiring him to take out £142,000 worth of additional life policies, and splitting the loan so that Phoenix led with a £80,000 share but the Clergy Mutual Assurance accepted £70,000 and the London Life £50,000. Lord Dudley also needed £152,000 of life policies to support his £112,000 loan.[232] A similar huge loan of £280,000 to Lord Ashburton was repaid in November 1912, while these other major assurance-secured transactions were being set up.

Within the largest class of loan, this type of aristocratic policy-based commitment became more common in the 1910s than the older style of property-based transaction. When the latter did occur, it was usually due to special conditions or connections. Thus, the Earl of Radnor drew a total of £90,000 from Phoenix in April 1912, against the ground rents of his Folkestone estates and property in Chancery Lane. The Directors minuted that this was 'on account of the value of the fire connection'; but, of course, there was also a more direct personal link between the Radnors and the Phoenix Board.[233] No such liaison underpinned a sequence of loans made to William Brass Esq. on property in Angel Court with an equity value of £328,000; by spring 1913, Brass held loans from Phoenix

[229] See vol. I, p. 654. [230] Directors' Minutes, 29, p. 333, 18 January 1911.
[231] *Ibid.*, p. 443, 5 July 1911; 30, p. 19, 8 November 1911.
[232] *Ibid.*, 30, p. 66, 7 February 1912; p. 379. [233] See above, pp. 37, 42–3.

amounting to a total of £110,000.[234] The money was advanced against what were clearly prime London sites, but, even so, the Board was sufficiently concerned in 1912 to launch another committee investigation into 'the present condition of the Company's transactions with Mr Brass'.[235] A suspicion was beginning to form that 'where there's brass . . .'. In these two unusually large cases, either a Board connection or the development potential of first-rate urban property provided the special reason for the Phoenix involvement.

The case of the Earl of Plymouth contained a wider mix of variables. This, in 1913, was another very big loan, of £204,000. The security was the Penarth and Barry Docks – and a number of life policies. And again, Phoenix was not to shoulder the burden unaided: once more, the Clergy Mutual would take a share. So this was not a standard estate mortgage. Rather, the Earl of Plymouth was a 'debt-funded developer', borrowing against the value of industrial or infrastructural assets. And he was having to offer assurance securities as well. And, finally, institutions were cooperating in order to reduce the risk to themselves.

These devices were a long way removed from the aristocratic mortgages which Phoenix and Pelican had tended to avoid in the late nineteenth century. And, indeed, it is instructive that the revival of very big loans to lordly names such as Hope, Dudley and Plymouth came immediately after the 1908 fusion between Pelican and Phoenix. The arrival at this time of loans secured against very large values of life cover is also significant. The suggestion must be that the Phoenix loan strategy was influenced by the inheritance from Pelican of a network of high-born life clients and an accompanying measure of assurance expertise with which to handle their expensive affairs.[236] Here it is less an attachment to traditional mortgage business than the Pelican's inclination towards the underwriting of noble lives which reintroduces gilded titles into the composite company's schedule of loans. This is a case where a revision in company structure affected the style of company investment.[237]

However, the values involved in lordly lending, though impressive on a unit basis, came nowhere near the amounts committed by Phoenix to its real investment staple of the period 1899–1914: the railways of America. Phoenix bought into these from 1892 – when a single block purchase of over £83,000 was made – and quite fiercely from August 1898 – when the company sold Massachusetts State Bonds to buy Illinois Central and

[234] Directors' Minutes, 30, p. 342, 28 May 1913. [235] *Ibid.*, p. 129, 8 May 1912.
[236] See vol. I, Chapter 10.
[237] See vol. I, pp. 613–15 for the Pelican's preferences in regard to aristocratic, as against middle-class, assurances.

Cleveland and Pittsburgh Railway gold bonds.[238] In June 1900, a similar conversion occurred when $0.3 million worth of US government bonds were sold in order to purchase 3% or 3.5% railway bonds in the Erie and Pittsburgh, Illinois Central and Chicago and Alton lines.[239] In November 1900, a further stake in the Baltimore and Ohio was added. Then, in 1905, the office made a massive commitment of over half a million dollars, starting in January with $100,000 split between the 4% bonds of the Lake Shore and Michigan Southern Railway and the Terminal Railroad of St Louis, going on to confer a similar amount on four more lines in September, and ending the year by dividing $350,000 between seven more.[240] While this was going on, at home the Phoenix was turning down the debentures of the Manchester Hippodrome and the Scientific Press Ltd. And Phoenix persisted with it, despite an unfriendly ruling by the Inland Revenue that tax was due on investment income generated in the USA, even if it was never remitted to the United Kingdom. In tax-year 1904/5, Phoenix was paying under protest and wondering whether to take on the Revenue in the courts.

In June 1898, Phoenix owned no named US railway stock, only the anonymous parcel purchased in 1892. By 1909 it held stock in no fewer than twenty-three different US lines, with a total balance-sheet value of £330,952.[241] At the end of the next year, US railways accounted for 56.1% of the non-government convertible securities within the Phoenix fire portfolio; by contrast British railways accounted for 4.3%, British breweries for 3.9% and other British industrials for 2.9%. When Phoenix found itself in possession of ordinary and preferred stock in British railways as a result of the investments acquired by the takeover of the Law Life Assurance in 1910, it moved rapidly to shed them; and invested the proceeds in more US railway bonds.[242] Of the 102 investment transactions carried out by the Phoenix in 1910, forty-four were in railways worldwide, half of these were in US railways and just six were in UK railways, mostly the underground companies, and including, ironically, the Baker Street and Waterloo Railway, against which Phoenix had protested because of the threat which its tunnels posed to the foundations of the office's West End Branch.[243]

238 Trustees' Minutes, 3 August 1898.

239 Directors' Minutes, A26, pp. 415, 423, 13 June and 4 July 1900.

240 Trustees' Minutes, 20 September 1905. The seven were: the Oregon Short Line, the Atlantic Coast, the Chicago and West Indiana, the Southern Pacific, the Long Island, the Louisville and Nashville, and the Norfolk and Western.

241 Revenue, Profit and Loss Accounts, 1903–9.

242 Directors' Minutes, 29, p. 204, 8 June 1910.

243 The more interesting of these transactions were in the Otago Harbour Board, the City of

In regard to these investment trends, the Phoenix was swimming with the same current that was moving the other offices; but, in some respects, it was swimming more energetically than most. Deterioration in the more conventional securities between the mid-1890s and the Great War – by 37% in price for UK consols, 40% for home railway preferred and debenture stock, and around 20% for colonial government stock – forced diversification upon all institutional investors. Rising UK interest rates brought severe depreciation for fixed interest assets and caused a mass evacuation from British government securities in particular between 1895 and 1914. On the eve of war, the insurance industry as a whole had barely 1% of total assets in home gilts, while Phoenix had virtually none (see Table 1.6).

By comparison, the attractions of US rail bonds – with yields holding at the very satisfactory level of 4–5% for the period 1895–1912 – were compelling.[244] The plunge towards them was by no means unique to the Phoenix. Indeed, the office was rather slow off the mark: the Scottish Widows' Fund had acquired the huge holding of £1.5 million in US railway gold mortgage bonds in the early 1890s and the Commercial Union had £0.7 million of them by 1900, while even the REA had over £0.25 million by 1896.[245] It is rather the proportion of the total fire portfolio which Phoenix was prepared to commit to US rail stock in the 1900s which probably picks the company out as unusual. At its peak around 1910 and 1911 this proportion was not far short of one-quarter of the Phoenix's entire fire funds.

In regard to foreign government securities, however, the Phoenix was much faster away from the line. Supple reports that in 1890 the insurance offices in general were still 'very suspicious of foreign securities', and, for instance, held a mere £3.5 million of the most accessible overseas assets, the paper issued by foreign governments.[246] Not so Phoenix. Already in 1883, the office had 27.5% of its complete fire portfolio devoted to several types of foreign asset, by 1890 32.7%, in 1900 52.2% and by 1910 reached its peak of commitment with 59.4%. Within these proportions, the imperial percentage was also rising, from 8.9% in 1890 to 14.6% in 1910 (see Table 1.7).

Phoenix's involvement with foreign securities was exceptional for

Porto Alegre, the Hyde Park Hotel, the Bengal and Northwestern Railway, Western Electric, the legendary Atcheson, Topeka and Santa Fe Railway, the York Hotel, the Chilean and Bolivian Railway, the Orient Steam Co., the Hokkaido Colliery and Railway Co., and the City of Tokyo.

244 R. W. Fogel, *Railroads and American Economic Growth* (Baltimore, 1964), p. 108.

245 Supple, *Royal Exchange Assurance*, p. 345. 246 *Ibid.*, p. 343.

Table 1.7. *Phoenix home and foreign investment: fire fund stock exchange securities as % of total portfolio, 1883–1914*

	Home investment			Imperial/foreign investment			
Year	Govt	Railway	Industrial & commercial	Empire govt	Empire railways	Foreign govt	Foreign railways
1883	22.6	2.4	–	1.0	1.2	25.3	–
1885	33.1	2.1	1.3	1.5	1.0	26.3	0.3
1890	33.2	10.5	–	6.3	2.6	23.6	0.2
1895	30.0	–	–	6.9	0.9	22.1	6.9
1900	18.2	2.6	1.0	12.5	0.8	25.4	13.5
1905	16.1	–	5.4	6.4	–	21.3	19.4
1910	2.5	2.0	7.2	12.2	2.4	19.9	24.9
1914	–	1.3	8.7	8.8	3.5	27.2	18.0

speed of entry as well as for share of portfolio. In 1890 all UK offices, fire and life, held only £3.5 million in the single sector of foreign government issues; Phoenix alone accounted for nearly £400,000 of that sum, or about 11% of the entire overseas investment in all foreign governments by the whole British insurance industry. Naturally, this share declined as the rest of the insurers woke up to the allure of overseas governments and municipalities. Thus, by 1900, Phoenix investment in foreign government paper represented some 4.8% of the industry's interest in the sector and, by 1913, about 2.8% – although none of these shares is by any means negligible for a single operator.

Similarly, if the whole of Phoenix's foreign investment is set against that of other insurers, or against the industrial standard, it looks impressive. Perhaps it could not compete with a big life investor, like the Scottish Widows', which by 1900 had £6 million of its huge total portfolio of £15.5 million in overseas mortgages, government bonds and railways. But by comparison with a company of similar age and venerability, the REA (which came late to insurance exportation, and by 1890 had only 10% of its investment holdings in capital exports), the Phoenix was years ahead.[247] Here, of course, the contrast is between an old company which had been slow to test the foreign insurance markets and an old company which had been an early specialist in insurance exportation, and, by 1910, had been reviving this specialism for nearly four decades. The emphasis on overseas insurances naturally led the Phoenix into a precocious interest in foreign investment. By 1914, British life offices – bigger and usually more adventurous investors than the fire offices – had about 40% of their

[247] *Ibid.*, pp. 345–6. The share was 14% in 1891, perhaps 45% by 1913.

Table 1.8. *Distribution of balance sheet assets by major sector: all offices, Phoenix and Pelican, 1900–10 (% share)*

	1900			1905			1910		
	All offices	Phoenix	Pelican	All offices	Phoenix	Pelican	All offices	Phoenix fire	Phoenix life
Mortgages	42.7	4.3	31.6	42.2	3.0	45.6	34.6	26.8	33.7
UK govt	2.5	15.5	–	2.4	13.8	1.6	1.5	1.5	0.8
Foreign govt	3.5	40.7	11.9	3.0	26.7	13.7	6.3	21.8	11.3
Debenture	19.2	9.7	29.3	18.8	16.8	16.9	23.2	27.5	21.8
Preference and ordinary shares	11.3	0.6	17.3	11.0	6.0	8.5	9.6	1.9	11.4
Land, rent, property	9.6	17.9	2.4	9.7	18.6	6.3	9.5	13.7	6.6

Note: Category definitions and total columns are not directly comparable with those in Tables 1.6 and 1.7. Trends are similar.
Sources: Calculated from Phoenix Balance Sheets and Red Account Books: D. K. Sheppard, *The Growth and Role of UK Financial Institutions, 1880–1962* (London, 1971), pp. 154–6.

funds invested abroad, thereby setting an industrial standard.[248] But around the same time, the Phoenix fire fund had almost half as much again of its portfolio placed outside the United Kingdom.

These patterns, and especially Phoenix's unusual foreign patterns, can be demonstrated in another way. Indeed, on this test, Phoenix emerges as a distinctly unconventional investor in the pre-1914 years (Table 1.8). Distribution of total balance sheet assets between major investment sectors can be calculated for all offices, for Phoenix, and for Pelican (and subsequently the Phoenix life department).

The Phoenix's disaffection with mortgages around the turn of the century shows through as exceptionally strong, although a larger than average holding is already evident in the related sector of land, property and rent. Phoenix mortgages moved some way back towards the norm between 1905 and 1910 but stopped well short of it. The fire office was much more reluctant to desert UK gilts wholesale than the industrial average, but then it was exceptionally attached to governments of all nations. Its share of foreign gilts was many times the industrial standard.[249] The Phoenix's relatively slow move towards debentures is clear in the 1900 figure, but its heavier movement is pronounced in the 1910 figure. Holdings of preference and ordinary shares by the fire funds were unusually light, as they were to remain for several decades.

[248] *Ibid.*
[249] Even Pelican's holding of foreign government stock, perhaps under the influence of the sister company, was 2–4 times the average. Broadly, the Pelican's investment pattern before 1910 emerges as more conventional than the Phoenix's. But it was in foreign gilts that it too was least conventional.

Supple argues correctly that figures such as the all-office columns for debentures and shares in Table 1.8 will understate the foreign interest of the insurance business in general, because many of these debentures and shares were vested in overseas companies.[250] But we already know that the Phoenix debentures were exceptionally weighted towards such ventures. And, on top of this, the figures do reveal clearly that Phoenix investment was also exceptionally slanted towards foreign governments. Whichever way the numbers are cut, it is clear that the Phoenix was a conspicuously active institutional participant in the great British foreign investment boom of the period 1900–14.

For the most part, too, the Phoenix investors were fairly fast on their feet over the longer period 1880–1914. Some big switches of emphasis were handled with speed. Thus, the adjustments out of property in the early 1880s, away from the UK government in the 1890s, and from the US government in the 1900s were all very swift. The build up in colonial government stock 1890–1914 was gradual, but the movement towards non-imperial foreign governments was densely concentrated in the period 1908–14, with a tripling of the total amount committed. By contrast, the interest in UK railway debentures, hovering almost always around 1–2% of the total portfolio, and in imperial railway stock, usually in the range 2–4%, look like tactical holdings or flank positions. On the other hand, the movement into foreign (here translating as heavily American) railway bonds – from 0.2% of the portfolio in 1890 to 24.9% in 1910 – marks a staggering overhaul of strategy. Even the emergence of UK industrials and commercials from traditional neglect in 1900 to an almost respectable 9% of the portfolio in 1910 indicates a heartening capability to revise stock opinions.

However, insurance companies do not only buy investments; they sometimes have also to sell them, whether they are home or foreign investments. Phoenix encountered two episodes of forced selling around the turn of the century. They came quite close together. As a result of bad business in the early 1900s, mainly deriving from punishing US loss rates,[251] Phoenix faced a spate of heavy claims and mounting bank debt. There were even rumours of a possible business failure and, in 1905, much speculation about mergers, takeovers and amalgamations, which the Board had firmly to deny.[252] The gossip was

[250] Supple, *Royal Exchange Assurance*, pp. 345–6. [251] See below pp. 287–90.

[252] The public statement was, 'No negotiations whatever had been initiated undertaken or entertained by any person acting with the authority, consent or knowledge of the Board, having for their object the amalgamation, absorption, fusion or merging of the company's business with, or into, that of any other corporation or institution.' Phoenix Directors' Minutes, 27, pp. 373–4, 18 October 1905.

mostly ill-founded, but what was certainly all too established was an expanding overdraft.

By November 1904, in order to reduce liabilities to their bankers of over £50,000, the Phoenix Trustees launched into an investment selling spree which shed the bonds of five governments – Newfoundland, India, Tasmania, Queensland and Egypt – and the stock of three industrial concerns – Commercial Cable, Imperial Tobacco and Ind Coope – and two railways – the Metropolitan and the North Pacific.[253] This was a fairly significant investors' retreat, but, even so, could not compare to the second evacuation which Phoenix was forced to undertake in 1906. Again, the need was to meet American claims, but this time of a more dramatic scale than merely indifferent business could produce. Rather, it was for a tragedy of global scope – the San Francisco earthquake of 1906 – that Phoenix, like many insurance companies, had to plunder its investment coffers.

The company was still purchasing enthusiastically in the spring of 1906 – a mixed bag of colonial government bonds, US railway stock and UK industrials, indeed replacing some of the sales of 1904 – but was forced radically to change position by the eruption on the American Pacific Slope. Between August 1906 and February 1907, securities with a face value of £254,000 had to be sold in the United Kingdom – with some British property having to go as well – while in the United States further assets valued at $330,000 were liquidated over a similar time span.[254] The sequel, later in 1907, was equally forced purchasing to make up the deficiencies in the portfolio, and this came in the shape of a medley of railway bonds and debentures, spread in many lots of £5,000, over the transport systems of the United Kingdom, India, Latin America and the United States.[255] Fortunately, however, this period of enforced replenishment came at a particularly low point in the market, indeed at the lowest point in the decade 1905–14.

Life funds, of course, were seldom if ever by the 1900s subject to such sudden assaults. In general, they could stand longer to fructify and accumulate, and because they were not subject to the same needs for crisis reserves as fire or accident funds, they – or at least a portion of them – might be directed towards investments of higher risk. Nevertheless, comparison for 1910 between the distribution of balance sheet assets for the Phoenix fire department and for the Pelican life department, which was absorbed into the main body of the new composite company some two years previously, throws up more similarities than differences (Table 1.9).

[253] Trustees' Minutes, 30 November 1904.
[254] *Ibid.*, 4 July 1907, and Directors' Minutes, 28, pp. 1–45.
[255] *Ibid.*, pp. 95–6, 14 August 1907.

Table 1.9. *Phoenix fire and life departments: distribution of balance sheet assets by major sectors, 1910 (%)*

	UK govt[a]	Emp. govt	Foreign govt	Deb stock[b]	Pref. stock[b]	Ord. shares[b]	Mortgages	Rents, property	Total (£m)
Life	0.8	8.6	2.7	21.8	6.8	4.6	33.7	6.6	10.2
Fire	1.5	7.2	14.6	27.5	1.3	0.6	26.8	13.7	3.2

Notes: [a] Central and local; [b] debenture, preference and ordinary shares are home and foreign. The first two are heavily rail-based. Category definitions and total columns are not directly comparable with those in Tables 1.6 and 1.7. Trends are similar.
Source: Phoenix Red Account Books.

By 1910 total life assets, having experienced no actuarial equivalent of Tooley Street or San Francisco, were considerably bigger than the fire funds. The shares of total holdings given to the UK and empire governments were broadly comparable, and the declining interest of insurers in home gilts is strongly evident in both accounts. The lower interest of the life department in non-empire governments follows logically from the fact that the assurers exported life policies to far fewer places than the revitalised fire insurers exported fire policies. Even so, the life assurers had clearly been influenced by their fire colleagues towards an interest in foreign gilts that was more pronounced than the industrial average (see Table 1.8).

Both departments still show a substantial interest in mortgage assets, the fire sector having rebuilt to more than 25% in mortgages proper, the life department retaining rather more, as was its long-term trend.[256] The fire department displays a stronger interest in rents and property which will also emerge as a long-run feature.[257]

There is a discrepancy in regard to preference and ordinary shares, with the life department showing as the more enterprising investor. This reflects the more generous risk margin available to the assurance funds and the greater need of the fire sector for instant access to dependable crisis reserves. Certainly, Pelican in its last years of independence had a greater willingness than Phoenix to confront preference rather than debenture stock, industrial-commercial openings, and even some equities, as well as foreign prospects that were not American railway bonds. However, this was a natural difference following from the divergent investment needs of the two sectors, if also perhaps from the Pelican's long-term record of craftier speculation.[258]

[256] See pp. 601–3. [257] *Ibid.*
[258] Pelican was distinctly more adventurous than Phoenix in its investment strategy for the pre-1870 years (see vol. I, pp. 662–6).

Anyway, that discrepancy is dwarfed by the convergence of choice towards debenture stock. In each case, this meant predominantly American railway bonds which were the favourite new investment for both portfolios. Clearly, the investment strategies of the fire and life sides were broadly similar around 1910, and a good deal more similar than they had been in the mid-late nineteenth century, indeed a good deal more similar than they had been in 1900 (see Table 1.7).

This is fortunate because, by the 1900s, the life funds were regularly tested for investment efficiency through the quinquennial valuations of the assurance assets.[259] For the period 1908–14 then, these valuations will form a proxy for the assessment of all Phoenix investment, given the similarities between the life and fire funds established above for the period around 1910. Two such valuations fell in the difficult investment period, 1905–14: the Phoenix Life Fund Valuation of 1911, covering the years 1906–10, and the British Empire Fund Valuation, an inheritance from the Pelican, falling in 1912, and covering the years 1907–11.

In his introduction to the Phoenix Valuation, General Manager Gerald Ryan reported that the Phoenix assurance portfolio had 'successfully stood the strain of the marked depreciation in high-class securities which has been such a conspicuous feature over the period'. He remarked in particular upon the Stock Exchange slide of 1907, before concluding, with satisfaction, that the Phoenix life portfolio had survived it more than handsomely.[260]

The British Empire fund had increased in value only from £2.94 million to £2.97 million between 1907 and 1911, after managing an advance ten times better than that in the preceding five-year period. But it achieved the modest increase of 1907–11, despite a decline in value of its UK stock exchange holdings of nearly £50,000.[261] Thanks to shrewd investment *outside* UK stocks, the British Empire was able to announce a bonus better by half than that of the previous quinquennium. As with the Phoenix funds, the investment managers had switched well into securities that had not deteriorated. Again, Ryan summarised with contentment that 'the results of the quinquennium are unexpectedly favourable'. The British Empire, like the other funds, had mostly US railroads to thank.[262]

In the end, one can only wonder what the contemporary observers who found insurance investment a 'laughing stock' had in mind. The really

[259] These valuations were introduced as a legal requirement by the Life Companies Act of 1870.

[260] Phoenix (Pelican) Quinquennial Valuation, 1911.

[261] British Empire Valuation, 21 February 1912.

[262] Special Committee on the British Empire Valuation, 21 February 1912; Directors' Minutes 30, pp. 81–8.

smart money amidst the investing circles of 1896–1914 would have been buying the highest quality industrial equities – the ordinary shares of heavy industrial concerns such as Vickers, Sons and Maxim or John Browns, among others, were often yielding 10–15% per annum in the 1900s and 1910s – but very little money in the United Kingdom was that smart. Indeed, if the same contemporary observers had found pronounced investment by the insurance offices in industrial equities, they would most probably – had they been City born and bred – have arrived at the same mocking conclusion by a somewhat different route. The London Stock Exchange in the 1900s dealt only in the most flame-proof industrial stock, and allowed even these only a fraction of its total capital, perhaps one-tenth of annual turnover around 1907. Most of manufacturing industry relied for capital either upon its own reinvested profits or upon the services of the provincial stock exchanges; and the local exchanges would deal only with established firms in the traditional industries of their localities. By the standards of an advanced industrial economy, or by the criteria of the investment banking systems of continental Europe, it was the British capital market itself that was a laughing stock.

From the perspective of a global investor, however, seeking not top yields but a combination of moderate return with good security, the London market offered endless choices. On the other hand, it tended to offer them in South Africa rather than South Shields, Brazil rather than Bradford, Minnesota rather than Manchester. Edwardian Britain still did not possess the financial institutions, credit structures or information flows competent to connect UK investors with the best UK investment opportunities. Instead, within the square mile of the City, it possessed an extraordinarily compact and highly sophisticated information network, able to offer the investor a global array of fairly attractive yields and fairly safe bets. This system was better at locating such a mix on the other side of the Atlantic than it was at finding it on the other side of Britain. Also, it was highly skilled at assessing railway securities.

Ever since the United Kingdom's own railway boom in the 1830s and 1840s, British investment institutions had leaned towards transport issues. Trained upon UK railway stock, they then pursued this interest overseas as other economies in their turn built their railway sectors. Just as Britain's mid-Victorian boom was centred around home railways, so Britain's late-Victorian spree in foreign investment was centred around other people's railways. No less than 40% of Britain's vast overseas lending 1870–1914 went into these railways, not to speak of the further 20% which went into associated projects such as harbours, docks and tramway systems. If yields within the rail sector are considered around

1900, home rail stock would yield lowest, then empire rail stock, with other foreign rail stock yielding highest.[263] Given the information flows circling the London insurance offices, and the institutional structure available to them, usually just down the street, a strong preference for non-UK rail stock seems entirely rational. American railway stock fell in the highest-yielding 'other foreign' category while the concentration, in type of stock, on gold bonds or debentures balanced the yield with a high level of protection. For an insurance investor of this vintage such a conjunction does not look especially risible.

8. AN EXCURSION INTO EDUCATION

One of Phoenix's exercises in mortgage lending or property investment had an outcome which no insurer or financier could have predicted or desired. It brought into uncomfortable and sometimes hilarious confrontation the very different values of the City and the schoolroom, the underwriters and the headmasters.

In 1890, Phoenix accepted a £40,000 mortgage on the grounds and buildings of Brighton College, in exchange for insurances worth at least £800 per annum. By November 1893, the College was three years behind with its interest payments; that is, it had taken the loan and paid almost nothing for it.[264] Nor, astonishingly, did the College appear to believe that it ought to pay the interest. Taking the academic high ground, the governors suggested to Phoenix that the company's right to anything as capitalistic as interest 'should give place to the other charges upon the College'.

This was not a good way to deal with the Phoenix Board. At first, they were dumbfounded – a big institutional borrower denying the basic principles upon which loans were conducted was a novelty for them – then they became irritated. The company solicitor was instructed to 'make peremptory application for the interest at the penal rate'.[265] But the College still could not pay. The only way which the Board could see towards achieving any restitution was to assume ownership of the College. In November 1894, the governors undertook to surrender to Phoenix, at the end of the next term, in April 1895, 'possession of the property including the Equity of redemption', but with the office allowing the College 'to carry on the Educational

[263] This, of course, assumes comparable types of stock, ordinary shares against ordinaries, preference stock against preference, and so on.
[264] Directors' Minutes, Z25, p. 117, 10 July 1890; Trustees' Minutes 23 November 1893.
[265] *Ibid.*, 24 June 1894.

arrangements in the meanwhile'.[266] Just as the fictional Phoenix of E. Nesbit's *The Phoenix and the Carpet* was an amiable guide to the young, so it seems that the real-life Phoenix of Lombard Street was inveigled into the business of educating them.

Between November 1894 and May 1895, the Phoenix Board tried to beat out a solution which would not involve them in becoming the unexpected proprietors of an unwanted school. In February, the company agreed to leave the College 'undisturbed' for five years if the College could amass a payment of £10–15,000. By mid-March, the Trustees agreed to cut their price still further: they would accept 'any reasonable proposal' for just £1,050 deposited against the arrears of interest. By late March, at the end of their tether, the Phoenix men said they would accept £500 as the price of keeping the school open until midsummer.[267] But the College did not have even £500 to its name, and on 16 May 1895, the Trustees decided that they must take possession of the property, while authorising the governors to continue the schooling. However, every aspect of the school's dealings were to be 'entirely subject to the control of the Company', and Phoenix would only pay a headmaster 'approved by them', at £600 per annum, for five years.[268] In this sequence of odd dealings, it is clear that the educationalists acted with great financial whimsicality and the financiers, bending over backwards in the cause of learning, with great legal restraint. Of course, the financiers were also bending over backwards in the attempt not to become educationalists, but to little avail.

During the late 1890s and 1900s, Phoenix made repeated attempts to dispose of its interest in the College. A good prospect seemed to arise in 1899 when one powerful public school perceived correctly that a financially weak public school was a fit subject for a sort of academic takeover: Fettes College made a bid to lease Brighton College for £400 per year, with an option to purchase at £20,000, over a ten-year period, and, in the meanwhile, to be responsible for all rents, repairs, expenses and scholarship charges. However, Phoenix was somewhat exasperated even by these more businesslike schoolmasters: in reply the Trustees pitched the cost of the lease at £500 per year, and the purchase price at £22,000, and pointed out, rather tetchily, that options to purchase do not come for nothing, and that this one would involve a deposit of £5,000. Fettes bridled at this display of financial punctiliousness and shied away.[269] Seven years later, the company was looking at possible ways of selling

[266] *Ibid.*, 15 November 1894. [267] *Ibid.*, 21 February, and 14, 21 March 1895.
[268] *Ibid.*, 16 May 1895. [269] *Ibid.*, 30 August 1899.

the Brighton connection by way of a terminable annuity. This project appeared to make reasonable headway in July and August 1906, although the Board was faced with the bizarre conjunction of trying to promote the new solution for Brighton while also clearing up after the disastrous earthquake at San Francisco. The insurers were trying to resign as educators while facing as underwriters one of the worst losses ever to affect their business. But this escape route also failed.[270]

In consequence, Phoenix became increasingly involved in the everyday detail of running a school. In 1903 they were directly financing necessary building work to the College's Chichester House, and in 1905, the luckless Bristow Bovill, as chairman, decided that he had better inspect the place for himself, only to conclude that further repairs were needed to Junior House and that the playing fields needed new changing rooms.[271] For the sporting Bovill, there was at least some interest in the latter issue, but he must have reflected, as he toured the corridors, that his task was a peculiar occupation for the chairman of a City institution. In 1907, the Phoenix Trustees were diverted from their consideration of losses in Japan and purchases of Grand Trunk Pacific Railway bonds to debate solemnly whether or not a sacked school clerk should receive a term's wages.[272]

A note of desperation is evident in these dealings. It was particularly pronounced in 1896 when a defaulting agent in the Brighton area was retained, despite his debt, 'as long as he co-operates with the Company in promoting the success of the College'.[273] Clearly, the Trustees felt they needed every supporting voice they could muster. However, no agent's support and no amount of avuncular school visits could solve the central financial problem. In 1900, the College's debt had to be written down from nearly £40,000 to £29,582 and in 1906 to £20,000, with accrued interest of £4,384 being written off, 'the amount never having been received'.[274] In 1912, the debt was rescheduled with a further mortgage on the property but Phoenix was still not getting its money.

By 1914, the Phoenix had been the reluctant owner of a public school for nearly twenty years and appeared to be no nearer shedding the liability than it had been in 1895. The Board could only conclude that mortgage business sometimes led in some very odd directions and into some very unpredictable obligations.

[270] *Ibid.*, 25 July, 8 and 15 August 1906. [271] *Ibid.*, 22 July 1903.
[272] *Ibid.*, 11 September 1907. [273] *Ibid.*, 19 March 1896.
[274] *Ibid.*, 10 January 1900; 17 January 1906.

9. STAFFING THE PHOENIX: LIFE IN THE OFFICE, 1870–1914

A Company of Clerks: the poor and the poorly, 1870–1900

As business expanded in the last third of the nineteenth century, so inevitably did the band of people required to transact it. Unfortunately, at the beginning of this period, the precise number of clerks and messengers who did the bidding of Phoenix's tiny group of administrative officers cannot be established, since the gentlemanly habit of inscribing each salary into the general ledger by name had died out earlier in the century. However, we do have the aggregate expenses of running Head Office, ranging from the costs of salaries and pensions to the bills for 'office beer' and 'office coals', and a good deal can be inferred from these.

It is not clear whether these general ledger journal entries represent the whole of staff and organisational costs – since it is possible that parts of these could have been charged to other accounts – but certainly the journals contain no other separable or identifiable figures attaching to these purposes. So it seems safe to assume that these entries capture at least the majority of staff and staff-related costs, and it is apparent that the series moves consistently over time.

Reinforcement from Minute Book entries concerning staff provides a background social, and a somewhat startling medical, history of those who worked at Phoenix House in the decades on either side of 1900.

In Table 1.10 increases in the home agency and home foreign staff between 1874 and 1877 (see above p. 5) are reflected in the rise in clerks' salaries for 1875/9, while the depressed business conditions of the early 1880s seem to have taken a while to work through into the lower expenditure on clerkly assistance for 1885/9. In general, however, the trend is clearly towards expansion, with a threefold increase in the recorded salary bill of clerks between 1870/4 and 1900/4. The huge increases in the period 1905/8 are produced by the company's reorganisation as a composite insurer in the middle 1900s. The increase in the administrative component of work is also nicely captured in the accumulative divergence between the totals for messengers' and clerks' salaries, although it is interesting that the Phoenix continued to require a high level of spruceness from its messengers and was prepared, as it remained until the end, to invest in this. The first sign of the 'secretarial revolution' appears with the initial salary payments to 'typewriters' in 1908.

Three lists of Head Office staff – which, of course, give names and numbers only for single points in time – exist for 1873, 1882 and, a probable date only, 1895. These suggest that Phoenix headquarters was

Table 1.10. *Phoenix clerks' salaries and office costs, 1870–1908 (average annual totals, £)*

	1870/4	1875/9	1880/4	1885/9	1890/4	1895/9	1900/4	1905/8
Clerks' salaries	517	730	882	587	1,306	1,982	1,586	6,205
Messengers' salaries	530	689	811	738	768	795	844	974
Messengers' uniforms	12	19	24	35	41	26	35	61
Typists' salaries	–	–	–	–	–	–	–	359[a]
Pensions	37	37	70	291	330	362	307	1,587
Beer	4	4	8	20	22	–	–	–
Gas	65	145	160	90	6	19	40	52
Coal	40	40	45	36	26	33	63	84

Note:[a] Single year, 1908.

run in 1873 by no more than forty-five individuals; that there was an increase to fifty-one in 1882; and then a small reduction to fifty in 1895. Clearly, the major increases in administrative scale had to await the switch to composite structure in the 1900s. However, the total salary bill was affected not only by numbers but also by age structure. In 1873, Phoenix had decided to 'conform with the practice of other first-class Fire Offices, and that the salary of junior clerks be increased by £10 per annum from the date of their being placed on the Establishment'.[275] A probationary junior clerk would still commence work for as little as £30–40 per year in the 1870s. And 'the Boy, Scott' who, in 1872, gave 'great Satisfaction' had his pay *increased* to £24 a year.[276]

Considerable disparities existed in the remuneration of those at Phoenix House. Figure 1.1 is a 'scattergram' recording Minute Book entries between 1870 and 1895 which attach a salary figure to a given post. It reveals the disparities very clearly. A clerk who completed his probationary period would enter the 'established' staff at a rate of £60 or £70 per year, and this modest figure scarcely budged over the quarter century. At the other extreme, Lovell and Broomfield as secretary both achieved £2,000 and the MacDonalds were not far off this figure.

There are three detectable bands within the scatter. The first, from £20 to £100, spans the great majority of clerks and messengers. It is likely that the data in Table 1.10 cover only this category of salaries. A clerk could, under the system of annual increments, work his way up to a total of £250

275 Phoenix Directors' Minutes, V21, p. 410, 9 September 1874.
276 Trustees' Minutes, 8 February 1872.

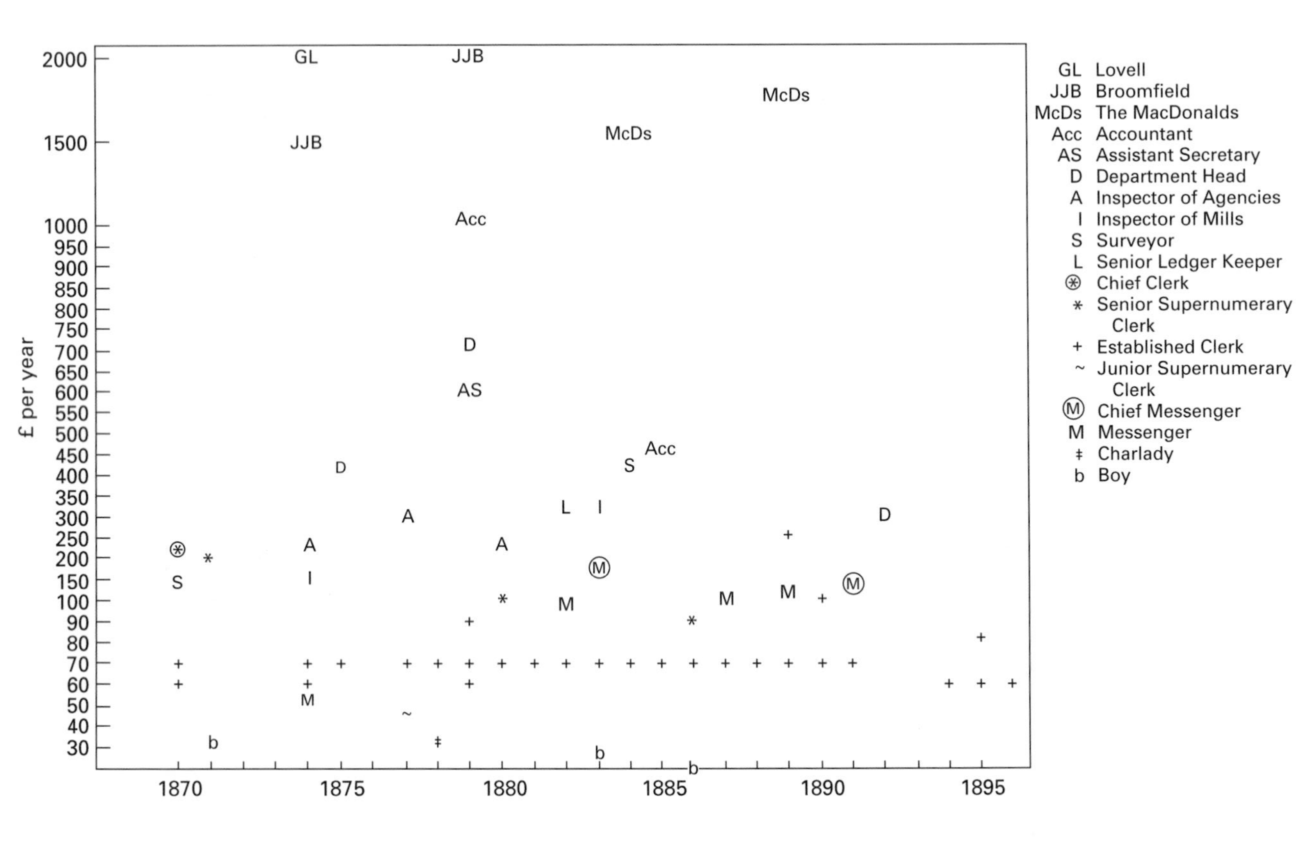

Fig. 1.1 Levels of staff salaries by type of staff, 1870–96

per year, but high levels of illness, resignations and sackings[277] tended to keep the staff structure bottom-heavy with a high turnover of junior members, of which there was a rich supply, with constant competition for entry.[278] Indeed, Phoenix kept a roster of *potential* probationary clerks and admitted them by turn.

The second band extends from about £150 to £400 and captures chief clerks, inspectors, surveyors, senior ledger keepers and the odd, untypically youthful departmental head (see 1892). By contrast, William Lovell, head of the town department could work himself well into the third band of £450 to £2,000 (see 1879), which covered the senior administrative officials, accountants, assistant secretaries, the older departmental heads, and, right at the top, the secretaries. The appointment of Musgrave Heaphy as inspector of agencies, as well as of Mills, shows up in the second band in 1877, as does the appointment of W. A. Harris as inspector of agencies in 1880 and of Arthur Thwaites as surveyor of metropolitan building losses in 1884, while F. B. MacDonald's rather economical appointment to assistant secretary registers in 1879. A sign for the future is provided in the appointment of E. A. Boston to an established clerkship in the foreign department in 1883 at all of £70, despite his 'perfect knowledge of German'.[279]

Some solace for the modest take-home pay of the underlings seems to have been offered, at least until the 1890s, in the provision of office beer, although it is unclear, given the absence of major changes in staff numbers, why consumption should have apparently doubled in the early 1880s, and doubled again in the later part of the same decade. Certainly, there are no known movements in beer prices, at a time of generally declining living costs, which could account for this.[280] Perhaps this too had something to do with age structure, or maybe it is related to the peculiar health profile of *fin de siècle* clerkdom (see below). At least, it could have had little to do with the third clerk in the guarantee department who was dismissed in 1879 'in consequence of his irregular attendance and intemperate habits'.[281] Clearly, he did his drinking elsewhere, and a lot of it before 1880.

It is also possible that the unusual health patterns are associated in some

[277] See below, pp. 97–103. Clerks who did reach the £250 ceiling were pensioned at half that figure.

[278] Clerks and chief clerks in the early branches were paid rather less then their colleagues in London. Junior clerks in a provincial branch received £30–50 per year in the 1880s, chief clerks £60–100, the latter maximum increasing to £120 by 1887 and £150 by 1889.

[279] Directors' Minutes, X23, p. 341, 2 May 1883.

[280] The price trend during the Great Depression years 1873–96 was generally downward and purchasing power advanced for those in work. Total dutiable production of beer in the United Kingdom fell slightly in 1882–6.

[281] Directors' Minutes, W22, p. 353, 8 January 1879.

way with the odd variations in the company's expenditure on fuel. The new technology of gas made great advances against the old technology of coal in the period 1875–90, but then fell off to almost nothing during a period when the expenditure on coal also declined. From the early 1890s until 1910, coal was again the dominant source of warmth for Phoenix employees.

The company's attitude towards its messengers and desk workers was strongly paternalistic. Pensions made their first appearance, for messengers, in 1871, and then, for clerks, from 1880, with widows' pensions being represented sporadically as the Board saw fit. Thus, in 1878, the widow of the former chief clerk of the country office was awarded £70 per year for ten years in order to help educate her two children.[282] More *ad hoc* were two contributions of 1876: one of £5 towards the funeral expenses of a Phoenix charlady who had died after twenty-six years of mopping up, and had secured the succession for her daughter, and one of £100 to a Blairgowrie millworker who had lost a hand while attempting to extinguish a blaze at a cotton factory insured by Phoenix.[283]

But, in relation to its own workers, it seems that Phoenix *needed* to be paternalistic : many of the payments and pensions were made in respect of those too ill to work or dying unseasonably. There were extraordinary numbers of these: between 1870 and 1895 the number of cases of illness, mostly serious, recorded in the Minute Books totalled sixty-eight. Given a total staff averaging around fifty, over a twenty-five-year period, this implies that a career at the Phoenix in the late nineteenth-century virtually guaranteed that the individual would contract something nasty. Since there is no reason to think that Phoenix was any different from any other large London institution, the implication is that the City of this era was a pestiferous place.

Some complained. One, Edgar Preston, junior clerk, and clearly a lad of refined sensibilities, objected more to his peers and his policies than to the pestilence, finding that 'my constant employment in copying policies was a degrading task, as well as being forced to associate with the very scum of the office whose habits and language, being distasteful and repulsive to my feelings, was a source of constant regret to me'. He was paid off with three months' salary.[284] But at least Preston left in full

282 *Ibid.*, p. 317, 22 May 1878.

283 Another Phoenix charlady in 1885 hailed from a family which had 'for three generations supplied a charwoman to the Company' (Trustees' Minutes, 24 December 1885).

284 This case inaugurated the system of requiring one month's notice and paying one quarter's salary on severance (Trustees' Minutes 21 and 28 December 1882). It is also worth recording that in 1884 three junior clerks were sacked from the country department for 'using bad language, swearing and otherwise misconducting themselves in the

health. Others worried about the threat to theirs, and, in May 1890, the Trustees recorded that there had been 'many complaints about the insanitary state of the office'. They decided that it needed a new drainage system costing some £510.[285]

But the state of the drains alone could not explain the variety of dangerous afflictions to which the Phoenix staff fell prey in these years. These included tuberculosis, typhoid and rheumatic fever, smallpox, diphtheria, enlargement of the liver, dropsy, quinsy, anasarca, and overwork, among others. Cases tended to cluster: there were eleven in 1876–8, the same number in 1883–4 and six in the single year, 1886. And they were no respecters of persons. After 58 years of surviving life in the office, without a single day lost to illness, Secretary Lovell was suddenly felled by disease, and died abruptly in May 1878.[286] A copy of the famous portrait of him[287] was hung in the boardroom by way of memorial. This did little to protect his successor, for J. J. Broomfield was forced into extended leave in 1879, 'after a severe attack of indisposition' hardly more than a year after assuming office.[288] But at least, both Lovell and Broomfield were in advanced years; more worrying was that their trials came after an extraordinary spate of sickness in the office.

Over scarcely more than two years, one clerk died of typhoid, another recovered from smallpox, eight were indisposed for sufficiently long periods to require the hiring of locums, one agency ledger keeper died after a 'long, continued and dangerous illness' and another was sent off to Australia to recuperate, probably from the same disease, which was almost certainly tuberculosis. Also in 1879, a clerk at the Charing Cross Branch was paid £25 to cover the expenses of his two children 'dying of diphtheria' and, two years later, the chief clerk of the Head Office Agency Department had to be given leave, being in 'a prostrate condition owing to the recent sudden deaths of *five* members of his family'.[289] This sequence suggests that around a quarter of Phoenix's main office staff were touched by serious illness at the turn of the 1870s and 1880s. Compared to this outbreak, the clerk who in 1872 went incurably insane after twenty-four years at the ledgers hardly ruffled the Board's calm, though it did provoke their charity. He was given £20 per annum and referred to St Luke's Hospital, of which Octavius Coope and George

Office as well as being careless and inattentive in their duties' (Directors' Minutes Y24, p. 3, 4 June 1884).

[285] Trustees' Minutes, 9 May and 16 June 1890.

[286] Directors' Minutes, W22, p. 307, 15 May 1878.

[287] Painted by E. J. Haynes at a cost of 150 guineas, and reproduced in vol. I at p. 691.

[288] Directors' Minutes, W22, p. 380, 21 May 1879.

[289] Trustees' Minutes, 25 September 1879, 3 November 1881. My emphasis.

Fuller were governors, on account of its 'moderate charges'.[290] But, by 1889, the Board was sufficiently moved by the string of disease attacks that it appointed medical inspectors, 'especially with the object of reporting on the health of absent clerks'.[291]

Working hours could not have helped. One veteran, looking back a half-century from the comparative safety of the late 1920s, remembered pay that was smaller, work that was harder and hours that were inhuman. His pay started at £10, and reached £25 by the fourth year; so he must have been very junior. But for him, Saturday half-days were the exception, sport was discouraged as detrimental to business, and his working week was extraordinary. 'Sometimes,' he recalled, 'I got away at 6pm, but two or three days a week, I worked up to 10, 11 or 12 o'clock. Sometimes I slept on the hearthrug in the private office.'[292] If he recalled correctly, it is little wonder that so many cracked under a pace of this severity.

Two further patterns of peculiarity underlie the spiral of ill-health. The first involves Phoenix's reaction to the frailty of its workers, the second adds a dynastic aspect to the cycle of affliction. In reacting to serious cases, company paternalism went beyond sick leave and illness allowances; often the patient was packed off on a restorative sea voyage. Thus, Arthur Long, agency department ledger keeper and a victim of 'chronic lung inflammation' was despatched on the long haul to Australia twice, in 1875 and 1881, only to resign immediately after his second landfall.[293] More modestly, the smallpox sufferer was sent to the seaside in 1877 and the quinsy sufferer to the countryside in 1886.[294] But, also in 1886, both Berkeley Broomfield, a junior clerk in the foreign department and the chief clerk in the town renewals department received the full treatment and were put aboard ship for a three-month return trip to the Cape.[295] Similarly, in 1888, Surveyor Musgrave Heaphy's overwork resulted in another maritime remedy.[296] Again, in 1892, the chief clerk in the guarantee (i.e. reinsurance) department was sent on a protracted errand to Genoa, partly on company business, partly for his health (although one can only guess what Genoa was supposed to do for him).[297] Both the degree of corporate care and the faith in the efficacy of sea air are in their different ways striking.

This is true also of the dynastic connections within the illness patterns.

[290] *Ibid.*, 30 May 1872, 6 June 1872. [291] Trustees' Minutes, 30 May 1889.
[292] *The Bird*, January 1928, p. 5. The witness was Mr Hargreaves, the London Marine secretary.
[293] Trustees' Minutes, 21 October, 29 September 1881.
[294] *Ibid.*, 10 May 1877, 16 September 1886.
[295] *Ibid.*, 28 October 1886, 18 November 1886. [296] *Ibid.*, 6 December 1888.
[297] *Ibid.*, 30 June 1892.

Of course, the dynastic links within the Phoenix organisation were significant, even without the additional bonds of infection. Thus, Arthur Shum, son of Phoenix shareholder Captain Shum, and bearer of one of the original Phoenix sugar names, was appointed a probationary junior clerk in September 1877, as was William George Lovell, grandson of Secretary Lovell, and son of William Lovell of the town department.[298] Similarly, around the same time, the son of another secretary, J. J. Broomfield, was admitted to the foreign department, the area of his father's original specialism. The family dimension to the business practice of the late nineteenth-century City is not perhaps especially surprising, except maybe for the slight whiff of downward social mobility in the case of the Shums.[299]

What is definitely surprising is the impact of ill-health on these descendants of the Phoenix mighty; disease drew no boundaries for them. Arthur Shum lasted only four years before succumbing to rheumatic fever in 1881, and, in 1893, his appointment was cancelled entirely owing to prolonged absence. More extraordinary was the fate of the Lovells and the Broomfields. Within months of joining the Phoenix, Stuart Lovell fell prey to tuberculosis – and was replaced in his clerkship by his brother, Charles Edward.[300] Less than a decade later, Berkeley Broomfield featured in exactly the same sequence: he joined Phoenix, contracted tuberculosis – and, in January 1887, was replaced by his elder brother, Gordon.[301]

The implication is that life in the late nineteenth-century City was not all high stools, loving copperplate and cheery coal fires. Other, largely unremarked features of the clerkly regime would seem to include predatory infections, dangerous drains and lethal coughs. If, as George Hurren's early history remarks, the staff of the Victorian Phoenix were increasingly moving out to 'what were then pleasant suburbs on the slopes of the Kent and Surrey hills and the Hampstead heights: Sydenham, Forest Hill, Norwood, Streatham, Beckenham, Finchley, Highgate',[302] the implication is not as comfortable as he assumed; they were running for their lives, and not always successfully. Clerking in a City office in the 1870s, 1880s and 1890s was not just workaday toil; if the Phoenix experience was anything to go by, it was a serious threat to life and limb.

Of course, there had also to be a happier side to life in the office. The centenary of 1882 brought a 10% bonus for everyone, with an additional 100 guineas for the secretary and the actuary, and 50 guineas for the

298 Directors' Minutes, W22, p. 245, 19 September 1877.
299 See vol. I, p. 674.
300 Directors' Minutes, W22, p. 286, 6 March 1878; *ibid.*, p. 415, 1 October 1879.
301 Trustees' Minutes, 6 January 1887. 302 Hurren, *Phoenix Renascent*, p. 126.

assistant secretary.[303] And, in respect of another centenary three years later, the foreign chief clerk, Newcombe was sent over to Hamburg with the Phoenix mace and emblem to mark the hundred-year connection between the Phoenix and the Hanbury-Behrmann agency. In 1883, the son of the Hamburg agent, H. Behrmann proved that dynastic connection was not invariably fatal for Phoenix clerks. He was appointed a temporary supernumerary clerk in November 1883 in order to acquaint himself with English insurance practice, served his time, and departed, apparently still in good health. His preparation was thorough, for he had already served two years' apprenticeship in a German fire office, and, when he had finished at Phoenix House, was passed on for a further bout of experience in the United States.[304] Others too must have liked working at Phoenix: in 1876 ledger clerk Alfred Hawkins had 'eighteen years service and [was] ... the fourth generation of his family as clerks in the office'.[305]

In 1884, perhaps to build up the resilience of those less robust than Behrmann or less pertinacious than the Hawkinses, Phoenix opened a subscription to the Insurance Offices' Cricket and Athletics Club, and, within a month, was persuaded by the indestructible sage and sportsman, Sir John Lubbock, to double it.[306] No doubt, too, the staff were heartened in the spring of 1887 by the company's decision to spend a 'moderate amount' – actually £35 – on the Queen's Jubilee Illuminations and to 'fit up the front of the Charing Cross office for the Royal Procession'.[307] And it is salutary to remember that science was not sleeping: in the *annus doloris* of 1886, as the clerks went down like flies, and poor Berkeley Broomfield was committed to the sea air, Phoenix's Liverpool office got its first telephone, for £20 a year.[308]

One other feature of staff behaviour which obtrudes from the record by its frequency is the incidence of fraud. When the clerks were not succumbing to the vapours of the office, they were, all too often, making off with its profits. At least this is true of the period 1870–1882; after this, if the clerks did not get healthier, they do appear to have become more honest.

Most, if not all, of the frauds of the 1870s were minor embezzlements by penurious clerks. Thus, in 1871 Mr Kendall had 'to make good his son's defalcation' and, a year later, still owed £16, which he could not

[303] Directors' Minutes, X23, p. 195, 18 January 1882.
[304] Trustees' Minutes, 1 November 1883.
[305] *Ibid.*, 14 December 1876. But this Hawkins ended in impropriety, debt to the company, resignation and 'abject poverty', before being reinstated as a supernumerary clerk (*ibid.*, 14 February, 1 August 1878). The impropriety was almost certainly minor fraud and Phoenix again showed startling generosity in reappointing.
[306] *Ibid.*, 28 February, 13 March 1884. [307] *Ibid.*, 6 January 1887.
[308] *Ibid.*, 9 September 1886.

pay.[309] In 1873, one of the Phoenix surveyors was sacked for participating in the fraudulent fire claim of a German wool warehouseman in London. He was paid off with six months' salary (£72) but not without dispute. It was from this disagreement that the principle first emerged that all clerks should accept, upon appointment, that their positions were terminable by the company at three months' notice.[310]

More serious were the outbreaks of the late 1870s. Well outside Head Office, the company's agent at Blackburn, F. M. Railton had developed a nice line in creative book-keeping. In 1877, this was detected and Railton fled to, and was apprehended in, Glasgow, whereupon he was committed for trial on a charge of forging the company's receipts.[311] But such things could also happen inside Head Office. In February 1878, the Trustees informed the Board that they had discovered a succession of frauds by a former agency department ledger keeper, Glover, amounting to some £2,000 over a four-year period. Amongst other things, Glover had made off with the balance of the Hackney account. Little could be done about Glover because he had died in the midst of his thievery. Indeed, here it took illness and death to reveal fraud. However, something could be done about office practice. Hackney got its just deserts as the agency commission was reduced from 10% to 7.5%. And the daily grind of the clerks was subjected to the immortal instruction that 'henceforth the use of erasers be forbidden in the Establishment and errors corrected by ruling out and rewriting only'. The MacDonalds also brought in new checks on the recording of monies received by each department.[312]

Less heinous than Glover's embezzlement was the double-dealing of Hobson, the principal clerk in the guarantee department. In the January of the next year, 1879, Phoenix discovered that Commercial Union, and a number of other offices, had been paying commission to Hobson on reinsurances laid off by Phoenix to them. This, of course, created an improper inducement for Hobson to cede insurances that could have made a profit for Phoenix. But the malpractice was a matter of playing the system rather than of robbing the company. Hobson was admonished and told to keep his mind on Phoenix business. However, the Board did consider it wise to be a little more generous with its reinsurance commissions, increasing them from 10% to the 15% employed by most other offices.[313]

[309] *Ibid.*, 8 June 1871, 13 June 1872.

[310] *Ibid.*, 4 and 18 December 1873. Later, in 1882, revised to one month's notice, as a result of the Preston case (see above, fn. 284).

[311] Directors' Minutes, W22, pp. 172–81, 24 January and 28 February 1877.

[312] *Ibid.*, p. 283, 27 February 1878; Trustees' Minutes 21 February, 30 May 1878.

[313] *Ibid.*, 21 January 1879.

Sin struck next at Charing Cross. A number of clerks in the old West End office fell to rooking the Phoenix in 1880 and 1881. In September 1880, one Brocklebank was sacked for stealing £63 and 12s; the sum was refunded, but he was still dismissed. With some cheek, he then applied for reappointment in the lesser position of supernumerary clerk, but was rejected. Six months later, a periodic financial review by the accountant caught his colleague, William Kerin, in a sad and similar misdemeanour. Eight renewal premiums, falling due at Christmas, and totalling £7 5s 3d, had been received but not entered by Kerin. He repaid the amount but went the same way as the more ambitious Brocklebank.[314]

These sackings seem to have cleansed the stables at Charing Cross, but scarcely were they enacted than similar iniquities broke out back in Lombard Street. This time Percy Selway, clerk in the much-attacked agency department, and previously well thought of, was found to have made 'false entries in the books'. Phoenix sacked him too and considered legal action. But the Selways were a Phoenix family and 'at the earnest request of his father, who has been an Agent for this Office for upwards of thirty years, and always correct and punctual in the payment of his Account, the Board consented to refrain from a prosecution which would bring ruin upon the family'.[315] Family connection, it would seem, could rescue even a fraudster.

But, once again a sterner regime followed upon the discovery of malfeasance. The senior ledger keeper in Selway's department, Colpoys, also ran an agency for Chelsea, and thus controlled both a stream of income and the means of recording its receipt. Now several times bitten in the agency department and mindful of Glover's exploits in the same post, the Board required Colpoys to raise a surety of £1,000 and to pay all premiums received from Chelsea directly to the accountant, making no entry for any Chelsea income in his own ledgers.[316]

Crime proved more resistible than disease. The remedies and safeguards against fraud kept the peace in the office from 1881 to the turn of the century. There are only three exceptions recorded by the Trustees and directors. In 1882, the ominously named William Crippen, principal clerk in the town renewals department, defaulted to the tune of £103 18s 7d and absconded. In 1887, the irregularities of Kenneth Lloyd, second clerk in the guarantee department, were mild by comparison: once he had put his own finances in order, the Trustees agreed that 'a further trial be given him in an inferior department'; but they still stopped his yearly

[314] Directors' Minutes, X23, p. 34, 2 June 1880; Trustees' Minutes, 2 September 1880; Directors' Minutes, X23, p. 101, 2 March 1881.

[315] *Ibid.*, p. 163, 28 September 1881. [316] Trustees' Minutes, 29 September 1881.

salary increases. Only Thomas Milnes, the local secretary for Newcastle, kept the standard of heroic dishonesty aloft. He was the most senior official of the era to be dismissed – or, in his case, permitted to resign – 'in consequence of financial irregularities'.[317]

Many characteristics already noted in regard to office life surface again in the phenomenon of clerkly fraud: low pay, the temptation offered to the very few individuals who handled premium receipts under the far from all-seeing eye of the small executive group, the permanent presence of sudden death, and the importance of family intercession, both to acquire position and escape punishment.

Corporate growth: the invisible hand writes on the wall

Once the century turned, some strong new patterns began to appear in staff affairs. The conversion of the Phoenix into a composite office between 1908 and 1914 revolutionised the size of the workforce as the company added life assurers, accident insurers and marine underwriters to its original fire specialists. The increasing complexity of the business required a more sophisticated arrangement of executive functions and the creation of a managerial elite with specialised roles. And, as the personnel expanded and were reorganised, so bigger and better premises were needed to house them. Yet it is noticeable that these aspects of modernisation did not succeed in securing a proportionate improvement in office health, although at a slower rate, improve it did. There was better luck with office crime, which virtually disappeared from the records between 1900 and 1914.

Around 1895, the old fire office was still being run by about fifty individuals. By 1910, the new composite office required a Head Office staff of 248; of these 150 worked the fire department, 45 the life and 21 the accident, while all of these were supported by a force of 32 messengers and 'typewriters'.[318] By 1912, the fire department had added two individuals but the workforce for the life and accident sections had grown to sixty-one and thirty respectively, and there were now thirty-two typists and twenty-eight messengers. Leaving aside the latter two groups, the average salary in the fire department was about £230, and a pound or so lower in the life department.

But, of course, there was a growing labour force (and increasing expenditure upon it) outside London and outside the United Kingdom. With

[317] Directors' Minutes, X23, p. 269, 2 August 1882; Trustees' Minutes 15 September 1887, 22 May 1890.

[318] *Ibid.*, 28, p. 273, 20 January 1909.

regard to these workers in the British provinces and the wider world, Phoenix remained more clearly a fire office. In 1913, the 302 staff at Head Office were reinforced by 159 in the UK branches, but, of these, only twenty dealt in non-fire business. While Head Office needed thirty-three lady-typists and twenty-six messengers to handle its paperwork, the branches could muster only thirteen typists between them. Overseas, in Phoenix's various foreign operations, there were 458 further staff but only fourteen of these were engaged upon non-fire business, and apparently not one of these 458 merited a typist. The total salary bill worldwide was £147,607 for fire business, £23,129 for life and £1,490 for accident. In addition, the need to maintain retired staff on pensions was costing Phoenix about £21,000 per annum on the eve of the First World War.[319]

The gentlemanly, broad-brush, all-round supervision practised by the Lovells or MacDonalds was insufficient to control a force of this size and these methods died, almost precisely, with the old century. In March 1899, W. C. MacDonald retired after fifty-four years' service with the Phoenix and on the highest pension awarded by the company to that point, £1,500 per year.[320] His brother, F. B., continued alone as chief secretary until this 'valued and respected servant' died in harness in April 1901.[321] Recognising the significance of the passing of the MacDonalds, the Board formed a committee 'to consider the changes which may be necessary in consequence'. In fact, some changes had been afoot since 1899. For, on the retirement of W. C. MacDonald, replacement was effected not by a single person but by three. While his ageing brother nominally kept the reins, H. B. Guernsey and Clement Hutt were appointed assistant secretaries for the home department and W. G. Newcomb for the foreign department. A new interest in specialisation and departmentalisation at the senior level was evident here.

This was carried further with the appointment in January 1902 of Guernsey as successor to Frank MacDonald. The new job carried a most significant change of title: where MacDonald had been chief secretary, Guernsey was to be *manager* and secretary.[322] Phoenix appears to have been something of a pioneer in the managerial changes occurring in the insurance sector at the beginning of the century. To be sure, the Liverpool companies had probably cut the track: the Liverpool & London & Globe had a general manager from as early as 1875, and at the Royal, professional

[319] The matching amount in 1984 was £1.1 million.

[320] Directors' Minutes, 26, p. 331, 8 March 1899. However, this grand sum was not paid for long since William MacDonald died in July 1900. W. H. Lovell also quit the scene by retirement, also after 54 years, in February 1900 (*ibid.*, p. 391, 21 February 1900).

[321] *Ibid.*, 27, p. 15, 17 April 1901.

[322] *Ibid.*, p. 72, 29 January 1902.

Plate 1.17 Office life before the Great War: a tempest of typewriters.

managers, not least the redoubtable Percy Dove, had been leading forces almost since the start, in the 1840s. On the other hand, the Royal Exchange had not solved the problem of central control, even in the 1910s, and compromised in 1911 by creating a Committee of Management consisting of three governors.[323] The Commercial Union, one of the most powerful offices in the market, appointed a general manager only in 1901.

And then they almost lost him. Some Board members at the Commercial Union held to the old orthodoxy that 'you must not allow your managers to be your masters'.[324] The manager in question, Roger Owen, probably the ablest fire expert of his generation, won the day for more forthright executive leadership by dangling an interesting threat over the head of his directors. He had received an offer from the Phoenix of the post of secretary, and, if he could not get his way at the Commercial Union, he was quite prepared to pursue it in the more congenial environment of the rival office. Two implications follow: first, the Phoenix Board around 1900 was interested in head-hunting a professional of the new breed – which throws an interesting oblique light on the recruitment of Gerald Ryan in 1908 – and, secondly, that Owen, as just such a professional, regarded Phoenix as a company committed to advanced managerial practice.[325]

[323] That is, members of the Board.
[324] E. Liveing, *A Century of Insurance: The Commercial Union Assurance Group, 1861–1961* (London, 1961), p. 77.
[325] *Ibid.*, pp.74–8; also see T. Yoneyama, 'The Rise of the Large-scale Composite Insurance Company in the UK', *Kyoto Sangyo University Economic and Business Review*, 20 (1993), pp. 14–15.

It was clear then that something new was intended in the redefinition of Guernsey's title in 1902. Even before the fusion with Pelican in 1908 transferred Ryan, the outstanding actuary of the day, from the leadership of the life company to that of the composite Phoenix, with the still more potent rank of general manager, control was handled differently. Guernsey did not hesitate to wield his expanded powers. Indeed he proved quite adept with the new broom. Within a month of his appointment, two clerks had been sacked and two more retired.[326] In a little over a year, William Newcomb had vacated the headship of the foreign department and two names that were to be important in the Ryan era were selected by Guernsey for top posts, E. A. Boston as chief clerk of the foreign department and A. W. Hardy as chief clerk of the town department.[327]

Guernsey set out particularly to strengthen the foreign department. No doubt, his perspective on this issue was affected by the indifferent trading results achieved by the company's overseas operation around the turn of the century. Not only did Guernsey carry Boston to prominence in the foreign section, he also actively pursued talent for Boston to deploy. In 1903, two officials were head-hunted from the Commercial Union; one, R. F. Kelly was appointed at £350 per annum and given fifteen years' seniority,[328] while the other, S. A. Slipper, was secured for £100 per year in consequence of Guernsey's conviction that the company now needed an official fluent in Spanish and Portuguese.[329] Further reinforcement for the foreign specialists was given when, in March 1904, E. A. Boston – he, of course, of the 'perfect German' – was promoted again, this time to assistant secretary.

There was one final, pleasing, loop of symmetry in Guernsey's run of appointments. It had taken Boston some twenty years from his first placement as a clerk in the foreign department in 1883 to reach the top of the tree. One of Guernsey's last independent appointments was of one Arthur Battrick to a clerkship in February 1907; again Guernsey had found him in another office, this time the Yorkshire. Somewhat over twenty years later, Battrick was to become an important accident manager for the Phoenix.

More generally, however, the managerial reforms of the period 1899–1907 appear to have been well founded. Certainly, when Ryan arrived as general manager, he did little to disturb them. He approved of Guernsey: while Ryan himself took the chief executive role, Guernsey was retained as fire manager and his salary raised to £2,000 per year.[330] Naturally, with the advent of composite status in 1908, the managerial structure of the

[326] Directors' Minutes, 27, pp. 83–4, 26 February 1902.
[327] *Ibid.*, p. 175, 11 March 1903.
[328] Trustees' Minutes, 14 October 1903.
[329] *Ibid.*, 9 December 1903.
[330] Directors' Minutes, 28, p. 137, 18 December 1907.

company needed further attention. Basically, Ryan divided the Phoenix's enlarged Board (the average attendance in the second half of 1907 was eleven members sitting; for the first half of 1908, sixteen sitting) into four committees – one each for fire, life, and accident business and one for finance – and attached an executive staff to each.[331] But he did not tamper with Guernsey's dispositions for fire operations, even after the latter's retirement, after forty-seven years' service, at the end of 1909.

True, early in 1910 Ryan did abolish the largely archaic distinction between the town and country departments of the fire business; in an increasingly urban and integrated Britain, a single home fire department was felt to be more suitable. But the official appointed as the Phoenix's first home fire superintendent was Guernsey's choice, A. W. Hardy.[332] Similarly, Ryan's selection for Guernsey's own successor as fire manager was Guernsey's protégé from the foreign department, E. A. Boston.[333]

The transition in management structure was rapid: within a decade Phoenix completed the move away from a system in which a tiny generalist 'executive' controlled small groups of clerks to a divisionalised system of large sectors each controlled by a specialist departmental manager and answerable to a general manager, each department in turn supervised by a matching committee of the Board.[334]

Of course, as branches expanded and received more staff and more space, other organisational implications followed. By 1906, better financial control over Phoenix's provincial units was becoming necessary. It was to be provided by a central auditing process carried out by Messrs Chatteris, Nicholas and Co., for 600 guineas a year, 'including travelling expenses'.[335] By 1908 the branches needed powers to write their own policies, since expanding volumes of business were making reference back to Head Office increasingly inconvenient. From January 1908, therefore, all fire policies were to carry the lithographed signature of Deputy Chairman Bristow Bovill, all accident policies that of the chairman, Lord George Hamilton, and all fire policies that of the fire manager, Guernsey. They would then be countersigned, either at the branch or at Head Office – with the exception of fire reinsurance contracts which were reserved to Head Office.[336]

[331] The finance committee replaced the Trustees as the company's investment group. The last meeting of the Phoenix Trustees – Avebury, Bovill, Ponsonby and Hodgson attending – took place on 1 January 1908.

[332] Directors' Minutes, 29, p. 106, 5 January 1910. [333] *Ibid.*

[334] The Fire Committee, for instance, reported to the full Board after 1908 as a matter of routine upon new fire losses, losses of other UK insurers, new fire policies over £5,000, and the monthly premium income and losses from the US Branch.

[335] Directors' Minutes, 27, p. 406, 21 February 1906.

[336] *Ibid.*, 28, p. 167, 29 January 1908.

Because of the pressure to gather business by aggregating different types of insurance within a single composite selling unit (in the hope that selling over a single 'counter' would increase the volume sales of all lines), the big insurers were among the leaders of the business community in adopting divisional methods of corporate organisation. And while they were executing this transition at the centre in the 1900s, the development of their branch organisations throughout the periphery turned them into genuinely national *and* divisionalised business systems.

The most imposing recent analysis of the modern business corporation, laid out in Professor Chandler's epic two volumes, *Strategy and Structure* and *Scale and Scope*, argues that the hallmark of twentieth-century big business is the appearance of a central and specialised executive staff.[337] As this central command structure develops, the firm divides into separate departments, each of which is answerable to the headquarters cadre. Such business organisations first developed in the United States in the years before 1914. In the interwar years, the global contraction of trade encouraged a further development: large enterprises split into distinct divisions and created branch organisations for handling overseas markets, the whole array again reporting back to, and directed by, the executive core. This distinctively modern version of big business was centred upon manufacturing industry. Its classical location was the United States, but Germany had created a similar (if less competitive) apparatus of large-scale business organisations over the same period. On the other hand, Britain, encumbered by an inheritance of small, family-based enterprises, was slow to effect the transition to Chandler's ideal business type. Although market and technological pressures are allowed a place in this development, the premier influence is reckoned to be the business leadership: the strategic choices which mould the new business form are taken by the captains of the executive cadre.

Do the Phoenix reforms of the 1900s therefore cast Ryan as a classic Chandlerian hero? Certainly, he created a multi-divisional structure, with a multinational spread, a branch system of organisation, and a central executive group. But the width of choice which he exercised may be open to doubt. And, by Chandler's standards, he is oddly located in both time – before 1914 – and place – the United Kingdom.

Indeed, the applicability of Chandler's formula to large business organisations in the services sector may be questioned. There are few attempts in his work to fit the master-pattern to the service sector in any

337 A. Chandler, *Strategy and Structure* (Cambridge, Mass., 1962); *Scale and Scope: Dynamics of Industrial Capitalism* (Cambridge, Mass., 1990).

country. Yet, in Britain, the multi-divisional composite insurance company, with multinational spread, was in full cry well before 1914. However inclined British manufacturing may have been towards unsuitably old-fashioned forms of family-based organisation, this had never been an option for the insurance ventures. Scale and scope had been an imperative here from the start. If the myriad of risks in a given field of insurance were to be covered effectively, a certain mass of resources was essential: this could come from a sizeable group of rich capitalists, a more sizeable group of partners in a given profession (such as sugar-refiners) or an even more sizeable group of the less rich (such as house-owners) clubbing together to find mutual relief from threat.

So the insurance sector does not make a suitable landscape for Chandler's strictures upon British enterprise. But had its divisionalised and multinational expression of scale progressed so far by 1914 that it may be reckoned to have stolen a march on Chandler's exemplars in American manufacturing? And, if so, why?

Certainly, it does not seem to have been as a result of dashing business leadership by Ryan and his peers. Rather, they were carried along by peculiarities of markets, costs and 'technology'. Insurance customers increasingly wished to cover their different types of risk – against fire, death, injury, burglary, etc., – in a small number of transactions. Convenience for the insured was to acquire the various types of product from the same insurer. High levels of competition and rising costs also made it economical for the insurer to group the different insurance lines within the same administrative structure. This was a classic, if early, instance of organisational change driven by transaction costs. 'The modern corporation', according to Oliver Williamson, 'is mainly to be understood as the product of a series of organisational innovations that have had the purpose and effect of economizing transaction costs.'[338]

Yet the 'technology' of the different lines of insurance did not cohere especially well; there was no strong 'production' logic which pointed in the direction of the composite form. Fire, life, marine and, more recently, accident insurance had developed, down to the 1900s, largely within different specialised firms and had created very distinct insurance practices and processes – in an industrial sense, quite *different* technologies. This is scarcely surprising since the tasks of insuring a ship's cargo, a domestic house or a human life involve quite different issues of title, risk appraisal and probability management. Viewed as products, as Supple

[338] O. E. Williamson, 'The Modern Corporation: Origins, Evolution, Attributes', *Journal of Economic Literature* (December, 1981), p. 1537.

points out, these different items have 'little more in common than, say, the respective purchases of clothing, furniture, gardening implements and food'.[339]

The institutional systems and skills built up to deal with these problems had not developed convergently. Therefore, if the different insurance technologies were brought under the same roof, there was effectively little choice but to organise them within a divisional structure: the divisions of fire, life, marine, accident did not have to be designed; they were ready-made. Here, the divisional layout is not the choice of the corporate strategist; it is presented to the corporate strategist by pre-existing markets; and then forced upon him by demanding clients and escalating costs.

Ryan and his contemporaries read the writing that these market forces left on the underwriting wall. It indicated not only that they should grow by diversification, but also how they should grow. The method was to be by external means – that is, the acquisition of new companies – rather than by internal means – that is, the development of new departments. Given that the technologies and skills of the various fields of insurance were so different, it made more sense to pursue them by purchase than by the re-education of existing staff. Of course, this was particularly true where 'new-type' insurance products, such as personal accident, employers' liability or, later, motor insurance were concerned. Phoenix, under Ryan, was to use the external method.[340] The companies which did so, including the Royal and the Commercial Union, were to achieve greater success in building multi-division composites than offices like the REA and the Alliance which attempted to amass new capacity by the internal method.[341]

However, a final cautionary note is needed in regard to the Phoenix's managerial revolution of the 1900s. It concerns the definition of its central executive. This was not a wholly modern feature. On the one hand, the emergence of General Manager Ryan, supported by a group composed of Fire Manager H. B. Guernsey – the fire manager remaining the senior departmental head – Foreign Fire Manager A. E. Boston, Home Fire Manager A. W. Hardy, Actuary E. R. Straker and Marine Manager J. Sandeman Allan was sufficiently clear-cut. But there were two problems. Firstly, the new hierarchy retained hard edges: the general manager dealt not with an executive committee of his senior aides but directly with each individual departmental chief. This encouraged a 'departmental mentality' which cut across the cooperative dynamic which the true modern

339 B. E. Supple, 'Insurance in British History', in O. Westall (ed.), *The Historian and the Business of Insurance* (Manchester, 1984), p. 1.
340 See Ch. 5 below.
341 Yoneyama, 'The Rise of the Large-Scale Composite Insurance Company', pp. 11–14.

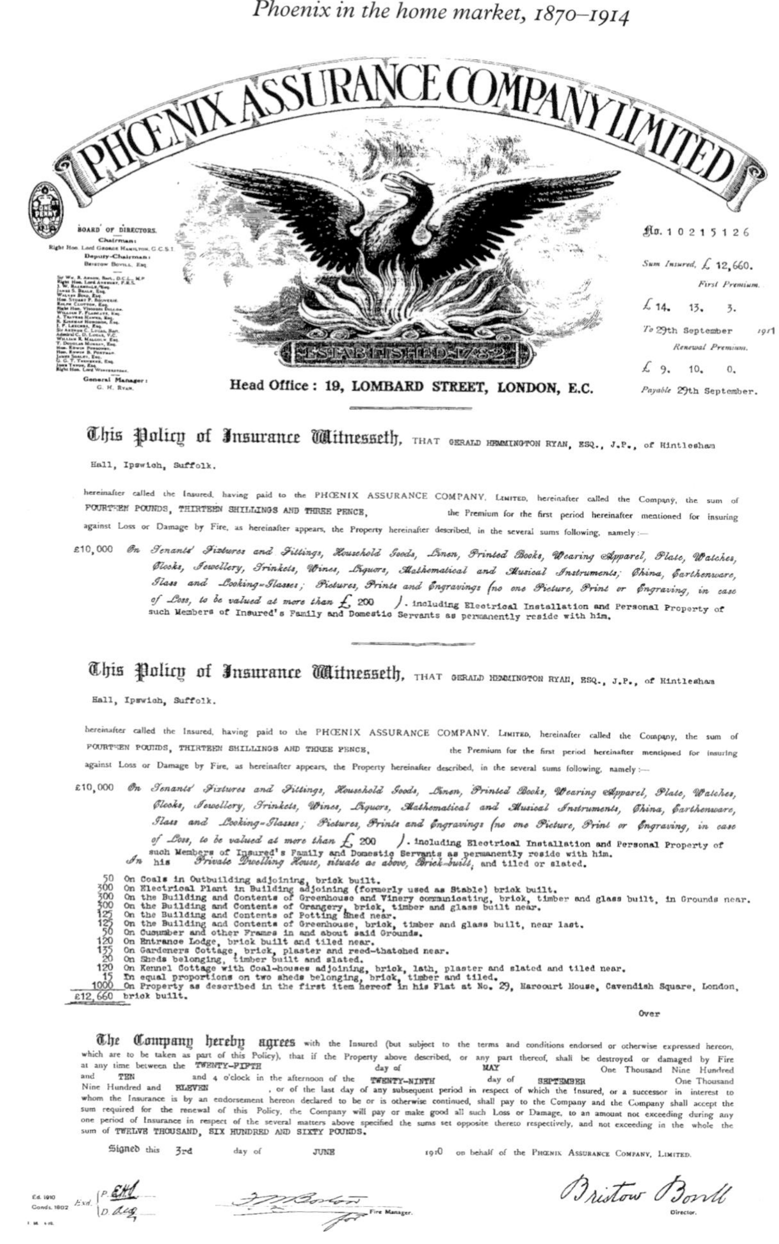

PHŒNIX ASSURANCE COMPANY LIMITED

ESTABLISHED 1782

BOARD OF DIRECTORS.

Chairman:
Right Hon. Lord George Hamilton, G.C.S.I.

Deputy-Chairman:
Bristow Bovill, Esq.

General Manager:
G. H. Ryan.

No. 1 0 2 1 5 1 2 6

Sum Insured, £ 12,660.

First Premium.

£ 14. 13. 3.

To 29th September 1911

Renewal Premium.

£ 9. 10. 0.

Payable 29th September.

Head Office: 19, LOMBARD STREET, LONDON, E.C.

This Policy of Insurance Witnesseth, THAT GERALD HEMMINGTON RYAN, ESQ., J.P., of Hintlesham Hall, Ipswich, Suffolk.

hereinafter called the Insured, having paid to the PHŒNIX ASSURANCE COMPANY, LIMITED, hereinafter called the Company, the sum of FOURTEEN POUNDS, THIRTEEN SHILLINGS AND THREE PENCE, the Premium for the first period hereinafter mentioned for insuring against Loss or Damage by Fire, as hereinafter appears, the Property hereinafter described, in the several sums following, namely:—

£10,000 *On Tenants' Fixtures and Fittings, Household Goods, Linen, Printed Books, Wearing Apparel, Plate, Watches, Clocks, Jewellery, Trinkets, Wines, Liquors, Mathematical and Musical Instruments; China, Earthenware, Glass and Looking-Glasses; Pictures, Prints and Engravings (no one Picture, Print or Engraving, in case of Loss, to be valued at more than £* 200 *).* including Electrical Installation and Personal Property of such Members of Insured's Family and Domestic Servants as permanently reside with him.

This Policy of Insurance Witnesseth, THAT GERALD HEMMINGTON RYAN, ESQ., J.P., of Hintlesham Hall, Ipswich, Suffolk.

hereinafter called the Insured, having paid to the PHŒNIX ASSURANCE COMPANY, LIMITED, hereinafter called the Company, the sum of FOURTEEN POUNDS, THIRTEEN SHILLINGS AND THREE PENCE, the Premium for the first period hereinafter mentioned for insuring against Loss or Damage by Fire, as hereinafter appears, the Property hereinafter described, in the several sums following, namely:—

£10,000 *On Tenants' Fixtures and Fittings, Household Goods, Linen, Printed Books, Wearing Apparel, Plate, Watches, Clocks, Jewellery, Trinkets, Wines, Liquors, Mathematical and Musical Instruments; China, Earthenware, Glass and Looking-Glasses; Pictures, Prints and Engravings (no one Picture, Print or Engraving, in case of Loss, to be valued at more than £* 200 *).* including Electrical Installation and Personal Property of such Members of Insured's Family and Domestic Servants as permanently reside with him.
In his *Private Dwelling House, situate as above, Brick-built,* and tiled or slated.

50 On Coals in Outbuilding adjoining, brick built.
300 On Electrical Plant in Building adjoining (formerly used as Stable) brick built.
300 On the Building and Contents of Greenhouse and Vinery communicating, brick, timber and glass built, in Grounds near.
300 On the Building and Contents of Orangery, brick, timber and glass built near.
125 On the Building and Contents of Potting Shed near.
125 On the Building and Contents of Greenhouse, brick, timber and glass built, near last.
50 On Cucumber and other Frames in and about said Grounds.
120 On Entrance Lodge, brick built and tiled near.
135 On Gardeners Cottage, brick, plaster and reed-thatched near.
20 On Sheds belonging, timber built and slated.
120 On Kennel Cottage with Coal-houses adjoining, brick, lath, plaster and slated and tiled near.
15 In equal proportions on two sheds belonging, brick, timber and tiled.
1000 On Property as described in the first item hereof in his Flat at No. 29, Harcourt House, Cavendish Square, London,
£12,660 brick built.

Over

The Company hereby agrees with the Insured (but subject to the terms and conditions endorsed or otherwise expressed hereon, which are to be taken as part of this Policy), that if the Property above described, or any part thereof, shall be destroyed or damaged by Fire at any time between the TWENTY-FIFTH day of MAY One Thousand Nine Hundred and TEN and 4 o'clock in the afternoon of the TWENTY-NINTH day of SEPTEMBER One Thousand Nine Hundred and ELEVEN, or of the last day of any subsequent period in respect of which the Insured, or a successor in interest to whom the Insurance is by an endorsement hereon declared to be or is otherwise continued, shall pay to the Company and the Company shall accept the sum required for the renewal of this Policy, the Company will pay or make good all such Loss or Damage, to an amount not exceeding during any one period of Insurance in respect of the several matters above specified the sums set opposite thereto respectively, and not exceeding in the whole the sum of TWELVE THOUSAND, SIX HUNDRED AND SIXTY POUNDS.

Signed this 3rd day of JUNE 1910 on behalf of the PHŒNIX ASSURANCE COMPANY, LIMITED.

Ed. 1910
Conds. 1802
Exd. P. EHL
D. deg

F M Boston
for Fire Manager.

Bristow Bovill
Director.

Plate 1.18 Ryan's own fire policy on his house at Hintlesham Hall. Much loved by Ryan, the house became, in later times, a celebrated restaurant, initially under Robert Carrier.

corporation requires. Secondly, many of the directors retained at least a semi-executive role. This may have worked quite well, but it permitted a certain diffusion of power which is not within the Chandlerian design. On the most demanding criteria for modern large-scale business, therefore, the Phoenix of 1914 was still a transitional form.

Rebuilding the nest

It stood to reason that all these new people and functions could not be housed within the old premises. Consequently, the period 1900–14 was a formative one for the Phoenix in the search for new buildings, some of which, especially the most important, it was to occupy for almost all of the rest of its business life. This era then is a crucial one, not only in terms of managerial and staff organisation – who was in the office and in which echelons – but in terms also of architecture, physical location and sense of place – where the office was, what it looked like, how grand it felt.

What was done first was not grand at all. In the autumn of 1900, a temporary wood and canvas extension was made to the roof of 19 Lombard Street 'to create more space for the clerks'.[342] But the clerks for whom space was being created had a sorry winter of it, and indeed a sorry couple of years. For it was not until February 1904 that the Head Office clerks were allocated rather more than £1,000 between them 'as a recompense for the loss and inconvenience occasioned by the recent building operations'.[343] Not long after getting a new roof over their heads, they received also a new way of conducting business: in March 1905, the Trustees agreed to spend £85 on 'installing a system of telephones' in 19 Lombard Street.[344]

In the provinces, the expansion of branch business produced an energetic quest for suitable buildings to lease or suitable plots to build upon. In Leeds, Bristol and Cardiff in this period, leases were secured and in Glasgow and Birmingham important buildings were built. In Leeds, Phoenix were prepared to offer £30,000 for the Philosophical Hall, both as an investment and for an office,[345] but eventually settled in 1901 for premises in South Parade at £11,500.[346] In the same year, £10,000 was offered and accepted on 22 Clare Street, Bristol,[347] and, in 1903, a lease was signed on 119 St Mary Street, Cardiff, as the branch office in that city.[348]

[342] Trustees' Minutes, 31 October 1900.
[343] Directors' Minutes, 27, p. 240, 10 February 1904.
[344] Trustees' Minutes, 15 March 1905. [345] *Ibid.*, 31 August, 19 October 1898.
[346] *Ibid.*, 13 March 1901. [347] *Ibid.*, 19 June 1901.
[348] Directors' Minutes, 27, p. 220, 28 October 1903.

In Glasgow and Birmingham, plans were more ambitious, and both of these branch redevelopments were launched after the mergers of 1908–11, so ambition was justified by the need to accommodate not just fire but also life, accident and marine departments. In November 1911, Phoenix found a site in Glasgow, on the corner of West Nile Street and Vincent Street and paid £35,000 for sufficient room to transact fire, life and marine business.[349] However, they chose to redevelop the space. By February 1912, A. D. Hislop had been selected as architect for a fine new building. It was to cost nearly £22,000 and to be constructed of Black Pasture stone, which impressed the Board, for this was the material out of which Glasgow's notable Post Office had been constructed. But, beyond this, the Board, struck by the dangers of excessive display, began to look for economy. They found it by opting for plain pillars rather than fluted ones, and were clearly pleased with this, for fluted pillars were quite extraordinarily more expensive than plain. Any sort of pillars purchased the necessary measure of civic grandeur, so why flirt with fluted ones?

The Board seemed to enjoy planning for the Glasgow building in 1912, but appeared much less engaged in the Birmingham project of 1914. Four architects were invited to tender in October 1913, and the plan proposed by Messrs Ewan Harper was accepted in March 1914.[350] In this case, the Board did not enthuse over the granite or delve into the economics of the columns. Perhaps the spring of 1914 was a less suitable season for thoughts about the concrete shapes of possible futures.

Meanwhile, however, all was not well with Phoenix's estate back in the capital. The old Phoenix home at 18/19 Lombard Street was proving too cramped for the new conglomerate, and neither it, nor the clerks inside it, would stand any more meddling with its roof space. The Pelican's abode at 70 Lombard Street had become redundant as soon as the 1908 fusion established the point that its purpose was to sell a full range of insurance over just one counter. And there were all sorts of trouble at Phoenix's old West End Branch at Charing Cross. This last supplied the most irksome of the pre-1914 property issues.

The Charing Cross site had first been acquired by Phoenix on 24 February 1803 for £3,500. As the company's title to the site was researched in the 1900s, the Board was surprised to find that, in previous incarnations, the address had sported the proud names of the 'Bull's Head', the 'Buffalo's Head', the 'Cardigan Head Tavern', and, finally, the 'Westminster Tavern or Coffee House'.[351] It is not clear why, over

[349] *Ibid.*, 30, p. 23, 15 November 1911.
[350] *Ibid.*, p. 409, 29 October 1913; 31, p. 7, 11 March 1914.
[351] *Ibid.*, p. 11, 11 March 1914.

time, the element of bull should have yielded to a more gentrified gloss, and the Board did not reflect upon the puzzle. But they did know that the prestigious and central location had provided both a suitable base for an aristocratic fire trade[352] and a convenient vantage point from which they could watch the royal processions and great events of the day. They had done this in regard to Queen Victoria's Jubilee and the Coronation of King Edward VII in the spring of 1902.[353] But it was precisely this centrality which, in the end, told against the West End office. First of all, the building of the London Underground sapped its foundations: excavations for the Baker Street and Waterloo Railway led Phoenix to press claims for £1,000 in respect of slippage in the subsoil and £5,000 for consequential damage to the structure.[354] But the building survived the railway. It was less fortunate with another onset of modernity: the West End Branch fell victim to an early outbreak of town planning.

In 1913, the London County Council was anxious to improve the Mall approach to the Admiralty Arch. The Council asked Phoenix to give up its site at 57 Charing Cross and accept instead a somewhat larger one, in a new position, across the street, on the west side, where the Council promised to erect a new building. Phoenix were incensed less by the enforced move than by the fact that the LCC proposed to install on the reduced site at No. 57 one of their competitors, the Liverpool & London & Globe. The Board, while professing itself willing 'to assist the authorities in their arrangements for improving the Mall approach', could not bring itself to accept 'a proposal which asks [us] to give up, not for the purposes of public improvement, but for the benefit and use of another company, the freehold property which has been in the possession of the Phoenix Assurance Co for nearly [sic] 100 years'.[355] By December 1913, the Board had taken steps to combat the Bill which would be proposed in the House of Commons for the acquisition of the old 'Bull's Head' site.[356]

The rejection of the Bill was moved in the House during March 1914 by two of Phoenix's MPs, the Hon. Michael Hicks-Beach, of Phoenix's West End Board, who was literally having the premises removed from under him, and Mr Arthur Dawes, from the firm of solicitors who had served Phoenix for decades. Predictably, this forlorn stand came to little, but it did ensure that there would be a Parliamentary Committee on the issue.

[352] See above, pp. 37, 54. [353] Directors' Minutes, 27, p. 88, 5 March 1902.
[354] Trustees' Minutes, 24 April 1901.
[355] Directors' Minutes, 30, p. 330, 7 May 1913. At this point the site had been in Phoenix's possession for rather more than 110 years.
[356] *Ibid.*, p. 439, 17 December 1913.

The Phoenix chairman, Lord George Hamilton, was interviewed by this Committee and even offered to forgo 15% of the compensation offered by the LCC if Phoenix were allowed to keep the reduced site at No. 57. But this too proved a lost cause as the governmental machinery rolled on. In May 1914, Phoenix was still contesting the Bill in the House of Lords. It was not until August 1914, some days after the outbreak of war, that the Phoenix Board admitted its own defeat, and withdrew opposition to the compulsory purchase, while maintaining claim to a full compensation of £75,000.[357]

While Phoenix was losing property in one part of London, it was seeking it elsewhere. But first it had to dispose of the Pelican's nest at 70 Lombard Street. Business had been so brisk at No. 19 after the fusion of 1908 that several departments of the Phoenix had been transferred to the Pelican's quarters. This not only had the old house creaking at the seams but fulfilled an astonishing literary premonition. Three hundred years before, the Elizabethan dramatist Heywood had written, of this same house,

> Here's Lombard Street, and here's the Pelican
> And here's the Phoenix in the Pelican's nest.

His Phoenix was King Edward IV and his Pelican's nest was the shop of the goldsmith Matthew Shore, which took the bird as its sign. Yet, as the insurance Phoenix overspilled into the office of its old sister company, this form of words became exactly correct for a second time. Even by the cyclical standards of the mystical bird, this was a trifle eerie. If the Phoenix directors of 1912 had known about it, maybe they would not have sold up. But as it was, they probably did not and they were short of space. Also, the site was highly saleable. Lombard Street was prime territory for the bankers and the bigger houses jockeyed for the position. Martins and Lloyds were bidding energetically late in 1912, at a price around £95,000, and Martins clinched the deal by a short £5,000.[358]

But the main need was to find or construct a building in London fit to house the entire central organisation of a new composite insurance office in suitable style. The core of a solution existed in Phoenix's inheritance, through the Pelican, of the old British Empire Life premises in King William Street. If Phoenix could lay hands on enough adjacent land, a new building might be put up in the sufficiently grand setting of one of the City's newer and more generously proportioned thoroughfares. The road

[357] *Ibid.*, 31, p. 88, 12 August 1914. They seem actually to have got £70,000. See below, p. 119.

[358] *Ibid.*, 30, p. 240, 18 December 1912. No. 19 Lombard Street was sold in 1917 to the London County and Westminster; see below, p. 118.

was cut as a wide avenue through the warren of City lanes from the Church of St Mary Woolnoth to St Swithin's Lane, in the 1830s, during the time of the 'respectable old Admiral' King William IV.[359] Until the 1910s, the buildings were of brick, faced with stucco, and the design 'uninteresting if harmless'.[360] Phoenix, however, was to change all that, with a major adjustment to tone and style.

Gathering the plots for a new development took some time and Phoenix had to embark upon a deliberate process of selected acquisitions throughout the period 1908–14. The first step was the purchase from the Fishmongers' Company for £30,000 of the freehold upon 6/7 King William Street, 'adjoining to the Company's property lately occupied by the British Empire Office'.[361] This was a quick move embarked upon almost immediately the fusion brought the British Empire's site within the Phoenix's grasp. Perhaps Ryan carried a fondness for it from his British Empire days. By early 1909, at any event, he had taken the Phoenix into negotiations with the Grocers' Company for the strategic adjoining site at 11 Abchurch Lane. The Board was prepared to offer the ground rents of other City property controlled by the Phoenix at 33/35 Eastcheap to the Grocers in exchange for the ground rents on Abchurch Lane.[362] In the late summer of 1909, agreement was reached, and, somewhat over a year later, Phoenix accepted from the Grocers' Company an eighty-year lease, at £1,718 per annum, to run from 1916.[363]

But it was not until early in 1913 that the finishing touches were put to the accumulation process. The purchase of 4–7 King William Street from the British Empire Trust was an internal transaction to regularise the formal ownership of assets, easily implemented in March 1913.[364] However, it was necessary also to purchase the lease of 3 King William Street, to run for ninety years, at a ground rent of £3,491 and to lease from the National Bank of Egypt, for 42 years, another plot on the corner of King William Street and Abchurch Lane, as well as sweeping up a remaining parcel at 18/19 Sherborne Lane. All but the last were secured by February 1913, but the final piece of the property jigsaw was not located until that July.[365]

359 The remark is from the Duke of Wellington. A statue of the king stood at the junction of King William Street and Gracechurch Street until being moved to more nautical surroundings at the Royal Naval College, Greenwich in 1936.

360 Hurren, *Phoenix Renascent*, p. 165.

361 Directors' Minutes, 28, p. 182, 19 February 1908.

362 The sum involved being in the region of £40,500.

363 Directors' Minutes, 29, pp. 28, 286, 18 August 1909 and 26 October 1910.

364 *Ibid.*, 30, p. 300, 19 March 1913. The value placed on these sites, for the book transfer, was £161,400.

365 *Ibid.*, pp. 278, 370, 19 February and 23 July 1913. And see Plate 8.22, p. 656.

On the block formed by these acquisitions, an extremely ambitious new building was planned. The architects were Messrs J. McVicar Anderson and H. L. Anderson, and they worked with some speed on the irregular site. Initial plans were produced by early May 1913, revised elevations a fortnight later, and a full model by mid-June 1913.[366] The builders were Trollope and Colls and construction work began in the summer of 1914.[367] In the course of the excavations for the foundations a number of archaeological remains were found, of Roman and medieval vintage, and some of these were displayed in the finished building from 1915 until 1982.[368] The structure that was raised on the foundations was remarkable. The steelwork, costing £16,810, was lavish and included steel grillages embedded in concrete for the foundations, a steel frame skeleton, and rolled steel joists for the floors. Plans of these dispositions were used again during the internal demolitions which were carried out during the great redevelopment of the building in 1983, which prepared it, in its present form, for occupation by Daiwa (Europe) Ltd. The resulting building, both in 1915 and in the 1980s, was and is remarkably solid, owing to both the steel and the widespread use of reinforced concrete in the basements. Fittingly, it conformed to the highest standards for fire-resistance and earthquake-resistance. This was to come in handy in the Blitz of 1940 and 1941, when the building took direct hits but withstood them.

Indeed, much about this Phoenix House proved extremely durable. Even the lifts, installed in 1915, were still functioning in the 1970s. And another feature, novel in the 1910s, endured into recent memory: the Phoenix pumped its own water supply from artesian bores 137 metres (450 feet) below the basement, although in later decades, the streams from the Hampstead and Highgate Hills did not replenish the underground lake as they once did.[369] A continuity more obvious to the eye was the marvellous entry hall of marble, mahogany and brass. Originally, this was the main business hall, and was given dimensions which made it the principal architectural feature of the building – 20 metres (67 feet) long, 17 metres (56 feet) wide and 6 metres (19 feet) high. At its centre stood an octagon which rose through two storeys, with its own arcaded gallery, and at the top a large light dome, 6 metres (20 feet) across and 12 metres (40 feet) above the visitor in the hallway. The Phoenix emblem was every-

[366] *Ibid.*, pp. 330, 337, 352, 7 and 21 May, 11 June 1913.

[367] *Ibid.*, 31, p. 49, 27 May 1914.

[368] In the year of the Phoenix's double centenary these remains were presented to the London Museum. The scope of the original collection was reduced by bomb damage in the Second World War.

[369] See Hurren, *Phoenix Renascent*, p. 168. From 1932, the depth of supply was extended to 183 metres (600 feet).

where, so much so that there was never an agreed tally of how many phoenixes there were in Phoenix House. Indeed the rumour arose that the Phoenix legend must be untrue: it could not be correct that the phoenix reproduced itself every few centuries or millennia; there were so many in Phoenix House, the wags protested, that the act had to be a nightly occurrence.

In other ways too, the detail was unusual in style and provenance. The first two storeys were generously decorated in grey, grey-green and white marble, which, however, did not have a fortunate career. Quarried in the Pyrenees, it was sent to Mons in Belgium to be worked, and thus into the cockpit of trench warfare. It could not be extracted until the Great War had concluded, and even then the last consignment from Spain was sunk as it crossed the Bay of Biscay. The panels which survived the First World War then fell prey to the bombs of the Second, and only skilful restoration work retained them, on a reduced scale, in the building of the postwar years. If the building was durable, parts of it had to fight to survive.

Back in 1915, Phoenix was not to occupy the whole of the new site. The two corners of the King William Street frontage were to be leased to banks, the Abchurch Lane corner, on three floors and two basements, to the National Bank of Egypt, which was given a miniature of the Phoenix lobby for its banking hall.[370] And the rear of the building and the churchyard area was still in the hands of tenants, including, most conveniently for the staff, the landlord of The Clachan hostelry. The Egyptian bank remained in place until Phoenix needed to absorb the space in the 1960s and the The Clachan survived as a local watering hole into the 1930s (see Plate 8.22).

The Phoenix moved into its new home during 1915. The company's securities were transferred to the King William Street vaults in October and the life department moved in on 1 November.[371] The first Board meeting in the new Phoenix House took place on 26 January 1916 and the first Annual General Meeting to be held there was that of 19 April 1916. At the end of the day, the total cost of the new building was £533,000, something under half of this being financed temporarily by the life department and the rest borne on Phoenix general funds.[372] This was defrayed by the value of the former office at 19 Lombard Street, which was sold to the London, County and Westminster Bank for £190,000 on 25 March 1917, and by the amount of £70,000 eventually raised from the London

[370] The British Bank of the Middle East later occupied this site.
[371] Directors' Minutes, 31, p. 304, 3 November 1915.
[372] *Ibid.*, 32, p. 78, 14 March 1917.

County Council in respect of the forced sale of the Charing Cross Branch.[373] The old Phoenix residence in Lombard Street endured until the late 1960s, when Natwest demolished it to make way for their new Lombard Street branch. Phoenix management and staff settled into the new residence in King William Street with alacrity: even in spring 1916 the Board was still telling the architects how much it liked it.[374]

It is not difficult to see why. The classical Renaissance styling of the main structure, with its Corinthian columns and pilasters, and its facade of Portland stone, made a powerful unifying presence on King William Street. This was needed. One architectural authority of the era complained that the brick-and-stucco medley of the street had wasted the opportunity for stylistic statement which the new thoroughfare had presented. J. Howard Barnes wrote in 1915, 'there can be little doubt that if the whole street could have been rebuilt in Portland stone to one complete design, a really fine and conspicuous architectural effect could have been obtained' but he thought the problems of coordination 'insuperable'.[375] However, his pessimism was misplaced and the effect of Phoenix House more influential than he guessed. For its impressive frontage – perhaps still the grandest in the street – gave a lead and drew others after it. Between the wars and after 1945, a number of other buildings in King William Street were redeveloped and had a standard to match. The result is a broad avenue of considerable dignity in which Portland stone does predominate and in which there is not a skyscraper to be seen.

The Phoenix House at 5 King William Street was a much-loved building, remembered by generations of staff.[376] It was a pleasingly eccentric place, with its vaulting lobby, curved staircases, and oddly located half-floors, which it was possible for the uninitiated to misplace entirely. The effect was to combine grandeur with homeliness in a very agreeable way. It provided a comfortable retreat for the Phoenix for nearly seventy years and almost no one who left it, whether the veteran official or the passing historian, did so without regret when, in 1983, the time came to redevelop and move to more modern quarters on the corner of King William Street and Cannon Street. For many decades the famous gold clock, with the full-winged Phoenix holding it aloft, projecting out over King William Street, was one of the most distinctive landmarks in the City.

The building produced very much the effect that Ryan had in mind; it was distinctly a symbol of Ryan's Phoenix. He had built the old fire office into a major composite and he needed premises fit for one of the nation's

[373] *Ibid.*, p. 54, 7 February 1917; 31, p. 86, 3 March 1915.
[374] *Ibid.*, 31, p. 399, 19 April 1916. [375] Cited by Hurren, *Phoenix Renascent*, p. 195.
[376] And even by this historian, from the commencement of this commission.

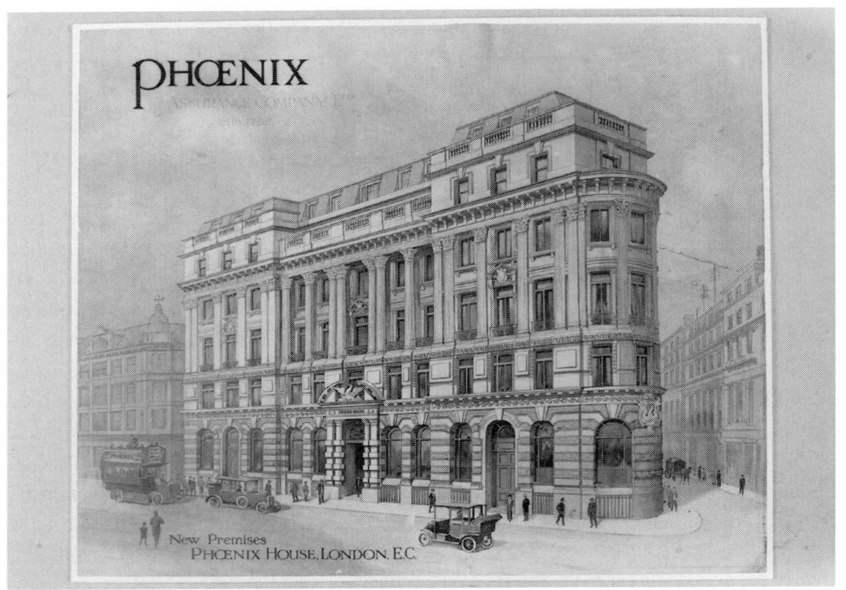

Plate 1.19 The new nest, 1915.

most powerful financial institutions. He planned, and achieved, a building that would act as a flagship during the company's period of greatest eminence. And not the least function of a flagship is to fly the flag.

For others too in this period the Phoenix and its abode were effective symbols. But it was the old Phoenix House at 18/19 Lombard Street which featured in E. Nesbit's celebrated children's story *The Phoenix and the Carpet*, first published in the *Strand Magazine* in 1903. At the midpoint of his magical, flying-carpet tour of the world, it was to the Lombard Street boardroom that the fictional Phoenix led his small charges. He found it 'my finest temple . . . with my image graved in stone and in metal over against its portal', while the children liked 'the beautiful hall, adorned with Doulton tiles, like a large and beautiful bath with no water in it'.[377] Intriguingly, however, Miss Nesbit's was not the first encounter between a story-book Phoenix and the impressionable young. Towards the end of the nineteenth century, the company itself published a short booklet, aimed at the children of existing and potential policy-holders, called *How and why the Phoenix came to live in London*. Here too the children are guests in the Lombard Street boardroom, at a board meet-

[377] E. Nesbit, *The Phoenix and the Carpet* (London, Puffin, 1994 edn), pp. 115, 122.

ing, and here too a genial Phoenix presides, though he does so in this account as chairman and in the costume of 1782. The similarities are sufficient, however, for one to wonder whether this was a case of unusually effective advertising material: a publicity handout triggers a minor literary masterpiece. Certainly, it would have been possible for E. Nesbit to have read the Phoenix booklet; and literary pedigrees have been built on less.[378]

However, Miss Nesbit's story is in itself proof of the Phoenix's stature as a national institution by the 1900s. Gerald Ryan was aiming to construct a building which made the same point for the 1910s. No. 5 King William Street lacked only a story-teller of genius to confer immortality upon it in its turn.

Persistent intimations of mortality: in the office and beyond

As staff numbers increased, management was modernised and accommodation was smartened, so the general wellbeing of those who worked for the Phoenix seems to have improved. But, in regard to health in particular, it took a surprisingly long time to do so. The prevalence of illness in the office, which was so marked a feature of the last decades of the old century, only begins to fade from the Minute Books in the late 1900s and 1910s. For a significant part of the pre-1914 era, the Board continued to project a high level of concern on this issue.

Around the turn of the century, the old patterns indeed seemed fully in place. One of the saddest cases was that of 'the boy Scott' who had given such 'great Satisfaction' in 1872 but had to be pensioned off in 1896, 'owing to the premature breaking down of his constitution after twenty-six years' service'.[379] And the pattern of insanity at the ledgers was still there, with Philip Bridgeman, after eighteen years' clerking, breaking down in 1900, 'owing to mental infirmity'. Another clerk in the Country Office, Frederick Pocock, suffered 'a severe attack of general eczema' in 1905 and had to be sent off for a course of sulphur baths at Schinznach in Switzerland. According to tradition, the Board gave him one month's leave and £20 towards the cost of the treatment.[380] It was perhaps in an attempt to reduce stress that the Trustees instituted in March 1907 a standard fortnight's holiday per year even for the most junior staff – clerks of under five years' service, probationaries and supernumeraries.

[378] However, Julia Briggs in *A Woman of Passion; The Life of E. Nesbit, 1858–1924* (London, 1987), p. 150, attributes the inspiration for the story to E. Nesbit's friend, Laurence Housman, brother of A. E.

[379] Trustees' Minutes, 8 October 1896. [380] *Ibid.*, 29 May 1905.

But such measures could scarcely address the most serious health problems. Tuberculosis, for instance, continued to wreak havoc after the turn of the century. In October 1903, A. E. Whiting was improving in a sanatorium in Bournemouth after an absence of almost a year. Only after extended treatment was he deemed fit to resume his duties, 'without fear of communicating the tubercular disease to others'. The Trustees were prepared to let him come back on the certification of the company physicians, Drs Hard-Wood and Crosby, but also recorded at the same meeting that another of Whiting's colleagues would require 'a prolonged stay at a sanatorium'.[381] Another clerk in 1904 was prescribed a year's open-air treatment at Darosplak, Switzerland, and was given the necessary leave, half of it on full pay, the rest on half-pay, while yet another was so ill that he had to be paid off with a full year's salary of £170.[382] The veteran of the Swiss cure was allowed to return to work in December 1905, but only on condition that Hard-Wood and Crosby examine him every three months. However, he barely lasted one month before deterioration set in and he had to retire after sixteen years' service.[383] And, by this time, two other clerks had gone down with the disease. One of these developed into a chronic case and had to be pensioned off in 1907, while, later in the same year, B. G. Broomfield, whose brother had contracted tuberculosis twenty years before, was obliged to resign owing to a breakdown in his health.[384] It is scarcely surprising that Phoenix had made a medical examination one of its conditions of employment by 1907.[385] Office life clearly still involved a substantial risk of office death.

Given the continuing disease and mortality patterns among the City clerks, it was also logical that the insurance employers should give some thought to their dependants. It is a sufficient comment on the average level of health in the offices of London that the industry created its own Insurance Clerks' Orphanage in 1902. Phoenix donated £100, and Lord Avebury consented to become vice-president.[386]

A similar logic appeared to be present in Phoenix's active support of the London hospitals. In 1905, the company made contributions to both the London Hospital and St Bartholomew's, in the latter case a generous present of 200 guineas to help with the new extension.[387] But here appearances were deceptive, for at least one other logic was operating. Phoenix was really after the fire insurance for Bart's, and, in July 1905, the

[381] *Ibid.*, 16 December 1903. [382] *Ibid.*, 17 August 1904.
[383] *Ibid.*, 6 December 1905 and 31 January 1906. [384] *Ibid.*, 10 April 1907.
[385] *Ibid.*, 27 February 1907.
[386] Directors' Minutes, 27, pp. 147, 149, 29 October and 5 November 1902.
[387] *Ibid.*, p. 356, 26 July 1905.

Trustees decided to *review* their annual subscription of 10 guineas to the London Hospital after Phoenix had lost 'a principal portion of the hospital business'.[388] Whatever these charitable contributions represented, it was clearly not only an altruistic reinforcement of the defences against the appalling health risks of the capital. Nevertheless, the Phoenix went on supporting the hospitals. In 1907, the Trustees donated 5 guineas to the Ilford Emergency Hospital but recorded dryly that Phoenix had £325,000 worth of Ilford Council fire policies. And the London Hospital had seen the light, and had maintained claim to its 10 guineas since 'during the past year, the hospital had given the company a substantial amount of business'.[389]

However, it is heartening to record that, in the last years before the Great War, the health of the Phoenix staff appears to have taken a turn for the better. Whether this was partly the effect of improvement to premises, or of better screening through the medical examination, or of improved standards of public health, or of the watchfulness of Hard-Wood and Crosby, or some combination of these, it is impossible to say. But, after the spate of tubercular cases and resignations around 1907, no further such cases were recorded in the period down to 1914. Before this point, however, the Phoenix evidence certainly emphasises, even within this small sample, the need for the debate over public health standards and the issue of 'nature versus nurture' which occupied much political attention in the 1900s.

Prior to 1914, the other major threat to longevity among Phoenix men was military service, and this was true even before the Kaiser's War of 1914–18. The outstanding occasion was, of course, the Boer War of 1899–1902. A small number of Phoenix staff volunteered to fight in South Africa, and three of them – an un-named messenger, Frank Godwin and I. O. Carson – unlike the majority of those recruited nationally, proved fit enough to serve. The fact that six out of every ten who offered themselves for service did not, and were rejected, was a direct influence on the debate about 'national efficiency' and public health, which continued throughout the next decade. However, the Phoenix trio left, fought and returned.

Phoenix took the South African War coolly. Little encouragement was given to volunteers, in contrast to the company's policy in 1914, and Messrs Godwin and Carson were merely given extended leave of absence for six months or until the end of the war, no pay being involved.[390] The messenger, however, received a better deal: he was the first Phoenix employee to join up, and this was marked by the voting of a half-year's

[388] Trustees' Minutes, 19 July 1905. [389] *Ibid.*, 26 June 1907.
[390] *Ibid.*, 13 February 1901.

salary and his job being held open for one year.[391] But in general this war raised few issues for Phoenix in London.

In South Africa it was a different matter. Here hostilities forced the withdrawal of the company's agent from Johannesburg to Cape Town, and then from Cape Town to London. Phoenix had to pay his removal expenses and an allowance until it was safe for him to return home.[392] Perhaps this lesson hardened Phoenix's heart against the enemies of the state, for, by 1909, the company was offering modest financial inducements to all of its staff willing to join the recently formed Territorial Force, which had been introduced by the Liberal Secretary of State for War, R. B. Haldane, in 1907. Possibly, the influence of an old sea-dog like Admiral Lucas or a former service minister like Lord George Hamilton, had left its mark upon the Phoenix Board. As all Europe became more warlike, this Phoenix policy of the late 1900s recalls the company's action in an earlier national crisis, when, during the wars against Napoleonic France, it had offered its firemen to the beleaguered nation as gunners. Certainly, rumours of war were affecting the Phoenix staff well before the guns of August opened up in 1914. But until 1914, these rumours were a good deal less troublesome than company mergers or office extensions and a lot less dangerous than the diseases of London.

10. SHARES IN THIS AND SHARES OF THAT

The capital of the new composite Phoenix was set in 1908 at £340,310 in shares of £5.[393] However, the fusion of 1908 had created two ways of arriving at this £5 value: the 'old' Phoenix shares had a face value of £50 but were only £5 paid (there were 53,776 of these in the hands of 1,684 shareholders), whereas the 'new' shares issued to cover the absorption of Pelican were £5 in value but fully paid up. Former shareholders in Pelican were allocated £71,430 of the composite's total capital in the new fully paid shares. The duality of status relating to shares of the same effective value was to cause confusion and misinterpretation. And, of course, it created two constituencies of shareholder: one liable for very substantial additional calls of capital and one entirely protected from this obligation.

Nevertheless, the distribution of capital in 1908 went smoothly enough. Only two Pelican shareholders decided to take cash from the liquidation of their holdings rather than accept shares in Phoenix, and it was dis-

[391] Directors' Minutes, 26, p. 380, 3 January 1900.

[392] Trustees' Minutes, 11 April 1900.

[393] The figure cited by Hurren, *Phoenix Renascent*, p. 109 is incorrect; it is the figure for the pre-merger capitalisation.

covered that the one Pelican share unaccounted for belonged to a shareholder who had died.[394] In passing, an unusual fact about the sociology of Phoenix shareholders came to light: of the pre-1908 shares, 26.3% by number were in the hands of women, while of the total roll-call of the pre-merger shareholders, 39.1% were women.

Further company acquisitions, as the composite design was filled out, required more additions to capital between 1908 and 1914. The takeover of Law Life in 1910 raised the paid-up share capital to £381,980 and the purchase of Union Marine in 1911 to £422,855.[395] To compound the confusion further, the former shareholders of Law Life were paid off in 'new' fully paid £5 shares, while those of Union Marine received 'old' £50 shares, one-tenth paid up.

This proved too much for one of the new directors from Union Marine. In January 1913, Helenus Robertson moved that the 'old' £50 shares should be divided into £10 shares, with £1 paid up, and the 'new' £5 shares divided into £1 shares, fully paid. He was unable to get rid of the distinction between partly and fully paid, but this proposal did create a much larger supply of small denomination shares, improving access and tradeability, and reducing the size of the uncalled liability on the 'old' shares. On 29 January 1913, the Board accepted this proposal and appointed a nine-man committee to implement it.[396] This remained the capital position until 1919.

The period of corporate development between 1908 and 1914 revolutionised not only the Phoenix's field of business but also its general financial strength in terms of reserves and assets (Table 1.11).

On the eve of the San Francisco disaster, the old fire company had a general reserve of £750,000 and total assets of just over £2 million. In the aftermath of the disaster, at the end of 1906, the reserve was down to £300,000 and the assets to £1.8 million. Recovery from this predicament was swift, with the general reserve replenished and the assets hugely augmented by the end of 1908. But this was almost wholly due to the fusion with Pelican and it was not achieved without complaints from the life company about submission to a weaker partner.[397] However, the rejuvenated Phoenix then proceeded to produce further marked growth in reserves and assets, with a 43% increase in reserves between 1908 and 1911 and a near-doubling of total assets, the latter being partly due to the

[394] Directors' Minutes, 28, pp. 281, 311, 12 August and 7 October 1908.

[395] See Chapter 5 below, pp. 331–59.

[396] Hurren, *Phoenix Renascent*, p. 110 gives May 1912 as the date for this reform, but the Minute Books are quite clear (Directors' Minutes 30, p. 260, 22 January 1913).

[397] See below, Chapter 5.

Table 1.11. *Phoenix Assurance: capital, reserves and assets, 1901–11 (current £)*

	Paid-up capital	General reserve	Total assets
1901	268,880	649,000	1,835,000
1905	268,880	750,000	2,092,000
1906	268,880	300,000	1,759,000
1908	340,310	700,000	7,569,000
1910	381,980	925,000	13,951,000
1911	422,855	1,000,000	15,375,000

infusions from Law Life and Union Marine. Composite acquisition, Ryan could argue by 1914, most surely paid.

With the assets and the reserves and the new companies came, necessarily, new sorts of business. However, some of the new types of business came before the acquisitions. This in itself emphasised how urgently Phoenix viewed the need for product diversification in the 1900s. The Trustees concluded in January 1907 that Phoenix was losing fire business as a result of not offering particular kinds of accident business, specifically workmen's compensation insurance. Accordingly, within one month in early 1907, Phoenix launched four new lines in the accident sector: workmen's compensation and burglary insurance from 9 January, personal accident from 16 January and fidelity insurance from 6 February.[398] This was almost a year before the Pelican life business was brought within the Phoenix net.

By 1911 Phoenix was well embarked upon accident underwriting. It was guaranteeing the Festival of Empire that its takings would reach not less than £200,000 by September 1912. After examining the winter racing seasons of 1908–10, it was insuring two-day steeplechase events against rain, flood, frost and snow. It covered the Pacific Steam Navigation Co. against the risk of losing a bag of precious stones bound for Antwerp. And, more adventurously, it was insuring the plate glass of London's shopkeepers against the brickbats of London's suffragettes. The range indicates what a vast opportunity for accident insurance a modern urban economy represented, both at work and play. But perhaps the most significant event of 1911 in the accident sector was in motor insurance: Phoenix was placed on the RAC's list of approved insurers.[399]

[398] Trustees' Minutes, 9 January 1907; Directors' Minutes 28, pp. 35, 37, 41–2; 9, 16 January and 6 February 1907.

[399] Accident Committee Minutes, Book 1, pp. 189–90, 12 April 1911; Book 2, pp. 16, 26, 45, 47; 4 October, 29 November 1911, 20 March, 3 April 1912.

The advent of Law Life in 1910 added further capacity in a field where the Pelican inheritance had already given Phoenix a considerable presence. But the arrival of Union Marine in 1911 transformed Phoenix's very modest maritime commitment. So much was this the case that early in 1912, the whole of Phoenix's marine work was transferred to Union Marine's base in Liverpool and centralised upon the specialist marine underwriters. This injection of expertise was similar to that provided for Pelican in the area of with-profits life business by the acquisition of British Empire Life in 1902.[400] But this time the effect was more sweeping as Phoenix implemented 'in effect the reinsurance of all Phoenix maritime risks with Union Marine'. The Liverpool subsidiary was even given its own 'Phoenix Marine' bank account so that it could pay claims without revealing that the parent company was not in fact underwriting the risks.[401]

These alterations in company size and business spread had major implications for Phoenix's ranking among the top insurance offices, which were the company's natural competitors. For much of the nineteenth century, indeed throughout the period 1790–1865, Phoenix had been the second largest fire insurer in Britain after the Sun, and by 1870 had already fought off serious threats to its market share from both the County Office and the Norwich Union.[402] However, in the last few years in which fire duty returns were available as measures of the total British market, new and ominous signs began to appear amongst the competition. In the period 1866–9, one Liverpool office, the Liverpool & London & Globe, knocked Phoenix out of its almost traditional second place and another, the Royal, was closing fast. In the ensuing three decades, the charge of the Liverpool offices represented a provincial assault upon market shares in the United Kingdom and export markets overseas, the like of which the insurance industry had never seen; and this was not beaten off.[403] By 1901, Phoenix ranked fifth among Britain's top fire insurers (and the Sun sixth), while three of the top four places were occupied by northern offices, with only the Commercial Union, in third place, keeping the flag flying for the underwriters of the City. Moreover, Phoenix in 1901 had missed a takeover which would have taken the company back to its number two position.[404]

It is little wonder that Phoenix turned to a composite strategy in the 1900s. Of course, other large offices, not least the Liverpool giants, were going in the same direction, and to have lagged at this point would have

[400] See Chapter 5 below. [401] Directors' Minutes, 30, p. 63, 31 January 1912.
[402] See vol. 1, Chapter 8, especially Table 8.2, p. 461.
[403] Trebilcock, 'The City, Entrepreneurship and Insurance'.
[404] See below, Chapter 5, Section 1.

incurred further competitive losses. But Phoenix had another reason: its market share in fire insurance was under siege and diversification into other types of insurance offered means of maintaining status and overall market presence which fire business alone could no longer give.

In a ledger entitled 'Results of Fire Offices, 1900–32', Phoenix kept track of the competition in a way which may be statistically eccentric but is probably satisfactorily comparative.

By it own reckoning Phoenix's rank among all fire insurers had slipped further to seventh by 1914, and among composite insurers with fire departments to sixth, and the company was not to improve upon such placings until the 1920s. By contrast, when total premium income is measured at the 1914 watershed, Phoenix's standing among the big composites is somewhat better than this, and when Phoenix is ranked against the other composites for life or marine business, it is, thanks to the inheritances from Pelican and Union Marine, better still (see Table 1.12). Strikingly, Phoenix is the only one of the pioneer offices from the eighteenth century to have employed the methods of composite diversification to remain among the biggest insurance players of the 1900s. The Sun and the REA are nowhere to be seen.[405]

Table 1.12. *The top six UK composite insurers by net premium totals, 1914 (£ million)*

Company	Total premiums	Rank	Fire premiums	Rank	Life premiums	Rank	Accident premiums	Rank	Marine premiums	Rank
CU	7.7	1	3.5	2	0.80	4	2.9	1	0.47	3
Royal	7.0	2	4.1	1	0.90	2	1.3	2	0.68	2
LLG	4.9	3	3.1	3	0.31	5	1.1	3	0.34	4
NBM	4.3	4	2.1	4	1.47	1	0.4	5	0.31	5
LL	2.8	6	1.7	5	–	6	0.9	4	0.24	6
Phoenix	3.1	5	1.4	6	0.89	3	0.1	6	0.71	1

Notes: CU = Commercial Union; LLG = Liverpool & London & Globe; NBM = North British and Maritime; LL = London & Lancashire
Source: Phoenix, Analysis of Companies' Reports, 1910–31.

The Commercial Union had reasserted a lead for the metropolitan insurers, but, with the exception of Phoenix, the rest of this top group were northern offices. Phoenix's pole position in marine work and its third position in life assurance made up for the modest performances in

[405] By contrast with Table 1.12, the matching numbers for the REA were, in £ million:

Total	Fire	Life	Accident	Marine
1.7	0.9	0.37	0.26	0.36

(Supple., *Royal Exchange Assurance*, p. 446).

fire and accident. Indeed, for all the interest and variety of Phoenix's underwriting in the latter sector, the measure of market penetration so far achieved was weak.

Phoenix's own examination of the premiums of the top twelve fire insurers in the United Kingdom for the period 1910–14 demonstrates the same capitulation of the City bourgeoisie to the northern bourgeoisie (Table 1.13).

Of the top nine companies, five were of northern origin and only two of the City insurers managed to penetrate the top half-dozen. London's trio of veteran eighteenth-century foundations ranked sixth, seventh and twelfth and even major 'second-wave' companies from the early nineteenth-century such as the Alliance and the Atlas were well down in the second half of the list. It is noteworthy that the REA, which had been knocked out of third place in terms of market share by the Norwich Union as early as the 1840s had slipped the furthest by 1914. But it is also striking that the great East Anglian provincial had been no more able to resist the northern challenge than the London veterans. Apart from northern origin, the other outstanding feature of the market leaders of 1914 was late date of foundation: with the exception of the North British they all hailed from the middle decades of the nineteenth century. And this was true of the one dominant force which was not of northern origin; for the Commercial Union had been launched in 1861.

Table 1.13. *The top ten fire insurers in the UK, 1910–14 (net premiums in £ million)*

Company	1910	1911	1912	1913	1914	Av. Rank
Royal	3.9	4.0	4.1	4.1	4.1	1
Commercial Union	3.1	3.2	3.2	3.4	3.5	2
Liverpool & London & Globe	2.8	2.8	3.0	3.1	3.1	3
North British	2.2	2.4	2.4	2.5	2.1	4
London & Lancs	1.6	1.6	1.6	1.7	1.7	5
Sun	1.5	1.5	1.5	1.6	1.5	6
Phoenix	1.4	1.4	1.4	1.4	1.4	7
Alliance	1.3	1.3	1.3	1.3	1.4	8
Northern	1.3	1.2	1.2	1.3	1.3	9
Norwich Union	1.1	1.1	1.1	1.2	1.2	10
Atlas	1.0	1.0	1.1	1.1	1.0	11
Royal Exchange	0.8	0.8	0.8	0.9	0.9	12

Source: Phoenix, Results of Fire Offices, 1900–32.

It is clear that Phoenix would have suffered great damage at the hands of competitors like these had it not sought energetically for diversification in the early years of the century. One other feature of the fire receipts given above underlines this: in the five-year period before 1914, there was remarkably little elasticity in the fire earnings of the biggest companies. For eight of the top twelve, the variation did not exceed £100,000 over the five-year period, and only the top four managed change of more than £200,000. Significantly, the Phoenix fire receipt line was the flattest of all.

But not all rankings show Phoenix fighting back successfully against competitive pressure by means of the composite strategy of Gerald Ryan. It is wise to end this survey of the half-century before 1914 on a note of warning. Unlike the Sun and the REA, Phoenix had diversified sufficiently to stay among the market leaders in terms of scale. But size of income was not the whole story. Phoenix recorded figures for its fire business against that of other leading companies for the period 1900–32 which allow ranks to be calculated, not only for premiums, but for fire funds, for trading surplus, for claims ratios and for expense ratios.

In terms of fire funds, Phoenix was well provided for. Despite ranking characteristically sixth or seventh in fire premiums in the years before the Great War, the company's ratio of fire funds to fire premiums placed it in a comfortable fifth place in 1914. This contrasts markedly with the experience of the top four fire insurers, which in regard to the fire fund/fire premium ratio, ranked respectively 10, 11, 7 and 12 in 1914. In fact, it was the next group of four companies by premium size, which included Phoenix, that proved to have the best ratios, and thus the best defences, as against those above and below them.

Where Phoenix fell down was rather in relative profitability. This does not mean that Phoenix was not profitable, nor that it could not pay a handsome dividend.[406] Instead, the figures suggest that many competitors were more profitable. Thus, in regard to trading surplus in 1914, Phoenix ranked only thirteenth among fire companies.[407] In terms of loss ratio, it ranked ninth with a fire claims to premium ratio of 56%, which was not too bad given that the Commercial Union and the London & Lancashire were only a mite better on 55.4%, and they were the first really large operators on the list (at rank seven). The really worrying news came in relation to the expense ratio. Out of the twenty top fire insurers, Phoenix ranked only seventeenth, with a ratio of expenses to premiums of 39%, whereas Commercial Union topped the list at 34.8%.

406 See above, p. 62.

407 With a result of 5.0%, whereas the Alliance led the pack with 19.8%, and the Commercial Union was the highest-ranking large office, at rank five, with a surplus of 9.8%.

Table 1.14. *The trading results of British fire offices, 1907–21 (% of premium and rank)*

	Underwriting Surplus		Claims		Expenses	
Company	% premiums	Rank	% premiums	Rank	% premiums	Rank
Alliance	18.1	1	41.6	1	39.1	14
Atlas	11.8	3	47.7	4	38.1	10
Caledonian	8.2	13	52.6	14	37.2	4
Comm. Union	10.8	5	49.9	7	36.8	3
Guardian	10.5	7	51.1	10	36.6	1=
London	11.4	4	46.5	3	39.4	16
London & Lancs	13.4	2	46.3	2	38.3	11=
Northern	8.6	11	51.3	11	37.8	8
North British	8.3	12	52.8	15	37.4	5=
Phoenix	7.1	15	49.6	5=	39.3	15
Royal	10.5	6	50.8	9	37.4	5=
Royal Exchange	7.2	14	51.7	12	38.8	13
Scottish Union	9.5	9	52.5	13	36.6	1=
State	5.5	16	54.1	16	37.7	7
Sun	10.4	8	50.2	8	38.3	11=
Yorkshire	9.0	10	49.6	5=	38.0	9

Source: Phoenix, Results of Fire Offices, 1900–32.

Much the same conclusion emerges from a longer-run survey of comparative underwriting surplus, claims and expenses experience which reaches somewhat beyond the end of this period (Table 1.14).

The Alliance again emerges as very profitable, even over quite a long haul. Commercial Union displays an enviable combination of good profitability, fair loss experience and very economical operation. The Royal and the London & Lancashire again fly a convincing northern banner, although, on these figures, the northern bloc is by no means solid. And the Atlas, which Phoenix just failed to take over in 1901, is confirmed as a property worth having. However, Phoenix itself, despite a very reasonable loss experience, proves very expensive to run and takes a good deal of punishment in its profit levels.

This is the first occasion when the expenses ratio rears its head as a problem in the operation of Phoenix as a composite office. Unfortunately, it is to be nowhere near the last. Certain features within the design of the Phoenix – not least its heavy orientation towards foreign, and perhaps especially American, markets – gave it a bias towards high costs which was to prove very difficult to correct.

CHAPTER 2

THE OVERSEAS DIMENSION RESUMED, 1: EVERYWHERE EXCEPT THE UNITED STATES, 1870–1914

I. THE GLOBAL SETTING FOR REVIVED EFFORT

During the years 1870–1914 Phoenix rediscovered a sense of purpose in its overseas dealings. While the mid-century decades had resounded to the mounting tempo of industrialisation in such major economies as the USA, France and the German states, Phoenix had preferred to take business quietly. As the world economy expanded, Phoenix accepted its modest share of the proceeds by the indirect process of reinsurance; much of its foreign income was made up of the cast-off business of other insurance offices.[1]

Paradoxically, Phoenix did better and performed more energetically as the world economy – at least from the British vantage point – became more treacherously complex. The years 1873–96 saw a cyclical downswing in the global economy, the first 'Great Depression'. It was a depression of prices, profits and rates of growth, rather than a matter of declining absolute levels of output; and in some economies – notably the German – there were even fewer signs of ill-health than this. On the other hand, the period was one of considerable imperial expansion and in some of these imperial or quasi-imperial possessions – India, Burma, the China ports – there was a strong burst of manufacturing as well as mercantile activity. Despite slower growth in some of the advanced economies, many distant regions that had been undeveloped in 1850 were notably more sophisticated by the 1890s.

Moreover, from the middle of that decade, the trend in the world economy turned upward. A long cycle upswing occupied the period down to the First World War and brought the experience of industrial 'take-off'

[1] See vol. 1, pp. 320–5.

to a new generation of economies, including Japan, Italy, Sweden and, very nearly, tsarist Russia.

For Britain, the precise severity of the trouble in the earlier of these phases has been much debated. But there is agreement that 'retardation' occurred. Growth rates of manufacturing output and industrial productivity fell; competitive pressure from the new industrial economies intensified and the expansion rate of British exports slackened, although record levels of absolute export values nevertheless were reached by 1913. But, as these indicators of British performance glowed amber, if not red, the measures of activity in the 'invisibles' sector of the economy – the export of capital, shipping services, and insurance – shone in more welcoming colours.

The entire period 1870–1914 was characterised by the domination of the world market in services by the city of London – and the city of Liverpool.[2] The dominant component in the United Kingdom's export of invisibles was, of course, the export of capital. But much of this capital created construction projects or other new assets which needed insurance. Certainly it raised the level of economic activity in many parts of the world and thus again created new opportunities for insurance. The absorption of British capital in the USA, especially the western states in the 1880s, the investment boom in Australia after 1885, the surge in South Africa in the 1890s, the domination of Britain's investments in Europe by Russian securities (which represented half the total by 1913), the enormous capital flows to the Argentine, Brazil and Canada after 1900 – all of these investment developments drew new maps for insurers to follow. After 1870, the Phoenix proved well able to track the expansion in the UK invisibles economy. During these years the veteran exporter rallied and made as positive a contribution to the late-century upswing in international insurance activity as companies such as the Royal or the North British had made to the mid-century expansion.

In the 1880s, and especially in the period of reform between 1890 and 1905, the Phoenix worked strenuously to rebuild its standing as a foreign specialist (see Table 2.1). Throughout the 1870s, foreign premiums accounted for only about half of total fire earnings. But, by the mid-1880s, the foreign proportion was very nearly two-thirds of the whole. During the 1890s it hovered just below 70%, and after the turn of the century climbed almost to 80%, maintaining this high trajectory continuously down to 1914, and even breaking the 80% barrier in 1911.

Phoenix's efforts were uniform across the fire markets of the world, but

[2] See Trebilcock, 'The City, Entrepreneurship and Insurance'.

Table 2.1. *Phoenix Assurance: total home and foreign gross fire premiums (five-year averages, 1871–1911; current £)*

	Home premiums	Foreign premiums	Foreign as % of total premiums
1871/2–1875/6	235,382	250,249	51.5
1876/7–1880/1	254,410	271,647	51.6
1881/2–1885/6	273,434	499,204	64.6
1886/7–1890/1	320,072	593,347	65.0
1891/2–end 1895[a]	329,326	745,349	69.4
1896–1900	362,905	826,044	69.5
1901–5	431,717	1,481,429	77.4
1906–10	434,030	1,494,331	77.5
1911 only	397,564	1,595,616	80.1

Note: [a]Change of accounting year in 1896.
Source: Annual Analyses of Business, 1871–95 and 1896–1925.

the results were not. The efforts consisted of a much greater emphasis on direct selling through agency strongpoints, the conversion of the best of these into full branches and the deeper penetration of markets by the expansion of up-country networks of sub-agencies. The clearest measure of this revival in selling commitment is given by the decreasing proportion of foreign premiums derived from reinsurance. Phoenix relied upon reinsurance acceptances for an annual average of 23.1% of its overseas income in the decade 1856–65,a staggering 57.8% for 1871–5 and a much more reasonable 17.1% in 1886–90; but by 1896–1900 this form of foreign operation had contracted further to a mere 6.0% of the total and by 1911–15 to 4.6% (Table 2.2).

The swing from nearly 60% to under 5% in the proportion of foreign income which Phoenix accepted from other insurers implies a fairly decisive alteration in the company's overseas strategy. The substance of the alteration was Phoenix's revival as an independent foreign operator of real stature.

Even so, in an increasingly intricate world economy, the results were not synchronised across markets. In the 1870s, there was major expansion in Phoenix's directly earned premiums from Europe, Australasia and the West Indies while income from Asia contracted; in the 1880s a vital resurgence in American takings began; in the 1890s Asia revived, Australasia built further, South Africa boomed, and Latin America continued to advance. In the 1900s, the USA continued to dominate, Europe, Canada

Table 2.2. *Foreign reinsurance acceptances as share total foreign premium*

	%		%
1856–65	23.1	1891–5	3.8
1866–70	48.8	1896–1900	6.0
1871–5	57.8	1901–5	5.2
1876–80	52.0	1906–10	4.5
1881–5	25.0	1911–15	4.6
1886–90	17.1		

Source: Calculated from Phoenix Review of Foreign Agencies, Books 1–4.

and Australasia maintained stable market shares, Asia expanded sharply and Africa lost ground (see Table 2.3).

The variables which controlled the success or failure of insurance selling in the distant markets in this period were basically threefold. The level of economic activity in the specific national or regional economy obviously had a bearing, and incoming capital flows were clearly relevant to this. But more worrying to the big British exporters was the intensifying competition from indigenous or foreign non-tariff insurers which was encountered almost everywhere in the later decades of the century.

These variables were interlinked. As the spread of economic development opened new markets so it opened new insurance competitions. Big offices from the advancing economies of Europe, especially Germany, chased the British veterans to the ends of the earth. And developing economies at the periphery quickly became home to developing insurers of their own, native offices willing to chance their arm from Argentina to New Zealand. It became increasingingly difficult for the old London specialists to impose their own discipline and rates upon distant markets when European interlopers and eager local offices had every interest in disturbing the accord and cutting the rate.

And where competitors did not cause problems, governments often did. The period 1870–1914 was one of increasing protectionism in world markets and the world insurance market was no exception. State administrations levied taxes on foreign insurers. Or, they would require increasingly large deposits of the insurer's assets, usually converted into their own government bonds, so that they held in their hands a guarantee of financial security and sound trading. Or, most aggressively of all, they could replace underwriting imports altogether by establishing state monopolies in insurance.

Table 2.3. *The Phoenix world map: premium income by master market area, 1871–1920 (£ and %, five-year averages)*

	USA		Europe		Canada		West Indies		India/Far East		Australia/NZ		Africa		Central/S. America		Total foreign
	£	%	£	%	£	%	£	%	£	%	£	%	£	%	£	%	£m
1871–5	43,248	18.4	112,084	47.7	31,456	13.4	12,021	5.1	17,078	7.3	–	–	1,560	0.7	5,269	2.2	0.23
1876–80	33,323	12.8	138,217	53.1	36,602	14.1	15,775	6.1	12,427	4.8	1,790	0.7	5,041	1.9	6,866	2.6	0.26
1881–5	192,442	43.1	141,509	31.7	46,164	10.4	15,090	3.3	12,188	2.7	11,981	2.7	6,574	1.5	11,007	2.5	0.45
1886–90	269,430	47.0	161,200	28.1	47,449	8.2	12,104	2.1	12,883	2.2	33,953	5.9	6,107	1.1	18,615	3.3	0.57
1891–5	373,931	48.7	180,906	23.6	60,474	7.9	13,293	1.7	16,355	2.1	50,356	6.6	32,205	4.2	22,258	2.9	0.77
1896–00	402,666	48.0	200,266	23.9	84,459	10.1	10,310	1.3	27,897	3.3	54,398	6.5	20,027	2.4	27,704	3.3	0.84
1901–5	561,178	48.8	229,954	20.0	143,772	12.6	10,764	1.0	39,093	3.4	74,838	6.5	40,483	3.5	30,952	2.7	1.15
1906–10	588,233	42.0	282,486	20.1	194,618	13.8	14,499	1.1	119,919	8.5	89,376	6.4	38,202	2.7	46,926	3.3	1.40
1911–15	719,409	45.4	254,773	16.1	222,098	13.9	17,046	1.0	132,193	8.3	118,930	7.5	29.195	1.8	57,444	3.6	1.59
1916–20	1,258,779	47.9	267,947	10.1	334,372	10.4	33,137	1.2	327,675	12.4	154,792	5.8	39,882	1.5	120,714	4.6	2.64

Note: Total foreign premiums do not tally with those in Table 2.1 because of different sources and accounting years, and the different balance of reinsurances in two sources.
Source: Review of Foreign Agencies, Books 1–4.

Naturally, institutions as powerful as the British insurance offices devised counter-measures to these irritations. But, against the new threats of the late nineteenth century, affable conversations between head offices in London or Liverpool were not enough. More effective was cooperation on the spot, within a problem market. This was provided by the local agents' association, a means of giving the representatives of the various UK offices a concerted voice and combined bargaining power at the point of competition. The Fire Offices Committee (FOC) in London would set tariffs for the distant markets, employing combination at the centre to police the periphery. But the FOC maintained a careful liaison with the local agents' associations and frequently accepted their judgement as to what the tariff rate should be. Thus expertise from the periphery was incorporated in the policing that was attempted from the metropole. This was a successful method of wielding the power of combination in both locations against the fractiousness of the further markets.

But, of course, there was a limit to the effectiveness of commercial combination against state initiatives. Although protection is a subject largely neglected in historical assessment of the late nineteenth-century insurance industry – much of which assumes that exports were there to be easily, if no doubt, gloriously picked – it is undoubtedly true that governments created real obstacles for the overseas strategies of the big corporate underwriters. Phoenix certainly experienced all these pressures in its attempts to reconstruct a dynamic foreign sales operation after 1870.

2. EUROPE 1870–1914: ESCAPE FROM THE HOME CONTINENT AND THE TROUBLE WITH REINSURANCE

For the entire span of volume I of this history, Europe had been the centrepiece and mainstay of Phoenix's overseas operation. As late as the decade 1866–75, the home Continent provided 48.7% of the office's foreign revenue against 27.8% for the whole of North America. Continued reliance on Europe, often by reinsurance acceptances rather than by direct trade, drastic cutbacks in the United States, and a certain lingering adherence to direct agency work in Canada composed the Phoenix approach to its major market areas during its mid-century period of retreatism.[3] Revival in the tone and muscle of overseas selling after 1870 depended much less upon Europe than upon the USA. Indeed, it is fair to say that, in one way or another, Phoenix's fortune and eventual fate in its second century were decided by its commitment to American business.

[3] See vol. I, pp. 305–10, 313–22.

This reversal of emphasis first became evident in the period 1870–1914. Over these years Europe accounted for a steadily declining share of total Phoenix foreign earnings, falling from just under one-half in 1871–5 to under one-sixth in 1911–15 (see Table 2.3). The relationship with the North American share was strongly inverse, as it rose from just under one-third in 1871–5 to not far short of two-thirds in 1911–15.[4] Nor can the near doubling in the North American share be attributed to any massive change in Canadian performance; in fact the Canadian share of total overseas earnings was rather stable, 13.4% of the total in 1871–5, 13.9% in 1911–15. So expansion in North America was procured increasingly in the USA.

Nevertheless, even in 1914, Europe was still the second largest export market for the Phoenix. And it possessed one other dominant, if not endearing, feature: it was certainly the most complex market. Whatever complication existed in the late nineteenth-century insurance business, Europe possessed it: industrial economies sufficiently advanced to generate large accumulations of hazardous risks; state administrations sufficiently centralised and confident to impose strict regulations upon the foreign insurer; native competitors sufficiently powerful to appropriate large slices of available custom; reinsurance facilities sufficiently sophisticated to baffle and ensnare the inexperienced; and, from the British underwriter's viewpoint, a number of agencies sufficiently grey-bearded and wise-headed to justify promotion to branch or general agency status, with supervisory power over their own organisations of sub-agencies.

Perhaps the most intricate and characteristic strand of all within the fabric of the European market was provided by reinsurance. The advance of European premiums 1850–70 had been largely due to the appearance of very big re-insurance agencies taking standard quotas of business from established native insurers such as Assurances Générales, Azienda Assicuratice or First Russian.[5] The retreat in the European share of total Phoenix foreign premiums after 1870 was associated with major changes in the type and distribution of reinsurance. It was not that Europe ceased to be the stronghold of reinsurance; rather Europe's hold on Phoenix's total turnover of reinsurance strengthened vastly. But this was due to the demise of reinsurance business elsewhere, rather than to continuing vitality within the European treaties.

Phoenix, of course, had re-entered the vital USA market in the late 1860s – while rivals like the Liverpool & London & Globe or the Royal were building a fortune by direct trade – upon the back of reinsurance

[4] Calculated from Phoenix Review of Foreign Agencies, Books 1–4.

[5] See vol. I, pp. 257, 31, 321–2.

arrangements, primarily with the North British.[6] Before this, Lombard Street's reinsurance business in the US market had been trivial: over the decade 1856–65, it provided an annual average 0.2% of Phoenix US premiums, while the matching proportion for European premiums was 55%. But between 1866 and 1879 reinsurance briefly supplied almost all of the average 13–14% of total foreign income that Phoenix was now able to draw from the USA. Then it stopped entirely. The reason, for neither the first nor the last time in this period, was government interference. In June 1879, New York State legislated to prohibit any insurance office with an agency on its territory from reinsuring 'with any other office not duly admitted by the usual deposit in state funds to do business there'.[7] Phoenix was such another office and its most important reinsurance connection with North British was shattered by the act. It was this development which forced Phoenix to start trading in the USA on its own account.

But forces other than the state could dampen the reinsurance tendency. In the West Indies, India and the Far East before 1900, Phoenix very seldom resorted to reinsurance largely because other forms of market control were being developed in these places. Outside Europe and the immediately post-bellum United States, only Latin America witnessed a massive resort to reinsurance by Phoenix after 1870. In the quinquennium 1871–5 no less than 96.8% of Latin American business was taken by the indirect method: but, even here, the share fell abruptly, sinking to 28.4% by 1886–90. In no other market did it scrape above 10% of earnings for any period of more than five years prior to 1900. The sharp reduction in Latin American reinsurance appears to have been deliberate policy rather than a response to state restrictions or a function of alternative methods of market control. Phoenix, in more dynamic mood, simply decided to pursue more of its own Latin American business – a business no doubt reacting to active British foreign investment in the region – rather than relying entirely on the leavings of others.

However, the effect of these changes was to make the European market virtually a monopolist of Phoenix reinsurance activity (see Table 2.4). Reinsurance also bulked large within Phoenix's total European premium earnings, always accounting for more than half before 1900 although tending to fall towards the half-way mark in the 1880s. The contraction in the share of reinsurance within total European income was associated with the contraction in the share of European premiums within total foreign premiums.

[6] *Ibid.*, p. 320. [7] Phoenix Trustees' Minutes, 26 June 1879.

Table 2.4. *Phoenix reinsurance by region as % of Phoenix total reinsurance*

	1856–65	1866–70	1871–5	1876–80	1881–5	1886–90
Europe	96.5	77.8	59.7	67.6	80.6	91.1
N. America	–	13.6	31.9	20.9	–	–
W. Indies	–	–	0.7	0.8	0.7	–
India/Far East	1.5	1.5	0.6	0.6	0.5	0.3
Middle East	–	–	–	1.1	1.5	1.5
Latin America	1.8	7.1	7.1	8.9	12.6	6.6
New Zealand	–	–	–	–	4.0	0.5

Why then does Phoenix's European trade alone display this long-term addiction to reinsurance? The answer is twofold: the intense levels of competition in this market and the fact that, under the pressure of this competition, the content of reinsurance changed. Reinsurance in Europe in 1900 was not the same as reinsurance in Europe in 1850. And European governments did not prevent the offices from introducing change. Though Continental states could, and did, amend the rules of practice, they did not, unlike their American colleagues, tear them up entirely.

So how did the content of reinsurance in Europe change? The practice of the period 1850–80, when Phoenix exports relied most upon acceptances from other offices, was notably orderly. Phoenix received agreed shares of total business from established and specific institutions, whether First Russian shedding Moscow business or Assurances Générales shedding Parisian business. In several cases, Phoenix acquired entrée to these agreements through the good offices of its peers and friends, as it did in Russia through the North British or in the Near East through the Sun.

But, as the volume of demand expanded, competition intensified and the number of native offices multiplied, these well-mannered exchanges became increasingly difficult to maintain. Specialised intermediaries became essential if the flood of applications for reinsurance was to be matched to companies in search of profitable acceptances.

From the 1880s, therefore, a new breed of international insurance broker began to appear in the most active parts of the European market. The broker's method of working was quite different from the company-to-company 'quota' reinsurance agreement by which a given proportion of an agency's business was passed on to another company. Instead, brokers operated 'surplus' treaties, collecting unwanted risks from many companies and drawing up agreements by which they were passed on to many other companies. The broker farmed out the work and negotiated his reward with the guaranteeing companies. Towards the end of the century, Phoenix, and many other companies, increasingly appointed brokers of this type as their foreign agents or 'correspondents'. Indeed, by 1898, Phoenix had employed arrangements like these in probably some fourteen centres, and all but one of these – New Zealand – was within Europe, or on its fringes in the Eastern Mediterranean.

Characteristically, this broker-mediated foreign trade was marked by heavy competition, fast turnover of contracts, quick losses and profits and high brokers' commissions. For the accepting office, the business looked very expensive, with commission charges commonly reaching 25% and more, against the 10–15% usual on ordinary agency business. Between 1870 and 1900, Phoenix paid 25% or more in twenty locations worldwide. Sixteen of these locations were in western Europe and all the rest were on the Eastern Mediterranean fringe. Only four of them recorded this level of charge before 1885. In reality, however, the cost of obtaining the particular sort of business that these commissions identify was not as astronomical as it looked. For the accepting office saved the overheads and many of the running costs associated with normal agency business. More worrying to such an office was the high level of losses to which this type of business proved liable.

It was probably pressure from reinsurance losses which led to the third adjustment in the operation of Phoenix's overseas selling from the late 1890s. This involved a reduction in the reliance upon reinsurance of all types and the conversion of the largest broker-agencies into regional branch offices with their own networks of agencies or sub-agencies.

However, there is no clear explanation for the map of reinsurance: why some agencies should have remained direct ones and others begun as, or become, the broker type. Within Europe, it was certainly not the case that Phoenix practised reinsurance only where it could escape adverse state legislation. Phoenix took reinsurance and no other form of business from markets like France, Italy and Switzerland, where there was little in the way of official interference, but from Gibraltar and Turkey, where there was equal freedom of operation, almost solely direct trade. In fact, most agencies handled both direct underwriting and reinsurance acceptances; it was the balance between the two that mattered. And this could be altered to suit changing conditions. Thus the Viennese agency began in 1875 as a reinsurance station, then converted briefly into a direct agency, then adjusted again to become a broker-mediated surplus reinsurance system in the late 1880s.

Possibly, reinsurance tended to be associated with the need to break into new competitive markets. Continental industrialisation was rapid and capital-intensive: the insurer needed to move fast in pursuit of the resulting business. The Hanburys in Hamburg or the Malms in Gothenberg, within their long-established strongholds, might regard reinsurance as a second string. But the best way into an unfamiliar and swiftly expanding market could well have been through a general broker with local expertise and wide-ranging connections. Alternatively, the suppressed growth of the European economies during the 1880s, the decade in which the effects of the Great Depression were most generally felt, could explain, if combined with high levels of insurance competition and low levels of underwriting profit, the increasing resort to surplus treaties during these years.

By comparison with the convoluted pressures emanating from the reinsurance markets of Europe, the difficulties created by European state administrations were moderate. Perhaps naturally, the tsarist autocracy set the most high-handed conditions – though not as high-handed as those of the libertarian United States. Until 1868 foreign offices were excluded from Russia and the First and Second Russian Companies were treated to a monopoly of the domestic market. Only by reinsurance could westerners do business in Russia, and that, by a quota arrangement, is what North British and Phoenix did. From 1871, however, foreign offices were permitted to trade directly upon depositing with the imperial government, securities worth the very considerable sum of 500,000 roubles (£64,583). Not surprisingly, having been forced into Russian reinsurances, Phoenix elected to stay there rather than pay through the nose for direct access.

Such deposits, usually in government bonds or public stock, were not uncommon in Europe. Often they formed part of a national policy of protectionism which became increasingly evident across the Continent as the Great Depression made itself felt. But the Russian version was probably the most expensive in Europe. In Germany, as Phoenix expanded its agency system throughout the industrial powerhouse of the Second Reich, it encountered the separate deposit requirements of many German states. The company purchased 4% consols for the purpose in Baden, Bavaria and Brandenberg between 1883 and 1886 and in Magdeburg in 1899. Yet these were for relatively modest amounts, some £30,000 covering all four cases, and a trifle against the underwriter's ransom demanded by the Russians or Americans. Similarly, in Spain in 1893 Phoenix had to provide deposits, but only in the humble sum of 7,000 pesetas. The Bulgarians did rather better in 1898 when they demanded, and received, £12,000 in 6% bonds. But not even this could be called exorbitant. Moreover, these were the only European countries where there is clear evidence that the Phoenix had to pay before it could insure.

Taxation was more pervasive. Phoenix operated in twenty-one European countries in this period and ten of them imposed upon insurers taxes of some kind: state, municipal, parochial, income or industrial taxes, or stamp duties on policies. Three of the four Scandinavian countries levied state and town taxes on Phoenix. Portugal, Holland, Belgium and Greece charged state or income taxes on insurance profits. Portugal and Belgium also had provincial and parochial taxes. To these Portugal – perhaps the most fertile in methods for rooking the underwriter – added an unusual industrial tax. Stamp duty was levied in Turkey, Belgium – and Portugal. A fire-fighting tax also existed in Turkey, Sweden – and Portugal.

A lesser nuisance was the official requirement for public declaration. Most governments stipulated that foreign insurers should issue a formal statement undertaking to submit their business conduct to native commercial law and the local courts. Certainly, Germany, Holland, Greece, Bulgaria and Finland, among others, insisted on this. Phoenix did not find it a difficult requirement to meet and often a simple declaration, legally drafted, satisfied the authorities. Official demands for the publication of accounts – part of the rule-book in Austria, Finland and Spain – presented knottier problems. But under the Phoenix Act of 1895, the office was required to publish its accounts in the United Kingdom. Any company facing this obligation could scarcely complain of foreign governments requiring the same level of information.

What effect then did government action have upon Phoenix's trade in Europe? Deposits impinged only in a few locations, and, for a rich company, did not sum to numbers that were embarrassing. Two reservations are in order. Firstly, if not rich companies, new entrants could certainly have been disadvantaged by the scale of prepayment required in Germany or Russia. Secondly, this valuation of deposits applies only to Europe; American requirements were quite enough to annoy even the rich. For Phoenix, European deposits were a minor nuisance, not a hindrance to trade, though its Russian policy after 1871 could well have been different in the absence of deposits. The standards of public declaration current in Europe created few difficulties for a company of Phoenix's rank. This leaves taxation as the potential drag on business. No one knows whether it was or not.

The totals paid out by Phoenix in taxation were small but in some locations accumulations of different taxes could look onerous against the receipts of individual agencies. It is worth remembering that, even in Britain before 1867, the stamp duty could double the cost of some insurances. Generally, however, the impression is that European fire markets in the period 1870–1914 were expanding so rapidly and so competitively that any negative effect of taxation upon this development was swept aside in the rout. But this is a speculative answer to an important question. In most of the literature the question of protectionist restraint of late nineteenth-century insurance markets is not even raised; the silence is deafening.

Even the dependable business histories of the Commercial Union and REA assume that entry to the European markets of this period was unproblematic.[8] Raynes' classic, *History of Insurance* refers to 'restrictive legislation' on the Continent, to 'troublesome conditions' in the German states and to the 'severest restrictions' in Austria; but his focus is almost entirely upon life offices and the troubles they encountered as a result of official demands for costly valuations and statistical returns.[9] Only Dickson, in his study of the Sun, senses that British fire offices found their 'agency business in Europe . . . hampered by government restrictions'.[10]

We must conclude that the proportion of cost added to British policies by foreign discrimination 1870–1914 is unknown and that this unknown represents an important lacuna in recent historical investigation of the industry. But that additional cost can only have made British insurance exports less attractive to European consumers. European protectionism limited British exports of insurance to the Continent, along with British exports of other commodities. Even if we remain ignorant of the amount of the limit, we need to recognise the fact. European business was not there simply for the picking.

3. THE AGENCY BALANCE OF POWER IN EUROPE

The interaction of these complex forces clearly altered the standing of Phoenix's European agencies relative to one another in the period 1870–1914. Historically, the outstanding European centres for Phoenix had been Hamburg and Gothenberg under the remarkable dynastic control of the Hanbury and Malm families. With slight adjustments to family organisation and major changes to agency organisation, this control survived down to 1914. But the environment in which it did so was much changed.

As Phoenix staged its belated return to transatlantic business in the 1870s and 1880s, the Hanbury agency continued, and even extended, its domination of the European trade, but its sway was exercised over an

[8] See Liveing, *Commercial Union Assurance*, p. 65; Supple, *Royal Exchange Assurance*, p. 243.

[9] H. E. Raynes, *A History of British Insurance* (London, 1964), p. 271.

[10] Dickson, *Sun Insurance*, p. 187. This source is an honourable exception to the general neglect of insurance protectionism.

Table 2.5. *Shares of major European outlets in total Phoenix foreign income, 1871–1915 (£000 and %)*

	Hamburg		Gothenburg		Paris[a]		St. Petersburg		Trieste	
	£'000	%	£'000	%	£'000	%	£'000	%	£'000	%
1871–5	15.5	6.6	2.9	1.3	31.9	13.6	23.7	10.1	14.7	6.2
1876–80	19.2	7.4	2.8	1.0	31.7	12.2	35.0	13.2	13.2	5.1
1881–5	23.2	5.2	2.3	0.5	26.3	5.9	49.4	11.1	2.9	0.6
1886–90	36.1	6.3	3.0	0.5	27.3	4.8	44.0	7.7	–	–
1891–5	46.3	6.0	2.4	0.3	28.4	3.7	41.0	5.3	–	–
1896–1900	62.8	7.4	3.7	0.4	32.8	3.9	27.6	3.3	–	–
1901–5	59.6	5.2	4.2	0.4	24.1	2.1	43.7	3.8	–	–
1906–10	97.1	6.9	5.3	0.4	0.5	0.03	43.0	3.1	–	–
1911–15	62.2	3.9	6.8	0.4	–	–	22.1	1.4	–	–

	Austria		Switzerland		Paris[b]		All Europe	
	£'000	%	£'000	%	£'000	%	£'000	%
1871–5	0.5	0.2	–	–	–	–	112.1	47.7
1876–80	5.7	2.3	–	–	–	–	138.2	53.1
1881–5	9.3	2.1	–	–	–	–	141.5	31.7
1886–90	10.3	1.8	–	–	–	–	161.2	28.1
1891–5	15.7	2.0	–	–	–	–	180.9	23.6
1896–1900	10.2	1.2	13.1	1.6	–	–	200.3	23.9
1901–5	5.6	0.5	25.0	2.2	8.8	0.8	230.0	20.0
1906–10	3.8	0.3	31.3	2.2	14.6	1.0	282.5	20.1
1911–15	2.5	0.2	38.1	2.4	20.3	1.2	254.8	16.1

Notes: [a] = Paris Old Treaty, [b] = Paris Treaties of 1902 and 1905.

increasingly sluggish total return to Head Office. Indeed, it is arguable (see Table 2.5) that the Hanburys were the only major part of the Phoenix operation on the home continent that was not drastically on the slide. The European economies may have been modernising, but there were too many insurance companies chasing the proceeds. Phoenix's outposts at Hamburg and Gothenberg, located in established and sophisticated markets, were particularly prone to the effects of this further advance in sophistication. Nevertheless, one coped much better than the other.

Alongside them, Phoenix maintained an increasing array of European agencies which did not supply much more than 1–2% of total foreign income and tended to slip further (see Table 2.5). The armoury deployed by the company against these hostile trends included conventional direct agencies, reinsurance treaties, the new style of broker-managed reinsurances, and, perhaps most effectively, the general agency commanding a string of sub-agencies across an entire market region.

The great quota reinsurance treaties established in the 1850s and 1860s were an early casualty of the 1870s. The Trieste treaty, after a brief burst as a substantial money-spinner, had burned out by the early 1880s. The Paris 'Old Treaty' of 1850 with Assurances Générales was the largest single source of Phoenix foreign premiums in Europe, and the second biggest in the world after New York in 1871–5. But it lost ground rapidly thereafter, being overtaken by the Russian reinsurances channelled out through St Petersburg in the later 1870s and by the agency business won by the Hanburys some ten years later. Although the Parisian takings in sterling fell by only one-quarter between 1871–5 and 1901–5, despite the strongly deflationary price trend for the majority of this period, this was sufficient to slash its share in Phoenix total foreign earnings by a factor of more than six. By 1910 the Paris 'Old Treaty' was dead and the new French treaties of 1902 and 1905 were trivial by comparison.

The Russian treaties held up rather better, topping Phoenix's world rankings in 1876–80 and coming second to New York in 1881–6 and 1886–90. This performance was a tribute to the strength of early Russian industrialisation in the aftermath of the mid-century 'Era of Reforms'. Receipts from St Petersburg formed Phoenix's biggest income flow in Europe for well over a decade (1876–90). Between the early 1870s and the later 1900s, the annual averages for these receipts almost doubled, but even this did not prevent their share in the office's total foreign earnings from falling by more than a factor of three. Nor did it prevent the Russian reinsurances, impressive as they were, from being outpaced by the Hanburys in the early 1890s. The Hanburys worked themselves up from third place in Europe in 1871–85 to the top position in 1891–5, and there they stayed until 1914. As the old quota treaties faded, the Hamburg agency re-emerged as Phoenix standard-bearer in Europe.

No other major source of European income managed to maintain itself in a style comparable to the Hanbury agency. Its share of all Phoenix overseas income in 1871–5 was 6.6% and the matching share in 1906–10 was still 6.9%. However, in order to preserve this uniquely secure foothold among the slipping European shares, the Hamburg dynasty was required to increase its remittances in money terms by more than sixfold over this period. And this was achieved against the background of an income flow from the whole of Europe which did little more than double.

The similarly venerable Malm agency at Gothenberg was quite unable to match the Hanbury result. Between the early 1870s and the early 1910s, it just about managed to double its average annual takings, but its share of total foreign receipts nevertheless fell from 1.3% to a meagre 0.4%. So traditional direct agencies, even with a certain measure of reinsurance tacked on, were no certain answer to the European problem.

On the other hand, the rise and fall of the Austrian returns made it clear that the new style surplus reinsurances were not foolproof either. But, on yet another hand, the Swiss results – again based on broker-led cantonal reinsurances – showed that this method could make ground against the tide, if perhaps for a limited period.

But none of these devices could keep the European slice of overseas revenue from crumbling. Nor could the multiplication of European agencies: where there had been only a dozen in the 1850s and early 1860s, there were thirty-one by the late 1880s. But, as the few great European income sources of the mid-century ran down – the Hanburys excepted – the new agency foundations did not produce successors of equivalent standing. In the early 1870s, only sixteen of the twenty-six Phoenix agencies operating in Europe reported takings of under 1% of total foreign earnings. By 1906–10, twenty-seven out of the thirty active European outposts were in this position. The proliferation of Continental agencies created a wide variety of relatively small-scale outlets and offered no replacements for the few large-scale goldmines of the earlier period.

The Hanbury agency maintained its own status as a goldmine by a variety of devices. One was territorial expansion as a general agency leading a force of sub-agencies. The first of these arrived with the appointment of Hirschfield & Co. as agents for the port of Bremen and its province in 1865, but this did not last long. More satisfactory arrangements for Bremen had to await the appointment of Schmidt and Boring in 1888.[11] Before this, Lubeck had been added with the appointment of Otto Gusmann in 1874.[12] But it was in the early 1880s, after a shake-up in their own leadership, that Hanburys showed themselves keenest to expand, particularly into southern Germany. They moved a sub-agency into the Grand Duchy of Baden in 1883 and the next year set up a Bavarian outpost to cover the important centres of Munich and Nuremberg. The Hamburg-based leadership liked the look of Bavaria, with ordinary rates at 4–6 shillings per cent, all insurances subject to average and lots of juicy brewery risks; they expected it to yield £20,000 per year in premiums when properly developed. With a lesser show of enthusiasm, they also moved quietly into Brandenberg in 1886.[13]

But the Hanburys did not content themselves solely with income growth achieved by organisational expansion. They also tried their hand

[11] Phoenix Directors' Minutes, U20, p. 65, 22 November 1865; Y24, p. 360, 21 March 1888.

[12] *Ibid.*, V21, p. 353, 25 February 1874.

[13] Phoenix Trustees' Minutes, 27 September 1883, 12 June 1884, 22 April 1886.

Table 2.6. *Reinsurance surplus treaties of the Hamburg agency, 1891–1905*

Acceptance from:	Span
General Insurance Co.	1891–5
Lancashire	1891–7
Lloyd Belge	1891–2
Norwich Union	1891–1905
Patriotic	1891–1900
La Rouennaise	1891–7
Société Anonyme de Réassurances	1891–1905
United (Palatine from 1894)	1891–9
Munich	1892–9
Western	1900
Gladbacher Ruckversicherung	1900–5
Norddeutsche	1903–5

Source: Hamburg Agency Notebook C19/21.

at the newer forms of reinsurance. Two unusual pieces of archive material, the Agency Memoranda of December 1893 and the Hamburg Agency Notebook, reveal that the Hamburg agency had joined the broker-mediated market on its own account by the early 1890s. The Agency Memoranda list as many as thirty-two companies with which the Hanburys had reinsurance dealings in 1893; about twenty of these were British, six were German, two French, two Irish, one Swedish and one Swiss. Eleven of the connections were specifically one-off facultative deals but at least a dozen, and probably more, were surplus treaties. Table 2.6 shows the offices from which the Hanburys took a regular premium income and the dates, recorded in the Hamburg Notebook, over which they were paid.

Whatever the form of their dealings, the Hanburys appear to have been especially proficient in handling the various German state governments. This was not a knack possessed by all British insurers: the Sun had experienced opposition from the Prussian government in 1837 but also as recently as the 1860s.[14] Phoenix, through the Hanburys, was more skilful at dealing with German bureaucracy. On Hanbury advice, Phoenix formed a committee of directors to deal with the application for the Bremen agency in 1865; they negotiated directly with the Bremen Court of Trade and were empowered to supply it 'with documents and certificates and

[14] Dickson, *Sun Insurance*, pp. 166, 169–71.

papers of every kind'.[15] In 1872 Hanburys asked Phoenix to supply them with a short pro forma version of their power of attorney, so that they did not have to yield up a fully certificated legal document every time a German state asked for proof of their credentials. This seems to have dealt successfully with the frequency of such requests. The long standing of this Hamburg mercantile dynasty and the excellence, and high social tone, of its German connections ensured that Phoenix's dialogue with the sometimes trying state administrators passed off relatively smoothly.

The special quality of the Hanbury agency was fully recognised in London. In this period, as in earlier ones, the family enjoyed a degree of autonomy that was allowed to few other Phoenix representatives. Thus, as early as 1872, the Hamburg firm was permitted to transact reinsurance business not only with British fire offices but with German ones as well. True, even Hanburys were not allowed to hold more than one-third of gross premiums as unremitted balances; the rest had to go to London and any losses larger than the balances had to be met by cash drawn as required.[16] True, too, that the Hanburys enjoyed their initiatives only against the hefty surety of a £4,000 bond. But both of these requirements reflected primarily the enormous cash-flow channelled through Hamburg. A better measure of the trust placed in this agency is provided by the readiness with which its powers of attorney were renewed regardless of changes in management.

In 1877, when H. J. L. Behrmann, for many years assistant to the senior partner, F. C. Hanbury, himself became a partner in the firm, Phoenix without demur appointed him joint-agent – although they did increase the bond to £5,000. When F. C. Hanbury died in 1878, Phoenix switched the joint-agency to Behrmann and Hanbury's German-born widow, Emma Henriette. They were no doubt influenced in this by the fact that Emma Henriette's German blood was tastefully blue; before marriage she was the Countess Holck.

Hanburys' long standing as a merchant house, and its considerable influence within the commerce of Germany's premier port, was heavily reinforced by the social eminence which the family had achieved. F. C. Hanbury's widow was the embodiment of this eminence, and no mean lady of commerce either. In 1886, Behrmann became 'General Manager of the Phoenix Assurance Company for Germany', a discreet recognition that Hamburg meant a lot more than a single North German city. It was also a recognition of something else, since in 1886 Behrmann's son, John William, joined the firm and the agency. In 1887 the renewal of the power

15 Phoenix Directors' Minutes, U20, p. 28, 18 April 1866.
16 Phoenix Trustees' Minutes, 19 March 1874.

of attorney was made to both Behrmanns and to Frau Hanbury; in 1899 Frau Hanbury was still going strong, the younger Behrmann had taken over from father, and the third recipient of the power of attorney was F. H. Schaechtel. In each case, Phoenix was happy to recognise, as a matter of routine, changes that had occurred within the internal management of the Hanbury firm.

There were other grace notes. When the Hanbury agency reached its centenary in 1885, Phoenix sent the chief clerk of the London foreign department, the section of Head Office which corresponded with the overseas outposts, to Hamburg, with the Phoenix mace and emblem, to add metropolitan dignity to the celebrations. Six years later, Phoenix bought 19-21 Rathausstrasse for the impressive sum of 400,000 marks (£20,000) as a new Hamburg home for its prize European agency. More materialistically, Phoenix paid the Hanburys a lot. Even in 1871, the basic commission rate for the agency, at 20%, was high; by the 1890s, at 33–35%, it was astronomical. Table 2.7 reveals both that the difficult and competitive conditions of the European markets had a tendency to push agents' commissions inexorably upwards and that there was a rough going rate for each era. But, even within this landscape, the Hanbury agency was exceptionally rewarded. Whatever blend of acumen and influence the Hanburys and the Behrmanns peddled, Phoenix clearly wanted it.

One explanation for the staggering shares of income that Phoenix was prepared to pay to the Hanburys may well lie in the pace and force of German economic growth in the high technology upswing of the 1890s and 1900s. Activity in the chemical, engineering and electro-technical sectors, as well as in the metals industries, was pronounced during these years and this must have boosted German demand for insurance. It is significant that the very high commission rates allowed to Hamburg were paid only after 1893.

A similar logic may well apply elsewhere in German territory, in Alsace-Lorraine. Of course, governmental power acted here in a particularly brusque way, by removing almost all the province into the orbit of the new German Empire after the Franco-Prussian War of 1870–1. Phoenix paid high commissions of 25–30% in Alsace from the 1880s and this important industrial region more than doubled its premium flow between 1882 and 1912.[17] Alsace, a much-disputed region of metal, mining and engineering industries, provided one of the stronger points among Phoenix's new continental outposts.

[17] From £8,028 to £19,986. This represented 2.2% of total foreign income in 1882 and 1.3% in 1912.

Table 2.7. *Rates of commission paid to European agents, 1865–1900 (%)*

	Hamburg	Alsace	First Russian	Anchor	Commercial	Salamander	Brandt	Vienna	Switzerland	Almindelige	Gothenberg	Spain
1865	–		12.5				3.5					
1868	–									12.5		
1869	–		15.0			15.0	3.5					
1871	20.0											
1872	–		18.0							15.0		
1873	–			18.0			3.5					
1874	–							25.0				
1877	–				18.0							
1878	–									20.0		
1882	–		15.0									
1886	–	25–30	18.0									
1887	–										20.0	15.0
1890	–		18.0				4.0					
1893	33–35									25.0		
1897	–								25.0			
1900	–						20.0[a]					20–27.5

Source: Minute Books. *Note*: [a]=Bless

At St Petersburg, the agent in Phoenix's second-ranking European money-trap – and until 1890 the leader even of the Hanburys – had a less active role to play, and was paid less for it. E. H. Brandt, agent from the 1860s until 1890, was effectively merely the collector and collator of the reinsurances laid off to Phoenix by quota treaty from the big Russian native offices. The commission structure reflected this. Before 1890, Brandt never received more than 3–3.5% of the valuable reinsurance stream passed on by the Russian companies. By contrast, First Russian, the most prolific of the ceding companies, enjoyed returns of between 12.5% and 18% in the period 1860–90. While Brandt took his usual humble slice, other Russian companies like the Salamander earned 15% and the Anchor and Commercial worked up to 18% in the 1870s and 1880s (see Table 2.7).[18] Brandt was succeeded in his long tenure at St Petersburg in 1890 by Gotthard Bless who kept the agency going into the 1900s.

It is striking that Phoenix relied so heavily for its Russian income on a treaty with a single Russian company; the compact with First Russian apart, Phoenix did not seek reinsurance arrangements with more than one additional partner at any one time: the dates of the treaties with Salamander, Anchor and Commercial are sequential. And these were tiny affairs compared with the returns from First Russian. In the period 1871–5, in which Phoenix had connections with six different outlets in Poland and European Russia, First Russian accounted for 78% of the total average annual premium from the region. Perhaps it is not surprising, therefore, that the relationship between the two companies should have been somewhat unusual. First Russian pressed continuously for higher rates of commission; Phoenix pressed for more and better business. Generally speaking, the Russians got their rates and the London office devised an ingenious scheme for getting superior risks.

During the 1890s, it is clear that a profit incentive scheme was built into the First Russian treaty. After First Russian had taken its 18% on gross premiums laid off to Phoenix and Bless his 4%, the profit on these premiums was calculated. Phoenix took the first tranche of the surplus up to a limit of 10% of the net premiums; then, if there were any further surplus, First Russian got the next tranche up to a limit of 3% of net premiums. Anything beyond 13% of net premiums accrued to Phoenix. Obviously, any business that earned above 10% of net premiums; once claims and hefty commissions had been met, must have been a high class of risk. First Russian was being offered a form of additional contingent commission to provide such risks.

[18] Phoenix Foreign Agents' Lists C19/16; 1 January 1889. Just before his replacement in 1890, Brandt's commission was raised to 4%.

However, after building strongly in the 1880s and early 1890s, Phoenix Russian premiums slumped in the last years of the century. Their best period was in the mid-1880s when, between 1884 and 1887, they exceeded £50,000 per year (see Table 2.5).This was twice the level of remittance from either Hamburg or Paris for these years, and outside New York, nothing in the Phoenix foreign network could touch it. After slipping somewhat in the later 1880s, the income stream from imperial Russia was back to over £45,000 by 1895. Then it collapsed, more than halving in 1896 and recovering to the 1895 figure only in 1903.

This is a most peculiar chronology. Tsarist Russia experienced substantial industrial growth between the mid-1860s and the mid-1880s, but the real acceleration came in the 1890s, during Count Witte's brilliant stint at the Ministry of Finance. This spurt produced growth rates in industrial output of around 8% per annum, the second fastest of the nineteenth century, trailing only Sweden's performance at roughly the same time, and made the Russian manufacturing sector the fifth largest industrial complex in the world by 1900. This growth faltered only in 1899 and then foundered entirely amidst the economic, social and political upheavals of the early 1900s which culminated in the abortive revolution of 1905. It resumed only in the period 1907–14. Thus Phoenix's income from Russia went down while the tsarist economy was still going up; and went up while the tsarist economy was coming down.

The Phoenix management was worried by this. The slipping returns of the late 1880s formed the prelude to Brandt's replacement by Bless. And the Phoenix downturn after 1895 produced a new system for rewarding the Petersburg agency. From 1 January 1900, the 22% commission rate was divided as before between First Russian and Bless, but Bless was also given a 20% contingency commission of his own (see Table 2.7). In all probability, this system replaced the former profit-sharing scheme, with Bless himself taking care of First Russian's appetite for a slice of the action in return for a handsome pay-off contingent on surpluses. Certainly, such an arrangement would have placed the Petersburg agency on a footing with most of Phoenix's other big European agencies. Apparently, also, it worked, for Phoenix premiums from Russia recovered, even in the early 1900s, when almost everything else in Russia was busy deteriorating.

Lombard Street's prospecting along the Neva proved effective. This was not the case for all British companies. Writing from the experience of the Sun, Peter Dickson concluded that Eastern Europe was 'a troubled and backward territory'.[19] Acting on the same belief, and what it saw as the poor Russian results of other companies, the Sun was reluctant to enter into Russian reinsurances. Phoenix's results were not poor and it acted in quite a different way and upon quite different assumptions.

For much of the period 1860–90, Russia was the biggest and most lucrative of all Phoenix's European markets, and one of its best on the global scale. Even in the 1850s, well before the major treaty was struck in 1864, Phoenix's home foreign department was recording the rates of native Russian insurers for cotton mills, hemp, timber and metal warehouses, glass dealers, druggists and sugar refineries in such centres as St Petersburg, Moscow, Cronstadt, Odessa and other major towns west of the Urals. That is, they were showing active interest in the sort of properties in which Phoenix was traditionally interested, well before they found a way of tapping this business for themselves. They were definitely not deterred by a 'troubled and backward territory'. When they achieved a Russian portfolio, it was – as it should have been, given the Phoenix pedigree – a good cross-section of Russian industrialisation. Whatever the Sun may have feared, the Phoenix decision was a sensible and profitable, and indeed enterprising, one.

Phoenix's approach to reinsurance in Russia was not passive. In the 1860s and 1870s, the office experimented with a variety of Russian treaties, rapidly discarding those which proved unprofitable. For the major ceding partner who did pass on rewarding business, First Russian, Phoenix boosted commission rates in the 1880s and 1890s and invented an imaginative profit-sharing scheme to keep the business rewarding. Management here was attentive and quick-footed. And it was determined: Phoenix continued to accept Russian industrial risks down to the eve of the Russian Revolution. The last was taken in March 1917. No doubt the Board were influenced by the long-term profitability of their dealings with First Russian. They would have held in mind, for instance, that, over the good period 1869–85, profits were recorded on business ceded by First Russian in twelve out of seventeen years and that the average profit on premiums in that dozen years was 20%.

Given the decline of the Paris Old Treaty, no other Phoenix outlet in Europe could compare with Hamburg or St Petersburg by the 1890s. The Paris connection was still producing nearly 4% of total foreign income 1891–5, ranking third in Europe after the German and Russian agencies (see Table 2.5). The fourth place was taken by Vienna and it controlled only 2% of the total, and this was to slip badly after 1906. Nevertheless, the Austro-Hungarian Empire did play an important part both in Phoenix income flow and in the development of foreign strategy in the final third

[19] Dickson, *Sun Insurance*, p. 183.

of the nineteenth century. Its two main centres for Phoenix, the Trieste agency, which serviced the Azienda Assicuratice treaty, and the Vienna agency ranked fourth and fifth in Europe in 1876–80, with annual average shares of foreign income at 5.1% and 4.1% respectively. This was the best shot from the region, however; by 1883 no further earnings were arriving from Trieste and by 1886–90, the receipts from Vienna were under 2% of all Phoenix overseas receipts.

Behind this pattern lies a diverting tale of agents with opposed convictions and differing tactics of reinsurance. The peak performance of the Austro-Hungarian agencies were recorded while both were under the same management, that of one Herr Vortmann. Between 1876 and 1880, the two Vortmann agencies went for turnover; they did this so successfully that together they averaged nearly £24,000 per year in takings at that time, when even the Hanburys were not reaching £20,000. Briefly, this put Vortmann alone as the biggest European earner for Phoenix after the great Russian and French treaties. But, in reality, only the pickings from the other treaty with Azienda kept Vortmann in business. He was on the high commission of 25% and he produced total charges which averaged 38% gross premiums 1874–8. With losses running at 60% and more of gross premiums at this time, Vortmann had nothing or next to nothing to remit to London. He proved that volume of business was not the answer in central Europe.

In 1882, Vortmann was replaced by Julius Kreil in Vienna and in 1883 Kreil took over Trieste as well. For reasons of close control rather than profitability, Kreil proceeded to run down the Trieste operation and concentrate his efforts upon the imperial capital of the Habsburgs. His was purely a reinsurance agency with an enormous geographical sweep which covered Austro-Hungary, Serbia, Romania and Italy. Over the years 1882–7, Kreil – and then, between 1887 and 1898, his successor, Nasir – turned Vienna into the archetype of the new surplus reinsurance agency. These two agents supervised at least a dozen treaties from Vienna on Phoenix's behalf. The results produced much smaller premiums – during its lifetime Kreil's agency averaged about a third of the income amassed by Vortmann in the late 1870s – but much larger profits. Kreil was able to send back an average £10,000 per year to London between 1882 and 1886 whereas his predecessor had often to present an empty account. This outcome appears a compelling argument for selectivity.

Nasir continued with this approach over much the same territory, with the addition of Bulgaria until 1891, and with much the same spread of treaties. In his turn, he was succeeded by the Viennese lawyer Stein in 1898. A more limited territory was allotted to Stein: he got Austria,

Table 2.8. *Treaties managed from Vienna, 1887–1904*

Company	Period of treaty	Termination
Austrian Phoenix (General)	1889–98	Cancelled
Austrian Phoenix (Sugar)	1890–6	Cancelled
Concordia	1883–1900	Run off
Dacia Roumania	1882–96	Cancelled
Donan	1882–1904	Cancelled
Fire Ins. Association	1882–92	?
Albion Fire	1893–5	?
Manchester Fire	1896–9	?
Nationala	1889–1900	Cancelled
North British	1882–1912	Cancelled
Vienna	1888–94	Cancelled
Securitas	1894–5	Cancelled
Generali	1893–6?	Cancelled

Hungary and Romania only. Bulgaria had been given its own Phoenix agency in 1891 and Italy, a richer prospect, somewhat earlier, in 1889. The identifiable cases of the Viennese treaties managed by the two men are listed in Table 2.8.

The pattern seems to have been one of frequent switches and ready cancellation. Results exist in some detail for about half of these cases (see Table 2.11) and these suggest that losses were also common. In fact, they seem to have become increasingly common in the second half of the 1890s and early 1900s. It is striking that all three of the most important and long-running treaties, those with Austrian Phoenix (General), Dacia Roumania and Donan were all cancelled by Phoenix between 1896 and 1904. Whatever magic Kreil had worked in the 1880s, it was clearly not a trick which could be long sustained. Selective acceptance on broker-mediated reinsurance did not enjoy extended profitability in central Europe.

However, the best documented example of a Phoenix broker-based agency was found not in the *locus classicus* of Austro-Hungary but to the south, in Italy. The 1889 agency was typical of Phoenix's European diversification in the era 1880–1914. At no point before the Great War did it earn as much as 1% of total foreign income, and for almost the whole period its characteristic level was about half that. It was thus similar in scale to the other several Phoenix initiatives on the home continent in these years: Bulgaria, Greece and the revised Austrian operation were all much the same size. But if Italy was small, it was also sophisticated; and that too was characteristic of the firm's European undertakings at this point. What is unusual is that we have in the archive the Phoenix agent's prospectus for Italy, and thus some notion of the workings of this sophistication.

From 1887 both Evan Mackenzie of Genoa and Arthur Hill of Athens held Phoenix powers of attorney for the Kingdom of Italy. Hill was Phoenix agent for Greece 1885–96 and his sons retained this post into the 1920s. There was clearly a business connection between Mackenzie and Hill, since Mackenzie was also managing Greek treaty business in the 1890s, nothwithstanding Hill's position as Athens agent. Nevertheless, Mackenzie was clearly the Phoenix presence in Italy.

But the point about Mackenzie's presence was that it was genuinely international; and that Phoenix was only one of many business ventures to make use of this fact. In 1875, Mackenzie established a general insurance agency, with its headquarters in Genoa, a branch in Paris and a sub-agency in London. By 1893, he dealt in a complete range of insurances: fire, life, marine, accident, burglary and fidelity, all in both direct and reinsurance modes. He held powers of attorney from ten British fire offices, two British life offices and one British marine insurer, as well as from six foreign offices, two Austrian and one apiece from France, Ireland, Italy and Greece. His claims department maintained contacts with forty-three insurance companies and with underwriters and shipowners' associations. This web spanned all continents: ten threads ran to Liverpool, nine to New Orleans, six to London, two each to Canton, Munich, New Zealand and Rosario, and one each to Amsterdam, Athens, Hull, Malmo, Newcastle, New York, Paris, Philadelphia, Shanghai and Singapore. Again to facilitate claims business, Mackenzie maintained 'special agents . . . in all ports of the Mediterranean'.[20]

It is difficult to believe that Hill in Athens,[21] let alone Hanbury in Hamburg or Malm at Gothenburg would have maintained an organisation less extensive than that of Mackenzie's relatively recent foundation. The inference may be that the rise of the broker-agent was one of the most influential features in the international insurance markets of the late nineteenth century, pre-eminently but not exclusively so in Europe.[22]

For Phoenix, the bulk of the business generated by Mackenzie's formi-

[20] Prospectus of Evan Mackenzie, General Agent and Insurance Broker, 1893. This is attached to one of the Agents' Lists in Foreign Agents' Lists C19/16. Mackenzie was also a crucial force in the foundation of the major Italian office, Alleanza Assicurazioni in 1898.

[21] Or Graham in New Zealand, see below, pp. 188–91.

[22] See Charles A. Jones in 'Competition and structural change in the Buenos Aires Fire Insurance Market: the Local Board of Agents, 1875–1921', in O. M. Westall (ed.), *The Historian and the Business of Insurance* (Manchester, 1984), pp. 114–29.

Table 2.9. *Reinsurance treaties operated in Italy, 1888–1927*

Company	Term	Years of loss
Fondiaria Old	1888–1904	6
Fondiaria New	1901–23	5
L'Union	1888–1911	5
Co-operativa	1889–1902	4
London & Lancs	1890–3	–
Milan	1888–1902	4
Anonima of Turin	1898–1927	5

dable network – just as with Kreil, Nasir and Stein in Vienna – was reinsurance. Mackenzie managed six reinsurance treaties operating in Italy (see Table 2.9).

Generally, these treaties were more successful than many of this era,[23] with the best of them, the latecomer of 1898, Anonima, suffering losses in only five years out of thirty and amassing an accumulated surplus of over 1 million lire by 1926.[24] Italy provides a good case of a rapidly expanding industrial market, with the economy achieving 'take-off' in the years 1896–1908, which was effectively tapped by an influential general agent. Mackenzie's local knowledge and far-flung connections allowed Phoenix to step quickly and precisely into this swiftly changing market.

Similar methods were tried in the rather different markets of Switzerland. The first Phoenix agency in this still largely pastoral economy was that of Mutzenbacher in 1890. Little is known of it, except that it was another general agency and that it did not thrive. Mutzenbacher launched five treaties in 1890, but all were showing excessive loss ratios by 1892. Not surprisingly, Phoenix beat a rapid retreat from this broker-agency. The office tried again in 1897 with Alfred Bourguin of the Bureau Général d'Assurances et Réassurances at Neuchatel. His role as a general broker was similar to that of Mackenzie at Genoa, and he was started at similar rates of 25% commission plus 10% contingency. The first treaty was signed with the canton of Neuchatel in 1897 and other cantonal agreements followed between 1898 and 1900 with St Gall, Fribourg, Soleure and Lucerne; Berne was added in 1905 and Vaud in 1910. These Swiss reinsurances, in various cantonal combinations, kept their position steadfastly in the pecking order of Phoenix foreign outposts between 1897 and 1914.

[23] See below p. 165. [24] *Ibid.*

Berne was the richest of these connections, averaging about 1% of total foreign income for a decade, before expiring in 1915. But the Swiss agencies were important only as an accumulation: together, they accounted for 2% of Phoenix total overseas receipts in 1901 and hit a peak of nearly 3% in 1905 and 1914. Not until 1916–20 were they afflicted by the long-run deterioration which seems to have ruined all arrangements of this type. But, of course, war will have had something to do with this.

While reinsurance dominated Phoenix affairs in Austria, Italy and Switzerland, new tendencies gathered strength on the European periphery, in Scandinavia and Iberia. Scandinavia presented a confusing picture. The great Malm agency at Gothenburg saw a continuous decline in both money premiums and share in the company's total overseas earnings from 1870 to 1885, and only the gentlest rally in the late 1880s. Takings fell by one-third between 1871–5 and 1886–90, ending as a tiny fraction of Phoenix's total foreign income.[25] The contrast with the early nineteenth century, when Gothenburg was surpassed among Phoenix foreign agencies only by Hamburg and New York, was painful.[26]

Elsewhere in the region, Helsinki, Oslo and Copenhagen all saw large increases in their money earnings between 1870 and 1890, but each also experienced contraction in its share of the company's total foreign income.[27]

Despite slipping shares, the Finnish and Norwegian agencies were enjoying some success, while the long-cherished Swedish operation was clearly in trouble. There were lessons in the differences. The doughty Norwegian performance was achieved by an 'old-style' reinsurance treaty from the mid-century period. This was the 'Storebrand' treaty with the Almindelige company which had been struck in 1862 and outlived every other arrangement of the kind, ending only in the inter-war years. In order to survive, Almindelige had to fend off a Phoenix attempt to establish a direct agency in Norway in 1876. Their logic was persuasive and Phoenix fell in with it. Faith was justified, but not by much. Almindelige was not able to continue the premium increases of the 1870s and 1880s into the new century. Nevertheless, Phoenix valued the Norwegian connection and demonstrated this in the commission paid to Almindelige, doubling the rate from 12.5% in 1868 to 25% by 1895 (see Table 2.7).[28] For a simple treaty reinsurance arrangement, Almindelige's was a remarkably durable record of success.

[25] About 0.3%. [26] See vol. 1, p. 199.

[27] Between 1871–5 and 1886–90, Helsinki's share fell from 1.4% to 1.0%; Oslo's from 0.7% to 0.5%; and Copenhagen's from 0.2% to 0.1%.

[28] Foreign Agents' Lists C19/4, C19/16.

In Finland and Denmark, the newer style of surplus reinsurance produced opposite results. It reinvigorated Copenhagen, quintupling the premium receipts to a modest average of some £4,000 by 1911–15. The turnabout appears to be connected with a change of agency in 1896 and a more extensive reliance on a brokerage strategy by this agency. The pattern from Helsinki was more like that from Oslo: roughly level or marginally slipping money earnings from the mid-1880s to 1914. Abdon Lindberg was Phoenix's representative at Helsinki throughout the period 1874–1914 and had to work hard for his 15% commission.[29]

The lesson for Sweden was that sterner measures were necessary if Gothenburg was to be rescued. They were provided by an initiative which, in 1887, promoted the Malms to be general agents for the whole of Sweden. Within two years, they controlled ten sub-agencies at Gothenburg, Helsingberg, Josskoping, Karlstadt, Kistinckaam, Malmo, Norrkoping, Ramslsen, Stockholm and Uppsala. By 1919 the array of sub-agencies had risen to sixteen. A reinsurance arrangement with the Svea company was maintained as a separate operation. The Malms got 15% on direct business and an extra 5% on all sub-agency business; on business remitted through Svea, they took another 5% while 20% went to Svea itself (see Table 2.7).[30]

The entire structure of the revised Malm agency was a clear imitation of the successful Hamburg system and was designed to arrest the decline of the equally venerable Gothenburg connection. To a considerable extent, the device worked. The decline of premium income from Sweden was arrested: the fall of 32% between 1871–5 and 1886–90 was succeeded by a threefold rise between 1886–90 and 1911–15.[31] This was better news in any language and a powerful advertisement for the virtues of the general agency system. Clearly, the point was taken in Scandinavia: by 1909 sixteen sub-agencies had appeared also in Denmark.

Phoenix's Scandinavian operations proceeded without much interference from governments. The most intrusive was the Finnish. In 1891, the Economic Department of the Senate set the conditions under which foreign insurers might operate within its jurisdiction: they were to apply for permission to transact business, submit copies of their company regulations, provide proof of existence over five years in the country of origin, validate the agent's power of attorney and admit the sovereignty of Finnish law. All accounts were subject to inspection by the Insurance

[29] Foreign Agents' List C19/4: Agency Memoranda of 1893.

[30] Foreign Agents' Lists, C19/4, 5, 16.

[31] Although even this managed only to raise Sweden's share of Phoenix foreign income from 0.3% to 0.4%.

Superintendant of the Handels und Industriexpedition. There is no evidence of equivalently tight supervision in Norway or Denmark. There were taxes to be paid everywhere, but they were scarcely onerous: income tax of £17 in Finland in 1872, total taxes of about £100 in Sweden by the late 1890s, a state tax of 2% and a municipal tax of 3% in Copenhagen by 1905.[32]

Scandinavian markets in the four decades or so before the Great War appear relatively sluggish. Reinsurance allowed Phoenix to make some headway in cash terms in three markets out of four. But in one case, the reinsurance tactic was of the older treaty type, in another it developed towards the broker type. Long-running associations, as with the Malms and Lindberg, continued to receive respect from Phoenix, although this did not prevent new forms being found for them. The most successful method of combining continuity with revived premium flow, in both Sweden and Denmark, was the general agency. However, the power of industrial growth to affect insuring fortunes is once more worth remarking. In the 1890s, the Swedish economy was achieving growth rates in industrial output which were probably the highest recorded by any economy in the nineteenth century. Recovery in the Malms' results owed not a little to this. The net result by 1914 was a market area moderate in size but acceptable in profitability, despite competition and a little light interference from governments.

At the other end of Europe, even in the absence of high industrial growth rates, the general agency still proved a useful instrument. In Portugal and its dependencies, business continued in highly traditional style. The wine trade sustained the fire market on the Atlantic seaboard of Iberia: Sandeman's wine lodges filled the Phoenix portfolio at Oporto and the wine connection ran out to Madeira – where J. F. Oliveira was sacked in 1878 for 'neglecting the agency over thirteen months', and was followed in 1889 by Leacock & Co., wine shippers – and through Madeira to the nearby Spanish possessions in the Canaries, also covered from the agency in Funchal.[33] Befitting such a traditional trade, premiums were collected by direct agencies in Oporto and Funchal, although a sub-agency was added at Lisbon in 1879. The major agency at Oporto came into the Archer family in 1882 and remained there for many decades. It accounted for a steady 0.4% of total foreign earnings through the 1870s and an even steadier 0.2% in the period 1881–1915. That is to say, it was respectable but the reverse of spectacular.

[32] *Ibid.*, also C19/17.

[33] Phoenix Trustees' Minutes, 4 April and 22 August 1878; Directors' Minutes Z25, p. 31, 7 August 1889.

In Spain, business was rather more interesting. Spanish law required foreign companies to publish their accounts, in all regions except the Basque provinces. Logically, the Sun office reacted to this stipulation by establishing its chief agency in Bilbao, and casting a net of sub-agencies east and south into the rest of Spain. Logically, too, in the 1870s, Phoenix dealt with the problem by going around it: the company took its Spanish business by reinsurance from the North British operation in Malaga. It also set up a small direct outlet in Bilbao but little came of this. However, Spain and Britain reached new commercial terms in 1883 and Phoenix's nerve for direct trade was anyway strengthening by the 1880s. In 1887 Phoenix converted to direct business in Spain: Prosper Lamothe became Phoenix agent in Malaga on a 15% basic and 20% sub-agency commission. As Phoenix juggled to get the difficult Spanish operation into an accurate trajectory, Lamothe was given more encouragement in 1897, together with a special rate of 27.5% for Catalonia, and in 1899, the same high rate for Madrid (see Table 2.7). By then, Phoenix must have become convinced that they had got it right, since, between 1899 and 1902, Malaga erupted into a classic cascade of sub-agencies. By 1902, there were thirteen of them: at Alicante, Almeira, Barcelona, Bilbao, Cadiz, Cartagena, Corina, Madrid, Orieda, Santander, San Sebastian, Seville and Valencia.

The upgrading of Lamothe's role to a general agency had the same desirable results as elsewhere. Spanish business taken through cedings from North British had dwindled to almost nothing by 1886–90.[34] The general agency arrangement stopped the rot and reversed the trend: by 1901–5 Malaga had recovered the proportion of total business that previously had come from reinsurance, and by 1911–15 had improved it to 0.4% of Phoenix total overseas receipts, the best result extracted from Spain since 1870.

As in Germany and Sweden, the Spanish experience suggests that by 1914 the general agency, underpinned by a network of sub-agencies, could provide an antidote to the declining shares of business that had come to be associated with the complex reinsurance arrangements of the late nineteenth century. The performance of the general agency in Europe was one of the few optimistic signs in markets increasingly beset by the penalties of economic sophistication: intricate urban development, much competition and a rising tide of legislation. It offered both a device for the future and a model for locations far removed from the home continent.

[34] From 0.3% of total foreign income in 1871–5 to well under 0.1% by 1886–90.

4. THE OUT-TURN IN EUROPE: REINSURANCES AND PROFITS

The high level of Phoenix activity in Europe had only a variable relationship with profitability. This was especially so in terms of reinsurance business. The company's Hamburg Notebook recorded a 'Recapitulation of Reinsurance (all Companies)' for the period 1888–99. The loss ratios (see Table 2.10) are astonishing.

Table 2.10. *All company loss ratios on Hamburg reinsurances, 1888–99*

1888	85%	1894	86%
1889	109%	1895	138%
1890	67%	1896	74%
1891	133%	1897	129%
1892	95%	1898	84%
1893	12%	1899	88%

But such losses were not unique. The results on Phoenix's Austrian treaties resembled the terrible record from Hamburg. Half of the biggest arrangements maintained by the company in Vienna reported average annual loss ratios in excess of 85% for periods within the time span 1887–1904 (see Table 2.11).

In the case of the Austrian Phoenix (General), Dacia Roumania and Donan treaties the severe damage came without exception in the last three years of the arrangement. This is not surprising since severe damage often formed the prelude to, and reason for, cancellation.

The reinsurance market in Austria was much like that in Germany: well-developed, fluid, wide-ranging and dangerous. One source of danger appears to have been what was usually a Phoenix speciality, large manufacturing policies. In Austria, and perhaps in Germany too, industrial risks could cost dear around the turn of the century: in 1906, Phoenix's Austrian treaty with North British recorded a loss ratio of 87%, with three-quarters of the damage in the first half of the year accounted for by claims on cotton, woollen and net spinning mills.[35]

Even the use of reinsurance to re-invigorate a highly traditional agency could come adrift in terms of profit. The Antwerp agency was in the hands of the Ellerman family from 1815 to 1879, and then passed, upon the resignation of Abraham Ellerman, to Eugene Van den Wyngaert. However, the new appointee was responsible only for conventional

[35] Phoenix Agents' List C19/19; Red Treaties Book.

Table 2.11. *Results of six Phoenix treaties managed from Vienna, 1887–1904*

Company	Period of treaty	Net outcome	Average annual loss ratio
Austrian Phoenix (General)	1889–98	Deficit £18,006	104.5
Austrian Phoenix (Sugar)	1890–6	Surplus £30,284	54.2
Concordia	1887–1900	Deficit £9,754	85.8
Dacia Roumania	1887–96	Deficit £1,219	97.7
Donan	1882–1904	Deficit £96,559	64.0
Fire Ins. Association	1887–92	Surplus £143	36.1

Sources: Phoenix Agents' List C19/16; Red Treaties Book.

mercantile risks in Antwerp. In September 1886, Arthur Bray was brought in specifically to create a network of reinsurance treaties for the region. He began immediately in the next month with a treaty linking Phoenix and Securitas and covering Belgium, Holland and Luxembourg. By December 1886, Bray had formed further agreements with the L'Escault, Union Belge, La Belgique and Compagnie à Primes offices. Phoenix must have wished that he had been less busy, for the results on six Belgian treaties 1887–97 rivalled the losses from Hamburg and Vienna in awfulness (see Table 2.12).

The Union Belge arrangement turned in losses in five years out of eleven and over the entire term achieved a negative balance of over 19,000 francs. La Belgique followed suit with losses in three years out of five and a net overall loss of over 4,000 francs and the L'Escault arrangement folded after four years in deficit. Securitas fared better and was in the black by nearly 6,300 francs at the end of 1897. But by no standard could this attempt to enliven Antwerp be counted a success. With results like these, it was scarcely surprising that the Phoenix reduced its commitment in the field in the 1900s.

However, it was true that results from Russian, Italian and Swiss reinsurances were better. Some Russian treaties came and went rather swiftly: the Salamander treaty opened in 1869, closed in 1870 and ran off in 1873; the Anchor treaty opened in 1873, closed in 1876 and ran off in 1879; while the Commercial treaty lasted from 1877 until 1880 and ran off in 1882. On the other hand, the First Russian treaty made profits from 1869 until 1914, if at declining rates in the 1900s and 1910s. The second attempt at a Swiss treaty system after 1897 established a tenuous but adequate grip.

Table 2.12. *Loss ratios of six Phoenix treaties managed from Antwerp, 1887–97*

1887	18%	1893	18%
1888	85%	1894	84%
1889	222%	1895	67%
1890	29%	1896	8%
1891	136%	1897	29%
1892	132%		

Source: Notebook on Belgian, Swiss and Russian Business, Phoenix Agents' Lists C19/20.

As a group, the Italian treaties were probably the most impressive (they are listed in Table 2.9). The Milan treaty was in the red on accumulated balance by 8,137 lire in 1902 and did not endure long thereafter; while the London & Lancashire arrangement was small beer that soon went flat. In contrast, the agreements with Union, Cooperativa, Fondiaria and, especially, Anonima positively sparkled. By 1900, the Union, Cooperativa and Fondiaria treaties had accumulated a total positive net balance of over 110,000 lire. By 1907, the running profit was 86,813 lire on the Fondiaria arrangement and 79,940 lire on the Union agreement. Though added late to the system, in 1898, the Anonima treaty recorded losses in only five years of its long life and accumulated a positive balance of over 1 million lire by 1926.

When heavy punishment was taken in Italy in the 1900s, it again emanated frequently from the industrial sector. A claim on a single sprinkler-protected cotton mill accounted for 58% of all losses in 1904; in 1905 two silk mills, one jute mill and a rope works produced 75% of all losses; and, in 1906,a brace of candle factories and a cabinet-maker ran up 51% of all losses.

Whatever the occasional attractions of Russian or Italian treaty results, it would not have been rational on these data to pursue reinsurance business for profit alone. Yet, judging by the high commission rates paid – commonly 20–25% even on German or Austrian business – the Phoenix and its colleagues clearly did choose to chase business of this type in the last decades of the nineteenth century. The suggestion is that reinsurance business was sought for connection and for market control in a highly competitive environment: the network of linkages built up between companies produced a certain measure of stabilisation in the market. It was better to take a certain proportion of business from Securitas or Anonima in friendship than to confront them in head-on competition. Even if reinsurances did not always provide gilded profits, the underwriters of the time had clearly concluded that life would have been worse without them. And there was the not inconsiderable point that substantial additions to cash flow might also be achieved while connection was being cultivated. However, in the end, the loss record would outweigh the arguments of liquidity and encourage the quest for a different method of obtaining market control: the direct branch organisation with its infrastructure of sub-agencies.

5. COMPETITION AND ENTERPRISE: FROM THE EASTERN MEDITERRANEAN TO WESTERN ASIA

The area bounded by Athens to the west and Smyrna (Izmir) or Alexandria to the east was an important one for the large insurers of the late nineteenth century. It contained a number of outstanding traditional entrepots, of which Alexandria and Constantinople were perhaps the greatest, but it was experiencing also a surge of mercantile and constructional activity, much of it related to the revolutionary transport developments of the period. On the fringe of Europe, the region shared some insurance characteristics with the home continent, most notably high levels of economic activity and rising levels of competition. On the other hand, the hubbub of the bazaar was never far distant, and insurance markets in this region were hardly more amenable to discipline than any other kinds of market. Subtle commercial games were no doubt a feature of the region but the particular subtlety of reinsurance did not find a ready home here. Intermediary between Europe and Asia, this market also stood intermediary between different types of insurance system. Moreover, for Phoenix it was an entirely new market in terms of agency presence: the first tiny premium receipts from Smyrna and Alexandria were recorded in the Phoenix Review of Foreign Agencies only in 1865.

For Phoenix, the area was perhaps more fertile in lessons than in revenue. The five main centres, Constantinople, Salonika,[36] Smyrna, Alexandria and Athens rarely managed an average annual return of more than 1% Phoenix total overseas revenue, 1871–1915 (see Table 2.13).

Furthermore, Phoenix entered the area with some circumspection. If the company was brave enough to avoid the backdoor method of entering a market via reinsurance, it selected the next best alternative in terms of caution: it appointed as agents experienced locals who were already

[36] Salonika and Macedonia remained a province of the Ottoman Empire until 1903. It then passed under a special administration controlled by the European powers. It became part of Greece only in 1913.

Table 2.13. *Premiums earned by east Mediterranean and west Asian agencies, 1871–1915 (£ and as % total Phoenix foreign premiums)*

	Constantinople		Salonica		Smyrna	
	£	%	£	%	£	%
1871–5	747	0.3	56	0.02	891	0.40
1876–80	1,279	0.5	111	0.04	754	0.30
1881–5	1,000	0.2	–	–	640	0.10
1886–90	2,755	0.4	877	0.10	1,225	0.20
1891–5	5,249	0.7	–	–	1,832	0.20
1896–1900	4,864	0.6	–	–	2,448	0.30
1901–5	4,965	0.4	–	–	1,660	0.10
1906–10	6,071	0.4	571	0.04	1,635	0.10
1911–15	10,614	0.7	–	–	398	0.04
	Alexandria		**Athens**		**Total**	
	£	%	£	%	£	%
1871–5	–	–	–	–	1,694	0.72
1876–80	1,458	0.6	–	–	2,144	0.84
1881–5	1,729	0.4	–	–	3,369	0.70
1886–90	1,525	0.3	830	0.10	7,212	1.10
1891–5	1,653	0.2	1,593	0.20	10,327	1.30
1896–1900	1,693	0.2	234	0.03	9,239	1.13
1901–5	2,002	0.2	–	–	8,627	0.70
1906–10	2,971	0.2	–	–	11,248	0.74
1911–15	2,977	0.1	–	–	13,989	0.84

agents for other major offices, primarily the Sun and the Royal. Phoenix's oldest agency in Asia Minor was opened at Smyrna in 1865 with the appointment of solicitor Henry Rose, Sun agent there since 1863. The Rose family continued to represent the Sun in Smyrna until 1907, and Phoenix employed no fewer than four of the Roses as agents between 1865 and 1886. In April 1870, as a joint venture with the Sun, Phoenix set up shop in Constantinople by appointing C. S. Hanson and Co. as agents and fixed their indenture limit 'as per Sun'. Following further in the orbit of its veteran colleague, Phoenix in 1873 chose another Sun agent for the Smyrna sub-agency in Salonika; this was Augustus Routh, the local manager of the Imperial Ottoman Bank. Similar recruiting tactics were followed in 1876 when the company wished to revive its connection in

Alexandria.[37] This time the Phoenix looked to Charles Moberley Bell who was not only the Royal's man in Alexandria but also *The Times*' manager for Egypt. Only in Athens, which Phoenix entered late, in 1885, after much hesitation, were there apparently independent appointments, first John Masson, a merchant of the city, and subsequently, from 1888, Arthur Hill, also a merchant from Piraeus. However, Hill was already known to Phoenix, since he had carried the firm's power of attorney for Italy from 1887 and was connected with the powerful Mackenzie brokerage in Genoa.

With considerable change in process in the region, Phoenix was perhaps wise to employ established expertise. Certainly, the Sun and the Royal played a pioneering role in opening the near eastern, especially Turkish, insurance markets to foreign underwriters. The reviving foreign operations of the Phoenix could only profit by following their example. There was plenty to be learned. Smyrna was by 1870, 'the chief emporium for Western Asia', exporting silk, cotton, wool, fruit and drugs to Europe and the USA. It was extensively improved during the 1870s with heavy reconstruction in the town and the addition of modern dock facilities.[38] Similarly the great port of Alexandria expanded rapidly during the 1880s, with much reconstruction in the old city and widespread development of the suburbs.

Most of these centres displayed, alongside marked commercial expansion, two other distinct characteristics: proliferation of sub-agencies and sharp non-tariff competition from outside the circle of established international insurers. In both, Phoenix was to find important lessons.

In 1886, when Francis Blackler took over from the Rose dynasty at Smyrna, on the same 10% basic commission but with a further 10% added for contingencies, he inherited not only the core agency but a string of sub-agencies at Mitilene, Chios, Rhodes, Samos, Dikili, Aivali, Chesura, Vourlah and Aidin. Phoenix had established another local network of representatives, here through the eastern Aegean and along the Izmir coast, but quite similar to those being created in Germany and Sweden around this time. The result was that Phoenix receipts from the 'chief emporium' of Smyrna more than doubled in money terms between 1886 and 1890, but the effect on the area's longer run share of total foreign income was scarcely perceptible.

Similarly, after a reputable stint at Alexandria, which had made it the richest outpost in the region, Charles Bell handed over to Francis Haseldon in 1890. Bell had started on a 10% commission and increased it to

37 A short-lived agency had been established in the mid-1860s. See vol. I, pp. 313, 321.
38 Dickson, *Sun Insurance*, pp. 188–91.

15%, but Haseldon apparently warranted 17.5% plus 10% contingency upon appointment.[39] Despite these early problems, Haseldon and Co. steered Phoenix through turbulent times in Egypt and were still holding the fort in Alexandria in the 1920s. They too seem to have made a genuine effort at expansion through sub-agencies during the 1890s with connections established at Port Said in 1891 and Cairo in 1893. As at Smyrna, the effect was welcome in cash returns but did little to alter Alexandria's standing among Phoenix agencies worldwide. Indeed, in the early 1890s Alexandria lost its regional pre-eminence to Constantinople and did not regain it before the Great War. Nevertheless, provincial markets in Egypt developed nicely during the 1890s and Phoenix tapped the development.

The pattern repeated at Constantinople. The Hanson family yielded to the short-lived agency of Klonarides and Cavafy in 1886. But in 1888 Henry Swan took over on 12.5% basic commission and 10% contingency allowance; ten years later Swan's basic rate reached the impressive level of 20%. This was not surprising: Swan's tenure in Constantinople produced the largest impact upon agency earnings of any achieved by a Phoenix representative in this region in the half-century before 1914. Swan nearly doubled Constantinople's share of total Phoenix foreign income (see Table 2.13). The method was again sub-agency expansion. The first satellite agency was set up at Panderma on the Sea of Marmara in 1889, another at Stamboul in 1899. By 1902, a bevy of merchants and bankers, mostly Greeks and Armenians, were running sub-agencies in the Dardanelles, at Angora (Ankara), Adabazar, Ismidt and Kerasunde. Rather earlier also, in 1890, Swan had assumed responsibility for supervising the new Phoenix general agency for Bulgaria, based at Varna, with J. M. Mavi, 'a Bulgarian subject and landed proprietor' as the local representative.[40]

Unfortunately, the pressure of all this proved too much for the energetic Swan who, in 1903, had to be removed to an asylum, 'leaving Mrs Swan and two children entirely unprovided for'.[41] Phoenix stepped into the breach, bailed out Mrs Swan with £100 and appointed K. Vartanian as the new agent for Constantinople.[42] This official proved well able to work the system created by the luckless Swan and in 1906 he was given full charge of it as general agent for Turkey in Europe and Asia Minor.[43]

[39] Phoenix Directors' Minutes, Z25, p. 97, 23 April 1890; Foreign Agents Book II.
[40] Phoenix Foreign Agents' Lists, C19/5 and 6; Directors' Minutes, Z25, p. 77, 5 February 1890.
[41] Phoenix Trustees' Minutes, p. 236, 3 February 1904.
[42] Phoenix Directors' Minutes 27, p. 203, 12 August 1903.
[43] *Ibid.*, 28, p. 28, 19 December 1906.

Only in Greece did Phoenix swing in another direction. Perhaps appropriately for the most western of these markets, it was a more European direction. For, in 1896, the Athens agency was cancelled and its incumbent, Arthur Hill, was appointed instead 'Phoenix Correspondent' in the Greek capital. Effectively, this meant that the connection was converted from direct business to reinsurance brokerage. It is probable that the Hill operation in Athens came to resemble the sophisticated Mackenzie business in Italy. The Athens agency thus succumbed to the strong tide of brokerage that affected some sectors of the global fire market in the pre-1914 years. But this did not imply any lack of robustness in Phoenix's presence in Greece. The sons of Arthur Hill succeeded him in the representation of the company in 1921 and the Hill family were still providing this service upon the absorption of the Phoenix into the Sun Alliance group in 1984.

If most of this regional market benefited from the development of the sub-agency system, most of it suffered under the pressure of competition from foreign offices who would not obey the discipline of the British tariff set by the Fire Offices' Committee in London, and could thus undercut the rates agreed by the big international insurers. This required the development of special counter-tactics.

From the mid-1880s non-tariff competition in both Alexandria and Smyrna was fierce. As both ports expanded, outsider companies fought for the insurances generated by new construction. In 1885, the Fire Offices' Committee created a sub-committee to examine the rates in Alexandria and the local agents of member companies were convened in the city to define the boundaries of the old town, 'not including the New Quarters'.[44] Similarly, British fire offices held regular meetings to interpret FOC tariff rates for Smyrna from the 1870s. In both cases, the response to the competitive threat was considered collectively in London and in the local market place. Cooperative initiatives by agents at the local level were to prove decisive.

In Smyrna the weapon used for market control was the fire brigade. Rose had started a volunteer force, using his own clerks and an ancient Sun engine, seconded from Barbados, in the late 1860s. In 1874, the British tariff offices, led by Sun and Royal, created a fully fledged joint brigade. The expansion of the port created opportunities for the big British offices to organise the market through the provision of fire-fighting capacity. The brigade was supervised by a standing committee of local agents. Respectable foreign offices, who would keep the British tariff,

[44] Fire Office's Committee Minutes (Foreign), 27 November 1885; 6 May 1886.

were encouraged to join but non-tariff competitors were rigorously excluded. To finance the brigade, the tariff offices imposed a 7.5% surcharge on premiums. It was effective interaction among local agents that produced and funded this ingenious closed shop.

However, it did not dispose of unruliness in Smyrna. A general meeting of agents in 1891, attended by representatives from sixteen British companies and one each from France, Germany, Holland and Italy, was still complaining of 'the daily growing competition from non-tariff foreign companies'. One speaker, while complimenting the port on its growth, 'its trade developed, its property increased, wealth and prosperity more equally divided, the streets much broader, our fire-extinguishing appliances greatly ameliorated, disasters limited', went on to bemoan that 'in the face of all that, the business of the United Offices remains stationary'.[45] However, the offices had an answer: they decided to reduce rates. And again this was decided at the local level.

Devolution of sovereignty of similar dimensions also proved necessary in Egypt. In 1895, the Alexandria and Cairo tariffs were suspended, after some British tariff offices were found to have been reinsuring non-tariff practitioners at less than tariff rates. The FOC in London responded by instructing local representatives to form their own fighting front, to 'constitute an Association of Agents for the protection of Insurance interests'.[46] The notion was that this combined local force should pressure the agents of non-tariff offices into an agreed system of rating fire risks. Effectively, this placed the management of market strategy in the hands of the local agents. The point was underlined in February 1896, when the local organisation requested that the head offices of member firms should not issue direct insurances in London upon Egyptian risks. The FOC was not prepared to go that far, but it did promise to encourage head offices, if they did take Egyptian risks, to do so only at a higher charge, 15% above tariff rates. All member firms had agreed to this by August 1896.[47]

Non-tariff competition appears to have been somewhat less severe in Constantinople. But there were problems in working the tariffs and similar devices were used to solve them. The most vexed issue of the era was the deferred payment of premium allowed to customers by most agents in this market. This raised major problems as to the balance of initiative between London and Constantinople. In 1896 the FOC tried to abolish the practice. The local agents, disliking the root-and-branch approach, proposed instead that insurance cover should not be supplied

[45] *Ibid.*, Smyrna, 11 August 1891. [46] *Ibid.*, Alexandria, 4 October 1895.
[47] *Ibid.*, Circular, 29 August 1896.

until 40% of the due premium was paid, and that the balance should follow within three months. The FOC argued that such a scheme would prove impossible to operate. The Constantinople agents thereupon demanded the power to suspend all or any of the local tariffs without reference to their head offices, and to form a local agents' association in which all companies insuring in the city could join. The FOC responded by executing a thorough overhaul of all agents' commissions, brokerage fees and discounts.[48] The outcome seems to have been about honours even. However, the amount of leverage applied by the fraternity of agents on the Golden Horn was considerable.

What Phoenix learned in the Near East was the virtue of well-applied localism. Premium income was increased by carrying sub-agencies into some very obscure places, often employing local businessmen from the heart of the bazaar. Market control, under the pressure of non-tariff competition, or even of creaking tariff rules, was preserved by the creation of local associations of agents. These men often showed more solidarity with one another than with their mother offices, or with the FOC, but their ability to apply coordinated expertise at the point of sale was swiftly appreciated by London. Overseas boards of agents proved crucial in regulating markets where tariffs were liable to come under pressure. In Europe, of course, where the complicated minuets of reinsurance created different types of joint interest, the cruder force of the agents' pack was less necessary. But there were plenty of other markets in the world which were also unlike Europe.

6. NEW MARKETS FOR OLD: GOVERNMENTS, COMPETITION AND COOPERATION IN THE WEST INDIES AND CENTRAL AND SOUTH AMERICA

Phoenix's operations in the Caribbean and Central and South America were on a far bigger scale than those in the Near East. Indeed, some individual agencies in this region were worth, at times, more than the entire Near Eastern market put together. But non-tariff competition was to be as much a problem in Latin America and the islands as it was in the Near East, and it was once again to require local cooperation by the agents of the big companies to contain it.

Latin America and the Caribbean did not form so homogeneous a market as the Near East. There was a clear bifurcation between the performance of the island trade and that of the mainland economies. The

[48] *Ibid.*, Constantinople, 2 May 1896; 3 July 1896; 1 October 1896.

Table 2.14. *Share of West Indian and Latin American agencies in total Phoenix foreign income, 1871–1915*

	West Indies			Latin America		
	Premiums (£)	% foreign income	Number of agencies	Premiums (£)	% foreign income	Number of agencies
1871–5	12,021	5.1	11	5,269	2.2	6
1876–80	15,775	6.1	14	6,866	2.6	6
1881–5	15,090	3.3	14	11,007	1.5	9
1886–90	12,104	2.1	14	18,615	3.3	12
1891–5	13,293	1.7	14	22,258	2.9	9
1896–1900	10,310	1.3	13	27,704	3.3	12
1901–5	10,764	1.0	10	30,952	2.7	6
1906–10	14,499	1.1	10	46,926	3.3	8
1911–15	17,046	1.0	9	57,444	3.6	7
1916–20	33,137	1.2	9	120,714	4.6	7

Source: Phoenix Review of Foreign Agencies, Books 1–4.

West Indies, of course, had been a traditional area of Phoenix concentration from the earliest decades of the company. The islands had earned more than 3% of total Phoenix foreign earnings in every decade between 1826 and 1875, and double that in the mid-century decades when the European and American staples had languished.[49] Caribbean agencies had been reinforced by additional appointments in the 1860s.[50] By the starting point of this volume, Phoenix had some eleven island agencies, mostly taking premiums by direct agency methods.

Yet, after peaking early, in the second half of the 1870s, the West Indian operation ran progressively downhill, ending the pre-war period with nine agencies and a mere fraction of total foreign earnings (see Table 2.14). Even in cash terms, takings fell by about one-third in the last twenty years of the nineteenth century. The venerable connections of the sugar trade, an economy of plantations and nabob gold, belonged to an earlier era. These old-style frontier markets were getting safer, but, at the same time, losing their ability to generate a convincing stream of income.

The only exception to this was Cuba. Here, one of the Phoenix's reinsurance arrangements yielded its first returns in 1865 and rich pickings by the early 1870s. But this connection was broken in 1885, and the income had effectively dried up four years earlier.[51] In keeping with the

[49] See vol. 1, p. 257. [50] *Ibid.*, p. 319.

[51] This was not before Phoenix's agents for Cuba, Messrs Schmidt & Panne, had protested that their operations were 'crippled by the continuation of the contract with the North British' (Trustees' Minutes, 22 October 1885).

company's more active exporting stance late in the nineteeth century, Havana was revived by direct agency work. By the late 1900s over three-quarters of all West Indian income was in fact coming from the single centre of Havana. However, Cuban affairs perhaps had more in common with the expanding business of mainland Latin America than with the patterns of the old island trade.

In contrast to most of the West Indian markets, the Central and South American region recorded a strong performance throughout the period, notably increasing its share of Phoenix world trade by the 1900s. Yet, like the Near East, it was an entirely new market for Phoenix in terms of direct agency trade, with the first premium receipts being recorded – from Valparaiso – in 1865. The number of agencies was variable, doubling in a definite market push between 1871–5 and 1886–90, then contracting again 1900–15 (see Table 2.14). But, unlike the West Indian experience, this contraction was around centres of strength. One market (Argentina) which did not possess even an agency in 1870 had the full-blown modern organisation of a branch office by 1900. Money returns from the region roughly doubled in each decade between the 1880s and the 1910s. Latin America clearly possessed promise for the Phoenix. And the promise was taken by increasingly enterprising means. The reformed Phoenix was seen to good advantage in this region.[52]

This was a very different tale from the West Indian story. Sugar and the plantation economy derived from an older style of empire. Railways, beef, wool or nitrates – some of the opportunities offered by Latin America – existed within a new sort of empire, the empire of global trade and massive international investment. This economic potential made Latin America a major focus of European, mainly British, commerce and finance in the classic era of High Economic Imperialism, 1870–1914. Argentina, Chile and Brazil attracted enormous amounts of British invisible exports, and insurance rode along with the capital and shipping services involved in these great transfers. By 1890 some £70 million had been invested on the London stock exchange in British-registered companies trading in Argentina and Uruguay alone. Naturally, the British-based directors of these expanding enterprises would seek to insure their Latin American property with British offices. The Caribbean islands were no longer 'hot spots' within the world economy in the same sense.

[52] Phoenix receipts from Latin America were large by the industrial standard. But Charles Jones is probably wrong to describe Latin American premiums as of 'marginal importance for all but a handful of British companies'. Phoenix was certainly one of the handful, but, as the big offices expanded and diversified worldwide, many regions accounted for only modest percentages of total income. See Charles A. Jones, 'Competition and Structural Change', p. 115.

The altering balance of power within the individual agencies of the region 1870–1914 reveals this pattern very clearly. In the 1870s, the richest direct Phoenix agency in the West Indies (with 1.2% of total overseas earnings) was still the venerable connection at St Thomas, scene of the inferno which had almost killed the Phoenix in 1806.[53] The most valuable source among all the Caribbean and Latin American markets was the reinsurance channel provided by North British through Havana, with 2% total overseas earnings. By the 1900s, St Thomas was hanging on as the largest reporter of premiums from the islands, bar Cuba, but now it could control only 0.2% of total foreign receipts and after 1909 remitted nothing at all. From the 1900s, no West Indian agency except Havana reached even 0.5% of total overseas income. That really did represent the end of an extended era.

Meanwhile, in Latin America, Argentina moved into the lead during the 1880s, with 1% total foreign income, followed by Chile with 0.7%. Throughout the 1900s, the Argentine branch was the most powerful earner in Latin America on 1.3% total foreign income, followed by Mexico on 1.0%

Beautifully symbolic of the expansion in Latin America was the appointment as Phoenix agent in Valparaiso in 1912 of Anthony Gibbs and Co.,[54] the City merchant bank and Chilean nitrate business. Gibbs acted, both as a channel for British investment in Chile and as a procurement agency for a raw material vital to the UK economy. Here Phoenix achieved a direct connection with a potent force in Britain's invisible export effort to Latin America. The Gibbs business by the 1900s was 'extraordinarily various and widespread', with major holdings in nitrate processing factories and Chilean railways.[55] It was not accidental that Phoenix's Chilean business surged after 1912, nor that Chile led even the Argentinian Branch in premium receipts in the period 1911–15.

Clearly, Phoenix operated with some thrustfulness in this market; there is little sign of the tendency to track more adventurous practitioners that was evident in the Near East. The Sun also experienced attrition in the Caribbean, with twelve agencies established there 1850–75 dwindling to six by 1914.[56] This was similar to the Phoenix experience. But the Sun seems to have been much warier in its Latin American dealings. Strict government conditions had deterred Sun from the Brazilian market in the 1860s, while similar problems caused it to retreat from Argentina for a full

[53] See vol. I, pp. 201–6. [54] Phoenix Directors' Minutes 30, p. 199, 9 October 1912.
[55] Vicary Gibbs, cited by S. D. Chapman, 'British-Based Investment Groups before 1914', *Economic History Review*, 38 (1985), p. 237.
[56] Dickson, *Sun Insurance*, p. 212–14.

decade after 1875. A Sun agency, opened in Venezuela in 1901, closed again in 1904 and no direct agency was risked in Uruguay until 1899.[57] Similarly, both the Royal and the Alliance withdrew in the face of the Argentinian tax law of 1875, the Alliance not to return for some twenty years.[58] The contrast favours Phoenix. The company appointed agents to Brazil in 1878, Uruguay in 1881 and Argentina in 1882. By 1900, Phoenix, not wary at all, had agencies in every South American country saving only Paraguay, Bolivia and Dutch and French Guiana.

So much for the positive action; on the other side were the problems. As in so much of the rest of the world, these were made up of governments disposed to protectionism and competing offices ill-disposed towards the British tariff.

Frequently, the large London offices, like the Sun, were deterred by the requirements of the region's governments in respect of the publication of accounts, insurance deposits and taxation levels. With the exception of Mexico, Central American regimes caused few problems and allowed the insurers a fairly free rein. But the South American countries erected a remarkable barrage of obstacles for the underwriter. Several of the London insurers had a tendency to retreat before these protectionist, sometimes xenophobic, measures, but Phoenix, with its very widespread network of Latin American agencies, defended itself as stalwartly as any office in the industry. As to the Caribbean markets, little has been written on their tendency to protectionism or otherwise.

However, the Phoenix archive does suggest that the islands were not immune to the gambit. Nowhere in the West Indies were insurance deposits required from the offices. Nor did many of the islands of the Eastern Caribbean even tax the insurers. But not all were so generous. Thus Jamaica imposed a scale of stamp duties in 1868 and in Trinidad a 2.5% tax was levied on annual premium income from the late 1860s. St Thomas charged a 2% impost on premiums in the early 1870s and the Bahamas had followed suit by 1882. In Puerto Rico, where Phoenix operated through its St Thomas agency, the state tax was increased from 3% to 3.5% in the 1890s. The inconvenience was real and the British offices did not care for it. On the mainland, in 1887, when the Demerara legislature resorted to fiscal tactics against the offices, the FOC instructed local agents 'to take united action towards obtaining, if possible, the repeal of the tax' and protested against 'the unfairness of imposing a tax of equal amount upon every fire insurance company'.[59]

However, within the decade, the FOC clearly became less disturbed by

[57] *Ibid.*, p. 219. [58] Jones, 'Competition and Structural Change', p. 115.

[59] FOC (Foreign) Minutes, 1 July, 4 November 1887.

taxation in the Caribbean region. Taxes were not extravagant; and the West Indian authorities restricted themselves to this form of nuisance alone. Besides, the burden could mostly be passed on to the customer. So West Indian tax barriers existed, but they were scarcely sufficient to explain the difficulties of this market or the decreasing attachment of the big offices to it.

Increasing competition, as in so many other markets across the globe, was probably a bigger worry. And it became sharper as the islands lost the 'frontier' qualities which had made them insurance material only for the expert and the brave early in the century. Better urban construction and, especially, better water supplies had improved risk levels but also made access easier. Both features exerted downward pressure on rates. The major offices were forced to concede 20% cuts in rates at Kingston in 1891, Montego Bay in 1894 and Port Antonio in 1895.[60] Even Guadeloupe, which had seen a devastating fire at Pointe à Pitre in 1871, was thought safe enough by 1896 for a 15% discount, 'other than usines, distilleries and factories' within the area of the 1871 blaze, 10% on other industrial risks and 30% on estates and plantations.[61]

As the erstwhile hell-holes became less fiery, the rates went down and the number of prospective insurers – especially European insurers – went up, the big British operators responded with two main tactics. All the major London offices recognised that the increasing complexity of the island markets could not be countered by independent action. They had found local associations of agents useful for confronting a variety of problems elsewhere and this method for concerting expertise in the individual marketplace proved no less relevant in the island context. The other device was equally collusive: to extend wherever possible the tariff agreed by the FOC throughout a regional market. As before the system called for a sensitive coordination of metropolitan and parochial influences. The FOC would set the tariff, but it would then be extended, altered, or even suspended according to the wisdom of the local agents. Thus, in 1896, European competitors were proving so troublesome in Puerto Rico that the FOC established a local committee to decide whether to amend or abolish the tariff.[62]

The Continental Europeans were clearly disturbing the British insurers in the entire Caribbean and Latin American market by the 1890s, much as European manufacturers were disturbing the long-maintained hold of British industrialists upon this and other markets at the same time. Even if the British exporters of invisibles played a straighter bat than the ex-

[60] *Ibid.*, 29 May 1891, 1 November 1894, 5 July 1895. [61] *Ibid.*, 15 October 1896.
[62] *Ibid.*, 29 November 1895, 1 May 1896.

porters of manufactures, and carried it for longer, they did not relish the bowling in the West Indies.

Much of this came from non-cricketing nations. Indeed, in 1896, the local agents' association in Trinidad was set up in the teeth of European disaffection, and particularly, the FOC noted, with 'the non-concurrence of the Netherlands'.[63] All was much as usual: in Trinidad, the Germans were making overtures while the Dutch were making difficulties; and, in the next match, and the next island, the roles would probably be reversed.

Insurance in the West Indies, afflicted by governmental whips and competitive scorpions, was simply no longer worth the trouble. The islands represented wealth in an old form, but many other markets were developing wealth in new forms much faster. The islands exhibited the modern problems – taxation, competition, reduced rates, difficulties of tariff management – but without the modern compensations. It was rational therefore that the most experienced offices should reduce their commitment to this traditional centre of fire insurance exports.

In the much richer markets of Latin America, rapid economic expansion did offset a further substantial helping of trouble. Though competition was by no means lacking here, much of the irritation was supplied by governments. The Peruvian government had levied a modest insurance tax in the 1870s, and the Argentinians in 1875 introduced the *patente* – an obligatory fee which bought a licence to insure – which had prompted the exodus of British companies from that market. But these were small beer compared to the mass outbreak of protectionism among the Latin American countries in the 1890s. In the first year of the decade, Brazil imposed a requirement that all offices insuring there should deposit securities with the government, and, in the same year, the Argentinian government imposed extremely stringent tax demands.

In the xenophobic aftermath of the financial crisis of 1890 – which had seen the near demise of Baring Brothers, the British merchant bank which was a main prop of the Argentine economy, and the subsequent collapse of the London market for Argentinian loans[64] – Finance Minister Vicente Fidel Lopez took vengeance on the foreign capitalist interests nearest to hand, the insurance companies. The Buenos Aires *patente* was doubled to $10,000, a levy on premium income of 7% was imposed and an insurance deposit of $50,000 to $100,000 (depending on agency size) was introduced.[65]

[63] *Ibid.*, 15 October 1896.

[64] In the 1890s it took an entire government to almost sink Baring Brothers; in the 1990s it took one foreign exchange dealer in Singapore to actually sink the bank.

[65] Jones, 'Competition and Structural Change', p. 125.

Within a few years similarly damaging controls had been erected by Mexico, Cuba, Peru, Ecuador, Chile and Uruguay. Mexico introduced insurance deposits in December 1892; Cuba increased state and municipal taxes in 1891 and resorted to deposits in 1894;[66] while Peru imposed *pro rata* deposits in 1896 and, like Argentina, inflicted increasingly strict conditions upon foreign insurers throughout the decade in an attempt to promote native offices. Chile failed to impose deposits in 1896 but finally passed the necessary legislation by 1904; the next year Phoenix received a demand for £22,500; and the year after that, as fate would have it, Chile suffered an earthquake which landed Phoenix with £15,000 in claims.[67] Uruguay was late in imposing fiscal penalties, but made up for it with a hefty deposit scheme in 1908.[68]

Initially, the offices made some effort to reverse this onslaught. No individual company, and certainly not Phoenix, could hope to stem the attack with its own resources; again, collective methods were called for. The method of defence was, once again, a campaign concerted between the FOC in London and local boards of agents in the markets. Amidst the difficult insurance markets around the century's turn, the local board proved repeatedly that it was the essential vehicle for the export of insurance.

In 1893 the local board in Mexico protested to the Ministro de Hacienda that the new deposit requirements 'would weigh very oppressively on Fire Insurance offices, as the amount of Fire Insurance premiums is very small in comparison with the sum insured, frequently not exceeding 1/8th of 1%' and requested that the amount of deposit be accordingly modified and 'should in no case exceed such an amount as $50,000 for those doing the largest business'.[69]

This response had the whiff of a humble petition and, indeed, most of the offices' approaches to government were moderate and conciliatory in tone. However, it scarcely mattered whether the tone was sweet or strident. Apart from a small abatement in tax demands conceded by the Argentinians in the 1890s, such resistance made little impact on government policy.

Although the local boards of agents were to succeed in other sorts of defence in Latin America, there was little that they could do to deter a state intent on protectionist measures, here or elsewhere. The usual outcome was for the local boards to recognise the *fait accompli* of higher fiscal impositions by a concerted decision to raise rates.

[66] Phoenix Trustees' Minutes, 3 May and 16 August 1894.
[67] *Ibid.*, 3 May 1905, 12 September 1906. [68] Dickson, *Sun Insurance*, pp. 217–19.
[69] FOC (Foreign) Minutes, 18 January 1883.

Competition, although uncomfortable, was absorbed with somewhat more success. The local boards acted against an excess of it by recruiting all companies operating within a market into a single tariff and protecting this from overseas attack by invoking the force of the London FOC. The metropolitan body, for instance, could protect the local board by imposing a considerable sanction: it could withhold a great proportion of UK reinsurance facilities from any maverick office which caused trouble at the periphery. The local and central cartels interacted to secure the desired orderly effect. Thus, in February 1885, the FOC instructed all agents of British offices in Buenos Aires, Rosario and Montevideo to follow the rates set by the Buenos Aires local board upon all business drawn from Argentina and Uruguay.[70] The next year the Rosario agents formed their own board.[71] In 1895 the Montevideo tariff was extended to the whole of Uruguay.[72] By the 1900s the FOC also maintained tariffs for Mexico, Brazil, Ecuador, Guatemala and San Salvador. The methods for holding the line were quite powerful.

In 1888 the FOC authorised its agents in Argentina to meet a new threat from 'outside companies'. The interlopers, mostly the native Argentinian office, the Estrella, and an assortment of Germans, had been attracting business by paying exorbitant commissions to the ever-growing fraternity of brokers in this market. In retaliation, the local board of agents was given licence to fix, by majority vote, whatever rate of brokers' commission they thought adequate to sink the opposition.[73] A similar reinforcement of local sovereignty was executed in Valparaiso in the 1880s. Here no tariff office was allowed to reinsure for any office that was not a member of the local board of agents, and, from 1885, the FOC banned from local board meetings any agents who were attempting to represent tariff and non-tariff offices at the same time.

Even such a staunch supporter of collective discipline as the Phoenix could fall foul of these increasingly detailed rules and the increasingly close attention that they were given. Thus in 1888 the Phoenix agent in Buenos Aires was fined for breaching the tariff set by the local board. Distancing himself and the company from such insouciance, the Phoenix Secretary assured the FOC that the Phoenix was 'anxious to support the Local Board of Agents and that the matter in question was under investigation'.[74]

[70] FOC (Foreign) Minutes, 19 February 1885. [71] *Ibid.*, 6 May 1886.
[72] *Ibid.*, 4 October 1895. [73] *Ibid.*, 13 January 1888.
[74] *Ibid.*, 4 May 1888. One local board, that in Buenos Aires, which, from the 1900s housed Phoenix's largest commitment in South America, has been studied in detail by Jones, 'Competition and Structural Change', pp. 121, 125.

Phoenix, of course, was obedience itself. The real trouble in Argentina and elsewhere were the Continental European offices, especially the Germans, and, most particularly, the Aachen and Munchen, the Hamburg and Magdeburg, and, pre-eminently the Transatlantica.[75] The latter caused such disturbance that there was palpable relief in the FOC's response to a suggestion of 1896 from Transatlantica that the European and British offices might cooperate in rating some classes of risk in the region. Displaying its over-anxiety, the FOC jumped to the conclusion that 'the Continental Companies are now willing to join with the British companies in observing all the Tariff Agreements which are already existing for various places in Central and South America'.[76] The Transatlantica's apparent conversion to quieter ways may have warmed the credulous heart of the FOC, but in fact the men in London were thinking wishfully: nothing so comprehensive was achieved during the 1890s.

However, that did not rule out tactical victories even against the Transatlantica and even in Argentina. Insurance competition had become especially fierce after the Baring Crash, and the ensuing financial crisis, in the early 1890s. Both German companies and local non-tariff offices had fallen into the practice of taking risks somewhat below the tariff, but, from 1892, the undercutting was severe.

The leading price-cutter was the Transatlantica and it was sternly and successfully disciplined by the local board of agents in Buenos Aires. After referring the matter to the FOC for permission, the local agents simply refused to accept reinsurance from the German freebooter. Bereft of cover, and foreseeing the prospect of severe contraction in premium flow, the Hamburg company capitulated immediately, promised to abide by the tariff and itself applied to join the board.

The locals were not so easily deterred. Offices like the Estrella enjoyed the fiscal advantage provided by the Argentinian state and viewed insurance premiums primarily as finance for lucrative speculation in the domestic economy; they were entirely prepared to boost commissions and cut rates in the pursuit of investment power. By 1896, they had provoked chaos in Buenos Aires rates, with all-round reductions running to 20%.[77]

Direct price-cutting apart, the local offices in Buenos Aires created two other related problems for the big British offices. General economic expansion in Latin America, as of course elsewhere, had created an army of wheeler-dealers and middlemen; many were general brokers and among the commodities in their capacious bags was insurance. Local companies would woo business from bands of these local worthies by

[75] Probably the Transatlantiische office out of Hamburg.
[76] FOC (Foreign) Minutes, 4 December 1896. [77] *Ibid.*, p. 123.

offering extravagant commissions. Secondly, the local worthies would often pass on part of their commission to the local customer, thus indirectly reducing the price of the insurance and undercutting the tariffs. It was exceedingly difficult for large international underwriters to penetrate these networks of connection.

Though the problem of the general broker existed wherever there were interesting markets in commodities, currency, real estate or insurance, it was particularly prevalent in Argentina. E. R. Owen of the Alliance complained in 1885 that business from Buenos Aires was 'getting more into the hands of brokers every year'.[78] However, the local board of agents suspected, correctly, that the problem was less the brokers than the use the Argentinian offices made of them: in Buenos Aires the broker connection had become a covert device for cutting rates. Therefore, the solution was not to chase the brokers but to strike a compact with the Argentinian offices, in the shape of their own cartel the Comité de Aseguradores Argentinos.

Accordingly, in 1889, conversations were opened with the intent of encouraging the local offices to observe the FOC tariff. By 1895, somewhat surprisingly, agreement on a 'joint tariff' had been achieved. By this time too, the war launched by the local agents in 1888 against excessive commissions was having effect: the Argentinian companies bound themselves to limit brokerage commissions to 15% and by a further agreement in 1901 moderated their position still further. The early 1900s saw regular meetings between committees of five delegates from the British agents' board and five from the Comité de Aseguradores, with powers to conciliate all issues of regulation, rates and brokerage. Though the joint tariff slipped in 1911, among the turbulent conditions and revived foreign investment of the pre-war boom, some resolution was achieved by 1915 and it endured until 1921. At that point a new structure of conciliation was introduced: the local board of agents was reconstituted as the Argentine Fire Insurance Association and the Comité as the Associacion de Aseguradores Argentinos, and the two were, once again, inter-related by a system of joint committees.[79] Given the sharpness, self-interest and complexity of Argentinian competition in the 1880s and 1890s, this was a tribute to the absorptive capacity and resilience of the local board of agents.

In the classic era of the invisible export trade between 1870 and 1914, the local board of agents was the distinctive feature of many foreign

[78] Guildhall Library, MS 18, 506; cited by Jones, 'Competition and Structural Change', p. 116.

[79] *Ibid.*, p. 124.

markets. Obviously enough, it was a device which reduced the power and initiative of the London head offices in the distant marketplace. But successful adaption to its collusive strategy was a qualification for staying in markets as difficult as the Latin American. Phoenix adapted very well and stayed in these markets with more consistency and persistence than many big operators. Nevertheless, this was the external structure *within* which Phoenix worked these markets: it tells us nothing about the internal workings of the company's export organisation for the region.

Two aspects of this were important: the switch from reinsurance to direct trade, and a subsequent attempt to find a superior form of administration for direct selling. The first switch was not restricted to Phoenix's West Indian adjustment of 1885, the evacuation of the previously impressive reinsurance position in Havana, maintained up to then by grace of the North British and replaced, from that point, by a conventional general agency. The same adjustment was repeated all over Latin America. In Chile, the reinsurance connection with North British, in place since 1863, was severed in 1885 with the appointment of Huth & Co. as agents at Valparaiso.[80] In Costa Rica, a loose facultative arrangement with North British, vintage about 1880, yielded in 1888 to an agency appointment in the form of J. R. R. Troyo & Co.[81] And the substantial cast-off trade that had emanated from Mexico through North British since 1872 was also replaced by a general agency appointment in 1888. Other general agencies covered Argentina and Uruguay from 1881, Ecuador and British Honduras from 1890 and Colombia from 1896. There is a clear concentration of this reform movement in the latter half of the 1880s.

The second adjustment, seeking a more effective form for the general agencies, was centred on Mexico and Argentina. A major programme of expansion was launched in Mexico in 1900 by setting up a network of full agencies in the most important provincial states. This resulted in new outlets in Mexico City, Veracruz, Puebla, Monterey, Saltillo, San Luis Potosi and Chihuaha. This was agency diversification on the basis of an existing metropolitan centre. In Argentina and Uruguay, the tactic was different. Here, instead of appointing commercial or professional men with their own trades and interests as insurance agents, Phoenix in 1900 decided to establish a full branch organisation, with a salaried professional manager and a permanent administration. The natural sequel was the creation, between 1900 and 1902, of a network of sub-agencies at Rosario, Tunuyan, Cordoba, Santa Fe, Mendoza and Bahia Blanca. The pioneering incumbent as manager in Buenos Aires was Edward Crispin,

[80] Phoenix Directors' Minutes, Y24, p. 84, 25 March 1885.
[81] *Ibid.*, p. 361, 21 March 1888.

appointed on a salary of £750 p.a. and a 5% contingency commission on profits; after a long stint, he was succeeded by R. W. Denton in 1908.[82]

The Argentinian initiative was Phoenix's first branch in the region and one of the first created by any major office in Latin America: the London & Lancashire seems to have been the only large-scale operator to have beaten Phoenix to branch status in Argentina, and by ten years, but such powers as the Royal, the Sun and the Northern did not achieve parallel scale until 1912, 1914 and 1916 respectively.[83]

Despite the technical differences in status, the strings of outlets in Mexico and Argentina were both supervised by a Phoenix managing official. But in Argentina the supervision was closer and more formal. The need for tighter control was a product of expanding economies and more intricate commercial relationships. Agents in busy marketplaces, men who were also merchants, lawyers or traders, had other than insurance fish to fry and might devote excessive time to these lines of interest.

The heyday of the direct agent was in earlier times, when trade was less frantic and much business came by way of trusted mercantile relationships, rather than by the quick-fire dealing of brokers matching anonymous clients with the agent who offered the swiftest underwriting pen, or the most lavish commission. So, in a sense, the agency relationship after 1870 was in an interim phase, no longer a wholly satisfactory mechanism for the distant trade, but not yet widely replaced by a more reliable mechanism. Phoenix felt this particularly keenly, since in the 1870s and 1880s, it was moving away from reinsurance connections and back into agency relationships.

Perhaps because of this, the company was relatively quick to apply the innovation of the branch system. It was employed in the new market of the Argentine only fourteen years after one of the most venerable of all Phoenix agencies, the 'Hamburg department', had been upgraded to the management of the entire German market. However, branch foundations in New Zealand in 1885 and Melbourne and South Africa in 1891 were faster still. Clearly, Phoenix wanted the extra powers of supervision that its own paid officials afforded. But, for all its advantages, the branch system could provide no escape from another enemy: the foreign state and its taxman.

The only way to achieve this was to go native, to take over a local office and thus purchase its tax exemption. In Latin America, which is important in providing a rich variety of pressures towards organisational sophis-

82 Phoenix Trustees' Minutes, 31 January 1900; Directors' Minutes, 28, pp. 305–6, 21 October 1908.

83 Jones, 'Competition and Structural Change', p. 126.

tication, Phoenix seems to have tumbled to this quite early. In Brazil in 1903 the company was considering acquiring a controlling interest in the Lloyd Americano Fire and Marine Insurance Co. of Rio de Janeiro but ended by bowing to a somewhat mysterious FOC ruling that 'it was not competent for this company to entertain the proposal'.[84] Not until 1920 was the device successfully applied when Phoenix, jointly with the REA and the Union, took over the Argentinian company, La Buenos Aires.[85]

So there were important lessons to be learned from the Caribbean and Latin America. Non-tariff competition and government fiscality existed in both, but the latter was immeasureably stronger in the independent and expanding economies of Central and South America. Local boards of agents at the periphery, reinforced by the FOC in London, offered defence against the competition, sometimes, as in the Argentine, to a good level of deterrence. Governments proved more difficult to resist: good lawyers gave some protection, but the superior method – absorption of native companies – had not been widely attempted before 1914. For its own part, in its retreat from reinsurance, its unwavering commitment to the region's markets, and later its sub-agency and branch tactics, Phoenix displayed a high level of enterprise in dealing with the problems off this market. Whereas in the Near East, it perhaps looked less impressive than some of its rivals, in Latin America, the tables were turned.

7. THREE DOMINION MARKETS: AUSTRALASIA, SOUTH AFRICA AND CANADA

Outside Europe and the United States, the most important Phoenix markets of the period 1870–1914, befitting its reputation as the era of high imperialism, were the 'white dominions' of Australasia, South Africa and Canada. Together these three regions never accounted for less than 13% of the company's total foreign income and at peak captured almost one-quarter (see Table 2.15). Their share increased progressively and without break from 1891–5 to 1911–15. But even these similar types of market were not synchronised in their behaviour through the period.

Canada saw almost a halving of its share of foreign income between 1871–5 and 1891–5 and almost a doubling between 1891–5 and 1911–15. South Africa's pattern was episodic with periods of sharp expansion and sharp contraction in the share. Australasia witnessed a powerful and almost smooth advance in its share throughout the period. Moreover the

[84] Phoenix Trustees' Minutes, p. 207, 8 July 1903.
[85] Jones, 'Competition and Structural Change', p. 126. La Buenos Aires was first acquired by London & Lancs in 1898.

Table 2.15. *Share of three dominion markets in Phoenix foreign income (£ and % of total)*

	Canada[a]		Australia & New Zealand		South Africa		Total	
	£	%	£	%	£	%	£	%
1871–5	31,456	13.4	–	–	824	0.4	32,280	13.8
1876–80	36,602	14.1	1,791	0.7	4,239	1.6	42,632	16.4
1881–5	46,164	10.4	11,981	2.7	5,767	1.3	63,912	14.4
1886–90	47,449	8.2	33,953	5.9	5,341	0.9	86,743	15.0
1891–5	60,474	7.9	50,356	6.6	31,568	4.0	142,398	18.5
1896–1900	84,459	10.1	54,398	6.5	18,653	2.3	157,510	18.9
1901–5	143,772	12.6	74,838	6.5	38,538	3.4	257,148	22.5
1906–10	194,618	13.8	89,376	6.4	37,355	2.5	321,349	22.7
1911–15	222,098	13.9	118,930	7.5	28,574	1.8	369,602	23.2
1916–20	334,372	10.4	154,798	5.8	38,141	1.5	527,311	17.7

Note: [a]Canada includes Halifax, Newfoundland, New Brunswick and British Columbia.
Source: Calculated from Phoenix Review of Foreign Agencies, Books 1–4.

markets were of quite different vintages. There had been a Phoenix presence in Canada since the earliest years of the agency system and an outpost opened at the Cape in the 1850s; but the Australasian market was wholly a creation of the period 1870–1914.

No doubt owing due to its clean start, Australasia was the first of these vital markets to show signs of adaptation to the new conditions of the late nineteenth-century export trade in fire insurance. Phoenix moved into the region with a rapid burst of agency creations in the second half of the 1870s and early 1880s: New Zealand in 1876, Melbourne and Sydney in 1878, Adelaide in 1879, Perth in 1880, Brisbane in 1882, and, somewhat later, Tasmania in 1900. This was about as quick as it was sensible to be. Australia and New Zealand had been colonised only in the 1830s and 1840s and even in the 1870s could scratch together a combined population of barely 3 million. Both economies revolved around sheep and only the marine companies were brave enough to insure the wool clip 'from sheep's back to London'.

These signs were read in similar fashion by both the Sun and the Commercial Union. The Sun resisted agency proposals from Melbourne, the most promising Australian city, for some twenty years before succumbing to temptation in 1865, only to close the agency in

1871.[86] The Sun went back into Melbourne in 1877, entered Adelaide in the same year, tied with the Phoenix by setting up in Sydney in 1878, beat Phoenix into the fruit and vegetable economy of Tasmania in 1891 and lagged behind Phoenix into Brisbane, a provincial town marooned in the fastnesses of Queensland, in 1888. Commercial Union also entered Australia through the preferred gateway of Melbourne in 1877, and, true to its very active policy of branch development, created branches there in 1880 and in both New South Wales and South Australia in 1881. In 1880 it also acquired two Australian subsidiaries, Sydney Fire and New South Wales Marine.[87] The Sun was always cautious and the Commercial Union was unusually forthright. But Phoenix was rebuilding an international export effort. Here its approach to a difficult but expanding market was rational.

Certainly, the market, though new, was not without attractions. In fact New Zealand was a good deal more attractive than Australia. Its climate was less aggressive; much of its population was of stout Scottish descent; its towns were conducted and constructed with propriety; the pacey features of brokerage were not much in evidence. Consistently with this, there was early tariff development: Canterbury had agreed rates and its own Fire Insurance Association from 1868, Nelson its own tariff from 1871; and there was a New Zealand Fire Underwriters' Association from 1879.[88] Where almost every seaport in the world had its Dead Man's Cove or Incendiary Point, Christchurch named its streets after bishops.

By contrast, Australia was hot, dry, big and unruly. The moral pecking order of the cities ran from sober and brisk Melbourne, the early capital of Australian insurance, through industrious Adelaide, with its many German settlers, remote Brisbane, isolated Perth, still an outback settlement, to a Sydney uneasily shedding the traces of its convict past. Tariffs in the 1870s were ineffective or impossible and an attempt to create a New South Wales Fire Underwriters' Association failed in 1880; it was achieved only in 1885. The Adelaide Fire Insurers' Association was founded in 1876, but did not even try to regulate rates. Competition from local offices was inexperienced and unscrupulous and closely keyed to the local market: some Australian companies, for instance, wooed the populace by offering advantageous mortgage services within their limited catchment areas. Unlike New Zealand, brokerage and discounting of rates was endemic, especially in Melbourne, Adelaide and Brisbane.[89] Nevertheless, heat and drought created an appetite for fire insurance. Population was increasing fast. And as the world transport revolution

[86] Dickson, *Sun Insurance*, p. 207. [87] Liveing, *Commercial Union*, p. 42.
[88] Dickson, *Sun Insurance*, pp. 203–6. [89] *Ibid.*, pp. 206–11.

created a global production system for primary products, the sheep and wheat economy of Australia became an important part of it.

The first British insurers to be attracted by these credit points were the Imperial, Alliance and Royal, all of which had agencies in Melbourne by the early 1850s. Within a decade, there were ten British companies locked in battle with the locals in the best Australian market. The Sun's foreign superintendant, G. S. Manvell, found it to have 'an amount of go in it quite refreshing'.[90]

In general, however, Phoenix displayed more 'go' than the Sun. This was especially true in New Zealand. Here the Sun's total premium income in the period 1878–95 summed to £67,000, whereas Phoenix over the same period amassed nearly £153,000.[91] Not that Phoenix enjoyed an easy landing in New Zealand. First attempts were fumbled. In 1876 Phoenix appointed to a general agency, Thomas Mabin, the Royal's representative in Auckland. In 1878 the agency was wound up with Mabin owing Phoenix £300, which they had to recover from his guarantors.[92] Tracking the Royal did not work. In 1880 Phoenix tried again. By April, the company had accepted a proposal from the Colonial Insurance Company of New Zealand that Phoenix should reinsure half of all Colonial's New Zealand risks, with expenses and charges to be covered by a commission of 20%.[93] This also looked like a return to the older, more conservative style of foreign trade by reinsurance.

But here appearances were deceptive: Phoenix was no longer prepared to play that second fiddle. Here the deal was rather a means of forming a connection with Colonial's general manager in Wellington, George Graham. By June 1880, Graham was Phoenix agent for New Zealand. His receipts for the first half of the 1880s were quadruple those of Mabin's last five years. The arrangement with Colonial generated premiums between 1882 and 1886 and was then allowed to expire, while from 1885 Graham was briefed 'to represent the company . . . in a more direct form than heretofore'.[94] Under initial impulsion from Graham, Phoenix's premium income from New Zealand climbed from £3,020 in 1882, remitted by

[90] *Ibid.*, p. 209.

[91] Phoenix Review of Foreign Agencies; Dickson, *Sun Insurance*, p. 205.

[92] In fact, genuinely first efforts were even earlier and more maladroit than this. For Phoenix actually appointed its first agent in New Zealand, J. S. Freeman, at Auckland in 1841. This was scarcely a year after the proclamation of British sovereignty in the colony and seems to have been wholly wishful thinking. No premium receipts were ever recorded. Compare Hurren, *Phoenix Renascent*, p. 52, with Review of Foreign Agencies I, 1787–1877.

[93] Phoenix Trustees' Minutes, 29 April 1880.

[94] Phoenix Directors' Minutes X23, p. 36, 9 June 1880; Trustees' Minutes, 12 February 1885.

Colonial, to £20,930 in 1900 and £42,779 in 1914, garnered by the agency. From as early as 1885, the Phoenix Review of Foreign Agencies records the New Zealand operation as a full branch with salaried manager and staff. The official appointed to run this establishment, R. M. Simpson continued to do so for the next thirty years.[95] These were firmer foundations.

However, if some New Zealanders were agreeably sober and upright customers for the insurer, other New Zealanders were sufficiently canny businessmen to cause problems as competitors. Phoenix was fortunate in its link with Graham and the Colonial, but by the 1890s there were quite enough local companies to pose a real threat to the British exporters, not only in New Zealand itself but throughout the Far East. The big British offices responded as they had in other markets beset by non-tariff competition or intrusive governments: they pressed for the creation of local associations of agents capable of enforcing the tariff. An FOC circular of June 1894 set its face against establishing a 'Resident Controlling Representative' in New Zealand but noted that British companies interested in this market were unanimous in wanting local tariff associations.[96] The next year, the FOC announced the intention of dissolving the New Zealand Fire Underwriters' Association and replacing it with separate local tariff associations for each of the main provinces. It was a condition of this scheme that *all* companies operating in New Zealand, including the locals, should enrol as members. And delegates of all British, Foreign and Australasian offices selling policies in New Zealand were summoned to an insurers' conclave in Melbourne in 1895 to be told so.[97]

However, they were not gathered together merely to emphasise the tactical merits of the local boards. The New Zealand companies had proved a problem not only in their own backyard but far offshore; they were summoned to Melbourne for an international wigging. In 1894 the FOC had observed dryly that, 'the competition felt by the British offices at certain important points in the East Indies and elsewhere through the action of New Zealand companies throws doubt on the question of co-operation with these same companies in the Colony'.[98] The threat now put to the New Zealanders was that they should behave themselves more decorously in the distant Asian markets or face a combined offensive by the large British and foreign offices in their own backyard. As the international insurance community began to organise the New Zealand market, they could use this disciplining process against competition emanating *from*

[95] Hurren, *Phoenix Renascent*, p. 86. The New Zealand Branch anticipated the Argentinian by fifteen years.
[96] FOC Circular, 6 June 1894. [97] *Ibid.*, 8 May 1895. [98] *Ibid.*, 6 June 1894.

New Zealand but impacting far away. The FOC initiative was successful and brought the New Zealanders to heel in 'Australia, India, China, Japan and other places in the East and in South America'.[99] Competition over a good part of the globe was ameliorated by this diplomatic coup.

In another sense, the accord came in the nick of time. For no sooner had the local competition been reined in than the other routine threat of the late nineteenth century manifested itself in New Zealand: government harassment. The colony was unusual in the region in this respect. Australian taxes were light and there were no deposit requirements before 1900, with the exception of a modest and discretionary one in Western Australia. Nor indeed did the New Zealand government impose directly any serious fiscal burden. What it did do in 1896 was to propose the formation of a state fire insurance department on the American model. The implicit threat here, of course, was of permanent hectoring, with a systematic and onerous deposit scheme on the horizon. Dealing with such a peril required a united front and the British offices were fortunate that they had just created one.

Just as they had done against the Transatlantica in Argentina, the massed British offices retaliated with the reinsurance weapon. The FOC immediately resolved 'not to accept any reinsurance whatever from, nor enter into any reinsurance contract with, the New Zealand government'.[100] All state insurances would have to face the typhoons of the Pacific bereft of a reinsurance shield. For the FOC tactic to work, it required the full participation of the native New Zealand companies. In February 1897, the British offices were relieved to hear that the lessons administered over the last three years had struck home and that 'the New Zealand companies will not follow the proposed state insurance'.[101] The effectiveness of a fully comprehensive local association was proved once more in New Zealand, just as it was at much the same time in the Near East, Latin America, India and the Far East.

Nevertheless, this was not the only point proved in New Zealand. For the state did not give up. In 1905 it imposed constraint in a different form, creating its own insurance capacity in an official fire and accident office, the New Zealand State Fire and Accident Insurance Company. The Commercial Union, which had invested heavily in New Zealand, purchasing the Colonial Insurance Co. in 1890, was badly affected by this démarche and its New Zealand Branch ran at a loss down to 1914. The buoyancy of Phoenix's premium returns – which stumbled slightly 1904–6 but recovered well in the later 1900s – suggests that the older office

[99] *Ibid.*, 8 May 1895. [100] FOC (Foreign), Memorandum, 12 October 1896.
[101] *Ibid.*, Note of 5 February 1897, appended to Memorandum.

withstood the pressure somewhat better. But the point was again made that government protectionism could harm even the largest of British insurers.

Much as in New Zealand, the first Phoenix approaches to agency business in Australia did not run entirely smoothly.[102] Perhaps this was not surprising. The planning of the city of Sydney was begun by Governor Macquarie only in 1811; South Australia was surveyed as a new settlement by Captain Light RN only in 1836; Melbourne was founded in the same year; while in 1880 Perth had only 5,000 inhabitants and the whole of Western Australia only 29,000. Nevertheless, railway development began to affect the economy of the interior from the 1870s and the next decade saw substantial growth in the woollen and mining industries.

The Australian 'settlements' in the 1880s still retained some of the frontier characteristics that Phoenix had been more used to in the 1810s and 1820s. And they could impose the same sort of punishment. Thus in 1882, Phoenix lost £15,000 on a single fire at Adelaide, within the confines of an agency established only three years before. The agent responsible for the excessive accumulation of risk in the city, George Cotton, forthwith abandoned underwriting to try his hand at selling policies of a different kind: he entered politics. Cotton was elected to the colonial legislature but there is little indication of whether he was any less dangerous in this area.[103]

By 1884, the Melbourne agency, established six years before, and already the heart of Phoenix's Australian operation, was in the hands of an experienced and well-recommended insurance broker, R. M. Taylor. The Phoenix Trustees found Taylor 'a thoroughly trained insurance official';[104] accordingly, his lament on the state of the Melbourne trade carries some weight. He wrote in 1884,

> I have to explain that it has been a Melbourne custom, for many years to allow a 'fixed discount' of 15% to everyone, both principals and brokers . . . years back the keen competition forced the extension of the concession to principals. The custom, a bad one no doubt, became established so firmly that all rates in Victoria are subject to a reduction of 15%. Since the abolition of the tariff, nearly all the leading offices allow their country and suburban agents 20% and I am compelled to do the same in order to obtain the services of reliable and energetic men.[105]

[102] Indeed, the symmetry is almost exact. After the Board had decided in 1839 that Australia was simply too far away for sensible insuring, they relented in 1840, so far as to permit an agency for South Australia as a retirement and emigration present to J. J. Duncan, formerly manager of the Metellus. The agency produced a brief flurry of premiums in 1841, then sank without trace. See vol. 1, p. 259.

[103] Trustees' Minutes, 21 June 1883. [104] *Ibid.*, 8 May 1884.

[105] Phoenix Foreign Agents Ledger, C19/4.

But not only Melbourne business was costly to acquire. Basic commission rates had reached 20% and more by 1894 in Sydney, Brisbane and Tasmania, a good deal above the going level encountered on most other continents. The myriad pay-offs required in the hurly-burly of this market – the contingent commissions, the sub-agency commissions, the brokerage allowances – made the Australian agency system particularly expensive to run. Exasperation with these conditions led the Commercial Union to desert the Melbourne tariff in the early 1880s, only to fall into loss for its pains. A semblance of order here came only in the next decade with the formation of a new Tariff Association.[106]

However, Phoenix spent much time as well as money on expansion in Australia. In 1890–1, William Newcomb, a promising Head Office official, was sent out from London on one of Phoenix's speciality expeditions (in the style of Jenkin Jones and J. J. Broomfield) but in a different direction. Newcomb was unleashed on the antipodes with powers to 'supercede and appoint agents . . . as he may find most suitable for the interests of the Company'.[107] He was paid an additional £150 in recognition of the arduousness of the task. What impressed Newcomb most was the cost of Australian agents. His recommendation to London was that a salaried manager and paid clerks might prove a better bargain. Also, an imposing branch office, proclaiming solidity in granite and mahogany, might do more for business than the endless hand-outs to the brokers. The early development of a branch system in Australia, a decade ahead of Argentina, owed much to the great expense of conducting business through traditional agencies.

Almost as soon as Newcomb made landfall back in England, the instructions went out from Phoenix for the erection of a branch structure in Australia. The senior appointment was that of J. Martin at Melbourne in 1891, while the Sydney agency was turned into a branch for New South Wales in the same year, Perth into Western Australia and Adelaide into South Australia in 1893. However, Martin had the over-riding control of all of these offices. He was succeeded by his son, R. W. Martin – on £500 salary and 5% profits – in 1899, and R. W. Martin enjoyed the same sweeping brief as his father.[108] After Edward Boston, Phoenix fire manager, returned from a somewhat more extensive and elevated tour of the Eastern hemisphere in November 1914, this brief was formalised and R. W. Martin received the title of Branch Manager for Australia. He held

[106] Liveing, *Commercial Union*, pp. 42–3.
[107] Phoenix Directors' Minutes Z25, p. 115, 9 July 1890; Trustees' Minutes, 3 September 1891. Newcomb became assistant secretary in the Phoenix foreign department in 1899.
[108] Phoenix Trustees' Minutes, 6 September 1899; Hurren, *Phoenix Renascent*, p. 86.

this post until 1924, thus completing a full quarter-century in overall control of Phoenix's operation in Australia.

During the 1900s Phoenix's business in Australia became progressively more sophisticated. There was an adverse side to this. The previously restrained attitude of the state became more complex: by 1909 Western Australia was sufficiently fashionable to require a £10,000 insurance deposit, while by 1914 Victoria had added a separate £5,000 guarantee for workmen's compensation business.[109] As befitted its growing status as a composite company, Phoenix had extended its newly formed accident department into the foreign field in the summer of 1907, and was thus vulnerable to both types of imposition.[110]

On the credit side, the organisation presided over by R. W. Martin greatly improved. Local directors were appointed to strengthen the branch system in 1905 and 1906. But, perhaps most important was a major catch for the agency system in 1906. As elsewhere, of course, agents were now supervised closely by the branch organisation. But a powerful agency connection could still be worth a mint to a branch. Or indeed to a national operation. For in 1906, Phoenix formed a link with perhaps the most powerful name in the agricultural and pastoral economy of Australia, Dalgety & Co. The link spanned the Commonwealth. Charles Hogendorf Campbell, Dalgety's managing director in Melbourne became agent for Victoria, and Dalgety's managers in Brisbane, Adelaide and Perth became agents for Queensland, South Australia and Western Australia respectively. The Dalgety name, influence, agricultural expertise and geographical span was a brilliant vehicle for working an economy like the Australian – as the near doubling of antipodean receipts between 1906 and 1915 testified. It was the loss of this connection, and the transfer of the agency to a British competitor in 1923 which was to be the source of Phoenix's troubles in Australia in the interwar period.[111]

Intermediate between the uproar of Australia and the well-controlled agency business of Canada was the valuable but volatile trade from South Africa (see Table 2.15). At peak, in 1893 and 1894 the area accounted for 5.8% and 6.1% of all Phoenix foreign income, yet between 1911 and 1915 it exceeded 2% in only one year.

Like Australasia, South Africa was a new market for British products and services. Captured from the Dutch during the Napoleonic Wars, it became formally British only in 1815; and even then disenchanted Boer farmers crossed the Vaal to create the semi-autonomous Transvaal Republic as late as 1836. The economy was similar to the Australian in its

[109] Phoenix Directors' Minutes 29, p. 16, 21 July 1909; p. 140, 9 December 1914.

[110] Phoenix Trustees' Minutes, 17 July 1907. [111] See below, pp. 757–73.

dependence on wool, grain, cattle, fruit and wine though the range was perhaps rather more diversified, rather earlier. Mineral strikes at Kimberley in the 1870s and Johannesburg in the 1880s certainly added a dash of enthusiastic instability at a sensitive point in the opening up of the economy. South African gold and diamonds came to the attention of the world economy just as it acquired superior means of reaching distant places.

The insurers were somewhat swifter in establishing a definite presence in South Africa than they had been in Australia. The Alliance office was busy in South Africa by the 1830s and 1840s.[112] The Sun was the second British office to establish an agency at the Cape, in 1852, and Phoenix was only weeks behind in 1853.[113] Both the older offices proceeded cautiously, but the Phoenix outpost did establish foundations and reported a modest but continuous stream of premiums between 1853 and 1870. By that time, there were nine British offices and five local competitors in the Cape Town insurance market.[114]

And before long, the revived Phoenix was proceeding in a more unbelted style. Where the Sun continued to instruct its agents to avoid manufactories and rejected risks in the Kimberley diamond fields, Phoenix like its former reinsurance partner, the North British, took full advantage of this first mining bonanza. Also, from the 1850s, Cape Town had featured increasingly as a natural staging post in the worldwide expansion of the transport economy. Commercial risks multiplied proportionately. Phoenix income profited from both effects: premiums won through the Cape went up from a mere £571 in 1873 to £6,225 in 1880. Clearly, in this market, Phoenix ran with the most enterprising and was tracking no one.

Major new opportunities in South Africa flowed from the gold and diamond strikes of the 1870s and 1880s. The Rand strike of 1884 generated considerable expansion in the ports of Cape Town, Durban and Port Elizabeth. By 1889, South Africa was raising £1.3 million worth of bullion, by 1893 £5 million, by 1898 £15 million. The big insurers needed to react to the resulting financial currents with structural changes. Sun was under pressure to make up for earlier conservatism and did so with a spate

[112] See vol. I, pp. 251, 254.

[113] Technically, in fact, Phoenix was the first of all into South Africa since it had appointed John Houghton and Alexander MacDonald to the Cape in its first bout of overseas expansion in 1806; but the times were problematic, Britain was at war and nothing came of the initiative. By contrast, the appointment in 1853 of Henry and Thomas Rudd began an unbroken line of descent to the agency firm of Graham Watson & Co., who were still representing Phoenix in its last decade. See vol. I, pp. 189, 312; Hurren, *Phoenix Renascent*, p. 24.

[114] Compare Dickson, *Sun Insurance*, p. 200.

of local company purchases in the 1890s, beginning with the Frontier Insurance Co. in 1891 and including three others by 1897.[115] Commercial Union followed a similar line, creating a Cape Town branch in 1890 and purchasing the Provident Assurance of Port Elizabeth in 1894 and the Colonial Assurance of Cape Town in 1899.[116]

Phoenix also found the early 1890s a turning point, but employed different tactics in the turning. The Cape agency soldiered on unaided through the 1880s and was taking by itself over 1% of all Phoenix foreign income by the end of the decade. But the 1890s saw a major diversification of the Phoenix operation. In 1889 the important Johannesburg concern of Becker Brothers had been appointed agents for the Transvaal and began reporting substantial receipts by 1891. Early in that year, the Becker agency was extended to cover Natal, Swaziland and Zululand. Natal commenced reporting a separate if modest premium flow in 1892. Delagoa Bay also opened a premium account in 1891. Roving further afield, Phoenix moved agencies into Pietermaritzburg and the Natal interior and into Durban and the coastal districts of Natal and Zululand in 1895.[117] By 1898 the movement had reached Rhodesia and spread into Matabeleland and Mashonaland.

This proliferating root system was itself fed by an expanding network of sub-agencies. The Cape Town agency controlled nine of these by 1902, mostly staffed by solicitors and extending through Cape Province, Orange Free State and Natal. Even the Rhodesian agency had sub-stations at Umtali, Gwelo and Salisbury by 1899, though it was noted in the next year that 'Umtali is degenerating'. Most important, the entire scatter of new agencies and sub-agencies was brought under central direction: for in May 1891, in another early branch innovation, Becker Brothers were created branch managers for all South African and associated territory.

As the new system came into operation, the old waned. The long-running agency at the Cape was taking only £3,159 in 1894, the new Transvaal outpost nearly three times that amount and the South African Branch over ten times that figure. The Sun, after taking only £5,000 from the Cape in 1891, was the first office to win £20,000 from this market, which it did in 1900. Its strategy of company acquisition clearly worked. So did the Phoenix strategy. The Johannesburg Branch alone took over £20,000 in 1902, over £30,000 in 1903.

Despite these considerable structural changes and the natural volatility of a mineral-driven economy, the advance of insurance in South Africa was relatively disciplined. Modest levels of agents' commission – almost

[115] *Ibid.*, p. 202. [116] Liveing, *Commercial Union*, pp. 60, 107–8.
[117] Phoenix Directors' Minutes Z25, p. 47, 9 October 1889; 26, p. 130, 6 November 1895.

always 10%, with nothing at 15% or above recorded before 1896 – tell their own story and contrast markedly with the 15% commissions which appeared in Latin America from the late 1880s and even more with the commissions of 20% and more required in Australia from the mid-1890s. Local rates committees developed early. By 1886 Phoenix was represented on the FOC subcommittee for the Cape tariff and, in the next year, the FOC drew up a fresh tariff for Cape Town, Simonstown and Port Elizabeth.[118] The 1880s saw the development of rate committees of local agents at four local centres – Cape Town, Port Elizabeth, Durban and Johannesburg – and by 1897 a fifth had been added at Pretoria. Crucially, the district rates they enforced were to be net, without any discounts or rebates, again a far cry from the Australian market practice. The interaction of local and metropolitan influences common in the world insurance markets of the period seems to have resulted in a particularly effective control of rates in the South African case.

This does not mean that competition was absent. A list of companies with agents in the port of Laurenzo Marques in 1903 reveals the presence of twelve other British offices alongside Phoenix, five German, two Dutch and one French. Against such opposition, it was vital to field high-quality agents and managers. Thus when M. J. Smith was placed in control of the South African Branch in 1901, Phoenix took up references from the Cape Town managers of the Alliance, British and Colonial, Southern Life and New Zealand offices. His successor, A. G. Twentyman Jones, was supported by references from the Standard Bank in Cape Town, officials of the Guardian and Sun and managers of 'about 34 mercantile firms'. Like R. W. Martin in Australia, Twentyman Jones had durability: he held the post from 1906 until 1927, yielding it then to E. B. Ferguson, later to become a pivotal general manager of the company.[119]

Nevertheless, despite the competitive presence, and no doubt helped by carefully chosen officials, the South African market developed between 1870 and 1914 in reasonable accord. This was largely true even of relations with government. Demands from this quarter down to 1914 were distinctly reasonable. The Cape government charged a licence fee of 0.5% of premiums between 1867 and 1883, but amended this to a flat rate requirement of only £50 per year in the latter year. It asked local agents to produce annual returns of premium, and, if the £50 levy represented too large a percentage of the total, it returned a share of the tax! Even a 2.5% impost, established in 1887, was costing Phoenix only £20 per year in 1895. This was much of a piece with the Rhodesian licence fee which was

[118] FOC (Foreign) Minutes, 19 November 1886, 13 May 1887.

[119] See below, pp. 878–92.

introduced at £30 per annum, 'to be retained at Bulawayo', in 1899. American or Canadian government officials would have viewed such fiscal behaviour with incredulity, although they might have recognised the slightly sterner line taken by South African administrations on the matter of deposits. In 1887, the Cape legislature required £1,000 in 4% Cape consols; from 1893, £5,000 in Transvaal bonds formed the entry price to that market; and the Orange Free State required a similar amount from 1897. American and Canadian officials would have applauded the principle but itched to increase the amounts by multiples.

The only way that governments truly caused trouble in the South African market of this period was by indulging in another form of official excess: they went to war. In 1899 the persistent tension between Boer settlers and British administration broke into open hostilities and continued in that vein, with much embarrassment to British arms, until 1902. The fighting occupied a third of a million British troops and cost the British Treasury about £200 million, about twenty times its initial estimates. Phoenix also experienced financial costs. The core of the South African Branch operation was in Johannesburg and that became a difficult place for British financial connections. Although premiums reported from the Cape went up in the period 1896–1900 and the Transvaal agency kept going, though with a little slippage, returns from the South African Branch itself entirely disappeared. When they resumed in 1901, they reached levels only one-third those of the boom years 1893 and 1894 and fully recovered only in 1904. Phoenix's South African Manager was evacuated from Johannesburg in 1900, sadly estimating that he would lose £2,000 per year in commission alone. That Phoenix paid his £75 removal costs to Cape Town and promised him £50 a month until the military had settled the matter could not have made up for this.[120]

Despite the rally in 1904, the returns to Phoenix from South Africa in the aftermath of the war did not recapture their earlier buoyancy. If they had grown by thirteen times from the early 1870s to 1900, they contracted by nearly half between 1903 and 1914. So too did the share of the region in total Phoenix foreign income, from above 4% to barely 2%. On the face of it, the inference is that the Boer War and its ensuing frictions proved the strongest adverse pressure encountered by Phoenix in this market in the half-century before 1914.

Fortunately, Britain did not go to war with Canada at any time in this period. At the commencement in 1870, this market was a vital one for Phoenix and Canadian business was very big business. While, in the

[120] Phoenix Trustees' Minutes, 11 April 1900.

1870s, the company was still maintaining extensive, if somewhat shallow reinsurance arrangements with North British throughout Latin and Central America, and its US income entirely depended on a solid treaty with North British, Canada was being run as it always had been, as a rumbustious direct trade. Nearly two-thirds of all North American business between 1866 and 1870 had come from agents in Canada, including Halifax, Newfoundland, New Brunswick and Vancouver Island. This proportion dipped to 42% in 1871–5 as New York business reconverted to direct agency trade but bounced back to 52% for the second half of the 1870s. Even after a massive resurgence of US business around the turn of the century Canada still accounted for 24% of all North American income.

By 1911–15, the relatively few Canadian outposts were taking average annual premiums of nearly £250,000; it required the several Phoenix subsidiaries in the United States and the massed agencies of Europe to beat Canada into third place in the rank order of Phoenix markets.

This pattern was in marked contrast to the Sun's performance: the oldest British fire office did not fully arrive in British North America until 1892.[121] Eleven other British offices, besides Phoenix, were less timid and were represented in Canada by 1869. By then, of course, Phoenix had maintained a Canadian agency for sixty-five years.

Not that Canada, even without war, was a safe place. Its experience in the early nineteenth century had been fiery and the market shed this tendency with reluctance in the late century. 'Canada', wrote R. T. Naylor, 'was notorious for its huge conflagrations, which wiped out large industrial areas, and, with them, in theory, threatened to destroy fire insurance profits as well.' Timber buildings, flimsy construction and the prevalence of standing forest were to blame.[122] And rising levels of economic activity multiplied the potential locations for disaster. The Canadian Pacific linked the coasts in 1885. Canadian exports nearly doubled between 1868 and 1891. And the Canadian population rose from 3 million in 1870 to 5 million in 1890, much of the increase representing immigration into rapidly expanding, wood-built towns.

Certainly, Phoenix had plentiful experience of the resulting Canadian conflagrations around 1870. In December 1867, the company closed its New Brunswick agency because of the unacceptable level of blazes in the

[121] Sun appointed a Canadian agency in 1841, wound it up in 1842 and refused eighteen different applications for a successor between 1851 and 1867 (Dickson, *Sun Insurance*, p. 220).

[122] R. T. Naylor, *A History of Canadian Business 1867–1914* (Toronto, 1975; 2 vols), p. 188. However, Naylor's unsympathetic treatment is surely implausible in suggesting that flimsy constuction was a *consequence* of the excessive rates charged by fire insurers.

vicinity.[123] And, within four months, it sustained another large loss on the Canadian Northern Railway on account of inflammable forest.[124] Its reaction here was indeed to increase smartly all rates for outlying stations on this line. The late 1870s were years of firestorm in Canada fit to rival those of the 1840s.[125] A decade before, in 1866, Quebec had been decimated, and then, in 1881, heavily damaged, by major fires. Even as late as the 1890s, the region proved capable of generating a truly traditional blaze: in 1892, for the second time in a half-century, St John's in Newfoundland erupted in a replay of the great inferno of 1846. Improvements to construction, fire-breaks and water supply had led Phoenix to 'anticipate that we could accept a larger amount of business with comparative safety'.[126] In reality, the St John's fire of 1892 imposed a bill upon all insurers of £3 million sterling, triple the cost of its predecessor. The Phoenix share of the 1892 disaster, at £124,000, was rather larger than its £114,500 participation in the event of 1846. However, the St John's attack was to be the last of its kind.

And, despite such reminders of hazard, Phoenix accepted very large single insurances in the Canadian market: $200,000 on the Grand Trunk Railway in 1867, $100,000 on two warehouses of the Montreal Warehousing Company in 1869.[127] The reason, according to Naylor, was that Canadian business was 'very profitable, despite the companies' protestations'. Displaying a splendid insensitivity to the costs of management, commission and expenses, he observes that,

> From 1867 to 1913, only once, after the great fires of 1877, did the annual losses paid exceed the premiums received. And the premium receipts were rarely less than 30% more than losses; frequently, they were double or even more than double the level of loss disbursements.[128]

Translated into a world where insurers incur operational costs as well as losses, this presumably means that the underwriting surplus for all offices was strongly negative in 1877 and that there was usually a margin of 50–60% of premium between losses and total receipts. Allowing an expenses level of around 30–35% of premiums, this leaves an average surplus in the Canadian fire market of 15–30% in the last third of the nineteenth century. This was scarcely excessive by nineteenth-century underwriting assumptions – which desired to make an *insurance* profit not to compensate for loss ratios in excess of 100% by fat returns on

123 Phoenix Trustees' Minutes, 12 December 1867. 124 *Ibid.*, 10 April 1868.
125 See vol. 1, pp. 293–5. 126 Phoenix Archive: Fire Loss Experience since 1788.
127 Phoenix Trustees' Minutes, 8 August 1867, 10 June 1869.
128 Naylor, *History of Canadian Business*, p. 188.

investment – and it would require superior management in such a market to hit this profit band. If the margin between total losses and total premium income was ever as low as 30% of premium, expenses would have consumed all of it. Dickson, indeed, much more soberly argues that most British offices did not possess superior management in Canada and that their business tended to run, not at an excessive profit, but, until the 1890s at least, at a loss.[129]

In this experience Phoenix did not share. Clearly, Canada Phoenix did have superior management. It came primarily in the form of the influential business of Gillespie, Moffat & Co. of Montreal and its descendants. Gillespie, Moffat were appointed agents in 1829 and served with distinction until 1887, when the partnership was dissolved. Between 1866 and 1887, the firm was always among the four leading foreign earners for Phoenix. Its dissolution did not see this talent run to waste – a Moffat relation, A. T. Paterson, was brought in to reconstitute the business and, incidentally, to found a managing dynasty for Phoenix. Gillespie, Paterson & Co. carried the Phoenix agency 1887–9 and Paterson & Co. took it on from 1889 until 1910, when, apparently belatedly, the Phoenix Canadian Branch was founded. It was then managed from 1910 to 1934 by two Paterson brothers. Between 1889 and 1909 alone the Patersons brought nearly £1 million in premiums to Phoenix. Moreover, in 1915 they created the first Phoenix foreign subsidiary company outside the United States. This was the Acadia Fire of Halifax, founded in 1868, and by the 1910s a substantial power in the Maritime Provinces.

The powers of attorney issued to Phoenix agents in Canada between 1874 and 1900 tell a revealing story (see Table 2.16).

They suggest that Phoenix's considerable Canadian business was run by a very select group of agents, dominated by the Gillespies, Patersons and Ceperleys. In particular, Gillespie, Moffat played a vital troubleshooting and expansionist role. When the St John, New Brunswick agency was revived in 1881, having been closed in 1867 after financial irregularity and fire damage, it was under the direct supervision of Gillespie, Moffat. A similar tale of excessive losses and indebted agents brought them into Halifax as avenging investigators in 1880; by the next year they were operating the agency themselves.[130] Yet this system was not expensive. Not until the 1890s did commission rates in Canada rise to the levels

[129] Dickson, *Sun Insurance*, p. 220. Dickson calculates also that 1881 saw a negative underwriting surplus for the massed British offices. However, longer-run measurement suggests that the Phoenix comfortably outperformed the standard suggested by Dickson, though never to the excessive degree imagined by Naylor.

[130] Phoenix Trustees' Minutes, 20 February 1879, 20 May and 22, 29 July 1880, 14 April 1881.

Table 2.16. *Powers of attorney for Canadian agents, 1874–1900*

Date	Firm	Place	Agency area
1874	Gillespie, Moffat	Montreal	Canada
1880	Gillespie, Moffat	Montreal	New Brunswick
1881	Gillespie, Moffat	Montreal	Halifax, Nova Scotia
1887	Paterson, Gillespie	Montreal	Canada
1889	Paterson & Sons	Montreal	Canada
1889	Ross & Ceperley	Vancouver	Vancouver, BC
1889	W. &. G. Rendell	St John's	Newfoundland, St Pierre, Miquelin
1890	H. T. Ceperley	Vancouver	Vancouver, BC
1892	G. H. Gillespie	Hamilton	Ontario
1894	G. F. Carruthers	Winnipeg	Manitoba
1898	British Columbia Land Investment Agency	London & Victoria	British Columbia
1898	L. A. Naret	Winnipeg	Manitoba
1900	T. C. Paterson	Toronto	Ontario

around 20% that had been reached in New York in the 1870s and in the major European agencies in the 1870s and 1880s. The late transition to a branch system in Canada is more apparent than real: in effect Gillespie, Moffat was a branch without the name.

There were other odd features in the Canadian market. Neither in Canada nor in the United States did the FOC manage to marshal the local agents of British and other offices into regional rate committees as it did in so many other places in the late nineteenth century. Probably, this was due in both markets to the proximity of independently minded American companies. Certainly, by the 1890s competition had brought Canadian rates to a level that the Commercial Union considered dangerously low. And relief came only by indirect, and characteristically Canadian, means: a spate of conflagrations between 1900 and 1904 burned out some of the competitors and levered up the rate level.

In 1900, embers from a burning village across the river lit Ottawa itself. In 1901 Montreal burned and in 1904 an electrical fault in a Toronto soap factory started a blaze which caused a neighbouring ammunition factory to erupt: the resulting blast destroyed 120 buildings and £1.5 million worth of property.

In itself, this combination of features would have required special managerial approaches from the successful British offices. But low levels of cooperation and high levels of combustion were not the only peculiar aspects of the Canadian market. Unlike almost all other colonial markets, there are signs here of the new-style surplus reinsurance arrangements that were so prevalent in Europe. No doubt, this too was related to the absence of the market-disciplining effect of the local rate associations. Certainly, the British Columbia Land Investment Agency, which received a Phoenix power of attorney in 1898, was a reinsurance brokerage: it worked on 20% commission with '5% overriding to Ceperley'.[131] Ceperley himself was clearly a broker. He was the manager of the Vancouver Loan, Trust, Savings and Guarantee Co. and by 1902 represented not only Phoenix but also the Liverpool & London & Globe, the Scottish Union & National and the British America.[132]

Here are features reminiscent of Europe: the contracts for surpluses with other companies, the proliferation of brokers, the high commissions sufficient to give the broker a chance to negotiate himself a profit. These commissions were a late development but they suggest that, around the century's turn, some features of the advanced insurance market were beginning to infiltrate Phoenix's longest enduring bastion of direct underwriting.

Nevertheless, the vast majority of Canadian trade down to 1914 came by the direct route. And Phoenix was very satisfied with it. In 1909 Phoenix business to the south, in the United States, was sufficiently troublesome to require a visitation from both Gerald Ryan and Edward Boston, the first of the regular transatlantic shuttles carried out by general managers and other senior executives for the rest of Phoenix's life. They found their American underwriting 'so much less successful' than their Canadian operation: 'our Canadian affairs have always been ably and successfully conducted and gave no grounds for anxiety'.[133] However, while Ryan and Boston were trying to diagnose the trouble in the United States, the senior Paterson, 'A. T', died in Montreal. This was considered a sufficiently serious event for the two senior officials to divert to Canada. They found the situation there 'eminently sounder and more satisfactory, partly owing to the fact that we have occupied the field since 1804 and have become a household name among the people'. The other part was that Phoenix had been 'exceptionally well represented' and consequently had gained 'the first position among British fire offices in Canada'. Despite a hazard level no better than the American, despite the absence of

[131] Phoenix Foreign Agents Ledger, C19/2, C19/17, Agency Memorandum 1898.
[132] *Ibid.*
[133] Phoenix General Manager's Report on USA and Canada interleaved Phoenix Directors' Minutes, 29, pp. 39–40, 4 August 1909.

the easy profits imagined by Naylor, and the real problems observed by Dickson, the resulting profit level for Phoenix was 'very gratifying'.[134]

But that, of course, had been in no small part due to A. T. Paterson. The problem now was what to do without him. By 1909, Canada was the *only* Phoenix outpost of major value controlled by a chief agent; every location of similar worth had been given over to a salaried branch manager and a permanent administration. The Sun had introduced branch organisation into Canada in 1892 and started buying into subsidiary companies in 1916. Commercial Union, true to its dynamic organisational policy, had maintained a branch organisation in Canada from as early as 1887. Armed with the Paterson organisation, Phoenix had simply needed no better weapon. But with the premier entrepreneurial figure in that organisation removed, Ryan and Boston reasoned that it was safer to replace individual brilliance with collective administrative power. That is, they applied the conventional structural wisdom of the day: in 1910, the Phoenix operation in Canada became a branch. But, even then, Phoenix did not sacrifice individuality, for the joint managers of Phoenix Canada for many years after 1910 were the two sons of A. T. Paterson.

Government did little to help in the profitable running of insurance business in Canada. Protectionist activity began early, with substantial deposit requirements being imposed by legislation in 1860, 1868 and 1873. The Registration Act of 1860 demanded a deposit of $50,000 and this was roughly the level maintained by Phoenix in Canadian government stocks and railway bonds down to 1900. Clearly, Canadian government took its cue from the punitive tactics of the American legislature: these were not the modest deposits to be found in other Commonwealth countries; they were seriously non-trivial. As in South America, it was the level of the state exactions, anyway much more harmful here, which frightened the Sun away from Canadian business for so many years. With interests much longer established in Canada, Phoenix could only wince and pay up. After 1900 both the pain and the expenditure intensified. Between 1901 and 1912, Phoenix was required to top up its Canadian deposits on no fewer than eight occasions and in sums totalling at least a further £85,000. Canadian insurance protectionism in 1914 was probably second only to the American in aggressiveness.

These apparently similar agrarian-colonial economies in reality proved very different insurance markets. New Zealand was a sobre and disciplined place, though with some troublesome local competition; Australia was the least disciplined of all, with a major brokerage and discount

[134] *Ibid.*

problem; South Africa was well controlled in insurance terms but less stable in general economic terms; Canada was highly traditional in its levels of agency activity and, occasionally, its levels of fire hazard, but rather modern in its incidence of surplus reinsurance and protectionist deposits. In three cases, local rates associations provided a vital market-controlling function; but not in Canada. In every case the branch organisation supplied the form for Phoenix's structural adaptation to increasingly complex markets, awash with intermediaries of all kinds; but this happened much later in Canada than elsewhere. However, in all these markets, and many others, the period 1890–1905 emerges clearly as an era of reform in Phoenix's foreign operation. Overhaul of agency appointments, proliferation of sub-agencies, promotion of local agents' associations, transition to branch operation mark these years as distinctive.

8. THE FAR EAST: VARIETY GALORE

Phoenix's operation in the Far East, or at least part of it, resembled the Canadian in deriving from an earlier phase of agency expansion. The company first entered this region with the appointment of Bruce, Allen & Co. at Calcutta in 1827. This was long before Dalhousie's subjugation of great tracts of India to explicit British domination, and long before the Mutiny and the assumption of Crown rule in 1858. Nevertheless, Calcutta proved the most promising insurance market in India and the Phoenix agency there reported an almost unbroken string of premium receipts – there were hiccoughs in the 1830s and in 1860 – throughout the period 1829–70. By mid-century, Phoenix was already expanding its Indian network with new appointments at Madras and Bombay in 1858 and at Karachi in 1864, while the long-running Calcutta agency was overhauled in 1862.[135] By contrast, the Sun, which Dickson presents as a pioneer in the eastern markets, did not establish its first agency presence in Calcutta until 1852.[136] On the other hand, the Commercial Union, active here as everywhere in branch organisation, had created a branch at Calcutta by 1870, within its first decade of life, and had added two more before the century's turn, one at Bombay in 1893, the other at Madras in 1897.[137]

However, the Far Eastern market, stretching from India through Ceylon and Burma to Siam and Cochin-China, from the Straits of Malacca through Java and the Philippines to the Chinese treaty ports and Japan, was too vast to be reduced to any single pattern. In the small matter of pioneering, for instance, the Sun beat the Phoenix into the vital

[135] See vol. I, p. 312. [136] Dickson, *Sun Insurance*, p. 192.
[137] Liveing, *Commercial Union Assurance*, p. 57.

insurance centre of Shanghai by six years (1852 against 1858), into the valuable one of Manila, also by six years (1865 against 1871) and into the much less important one of Hong Kong by ten years (1852 against 1862). But, in return, Phoenix outpaced the Sun into Singapore by eleven years (1855 against 1866), into Java by five (1852 against 1857), into Penang by four (1861 against 1865), and into the overwhelmingly significant location of Yokohama by about twelve months (1863 and 1864). Yet by 1870 Phoenix did not possess a consistent presence throughout the region: part of its network was of venerable pedigree, part very recent, part still to be established. By 1914, following from this, the office was represented here in a variety of ways: there was a major Far Eastern branch centred on Shanghai; there were chief agencies, notably in Japan; there were strings of general agencies.

The great geographical span and economic heterogeneity of the Indian Ocean and Pacific Basin markets was reflected also in the rapid multiplication of Phoenix outlets: there were eleven in 1870, fifteen in 1880, seventeen in 1890, twenty-one in 1900, thirty-seven in 1910. Some were appointments in new places, such as Samarang in 1882, Rangoon in 1883, Padang in 1893, Bangkok in 1898 or Iloilo in 1901, others represented doubling up or tripling up of agencies in key centres such as Calcutta, Shanghai, or, soon after the initial appointment, Rangoon. Again, as in many other markets, a spate of reformist activity is clearly located around 1900. However, the emphasis here seems to be on an intensification of existing capacity. New creations in the 1890s and 1900s were concentrated upon Indo-China and South-East Asia. There was no further locational initiative in the Indian subcontinent after the creation of the Kandy agency in 1884, while in China only Tientsin in 1893 and in Japan Kobe in 1903 rated fresh and full agency appointments. Much of the intensification came in the form of networks of sub-agencies and broker connections.

The disparities of position and prospect among the economies of this huge area makes any generalisation about trends in trading opportunities distinctly problematic. The apparently enticing commercial possibilities such as the natural entrepots of Hong Kong, secured as a Crown Colony in 1843, or Singapore, which came under direct Colonial Office rule as part of the Straits Settlement in 1867, proved disappointing. Although they certainly became increasingly busy and sensitive cross-roads in the worldwide expansion of trade, they did not achieve commensurate rank as centres of insurance before 1914.[138] The Chinese Treaty Ports, exposed

[138] This was not true for the Commercial Union which selected Singapore as the centre for its Far Eastern Branch in 1894. *Ibid.*, p. 58.

to international commerce by the classic gunboat diplomacy of the mid-century, were within decades providing efficient conduits for outgoing tea and incoming capital and manufactures. Perhaps surprisingly, they also proved first-rate fire insurance markets: Shanghai, for instance, became a metropolis for both Sun and Phoenix and for many other offices.

Yet, generally speaking, the richest business in these markets was generated by industry rather than by commerce. No doubt from the 1860s the British offices were following the adventurous trail blazed by German and Dutch, as well as British, merchant houses to Siam, Java or the Philippines in search of spice, timber, sugar or coffee; but they netted more receipts where the tempo was dictated by loom or lathe. That was true even of the treaty ports, where much western capital went into creating enclaves of modern mill technology, almost entirely quarantined from the handicraft trades and peasant cultivations of the interior. It was true too of industrial prospects in some apparently unlikely places: saw mills in Burma, rice mills in Siam, paper mills in Batavia. The FOC expended many hours head-scratching between 1885 and 1900 in the attempt to rate such installations. But it was most true of the increasing manufacturing capacity of India and Japan.

Here the limited and familiar lines in warehouse and residential risks, the stock-in-trade of the less developed economy, were entirely overtaken by the upsurge of factories and workshops mass-producing cheap goods for the markets of Europe and America. The 'goods for export, consisting of cocoa-nut oil and fibre, and a little cotton' derived from the Rajah of Travancore's territory on the southwest coast of Hindustan in 1858 had become a lot of cotton derived from many Indian locations by the 1880s. During that decade and the next, the FOC was permanently attentive to the rating of Indian manufacturing risks, whether they were jute or cotton presses, screwhouses or ginning factories in Calcutta, or, for domestic consumption, corn or flour mills in Bombay or Bengal. During the 1880s as well British trade into India swelled to proportions which established the Raj as one of the motherland's most vital markets.

Yet India in 1914 was still a semi-industrialised satellite economy. Japan, by contrast, stood in that year as the first heavily industrialised economy in Asia. Opened to western influence after the Meiji Restoration and the end of feudal rule in 1868, Japan witnessed the effects of economic imperialism in China and declined to go down the same road. The most effective way to evade colonialisation at the hands of the industrial powers was to industrialise on one's own account. Accordingly, the reformers of the Meiji Era (1868–1912), built a new economy based upon the export of cheap cottons, raw and reeled silk and Japanese handicraft

Table 2.17. *The Far Eastern market: average annual premiums and share in Phoenix total foreign income, 1871–1914*

	Average premium (£)	% Total of total foreign income
1871–5	17,078	7.3
1876–80	12,427	4.8
1881–5	12,188	2.7
1886–90	12,883	2.2
1891–5	16,355	2.1
1896–1900	27,897	3.3
1901–5	39,093	3.4
1906–10	119,919	8.5
1911–15	132,193	8.3

Source: Calculated from Review of Foreign Agencies, Books 1–4.

products. Between 1880 and 1910, in one of the most rapid exercises in technological absorption on record, Japanese industrialists borrowed exactly and brilliantly from western manufacturing practice. By the 1880s the Japanese economy was accelerating fast. By the 1900s, it was moving into the heavier and machine industries such as steel and shipbuilding. By 1910, on any reckoning, it had successfully 'taken off'. This was the strongest economic performance in the Far East in this half century. It created much that needed insuring.

Despite these forceful developments, however, the pattern of Phoenix's premium earnings from the Far East 1870–1914 was not one of uniform advance. Indeed, the Great Depression of 1873–96 seems to have had a more marked effect on this market than on any other, remarkably in view of its great diversity (see Table 2.17). Decline in the world demand for silk, indigo and opium cut a swathe across economies of many types and the insurers were among those to suffer. For Phoenix, both average money premiums and the region's share in total company earnings dipped sharply after 1875 and witnessed no secure recovery before 1905.

Unfortunately, too, there was little diversity in the way widely separated outposts reacted to these troubles: almost all Phoenix's leading agencies in the region witnessed severe contraction in the late 1870s and stagnation throughout the 1880s. Again the great majority of individual agencies saw retreat in both their currency takings and their shares of Phoenix total foreign income (see Table 2.18). The downturn was particularly severe in

Table 2.18. *The five leading Phoenix agencies in the Far East, 1871–1914 (£, average annual premiums; % total Phoenix foreign income)*

	Yokohama		Shanghai		Calcutta		Bombay		Rangoon	
	£	%	£	%	£	%	£	%	£	%
1871–5	6,185	2.6	2,482	1.0	2,775	1.2	1,399	0.6	–	–
1876–80	3,863	1.5	1,682	0.6	1,796	0.7	1,627	0.6	–	–
1881–5	3,422	0.8	999	0.2	2,328	0.5	1,679	0.3	173	0.04
1886–90	2,944	0.5	562	0.1	2,410	0.4	2,837	0.3	723	0.1
1891–5	3,528	0.5	722	0.1	4,657	0.6	2,763	0.4	1,641	0.2
1896–1900	5,724	0.6	3,073	0.4	8,109	0.9	5,191	0.6	2,585	0.3
1901–5	10,531	0.9	6,642	0.5	8,097	0.7	4,497	0.3	3,483	0.3
1906–10	28,986	1.9	11,189	0.8[a]	11,179	0.8	6,556	0.5	7,144	0.5
1911–15	23,853	1.5	11,260	0.7[a]	7,836	0.5	13,224	0.8	9,538	0.6

Note: [a]In addition, the new Far Eastern Branch at Shanghai produced takings of £37,423 for 1906–10 and £45,938 for 1911–15.

Shanghai and only Bombay showed any ability to resist. However, the recovery was strong after 1891; and it was equally well spread. Indeed, the industrial drive in Japan, a further manufacturing upswing in India and commercial expansion in China brought results from Tokyo, Calcutta, Shanghai and the Shanghai-based Far Eastern Branch that were little short of spectacular.

If total Phoenix foreign income is broken down by agency groups for the quinquennium 1911–15, the Far Eastern Branch alone ranks fifth, after the United States, Canadian, Australian and German groups and ahead of the New Zealand and Russian; and Japan alone ranks eighth after Russia. If the comparison is organised by entire market areas, the aggregate for the Far East in 1911–15 ranks fourth, after the United States, Europe and Canada. After dwindling to a meagre 2.1% of total company overseas income in 1891–5, the Far East market rebounded to a peak of nearly 9% in 1906–10. Within the sector, it is significant that the Japanese operation ranked first or second among the Far Eastern agencies in every quinquennium between 1871 and 1915, being outstripped towards the end of the period only by the full Far Eastern Branch. Thus in 1910, when the branch achieved its pre-war peak of premiums with takings of £48,810, the Phoenix organisation in Japan surpassed the combined totals of India, Burma and Ceylon (£24,039) to take second place with £34,615.

Furthermore, Phoenix appears to have been a market leader in the region. Dickson records that the Sun took about £11,000 per year from Calcutta, the most promising Indian market, in the early 1900s. Here Phoenix was close, on about £9,000, and reached the same levels as the Sun in the later 1900s. But in 1910, when the Sun was taking a further £5,000 from a string of eastern agencies in Siam, Cambodia, Indo-China, Malaya, Java, Sumatra and the Philippines, Phoenix was netting almost a third as much again from these places, not to speak of the much larger sums coming in through the Far Eastern Branch.[139]

Phoenix put much thought and energy into this push towards the Orient. This was seen particularly in the way Indian representation was handled during the general foreign reform movement around the turn of the century. With full agency representation already centred on Calcutta, Bombay and Madras, the main requirement was to get more geographical scope and penetration. The answer to this problem, here and in similar locations, was to employ a network of sub-agencies to handle the proliferation of small markets which existed in 'upcountry', 'interior' or 'outback'

[139] Dickson, *Sun Insurance*, pp. 192, 196.

situations. Thus, in 1898, Phoenix made five appointments in the Bombay Presidency alone: they went to a trio of mill agents, a broker and a representative of the Bombay Flour Company. In addition, another sortie established an outpost in Hyderabad for the Nizam's dominions. The next year, three more firms were enlisted to work the Bombay market; no doubt, this was a factor in Bombay's replacement of Calcutta as Phoenix's leading centre in India during the 1910s. At the same time, an additional cordon of influence was thrown out through three agencies ranging widely across Kathiawar, Ujjain, Indore, Bhopal – later to become infamous owing to an industrial risk of a 'higher' technology – Ruttam, Mundessour and the district of Ahmedabad.[140]

Almost all of the Phoenix men in such locations were Indians. Some, like Jamseljee Dorabjee Chinory, a broker in Bombay, were referred to as 'canvassers' and paid a special allowance by the major agency of the region. Chinory himself got 33 rupees a month in 1899, paid through the premier agency in Bombay, Graham & Co. Evidently, Calcutta was more expensive, for 'canvassers' there drew 60 rupees per month, further evidence of this city's status among the insurance markets of India. The major agencies, like that of Graham, would take 20% commission by 1900 on business they drummed up themselves, a net 10% on the 'up-country' sub-agency work, after the canvassers' allowances had been deducted, and a net 15% on similar work reported in from Bombay and its own environs. The strings of sub-agents run by such centres could be numerous. By 1900, the Phoenix centre in Madras was answerable for eighteen sub-agencies scattered throughout the Presidency. Such methods gave good penetration in interiors that were more or less dependable.

Dependability in the centres that ran the sub-agencies was also clearly vital. The institution that provided the highest level of dependability was the large European trading house, well settled into a structure of local expertise, custom and contact. Within economies that were both less developed and complex, information costs inevitably were high. Here sensitive colonial hands were needed to play the useful connections among the indigenous community, to follow the ins and outs of the local markets or quaysides, and at the same time, to maintain as wide a range of relationships as possible with the western interests operating within and through major ports or railheads. A classic case is provided by Phoenix's Madras agents from 1875, Binney & Co. This celebrated merchant house by 1902 represented a shrewdly balanced array of insurance offices, the

[140] Phoenix Directors' Minutes, 26, pp. 255, 293, 295, 317, 19 January, 3 and 17 August, 21 December 1898.

Singapore Insurance Co., the China Fire, and the Netherlands Sea and Fire, all no doubt because of trading connections within the greater eastern market, but also a generously imperial selection of British companies, the Lion, the Manchester and Palatine, the Atlas, the Scottish Union and National and the Yorkshire as well as the Phoenix, a far greater power than any of these.

At the much more valuable outpost of Rangoon, among Phoenix's top earners in the Far East – which Madras was not – another mercantile enterprise, Finlay Fleming & Co., played a comparable role. Perhaps because they were better at it – the Phoenix returns from Rangoon suggest either this or a richer market – Finlay Fleming represented a more formidable group: not only Phoenix but also the Royal Exchange, the Lancashire, the Manchester and the South British, as well as the Batavia Sea & Fire.

However, the case we know most about, for the accidental reason that a company prospectus survives, is Carson & Co., merchants and Phoenix agents of Colombo. For similarly accidental reasons, a surviving prospectus gave us an insight into the dealings of the Mackenzie agency in Italy. Carsons were not in the same league but they do provide a matching porthole onto an oriental scene. Beginning as a small merchant venture in 1857, Carsons rated themselves by the century's end as 'one of the leading and most substantial businesses in Ceylon'. They maintained offices in Australia Buildings, Columbo, a depot at Kew Lane, Slave Island and a senior partner to represent the firm's interests in London. They styled themselves 'Import and Export Merchants and Steamship Agents'. They imported Australian hardwood, Welsh and Indian coal for the steamships and Manchester piece-goods on the largest scale; and they were a force in the export of tea, representing six tea companies, mostly London or Manchester firms operating plantations in Ceylon. Their marine interests included one of the institutions of the Indian Ocean and the Bay of Bengal, 'so extensively patronised by Ceylon and Southern Indian passengers', the 'Bibby Line' (H. C. Bibby was one of Carsons' resident partners in Colombo); it also included another legend for efficiency, the Nippon Yusen Kaisha (Japan Mail Steamship Company). These connections were important for 'both lines are favourites with the Ceylon shippers, owing to the strict regularity of their respective services, and annually convey a very large proportion of the island's produce'. On top of this, Carsons also represented two powerful Liverpool shipping interests, Ismay Imrie and White Star. For good measure, they held twenty-two agencies of a more general sort. They could fairly be said to have penetrated the grain of the trade in and out of Ceylon.

Phoenix encountered Carsons in 1880 when they sacked their earlier agents in Colombo for having remitted no business, nor answered any letters for the previous four years.[141] The company must have been pleased with the change. Before 1914, business from Colombo was never lavish. But in the 1870s it had run only to pence; by the 1900s it was in hundreds of pounds; and by the 1910s in thousands. In the process, Carsons became modest specialists in insurance, adding not only Phoenix but also London Assurance, Union Marine and Tokyo Marine to their catholic array of agencies. Here again,it is interesting to see the maritime and Japanese connections surfacing among the insurance commitments. It was, of course, precisely such links arising out of other mercantile interests that the insurers were trying to tap.

Phoenix did so with a will right across Asia. They chose a solicitor for Kandy in 1883 and mill agents at Bombay in 1898 but they appointed merchants by the dozen: to Bombay in 1873, Singapore in 1882, Rangoon in 1883, Foo Chow in 1892, Padang in 1893, Madras in 1895, Iloilo and Hankow in 1900 and the Dutch manager of the Merchants' Bank in Java in 1882. The logic is clear and well symbolised by the careers of the Binneys, Finlay Flemings and Carsons.

Within this logic fell the most important appointments of all. By the 1900s some parts of the Indian networks were beginning to require more discipline. The Sun, although somewhat late into the market, was characteristically quick to see the organisational point and responded in characteristic style: in 1897 it purchased a local subsidiary, the Asiatic of Bombay and employed it as the nucleus for a new branch structure.[142] From January 1903 Phoenix also maintained a Branch in India with managerial powers over the Bombay Presidency, Northwest Province, Oudh, Punjab, Bangalore and Calicut. Phoenix's logic was different from that of the Sun, for this brief went to an organisation in the mould of Finlay Fleming or Carsons, the Bombay merchant house of W. Graham & Co.[143]

The China trade of Phoenix was also dominated by merchants, general and specialised. A handful of long-standing merchant connections provided the vanguard for Phoenix's operations among the ports of coast and river from the 1870s and 1880s and into the 1900s. Over this period a stream of powers of attorney maintained relations with this group: with Evans, Pugh & Co., merchants of Hankow, well up the Yangtze, deep in

[141] Phoenix Directors' Minutes W22, p. 444, 4 February 1880; Trustees' Minutes, 29 January 1880.

[142] Dickson, *Sun Insurance*, p. 193.

[143] Phoenix Directors' Minutes, 27, p. 167, 28 January 1903.

the interior of Wuhan Province;[144] with W. S. Ward & Co. and Hatch & Co., general merchants at Tientsin, in the Gulf of Chihli,[145] on the North China coast; with H. S. Brand & Co, merchants at Foochow, at the mouth of the Formosa Strait;[146] and with Westall, Little & Co.[147] and the China & Japan Trading Co.[148] for the great harbour of Shanghai in the estuary of the Yangtze Kiang. These agencies were potentially valuable but widely dispersed; they were the classic outposts looped along an extended coastline and up great rivers; and they needed more coordination. This time Phoenix provided it by infiltrating their own man into the merchant community of Shanghai, a city viewed as 'the lodestone of the Orient' or the 'Whore of Asia' depending on perspective.

The company had appointed W. H. Crombie as a Foreign Inspector 'chiefly for the East' in 1903.[149] Late in 1905 he was inspecting in Australia. At about the same time, Phoenix was deciding to create a Far Eastern branch with its headquarters in Shanghai and Crombie as manager.[150] Shanghai had been the first of the treaty ports to experience the enforced concession of western trade, at the hands of the British immediately after the end of the first Opium War in 1842, and of the Americans and French from 1843. By the 1900s the great banking palaces and merchant houses along the Bund were rooted in granite and marble and the many factories were well embarked on the process which made Shanghai what it still remains: the premier industrial city of China. Symptomatically, also, its riverside park from 1885 had sported the infamous notice: 'No admittance to Dogs and Chinese.' It was imperial Britain's sea-gate to the East.[151]

For Phoenix, the Shanghai station was intended to give organisational coherence to the agencies in Siam, Borneo, Cambodia, the Dutch East Indies, the Philippines, Malaya, Indo-China, Hong Kong, Korea, Japan and the China treaty ports. Not surprisingly, the manager's job entailed much travelling on slow boats to and from China; and on some of these the only way to avoid cholera, or something as bad, was a religious diet of Scotch and hard tack. Nevertheless, Crombie survived in the post from 1906 until 1927, and was very successful. Here the Sun followed an

144 *Ibid.*, V21, p. 321, 8 October 1873; 26, p. 410, 9 May 1910; 28, p. 17, 14 November 1906.
145 *Ibid.*, Z25, p. 224, 2 September 1891; 26, p. 328, 15 February 1899; 27, p. 184, 29 April 1903; 30, p. 311, 9 April 1913.
146 *Ibid.*, p. 318, 10 August 1892; 27, p. 79, 19 February 1902.
147 *Ibid.* Y24, p. 155, 9 December 1885; Z25, p. 445, 31 January 1894; 27, p. 124, 26 February 1902.
148 *Ibid.*, 27, p. 292, 19 October 1904.
149 Phoenix Trustees' Minutes, p. 210, 29 July 1903.
150 *Ibid.*, p. 292, 25 October 1905.
151 Colin Thubron, *Behind the Wall* (London, 1988), ch. 5.

identical pattern: it too created a Far Eastern branch, also in Shanghai, also in 1906. The Commercial Union followed suit two years later.[152] No doubt, too, their managers spent many weeks on slow boats, fending off disease.

Crombie and the Far Eastern Branch were very active in their first decade. More merchants, often with more than one home base, were brought in to give additional capacity in existing Phoenix locations: Shewan, Tomes & Co. of Hong Kong and Tientsin, at Tientsin in 1908,[153] Liddell Brothers of Shanghai, Tientsin and Hankow, 'Press-packers and Merchants', for Hankow and district in 1908,[154] and Welch, Lewis and Co. at Shanghai in the same year,[155] Roughly contemporaneously with the creation of the branch, further merchant-agencies were set up in new locations: Messrs E. Bollweg & Co., merchants of Hamburg and Tsingtau, for the Shantung Peninsula on the northwest coast of the Yellow Sea in 1905;[156] E. Meyer & Co. for Tsingtau, on the southern side of the same peninsula in 1908;[157] J. Jasperson & Co. for Newchwang on the Manchurian coast also in 1909.[158]

The period 1905–8 was clearly one of reorganisation and expansion in Phoenix's China trade. And, clearly, it paid off. In 1905, Chinese takings came from four ports and totalled slightly more than 1% of Phoenix overseas earnings. By 1915, receipts were gathered from eleven separate Chinese agencies and totalled nearly 4% of the company's overseas earnings. Back in London, the Board were themselves sensitive to the value of these Chinese developments: in October 1908 they 'received the Chinese Ambassador, Lord Li Ching Fang, accompanied by his Secretary, Mr Ivan Chen, and entertained them to luncheon in the Library of Phoenix House'.[159]

The China hands, India hands and island hands, despite the variety of locations and economies in which they found themselves, confronted some similar problems. For a start, customer resistance to insurance could be pronounced among native communities. The Chinese, members of a society in which fatalism and secret clan organisations were the norms of life, did not take to the idea. And elsewhere there were theological reservations: the Sun found in Java that, 'the Natives, being Mahomedans, it is contrary to their creed to insure'.[160] Such influences had the effect in many locations of producing segregated markets: a native

[152] Liveing, *Commercial Union*, p. 108.
[153] Phoenix Directors' Minutes, 28, p. 256, 1 July 1908.
[154] *Ibid.*, 28, p. 293, 9 September 1908. [155] *Ibid.*, 28, p. 229, 13 May 1908.
[156] *Ibid.*, 27, p. 348, 28 June 1905. [157] *Ibid.*, 28, p. 159, 15 January 1908.
[158] *Ibid.*, 28, p. 200, 18 March 1908. [159] *Ibid.*, 28, p. 326, 28 October 1908.
[160] Cited by Dickson, *Sun Insurance*, p. 194.

market in which comparatively little business was written and a European, largely mercantile or manufacturing, market where the bulk of trade was sought. This bifurcation was often reinforced by divergent standards of construction in the two markets. At the beginning of the period, risks at Bombay were divided into three classes: country houses; property in the native part of the fort; and property in the European part. Madras had four classes and had been reminded of their necessity by a fire of 1856 which had destroyed £200,000 worth of buildings in the 'Mogul or Native portion of the Town, quite distinct from the European part, and from the merchants' stores. No loss was thus sustained by them . . . the English stores are all stone and each firm has its own compound.'[161] Such problems were long lived. In 1896 the FOC refused a request from the Pondicherry Chamber of Commerce to rate godowns in the European quarter of Madras at the ordinary town rate and godowns (warehouses) elsewhere at the rate for the native quarter; the distinctions were reckoned to be more complex even than this.[162] Equally complex shadings occurred in Burma, Hong Kong, Indo-China and the treaty ports.

The extension of industrial risks into such locations added another dimension of intricacy. As factories multiplied within less developed economies, they produced insurance problems which were uncanny echoes of those generated by the early phases of the British Industrial Revolution. Thus, in the 1890s, jute or cotton manufacturers in India, faced with seasonal patterns of activity, made the same pleas for the reduction of premiums on behalf of their 'silent mills' as had emanated from their British counterparts a half-century and more before. The underwriters returned the same answer: no concessions.[163]

Another industrial reprise was multiple tenure: the development of multi-purpose buildings occupied by sundry manufacturers and merchants. This problem had first arisen in the British industrial heartland at the end of the eighteenth century, but it was widely reiterated in the Far East at the end of the nineteenth. In Hong Kong and Shanghai in 1896 the FOC took its usual stern line on this point too: the highest rate applicable to any one risk should be charged for the whole. Stern also was the response of the British offices to the persistent requests from merchants and manufacturers in oriental climes for the financial support of fire brigades. In Madras in 1887 the tariff offices flatly refused to contribute; and in Manila in 1895 a suggestion for a fire-fighting subsidy financed by a deduction from premiums was turned down by the FOC, 'it

[161] Note from Northern to Phoenix, undated, 1856.
[162] FOC (Foreign) Minutes, 31 October 1896.
[163] *Ibid.*, 11 May 1894. See also vol. I, pp. 357–60, 411–12.

being contrary to the practice of the offices'.[164] This resistance, of course, also repeated – somewhat more authoritatively – a reluctance which the insurers had displayed at home earlier in the century.

The march of technology did not only complicate the problems of climate and place; it also offered some remedies. Fire-proofing, extinguishers and automatic sprinklers all came into increasing use in the 1880s and 1890s. But, inevitably, these also carried their own complications, mainly in the form of pressure, once more, for reduced rates. During the middle 1890s the FOC was occupied in almost permanent discussion of whether allowances should be made in respect of sprinklers in Burmese rice mills, East Indian cotton factories, Calcutta jute presses or Bombay corn mills.[165] Their reservations were understandable. In 1895, they wrote more in sorrow than in anger to the Ahmedabad Ginning and Manufacturing Co. enquiring as to why the firm's sprinklers had failed to go off during a recent fire.[166] A similar question posed in Shanghai in the next year received a straightforward answer: they could not be connected to the town's water supply. A proposal that they should use instead unfiltered river water was met with horror.[167] Presumably, the offices did not regard the substitution of fire hazard by cholera hazard as a reasonable exchange.

All of these features were related, of course, to the relatively less developed status of most Far Eastern markets at this time. However, this level of development also carried some credit features for the western insurers. For a start, these markets were not expensive to run. Commission rates were modest and rose slowly. From the 1860s until the mid-1890s, Phoenix paid its agents right across Asia only 10% on premiums and only a handful of them received additional commissions contingent on profits before the 1880s. After 1895, in step with accelerating activity in the oriental market, there was a general rise in commissions to around 15% and a slight increase in the frequency of contingencies. But, by European or North American standards, this was distinctly restrained. The reason was clearly not lack of competition; there was plenty of that. Rather, perhaps, it was a relatively lower density of intermediaries and brokers in somewhat less sophisticated markets. Also, no doubt, the wide scatter of many discrete, often small, sometimes isolated, insurance markets in this region damped tendencies towards the escalation of commissions.

For the offices, a still more valuable characteristic of the region was the

[164] *Ibid.*, 4 November 1887, 3 May 1895.
[165] *Ibid.*, 4 November 1892, 12 May 1893, 4 October 1895, 31 January and 1 May 1896.
[166] *Ibid.*, 5 July 1895. [167] *Ibid.*, 15 October 1896.

low level of government interference. India charged stamp duty from 1879 and income tax from 1886; Singapore also had stamp duty; and from 1892 the Philippines imposed a tax on profits. But, generally, taxation was light; there was little pressure to publish accounts; and, before 1900, deposits were not in evidence. Fittingly, the most developed economy in the region, Japan, opened the serious bowling for the government side with the introduction of a deposit scheme in 1903. This was enough to frighten the Manchester Fire out of the Japanese market. But Phoenix, more inured to such impositions, paid up – and took over Manchester's Japanese account.[168] This seems anyway to have been an isolated offensive on a batsman's wicket. Dickson, who is commendably sensitive to the issue of protectionism, makes no mention of its presence in India, South-East Asia or China and the Phoenix archive adds only a little of substance. For most of this period, the inference is that the greater part of Asia was effectively a free trade area for the insurer.

As with many regions where moderate levels of economic development, modest costs and restrained government tactics combined, the over-riding problem for the insurance exporter was provided by other insurance exporters. In some of these discrete eastern markets, there could be very many of them. In the relatively limited market of Java by 1862, for instance, there were nine British and fifteen Dutch offices. A proliferation of agencies and a Dutch ascendancy made the going hard for all British competitors. In Singapore at the same time, the proportions were different – eighteen British and nine Dutch – but the problem was the same, and worsened in the 1870s and 1880s with further multiplication of agencies.

Here, too, new formations of local companies added to the problem. One, the Anglo-Chinese Singapore Insurance Co. of 1885, was much feared since it drew on both British and Chinese capital and 'nearly everyone has become a shareholder';[169] but it lasted only seven years. The pattern was the same in Hong Kong. When the Sun set up shop there in 1852, it made up a foursome of British offices. By 1865, almost every British company worth its salt had a Hong Kong agency, and Phoenix had joined this elite. Many of its members then used Hong Kong as a base from which to sprinkle sub-agencies along the coast to Macao, Foochow or as far as Tientsin.[170] Local offices had their say here as well. Often they were backed by great merchant interests like the Sassoons, Jardines or Mathesons who were impatient of the caution of the London offices, finding that it sometimes impeded their own ability to obtain cover.

[168] Phoenix Trustees' Minutes, p. 212, 12 August 1903.
[169] Cited by Dickson, *Sun Insurance*, pp. 194–5. [170] *Ibid.*, p. 193.

The only way of making sense of this ferment, particularly in areas of high natural hazard, was by cooperation among the hosts of local agents. The Far East was a classic terrain for the local agents' associations. Cooperation began very early. Regular conversations to concert rates and interpret tariffs were held by the Indian agents of British offices from the 1860s. Similar discussions were held in Shanghai and Hong Kong in the same decade. Those companies early into Japan – which included Phoenix in 1863 and Sun in 1864, both at Yokohama – were greatly encouraged to compare notes by the Yokohama fire which destroyed the port in 1866, soon after their arrival. Even without such forceful persuasion, conversations rapidly grew into regular associations: Bombay had a formal agents' association by 1882, Calcutta by 1888, Madras, Rangoon and Nagasaki by 1890.

China had experienced very low premiums and heavy competition from local Hong Kong based offices in the 1870s and 1880s; and the FOC had retaliated by suspending all tariffs. This was sufficient to produce first consternation, then cooperation at the local level: agents' associations were formed at Shanghai and Hong Kong in the early 1890s. In Japan, where the earthquake hazard was a standing inducement to coordination among agents, a Fire Insurers' Association was formed at the underwriting centre of Yokohama in 1896. Almost simultaneously, the Singapore market – which, like Hong Kong, had experienced much activity from local offices financed by dissatisfied mercantile interests – decided that such an association might 'do away with the "cutting out" war which has been carried on more or less for years'.[171]

The middle 1890s saw a massive overhaul of its Far Eastern organisation by the FOC. Around 1895–6, agents' associations were either founded or reinforced at a great string of locations right across the East, from Madras to Nagasaki. Partly, this was to consolidate a successful defence against a 'merchants' revolt' in some centres, partly it was to take stock of a few powerful local offices which had survived the defence. Many of these offices were connected with big western merchant houses. Although, the London insurers appointed outstanding merchants as their agents in many Far Eastern markets, in some like Hong Kong and Singapore the very biggest merchant ventures resented both the intrusion and the prudence of metropolitan capital. These houses had wealth and local knowledge; they believed that they could cover more risks, with more safety and less hesitation, than the London offices.

For the most part, they were wrong, and many of the merchant-backed

[171] Cited by Dickson, *Sun Insurance*, p. 195.

competitors, such as the Singapore Insurance Co. or the Victoria of Hong Kong were driven into the ground by the tariff offices. Some, however, like the China Fire Insurance Co., launched in 1870 by the doyens of the Hong Kong trading community, were not so easily disposed of. Nowhere was it comfortable for the London offices to encounter the highest of the colonial plutocracy, the mighty Mathesons, Sassoons, Dents, or Whittalls, from the wrong side of the market. Accommodation with this sort of competition – as with other local competition, and with foreign competitors like the Germans, who arrived in the China market in the 1880s – was the purpose of the association movement of the 1890s. The unusual collision between British metropolitan capital and British colonial capital was only one phase of this sequence but a most interesting phase.

Just as in the other markets where local associations predominated, the structure of underwriting which emerged was a three-tier system. The FOC in London devised the initial guidelines; the local association coordinated the holding of the line in the market; the agent presented the result at the point of sale. If there was trouble in the market, the association and the FOC cooperated to deliver counterfire in both metropolitan and peripheral locations. In practice, too, the guidelines were defined by an interplay of influences between London and the distant market. In the special conditions of the Far East, London often had to take the local association's word for it and trust to local expertise. The association would set tariffs which would then be adopted by the FOC. This happened frequently in China and Japan, as at Shanghai in 1895 and, in the active year 1896, at Tientsin, Hankow and Chefoo in the one case, and at Nagasaki, Kobe and Yokohama in the other.

Sometimes, of course, London would insist. In China in the 1880s, at Singapore in 1886 or at Hiogo in 1887, when the competition of local non-tariff offices became too sharp, it simply ordered the suspension of the tariff.[172] Similarly, at Calcutta in 1889, when the problem was again local competition, the association of agents was minded to meet the non-tariff operators half-way with a discretionary 10% discount; but the FOC was not inclined towards such weakness and flatly refused.[173] Discounts in any form drew the wrath of London, although local interests might sometimes favour them for the purpose of a quick advantage. As at Calcutta in 1896, the FOC was liable to ask a local association to 'fully investigate' any suspicion that agents were achieving a covert discount by sharing their commission with the insured.[174] Indeed, in that year the Phoenix agents at Calcutta were caught in the act of allowing a 5%

[172] FOC (Foreign) Minutes, 19 November 1886, 1 August 1887.
[173] *Ibid.*, 22 November 1889. [174] *Ibid.*, 4 December 1896.

discount to a local jute press owner. The agents' association came down on them with a stern reprimand, and the FOC in London – including Phoenix, in a characteristic disavowal by a head office of an undisciplined subordinate – united 'in condemning this unauthorised proceeding'.[175]

Further, the FOC could order the deployment of the reinsurance weapon, as it had in Argentina and New Zealand. This was a way both of hurting local competitors who needed this service and of preventing excessive fraternisation by the agents of tariff offices. Thus resolutions of 1884 and 1887 forbade associations in the East Indies from providing reinsurance services for non-tariff offices. And in the 1890s a ban was imposed on reinsurance transactions with Bombay and Calcutta offices which were not members of the associations for those cities. However, such restrictions were often disliked by agents who saw reinsurance arrangements as part of the necessary diplomacy of give-and-take in distant markets, and London came under increasing pressure to show flexibility in this respect. By 1895 the Calcutta association was justifying reinsurance transactions between tariff and non-tariff offices on business that both parties transacted at tariff rates. And London accepted the point. Over time it did so increasingly. Associations were left to meet non-tariff competition by discreet manipulation of local tariff regulations and to take the critical decisions in the light of the prevailing tactical realities at the point of sale.

This tacit migration of initiative to the periphery was somewhat complicated, especially in the many markets of the Far East, by a technological miracle: the electric telegraph. Hypothetically, this improvement in business communications gave London greater ability to track and control developments almost anywhere. Ironically, however, the telegraph at first introduced as many problems as it resolved. FOC members receiving tariff information by telegraph from London were placed at an advantage above members of local agents' associations who were not members of the FOC. This introduced a new game: speculation against impending rate changes and 'forward contracts' with favoured clients. The FOC set its face against such high-technology wickedness and in 1896 sent warnings to a suggestively wide range of places – Bombay, Calcutta, Hong Kong, Karachi, Madras, Manila, Rangoon, Shanghai, Singapore, Tientsin and Yokohama – that it would take a dim view of this new malpractice.

Rather than risk disturbing the precious local unity of the associations, the FOC deployed the telegraph with a prudent and gentle touch – which

[175] *Ibid.*, 2 October 1896.

is not to say that it could not sometimes use the transmitter with force. Undoubtedly, the instrument did allow finer tuning of tariff rates to market conditions. A case in point arose in Yokohama in 1885. The FOC authorised its agents there to deal with troublesome local and non-tariff operators by following their rates down to a new FOC tariff line. Instructions went out by telegram and the response came back by wire:

Tariff agreed. Basis local rates. Majority agents resolved allow 33 discount.

This was the good news. The bad followed:

Locals follow increased discount. Maintain annual bonuses. Conflict inevitable.

This did arouse the FOC to a bout of telegraphic authoritarianism. It was the underwriter's equivalent of *non pasarán*, and just as terse: 'Go no further.'

Generally, however, the head offices accepted the constraints of distance and the word of their agents. The local associations were usually formed upon the initiative of the agents, although with the real if distant approval of the FOC. They were then invited to affiliate to the FOC. The tariffs that were generated came to be framed more by local than by metropolitan influence and were usually taken aboard wholesale by the FOC. The working of the tariff would be monitored both by the association and by the FOC; and the latter would certainly hold and express views on the conduct of the managed market. But most tariff offices recognised most of the time that the association was a better way of reading the foreign trade than the long-distance translation from London. The relatively low level of commissions in the Far East suggest that the associations were indeed effective in controlling competition and preventing the proliferation of intermediaries and discounts that were increasingly the rule in other markets.

Like Canada and Australia, the Far East in the late nineteenth century retained some of the characteristics of the frontier markets in which Phoenix had proved adept from its earliest years. As the great clippers, the many schooners, the spreading railways and the increasingly numerous steamers worked the shores and islands of this newest sector of world commerce, so the underwriters with their agents, local associations and branch offices worked the insurance markets which, even more surely than the flag, followed trade. Phoenix was as adventurous as any London insurer, and certainly as active an orientalist as the Sun, in exploiting this new source of demand. Indeed, the Phoenix Far Eastern Branch by 1914 was a powerful vehicle of insurance, by the standards of any competitor.

9. EVERYWHERE EXCEPT THE USA: CONCLUSION

Phoenix resumed an active foreign policy during a period of transition in both world and insurance markets. Global commerce and investment experienced a phenomenal period of expansion between 1870 and 1914. And the methods of selling insurance worldwide – beginning with agency representation and simple treaty reinsurance and ending with agents' associations, branches, subsidiary companies and broker-directed surplus treaty reinsurance – also underwent great change. Naturally, these two streams of development were related. As distant markets became more specialised, fragmented and complex, as well as richer and busier, so the traditional insurance agent became less able to penetrate to the demand, and, with many more interests available to financial and commercial intermediaries, less committed to doing so. Individual contacts could reach only so far in such markets. Larger scales of organisation were necessary, not only to deal with the competition which greater economic sophistication brought with it, but also to handle the greater volume and width of information. Collective action by agents could usually cope with the niceties of tariff rating and with most of the implications of competition. But branch managers and salaried clerks became increasingly necessary for commitment, width of contact and the daily processing of the information flow.

In no place outside the United States before 1914, did Phoenix follow this logic to the conclusion of acquiring full foreign subsidiaries.[176] A parallel logic did lead it to acquire the foreign business of a small British office, the National Union of Bedford, in 1907. The cost – £3,100 – was trivial but the augmentation of contact and administrative capability was not,[177] for the National Union organisation included about a dozen outlets concentrated in Russia, the Near East, Australia and the Far East.[178] It was not accidental that the biggest of these was in Shanghai. Together National's foreign agencies netted about 0.6% of Phoenix total overseas income over the period 1906–10, about as much as a single substantial agency within Phoenix's own foreign network. Clearly, it was density and range of contact that appealed to Phoenix. And it was

[176] The Patersons' acquisition of the Acadia Fire of Halifax took place in 1915–16. The first recommendation that the company should be acquired at a cost of $60 per share for 10,000 shares was made in July 1914, but the interruption by war delayed completion of the purchase into 1916. Fire Committee Minutes, Book 2, p. 117, 1 July 1914.

[177] Phoenix Directors' Minutes, 28, p. 84, 10 July 1907.

[178] Russia, Constantinople, Smyrna, Alexandria, New South Wales, Victoria, Manila, Rangoon, Singapore, Shanghai, Hankow, Tientsin. The home fire and accident business of the National Union was sold to the London & Lancashire in 1906. The Bedford company went into liquidation in 1907.

significant that much of the National Union's structure was immediately absorbed as building material for Phoenix's Far East Branch.

The three basic tenets of Phoenix foreign policy in this period were: resist and withstand government protectionism; promote membership of local agents' associations; form general agencies supervising strings of sub-agencies wherever possible and transform these into branches where feasible. Foreign subsidiaries for the most part came later, and in this Phoenix was slower than the Sun.

Government protectionism, primarily in the form of insurance deposits, was an under-rated constraint on all British exporters of insurance, particularly in Germany, Canada and the United States. Here Phoenix showed notable hardihood, persevering where others, from the Sun to the Manchester Fire, displayed fainter hearts. Phoenix left no market and was deterred from entering none by the worst that pre-war governments imposed; and that was more than could be said of many offices.

Like all committed exporters, Phoenix forced on the growth of agents' associations wherever they could be persuaded to take root. Outside Europe, where the brokers and the calculus of reinsurance dominated the markets, the growth was prolific, all the way from South America, through the Near East, South Africa and Australia to the Far East, though some soils, like that of Australia, remained resistant and others like that of Canada definitely stony.

The general agency, sprouting arrays of sub-agencies, also proved widely adaptable, thriving in climates as widely different as the Scandinavian, Spanish, Indian and Chinese. Branch development too was strong, with the central cluster of initiatives including Argentina, Australia, New Zealand, South Africa and Bombay falling in the reform period 1885–1903, Shanghai providing a powerful burst of growth from 1906, and Canada, for very good reason, providing a late autumnal yield from 1910. Seven full branches outside the United Kingdom and United States by 1914 was a very creditable harvest. By the late 1900s also, some of the provincial centres were being reinforced by Local Boards of Directors. The minutes of the first Indian meetings in November and December 1907 were read out to the London Board in January 1908; and there were also Australian and Canadian Local Boards by this time.[179] These committees of local dignitaries were intended to gather influence rather than make policy, but they were useful adjuncts to the branches in a context where every little helped. The philosophy in London was: if initiatives in rating and administration

[179] Phoenix Directors' Minutes, 28, p. 150, 1 January 1908.

had to be devolved to the periphery, then initiative might as well be made effective at all levels.

If the period 1870–1914 was a transitional stage in the history of insurance exportation, it was also a discrete stage in Phoenix's corporate development. The office, like most big British insurers, was by 1870 already a fully international business, and, as the pioneer of exportation in fire insurance, had been so for longer than any other office. However, in the 1870s and 1880s the insurers relied predominantly on agency representation overseas, and businesses which did this, rather than operating directly owned manufacturing or service bases overseas, were not strictly multinational companies. On the other hand, as the requirements of managerial supervision pressed them increasingly towards the creation of overseas branches, they approached nearer to this status. Yet they still differed from the true multinationals in explosives, oil and armaments that were developing in the manufacturing sector around the turn of the century.[180] A further stage was needed to make the resemblance closer. As fiscal protectionism sucked the underwriters further into the foreign markets, to the point where they absorbed whole foreign companies, their offices became multinationals by the most demanding criteria. Phoenix had experienced all of these pressures by 1914. Within the American market, it had already graduated to full multinational status. Elsewhere, notably in the Argentine and Canada, it trembled on the brink of corporate acquisition.

But this was not the only way in which the Phoenix overseas sales effort carried important implications for the office's corporate evolution. The agency system on which Phoenix and other large insurers relied for the bulk of their foreign underwriting in 1914 was already yielding to branches and subsidiaries. Nevertheless, it could be a sales weapon of great strength. This of course depended on the quality of the individual or the form of the enterprise to which the agencies – especially general agencies – were awarded. It is clear in the case of Phoenix that the choice between 1870 and 1914 often fell on merchant houses of the first rank, and indeed, more than that, on leading practitioners of the 'managing agency system' and even on what S. D. Chapman has dubbed 'the British-based investment group'.[181] General agencies, of course, could operate within Europe, but the managing agencies and the investment groups usually roved further afield.

The aim of the managing agency was diversification in production,

[180] Examples are the Anglo-German Nobel Dynamite Trust, Standard Oil, Dunlop, Vickers, Armstrong. All these controlled foreign manufacturing subsidiaries by 1914.

[181] Chapman, 'British-based Investment Groups', p. 235.

trade and financial services: it strove to monopolise as much of the industrial, commercial and financial business of a given region as possible. As well as its own production, trading or shipping activities, such a house would amass as many agencies as possible across as many trades as possible. For this reason, the system was more fitted to the developing economies of Latin America, India and the Far East than to the already crowded economies of Europe. Thus the span of the multipurpose agency house in such places was quite different from the span of Mackenzie's specialised insurance operation in Italy, impressive as that was.

An excellent instance of the professional agency-collecting venture in the long-distance trade is provided by Blyth Brothers, Phoenix's venerable merchant representatives in Mauritius: by 1914, Blyths held no fewer than fifty-five agencies; thirty of these were banks, nineteen of them British, five American, two French and one each from Sweden, Switzerland, South Africa and Hong Kong; eight of them were steamship lines; two were oil companies; one, Daimler, was an automobile company; and nine were insurance companies, five marine offices and four fire offices. Similarly, the firm awarded the Phoenix agency for Matabeleland and Mashonaland in 1898, the Anglo-American Trading Co. of Bulawayo, boasted some big names on its varied roll, including Standard Oil and Josson's Portland Cement.

Often membership of the roll implied a definite strategy, with agencies selected for their ability to reinforce one another: thus oil, metal, tea, cement, coal or timber were traded by agents who also represented the steamship lines which carried these commodities and then promoted the services of financiers and insurers who could fund or underwrite these activities. Reinforcement also could operate internationally. Many of the big agency houses had a British base and a number of 'correspondents' in distant places. Thus, Phoenix's important agents in Bombay, Messrs William & Alexander Graham were correspondents of W. & R. Graham & Co. of Glasgow and affiliated to Messrs Graham & Co. of Calcutta and Messrs Donald Graham & Co. of Karachi.[182]

But even these powerful operations did not rival the reach of Phoenix's most formidable pre-war agencies. These were the investment groups, the super-merchants with a British base and with enough investment power to operate at the extra-European periphery not only as agents, but also as direct financiers for a range of manufacturing, mining, plantation, financial or shipping enterprises. Of the thirty cases identified by

[182] Power of attorney granted 25 June 1884 and still current into the 1910s (Phoenix Directors' Minutes, Y24, p. 11).

Chapman worldwide (although, undoubtedly, more existed), Phoenix had direct dealings with four. One, Matheson & Co., joined the other side and put some of its massive capital into promoting local non-tariff insurance competition in Hong Kong.[183] The three others worked for Phoenix. The great Indian agency house of Finlay Muir, a major operator in the cotton and tea trades, took on the company's general agency for Bengal from 1877.[184] Binney & Co. of Madras held the Phoenix power of attorney, among many others, from 1875. And Antony Gibbs & Co., originally textile merchants, later monopolists of the Peruvian guano trade, later still speculators in Chilean factories and railways and merchant bankers of London, were perhaps the supreme example of the multi-sector investing, banking, trading and agency operation; they acted for Phoenix in Chile, with effect, from 1912.

Many other Phoenix agencies of the late nineteenth century, if not quite up to this strength, carried weight enough. Carsons of Colombo, with their plantation and shipping connections, bear more than a passing resemblance to Chapman's classic cases. And Dalgety in Australia proved a power that could make or break an antipodean service trade. Many of those who sold insurance also headed truly comprehensive and international business enterprises.

There are implications here for the general economic history of late nineteenth-century Britain. Between roughly 1850 and 1890, it is true that Phoenix suffered from a certain conservatism in its foreign policy. This was the product of 'corporate memory', an undue dwelling on the disasters of the past, a consequent impulse to 'purify the books' and an over-reliance on reinsurance.[185] True also, the effect was most marked in the United States, and, even before 1890, the company proved capable of promoting growth in other markets, notably Europe and Australia. Nevertheless, before 1890 Phoenix provides an unusual case of entrepreneurial frailty in the service sector of the economy. This suggests parallels with the widely debated managerial weakness in Britain's manufacturing industries during the Great Depression of 1873–96. But it contrasts strongly with the accepted interpretation of performance in the UK financial sector over the decades down to 1914; this is generally thought to have been powerful. However, where superior export results were achieved in insurance they came largely through the efforts of newer, and frequently northern, offices; the classic case was the Royal

[183] The Canton Fire Office (1836); The Hong Kong Fire Insurance Co. (1868).

[184] Phoenix Directors' Minutes W22, p. 260, 21 November 1877; Chapman, 'British-based Investment Groups', p. 234.

[185] See vol. I, pp. 290–331; also Trebilcock, 'The City, Entrepreneurship and Insurance'.

Insurance of Liverpool. Older offices like the Phoenix were as prone to technological obsolescence as Britain's venerable manufacturing industries.[186]

This argument has utility. But it cannot be extended beyond 1890 in any Phoenix market. Unlike many of its industrial contemporaries, the company contrived a managerial and export revival in the late Victorian period. The worldwide reform movement in the Phoenix agency and branch structure at the turn of the century is the clearest sign of this. But even before that point, export sales in some markets – Italy, India, Ceylon, New Zealand – had fallen into notably active hands. Finlay Muir were appointed to Bengal in 1877, Carsons in Colombo in 1880, George Graham in New Zealand in the same year, the Graham brothers in Bombay in 1884, Evan Mackenzie at Genoa in 1887. In Australia, Dalgety came later in 1906, and Gibbs in Chile, later still in 1912.

In the manufacturing sector, throughout the period 1870–1914, the British reputation for export salesmanship is – probably deservedly – questionable.[187] The promotion of industrial exports has been presented as amateurish, slipshod, linguistically illiterate and culturally dogmatic. British salesmen abroad were too few in number, spoke loudly in the wrong language, cited inappropriate weights and measures, and did not cooperate with one another. British consular officials did not like them or their efforts and said so. By contrast, much of the insurance selling reviewed here was conducted by extremely impressive mercantile agencies combining international reach with massive local expertise. There was little pinched nationalism, no lack of cosmopolitanism in Phoenix's selection of agents: the company employed Dutchmen in the East Indies, Swedes in Sweden, Frenchmen in Paris, Scots and Indians in India, and, if advantage offered, Hamburgers in China.[188] And the agents' associations gave all these a cooperative capacity that is evident in few, if any, lines of industrial marketing before 1914.

[186] *Ibid.*

[187] The literature is enormous. But see D. H. Aldcroft's classic statement in 'The Entrepreneur and the British Economy, 1870–1914', *Economic History Review*, 17 (1964); A. L. Levine, *Industrial Retardation in Britain 1880–1914* (London,1967); and R. P. T. Davenport-Hines, *Markets and Bagmen* (Aldershot, 1986). For a contrary view, see S. J. Nicholas, 'The Overseas Marketing Performance of British Industry, 1870–1914', *Economic History Review*, 37 (1984).

[188] It is also striking that many appointments of this vintage possessed remarkable endurance: the Netherlands agency of the de Castro family, established in 1868, lasted for more than a century; while the Archer family at Oporto, recruited in 1862, did better still; both major Spanish agencies, the Lamothes at Malaga (1887) and the Parages at Madrid (1893) survived into the late twentieth century, as did the major Athens agency of the Hill family, first established in 1887, the Madeira agency of Leacock & Cia, and the Mulhouse agency of the Wintzer family, both commenced in 1889.

So, if Phoenix's export performance in the middle third of the nineteenth century makes the point that older service ventures could falter just as readily as older industrial ones, the discrete phase in the company's foreign development after 1870, or, more generally, after 1890, makes some quite different points. It demonstrates that an older service venture could revive; that in reviving it employed selling tactics which appear far superior to those current among its industrial peers; and that, in developing a framework to coordinate these tactics, and the agents who wielded them, it produced increasingly sophisticated institutional forms. In the non-American world, the Phoenix's equipment of sub-agencies, general agencies, branches, and, in common with its FOC partners, agents' associations, represented a highly creditable determination to adapt to new markets. This was a great deal better than Phoenix's wary mid-century preoccupation with reinsurance.

But such adaptation means little unless it is put in a comparative context. Data of a comparative kind exist, though in varying degrees of quality, for three other major companies, two veterans and one mid-century newcomer: the Sun and the Royal Exchange, and the mercantile innovator from the 1860s, the Commercial Union. Clearly, Phoenix was slower to employ branches and subsidiaries than this group. Phoenix had seven overseas branches, but no overseas subsidiary companies, outside the United States, by 1914. In contrast, the much-needed overhaul of the REA's foreign operations after 1890 had created twenty-seven branch operations outside the United States by 1910, though the Corporation was no quicker than Phoenix to latch onto directly controlled subsidiary companies. The dynamic Commercial Union, Britain's second-ranking insurance company in 1900, was the most active exponent of both techniques. By 1914, it possessed twenty-one branches and eight subsidiary companies outside the United States.[189] The Sun's pattern was more similar to that of Phoenix. Like Phoenix, the Sun had seven overseas branches outside the United States by 1914, but it had also resorted to the purchase of foreign companies in Canada, South Africa and India.[190]

However, this is not as much to the disadvantage of Phoenix as first appearances may suggest. The REA had a foreign operation to create effectively from scratch and was doing so in an era when the branch was the coming technology. For the REA, the branch system was a necessary

[189] Calculated from Liveing, *Commercial Union*. Three of these branches were created very early, in the 1870s, four in the 1880s, eight in the 1890s and the remaining five between 1900 and 1914. Of the subsidiaries, three were acquired in the 1880s, five in the 1890s. The emphasis in this structural adjustment was concentrated, therefore, as it was for Phoenix, around the 1890s.

[190] Dickson, *Sun Insurance*, p. 232.

Table 2.19. *Foreign fire earnings, four companies, 1885–1905 (gross premium £,000)*

	1884	1889	1891	1905	1914
Commercial Union	591.7	789.5	–	1,556.0	2,115.0
Sun	432.5	399.4	551.9	–	–
REA	3.0	–	–	476.0	745.6
Phoenix	527.9	557.7	733.5	1,316.7	1,538.2

Sources: Commercial Union: see Liveing, *Commercial Union*, pp. 45, 54, 110. Proportions as suggested by Supple, *The Royal Exchange Assurance*, p. 214 to convert total fire premium to foreign fire premium for 1905 and 1914.
Sun: see Dickson, *Sun Insurance*, p. 305. Premiums before 1889 adjusted to gross, using Dickson's suggested proportions, p. 301.
REA: Supple, *Royal Exchange Assurance*, pp. 240, 243, 470. Premiums for 1913 converted to gross using proportions suggested by Dickson.
Phoenix: Review of Foreign Agencies, Books 2–4.

means of catching up; and many of its branches were created late in the period: Brussels, Amsterdam, New Zealand, the Far East and Canada all coming after 1905. Similarly, the Sun frequently purchased a subsidiary company merely to convert it into a ready-made branch whereas the Phoenix technique was to establish the branch from its own materials, frequently drawing them from an agency system that was already in place. Often, too, the Sun employed the acquisition device to develop strength quickly in a market which it had entered late. The Commercial Union, too, needed to make ground swiftly in many markets where Phoenix was already represented. The longer foreign experience of the Phoenix included an extended acquaintance with the agency system, and a larger number of strong agency bases. Given this inheritance, its measure of structural adjustment within its overseas selling organisation between 1870 and 1914 was probably about right.

Certainly, the premium results suggest as much. In 1885 the REA's foreign premium struggled still at a derisory level and the Sun's takings, though much more substantial, were comfortably outclassed by those of the Phoenix (see Table 2.19). In 1891, the last year for which Dickson can cite exact figures for the Sun, Phoenix's margin of advantage had widened from a 22% superiority to one of 33%. Even the revitalised REA could not approach one half of Phoenix's takings by 1905. Yet these are comparisons with the weaker foreign exporters. In fact, Phoenix could hold up its head in the presence of the best. The massive Commercial Union

Table 2.20. *Distribution of total fire income: UK, US, foreign: four companies, 1891–1913 (gross premium £,000 and %)*

		UK		US		Rest of World	
		£'000	%	£'000	%	£'000	%
Sun	1891	405.5	42.3	361.3	37.7	190.6	19.9
Phoenix	1891	420.0	36.4	370.7	32.1	362.8	31.4
REA	1905	273.5	36.4	250.6	33.4	225.4	30.1
Com. Union	1905	519.0	24.0	1,017.0	50.0	540.0	26.0
Phoenix	1905	410.0	23.8	625.0	36.2	690.8	40.0
REA	1913	289.3	27.9	393.6	38.0	351.6	34.0
Com. Union	1913	705.0	24.0	1,380.0	50.0	734.2	26.0
Phoenix	1913	400.5	19.6	701.5	34.8	938.8	46.0

Sources: As for Table 2.19 above.

extracted growth of 163% from its favoured foreign underwriting sector between 1884 and 1905; but Phoenix managed growth of 149% over this period and the absolute size of its takings were not disgraced by the CU figures.

Moreover, the spread of Phoenix's revived foreign business was superior to that of its competitors. By the 1900s, it was common for British offices to be taking a good deal more than half of their total fire income from the world's biggest insurance market, the United States.[191] This could be extremely dangerous. Thus, the REA lost over £600,000,more than its entire overseas income, to the San Francisco earthquake of 1906, largely through pinning too much of its own foreign recovery on American risks. Although Phoenix's overhaul of its foreign operation from the 1870s included a deliberate renewal of exposure to American business, and although this exposure was to be a crucial variable in the company's fortunes over the long period 1879-1984, the management of the pre-1914 years did not put all of the old Bird's eggs into the transatlantic basket (see Table 2.20).

The striking feature of these numbers is the persistent strength of Phoenix in the non-US sector of foreign trade. The company was markedly more powerful here than either REA or Sun, but, more importantly, both in 1905 and 1913, it could outpace even the Commercial Union in these markets. Indeed, in the 1900s, the only major sector in which the

[191] Supple, *Royal Exchange Assurance*, pp. 214, 243.

Commercial Union was distinctly stronger than Phoenix *was* the United States. It was Phoenix's long-term strength in Europe and its fondness for frontier markets like the Canadian or the Far Eastern which gave it this superior balance. Much later in the company's career, in the 1970s and 1980s, Phoenix would need to seek once again a balance of this quality.

Clearly, too, this pattern of expansion served to resurrect Phoenix as a foreign specialist. By the 1900s, its commitment to the UK market was lower than that of the other companies sampled here. After its mid-century retreat from foreign fields, the home market had reclaimed as much as one half of Phoenix's total income; this share fell to around one-third through the 1880s and 1890s and dipped below 30% by the end of the century. But then it continued to retreat during the later 1900s and, in the years before the Great War, could not prevent foreign trade absorbing some 80% of the office's total fire income. Probably, not even the Commercial Union managed to gather such proportions of its fire revenue from the overseas sector.

Moreover, these foreign shares of Phoenix's total fire business were far larger than those achieved during the office's previous era of foreign specialisation between 1811 and 1830. Indeed, the average foreign share for the period 1901–10 exceeded 77% (see Table 2.1) contrasting with the results in the range 46–51% achieved in the first third of the previous century. Clearly, by the 1900s, Phoenix's return as a foreign specialist was emphatic. If a few major fire insurers outsold it abroad, very few indeed outsold it outside the United States, and almost none could match its share of income drawn from outside the United Kingdom.

CHAPTER 3

THE OVERSEAS DIMENSION RESUMED, II: THE PHOENIX RISES IN THE UNITED STATES

I. THE ATTRACTIONS AND DISTRACTIONS OF AMERICA

By the late nineteenth century, the United States was the most important insurance market in the world. It offered enormous volume, enticing profit opportunities and horrendous losses. It combined an industrial potential greater even than that of the advanced European economies with a propensity to burst into flames or seismic tremors quite as emphatic as that of the more obviously frontier markets such as Canada, Australia or Japan. It was a market which British underwriters could not afford to stay out of – and one where they could sometimes scarcely afford to stay in. And, as British insurers added accident business to their export range in the 1900s, the United States added to its other tendencies an inclination also to burst into litigation.

The short period between the end of the Civil War in 1865 and the opening date of this volume saw a massive industrial acceleration in the United States. Over the period 1868–72 a phenomenal 25,000 miles of new railway track came into operation, including the vital Union Pacific Line which established the first transcontinental rail link in 1869. Manufacturing capacity grew more rapidly between 1865 and 1870 than in any comparable period of the American past.

Many of the more enterprising British insurers – primarily those based in Liverpool – were already in place in the United States with agencies poised to tap these developments. In 1851, for instance, the Royal Insurance established its first outposts at New York, in the cotton-shipping centres of Savannah and Charleston, at Baltimore, the sea-gate to the mid-Atlantic states, and at Philadelphia, America's fourth largest city and a major industrial centre. In 1852 and 1853, further appointments followed at Boston, Cincinnati, Louisville, Mobile, New Orleans and San

Table 3.1. *Phoenix gross premium earnings from the United States, 1865–1914 (£ and % of total foreign income, five-year averages)*

1866–70	11,234	7.1
1871–5	43,248	18.4
1876–80	33,278	12.8
1881–5	192,442	43.1
1886–90	269,430	47.0
1891–5	373,931	48.7
1896–1900	402,666	48.0
1901–5	561,177	48.8
1906–10	588,233	42.0
1911–15	719,409	45.4

Source: Phoenix Review of Foreign Agencies, Books 1–4.

Francisco. Boston was the maritime access for the mills of New England; Cincinnati was a major meat-packing centre and flourishing port on the Ohio River; Mobile and New Orleans were the ports of the Gulf, San Francisco of the West. The Royal was just beaten into San Francisco by its northern colleague, the Liverpool & London.

Phoenix, of course, had not matched these accurate strokes. It had pioneered the first British invasion of American insurance markets many decades before, but it took little part in this second onslaught. The company had been battered by early American losses, seen its long-established centres, mainly in the Old South, savaged by the Civil War, and failed to detect the industrial rhythm of a new America.[1] Accordingly, Phoenix began this period by handling the American trade with tongs. From 1866 it had established reinsurance arrangements which gave it the surplus trade from San Francisco and Oregon laid off by the Edinburgh-based North British and Mercantile (NBM), one of the three largest British operators in the United States.[2] More importantly, in 1867 the Phoenix had signed a reinsurance treaty with the North British to cover the New York market. This provided the staple of Phoenix's US trade until 1878. The breaks in trend as the New York treaty went in and out of Phoenix's American income flow are clearly visible in Table 3.1. And only once direct agency trade was resumed after 1878 did Phoenix begin to take anything like its proper share of the American insurance bonanza.

[1] For an extended comparison between the first and second generation of insurance exporters to the USA, see C. Trebilcock, 'The City, Entrepreneurship and Insurance'. Also see vol. I, pp. 320–31.

[2] The others were the Liverpool & London & Globe and the Royal.

2. CONFLAGRATION AND REINSURANCE, 1867–78

Indeed, it is a small wonder that Phoenix ever reverted to direct insurance in nineteenth-century America. For the company had adopted the reinsurance gambit owing to bad experience and bad memories in earlier direct trade in the United States. And then, immediately it had done so, the American market gave a spectacular demonstration of its ability to generate still more bad memories. Within three years of this volume's opening date, not one but two major American cities had suffered calamitous fires, the first in Chicago in October 1871, the second in Boston in November 1872.

The Chicago Fire was one of the insurance disasters of the century and the largest blaze seen in the United States before 1900. Accounts of its inception on 9 October 1871 vary from a more than usually ambitious, or uncontrolled, demonstration by the Ku Klux Klan, through an incendiary attack by southern terrorists, to a collision between a cow and an oil lamp. The outcome, however, brooks no argument: 18,000 buildings, five square miles of city and £33–40 million in property were destroyed.

Whatever the origin of the first spark, the mechanism which converted it into a firestorm was a classic feature of this city: wind. In the estimation of G. H. Burnett, the foreign superintendant and roving troubleshooter of the North British, the sparks started among Chicago's 'inferior buildings, a great source of danger to the solid heart of the city, where the greatest portion of its immense commercial wealth was stored... seized the Lumber Yards and Bridges and were carried by the fearful wind with incredible force upon the solid blocks'.

Chicago in 1871 was no frontier shanty-town but a city of over 30 square miles (80 km^2) and a population of 334,000. It possessed wide streets and modern city blocks, 'about the size of the Bank of England', and its business centre was 'one of the most imposing brick and stone quarters in the world'. Together with the northern suburbs, it was precisely this that was gutted, an area 'equal in extent to the City of London within the walls... entirely destroyed'; Burnett amidst 'the very picture of desolation' could find 'hardly a trace of it'. What burned at Chicago was the business heart of an up-to-date commercial metropolis. This was as bad as Hamburg in 1842: another unthinkably primitive visitation upon a most modern centre of urban wealth.[3] Faced with the stupefaction of his masters back in London, Burnett needed to emphasise

[3] Compare vol. I, pp. 284ff.

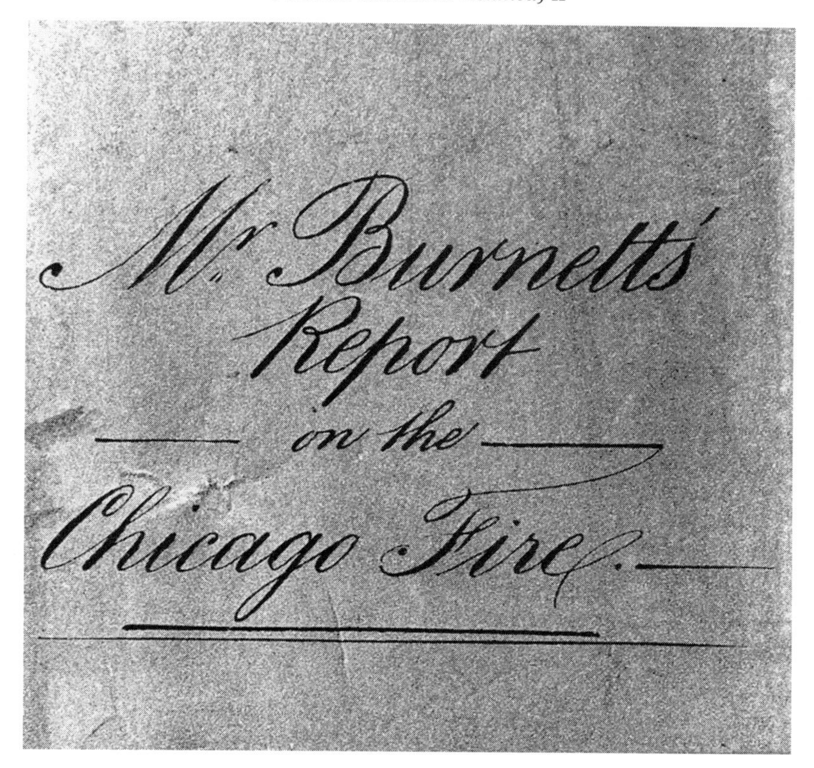

Plate 3.1 Title page to disaster: Burnett's Report on the North British Losses in the Great Chicago Fire of 1871.

Chicago's proneness to natural malevolence. Its situation, 'with the great sweep of Prairie Land on the one side and the Broad Lake on the other particularly exposed it to the draught of fierce winds'; on 9 October 1871, it was a 'hurricane wind', having the effect 'of a blow-pipe to direct the flames upon the different blocks'. He gave what comfort he could: 'All ordinary calculations for dealing with a large conflagration were entirely upset.'[4]

Further calculation revealed that total insurance losses from this lethal hot blast, reflecting the quality of what had been destroyed, were £20 million and that the British offices bore £1.2 million of it. The effect was

[4] Manuscript copy of Mr Burnett's 'Report on the Chicago Fire of 1871' to the General Manager, North British and Mercantile Insurance Company, 23 January 1872 (Phoenix Archive PX1182).

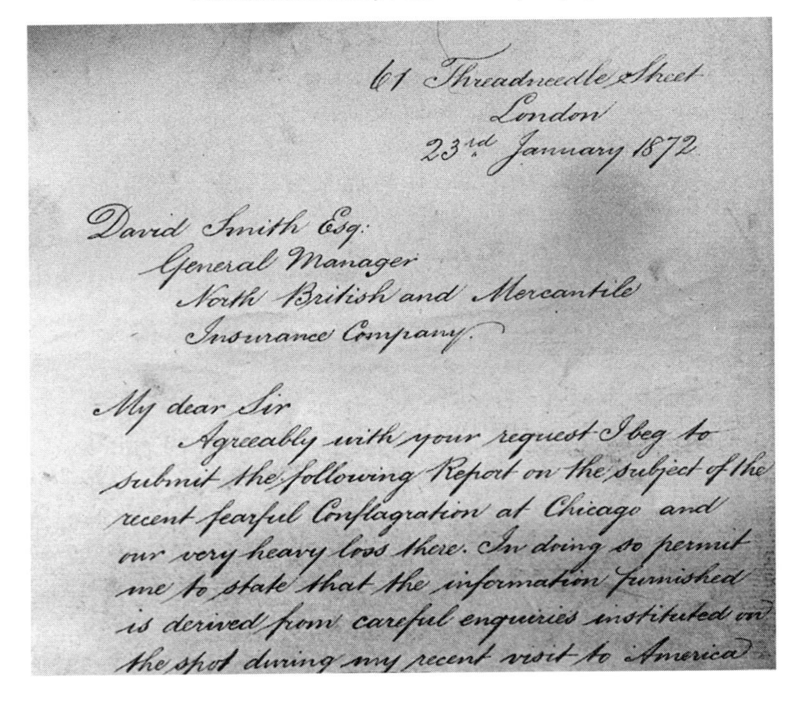

61 Threadneedle Street
London
23rd January 1872

David Smith Esq:
General Manager
North British and Mercantile
Insurance Company.

My dear Sir
Agreeably with your request I beg to submit the following Report on the subject of the recent fearful Conflagration at Chicago and our very heavy loss there. In doing so permit me to state that the information furnished is derived from careful enquiries instituted on the spot during my recent visit to America

Plate 3.2 Burnett's copperplate regarding 'the Fearful Conflagration at Chicago'.

sufficient to inflate the loss ratio for the entire British fire insurance industry from about 58% in 1870 to over 70% for 1871.

Phoenix received some protection from its reinsurance shield with the North British, but not much. North British lost about £300,000 in Chicago, Phoenix some £99,060. This was much less than the £600,000 lost by the worst British sufferer, the Liverpool & London & Globe, and even the NBM's sacrifices were less than those of the big American offices. Phoenix's choice of reinsurance partner had been shrewd: NBM's acceptance ceilings for Chicago districts had been much more rigorous than most insurers and, most prudently, they had been scaled down as recently as 1869.[5] Nevertheless, the damage to Phoenix was real. Table 3.2 shows the effects both of Chicago and Boston upon Phoenix's American loss ratios in the first half of the 1870s. Indirect trade was clearly no magic spell against the terrors of insuring in America.

[5] *Ibid.*, p. 4.

Table 3.2. *Phoenix losses on American insurances, 1870–5 (gross premiums, £ and %)*

Year	Premium	Loss	Ratio
1870	22,762	6,483	28.5
1871	36,348	23,247	64.0
1872	30,089	116,740	388.0
1873	66,910	63,421	94.8
1874	39,802	29,367	73.8
1875	43,044	15,293	35.5

Source: Phoenix Review of Foreign Agencies, Book 1.

The Boston fire was about half as bad as Chicago, but that was quite bad enough. There was no mystery about its origins or severity. It started in the boiler room of a dry goods store on 9 November 1872 and burned through 750 buildings, and 60 acres of streets, including most of the business district. It was assisted by the forces of both nature and technology. The stables of Boston were afflicted by horse 'flu and the draft power of the fire brigades were so sick that they could not pull the engines; the pumps were dragged by the firemen themselves but scarcely at a gallop. Boston also had modern technology in the shape of gas mains; these exploded. Slow fire-engines and fast flames produced insurance losses of £15 million sterling of which the British offices bore £1 million.

The effects of these blazes on Phoenix – as with Hamburg or Tooley Street in earlier decades – were complex.[6] The most straightforward outcome was the realisation that reinsurance was a frail defence in this market, more wish even than prayer. Proof was provided by the company's American loss ratios, which did not settle to anything approaching stability before 1875. But the way in which Phoenix had deployed reinsurance in America before the Chicago disaster had not been entirely faint-hearted: it had been a positive wish rather than a quavering prayer. There is evidence of very large warehouse acceptances in 1867–9, with Phoenix raising its ceilings to take increasingly big commercial risks from North British. By the time of the blaze in Chicago, NBM had about 1,000 risks in the city, spread over some 115 blocks, and Phoenix had accepted a share in 250 of these. Yet, after the disaster, the company responded to the implications of this exposure with more fortitude than it had managed in the wake of the Hamburg firestorm some three decades before.

[6] See vol. 1, pp. 287–91, 426–9.

The reaction was double-barrelled. The first was to trigger swift and full payment. Two days after the fire, the Phoenix directors resolved 'to place in the hands of that company (NBM) . . . such sums as should appear necessary for a prompt discharge of this Company's obligations under the reinsurances granted by them on risks at Chicago'.[7] They remembered that reputation and affection were effectively purchased by generosity at this stage of loss adjustment. But at Chicago this point scarcely had to be remembered since circumstances emphasised it most forcefully. The American companies were in trouble and some could not pay their losses.

Burnett reported, 'the distress among the American Societies is very great. A host of them are wound up, while even the strongest are obliged to call up Capital'; and, as he usually did, he saw the logical sequel: 'The British offices have now the ball at their feet.'[8] Clearly, the route they should take with it was down the path of quick settlement. To NBM alone, this was 'of itself worth many thousands of pounds . . . the manner in which the loss was settled cannot fail to do us an infinitude of good and create for us a position which it would otherwise have taken us a long series of years to make; new business is pouring in.' So rapid was the movement of custom to the British offices that Burnett expected to recoup his company's whole loss 'within no distant date'.[9]

Disaster at Chicago then was a mixed catastrophe for the insurers, as in the nineteenth century it often was. Great fires imposed heavy losses, but they also removed competitors, raised rates, frightened new clients into the market and transferred business to those offices sufficiently well-heeled to secure a good (or even better) name by rapid payment of claims. Phoenix had fired the barrel of quick settlement at Hamburg but had balked at collecting the bag. After Chicago, Phoenix settled quickly, and then fired the second barrel of enlarged capacity – and went looking for the game. They were not alone. 'So far from inducing the English offices to restrict their business', observed Burnett, 'those before established are all doing much more than formerly, while others not previously in the field are preparing to take advantage of the opening.'[10] The failure of the American offices had rocked the confidence of the American insuring public and the ensuing rush into the arms of the English insurers had been 'quite unexampled in history'.[11]

The form in which Phoenix took advantage was by accepting more from NBM. As early as mid-November 1871, NBM telegrammed Lombard Street that they were now insuring an increased amount of £750,000

[7] Phoenix Directors' Minutes, V21, pp. 135–6, 11 October 1871.
[8] Burnett, 'Report', p. 19. [9] *Ibid.*, pp. 15, 18. [10] *Ibid.*, p. 17. [11] *Ibid.*, p. 20.

Plate 3.3 Artist's impression of the Chicago blaze.

on the unburned sections of Chicago. Phoenix took £250,000 of this, increasing its acceptance proportion of business generated by NBM from one-quarter to one-third.[12] Both parties avoided the burned parts of the town, where shanties were temporarily springing up. Also, early in 1872, Phoenix informed NBM that they were willing to increase their acceptance level for New York and other American cities. In New York, Phoenix would take up to £100,000 in each of the city's districts and in other centres would fix their ceiling at half the amount retained by NBM.[13] The effect of this was to boost Phoenix's American takings immediately from £36,255 in 1871 to £66,796 in 1873, before they settled to £42,968 in 1875. Here the outcome of disaster, unlike the Hamburg case, was that Phoenix did choose to take its share of the resulting cascade of business. After Chicago, the British export effort to insure America won an increased share of the US fire market, and Phoenix, by closer cooperation with NBM, contributed to this success.

However, Phoenix showed due discrimination in assuming these larger obligations. One of the company's first demands upon NBM after the Chicago blaze was for details of other large American cities and their

[12] Phoenix Trustees' Minutes, 8 November 1871. [13] *Ibid.*, 15 February 1872.

liability to 'extensive fires', a prudent thought in view of the calamity that would befall Boston a year later. Indeed, a major consequence of the Chicago experience was to force the big British offices, who were the major beneficiaries of the surge in the market after 1871, to find better methods of managing the risk levels in all American conurbations. Thus by December 1871, NBM had decided that the way to handle Chicago was to divide it into five zones and to accept insurances of $100,000 to $500,000 in each up to an overall exposure of $1.5 million. It was within this set of rules that Phoenix agreed to take one-third of the consequences.[14] Subdivision of risks, already familiar in commercial insurance practice, was extended to thousands of acres of urban sprawl. In 1872, Phoenix decided to subdivide its liabilities in Philadelphia – where it was covering some £180,000 – into zones which were not to contain more than £50,000 apiece. The same was done in Brooklyn and Charleston by the end of the year.[15]

The general impression is that, in the aftermath of Chicago, Phoenix followed NBM through uproarious American markets, acquiring much expanded business and much refined practice as it went. But, if the directors were more stalwart in this action than ever they had been in the aftermath of Hamburg, they were not immune from hesitations. The outbreak at Boston in late 1872 made them wonder if they were following NBM too slavishly. At this time a note of caution about over-rapid expansion in the United States understandably intruded. In the autumn, NBM had arranged a co-insurance scheme with two American offices, the Home Insurance and the Phoenix of Hartford, by which the three would pool business and share risks equally on acceptances from the Pacific Coast districts of California, Oregon and Washington State; it then asked the Phoenix of London to provide the reinsurance cover for all three offices in the scheme. This proved too much for Lombard Street. Although the decision was reversed in 1873, the Phoenix Trustees decided in October that 'it is not advisable to open new reinsurance connections in the United States', and they rejected the NBM proposal.[16]

Perhaps, the Phoenix managers were worried about a general excess of pace in their American advance. Or they may have been disturbed by the enlargement of commitment in the Pacific market. Certainly, it was not the last time that this region caused heart-searching and hair-tearing among the London underwriters. But, in any event, within a month of the rebuff to NBM, the second disaster at Boston gave prudence irrefutable

[14] *Ibid.*, 14 December 1871. [15] Ibid., 21 November 1872.
[16] *Ibid.*, 10 October 1872.

Plate 3.4 The reality: the remains of State Street, Chicago.

reinforcement. One disaster might stimulate expansionary thoughts, but two in hardly more than a year necessarily challenged confidence.

In November 1872, the Board requested the Trustees to review all Phoenix engagements in the United States. The timing of this initiative makes clear the source of doubt: it came four days after Boston burned.[17] The Trustees reported carefully upon the working of the arrangement with NBM over its five-year term. They brought out the magnitude of the fees that had to be paid to NBM for acquiring the business, effectively the equivalent of management charges, expenses and commissions in direct trade. These had amounted to 26.5%, latterly rising to 27.5%, of gross premiums. The Trustees seemed to find this rather a lot, though in fact it compares well with the commission and charges incurred in the first five years of the revived agency trade in the USA between 1881 and 1885. The

[17] Phoenix Directors' Minutes, V 21, p. 239, 13 November 1872.

Trustees of 1872, of course, had no means of guessing what these were going to be; but actually they would amount to 30.5%.[18]

Quite rightly, however, the Trustees were more disturbed by the losses. The five-year US account to Michaelmas 1872, including the Chicago loss, but excluding Boston, showed losses of 195% on net premiums. If the Chicago claims also were excluded, the loss ratio would have been 71% on net premiums, and a small profit would have resulted. In the year after Chicago, in the brief interval between the two blazes, the Phoenix, after paying its dues to NBM, received £31,497 in net US premiums and paid out £23,064 in losses. This was a net loss ratio of 76.5%. The trustees were left with mixed impressions.

Historical assessment suggests that the rapid post-Chicago expansion in insurance involved quantity of business rather than any major advance in quality. And of course it was bracketed by two catastrophes. The Trustees' mixed impressions were not dissimilar. On the one hand, they reflected, American rates were high, perhaps five times the British level, and great fires took them higher. And they respected the sheer volume of American trade. But they could not ignore the catastrophes. So they ruled:

> in considering a large business, especially good and remunerative under ordinary circumstances, but shown to be exposed to the gravest dangers from the possibility of unusually extended conflagrations, the Trustees are not prepared to recommend its sudden abandonment.[19]

This, of course, reveals that 'abandonment' was in the air after the second disaster had struck. But it also raised the question: if 'abandonment' was not to be the course, how were circumstances to be made sufficiently 'ordinary'?

The Trustees had a strategy for this. If the Phoenix were not to evacuate America entirely, it must do the following: report quarterly on its gross liabilities in every city where it held cover of more than £50,000; divide more cities into zones with assigned acceptance ceilings; reduce these ceilings in key locations. Given such precautions, the Trustees felt that 'hope of a large and profitable business in the USA might be reasonably entertained'.[20]

Certainly this strategy was followed. In 1872 Phoenix cut its risk ceilings per district in New York by half. And in the February of the next year, it accepted NBM's revised plan for Chicago, adding two new

[18] Calculated from Phoenix Review of Foreign Agencies, Book 1.
[19] Phoenix Private Minutes, Report of Trustees on US Business, 14 November 1872.
[20] *Ibid.*

districts to represent the reconstructed sector, making seven in all; but Phoenix limited its overall cover for Chicago to £136,700, contrasting with the £250,000 which it had accepted on the unburned five sectors in the immediate aftermath of the fire. Also in 1873 and 1874, new subdivision schemes were applied to New York and eight other major US cities.[21] Although Phoenix continued to cooperate closely and fully with the NBM – even to the point of providing reinsurance from August 1873 at least for the San Francisco policies of the Pacific consortium maintained by NBM, Home Insurance and Phoenix of Hartford – its more rigorous approach to divisions and ceilings had the effect of restricting its total US income in the second half of the 1870s.

Thus reported American premiums fell progressively from £42,968 and 16.1% of total foreign income in 1875 to £27,418 and 10.3% of total foreign income in 1879, before collapsing to £18,427 and 6.9% of total foreign income in 1880. Nevertheless, profits appear to have been reasonable: for the four years of the middle 1870s, 1873–6, the Foreign Agents' Ledger records surpluses on net premiums of 20%–33%.[22] This was consistent with the good profits achieved by the stronger American companies, such as the Insurance Company of North America, at this time.[23] Phoenix, then, could afford to be pleased, in the late 1870s, both by its relationship with NBM and by its own post-conflagration policy.

The evidence suggests that it was indeed content. The test was Chicago in 1878. By this time the city had recovered; in the next year Robert Louis Stephenson found it merely 'great and gloomy'. And, hungry traveller that he was, he reflected upon the fire eight years earlier,

> I remember having subscribed, let us say, sixpence towards its restoration . . . and now, when I behold street after street of ponderous houses and crowds of comfortable burghers, I thought it would be a graceful act for the corporation to refund that sixpence, or, at least, to entertain me to a cheerful dinner.[24]

Phoenix must have shared Stephenson's optimism about the reconstruction – if not about the prospects of a free dinner – for in 1878 it took £50,000 on the new business sector of the city and thus raised its total liability in Chicago once more to £180,000.[25] However, this was one of the company's last policy acts within the reinsurance compact with NBM.

[21] Phoenix Trustees' Minutes, 6 and 20 February 1873, 15 and 22 May 1873.
[22] Foreign Agents' Ledger C19/4.
[23] Marquis James, *Biography of a Business: The Insurance Company of North America, 1792–1942* (New York, 1942), pp. 161, 170–1.
[24] R. L. Stevenson, *The Amateur Emigrant* (London, 1984 edn), p. 103.
[25] Phoenix Trustees' Minutes, 22 August 1878.

Neither Phoenix nor NBM had any wish to dissolve this compact. But it was dissolved in June 1879 – by act of state. NBM had to explain to Phoenix the dire implications of the legislation introduced by the State of New York. This most protectionist of American states had realised that insurance companies accepting reinsurance from other principal foreign offices were in effect evading the obligation to pay insurance deposits which the state imposed upon the principals. Accordingly, it ruled that no office which maintained an agency in New York, and which had fulfilled the deposit obligation, should reinsure with any company which had not met the deposit requirement.

At one stroke this removed Phoenix's livelihood in the United States. Its response was to immediately set about investigating the establishment of a direct Phoenix agency in New York. It had no choice. There is irony in the fact that Phoenix's fateful re-involvement in direct American underwriting, the dominant factor in its twentieth-century fortunes, was a forced decision.

From another standpoint, it is also worth emphasising that it was an act of state protectionism which impelled one of history's great insurance exporters back into the big time in the world's biggest insurance market. Though epochal for Phoenix, therefore, it could scarcely be deemed very efficient protectionism.

3. PHOENIX RISEN: DIRECT TRADE AND THE IRVING AGENCY, 1879–1897

No doubt, it was knowledge of the American market, gained in tracking NBM, which allowed Phoenix to replace the NBM treaty with such rapidity. Informed of the legislative constraint late in June 1879, the office had found an alternative by the end of July.

Much of the necessary information came through personal connection. Phoenix's long-standing relationship with Barings of London had extended to the appointment of the related house of Baring, Magoun & Co. as Phoenix's bankers in New York. The financiers were immediately asked to look out for a suitable American agent for the insurance company. But a much closer connection, the veteran Phoenix director, Octavius Edward Coope, brewer, parliamentarian and philanthropist,[26] undertook to inquire among his friends in the House. The lobby produced one good idea, an introduction to Alexander Duer Irving, of Irving, Frank and Dubois of New York, insurance agents, and, probably, bro-

[26] See vol. I, pp. 676–7. Coope sat on the Board for the long period 1845–86, and was currently MP for Middlesex.

kers. This insurance Irving (Alexander) was the nephew of the great literary Irving (Washington). References were sent through Barings from 'first-class merchants' in New York; they proved 'highly favourable', supporting Irving as 'a person to whom the Phoenix Co. might with interest and advantage entrust the management of their United States Agency'.[27]

Phoenix was convinced: the Board appointed Irving as agent for New York on 30 July 1879.[28] It was an unusual dual appointment. Not only was he appointed as Phoenix representative for New York State; the firm of Irving, Frank and Dubois was appointed also as branch agent for the whole of the United States.

From this point, Phoenix clearly intended to create an American Branch, as well as an array of individual agencies. Here the office was in a position analogous to that of the Sun in South Africa or the Commercial Union in Australia. For very special reasons, it was in a sense a latecomer in America, and, consequently, it needed to catch up by employing the latest organisational technology. Thanks to its concentration since the 1860s on a reinsurance approach to this market, it could not gradually develop a branch capacity out of existing agency expertise. Instead, it needed to put into place in short order a string of new agencies and a system to control them.

Within six months, individual appointments were made for Baltimore, Philadelphia, Massachusetts, Chicago, Detroit, Missouri, St Paul, California and Louisville. One of these, Robert Critchell at Chicago, clearly thought it tactful to allude to the literary associations of the Irvings: he cited Mark Twain among his referees.[29] Between 1882 and 1885, further appointments were made for Philadelphia, Connecticut, Missouri, New Orleans, Indianapolis, New York and Vermont. Then, between 1887 and 1893, another set was installed in Rhode Island, New Orleans, Wisconsin and Wyoming. In six states, the named agent was the insurance commissioner of the state. The individual states were interested in securing the nomination of a legal personality against whom claims upon the company could be brought, and, from the Phoenix standpoint, the device offered a quick and dependable means of extending the company's representation.

The American insurance code, fearful of the power of alien financial institutions and protective of the interests of native policy-holders, set out to ensure that the American operations of foreign offices were precisely constituted and firmly under the thumb of the courts. However, despite

[27] Phoenix Trustees' Minutes 17 July 1879; Directors' Minutes, W22, pp. 394–5, 23 July, 30 July 1879. [28] *Ibid.*, 30 July 1879.

[29] R. S. Critchell, *Recollections of a Fire Insurance Man*, Ch. 23, MS, Phoenix Archive.

these restrictions – and, indeed, with the participation of the state commissioners – Irving's agency network proliferated with great rapidity, from the eastern seaboard to the Mid-west by 1880, to the south by the mid-1880s. Well within a decade, Phoenix established a comprehensive direct selling operation in the United States. By 1900, Phoenix controlled twenty-five separate US agencies.

If it took forcefulness to achieve this, it also took a deep purse. The worst aspect of the states' activities lay not in the registration procedures but in the insurance deposit requirements. The initial deposit paid out by Phoenix merely to start direct trading in the USA was no less than $300,000 in US Treasury 4% bonds. The spirit in which this was paid in 1879 contrasts markedly with the hangdog acceptance with which the old Savannah agency was closed in August 1869 'as the State required us to invest money and publish a balance sheet'.[30] Even so, the repeated demands for more and more deposits were a constant drag on enterprise. The states dunned Phoenix incessantly: Ohio for $100,000, Georgia for $25,000, Virginia for $20,000, all in 1880, and Oregon and North Carolina for $50,000 and $10,000 respectively in 1882. But New York trumped them all: at the end of 1882, Phoenix deposited another $100,000 there in order to meet the latest alteration in state regulations.[31]

The directors paid up stalwartly, but their patience was not inexhaustible. In July 1891, Phoenix was faced with yet another, especially large, demand for further increases in the 'net surplus' required under US law. This time the Board debated seriously whether they should pay. It took a visit by Irving to Lombard Street before the Board agreed to put up the extra £80,000.[32] By 1898, the total amount consumed by American deposits was an enormous £700,000.[33]

This enforced interest in US securities did have one positive outcome: it initiated Phoenix's long-lived involvement with the US investment market. Having to deposit securities encouraged Phoenix to consider which might be the most efficient securities. Thus, in the 1890s there was substantial switching of the funds and assets which represented the deposits. In 1897 $200,000 worth of Treasury 4%s were withdrawn from the New York State Insurance Department at Albany and replaced by $200,000 worth of New York 3½% gold bonds. This deposit was reckoned good 'both for legal and commercial considerations'.[34] Similarly, the

[30] Phoenix Foreign Agents Ledger C19/4.
[31] Phoenix Trustees' Minutes, 14 December 1882. The New York legislature had decided that it could no longer take account of deposits in other states when assessing the overall security of a foreign insurance office.
[32] *Ibid.*, 23 July 1891. [33] Phoenix Directors' Minutes, 26, p. 268, 16 March 1898.
[34] Phoenix Trustees' Minutes, 19 August 1897.

extension to the deposits which caused so much debate in 1891 was placed, once agreed, in the bonds of nine different railway companies. Railway investment was particularly active in 1900, with as much as $380,000 going into railroad bonds in that year.[35] Clearly, if Phoenix was stimulated to shop around for the best-yielding American securities for its legal deposits, the expertise which resulted could as easily be applied for the company's own investment purposes.

To begin with at least, the Irving administration seemed well able to provide the income needed to finance this scale of investment. In 1880, Irving handed over $90,000 for conversion into securities. His profits on net premiums for the early years were: for 1879–80 24.5%, for 1881 3.3%, and for 1882 5.2%. But the increase in the scale of the premiums on which they were earned was very striking. Gross income from the United States soared in the early 1880s (see Table 3.1), as did the US share in total foreign earnings. By 1885 this stood at a remarkable 50.3%, very nearly the highest American share for the entire period 1870–1914 (the actual peak was 50.5%, scaled in both 1891 and 1901), and one of the highest in the company's extended history of US trade. That this should have been achieved within six years of relaunching direct trade in the USA was impressive. Thereafter, in the thirty years between 1885 and 1914, the US share in Phoenix total foreign income never fell below 40%; and that too was impressive.

Clearly, such a record required unusual commitment and industry and Phoenix recognised as much. In 1881 Irving's commission on profits was increased from 5% to 19%, and he was appointed formally as US manager, with the Philadelphia agent, E. B. Clark as assistant US manager.[36] The Trustees agreed that Irving had 'successfully established the business of the agency with great energy throughout the several states by the selection . . . of influential and suitable sub-agents and satisfactorily conducted the business from the commencement'.[37] Next year Irving was invited to London to brief the full Board on his transatlantic successes. He enjoyed pointing out on a large map 'the position of the most important Cities and Towns in which active Agencies were in operation'.[38]

This was the honeymoon period. By the middle 1880s American affairs did not look so rosy. The US business cycle had turned down, and, from the last months of 1882, insurance losses turned sharply upwards. In the big cities, the insurance bogey which conventionally hunted with the

[35] *Ibid.*, 14 March, 24 October, 28 November 1900.
[36] Phoenix Directors' Minutes, X23, p. 153, 3 August 1881.
[37] Phoenix Trustees' Minutes, 16 June 1881.
[38] Phoenix Directors' Minutes X23, p. 250, 14 June 1882.

hounds of economic recession – arson – reappeared to such effect that it became 'a means of permanent employment for professional criminals'.[39] In this phase Irving could point only to 'careful and satisfactory management . . . during a period of considerable depression'.[40]

The Board were not pleased. In February 1884, they refused to buy Irving a new head office on Wall Street, which he had coveted, and he had to wait another ten years before he was re-housed.[41] In November, the monthly announcement to the Board of US losses was replaced by a regular weekly set-aside of £3,000 to cover US losses, increased to £4,000 per week in April 1885.[42] Amidst what was perceived in London as deepening crisis, two of the Trustees, Walter Bird[43] and Sir John Lubbock were briefed to review the past five years of American trade. They reported within one week. Firstly, they concluded that five years was too short a period from which to draw any conclusions. Secondly, they concluded that this five years had been profitable: the surplus of receipts over outgoings had amounted to £65,000.[44] But they remained uneasy. The problem was the amount of money that had to be deposited in the United States before the surplus could be harvested: 'Important questions remain both as to the extent of this gain and as to the locking up for the sake of it, a large part of the Company's capital.'[45] At this point, the unease was such that the Trustees decided to send Walter Bird, who, as an old-style London merchant, had American business interests of his own, to view the US problem at first hand.

However, there is no evidence that Bird ever went. In January 1886, Coope and Lubbock were still quizzing him on his proposed trip and he was replying that he was 'not unwilling' but had 'no personal business need for going there at present'. As he dallied, Phoenix's corporate need also abated. By early 1886, the American results were looking better (see the surplus for 1885 in Table 3.3) and the Trustees decided to indulge their travel-shy colleague, agreeing that 'it would not be desirable to press forward Mr Bird's intended mission'.[46]

Oddly, this cycle of concern did not synchronise well with the cycle of actual business performance. Measurement of the net underwriting surplus on the American trade does indeed reveal a decline from high levels

[39] James, *Biography of a Business*, p. 181.
[40] Phoenix Directors' Minutes, X23, p. 430, 19 March 1884.
[41] *Ibid.*, p. 418, 4 February 1884.
[42] *Ibid.*, Y24, pp. 52, 86, 19 November 1884, 1 April 1885.
[43] Phoenix director 1884–1921. Bird was similar to the anonymous appointees of the 1850s, and thus an 'old-style' director by the time of his appointment in 1884. He gave his business as 'W. Bird & Co., Merchants of 7 East India Avenue. E.C.'.
[44] Phoenix Trustees' Minutes, 30 July 1885. [45] *Ibid.* [46] *Ibid.*, 14 January 1886.

Table 3.3. *Net underwriting surplus on US fire business, 1880–90*

Year	Gross premium (£)	Loss ratio (%)	Underwriting surplus (%)
1880	25,149	9.9	59.8
1881	93,723	40.3	29.5
1882	140,652	61.1	7.7
1883	193,084	64.6	5.0
1884	247,240	59.4	10.0
1885	287,696	58.2	11.4
1886	292,457	70.0	6.9
1887	269,502	61.5	7.0
1888	274,617	69.7	0.03
1889	254,237	75.7	−5.9
1890	255,955	77.2	−7.3

Note: Modern practice would deduct payments out of the premium reserve funds from *written* premiums to produce *earned* premiums. Similarly, if it is necessary to increase the claims reserve fund in the course of the year, modern practice adds that increase to *losses paid* to produce *losses incurred* in the year. However, premium reserve fund data cannot be secured for historical periods. And there is justification for the historian in following contemporary practice. Although transfers from reserves to cover unpaid losses were common enough, most nineteenth-century insurers were guided by the underwriting surplus outcome, produced by premiums less expenses and losses paid, as displayed above.
Source: Calculated from Phoenix Review of Foreign Agencies, Book 2, p. 187.

after 1880, a trough around 1883 and a rally around 1885. But the rally is modest and is not sustained: surpluses revert to lean dimensions after 1886, to trivial dimensions after 1888, and convert into outright loss in 1889 and 1890 (see Table 3.3).

Table 3.3 at first seems to suggest that, as the premiums climb, so the surplus out-turn gets worse. Then, as the premiums are trimmed back in the late 1880s, the results get worse still. And these are results affecting about half of all Phoenix overseas income. A list of US profits interleaved at folio 53 of Review of Foreign Agencies, Book 3 (shown as Table 3.4) indicates that the Phoenix management was aware of the problem.

There is no indication of how the contemporary overall profit figure was calculated, but it is reassuring for the historian that the contemporary measurement also shows the Phoenix American account dropping into the red in the late 1880s. Yet the Board, which had good reason to be

Table 3.4. *Phoenix calculation of US profits, 1880–9*

	Profit (£)	% Gross premium
1880	26,284	104.5
1881	4,212	4.5
1882	8,861	6.3
1883	10,163	5.3
1884	3,028	1.2
1885	26,203	9.1
1886	28,762	9.8
1887	−5,303	−2.0
1888	−2,933	−1.1
1889	−13,179	−5.2

Note: The percentage calculations have been added to the contemporary note, by expressing the raw figures as percentages of premiums listed in the same source. The aberrational figure for 1880 is probably produced by a carry-over. The overall pattern is not dissimilar from our calculations of underwriting surplus (above, Table 3.3).
Source: Phoenix Review of Foreign Agencies, Book 3, p. 53.

agitated late in the decade, is at its most worried in 1884 and 1885; there is no similar litany of doubt in the minutes for the later 1880s and no plan to send Bird, or anyone else, to the United States

Perhaps some directors were reassured by the fact that the whole-decade result for the 1880s, despite the losses of the last years, was a net cumulative profit of £86,100. By contrast, others may have reflected that this represented a gain of 3.7% on a decadal turnover of £2.3 million, for which the company was locking up £700,000 of its capital in copper-bottomed, and necessarily low-yielding, US securities required by the government as insurance deposits. All will have realised that deposits were a considerable nuisance in America, and that underwriting profits there were subject to very considerable instability.

If any of them were still wondering about this pattern by 1890, the ensuing decade must surely have put the matter beyond question. The results of the underwriting surplus calculations for the period 1891–1903 again show an upward sweep for 1895–8 and steep downturns in 1894 and after 1899. The turn-of-century cluster of bad results in 1899–1902 is particularly striking (see Table 3.5).

Here initial improvement appeared to be obtained by writing more premiums and achieving lower losses; but later still higher premiums were associated with some very punishing claims ratios.

Table 3.5. *Net underwriting surplus on US fire business, 1891–1903*

Year	Gross premium (£)	Loss ratio (%)	Underwriting surplus (%)
1891	336,150	53.7	14.9
1892	380,793	64.1	6.0
1893	402,521	65.4	5.6
1894	347,439	75.3	−6.8
1895	368,716	64.8	4.7
1896	383,788	59.8	8.5
1897	384,510	54.9	13.7
1898	377,233	62.6	5.5
1899	393,467	70.7	−1.6
1900	424,993	77.1	−7.9
1901	495,061	68.7	0.7
1902	490,905	79.4	−9.9
1903	496,962	59.3	9.0

Note: These results refer to the US Branch alone. Inclusion of the results of Pelican of New York from 1899 would not alter the general pattern. The combined outcome for Branch and Pelican for the five years 1899–1903 gives loss ratios of: 69.1%; 75.7%; 66.9%; 77.6%; and 58.7%; and surplus/deficits of: 0.16%; −6.5%; 2.6%; −8.0%; and 9.3%.
Source: Calculated from Phoenix Review of Foreign Agencies, Book 2.

Again, the contemporary record confirms this outline. Phoenix kept its own comparative account of the branch premium and branch profit performance of the leading British players in the US market for the 1890s. The profit results are converted into graph form in Figure 3.1 and tabulated in Table 3.7; and comparative premium earnings are given in Table 3.6. These data immediately reveal two striking effects. One is that the further, and very large, increase in Phoenix US premiums in the 1890s was enough to promote the office into the company of the very biggest British operators in the transatlantic market. Phoenix began the decade in seventh place and ended it in fifth. Its increase in US premium in the period 1890–1900, at 29%, was bettered only by Norwich Union. The second was the extreme variability of profits, as measured by Phoenix,[47] not only for itself but for all leading British companies. Allowing for lags and slightly different reporting periods, the manner of the variation for

[47] Here the method of calculation can be inferred. Profit appears to be defined as premiums net of reinsurances, less all losses and expenses, plus or minus the difference between unpaid losses of the previous and current year.

Fig. 3.1 The profitability of US branches of leading UK fire offices, 1890–1901

Table 3.6. *US premiums of major UK insurers, 1890–1901 ($)*

	1890	1891	1892	1893	1894	1895	1896	1897	1898	1899	1900	1901	Premium income % increase (approx) 1890–1900	1897–1900
LLG	4,496,999	4,813,522	5,393,150	5,690,877	5,651,713	5,633,321	5,473,606	5,185,885	4,979,422	4,717,490	5,001,988	5,502,416	11	−4
Royal	3,574,840	4,027,911	4,731,855	4,925,130	4,931,919	4,863,197	4,823,512	4,627,028	4,268,991	4,008,029	4,013,709	4,062,437	12	−13
CU	2,724,387	2,909,193	2,786,840	2,837,428	2,682,371	2,258,962	2,373,035	2,299,942	2,235,875	2,361,596	2,435,469	2,816,675	−11	6
NBM	2,092,754	2,159,207	2,369,178	2,402,078	2,311,482	2,330,518	2,369,884	2,480,623	2,389,949	2,322,457	2,677,481	2,828,180	28	8
LL	1,740,297	1,813,330	2,140,269	2,034,618	1,931,211	1,850,223	1,740,947	1,810,477	1,752,511	1,640,526	1,611,199	1,727,068	−7	−11
Lancs	1,657,056	2,804,298	2,721,858	2,085,214	1,872,096	1,883,146	1,898,060	2,001,796	1,978,738	1,799,210	1,886,781	–	14	−6
Phoenix	1,652,698	1,853,470	1,889,684	1,860,874	1,815,990	1,926,891	1,940,634	1,911,714	1,864,620	2,031,142	2,134,644	2,468,690	29	12
Sun	1,455,217	1,755,176	2,157,562	1,981,608	1,610,990	1,561,441	1,575,596	1,629,170	1,579,258	1,405,683	1,480,742	1,815,094	2	−9
NU	1,223,029	1,371,540	1,567,671	1,535,786	1,580,511	1,563,298	1,503,337	1,491,151	1,471,814	1,484,329	1,643,496	1,779,733	34	10
Imperial	1,103,813	1,159,576	1,241,009	1,160,734	1,137,802	1,161,389	1,075,199	1,144,257	1,147,181	–	1,286,499	1,180,765	17	12
Northern	1,070,766	1,117,127	1,219,973	1,252,373	1,196,111	1,251,841	1,134,241	1,00,8134	988,597	1,031,510	1,189,079	1,529,918	11	18
London Assurance	1,021,311	1,103,654	1,109,890	989,485	898,876	844,127	1,029,252	890,961	824,597	801,632	854,631	1,053,025	−16	−4

Key: LLG = Liverpool & London & Globe
CU = Commercial Union
NBM = North British & Mercantile
LL = London & Lancs
NU = Norwich Union
Source: Phoenix Review of US Business.

Table 3.7. *US profits of major UK insurers, 1890–1901: loss or gain as % of premiums*

	1890	1891	1892	1893	1894	1895	1896	1897	1898	1899	1900	1901	Annual average 1891/1901	Ranking
LLG	+13.7	−2.0	+8.9	+4.3	+10.4	+15.6	+18.9	+16.0	+7.4	−7.2	+0.1	−2.1	+8.1	1
Royal	+12.7	−2.4	+5.2	+2.8	+7.9	+14.2	+13.2	+11.6	+2.3	−9.6	−5.4	−0.9	+5.0	3
CU	+11.7	+0.5	−3.1	−5.3	+6.3	+4.1	+12.9	+16.1	+6.3	−1.6	+0.2	−1.8	+4.0	6
NBM	+6.7	−7.0	−4.5	−10.4	−4.8	+11.2	+14.5	+18.7	+8.4	−7.3	−1.4	−0.9	+3.0	7
LL	+14.3	−4.2	+2.9	−1.3	+9.5	+14.3	+15.4	+20.6	+6.7	−2.9	+5.1	−1.7	+7.2	2
Lancs	−0.5	+8.7	−32.0	−23.1	+4.6	+7.6	+10.5	+13.3	−2.2	−22.9	−8.4	–	–	–
Phoenix	+15.0	−4.5	+3.8	−2.3	+7.3	+11.0	+12.4	+13.4	+6.4	−6.3	−4.6	−9.5	+4.4	4
Sun	+12.8	−1.1	−3.6	−16.1	+2.5	+8.3	+14.8	+13.5	+1.6	−15.1	−11.6	+5.2	+0.2	10
NU	+14.8	+2.7	+1.0	−10.9	+9.4	+7.7	+9.6	+12.3	+4.9	−1.2	−1.1	−17.3	+4.1	5
London	+14.2	−10.3	−7.6	−14.4	+3.0	+10.0	+11.7	+27.1	−0.9	−6.8	−1.9	+8.2	+1.0	8
Northern	+9.0	−13.4	−5.6	−11.7	+7.3	+8.1	+11.2	+5.5	+5.3	−7.1	+2.4	+3.1	+0.9	9

Key: LLG = Liverpool & London & Globe
CU = Commercial Union
NBM = North British & Mercantile
LL = London & Lancs
NU = Norwich Union
Source: Phoenix Review of US Business

Phoenix is very similar to the result achieved by our calculations of underwriting surplus. But, again, over the entire period 1890–1900, the cumulative out-turn was a profit of £190,723. However, on accumulated premiums of £4,296,782, this was, once more, a yield of only 4.4%.

Perhaps the Board simply learned to live with the variation, learning too that there was usually a surplus at the end of the day. But, in fact, this will not wash since their doubts about the American operation continued into the 1900s.[48] A more plausible interpretation of the Board's panic in the mid-1880s, and its periodic agitation thereafter, is drawn less from the profit record than from the Board's reaction to Irving's behaviour as manager. This was in the best tradition of thrusting American enterprise. To begin with, Irving increased American premiums, so suppressed for many years, at a speed that left many directors breathless. But this was as nothing compared to the high-handedness with which he ran his big accounts. The most damaging episode occurred in January 1885.

At the turn of 1884 and 1885, Irving took over the liabilities of the Manufacturers' Insurance Company of Boston, paying for them some $300,000. He did this off his own bat, without first consulting the Board in London, and in clear violation of his power of attorney. The directors were aghast. Managers of branches were not supposed to stalk the far corners of the globe buying without notice large chunks of other people's insurance companies. Or, if they were, what kind of innovation had Phoenix fallen into? The Board decided that they were not, that Irving was *ultra vires*, and that a stiff reprimand should be addressed to the American manager.

Irving replied, apologising for his 'presumptive [sic] telegram' – which had simply told the Board what he had already done – and explaining that the advantage had needed to be seized swiftly; there had been no time for debate with London. The Board did not note, but might well have done, that Irving's original disclosure of the *fait accompli* had come by wire. But the advantage that decisive action had acquired was real enough, 'an excellent business in Boston and other cities'. In the end, the Trustees accepted Irving's coup, 'demurring to the reasonableness of the explanation'. But they also sent him a 'cautionary letter' warning him that a second display of transatlantic autonomy would not be tolerated.[49]

This stroke of managerial independence, more than any other factor, triggered the Board's unease about US business in the mid-1880s. Significantly, the Lubbock–Bird Report on American Business of July 1885, coming well after the Board's acceptance of the initiative, and well after

48 See below, pp. 259–66.

49 Phoenix Trustees' Minutes, 29 January 1885; Directors' Minutes, T24, pp. 71–2, 4 February 1885.

tempers should have cooled, still recorded that Irving's actions had 'to some extent, weakened the Directors' confidence in him'.[50] This seemed to be a lasting effect, since nearly twenty years later, when Irving again took a major independent initiative, this time over rate increases in 1902, he was immediately checked by London.[51] By that time, the Phoenix Board feared that its American business had 'fallen into a groove'. It may have been unfortunate, therefore, that an early contretemps in the relationship between Phoenix in London and their manager in America worked to limit the enterprise of the latter. For it was scarcely consistent of the Board to complain of an excess both of entrepreneurial risk-taking and of administrative routine.

However, for much of the period 1885 to 1897 it was clearly what their powerful US manager might do on his own account which most disturbed the Phoenix Board. To these worried men, America appeared to be a place of spiralling premiums, loss ratios above 70% and managers who acted as if they were Boards of Directors. Clearly, some of them began to wonder just what had been restarted in the USA.

4. ANOTHER BIRD FLIES IN: PELICAN OF NEW YORK, 1897

In January 1897, Alexander Irving, in his sixteenth year as Phoenix US Manager, took ship for England. Ostensibly, his purpose – or at least the only one minuted – was to ask permission to add his profits for 1896 to his net surplus in the USA, so as to bring it up to a total $750,000.[52] In reality, he was probably taking his first soundings about a much more radical proposal. Given the Board's views on America and American managers, Irving must have known that he needed the most comprehensive sanction for what he intended. No doubt, however, the presence of a large surplus in the United States was not irrelevant to his calculations. In October, a second visit to London by Irving's equally long-serving deputy E. B. Clark revealed more clearly what these were. The Americans were proposing that Phoenix should procure a New York charter empowering the company to launch an independent American subsidiary, 'a course similar to that already adopted by our British competitors'.[53]

There were two main purposes: to achieve a stronger foothold among rising competitive tides; and 'to protect our business from undue taxation by the establishment of a local company in the state of New York',[54] a

[50] Phoenix Trustees' Minutes, 30 July 1885. [51] See below, p. 261.
[52] Phoenix Trustees' Minutes, 7 January 1897.
[53] *Ibid.*, 14 October 1897. The Royal, for instance, had established the Queen as its US subsidiary in 1891. [54] *Ibid.*

means of side-stepping the continuing torrent of American deposit requirements. One powerful native competitor, the Insurance Company of North America, reported in 1899 on the bareknuckle state of the American insurance market:

> The difficulty of reform is very great owing to the large number of companies which refuse to join any agreement but remain outside with the hope of making a profit by shading premiums fixed by the old line companies and also by the payment of larger brokerage and agency commissions.[55]

The USA was not one of those markets, worked so assiduously by Phoenix worldwide, where a dependable tariff and the disciplined cooperation of local agents' associations provided effective antidotes to mayhem and misrule. In the United States, insurance business consisted of mayhem and misrule.

Much of it, as the North America also stressed, was official in origin:

> Adverse legislation in almost every state of the Union is also an important factor, and the conduct of the business is attended with more and more difficulty. The average legislator fails to recognise the difference between Trusts, which are inimical to public welfare and an agreement between insurance companies to charge certain fair rates for their policies.[56]

Also, of course, the average legislator gave 'adverse legislation' a special costly twist when dealing with foreign insurance companies, a refinement with which the North America did not need to concern itself. Immunity from the refinement was precisely the state which Irving and Clark wished Phoenix also to occupy.

No doubt because American deposits had hurt so badly, the Trustees took the point relatively quickly. They decided that an American cousin should carry the same name as the sister office on the other side of Lombard Street. It should be established on capital of £50,000 maximum, 'denominated the Pelican Assurance Company... worked by our present US staff... any necessary surplus provided from our US Assets'.[57] Not that dissent was entirely lacking. Lubbock, wary neither for the first nor the last time of the American 'entanglement', stressed that £700,000 had been invested in the American business already and objected to sending still more British money chasing after this.[58] Tactfully, the Trustees informed Irving that the Board was not minded to 'send over' any further funds to float any subsidiary but were still prepared to contemplate solutions which did not involve further capital exports. This, no

[55] Quoted by James, *Biography of a Business*, p. 208.
[56] *Ibid.* [57] Phoenix Trustees' Minutes, 14 October 1897.
[58] Phoenix Directors' Minutes, 26, p. 268, 18 March 1898.

doubt, was where Irving's surplus came in. With more than a hint of his old independence, he replied that he could find the necessary £50,000 from among the current US investments of the office. The Board settled for that; Lubbock curbed his tongue; and the scheme went ahead in the spring of 1898. It was Phoenix's first major overseas subsidiary.

The management was to consist of three Trustees and ten directors, each of whom was required by law to hold at least $500 of Pelican stock. Despite an attempt by the prospective directors to cajole Phoenix into lending them the necessary shares, the company insisted that candidates should find the qualifying amount for themselves.[59] The capital of the New York Pelican was to be $200,000, of which the directors held $6,500 and Phoenix controlled $193,500.[60] Shop was to be set up at 31 Liberty Street, New York.

There were strong financial and familial elements to the composition of the Board. The first were provided by the Phoenix link with Barings, the second by the extended clan of Irvings. The three founding Trustees were: Joseph A. Dean, Chairman of the Oil and Coke Company, George F. Crane of Baring, Magoun & Co., bankers, and the solicitor, John Duer, a relative of Irving. The executive directors were: A. D. Irving, president of Pelican and US manager, E. B. Clark, vice-president and assistant US manager, L. P. Bayard, second vice-president and secretary and deputy assistant US manager, and A. D. Irving Jnr, assistant secretary and US branch secretary.[61]

The Pelican took its first premiums, some £11,543, in 1899 and more than quadrupled this, to £54,869 by 1903. In the period 1904–13 takings ran in the £60,000s and first rose above £100,000 in 1915. In the year before this, the Pelican changed its name to the Imperial Assurance Company. The Phoenix US Branch continued to report its income separately from that of Pelican/Imperial and it continued to earn much more. Average income of Pelican for 1901–5 was just over 10% of the Branch average receipts, nearly 13% for 1906–10 and nearly 12% for 1911–15. Clearly then, the subsidiary served as additional and auxiliary capacity, taking much of the increase in Phoenix's American trade, rather than as a replacement mechanism for the existing organisation.

The USA was the market in which Phoenix experienced the most rapid organisational transition of its late nineteenth century career. Bereft of the

[59] Phoenix Trustees' Minutes, 21 December 1898. [60] Foreign Agents Ledger C19/4.

[61] The other directors were: R. B. Whittermore, A. P. Whitehead, G. A. Strong, L. R. Warren and yet another Irving (W.) and another Bayard (L. P. Jnr). Dean was replaced by H. H. Treadwell of Tiffany's, the renowned jewellers, in 1904 and two more members of the Whitehead family filled vacant seats in 1904. Also in that year of upheaval, E. B. Clark resigned amidst yet another inquiry into US affairs by London Head Office.

reinsurance structure and the agency traditions, which remained the staples of support in Europe, the company resorted to a full branch operation almost immediately direct trade was re-established in the United States. Then, the special conditions of the US market – heavy losses, cut-throat competitors, and, above all, aggressive state governments – forced Phoenix within twenty years into what was for it an early example of the classic administrative graduation from branch to subsidiary company. Naturally, it was not accidental that the USA was both Phoenix's biggest market and one only recently rebroached. Where elsewhere, outside Europe, long-established agencies and the new agents' associations sufficed, America needed the most up-to-date combination in insurance technology, both subsidiary and branch.

5. YET MORE DOUBTS: TROUBLE IN THE 1900S

Despite the apparently profitable out-turn on each of the previous decades of direct trade in the USA, the Phoenix Board in the 1900s continued to gnaw at the bone of discontent. Probably, their ache originated in an imbalance: the United States now provided so much income that the balance of an enterprise used to a truly global spread was thrown out of true.

However, the directors themselves contrived far more complex rationalisations than this. One was that the previous decades had not really been profitable at all. A Head Office analysis of all Phoenix and Pelican of New York results for the period 1879–1901 added the modern assumption that there should be a 40% premium allowance against unexpired risk and concluded that, on this assumption, the twenty-two years of the revived American trade actually showed an absolute loss.[62] The New York office protested that inclusion of the unexpired risk allowance should be balanced by the inclusion of the income earned on American investment.[63] This point went unheeded.

Examination of the comparative record does not suggest that the critical attitude of Head Office towards the American trade in the first years of the century was particularly well founded. Ironically, it may have become more firmly founded as the 1900s wore on. But the Phoenix record for the 1890s looks respectable against that of other companies. To begin with, of course, Irving's premium drive had reinstated Phoenix among the largest British insurance exporters to the USA. And, if its premium ranking had improved substantially during the decade, its profit ranking had done even better: by 1900 the company ranked fifth in terms

[62] Phoenix Head Office to New York office, 6 February 1902.
[63] Phoenix New York to Head Office, 7 March 1902.

of its American income level, but fourth in terms of its average annual advance in profits 1890–1901 (see Table 3.7). As late as 1899, Phoenix's results, though showing a loss in that year, were better than those of the Royal, the Liverpool & London & Globe, and the North British. Moreover, it is striking that all the big British offices experienced the profit upswing of 1893–7 and the collapse in profits between 1897 and 1901 (see Figure 3.1). These data hardly support the notion that there was something specially amiss with Phoenix's American management.

The point made by the New York office about investment income was also valid. The premium flow in the USA was sufficient to fund the immense deposits required by the state governments. And the investments providing these guarantees were of increasingly effective composition as experience led to switching of securities towards higher yielding stock. After twenty years, the deposits could surely be viewed as a form of forced saving, upon which a useful income was payable. It was inconsistent to consider the entrance fee a burden upon American insurances, then to exclude the resulting yield from consideration as insurance income.

It is likely that the immediate stimulus to the Board's renewed agitation in the 1900s was less consideration of the long-run results of the Irving administration than the short-run crisis in American earnings since 1897. Just as in 1885, they were alarmed by an unexpected development rather than by an unappealing perspective. And they were further confused by a lack of synchronisation between the American economy and the insurance economy: the peak in insurance profits in the mid-1890s had coincided with a somewhat suppressed phase for the US economy generally, while the insurance downturn at the end of the decade ran alongside a phase of accelerated economic activity, 1899–1902.[64]

Whatever the origins of the Board's discontent, they were determined to give full vent to it. Late in 1901, Head Office called for a special report from New York on the US Branch's expenses and losses for 1899–1901, and, from the beginning of the next year, instructions went out for a selective reduction of risks in the USA 'that offer little hope of improvement'. American business was about to be treated to one of Phoenix's periodic 'purification of the books'. This had caused problems in the nineteenth century but it was deeply embedded in the corporate memory. The notion of 'smaller but better' as an underwriting approach was a reflex response to difficult conditions. Here it reappeared to little better effect than on previous occasions.

London now looked askance at the increase of £160,000 in American

[64] *Ibid.*, 25 February 1902.

income over the previous ten years, a 50% advance on the level for 1890, and took a sinister view of the fact that this was 'above the average as compared with other leading British offices'. The stated aim was 'to arrest the swelling of premium income'.[65] This was to be done, despite recent widespread rate increases which had pushed all fire insurance prices east of the Rockies up by a full 25%. Such increases affected about 40% of Phoenix's US income. Yet, 'even allowing the 25% increase', ruled Lombard Street, '1902 figures *must* go below 1901 . . . Until things mend considerably, a free hand can no longer be given.'[66] Indeed, the effect was meant to be lasting: 'The reduction of US liability is no mere transitory thing.'[67]

Particular ire was reserved for American railway risks, which in 1901 had generated one-sixteenth of premium income from the USA but incurred one-half of all US losses. These were drastically pruned. Business was also scrutinised on a state-by-state basis. In February, Irving's office reported that, leaving railways aside, nineteen states were showing losses, twenty-five showing profit. The out-turn was not helped by a major blaze at the fashionable holiday resort of Jacksonville in May 1901 when a four-hour outbreak on a sunny day burned out 148 blocks, destroyed property worth £1.5 million and promoted Florida high on Phoenix's list of dangerous states. To such places pruning was also applied.

Head Office emphasised to New York in March 1902 that of 'nine bad states' previously identified, six appeared again in the offenders list for 1901.[68] The result was that during 1902 Phoenix withdrew completely from Delaware (excepting Wilmington and Newcastle), Indian Territory and New Mexico and partially closed down its operation in North Dakota, Ohio, Tennessee, Michigan and Missouri. In Pennsylvania farm risks were cut back and three agencies closed in New Hampshire.

In the midst of this general surgery, Irving's third in command, L. P. Bayard, reckoned a competent but 'somewhat conservative underwriter', was summoned to London so that the Board might obtain a more personal view of the patient. He did not have a pleasant trip. Bayard met the Phoenix fire manager and secretary, H. B. Guernsey on 5 May and, on 6 May, a group of directors, led by the chairman, Bristow Bovill, and including Newcomb and Bird, still thought to possess American expertise, and assisted by Guernsey. The first session was supposed to be 'a long general talk over the remedial measures instituted by the Directors to place our American business on a profitable basis'.[69] In fact, Bayard was pressed hard on how much Irving had managed to cut out of the

[65] Phoenix Head Office to New York office, 6 February 1902.
[66] *Ibid.*; also 2 April 1902 (emphasis in original). [67] *Ibid.*, 19 March 1902.
[68] *Ibid.* [69] Guernsey, Notes on the Visit of US Manager, 5 May 1902.

American business. He replied that they could not excise whole classes 'except where persistently bad' – such as farms and railway risks – but they were weeding out 'individual risks in the various bad classes'. This was being effected by special roving agents, senior officials who monitored entire districts for poor business, reporting back to New York in person, by the month, or from the South and West, by the half-year.

Discussion at the larger meeting was still more pointed. Bovill asked if it might not benefit the Phoenix to separate off the Pacific Slope business from that supervised from New York. Well before the disaster at San Francisco in 1906, the Pacific market was problematic: in the first half of 1903, for instance, Phoenix's entire US operation showed a profit of $26,139, while the West Coast made a loss of $12,572.[70]

In public, Bayard reacted strongly against the idea of separation, arguing that, 'decentralisation would be no advantage to the Company . . . and that Messrs Irving had spent large sums in organising and building up the business'.[71] In private, Bayard let it be known that he 'was greatly upset' by the proposal for a separate Pacific Coast operation. Having thoroughly raised tempers and muddied waters, the Phoenix central management then performed a manoeuvre which became characteristic of these American investigations: they withdrew. Guernsey discussed Bayard's reaction with Bovill and a select group of directors; and they decided to press the US management no further.

It is unclear what was gained here. Phoenix Head Office first became alarmed by a set of conditions that was affecting all British insurers in the USA. The leadership decided to *rejudge* the US management of the previous two decades by changing their criteria of profitability. Transatlantic relationships were adversely affected by this. Having risked this much in the cause of 'purification', Head Office had no real choice but to proceed to further reform. Instead, it was deterred by the American response and did nothing. Surely, the only outcome was the worst of both worlds.

Perhaps unsurprisingly, it seems that American management actually did deteriorate under these conditions. Whatever its state when Head Office began to investigate it, the process of investigation did it no good. Thus even Phoenix's unbreakable determination to drive the 1902 US premiums below those of 1901 succeeded only for that one year; by 1903 the combined income of Pelican and the US Branch was well above that of 1901 and by 1905 it was nearly 20% above. Profits did not travel in the same direction: the out-turn for 1903, a surplus of $188,752 was well

[70] Phoenix New York to Head Office, 4 August 1903.
[71] Guernsey, Notes, 6 May 1902.

below the Irving administration's average since 1879 of $237,863.[72] The first half of 1904 was again poor and prospects for the second half were no better. This was a notably weak return upon an exercise in correction which by mid-1902 had closed ninety agencies in eighteen separate states at a sacrifice in premium income of about $0.3 million. The mood of the US management which was being forced to implement these policies may be judged by their response to the constant stream of inquiries, requests for information and expressions of concern emanating from London: in late 1903 and through 1904, the proportion attracting no answer rose significantly.

Neither the mood in New York, nor that in London was improved by one other feature of the 1900s in America: the spectacular incidence of calamities. Jacksonville had been bad, but it was merely a foretaste. On 7 February 1904, the great port of Baltimore burned, and on a scale that invited comparison with Hamburg or Chicago. An electrical fault in a wholesale store on Hanover Street, in the centre of the city's highly inflammable maritime dry-goods trade, started a tinder trail which ignited a gasoline tank and two nearby chemical works. The resulting explosion and fire reached deep into the business sector, causing twenty-storey skyscrapers to crumple, as one observer exactly caught it, 'like birdcages in a furnace'.[73] These birdcages were framed in steel and clad in granite, but they crumpled nonetheless. Among them were the offices of some very grand organisations: the Baltimore Stock Exchange, the Customs House, the headquarters of three railway companies, including the Baltimore and Ohio, the Western Union Telegraph building, the offices of the Continental Trust and the Equitable Life, as well as virtually all the banks. Over a hundred trading vessels were driven by the flames from Baltimore's quaysides, slipped their moorings and stood out into Chesapeake Bay; but at least they could get away. Again, a modern city proved mere kindling for a primitive terror.

What did not get away from the Baltimore conflagration included seventy city blocks and 2,500 buildings. They burned for two days, despite the presence of four metropolitan fire brigades. As at Chicago, wind was a vital factor. But it did not have to blow so fiercely at Baltimore: where Chicago's broad boulevards failed to stop a flaming gale, Baltimore's narrow streets fed an advancing bonfire. Baltimore was not badly built; it was too cosily built. Its embers provided a global advertisement for wide streets. The total insurance loss was £15 million, of which the British offices carried about £1.2 million. Of this the Commercial Union

[72] Phoenix Head Office to Phoenix New York, 11 February 1904.
[73] Cited by Liveing, *Commercial Union*, p. 97.

had £120,000 and Phoenix was not far behind with £110,000. The Phoenix Board were so disenchanted with the USA by this point that they did not even record the loss in their minutes, although they did bring themselves to tell their shareholders at the next AGM.[74] But, of course, there was much worse yet to come.

Baltimore must have increased Phoenix's worries about the American trade. The Board minutes are silent. But there are tell-tale signs in the correspondence between London and New York. In March, Head Office requested a general inquiry into the conflagration hazard in the USA. Ironically, Washington Irving undertook to provide an assessment of the conflagration risk in San Francisco.[75] By May instructions had gone out to close three more agencies, prevent increases in liabilities, improve the quality of risks and pay special attention to Chicago.[76] The account books also have tales to tell. The combined underwriting result for the US Branch and Pelican of New York in 1904 shows a loss ratio of 78.6% and a net deficit on premium income of 13.4%, worse even than 1900 or 1902.[77]

It was the way in which the Baltimore disaster fitted into the sequence of American troubles, rather than the single crisis itself, which decided the Phoenix management in autumn 1904 to send senior representatives to see for themselves. Given that Walter Bird had not made the trip in 1885, this was the first major Phoenix embassy to the USA since the days of J. J. Broomfield; but it was also the precursor of many directorial crossings.

This one was made by the fire manager, Guernsey, and the assistant secretary, E. A. Boston, in October 1904. In some ways their report maintained the critical tone which Phoenix had employed in the discussion of its American business since the turn of the century. Thus, their key finding was that, 'things, to our mind, have been allowed to get too much into a groove in the Office; there appears to be room for a shaking up of the men and a revising of ideas'.[78] No matter that Irving protested that on the two major occasions when he had displayed special initiative – the 1885 acquisition of Manufacturers of Boston and the big increase in rates in 1902 – he had been 'strongly checked by the Head Office'. No matter that his deputy, the able E. B. Clark, should so dislike London's intervention that he should provide his own 'shaking up of the men' by resigning in the middle of the 1904 investigation. The men from Head Office were convinced that the trouble was 'due principally to the fact that

[74] Chairman's Annual Report, 1905. This also revealed a loss of £40,000 at Toronto in the same year.

[75] Phoenix Head Office to New York office, 15 March 1904. [76] *Ibid.*, 25 May 1904.

[77] Calculated from Phoenix Review of Foreign Agencies, Books 2 and 3, pp. 53, 63.

[78] A Memorandum on American Business for the Trustees, 31 October 1904.

matters have been allowed to go on unaltered, and with the Agents' ideas of their position unreviewed for a quarter of a century'.[79]

Then, as before, they proceeded actually to alter very little. They judged that the company had 'on the whole, a fine connection which certainly ought to be capable of being turned into a paying asset' and that although it was

> by no means in the forefront of the movements of which one hears on this side – such as the propositions for general rate increases and so forth – still it has a very high reputation for honourable dealing with other Offices, Agents and Brokers and the Public.

Despite the critical remarks about gingering up the management and revising its ideas, the bulk of the report in fact circles comfortably around the status quo. This is true even of the loss of Clark. Here the remarkable opinion is delivered that,

> If it were decided that a push ought to be made for a largely increased volume of business, the loss of Mr Clark would undoubtedly be felt; but so long as the motto continues, as now, to be 'little and good', our interests will be adequately represented by Messrs Irving and Bayard.

So, on the one hand, the management wishes to 'shake up' the men; on the other, it swiftly accustoms itself to the defection of its most thrusting US official. Certainly, it did not proceed to shake up those who were left. For Bayard is seen as 'capable but somewhat too conservative'. And the verdict on the frequently maligned Irving resounds neither one way nor the other. If 'he is not quite well up in details', the visitors found that 'his judgement, firmness and character are of high order'. Just why Irving should have been 'strongly checked' is not made clear by Guernsey and Boston. Nor was it clear to Irving; and, as the London offficals noted, 'the effect is plain in his present attitude'.

At the end of the day, the visiting firemen concluded somewhat limply, 'that there was no adequate reason, and that it would not be desirable at this date, to make a change in the personnel of the Management'. They recommended continuation of the US business – implying once more that there were weaker spirits back in Lombard Street who preferred complete evacuation – but also, with the ambiguity that ran through the whole of this analysis, that 'it should be somewhat more fostered and controlled from London than was the case in the past'.[80] Control from London had been precisely the factor that had alienated the US manager. Yet it had apparently done little for the purity of US business.

[79] *Ibid.* [80] *Ibid.*

It is difficult to escape the impression that if there was indecision present in the handling of Phoenix's US operation, it was located in London rather than elsewhere. Head Office did not seem clear as to what it expected from the US Branch. It appeared overawed by the size of its largest overseas venture and unsure how to proceed with an offshoot both so foreign and so big. The inclination was towards caution, but there was no clear vision of how to be cautious. The traditional remedy of purification was applied, but with little conviction. Despite stern admonitions that the scaling down of American liability was to be 'no mere transitory thing', it was precisely that. Within a few years, Ryan was to assess the purification policy of this phase as misguided.[81] He was also to have views on the 'shaking up' of the men. In its handling of the American market before 1906, Head Office did both too much and too little. Management in London should either have given Irving his head or replaced him and set a strong controlling brief on his successor. But, in reality, it lacked sufficient confidence to do either.

Its difficulties inaugurated a tradition. Communicating effectively with 'the American side' was to be a besetting problem for the twentieth-century Phoenix.

6. DISASTER AT SAN FRANCISCO, 1906

The city of San Francisco was a Gold Rush shanty town in the 1840s, a conurbation of 400,000 people by the 1900s. Early on, it was no stranger to fire, suffering a half-dozen major outbreaks in its first few years. It was rebuilt so frequently in this period that it adopted the sign of the phoenix bird as its emblem. This, and no doubt other measures, proved effective and, by the late nineteenth century, San Francisco was a safe town. Over the period 1881–1902 it imposed on the fire offices a loss ratio of only 28.7%. For Phoenix, ironically, San Francisco before 1906 did not contribute to the general problems of the Pacific Slope trade.

Even more ironically, the city was surveyed by the US National Board of Fire Underwriters in 1905. Much of it was built on land reclaimed from the sea, and so of indeterminate stability. About 90% of construction was timber-framed, the majority using the easy-burning redwood. Nevertheless, a few strictures on the water supply apart, the Board's engineers were satisfied. Certainly, they did not perceive an earthquake hazard. At the time, a geological fault in the vicinity of the San Andreas reservoir was known; but it was not thought to be serious. The engineers reported that

[81] See below, p. 284.

Plate 3.5 Earthquake at San Francisco, 1906: a panorama of destruction.

'slight earthquake shocks are not unknown, but their effects on walls is not noticeable and reported to be of little consequence'.[82] Similarly, Bayard reported to Phoenix that, 'while slight tremors had occurred from time to time, these were satisfactorily accounted for by the scientists, and no fear was entertained of any serious seismic disturbance'.[83]

The shock that hit San Francisco at 5.15 a.m. on the morning of Wednesday, 18 April 1906 was serious. Not only did it wreck buildings and kill people, it also destroyed the means of relief. The tremors which rippled through soft, reclaimed subsoil easily toppled buildings, but, worse still, they cracked open water mains, disconnected the telephones and ruptured gas and electricity lines. Within the first hour, they also killed the fire brigade chief, D. T. Sullivan. Supplies of information, direction and water were immediately disrupted. Fire followed.

No assessment of the conflagration hazard in San Francisco had anticipated the simultaneous eruption of hundreds of small or medium fires. But that is what a myriad of lesions in the gas and electricity mains produced on 18 April 1906. The first emitted clouds of explosive vapour,

[82] A. S. Reed, *Special Report to National Board of Fire Underwriters*, 1905.
[83] Bayard to Head Office, 29 May 1906.

the second the sparks to detonate them. Tottering buildings spilled additional fuel into the resulting fires. The fire-fighting forces, bereft of leadership and water, could not cope. Inexperienced soldiers, brought in under martial law to form firebreaks by dynamiting buildings, added to the destruction. Faced with the magnitude of the attack and the confusion of the response, the populace panicked – and so compounded the losses. Under these conditions, a full-scale conflagration developed and reigned unchecked for three full days, dying away at last – possibly owing to rainfall – on Saturday 21 April.

Between Nero's burning of Rome and the Allied bombing of Dresden or Hiroshima probably no city suffered such extensive devastation as San Francisco in the spring of 1906. Four-fifths of the city was destroyed, an area of nearly 5 square miles (13 km^2), a space equivalent to that portion of London between the limits of Regents Park, Dalston Junction, Battersea Park and Peckham High Street. Nearly 500 citizens died, 1,500 were injured and 250,000 were left without homes. The total fire insurance liability at San Francisco was between £45 million and £54 million, of which about £40 million was paid. The loss was equal to the total worldwide surplus of all fire insurers operating in the USA in 1906 and wiped out in three days the entire underwriting profit on all US fire business over the previous thirty-five years.

Just how much damage was caused by the earthquake and how much by the fire is unknown. The use of explosives both to create obstacles to the blaze and to demolish buildings left unsafe by the shock further obscured the issue. Yet the distinction was vital. For, technically, fire offices were not liable for fire damage to buildings already 'fallen' as a result of other forces. Even more pertinently, some companies, among them four British ones, included 'earthquake clauses' in their contracts, specifically repudiating obligation in the case of fire associated with shock damage. An indulgent reading of these clauses would have held these offices immune to claim. But, of course, indulgence is unlikely under such circumstances. In reality, bitter controversy formed the context for the settlement of the San Francisco claims. It was composed of four main elements: the impossibility of determining at which point fire damaged which buildings; the inability of some companies to meet their vast losses; the perception by others that generous settlements were good for business; and, above all, a clamorous public demand for hefty compensation.

To begin with, there was much confusion. Communications between San Francisco and the outside world were cut, and for some days, while the press imagined an even worse disaster than the one that had happened, the insurance community had no idea of the extent of its losses.

Plate 3.6 Fire after the shock: San Francisco burns.

Many offices set up temporary headquarters across the Bay, in Oakland, but could not send telegrams out. Most agents could not get at records incarcerated in vaults or immolated in the flames. Phoenix in New York could not contact its chief agent in San Francisco, Washington Irving, because the telegraph link with his home in Berkeley was sundered. On 21 April, New York received news that Irving was safe and the message,

> Wholesale, retail, financial districts burned; office gone; cannot determine liabilities . . . make uncertain estimate . . . amount at risk both companies from $3,000,000 to $3,500,000; this may be much altered; will cable again Monday.

Irving needed his key files, but they were in the Phoenix vault and 'I cannot reach it . . . until the ruins cool'.[84] However, although charred, the papers survived and, after some days, were retrieved; once treated with chemicals, they were able to assist Phoenix in the management of the settlement.

Before this point, however, Phoenix, like other offices, was operating largely in ignorance. On 22 April, Washington Irving told New York that he was accepting only business that could be carried net, partly because of 'the disquieting rumours concerning the solvency of the companies from whom I would have to obtain reinsurance covers' and partly because the fire

[84] W. Irving to New York office, 22 April 1906.

Plate 3.7 Artist's impression of the San Francisco fire at street level.

had destroyed all his maps.[85] But at least the offices decided to pool what little they did know. By 22 April, they had already formed a Fire Underwriters' Adjusting Bureau equipped with an Executive Committee upon which a Phoenix man sat alongside representatives from the Aetna, the Hartford, the German American and the Norwich Union, among others. Despite this show of activity, however, Irving had to report that 'there will be nothing done, of course, in the way of adjustment for some weeks'.

In the meantime, the British press occupied itself in guessing games as to what the London offices might owe. On 21 April *The Economist* overestimated the Phoenix liability (which was to turn out at £624,241) by a factor greater than two; it guessed £1,544,000, while the *Daily Telegraph* speculated more modestly on £869,000.[86] With rather more certainty, *The Economist* also showed the effect of the conflagration on insurance shares: between March 30 and April 26, the average fall was 12%, but, as a large American operator, Phoenix suffered more, with a fall of 17%. But, as the papers guessed and the shares fell, the insurers themselves had no idea of what their losses actually were.

On May 1, Phoenix Head Office cabled New York inquiring whether the figures roughly estimated in Irving's first message from San Francisco after the disaster – $3.5 million (£721,649) gross, $2.7 million (£556,701) net – still stood. But Irving's information was still deficient: the insurers were not allowed back into the ruins until 5 May. Some, like the German American and the Firemens' Fund, found nothing but ashes. Phoenix was luckier. However, fortune had its limits. When Phoenix New York was able at length to submit more considered estimates on 7 May, the figure for the likely net loss had risen to $3.25 million (£670,103). The London management was not pleased: Fire Manager Boston wrote back, 'we had not educated ourselves up to the point of expecting a further $550,000; and our Directors were somewhat disturbed at today's Board Meeting'.[87] They were alarmed that 'as the particulars come in, the disaster seems to grow in magnitude... setting aside the first wild reports'.[88] In the end, they were to receive some solace. In the last days of May, L. P. Bayard – who had declined to visit San Francisco until 'the hysterical conditions' there had abated – was able to make his own survey of the damage. His estimate for Phoenix's share of it, at $3.08 million (£635,052) revised the liability downwards again.[89] It had taken Phoenix more than a month to achieve an acceptably accurate measurement of the office's single biggest monetary loss.

[85] *Ibid.* [86] *The Economist*, 21 April 1906; *Daily Telegraph*, 23 April 1906.
[87] Boston to A. D. Irving, 9 May 1906. [88] *Ibid.*
[89] Bayard, Report on the San Francisco Conflagration, 29 May 1906.

Table 3.8. *British companies at San Francisco, 1906: the ten biggest losers (after reinsurance and salvage, £)*

Company	Loss
Royal-Queen	1,193,356
London & Lancs	872,107
CU-Palatine	848,718
London	828,138
London & Liverpool & Globe	824,330
North British	621,134
Phoenix-Pelican[a]	579,034
REA	544,240
Northern	425,552
Atlas	366,637

Note: [a]By this time, salvage had further reduced the 'final' Phoenix loss of £624,241.
Source: *The Economist*, 11 August 1906.

The gross loss of £624,241 represented 83% of Phoenix's General Reserve as it stood in 1906, 40% of the entire premium income for 1906 and 35% of the company's total assets. The office's 'grand reservoir' of £750,000 was reduced to £125,759 and the Profit and Loss account had to be raided to make it up again to £300,000. The strain of this pushed the Phoenix dividend for 1906 down from 23 shillings per share to 18 shillings. However, not even the scale of the largest disaster yet suffered by the Phoenix could threaten the company as the earlier firestorms at St Thomas or Hamburg had done: these had consumed 126%, and 105% of global annual premiums respectively.[90] The difference measures the greater resilience of the modern international insurance office by 1906.

Moreover, Phoenix's loss at San Francisco was smaller than it could have been. Although Phoenix ranked fifth among British insurance exporters to the USA, it did not rank equivalently among the losers in 1906. Indeed, it did better than its weight of American business would have suggested: six British offices suffered heavier losses than Phoenix and Pelican combined (see Table 3.8).

The main reason for this was the close scrutiny of the Californian market maintained by Washington Irving. Irving gained in stature throughout the San Francisco crisis. In 1904, he had surveyed the city and

[90] The Chicago disaster consumed 22% of the total premium income of 1872.

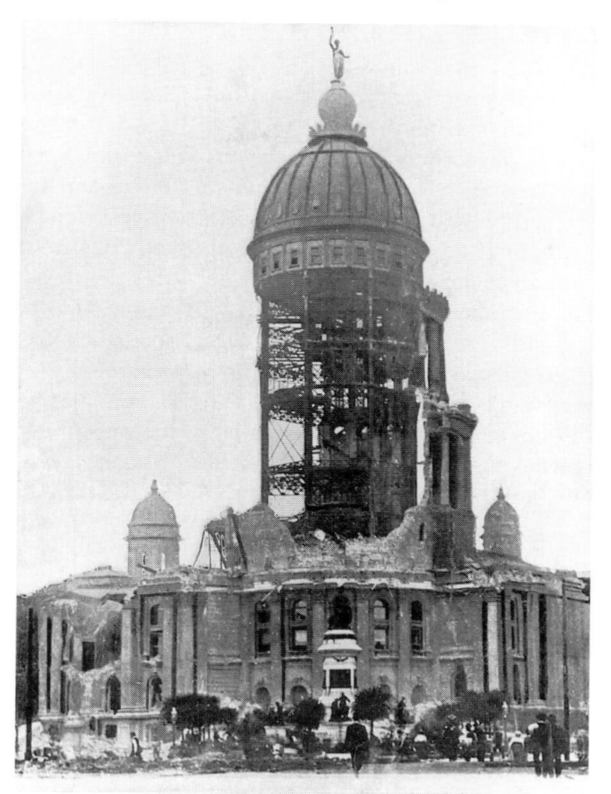

Plate 3.8 Liberty survives at San Francisco.

proposed more rigorous insurance limits per block. In April 1906 he could report that, 'These limits have been very strictly observed and I have in no case . . . exceeded two-thirds of the authorised block limit.'[91] Even before the true results became known, Phoenix could guess that they had not done as badly as many others.

However, the management had done more than merely worry and thank their stars for Washington Irving in the interval between the occurrence and the measurement of the catastrophe. They had begun to set up a war chest for the payment of claims. On 25 April they transferred $200,000 from Phoenix funds to Pelican of New York's surplus account, and two days later Phoenix's Trustees in the USA were requested to deliver up a

[91] W. Irving to New York office, 22 April 1906.

further $200,000 to Pelican.[92] Probably, Phoenix was concerned to build up Pelican's paying power since the subsidiary's investment assets were spoken for as insurance reserves. Also, the US Branch management needed to conserve its investments in the USA in order to meet government's deposit requirements; accordingly, it was empowered to draw funds on London so as to leave a net surplus in the USA of $1 million.

The mother company, however, could sell its investment holdings in the United Kingdom in order to release funds for the payment of claims. Such selling began as early as 25 April, a week after the disaster. By the time that it was completed, Phoenix had cashed in some £250,950 worth of stocks and bonds across a very wide range of securities, from US and South American railways, through Colonial government stock even to British property and brewery debentures. The San Francisco earthquake therefore hit Phoenix in the strongest sectors of its investment portfolio. In one way, however, the timing was kind: the market was high during the period of selling by insurance offices and low by the time they needed to restock their portfolios in the next year. Moreover, Phoenix was now sufficiently rich that even selling of this scale represented only 12% of the pre-disaster portfolio. This was a far cry from the days when a crisis like the St Thomas inferno, almost exactly a century before, could virtually empty the coffers.

After the insurers had girded their assets and estimated the claims they had to adjust, they faced a still more intractable problem: on what principles to pay the claims? How to distinguish fire damage from earthquake damage or explosion damage? Whether to escape claims that were really earthquake claims? Whether to pay 100% of claims to earn goodwill, or what percentage for what effect? To begin with, the British offices, or at least their head offices and representative bodies in London, tried to take a strict line. On 2 May, the Fire Offices Committee instructed its members not to exceed their contracts by recognising liability for damage by shock where no fire had ensued, nor for fire damage to fallen buildings, nor for buildings dynamited by the military.[93] Phoenix Head Office was similarly minded. Boston wanted united action: 'individual offices should not compromise on their own account, as what might be thought . . . advantageous in a particular case might give away some principle of great general interest'. He enjoined close examination of every claim and warned against 'misplaced liberality'. Close examination included establishing the value of shock-damaged buildings before they caught fire.[94]

[92] Bayard to Phoenix, London, 27 April 1906.
[93] FOC (Foreign), Memorandum of 2 May 1906.
[94] Boston to A. D. Irving, 9 May 1906.

Even in late May, Boston cabled New York 'to pay only where legally advised no chance successful resistance'.[95]

These were counsels of perfection and had little to do with what was going on in California. There, both press and political weaponry had been trained upon the insurers and, thus encouraged, the dispossessed public was baying for dollars. No doubt, some offices were guilty of sharp practice and evasion of due responsibility. But no doubt also, pressure on the underwriters was extreme, and in some cases, unscrupulous.[96] Within the city, the 'San Francisco Earthquake' was rapidly rechristened the 'San Francisco Conflagration', and there were remarkably few eye-witnesses of shock damage. The Governor of California and the Mayor of San Francisco spoke for the victims of the fire – not of the earthquake – by telegraphing to the Head Offices of all major companies the stirring invocation,

> We appeal in our misfortune to your manhood, business integrity and sense of justice to interpose your veto on the disreputable tactics of certain agents, who are driving our people to the point of exasperation.

But the people were not the only parties to be exasperated. Whatever the state of their manhood, the major underwriters calculated that the chances of local courts upholding the distinction between shock damage and fire damage under these conditions was slim indeed.

Under the threat of a blanket liability, some offices – four of the fifteen European companies operating in San Francisco, all of these with big liabilities, and fifteen of the ninety American companies represented there – repudiated all responsibility and defaulted. Some of these were indeed 'welshers and shavers' who took advantage of the California bankruptcy laws and 'like the Arab . . . folded their tents and silently stole away'.[97] But others were genuinely overborne by the breadth of the indemnity which threatened or the speed with which it was necessary to meet the demands for settlement. British offices were not overborne: of the eighteen operating in San Francisco not one defaulted.

However, even those who stood firm were not agreed on where they should stand. On 31 May 1906, the managers of the US branches of the large UK insurers met in conclave: they resolved to resist claims on buildings that had fallen before the fire or had been destroyed by the

[95] *Ibid.*, 23 May 1906.

[96] R. K. Mackenzie, 'The San Francisco Earthquake and Conflagration', *Proceedings of the Insurance and Actuarial Society of Glasgow*, February 1907. Mackenzie was sub-manager of the State Fire Insurance Co. Ltd.

[97] G. Brooks, *The Spirit of 1906: An Account of the San Francisco Earthquake and Fire* (San Francisco, 1921), cited by Liveing, *Commercial Union*, pp. 99–100.

Table 3.9. *The San Francisco conflagration: how claims were met*

Type of payment	UK offices	US offices	European offices	Colonial offices
100%	2	3	–	–
Full less 1% for cash	1	2[a]	–	–
Full less 2% for cash	8	13[a]	–	1
Full less 2–5% for cash	1	7	–	–
90%+	1	7	–	–
75%	2	20[a]	4	–
50–75%	3[b]	1	–	–
50%	–	2	–	–
40%	–	1	–	–
30%	–	1	–	–
Portion, by instalment	–	1	–	2
Bankrupt	–	4	–	–
Paid nothing	–	1	4[c]	–

Notes: [a] three waived the earthquake clause
[b] all with earthquake clause
[c] one with earthquake clause.

authorities but to propose 'reasonable compromises' where there was no certainty of damage by earthquake or dynamite. The San Francisco managers of all interested offices, British and American, met at Reed's Hall, Oakland on 7 June 1906 to consider these and other proposals. The meeting was animated on the subject of reasonable compromise. The majority argued that since all property had been more or less affected by earthquake shock, all claims should be settled on the basis of 75% face value. Others saw this as a 'horizontal cut of twenty-five cents' in every dollar.[98] The minority proposed that an estimate should be made of the difference between the sound value of the building and the value after shock damage and the fire policy paid in full up to this amount. Since most buildings were under-insured, this effectively constituted payment in full, or 'dollar for dollar'. Sixty-one offices voted for the 75% strategy, thirty-two dissented, eighteen abstained and nine did not attend. The minority formed themselves into the General Adjustment Bureau and set about implementing the 'dollar for dollar' approach.

In the event, an enormous variety of settlement tactics were employed by the various offices. Table 3.9 summarises many of these.

[98] Cited by Liveing, *Commercial Union*, p. 99.

The British, including Phoenix, did very well out of this. The three UK offices with the earthquake exclusion – Commercial Union, Norwich Union and Palatine – all offered reasonable *ex gratia* settlements, whereas the one German company with this protection paid nothing. All eighteen British offices clustered at the top end of the payment range, whereas the American 'tail' was pronounced. In the event, despite the initial rigour of Boston's attitude, the Phoenix paid in full with a 2% discount for cash payment. Besides Phoenix, the British offices employing one or other variant of the payment in full were: Atlas, Law Union, Liverpool & London & Globe, London Assurance, North British, Northern, Royal, Scottish Union, Sun and Union. When, on 19 April 1907, a year and a day after the disaster, the *San Francisco Express*, promoting the angels for once, carried an 'Insurance Honour Roll' of thirty-nine companies which had distinguished themselves by their payment policy, eleven of them were British. Phoenix and Pelican were prominent on the list. As at Chicago, the British reputation for fair settlement acted as a good advertisement for the post-disaster trade.

Nevertheless, it is salutary to recall that, at Phoenix House, the staff had feared for their jobs in 1906 and that from then until 1925 the wall of the fire manager's room bore a photograph of the devastation at San Francisco as a reminder to all incumbents – especially home fire managers – of the perils of foreign business.[99]

7. THE LEGACY OF SAN FRANCISCO, 1907–14: THE PENALTIES OF PURIFICATION

As usual, disaster created its own opportunities. It ruined the reputation of sharp or ungenerous insurers and promoted the standing of the solid and even-handed. The weakest were destroyed entirely. It raised rates, commonly by 25% on the Pacific Slope and in the congested parts of the western cities. It forced rebuilding to fireproof and shock-resistant standards. More generally, it reinforced faith in insurance itself. The jibes of the press in 1906, likening the underwriters to gamblers meeting in solemn and petulant council to discuss what proportion of their losses they might deign to pay, had been proved unjust: about 80% of all insurance cover at San Francisco was recognised and paid. As one contemporary expert summarised, 'The whole system of joint-stock fire insurance has been put to a searching test, and it must be admitted to have justified itself.'[100]

[99] Hurren, *Phoenix Renascent*, p. 96.

[100] Prof. A. W. Whitney, *A Report on Insurance Payments in Relation to the San Francisco Fire and Earthquake* (San Francisco Chamber of Commerce, 1907).

If it was true, as the same observer argued, that the offices had applied a philosophy of settlement, rather than of adjustment, to the disaster, and, 'taken all in all, have done remarkably well', the British offices had emerged as the most reliable settlers and had scored best of all in public acclaim. Accordingly, they should have been best placed to exploit the post-disaster market. Some clearly did so effectively: the London & Lancashire extracted a 15% trading profit from the USA in 1911 and over 12% in 1912; the North British managed 14.6% and 6.1% in these two years; and Commercial Union even squeezed 15% out of the adverse conditions of 1914.[101] But Phoenix was to experience problems – and trivial profits – in this phase, just as it had in the more difficult phase of underwriting between 1899 and 1906.

Very early on, Washington Irving had perceived the openings among the rubble of San Francisco. Four days after the earthquake, he felt 'a very hopeful determination' about the possibilities of reconstruction. His general diagnosis was that 'the material prosperity of the Coast can only be retarded temporarily; it cannot possibly be stopped'. The specific insurance perspective, he thought, offered 'a wonderful opportunity to select and scatter liability, obtain very high rates, and, consequently, large profit'.[102] He, like most other underwriters and Californians, discounted the possibility of a repeated earthquake hazard. Albert Reed's Report for the National Board of Fire Underwriters omitted 'for the present, any consideration of apparently well-founded theories on the existence of a fault or line of weakness running through the solid formations, on a line from Lake Merced to, and through, San Andreas Lake, which line of weakness should be avoided by future conduits'.[103] So was the San Andreas Fault assessed in 1906, the subject of well-founded theories and a good place for the water board to avoid.

Such undiluted optimism was not shared at Phoenix House in London. There, a classic post-catastrophe debate ensued, much like that after the Hamburg disaster of 1842, between those who wished to cash in on expanding opportunities and those who wished to shy away from proven hazards. Following the San Francisco crisis, the Board became even more sensitive to every peculiarity of American business. Their first thought was to reduce their liability in America, and especially in the Californian cities. In July 1906, the US managers were instructed to report on all locations where conflagration hazard existed, and where Phoenix, given its existing levels of cover, might suffer a further loss of above £200,000.

[101] Phoenix Analysis of Companies Reports, 1911–31.
[102] W. Irving to Phoenix, New York, 22 April 1906.
[103] A. S. Reed, *The San Francisco Conflagration of April 1906: Special Report to the National Board of Underwriters' Committee of Twenty* (New York, 1906).

The purpose was to fix new insurance limits allowing for the recurrence of earthquake and guarding against any future loss from this direction. Influenced by heavily cautious submissions from Avebury, the directors thought that liability might be limited to £0.5 million in any area of 2 miles diameter. On 19 December, they agreed on new US limits: no one risk to exceed $10,000, no one block to surpass $150,000. An aggregate ceiling for all US business was fixed at $2.75 million (roughly £570,000). In view of the 'drastic alterations and revisions' to US liabilities since 1902, and the improving standards of fireproof construction, Bovill thought that these limits were safe, and even Avebury, the Board member least sympathetic to US business, did not dissent.[104]

Somewhat earlier, in mid-November, Phoenix decided to insert an earthquake clause in its West Coast policies; this was a line of thought shared by several[105] other British offices around this time. Phoenix decided to follow it – 'disclaiming liability for loss caused directly or indirectly by earthquake or volcanic action' – even though the Board recognised that it 'might lead to loss of business' or 'even to our retirement from this field of operations'.[106] This was the classic minimalist line, frequently encountered in the aftermath of a heavy loss.

The first stage of the battle of the Pacific Slope followed from these decisions and was waged between the 'earthquake clause' companies and the California legislature.

Both houses of this body by early spring 1907 had approved a Bill embodying some of the harsher thoughts about insurance companies that had circulated in San Francisco a year before. By the end of March, the Bill awaited only the Governor's assent. The Phoenix Board found that this threat confirmed their fears about the Pacific market in general and decided 'in the event of the Bill becoming law, to *at once* discontinue business in the State of California'.[107] However, the FOC let the Governor know that all major British operators in California were likely to take a similar position. Faced with a wholesale evacuation from his state by the insurers who had treated his worst disaster most honourably, the Governor wisely withheld his signature. So, governmental forces were not permitted to convert the post-disaster opportunities into post-disaster obstacles; in the contest between the international insurers and the US state administrations, this was a rare victory for the offices.

However, it was not joyfully received by an influential group within

[104] Phoenix Directors' Minutes, 28, p. 30, 19 December 1906.
[105] Actually four: Caledonian, REA, Scottish Union and State.
[106] Phoenix Directors' Minutes, 28, p. 18, 14 November 1906.
[107] *Ibid.*, p. 55, 20 March 1907.

Phoenix. These directors wished to discontinue business in California, and probably in the USA, anyway; and would have welcomed an outcome of this kind dictated by external influences. Bereft of this outcome, they turned the issue into a fierce internal debate; this was the second stage of Phoenix's battle of the Pacific Slope. The conservatives, led by Lord Avebury, launched a major offensive in May 1907. On 1 May, Avebury put the question to the Trustees as to whether Phoenix should continue to transact business in the earthquake zone of California. The other Trustees wished to refer the question to the whole Board, but Avebury insisted that his opinion – that Phoenix should abandon 'the earthquake zones of North West America' – be placed on record. The Trustees discussed the matter again on 8 May, and this time succeeded in postponing it and transferring discussion to the Board.[108]

The full array of directors confronted the issue on 29 May. Avebury again pressed for withdrawal, arguing that, in the aftermath of the disaster, the American courts had afforded the insurers no protection and that they had been fleeced by tainted evidence. Phoenix, said Avebury, 'had in the late disaster, paid much more than it ought to have done owing to fraudulent claims'.[109] The chairman and the executive officers were not prepared to draw the same conclusions as Avebury, but they did concede that, if the British offices could not agree and enforce a common earthquake clause, Phoenix might have to retire from the field. On the other hand, Edgar Lubbock wrote in that Phoenix should 'do nothing more at present' and Portman telegrammed his opposition to 'hasty action'. This was the refrain picked up by the more enterprising spirits. Treherne moved the amendment that Phoenix should do no more until: (1) the Pacific Board of Underwriters had formed a view; (2) until the judgments on the San Francisco cases referred for appeal in the Supreme Court were known; (3) until the state of legislation in California was settled; (4) until an effective earthquake clause was agreed.[110] This comprehensive gambit bought the necessary time.

From this point the conservative lines suffered a creeping erosion. On 10 July the Board accepted as a necessary step in 'protecting the company's position against competition' that Phoenix should take insurances from the earthquake zone.[111] Four months later, they agreed to waive the earthquake clause entirely, except in the defined conflagration districts of San Francisco, Los Angeles and Oakland, or in towns where the office had more than £20,000 in high-risk areas.[112] In December Bayard visited San

[108] Phoenix Trustees' Minutes, 1 and 8 May 1907.
[109] Phoenix Directors' Minutes, 28, p. 72, 25 May 1907. [110] *Ibid.*
[111] *Ibid.*, pp. 85–6, 10 July 1907. [112] *Ibid.*, p. 125, 13 November 1907.

Franciso again and re-zoned it along optimistic lines. The city was divided into nine zones. On six of these, the Board accepted that there should be no fixed ceilings and that they should receive only an annual return of the details. On the remaining three hazardous zones, the aggregate limit, fixed at $2.75 million late in 1906, was raised to $3 million. Bayard also proposed that the earthquake clause should be attached only to insurances in the congested sections of towns, so that Phoenix might pick the better risks on the outskirts without imposing the clause. Bayard expected that these amendments, together with the movement of the western market, would produce a considerable increase in premium income from the Pacific Coast.[113] This was a long way from the spirit of Avebury's proposals.

However, the Board did not banish this spirit entirely. In July 1908 they were still asking Washington Irving for reassurance about the West Coast market.[114] They wanted to know about the levels of prosperity, investment, 'social order' and corruption. Irving, who had impressed London with his handling of the disaster, and received a promotion to 'Agent and Attorney' in June 1907,[115] was even more sanguine than he had been in 1906. Then, he had foreseen the prospects for increasing business, even before the tremors had died away. By 1908, he could argue,

> Probably no part of the United States is increasing in material wealth and prosperity as fast as that section between the Rocky Mountains and the Pacific Ocean . . . the situation is even more healthy than a few years ago.

Moreover, since the conflagration, loss ratios in the state had been very low; building standards had greatly improved; Phoenix had anyway greatly reduced its liability; and, as for corruption, 'the affairs of the community are moving satisfactorily upon a high moral plane'.[116]

Washington Irving also made some play with the tactics of Phoenix's competitors. Most British offices doing business on the Pacific Coast, he pointed out, had not altered their underwriting policy, other than by limiting liability in congested areas, and most of them were willing to hazard more than Phoenix. By the time of Irving's report, only two British offices retained the earthquake clause for California: one was the Caledonian and the other was Phoenix. Irving's message was that Phoenix needed to relax its restrictive approach if it was to measure up to the British competition in California.

The Board response to this was a masterpiece of temporisation. Its Fire

113 Bayard to Phoenix, London, 18 December 1907.
114 Phoenix Directors' Minutes 28, p. 270, 29 July 1908.
115 *Ibid.*, 28, p. 79, 26 June 1907.
116 W. Irving to Phoenix, London, August 1908.

Committee considered the report on 30 September 1908, and decided that Irving was right. It resolved that Phoenix policy should be to operate wherever the largest British offices operated and on the same terms, 'omitting the earthquake clause in countries where it is not generally adopted'.[117] However, the Lords Avebury and Winterstoke dissented from this. So, in order to placate them, the Board agreed to the general proposition that 'in the matter of limits . . . and individual risks, the foreign business of the Company should be conducted on a more conservative and cautious basis'.[118] Then, at its meeting on 25 November 1908, the Fire Committee blandly increased the San Francisco limits by $0.25 million per district. The language was for the conservatives, the actions were addressed to the realities of the market.

But it seems likely that Phoenix was slow in coming to terms with these. Again the company fell between two stools in its approach to American insurances. It did not pursue the expanded business which Irving had detected on the far side of the earthquake; rather, it picked at it with fastidious distrust. Gross premiums for the US Branch and Pelican of New York combined fell by over 17% between 1906 and 1908, and the pre-earthquake peak was not reached again until 1911. On the other hand, the office did not grasp the nettle and get out of the USA. This was a wholly possible course. Neither the expense nor the profit outcome for Phoenix in the USA between 1900 and 1914 was in itself a justification for being there (see p. 288 Table 3.10). The two sensible alternatives were to be there more energetically or not to be there at all. The problem was that the second argument was propounded from the wrong mouths. For, given the size of the US cash-flow, the necessary sequel to abandoning the USA was to promote an equally large business in a number of more profitable places very swiftly. But neither Lord Avebury nor any other Phoenix conservative propounded this alternative. Conservatism was limited to getting out of the USA, enterprise limited to staying there. A keener spirit was needed.

8. THE RISE OF A KEENER SPIRIT: GERALD RYAN AND THE USA 1908–14

It is perhaps significant that Phoenix's insistence upon purification and the earthquake clause abated during 1908. This was partly because of market forces in the USA. It was also partly because of what was happening to Phoenix back in Britain. In the second half of 1907 Phoenix was under three major pressures: the competition of composite offices; a

[117] Ratified by Phoenix Directors' Minutes, 28, pp. 313–4, 7 October 1908. [118] *Ibid.*

related need to diversify, not least into accident insurance; and a need to rebuild its fire reserves after payment of the San Francisco claims. Willed or not, this predicament forced innovational thoughts and innovatory personalities into the foreground of the Board's attention. These found partial expression, of course, in the merger between Phoenix and Pelican early in 1908. And it was not accidental that the new composite's preoccupation with purification weakened as Gerald Ryan assumed closer control of Phoenix from January of that year.

Just over eighteen months later, Ryan visited the USA to inspect his biggest fire market at first hand. He had been given sweeping powers to execute reform; and these fully reflected the Board's earlier reservations about insurance in the USA. The Phoenix chairman, Lord George Hamilton, briefed Ryan: 'I want you to have this contingency [that Phoenix might abandon US trade] ever present in your mind, especially if you encounter local or personal opposition to changes which, in your judgement, are essential for the betterment of our organisation.' Hamilton described the Board's worries as twofold: 'return in profits . . . inadequate to the amount of business done' and the memory of the San Francisco losses. 'Putting the two factors together, there is undoubtedly a disposition on the part of a section of my colleagues to close up the American business.'[119] So the Avebury view of the Pacific Coast endured more than three years after the earthquake. By contrast, Ryan proceeded to find the US market thriving, San Francisco to have been sturdily rebuilt and the competition of British offices for Californian business to be fierce. Phoenix, he judged, was insufficiently committed to this market.

The brief that he set himself was 'to ascertain the causes that led to our Company being so much less successful than its leading competitors'. His diagnosis of the trouble revolved around three variables: weakness in the New York management; a defect in central policy-making; and an inferior organisation of agents and inspectors. He rejected the last hypothesis, finding that the field force ranked 'second to that of no other British company transacting fire business in the States'. He reserved a certain amount of mildly censorious comment for the US management. A. D. Irving, at least in recent years, had allowed his attention to wander: 'a series of family troubles and increasing years had told severely upon . . . our manager'.[120] Consequently 'the Chief Office is noticeably behind its Chicago and San Francisco Branches'.[121] So, in 'a harmonious

119 Hamilton to Ryan, 28 August 1909.
120 Report of General Manager to Chairman and Directors on Business in the USA and Canada, 4 August 1909.
121 Ryan to Phoenix, London, 27 July 1909.

and amicable manner', the retirement of A. D. Irving was arranged. He was to be replaced by a joint appointment. L. P. Bayard would constitute one half of it, Percival Beresford, formerly the company's manager at Hull, and now transferred to New York at a salary of $10,000, would provide the other half. Both were reminded that 'greater smartness and a closer grip are needed'.[122]

At this point, however, it is clear that Ryan considered the major culprits to be the policy-makers in London. He recognised that high deposits and poor results had predisposed the Board to curbing the US trade: 'it was doubtless thought that the inconvenience of parting with the control of so large a portion of the Company's funds was scarcely compensated for by the meagre profits of the business'. And then came the earthquake which 'probably induced the Board to fix a definite limit to the extent of the United States Business'. So far, so good. But beyond this point, a keener spirit judged differently: 'this policy . . . has not operated in the direction anticipated'. A 'restricted business' had not equated to 'a superior class of business'; little was not the same as better; yet again purification had failed to deliver the goods. The problem was that brokers and agents shied away from a company that would only accept the best risks; and, consequently, it did not get the best risks. Indeed, the reverse of what was intended was actually achieved. Ryan chose the agent for Baltimore as the most eloquent spokesman for the Phoenix representatives in almost every city: 'On risks that burn, the Phoenix seems to have about as much as the other companies: but, on those that don't, it only has a fraction of their holdings'.

The agents were upset that they missed the best business because the Phoenix 'issued such small policies' and because the brokers preferred to deal with offices which accepted larger lines. Everywhere, Ryan found 'a cry for greater facilities in regard to the amounts permitted to be written'.[123]

Given the increasing prevalence of fireproof construction, Ryan concluded, the Phoenix's position must be less safe, and its loss ratios higher, than those of its major competitors. His remedy was to jettison the aggregate ceiling on US business, relax the local limits and take more business. Block limits, set at $150,000 in 1906, should be raised to $250,000; limits on individual risks, fixed at $50,000 in 1906, should be doubled.[124] The Board, then, had done no better, and possibly worse, than A. D. Irving in earlier times had managed by himself.

As for San Francisco, Ryan found that it had undergone a 'marvellous recovery'. Its large areas of reconstruction, fireproofed and shock-

[122] Report of General Manager, 4 August 1909.
[123] Ryan to Phoenix, New York, 27 July 1909. [124] *Ibid.*

protected, compared well 'with the finest new structures of any American city'.[125] It gave now 'a highly favourable impression as a field for insurance'. The risk of another earthquake catastrophe, under these conditions, was not rated high. As evidence Ryan cited the case of a leading US office, the Home Insurance Company which had done little trade in San Francisco before 1906 but which was now chasing it avidly; and he could point too towards the municipality of Oakland which was even considering entering the insurance business on its own account. In general 'American and British offices are pressing for business with increased activity'.[126] Ryan was anxious that Phoenix should get its proper share of cover on the city's new buildings.

In 1909 Ryan's conclusions on the US trade were optimistic. He recognised that the market posed special problems. Poor insurance results could be traced to a climate that produced intense dryness in summer and heavy snow in winter; the first increased fire hazard, the second impeded fire engines. Also, the working class was prone to 'a want of thoroughness and of the sense of responsibility', especially when carrying out electrical installations. Fire-waste was clearly excessive. But Ryan believed that the fire-waste had attracted the attention of the appropriate experts and that remedies were well under way, similarly that the carelessness of the workers was being attended to. Summing up, he thought that 'the conditions (save the climate) are steadily becoming more favourable to our business'.[127] He saw no reason why, under new assumptions, Phoenix results should be any poorer than anyone else's. 'Our past experience in the United States is no sure guide to the measure of success that we ought to achieve in the future.'

For a while confidence ran sufficiently high for Phoenix to look some of the worst American risks fully in the eye. In view of 'certain offices' accepting insurance in San Francisco, including earthquake risk, the company decided to follow suit 'to a limited extent, as a defensive measure'. But they did not follow with a faint heart: in July 1913, they provided cover on City Hall, Oakland. The distance between this spot and the epicentre of 1906 could be counted in yards.[128] It is as good a measure as any of Ryan's attempt at a bullish reinterpretation of the US market.

Sadly, by 1914, he could not be so sure. In that year, 'the poor results of our business during the five years elapsing since the revision of our policy' drove him once more to the USA for a second investigation. That Phoenix 'should continue to hold an unsatisfactory position compared with the

[125] Report of General Manager, 4 August 1909. [126] *Ibid.* [127] *Ibid.*

[128] Fire Committee Minutes, Book 2, pp. 73, 137, 30 July 1913, 25 November 1914.

great majority of its British rivals in the United States' was by this time causing 'no little anxiety and disquietude in the minds of the Head Office Executive'.[129]

Most companies writing fire business in the USA over the period 1870–1914 had been adversely affected by two separate processes: conflagrations in new, sometimes indifferently built and overcrowded cities, as with Chicago in 1871, Boston in 1872, Baltimore in 1904 or San Francisco in 1906; or cyclical downturns in the economy, as in 1871–3, 1878, 1893 or 1897–8. But, in the period 1899–1914, Phoenix appears to have marched to a more doleful rhythm of its own.

During his 1914 tour Ryan did not subject this phenomenon to the same detailed analysis he gave it in 1909. Rather he appears to have decided that if the careful examination of variables in 1909 had not done the trick, if the gingering up of central policy had not reversed the decline, the answer must lie after all with the American management. So he made a clean sweep of it, or almost a clean sweep. Bayard was retired, though at sixty-seven scarcely prematurely. His son and A. D. Irving's son (L. P. Jnr and A. D. Jnr), who had been respectively company secretary and agency secretary since 1909 – both tolerated rather than approved by Phoenix in earlier years – were now ejected: each was 'too imbued with old traditions and methods'. With A. D. Irving Jnr went his deputy, O. Dellavie, 'a weak, amiable man of failing powers'. Chicago got the same treatment: the agent there proved 'another man of the old school . . . no longer fit to represent the Company'. Never short of an apt slogan, Ryan proclaimed that 'New measures require new men, and no Company ever wanted a change of regime more than the Phoenix does.'[130] Certainly, he cut a swathe through the old men.

Among the major figures, only Beresford escaped. Ryan was prepared to be sceptical here as well, or, as he put it, 'uncommitted'. But Bayard spoke up for Beresford as 'a most capable and energetic man [who] had assimilated the best traits of American management and . . . was extremely popular with the outside men'. Ryan asked around, but found nothing but 'favourable testimony'. So Beresford survived the sabres – at least this time around – and was confirmed as the new, and sole, Phoenix US manager.

There is disillusion evident in Ryan's root-and-branch approach. And a certain lack of consistency. He was clear in 1909 that underwriting policy was a more important variable than the American officials. If the correct

[129] General Manager's Report to the Board on American Business, 25 June 1914 (Ryan's draft).

[130] *Ibid.*

approach really was the unsheathing of the long knives, it is a pity that they were not unsheathed earlier. For by 1914, when war and a multitude of entirely new variables intervened, measurement of whether this new approach made any difference becomes impossible. One is left only with a certain resistance to the thesis that old men were not the problem in 1909 but had become the problem by 1914. Perhaps dealing with Head Office between 1899 and 1914 made men grow old quickly.

Ryan concluded that the blood had been shed to good effect: 'we are now, I believe for the first time in the United States, in a position to earn our fair share of success'.[131] It was of course the second time that he had believed this.

9. THE UNDERWRITING RESULTS 1899–1914

Nothing really worked for Phoenix over this period in its largest fire market. Ryan's explanation of 1909 as to why nothing worked is probably the most convincing available, but it is, to say the least, historically inconvenient that his own remedies worked only slightly better.

The sequence seems to be that Phoenix started looking for an American problem around 1900 when in fact the company's transatlantic predicament was little worse than that of other British offices. But then, while the investigation proceeded, the predicament became, and stayed, worse. The temptation is to ascribe the developing difficulties to the method of investigation itself.

Certainly, the underwriting surplus results for the United States show an improvement in the second half of the 1890s (see Table 3.10). On this evidence, the Board had only the shortest-term justification for alarm as the century turned. Then, the surplus results deteriorated as the managerial inquiry probed deeper, upsetting the US managers and limiting the lines they could write. The San Francisco disaster plunged the results for 1905–9 deeper into deficit, although individual years such as 1905 and 1909 looked healthier with surpluses of 8–11% (see Table 3.11).

A period of greater stability followed after 1907, with a sustained run of modest surpluses. The effect of the earnings curb of 1906 is very clearly visible in the premium returns, as is Ryan's reversal of this policy in 1909. The restriction of 1906 bit much more deeply than the earlier attempt to hold down income in 1902. There is some slight suggestion in the figures that Ryan's revised strategy had the capability to produce surpluses that were above the Phoenix trend for America (see 1910, 1911, 1913), but the

[131] *Ibid.*

Table 3.10. *Phoenix net underwriting surplus, fire business: US Branch and Pelican of New York, 1890–1914 (five-year averages %)*

1890–4	2.5	1905–9	−14.9
1895–9	6.2	1910–14	5.5
1900–04	−3.2		

Source: Calculated from Phoenix Review of Foreign Agencies, Books 2–4.

Table 3.11. *Phoenix net underwriting surplus, fire business: US Branch and Pelican of New York, 1899–1914 (annual results)*

Year	Gross premium	Loss ratio (%)	Expense ratio (%)	Underwriting surplus (%)
1899	403,525	69.1	30.7	0.2
1900	449,407	75.7	30.7	−6.5
1901	528,931	66.9	30.5	2.6
1902	537,091	77.6	30.4	−8.0
1903	551,031	58.7	32.1	9.3
1904	582,215	78.6	34.7	−13.4
1905	625,906	54.0	35.3	10.7
1906	659,619	165.3	35.3	−100.6
1907	580,974	57.7	37.4	4.8
1908	544,675	59.6	38.3	2.1
1909	561,329	53.0	38.7	8.4
1910	594,570	51.9	38.7	9.5
1911	666,011	56.2	37.2	6.6
1912	635,934	58.4	39.7	1.9
1913	671,217	51.2	39.3	9.2
1914	688,772	58.6	41.1	0.2

Source: Calculated from Phoenix Review of Foreign Agencies, Books 3 and 4.

effect was neither satisfactory nor stable (see 1912, 1914). Phoenix's attempt to do a 'limited profitable business' in the USA was achieved neither by limiting it, nor by releasing the limits.

What was still more worrying to Ryan was that other companies were obviously doing better. Where Phoenix's profit out-turn for the 1890s was similar to that of most large British operators in the USA, and rather better than many, the office's results for the 1900s and 1910s were undoubtedly worse than those of its peers. The company attempted to

Table 3.12. *Selected British offices: trading profit on US business, 1911, 1912, 1914 (%)*

Company	1911	1912	1914
Atlas	2.0	9.2	3.3
Caledonian	7.3	1.2	−7.3
CU	7.9	7.5	14.9
Liverpool & London & Globe	11.4	9.2	1.7
London	10.3	12.0	−3.3
London & Lancs	15.0	12.0	4.4
North British	14.6	6.1	−2.9
Northern	4.7	6.9	0.2
Norwich Union	5.1	4.6	−2.9
Phoenix	1.5	0.3	−3.6
Royal	10.9	12.3	2.3
REA	4.2	8.0	−1.4
Scottish Union	3.2	9.9	1.1
Sun	7.2	5.6	3.8

Source: Analysis of Companies' Reports 1911–31.

keep track of the comparative record and its American figures for a group of British insurance companies have survived for the years 1911, 1912 and 1914 (see Table 3.12).

According to the longer-range data presented in Table 3.12, 1912 and 1914 were clearly particularly bad years for Phoenix, although 1911 is a little better in both series. According to the Review of Foreign Agencies series (Table 3.11), 1914 saw a bare profit on net underwriting surplus; but according to the comparative data for trading surplus the year witnessed a small deficit. By either measure it was a poor year for Phoenix. But that is not the point. The issue is rather Phoenix's performance in relation to its competitors. Here Phoenix came bottom of the league of fourteen British operators in the USA in 1911 and 1912 and next to bottom in the generally adverse year of 1914. At this point, Phoenix was still the seventh-ranking British insurer in the USA, but the least profitable of the senior exporters to this market.

The figures do not make clear what had gone wrong, but they offer some suggestions. Table 3.11 indicates that the main influence on profitability in the period 1899–1906 was the loss ratio: fortunes were dictated primarily by the selection of risks and the incidence of catastrophe. After 1906 the limitation on premiums accepted does accompany a calmer phase for loss ratios, although Ryan believed that the 'purification' policy still produced higher loss ratios than those achieved by companies writing more generous lines. Certainly, the retreat from purification after 1909, as Ryan manoeuvred Phoenix itself into a more generous position, had little perceptible impact on the loss ratios, and no adverse one.

In the period 1907–14, the expenses ratio exerted a stronger depressant effect on profits than did the loss ratios. The irony is that as Phoenix investigated the American management, so the American management became progressively more expensive in relation to premium earnings. This first became true during the inquisition of the early 1900s, and it continued unchecked through both purification and the retreat from purification. The expense ratio had remained stable around 30% throughout the period 1885–1902, but thereafter it climbed progressively, with an increase every year except 1911, until it ended in 1914 a full one-third higher than in 1902. This may well have been the statistical effect underlying Ryan's decision to clean out the American management. The managerial costs of Phoenix's American policy 1899–1914 were high.

Those who argued that Phoenix should have abandoned US business in the 1900s had a point: it was a costly way to earn a very modest profit. However, that point would have been sustained only if the spokesmen for this viewpoint had proposed to push Phoenix energetically into new areas where a half-million in sterling premiums could be earned at lower levels of deposit and improved levels of profit. This was perfectly possible. Phoenix's surplus results from other markets show that the company was capable of picking much higher profit levels from other quarters of the globe (see Chapter 4). And it was a relevant and sobering thought – and surely not one unknown to contemporaries – that the most consistently profitable insurance company of this era was the Alliance; and the Alliance did no business in the United States. However, the men who argued for Phoenix to leave the USA did not proffer other markets where a half-million was to be had.

Both in 1909 and in 1914, Ryan was optimistic regarding Phoenix's future in the USA. In reality, at few points in the twentieth century was there cause for cheer on this score. Even before 1914 both losses and expenses on US business looked threatening. But US expenses, which first sounded a warning rattle in the 1900s, were to prove deadly for more than one generation of optimists.

CHAPTER 4

PHOENIX AND PROFIT-MAKING IN THE FOREIGN MARKET: THE WORLD MAP, 1870–1914

If Phoenix was engaged in almost every insurance market on the globe's surface in 1914, the profitability of these various locations was nowhere near as uniform as the company's physical presence in them. Nor even did the Phoenix's largest overseas commitments correspond especially well with the centres of best profitability. The reasons for this, of course, were primarily historical, competitive and developmental. That is, earlier penetration of a market could leave an insurer with an expensive selling network and substantial sunk costs upon which a return had to be sought in the medium-to-long run whatever the prevailing loss or cost situation. Similarly, the presence of major competitors might force a player to maintain a commitment even in the face of short-run adversity. And a market entered for its developmental potential could in fact develop complications for the insurer. The USA indeed played all of these roles for many British exporters of insurance.

The levels of underwriting profit displayed in Table 4.1 correlate almost inversely with the size of the Phoenix operation in the market concerned. By the 1910s, the four largest groups of foreign agencies and branches in descending order were the American, the Canadian, the Australian, and the German, while the Far Eastern array of agencies came fifth. Yet, on the average of the quinquennial results between 1878 and 1917, the United States and Germany and the Australia–New Zealand group returned the lowest surplus scores, and only Canada maintained a steadily respectable performance. By contrast, the Far Eastern outposts, which Phoenix did develop rapidly in this period, performed very well. The three main concentrations of agencies in this theatre, based on India, Shanghai and Japan, easily and consistently outpaced the rest of Phoenix's world in their ability to generate underwriting profits.

If those who had argued for the Phoenix's withdrawal from the US market in the early 1900s had thought more constructively and sought an

Table 4.1. *Phoenix net underwriting surplus by major market areas, 1878–1917 (five-year averages)*

	Germany	USA	Canada	Argentina	Australia	New Zealand	South Africa	India	Shanghai/ Far Eastern Branch	Yokohama/ Japan Branch
1878/82	11.2	32.3[b]	27.7	–	55.3[a]	44.4	48.6	79.7	85.2	23.4
1883/7	16.7	8.1	13.8	28.1	−96.4	−1.1	7.3	42.1	84.2	18.9
1888/92	1.1	1.5	32.6	18.7	−19.4	−2.2	17.1	42.6	23.9	75.5
1893/7	−2.8	5.2	−22.4	36.1	9.5	2.2	14.1	28.0	−83.1	17.7
1898/1902	8.1	−2.6	31.0	−18.0	4.0	13.2	−38.8	55.8	49.6	29.9
1903/07	19.0	−17.8	24.8[a]	−3.3	15.1	6.3[b]	12.2	−40.2	26.2[b]	49.4
1908/12	14.6	5.7	21.4	18.5	16.9	19.5	22.8	0.1	16.7	41.3
1913/17	–	8.5	13.9	21.7[c]	14.1	15.2	14.9	35.6	33.6	13.5
Average	9.7	5.1	17.9	14.5	0.1	12.2	12.3	30.5	29.5	33.7

Notes: [a]4 years only, [b]3 years only, [c]2 years only.

Table 4.2. *Phoenix net underwriting surplus, aggregate of all foreign agencies, 1878–1902*

1878/82	22.7
1883/7	14.5
1888/92	6.5
1893/7	2.8
1898/1902	3.0

alternative from which a replacement income of £0.5 million might more profitably have been drawn, they could have done worse than look to the east. However, without that reinforcement, the results for the aggregate underwriting surplus from *all* foreign agencies – which are available only for the period 1878–1902 – reveal a disturbing downward slant (see Table 4.2).

Although in some places and at some times – as on the American Pacific Slope between 1880 and 1910 – loss ratios were clearly the major determinant of the profit outcome, the more enduring effects were generated by the expenses of getting the business in the first place. Most notably, the places that were most consistently profitable were those where business could be whipped in most economically. In such places, the odd disaster could be afforded.

Clearly, the cost of getting business rose progressively in almost all foreign markets in the half-century before the First World War. In the worst cases, such as Australia and South Africa between 1880 and 1920, it more than doubled. Certainly, it was not accidental that one of the most expensive markets to operate in, Australia – where commissions ran riot from the 1890s and the expense ratio exceeded 45% by 1918 – was also the market to produce the lowest average in trading surplus between 1878 and 1917. But in 1914 there were still major differences between markets in acquisition costs. As between Australia or the USA on the one hand and the Far Eastern markets on the other the difference could easily exceed ten percentage points.

However, beyond the generalisations regarding the importance of getting business cheaply wherever one could lies an inconvenient untidiness. It is that expense ratios and loss ratios *combined* to very individual effect in most important markets. Two massive market areas bracket loosely together. The German operation was costly to run, but it was also dangerous. Losses were uniformly high, falling below 50% of premium income in only six years between 1878 and 1903. Performance improved somewhat in the period 1904–13 with a defiantly symmetrical string of six years managing to stay below 50%. But the average losses per decade were 54.5% (1881–90), 65.7% (1891–1900) and 46.7% (1901–10). The USA was similar in expensiveness of operation but even more prone to add the insult of high claims to the injury of high costs: losses were awesomely but unattractively consistent – 63.8%, 64.8% and 72.3% for the three decades between 1881 and 1910. With operating expenses spilling over 30% of premium income, such places left little margin for error or mischance. Yet in complex urban-industrial environments, with the possibility of riot, hurricane or the odd earthquake thrown in, there was plenty of room for either.

By contrast, the expensive operating area of Australia–New Zealand displayed a quite different risk pattern. Loss ratios were very high in the 1880s and 1890s – *averaging* 90.2% for Australia and 71.7% for New Zealand in the period 1884–96 – but then fell sharply from the late 1890s. They did this to such effect that between 1905 and 1920 claims against premium income remained around or below 50% in eleven years for New Zealand and in no fewer than fourteen for Australia. In these markets, there appear to have been two quite opposed phases of risk but steadily mounting levels of operating cost.

Two other 'white dominion' markets, Canada and South Africa, were as different in underwriting outcome as Australia and New Zealand were similar. South African costs went from relatively cheap to relatively expensive, but the loss ratio was markedly erratic. It notched up levels above 70% and frequently above 90% in clusters of bad years: 1879, 1883–5, 1890–2, 1894, 1897–8, 1900, 1902, 1905. This volatile performance persisted through three decades, but it too was subject to quietening influences in the period 1905–20. And it is noticeable that the only quinquennium which produced a negative outcome in respect of surplus was the one that contained the Boer War (1899–1902).

It is striking that the maturing of a branch system in South Africa, as in Australia, seems to have exerted a checking influence more upon claims than upon costs. However, it is also relevant that the better loss ratios after 1905 – only on two occasions worse than 60% – were achieved on volumes of business much reduced in the aftermath of war. Of course, both influences may have worked in the direction of a better selection of risks.

Canada, by the test of trading surplus, was the cleanest Phoenix operation in the white dominions. It was not only big; it was also efficient. And belying its rumbustious frontier past, it was, in the period 1870–1914, even becoming significantly safer. Table 4.1 reveals that Phoenix lived up particularly well to the test of the Canadian market. If the target for a well-managed insurer in that market was a trading surplus of around 15–30% of premium income,[1] Phoenix achieved results within or better than this target band in five of the eight quinquennia covered by the table. Its cost record was good: Canada began the period 1880–1920 among the less expensive of the Phoenix's major non-oriental markets and ended as the least expensive of this group (see Table 4.3). But, surprisingly, in view of its past, its damage record had also improved markedly. True, the St John's blaze of 1892 left a highly traditional loss ratio of 276.6% in its cinders, but, between 1878 and 1920 only two other years – 1884 and 1887 – produced losses above even 70%. The average loss levels for the four decades between 1881 and 1920 ran at almost tranquil numbers: 55.3%, 67.5%, 47.0% and 49.4%. Clearly, the level of fire hazard in late nineteenth-century Canada can be exaggerated. Equally clearly, the exaggeration follows from the assumption that what was once true continued to be true.[2]

In Canada, then, both costs and claims were conspicuously well controlled in the long term. Dickson's argument that most British insurers in Canada operated at a loss, at least until the 1890s, will not hold for the Phoenix; indeed only in the quinquennium of the St John's fire was the trading result negative. Equally, in no quinquennium was the profit excessive. But it is little wonder that the visiting grandees of 1909, Ryan and Boston, were well pleased with their 'Canadian affairs'.

Argentina, on the other hand, was an example of a different and rare kind of market, less a developing economy than one in which development was poised in the tricky band between success and suspension. In the event, it would be suspended. Around the turn of the century, however, Argentina seemed to present the aspect of a coming economic power. An observer of speculative habit, composing a book at this time on the prospects of which country might become the second major industrial economy in the Americas would have given short odds on Argentina.

Insurers, however, found other ways to lose money here. Buenos Aires was considered the Paris of Latin America and its fashionable inhabitants, forgetting the intervening expanse of water – and of industrial experience – were apt to compare their homeland favourably with 'the rest of Europe'. Certainly, the hazard levels for the Phoenix were not high and it did not lose money on these. Loss ratios averaged 51.3%, 53.9% and 45.7% for the three decades between 1885 and 1914. These could be

[1] See above, Chapter 2, Section 6, pp. 199-200.
[2] See, for example, R. T. Naylor, *A History of Canadian Business* (Toronto, 1975).

Table 4.3. *Phoenix foreign expense ratios by major market area, 1881–1920*

	Germany	USA	Canada	Argentina[a]	Australia	New Zealand	South Africa	India	Shanghai/ Far Eastern Branch	Yokohama/ Japan Branch
1881/90	33.3	29.8	20.5	23.1	19.5	26.8	16.6	23.4	16.4	15.1
1891/1900	34.5	30.9	26.0	37.6	37.0	35.3	21.9	24.9	20.0	16.5
1901/10	33.7	35.1	27.8	41.8	38.2	33.3	30.8	28.4	25.2	20.6
1911/20	–	38.9	32.1	–	41.9	34.4	35.8	28.6	28.8	24.7

Note: [a]The time-periods for Argentina are 1883–90, 1891–8, 1905–14.

1 Sir Winston Churchill in a tube: a double centenary advertisement.

2 The ruins of City Hall, San Francisco, April 1906.

3 Portrait of Sir Gerald Ryan by Sir William Llewellyn, 1932.

4 Ralph Sketch at work.

5 Sir Edward Ferguson.

6 The Phoenix Golf Tournament, 1981. The players, from left to right: Nancy Lopez (USA), Sally Little (South Africa), Jerry Pate (USA), Johnnie Miller (USA). (See pages 975–7.)

absorbed. Less acceptable were the expenses of operating in the Paris of Latin America. For the precocious cosmopolitanism of the Argentine Republic extended to a ferociously advanced level of costs. Of the major Phoenix foreign outposts, the Argentinian operation, the company's flagship in Latin America, was already the most expensive of all by the 1890s and it retained this unenviable distinction into the new century. The complexity of broker relations, commissions and incentives in Buenos Aires could only mean high costs. In two of the quinquennia covered by Table 4.1 Argentina did not manage to produce any surplus at all and its average result was not much better than those of some much more dangerous places. The *chic* of Buenos Aires was thus expensively purchased.

The most profitable markets of all, in India, China and Japan, shared three characteristics: they were all cheap to run, their average loss ratios were usually low, but they all combined very high losses in occasional years with very low losses in most years. Two out of these markets had exceptionally low costs in the 1880s; but by the 1910s all three looked most economical by the standards of Phoenix's other large overseas operations. Episodically, losses could be spectacular; but Yokohama produced levels over 100% in only four years between 1880 and 1914, India five times in this period, and Shanghai just twice, once each in the 1880s and 1890s.[3] Yet trouble was episodic only: the long-run loss ratios were very modest. Thus in India, they exceeded 40% on only ten occasions between 1878 and 1920; on a similar test, Yokohama suffered more than 40% in only five years between 1878 and 1903; while Shanghai took losses of more than *20%* only six times between 1878 and 1903.

Table 4.4 gives the average decadal loss ratios for these three highly profitable locations. Here again the profits flowed from economical working combined with a very particular risk pattern.

It is clear, then, that the map of the Phoenix's energetic overseas recovery in the half-century before the First World War was not the same as the map of its overseas profitability. An overlay traced upon the globe and shaded for profits would have assumed a quite different shape from an overlay shaded for priority in export policy. Only in a few locations, with Canada pre-eminent, would the two outlines have coincided exactly. It is tempting to believe that, had the Phoenix managers of the day processed the available information – and they certainly had the information discussed above – in the same way as we have done here, they would have concluded that the overlay for policy needed to be redrawn so as to capture

[3] However, these were 185.9% in 1889 and 811.9% in 1894 (see Table 4.4).

Table 4.4. *Decadal loss ratios: India, Shanghai, Yokohama, 1881–1920*

	India	Shanghai	Yokohama
1881–90	27.5	26.2	43.0
1891–1900	37.3	95.3	45.6
1901–10[a]	71.1	41.8	39.4
1911–20	54.1	42.2	50.6

Note: [a]Eight years only.

more of the high profit areas and less of the low. Or perhaps they would have done so had they been prepared to discount the cost of established administrative capital, existing agency networks, the value of investments in various national securities and whatever it was that the competition was thought to be doing. However, the suspicion is that they would have been wise to discount at least some of this.

CHAPTER 5

THE QUEST FOR A COMPOSITE INSURANCE COMPANY

I. GERALD RYAN, FIRST THOUGHTS AND THE ATLAS AFFAIR

Just as the Phoenix had needed revival and renovation abroad in the last quarter of the nineteenth century, so before long it needed modernisation at home. In foreign fields, simple enterprise had not been enough; new structures in the form of multiple sub-agencies and branches had already been required and the prospect of foreign subsidiary companies was not far off. Over the period 1870–1914, Phoenix had moved a considerable distance towards becoming a genuine multinational corporation. On the home front, similar adjustments to enterprise and structure were required. Much of the enterprise went by the name of Gerald Hemington Ryan.[1] The adjustment in structure ran towards the multi-division 'composite' office which has dominated the insurance markets of the present century.

By the early 1900s, the rationale for the specialised, single-purpose insurance company was less firm than it had been. As company reserves grew to plutocratic proportions, the insistence of Stonestreet and the other prudent founders of the insurance business that different lines of business should be protected by distinct and separate allocations of investments lost some of its force.[2] Similarly, as the underwriting market became more complex – containing by the 1900s accident, travel, burglary, and industrial insurances, as well as the venerable staples of fire, life and marine – there was less reason for retaining the separation of function that had served well when the whole of the business had been devoted to

[1] In 1911 he became Sir Gerald Ryan; and in 1919, he was made a baronet.

[2] This was true in regard to most classes of business, but not in regard to life assurance. That class could be offered across the composite counter, but separate funds would always be required to secure it.

the cover of buildings, lives and ships. The new lines blurred the old distinctions.

Alert insurance men began to argue that the way to boost premiums was to offer all the industry's 'commodities' across a single 'counter'. Then, one could draw life or accident or, later, pension business from one's fire risks, home protection policies from life risks, marine business from industrial business, and so on. Typically, a manufacturer seeking fire cover might also be sold accident cover for his workshops and group insurance for his workforce. By July 1907, even *The Times* was using the fashionable analogy to describe the change: 'Insurance offices are rapidly losing those specialist features which at one period were carried to excess and are becoming stores at whose counters all kinds of insurance are retailed.'[3] As the underwriting processes became more diversified, it made good sense to reflect that diversification within the structure of insurance companies.

It is arguable also that, with the transition from the single product office of the nineteenth century to the composite office of the early twentieth, the insurance business produced a pioneering form of the corporate structure subsequently adopted by many of the largest manufacturing concerns. To be sure, the idea in insurance was to sell a wide range of insurance products through a single marketing organisation. But behind the single marketing organisation were a number of specialist 'divisions' – life, fire, accident, marine and, later, aviation – each with its own expertise and 'technology'. As in many other industries, the pressure towards product diversification was the shaping influence behind the divisional system.[4]

Phoenix felt its way towards these insights in the first years of the century. In this process, it had one true guide. On 1 January 1908, Gerald Ryan became general manager of the Phoenix and continued in the post of chief executive until 1920; he then became chairman of the company and served an active term in this role until 1931; even after retiring from the chair, he remained on the Board until his death in 1937.

For thirty years Ryan dominated the Phoenix. Undoubtedly, he was one of the major influences upon its development in this century and perhaps the strongest influence of all. Between 1907 and 1922, Ryan transformed an office which had prided itself on its specialisation in fire

[3] *The Times*, 11 July 1907.

[4] This idea developed from a discussion forming part of a conference on the theme, 'Organisational Change in the Corporate Economy' held at the University of East Anglia in September 1987. I am grateful, in particular, to Dr Oliver Westall and the late Professor Donald Coleman for sparking these thoughts.

business into a complex underwriting organisation able to offer a full service across the life, accident and marine, as well as fire, markets. He did so primarily by buying capacity: the period 1907–22 saw a string of acquisitions by Phoenix. Starting relatively modestly with the full absorption of the Pelican and British Empire, the sister life office, in 1908, the Phoenix shopping list went on to incorporate the Law Life Assurance in 1910, the Union Marine Insurance in 1911, and the Northern Maritime Insurance in 1917 before achieving its most ambitious purchases with Norwich Union Fire in 1919[5] and London Guarantee and Accident in 1922.

The most surprising aspect of this spate of mergers and takeovers is perhaps that its architect at the start of the process was not even an employee of the Phoenix; in 1907 Gerald Ryan was general manager of the Pelican and British Empire. And he had been in this job only five years; until 1902 he had been secretary of the British Empire Mutual Life. Ryan was an actuary by training and he turned out a brilliant practitioner. His first major post was as actuary of the Marine and General in the early 1880s but his first opportunity to make a real mark came when he was appointed actuary of the REA, at the age of twenty-nine, in 1888. Before Ryan, the REA was a by-word for conservatism in the life business. Under Ryan, the REA was given lower policy costs, interim bonuses, guaranteed surrender values, faster settlement, district inspectors and a growing branch organisation; new life business attracted by the REA nearly doubled and the life department rightly considered itself transformed.[6] Similar surgery was applied to the British Empire after Ryan's arrival in 1893. This office had made mistakes in the past but was galvanised by Ryan into remarkable progress, not only in magnitude but in the still more important features of much stronger reserves, economy in expenditure and improvement in bonus results and bonus prospects.[7]

Soon after this, rather oddly, Ryan seems to have lost interest in his skills as a life insurer. Certainly, he never meted out to the Pelican or Phoenix life operations treatment anywhere near as drastic as that experienced by the REA or the British Empire in the 1890s. The suspicion is that he had other fish to fry and that the largest of these swam in the pool of corporate diplomacy.

It would be too much to say that Gerald Ryan in the early 1900s had a

[5] This purchase left Norwich Union Life as a separate and independent venture. Norwich Union Fire was sold back to Norwich Union Life in 1925. The story of this astonishing lost opportunity is told below, pp. 469–85.

[6] See Supple, *Royal Exchange Assurance*, pp. 253–4.

[7] *The Saturday Review*, 22 November 1902.

grand strategy aimed at the creation of a composite insurance company. No individual could have had such a fully understood strategy at this time. What he did possess were four relevant qualities: an ambition to promote the expansion of certain offices between which he discerned useful connections; a pragmatic response to the opportunities thrown up by expansion and an ability to exploit the advantage rapidly; realisation after a few years that the results of this process were pointing towards a composite solution; and, consequentially, an enthusiastic acceptance and promotion of this outcome.

On the formal record the first contact between Ryan and any Phoenix personnel came about circuitously in 1895 when Ryan was asked to give an expert outsider's evaluation of a proposed merger between Pelican and the Scottish Life Assurance Co. Nothing came of this scheme, but it did establish relations between Ryan and the Pelican Board, many of whom were also Phoenix directors.[8] Beyond this, of course, it allowed Ryan to go over the Pelican books with a fine toothcomb. That was probably more significant, since, as it turns out, the formal record has not captured the full range of the early contacts between Ryan, Pelican and Phoenix.

Ryan had moved from the REA to become actuary and secretary of the entrepreneurial mutual office, the British Empire, in July 1893. But two months before this, he had, on his own account, begun buying shares in Pelican. Within the circle of Pelican shareholders, 700 shares defined the lower boundary of substantial investors: by spring 1896 Ryan held 500 Pelican shares; by July 1904 he had 980. At that time, twenty-four individuals held between 1,000 and 2,000 Pelican shares, and fifteen more held between 700 and 1,000. These were £10 shares, £1 paid, and they were costing Ryan about £2 each in the mid-1890s. His early purchases were acquired from big names, the first 100 from the executors of Lancelot Holland, the former and famed governor of the Bank of England, the next 100 from Mary Streatfield, member of an important Phoenix dynasty, and the next block from the executors of W. C. Toulmin, a relative of the Phoenix director, H. H. Toulmin.

The rapidity and the pattern of the accumulation suggest that Ryan may have had his eye upon the share qualification for a directorship in Pelican long before the merger which he was to effect between Pelican and British Empire in 1903.[9] It is especially suggestive that Ryan attended every Annual General Meeting of the Pelican from 1894 until 1902 and was an assiduous speaker and seconder of motions among the select group of proprietors with the taste or stamina for such encounters. Nor

[8] See Hurren, *Phoenix Renascent*, p. 66.
[9] See below, pp. 308–17.

can it be irrelevant that the British Empire Trustees also commenced buying Pelican shares on the mutual office's account in October 1896 – almost always with Ryan as witness or intermediary to the transaction – and had built up a substantial holding of 2,100 shares within six months. At this point, five years before the merger, Ryan and British Empire together must have represented the biggest single interest within the Pelican proprietorship. Whether or not a grand strategy was in play here, a set of tactical options was clearly being established.

Yet outline options they remain. At this point, Ryan had no unobstructed view of his final objective. Despite the apparently deliberate pattern to these share acquisitions, an event of 1901 suggests that Ryan's thinking on the *shape* that insurance expansion should take was, if not equivocal, at least still evolving. The event was the proposed three-way merger of the Phoenix *and* the Pelican with the long-established Atlas Assurance (founded in 1808); this last had once been, under Charles Babbage, a major innovator in the life insurance market of the mid-nineteenth century and was still 'a steadily and vigorously progressive company'.[10]

Late in 1901 correspondence began between Samuel Pipkin, general manager of the Atlas, Bristow Bovill, his opposite number at Phoenix, and Ryan. Technically, Ryan was an interested outsider. He was a substantial shareholder of the Pelican but also an official of the British Empire, which was still a competitor of both Pelican and Atlas. He acted as consultant, adviser and broker of ideas in the negotiations and he was treated with deference by the main protagonists.

The attractions of Atlas to Phoenix were clear. Its fire business, which had advanced from an annual premium income of £100,000 in 1896 to nearly £500,000 in 1901, would make a tidy addition to the Phoenix fire account of over £1.3 million per annum. *The Times* caught the Phoenix thinking very well:

> It was quite obvious that the Phoenix Company could not possibly obtain so great an accession of business in any other way than that now proposed, because it had never been their policy to do a cutting or pushing business. Without anything of that nature, however, the amalgamation would give them a very large increase of business.[11]

For the life side the benefits were more mixed. Although much smaller than Phoenix, Atlas was about the same size as Pelican (see Table 5.1).

The assets of the Atlas life side were £1,672,440, but Pelican could not touch them, since, after the merger, they would constitute a closed fund

[10] *The Times*, 24 October 1901.
[11] *Ibid.*

Table 5.1. *Capitalisation of the Phoenix, Pelican and Atlas, 1901*

Company	Nominal capital	Paid-up capital
Phoenix	£2,688,800	£268,880
Pelican	£1,000,000	£100,000
Atlas	£1,200,000	£120,000

for the participating policy-holders of the original Atlas. Pelican could reinsure with this 'Atlas Fund' but could not write new policies against it.[12] This was a device to protect the interests of participating policy-holders and one increasingly encountered in mergers of this type.[13] Pelican shareholders were told by circular of the advantages they would get: 'the broader base secured for . . . operations and the substantial increase of connections thus acquired by the Pelican and Atlas offices'.[14]

However, the Pelican tone was cool; the merger was more in the interests of the Phoenix Board than of the Pelican Board and the one felt that it was being led by the other. As for the Atlas interest, there were more grounds for enthusiasm. Ryan, who did the actuarial report on the merger for Atlas, argued that it would benefit Atlas life policy-holders 'both from the extended funds securing their policies and from the prospects of enhanced bonus payments consequent on the reduction of management expenses'.[15] Furthermore, Phoenix was willing to pay a good price for its side of the transaction.

Phoenix proposed to consummate the merger by issuing 18,000 new £50 shares (£5 paid) ranking on a par with existing Phoenix shares and then to award Atlas proprietors three of these shares for every four of their Atlas shares. The Atlas share price had almost doubled between 1896 and 1901; but even so, the Phoenix offer represented an effective premium of £2 on its current market value. Furthermore, the recipients of these new shares would earn higher dividends and face lower liabilities: in 1900 four Atlas shares had earned 96 shillings while three Phoenix shares had netted 105 shillings; similarly, the uncalled liability on four Atlas shares was £176 whereas on three Phoenix shares it was only £135.

In return for its generosity, Phoenix was hoping to achieve an enlarged fire office with over £3.5 million in nominal capital, £2.1 million in assets

[12] Phoenix Actuarial File 853.
[13] See below, p. 313 for the similar provision written into the Pelican–British Empire merger agreement as protection for BE's mutual policy-holders.
[14] Pelican Circular to Shareholders, October 1901.
[15] Actuarial Report on behalf of the Atlas Assurance Company Ltd by G. H. Ryan, 29 September 1901.

Plate 5.1 The Bird and the World: artwork for the Phoenix–Atlas merger.

and a further uncalled capital of £3.2 million.[16] If this merger had succeeded – which it did not – the increment to Phoenix income would have promoted the office from the fifth-ranking to the second-ranking British insurer against fire (see Table 5.2). This would have achieved one of the most rapid changes in status in the Phoenix's history. So it is not surprising that Bovill and his colleagues were ready to pay a good price.

These proposals travelled an exceptional distance towards completion before eventually failing. A final draft of a provisional agreement was ratified on 25 September 1901, and printed. Artists were even set to work on the design of new policy headings for the Phoenix and Atlas Office (see Plates 5.1 and 5.2). Pelican shareholders were circularised on 29 September, confirming approval of the provisional agreement and two Extraordinary General Meetings were called to settle the Special Resolutions attached to the agreement. On 25 November Phoenix discharged its auditors since the new agreement called for professional auditors only. Two days later Bovill and Admiral Lucas sealed the final form of the agreement on behalf of Phoenix.[17]

[16] Phoenix Actuarial File 853.
[17] Phoenix Directors' Minutes, 27, p. 53, 27 November 1901.

Table 5.2. *The top ten UK fire insurers, by premium income, 1901*

Company	£	Rank	Company	£	Rank
Royal	2,509,700	1	Sun	1,165,300	6
LLG	1,788,200	2	LL	1,143,200	7
CU	1,664,400	3	Norwich	1,036,000	8
North Brit.	1,624,000	4	Northern	752,000	9
Phoenix	1,385,000	5	Scot. Union	583,000	10

Key: LLG = London & Liverpool & Globe
CU = Commercial Union
LL = London and Lancashire
Source: Calculated from Phoenix Analysis of Companies Reports, 1901–31.

Nevertheless, Atlas was not able to reciprocate. By mid-December, two problems had developed. Somewhat belatedly, the Atlas Board discovered that, under the company's existing constitution, they did not possess the powers to transfer ownership to another body; the company would have to go into liquidation before its business could be allocated to Phoenix or any other office. This gave pause for thought but could have been circumvented. Phoenix readily agreed in cooperating to promote an Act of Parliament which would extend the powers of the Atlas Board in the desired direction. But the Atlas Board had paused also on another matter. They now wanted the right reserved to 'determine', that is, to terminate, the agreement at any time. Understandably, the Phoenix Board could not agree to this 'highly inconvenient' condition.[18] This became the sticking point. A conference on the extension of the Atlas powers, scheduled for 17 December 1901, never took place and the negotiations were dropped.

At the eleventh hour, Phoenix lost its chance to regain its position as the second largest fire insurer in Britain. In the much longer run, the Atlas fell to the REA in 1959 and became part of the Guardian Royal Exchange group in 1968.

The cliff-hanging conclusion to the Phoenix–Atlas talks was not their only extraordinary feature. For the basic assumption of these discussions totally contradicted the premise that the composite office was the coming thing in the insurance market. The intention from the start was to *divide* the Atlas between Phoenix and Pelican. Atlas would pass to Phoenix by amalgamation and then its life business would be transferred by Phoenix

[18] *Ibid.*, p. 61, 18 December 1901.

Plate 5.2 More artwork for a non-event.

to Pelican. Effectively, the negotiators had two distinct mergers in mind. Even the Atlas name was to be memorialised in two separate companies: the Phoenix and Atlas Fire Office Ltd and the Pelican and Atlas Life Office. There is little trace of composite thinking or single 'counters' here.

Samuel Pipkin had insisted on the division, and the transfer of Atlas life business to Pelican was written into the provisional agreement as 'part of the terms of the amalgamation'[19] between Atlas and Phoenix. His circular to Atlas shareholders on 23 October 1901 stressed that it was 'thought preferable to maintain *separate organizations* for the Fire and the Life businesses'.[20] He also told them that 'the Pelican is the oldest Joint Stock Company in the world, and is also one of the strongest'. It is significant that it was Pipkin, and not Bovill or Ryan, who had been selected as the new general manager for the Phoenix–Atlas company. However, Phoenix can scarcely be said to have disagreed with Pipkin's logic. At an Extraordinary General Meeting on 23 October 1901, Lord Avebury explained to the Pelican shareholders that, 'The Phoenix had been solely a fire office and their directors naturally did not feel disposed to embark upon a new

[19] Provisional Agreement between the Atlas Assurance Co. Ltd and the Phoenix Assurance Co., 25 September 1901, p. 1.

[20] My emphasis.

line of business. They had therefore suggested that it might be advantageous to the Pelican company to take over the life business of the Atlas company.'[21] He managed to sound disgruntled that the suggestion was ever made but appeared to accept the force of the argument coming from the Phoenix Board.

At the heart of these negotiations – advising both Phoenix and Atlas, and holding shares in Pelican – was the man who would become the architect of Phoenix as a composite company. Yet at no point did Ryan contradict the case put most strongly by Pipkin. Perhaps he saw the matter as primarily a Phoenix affair, and in regard to that company he had no formal standing outside that of consultant. Perhaps he realised that, as long as Phoenix and Pelican remained separate ventures, there was little that could be done by acquisition but to expand them separately. Perhaps his ideas in regard to the 'single counter' were in an early stage of evolution.[22]

Whatever is the truth, it was as well that the Phoenix–Atlas scheme came to nothing. The completion of the Pipkin design, strengthening the separate wings of fire and life, would have imposed a major restriction upon Phoenix–Pelican on the eve of the industry's adjustment to new, integrated forms of enterprise. It would have made the building of a composite office on the Phoenix base a very untidy affair. And it would have denied the old fire office both the managers and the structures needed to ease its adjustment to the modern market. This was an opportunity most fortunately lost.[23]

2. RYAN AND THE LIFE MERGERS

It was the next year, 1902, which saw the start of the three-stage process that really was to convert Phoenix–Pelican into a genuine composite office. In the first stage, Ryan connected together the Pelican and the British Empire. For the first time, this brought him, securely and professionally, within the inner councils of Pelican and thus Phoenix. He now possessed standing which allowed him to include the fire office within his

[21] *The Times*, 24 October 1901.

[22] Or perhaps he was simply playing a waiting game, calculating that it was worth accepting the segregation condition, in order to get the UK business of the Atlas as a counterbalance to the Phoenix's rapidly expanding US trade, and hoping that Phoenix could tidy up later.

[23] However, it is noteworthy that the corporate pattern of the 1970s and 1980s ran towards umbrella holding companies with separate life and general subsidiaries, as with Royal and Sun Alliance. Such a pattern could have incorporated Pipkin's design, but there were, of course, many corporate fashions in between.

designs. It was not chance that, in the second stage (1907-8), Phoenix absorbed its sister, the Pelican. This created a dual-purpose office on a single base to which other purposes progressively could be added. In the third stage, the enlarged Phoenix went in quest of the specialised components it lacked (1910–25).[24]

By this time the young composite was in good company; for the 1900s witnessed one of the periodic bursts of concentration within the insurance industry as a whole. No less than 101 acquisitions were made by insuring offices during the period 1900–14 and about 60% of these purchases involved diversification away from the stock-in-trade of the initiating venture.[25] The Royal Insurance headed the pack of predators with eleven acquisitions, Commercial Union came next with ten, and Yorkshire Insurance and Alliance equal third with nine apiece (see Table 5.3). A glance at the company titles of the offices absorbed by some of the major predators of the period 1900–14 makes plain the strategy of diversification across the 'single counter' (see Table 5.4). In general, however, the five acquisitions made by Phoenix–Pelican were more substantial than the often small and specialist offices singled out by their competitors for consumption.

The route by which the Phoenix entered the company of the predators lay through the life business. The first step along it was taken not by Phoenix itself but by the British Empire. In 1895, in a preparatory exercise for the sequence of manoeuvres which would make Phoenix a composite, Ryan launched the British Empire into a takeover of the Positive Government Security Life Assurance Co. Ltd (founded in 1870). This was a small life office with a paid-up capital of nearly £70,000 but with assets of nearly £500,000. It also interested the British Empire because of its specialisation in Canadian and Indian life policies. In 1895 adverse court decisions preventing the company from reorganising its Indian trusts caused its share price to tumble from its usual level around 40 shillings to 27s 6d. At this point, Ryan swooped. Prevented from using the income from its Indian securities as freely as it needed, the Positive was a lame duck. However, Ryan scented the prospect of useful diversification in its Indian business. After several brisk exchanges with the Positive management, he bought the office for the sharp price of £85,244, goodwill included.

The incident is important for the pointers it offers to Ryan's takeover style. His appraisal of the Positive's resources was lucid. His bargaining

[24] Or, arguably, 1910–84.

[25] Calculated from H. A. C. Cockerell and E. Green, *The British Insurance Business 1547–1970* (London, 1976), pp. 76–118.

Table 5.3. *Number of insurance offices absorbed by major offices, 1900–14*

Acquiring office	Number acquired	Rank
Royal	11	1
Commercial Union	10	2
Alliance	9	3=
Yorkshire	9	3=
London & Lancashire	8	5
General Accident	6	6
Phoenix–Pelican	5	7=
Northern	5	7=
Royal Exchange	4	9
North British	3	10=
Liverpool & London & Globe	3	10=
Scottish Union	2	12=
Norwich Union Life	2	12=
Norwich Union Fire	1	14=
Sun	1	14=
Sun Life	1	14=
Miscellaneous	21	
	101	

Source: Calculated from Cockerell & Green, *The British Insurance Business*, pp. 76–118.

on price brooked no nonsense; if fair, it was also hard. His method with the policies of the smaller office, once acquired, was to protect them with a closed 'Positive Fund' on which no new business could be created. This device was to recur in the Atlas negotiations and also in Pelican's absorption of the British Empire.

However, the Positive episode was merely a training exercise compared with what was to follow. The connection of the enlarged British Empire with the Pelican in 1902 was the key step. But to many contemporaries, it was not an obvious step. Indeed, it was rather an odd one. To begin with, the first proposals at the public level apparently originated not with Ryan's enterprising and zestful office but with the more conservative Pelican. In all probability, Ryan prompted the thinking within Pelican, but this did not show on the public level. Secondly, it was Pelican and not the larger, more prosperous and more dynamic British Empire which gained the better part of the deal. The financial press could not understand what was going on. Only the *Financial Times* offered any insight and even then it was an irritable insight: it portrayed the absorption of the

Table 5.4. *Acquisitions by three major offices, 1900–14*

Commercial Union	Royal	London & Lancashire
Palatine 1900	Lancashire 1901	Equitable Fire & Acc. 1901
Vehicular & Gen. 1901	Kent Fire 1901	Scottish Employers Liability 1904
Globe Accident 1901	Unit. Kent Life 1901	Law Acc. 1907
City Accident 1906	Northern Accident 1906	Standard Marine 1907
Amal. Accident 1906	Textile Mutual 1905	Amal. Albion Fire 1907
Scottish, County & Mercantile 1907	Durham & Yorks 1906	L & L Guar. & Accident 1908
Ocean Accident 1910	Post Office Employer Guarantee 1908	Ulster Plate Glass 1908
Alliance Plate Glass 1910	British & Foreign Marine 1909	United London & Scottish 1912
City of London Plate Glass 1910	Derby Building 1912	
Liverpool Victoria 1913	British Engine Boiler 1912	
	Warden 1913	

Source: Cockerell & Green, *The British Insurance Business*; Liveing, *Commercial Union Assurance*.

British Empire by Pelican as a needless and abject surrender to inferior forces.[26] The newspaper thought the terms 'outrageous' and presented the Pelican, not in its usual maternal role, but in the harsh plumage of the hunter, under the screaming headline: 'Voracious Bird Swallows the British Empire'.[27] What was Ryan up to?

The press made much play with Ryan's startling reforms at the British Empire over the preceding decade and complained that he was throwing his achievements away. The *Financial Times* even suggested that it was about time that insurance managements stopped treating their companies like 'feudal possessions' and openly lamented the loss of 'one of our most promising Mutual Offices'.[28]

Almost every commentator noted the disparity in style and size between the two offices. The British Empire had witnessed 'a vast improvement...in financial strength', 'its development during late years...a very marked feature of contemporaneous insurance history'; it was 'instinct with life of the most active kind'.[29] But if Ryan's overhaul of the British Empire was seen as one of the insurance success stories of the 1890s and 1900s, Pelican was viewed more gloomily: 'has perhaps

[26] *Financial Times*, 26 November 1902. [27] *Ibid.* [28] *Ibid.*
[29] *The Statist*, 15 November 1902; *Financial Times*, 26 November 1902.

lacked . . . vigour of management', 'a thoroughly respectable old proprietary company of no great impetus'.[30] Certainly, these differences showed at the level of assets and income.

Broadly, the British Empire was about twice as big as the Pelican. In 1901, Pelican possessed £1,296,331 in life funds, attracted some £300,000 in new sums assured and earned a total premium income of £121,779. By contrast, British Empire had £3,014,940 in funds, won £550,000 in new sums assured and took premiums of £272,834. Little wonder that outsiders puzzled over who was absorbing whom and why. The *Financial Times* summed up most harshly, though not, given the outside viewpoint, inaccurately: 'The operation is really not a partnership but an advised suicide, with retention of the present assets of the deceased for the benefit of his family and the transfer of his valuable going business to the man next door.'[31]

One answer, of course, as to why the Pelican was taking over the British Empire, and not *vice versa* was that the British Empire was a mutual office, and thus had only partners, while the Pelican was a proprietary company with share-owners. The legal intricacies of so mixed an amalgamation made it easier for the proprietary company to do the purchasing. But the real reason was that Ryan wanted it this way. *The Saturday Review* came close to realising this when it pondered:

> as the manager of the British Empire is to become the manager of the future Pelican and British Empire Life Office, while the (former) manager of the Pelican becomes a director of the new company, it is perhaps more likely that the policy for the future will resemble more closely that of the company which is taken over than that of the office which is nominally the purchaser.[32]

Meanwhile, as the press comment clattered on, the manager in question was quietly building up his own share interest in Pelican. His holding had fallen to 280 shares by August 1899, but, during 1902 and early 1903, the period of the merger negotiations, he built it up rapidly until it reached 722 shares in January 1903, putting him well among the substantial shareholders in Pelican. For most of 1902, British Empire retained its 2,100 further Pelican shares, but began shedding them in December, presumably as the increasing firmness of the agreement between the two companies rendered the voting power unnecessary. Together, the British Empire and Ryan holdings in Pelican composed the most powerful single interest in mid-1902, but, even so, this amounted to only about 3% of total Pelican equity. However, Ryan could probably have called upon a

[30] *The Saturday Review*, 22 November 1902; *Financial Times*, 26 November 1902.
[31] *Ibid.* [32] *The Saturday Review*, 22 November 1902.

much larger block of 'allied' holdings if he had needed them. But in the event, he did not.

That is not to say that Ryan had everything his own way. The British Empire's partners, many of whom were as sceptical as the journalists, had to be convinced that the deal was in their interests. This was not easy. Ryan tried by offering them two benefits. Upon takeover, the British Empire policies would be taken into a closed fund within the Pelican, much as British Empire had done with the Positive business. No new business would be permitted on this fund. Here, it was an essential device for protecting the mutual element within a mixed amalgamation. But it was also a device which could be administered very cheaply. In place of the 16% of premiums which were consumed in the running of the existing British Empire organisation, the projected Pelican and British Empire Life Office (PABELO) could run a British Empire fund for 10% of premiums. And the freed surplus would go in larger bonus payments to British Empire Fund members. Secondly, the accretion of Pelican financial resources would give British Empire policy-holders even better protection than they already enjoyed.[33] In a letter to a disgruntled partner, Ryan combined these points very neatly: 'In effect our members will form a Mutual section in a Proprietary Company, they having the advantage of their expenses being reduced and limited to 10%, while in addition, their liabilities are fully guaranteed by the capital of the Proprietary Company.'[34] Also evident in his thinking, but not stated publicly, was the expectation that the wide connections of British Empire would win a greatly extended business for PABELO.

The stated benefits attracted widespread criticism. British Empire members and journalists alike made hay with Ryan's figures. They pointed out that new business might cost more than 16% of premiums to acquire, but that renewal business cost much less than 10%; and the British Empire Fund was not going to be writing any new business. In fact, PABELO itself did not turn out to be especially cheap to run; in the post-merger phase 1903–6, the expense ratio for the whole company ran at 14–16%, not very different from the 12–17% managed by Pelican alone between 1884 and 1902. Nor were the attractions of greater capital protection universally appreciated. British Empire policies were already more than amply protected by British Empire's own £3.0 million of funds; they did not need the additional consolation of Pelican's meagre £1.1 million.

Once challenged, Ryan moved away from these points with a speed

[33] Ryan, Circular Letter to British Empire Members, 13 November 1902.

[34] Ryan to J. B. Leach, 18 November 1902; British Empire Guardbook.

that suggests tactical argument and other objectives rather than deep commitment. In internal papers of 1902 and 1903 the true direction of his thinking about the amalgamation becomes apparent. He is much more concerned with expansion of business than with lower costs or better protection. And there are some indications that he is looking for expansion even beyond the confines of PABELO.

A memorandum of 26 November 1902 by James Sorley, the Pelican Manager, reveals that, before the issue of the merger overtook all other business, he was considering a reform of the method by which Pelican distributed profits. The existing system was unusually generous to shareholders: they received the whole of the profit return on non-participating policies, as well as a share of the return on with-profits business.[35] Sorley wanted to reduce the shareholders' 100% claim on non-participating profits to 10% and put Pelican on a footing with other leading life assurers such as the Sun, Equity & Law, North British and Prudential.

As well as confirming a contention of volume I – that Pelican distributed too much of its profits in dividends – this defined a notable opportunity for Ryan. Indeed, the fact that there was great scope for *reducing* the share of Pelican profits flowing to its proprietors may have been one of the features which so attracted Ryan to the office in the first place. For, of course, profits saved from distribution could be employed for more entrepreneurial purposes.

In a confidential note of his own on 8 December 1903 Ryan summarised Sorley's arguments and showed how they connected to his own analysis. The drastic reduction advocated by Sorley in the share of profits claimed by Pelican shareholders would no longer be necessary in the newly enlarged PABELO. So, Ryan reasoned, the distribution of benefits between shareholders and policy-holders could be adjusted in a different way. His idea was to reduce the entitlement of PABELO shareholders to profits from the *participating* sector of the life business and convert the savings into larger bonuses for participating policy-holders. Ryan wished to use any income surrendered by shareholders to boost the appeal of the most commercially attractive sector of PABELO's activities. He concluded, 'the advantages gained by the Company in competition will be so important as ultimately to overshadow any temporary sacrifice'.[36]

But, in reality, sacrifice even for the shareholders could be minimised. Ryan calculated that the balance of profitability between the participating

[35] Non-participating policies did not earn bonuses, i.e. they did not receive a share of investment profits. The opposite was true of participating or with-profits policies.

[36] Ryan, Confidential Memorandum on Proprietors' Dividends, 8 December 1903, citing Sorley's Memorandum of 26 November 1902.

and non-participating branches of the new company's business was such that the proprietors could be guaranteed a fixed 15% dividend on paid-up apital financed entirely from the non-participating sector while the entirety of the profits from the participating sector could be returned as bonuses to its policy-holders. The planned dividend represented an advance on the usual $12\frac{1}{2}$% yield but it was to be raised no further unless the increase could be wholly funded from the non-participating business. But should the yield on the non-participating branch fall below 15%, the profits on the participating sector could be drawn upon to achieve the guaranteed level.[37]

The rationale for these tactics was market share. Even before the merger, Pelican had recognised the superior appeal of bonus business and wished to build up its stake in this sector. The arch-distributor of dividend, it was even prepared to trim proprietor's profits in order to do so. British Empire offered not only a dynamic selling reputation but, as a mutual, great experience in the working of bonus schemes. Ryan then saw how the combination of diverted proprietorial profits and the mutual company's skills could be used to combat *both* corporate competitors, which had 'in modern times . . . generally reduced the share of the profits taken by the Proprietors'[38] (but lacked the mutual element) and successful mutuals (which, however, lacked proprietor's profits).

Naturally, the marriage between a proprietary and a mutual office was not easy to arrange and a new Act of Parliament had to be sought to solemnise it. The Bill was filed on 17 December 1902 and received the Royal Assent on 30 June 1903. But even this most formal part of the procedure had a competitive content. The 1891 Act which governed Pelican's dealings down to 1903 had proved restrictive and forestalled other attempts at expansion, forcing Pelican 'to allow desirable transactions to go past us to other offices'.[39] Ryan was not prepared to tolerate such impediments. The new Act gave PABELO the power to transact business not only in its established life markets but also in the additional ones of accident, employer's liability, workmen's compensation and fidelity guarantee. Ryan clearly intended to use his larger resources to widen

[37] Even this residual charge upon participating profits was removed in the next Phoenix–Pelican merger, and they became wholly reserved to policy-holders; see pp. 324–5 below. However, this manipulation of profits was not to prove auspicious in the longer run. The generous treatment of policy-holders – a product of Ryan's experience at the mutual British Empire – was, in a later era, to curb dangerously *shareholder* interest in the expansion of life business. See below Ch. 12. And the older 100% allocation of profits from non-participating business to shareholders was later to prevent adequate *reinvestment* in this sector and to damage competitiveness.

[38] Ryan to Messrs Herne and Mackinnon, 27 April 1904.

[39] Ryan to Extraordinary General Meeting, 27 January 1903.

the fighting front on which PABELO operated. The assault on bonuses was part of a bigger battle.

It was for these prospects of expansion that Ryan dragged his sometimes protesting British Empire members into the merger. To do so, he had to conceal from them that they did not need to go, for their own office was perfectly viable as an independent operation. The British Empire partners could have stood out for independence. Indeed, if the broadside from the *Financial Times* had come at an earlier point, there could well have been a partners' revolt. As it was, Ryan collected as many proxies as possible for the Extraordinary General Meeting on 27 November 1902 because he feared just that eventuality.

The British Empire partners got their somewhat reduced costs and their somewhat improved protection. But they gave away for a song the valuable connections of their office. As the *Stock Exchange Gazette* commented, 'If the British Empire were not a mutual company, they (the Pelican) would have to buy out its shareholders in order to acquire these connections.'[40] Yet Pelican did not get, in any sense usual in insurance mergers, the British Empire premium income or the investments for securing British Empire policies, for both of these were tied to the closed and frozen fund buried in the vaults. Only new business drawn from former British Empire clients or connections could count as additions to Pelican business arising directly out of the merger. And only investments surplus to the cover of British Empire liablities, and thus outside the closed fund – there were some useful mortgages – could be absorbed into the Pelican's general ledgers.

It was a remarkable achievement on Ryan's part to carry off the merger against a background of such apparently unattractive 'advantages'. But closer study reveals that they were not the objective of the merger. The true objective was the much-enhanced combat power of the proprietary–mutual blend. This gave new life to an old proprietary office. And it gave mutual managers new markets – which otherwise they could not have penetrated – upon which to test their skills. The new competitive strength of PABELO is evident by 1906. In April the company announced a handsome Reversionary Bonus 'which is a matter of gratification at the present time, seeing that a number of leading companies have been compelled to reduce their Bonuses . . . there are bright prospects of still more satisfactory results in the future. The present great prosperity of the Office and the promising outlook should prove very attractive.'[41]

There are even hints that, during the negotiations for PABELO, Ryan

[40] *Stock Exchange Gazette*, 29 November 1902.

[41] PABELO Circular to Agents, 30 April 1906.

had achieved at least some glimpses of a still wider panorama. Possibly, he was viewing the Phoenix perspective along the sight line provided by Pelican. As early as July 1903, he wrote to all Pelican and former BE agents stressing how life business could be assisted by the possession of a fire connection and asking whether they would be prepared to act also as Phoenix agents. He reported too that 'arrangements have been made with the Phoenix Fire Office by which the two companies will render to each other as much assistance as possible in extending their connections throughout the country'.[42] This was more than four years before the Phoenix–Pelican fusion.

Similarly, when having to defend to more irate British Empire partners the primacy of the Pelican name in the PABELO title, Ryan used a highly significant argument. After pointing out, somewhat tendentiously, that Pelican was the older company, he came closer to the mark: 'Because the close tie between the Pelican Co. and the Phoenix Fire Office would have been weakened had the title not been arranged as it is, and from this connection a great deal of new business is expected in the future.'[43] From an early point, therefore, Ryan had seen the advantages of the tie with Phoenix, the rewards to cooperation and the relevance of Phoenix to the health and power of the life business.

By 1903 Ryan was clearly more alert to the possibilities of a composite strategy than he had shown himself in his approach to the Atlas project in 1901. This was natural: the terrain opened up to him ridge by ridge. The perspective – refined as the sequence British Empire, Pelican, Phoenix – presented itself.

3. THE PHOENIX–PELICAN MERGER: A UNION OF RELATIVES

On the face of it, the next step looks easy to predict, and, in retrospect, many found it so. In 1903, Ryan had stressed the importance to PABELO of its 'arrangements' with Phoenix and had cultivated the common ground between the two companies. He had clearly detected the potential for enlarged life sales that lay within the extensive connections of the fire office. It required no great imagination to conclude that a closer association with the Phoenix would bring these connections more firmly under PABELO's control. Indeed, the trade press in 1907 considered the talk of union between the two sister offices so predictable as to possess little news value.

Phoenix and Pelican had been separate but affectionate ventures, with

[42] General Manager's Circular to Agents, 7 July 1903.
[43] PABELO to J. B. Sluman, undated January 1903.

directors in common, ever since the launch of Pelican in 1797. They had always worked closely together, so what was more natural than that they should follow the tendency of the age and move under the same roof and the same title? Outsiders saw this manoeuvre as no more than a domestic rearrangement conditioned by external influences: that is, the rise of composite offices in other quarters. *The Times* called it 'to some extent a family affair' although it noted 'a wider significance in that it emphasises the composite tendency to which we have frequently drawn attention'.[44] Similarly, *The Policyholder* thought that the merger merely 'verified a favourite prophecy. The two ancient birds of Lombard Street have been mated by rumour more often than one cares to count and the announcement that they had at last decided to join forces was therefore not in the nature of a surprise.'[45] Even where the modern 'tendency' was perceived as a competitive one, this merger was still seen as a rather cosy method for old companies to deal with newfangled problems. The *Insurance Record* described it as 'a better way for our ancient offices to put themselves in a position to resist modern competition . . . to stand alongside the powerful formations of more recent years'.[46]

This blasé acceptance of a 'predictable' and comfortable outcome was mistaken. If it was natural, the Phoenix–Pelican merger was much more complex than a mere shuffling of household effects between the two sides of Lombard Street. And it was also a good deal more contentious.

One striking feature of the merger was that it was originally a design for the fusion not merely of the sister offices but of *three* insurance ventures. For, even in 1907, Ryan was considering seriously the acquisition of an accident company and his choice had lighted upon the London Guarantee & Accident. In the event, he had to wait another fifteen years before he was able to claim it for the Phoenix. But the plan of 1907 was a clear attempt to offer, across a single counter, capacity in life, fire and accident insurance. Nevertheless, it is probably still too much to claim that Ryan had arrived at an explicit composite strategy. The realities were more workaday than this.

To begin with, Ryan's war-horse, PABELO, had less immediate need of the merger than the other two participants in the negotiations. By the mid-1900s, the life office was healthy and fully recovered from the doldrums of the previous century. Ryan reported to the Pelican Board in February 1907 that, 'The business has shown a steady improvement over a period of several years and indicates that the Company's holding upon the insuring classes in the country has improved.' Consequently, Pelican

[44] *The Times*, 11 July 1907. [45] *The Policyholder*, 17 July 1907.
[46] *Insurance Record*, 19 July 1907.

was 'in a prominent and highly satisfactory position and need fear no diminution of business as a result of the pressing competition of the day'.[47] Even twenty years before, a merger with Phoenix could have been seen as a means of rescuing a lame Pelican, but, by 1907, the life office had no need of rescue.

Ironically, there was by then more need to bolster the Phoenix, despite its traditional role as the senior and stronger of the sisters. Although Phoenix had suffered less than some UK insurers from the consequences of the San Francisco earthquake, that disaster had left the company poorer by nearly £650,000 and the fire reserves in a sensitive state. In contrast, Pelican's absorption of the British Empire assets, and through this, the Positive assets, had pushed the life office's reserves to a historic peak.[48] To the eye of the wounded Phoenix, the Pelican strutted a little too proudly. The older bird needed to restore the accustomed pecking order. So some pressure for the merger followed from sudden changes in the long-accepted balance of power between the two associated offices.

But, apparently, Phoenix was more interested in funds than in status. Its managers had noticed the huge imbalance in the assets to capital ratios maintained by the two companies: 1.9 for Phoenix, even before full allowance for the San Francisco disaster, against 23.0 for the life company (see Table 5.5). Their disquiet was reinforced by the effect of San Francisco on the Phoenix reserves.

Lord George Hamilton wrote to Ryan on 16 June 1907, 'The fire reserve is low, and I assume that, if no amalgamation took place, a reduction in dividend might be necessary to the Phoenix shareholders until the reserve is brought up to the necessary level.'[49] By contrast with such distasteful strategies, the device of amalgamation would produce a company with assets of £7.5 million, premiums of £2.4 million and an asset to capital ratio of 5.7. Even if London Guarantee were omitted from the scheme the numbers were still very attractive: assets, £6.8 million, premiums £2 million and a ratio of 7.6. Considered any way, this was better news than a dividend cut.

However, it is likely here that worried directors were more concerned with appearances than realities. Modern insurance opinion would not be happy with comparing a general office with a life assurer in terms of asset ratios. Life companies necessarily carry substantial assets in the shape of

[47] PABELO, Report of Chairman and General Manager, 6 February 1907; Confidential Memorandum, 14 June 1907.

[48] This was, of course, largely a paper effect since most of the British Empire assets were locked in a closed fund.

[49] Phoenix Guardbook B4/40, Directors' Correspondence on the Phoenix–Pelican Merger.

Table 5.5. *Capital disposition of Phoenix, Pelican and London Guarantee & Accident, June 1907*

	Phoenix	Pelican	LGA	Total
Proprietors' funds				
Capital	268,880	100,000	75,000	443,880
Reserves	494,000	133,000	260,000	887,000
Total	762,880	233,000	335,000	1,330,880
Premium income	1,533,000	429,000	395,000	2,357,000
Interest income	57,000	208,000	21,000	286,000
Total	1,590,000	637,000	416,000	2,643,000
Total assets	1,462,000	5,353,000	735,000	7,550,000

Source: Guardbook on Phoenix–Pelican Merger, p. 9.

policy-holders' accumulated savings, while the assets of a general company consist of the premium reserve backing and the loss reserve cover. Probably, the Phoenix directors of 1907 believed that the 'technical reserves' were too low and needed bolstering. But to rely upon the assets of a life company for comfort in this respect could be seen as cosmetic at best.

However, the plans to create an amalgamated company did not begin with Phoenix's reserve problem, nor even with the 'predictable' attraction between the two related offices. Informed City talk had noted that Phoenix was eyeing the accident market. *The Financier* was convinced that Phoenix's merger ambitions were derived from a rationale featuring accident insurance.[50] Neither the gossips nor the journalists knew just how right they were, nor were they to know.

The Workmen's Compensation Act of 1906 had defined and dramatised the market opportunity for workplace insurance and Phoenix responded by writing its first accident policies in January 1907. From his base at PABELO, Ryan had long seen the opening. Moreover, Pelican had accepted accident reinsurances from Phoenix in April 1907, within weeks of the fire office entering the trade. No doubt, too, both companies were keeping a weather eye on the activities of the other veteran offices: the REA had first broached the accident market in 1898 and joined the Accident Offices Association in 1904, while the Sun set up a specialised Accident Department in 1907.[51] Both Phoenix and Pelican had taken an early guard against such initiatives. The Phoenix Act of 1895 and the

[50] *The Financier*, 13 July 1907.

[51] Supple, *Royal Exchange Assurance*, pp. 262ff; Dickson, *Sun Insurance*, p. 194.

PABELO Act of 1903 each provided the necessary powers to transact accident business. However, by 1907 Ryan and his colleagues at Phoenix calculated that they needed additional capacity and expertise in the field if they were to match the diversification policies of their peers. It was in the attempt to procure an accident business *larger* than any which Phoenix and Pelican could support that one of the most important mergers in Phoenix's history began.

For it seems that the initial target in 1907 was not the 'predictable' fire–life merger but the acquisition of the London Guarantee & Accident by the Phoenix. The LGA felt itself to be in a vulnerable position. As a specialist accident company, it had suffered a paradoxical blow at the hands of the Workmen's Compensation Act. In consequence of this legislation, the LGA directors informed their shareholders that 'most of the leading Fire Insurance Companies are now undertaking Personal Accident, Workmen's Compensation and Burglary Insurance. They no doubt will be formidable competitors.'[52] The Board was particularly concerned about the effect of this development on the large number of LGA agents who were also agents for fire companies. Doubtless, they also had in mind the parlous state of the market in the United States where much of their business was, then as later.[53] Their first thought for a remedy was a direct return of service: instead of waiting to be assaulted by incoming fire offices, they would attack by entering the fire market on their own account. However, shareholder unrest both on this issue and on the failure of the dividend to rise spoiled the shot.

In March 1907, shareholders representing about one-third of LGA equity, protested at the design of the balance sheet: 'It is, as it always is, excellent, but it is set out in such a way as to prevent the majority of shareholders from understanding it properly.' What they were being prevented from understanding was that the Board had been salting away profits to reserves for years rather than increase the dividend. If this same Board were allowed to go into fire risks as well as accident risks, how much *more*, asked the rebels, would they consider it prudent to salt away? The outlook for the dividend was not deemed to be bright. The shareholder propaganda was effective; it forced the LGA directors to seek an alternative method of protecting their business. Again they adopted a direct tactic: a frontal approach to a fire office, which, by merger, would 'keep their business together'.[54] The initiative was taken when LGA put this proposition to Phoenix in May or early June 1907.

By 12 June Phoenix and PABELO had appointed a joint committee to

[52] LGA Circular to Shareholders, 8 March 1907.
[53] See below, pp. 443ff.
[54] PABELO Confidential Memorandum, 14 June 1907.

consider the possibility of a three-way fusion. It produced its first report on 14 June. The introductory paragraph of this report makes clear that the issue of fusion had been raised by the prospect of acquiring accident capacity in which both Lombard Street offices would possess interest. By the end of June the Committee had produced a financial outline for merger: Phoenix should increase its capital to £3 million by the issue of 62,240 new shares of £5 each; about 15,000 of these, fully paid, would go to acquire Pelican, and about 20,000 to secure LGA, also fully paid, at the rate of four Phoenix shares for every five LGA shares. LGA boasted an authorised capital of £250,000, of which £150,000 was issued. When preference shares were taken into account, the Phoenix offer price was £132,500. The device of financing the merger by the issue of new £5 shares, fully paid, and ranking for dividend alongside existing shares followed contemporary fashion and particularly 'the precedent of the recent issues of capital made by the Alliance Company'.[55]

With great swiftness, a provisional agreement was beaten out, and signed, by mid-July. Just before this, on 29 June, A. R. Kirby of LGA wrote to Ryan, 'I would join on reputation and your published figures . . . one reason [is] that I believe the Combined Company will be able within a reasonable period, to be able to double the business we have now. But I have to convince others . . .' (though he added, scarcely reassuringly, 'I return your letter to enable you to have a copy made. I am sorry to say I never keep a copy of any letter I write, with the result that I never write if I can help it').[56] An interview between Ryan and Kirby two days before had stressed the attractiveness of LGA's profit levels: just under 9% for the US market, which provided about three-quarters of all premiums, 10% for UK business, 20% for Canadian lines and 30% for Australian.

Despite Kirby's sales talk, however, doubts were beginning to spring in Lombard Street. Although LGA's US profits had risen between 1903 and 1906, the current year promised to be a miserable one with securities depreciating in New York and London. And Phoenix, of course, had just taken the hammering of a lifetime in America. A company which depended as heavily as did LGA on the US market would not have been at its most alluring in 1907. But even more damning was a legal query which had surfaced by early July. Doubt had arisen as to whether any successor company to LGA would be empowered to retain the benefit of its American accident trade. The prospect of LGA with its American portfolio was bad enough. But the prospect of LGA without its American portfolio was

55 Phoenix–PABELO Committee on Fusion, Report of 24 June 1907.
56 Phoenix Guardbook B4/40, Directors' Correspondence, Kirby to Ryan, 29 June 1907.

not worthy of attention from the birds of Lombard Street. Between 15 and 17 July they terminated negotiations with LGA.

In the longer perspective, the flirtation with LGA was a fateful one for the Phoenix. For its – or possibly Ryan's – ambitions for an accident acquisition became somewhat unhealthily concentrated on LGA. The flirtation became a fixation. Phoenix returned to it in the 1920s when it would have done better to remember its doubts about the relationship between the LGA and the United States.

In the shorter perspective of 1907, Phoenix and Pelican were left gazing at one another over the wreckage of a beautiful idea. But the time was still ripe for a fusion. The *Insurance Record* thought July 1907, 'the most favourable moment that could be found for the formation of a strong combination to transact fire, life and accident business'.[57] Nor had the threat of competing composites evaporated as readily as the prospect of taking over the LGA. After reviewing the advantages of life in the composite style, a Phoenix–PABELO memorandum of June 1906 had found a more sombre argument for action: 'Recent events in the insurance world would appear to show that what might be argued upon the foregoing lines, to be a matter of policy is becoming more or less a matter of necessity for Offices who wish to retain their position under present circumstances.'[58]

Even before the LGA prospect had been abandoned, this logic had pointed to a twinning of Phoenix and PABELO. The first report of the joint committee on fusion, after explaining the reasons for the planned fire–accident merger, had continued,

> The *inclusion* of the Life Office in the amalgamation was deemed to be a desirable and opportune course, for very much the same reasons as mentioned above. When refined, these were that, a Life Office *standing alone* will no doubt feel very acutely the competition of those large offices who are in a position to offer the general public, facilities for transacting all classes of insurance.[59]

Clearly now, Pelican could not be left to 'stand alone'. If there was not to be a three-way merger, there would have to be a two-way merger. It was in this way, through the mediation of a failed acquisition of a much younger company, that the Pelican and the Phoenix actually came to move into the same nest.

By mid-June 1907 the fact that Phoenix and PABELO were negotiating was anyway 'a matter of open rumour',[60] although the news that the talks

[57] *Insurance Record*, 19 July 1907.

[58] Phoenix–PABELO Memorandum, 17 June 1907, Guard Book on Phoenix–Pelican Merger.

[59] Phoenix–PABELO Committee on Fusion, Report of 14 June 1907 (my emphasis).

[60] *Ibid.*, Report of 12 June 1907.

were at that time tripartite apparently did not get out. The rumours made for some urgency of treatment, whether or not the merger was to be a dual or triple affair. The joint committee of Phoenix and PABELO directors appointed on 12 June (Gorst, Avebury, Bovill, Bird, Hawes and Phillips, with Guernsey from Phoenix and Ryan from PABELO as secretaries) possessed the musculature to move fast, and the comprehensive memorandum it produced by 14 June was a remarkable achievement. This document was accepted by all parties as the basis for a Provisional Agreement by 26 June. The Agreement, now with only two parties, was signed on 31 July. A new committee to handle the details of the amalgamation was launched on 16 October. It produced draft regulations for the new company by 6 November and its Memorandum of Association, based generally on the model of the PABELO Articles, by 28 November. Legal sanction for the fusion was obtained in Chancery on 27 November. The Provisional Agreement became absolute on 18 December and the voluntary winding up of PABELO was announced to its shareholders by Ryan on 29 January 1908. The pace proved sufficient to outstrip any damage that the rumours may have done.

However, speed did not equate with ease. There were some tricky issues in the negotiations between relatives. The advantages for the fire side were, if anything, too clear. San Francisco had wrecked the reserves; PABELO would repair them, or at least, so it would appear; and the capital base would be strengthened. The key memorandum of 14 June 1907 stressed that, for Phoenix, 'the percentage of Funds-in-hand to Premiums is very much lower than used to be general . . . these Reserves are proportionately smaller than is the case with many of the great Fire Offices'. By contrast, amalgamation would boost the fire fund to a level equal to a full year's premiums – in place of the 75% level prior to amalgamation – and provide 'reserves, outside Capital, according to a high standard'.[61] Other gains such as savings on expenses, the 'attractive power' of larger resources and the additional premiums to be won by extended connections were listed as clearly subordinate, if real, considerations.

The advantages to PABELO were more difficult to explain. The memorandum recognised that policy-holders and proprietors of PABELO had to be given 'a reasonable inducement . . . an obvious improvement in their position' if they were to surrender their separate existence. Under the terms of the earlier PABELO merger, holders of with-profits policies could lose part of their profits under the constitutional obligation to make up the proprietors' dividend to 15%, if this

[61] *Ibid.*, Report of 14 June 1907.

could not be done out of other trading profits. So the inducement designed in 1907 was to convert the participating fund into a genuinely mutual arrangement with 100% of the profits earned by the fund reverting to its policy-holders. Moreover, the PABELO life operation was to be taken over as a going concern, becoming the life department of Phoenix, not as a closed fund in the style of the British Empire arrangement of 1903. So PABELO policy-holders could look forward to expanded business as well as a tighter hold on profits.

This provision in regard to assurance profits was to cause trouble after 1945, since it worked to discourage the interest of shareholders – and some managers – in expanding the life business. But in 1907 it seemed a cunning way of encouraging PABELO policy-holders to whip up an interest in a merger which otherwise they might too easily have seen as serving primarily the needs of Phoenix proprietors.

PABELO policy-holders were also offered the additional security of guarantee funds totalling £2.8 million. However, it cannot have escaped them that their current guarantee was quite adequate for the scale of their business. Here they would be excused if they could not find the cake for the icing.

More to the point was the third sweetener. This was directed at PABELO shareholders. Shares in PABELO were £10 shares, one-tenth paid; so proprietors were liable for further calls of £9 per share. The Phoenix offer for PABELO was couched in newly issued £5 shares in the freshly titled Phoenix Assurance Co. Ltd, fully paid, and ranking for dividend equally with the existing shares of the Phoenix. They received one of these £5 shares for every seven £10 shares (but only £1 paid) in PABELO. Given current share values, this meant that PABELO shareholders received a consideration of about £4 11s. per share against prevailing market value of about £3 15s per share. Also they could look forward to an improvement in their dividend earnings of about 42%. Most of them detected this, correctly, to be a good deal. Indeed PABELO submitted the Phoenix proposals for the analysis of two eminent actuaries, F. B. Wyatt (then president of the Institute of Actuaries) and C. D. Higham (then chairman of the Life Offices Association). They too thought the deal a good one.

But not everyone, indeed not everyone on the PABELO Board, was so content. The merger which the press found so natural actually caused feathers to fly.

One of the ablest of the Pelican Board, the shrewd solicitor, John Tryon, perceived clearly that the life office was currently the healthier of the two relatives and queried whether the amalgamation was in its best interests. He stressed that the merger was a danger *for Pelican*: 'Had there been a proper reserve, there would have been no appreciable risk . . . but it is rather a different thing in the case of a very depleted reserve.' He concluded that, 'The Pelican is undoubtedly financially the stronger institution and in my opinion ought to have a voice in the management disproportionate to its share in the capital.'[62] Presumably, this point was recognised as dangerous by the advocates of the merger. For it was met, and those of Tryon's persuasion mollified, albeit by a device that might have been predicted on other grounds: Ryan was selected as general manager of the new Phoenix Assurance.

However, this was not Tryon's only criticism. He also resented the secrecy with which the Pelican merger committee (Gorst, Hamilton, Hawes, Phillips, Ryan) conducted its business; there were suspicions that the merger with Phoenix was being railroaded through the Pelican Board. Tryon spoke for those who believed that the Pelican directors, as the true decision-making committee, were not receiving sufficient detail on which to base sensible decisions:

> I should ask for a statement of actual profits for a period of years . . . It seemed to me to be a strange proceeding when in the one week the Chairman, in a three-minute speech, mentioned the proposal, and, in a week or so afterwards, sent a memorandum saying that the matter was of the greatest importance, but giving no data whatever as to Phoenix profits in the past, and then, next day, moved a resolution that he should agree to a document containing unknown terms, that is, unknown to almost everyone asked to vote on it.[63]

This was not gratuitous trouble-making. Tryon later served with distinction on the Board of Phoenix Assurance; his contributions over many years provide clear evidence of integrity, clear judgement and a quick mind. In contrast to some of his colleagues, Tryon could be recommended for a top job, with, as the academic referees tend to write, 'no reservations'. It is significant that he held, and expressed, serious reservations of his own regarding the merger with Phoenix. After doing so, it is also significant that he wrote to Ryan: 'Having expressed my feelings, let me add that my belief in the amalgamation rests on your own support of it, and on the fact that you will manage it. I sincerely wish it every success and yourself satisfaction in conducting its affairs.'[64] This is evidence that Ryan was a moving spirit, and one who commanded confidence in the best quarters; but it is also evidence that some of the keenest thinkers at Pelican considered the Phoenix merger as a long way removed from 'natural'.

[62] Phoenix Guard Book B4/40, Directors' Correspondence, Tryon to Ryan, 1 July 1907.
[63] *Ibid.*, Tryon to Ryan, 12 July 1907. [64] *Ibid.*

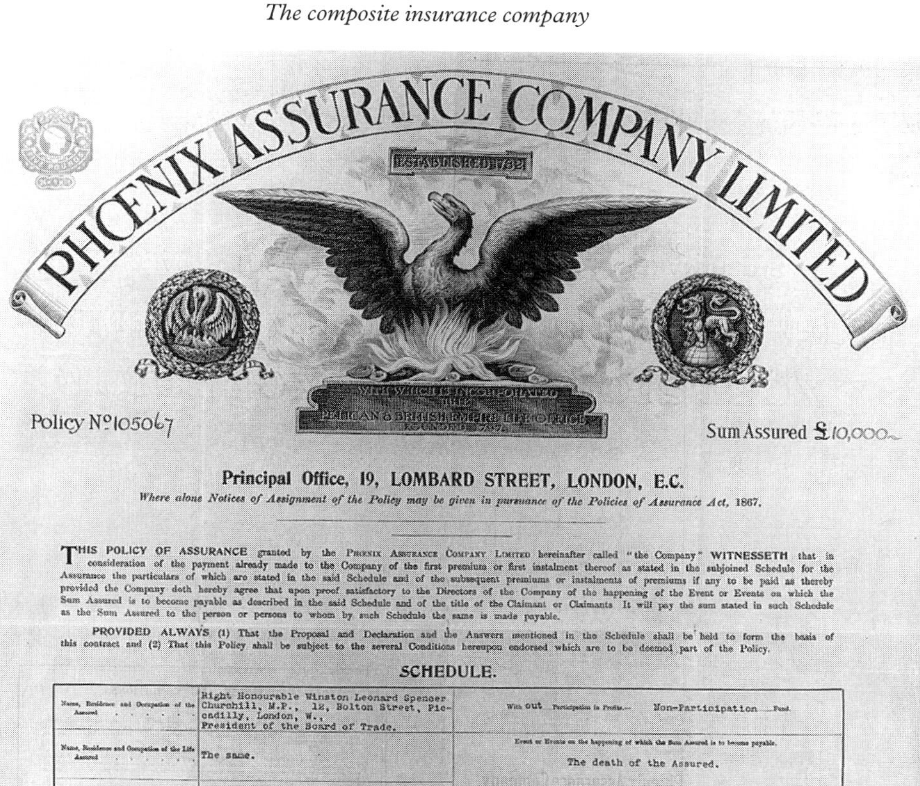

PHŒNIX ASSURANCE COMPANY LIMITED

ESTABLISHED 1782

WITH WHICH IS INCORPORATED THE PELICAN & BRITISH EMPIRE LIFE OFFICE FOUNDED 1797.

Policy No 105067 | Sum Assured £10,000

Principal Office, 19, LOMBARD STREET, LONDON, E.C.

Where alone Notices of Assignment of the Policy may be given in pursuance of the Policies of Assurance Act, 1867.

THIS POLICY OF ASSURANCE granted by the PHŒNIX ASSURANCE COMPANY LIMITED hereinafter called "the Company" WITNESSETH that in consideration of the payment already made to the Company of the first premium or first instalment thereof as stated in the subjoined Schedule for the Assurance the particulars of which are stated in the said Schedule and of the subsequent premiums or instalments of premiums if any to be paid as thereby provided the Company doth hereby agree that upon proof satisfactory to the Directors of the Company of the happening of the Event or Events on which the Sum Assured is to become payable as described in the said Schedule and of the title of the Claimant or Claimants It will pay the sum stated in such Schedule as the Sum Assured to the person or persons to whom by such Schedule the same is made payable.

PROVIDED ALWAYS (1) That the Proposal and Declaration and the Answers mentioned in the Schedule shall be held to form the basis of this contract and (2) That this Policy shall be subject to the several Conditions hereupon endorsed which are to be deemed part of the Policy.

SCHEDULE.

Name, Residence and Occupation of the Assured	Right Honourable Winston Leonard Spencer Churchill, M.P., 12, Bolton Street, Piccadilly, London, W., President of the Board of Trade.
Name, Residence and Occupation of the Life Assured	The same.
Date of commencement of Assurance	9th September 1908.
Sum Assured. Amount	Ten Thousand Pounds.
Sum Assured. To whom payable	The Executors, Administrators, or Assigns of the Assured.
Sum Assured. Where payable	At the Company's Principal Office in London.
Premiums. Amount per annum and how payable	£137: 18: 4 during the first five years. £261: 5: 0 yearly thereafter.
Premiums. Date or dates when due	9th September.
Premiums. Period during which payable	The whole duration of the Assurance.
Premiums. Final payment due	– – – – – –

With out Participation in Profits.— Non-Participation Fund.

Event or Events on the happening of which the Sum Assured is to become payable.

The death of the Assured.

Date of the Proposal and Declaration, and by whom made	31st August 1908.	The Assured.
Date of the Answers to questions put by the Company's Medical Examiner, and by whom made	31st August 1908.	The Assured.
Date of Birth of the Life Assured, as stated in the Proposal	30th November 1874.	
Whether admitted or not	Not Admitted.	
Conditions as to Foreign Travel and Residence, and as to Occupation	See Memorandum below.	

Special Provisions, if any.

IN WITNESS whereof the undersigned being two of the Directors of the Company have for and on behalf of the Company hereunto set their hands this Ninth day of September 1908.

Arthur F. Lucas
Directors.

Actuary.

Plate 5.3 An early client of the composite: life policy of Sir Winston Churchill, 1908.

This is also suggested by the difficulties surrounding the transfer of Pelican directors to the new fire–life company. Anyone who wished was welcome to trans-ship. Some did not wish. Some wished too much. Some of the difficulties were merely funny and concerned the latter group. One septuagenarian Pelican director, Judge Bompas, was concerned – the ungenerous might say with good reason – that Phoenix Assurance would not want him. He was so anxious that he sometimes sent the Pelican chairman more than one letter a day on the subject, largely because he was not good at remembering whether he had sent the first. Nevertheless, despite the confusions of his postal arrangements, and of his prose, he established an interesting defensive position:

> I am, as you know, one of the oldest Directors . . . I know that I have been slack in my attendance at the Pelican Board lately, but I expect before very long to retire and should then be able to give whatever time might be required . . . I do think now that I ought to receive £700 a year as compensation. I think any jury would give it and though I do not want to be greedy, under the special circumstances, I think that I am entitled to it.[65]

In the event, Phoenix calmed Bompas' worries, graciously gave him a directorship and avoided the issue of compensation. Judge Bompas died in 1909.

But not all Pelican directors were so eager to continue with the new company. Four of them – Avebury, Hodgson, Ponsonby and Treherne – already held Phoenix directorships alongside their Pelican posts, and so were unaffected. Seven of them – Hamilton, Dillon, Hawes, Sorley, Tryon, Winterstoke and Bompas – voted to join Phoenix. But the remaining four – Gorst, Bouverie, Phillips and Young – elected to retire. Of these, Bouverie and Phillips certainly expressed doubts about the wisdom of the merger.

Despite these doubts, Phoenix Assurance Co. Ltd came formally into existence on 1 January 1908. Achieved with speed, smaller in scope than originally planned, and peppered with disappointments and difficulties at which few guessed, the negotiations nevertheless created the essential structure for the modern Phoenix. After January 1908, Phoenix Assurance could grow only by adding more sections to its single 'counter'. With the absorption of Pelican, the strategy of specialisation insisted upon by Stonestreet more than a century before yielded to the exactly opposed strategy of composite expansion.

Ryan had been led to this destination by a curious variety of pointers: the actions of other companies, the level of competition, perhaps, above

[65] *Ibid.*, Bompas to Gorst, 27 June 1907; and to Ryan, 2 July 1907.

all, the appetite for accident capacity. It could not be said that the Phoenix arrived at the composite strategy by a single flash of entrepreneurial insight. Rather it got there by a series of diligent responses to a sequence of differing needs.

Gerald Ryan was clearly the force behind the responses. He did not dominate proceedings. The correspondence suggests neither a brilliant autocrat nor a master diplomatist. He put his arguments forcefully but courteously, took a close interest in all departments of business, worked like a Trojan. The approach was by no means dashing; he was meticulous, almost schoolmasterly, with every detail of the merger. However, the letters to him from his own directors, particularly those from Hamilton or Tryon, were notably respectful and expressed faith in the scheme – even where there were also misgivings – largely because Ryan had faith in it. The Pelican directors acceded to the proposals precisely because they were Ryan's proposals.

From the moment they did so, Gerald Ryan became the most important figure in the second century of Phoenix's existence. He was as much the architect of the twentieth-century Phoenix as Stonestreet was the architect of the nineteenth-century Phoenix. And the merger of 1908, circuitously achieved as it was, served as the foundation upon which he was to construct, with more obviously deliberate intent, a classic, multi-division composite insurance company.

4. THE SEQUEL: RYAN AND THE LAST MERGERS OF PEACETIME

The takeovers and mergers of the period 1892–1908 had created the cortex and spine for a composite. Those of the years 1908–31 – dates defined by Ryan's appointment as general manager, and his retirement as chairman, of Phoenix Assurance – added the limbs and flesh. Generally, the additions of the pre-1914 era were not as substantial as those of the 1920s, and, mercifully, did not entail the major surgery that these later exercises in company doctoring required.

By the late 1900s, it was clear that the Phoenix–PABELO foundation merger had left several functions in need of particular attention: the new Phoenix still lacked genuine capacity in marine insurance; it would profit from greater volume in life assurance; and it absolutely required a substantial operation in accident insurance. Ryan himself had begun to think in terms as explicit as these and had turned thought into action in all these areas, bar accident, by 1914, and the last was not for want of trying.

In preparation for his second wave of acquisitions, he wrote in 1910,

PHŒNIX ASSURANCE COMPANY, LIMITED.

Phœnix Fire Office,

Telephone Nos. 8157 Central
8158 „

19, LOMBARD STREET,
LONDON, *March*, *1907*.
E.C.

To the Agents,
Phœnix Assurance Company, Limited.

Dear Sir,

I have much pleasure in advising you that the Directors have decided to increase the sphere of usefulness of the Phœnix Fire Office, by adding an Accident Department, to enable our clients to place their **Burglary, Accident, Fidelity Guarantee** and other **Contingency Risks** with the one Office.

The new Workmen's Compensation Act, 1906, including as it does **Domestic (Indoor and Outdoor) Servants, Shop Assistants** and **Clerical Staffs,** will affect practically the entire community.

Prospectuses, &c., are enclosed giving particulars and rates, and all further information will be given at our Offices throughout the United Kingdom or I shall be pleased to arrange for a representative to call upon you to go thoroughly into the subject.

The Agents' remuneration will be as follows:

WORKMEN'S COMPENSATION AND EMPLOYERS' LIABILITY:

Single Premiums.

Not exceeding £ 50.	Between £ 50 and £ 100.	Between £ 100 and £ 200.	Between £ 200 and £ 300.	Above £ 300.
15 per cent.	15 per cent. on 1st £ 50.	12½ per cent. on 1st £ 100.	12½ per cent. on 1st £ 100.	12½ per cent. on 1st £ 100.
	10 per cent. on 2nd £ 50.	7½ per cent. on the balance.	7½ per cent. on 2nd £ 100.	7½ per cent. on 2nd £ 100.
			5 per cent. on the balance.	5 per cent. on 3rd £100.
				2½ per cent. on the balance.

PERSONAL ACCIDENT, FIDELITY GUARANTEE AND BURGLARY.

On New Premiums ... ... 15 per cent.
On Renewal Premiums ... ... 15 per cent.

In all other respects the Agency terms and Conditions will be the same as those which apply to the Fire Agency.

If you kindly inform me how many circular letters and prospectuses similar to the enclosed specimens you will require, based on the number of Insured in your Agency, I shall have pleasure in ordering the necessary supplies to be sent.

I trust that this extension of the operations of the **"Phœnix"** will be appreciated, and that our Fire Clients will largely avail themselves of the new facilities to the mutual advantage of the Company and yourself.

I am, Dear Sir,
Yours faithfully,
H. B. Guernsey
Manager and Secretary.

Encl.:
Abridged General Prospectus.
Workmen's Compensation Prospectus for General Risks.
Special (Reply Card) Prospectus for Servants.
Burglary and Theft Prospectus (Private Premises).
Business Form in active preparation.
Specimen Circular to Policy Holders.

N.B.—Agents affiliated to Branches are requested to communicate as to the above with their respective Branch Managers, as in the case of Fire business.

Plate 5.4 Phoenix enters accident without the LGA.

It is probably unnecessary to adduce arguments in favour of the endeavour to build up the business of a Company . . . by means of purchasing the business of other Companies. Among banks and insurance companies, the process continues with no visible abatement. The leading institutions are eager to safeguard their interests, present and future, against the competition and inroads of their rivals. The home field is regarded as the richest and most desirable ground to occupy. *One by one, those companies who cultivate a single class of insurance business are disappearing from the active list, and the chances of increasing one's strength and power by these means are dwindling year by year.* Everyone connected with our Company will be desirous that it shall have an absolutely secured position among the leading companies of the future, that its clientele shall be *so widely spread* that, come what may, it will, as in the past, remain in the forefront of the powerful and prominent insurance Institutions. To promote this object, the acquisition of a fine old home Company would be useful.[66]

The experience of the period 1892–1908, and especially the complex experience of the three-pronged merger attempt of 1907, had made its mark: Ryan was now in no doubt regarding the proper insurance vehicle for the times.

5. PHOENIX AND LAW LIFE, 1910: A MERGER FOR PROFESSIONALS

The first successful acquisition in the new mode came two years after the marriage between Phoenix and Pelican. The negotiations which brought the Law Life Assurance Society into the Phoenix family were straightforward, although this dignified life office was by no means itself a simple concern.

To the Phoenix eye, 'a first-class life office established eighty-six years ago' (in 1823), Law Life was precisely the sort of 'fine old home Company' that Ryan had envisaged. Indeed, it was exclusively a home company and by the late nineteenth century there were few finer: in 1870 Law Life boasted total funds of £5.5 million, making it the richest life office in Britain. By this measure, it was $4\frac{1}{2}$ times bigger than the Pelican of 1870 and a good deal more than ten times bigger than the British Empire (with £0.48 million) or the infant Prudential (with £0.36 million). When measured by its life reserves alone, Law Life then occupied second rank among all British companies, dipping its pennant only to the Scottish Widows' Fund (£4.4 million against £4.9 million). However, it did not continue at such levels of strength. The *Post Magazine* warned in 1874

[66] Phoenix Law Life Guard Book No. 1, General Manager's Memorandum for Directors, 8 November 1910 (my emphasis).

that the office was approaching that difficult age 'when claims fall in and cause heavy reductions in premiums receivable, so that very great exertions are necessary to prevent a positive decrease in the income of the company, [but] ... energetically pushed, the new business of the company would, in a very few years, equal that of the Scottish Widows' Fund'.[67]

Unfortunately, energetic pushing did not occur and the mortality cycle took its toll on Law Life. By 1880, its funds had slipped to third place in the pecking order of offices, by 1890 to twelfth, and by 1900 they had fallen off the list of the top sixteen. PABELO had built its funds to a level better than £5 million by 1907, while Law Life had watched its own assets drop to a level slightly above £4 million. These funds were carried on a modest equity: 50,000 shares of £20 each, giving a total approved capital of £1 million, but, with only £2 of each share paid, the subscribed capital amounted to a mere £100,000. By the time Law Life caught Ryan's eye, its premium income was about £290,000 per year and its net earnings from interest a further £200,000. All this made it a middle-size company with assets well worth plucking.

It also possessed some attractive special features. Current profitability would be attractive to any predator: it had run at £100,000 p.a. during the 1890s and was still making £60,000 p.a. in the 1900s. In his final report, Law Life's chairman emphasised this profit record, 'even in the bad times through which capitalist companies have been passing, say in the last fifteen years'.[68] So, even if Law Life had not been managed to the best of its abilities, it was still a milch cow of some girth. Certainly, in the 1900s it was no mean performer as a profitable assurer of lives.

Profits mattered to Phoenix, but at this time a peculiarity of the Law Life's clientele counted most with the older office. Law Life enjoyed 'a very large Home connection' at a time when the UK market offered 'the most desirable class of business', and it did so through 'a special class of the community ... upon which the Phoenix has not hitherto had any special hold'.[69] From its beginning Law Life had focused upon a certain band of wealth, homing in with all due decorum on the professionals of army, navy, church and, above all, law. It had developed a speciality in life business for solicitors and by the 1900s boasted 'an intimate connection with the Legal Profession'. It took Ryan no time at all to identify this as 'a unique opportunity to cultivate a new and important field for *all* classes of

[67] *Post Magazine and Insurance Monitor*, 7 February 1874.
[68] Law Life Assurance Society, Annual Report 1909.
[69] Phoenix Chairman's Speech to Shareholders' Extraordinary General Meeting, undated, probably February 1910.

business'.[70] A special relationship with the lawyers would clearly bring gains not only to life but also to fire, accident, burglary and leasehold branches. Even Law Life's head office was situated conveniently close to the Law Courts, in Fleet Street.

Ryan wished to use the home market for Phoenix's first massing of forces as a composite: it was 'the richest ground to occupy'.[71] And, as he had seen, Law Life provided a legal introduction to a range of UK insurance custom. Nevertheless, even within the narrower perspective of the life sector, Law Life was a suitable partner for Phoenix. The Pelican life operation had always concentrated on the top end of the market and the larger policy.[72] Law Life also sought the carriage trade: its average size of policy in 1902 was £947 (against a matching average for PABELO in 1903 of £929) and this rose to £1,013 by 1908 (against a figure for PABELO in 1909 of £886). Throughout the negotiations, the Phoenix men laid much stress on the high quality of lives and reputation enjoyed by Law Life. By 1914, Phoenix, now incorporating these Law Life assets, maintained the highest average policy value of all the twenty-five largest UK life assurers.

The market trend of the 1900s was, of course, the other way: increasing middle-class wealth, widening habits of insurance, and rising life expectations all pointed towards a mass market for lower value policies, especially endowments. Ryan may have calculated upon using other means to tap this market. But the Law Life takeover had a different and older rationale: it aimed to cement Phoenix's hold over the prestige sector of the life trade, expanding a traditional Pelican staple to a scale suitable for the new composite status of Phoenix Assurance.

For Law Life the takeover represented a flight to security. Even though the company remained profitable, it had taken some hard knocks. The total dividend on the £20 ordinary share had declined from 9.5% in 1900 to 4% by 1909, although a bonus was managed as late as 1905. The hardest knocks were dealt to investments. The very quality of the Law Life holdings, forced by the impeccable connections of the office into the most secure of securities, proved a liability as government stock hit choppy seas in the 1900s. With Law Life holdings caught in the eye of the investment storm, the office was driven into punishing levels of write-off. Altogether, the book value of Law Life's holdings declined by a fraction under £0.25 million between 1884 and 1909. Correspondingly, the shareholders' proportion of the quinquennial surplus, allowing for the investment out-turn, fell by more than half between 1889 and 1909.

[70] Phoenix Law Life Guard Book No. 1, General Manager's Memorandum for Directors, 9 November 1909. My emphasis.
[71] *Ibid.* [72] See vol. 1, Chapter 10.

Though by no means on their uppers, the Law Life directors were unconvinced of their ability to stop the rot. Indeed, the manager and secretary expressed anxiety that the conclusion with Phoenix should be swift; he wrote to Ryan on 13 February 1910, 'Pray press this on – there is nothing so far as I can see between us in principle – but there are many people to gnaw at this grand legal bone.'[73]

In fact, Ryan *had* pressed on. He had made the first written approaches on 1 and 4 November 1909, returned with slightly improved terms by 24 November and secured Law Life's initial agreement to them by 29 November. The newspapers were told on the same day. A formal Provisional Agreement was signed on 1 January 1910 and the transfer was sanctioned in Chancery by Mr Justice Warrington on 5 March 1910. Phoenix planned to erect its sign over the Law Life office at 187 Fleet Street – which was to serve as the Law Courts branch of the Phoenix group until 1968 – on this day and to commence writing insurance there on 7 March 1910.

The dealing was fast. Indeed, Law Life accepted the Phoenix proposals almost in their virgin form, and may fairly be described as having jumped at them. Although the bargain involved large sums, it was struck with notable ease. The Phoenix chairman told his shareholders, 'the combination we are asking you to sanction is a large one, but it has been effected without an atom of friction, dispute or controversy'.[74]

Following from this, he argued that the details of the arrangement involved 'no very complicated matter of finance.' The basic principle was that the Phoenix should purchase the Law Life by an issue of £1 million in 4% debenture stock and £8,334 in Phoenix £5 ordinary shares, fully paid. The bulk of the price was delivered in debentures because an unusually high proportion of the Law Life shares were held by Trustees, again reflecting the professional bent of the proprietorship. Ryan calculated that an offer couched in the ordinary shares of a company previously known as a fire office would provide insufficient security for vendors of this class. Moreover, since Phoenix would absorb by the purchase Law Life's guarantee fund of £1 million, any issue by Phoenix needed to reflect in full measure the highly protected nature of this reserve. Ordinary shares did not supply sufficient protection.

In this and every respect, Ryan took great pains to ensure that the Law Life shareholders would accept the bait on the first cast. Price was, of course, a major respect. It could not be faulted. For every six Law Life shares of £20 nominal value, proprietors would receive £120 in Phoenix

[73] Phoenix Law Life Guard Book No. 1.

[74] Chairman's Speech to Extraordinary General Meeting, probably February 1910.

debentures and one fully paid Phoenix £5 ordinary share. The net outcome, with the Phoenix ordinary share commanding a market value of £36, was a purchase price for one Law Life share of £26. Since the best that this share achieved in 1909 was £21, and in the previous half-decade only 10 shillings beyond that, the Phoenix offer represented a handsome premium. Nor was this all. Law Life shareholders and policy-holders were offered special incentives on dividends and costs.

Ryan was keenly aware that his prospective new shareholders were not of the kind to be careless about future earnings. He informed his directors that 'it is a *sine qua non* of any overtures that at least as high an annual dividend shall be offered as that currently earned'.[75] The Phoenix debentures and equities were arranged so as to yield an annual income fully equivalent to the dividend on the Law Life share (about £1 per annum) and for 1910 an 'extra inducement to approve the Scheme' (£1 8s for the year) was promised. It was this incentive which formed the substance of the improved terms of late November 1909.

To complete the cast, Ryan offered an exceptional deal on costs. He studied a dozen amalgamations projected or completed around the turn of the century and found that the expense ratios of the target companies varied between 11.96% and 20.21% of premiums. By 1909 most of the completed amalgamations had reduced the expenses on the business acquired to around 10%, but none had got below 10%. Law Life was scarcely extravagant as an independent company, with an expense ratio running between 11% and 13% in the years 1904–8. And since it possessed no branch organisation, there appeared to be little scope for further economies.

Nevertheless, Ryan proposed to absorb the Law Life assurance account in a way that would reduce life acquisition costs to 9%. This, he claimed proudly to Secretary Holt of Law Life, his major correspondent in the negotiations, was 'the lowest rate I believe ever adopted in an amalgamation'.[76] Lower costs, of course, meant more profits for policy-holders and more intrinsic value for anyone with a long-term interest in the composite Phoenix. With his projected 9%, Ryan rather deliberately placed a red ribbon on the golden package of the Law Life purchase. The Law Life shareholders accepted with alacrity, though not without a swift glower in the direction of a minority of dissenting policy-holders ('two solicitors in Newton Abbot insured with us for £500 each')[77].

Not, of course, that Phoenix stinted itself in this deal. Since the £1

[75] Phoenix Law Life Guard Book No. 1, General Manager's Memorandum for Directors, 9 November 1909.

[76] *Ibid.*, Ryan to Holt, 1 November 1909.

[77] *Ibid.*, Holt to Ryan, 13 February 1910.

million in Phoenix debentures was balanced by the £1 million in Law Life's guarantee fund, the real charge to Phoenix for the acquisition of Law Life amounted to the price for goodwill and costs: Ryan calculated these to work out at about £7,000 p.a. But even this was covered: as the Phoenix Chairman reported, 'we estimate to receive in interest and profits the same sum as we are paying out'.[78] Even given the cost of the debenture issue, Ryan was confident that Phoenix was in such a strong position that it could maintain its own dividend at its accustomed level. Also, of course, Phoenix was better placed than Law Life to wait upon the under-performing gilts: the directors thought that 'the future might have a better tale to tell in the matter of marketable securities'[79] and expected in due time to extract advantage from the portfolio that had sunk the weaker office.

But what Phoenix most wanted from the acquisition was an increase in scale and an increase in business. This the combined company certainly offered. Its total capital would be £1.3 million and its total funds £12.7 million. Most critically, Phoenix's life funds would almost double, from £5.3 million to £9.6 million. There would also be a welcome boost to new business. Despite its lack of push in earlier years, the Law Life had succeeded in dragging new net premiums up to a very creditable proportion of total net premiums in the 1900s.[80] Phoenix expected before long to gather an additional £1.5 million per annum in new sums assured from this source. A figure of these dimensions would make Phoenix a leader in the life market, 'placing the Company amongst those of the first rank as regards the magnitude of new business transacted'.[81] Even in the short term of the takeover year, 1910, Phoenix new sums assured improved by about £0.6 million or over 60% in gross acceptances.

The injection of Law Life capacity had a striking effect upon the standing of life business within the structure of Phoenix Assurance. In 1906 life earnings made up 29.4% of joint Phoenix–Pelican earnings; in 1908 the life operation of the composite Phoenix Assurance contributed 30.9% of total group revenue; by the end of 1910 the Law Life acquisition had pushed the share of life earnings in total group income up to 45.3%. The strength of the life department in the period 1910–14 – when its yearly average contribution to group earnings floated just below 40% – represented a historic peak.

Never again in the career of the Phoenix were life premiums to stand so high in the composite's earnings. It is probable that no other event in the

[78] Chairman to Extraordinary General Meeting, probably February 1910. [79] *Ibid.*
[80] From 8.91% in 1902 to 9.4% in 1908 (against a figure for Phoenix in 1908 of 7.75%).
[81] General Manager's Memorandum for Directors, 8 November 1909.

extended story of Phoenix–Pelican could match the Law Life takeover for the sharpness of improvement to the relative standing of the life department. Even the great revival of life business after 1950 took the share of assurance earnings in total group income from a trough of 12.1% in 1953 to a peak of 25.9% in 1981; and this took nearly thirty years.

The corporate arrangements of the scheme which so altered the status of life business for Phoenix clearly require attention. The basic design was very much in the Ryan style. Law Life's policies were to be assumed by Phoenix but grouped in a closed fund, kept separate from all other funds, just as the Positive and British Empire Funds had been. Against this new liability was to stand a guarantee fund, providing a double reserve for the assurance fund. This was to convince Law Life policy-holders of the ultimate security that was being offered them. During the negotiations, the guarantee fund had been taken to consist of Law Life's £100,000 of paid up capital, plus some £897,000 of accumulated Law Life profits; Phoenix undertook to maintain it at around £1 million. That took care of existing business. New business was to be pursued, not in the name of Law Life, but under the emblem of Phoenix; however, the Law Life connection – the point of the takeover – was to be cultivated assiduously.

Most important, perhaps, was the treatment of the profits from the participating and non-participating, or the with-profits and without-profits, branches of Law Life's operation. Under the office's previous conventions, shareholders had been entitled to between one-fifth and one-seventh of the combined profits from the two branches; but the proportion declined seriously during the 1900s as the value of the company's securities depreciated. In order to rectify this, and to create symmetry with the Phoenix's existing life business, Ryan proposed a different division of the spoils.

Firstly, all profits from participating business should revert to the policy-holders. So this potential source of income was denied to the Phoenix shareholders. However, it was a form of deprivation to which they were accustomed, since the Phoenix–PABELO fusion had contained the same provision. Indeed, it was the follow-through from this earlier stroke of corporate strategy which, for consistency's sake, necessitated the adjustment to Law Life's bonus arrangements. In recompense for their sacrifice, shareholders were to receive the whole of the profits from the non-participating department; this would more than make up for the fraction of combined profits that they had received under the original Law Life dispensation. Ryan entertained high hopes of this provision, since Law Life's non-bonus business had been expanding rapidly prior to the takeover and in 1904 had reached nearly one-quarter (23.3%) of its assurance business. He foresaw good prospects for further expansion in this direction.

In the long run, however, this method of distributing assurance profits reinforced the divergence of interest between policy-holders and shareholders over the yield from participating business. Basically, the shareholders were not given sufficient reason to be interested in with-profits business. Although he did not perceive it, Ryan, in his moves of 1908 and 1910, created the potentially dangerous situation in which shareholders – and, by extension, managers – were given cause to play down an important sector of assurance activity. The handling of the Law Life takeover strengthened this tendency and placed much weight on managers' ability to detect opportunities in the *non-participating* sector. However, these *were* problems for the future.

Back in 1910, policy-holders and shareholders duly mollified, it remained to sort out the Law Life directors and staff. This was done in the gentlemanly style of the times. Ten of the nineteen Law Life directors had no conflicting insurance interests and were invited to join the Phoenix Board. There they were to form a separate supervisory echelon, composing a distinct Law Life Committee and excused from all other Phoenix committees. Secretary Holt, who had greatly assisted Phoenix in the takeover, was to manage the Law Life fund over its first twelve months in its new home; in return, he was to receive his full salary of £2,750 until age sixty-five and then a pension of £1,500 for life. Similarly expansive provision was made for the Law Life actuary. And not least, Ryan promised, 'all other officers and employees (indoors and outdoors) would be maintained in their present positions and remunerations'.[82]

A modern takeover would shed staff; early twentieth-century takeovers sometimes went surprisingly far in the opposite direction. In a characteristically paternalistic touch, Holt drew Ryan's attention to the chief clerk of twenty-four-years' service: 'I am sorry to say that he has just lost his wife and he has twenty children.'[83] Ryan's response to this combination of long service and fecundity is not on record; but no doubt it was generous.

That is more than can be said of Ryan's way with information regarding the Law Life affair. By 1909 he was very much in control of Phoenix and the Law Life takeover was unmistakably his own initiative. Indeed, his manner verges on the high-handed. Despite the fact that he had been considering the Law Life project since the spring of 1909, had composed a detailed memorandum by October and had been talking to Holt well

[82] *Ibid.* [83] Holt to Ryan, 13 February 1910.

before his formal overtures of early November, he nevertheless admitted, almost as a postscript to his letter of 1 November, 'I have reason to believe that such a scheme would be supported by my Chairman and Deputy Chairman, *though this matter has not been mentioned to the Directors*.'[84] Ryan was not disturbed by the omission and clearly did not need to be: his directors did as they were told.

The Law Life acquisition was smoothly handled from beginning to end, although, technically, the end was much later than any participant could have expected. It was not until 1972 that the 4% debenture stock issued in 1910 was redeemed; by this time, only £193,000 of the £1 million was still outstanding. However, the manner of the redemption still struck some as smooth. For Phoenix proposed to buy out the remaining stockholders by exchanging for every £100 nominal of the debentures – this having a market value of £40.50 in 1972 – an equal amount of War Loan – worth about £40.50 for each £100 nominal – plus £2.50 in cash.[85] The *Evening News* was much impressed, on the grounds that the exchange of one stock for another created no liability to capital gains tax; the paper hailed Phoenix as a pioneer and confidently anticipated a spate of entrepreneurial takeovers all framed in tax-efficient War Loans. Equally smoothly, Phoenix thanked the *Evening News* for its compliments and pointed out that, by the company's reading of tax law, redemption (whether in War Loan or any other medium) still counted as a disposal for tax purposes. Nevertheless, even to be thought this clever constitutes an agreeable postscript to an impeccably managed transaction.

Clearly, the acquisition of Law Life was a major step in the development of Phoenix's life business, and perhaps one insufficiently appreciated in the conventional understanding of the company. Yet, the outcome was not without ambiguities. The effect upon the volume of Phoenix life transactions was so marked that it may have encouraged Ryan to be satisfied with the traditional up-market *content* of the Pelican–Law Life portfolios and so turned his attention away from the generation of life products more suited to the rapidly expanding mass market for cheaper assurance. The episode gives substance to the notion that the Phoenix–PABELO merger of 1908 represented a watershed in Ryan's thinking as he moved from a product-related to a company-related strategy. There were dangers here. It is arguable that some insurance strategists of this century, and some of them at Phoenix, came to think too readily in terms of corporate mechanisms, in company-shapes and administrative costs, and not readily enough in terms of product-

[84] Ryan to Holt, 1 November 1909 (my emphasis).

[85] The *Evening News*, 1 May 1972.

shapes and marketing advantage. If so, the exotic fruit discovered by Ryan in his heyday as a cultivator of composites contained a nasty and long-lived worm.

6. BACK TO THE SEA: PHOENIX AND MARINE INSURANCE IN THE 1900S

The early twentieth-century currents in insurance also carried the largest offices seawards. Those who sought composite status displayed a remarkable acquisitiveness for the brass-bound ledgers and mahogany-lined boardrooms maintained by the specialist marine underwriters of Liverpool and London. Thus, between 1900 and 1910, a clutch of big generalists, obeying the pressure of composite logic, bought corporate interests in the maritime market: the Alliance took its sister the Alliance Marine under the same roof in 1905; the London & Lancashire Fire took over the Standard Marine in 1907; and the North British absorbed the Ocean Marine also in 1907. Of the sixteen specialist marine companies reporting in 1900, eight had yielded to composite predators by 1914.

The attackers had almost always begun as fire offices. *The Times* described 'the battle-cry of the fire offices' attack on the marine insurance citadels' as 'one of the most interesting insurance movements of the time'. According to the newspaper, the underwriters' motive was less an appetite for marine profits – which was just as well – than the hope of augmented fire business, 'the extending of home fire insurance connections'.[86] Phoenix's specialist adviser on marine insurance, T. J. Storey, underwriter of the British and Foreign Marine, agreed but feared that, 'if all the Fire Companies wish to go into the Marine business, there will not be enough Marine Companies to go round'.[87] To the eye of another marine insurer, Helenus Robertson, chairman of Union Marine, the fire-fighting composites were 'spreading over... the whole business globe'.[88]

Phoenix, of course, had no more than trifled with seaborne insurances in the previous century. Deterred by the duopoly of the chartered marine companies, Royal Exchange and London Assurance, in the 1800s, Phoenix had restricted itself to covering vessels in harbour or under construction and cargoes in transit but had risked little on the high seas.[89] In the decade 1861–70 marine premiums of this limited type had accounted for a meagre annual average 0.6% of Phoenix's total gross premium, and by

86 *The Times*, 16 June 1911. 87 Storey to Ryan, 13 November 1908.
88 Reported by *Liverpool Journal of Commerce*, 21 June 1911.
89 See vol. I, pp. 384, 431–3, 721–3.

the period 1901–5 the marine component recorded alongside gross fire premiums scored an annual average 0.01% of worldwide earnings.[90] By the later 1900s marine earnings had virtually disappeared, such as there were swallowed up largely as transit risks within the separate maw of the Phoenix accident department. By 1911 the Phoenix management itself placed such a discount on these operations that its press hand-outs described marine insurance as the only form of insurance *not* offered by the company.

Clearly, however, contemporary style required that any self-respecting composite should sport a marine capability of some size. The problem was that although the 1900s may have been a good decade for composites, they were poor years for the marine underwriters. Between 1905 and 1908 the outstanding nine specialist marine offices reported an aggregate loss of 2.3% of total premium income.[91] Ryan himself recorded in 1911 that, 'marine insurance has passed through an exceptionally unprofitable period during the last five to ten years'.[92] For much of the previous decade seaborne insurances wallowed with a bad-tempered swell.

In a review of maritime prospects undertaken for Ryan in 1908, Storey was not impressed by the case for an acquisition. He analysed three cases in which a major fire office had recently absorbed a marine company and concluded that in no case was the balance of advantage clearly in favour of the fire office. There was little to be learned from the family affair between the two Alliances. But the transaction between the London & Lancashire and the Standard turned out to be a family affair in a somewhat unexpected way since 'the Deputy Chairman of the London & Lancashire was father-in-law to the underwriter of the Standard who, for a long time had been anxious to get out of his large holding of shares'.[93] However, the real significance of the deal was that it proved 'an extremely bad bargain for the Fire Company' since the Standard's business was not sufficient to justify the large settlement for goodwill, which no doubt did the underwriter's shares a power of good. Again, the takeover of the Ocean by North British was 'keenly criticised in the Market'. The feeling was that,

> if Marine business improved, the Fire Company had made a good bargain, but if it did not improve, then the Ocean Company had made a good bargain. Up to the moment, no improvement having taken place, people are disposed to say that the Ocean Company have 'got ahead' of the North British, but if a change comes over

90 Calculated from Phoenix Annual Analysis of Business of all Departments.
91 *The Times*, 14 March 1913.
92 Ryan, Memorandum respecting the transfer of the B. Insurance Co. to the A. Insurance Co., 12 April 1911.
93 Storey to Ryan, 13 November 1908.

our business in a few years, we shall doubtless be told that the Directors and Managers of the North British were a long-headed, far-seeing lot of men and that the Ocean people were duffers.[94]

Storey's tough and lively opinion was that the marine market was too uncertain to justify expansionist purchases by fire companies. He proposed a superior solution which would give Phoenix entry to the marine business – an influential thought this – 'without spending one shilling on good will'. Marine business was now excellently serviced by brokers. Phoenix should engage an experienced marine underwriter and conduct its own marine business through the brokers, for whom the Phoenix name would be a sufficient drawcard in its new undertaking. 'Years ago, this would not have been the case, but now, when almost all the business is placed through brokers, any good underwriter commands the business he wishes to have.'[95] There was no need for a special corporate structure and, by side-stepping the current, Phoenix would 'save itself thousands'.

This was a logic which clearly had some appeal for the Phoenix Board but conspicuously less for Ryan. The general manager wanted a marine company. His quest for one, beginning in 1908 and ending in an exceptionally adroit and calm takeover in 1911, is interesting less for the drama of the hunt than for four other features: the independence of the line pursued by Ryan; his circumvention of alternative solutions; the cheapness of the consummated deal (thus undercutting Storey's reasoning); and, once again, as with Law Life, the striking effect upon the pattern of Phoenix earnings.

In 1908, the object of Ryan's appetite was a company conceded by Storey to be 'in every way tip-top' and possessing 'an underwriter of very great experience who undoubtedly knows his business from A to Z'.[96] Ryan also judged that 'its Directors have been drawn from the highest circle of City men and its connections are of long standing and excellent character'.[97] The company was the Indemnity Mutual Marine, first launched in 1824. Ryan saw close parallels between the proposed Phoenix–Indemnity takeover and the North British–Ocean connection of November 1907 and intended to handle the deal along the same lines, while using the Law Life takeover as the model for his financial arrangements.

In October 1908 Ryan and Bovill had heard from the Phoenix director Kirkman Hodgson that Indemnity Marine 'would not be indisposed to consider a proposal for a combination of the two companies'. Late in the month, the chairman of Indemnity invited an informal committee from Phoenix (Avebury, Bird, Clutton, Hawes, Tryon) for exploratory talks.

[94] *Ibid.* [95] *Ibid.* [96] *Ibid.* [97] Ryan to Hamilton, 3 November 1908.

This group recommended to the Phoenix Board that the office should follow the North British precedent and snap up Indemnity.[98] A second official committee of the Board (Hamilton, Bovill, Bird, Tryon) was sent to meet a negotiating team from Indemnity and it got as far as framing an offer and sending an official letter. Indemnity Mutual was a substantial marine company with £870,000 in assets and a recent profit record of some £20,000 per annum. The committee proposed to pay for it by the same device as was used for Law Life: an issue of 4% debenture stock, this time summing to £887,750 in value. However, before the committee could clinch these terms, there was 'a subsequent intervention by certain directors dissenting from the majority' and this 'resulted in the offer being nullified'.[99] The interveners were Sorley and Avebury who had not been able to attend the first informal discussion.

In response, Indemnity Mutual said that it could deal only with a united Phoenix Board. The Phoenix takeover committee wished to persevere but could not do so under these conditions. Accordingly, it 'resolved, but with regret, that the negotiations should be allowed to lapse'.[100] Indemnity Mutual survived almost another decade before being absorbed by Northern Assurance in 1917 and then passing, with Northern's baggage train, into the Commercial Union empire in 1968. Ironically, in view of later events, Indemnity was also being pursued in 1908 by the somewhat larger Liverpool marine specialist, Union Marine. However, Union's £937,000 worth of funds were insufficient to meet Indemnity's price.

The failures of Phoenix and Union Marine to pick the Indemnity were providential since it left these two companies to pick one another in the much better balanced, and much cheaper, takeover of 1911. The interveners on the Phoenix Board were clearly right, while the takeover committee almost put Phoenix into the ranks of the fire offices which acquired their marine capacity the expensive way. There were two problems: information leakage and goodwill. The Indemnity share stood at £9 prior to the negotiations with Phoenix; by the time the fire office had delivered its offer it had jumped to £11. But goodwill proved much more expensive. Storey calculated that the break-up value of Indemnity was about £650,000, implying that Phoenix was being asked to stump up over £200,000 for maritime goodwill. As Storey saw, this number 'would be a nasty looking item in your accounts'. He put the crucial question to Phoenix: 'are the prospects for Marine Insurance in the future sufficiently good to justify . . . paying such a large sum for goodwill?'; and then

[98] *Ibid.* [99] Phoenix Secret Minutes, pp. 3–4, 11 November 1908.
[100] *Ibid.*, p. 5, 18 November 1908.

answered it himself, 'in my opinion, the prospects are not sufficiently good and the risk is too great'.[101]

It was just as well that the interveners took Storey's part, for, in the event, Phoenix was to get a larger marine office without paying a penny for goodwill. In the interim, however, between 1908 and 1911 there ensued a period of intricacy and delicate footwork. Throughout it, Ryan maintained his determination to have a marine company. But he needed to maintain it while keeping, or appearing to keep, his options open. These were: to follow Storey's advice and to go into marine via a broker's connection only; to snap up a London marine specialist; or, better, to snap up a Liverpool marine specialist, together with the multifarious northern commercial linkages that this would bring for the fire side; or, perhaps best, to snap up both types of marine specialist. Ryan's main problem during this period was, clearly, that his Board leaned towards the shrewd minimalism proposed by Storey.

In the spring of 1910 Ryan was drawn towards the Liverpool connection. He had good personal contacts with Helenus Robertson, chairman of Union Marine, and he was provided with a stream of information and proposals by Arthur Hargreaves, a marine broker who was also a large shareholder in Union Marine with reasons of his own for fostering a takeover. The Liverpool company itself was very desirable. Founded in 1863, its Board by the 1900s was rich in connection, decorated with shipping luminaries from the lines of Cunard, Allan and Booth. Although, on Hargreaves' admission, Union Marine, like most of the mariners, had taken 'heavy losses' in recent years, its 'new underwriters had made a clean sweep of former arrears'.[102] It was capitalised at £163,500, possessed assets of £543,738, earned in 1910 premiums of £408,461 and boasted total funds of £937,000, and its shares at just over £6 were, according to its Chairman, 'very cheap'.[103] More substantial than Indemnity Marine, it also made more of a stir in the maritime market: the local press thought it, 'one of the foremost concerns of its kind in the world';[104] the less partisan *Times* acknowledged it as 'one of the few strong independent marine offices' though noting that it had 'suffered severely in recent years';[105] while Ryan placed it as 'one of the most powerful of the Liverpool Marine Offices'.[106]

Clearly Ryan was tempted, but, in 1910, his Board was pulling the other way. Nevertheless, it was a serious struggle. For, as early as April 1910, the insider Hargreaves had come up with the proposal that was to be the key to the eventual absorption of Union Marine by Phoenix. He

[101] Storey to Ryan, 13 November 1908. [102] Hargreaves to Ryan, 21 April 1910.
[103] *Ibid.* [104] *Liverpool Journal of Commerce*, 1 June 1911.
[105] *The Times*, 1 June 1911. [106] Ryan, Informal Memorandum, 25 May 1911.

Plate 5.5 Sir Helenus Robertson of Union Marine.

was convinced that Union Marine wanted to be taken over so much – its Board had been shaken by the storms of recent years and now saw no future outside an amalgamation, indeed had concluded that 'the marine company without the backing of a powerful fire company would in the future be seriously handicapped'[107] – that the company would offer itself for sale to the right bidder at effectively zero cost. The bidder would issue shares solely for the value of Union Marine's assets. These shares would necessarily impose a dividend burden on the bidder. But the interest receipts on Union Marine's funds would finance these dividends; and

[107] *Liverpool Journal of Commerce*, 21 June 1911.

'thus you would get the business and connection free of cost'.[108] Crucially, there would be no payment for goodwill. But, at this stage, the Phoenix Board, also wary of the recent storms in maritime insurance, would have no truck even with terms as seductive as these.

A Special Committee on Marine Risks was briefed to produce a consensus line and reported to the Board on 22 June 1910.[109] It argued that the increasing tonnage and swelling cargoes of modern vessels had produced under-capacity in the marine insurance market; this promised a future of attractive rate levels and relatively weak competition. A powerful office like Phoenix should achieve a good share of these pickings on remunerative terms. However, it should pursue them not in the high-risk vehicle of a purchased marine company but in the safer conveyance of a broker connection. The Board accepted this logic and appointed Messrs Leslie and Godwin, brokers, to accept marine risks on their behalf and to submit to them a weekly bordereau against a 25% commission. The first of these, marking Phoenix's re-entry to, or, upon a stricter reading, its first-ever penetration of, the high seas market was tabled on 13 July 1910.

Even before this, however, in May 1910 Ryan had to tell Hargreaves that his Directors had stamped on the takeover proposal.[110] Deterred neither by this, nor by Phoenix's initiative with the brokers, Hargreaves returned to Ryan in July 1910 with more news of Union Marine's glowing prospects.[111] This time, Ryan was forced to tell him, rather curtly, to go away.[112] But still Ryan did not discourage Hargreaves from developing his calculations of the terms on which Union Marine *might* be taken over. Clearly, despite the directive of his Board, Ryan continued to hold his *own* options much more open than they would have liked.

While the Phoenix Board believed that it had entered the marine trade through the broker connection, Ryan did not abandon his plans for acquiring a London or Liverpool company, or even both. By early 1911, the metropolitan option had taken concrete shape in the form of the London and Provincial Marine and General Insurance Company, a medium-sized marine specialist that had suffered by the troubled state of shipping insurances in the 1900s and offered itself for absorption. At almost exactly the same time, Ryan resumed informal and confidential discussions with Helenus Robertson, chairman of Union Marine (and also of the Mersey Docks and Harbour Board). Between summer 1910 and spring 1911, Ryan had clearly kept an eye upon Union Marine's

[108] Hargreaves to Ryan, 21 April 1910.
[109] Phoenix Directors' Minutes, 29, p. 216, 22 June 1910.
[110] Ryan to Hargreaves, 6 May 1910. [111] Hargreaves to Ryan, 15 July 1910.
[112] Ryan to Hargreaves, 20 July 1910.

improving trade, mindful of Hargreaves' claim of July 1910 that 'we have turned the corner'.[113] By March 1911, Ryan was beginning to believe that this might be true.

On 26 March, despite difficulties in booking a table, the morrow being Boat Race Day, Robertson invited Ryan to dine at the Union Club. Robertson was intent on getting to the river and Ryan had to be fitted in beforehand. The invitation came shortly before Ryan was due to depart upon one of his periodic inspections of the American market and he could not take it up. Nevertheless, time was found for a meeting and a rapid exchange of letters. At this stage, negotiations were exclusively between the expansive Robertson and the punctilious Ryan; and the personal relationship between the two men was to be an important influence upon Phoenix's eventual takeover of Union Marine. The early exchanges circled around two possibilities: that Phoenix might take the *London* end of Union Marine's operation, and, that this project might be combined with a full takeover of London and Provincial. Certainly, Ryan's designs upon London and Provincial were discussed with Robertson. The two men then consulted Union Marine's chief executive official, Sandeman Allen, on this point. Both Union Marine representatives agreed that London and Provincial possessed 'some good merchant accounts in London and some good Foreign Agency business', and consequently that 'the scheme is well worth consideration'.[114] Ryan even informed Robert Ward of London and Provincial that he had met 'the Representatives of the *other parties* to our proposed negotiations' and 'had a short conversation of a non-committal character'.[115] Just before taking ship, Ryan asked Ward to postpone a decision for two months and await his return from the United States. At this point, therefore, Ryan was clearly considering a *three-way* marine arrangement and he was deliberately keeping Ward and London and Provincial on ice, against the possibility of executing this coup.

When Ryan did get back from America, the pace of events quickened markedly. By 31 May, the Phoenix Special Committee had reversed course and recommended an outright purchase of Union Marine's complete operation; Storey too now backed this line of approach. On the same day, the Phoenix Board accepted the Committee's recommendation and signed a Provisional Agreement with Union Marine. Circulars to shareholders went out on 8 and 9 June and the first joint meeting of Phoenix and Union Marine shareholders took place on 20 June. This day marked

[113] Hargreaves to Ryan, 15 July 1910.
[114] Confidential Memorandum by Sandeman Allen for Robertson and Ryan, 8 April 1911.
[115] Ryan to Ward, 6 April 1911 (my emphasis).

the full legal sanction of the takeover. With immaculate timing, the king also chose it to confer a knighthood upon Gerald Ryan for services to the world of insurance.

Meanwhile, on 1 June, a penultimate rebuff had been administered to London and Provincial. Back in March, Ryan had warned Ward that Phoenix might not find it 'expedient to take over a business like that of your company unless they were certain of obtaining the services of an experienced Underwriter. After seeking independent advice, the Directors have not been satisfied on this point.'[116] In June, Ryan told Ward that the acquisition of Union Marine was causing so much work that, 'we could hardly expect our new Marine advisers at once to take up the question of the proposed working arrangement with your Company' and added somewhat disingenuously, 'the present situation has developed rapidly and could not have been anticipated when pourparlers were started between you and our Directors some months ago'.[117] He thanked Ward for his patience and courteously signed off. This was not quite the end of the London and Provincial proposal. Ward was not happy with explanations given him. So, even more circuitously, Ryan wrote to Sandeman Allen of Union Marine asking for a 'a letter from you stating that, as a result of further consideration, *you advise us* that the transaction is not one which it is in our interest to entertain'.[118] Allen duly obliged and Ryan finally placed the matter beyond discussion on 2 August 1911.[119] What had caused this sudden onset of decisiveness?

Hargreaves' plan for a cost-free acquisition by Phoenix had looked attractive from the start. It was a difficult deal to refuse. Above all, it had circumvented the obstacle to the Indemnity Marine proposal which had given a wide spread of opinion, ranging from the conservatives on the Board to the perceptive Storey, a legitimate reason to oppose a marine acquisition: the high cost of the goodwill. A further obstacle was removed by Union Marine itself: it had indeed turned a corner in profits. What had still looked problematic in 1910 presented a much rosier aspect by spring 1911. Ryan clearly wished to see Union Marine's profits for 1910 before pushing further. After making losses which reduced reserves by £100,000 in the period 1903–8, Union Marine recorded an underwriting profit of £14,485 in 1909 and another of £12,274 in 1910; the surplus of 1910 represented a 3.0% return on net premiums and this was bettered again in 1911 with a figure of 7.5%.[120]

But these figures had a double value: if they confirmed Ryan's better

[116] Ryan to Ward, 24 March 1911. [117] Ryan to Ward, 1 June 1911.
[118] Ryan to Allen, 21 July 1911 (my emphasis).
[119] Ryan to Ward, 2 August 1911. [120] *The Times*, undated.

expectations, they also attracted predators. By 1911 rumours abounded among the Liverpool marine community that at least one big fish was pursuing Union Marine; and local gossip named the raider persistently as the Liverpool & London & Globe.[121] This worried Phoenix. Not only had the rumours immediately begun to talk up the price of the Union Marine share – it moved from its 'equilibrium' level of about £6 to £8 as early as April 1911 and was headed towards £9 by June – but they carried unpleasant implications for any London-based company. For, if Liverpool & London & Globe was really interested in Union Marine, few southerners would stand much of a chance against its combination of wealth – in 1911 it stood sixth in the rank order of composites by assets to Phoenix's fifth – *and* local connection.

Certainly, Ryan feared an attack from within the Liverpool financial community. On 1 June, he explained to Kirkman Hodgson,

> Our hands were forced at the last moment by a definite statement that the Liverpool & London & Globe were acquiring the Union Marine at £9 a share, and speculation threatened to advance the market price beyond the point where our terms would give any advantage whatever to recent purchasers. To check and prevent such speculation, both sides thought prompt action necessary.[122]

Having exercised a proper prudence when Union Marine's attractiveness was not clear, Ryan did not wish to lose the prize to others just as clarity was established.

Probably, the Liverpool & London & Globe scare was a fiction, possibly a deliberately contrived goad to hurry Phoenix along, but, in any event, it added a powerful reason for swift action to the existing arguments provided by the Hargreaves plan and Union Marine's improving balance sheets. The combination decided the Phoenix Board that they should have the whole of Union Marine.

The prospective advantages for shareholders were well distributed on either side of the transaction. Of course, Robertson's prognosis that a lone marine specialist was unlikely to prosper in the markets of the future implied that, in a general sense, Union Marine shareholders could find profit *only* within the haven of a composite. But association with the Phoenix did offer his proprietors more specific gains. Under Union Marine's shareholding arrangements, each £20 share was partly paid, leaving it liable to further calls of up to £17 10s. Under Phoenix's scheme of purchase – half in 4% debentures worth £277,950 and half represented by 8,175 Phoenix ordinary shares worth an equivalent amount – the

[121] *The Times*, 1 June 1911; *Glasgow Herald* 2 June 1911.
[122] Ryan to Hodgson, 1 June 1911.

outstanding liability of the Union Marine shareholder was reduced by 68%.[123] Moreover, the Phoenix offer attributed a value of £8 10s to each Union Marine share, whereas the pre-negotiation market value was £6 10s; so each Union Marine shareholder walked away with a profit of £2 per share. It is not surprising that there was little dissent.

Robertson had wished the purchase to be effected entirely in Phoenix shares; Phoenix had wanted to pay entirely in debentures, as had become Ryan's style in the takeovers which made the veteran fire office into a modern composite. But the system used for Union Marine was a compromise which served both interests well. The vendors were paid in a good balance of high-class securities. And Phoenix received the benefit – which Ryan conceded as well worth having – that an active Liverpool market in Phoenix shares was created.

For Phoenix shareholders, the advantages were almost embarrassing. A genuine marine capacity was, as the *Liverpool Daily Post* stressed, 'the missing link' in the chain of Phoenix departments.[124] It was now supplied by a company earning premiums of nearly £0.5 million per year from its home base in Britain's leading provincial port, from its 115 foreign outlets and from its connections with American and Canadian companies, including an £134,000 interest in its subsidiary, Columbia of New Jersey. The underwriting expertise which became available to Phoenix in London and Liverpool was formidable, with Sandeman Allen in particular occupying a commanding position among marine insurers. Yet, even more to the point in Ryan's mind, were the opportunities offered by Union Marine for strengthening links which Phoenix already possessed. To his eye, 'the Liverpool connection' was a potent source of enlarged business on the fire and accident accounts.

In this connection much was hoped from 'the very influential Directors' of the Union Marine.[125] This was a reasonable hope since the Union Marine Board contained, alongside representatives of the Booth and Allan lines, three senior members of the Mersey Dock Board – its chairman, Robertson himself, its deputy chairman, J. H. Beazley, and Robert Allan – and two members of the Cunard Board – its deputy chairman, Tom Royden, and Beazley again. Ryan calculated that such cumulative muscle would 'greatly strengthen our position in the commercial centres of Liverpool, Manchester and London. *Great stress is laid on the last-*

[123] For every eight Union Marine shares, the proprietor would receive £34 worth of Phoenix debentures and one Phoenix ordinary share, £5 paid, also worth £34; the nominal value of this share was £50, so a potential liability of £45 remained, but the potential liability on eight Union Marine shares had been £140.

[124] *Liverpool Daily Post*, 1 June 1911.

[125] Report of Phoenix Special Committee on Marine Risk, 23 May 1911.

mentioned result of the transfer as affording the Phoenix the opportunity of securing a position in Liverpool and Manchester which it does not now possess and cannot easily acquire.'[126] Clearly, the Union Marine merger was intended to produce a more than purely marine advantage. Indeed, Ryan is here using the tactic of acquisition to break into an entire regional market. In this respect, the Phoenix absorption of Union Marine in 1911 is a direct descendant of the Phoenix absorption of the Glasgow Fire Office in 1811.[127] But this time, of course, the regional market into which Phoenix was breaking was not for one insurance product but a whole range.

It is obvious from the Phoenix's stress upon Union Marine's capacity, expertise and connections that the veteran office expected to derive major *trading* advantages from the acquisition. But, under the Hargreaves formula, it achieved these advantages virtually cost-free, indeed at an immediate *investment* profit. For the cost to Phoenix of raising the capital for the purchase was about £21,000 p.a. whereas a conservative estimate of the earnings on the securities handed over by Union Marine was £26,000 p.a. Thus, with no goodwill to finance, Phoenix was ahead by £5,000 p.a. in interest earnings before it ever commenced to trade. It appears that the Phoenix Board did have the grace to be embarrassed by the richness of these bounties. The Phoenix secretary reminded Ryan on 7 June 1911 'that there was a Clause in our circular to Shareholders stating that the amount of Free Assets transferred covered the cost of (acquiring) the business. Mr Bateson and Mr Allen were both of the opinion that this fact, if known, would be commented upon by their Shareholders and might cause trouble. I have therefore deleted it from our circular . . .'[128] However good the deal for the Union Marine shareholders, it was clearly felt that the princely handout to the Phoenix shareholders might stretch Liverpudlian tolerance, or perhaps credulity, beyond reasonable bounds.

Once the balance of advantage was settled, and, with a little discreet engineering, found convenient, the takeover was a very straightforward matter. Financially, its simplicity was a function of the Hargreaves formula: Phoenix shares and debentures to the value of Union Marine equity. Almost all Union Marine shares were bought out, with the exception of a few retained by former Union Marine men like Sandeman Allen, 'for sentimental reasons'. Administratively, simplicity followed from Phoenix's desire to take over 'our offices, directors and staff . . . bodily'.[129] Union Marine would operate as a separate company under its existing

[126] Ryan, Memorandum respecting the Transfer, 12 April 1911 (my emphasis).
[127] See vol. 1, pp. 468ff. [128] Memorandum, Secretary to Ryan, 7 June 1911.
[129] Robertson to Union Marine Extraordinary General Meeting, 20 June 1911.

name and constitution, although Phoenix reserved the right to absorb it or change the constitution at pleasure. As Sandeman Allen himself put it, 'Union Marine will remain as it is, an old Liverpool company with its existing organisation undisturbed and its Head Office in Liverpool.'[130] Management would remain in the same hands, with Sandeman Allen continuing as general manager. Phoenix's existing marine business – which *The Times*, while crediting Phoenix more recently with 'distinct marine leanings', dated only from July 1910 and placed 'on a very modest scale'[131] – was to be transferred to Liverpool. Effectively, Union Marine was to become the marine department of Phoenix. Policy coordination would be achieved by Allen visiting London weekly and Ryan visiting Liverpool once a quarter. In Allen's judgement, 'the fusion and these subsequent arrangements are unusually simple'.[132]

Indeed, they were so simple that some sections of the press argued that they composed 'not strictly an amalgamation, as both companies will retain their separate identities'. However, the same commentators congratulated Phoenix for keeping up with the fashion since 'it is an arrangement which has been much favoured of late between insurance offices where a controlling interest has been acquired'.[133] In fact, the tactic chosen by Ryan for dealing with Union Marine reflected not fashion but particular Phoenix needs. Quite different approaches had been taken with Pelican and Law Life, both of which had been entirely absorbed. In each case the field of expertise and type of connection had been familiar to the Phoenix Board. But in the case of Union Marine, Phoenix was, quite specifically, buying an independent expertise.

Ryan had ensured that it was the right kind of expertise. He 'went carefully into the figures... and considered the Agency results, Home and Foreign, very satisfactory, as also the recent Head Office results'. More to the point, he approved Union Marine's style. He found it, like his own, 'averse to large ideas or big London Underwriter ways... [wary] of the market business there... but not afraid of the Broker'. He preferred cargo risks, which ran off in a few weeks, to annual hull insurances, which required heavy reserves, and was glad to find in Sandeman Allen a professional of similar inclination. Consequently, Allen was able to report with satisfaction that 'the present line of policy has his (G.H.R.'s) strong approval'.[134] This indicates a very careful, hands-on approach to acquisition. But, having rummaged through Union Marine's skills and found what he wanted, Ryan was prepared to allow them a free run. Naturally,

[130] Allen, Confidential Memorandum, 8 April 1911.
[131] *The Times*, 1 June 1911. [132] Allen, Confidential Memorandum, 8 April 1911.
[133] *Morning Leader*, 1 June 1911. [134] Allen, Confidential Memorandum, 8 April 1911.

too, the northern business connections which he coveted would accrue most readily if Allen and his illustrious sea-dogs were to retain their independent status as Liverpool capitalists.

Once again, it is clear that the acquisition is a product of Ryan's personal strategy. It was the connection between Ryan and Robertson which set up the deal, and kept it up despite the initial scepticism of the Phoenix Board. And it was the connection between Ryan and Sandeman Allen – expressed in the mutual regard of experts shining through their correspondence – which clinched the deal. The Phoenix Board sat – or, in some cases, slumped – on the sidelines, applauding fairly quietly when a piece of information came their way. By 1910, this was an ageing Board and its level of activity was not high. K. D. Hodgson, who had introduced the Indemnity proposal in 1908, had to cry off two crucial meetings of the Phoenix Special Committee late in May 1911, the first because he was 'in the middle of a "cure"' at Llandidrod Wells and the second because, upon return, he 'came under strict instructions to betake myself to the country forthwith'; he went on to apologise for 'being so useless at present'.[135] At the same time, another member of the Special Committee, Ralph Clutton was similarly engaged at the Hôtel Royal Excelsior (250 chambres; 75 salles de bain), Aix-les-Bains: he did not know who the directors of Union Marine were, but he was happy to support Ryan.[136]

Indeed, both Hodgson and Clutton – and, no doubt, others – were heavily inclined to let Ryan get on with it. Hodgson wrote on 19 May, 'no doubt there are excellent reasons for the methods adopted, and, as you do not foresee any difficulty, I am quite reassured'. One week later, he consoled himself, 'everything seems to be going so smoothly that I hope the Committee will be more a formality than a discussion of principle, and I anticipate that there will be no doubt of the approval of the Board'.[137]

Hodgson, of course, was right: the Board followed Ryan. But that two directors appointed to a Special Committee entrusted with the management of a major takeover should in reality be so removed from events is powerful testimony to the autonomy of the Phoenix general manager. Not that autonomy was achieved without strain: the American trip and the Union Marine takeover so tired Ryan that he too needed a 'cure' by August 1911; he took his at Carlsbad. As a contrast in après-acquisition styles, Sandeman Allen spent his 1911 holiday visiting Union Marine agents in Scandinavia.

Although fatigued, Ryan was widely applauded. For the Union Marine

[135] Hodgson to Ryan, 19 May 1911, 27 May 1911. [136] Clutton to Ryan, 21 May 1911.
[137] Hodgson to Ryan, 27 May 1911.

scheme was welcomed almost as warmly by the press as by the Phoenix directors. Its impact is measured by the fact that during June 1911 no fewer than forty-one newspapers and journals carried comment on the takeover. The financial journalists portrayed Phoenix as a pioneer in composite expansion into the marine market. The *Standard* confined itself to describing the Union Marine scheme as 'a further step in the policy of expansion which has been adopted in recent years by the Phoenix Company', but the *Financial Times* caught the more general mood with its argument that the scheme was 'of more than usual importance and entirely eclipses all recent insurance absorptions in the far-reaching nature of its effects'.[138]

These, the newspaper felt, would entail a change in the balance of power within the marine insurance market. 'Marine underwriters at the Mersey port', it reflected, 'are inclined to patronise their confreres in London, and recently there has been a tendency to regard the northern city as the true home of marine insurance.' By setting up its own London operation 'in the heart of the City' where it 'made itself felt . . . a factor to be reckoned with', Union Marine brought the Liverpool challenge into the London market. But, by absorbing Union Marine in London, and by establishing its own bridgehead in Liverpool, Phoenix had tipped the balance back in favour of the great metropolitan insurers. The result, opined the *Financial Times*, was that the Phoenix which 'has grown more vigorous with advancing years' . . . but had 'not hitherto ranked as a power in the marine insurance market . . . in future will certainly do so and will be classed in much the same category as the London [Assurance] and Commercial Union Companies'.[139] To be placed in such company, of course, implied that Phoenix had joined the first rank of the corporate marine insurers.

Certainly, in the aftermath of the takeover, Union Marine bulked large, both within the marine market and within Phoenix. After the turn of 1909 the maritime market rose to 1914. Even the loss of the *Titanic* – which cost several marine specialists about 4% of their annual premium income – and a number of other formidable shipping disasters in 1912, not to speak of the increasing size of vessels and rising commodity prices, failed to restrain the profitability of sea-borne insurances. High levels of trade activity and the enhanced rates of marine premium charged to cover rising shipyard repair bills proved more than equal to heavier risks and higher costs. Although not as prosperous as the better years of the late nineteenth century, this phase was more favourable than anything the marine insurers had seen for a decade.

138 *Standard*, 1 June 1911; *Financial Times*, 1 June 1911. 139 *Financial Times*, 1 June 1911.

Plate 5.6 Publicity for the maiden voyage of the *Titanic*.

Union Marine achieved more than its fair share of this improving trade. Among the top ten specialist marine companies, Union Marine ranked second only to British and Foreign Marine in premium income for 1910, with net takings of £403,461; and, helped by energetic expansion in the Pacific and Far East, it was second to no company in 1911 and 1912. What was Phoenix's marine department had become the largest specialist mar-

Plate 5.7 *Titanic* on a plate.

ine company in the UK economy by 1911, and, with £513,527 in premiums by 1912, it enjoyed a 10% advantage over its nearest rival. Between 1911 and 1914 its premium income advanced by no less than 50%.[140] Moreover, its profit record was good, with a 7.5% return on net premiums in 1911 and a further sharp increase in 1912.[141]

The Union Marine takeover appears to have been a most effective way for a composite office to do marine business in the early 1900s. By contrast, the REA, a marine specialist of great antiquity but also a composite office by the 1900s, managed average net premiums on its

[140] *The Times*, Review of Marine Insurance Companies, undated March 1913; *Post Magazine and Insurance Monitor*, 7 March 1913. [141] *Ibid*; *The Statist*, 8 March 1913.

marine account of only £199,300 (1906–10) and £253,047 (1908–12).[142]

Ryan could be forgiven for believing that he had achieved a major bargain. For Union Marine did notably well even before the enormous bonanza in marine insurance which developed upon the outbreak of the First World War. He could also have congratulated himself upon having let the London and Provincial Marine pass by in the night: where the top ten mariners recorded an aggregate profit of 9.7% of net premiums on the underwriting account for 1911, London and Provincial managed a loss of 4.5%. Phoenix's doubts about the underwriting capability of this office had clearly been well directed. When London and Provincial was bought out by another maritime specialist, World Marine, in 1911, Ryan could only have judged that the purchasers were more than welcome. On the other hand, there must have been regrets at Phoenix over Indemnity Marine. When the 1911 account was closed, Indemnity headed the underwriting results of the ten specialists with profits on net premiums of no less than 19%. However, Indemnity was wont to tack between very favourable and very unfavourable results, so Phoenix could be well pleased with the quality of the company it had purchased. After his initial doubts about the purchase of *any* company, Storey was proved right in his conclusion that 'the Union would be the *best* company for us to acquire'.[143]

Naturally, the impact of Union Marine's success in the marine market registered upon Phoenix's general business performance. In terms of premium earnings, the impact was similar to that produced by the acquisition of Law Life. That takeover gave the life department an additional 10% of *total* Phoenix premiums. In 1910, the marine premiums earned through the brokerage arrangement summed to only 0.4% of total Phoenix premiums. In 1911 the marine earnings taken through Union Marine amounted to 15.3% of total Phoenix net premiums and the percentages for 1911–13 stayed in the range 15–18%. Again, as with the Law Life out-turn, these numbers defined an historic peak. The two world wars produced extraordinary marine shares in total group earnings: an annual average of 27.1% of total premiums for 1914–20 and 14.5% for 1940–8. But in no other peacetime years between 1911 and 1967 did marine net earnings move outside the boundaries of 5–11% Phoenix net group premiums.[144]

Like the Law Life acquisition, therefore, the takeover of Union Marine altered the internal balance of Phoenix Assurance in a fundamental way.

[142] Supple, *Royal Exchange Assurance*, pp. 239, 261.
[143] Cited by Ryan, Notes for Chairman, 23 May 1911 (my emphasis).
[144] Calculated from Phoenix Annual Reports and Accounts.

7. A SMALL MARINE ADDITION: NORTHERN MARITIME 1914–17

There was a postscript to the Phoenix absorption of Union Marine. The Liverpool office had run an expansionist ship throughout the 1900s and this continued into the 1910s. Union Marine had opened its first overseas branch in New York in 1904, and followed this with an Australian Branch in 1908, a Far Eastern Branch in 1910, a Pacific Branch in San Francisco in 1911.[145] Joint operations were launched in New York in 1915 with the Phoenix, the Thames and Mersey and the Liverpool & London & Globe.[146] But possibly Sandeman Allen's most expansionary move within his first few years at the helm of Phoenix's maritime department was the acquisition of Northern Maritime.

This was a small marine office, specialising in insuring coal cargoes on the Newcastle–Cardiff run. Based in Newcastle, it had been founded there in 1863, and thus shared a birth date with Union Marine. However, it shared little else. Its sponsors were a mixed crew of merchants, shipowners and bankers, quite unlike the underwriting and broking professionals who were active in company promotion in Liverpool and the moving spirits behind Union Marine. Northern Maritime was a brave attempt to compete with the many mutual marine clubs which handled the insurance of Tyneside's collier brigs in the later nineteenth century. Such business was far removed from the long-distance hull and cargo trade which needed insurance out of Liverpool. Also, Northern Maritime was tiny, launched on a capital of 10,000 £5 shares but with each share only 10 shillings paid; this yielded a total starting capital of a mere £5,000. Nevertheless, Tyneside was an important market for the marine insurer. And, by 1914 Northern Maritime could boast a paid-up capital of £30,000.

Sandeman Allen had informed James Ferguson, secretary of Northern Maritime, probably early in 1914, that Union Marine might offer a friendly hand if the Tyneside firm should ever contemplate absorption. In May 1914 Ferguson reminded Allen of this and told him that Northern Maritime had been approached from 'an undesirable quarter'.[147] Ferguson was anxious for the friendly hand. Negotiations commenced immediately and ran through June and July 1914. They were at an advanced stage when war broke out. However, the enormous upheaval created in the marine market by naval hostilities appear to have driven all

[145] And later a Spanish Branch in 1917.
[146] And later in San Francisco in 1919 with the Norwich Union.
[147] Ferguson to Allen, 21 May 1914.

other thoughts from the minds of the participants: the negotiators fell silent.

Three years later, just as suddenly, they picked up where they had left off. By early October 1917, Union Marine had agreed to buy the smaller mariner for five-year's purchase of pre-war profits plus the value of its free assets.[148] The price, agreed by early December, was to be £17 10s in 5% War Loan for each £5 share (£3 paid-up).[149] No doubt, the vast expansion of marine business during the war explains the high cost, and Union Marine's sustained interest.[150] Certainly, Stanley Mitcalfe, Chairman of Northern Maritime, could scarcely comprehend the changes in his company's results, 'so far beyond my life-long experience of underwriting ... in the near future the new accounts from Liverpool, London and Australia will far exceed our pre-war figures ... from Newcastle, Cardiff and elsewhere'.[151]

Mitcalfe found the conditions so different that he wanted to retire. But, interestingly, the same model of acquisition was applied by Phoenix–Union Marine to Northern Maritime as had been applied by Phoenix to Union Marine. That is, management was to remain independent; Northern Maritime was to continue as a separate company; it was to retain its Newcastle base and connection.

The style is that of a Phoenix maritime acquisition of the 1900s. But, unfortunately, Northern Maritime did not turn out as well as Union Marine. It did add an extra element of capacity and connection to Phoenix's marine operation. But the takeover, delayed by war, then fell upon a crest in the marine market, and a particularly vicious and deceptive crest shaped by highly distorted wartime demand. Once peace returned, the marine insurers faced a selection of horrors: contracting world trade, overbuilt shipyards, idle fleets. Northern Maritime took a mere £17,113 in gross premiums in 1921,a derisory £8,619 by 1926. Phoenix had stripped it to a shell by the mid-1930s.

8. THE PHOENIX COMPOSITE IN 1914

The year 1914 is an obvious watershed for the British economy, as it was for British society, and as it was, of course, above all, for an entire misplaced generation. Within the economy, the Great War divided the Edwardian summer, all rising exports and long dresses, from the interwar winter of rising unemployment and short skirts. It would be a major

148 Phoenix Directors' Minutes, 32, p. 152, 10 October 1917.
149 *Ibid.*, p. 171, 21 November 1917; p. 182, 5 December 1917.
150 See pp. 372–89 below. 151 Mitcalfe to Allen, 15 November 1919.

Table 5.6. *The top fifteen composite insurance offices in 1911*

Company	Departments[a]	Assets (£ m)	Rank
North Brit. & Mercantile	F,L,A,M	23.8	1
Commercial Union	F,L,A,M	22.3	2
Royal	F,L,A,M	19.3	3
Alliance	F,L,A,M	18.4	4
Phoenix	F,L,A,M	14.0	5
LLG	F,L,A	11.5	6
Law Union & Rock	F,L,A	9.1	7
Northern	F,L,A	8.0	8
Guardian	F,L,A	6.6	9
REA	F,L,A,M	6.1	10
London	F,L,A,M	4.6	11
Atlas	F,L,A	3.8	12
Caledonian	F,L,A	3.7	13
London & Lancashire	F,A,M	3.6	14
Yorkshire	F,L,A,M	3.0	15

Note: [a]F=Fire, L=Life, A=Accident, M=Marine.

surprise if it were not also a hiatus for large insurance companies. So, in the expansion of a composite insurer, it is an apposite moment for stock-taking.

Undoubtedly, the two decades before 1914 represent a key period in the history of insurance amalgamation. As *The Times* put it in 1911, 'The assertion that this is the day of the composite is becoming more and more insistent.' The paper did not consider this entirely good news, for it feared that the vast extension in the scale of insurance ventures would encourage management to treat some departments – it mentioned marine – as loss leaders in order to maintain position elsewhere. However, it acknowledged that, 'among the giants the competition gets keener', and thus that the pressure towards composite forms of organisation could only increase.[152]

In this formative period, Phoenix was clearly one of the leading giants. However tentative and pragmatic Ryan's approach to composite strategy may have been before 1908, his corporate diplomacy became premeditated, direct and deliberate in the period 1908–14. Both he and the

[152] *The Times*, 1 June 1911.

Phoenix were identified correctly by the financial press as pioneers in composite company promotion, most particularly in relation to the Union Marine acquisition. There is both substance and justice in the notion that Gerald Ryan should be 'considered as a second founder of the Company's fortunes, of the same calibre as George Griffin Stonestreet'.[153]

Within four years from 1908 Phoenix had been transformed from a simple fire office into a multi-divisional composite transacting as well life, marine and accident business. With the exception of the last, which depended on internally generated capacity – though not for lack of trying to acquire external capacity – the diversification had been achieved by amalgamation or takeover. After absorbing Law Life, Phoenix boasted a total capital of £1.3 million and total funds of £12.7 million; after absorbing Union Marine its total capital was £3.2 million and its total assets £14 million. Among the fifteen composites which offered three or more main types of business in 1911, Phoenix ranked among the very top flight (see Table 5.6). It is striking that Phoenix was the only one of the original 'first generation' offices to achieve such a place among the composites. Fellow veterans such as the REA and London trailed far behind and the Alliance was the only company of even comparable vintage to achieve a similar status. With these two exceptions, all other composites in the top-half dozen were relative latecomers, dating from the second half of the nineteenth century.

It is noteworthy that the companies in Table 5.6 which lacked marine capacity tended to have low ranks for assets. However, three companies possessed all four main departments and still achieved low ranks for assets. Very significantly, two of these were Phoenix's eighteenth-century colleagues, REA and London.

A similar pattern is achieved if the measure employed is total premium income (refer Table 1.12). Among the top six composites, Phoenix again ranked fifth. And within this group of six, Phoenix ranked first for marine premium and third for life premium. But all of the four offices which outstripped Phoenix in total premiums were late-generation ventures; once more, Phoenix was the only veteran and metropolitan office within the first flight. The conclusion would seem to be that Ryan's takeovers allowed Phoenix to escape the relative decline affecting its age cohort of insurance companies.

Phoenix compared most strongly in the markets where its acquisition policy had been most active, and most feebly in the area where acquisition

[153] Hurren, *Phoenix Renascent*, p. 71, and see vol. 1, Chapters 2 and 3.

had failed. Leaving aside the fundamental – but also fundamentally 'soft' – merger with sister Pelican, the Phoenix's relative strength in 1914 had been achieved by means of two model takeovers. There were marked similarities between the two. Each featured strong companies which had taken hard knocks, were looking for refuge but remained viable. Both takeovers were fast, friendly, simple and cheap. Once seriously launched, they were completed within weeks. They involved few cross words and virtually no aggressive tactics. Neither displayed any complicated feature of finance. Each of the purchases was denominated in debentures and ordinary shares, although the fraction of the total price represented by Phoenix shares was much smaller in the case of Law Life than in that of Union Marine, one quarter against one half. Each purchase was organised so that the acquisition paid for itself: although there was goodwill to be financed in the Law Life deal, Ryan calculated that future interest on Law Life funds and profit on Law Life policies would meet this cost; in the case of Union Marine, there was no goodwill to be funded. Both acquisitions were designed to extend connections and so to expand capacity both within *and* outside the life and marine markets.

But the feature that stands out in regard to both takeovers is the excellence of Phoenix's timing. Phoenix went for Law Life long after it had ceased to be a premier life office but long before it became a lame duck. Phoenix took Union Marine just as the marine market bounced. Shares in the sector were low after a period of heavy losses and Union Marine's shares were especially low due to managerial strategy. Ryan bought only when he was sure that recovery had commenced. The market turned in 1909; Ryan investigated Union Marine's improving profits in 1910; purchase was complete by 1911. Judged merely as a foray into the stock market, this was a shrewdly handled operation.

The case of Northern Maritime, of course, will not fit this pattern, and it must be seen as exceptional. Strictly, it was, anyway, a takeover initiated by Union Marine and not by Phoenix. Moreover, it was originally timed for 1914, and, had it been completed prior to the outbreak of war, Union Marine and Phoenix would have benefited from Northern Maritime's expansion in the exceptional wartime markets for marine insurance. That the acquisition was completed only in 1917 was an accident produced by the rush of war business. And that the marine market would be wrecked after 1920 could not have been foreseen in 1917. Fortunately, the accident featured only a tiny company.

For diplomacy, rapidity and economy, these manoeuvres would be difficult to beat. But they were expansionary moves executed in rising markets. It could be an open question as to whether the same entrepreneurial gifts of amicable negotiation and fine timing would serve as well in unfriendly markets and flagging trade. Would the devices of 1900–14 prove suitable for the trading conditions of the 1920s? Or would Gerald Ryan rank among those many businessmen who did their best work in the Edwardian heyday and proved unable to devise tactics appropriate to the harsher markets of the interwar years?

CHAPTER 6

INSURANCE AND TOTAL WAR, 1914–1918

1. THE SURPRISING RESILIENCE OF CAPITALISM

Britain declared war upon Germany on 4 August 1914. The Phoenix Board was due to meet on the 5th. It did not do so, most minds being distracted from business. Instead, it met a week later, on 12 August, and decided to hold only fortnightly sessions for the duration of the conflict. The meeting on the 12th was understandably jittery.

In the autumn of 1914, many economic observers expected that the advent of a new type of warfare would wreck capitalism as they understood it. Continent-wide hostilities between nations able to call upon mass manpower through the technology of conscription and upon mass-produced munitions through the technology of repeat engineering defined a new scale of conflict. Many contemporaries believed that it would smash the delicate mechanisms which exchanged goods, capital and services within the newly globalised economy. The connection between leading currencies – pre-eminently sterling – and gold would not be sustainable in such a war; and when this connection broke, the economic firmament, it was expected, would crumble.

Experts in insurance shared fully in the cataclysmic vision: their international service industry, rich in export flows, intricately linked by reinsurance arrangements with offices in many different lands (and not least in Russia and Germany), must surely run aground on the reefs of European conflict. The only glint of optimism in these economic jeremiads was the conviction that such a war at least could not last long: indeed such thinking among financiers and industrialists provided strong support for the short-war illusion. If the capitalist economy of Europe could not stand the strain of total war, then it would collapse; and, in collapsing, it would bring conflict to a standstill; and the war would really be over by Christmas.

For good or ill, European capitalism of course proved a great deal more resilient than this, not once but twice in a sadly battered century. In 1914, the pound left gold and the economic firmament did not crumble. Complex, far-flung relationships reassembled themselves into more nationally based relationships. Large proportions of manufacturing industry – engineering, automobiles, fertilisers, and many others – converted from civilian to military production. Some capital markets – outstandingly, the City of London[1] – proved as adept at supporting beleaguered governments, and placing their war bonds, as they had previously been at financing the outposts of empire or the railways, mines and plantations of the developing world. In Britain, the biggest stock exchange in the world did a smart about-turn and set itself to providing a war-winning financial advantage for the home front.

In short, it would take more than world war to lay out world capitalism.[2] The latter was surprised by this, but was not slow to adjust to new demands. The insurance sector of world capitalism was no exception.

To begin with, of course, there was deep pessimism everywhere in the City, and the Phoenix men were as pessimistic as anyone. In April 1915, the company's chairman, Lord George Hamilton, lamented a war which 'had not only compelled us to fight for our national existence but had, incidentally, cast our commercial system into confusion'. He foresaw, for financial institutions, administrative systems failing through losses of manpower and resources decimated by soaring taxation.[3] By 1916, however, a somewhat stunned City was beginning to realise that it was not only withstanding the strains of war, but actually doing so in some style.

Observing a key indicator of London's international standing, Hamilton commented that, 'the steadiness of the American Exchange, in view of our enormous purchases [from the USA] for carrying on the War, is quite remarkable'. And he then forestalled modern economic historians with the insight that one of the features of British strength 'which have most disconcerted our enemies . . . is the marvellous response of our financial system'.[4]

It is only recently that detailed research on the British war economy of the First World War has proposed that one of its fundamental advantages over the German economic system was the capacity of the City to mobil-

1 T. Balderston, 'War, Finance and Inflation in Britain and Germany, 1914–18', *Economic History Review*, 42 (1989).

2 Now that the Soviet experiment of 1917–89 is apparently over, it would take even more than a historian of, say, the 1950s or 1960s might have calculated.

3 Annual General Meeting, Chairman's Annual Report, 28 April 1915.

4 *Ibid.*, 19 April 1916.

ise war funding by the mass flotation of government paper. By comparison, the Berlin stock exchange was poorly developed, and the depth of purchasing for German war loans shallow.[5] Unable to lay its hands on the other major alternative for war finance – sufficient taxable resources – the Imperial German government was forced towards the lethal third choice: the printing press and an inflationary expansion of the monetary supply.

However, the leaders of Phoenix were impressed not only by the debt-funding capacity of the City. They found also 'of all the exhibitions of national strength . . . the figures of our present Budget are the most remarkable. We are raising nearly £300 million in excess of our taxation two years back.' Hamilton then went on to give his part of the City a pat on the back. 'May we not say that one of the contributory causes to this massive structure of accumulated wealth is the work and development of Insurance in this country – the confidence it has given, the losses it has averted, the thrift it has promoted.'[6]

But, of course, the insurance sector had gone through the same sequence of self-doubt and surprised resilience which had affected the rest of the City. In 1917, Hamilton recalled that, three years before, 'those experienced in insurance were very anxious about the likely effects of the War'. But, by April 1917, he could find 'little in our accounts indicative of the tensions imposed upon the financial and commercial resources of the country by the most gigantic war the world has ever known'.[7] Whatever worries the insurers had felt about the fragility of their part of the capitalist system in wartime, the actual trading results were turning out 'such as to be considered favourable even in peacetime'.[8]

The path marked out by trading profits during the war leaves Hamilton's meaning in no doubt (see Table 6.1). But, if the returns on insuring in wartime had soared, so had the drains upon the profits. There were two in particular which siphoned huge sums out of the company: increased taxation (on both income and excess profits) and the inevitable wartime deterioration in investment values. Of these the latter made the earlier inroads, being concentrated in the period 1913–16, while tax pressures intensified from 1915.

Falling stock markets on the eve of war in 1913 had necessitated major write-offs of investment values in the accounts of April 1914, and these

[5] The glory of German high finance in the late nineteenth century had been the Great Banks, or Kreditbanken, the investment houses which had supported the development of German advanced technologies. This high-pressure bank credit had reduced the need for a stock *market*, but, ironically, in a national crisis, it provided little effective substitute for the mass placement of government paper across a wide swathe of the investing public.

[6] Annual General Meeting, Chairman's Annual Report, 19 April 1916.

[7] *Ibid.*, 25 April 1917. [8] *Ibid.*

Table 6.1. *Phoenix group gross trading profit, tax payments and investment write-offs, 1913–18 (as at end December)*

Year	Trading profit (£)	Income & excess profit tax (£)	Written off against investments (£)
1913	121,158		91,749
1914	176,000		525,282
1915	284,000		390,000
1916	305,800	218,000	86,000
1917	379,411	260,000	140,000
1918	655,999	481,440	

Source: Chairman's Annual Reports.

grew markedly in the ensuing two years of hostilities, as capital values continued to spiral downwards. The Stock Exchange was reacting, of course, not only to the outbreak and course of the war, but also to the vast helpings of government paper that were soon served up to investors. By comparison, American investment values held up well in the face of the European crisis, but only for so long as America kept out of it. As soon as the United States committed itself to fight, huge issues of War Loan in 1917 set American asset values on the slide as well, and the £140,000 written off by Phoenix in the accounts of April 1918 was largely in respect of depreciation in the company's US holdings during the course of 1917.[9]

But, equally, Phoenix itself *bought* its share of war stock. From early on, the company sought large allocations of the government's National War Loan, starting with a claim for £50,000 worth in November 1914 and amassing a tally of £352,000 received by mid-July 1915.[10] In 1916, further large applications were made and a total holding accumulated of £3.3 million. Phoenix even encouraged its staff to buy War Savings Certificates by advancing loans for the purpose, at 5% interest.[11]

One of the major investment devices of the war, and a powerful influence in increasing Phoenix's holdings of His Majesty's Government paper, was a Treasury initiative of late 1915. The department approached financial institutions 'with a view to obtaining, a temporary deposit of

[9] Depreciation of investments was not the only wartime loss of value which required writing off by the company. In 1917, Phoenix decided that in prudence they should write off also all outstanding balances due from agencies or companies in markets affected by hostilities, whether or not these were long-standing connections (as many were), from which Phoenix might expect redress after the war.

[10] Directors' Minutes, 31, pp. 138, 250, 18 November 1914 and 14 July 1915.

[11] *Ibid.*, 32, p. 447, 2 August 1916.

American and Canadian securities', and in return for securing these in government hands, promised to pay an additional 0.5% interest on the nominal amount deposited.[12] The purpose was to accumulate as many dollar-denominated assets as possible. Phoenix did its best to support 'the American Exchange', by selling over £1 million worth of dollar securities to the Treasury and transferring most of it into UK government stock. Again, in early 1916, the Treasury bid for a further £0.3 million of Phoenix dollar holdings and the company took 5% UK Exchequer Bonds in return.[13] In addition, the company loaned to His Majesty's Government a further £700,000 worth of US securities. Certainly, Phoenix did its bit: about £2 million worth of company assets were actually involved in transactions of this kind during the war and Phoenix had offered as eligible for deposit in December 1915 as much as £4.6 million.

Nevertheless, the company drove a shrewd bargain. It specified that, if the government should sell the securities deposited, the proceeds, together with a 2.5% bonus, should revert to the original owners. More to the point, the company should have the right to ask the government to sell the deposit on its behalf – thus, of course, securing the 2.5% bonus, rather than the 0.5% commission.[14]

Under pressures of this kind, holdings of home government stock rose from close to zero in 1914 to above the £1 million mark by end 1915. Counting securities loaned to the government and holdings in Allied and Colonial Government War Loans, the commitment of the Phoenix to funding the war effort through the markets amounted, by the end of 1916 to over four times this amount and about 26% of the company's total portfolio. More generally, holdings in UK and imperial government stock of all kinds represented 8% of general fund assets in 1914, 29% in 1916 and 36.0% in 1918. For the life fund, the matching proportions were 12.1%, 28.0% and 36.0%. In both funds, there was a major move – by about half – away from the 'railway and other' debentures and preference shares which had dominated investment activity before the war (see Table 6.2). Fortunately, as Hamilton pointed out, government stock was, for the present, again, 'an investment which yields us an excellent rate of interest'.[15]

[12] *Ibid.*, 31, pp. 317, 321, 24 November and 1 December 1915.

[13] *Ibid.*, p. 352, 2 February 1916.

[14] *Ibid.*, p. 321, 1 December 1915. Equally shrewdly, dealing with a different government in January 1917, Phoenix elected to take cash for £10,000 Russian government sterling Treasury Bills, and, presciently, to make no application for the new issue worth £10 million. This was possibly the last ever issue of the doomed tsarist government. *Ibid.*, 32, p. 49, 24 January 1917.

[15] Chairman's Annual Reports, 19 April 1916, 25 April 1917.

Table 6.2. *Phoenix general and life funds; major trends in distribution by type of investment, 1914–18*

	Total securities (£m)		% of holdings in UK and imperial government stock		% of holdings in railway and other stock	
	General funds	Life funds	General funds	Life funds	General funds	Life funds
1914	2.8	7.9	8.0	12.1	60.0	46.0
1915	3.1	7.8	19.0	21.0	53.0	36.0
1916	3.4	7.9	29.0	28.0	45.0	31.0
1917	4.0	8.6	32.0	36.0	32.0	28.0
1918	4.6	8.7	36.0	36.0	31.0	27.0

Source: Phoenix Assurance Statistical Survey of WWI.

Nevertheless, the need to write down the depreciating values of investments which were not new government paper hurt the Phoenix. Between 1906 and 1914, the company's General Reserve had grown by £900,000, by way of transfers from profits, and the total that had been set aside for writing down investments in these nine years had been £144,000. The company tried, in this period, to set aside £100,000 per year out of profits for the General Reserve. Between 1913 and 1918, the full amount could be afforded only once, in 1915, and in 1916 and 1917 only smaller amounts of profit, £50,000 and £37,000, could be rescued for the Reserve. On the other hand, the amount that had to be dedicated to the depreciation of investments was nearly ten times that of the period 1906–14, at over £1 million.

As the capital values of investments declined, the wartime yield upon stocks and shares went up, and investment interest became a strong feature in the company accounts of financial institutions. The Phoenix directors were somewhat defensive on this score, as with some other aspects of their war economy. Hamilton spoke for them in April 1916: 'It is a common thing to hear people dilate upon the improved yield of capital at the present time, from which it is too often inferred that capitalist institutions like our own are enjoying in this respect a prosperous time.'[16] Phoenix did not wish the merest whiff of war profiteering to attach to itself, nor to appear to be profiting from the misfortune of

[16] *Ibid.*

Table 6.3. *Phoenix non-life trading profits (fire, accident, marine) and tax liabilities, 1914–18*

	Trading profit (£)	Tax liability (£)	Effective rate
1914	121,158	10,754	8.9
1915	259,044	38,198	14.7
1916	305,800	99,337	32.5
1917	379,411	230,150	60.7
1918	655,999	481,440	73.4

others. Its strongest defence against such implications was to emphasise its soaring contribution to the Inland Revenue.

Gross investment earnings for the Phoenix Group in 1914 were £654,153 but the taxman removed £46,000 of this; by 1915 the yield was £667,602 and the Revenue took nearly £73,000 of that sum. Life investment yield rose from £30,633 in 1914 to £109,036 in 1918, but the effective rate of tax upon these interest earnings moved from 6.6% to 20.7%. But the impact of income tax, excess profits tax and other government levies upon trading insurance profits was far more severe than the drain on investment earnings (see Table 6.3).

Trading profits took a hammering, especially in the second half of the war. In 1918, taxation left the Phoenix's net trading profit at about one-quarter of the gross result. Insurance companies, as Hamilton stressed in 1919, had contributed handsomely to the 'sinews of war'.[17] Earlier, he had elaborated the point with an enthusiasm, in which it is tempting to read an excess of sensitivity: 'As good patriots, we shall contribute to the Exchequer with the utmost pleasure, whatever sum may be found to be payable by us.'[18] This turned out to be a large aggregate number: of the total £1.62 million paid by the Phoenix in taxation in the decade 1910–19, 95.7% represented wartime liabilities.[19]

Pleasure might not be a company's first response to the knock of the taxman, even in wartime, but it must surely have been the reaction of Phoenix's shareholders to the arrival of their dividend envelopes. In 1913, the usual 40% dividend had been easily maintained, its cost of £207,000 being met almost wholly from investment earnings and life receipts, with a draw upon profits of only £25,000. But, in 1914, the first war year, the dividend was held, with scarcely more strain, with no more than £50,000 being transferred from profits; and it was the same again in 1915, with

[17] *The Times*, 1 May 1919. [18] Chairman's Annual Report, 19 April 1916.
[19] *Ibid.*, 28 April 1920.

Table 6.4. *Phoenix Assurance: total assets, income and profits, 1908–17 (in current and 1913 prices)*

	Total assets (£m)		Total income (£m)		Total profit (£m)	
	Current value	Real value	Current value	Real value	Current value	Real value
1908	7.4	7.7	2.2	2.3	267,556	279,870
1916	17.4	11.8	4.3	2.9	305,800	206,901
1917	19.0	10.7	5.6	3.1	379,411	212,913

Source: Phoenix Annual Accounts; values deflated by the London & Cambridge Economic Service, *Key Statistics*, 1900–64 (London, 1965), Table C, recalculated on a base of 1913=100.

£40,000 taken from profits and £100,000 given to the reserves; and in 1916, with only £28,000 of the £180,274 cost of the dividend coming from profits. But, in the record profit year of 1917, the customary 40% dividend of 8 shillings was raised to 9 shillings, with virtually the entire cost of the dividend and the debenture interest met from investment earnings. And, in 1918, when the record was immediately broken, the dividend went up to 10 shillings per share.[20]

Between Phoenix's launch as a composite insurer and the last years of the Great War, the company's overall financial position was, at least apparently, transformed (see Table 6.4).

On the asset side, total fire funds rose from £1.86 million in 1914 to £2.2 million in 1918, passing the £2 million mark in 1916. Life Funds advanced much less over this period, from £11.4 million to £11.6 million, after actually declining slightly in 1915. The biggest proportionate rise, however, was within the marine fund, which soared from £530,440 in 1914 to £1.2 million in 1918. Lord George Hamilton judged that, 'few companies can show a like progress in the same short space of time' and concluded in 1919 that, 'we enjoy a position of great financial strength and exceptionally bright prospects'.[21]

In similar vein in 1918, Gerald Ryan was moved to reflect on his quarter-century long association with the Phoenix: then, in the early 1890s, there was no insurance company with even half Phoenix's income for 1917, and only one office which held more than Phoenix's assets of 1917. By 1917, Phoenix ranked fifth among all UK corporate insurers. It was largely the wartime financial results which led Ryan and Hamilton

[20] *Ibid.*, 1914–19. [21] *The Times*, 1 May 1919.

and their colleagues to the misplaced conviction that they could approach the postwar era with 'unqualified equanimity'.[22]

Money illusion seems to be present here. Table 6.4 reveals that, in real terms, total assets and income had advanced much less than in money terms 1908–17, while annual profit had actually declined. Wartime inflation had consumed much of the apparent gain. It is more than slightly alarming that the Phoenix archive is entirely silent on this aspect of the war economy.

The response of the Phoenix Board to the pressures of the First World War ran the gamut from initial pessimism through startled resilience to a final and slightly guilty euphoria. It is not implausible that this last state led on to overconfidence. If the Phoenix could withstand the strains of this 'gigantic war' in such shape, what did it have to fear? One answer perhaps was ill-judged company acquisition in the postwar depression. Another was a failure to allow sufficiently for the difference between current and real values; for this sent the Board into the postwar period believing that they were richer than they actually were.

It is possible to see why Gerald Ryan believed that the unexpected wartime bonanza could be translated into yet another phase of swashbuckling corporate diplomacy. Once the commerce raiders had been dealt with, the corporate raiders could return to the City. And it seemed that the war had given them the resources to do so. It is true that, even when deflated for price changes, the increase in Phoenix's total assets was large. But it is also tempting to suppose that Ryan may have omitted to deflate.

2. INSURING AGAINST THE WAR AT SEA

Apart from a number of Zeppelin and aircraft raids, and some target practice on the part of the German navy, mainland Britain in the First World War remained more or less free of direct war damage.[23] This meant that insurances of assets which stayed in the United Kingdom were comparatively little affected by hostilities. Bombardment by aircraft and rocket would change this drastically in the Second World War, as the home front and the fighting front effectively merged into a single war zone, but in 1914–18 the technology which would produce this lethal transition was not fully formed. So, it was the assets which moved outside the United Kingdom which were most at risk and raised new problems of insurance in the First World War. These assets were ships and lives. Perhaps surprisingly, the second saw fewer changes than the first; and, for

[22] Hamilton, Chairman's Annual Report, 26 June 1918.

[23] There were 108 raids altogether from January 1915 to June 1918.

Phoenix at least, war mortality did not add greatly to normal anticipated mortality among the assured population.[24]

Consequently, marine insurance emerges as the sector of the business which not only profited most from the war in economic terms, but was also most directly affected by the conditions of combat. Hulls and cargoes succumbed to torpedoes and shell-fire, and sank with a frequency that Mother Nature, at her worst, could not rival. But, further, new markets were opened, because the enemy inflicting this damage had been, before the war, a great competitor in marine insurance. Now, its powerful marine offices, if not its submarines and commerce raiders, were swept from the seas, or at least out of the way of the British offices. Yet that in itself imposed a complication, since, in a particularly international insurance trade, much reinsurance business had been transacted before the war between British and German marine offices. Now such transactions would rank as trading with the enemy and were proscribed. It follows from these special conditions that, of all sectors of the UK insurance industry, marine had most contact with the wartime government, with the enlarged and beleaguered state produced by the requirements of total war. The markets of the fire and life insurers were scarcely untouched by war; but that of the marine underwriters was revolutionised by it.

British governments of the early twentieth century recognised that an unimpeded flow of imports was a necessity for an industrial island nation. The maintenance of shipping resources was a crucial factor of national interest and the provision of adequate insurance for vessels and cargoes was a crucial factor of interest for the capitalists who ran the ships. Indeed, without sufficient protection from risk they would not run them at all; and then there would be no British war economy. However, in wartime, private insurers of ships wish to cover only good risks. Yet, in wartime, it is precisely the poorest risks – the most explosive cargoes or the most perilous voyages – which may be of the greatest strategic value. Between 1914 and 1918, it was essential that the poorest risks should continue in operation. Some answer to this insurance conundrum had to be found that would allow them to do so.

In the navalist decades on either side of 1900, when the survival of nations depended more heavily upon whether or not the freighters got through than in any period before or since, the puzzle of marine insurance in wartime was much discussed. The issue was sharpened by a Lloyds decision of 1898 to exclude war risk from the standard marine policy, which, traditionally, had included it. Lloyds was reacting to the recent

[24] Although the war created plenty of other difficulties for life insurers. See below pp. 403–14.

enormous advances in the potency of naval weaponry.[25] In 1905, a Royal Commission on the Supply of Food and Raw Materials in Time of War proposed a remedy in the form of a state indemnity for all ship owners: they should pay no premiums and carry no policies against war risks but should receive automatic compensation from the state if their ships and cargoes were lost to enemy action.[26] By 1907, as Britain geared itself up for the final sprint in the pre-war dreadnought race, a more aggressive (and misplaced) confidence was in evidence: a Treasury Committee on a National Guarantee for the War Risks of Shipping, under Austen Chamberlain, concluded that indemnities were no match for battleships and that the Royal Navy was the best guarantee for the ship owners; they required no further assurance.[27]

By 1913 the capabilities of the German High Seas Fleet clearly threw this logic into jeopardy. So too did the attitude of Lloyds underwriters who, in the cause of professional obligation, expressed themselves willing to pay out on *German* ships, whether or not hostile. It required pressure from the Admiralty before they would concede even that compensation was not payable on enemy vessels captured by the Royal Navy![28] Cross-currents of this kind required the appointment in May 1913 of a further inquiry, this time a subset of the Committee of Imperial Defence, chaired by the Rt Hon. F. H. Jackson and including strong representation from the ship owners and Lloyds. Its terms were much more realistic: to devise a scheme that would ensure that British steamer traffic was not 'interrupted' for lack of insurance; that this insurance should be reasonably priced; and that the ship owners should make reasonable contributions to the costs.[29]

The subcommittee, reporting in April 1914, found that the ship owners had already set up their own mutual hull insurance schemes for the protection of vessels entering war zones. This was an indication of the troubled state of the world in the months before the outbreak of pan-European conflict. Three principal associations, the North of England Protection and Indemnity Association, the London War Risk Association and the London and Liverpool War Risk Insurance Association covered, in roughly equal shares, a total of £87 million worth of hulls by the spring

[25] Quick-firing guns, long-range artillery, effective torpedoes, operational submarines formed part of an innovational 'cluster' in armament technology around the turn of the century. See Trebilcock, *The Vickers Brothers*.

[26] Cd 2643, xxxlx, 1905. See also D. French, *British Economic and Strategic Planning, 1905–14* (London, 1982).

[27] Cd 4161, lviii, 1908.

[28] P. Kennedy, 'Strategy and Finance in Twentieth-century Britain', in P. Kennedy (ed.), *Strategy and Diplomacy 1870–1945* (London, 1984), pp. 89–106.

[29] See Sir Norman Hill (ed.), *War and Insurance* (London, 1927), p. 13.

of 1914. But the value of UK tonnage covered for ordinary non-war marine risk was £127 million. So the majority of British hulls did not carry war cover in 1914. And most underwriters would not offer war terms for *cargoes* at all because they calculated that no level of wartime premium would reimburse them for the forced sale of depreciated investments which wartime losses would require of them.

The subcommittee proposed that the structure of the Associations should be employed to provide a comprehensive system of cover in any major war, combining private underwriting with state guarantees, and giving the ship owners the vital incentives to continue putting out the boats. In regard to hulls, the Associations would act as principals for all war risks, accepting insurances at rates of premium fixed by the state. The state would then reinsure the Associations, at the same rates, for 80% of the risks, leaving the private mutuals to cover the remaining 20%. For cargoes the state would offer a flat, fixed rate, regardless of the risk of the voyage, leaving the ship owner free to insure with the state agency or with a private underwriter. On the one hand, the state would cover risks which the private sector would not contemplate at any price, at the flat rate. On the other, the private sector could offer prices below the official rate for the safe voyages that remained even in wartime, and the ship owners would no doubt prefer this bargain for such journeys.

Hull insurance was not compulsory in the initial scheme,[30] but cargoes could not be covered for war risk by any party unless the hull insurance had passed through the Association system. Nor was war insurance for cargo compulsory but it would not be supplied by either the state or the private sector unless the freight had first been covered for ordinary marine risk. The effect of these provisions was that the very dangerous risks passed automatically to the state, while the private sector, including the great corporate insurers, could pick off the better risks. The big offices in particular could continue with ordinary hull and cargo business, pass entirely on war risks for hulls, and target the best and most lucrative war risks for cargo.

This system went into force on Tuesday 4 August 1914, and the State Cargo Insurance Office was opened on 5 August, a matter of hours before hostilities commenced. The dual structure for both hulls and cargoes continued until August 1917. By that time, two influences had combined to render it unsuitable for hulls: submarine attack proved beyond doubt that the Royal Navy's big ships could not provide effective protection for the merchantmen and inflicted punitive losses upon them; and, partly in

[30] It became so in December 1916.

consequence, the government took control of virtually the entire merchant fleet. It followed that the state should also assume responsibility for 100%, rather than 80%, of hull losses. At the same time, the authorities tried to establish a similar monopoly of cargo risks. Here, however, the interest of the private underwriters lay in retaining their share of a very lucrative business and the state's initiative was vigorously opposed. The government introduced a modified scheme in March 1918, aiming to make official cargo insurance more competitive, and to achieve a break-even result; but a two-tier system of cargo insurance persisted throughout the war.

The official commitment to marine insurance cost the state millions. Of the £18.5 million worth of hulls lost between August 1914 and August 1917 – the vast majority in the period of intense submarine warfare which occupied the twelve months after August 1916 – the state paid out £14.8 million. Cargoes produced £65 million in claims upon the State Insurance Office, and an overall loss of £10 million. Meanwhile as the state agency accepted, and never declined, the worst cargo risks – which made up slightly over one-quarter of the wartime total – the private sector was coining profits on the three-quarters which could safely be covered at premiums below the government's rate.[31] Its loss ratio for this business was well below 3% of that on the state scheme.

Phoenix was no exception to this pattern. Like other marine insurers, Union Marine, which operated effectively as Phoenix's marine department, had found hull insurance a variable business in the pre-war years.[32] Its manager, Sandeman Allen had reported to Phoenix, as early as 1912, that the 'lower-rated cargo business... is the most profitable portion'.[33] In general, the marine underwriters entered the war from a weakening hull market and with an established preference for cargo business. However, at the start of hostilities, Union Marine was fairly well protected

[31] Total war cargo risks exceeded £8,219 million.

[32] There was some reorganisation of the direction of Phoenix–Union Marine marine work during the war. The building of the new Phoenix Head Office in King William Street had contained the objective of consolidating all branches on a single site. This made it anomalous that the main channel for marine business should be in Liverpool. From January 1916, a mechanism was sought which would improve Head Office participation in marine management. A second Union Marine director, Sir Thomas (later Lord) Royden, was brought in to join Helenus Robertson as a director of Phoenix. Within Phoenix, a Marine Committee was formed, with Robertson (chairman of Union Marine) presiding and Royden as his deputy. Both Gerald Ryan and Sandeman Allen, as the chief executives of the two companies, would attend the Committee. This body supervised all Phoenix–Union Marine marine business from this point. Phoenix Directors' Minutes, 31, p. 342, 12 January 1916. For the administrative structure employed during the period 1911–16, see above pp. 354–7.

[33] Union Marine General Manager's Report, 27 March 1912.

from war risks. Before the outbreak of fighting in Flanders, the company was committed to hull insurance on only two fleets, and both of these were heavily reinsured. Most of its cargo business, with the exception of the eastern trade, was written free of war risk, and this form of insurance was supplied only when required by existing clients.[34]

Nevertheless, after the start of the European conflict and the institution of the government schemes, Union Marine quickly saw the prospects for good war cargo risks. By mid-August, Allen had secured permission to write desirable war cover even when the company did not have a line on the original marine risk. Rates were stiffened by the operations of the commerce raiders *Emden* and *Karlsruhe*, and the first submarine sinking late in 1914, while the increasing U-boat threat, especially to traffic in the Dover Straits and North Sea, pushed them up further early in 1915. Soaring demand and rising rates produced rapidly expanding premium flows. By October 1915, the increase in the volume of Union Marine's cargo business was so sharp that the Phoenix chairman took fright, and Ryan, in order to calm him, proposed a halving of Union Marine's retentions on war risks. The war risk receipts which had averaged £20,000 per fortnight during the year, were cut to £12,000 by early November.[35] Allen reported in March 1916 that he favoured continuing with a conservative policy long before the submarine menace became acute in the later part of that year.[36]

The accounts presented in April 1916 were the first to show the results of Sandeman Allen's war strategy. Marine profits for 1915 were £100,000 against the £40,000 of 1914 and the £20,000 of 1913, while premiums had moved from £712,774 in 1914 to £1,053,614 in 1915. War risks had been written less with an eye to the main chance than, as Lord George Hamilton put it, 'to keep together our general connections' and the premium surge had followed less from a desire to write a greater business than from 'the marked increase in the values of shipping and merchandise'.[37] This note of defensiveness in regard to the writing of explicit war insurances, in apparent danger but to actual profit, reappeared again in Hamilton's résumé of 1916, when marine profits moved up a further notch to £150,000.

Commenting in April 1917, at the height of the U-boat attacks, Hamilton was defensive also in another sense. His earlier experience as First Lord of the Admiralty, and his continuing naval contacts, did more to excite than to assuage his fears. Losses to the torpedoes could 'only be

[34] Union Marine Directors' Minutes, vol. D, p. 48, 5 August 1914.
[35] Union Marine General Manager's Report, 2 November 1915.
[36] *Ibid.*, 8 March 1916. [37] Phoenix Chairman's Annual Report, 19 April 1916.

surmounted by strict frugality and self-denial on the part of all classes of the community. Speaking as one who has, in various ways, accurate information upon the subject, I wish to give you this emphatic note of warning.'[38] His earlier service as a 'building' First Lord, concerned with the weaponry aspects of naval competition, led him to strike an unusual note for an insurer.

In 1917 Union Marine's profit was £185,000 and in 1918 £392,000. Premium income, sharing in the phenomenal expansion of the chief companies, rose from £1.3 million in 1916 to £2.4 million in 1917 before returning to £1.3 million in 1918. War demand could now cause swings in annual premium of a full £1 million. Before 1914, a marine income of £1 million was virtually unknown among the corporate insurers; by 1917, Phoenix–Union Marine was one of the few offices to have doubled the largest pre-war receipts.[39] Its profit out-turn was also one of the best. Once more, Hamilton took pains to trace these lucrative results to 'the necessities of the abnormal situation', 'a necessary temporary inflation', and he warned of the inevitable downswing to come. Indeed, this would come even before the war ended due to 'the more successful counter-action of the submarine peril'. Hamilton had clearly concluded that the world was an unsafe place: the marine insurer was beset either by rampaging submarines or by subsiding profits. Meanwhile, he continued to explain rising premiums by the inflated value of ships and cargoes and the inflated cost of repairing ships – nearly quadrupled since 1914 – that had been damaged but not sunk.

Losses to ships insured by Union Marine were, in absolute terms, inevitably high. In the last peacetime year, they were around £0.25 million. By 1916, war conditions had doubled this figure and by 1917 almost quadrupled it to £0.9 million, before the convoy system and improving command of the seas returned the level of loss to £0.5 million in 1918. On the other hand, the demand for the insurance of seaborne trade was also very large. It had made marine the biggest sector of Phoenix's business by 1917: marine premiums were 42.6% of fire premiums in 1913, 89.4 % in 1916 and 141.1% in 1917 (and, in 1918, 63.9%). This was sufficient to promote the marine department from the 15–18% share of total Phoenix income which it had supplied in the period 1911–14 to an average of 30.6% for the war period and a peak of 44.4% in 1917.

The marine department had never before occupied such a pre-eminent

[38] *Ibid.*, 25 April 1917.

[39] Surprisingly, there is little sense in the contemporary record of the effect that wartime price inflation was having on premium values, although its impact on profits and repair costs was noted.

position in total earnings, and would never do so again: the 1917 share of total premiums won by the marine department marked a zenith within the entire history of the company. And in money terms the £2.4 million taken in marine premiums in 1917 was not surpassed until 1951 (£2.7 million). Even more to the point, the marine department was clearly the Phoenix's biggest money-spinner for the war period: in 1916 it accounted for 50% of group non-life profits, in 1917 49% and in 1918 60%. For the period of the war, Union Marine was the brightest star in the Phoenix galaxy.

It burned brightly too in the wider universe of marine insurance. Even before the war, Union Marine had been a considerable force among the ship insurers. Its net premiums for 1911–14, at an average of £604,703 per annum, exceeded those of the veteran mariners, the London Assurance, at just over £400,000 and the Royal Exchange, at just over £300,000. But Sandeman Allen's manipulation of war risks took Phoenix–Union Marine to the very top of the marine league, among composite insurers, and indeed to the top of all non-Lloyds marine dealing. Table 6.5 shows Phoenix–Union Marine ranking first among the composites in 1914 and 1917, second in 1915, slipping to third in 1916, and falling out of the top half-dozen only in 1918, as the company's business contracted more sharply than that of most offices in the final months of the war. This is itself indicative of a special focus upon war business, since war risks, often attaching to a single voyage, run off far more quickly than conventional marine risks. Phoenix–Union Marine marine premiums almost halved between 1917 and 1918, leaving the group ranking seventh among the ship insurers, with £1,273,367 in earnings (see Table 6.5).

One or two specialist marine insurers outdid the composites in some wartime years – as did the Indemnity (taken over by the Northern in 1917) with premiums of over £1.8 million in 1916 – but, broadly, Table 6.5 displays the dominant forces in the corporate marine market of the war period. Phoenix–Union Marine is conspicuous in the vanguard. Not only was this true in volume, for Sandeman Allen stood out also in the test of comparative profitability.

Among eleven leading marine insurers assessed over the underwriting years 1916 and 1917, Union Marine ranked third; and in 1918 Phoenix produced the best profit out-turn (30.8% of premiums against an average of 17.2%) of some sixteen maritime operators.[40] It was no mean achievement to extract such results even from the favourable wartime risks left in the market by the government schemes.

[40] *Journal of Commerce*, 27 August 1919.

Table 6.5. *The top six composite marine insurers, 1914–18: net premiums and ranks*

1914			1915			1916		
	Net premiums (£)	Rank		Net premiums (£)	Rank		Net premiums (£)	Rank
Phoenix-UM	740,388	1	Royal	1,164,351	1	Royal	1,764,685	1
London Assurance	465,106	2	Phoenix-UM	1,111,954	2	British Dominion	1,484,810	2
British Dominion[a]	404,109	3	British Dominion[a]	1,020,354	3	Phoenix-UM	1,391,054	3
REA	359,008	4	REA	854,124	4	REA	1,331,913	4
Thames & Mersey[b]	337,016	5	London Assurance	794,790	5	Alliance	1,304,653	5
Alliance	290,064	6	Commercial Union	759,791	6	London Assurance	1,157,702	6

1917			1918		
	Net premiums (£)	Rank		Net premiums (£)	Rank
Phoenix-UM	2,411,564	1	Northern	3,019,706	1
Royal	2,154,057	2	London & Lancs	2,910,720	2
Alliance	2,083,943	3	Royal	1,812,614	3
Eagle Star/British Dominion	1,909,792	4	Eagle Star/British Dominion	1,675,908	4
REA	1,799,400	5	Alliance	1,628,583	5
London Assurance	1,743,928	6	United British	1,568,870	6

Note: [a]absorbed by Eagle Star, 1917; [b]absorbed by Liverpool & London & Globe, 1911
Source: *Journal of Commerce*, 1914–18.

However, the good wartime profits, experienced in some measure by most marine insurers, were not easy to keep. For where there were wartime profits, there were also tax collectors. Marine profits raised particular issues in relation to excess profits tax. Marine accounts were run over more than one year[41] and war risk profits were drawn from an obviously perilous trade at the very centre of the war effort. Were they therefore fair prey for excess profits tax? Marine underwriters thought not and argued that they constituted a special case under the terms of the war taxes. They asked for a pre-war standard of profit to be applied to a percentage of premium income and that investment earnings should not be included in the calculation of marine profit. Representations were made to the Board of Referees of the Inland Revenue in May 1916, and, early in the new year, a part of this case was conceded. The Referees agreed to treat marine premiums as capital for the purposes of excess profits tax and to measure taxable premium from a benchmark related to a pre-war standard.

If the government proved sympathetic to the special tax problems of marine insurers, it proved much less forgiving in respect to many of their other activities. In some indeed it was intrusive to a quite surprising degree. Of course, the principles of *laissez-faire*, however fervently held by the Victorians and Edwardians, had always yielded to the demands of national security. Moreover, one of the strongest of those demands was the prohibition against trading with the enemy; here the notion of free trade gave way naturally to the requirement that no assistance be afforded those who threatened the safety of the realm. Nevertheless, the energy invested by the Board of Trade, and other departments of state, in ensuring that British marine insurers maintained no contacts with German insurance agents or companies was remarkable.

Obviously, after August 1914, no British insurer could maintain a marine (or any other) agency on German soil, and clearly also the extensive pre-war reinsurance arrangements between the marine underwriters of London, Liverpool, Bremen and Hamburg had to stop. But British insurers were required also to avoid all dealings with German nationals in neutral countries and even with neutral nationals in neutral countries who could have German affiliations. This was a tall order in a service trade which had developed very complex international ramifications, and in which German companies had built up a considerable presence. On the other hand, of course, this was precisely why the Board of Trade gave it such close attention. The level of scrutiny is a tribute to the thoroughness

[41] Hence the lag between the premium peak in 1917 and the profit peak in 1918 above.

with which a liberal state can wage economic warfare.

Direct agencies in hostile territory raised few issues for Phoenix–Union Marine. In autumn 1914, Union Marine had only two agencies in Germany, at Bremen and Hamburg, and neither did much business; both were suspended until the end of the war. The Antwerp agency in occupied Belgium was effectively transferred to the United Kingdom.[42] And the Beirut and Smyrna agencies, within the Turkish orbit, were closed for the duration from January 1915. Similarly, hull reinsurance connections with offices in enemy lands were given short shrift. At the outbreak of the war, Union Marine had no reinsurance contracts with German offices and swiftly decided to cancel all other hull reinsurance arrangements, though with a prudent eye to postwar prospects, they decided to do so gently: 'we shall have to be extremely careful . . . to do everything most correctly so as to avoid every possible excuse for repudiation on the termination of the war'.[43] Like most commercial interests in the United Kingdom, the marine insurers expected the war to be short, viewed it as a regrettable interruption of normal business, and kept in mind the need to resume trading once the interruption was over.[44] Nevertheless, by the end of 1914, Union Marine had replaced all German reinsurance links with regard to the important British, Norwegian and Russian markets.

More heart searching occurred in regard to the Specie Pool and the reinsurance of cargo risks. The Specie Pool had been created in 1909 to share risks on the insurance of hulls carrying bullion. It was a valuable facility for handling a highly vulnerable business. But it was managed by a German venture, the influential Mannheim and Co. Reluctantly, Union Marine decided that it must run off all its current risks and make up the account at the end of the war.[45] In respect to cargo risks, the pain was even worse. For Union Marine had been deeply involved with German offices in this department, ceding most of its cargo reinsurances by a treaty which, through the prominent financial house of Bleichroder, gave half of the business laid off to a group of eight marine insurers in Hamburg, Bremen and Cologne.[46] This arrangement was fundamental to Union

[42] Phoenix Marine Committee, Book 1, p. 8, 23 February 1916; *ibid.*, p. 23, 17 May 1916. The arrangements were that W. van Erkal was appointed marine agent at Antwerp to take up the business when it was possible to return to the city, while, in the meantime, the Belgram Brothers in London agreed to credit a share of their risks to this non-operational agency. [43] Union Marine Directors' Minutes, vol. D, p. 49, 10 August 1914.

[44] See C. Trebilcock, 'Legends of the British Armaments Industry', *Journal of Contemporary History*, 5 (1970), pp. 3–19.

[45] Union Marine Directors' Minutes, vol. D, p. 48, 10 August 1914.

[46] Bleichroders traditionally had extremely close connections with the Imperial Government. See F. Stern, *Gold and Iron* (London, 1977). Under the terms of the treaty, the Nord Deutsche and the Nord West Deutsche offices, both of Hamburg, each received a

Marine's pre-war operations and measures well the heavy interdependence of the principal British and German marine insurers. Yet the Union Marine directors decided on 10 August 1914 that,

> as it is quite impossible to communicate with Germany during the war, or even to get into touch with the Head Offices of these companies . . . it is quite useless to attempt forwarding documents, and, of course, remitting or receiving money from them is equally out of the question.

By 5 October 1914, Union Marine had terminated all cargo reinsurance contracts for sailings after 31 December 1914.[47] The Union Marine Board, meeting on 10 August 1914, took a lot of hard decisions about the basis of wartime trading; but they were taken rapidly, within days of the declaration of war, and cleanly. In all of these cases, the battlelines were clear and Union Marine acted in accordance with them, however deep the disturbance to its business. Other cases were much less cut and dried. The really difficult issues involved governments and markets with particularly demanding criteria for what constituted a German company; or foreign agents in neutral markets with suspected, or real, German sympathies; or agents in neutral markets who proved, or were deemed, to be of German extraction. Such cases particularly excited the interest of the British government.

Its blacklists were certainly sufficiently demanding. Phoenix–Union Marine encountered difficulties on this score in at least four different markets: Norway, Spain, Cuba and the United States, of which the first and the last were important and valuable ones. In the cases of Norway and Spain, the problem arose because of the dealings or sympathies of Norwegian and Spanish agents. In Cuba and the United States, they stemmed from the presence of agents who were themselves of German extraction.

Spain presented the simplest issue. After a relatively quiet war, Union Marine's Spanish agent in 1918 suddenly broke into a correspondence actively attacking the United State's entry into the war. Unfortunately for him, he conducted it on Union Marine notepaper and the US Censor intercepted the results. This was clearly beyond the pale and the agency was abruptly cancelled.[48]

In Norway, by contrast, few things were clear. However, the value of business in a major seafaring nation, from which powerful German com-

10% share of the ceded Union Marine business, while 5% shares went to the Neptunus, the Hansa Allgemeine, the Albingia, and the Assecuranz Union, also all of Hamburg, and to the Deutsche Insurance of Bremen and the Agrippine of Cologne.

[47] Union Marine Directors' Minutes, vol. D, p. 49, 10 August 1914.

[48] Phoenix Marine Committee, Book 1, p. 155, 31 July 1918.

petitors had vanished, was obvious enough. Sandeman Allen reported on this phenomenon early in the war and opined that Phoenix–Union Marine should be able to develop its Norwegian business strongly in both war risks and ordinary lines.[49] However, The Board of Trade had reservations about the company's Norwegian operation: the officials objected to Union Marine's agent in Christiania, P. Th. Duborg & Co., on the grounds of a dubious but unclear German connection. In view of the value of the market and the power of Duborgs as representatives, Phoenix took the government's threat to a potentially lucrative trade very seriously. Allen's deputy, John Ferguson[50] was sent to Christiania to ensure that arrangements there did indeed conform with His Majesty's Government's requirements, and one of the Duborg partners was hauled across the North Sea for a thorough grilling at Head Office.[51] Ferguson found nothing out of the way and the Duborg man denied that there was any foundation to the allegations made by the British government.

However, this did not satisfy the Board of Trade. Early in 1916, the Admiralty seized a number of bordereaux regarding Phoenix reinsurances with Duborg and requested that the business be discontinued. Union Marine was forced to open up direct dealings with Norwegian companies and to transfer its claims agency into other hands, while all accounts with Duborg were cancelled.[52]

Yet the government itself vacillated in its blackballing of Duborgs. For, in May 1916, the Foreign Trade Department changed tack and removed all restrictions on the Norwegian agents. Thankfully, Union Marine resumed contact and restarted trade. But, astonishingly, the company's relief proved premature. By September 1916, Royden reported to the Marine Committee that Duborgs had once again been placed on a secret government blacklist. By the end of September Phoenix–Union Marine had to repudiate Duborgs for a *second* time. A temporary agent was appointed in Christiania in their stead.[53]

This episode is striking in a number of aspects. It occupies a great deal of space in Phoenix–Union Marine's wartime minutes and reports; the company clearly considered it important. Further, they went to extraordinary lengths to satisfy the government, even when official requirements appeared tergiversatory or even whimsical. Communication with govern-

[49] Union Marine General Manager's Report, 5 October 1914.

[50] This Ferguson succeeded Sandeman Allen as marine manager 1920–2 and should not be confused with Edward Ferguson, successor to Ryan and Sketch as Phoenix general manager (see below). The latter was on war service in Egypt at this time.

[51] Union Marine General Manager's Report, 7 September 1915.

[52] Phoenix Marine Committee, Book 1, p. 10, 8 March 1916; *ibid.*, p. 13, 22 March 1916.

[53] *Ibid.*, p. 22, 3 May 1916; *ibid.*, p. 47, 13 September 1916; *ibid.*, p. 49, 27 September 1916.

ment departments was, by pre-war standards, remarkably direct and frequent. But most arresting of all is the extent and force of Board of Trade interference. No direct allegations against Duborg were ever made or substantiated in written form. Yet a major corporate insurer was made to cancel business dealings with an agency in a friendly state, effectively at the behest of the varying currents in bureaucratic sentiment or, perhaps, military intelligence.

By comparison, the official position in the Cuban affair was explicit, and Phoenix reacted immediately to the government's lead. Phoenix's marine agent in Havana was a German and the Foreign Office misliked this. The diplomats requested that he be replaced with a British representative and the British minister at Havana was able to recommend one. Phoenix simply accepted the suggestion.[54] Yet, in 1917, the Foreign Trade Department still complained to Phoenix that the Marine Committee had not cut all links with the celebrated Havana merchants, Upmann & Co., who had acted for the company in the years before the war.

Even more important to Phoenix–Union Marine, and even less escapable, was governmental pressure upon their arrangements for marine trade in the United States and Canada. This was a vital regional market for Union Marine and was given much attention – with frequent transatlantic trips by Sandeman Allen – upon Phoenix's absorption of Union Marine in 1911. Allen succeeded in setting up American trade for Phoenix–Union Marine upon a strong base, but at an unforeseen cost. At the time of the merger, the agents already acting for Union Marine in the United States were Messrs F. Herrmann & Co. of New York, a venture of German origin and strong German connection. In 1912, Allen travelled to New York to arrange for Herrmann to take over representation of all Phoenix–Union Marine marine business in the United States and Canada. It was hoped also that Phoenix and Herrmann could trade introductions for fire business. In August 1912, the Union Marine link and Union Marine's American subsidiaries secured Phoenix access to a US pool agreement for cargo business. But in this pool were not only the Firemen's Fund, with a 25% share, and the Phoenix–Union Marine–Columbia connection with 35%; the biggest participant, with 40%, was the ubiquitous Mannheim interest. Allen sailed to the United States twice more, in 1913 – when he found Herrmann acting also for the Nord Deutsche of Hamburg – and in 1914 before he was satisfied that the arrangements were suitable for a company of Phoenix's standing. By May 1914 he was confident that they were.[55]

[54] Union Marine General Manager's Reports, 5 October and 9 November 1914.
[55] *Ibid.*, 16 May 1914.

In commercial terms, no doubt he was correct. But, by August 1914, Phoenix–Union Marine was represented in New York by a joint office, containing the Firemen's Fund, the Mannheim group, and the Nord Deutsche, all under the management of Herrmann. In political terms, this did not inspire confidence; it was embarrassing. By 10 August 1914, Union Marine had recognised that the British government's Proclamation on Trading with the Enemy had made it necessary to reorganise their American commitments, 'as amicably as possible . . . with a view to the future of our business . . . due regard for our financial position . . . and our duties as British subjects'.[56] However, even this formulation suggested a *balance* of interests, among which the war was seen as one consideration, a temporary disruption requiring temporary adjustments. Some of these could be managed quickly. Within the month, marine representation for Canada had been transferred to Phoenix's long-standing connection for fire and life business with the Paterson organisation.[57] But there were no such easy alternatives in the United States, and Phoenix–Union Marine was not in a hurry to abandon Herrmann. At the end of August, cables were exchanged with the American agents confirming that favourable arrangements had been made for Phoenix–Union Marine to continue within the American cargo pool for the next season.

It was not until March 1915 that the Board of Trade wrote pointing out that this would not do.[58] The Union Marine Board sent Allen again to New York in May and June 1915 to scout for an alternative scheme. But the pace was not urgent and the British side was anxious for a friendly unravelling of the existing agreements. Upon his return from the United States, Sandeman Allen, together with Royden, saw Walter Runciman, the president of the Board of Trade, and received some reassurance that this approach was not inappropriate. For Runciman had 'stated that, unless some specific charge could be established against Mr Herrmann, we should probably hear nothing more in the matter'.[59] However, Phoenix–Union Marine did hear more: either the department proved more draconian than its minister or more information was laid against Herrmann. By late July, Phoenix–Union Marine had agreed to separate from Herrmann for the duration of the war and a power of attorney was generated permitting Percy Beresford,[60] at Pelican of New York, to take over all Phoenix–Union Marine marine business in the United States.[61]

[56] Union Marine Directors' Minutes, vol. D, p. 49, 10 August 1914.
[57] *Ibid*, p. 50, 24 August 1914. [58] Board of Trade to Union Marine, 23 March 1915.
[59] Union Marine Directors' Minutes, vol. D, p. 62, 5 July 1915. [60] See above p. 286.
[61] Union Marine Directors' Minutes, vol. D, p. 63, 19 July 1915; Phoenix Directors' Minutes, 31, p. 261, 21 July 1915.

Nevertheless, this was still viewed as a stop-gap measure, and in September 1915 two partners in Herrmann & Co., who did not have German names,[62] travelled to Liverpool to discuss a friendly change in the basis of the agreement. However, they did not succeed in saving Herrmann's power of attorney which was revoked on 22 September 1915, more than a year after the declaration of war.

Up to this point, Phoenix–Union Marine had acted circumspectly and had tried to retain as much as possible of existing connections by a number of tactical adjustments. Beyond it, increasing pressure from the Board of Trade made clear that removing power of attorney from Herrmann and appointing temporary replacement agents was not sufficient. From September 1915 the Board pushed Phoenix–Union Marine to make an absolute break with Herrmann, and to this initiative the company had to react in a great hurry. The need for a formal break became insistent because the Board was able to charge, as it did not with Duborg in Norway, that Herrmann & Co., 'were actively supporting German interests'.[63] No doubt Herrmann's obvious affinity with Mannheim and Nord Deutsche made them more vulnerable than Duborgs. On 5 October, the Union Marine directors packed poor Sandeman Allen off to New York again, to find a more permanent solution than simply loading the work upon Percy Beresford. The next day, the Phoenix directors cancelled the Herrmann agency outright and voted Herrmanns $100,000 compensation.[64]

The more permanent solution engineered by Allen was born out of Liverpool rather than Hamburg. It came in the form of an agreement with Harry Keedwell Fowler, already the marine manager and underwriter in the United States for the Thames and Mersey and the Liverpool & London & Globe. Phoenix–Union Marine were brought within this operation by formal agreement on 8 December 1915 and Columbia tagged along in January 1916.[65] As America prepared to enter the war and put its own Trading with the Enemy Bill before Congress early in July 1917, the scope for German insurance operations in the United States narrowed rapidly and the scope for British operations commensurately widened. Accordingly, the Fowler stable was enlarged by the addition of the

[62] They were called Wall and Dean.

[63] Union Marine Directors' Minutes, vol. D, p. 66, 5 October 1915.

[64] Phoenix Directors' Minutes, 31, p. 288, 6 October 1915.

[65] Although Fowler had acted as agent for Phoenix–Union Marine from the point of rupture with Herrmann & Co. This arrangement stayed in place until 1924, when Phoenix–Union Marine recreated independent representation in the United States, with the appointment of W. C. Spelman as manager, Phoenix marine department, New York. *Ibid.*, 34, p. 350, 18 June 1924.

Norwich Union in August 1917. This new alliance, a fair substitute for the Herrmann cartel, gave a 40% share to Phoenix–Union Marine–Columbia, a further 40% to Thames and Mersey and Liverpool & London & Globe, 15% to Norwich Union and 5% to the North China.

Fowler in fact harboured more ambitious plans still. He had seen the danger of intensifying German marine competition in the spring of 1917 and then the opportunity created by the impending German retreat in the autumn.[66] His proposal was the same for either set of conditions: a 'British group', with himself acting as underwriter for a considerable combine, which would dig into the rich US market and prevent a recrudescence of German insurance power in the postwar period.[67] As a plan for bridging the war economy and aftermath phases, in one of the world's biggest marine arenas, this scheme seems to have possessed some merits. However, neither Phoenix nor Fowler's original Liverpudlian masters detected them. None of the three was willing to submerge direct representation in the anonymity of a 'British group'; and all of them seem to have distrusted Fowler's tendency to think in a radical way.[68] Anyway, little came of what may have been a bright idea.

The American ban on German insurers more or less concluded Phoenix's experience of the government-designed chicanes in its largest earning sector of wartime insurance. But not quite. The Russian provisional government had fallen to revolution in October 1917, some weeks before the US government threw German insurers out of America. Nevertheless, the repercussions lasted rather longer. Phoenix had worked for a considerable while with the Russian Salamander company, and in December 1917, two months into Bolshevik rule, was still trying to put its marine treaties on a more satisfactory footing.[69] Three months later, however, having seen the light, the office was 'trying to terminate, as expeditiously as possible, all marine treaties with Russian companies'.[70] The Phoenix chairman realised, accurately, that the events in Russia of October 1917 had created 'a social, economic and financial gap in the structure of the world', and the further Phoenix was away from it, the better.[71]

But even the occasion on which Hamilton offered these comments (his annual report for 1918), had been delayed by another direct consequence of the war. This happening was an unpleasant reminder both of the

[66] The US government instructed all insurance companies owned by German or Central Power interests to liquidate their affairs and quit the United States on 5 December 1917. There was a stay of execution for life assurers.

[67] Fowler to Phoenix Marine Committee, 2 March 1917.

[68] Phoenix Marine Committee, Book 1, p. 96, 15 August 1917.

[69] *Ibid.*, p. 114, 5 December 1917. [70] *Ibid.*, p. 130, 27 February 1918.

[71] Phoenix Chairman's Annual Report, 21 June 1918.

importance of the American market and of the vulnerability of marine insurance. En route from New York to London, the Phoenix US accounts for 1917 were lost to enemy action; as Hamilton put it, 'they were in the sea, when they ought to have been in the hands of our auditors'.[72] Although marine profits for corporate insurers remained substantial into 1918, there could have been few more graphic illustrations of the risks that underlay them.

Apart from size and profitability, the outstanding feature of marine business during the First World War is the dominant influence upon the corporate insurers of government policy. The degree of control achieved by the officials over the business connections of British capitalists was remarkable. The contrast between the Board of Trade's ability to sway Phoenix in regard to the Herrmann case, or even more in regard to the Duborg case, where its evidence was much slighter, and the German government's inability to prevent even the export of such a strategic commodity as steel plate provides a striking summary of two very different types of war economy.[73] That of the liberal democracy was by far the more authoritarian, and Phoenix had its taste of this unusual truth.

It is not surprising even in this context that it took until late 1915 to unravel Phoenix's links with German marine insurers in the best markets. Consider an industrial parallel. Before 1914, German interests had been even more dominant in the international chemical trade than in the international business of marine insurance, and Anglo-German connections were at least as dense here, and in a sector quite as closely related to the war effort. The complicated cross-shareholdings and technological flows of the Anglo-German Nobel Dynamite Trust were not disentangled, despite strenuous efforts, until September 1915 and only then were 'its former subsidiaries in Glasgow and Hamburg... free to go their separate ways'.[74] Germany and Britain were the two strongest economies in Europe in 1914, and the Continental economic system had developed powerfully since 1890. It was natural that the most sophisticated service and manufacturing industries in the biggest economies should have ramified and inter-woven outside national boundaries. Unthreading them was not easy and took time.

[72] *Ibid.*

[73] On the many shortcomings of the German war economy, see G. D. Feldman, *Army, Industry and Labour in Germany, 1914–18* (Princeton, 1966).

[74] W. J. Reader, *Imperial Chemical Industries, A History*. Vol. I: *The Forerunners, 1870–1926* (Oxford, 1970), pp. 307–9.

3. FIRE AND DESTRUCTION: FOREIGN BUSINESS, HOME FRONT AND AIR RAIDS IN THE FIRST WORLD WAR

At first sight a war ought to offer no more promising prospects for fire insurance than for life business. However, the First World War and Phoenix possessed special characteristics which certainly did not make 1914–18 a particularly difficult time for the company's oldest line of trade. Wartime inflation pushed up the values which needed to be insured. Of course, it also pushed up the cost of restoring fire damage, but, if the loss ratio could be controlled, there were gains to be had. Then again, despite some initial fears, the home front in the First World War, in striking contrast to its vulnerability in the Second World War, proved a fairly safe place to be.

By the late 1930s, the bombers would get through, and if not always, as some argued, at least often enough to turn significant proportions of the home front into flame and rubble and significant numbers of its civilian population into wartime casualties. But the Zeppelins of 1914 were not the Dorniers and Heinkels of 1940 and the craters left by their bombs were, relatively speaking, few and far between. The big guns of the Imperial German navy were another matter, but, for the most part, with the odd terrifying exception, they remained well out to sea or locked up in port. Finally, Phoenix's global diversification in fire business generated some advantages in wartime. In particular, the American market came in handy during this period. It had caused problems in the 1900s, both before and after the San Francisco earthquake, but the careful work carried out at that time yielded benefits in the late 1910s. America would be a problem again in the disturbed economic conditions of the interwar years, but it offered Phoenix some timely compensation during the great European war.

Of course, there were some major disruptions. German offices had supplied important reinsurance services for Phoenix's fire business, and, as in the marine sector, these had to go. But, in an area of less strategic significance, the company did not come under such overt government pressure. The Board decided in October 1914 to terminate its treaties with German companies and 'to obtain other companies in place of these'; but even then, it was able to give six months' notice.[75]

Fire prospects in the last phases of peace had not looked particularly attractive for Phoenix. In 1913, more business had been won at home and in most foreign places than for several years, but the medicine applied to the US market had produced, in the short term, a reduction in premium

[75] Directors' Minutes, 31, p. 112, 14 October 1914.

income. Overall loss ratios were satisfactorily stable but expenses were still rising and both taxation and competition levels in foreign markets indicated that the trend was set to continue. If anything, 1914, Phoenix's last year in its Lombard Street office, looked worse. A corner was turned right in the middle of the war. It was in 1916 that the company's leaders noticed a change. Although fire premiums had expanded modestly, the trading profit had touched the 'highly satisfactory ratio' of 10% of premiums, better than in any year since 1910.[76] In 1916 also, 'contrary to recent experience' the US operation turned in a favourable performance, attributed by Hamilton to the 'special and increasing attention' which the management had lavished on this market over the preceding decade. The American out-turn was the main influence behind a surge of £75,000 in total fire premium, and the lowest loss ratio since 1907. It was this premium surge which allowed the Fire Reserve to wind up to the £2 million mark.[77] The next year saw a substantial increase in fire profit – by £41,000 to £176,000 – and a further fall in the loss ratio to 47.6%. This was attributed to the inflationary pressure on insured values and the fact that Phoenix had been untouched by a great wartime disaster – the huge fire at Salonika in 1917 – which hurt many insurers.

The Salonika catastrophe was an indirect – or, if conspiracy theories are credited, a direct – effect of war. Salonika was the headquarters of the Allies' Balkan campaign which was launched at the end of 1915, and, after a long grind, eventually produced a successful advance. The city suffered a severe conflagration on Saturday 18 August 1917. The conspiracy theory holds that it was the work of enemy agents; but this has never been substantiated. A more likely explanation is the 'one-damn-thing-after-another' factor which bedevils any large-scale military operation. In normal times, the Salonika water supply would have been sufficient to put the fire out. But not with British and French troops billeted en masse within the city; their requirements had consumed the margin needed for fire-fighting. And, on a sweltering day, the sirocco ripped the flames through a square mile of the native and commercial quarters in a matter of hours. The total loss was over £4 million, with half of that amount falling on British offices, and more than a quarter upon the North British. Phoenix was exceedingly fortunate not to be involved.[78]

The final phase of the war brought the lowest loss ratio and the highest profit in fire business for many years. The higher level of business was

[76] Chairman's Annual Report, 19 April 1916. [77] *Ibid.*, 25 April 1917.

[78] Liveing, *Commercial Union Insurance* pp. 272–3: H. Collinson Owen, *Salonika and After* (London, 1919), pp. 90–104. To the chagrin of this resident newspaperman, the fire claimed the English Club and the Hotel Splendide.

Table 6.6. *Phoenix Assurance: fire loss ratios and underwriting profit, 1913–18*

Year	Loss ratio %	Underwriting profit
1913	–	9.1
1914	56.1	4.9
1915	50.1	10.2
1916	48.9	8.8
1917	47.6	10.3
1918	44.6	12.3

attributable largely to price movement rather than to any special success in selling for, as Hamilton pointed out, 'the war had usurped . . . the services of many of our propagandists'.[79] However, a good part of the improvement came from adjustments to the Phoenix's US operation, and these did have real substance. Lord George was proud that, 'by incessant work and supervision, our operating machinery there has been improved, and the good return of the past two years is not, in my opinion, an evanescent gain'.[80]

Improvements in the United States were largely to thank for the decline in the company's fire expense ratio from an average of around 39% of premiums for the period 1913–16 to 37.4% in 1918. Gains in organisational efficiency, through improved selection of risk, also probably in foreign markets, may again help to explain the sharp fall in fire loss rates 1914–18 (see Table 6.6). Under the influence of these two pressures, underwriting profits as a percentage of premium income improved substantially on their peacetime levels.[81]

As part of the general tightening and tidying of fire business which these advances allowed, the fire reserve for unexpired risk was also taken in hand during the war. Previously, it had been kept at a level of £650,000 and topped up to this figure whenever necessary. It was in 1917 that it was established at the conventional modern ratio of 40% of premium income. This reform had the effect of raising the reserve to £684,000 in 1917 and to £798,000 in 1918. It is definitely paradoxical that Phoenix's fire busi-

[79] Chairman's Annual Report, *The Times*, 1 May 1919. [80] *Ibid.*

[81] As Phoenix was lucky in Salonika, so too it took only light losses in a transatlantic disaster of 1917: yet another devastation of Halifax, Nova Scotia. Phoenix lost only £13,000, but, because of its connection with the Acadia Co., donated a further 1,000 guineas to the Canadian Relief Fund (Directors' Minutes, 32, p. 183, 12 December 1917).

Plate 6.1 The shelling of Whitby Abbey.

ness should have become safer and better defended in the middle of major war; but that was the outcome.

A possible heavy threat to this security never materialised in this war. Aerial or long-range bombardment could rain fire and destruction from the heavens; but, by and large, it did so only rarely. On 16 December 1914, a German cruiser force shelled the Hartlepools, Whitby and Scarborough, wreaking considerable devastation and leaving 137 dead and 592 injured. In spring 1915, the much-feared Zeppelin attacks began. On 31 May ninety bombs were dropped on London causing twenty-four fatalities, and there were further serious raids in June and October. Air attacks intensified in 1917, reaching a peak on 13 June when 162 died and 432 were injured. In the period between January 1915 and June 1918, mainland Britain suffered fifty-one Zeppelin attacks, which caused 1,913 casualties, and fifty-seven attacks by winged aircraft, which caused 2,907 casualties.

The total civilian death toll from air bombing in the First World War for the whole of the United Kingdom was 1,413 lives.[82] In London the bombs of 1914–18 claimed some 500 lives, about the same number as

[82] A. Marwick, *The Deluge* (2nd edn, Basingstoke, 1991).

those lost to aerial bombardment in the apparently more vulnerable city of Paris. By contrast, in the terrible months of September, October and November 1940 the London region alone suffered the loss of 13,000 civilian lives and 20,000 injuries. The German airforce of the First World War did not lack teeth, but they did not compare with the fangs of 1940.

However, they were quite sharp enough to raise fears about the insurance of property from air attack. Accurate prediction of the level of threat from the air proved difficult. Some believed that the technology of 1914 was capable of mounting a blitz of near 1940 proportions. The fire manager of the REA envisaged craft which 'travel so quickly that a few of them might drop bombs charged with inflammable materials into more than one congested area . . . we can hardly say what the limit of possible destruction may be'.[83] Generally, opinion among financiers and insurers was cooler and nearer the mark.

The government's Aircraft Insurance Committee, briefed with investigating a method of securing property against such attacks, reported on 9 July 1915 that it was not

> practicable to fix rates which would cover the State against loss in the event of raids by hostile aircraft, resulting in a series of general conflagrations in congested areas. The possibility of any raid having such serious results is a matter on which we can form no opinion and it is a risk which we think the State must be prepared to accept.[84]

This Committee aimed for a level of premiums which would 'cover the cost of sporadic raids of the kind already experienced'. They did not hope to cover the losses which might arise from a mass raid by an air armada. They found it 'impossible to estimate the probability of such an event';[85] but they clearly did not believe it high.

Nevertheless, it was the big raid on London on 31 May 1915 and the repeated attacks a week later which lit public interest and spurred the government to rapid action. Where the naval bombardment of December 1914 was interpreted as an aberrational incursion, against which the Royal Navy would normally offer sufficient defence, the air attacks of early summer 1915 were seen to threaten more successful penetration and much greater expanses of the kingdom. The official committee to investigate anti-aircraft insurance had been appointed within a fortnight of the 7 June raid and had reported within hardly more than another fortnight, on 9 July 1915.

[83] Supple, *Royal Exchange Assurance*, cited p. 415.
[84] Report of the Aircraft Insurance Committee, (Cd. 7997, xxxvii, 1915) p. 3.
[85] *Ibid.*, p. 6.

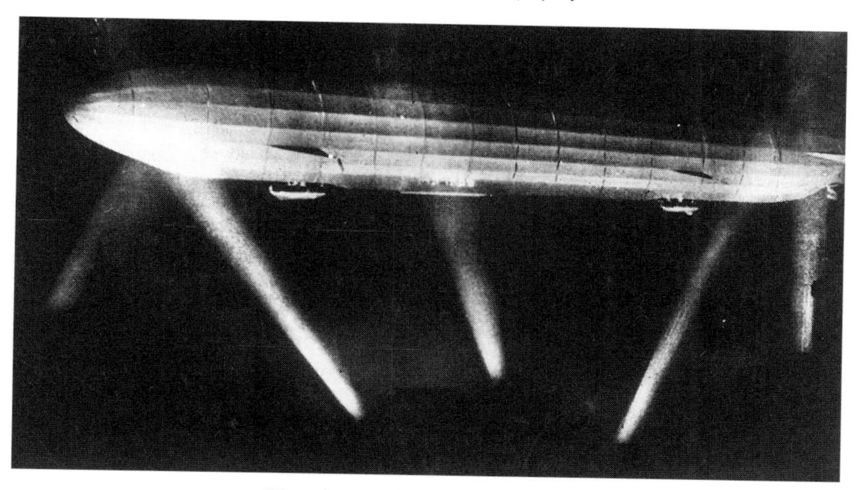

Plate 6.2 Zeppelin night attack.

Just four days after that report, the Board of Trade wrote to the offices asking them for their assistance in the running of a state insurance scheme against air and bombardment risks,

> If the Government is to establish an insurance scheme of this kind at all, it is essential that it should be established without delay, and it is hoped that if your Company are willing to co-operate with the Government in the matter, they will be able to arrange the scheme *to come into operation on Monday next, the 19 July.*[86]

The Board was much concerned that the reaction to public alarms should be handled with speed and simplicity. In this they were conspicuously successful. The rapidity with which a coordinated bureaucracy, with public alarm behind it, can operate in wartime is sometimes, as on this occasion, impressive.

The scheme offered by the Aircraft Insurance Committee proposed two kinds of insurance against aerial attack. One would cover property against damage caused by aircraft of any kind, including 'own goals' perpetrated by friendly aviators or falling shell fired at enemy ones. The second provided cover against all air risks *and* against bombardment by distant guns or other offshore engines of destruction such as submarines, torpedoes and drifting mines. Neither scheme offered protection from invasion or guns landed by an invading force. Both charged a flat rate.

The Committee had settled upon the dual policy strategy after considering carefully, but then rejecting, the possibility of identifying

[86] Board of Trade to Phoenix, 13 July 1915 (my emphasis).

graduated zones of danger in the United Kingdom, and matching the premiums to the danger level. They concluded that,

> although it might be possible to express the view that the East Coast of England was more liable to attack than the West Coast, we felt that any attempt at scientific 'zoning' was impracticable. On the other hand, it was felt that if a flat rate were fixed for the whole country at a figure which might be expected to cover loss from both air-craft [sic] and bombardment, it would deter a large number of people who considered themselves relatively immune from attack, from taking advantage of the scheme.[87]

Hence the canny notion of proposing both 'aircraft only' and 'aircraft plus bombardment' policies. Citizens in the more exposed areas could opt for the second while the more fortunately located could select the first.

The scheme would be wholly one of state insurance, with a panel of approved fire companies acting as agents for the government. Customers for the air-bombardment policies would be divided into those already holding fire policies with the approved companies; those holding fire policies with non-approved companies; or those with no fire polices at all. No approved company was allowed to accept air bombardment proposals from the fire clients of other approved companies. The air bombardment policies would only cover risks not covered by existing fire polices. The band of approved companies would take a 10% commission for collecting and operating costs. All premiums would be paid though to the state and it would pay all the losses. On these scores the Committee was moved by two clear principles. In contrast to the state's arrangements for maritime insurance, the participating companies were not permitted to accept aerial or bombardment risks on their own account: 'without this stipulation the Company would be free to retain the good risks and only give the State the bad risk'.[88]

However, a monopoly of bad risks was precisely what the state had accepted in the apparently related field of wartime insurance of shipping.[89] The divergence implies a different estimation of risks and demand side conditions. The worst risks in marine insurance were unacceptable to any commercial insurers but the demand for covering them had to be met in the national interest. On the other hand, the state did not wish to take on responsibility for the whole of the enormous maritime sector. The worst risks in the sector of air and artillery were not yet provenly so bad, and the state's role here was to bolster public confidence rather than to maintain a vital line of national supply. In these demand conditions there

[87] Report of Aircraft Insurance Committee, p. 7. [88] *Ibid.*, p. 4.
[89] See above, pp. 374–9.

was no clear reason why it should shoulder a disproportionate share of the bad business. Perhaps too, it, or its close advisers, had learned something from the way in which the risk differential had operated in marine business.

The second principle was that the state should create its own Insurance Office, to administer the scheme, as it had in the marine business with the War Risks Insurance Office. Although the first principle was firmly enacted, the second was not. Originally, the Committee had feared that those holding fire policies with Lloyds or non-approved companies would express 'considerable opposition' to a scheme requiring them to obtain war insurance through a restricted group of elite companies; therefore, they felt, a state office was needed to cater for this section of demand. In wartime, however, the Board of Trade was not minded to indulge such delicate market sensitivities. By 15 July, it had decided that 'if, as is hoped, the Government receives the cordial co-operation of the Fire Insurance Companies, the majority of the insurance effected under the scheme will be effected through the agency of the Fire Offices . . . it will not then be necessary to establish a special State Insurance Office'.[90] Instead it proposed to feed its premium and claims flows through the state insurance office it already had: the maritime War Risks Insurance Office would also handle all official transactions for air and bombardment insurance. Conveniently for Phoenix the War Risks Office was situated just down the street at 33–36 King William Street.

The links between conventional fire insurance and the air-bombardment insurance scheme were strong. Damage from bomb or shell was highly likely to involve fire and the need for additional protection grew in the first place out of the need to cover risks not normally covered in fire policies. The most common, and expected, transaction in this market was that a holder of a fire policy with an approved company would apply to the same company for a war-protection policy. The policy values employed under the air-bombardment scheme were then taken from the values given in the fire policies.[91] Within Phoenix, all air-bombardment work was directed by the fire manager, and all business on properties covered by both fire and air-bombardment was handled by the fire department. Such arrangements were typical of most offices.

Despite the fact that some companies had offered independent protection against air risks before 1915, and some, like the Hearts of Oak operating outside the state scheme, continued to do so after the

[90] Board of Trade to Phoenix, 15 July 1915.

[91] Where there was no fire valuation, the insurance was accepted at any value proposed by the insured.

government had organised most of the market, most FOC members preferred to avoid *direct* involvement in air business. Indeed, most had been hostile to this idea, even when a government guarantee against catastrophe had been floated in connection with it. The company view thus chimed well with the official argument that the companies should act as agents to a state scheme.[92] However, the big offices were anxious that in doing so, they should not act against the interests of their peers: hence the stipulation that an approved company should not accept air-bombardment proposals from the clients of another approved company. This restriction was seen as necessary for the maintenance of solidarity among the first–line insurers. It was not surprising that a high degree of convergence was achieved between these corporate preferences and the recommendations of the Committee of Aircraft Insurance. Of its five members, two were members of Lloyds, and one was a banker; but two came from the biggest corporate insurers. One was E. R. Owen from Commercial Union; the other was Gerald Ryan from Phoenix.

Nevertheless, not all insurers joined in this display of solidarity and other interests were served outside the state scheme. The Hearts of Oak, for instance, became somewhat of an independent specialist in air risks. It supplied a simple aircraft protection policy, but its air and bombardment option offered the additional enticement of invasion cover – possibly the most desperate and least reassuring of all insurance concepts – as well as a rather more sensible combination of aircraft and personal accident protection. Where its policies equated to those in the state scheme, it was consistently cheaper. This outcome also fitted well with the Committee's expectation that leaving a partial free market in existence would 'provide a very important [service] by affording facilities for insurance in the special cases for which no provision is made in this scheme and for tempering the rigid lines of a flat rate system'.[93]

Where the Committee had wanted the participation of as many approved companies as possible in order to spare the load on the State Air Insurance Office (which was never created), the companies wanted as many approved participants as possible in order to equalise the load of administration. The insurers expected the public response to be dramatic; and they were correct. But a good number of them did come forward to handle it: by 19 August 1915, there were fifty-six approved companies, by 7 July 1916 nearly eighty.

Among customers, the response was less uniform. Those who flocked to insure were the more substantial property-owners; the smaller fry were

92 Minutes of Emergency Sub-Committee, Fire Offices Committee, 2 July 1915.

93 Report of Aircraft Insurance Committee, p. 5.

ZEPPELIN & ACCIDENT
INSURANCE.

We have effected an Insurance Policy with
The Phœnix Assurance Co., Ltd.
Principal Office,
Phœnix House,
King William-st.,
London, E.C.

(To whom notice in case of injury must be given within 7 days after the accident, and in case of death within 14 days after the accident), which gives our readers the following benefits:—

ACCIDENT

£1,000 (or **£100** per annum for 15 years*) — to the legal personal representative of the bona fide holder of this Coupon-Insurance-Ticket if such holder shall be fatally injured by an accident within the United Kingdom to a passenger-train, passenger-steamer, public omnibus, tramcar, or cab (which is being driven by a licensed driver plying for public hire), in which such holder is at the time of such injury travelling as a ticket (or pass) bearing or fare-paying passenger, or will pay to such holder should such accident cause non-fatal injury to such holder:

£1,000 (or **£100** per ann. for 15 years*) — for the Loss of Two or more Limbs by actual separation at or above the wrist or ankle or of Both Eyes or the loss of One or more Limbs as above defined, accompanied by the Loss of One or Both Eyes; OR

£500 (or **£50** per annum for 15 years*) — for the Loss of One Limb as above defined or One Eye only; OR

£1 10s. per week. — during total disablement from earning a livelihood.

*If such holder shall so long live.

Provided that the above undertakings are subject to the further special conditions as published in "The Daily News" on Saturdays, which are of the essence of the contract.

AIRCRAFT & BOMBARDMENT

"The Daily News" will pay:—
£250 In the case of damage by Aerial Attack.
£25 in the case of damage by Bombardment from the sea or by our own anti-aircraft guns.

To obtain the above benefits the reader must order "The Daily News" from his Newsagent, and comply with the form of receipt as published on Saturdays.

A reader who has not complied with the conditions of the form of receipt, but who has prior to the accident written his usual signature in the space provided below, will be insured only for the Accident benefit for 24 hours (except in the case of Saturday's issue, which is available for 48 hours) from 6 a.m. on the day of issue, subject to the conditions appertaining to such insurance.

Signature ....

Postal Address ....

Plate 6.3 The Phoenix response.

less easily netted. In November 1915 the state did set more bait by offering low-cover policies, up to £75 in value, for sale through post offices. But the raids of 1917 proved this stratagem inadequate. In February of that year, the government introduced a 50% rates discount on the original measures of July 1915 which brought the minimum premium down to two shillings (buying cover on £200 worth of property).[94] No doubt this partly reflected low claim rates to this point; but it was also intended to catch the smaller householder. This again it apparently failed to do. Amidst the punishing raids of summer 1917, the mayor of Walsall reported that much damage had been done to uninsured property in the Midlands before it was realised that attack so far inland was a real threat.[95]

Reacting to the same series of attacks, Prime Minister Lloyd George replied to a delegation led by the Lord Mayor of London on 13 July 1917 that the government accepted the principle of *compensation* for uninsured property owners suffering loss by air raid. Consequently on 5 November 1917, measures were announced in parliament providing for the reimbursement of those whose uninsured property had been damaged by bombing. The compensation limit was £500 payable 'to persons the whole of whose property in the U.K. does not exceed £500 in value'. For those with more than this, the government would pay the first £500 without asking for a premium, provided that all property above £500 was insured under the state scheme. Phoenix advised all policy-holders to continue insuring for the full amount in order to retain a clear and unsullied contract with the government.[96] But the real purpose of the move was 'to give relief and protection to the poorest section of the community'.

For the offices, the working of air damage insurance was not simple. Although overall claims levels were not high, they were heavily concentrated in the periods after raids and individual attacks could produce disproportionate effects upon demand levels. In advance of the scheme's initial launch, Phoenix had written to its branches on 6 July 1915, 'The work will be quite simple, and relatively light . . . the numbers of proposals you may receive will, however, probably be considerable.'[97] But after a large raid, the workload was anything but light; it swamped local offices. The attack on Ramsgate on 17 June 1917 drew a letter from

[94] War Risks Insurance Office to Phoenix, 16 February 1917.

[95] *The Times*, 14 July 1917. The raids of 1917 changed perceptions in several ways. It was not until June 1917 that Phoenix decided to insure all its London officials against injury or death from air attack (Directors' Minutes, 32, p. 122, 27 June 1917).

[96] Circular to Agents, 21 November 1917.

[97] Circular to Branches, 6 July 1915.

agents of approved companies to the Fire Office Committee complaining that, with depleted and inexperienced staff, 'the additional work involved a very great strain'. Even as late as spring 1918 an escalation in metropolitan damage – this time the shelling of Paris by long-range German artillery – could generate a mass demand for the conversion of policies from 'air attack only' to 'air attack plus bombardment'. Such unpredictable peaks in demand were complicated by uncertainty about the need for policy renewals. These were always left until the last moment 'as a conclusion of the War at any date before December may render the process unnecessary'.[98]

The total demand which emerged from these and longer-term worries were considerable. The government's own estimate of 1919 put the premiums paid over the duration of the war at £13.6 million, while an independent assessment of 1938 put the total income of the scheme at £16.5 million.[99] The Aircraft Insurance Committee of 1915 estimated the total gross sum insured under fire policies in the United Kingdom, in summer 1915, at £6,000 million and the annual revenue from the fire premiums at £9 million.[100] The air-bombardment insurances had netted £13.6 million in premiums over the life of the scheme, suggesting an annual premium income of about £4 million. This implies that air-bombardment insurance in the First World War achieved a market which was not much smaller than a half of the total fire insurance market. Given that there must have remained significant tracts of the United Kingdom which were considered to be genuinely beyond the range of German bombs and shells, this is a remarkably high rate of coverage for a conflict in which, conventionally, the home front was not thought to be substantially at risk.

In terms of insurance outcome, however, if not of client perception, the convention proved correct: the loss ratio was notably low. Total claims, according to the 1919 official estimate, summed to nearly £3 million (22% of premiums), total expenses according to the 1938 calculation to £5.6 million (33.8% of premiums). Even allowing for the 10% commission paid to the approved companies (included in expenses), and the reduced premiums of 1917, the state made a handsome profit out of air-bombardment insurance. This offered at least some solace for the fortune paid out on marine losses.

Some time after the war, in 1925, the Phoenix management returned to

[98] Phoenix Internal Memorandum, March 1916.

[99] Government War Insurance Schemes, Preliminary Statement of Results (Cd. 98, xxxii, 1919); *The Review*, 3 April 1938.

[100] Report of Aircraft Insurance Committee, p. 6.

Plate 6.4 Zeppelin in retreat.

the air-bombardment issue and reviewed the wartime provisions. They congratulated themselves that direct payment of claims by the state in 1915–18 had 'opened the eyes of the public to the liberal treatment usually accorded by the Fire Offices and incidently proved a good argument against state insurance'.[101] Perhaps they were reflecting upon the official reaction to the severe raid on Great Yarmouth in November 1917, when the War Risks Insurance Office, faced with heavy total losses, sent in inspectors to investigate 'whether any special reasons exist for greater liability of buildings in Great Yarmouth and district than in other East Coast Towns, to damage from concussion, such as the nature of construction of the buildings or the nature of the ground on which they are built'.[102] In looking back, Phoenix could disapprove of the state's niggardly way with claims. In looking forward, the office expected a much bigger demand for insurance against air attack in any future war. Even in 1925 public fears of the consequences of air raids were reckoned to be much higher than ten years before. Phoenix calculated that an air insurance scheme would draw £7 million in premiums in the first year of any new war. On the other hand, the managers believed that bombardment rates

[101] Phoenix Notes on Insurance against Air Attacks, March 1925.
[102] War Risks Insurance Office to Phoenix, 22 November 1917.

could probably be much reduced 'as there is not likely to be any strong European Navy in the near future'. Admiral Doenitz's submarines and battle cruisers would in time dispose of that notion, but once again, in the Second World War, the German navy would do little damage to property on the mainland. In the second great conflict that could safely be left to the Luftwaffe. Independent assessors, like the Phoenix managers, foresaw this. *The Review* of April 1938 chose a timely moment to reflect on the air-bombardment insurances of the First World War and concluded that they succeeded because defence proved superior to attack; but also that such profits would not be made again.[103] That journal article was among the papers found by another set of Phoenix fire officials when, in July 1939, they called for the file containing the résumé of the First World War scheme. With the Heinkels and Dorniers of the late 1930s in their minds, they re-read the accounts of the damage wreaked by the Zeppelins and Fokkers of the 1910s.

4. LIFE ASSURANCE AND WAR MORTALITY, 1914–1918

Warfare is scarcely favourable to the cause of life assurance. The most obvious reason is that warfare kills people. A less obvious one is that in war the age structure of death changes: mortality swings away from its usual concentration on the very young and the elderly towards the military-age groups which, in normal times, are most resistant to it. In itself, this destroys the established patterns from which the actuaries predict the likely incidence of death. But war also brings inflation, falling investment markets and soaring taxation. For life companies, these are almost as damaging as the operations of the Grim Reaper, and in some ways and cases, perhaps more so. Premium increases may not match price increases and so earnings will deteriorate in real terms. Valuations of life funds will be depressed as stocks depreciate. Already straitened profits will be squeezed by the taxman's insistent demands for more war finance.

For all these reasons, and more, it is orthodoxy that the Great War was a gruelling time for the life companies. Thus, Supple writes of offices having to maintain assurance liability on pre-war policies, which had been issued 'free and unconditional' on civilians, and then bear the losses on soldierly deaths as these civilians donned khaki. Life cover had to continue 'in the midst of a holocaust whose terrible dimensions exceeded the worst imaginings of actuary or policy-holder a mere

[103] *The Review*, 8 April 1938.

Table 6.7. *The life assurance market, 1914–1918: The twenty biggest companies*

1 Company	2 Renewal premium. 1914	Rank	3 % all companies' renewal premium	4 Renewal premium 1918	Rank	5 % all companies' renewal premium	6 Sum assured 1914	Rank	7 Sum assured 1918	Rank	8 4 as % of 2	9 7 as % of 6	10 Av. policy value 1914	11 Av. policy value 1918
Prudential	425,717	(1)	16.7	1,293,182	(1)	29.2	6,849,224	(1)	13,846,213	(1)	304	202	96	164
NU Life	206,970	(2)	8.1	163,291	(4)	3.7	5,356,785	(2)	4,259,470	(3)	79	80	459	540
Refuge	198,035	(3)	7.7	265,031	(3)	6.0	3,353,006	(3)	3,663,588	(4)	134	109	60	96
Scottish Wid.	127,629	(4)	5.0	78,960	(6)	1.8	3,223,937	(4)	1,729,349	(6)	62	54	563	659
L & G	108,263	(5)	4.2	107,353	(5)	2.4	2,744,070	(5)	2,055,552	(5)	99	73	514	527
Pearl	104,066	(6)	4.1	472,794	(2)	10.7	2,331,261	(6)	5,733,183	(2)	454	246	83	130
Sun Life	98,590	(7)	3.9	74,087	(8)	1.7	2,603,454	(7)	1,673,093	(8)	75	64	361	602
NBM	96,131	(8)	3.8	76,727	(7)	1.7	2,528,596	(8)	1,680,991	(7)	80	76	537	550
Standard	84,760	(9)	3.3	63,227	(11)	1.4	2,189,323	(10)	1,170,406	(13)	75	47	545	616
CU	70,842	(10)	2.8	57,941	(13)	1.3	2,349,388	(9)	1,607,769	(9)	82	68	520	569
Alliance	65,763	(11)	2.6	42,514	(16)	1.0	1,798,087	(11)	948,386	(16)	65	53	656	732
Royal	62,756	(12)	2.5	68,474	(9)	1.5	1,753,891	(12)	1,547,536	(10)	109	91	468	613
Scottish Prov.	56,086	(13)	2.2	59,000	(12)	1.3	1,652,235	(13)	1,300,209	(12)	105	79	648	857
UK Temp.	54,765	(14)	2.1	42,114	(18)	1.0	1,426,284	(14)	1,001,655	(15)	77	70	370	439
Phoenix	48,086	(15)	1.9	66,550	(10)	1.5	1,356,053	(15)	1,420,418	(11)	138	105	690	709
Wesleyan & General	39,039	(16)	1.5	24,181	(26)	0.5	663,027	(20)	355,938	(20)	62	54	47	90
Law Union & Rock	35,826	(17)	1.4	41,105	(19)	0.9	1,076,404	(16)	1,057,084	(14)	114	98	454	555
REA	31,784	(18)	1.2	40,240	(20)	0.9	990,752	(17)	806,388	(17)	127	81	439	589
Scottish Amic.	30,432	(19)	1.2	42,245	(17)	1.0	897,435	(18)	728,377	(18)	139	81	591	777
National Prov.	29,340	(20)	1.2	29,977	(24)	0.7	714,175	(19)	603,983	(19)	102	85	407	563

Sources: Insurance Directory, Reference and Year Book 1916 and 1920; Parliamentary Papers 1914, lxxiv, Summary of New Life Assurance.

generation before'.[104] The additional death strain falling upon the assurers as the result of war-generated mortality cost them about £13.6 million.

Certainly, too, at the start of the war, the life offices *thought* that they were facing crisis. They were alarmed that there could be a sudden onslaught of mortality or a catastrophic loss of financial confidence; and the Life Offices Association actually approached the Treasury in search of support for policy loans and surrender values, 'should any undue demand arise'. They also sought, and achieved one year's postponement of the government's requirement for the companies to submit regular balance sheets and valuations.[105]

What is not generally recognised, however, is that the life offices reacted to the stresses of war, as they developed, in very different ways and experienced exceptionally divergent fortunes. Phoenix, in fact, fared among the best of all and notably improved its standing among the top twenty life insurers (see Table 6.7).

Despite the boost given to capacity by the acquisition of Law Life in 1910, the company's life performance in the period immediately before the war was a little suppressed. Phoenix's total number of policies declined for both home and foreign business between 1911 and 1914, and in both markets underperformed the industrial standard. The effect was less obvious in total sums assured or premium income but neither of these was buoyant and the Phoenix trend was again weaker than the average for all companies.[106] The out-turn in wartime was much stronger. In both sums assured and premium income, Phoenix matched or out-performed the industrial standard in three years out of five on British policies, and in four years out of five on policies outside the United Kingdom (see Table 6.8 and compare Table 6.7).

[104] Supple, *Royal Exchange Assurance*, p. 417. These pre-war policies included no provision for raising premiums in the event of war. Moreover in 1914, the Life Offices Association agreed to charge no additional premium on territorials or volunteers who joined the colours. Industrial life companies which had not issued unconditional policies nevertheless decided to impose no war surcharge on policies issued before 4 August 1914. Before 1914, regular soldiers and sailors had paid a moderate annual supplement above normal rates, and these policies did allow some room for wartime increases. Accordingly, on the outbreak of war, their rates were raised to 5 guineas per £100 for combatants and 3 guineas for non-combatants. For new policies, there were huge increases, to 7 guineas per £100 for combatants and 5 guineas for non-combatants. But it was widely believed that no increase in rates could cover the spiralling increase in risk. See also S. O. Warner, 'The Effect on British Life Assurance of the European War', in Hill (ed.), *War and Insurance*, pp. 101–68. [105] Directors' Minutes, 31, p. 92, 26 August 1914.

[106] Although new net life assurances in 1913 were bigger than ever before and were met with 'unqualified satisfaction' by Hamilton in his Chairman's Annual Report of 29 April 1914. So Phoenix's superior wartime results did not lack a foundation.

Table 6.8 *Policy numbers, sums assured and yearly premiums: Phoenix and all companies, 1911–18 (index numbers)*

a) *Assurances within the United Kingdom*

	No. of policies		Sums assured		Yearly premiums	
	All companies	Phoenix	All companies	Phoenix	All companies	Phoenix
1911	100	100	100	100	100	100
1912	107	96	106	102	108	101
1913	124	91	119	115	124	116
1914	107	92	106	106	114	125
1915	99	67	88	72	105	92
1916	83	67	88	90	105	116
1917	105	121	104	108	142	169
1918	121	97	136	128	208	168

b) *Assurances outside the United Kingdom*

	No. of policies		Sums assured		Yearly premiums	
	All companies	Phoenix	All companies	Phoenix	All companies	Phoenix
1911	100	100	100	100	100	100
1912	98	91	100	101	101	96
1913	103	82	105	93	104	88
1914	86	65	87	90	82	83
1915	50	54	53	63	49	60
1916	48	52	52	56	51	58
1917	45	32	54	32	52	37
1918	51	46	66	70	87	100

Sources: For all companies, see Warner, 'The Effect on British Life Assurance of the European War', p. 125; for Phoenix, Annual Reports.

In underwriting terms, war hit the insurers by deterring new business, damaging foreign markets and increasing 'death strain'. From the client's perspective, the uncertainties of war discouraged the assumption of new obligations; unless, of course, the client was a combatant, in which case he would encounter the assurer's wariness of extending cover to men on active service. Falling real incomes in the first half of the war also argued against the commencement of new policies. On the other hand, for those whose resources were relatively little affected by current price trends, war offered new investment prospects – such as War Loan – which competed with investment products. Life business overseas, of course, was directly damaged by enemy operations as communications were disrupted, agents lost or withdrawn and local competition left to run free. And death strain was all too evident in the sorry roll-calls of the Marne, Ypres, the Somme, Passchendaele and the rest.

Phoenix experienced its fair share of most of these effects. The company certainly felt the downward pressure on new policies which was common to all offices. Like all assurers with substantial overseas commitments, the Phoenix experienced trouble. The impact of war upon the export of life assurance is vividly seen in Table 6.8. True to its international traditions as a fire insurer, and indeed to the Pelican's long-standing commitments to the global trade, Phoenix's assurance dealings of the 1910s inclined more heavily than was usual for a United Kingdom company towards the foreign market. Where the company held 1.9% of the sums assured by all British offices on lives within the United Kingdom in 1914, its share of the sums assured on lives outside the United Kingdom was 3.4%. In wartime the company suffered for this. Where Phoenix's lowest value of sums assured on UK lives during the 1914–18 conflict, measured against a base of 100 in 1911, was 72 in 1915, the matching nadir on non-UK lives was a paltry 32 in 1917 (see Table 6.8). Yet, on the other hand, direct war mortality treated Phoenix relatively gently (see Table 6.9).

Table 6.9. *Phoenix Assurance: all death claims and war death claims, 1915–18*

Year	(1) All death claims	(2) War death claims	(2) as % of (1)
1915	698,570	63,777	9.1
1916	641,692	91,718	14.3
1917	631,756	70,530	11.2
1918	562,893	62,565	11.1

The personal tragedies represented by an average annual increase in mortality of around 11% were many and various, but, in underwriting terms, this was a burden which Phoenix did not find it difficult to absorb. By the end of 1917, the worst that Hamilton had to report was that death claims arising from hostilities had wiped out the profit that could normally be expected from 'favourable' mortality. That is, to this point, the deaths from the trenches, for Phoenix, constituted no more than the difference between conservative actuarial prediction for all deaths in normal peacetime and the average annual *outcome* for all deaths in normal peacetime, the outcome being usually a good deal better than the prediction. The Quinquennial Valuation of 1920 attributed £172,000 specifically to deaths in action in the calendar years 1916–20, of which £120,000 represented a loss on predicted mortality. But this was scarcely more than a third of the damage done to Phoenix's life business by stock market losses over the same period.[107]

This underwriting result seems to have been achieved by a selective policy of acceptances. Realising that strict actuarial assessment of new risks in wartime would have produced prohibitive rates, Phoenix introduced instead a system for automatically limiting the total volume of sums assured for the duration of the war. This method of rationing proved successful in controlling the level of total claims. Here, there is a clear contrast between Phoenix and many other assurers, for whom the life specialist, Standard Assurance, must stand as representative (see Table 6.10).

Standard suffered significantly more throughout, especially in the early stages of the conflict, and matched Phoenix only once, surpassing the non-specialist not at all.

Comparative figures of wider sweep also place Phoenix in a prominent position as a wartime insurer of lives (see Table 6.7). Only half of the top twenty life assurers, and only four of the top ten, ranked by renewal premiums, managed to increase this vital flow of income in the period 1914–18; and Phoenix was one of these. Only four of the top twenty managed to raise the aggregate of sums assured over the war period; and Phoenix was one of these. Only two of the twenty succeeded in improving their ranking as to renewal premiums by four or more places: the Pearl which rose from 6th to 2nd and Phoenix which moved from 15th to 10th. And the same two were the only ones to improve rankings in respect of total sums assured by four or more places: the Pearl again from 6th to 2nd and the Phoenix this time from 15th to 11th.

The total life market expanded during the war, but in no simple manner. Between 1914 and 1918, the total yearly renewal premiums of all offices increased in value by 74%,[108] but the number of policies issued rose by only 10% and the total sums assured by 22%. This suggests that the increase in premiums necessary to meet war conditions was considerable. However, the Phoenix policy of underwriting effectively through

[107] See below, pp. 412–14. [108] But this hardly matched inflation.

Table 6.10. *Relative claims levels, 1914–18: Phoenix Assurance and Standard Assurance (1910=100)*

Year	Phoenix	Standard
1914	104	112
1915	116	123
1916	107	115
1917	105	105
1918	94	98

Sources: For Standard, J. Butt, 'Life Assurance in War and Depression: the Standard Life Assurance Co. and its Environment, 1914–39', in Westall (ed.), *The Historian and the Business of Insurance*, pp. 155–72. For Phoenix, Annual Reports.

self-constraint shows up strongly against these trends, for Phoenix's renewal premiums rose by 38.4%, its total policy numbers by 2% and its sums assured by 5%.

Almost all companies suffered reductions of market share, measured by proportion of total renewal premiums, during the war; the only exceptions were the Prudential and the Pearl which expanded their market share, in the first case, quite massively from 16.7% to 29.2%, in the second case from 4.1% to 10.7%. It is notable that the three market leaders of 1918 displayed three out of the four lowest average policy values. Quite clearly, the 'industrial' assurance offices significantly tightened their hold on the market during the war, at the expense of almost all other offices.

The implication is that the big 'industrial' companies soaked up the major part of the new low-value policies that the men of Kitchener's New Armies and their families wanted. For Phoenix to have matched in its improvement of rankings the fastest rising of these 'industrial' offices, the Pearl, was an extraordinary achievement for a traditional office at the other end of the range in average policy value.

Within this bracket, high average policy values were certainly not a universal recipe for success and were associated with very divergent fortunes. Four companies offering policies at an average value of above £600[109] suffered declines in their renewal rankings (Scottish Widows',

[109] However, with retail prices moving from 100 in 1913 to 204.3 in 1918, a high value policy of £600 was certainly less high in 1918 than in 1913.

Sun Life, Standard and Alliance), while four enjoyed improvements (Royal, Scottish Provident, Scottish Amicable, and Phoenix). The oddity is that all those which suffered declines in ranking had been among the very biggest offices of 1914, while all those who did well in wartime with high policy values came from the bottom half of the 1914 rankings.

Also striking is the major change in the overall shape of the life market which occurred during the First World War. The Prudential's dominance of renewal business, which was big enough in 1914, was almost doubled by 1918. At each end of the war, it was flanked by a pair of lesser, but formidable, competitors: the Refuge and the Norwich Union Life in 1914, the Refuge and the Pearl in 1918. In 1914, however, there was a clear second division of six offices controlling market shares of between 3.3% and 5.0% and distinguished from a third division of eleven companies with shares between 1.2% and 2.8%. By 1918, this distinction had almost disappeared. The second division had shrunk to a club of two, Norwich Union Life and Legal & General, and *all* other companies were covered by market shares of just 0.7–1.8%. The huge ascendancy of the 'industrials', which the war period had witnessed, had flattened the market for almost all other operators.

But by no means all 'industrial' companies prospered. Those which achieved the largest increases in renewal premiums were the very largest, the Prudential (204%) and the Pearl (354%), and the very smallest, the Cooperative (667%) and the City Life (323%). All of these also showed considerable increases in sums assured between 1914 and 1918. The implication is that they were varying their business by offering a range of policies and terms to meet the war conditions. In particular, the Prudential and Pearl were by 1918 at the very top of the range of average annual premiums per policy for the 'industrial' group and much further away from the middle of this price spread than they had been in 1914. By contrast, those small industrial companies which, in 1918, still asked only a few pounds per year for their average policy had experienced a miserable time during the war. Thus the Wesleyan and General, the Abstainers and General, the London and Manchester all experienced sharp falls in their business.

Amidst such varying fortunes and such a strong showing by the big 'industrial' offices, Phoenix's strengths seemed to stem largely from the handling of new business. Given that Phoenix policy was to hold back deliberately on total sums assured, new annual premiums performed surprisingly well. An exception must be made for 1915, which in many ways was Phoenix's worst wartime year. But the 1913 figure was comfortably exceeded by 1917, well before the end of the war (see Table 6.11).

Table 6.11. *Phoenix Assurance: new life business, 1913–18 (current prices and 1913 values)*

Year	New net annual premiums (current £)	Retail prices	New net annual premiums (1913=100)
1913	48,086	100.0	48,086
1914	50,351	104.3	48,275
1915	36,974	126.1	29,321
1916	44,850	147.8	30,345
1917	59,747	178.2	33,528
1918	66,550	204.3	32,575

However, in real terms, of course, it was a different story, with new annual premiums struggling to keep above £30,000 in every year after 1914. But the problem of acquiring new business amidst international strife and inflating prices was a difficult one for all offices. And, by the comparative test, Phoenix again did well.

In new business acquisition, the contrast between Phoenix and the specialist life office, Standard Assurance, was again marked (see Table 6.12). Phoenix was notably stronger in new premiums, whereas the *total* premium flow of Standard retained the advantage. This again suggests that Phoenix improved its underwriting performance during wartime, and that its short-term performance was more solidly based than its medium-term performance.

The average value of the Phoenix policy (see Table 6.7). remained on the high side throughout, though falling in real terms, so it would appear unlikely that the success with the new business was achieved by moving towards a different band of demand. The offices which began the war in 1914 with high average policy values (£500 and above) increased those values down to 1918 by very variable amounts (ranging from 2.4% for North British to 32.3% for Scottish Provident).[110] No clear pattern in the fortunes of this group can be correlated with the movement of their average policy values (see Table 6.7). Large increases did not prevent Scottish Provident or Scottish Amicable from slightly improving their

[110] The increases for other high value companies were: Scottish Widows, 17.1%; Legal & General 2.5%; Standard 13%; Commercial Union 9.4%; Alliance 11.5%; Phoenix 2.8%; Scottish Amicable 31.5%. Retail prices, of course, easily outpaced all of these (see Table 6.11).

Table 6.12. *Phoenix Assurance and Standard Assurance: new and total life business, 1914–20*

	New premium income		Total premium income	
Year	Phoenix	Standard	Phoenix	Standard
1914	100	100	100	100
1915	69	65	73	94
1916	86	68	72	89
1917	122	66	74	87
1918	123	82	76	93
1919	160	136	81	92
1920	190	154	86	96

Sources: For Standard, Butt, 'Life Assurance in War and Depression'; for Phoenix, Annual Reports.

market shares. Those offices which increased policy values least did tend to retain high stable market shares (Legal & General, North British) or improve share significantly (Phoenix). But it would be unwise to infer any particular market strategy from this. Among this group of offices with high average policy values, the best indicator of likely wartime success seems to be the market share of 1914: those with the lower starting positions were likely to do better.

However well Phoenix may have done in the assurance of war, the pressures placed upon the life offices by taxation and plummeting investment values was universal; no levels of skill would serve to escape these. Existing tax provisions which fell upon interest earnings or upon trading profits, whichever was the greater, caused particular difficulties under war conditions, and especially at tax rates as high as the 6 shillings in the £ which was in force by 1918. As profits diminished, tax demands hit hard upon interest earnings which were already under pressure from sliding stock markets. Actuarial forecasting depended on accurate estimation of interest returns and unpredictable tax regimes made this impossible. These were sore points with the offices throughout the war. They were to come up before the Royal Commission on Income Tax in 1919–20, but that was scarcely soon enough for Hamilton, who was still complaining about 'heavily and unfairly apportioned taxation' in May 1919. He pointed out that tax on interest earnings was not the only issue. Life offices were particularly vulnerable to changes in fiscal policy, since their contracts were long term ones with fixed premiums. With fire or accident policies the rates could be changed to defend against alterations in external requirements; but the life assurer could not manoeuvre to escape the fiscal scourge. And he had suffered for it during the war.

However, the most stunning blow was delivered early in the conflict. The reaction of the stock markets to European warfare was violent and was exacerbated by the decontrol of prices on the London Stock Exchange in 1915. At the Annual General Meeting on 19 April 1916, the first to be held at the new offices in King William Street, Hamilton was able to report that the Valuation of Phoenix Life Funds for the quinquennium 1911–15 had produced a bonus of 7.5%, against the 8.5% recorded for 1906–10. It was, he thought, given the times, a 'trifling reduction' and the life business had 'passed through the trials and difficulties of an exceptionally anxious period with surprisingly little shrinkage of bonus'.[111] But this was due only to impressively accurate underwriting. This had been on course for a really exceptional surplus, even accepting war mortality, until the stock market had collapsed. Actuary Straker reported to Gerald Ryan in March 1916 that the gross depreciation on Phoenix life funds since war began was a punishing 15.8%; in money terms, almost exactly a third of a million pounds had been wiped off the Phoenix's life assets. Special reserves held against stock falls reduced the net damage to about 8%, but it was still enough to cancel out the assurance gains.[112]

Yet the fact that the 1915 Annual General Meeting had been the last to be held in Lombard Street proved a blessing in disguise for Phoenix. For the sale of the Lombard Street property also supplied an off-set against the losses in securities.[113] The old houses did Phoenix the final courtesy of bequeathing the company a much smaller net depreciation in 1915 than was suffered by most other assurers.

Denied such fortuitous assistance from the property sector, and valued at a later date, in December 1916, the securities of the old British Empire fund, still maintained in a closed form by Phoenix, fared much worse. Its Stock Exchange holdings suffered a 16.3% fall in the five years to December 1916, and, in the end, some 6% of the entire Fund had to be written off. Ryan ruled that its bonus for 1912–16 had better be frozen.[114]

In due time, of course, the stock market revived and these values were recovered. But it took until 1920 for this to happen, and during the war period the assurers received little help in maintaining their asset values from stocks and shares. Interest earnings might rise but capital values

[111] Chairman's Annual Report, 19 April 1916. [112] Straker to Ryan, 20 March 1916.

[113] The total profit on the sale of 70 Lombard Street and 57 Charing Cross was £104,704 of which the life funds received £66,000.

[114] Observations by the General Manager on the Actuary's Report, 7 March 1917.

remained depressed. Investors, along with most of Europe, remained pessimistic.

The Phoenix Quinquennial Valuation of 1920 counted the cost to the company over the second half of the war. Loss on war mortality had amounted to £120,000 but losses on stock market deaths, due to depreciation over this period, totalled £330,000. The resulting 'exceptional strain' led to a five-year profit of only £84,000; so the directors decided to declare no bonus. However, it is striking that three-quarters of Phoenix's exceptional strain had followed from losses in securities rather than in soldiers.

5. PHOENIX STAFF IN WARTIME: OFFICE LIFE AND BATTLEFIELD DEATH

The nervous board meeting of 12 August 1914, the first of the war, occupied itself with acts of topical charity and the competing demands of nation and company upon the manpower in the Phoenix's employ. It donated £500 to the Prince of Wales's National Fund for the Relief of Distress in War. And it granted one of its own number, Lt. Col. the Hon. Stuart Pleydell Bouverie, special leave of absence from its meetings, for a six-month period, so that he might attend to the larger business across the Channel.[115]

Thus closely reminded by the predicament of a colleague, the directors then legislated for all staff who had been 'called out' on national service: with befitting generosity, the Board voted these first volunteers to the colours their full Phoenix salary and promised that their insurance jobs would be kept open for them until the fighting was done.[116] The allowance of Head Office directors absent on war service was not settled until 9 September; they were to get £300 per annum.[117] But both Bouverie's initial leave and the lavish provisions for staff were based on the assumption that it would all be over by Christmas.

During the rest of 1914 and the early part of 1915, much of the Board's war business was taken up with giving money to worthy causes related to the fighting. In September 1914, £250 went to the Canadian War Relief Fund and consideration was given to similar pleas from India, South Africa, Australia and New Zealand.[118] Perhaps more immediately constructive was the £200 subscribed to the Lord Mayor of London's Fund

[115] Regrettably, this six-month leave had to be renewed on many subsequent occasions. Fortunately, Bouverie survived all of them.

[116] Directors' Minutes, 31, p. 89, 12 August 1914.

[117] *Ibid.*, p. 99, 9 September 1914.

[118] *Ibid.*, pp. 106–7, 23 September 1914.

for Armoured Cars so that the London Mounted Brigade might drive into battle adequately protected.[119] Also direct in application was the £250 donated to the British Red Cross, which, after due comparison with the amounts given by other companies, was speedily converted into £500 in January 1915 and made up to £1,000 by June.[120]

By then, however, Phoenix staff were beginning to suffer directly. The company's first war casualty was probably Frank Potter of the accident department who died on 27 February, of cerebro-spinal meningitis contracted while serving with the London Rifles in Flanders.[121] The first death in action was that of F. R. Smith, also of the accident department, and subsequently of the 23rd Battalion, the London Regiment, on 26 May 1915. However, in the late summer of 1915, the Dardanelles offensive took a heavier toll: at least three Phoenix men died at Gallipoli, one the accountant of the Sydney Branch, serving with the 2nd Battalion Australian Infantry, and two with the City of London Yeomanry's Roughriders.[122] In October, the Board sent 100 guineas to the Fund for the Sick and wounded of the Dardanelles; but it was too late for some of their own former employees.[123]

On the first day of June 1915, Phoenix employed 366 staff of military age in the United Kingdom and 169 of these had already joined up; by mid-November the equivalent numbers were 363 and 198. This represents military participation rates of 46.2% for June and 54.5% for November, and was a high rate of enlistment. Nationally, however, the level of recruitment under the system of voluntary service was proving unequal to the level of attrition in the trenches. Between October and December 1915, the scheme of mobilisation designed by Lord Derby[124] proved to be the final bid for voluntarism. Despite long hesitation and agonised debate over the issue of compulsory call-up, military conscription came into being in Britain with the first Military Service Act of 27 January 1916. The voluntary system provided 2.5 million men willing to fight and that was its limit, reached in December 1915.[125]

By then, the Derby scheme had canvassed the numbers of those willing to enlist if called upon (and had received the disappointing answer that

119 *Ibid.*, p. 129, 18 November 1914.

120 *Ibid.*, pp. 152, 238, 6 January and 9 June 1915.

121 *Ibid.*, p. 185, 3 March 1915.

122 *Ibid.*, pp. 235, 285, 315, 2 June, 22 September and 17 November 1915.

123 *Ibid.*, p. 292, 13 October 1915.

124 This was a two-stage process by which the government first identified all eligible males, and then *asked* them if they would be willing to serve, if called upon. So enrolment in the scheme did not constitute enlistment in the services until the call was made.

125 I. F. W. Beckett, 'The Nation in Arms, 1914–18', in I. F. W. Beckett and K. Simpson (eds.), *A Nation in Arms* (Manchester, 1985), p. 12.

Plate 6.5 Londoners responding to Lord Derby's call.

only 1.2 million out of 2.2 million eligible single men *were* willing; hence the resort to compulsion). Around the same time, in the last months of 1915, the Phoenix Board discovered that they had 165 men liable to the terms of the Derby scheme.

The distinction between the two Phoenix military echelons – those who joined up early and those who were polled by the Derby scheme – is notable. The average salary of those enlisting in the early part of the war was £118; while the average salary of those not yet enlisted in November 1915 was a full one-third higher, at £177.

Of course, it is no longer believed that the remarkable growth of Kitchener's New Armies of 1914–15 was formed by a simple patriotic stampede to join the colours. In fact, the pattern of recruitment was progressive and stepped, and the forces behind it ranged from nationalistic fervour to boredom with urban life or rural employment. Many without commitments joined up quickly. Others with responsibilities took time to put their affairs in order. Still others needed to be convinced of the necessity before acting. Some wished to retain the respect of social equals or fellow workers and a certain interval was necessary before such peer group pressures could take effect. The 'Pals' Battalions', which were

Plate 6.6 London buses in service, near Compiègne, late in 1914.

one expression of such pressures, were particularly prolific in the City. Among the earliest to join up were young single men in junior positions seeking some adventure – and lacking any way to measure its dreadful cost – away from the drudgery of a factory job or the routine of office life.[126]

No doubt, Phoenix had its share of such recruits. But no doubt also, it had its complement of those who made an economic calculation. Many employers in the last quarter of 1914, believing that the war would be short, offered inducements to their staff, in the shape of guaranteed jobs upon return or supplements to army pay, with the object of promoting enlistment. Phoenix offered both, and indeed more. For the company's first position was to furnish recruits with full salary and a secure job upon return. With army pay and allowances on top of this, and without knowledge of what awaited them in the field, Phoenix men

[126] For a particularly cool appraisal of the motivations for joining up, or avoiding joining up, see D. Winter, *Death's Men* (London, 1978) or R. Blythe, *Akenfield* (London, 1969). In the latter, bad weather and a lack of harvest employment give two farm labourers a particularly earthy reason for enlistment. See also, among many possible perspectives, that by P. Barker, *The Regeneration Trilogy* (London, 1991–5).

could easily believe that they were better off in khaki than in business suits.

For Phoenix, however, as for the government, the end of 1915 represented a turning point in the treatment of enlistment. And for the insurers this included a change in the level of corporate generosity they could afford to extend to it. The war had not been over by Christmas 1914; and it was clearly not set to end by Christmas 1915. Moreover, further voluntary enlistment, such as Lord Derby envisaged, would stretch already strained office workers beyond endurance; and conscription would do worse still.

The insurers were no longer in a position where they could afford to encourage their workers to join up and then pay them full salaries for extended periods of absence.[127] However, the Derby scheme did at least allow employers to protest to the government in the interval between a valued employee's enrolment in the scheme and his enlistment in the services. Thus, in November 1915, delegates from the big insurance offices saw Lord Derby in order to argue their corner in the contest for manpower. After the meeting, they agreed to,

> encourage the enrolment of their staff of military age . . . under the group system, relying on the promises of Lord Derby to assist the companies . . . to retain in their present position enrolled men whose services cannot be dispensed with, having regard to the public responsibilities and obligations of the companies.[128]

Accordingly, Phoenix decided to give permission freely to those who wished to join the Derby scheme but to require a special permission for those who wished to enlist immediately.

The financial terms for volunteers were also revised. Instead of the full pay voted in August 1914, significant reservations were now made. Even in June 1915, Phoenix had decided to adjust its full-salary deal for volunteers to full salary *less* army pay, but undertook to pay this lesser amount for the whole of the war. Under the Derby scheme, the scale of the company's commitment was taken down another notch. Married Phoenix men, enrolled or enlisted, were to get full salary less service pay. Single men were to revert to half-pay upon joining the colours, but were allowed their army pay above this, without adjustment. However, a nice socio-economic distinction was made in favour of single men who achieved commissioned rank: they too had their service pay made up to full salary;

[127] When Hamilton had referred to 'the company's system for assisting members of the Staff to be absent from their ordinary duties' in his Chairman's Annual Report of 28 April 1915, the anticipation was that it would work in the national interest, not against the company's interest.

[128] Directors' Minutes, 31, pp. 313–15, 17 November 1915.

the King's Commission had the same effect as a marriage licence. But in no new case of enlistment was the full *premium* for joining up, which had been represented by army pay plus Phoenix pay, permitted beyond November 1915: although all engagements under the terms of August 1914 were honoured.

By June 1916, 106 of the 165 Phoenix men who in November 1915 had been liable to the provisions of the Derby scheme had become participants in it. Of these, 56 had gone off to war, while Phoenix had succeeded in achieving postponement of the call-up for the remainder. And from the start of 1916, Phoenix had a further category to cope with: those unfortunate enough to be conscripted. They were unfortunate not only because of the disruption in their lives, but also because of the still more modest financial commitment that employers were prepared to make to them. Phoenix undertook to keep their jobs open; but they were to be paid no salary in their absence; in its place went a £10 leaving present upon joining the colours.[129]

The effects of these enlistment patterns for Phoenix are shown in Table 6.13.

Three features emerge particularly clearly. One is the effectiveness of the encouragement to early enlistment, including no doubt both patriotism and the Phoenix premium. A second is the impact of the Derby scheme upon Phoenix men: where it achieved a positive response from only 55% of the national constituency, the Phoenix rate of scoring was over 64%. The third was the relatively minor impact of conscription: the net of compulsion yielded only twenty additional recruits. This more or less reflected the national picture.[130]

Once in uniform, Phoenix men served with distinction. The first major decorations were produced by the murderous battles of the Somme in summer and autumn 1916: Capt. E. W. Hughes and Lt. W. R. Moore were both awarded Military Medals in June 1916, and Private P. B. Titterington received the same medal in September and a bar for it in December.[131] The year 1917 produced six major decorations and eight

[129] *Ibid.*, p. 421, 7 June 1916. This overall salary scheme, allowing for the different points of enlistment, remained in place for the remainder of the war, with one exception. The adjustment was necessitated by the increases in army pay for all ranks early in 1918. Under the company's formula of 'Phoenix pay less army pay', this would have produced financial gain for Phoenix. In order to avoid this, the element to be subtracted was defined as a fixed sum smaller than the new military pay scales.

[130] Beckett and Simpson, *A Nation in Arms*, p. 13. Between 1 March 1916 and 31 March 1917, 371,500 men were conscripted, but 779,936 exempted for a variety of reasons.

[131] Directors' Minutes, 31, pp. 422, 430, 7 and 28 June 1916; *ibid.*, 32, p. 36, 6 December 1916.

Table 6.13. *Phoenix salaries paid to enlisted men by categories (current £ costs per annum at January 1918)*

No. of enlistments	Full salary to end of war	Full salary less army pay to end of war	Full salary less army pay (Derby)	Half salary plus army pay	No salary	Date of Phoenix Board minute
141	16,671					12.8.14
21		1,740				2.6.15
61			13,134			17.11.15
28				2,705		7.6.16
						20.12.16
20					1,011	7.6.16

Source: Directors' Minute Books, 32, p. 203, 23 January 1918.

mentions in despatches.[132] Hughes, of the 6th London Rifles was a major by May 1917 and distinguished himself for a second time, by a mention in despatches, and then added a DSO in 1918. A. C. L. Nicholson was a 2nd lieutenant in the East Kents in June 1917, when he was mentioned in despatches, but a captain by October, when he was awarded the MC.[133] A similar pattern was repeated in 1918, when there were four important decorations and three mentions in despatches. R. H. Rowland was a captain when he was mentioned, early in 1917, but a lieutenant-colonel, commanding the 8th Battalion, the Queen's Royal West Surreys, when mentioned for a second time in June 1918.[134] Senior officers from Phoenix backgrounds were also conspicuous among the medal winners. The much-absented director, Lt. Col. Bouverie, Royal Field Artillery, won the DSO in January 1917, at the same time as his Phoenix subordinate but gunner colleague, Lt. Col. N. L. Roberts, of the same regiment, won the MC.[135] A third Phoenix colonel, C. M. Robertson, the secretary of the Glasgow Branch, and yet another artilleryman, achieved two mentions in despatches before winning the DSO in January 1918.[136] Probably the most elevated of Phoenix's military men, Brigadier-General the Hon. C. S. H. D. Willoughby, in more peaceful times chairman of Phoenix's West End Board, was mentioned in despatches before being awarded the CMG and CB, also early in 1918.[137] Decorations conferred after the end of the war included three more Military Crosses, one DSO (to Rowland again), one Distin-

[132] The awards were Military Medals, Military Crosses and Distinguished Service Orders.
[133] Directors' Minutes, 32, pp. 107, 114, 160, 16 May, 6 June, 24 October 1917.
[134] *Ibid.*, pp. 49, 258, 17 January 1917, 5 June 1918. [135] *Ibid.*, p. 41, 31 January 1917.
[136] *Ibid.*, p. 197, 9 January 1918. [137] *Ibid.*

Table 6.14. *Phoenix deaths and decorations in war service, 1914–19*

Year	Deaths	Of which officers below captain	Decorations	Phoenix men serving
1914	0	0	0	–
1915	7	1	0	214
1916	17	9	4	283
1917	10	7	14	366
1918	10	8	7	336
1919	1	1	15	–

Source: Directors' Minute Books.

guished Flying Cross, one Air Force Cross and the Croix de Guerre (to Robertson again).[138]

The number of these awards for gallantry is strikingly high. About 10% of the Phoenix men who served in the First World War achieved major decorations or mentions in despatches. The next most arresting characteristic is the pattern of repetition: men who were rewarded for bravery once were likely to be rewarded for it more than once. Perhaps least predictable of all is the connection between bravery and survival. All but one of Phoenix's highly decorated soldiers appear to have seen the Armistice in.[139] Perhaps brave soldiers were also often the most skilful soldiers. In any event, they almost justified Hamilton's rhetorical flourish, in his Chairman's Annual Report for 1917, when he inquired, 'Does it not send through all of us a thrill of pride to know that our City businessmen and boys have shown themselves, in the field, to be a match – and more than a match – for the best fighters of the much-vaunted Prussian Army (Cheers)'.[140]

Many of those who left Phoenix offices for the front were not as fortunate as those who fought bravely and lived to tell the tale. Table 6.14 gives total deaths in action, alongside total decorations, as listed in the Directors' Minute Books. The figures for Phoenix men serving come from Hamilton's Chairman's Annual Reports. From the Minute Books it is possible in most (but not all) cases to establish the rank of the casualty.

[138] *Ibid.*, 32, pp. 350, 402, 407, 5 February, 4 and 18 June 1919.

[139] The sad exception was 2nd Lt. H. J. Dawes, MM, 2nd Battalion the Yorkshire Regiment, who was killed in combat in France on 8 May 1918 (*ibid.*, 32, p. 257, 5 June 1918).

[140] Chairman's Annual Report, 25 April 1917.

Plate 6.7 Irish advertising in wartime: Uncle Sam joins the War.

The final outcome, according to Hamilton's Annual Report of 1 May 1919 was that 'more than 400' Phoenix men served and 57 died. This suggests a Phoenix mortality rate of around 14% of those enlisting. The Directors' Minute Books list a total of 44 Phoenix deaths for 1914–18, which, taken against the average annual number serving, suggests a mortality rate of around 14.7% for this shorter period. However, the Phoenix War Memorials give a total of 65 war dead for the period 1914–19, and a complete roll-call of all Phoenix men enlisted, from all departments, home and foreign, of 504.[141] The mortality rate produced by these figures is 12.9%.

The discrepancies in the numbers of war dead between the different sources is probably accounted for by time-lag effects. Some men listed as missing were confirmed dead after the end of hostilities; some died subsequently of wounds sustained in the last phases of the fighting; and some expired, while still in service, from the great influenza epidemic of 1918–19. Whichever way it is measured, the overall Phoenix mortality rate for the First World War, at around 13–14%, contrasts starkly with the fewer than 6% of Phoenix servicemen lost in the Second World War.[142]

The Phoenix mortality rate for the First World War was in fact high by national standards. For British military formations as a whole, the heaviest death toll of 12% was suffered on the Western Front.[143] The Phoenix figure was higher than this, yet Phoenix men did not fight only on the Western Front.

Indeed the map of Phoenix war deaths stalks the overall pattern of British strategy. The Mesopotamian campaign, which decimated some British units, like the Hampshires, in late 1915 counted Phoenix men, like 2nd Lt. Arthur Wheate of the East Lancs Regiment, among its victims; another 2nd lieutenant, A. C. H. Field, of the Royal Fusiliers, died on the Tigris; and a third, Lt. the Viscount Quenington, a director of Phoenix's West End office since July 1908, succumbed to wounds suffered in the Egyptian campaign.[144] Gallipoli left a similar mark.[145] But nothing for Phoenix was as lethal as the Somme: it produced in the summer and autumn of 1916, many decorations but a sad number of fatalities. At least a dozen Phoenix men fell here, no fewer than four of them from the Union Marine contingent which had enrolled in the 17th Battalion, the King's Liverpool Regiment, which took particularly heavy punishment. The final British offensives, which were generally costly, also hit Phoenix hard:

[141] The period here covers the whole of 1919. The memorials, cast in bronze by Sir George Frampton, form an important historical source. The two plaques, one a tribute to those who fought and survived, the other commemorating the war dead, were first erected in 5 King William Street in 1921 and then removed, during the redevelopment of the building, in 1985. The second of these was restored to a fitting place alongside the Alliance Assurance's memorial on the second floor of the Sun Alliance headquarters at 1 Bartholomew Lane, in March 1993. That commemorating the survivors has been located on the first floor next to the two marble Rolls of Honour in memory of the staff from the Sun Insurance Office who fell in the two World Wars.

[142] If mortality in the Second World War is taken as a percentage of those serving, not merely in the armed forces but also in the Home Guard, ARP, Civil Defence, etc., the figure falls further to around 3%.

[143] Winter, *Death's Men*, pp. 192–3.

[144] Directors' Minutes, 31, pp. 395, 404, 12 April, 3 May 1916.

[145] See above, p. 415.

six died in April and May 1918 alone. Some of the last deaths of the war were marked by technology and pathos. A captain in the RAF was shot down in September 1918; another from the Royal Tank Corps died in his armoured vehicle in the same month.[146] The last of all the clear battlefield casualties, yet another 2nd lieutenant, who died on 9 October 1918, left a young widow who made a unique appeal to the company for help in educating her young daughter.[147]

Amidst this carnage, there were clear patterns. The most lethal rank was that of lieutenant. The junior officers of the lost generation, who died in droves leading platoon attacks, are appallingly over-represented in the Phoenix roll of mortality. Table 6.14 shows clearly how high a proportion of Phoenix casualties came from these echelons. In general terms, the myth of the 'three-week subaltern' has been subject to legitimate revision, but the history of a specific institution such as Phoenix still reveals with force just how dangerous it was to hold junior commissioned rank.[148] Indeed, this is probably the single major explanation of Phoenix's above-average war mortality. Despite the fact that Phoenix men fought in many theatres of war, their death rate exceeded the average for the worst theatre. The most likely reason is that young men sufficiently educated to attain position in a major City office had a higher than average probability of achieving commissioned rank. And then of dying in a platoon attack.

A further irony was that, as many of the young died in the field, many of the directors died at home, from less unnatural causes. By coincidence, the First World War marked one of those phases when the boardroom experienced one of its periodic generational upheavals. Admiral Lucas died in August 1914, John Baxendale and Sir Arthur Lucas in June 1915, Sir Thomas Bland Royden of Union Marine in September 1917, and Sir Helenus Robertson, after losing his own subaltern son to the trenches, in March 1919. A particular link with the past was snapped in June 1917 when William Henry Lovell, son of Secretary G. W. Lovell, died at the age of 87. George Lovell had started with the Phoenix in 1820; William Henry had retired in 1900, after fifty years' service.

Life for those left behind in the office of the wartime City – and it should be remembered that from late 1915 Phoenix laboured to *keep* as many as possible behind – was very different from the routine of peace-time. For one thing it was extremely expensive. From 1915 inflation was such that repeated bonuses to salaries had to be paid 'in consideration of

[146] Directors' Minutes, 32, pp. 290, 294, 11 and 25 September 1918.
[147] *Ibid.*, p. 302, 16 October 1918. Phoenix paid six months' salary as a compassionate gesture. The war ended on 11 November 1918.
[148] Keith Simpson, 'The Officers', in Beckett and Simpson, *A Nation in Arms*, p. 86.

the rise in price of the necessaries of life'; these were paid at the rate of 5% in December 1915, 10% in October 1916, and, when this did not suffice, a further 10% in June 1917 and 15%, on salaries below £1,000, in autumn 1918, on account of 'the continued rise in the cost of living'.[149] For another, the number of women employed by the company increased markedly. This, of course, was true of many large City institutions. But Phoenix noticed it most particularly. By early 1917, the company was desperately short of male clerks, to the extent that the director-general of recruiting was told that the Board could no longer 'advise their employees to enrol under the National Service Scheme . . . seeing that the time of all members of staff of the companies is now so fully occupied upon work which is of national interest'.[150]

Effectively, Phoenix was saying, as were many civilian employers, that if the war machine was to work, the general economy needed also to work. As with so much of the home front economy, whether in the agricultural, manufacturing or service sectors, Phoenix turned to women to make its business work. By January 1917, Head Office was being run with only 130 permanent male staff, about half its pre-war complement, the UK branches with 138 men, and, relatively untouched, the foreign branches with 225 men.[151] Women staff filled the empty desks. In the old days, Hamilton reminisced (to his credit entirely cheerfully), it had been rare to see anything other than males in the office, but 'now there is a preponderance in some departments of females'. At the end of 1913, King William Street had employed only thirty-three women; by late 1916, there were 132 of them. Throughout the Phoenix organisation the numbers of women employed by early 1917 were: at Head Office 178 temporary clerks and typists, in the UK branches 49, and an additional 77 in the foreign branches.[152] No male chauvinist, Hamilton concluded, 'There is little reason to doubt that the employment of women in the great City offices will be much more general in future. They have won for themselves the right to a place in the organisation of commercial industry.'[153] These noble sentiments were not misplaced. Female employment in the City went down again after the First World War, as the men returned to claim

149 Directors' Minutes, 31, p. 471, 4 October 1916; *ibid.*, 32, pp. 177, 298, 28 November 1917, 9 October 1918. Compare the retail price index in Table 6.11.
150 *Ibid.*, 32, p. 84, 21 March 1917.
151 *Ibid.*, p. 51, 24 January 1917. This throws an interesting sidelight on the larger fact that over 80% of the manpower and finance for the British Empire's war against the Central Powers was provided from the United Kingdom alone. See P. K. O'Brien, 'The Costs and Benefits of Empire', *Past and Present*, 120, (1988), pp. 163–200.
152 Directors' Minutes 32, p. 51, 24 January 1917.
153 Chairman's Annual Report, 25 April 1917.

the jobs kept open for them,[154] but the war period marked a potent and irreversible stage in the secretarial revolution.

The period of European upheaval held one final tribulation for the home front: influenza. The Spanish 'flu that sent another apocalyptic horseman across the Continent in the tracks of his warrior colleague proved a scourge for office workers and troops alike. In November 1918, within days of celebrating the Armistice, about one-sixth of Phoenix staff were laid out by the virus, with the proportion of women affected roughly twice that of the men (39 out of 184 women, 16 out of 171 men).[155] After warfare had claimed so many Phoenix lives, it was ironic that disease should claim two more in the same month that the war ended. That irony was repeated right across Europe. The story of the Phoenix staff in wartime presents an effective microcosm of a society under many types of damaging strain.

154 Fire Manager Boston lamented in 1919 that, 'we shall be losing most of our ladies, and we shall lose them with regret' (Phoenix Annual General Meeting, reported in *The Times* 1 May 1919).

155 Directors' Minutes, 32, p. 320, 27 November 1917.

CHAPTER 7

THE EXPANSION, AND STRANGE CONTRACTION, OF A COMPOSITE OFFICE

In its quest for further corporate growth in the interwar years Phoenix participated in one of the oddest incidents in modern insurance history. For the veteran of King William Street acquired two major offices, one each in the fire and accident sectors, within five years of the Armistice, and lost one of them within six. The offices acquired were the Norwich Union Fire and the London Guarantee & Accident. The office sold on was the Norwich Union Fire. This was a fateful decision. For the dominant constraint upon the Phoenix in the post-1945 era was its inability to secure a major acquisition from among the leading offices of the day. Phoenix surrendered during the 1920s an asset of the kind that it most needed during the 1960s. Had Phoenix managed to keep Norwich Union Fire, this history might not have ended in 1984. Ryan, it transpired, could make mistakes.

I. MORE ATTRACTIONS OF FIRE

In 1914, and still in 1918, Phoenix compared poorly with the other great composites in two areas of insurance activity (see Table 5.7, p. 362). These were the fire market – ironically, for this was the Phoenix's birthplace – and the accident market. If Ryan's strategy of advance by acquisition was to be sustained, these were the natural target zones for the next offensive. But, of course, offensives of a different sort had occupied the hearts, minds and energies of the nation between 1914 and 1918.

Corporate takeovers in the midst of a world war were only for the foolhardy. Obviously, this would be less true in an area of underwriting especially affected by war demand. Thus Union Marine's acquisition of Northern Maritime in 1917 could be excused by the exceptional wartime conditions in the marine insurance market. But equivalent conditions did

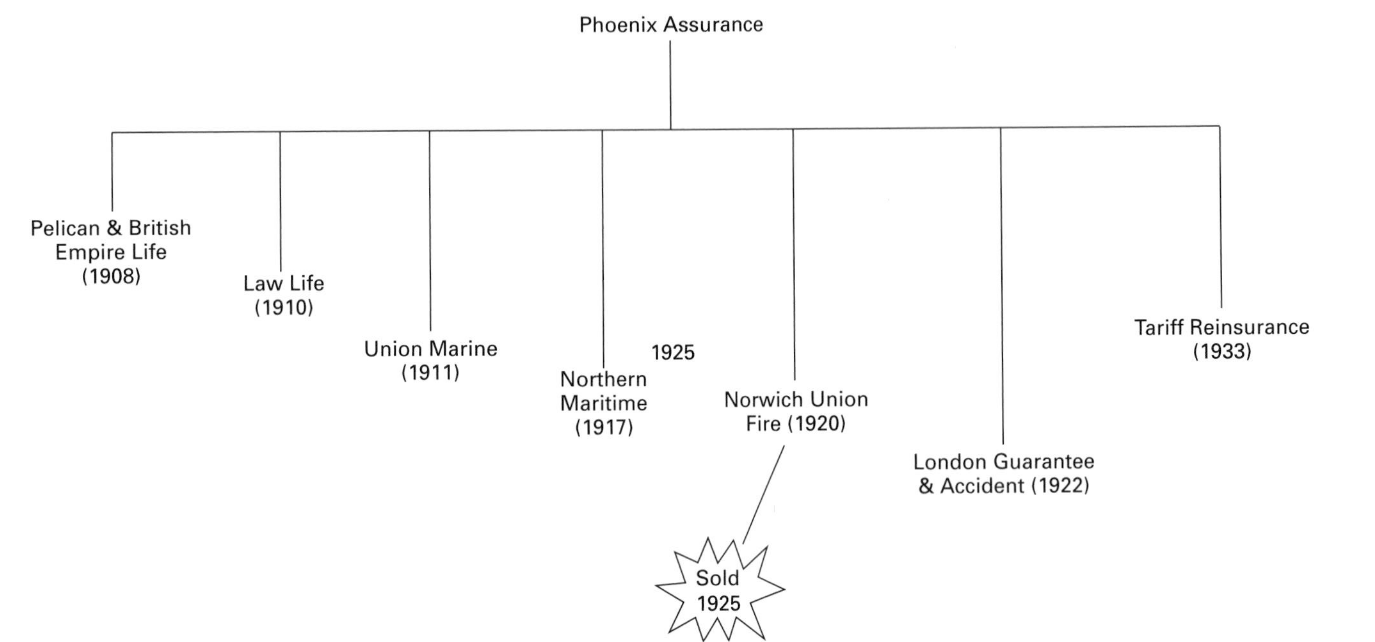

Fig. 7.1 The Phoenix Group in the United Kingdom: acquisitions, 1908–39

not exist in the fire or accident markets of 1914–18. Whereas marine premiums had risen by 238% from 1914 to the peak of 1917, fire and accident returns rose over the same period by 19.7% and 18.9% respectively.

It is therefore a major surprise to find that Phoenix had planned the acquisition of a Tariff Fire Office in *November 1916*. Indeed, a Special Committee of the Board was sent out to find such an office in the middle of the war.[1] Nothing came of the initiative at this time but it is extraordinary that it was ever undertaken. Certainly, it throws an interesting light on the postwar events which did bring into Phoenix's possession a fire office of the finest calibre. Perhaps too it suggests the merest whiff of undue haste?

It is striking that, in the immediate aftermath of the First World War, Phoenix's appetite for acquisition was sustained virtually irrespective of economic conditions; there was no sign of any abatement from pre-war levels. On the contrary, two of Ryan's most ambitious coups were tried during this period, one in 1919, the other in 1924. In general economic terms, it is perhaps easier to understand the first than the second.

For the economic phase which followed the Armistice did deliver the restocking boom which all good capitalists had been anticipating ever since the war began. Investment levels were high and there was much speculative activity in the promotion and amalgamation of companies; shipping and cotton textile firms were prominent in the sharper aspects of this activity. But financial and insurance ventures did not escape attention. Ryan observed in January 1920 that 'during the last few months, the market for insurance shares has become active and speculative and . . . (has) forced prices up to a very high level'.[2] The market peaked in October–November 1919. The expansionary optimism of this period encouraged many schemes of corporate reconstruction.

According to the chairman of the Norwich Union Fire Insurance Society, Hustler Tuck,

> it was the war [which] has brought its lessons home to us – that, in the long run, size and strength must prevail. Since the signing of the Armistice, we have seen a determination among all mercantile and industrial enterprises to increase in strength and size.[3]

No doubt, uppermost in his mind were the recent efforts of the Royal Insurance and the London & Lancashire to 'increase in strength and size':

[1] Phoenix Secret Minutes, p. 29, 22 November 1916.

[2] Ryan, Chairman's Speech to Phoenix Extraordinary General Meeting, 20 January 1920. This was his first address to shareholders as chairman.

[3] Tuck to Norwich Union Fire Extraordinary General Meeting, 20 January 1920.

the former had purchased a sizeable interest in the Liverpool & London & Globe at the end of October 1919 and the London & Lancashire had absorbed the Law Union & Rock at around the same time. But then the managers of the Norwich Union had themselves shown more initiative than merely noting the trend among their competitors.

Late in 1919, R. Y. Sketch, general manager of Norwich Union Fire (NUF), put a proposal to Ryan which the Phoenix general manager found highly congenial: it concerned a plan for the fusion of the two old offices – Phoenix was by then 137 years old, Norwich Union 122 – on equal terms.[4] Norwich Union, a rich and successful but deeply provincial, office was probably looking for better defences in a confusing postwar world of rising competition and intensifying amalgamation. As Chairman Tuck put it, 'some allowance is necessary for the old Norwich Union to enable it to maintain its prosperous career'.[5] There are suggestions also that Sketch wished to give his stalwart East Anglian veteran a little of the metropolitan gloss displayed by Ryan's Phoenix. And it is unlikely that Sketch, any more than Ryan in his British Empire days, missed the potential advantage to be had as the conductor of a larger band.

Indeed, there are some hints of head-hunting in Ryan's handling of Norwich Union and Sketch. In 1919, Ryan was fifty-eight, had achieved all that he might reasonably have expected, and was looking forward to a lighter non-executive role. His appointment as chairman of Phoenix was announced on 28 November 1919 – inaugurating an era for the company quite as distinct as 'the inter-war years' were for the economy as a whole – and Phoenix needed a general manager. There was no obvious candidate within the Phoenix. It is surely significant that, upon completion of the Phoenix–NUF agreement, Sandeman Allen telegrammed his congratulations to Ryan, 'Scheme *and man* are all that could be desired.'[6] For Phoenix, Sketch's appearance in 1920 seemed providential: he provided the succession to Ryan, following him as general manager 1920–35, managing director 1935–40 and chairman 1940–8.

Sketch was a burly Welshman of sporting interests – in his day, captain of the national water polo team and oar for Penarth and, in more mature years, captain of the Royal Wimbledon Golf Club – and varied career. His first major insurance post was as manager of Ocean Accident's operation in South Africa; this he secured, aged twenty-six, in 1903. By 1910, he was

4 Sketch may have been encouraged in this direction. It was a habit of Ryan's to put his better ideas into the minds of others and then welcome them when they returned homewards.

5 Tuck to Norwich Union Fire Extraordinary General Meeting, 20 January 1920.

6 Allen to Ryan, 9 December 1919 (emphasis in original).

Plate 7.1 Ralph Sketch in 1932.

back in London as foreign manager of General Accident, later its London manager. He transferred to Norwich Union Fire as accident manager in 1914 and moved up to assistant general manager in 1916. He had been general manager, at the age of forty-two, only a matter of months when the idea of the Phoenix–NUF fusion came to him (or Ryan). Within the insurance business, Sketch's reputation was high. The City, through which he had passed en route from South Africa to Norwich, clearly remembered him, *The Times* reporting that

> many believe that he will be quick to occupy a place among the leading fire managers of London . . . The great composite insurance companies have now become vast organisations with worldwide ramifications and men with exceptional qualifications are now required at the helm.[7]

Nevertheless, Ryan did not go after Norwich Union simply to get Sketch. There was much emphasis on the naturalness of a marriage between two veterans in difficult times. Ryan described the notion as 'an ideal

[7] *The Times*, 18 December 1919.

one . . . cementing the alliance of two old friends',[8] while *The Times* agreed that 'the offices have long worked very harmoniously together'.[9] Similarly, a Special Committee of the Phoenix Board, briefed to consider the proposal, was told that it was 'a transaction of the first magnitude with . . . an old-established institution transacting business all over the world on much the same lines as the Phoenix'.[10]

But there was more to it than that: in the welter of speculative amalgamation after the war, *both* Phoenix and Norwich Union Fire were potential targets for the biggest predators, and particularly for the two which furthest outstripped Phoenix in premium income, the Royal and the Commercial Union. Ryan was well aware that Phoenix and Norwich Union shared an interest in keeping themselves off the menu of these offices.

However, the explanation that the number five office was laying plans to escape the clutches of numbers one and two was not easily voiced in the public domain. Nor were such niceties as the shared marine agencies in the United States or a century's worth of cordial conversation really compelling reasons for amalgamation. Ryan was fortunate that still nicer elements were present.

It did not escape him that these 'brothers in arms, grown up together in health and strength',[11] as Hustler Tuck characteristically called them, were also remarkably prosperous brothers. Their equality was of the plutocratic variety, for each of them could dispose of some £2 million in free assets. The accretion of financial power that this represented to Phoenix – and the debilitating loss, should it be misplaced – was awesome. Ryan was duly impressed. Nevertheless, he found other arguments to assist his directors. On 8 December 1919, he listed these for the Special Committee. In the fire market, Phoenix would 'acquire a very large accession of profitable business of all classes in all parts of the world'. Indeed, since between 1913 and 1919 NUF took over 70% of its premium income from the foreign sector, it would powerfully reinforce Phoenix's great historical specialism as an exporter (see Table 7.1).

Within the United Kingdom, the company's position would also be greatly strengthened, 'especially in places and districts where the Phoenix is not at present strong'. So if Phoenix's City lore would add polish to Norwich Union, the Norwich office's provincialism would create a complementary asset for Phoenix. Then, somewhat disingenuously, Ryan added,

[8] Ryan to Sketch, 12 December 1919. [9] *The Times*, 18 December 1919.
[10] Phoenix Special Committee, 8 December 1919.
[11] Tuck to Extraordinary General Meeting of Norwich Union, 20 January 1920.

Table 7.1. *Foreign fire earnings of Norwich Union Fire, 1913–19*

	Total NUF premium £	Foreign % total	Foreign loss ratio %	NUF foreign premium £	Phoenix foreign premium £
1913	1,187,670	73.3	57.6	870,582	1,640,299
1914	1,212,612	72.9	63.2	885,083	1,538,238
1915	1,188,767	70.6	50.7	838,858	1,658,178
1916	1,292,779	71.0	53.9	917,862	1,813,183
1917	1,365,245	73.7	47.9	1,006,319	2,106,954
1918	1,602,968	73.1	45.4	1,172,487	2,476,386
1919	1,921,202	71.6	43.2	1,375,299	3,075,337

Sources: NUF Fire Manager's Account Book; Phoenix Foreign Agencies Book 4.

Incidentally also, the Phoenix will obtain a means of starting an Accident business in the United States by reason of the other company having machinery and funds available there for the purpose. For a long time we have desired to enter the American field for casualty business, but it would require transmission of funds to America in order to put up the necessary capital and reserves and this is quite impracticable in the present state of the exchange.[12]

NUF possessed a sizeable accident account, and, given Ryan's strategy of diversification by acquisition – given especially his failure to acquire an accident company in 1908 – it is difficult to see this factor as merely 'incidental' to the negotiations of 1919–20. Nor, surely, was it fortuitous that Sketch by training was an accident specialist. Indeed, accident business, and, most unfortunately, American accident business, was to remain central to Ryan's thinking throughout the 1920s. It was a powerful influence on Phoenix's appetite for NUF, even to the point perhaps of compulsive eating.

The first attempt to satisfy the craving was an oddly ingenious scheme for integration on entirely equal terms. Ryan described it as 'a somewhat novel method of bringing together the business and influence of two leading composite companies'.[13] The notion was to create a third insurance venture, a holding company – to be called the British Empire Insurance Co., perhaps a nostalgic whim of Ryan's – which would control both Phoenix and Norwich Union. Ryan was to be chairman of all three companies, Sketch general manager of all three and the Board of the

[12] Ryan to Phoenix Special Committee, 8 December 1919.

[13] Ryan to Sketch, 4 December 1919. The correspondence concerning this scheme is in Phoenix Red Box File 53.

holding company to be composed of six directors apiece from the London and Norwich offices. Ryan emphasised that, 'One policy would be pursued throughout the three companies, the control being unified by the common Chairman and General Manager. Thus the business of the two companies could be worked together with very great advantage in many directions.'[14] The combined capital of the three units would be £2.9 million and the total funds an impressive £21.9 million. Shareholding in the superstructure company was to be split exactly between Phoenix and Norwich Union Fire and – in a stipulation that was to prove fatal – it was to be purchased at the ruling share price of the other company. That is, NUF would buy its half-share of the holding company equity at the current Phoenix share price, and *vice versa*.

Neither office wished to pass out of existence or become the subsidiary of the other. The British Empire device protected this desire for autonomy beautifully, leaving the two original companies, names and styles intact. Moreover, it defended a flank vital to NUF: its special relationship with Norwich Union Life. Originally, in 1808, the life office had been an offshoot of the fire office, which was then itself a mutual office. However, in 1821 NUF became a proprietary company while NUL stayed a mutual. Subsequently, the two Norwich offices developed as separate ventures in capital and organisation. Nevertheless, over many decades they maintained a close collaboration, sharing directors and agencies, handing on business and enjoying a high reputation within their home city. In its relations with other companies, NUF could not afford to compromise the Norwich identity, sacrifice its own name or divert business from NUL; within the local economy the consequences would have been dire. However, a joint interest in the British Empire Insurance would have enlarged the scope of NUF's operations without risking any of these outcomes.

It is not surprising, then, that Sketch found the British Empire proposal, 'the one that appeals to us, in fact it is the only one to concentrate on'.[15] It fitted the Norwich calculus. But it also fitted the Ryan composite strategy. He reflected upon the neatness with which the NUF project conformed with the current flow in the multiple insurance market:

> The present feature of insurance business is the movement in the direction of large combines which constitute a very powerful rivalry to those undertakings which maintain an isolated existence. The scheme . . . provides a means of defending the interest of two of the oldest Companies while fully preserving their separate identities.[16]

[14] *Ibid.* [15] Sketch to Ryan, 26 November 1919.
[16] Ryan to Sketch, 4 December 1919.

Ryan had in mind growth, competition, defence – and, of course, accident.

Yet despite the rapid construction of an accord between Ryan and Sketch – in a flurry of letters, at a rate of several per day, they progressed from introductory remarks to the full-blown holding company scheme within the space of two weeks (between 25 November and 4 December 1919) – and despite the obviously warm personal relations between the two men – reinforced by Sketch's trips from Norwich to Ryan's conveniently situated mansion at Hintlesham Hall – the proposal was not accorded an equally swift or rapturous reception by the Phoenix Board.

The fall in insurance company shares in late 1919 did not help, for, in a bear market, it would be more difficult to promote the equities of a new holding company than those of two old dependables. But these were not the only worries over shares. Sharp eyes detected evidence of over-eagerness in the financial arrangements especially. John Tryon pointed out the flaw in the proposed scheme for the purchase of joint shares in the holding company: the NUF shares stood at £90, the Phoenix shares at only £15. If Phoenix were required to buy its half of the equity at £90 per share and NUF its half at £15 per share, the London company would end up £2.2 million out of pocket, to the profit of the Norwich office. Yet, as Tryon stressed, 'our free capital is at least £1 million, not to say £2 million, bigger than the Norwich Union. Our premium income is bigger. Our profits are bigger.'[17]

The only inference to be drawn from Ryan's apparent willingness to accept such financial sacrifice is that he was desperate to have NUF in the Phoenix fold. Certainly, his regard for the sharp price, so evident in his pre-war acquisitions, is notably absent here. So too is his ability to carry the Board. Although the introductory stages of the negotiations had been carried out with Ryan's customary secrecy – his directors had no inkling before early December – the Phoenix Board, when they did find out, declined to let him have his way at this price. Another way had to be found. But, even when it was, it is worth recalling that another Phoenix director, J. F. Lescher, believed that the NUF shareholders had been 'uncommon well treated'.[18]

The second way was found with enormous speed. Tryon had hammered the coffin nails into the holding company scheme on 6 December. On the same day, Sketch and Ryan met again at Hintlesham. Their discussion produced the framework for a full fusion between the two companies; the formal notes of these talks are virtually a draft of the final

[17] Tryon to Ryan, 6 December 1919. [18] Lescher to Ryan, 9 December 1919.

agreement between Phoenix and NUF. When Ryan told the Special Committee about the NUF proposal on 8 December, it was the fusion scheme that he put before them. Also on 8 December, the NUF Board agreed to receive an offer couched in these terms and to recommend it to their shareholders.[19] Two days later the scheme was approved by the full Phoenix Board, and the press announcements went out on 12 December. Shareholders got the details by circular on 17 December. The memorandum of agreement was signed on 12 January 1920, although the arrangement was actually to run from the first day of the new year. Both companies held Extraordinary General Meetings on 20 January and final confirmation was achieved on 18 February 1920. Ryan clearly was in a hurry. As he told the Special Committee early in December 1919, 'Negotiations have only been pending for a few days, and, as you will readily perceive, despatch and secrecy are essential.'[20]

Despatch was certainly achieved, but one of Ryan's worries was that secrecy was under threat. There was considerable speculative dealing in the shares of both companies in late November and early December. The market executed the classic minuet for a bid rumour: NUF shares rose as Phoenix shares dipped. Ryan found the leaks 'most annoying', especially as 'I do not think we have lost a moment's time'. He thought it a reason for informing shareholders posthaste.[21] Sketch could not 'trace any leakage of information from this end' and thought that 'the marking up of our shares is more the result of intelligent anticipation than of actual knowledge'. However, he did add, in a possible reference to Union Marine, that 'it would appear as if Liverpool had some knowledge beforehand'.[22]

Nevertheless, this was a relatively small imperfection in a scheme apparently executed with all Ryan's old panache. Its general design retained many of the guiding principles of the British Empire device. As *The Times* realised, the intention was 'a real fusion . . . not a mere absorption . . . [but] a new career of the closest joint working'.[23] As before, each company was to pursue business under its own name, its own organisation and its own Board. The individuality of each office was to be emphasised, while 'gaining advantage from joining with the other'. Capital in the new venture was again to be held equally by Phoenix and NUF shareholders. The same power structure as envisaged in the British Empire scheme was to be retained since the chairman of Phoenix (Ryan) was to become the chairman of both Boards, while the general manager of NUF (Sketch) was

[19] NUF Private Minute Book, 8 December 1919.
[20] Ryan to Special Committee, 8 December 1919.
[21] Ryan to Royden, 13 December 1919. [22] Sketch to Ryan, 13 December 1919.
[23] *The Times*, 18 December 1919.

to become the general manager of both units within the fused company. There was to be an exchange of directors with five NUF directors (Tuck, Buxton, Chamberlin, Large, Walter) joining the Phoenix Board and five Phoenix men sitting on the Norwich Board. At this point, the question of travelling and hotel expenses for the Norwich directors caused some consternation, but it was decided that the larger good justified the costly shuttle between East Anglia and the City. Amidst smiles all round, Hustler Tuck was made an additional deputy chairman of Phoenix.

Perhaps most important was the renewed – indeed strengthened – concern about Norwich Union Life. With NUF effectively absorbed by Phoenix – whatever the disclaimers – this was obviously a sharper worry than that raised by the proposal to incorporate NUF within the British Empire scheme. So the safeguards were stringent. The long-standing community of interest between NUF and NUL had to be protected.[24] Thus Phoenix was not to compete in the life market with NUL, and NUF was not to pass life business to Phoenix. Here a major principle of the fusion, and of all Ryan's acquisitions, to generate non-fire diversification, was abrogated in favour of NUL. Just to be on the safe side, two of the five directors recruited from NUF to the Phoenix Board were to be directors also of NUL (Tuck and Chamberlin). Sketch was very exercised that his back should be protected in Norwich: 'Our income here is a very substantial, profitable one and anything that safeguards this should be done. Our competitors here will not be slow to try and foster the idea that we are no longer *the* local choice.'[25] Proper handling of NUL was indispensable to remaining the local hero.

Hustler Tuck was exceptionally careful to spell out the special conditions accepted by Phoenix when he faced his shareholders at the NUF Extraordinary General Meeting on 20 January,

> Provision is also made for the maintenance of our close association with our old friend the Norwich Union Life Office. An association of such a nature is not lightly set aside . . . although the Phoenix will carry on life business, they would place no obstacle in the way of the continuation of such relationship – but, on the contrary, they have assisted in cementing it.[26]

Clearly, there were problems in absorbing a major provincial office that were a good deal thornier than meeting the directors' travelling expenses. Some, however, though unexpected, were almost endearing. Thus Sketch has to warn the Phoenix secretary about the special nature of transaction costs in East Anglia:

[24] It had been codified by an important agreement of January 1908. See below, pp. 471–2.

[25] Sketch to Ryan 19 December 1919 (emphasis in original).

[26] Chairman's Speech to NUF Extraordinary General Meeting, 20 January 1920.

My fear is that a number of our somewhat old-fashioned shareholders would be thrown into a turmoil if they were to receive an envelope containing all these documents at once. I am quite in agreement with you from the businessman's point of view . . . but hardly feel that this procedure would assist in making matters go smoothly.[27]

Phoenix bowed to local lore and the investors of Norwich were not baffled.

Yet there was a sequel. The Norwich officials *were* baffled by the newspapers and Sketch had to enlist the assistance of metropolitan lore in dealing with the gentlemen of the press.

In one respect, any observer of the Phoenix–NUF fusion could have been excused for suffering bafflement. The respect was financial. The share arrangements for the fusion were not simple. Prior to the fusion, Phoenix capital stood at £3.2 million, divided into 309,775 shares of £10 denomination (£1 paid) and 113,100 Phoenix (Pelican) shares of £1 denomination (fully paid). NUF's capital stood at £1.1 million divided into 44,000 shares of £25 denomination (£3 paid). In order to buy out the NUF shareholders Phoenix agreed to issue 440,000 new Phoenix (Norwich Union) shares of £1 denomination (fully paid). NUF shareholders were to get ten of these new shares for every one old NUF share they held. But this left Phoenix proprietors with less than a half share in the total capital while the agreement demanded equal shares. So Phoenix was forced to issue a further 17,125 shares to its own shareholders in order to achieve the grand total of 440,000 for each team. The Board chose to make these additional shares Phoenix (Pelican) £1 shares because these were most like the new Phoenix (Norwich Union) £1 shares. At the end of all this, Phoenix boasted a total nominal capital of £3.7 million, divided into three different types of ordinary share. By the end of March 1920, Phoenix had acquired 95% of NUF capital. That was a tidy conclusion, but the capital scheme which achieved it was scarcely elegant in construction.

However, untidiness was not the major flaw within these financial dispensations. The issue rather was the balance of monetary advantage between existing Phoenix shareholders and NUF shareholders. Phoenix bound itself to maintain the dividend that NUF shareholders had previously enjoyed. This would consume £129,000 of trading profit every year, but then the company's average annual trading profit for 1913–18 had been £330,000, so this did not seem a great worry.

The real problem lay in the relative share values. NUF shareholders had previously faced a potential call of £22 per share, since only £3 had been

[27] Sketch to Winter, 6 January 1920.

paid on the NUF share; they were now discharged of all liability since they were to receive *fully* paid Phoenix (Norwich Union) shares. Moreover, they were to get ten of these £1 shares for every one NUF share; but at the start of 1920 ten Phoenix £1 shares had a market value of about £150 while one NUF share commanded about £90. So, NUF shareholders, on market prices alone, received an immediate profit of around £60 per share, to go with their extinguished liability and their guaranteed dividend.

By contrast, the Phoenix shareholders were promised 'a very large accretion of business' and received an effective bonus of 10 shillings per share through the issue of the new fully paid shares plus an increased dividend. These gains do not compare in weight with the birds already in the hands of the NUF shareholders. Even worse was the perceived disadvantage of the 'old' Phoenix shareholders with the £10 shares, only £1 paid. The agreement turned this group, previously the majority of Phoenix shareholders, into a minority, and a minority which retained a liability of £9 per share. In effect, NUF shareholders were discharged of liability at the expense of the existing Phoenix shareholders who were now the only group to retain it. This was surely a fertile area for discord.

Viewed in another way, Phoenix secured NUF for a 30% premium. The joint market capitalisation of the two companies on the eve of the fusion was £10.3 million. NUF's share of this was £3.96 million.[28] But Phoenix paid half of the joint sum to get NUF into the fusion, i.e. £5.15 million; hence the premium. The Royal had paid a 30% premium to take Liverpool & London & Globe at the top of the market in 1919. The London & Lancashire paid a more modest 27% to get the Law Union in 1919. It was thus the tenderness towards NUF shareholders in regard to uncalled liability, together with the premium paid in a *falling* market, rather than the recent track record in asking prices, which singled out the Phoenix–NUF deal.

Lescher was not the only one to believe that the Norwich shareholders had been 'uncommon well treated', although he did supply a reason in the 'need for close husbanding of forces when so much fierce competition is ahead'.[29] Others were more forthright: the *Evening Standard* reported that, 'Evidently some shareholders of the Phoenix Assurance fail to enthuse over the absorption of the Norwich Union . . . [feeling] that the Norwich Union has had the best of the bargain.'[30] Another Phoenix director, R. K. Hodgson, recovering from his annual attack of influenza, warned Ryan in only semi-jocular style that he could only 'hope yet to

[28] NUF's pre-fusion market worth was 44,000 × £90 shares = £3.96 million; Phoenix's was 422,875 × £15 = £6.34 million.

[29] Lescher to Ryan, 9 December 1919.

[30] *Evening Standard*, 31 December 1919.

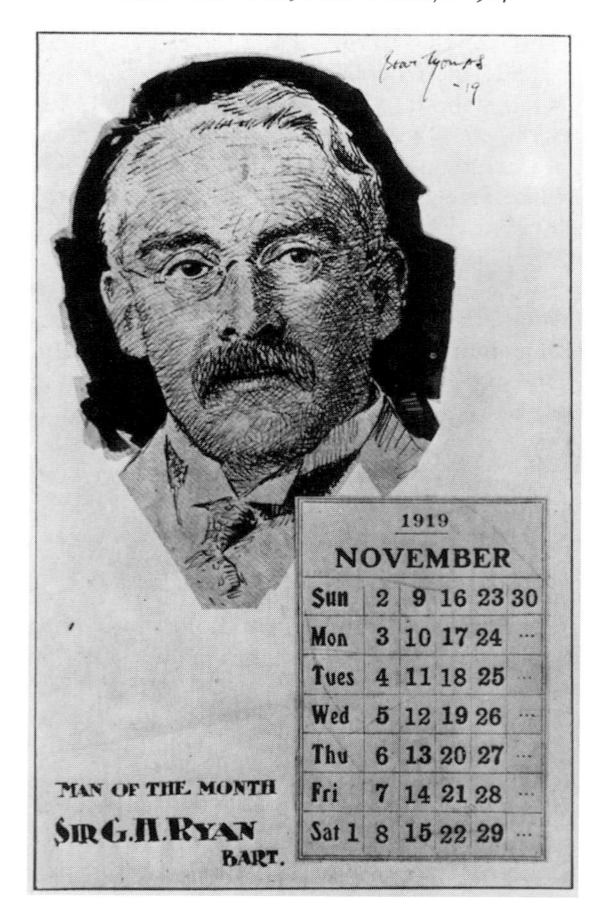

Plate 7.2 Gerald Ryan as Man of the Month, November 1919.

face our infuriated shareholders'.[31] Over-eagerness seemed once more to be expressing itself in the form of an improbable financial largesse.

Nevertheless, Ryan sailed on. He attended his first Board meeting in Norwich on 29 December 1919 and was 'highly gratified at the kindness of my reception'.[32] This was scarcely surprising: in Norwich, Ryan was regarded as a metropolitan Merlin, the underwriting equivalent of the man who had discovered the philosopher's stone. When addressing his first joint shareholders' meeting as chairman at the end of January 1920,

[31] Hodgson to Ryan, 27 January 1920. [32] Ryan to Sketch, 1 January 1920.

he stressed the familiar themes, 'a natural development of an old alliance... the considerable margin of surplus profit accruing in the future... the greater powers of defence against competition', and, certainly not least in his mind, 'the cooperation of two powerful companies [which] will open up a wider field of enterprise in that important part of the world'.[33] By the last he meant, of course, the United States.

However, even amidst this optimistic and congratulatory review, he did find it necessary to concede that 'a few unfavourable comments have reached the Board, based upon the view that the terms are too liberal to the Norwich Union shareholders'. But he defied their mathematical logic, and, concentrating upon the future gains to capacity, ended with his own rousing approach to the figures, 'If I had not great respect for the laws of arithmetic, I should say that, in this case, 2 and 2 do not make 4 but 5 or some higher number.'[34] Yet there were some who muttered that this was precisely the kind of arithmetic that he must have applied to the NUF share values.

The Phoenix–NUF fusion has some of the old Ryan magic. It was done with great speed, yet across an enormous sweep of detail. His control of the detail was formidable, as was the ability to rework it to create within days an alternative to the failed British Empire proposal. As before, he prided himself, justifiably, upon the standard of negotiations conducted 'in the most amicable and harmonious spirit'.[35] He was right too about the boost to capacity. Total Phoenix premium income more than doubled between the earning years 1919 and 1920. Fire and marine earnings rose by similar amounts (128.4% and 117.4% respectively), while accident earnings, reflecting significantly on Ryan's priorities, rocketed by 852.8%. Life income provided something of a control since NUF could not transact this type of business: it rose by 2.1% only. Taken all round, Phoenix was about twice as big at the end of 1920 as it had been towards the end of 1919.

There are perhaps three pauses for thought. The negotiations were marked by a kind of financial over-optimism, even a type of rashness that was new in Ryan's handling of major acquisitions. NUF was clearly worth having, but it would have been more reassuring had Ryan sought to have it at a keener price. A second doubt follows from the first: despite the ready acceptance of a high price for NUF, the negotiations considered few *other* aspects of the deal than the financial. There was a little, but not much, discussion between Ryan and Sketch on the business implications of the fusion and even less upon its possible administrative repercussions. This relative nonchalance about administrative detail carried

[33] Chairman's Annual Report, 28 January 1920. [34] *Ibid.* [35] *Ibid.*

some penalty in regard to the NUF acquisition but was to prove positively lethal in regard to the next item on Ryan's shopping list, London Guarantee & Accident. Lastly, there is a serious reservation concerning Phoenix's growing preoccupation with accident business and particularly American accident business. Again, this was a feature which proved reasonably safe in the NUF fusion but enormously destructive in the takeover of London Guarantee & Accident.

Nevertheless, an optimistic reading would concentrate on what NUF brought to Phoenix. By 1925, Phoenix would have been a great deal poorer if it had *not* possessed NUF. Indeed, it would have been poorer to the tune of about £2,228,260 or 41.5% of its fire account, by about £2,152,705 or 35.2% of its accident account and by about £506,995 or 48.7% of its marine account. Altogether in 1925 Phoenix would have been a smaller operation by some 30% had it not possessed NUF. We know these counterfactual proportions so exactly because, unfortunately, by 1925 they were not counterfactual at all. By 1925 an optimistic reading was not possible because Phoenix no longer possessed NUF and *was* poorer by exactly these amounts and proportions. The reason was that Ryan's final acquisition – London Guarantee & Accident – went so badly wrong that his successful penultimate acquisition – NUF – had to be sold to cover the cost of the damage.

2. AN AMERICAN ACCIDENT IN LONDON

The acquisition of London Guarantee & Accident (LGA) in 1922 was one of the worst things to happen to the Phoenix in the twentieth century. In the short term, it was a financial disaster. Before long it became a corporate disaster, requiring the shedding of Norwich Union Fire. In the longer run, its effect on corporate memory, especially the contribution to it of former LGA men, like Edward Ferguson, was the inculcation of an unwarranted caution, long after the time when caution was actually needed had passed. Responsibility is difficult to allocate. Ryan, though a non-executive chairman, was much involved in the deal and many of his long-running interests were centrally in play. The power, range and vivacity of his Chairman's Annual Reports in the early 1920s establish beyond doubt that Ryan remained a central power in Phoenix's affairs.[36] Sketch, though very proficient in the subsequent damage control, displayed a good-natured innocence in the earlier financial negotiations that sometimes beggars belief.

[36] See Chapter 8 below.

PHŒNIX ASSURANCE COMPANY LIMITED

BOARD OF DIRECTORS.

Chairman:
Right Hon. Lord George Hamilton, P.C., G.C.S.I.

Deputy-Chairman:
Bristow Bovill, Esq.

General Manager:
G. H. Ryan.

Policy No. MR 130892

Renewable Michaelmas 1911

Annual Premium ... £21 : 5 : -
Odd time to

Quarter Day ... £ - : - : -

First Premium ... £23 : 8 : 8

Head Offices: 19 & 70, LOMBARD STREET, LONDON, E.C.

MOTOR POLICY.
(PRIVATE CAR.)

Whereas GERALD HEMMINGTON RYAN ESQ. of 29, Harcourt House, Cavendish Square, London, W. (hereinafter called "the Insured") has made to the PHŒNIX ASSURANCE COMPANY, LIMITED (hereinafter called "the Company") a written Proposal and Declaration containing certain particulars and statements which it is hereby agreed shall be the basis of this contract and be considered as incorporated herein.

Now this Policy witnesseth that in consideration of the payment to the Company of the above-mentioned Premium in respect of the First Insurance Period commencing at noon on the 24th June 1910 and ending at noon on the 29th September 1911 it is hereby agreed that the Company whilst this Policy is in force shall indemnify the Insured as hereinafter mentioned during the said First Insurance Period and also (subject to this Policy remaining in force) during any further period for which the Insured shall pay and the Company shall accept an agreed sum as Premium, namely:—

(A) Accidental Damage. The Company shall pay or make good any damage caused by accidental means to any Motor Vehicle belonging to the Insured and described in the Schedule hereto whilst such Motor Vehicle is in the custody of the Insured or of the Insured's paid and duly authorised and licensed male driver (including damage to Rubber Tyres and Accessories in the event of the Motor Vehicle itself being damaged) and also any accidental damage in transit during carriage on any road railway or inland waterway but always only to the extent of the sum of Four Hundred Pounds in respect of any one "accident." The word "accident" shall include a series of accidents occurring in connection with or arising out of one event.
Exclusions. Provided always that this Clause shall not cover Wear and Tear or Depreciation or damage from or arising out of Fire or Explosion or Self-ignition or Mechanical Breakdown.

(B) Claims by the Public. The Company shall indemnify the Insured against all sums which the Insured shall be liable to pay and shall pay in respect of Accidental Injury to any Person or Accidental Damage to any Property caused by any Motor Vehicle belonging to the Insured and described in the Schedule hereto whilst in the custody of the Insured or of the Insured's paid and duly authorised and licensed male Driver but always only to the extent of the sum of Unlimited in respect of each "accident" which word "accident" shall be held to include a series of accidents occurring in connection with or arising out of one event whether the said accident shall cause injury to one or more persons and/or damage to one or more items of property and the Company shall in addition be liable for the expenses of litigation incurred by or with the written consent of the Company. Provided always that where any sum is recovered against the Insured in respect of accidental injury and/or accidental damage in excess of the said sum of Unlimited the Insured shall be liable for such excess and shall also pay such a proportion of the costs and expenses of the proceedings as the said excess bears to the total sum recovered.
Exclusions. Provided always that the Company shall not be liable under this Clause for injury to any Person driving or being driven in or mounting into or dismounting from any such Motor Vehicle or to any Person in the Insured's service or acting on behalf of the Insured or for damage to any Property belonging to or held in trust by or in the custody or control of the Insured.

(C) Injury to Owner. If the Insured shall sustain any bodily injury by accidental external and visible means directly arising in connection with any Motor Vehicle belonging to the Insured ...

Plate 7.3 Accident protection: Ryan's motor policy for 1911.

Of course, Ryan had tried to buy London Guarantee once before, in 1907; but the LGA had priced itself out of the deal. Also, Ryan had then been properly wary of the gains to be had from the American market; and it may be that he would have done better to maintain this wariness. He had wanted an accident company in 1907. And in 1922, Phoenix still lacked a specialist accident company. Yet to go back to the same accident company in 1922 could argue for a certain lack of imagination. Why should diversification into accident equate to diversification into LGA? At this point, Phoenix seems rather to have been running on rails. The explanation for this lies in a peculiar saga that centres on the years 1912–22.

It must be conceded at the outset that the LGA of early 1922 was a very different company from the LGA of 1907. Its total premium income had risen from £395,160 to £5,139,885, over three-quarters of it drawn from the United States at each point. However, by 1922 it also took business from eighteen other countries. It had enjoyed particularly rapid income growth during the war period and in the immediate aftermath, especially in US general accident business.

But these major increases in scale did not depend on accident or America alone. In 1909 the company had diversified into UK and European fire insurance and from 1920 added an American fire trade through its purchases of the North Empire Insurance Co. of Canada (1920) and most of the equity of the important United Firemen's Insurance Co. of Philadelphia (1921). Furthermore, in 1915 it had launched into marine business and in 1919 into life assurance. London Guarantee's authorised capital had remained at £250,000 since the company's inception in 1869 but was increased to £375,000 in 1920, 52% paid up. Total assets had soared from their pre-war levels, of £1.0 million in 1911 to £6.25 million in 1920.

Undoubtedly then, LGA had become a much bigger, and, apparently, richer prize, and one that had gone through its own process of evolution towards the composite form in the 1900s and 1910s. By 1920, its diversified income flow of over £5.1 million was not inconsiderable even by the standards of Phoenix's diversified income flow of £9.9 million. But it was LGA's accident business which remained the lure for Phoenix. Around 1909, LGA's accident account had dwarfed Phoenix's own by a factor of ten but by 1919 the disparity had worsened to a factor of seventeen. This was before Phoenix got its talons into the accident income of NUF; but, even after it had done so, LGA retained a superiority of better than two-to-one, with total accident receipts in 1921 of £3,486,805 against the Phoenix-NUF figure of £1,666,263. If the Phoenix of 1921 was roughly twice as large as the LGA in terms of total earnings, the LGA's accident account remained double the size of Phoenix's own, despite the latter's best efforts and a major amalgamation.

The position of LGA in the American accident[37] market looked similarly impressive. In 1920 it took $14 million in US accident premiums, making it the third largest UK operator in this business;[38] only the Employers' Liability and Ocean Accident did better. It seemed therefore that the enlarged LGA offered Ryan what he had wanted since the early 1900s – the possibility of becoming an outstanding force in the accident market. LGA had size, rich assets, useful subsidiaries and geographical spread.

But LGA was a company of appearances. Many of the realities were much less appealing. Profitability was one of these realities: there were difficulties here from the 1900s, and they did not diminish with time. Even in 1906, the United States was yielding a gross profit on premium income

[37] The US usage is, of course, 'casualty' rather than accident, but, with UK companies writing US accident business, matters become confusing, and it seems best to retain 'accident' as the standard form.

[38] Memorandum of R. Y. Sketch on London Guarantee & Accident, 27 October 1921.

Table 7.2. *Net underwriting profit of London Guarantee & Accident, 1912–20 (% net premiums)*

	General business	Accident	All business
1913	1.6	2.4	1.3
1914	0.8	0.3	0.9
1915	1.1	0.3	0.9
1916	1.1	0.3	1.3
1917	1.8	4.4	2.1
1918	3.1	2.8	3.0
1919	–	–	8.4
1920	–	–	0.8

Sources: Phoenix Translation of LGA Accounts, 1913–18; Sketch Memorandum on LGA, 27 October 1921 for 1919 and 1920.

of 9% against 10% for the United Kingdom, 20% for Canada and 30% for Australia; and LGA was devoted to American business. The results for the company's net underwriting surplus for 1913–18 were even more worrying (see Table 7.2); and the average trading surplus for all departments over this period was a paltry 1.89% on net premiums. During the negotiations between Phoenix and LGA in 1921, Sketch was in possession of figures which gave a scarcely more impressive result of 2.76% for the years 1916–20.[39] If LGA's American business grew strongly during the war, so did LGA's American losses: exceptionally heavy claims on liability business extinguished all profit from that department between 1912 and 1916.

Consequently, at no point in the pre-war years or down to 1920 was there much left over for the proprietors. LGA suffered much shareholder discontent on this score: the passing of the dividend in 1912 and the meagre distributions of profit in subsequent years produced sheaves of angry letters. And comment was not restricted only to insiders: as early as 1915 a senior Phoenix official had detected that LGA's 'trading profit is . . . a dangerously narrow percentage of premiums' and he concluded prophetically, 'it is not a figure that would justify anyone in forming very optimistic views for the future'.[40]

However, it was not simply the profit record which ran up warning signals over LGA. It was also the treatment meted out to insurance reserve funds, largely as a result of poor profitability. This danger flag first

[39] *Ibid.*

[40] Memorandum of A. T. Winter, Phoenix Life Manager for General Manager, 15 May 1915.

fluttered in 1912, but it was to fly continuously for the best part of the next two decades. Reserves against three dangers of the trade – unearned premiums, unexpired risks and claims – were to be the heart of the LGA crisis for Phoenix. In 1912 LGA suffered an appalling year: the *Titanic* sank, the US authorities demanded bigger insurance deposits, and US employers' liability claims were punitive in the extreme. Shares halved and the dividend evaporated. Under such withering fire, LGA turned to accounting devices that were either unfamiliar by British standards, or unhealthy by any standards.

By the 1910s, British and American practice for dealing with one aspect of insurance reserves – the reserve against unearned premiums – already differed. All insurers of the modern era require a reserve against the portion of premiums that the client has paid or contracted to pay but for which the risk has still some time to run at the normal balance sheet date. The British approach of the 1910s – and it remained the British approach until the 1960s – was to establish an across-the-board reserve of 40% of gross premiums written. The American system was to gear the reserve *pro rata*, on a monthly basis and on each contract, to the proportion of the gross premium written but not earned.[41] Since the effect of this is to include in the unwritten premium reserve an element representing expenses which in reality have already been paid in acquiring the business, the outcome is to create a portion of 'artificial equity' – perhaps as much as 30–35% of the fund – in the reserve. This more 'scientific' method can generate considerable financial strength for the insurer, as long as premiums are rising well.[42]

For LGA, however, there is surely significance in the fact that it first turned to this method in its *annus horribilis* of 1912. Presumably, the attraction was that, instead of any given percentage of total premiums written being drafted straight to the reserves, smaller allocations could be made *pro rata*;[43] thus, quite modest sums could be presented as secure percentage reserves. This *was* American practice, and, subsequently, British practice. So, there was some force in the complaint of LGA's Chairman, A. W. Tait, in his Report for 1914, that 'unjust criticism' had been levelled against his company, simply because it did not calculate its unearned premium reserve against total premiums written.

41 More recent practice, in a world where information travels faster, is to revise the reserve on a daily basis.

42 And as long as the anticipated loss ratio used in calculating the original rate for the insurance is not exceeded. Of course, if gross written premiums begin to fall, the boot is on the other foot.

43 This requires the manipulation of the start, or renewal, dates of contracts.

Plate 7.4 'Insure your car with the LGA.'

The snag was, of course, that the vast majority of British insurers remained puzzled by the 'American' method, if they thought about it at all, for a further half-century. So, it was natural that, between 1912 and 1914, eyebrows should be raised. A pair of these belonged to an active and well-informed shareholder who, in commenting on the 1913 results, complained to LGA's General Manager, 'I cannot find any improvement on those for 1912, and I fear that you have not earned any dividend . . . *The provision for unearned premiums . . . points to increasing weakness – indeed this*

Table 7.3. *Reserves against unexpired risks as % general premiums: seven companies, 1902–20*

	1902	1912	1920
Century	–	138.0	49.0
Commercial Union	85.1	43.1	48.3
Employers' Liability	–	–	40.0
Guardian	46.6	43.3	48.5
Ocean	31.3	36.3	58.0
Royal	40.8	40.0	40.0
LGA	58.5	37.4	37.1

is so serious that it calls for some explanation now.'[44] Of course, he may also have detected that a whiff of implausibility attached to Tait.

Nevertheless, in respect to the unearned premium reserve, LGA could cite American practice. It is far more difficult to defend the company's habits in regard to the reserve against unexpired risks. Phoenix had formally converted in 1917 to the convention that the unexpired risk reserve should set at 40% of premiums written. LGA's reserve hovered around this level in 1908 and 1909 but fell to 29.3% by 1913; and was still below the convention in 1920. Here no comparative test afforded Tait any defence. Certainly, no redefinition of practice could make LGA's tactics look respectable by the standards of its British peers (see Table 7.3).[45]

At the least, Tait's defence of LGA's reserve policies was disingenuous. He must have known perfectly well the financial reasons that had pushed the company into these policies. In fact LGA's dividend in 1911 had been maintained only by financing it from the reserves. This took the real unexpired risk reserve down to 36.1%. Then the 1912 results produced, but only to the discerning eye, a trading loss of £96,797. By 1913, there was a tremendous crash in the real reserve to 29.3%. It was caused by a further trading loss of £30,000 but this did not show in the books at all; instead these displayed a surplus of over £18,000. The reason they did so was that £48,738 had been pillaged from the reserve in order to prettify the profit and loss account.

Such audacious financial tactics did not go unremarked, least of all in 1912. The *Financial News* commented that 'the progressive policy fa-

[44] J. H. Coles to H. C. Thiselton, 30 September 1912 (my emphasis).

[45] Technically, LGA's levels of claims reserves *could* have been sufficient had the anticipated loss ratio remained low (say below 30%). But this was rarely the case for US accident business 1910–41.

voured of late years by the directors has led to a large increase in business' but concluded, rather mildly, that 'the quality of the business has suffered'.[46]

The underlying reality was that a mixture of statistical manipulation, reference to American practice and selective representation, if not outright misrepresentation, of profits and reserves became, and remained well into the early 1920s, the distinctive house style of the LGA. Many were confused by it.

Phoenix could surely not have been among them. For by an extraordinary connection, the harshly critical shareholder of 1912 was provided with information by the discerning eye which had followed the strange highlights through the LGA accounts. And the eye belonged to a Phoenix man. Indeed, this is the sole reason that we have such exact knowledge of LGA's unusual past, prior to the Phoenix takeover. In 1910, the shareholder, J. H. Coles, worried by LGA's performance, approached Ryan for advice. Always interested in LGA's performance, Ryan set Phoenix's best actuarial brain, Life Manager A. T. Winter, upon the LGA accounts. Winter reported upon them continuously, for both Coles and Ryan, from 1910 until 1917. If any office was in a position to judge the possible shortcomings of LGA, it was Phoenix.

Winter certainly found plenty of them. He picked up the initial fall in the reserve against unearned premiums almost immediately, in March 1911. To begin with, he thought that it might be due to variations in the average renewal dates, but warned: 'If, however, this is not so, and it is a weakness in the Reserve, it is, of course, a very important feature of the accounts.'[47] Winter, of course, was applying British conventions. The 1913 balance sheet left him in less doubt; there he found clear manipulation of the unexpired risk reserve: 'The serious feature of the Accounts is the large fall in the percentage of Premiums reserved for unexpired risks.'[48] He put the reduction at no less than £80,000. And, one year later, it was Winter who judged that LGA profit was 'a dangerously narrow percentage of premiums'.[49] The 1915 account he thought to be 'very poor' and its successor of 1916 only 'slightly more satisfactory'.[50]

Most important, Winter knew beyond a shadow of a doubt that LGA was in the habit of doctoring the reserves in order to conceal current trading losses. Not only the losses but the way of presenting them should surely have warned Phoenix off, especially as the company was in the remarkable position of being able to scrutinise both as they were perpetrated.

[46] *Financial News*, 30 September 1912. [47] Winter to Ryan, 15 March 1911.
[48] *Ibid.*, 27 March 1914. [49] *Ibid.*, 15 April 1915.
[50] *Ibid.*, 20 April 1916; 17 April 1917.

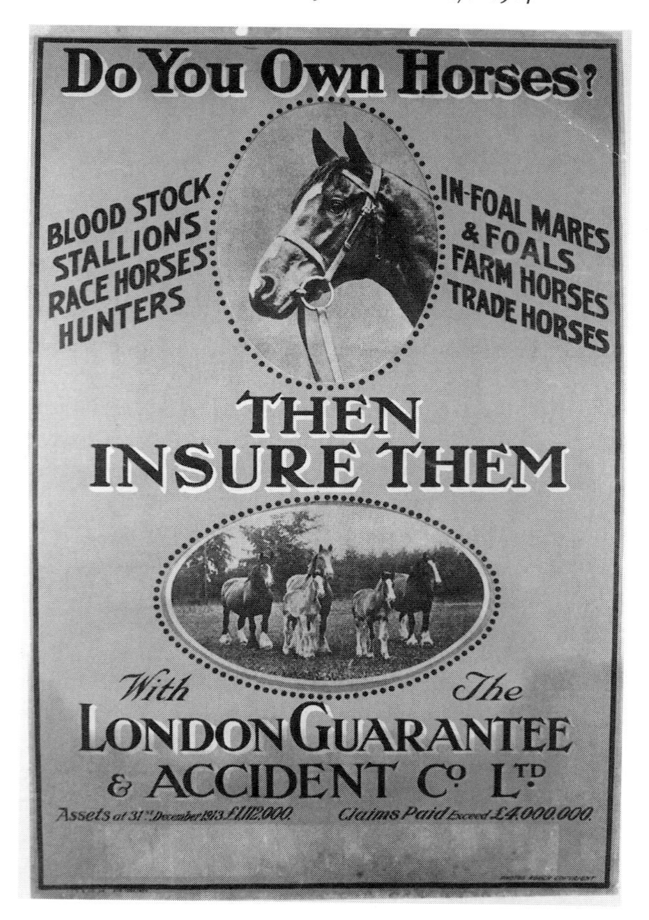

Plate 7.5 'Insure your horse with the LGA.'

It is astonishing, in these circumstances, that Phoenix should have retained its buying interest in LGA. One has to struggle for explanations. Possibly the argument was that Phoenix at least knew LGA better than it could know any other accident company. This knowledge may have convinced Ryan and Sketch that they could reform LGA and clear a good profit. They may have embarked upon this course, only to be blocked by increasingly adverse markets or unrevealed weaknesses in LGA. If Ryan had been carried along by the general burst of market speculation in 1919, this could scarcely have been true in the very different circumstances of autumn 1921. More likely, perhaps, is the possibility that Ryan and Sketch simply believed the reassurances given them by the LGA team. The Phoenix men had the correct doubts and these were robustly corrected by Tait and his colleagues; impressed by this forcefulness, Ryan and Sketch failed to detect that there was still more to doubt.

Consistent with this last position is a preoccupation of Sketch's which is the most frequent refrain in the documents. It is his desire to obtain the *interest* earnings of LGA. He had noticed that LGA drew on very little of these earnings to pay its dividend. The remaining large margin of interest could be brought into the Phoenix accounts to strengthen its dividend-paying position. This was particularly attractive since the fusion with NUF had been conducted entirely through an exchange of shares and, in consequence, Phoenix was somewhat less well placed than before in meeting dividend obligations from interest earnings. If the interest earnings of LGA could be captured, any strain could be eased and any risk of reducing the dividend escaped.[51] Sketch later recorded this as the 'main object' of the LGA purchase.[52] This potential investment advantage and matter of financial 'face' seems to have bulked larger in Sketch's mind than it should have done.

The attractions to LGA of a buy-out from Phoenix are simple by comparison. The American market was not running smoothly and there were signs that it would become rougher still. There were reserve problems. There was a profit problem. Trading profit in 1920 and 1921 was still only fractionally above 2% of total net premiums and that total in 1921 was 11.2% down on the 1920 figure. And there was a debt problem. LGA had never been flush with funds, but its resort to temporary loans increased massively after 1918 (see Table 7.4).

The main reason for this illiquidity, before the onset of the American problems, was LGA's singularly ill-judged expansion of marine business

Table 7.4. *LGA: total temporary loans incurred per annum*[a]

1912	63,000	1916	17,000	1920	231,000
1913	17,200	1917	10,000	1921	970,000
1914	0	1918	31,000	1922	437,000
1915	3,000	1919	94,000		

Note: [a]Gross of repayments.
Source: LGA Minute Books.

[51] In fact, Phoenix was very successful in maintaining dividend payments during the 1920s. See below, pp. 494, 496, 502.

[52] Sketch to Walters, 23 October 1920.

Plate 7.6 Pre-feminist insurance by the LGA.

from 1917, at a time when the shrewd operators, Phoenix among them, were cutting back. By the end of 1921 LGA was having to consider increasing its borrowing powers up to the full amount of its authorised capital, and this was carried out in 1922. But the debt was still rising during the period of the takeover negotiations: by June 1922, it had reached an accumulated total of £368,000, only £6,000 short of the new limit, and more heavy payments on the marine account were imminent. LGA had every reason for presenting itself seductively to Phoenix.

So, for a complex of reasons, Phoenix and LGA were once again negotiating by August 1921. These negotiations were very private, and the press which reported fully on Phoenix's eventual acquisition of LGA in mid-May 1922, never got wind of these talks. They were restricted, very much in the Ryan style, to a cast of six: for the Phoenix side, Ryan, Sketch and Southam (the accident manager of NUF), and, for LGA, the chairman (A. W. Tait), the general manager (H. C. Thiselton) and Ryan's contact on the LGA Board, Whittall. True to form, at no time in 1921 did Ryan even tell his deputy chairman what was afoot.

It may not be irrelevant to the character, nor to the outcome, of these talks that Tait, who held twenty-four industrial directorships, fell foul of a public scandal in 1925 and was moved to resign from many boards, including the chairmanship of the British Aluminium Company and the Phoenix seat which he had gained through the LGA takeover. Tait was a highly placed accountant, partner in Messrs George A. Touche & Co., reconstructor of companies and one of the influences behind the formation in 1916 of the Federation of British Industries.[53] Yet, early in 1925, it was revealed in the High Court that the British Trusts Association Ltd, of which Tait was also chairman, and which was Trustee for the debenture holders of the Magadi Soda Company – a company under offer from Brunner Mond – had failed to defend the interests of these debenture holders or even to answer properly their inquiries concerning the bid, while itself purchasing the debentures at knockdown prices. In a scathing summing up, Mr Justice Eve revealed a clear abuse of powers and found the action of the trustees in 'the deliberate concealment of matters vitally affecting the value of the beneficiary's interest... unsavoury and discreditable'. Tait was deeply implicated and was judged to be in 'grave dereliction of duty'.[54] In view of the difficulties caused to Phoenix by the LGA acquisition, the conjunction is at least unfortunate. So too was the fact that the secrecy of Ryan's negotiations eliminated from the early discussions the man who knew most about LGA's closets, A. T. Winter.

Nevertheless, even without Winter's guidance, Phoenix gave little sign of over-keenness in 1921. Southam's eye was no less sharp than Winter's and it spotted trouble. This time it lay in a third area of reserves. Southam thought that LGA's American figures 'have been to some extent "doctored" in the General Balance Sheet, especially as regards Claims Reserves'.[55] He judged that these were £110,000 short of a safe figure.[56]

[53] See R. P. T. Davenport-Hines, *Dudley Docker, The Life and Times of a Trade Warrior* (Cambridge, 1984), p. 108.

[54] *The Times*, 13 February 1925; *Daily Mail*, 14 February 1925.

[55] Southam to Sketch, 3 August 1921.

[56] Southam, Memorandum on Company X, 5 August 1921.

Alongside the doubts provoked by LGA's handling of its reserves, Phoenix also began to suspect that the accident men were again tending to overprice themselves. By August 1921, they were asking two Phoenix shares for one LGA share, whereas the most Ryan was prepared to offer was three Phoenix for two LGA. After two months of talking around these numbers, Ryan was all for withdrawing 'with a bow and an apology'.[57]

However, LGA was not prepared to give up so easily, and, towards the end of October, Thiselton came back with a very hard sell: that 'the Accounts as published did not disclose the full strength of the company . . . the business was capable of producing a greater profit than their past record would appear to justify'.[58] Sketch was actually satisfied 'that there were undisclosed assets for a substantial amounts';[59] but it does not seem to have crossed his mind that there might also be more undisclosed liabilities. Nevertheless, for all its energetic puffing, LGA was not disposed to move on its price and by December 1921 the negotiations were effectively stalled. Ominously, however, Sketch let slip how impressed he was with Thiselton's 'thorough grasp . . . of the American position' and Tait returned from America in December 'full of enthusiasm as to the future prospects for their business over there'.[60] Clearly, the Phoenix men were still vulnerable to the call of the transatlantic market.

This impressionability surfaced again when negotiations restarted in earnest in spring 1922. The critical talks took place in Tait's quarters at Touche's and were concluded very rapidly between 5 and 17 May. It is unclear why the process should have recommenced so abruptly and concluded so quickly. Conceivably, publication of LGA's results for 1921 provided the trigger, but, with premium income down by over 11%, it could not have been because they were especially good. Nevertheless, to the historian's eye, these 1921 accounts are unintentionally revealing in regard to LGA's methods of thought and presentation. They are spectacularly unhelpful. Premium receipts of a few hundreds or thousands of pounds are cited for UK business in accident, employers' liability and fire. By contrast, the anonymous heading 'Other Classes' is attributed over £3 million worth of income; almost all of this was unspecified American income. The accompanying note merely says, 'In this account is included the Workmen's Compensation and Employers' Liability business in the United States, which has shown satisfactory results.' This

[57] Ryan to Whittall, 10 October 1921. [58] Sketch, Memorandum, 27 October 1921.
[59] *Ibid.* This was a major error. LGA was showing 'savings' on its US reserves as assets.
[60] Sketch to Thiselton, 27 October 1921; Sketch to Ryan 28 December 1921.

Plate 7.7 LGA as a global insurer.

formula, used yearly, in fair weather and foul, concealed on this occasion a loss ratio in excess of 60%. Naturally, Phoenix had means of obtaining better information than LGA's luckless shareholders. But, even so, the bland distortion of these public documents is instructive.

From the LGA viewpoint, it was very likely that it was an element on display – the reduction in premium income – that produced a greater willingness to accept a keener bid price. And a further privately conceded element – a loss on LGA home business of £90,000 – would have reinforced this effect. Sketch knew about this loss but was glad to accept that it was 'due to high expenses incurred in maintaining their home organisation in competition with the large composite companies', a feature which, of course, would disappear once LGA was itself part of a large composite company. From the Phoenix viewpoint, there may well have been relief that the figures were not worse. The American results were undeniably poor, but this merely provoked the major misjudgement from

Ryan that they constituted 'a mere incident, only a bad start'.[61] Indifferent results were greeted with an outbreak of optimism in the Phoenix camp.

But the rapidity with which optimism was expressed in action did not lead to a lack of care. After all, Phoenix had been asking careful questions about LGA for some fifteen years, and they were not about to stop. As late as 3 May 1922, R. K. Hodgson, circling for the umpteenth time the problem that Winter had first identified a decade earlier, calculated that a full reserve for unexpired risk would have reduced the profit shown in the LGA account for 1920 by £51,877 and that shown in the 1921 account by £115,425. On 9 May, Sketch was still asking for 'proper evidence' as to the way the reserves were calculated in the accounts. Phoenix scarcely jumped with its eyes shut.

And it jumped at a convincing price, certainly less lavish than that offered to NUF. Ryan shrewdly recommenced negotiations on 5 May with a bid that was defined by Phoenix at the outset as a maximum; if LGA would not accept it, there would be no more talking. This offer was one Phoenix share for one LGA share, plus the issue of £1 million worth of Phoenix debentures. Since LGA's paid up capital in 1922 was £125,000, this meant that Phoenix needed to create 125,000 £1 ordinary shares and the debentures. Each LGA share, then selling at £10 5s, would receive one Phoenix share with a current market worth of £11 and £8 in debentures. This total bid price of £19 appeared a good deal lower than the £22 (two-for-one) insisted upon by LGA in 1921, but somewhat up on the £16 10s (three-for-two) offered by Phoenix at that time. A more sombre reading of its prospects by LGA may have underlain the 1922 price.[62]

The new Phoenix shares and debentures would require servicing in dividend and interest to the tune of £125,000. But this would leave, to Phoenix's credit, £71,000 in free interest on LGA assets and the whole of the LGA trading profit. Superficially, this looked a much tighter deal than the NUF fusion. But, of course, much depended on what the trading profit actually was and how much of it, under proper management, would need to be dedicated to the reserves. Nevertheless, in 1922 it looked as if Phoenix had laboured effectively to strike a good price.

Once the outline of an acceptable financial deal was fixed, and only then, did Ryan and Sketch draw their directors into their confidence. A Special Committee of the Phoenix Board, comprising ten directors, met to consider the matter on 10 and 11 May. These meetings immediately provided Ryan with some justification for his insistence upon secrecy: on 11 May the

[61] Phoenix Special Committee Minutes, p. 18, 10 May 1922; Ryan's notes on agenda for meeting at offices of G. Touche & Co., 9 May 1922.

[62] The LGA Minute Books are studiously quiet on the details of the negotiations.

LGA share stood at £10 10s; on 13 May it topped £16 and Thiselton had to circularise shareholders telling them not to sell. Despite the leaks, however, the Committee addressed the right points. Correctly, it approved the financial details of the bid. Concern was voiced about uncertain conditions of trading and fierce official regulations in the United States. It was met by reassurances from Ryan and Southam that the powers of individual states there rendered remote the prospect of any uniformly adverse regulation. Wary on this point, the meeting on 10 May, nevertheless, expressed itself generally content and did not raise the issue of the reserves.[63]

The next day, however, with Tait, Thiselton and Heron from LGA in attendance, the wider forum did address this problem. It is scarcely surprising that the question of insurance reserves should have been in the minds even of contemporaries who had not studied the accounts of LGA in depth. A major insurance scandal early in 1922, the collapse of the large reinsurer City Equitable, had dramatised this issue among many. As scandals go, this one had everything to frighten the insurance man.

City Equitable had been a cautious, modest affair before 1914 but had expanded greatly during wartime and turned to highly speculative investment from 1916; it was over-committed to marine business when others were pulling back and over-exposed to equities when markets were on the turn. Its speculation included insider dealing by at least one director. Two board members were charged with malfeasance, another with conspiracy and the chairman – who was sufficiently conventional to flee the country when twigged – with fraud. The collapse of City Equitable shares late in January 1922 exerted downward pressure on all insurance shares in the following month.[64] Reinsurance reserves became a matter of rapt scrutiny for many underwriters. Phoenix directors encountering the LGA proposition in May had thus only recently experienced sharp confrontation with the question of the reserve level maintained by a specialist insurer expanded by war and inclined to speculative practices. If by any remote chance they had missed the parallel, the fact that Sketch served on the committee of inspection for the City Equitable fiasco must have forced it home. The insurance business was unusually sensitive to the matter of reserves in the spring of 1922 and Phoenix was more sensitised than most.

So the Phoenix Special Committee came to the matter of reserves with something like a head of steam behind it. The LGA representatives handled this phase brilliantly. At a preliminary meeting between Ryan, Sketch, Tait and Thiselton on 9 May, Thiselton had made the major tactical move, disarming much criticism, by suggesting that 'he would be

[63] Phoenix Special Committee Minutes, pp. 17–20, 10 May 1922.
[64] *Financial News*, 4 April 1922; *Statist*, 28 January, 4 and 11 February 1922.

prepared to touch on all the weak spots he could think of in the Accounts so that there should be no necessity for long and detailed investigation'.[65] This deliberate stroke of self-revelation was very effective. When the LGA men encountered the inevitable questions about their level of reserves on 11 May, they replied sturdily that they observed strictly the 40% requirement on short-term policies but adopted lower standards on annual or more-than-annual policies.[66] Thiselton and Tait gave further assurances that the American reserves were sufficient to cover outstanding claims – and Sketch, apparently disarmed by Thiselton's baring of the LGA soul two days previously, proclaimed himself satisfied! Again, one can only wonder if Sketch's financial acumen was equal to his talents in other fields.[67]

Infected by the general enthusiasm, Southam decided that the amount of £1.7 million set aside by LGA for outstanding losses was adequate. Extraordinarily, Winter, who *was* present at this meeting, was restricted to commenting on the worth of LGA's Stock Exchange investments; he found these adequate too. Lord George Hamilton decided that Tait and Thiselton were splendid fellows and Sketch contributed the valuation that the final stages of negotiation had 'increased our confidence in the other side – they certainly seem good people.'[68] By this point the Phoenix leadership seems to have been lulled, most skilfully, into a romantic sense of reassurance. On 15 May the NUF directors were informed and on the 17 May the Provisional Agreement was confirmed.

It is worth noting, however, that the press also applauded. The *Liverpool Post* thought that Phoenix had struck 'a good bargain in acquiring the London Guarantee on these terms' and even the *Financial Times* thought that 'the price now to be paid is by no means excessive'. Even more to the point, it judged that this price had been achieved by LGA having been 'very closely scrutinized, not only by the Phoenix, but by independent experts of acknowledged standing'.[69] *The Policyholder* saw a fair exchange: LGA received a greatly increased capital value for its shares, an enhanced dividend and 'partnership in one of the oldest, strongest and most progressive composite offices'; while Phoenix acquired 'one of the pioneers of accident business' and thus 'a very strong

[65] Sketch, Notes on Interviews, 10 May 1922.

[66] Modern practice would ask for a *larger* premium reserve on annual policies than on lesser periods as, in the latter case, there is greater likelihood that the premium would be fully 'earned' by the accounting date.

[67] Namely administration, underwriting and the management of honest people.

[68] Phoenix Special Committee Minutes, pp. 20–22, Sketch to Walter, 16 May 1922.

[69] *Liverpool Post*, 18 May 1922; *Financial Times*, 18 May 1922.

position in the American accident world'.[70] The emphasis chosen by the journalists was very much that Phoenix had at last bought in a major accident capability.

Interestingly, the Phoenix management was not so confident on all fronts. It maintained a firm and successful pose in regard to its own directors. And the press did it proud. But it expected trouble from its shareholders, most notably at the Extraordinary General Meeting arranged for 7 June 1922. In anticipation of this, the executive prepared a draft of the awkward questions shareholders might ask. These are very revealing. The list included: 'Have you satisfied yourself that the £700,000 reserved for the purpose is amply sufficient to meet liabilities on reinsurance treaties in view of the recent scandals?' and 'Does not the "arrears" position of the LGA compare unfavourably with that of the Phoenix?' Perhaps most tellingly of all, the executive imagined the chairman being asked, 'Is it wise to take over a business on these terms, largely comprising American casualty premiums which adverse legislation may prejudicially affect at any time?' Unfortunately for the historical record, the prospective answers were not spelled out. And, fortunately for the executive, the shareholders were more peaceable than had been feared and the most difficult questions were not put. The extraordinary meeting went off smoothly, with the Phoenix shareholders ratifying the agreement on 7 June. Now all that remained was to count the real cost.

This became apparent only gradually. But the damage was spread over a remarkably broad front. Phoenix encountered financial trouble from LGA in no fewer than four main areas: reserves, premium growth, American premises and company debt.[71] The first inklings were produced by the task of conciliating LGA accounts with the Phoenix accounts. This operation revealed that the issue of the suspect reserves had deserved every doubt that had been levelled at it. By late 1925 Phoenix was at last sure of this. Southam, the accident manager, who visited America at least yearly during the 1920s in an attempt to pick up the pieces of the LGA operation there, reported home his definitive conclusion from the site of the crisis: 'After exhaustive examination, I concluded the reserves set up for outstanding compensation and liability claims . . . were insufficient.'[72]

But suspicion had been hardening from as early as August 1922, merely

[70] *Policyholder*, 24 May 1922.

[71] There was more trouble to come in the handling of US business acquisition. See Chapter. 9.

[72] Accident Manager's Report on Visit to USA, submitted to Phoenix Board, 9 December 1925.

Plate 7.8 LGA: a steal at the price.

weeks after the agreement was finalised. On 29 August, Dr Heron, secretary of LGA, wrote for Sketch a memorandum on 'The Hidden Liabilities and Assets of the London Guarantee'. This followed from Thiselton's claims during the negotiations concerning undisclosed assets. Poor Heron – until 1915 an academic statistician of some standing – now had to own up that these assets of £173,291 were composed largely of allowances for reserves that had not been used in past years. But, much worse, he had also to show how the current reserves stood. The 37% reserve for unexpired risks shown in the 1921 account turns out to have been produced by an 'arbitrary transfer' from the General Claims Reserve. Before this robbing of Peter to pay Paul, LGA's real reserve against unexpired risks was only 30.6%. Even Heron had the grace to concede that this was 'window-dressing'. Phoenix's leaders began to realise the cost of filling the window: in 1922, the price of establishing full 40% reserves at LGA would have been £355,423.[73]

Then, in 1924, the US government did precisely what Sketch and Southam had calculated it was unlikely to do: introduced an across-the-board stipulation affecting all insurers. It required them forthwith to increase their level of reserves against outstanding claims. This, of course, hit LGA in one of its vulnerable areas. The Commissioner of Insurance for Boston, Massachusetts showed that on 31 December 1923 the American branch of LGA suffered from a deficiency between its specific and its statutory reserves of over $2 million. Phoenix's share in rectifying the shortfall cost the company £181,521. At the same time, Sketch decided that the lingering affliction of the unexpired risk reserve had best receive treatment. A transition to a full 40% in one dose was ruled out as too expensive for 1924. So the palliative of 33.3% was adopted. But even this cost £320,000.[74]

However, it was just as well that Phoenix applied the medicine, even if the relief was only partial. For, as Sketch found on his own visit to the United States in 1925, the American authorities had no love for LGA: the New York Superintendent of Insurance emphasised to him that 'the leading American and British casualty companies doing the same volume of business as LGA have *much more substantial surplus and capital than LGA*.' All that Sketch could retort was that the Phoenix staff were working assiduously 'to repair the errors under the old regime'.[75]

To begin with, Phoenix took the cost of the repairs fairly nonchalantly. They were, said Sketch, 'merely transfers from one hidden reserve to another [and] . . . will greatly improve the appearance of the accounts without weakening the reserves'.[76] But within months, he was singing a different tune, stressing 'the tightness in regard to liquid assets that has arisen from the necessity of such large deposits abroad'.[77] Every suspicion

[73] Heron to Sketch, Memorandum on Hidden Liabilities and Assets of the London Guarantee, 29 August 1922.

[74] Phoenix Special Committee Minutes, pp. 55–6, 18 March 1925.

[75] General Manager's Report on Visit to USA, submitted to Phoenix Board 25 November 1925 (my emphasis).

[76] Phoenix Special Committee Minutes, p. 56, 18 March 1925.

[77] *Ibid.*, p. 66, 18 June 1925.

that Phoenix had nurtured about the LGA reserves was well founded; every reassurance from LGA had been baseless. Phoenix had been taken for a ride.

Nor was the price of the ride made up by a surge in earning power. There is no detectable effect upon Phoenix fire, life or marine receipts as a result of the LGA takeover, although, of course, group accident premiums increased sharply – by 223%, from £1.7 million to £5.4 million – between 1921 and 1922. The trouble lay in the content of these premiums and the *reduction* in earnings that this necessitated; and also in the low or negative profitability that they commanded. On his 1925 visit, Sketch found, somewhat belatedly, that LGA was a by-word for reckless growth, and in New York, 'the most dangerous of any business in the States' had pursued a policy of 'unbridled expansion'.[78]

The result was that Phoenix had to embark upon its historic transatlantic remedy, 'purification of the books': this shedding of the worst risks was a powerful influence in the reduction of LGA's American premium writings by 30% between 1922 and 1928 and by 50% between 1922 and 1934 (see Table 7.5). Similarly, the big numbers did not guarantee big profits. After ostensibly averaging, over the five years down to 1920, a profit on American liability business of $660,000 per year, the LGA account fell into the red in 1921 and stayed there for many years.

By 1924, Southam concluded sadly that 'under present conditions and rates, it is almost impossible to write casualty business at a profit on risks situated in the City of New York'. In 1926, the combined accident account of Phoenix and LGA in the USA recorded a loss of £275,000 on a premium income of some £4 million. At this time the loss ratio for this class of business in the USA was 67% while the matching figure for the UK market was 54.4%. Southam even contemplated reinsuring the *whole* of the group's American accident business and desisted only because of the likely effect on Phoenix's reputation.[79] The worst hit sector was the largest transacted by LGA, workmen's compensation insurance, which suffered astronomical loss ratios throughout the 1920s and into the mid-1930s (see Table 7.5). Southam's verdict for 1926 that 'we have to face the fact that the trading results of the past two or three years have been disastrous' could have been repeated in many of these years.[80]

Of course, it was not diffcult to lose money on accident insurance in the America of the Depression decade. Indeed, of the sixty casualty companies operating in New York, forty-one suffered serious financial losses

[78] General Manager's Report on Visit to USA, 1925.
[79] Accident Manager's Report on Visit to USA, 1924, 1927.
[80] *Ibid.*, Southam to Berger, 25 November 1926.

Table 7.5. *LGA total US premium, 1922–40*

	Total premium ($)	Total loss ratio	Workmen's compensation loss ratio
1922	14,185,884	51.0	65.4
1928	9,677,435	50.8	71.8
1929	9,633,373	52.9	69.9
1930	8,781,382	60.0	76.7
1931	8,323,387	n.a.	76.5
1932	7,576,877	55.2	74.4
1933	7,330,538	53.4	73.9
1934	7,189,244	54.3	70.8
1935	7,042,769	48.2	58.4
1936	7,730,329	42.3	52.6
1937	8,467,063	38.7	49.1
1938	7,497,578	44.2	51.0
1939	7,062,315	42.3	55.0
1940	6,941,082	39.9	53.9

Source: Calculated from LGA Annual Statements to New York Insurance Department.

during the 1920s. But the state of the market alone does not explain the state of LGA before 1929.[81] Nor was it simply bad luck or bad judgement that put Phoenix into this market at such a time. The true state of LGA was revealed by a report from the United States which was not formally discussed by the Board.

In June 1926 Sketch sent B. H. Davis to conduct an undercover scrutiny of all Phoenix's operations in the United States. It lasted until November and Davis kept a meticulous day-by-day diary of the astonishing malpractices that he found. On the 'administrative shambles' at LGA, he is scathing:

> the impression I got . . . was that in the past the whole organisation was hopeless and that even now the leaks in the sieve are not all discovered and stopped up, the office wants reorganising almost throughout.[82]

Clearly, part of LGA's problem was rotten management. So why did Phoenix buy an inefficient, inept and disorganised accident insurer just as it moved into a phase of severe losses?

[81] See below Chapter 9, Section 4 for the cure of LGA.
[82] B. H. Davis, American Diary, pp. 55, 79, 2 and 7 August 1926.

Neither luck nor judgement had much to do with this; but information did. The full implications of LGA's marine losses were not revealed to Phoenix. There was endless obfuscation on the matter of reserves. Moreover, the LGA management must have known, during the negotiations of 1922 that their results for that year, were going to be bad; but they did not tell Phoenix. Not until Heron's memorandum for Sketch in August 1922 was there a hint that the final account 'may show a loss'[83] and by that time LGA was in deep trouble. Its senior officials had known for months that they faced major losses. All that they did not know was precisely how major. Left to its own devices, it must be doubted whether LGA could have survived the period 1922–9. The Davis diary reveals that the LGA managers shared these doubts: it records the views of one who 'does not know how the company held together'.[84] The answer, of course, is that they persuaded Phoenix to take them over. But one of the reasons that Phoenix bought such a pig in a poke is that the pig was busily manufacturing its own silk purses throughout the talks. Or, put another way, it was hinting at hidden assets while concealing hidden liabilities.

A paradigm of this sorry affair is provided by the saga of the Fort Dearborn building, LGA's imposing new headquarters on the Chicago waterfront. Built at great expense on the site of the old fortress, this twenty-one storey prestige block symbolises the inattention to detail, bad judgement and crass timing that afflicted LGA in its final phase. The lease upon Fort Dearborn was signed by LGA *four days* before the takeover talks with Phoenix were recommenced. LGA was to take the head lease and find tenants for the majority of the building that it would not occupy. There were two problems: the terms of the lease and the tenants – too demanding as to the first, too few as to the second.

When the Phoenix management discovered the provisions, they registered 'the keenest disappointment' and concluded that 'there seems to have been an utter lack of control and foresight'.[85] This included the acceptance by LGA of a clause requiring them to fit out the whole building – at a cost of £133,470. By 1925 a total of £300,000 had disappeared into Fort Dearborn. The return was paltry since LGA contrived to sign the lease just as the American letting boom collapsed. Phoenix had been 'overwhelmed with assurances' by LGA 'as to the tenants who were simply waiting to come in on terms very remunerative to us';[86] but, by 1929, there were 4 million square feet (370,000 m^2) of excess office space in Chicago. Fort Dearborn was never fully occupied

[83] Heron to Sketch, 29 August 1922.
[84] Davis, American Diary, p. 171, 14 September 1926.
[85] Swanson (Phoenix overseas accident manager) to Heron, 5 June 1923.
[86] *Ibid.*

Plate 7.9 White elephant at Fort Dearborn.

throughout the 1920s and the Crash, of course, made matters worse. After 1929, it was impossible to attract new tenants and by the end of 1931 many existing tenants had stopped paying rent. Fort Dearborn was a colossal white elephant.

Phoenix's reaction to the débacle was to flee Chicago. Sketch wanted to sell the lease, surrender the fort and decamp. But in the conditions of the 1920s, there was no market for the lease. So, in order to save face, Phoenix had to invent the argument that an insurance multinational operating in the USA needed to maintain its headquarters not in Chicago but in New York. Consequently, the American head office moved east in September 1923. This in itself cost a further £96,662. The only possible approach to the Chicago building was to treat it as an investment, and rent out as much of it as possible until the lease could be sold. Rentals did improve from the mid-1930s, but no final solution to the Fort Dearborn bungle was found until a buyer eventually came forward for both the site and the lease – in 1946.

Nor was Fort Dearborn merely an object lesson in how not to play the American property market. For it had a direct bearing on another feature of LGA in which Phoenix had an overpowering interest: the accident company's level of debt. In 1925, the New York Insurance Department refused to recognise a loan to LGA from the developers of the Fort Dearborn site, against the value of the lease, as an insurance asset. Coming at a time when LGA, under insistence from Phoenix, was struggling to improve its level of reserves, this rebuff caused a severe liquidity crisis. Like it or not, Phoenix had to bail LGA out with a loan of $1 million. But the parent company did not wish a loan of this size to stand indefinitely and cast about for an alternative method of funding it.

The Phoenix managers realised that the LGA books would look better if a way could be found of absorbing the loan in a rearrangement of the smaller company's capital. At the end of the day, the cost of this operation imposed a further surcharge of £650,000 on the price Phoenix paid for LGA. It was financed only by the release of funds obtained by the sale of Phoenix's valuable holding in Norwich Union Fire.[87]

Nor was it surprising that this chain of events should have attracted criticism inside Phoenix. The elderly Lord George Hamilton, who had thought Tait and Thiselton such fine fellows in 1922, had changed his view by 1925. He wrote to Sketch in July,

> I am much obliged for the papers you sent me relative to the London Guarantee and Accident. When shall we get to the bottom of our actual and prospective losses in connection with this unfortunate venture? [Your visit to the USA] . . . is the best method of clearing up the mess. As you know, I have never liked our heavy commitments through the agency of the London Guarantee . . . and I approve of every step you have taken to extricate the Phoenix from the tentacles of that organization.[88]

In 1930 there was similar criticism from two prominent Board members, Walters and Tryon. The latter calculated that the real cost of acquiring LGA was about £800,000, probably an underestimate.[89] If the figures involved in the reserve adjustments, the Dearborn costs, the shift

[87] Phoenix Special Committee Minutes, pp. 86–8, 5 and 14 December 1925. And see pp. 469–85 below.

[88] Hamilton to Sketch, 28 July 1925.

[89] Tryon to Sketch, 27 November 1930.

of American head office and the debt funding are summed, a figure nearer £1.4 million is reached, and that is on top of the purchase price. All that Sketch could say in reply was that Phoenix *had* captured the investment interest earnings of LGA and that it had worked to put LGA's house in order. The last point has some force.

By 1927, Phoenix had shed the worst of the workmen's compensation risks and by 1929 LGA was looking reasonably fit by the standard of most American accident operators. Also, even in its slimmed state of the late 1930s, LGA was by far Phoenix's largest operation in the United States, double the size in premium earnings of all other subsidiaries put together. The *United States Review* found in 1931 that LGA was 'conservatively managed and with a goodly premium volume [and] . . . in spite of all the troubles coincident to the depression, has demonstrated that it can make commendable headway'.[90] Phoenix standards of management had worked to good effect. But it had taken many tribulations – and a ransom in resources – before LGA's improved state was attained. Ryan by now was in failing health. The remaking of LGA was Sketch's work.

Clearly, the US accident market in the 1920s was a jungle. It featured falling premiums, rising claims ratios and, consequently, increasing government interference. As well as economic depression, earthquake and hurricane took their toll. But probably the worst damage followed from the ruinous loss ratios on workmen's compensation policies: as rising unemployment led to falling payrolls, so the claims proportion rose inexorably. Why then did Phoenix choose to enter the jungle? One answer is simply that the jungle grew up very fast. The years 1918–20 were very good ones in the American accident business; for Phoenix, prosperity here seemed to offer a prolongation of the euphoric expansion which had affected the UK economy in the months after the Armistice. Certainly, Phoenix was not alone in feeling the attraction of the apparently insatiable demand from the US accident sector. British companies led the rush to meet it and American offices followed. One major player, the Insurance Co. of North America, undertook one of the largest initiatives by launching the Indemnity Insurance Co. in 1920 – and then took heavy losses.[91] The critical turning point came only in 1921/2, and it was precisely at this point that Phoenix chose to jump. There had been no warning of what was to come and Phoenix could be seen simply as the victim of a capriciously damaging chronology.

Yet it is impossible to suppress the suspicion that elements of bad judgement were also present: that senior management had wanted an

[90] *United States Review*, 15 December 1931.
[91] Marquis James, *Biography of a Business, 1792–1942: The Insurance Company of North America* (New York, 1942).

accident company for too long and, by the 1920s, were over-anxious to acquire one. Perhaps they suffered also from an expectation lag: their expectations took over-long to adjust to the new circumstances of the postwar markets. Certainly, Ryan misread completely LGA's results for 1921: they were not merely 'a bad start'; instead the workmen's compensation market did not settle for another fourteen years. And Sketch in 1925 rather pathetically emphasised Phoenix's original motivation, its current disappointment and its still inaccurate anticipation: 'We look forward to a return to that prosperity in the casualty business which made the purchase of LGA a desirable transaction for the Phoenix.'[92] Phoenix had to wait a long time for this outcome. Moreover, it is possible that Phoenix's appetite for LGA's interest earnings was seriously misplaced. Insurance acquisitions which go wrong often prove to have been purchased on the grounds of 'good investment return'; omitted from these grounds is a sufficient concern with the business actually transacted.

On the other hand, if Phoenix had been given accurate information in 1921, Ryan and Sketch no doubt would have adjusted their expectations and desisted from entering the jungle. They were prevented from escaping the effects of a threatening chronology largely because they were misled. But, on yet another hand, if they were misled, they also had sufficient information of their own to detect the deception.

The LGA affair is an immensely complex problem. Probably, it is fairest to say that the result was determined by an interaction of unfortunate timing, miscalculation and misrepresentation. Undoubtedly, it was Ryan's worst takeover and it proved bad for his heart. He was ill for much of 1926, took leave from the chairmanship in the winter and was not fit enough to return until May 1927. The LGA fiasco and Ryan's failing strength combine to convey the impression that a distinct era was coming to an end.

It says much for the feelings of the Phoenix management about the disarray they had found in LGA's organisation at home and abroad that no immediate attempt was made to integrate the two head office organisations. Indeed, the attitude taken by the Phoenix leadership was to keep them as far apart as possible. More exactly, Sketch kept the LGA organisation at 20 Lincoln's Inn Fields (the former historic Inns of Court Hotel, and, subsequently, during the Second World War, the headquarters of the Royal Canadian Air Force), a brisk walk from King William Street. Not until a decade had passed were the LGA staff permitted a tenancy in the enlarged Phoenix House. Perhaps Sketch calculated that, by then, the contagion must have passed.

[92] General Manager's Visit to USA, 1925.

3. A LOSS OF SUBSTANCE: THE SALE OF NORWICH UNION FIRE

Phoenix fused with Norwich Union Fire in 1919 and decoupled in 1925. The first action was willed, the second was forced. Whilst it included NUF, Phoenix ranked third among the UK composite offices with £12.9 million in premiums. Without NUF, Phoenix still ranked third by the end of 1925, but with the reduced premium income of £9.0 million. However, for the future the loss was incalculable. One can only speculate on the possible standing of the Phoenix in the post-1945 insurance market had it been able to hold on to the growth capacity of the Norwich office.

The compulsion that forced Phoenix to surrender NUF was its acquisition of LGA. The cost of that acquisition had weakened the Bird. Before long, this showed in its own level of reserves. By 1923 the ratio of reserves to total premiums was significantly below the level considered wise by the senior offices; in fact, the proportion was hardly more than half that of the best-protected office, the London & Lancashire (see Table 7.6). Somewhat disingenuously, Sketch gave as the reason for this uncharacteristic weakness, 'the necessary strengthening of our American reserves during the last ten years which has left our General Funds with a very small margin of liquid securities in other countries, particularly at home'.[93]

No doubt, reserves had been a problem in the United States for a decade, but the real issue was two years old rather than ten. Nevertheless, whatever the time span, such a disparity was clearly dangerous and could not be allowed to persist.

But how to eradicate it? An obvious, if drastic, ploy would be to sell the company which had done most damage to the reserves. But to shed in 1924 or 1925 a company purchased in 1922 would have had catastrophic effects on public confidence in Phoenix as well as imposing a severe financial loss upon the transaction. And there was the problem of finding a buyer: if Phoenix did not want LGA, who else would?

This sequence of thought prompted the notion of realising capital by selling Phoenix's shares in NUF. But here too there was a dilemma. How could the need for the sale be presented? Phoenix could scarcely announce that it needed to sell NUF shares in order to cover the financial crisis caused by its acquisition of LGA. Such a revelation would also wreck confidence in Phoenix. The only way of justifying a sale would be by receiving a bid that was simply too good to refuse. But how could such a bid be provoked? Phoenix could scarcely invite offers. And, even if it could, its need for a high price would surely deter buyers. A low price

[93] R. Y. Sketch, Private Memorandum on the Norwich Union Fire and Life Offices, 22 July 1924.

Table 7.6. *Top seven offices in 1923; reserve funds against premiums (%)*

	Premium income £	Reserves £	%
Royal	20,952,159	21,430,959	102.3
Commercial Union	14,556,101	13,377,141	91.9
Phoenix	12,893,100	7,727,250	60.0
London & Lancashire	5,769,875	6,886,881	119.4
North British	5,499,605	6,425,436	117.0
Employers' Liability	5,022,103	4,605,094	91.7
Northern	5,019,218	5,758,298	114.9

Note: Reserves = capital and free reserves. Premium excludes life premium.

would attract them. But it would not solve the reserve problem; it would not justify the sale to shareholders or directors; and it would again damage confidence in the vendors. The only feature of the sale that was clear was that at least one potential buyer existed. There was no problem about who might want NUF if Phoenix did not want it: its old partner in Norwich, Norwich Union Life ought to want it. So the crucial issue was to persuade Norwich Union Life to offer exactly the sort of price which would allow Phoenix to raise the wind on its NUF shares without loss of face. Still better if this contrived bid from NUL could be presented as an independent offer inspired from Norwich.

If this could be carried off, it would stand as a brilliant stroke of damage control; but it was a very tall order indeed. The Phoenix directors would not be anxious to shed such an enormous portion of the company's substance. The NUF directors would question why such a recent and successful amalgamation was being so abruptly overturned. The NUL directors would wonder what was in it for them and why they should bestir themselves, apparently on Phoenix's behalf. Certainly, Phoenix would have to take the greatest care not to appear over-eager in their eyes. Here, too, there was the added complication that the NUL Board was known to have been 'bitterly antagonistic to the linking up of the two Norwich offices'[94] in 1919, when Phoenix was planning the fusion. And both shareholders and the market could easily turn sour if the least hint of Phoenix's true reasons for a sale got out. It is a tribute to Sketch that he did successfully negotiate these hazards; and also that he did not expect to get away with it. Presentation, of course, was everything.

[94] Sketch to Beresford (American Branch manager, Phoenix–NUF), 9 July 1925.

Sketch's first attempt at justifying disengagement was to contrive the argument that the Phoenix–NUF merger had not really taken. He suggested that the connection between NUF and NUL prevented Phoenix from exploiting its relationship with NUF to the full. The main impediment was the formal agreement struck between NUF and NUL in 1908; this barred the life office from diversifying into the fire trade and denied the fire office access to life business. By the terms of its purchase of NUF shares, Phoenix was bound to honour this agreement. But by 1924, for pressing reasons of economy, Phoenix wished to integrate NUF more fully into its administrative structure. It found itself restricted by the separation of functions written into the 1908 agreement. Sketch expressed himself frustrated by the need to preserve the specific East Anglian identity and limited function of NUF.

A refinement to this line of thought was the notion that NUL might even constitute a threat to Phoenix's wellbeing, since life offices were themselves under increasing pressure to diversify. Should NUL conform to this pressure, which it could do without infringing its undertaking to NUF (for instance, by developing accident capacity), then obviously Phoenix's business would suffer while the company would be inhibited from retaliating by its obligations inherited from NUF. Even more galling to Phoenix was that NUF clearly had the capacity to transact life business. Indeed, it had long ago taken powers to do so; only the 1908 agreement prevented the company from using them. So, if the undertaking was honoured, Phoenix lost business. If it was infringed, then, in Sketch's words, 'something approaching fratricidal warfare threatened'.[95] He argued, in a somewhat opportunistic way, that 'in years to come, given any unfriendliness in the respective managements, there was every opportunity of serious trouble arising'[96] from the direction of NUL.

One answer to this type of problem, fairly obviously, was not to sell NUF but to buy NUL. If the agreement between the two Norwich offices was a problem, if NUL looked like becoming a threat, why did not Phoenix simply take the second, logical bite at the Norfolk cherry? This may have been considered. It is quite likely that Ryan, given his special taste for corporate acquisition, had seen NUF as a possible bridgehead into a larger Norwich connection. But, by 1924, Sketch had had four years in which to consider this proposition; and it had come to seem too difficult. The major complication was that NUL was a mutual society. Such offices distributed all their profits to their policy-holders. So there would be no pay-out for the shareholders of any proprietary company

[95] *Ibid.* [96] Sketch to Royden, 23 July 1925.

which acquired an office of this type; but there would be an obligation to finance the bonus that mutual policy-holders expected as of right. Absorption of the British Empire by the Pelican – a technical problem in its day and a worse problem in time – had given Phoenix due warning of these complexities. So Sketch steered clear.

The natural remedy, he suggested, was that NUF and NUL should get together more permanently. Because NUL was a mutual and NUF no longer was, the only practicable method was for NUL to buy NUF.

Sketch's arguments were of variable virtue. Take first the true balance of advantage for Phoenix. It is difficult to believe that the massive overseas capability of NUF – including its sizeable American accident department – was outweighed by domestic administrative entanglements. Surely the Norwich factor was not that potent. Several of the sharper minds at Phoenix certainly saw that it had not become *more* potent since 1920; every administrative reservation which attached to the Phoenix–NUF fusion in 1924 had been present and known in 1920 – but had not been considered sufficient grounds for cancelling the operation at that juncture. Indeed, Ryan, in his second Annual Report as chairman of NUF had gone to some pains to stress 'how happily the two businesses dovetailed into one another'.[97]

Nor had NUL, in the decidedly lethargic hands of its general manager, N. M. Lees shown any convincing sign of aggressive market behaviour. However, there were undoubtedly benefits for NUL in achieving a freer field of manoeuvre – if only it could be brought to realise this. Lees did not rush to make the perception. Quite belying the statements by Sketch and Ryan that the idea came from NUL – witness for instance Sketch's paper of July 1924 where he writes 'we have been approached by the Life Office with a view to their purchasing from the Phoenix the original shares of the Norwich Union Fire Insurance'[98] – Sketch was having major difficulties by summer 1924 in his attempts to cajole Lees into considering it. Sketch first broached the proposal to Lees in the first week of May 1924 and did not secure even his provisional agreement until the very end of June. Before Phoenix were 'approached', their general manager had to build the path with his own hands; his sense of relief is painfully evident when he learns after his first overture that Lees is 'as nearly enthusiastic as he can be.'[99] Nevertheless, Sketch spent a considerable part of that summer in further attempts to galvanise Lees into thinking up a suitable price for

[97] NUF Chairman's Annual Report, May 1920.
[98] Sketch, Private Memorandum on the Norwich Offices, 22 July 1924. We have, of course, encountered this ploy before (see above, pp. 302, 310, 430).
[99] E. F. Williamson (manager, NUF) to Sketch, 7 May 1924.

the NUF shares. Lees preferred a quick round of golf – to which Sketch was expansively invited – to the tedious business of share calculations. The correspondence crackles with Sketch's barely concealed exasperation.

A more plausible explanation of an administrative kind derives from the organisational distortions produced by the introduction into the Phoenix Group of LGA itself. These were far worse than any lack of fit on the part of NUF. Firstly, the great accretion of LGA's accident accounts unbalanced Phoenix's operation in the United States towards liability, and especially workmen's compensation, business. Secondly, the acquisition complicated still further Phoenix's intricate array of ventures in the United States: it added the chaotic LGA structure, together with its satellite United Firemens', to Phoenix's own fire business, Pelican of New York, the Union Marine subsidiary, Columbia and the recently created Phoenix Indemnity with its affiliated concern, Norwich Union Indemnity. The untidiness of LGA's home operation also caused major problems of control in the United Kingdom, as well as drawing a rich stream of abuse down upon LGA's headquarters in Lincoln's Inn. This sort of disarray did require rationalisation. However, it is significant that Sketch set about providing it and clear that he regarded the distortions requiring treatment as irritating blemishes rather than lethal wounds. But it is still more significant that he did not embark upon his remedial campaign until 1925, after his first attempt to sell NUF the year before had failed.

Both Phoenix's internal discussions of the sale proposals of 1924 and the reasons for their failure offer strong suggestions as to the prime motives for the disposal. As Phoenix liquid assets came under increasing pressure – due, Sketch was arguing by the middle of 1925, primarily to the running off of unfavourable marine accounts at Phoenix and LGA – so it became increasingly obvious that other units in the Phoenix Group, notably Union Marine and NUF, possessed temptingly ample liquid assets. Under existing conditions, Phoenix could be tempted but could not touch.

NUF was particularly alluring. Its share capital of £5.28 million, was divided into a mere 44,000 shares which were only £3 paid but possessed a potential market value of £120. The office had free assets of £2.0 million, and if twenty-five years' purchase of its average annual trading profit (about £200,000 per year) were added to these, the total notional purchase price for the company came out at £7 million or £160 per share. Sketch obligingly worked out a scheme by which NUL could finance acquisition on these terms, at minimum cost to itself. At this point, one

Table 7.7. *Phoenix reserves with and without NUF in 1923*

Company	Premium (£m)	Reserves (£m)	Reserve/premium (%)
Phoenix 1923	12.9	7.7	59.9
Phoenix less NUF	9.0	11.0	123.0

Note: Definitions as Table 7.6.

might be forgiven for concluding that Sketch had lost sight of any interest other than Phoenix's own. His view was fixed on one objective: 'the transaction would . . . place the Phoenix in an exceptional position as regards free funds.'[100] More precisely, over £3 million would become available immediately for the reserves. Any loss in premium income that NUF took with it would be compensated by this massive gain in security. At one stroke Phoenix could be transformed from the worst-protected to the best-protected of the big offices (Table 7.7).

Others were not so blithe. The NUF directors on the Phoenix Board were kept in the dark about the sale proposals throughout the period May–December 1924, so they did not have the information to be blithe or otherwise. Indeed, in the approved Phoenix style, the negotiations were highly confidential: Ryan and Sketch took their own decisions; at NUL, Lees talked to a small group of his directors; at NUF, the manager, E. F. Williamson was in Sketch's confidence but worked independently of his Board. However, by July 1924 Ryan and Sketch realised that they must let some other players into the game. Sketch had been pressing NUL hard since June because 'circumstances have so conspired that we have to make progress, one way or the other'.[101] As he pressed, one player increasingly came to compromise the Ryan–Sketch preference for secret diplomacy: Sir George Chamberlin was the one director who sat on all three boards, NUL, NUF and Phoenix. Once Chamberlin knew, Ryan needed to tell the other Phoenix directors, excluding, of course, the delegates from NUF. Ryan knew that a NUL Special Committee would meet to consider the matter on 17 July 1924. So he summoned a Special Committee of the Phoenix Board for 23 July 1924 which pointedly included all Phoenix directors and Buxton – who, as deputy chairman, could scarcely be left out, despite his NUF origins – but no other NUF man. Ryan contrived to give the impression that the initiatives were

[100] Sketch, Memorandum on the Norwich Offices, 22 July 1924.
[101] Sketch to Lees, 27 June 1924.

coming from NUL and the Committee did not really form a clear idea of the way negotiations had developed.

But this gathering was certainly not blithe. It gave Sketch authority to explore further, but it showed little enthusiasm for reducing the size of the Phoenix Group. As Sketch himself reported to Williamson, on the day of the meeting, 'there was a good deal of dislike to [sic] any question of selling any part of our business, and it was only the peculiar relationship between the two Norwich offices that induced the Directors to consider the matter'.[102]

Nor was there any rush of enthusiasm at NUL. The inner circle of directors, Sketch thought, wished 'to tackle the subject, but when they get near to the figures, they begin to fear the difficulties'.[103] Two sets of figures in particular gave them difficulties. Firstly, the purchase of the NUF shares would mean the surrender of gilt-edged securities which earned NUL more income than they could hope to derive from NUF in the short term. Lees had the difficult job of selling present sacrifice in exchange for future gain. Secondly, they did not like Sketch's attempt to get the highest possible price for Phoenix's NUF shares. During a meeting between Sketch and Lees on 18 August 1924, Lees suggested – surely mischievously – that the proper price was not the £180, which was the best that Sketch could imagine, but nearer £100, which was less than the market rate. However, Lees gave fair warning that some number 'considerably less' than the Sketch number would be necessary 'before anything could be done'.[104]

During August, legal difficulties arose as counsel began to doubt whether NUL possessed the powers to carry out the proposed operation. Coupled with the NUL scepticism as to price, these problems caused Sketch to lose heart. Early in the month, he organised a family holiday at Overstrand, near Cromer, so that he would be conveniently situated for the dash to Norwich. But both he and the negotiations fell into the doldrums and, within a fortnight, he was considering breaking the whole thing off. In the last week of the month, it was left to Ryan to rally Sketch and to ease matters forward again. He wrote to Sketch that any breaking off must be by mutual consent: 'I should not like Lees to go to his Board and say that, after all the trouble he and they have taken, you coolly write and suggest that the whole affair should be put an end to!'[105] The tone of the rebuke is perhaps a measure of Ryan's continuing influence as chairman.

But even Ryan's closer involvement could not keep the proposition

[102] Sketch to Williamson, 23 July 1924. [103] *Ibid.*, 6 May 1924.
[104] Sketch's Notes on Interview, 20 August 1924. [105] Ryan to Sketch, 23 August 1924.

alive. Phoenix was unable to show any flexibility on the matter of price. And its only other bargaining point – the implied threat to the special relationship between NUF and NUL – began to look increasingly weak as the autumn wore on. During November, arrangements were made for a meeting at Hintlesham between subcommittees of the Phoenix and NUL boards. This took place on 4 December. Despite Ryan's best efforts as host, the two sides could get no closer on the matter of price. Sketch's campaign for the most handsome bargain finally exhausted the patience of the NUL team and the negotiations broke down after only two hours of talking. Several Phoenix directors were far from displeased. Their attitude was made up of regret that the gambit should ever have been necessary, recognition that Sketch had to try it, relief that it had failed and sympathy for Sketch upon the negation of his efforts. White Todd caught this mood when he wrote to Sketch: 'It is a satisfaction to me to know that the proposition that was on the tapis is now a thing of the past as I should in principle have disliked seeing our dear Company, as it were, shorn of its magnitude.'[106] Sketch's comment was somewhat more sour: 'NUL did not put the same value on the proposition as we did.'[107] But, of course, there was no reason why they should have done.

If the NUF sale had been a vital interest for Sketch, he did not let its failure impede the search for alternative solutions. If he could not deal his way out of trouble, he determined to rationalise his way out. Recognising that recent acquisitions had thoroughly muddled the command structure of the Phoenix Group, he began the new year with a thorough overhaul. In 1924, the only managerial connections between the major companies of the group at senior level were Sketch himself as general manager of Phoenix and NUF and director of all the rest and H. E. Southam as accident manager of Phoenix, manager of NUF and director of LGA. Sketch decided to remedy this in January 1925 by introducing a system of divisional control: Southam was to have overall command of the accident business of all Phoenix companies, J. Swanson to control the foreign accident business of all companies and A. Battrick to govern the home accident business of both Phoenix and LGA. NUF accident business was the exception; it would continue to run independently out of Norwich. To these measures, Sketch made important additions in the spring of 1925. In a scathing memorandum of mid-March, he mapped the duplicated and crossed lines of control within the group. This document went to the Phoenix Special Committee in late March and to the NUF Board a month later.[108]

[106] White Todd to Sketch, 8 December 1924. [107] Sketch to Beresford, 9 July 1925.
[108] Sketch, Memorandum on Internal Organisation, 19 March 1925.

It was significant that the pioneering initiative in the rationalisation exercise came in the accident sector, where Phoenix had been most harassed in recent times. And it is significant that Sketch explicitly connected the need for rationalisation with the advent of LGA: 'The question of unified control in each department of the business of the Group has been forced on me more and more since the association of the Phoenix and the Norwich Union and still more strongly since the London Guarantee came into the Group.'[109]

After commencing with the unification of departmental control, Sketch progressed to a rationalisation scheme for the overseas organisation of the group. A series of important foreign markets – Australia, India, China, Japan and Singapore – were each given a general manager who would handle operations for the three main companies, Phoenix, NUF and LGA. His third preoccupation was with linking the management of home and foreign business. The approaching retirement of E. A. Boston (the Phoenix fire manager) presented 'an opportunity of following the same general principles as to control' by the creation of the post of group fire manager for all companies and all business, home and foreign. Sketch proposed Williamson, the joint manager of NUF (with Southam) for this key job. It is significant that Sketch mostly chose as his centralising officials men whom he had known from his old team at NUF. Clearly, at this point he was thinking of a solution which would *include* the resources of NUF; and he would not have wished to sell the human capital that was to carry it out. Moreover, he thought that it would work, 'I feel convinced that, if the scheme which I have outlined above is adopted, it should make for efficiency and economy.'[110]

Of course, the special problem of the Norwich identity remained. The Phoenix directors did not relish the monthly trek eastwards for the NUF Board meetings; this consumed a whole day and involved a round trip of 200 miles. In 1925, such a pilgrimage was thought excessive and Sketch set out, among other objectives, to save his colleagues the time and trouble. He did so by proposing further streamlining and presenting the issue as part of the necessary policy of concentration and coordination: all foreign business could be handled by a Special Committee of Phoenix directors in London, all home business by a matching committee in Norwich and the Phoenix directors would surrender the adventures of travel. This elicited some predictable noises from Norwich. The NUF secretary, Frank Botting, was anxious to 'maintain the existing standing... in the eyes of the public' of the NUF Board, 'we can hardly be too

[109] *Ibid.* [110] *Ibid.*

careful not to run counter to local sentiment in a corner of England which is historically tenacious and slow to change'.[111] Nevertheless, he agreed the specialisation of the committees on Norwich and London. Norwich directors were still to attend London meetings, but it was conceded that Phoenix nominees could be excused appearance in Norwich without irrevocable damage to the local credibility of NUF.

Up to this point, through the first half of 1925, two themes had run through the correspondence of Sketch and his senior officials: the need for centralisation of group administration and doubts about the true state of LGA. So far the latter had not proved sufficiently powerful to call into question the practicality of the former. But from June 1925, the doubts began to grow in intensity. Deputy chairman Buxton wrote to Ryan from holiday in Sutherland, 'I have been reading all the letters between us and New York, which are not very cheerful'; he thought that Phoenix might well need 'an issue of sorts' to get out of trouble.[112] On 10 June, the Phoenix Board reluctantly approved the remittance of $1 million to maintain LGA's American reserves.[113] From this point, the questions of reorganisation and LGA's indebtedness became not only closely but crucially entwined. The concern that had existed over Phoenix's reserve position in 1924 sharpened accordingly.

But Sketch did not return in haste to the notion of selling the NUF shares. Rather his first response was to direct his new weapon of rationalisation at the worsening financial crisis. The Phoenix–NUF Finance Committee was turned into a Special Committee to investigate the LGA debt and the general financial organisation of all Phoenix companies. Sketch wished to see what could be done by streamlining and concentrating finances as well as administration: if surpluses existed in some parts of the group, 'it became advisable to see what machinery could be evolved in order to realize them'.[114] Sketch defined his thinking on financial coordination most exactly in a memorandum prepared for the Special Committee meeting on 18 June: 'The question of the general finance of the Group has reached a stage when a review of the relations between the Phoenix and the allied companies in this respect has become desirable.' He was equally precise about the reasons for this, although he does not quite point the finger at LGA.

Our liquid assets have been further considerably restricted by calls made upon them on behalf of allied companies . . . The difficulty is accentuated by the state of affairs in America, where the attitude of the Government administration is such

[111] Botting to Sketch, 21 May 1925. [112] Buxton to Ryan, 5 June 1925.
[113] Phoenix Directors' Board Minutes, 10 June 1925.
[114] Sketch to Royden, 23 July 1925.

that profits and interest of British companies seem destined to be required for investment in that country.[115]

It is a moot point here as to which is the bigger villain, the 'allied company' or the American government.

But the remedy, Sketch still believed, was 'placing the Central Administration in closer command of the assets of all the Companies'.[116] He considered that this might be achieved most flexibly by amending Phoenix's rights as a shareholder in its dependent companies: Phoenix should forgo its limited liability as a shareholder and accept the obligation to pay all losses and expenses of the allied ventures but should receive in return the income and profits of all companies. This would achieve full control over assets and management without impairing the goodwill enjoyed by individual company names.

Thinking was proceeding on these sensible lines, when an entirely unexpected development occurred: Chamberlin, the director with a foot in the camps of Phoenix, NUF and NUL, reported that the life office had undergone a change of heart and was once more interested in buying the NUF shares. When Sketch expressed interest, Chamberlin telegrammed Lees to return from holiday in Scotland so that serious talks could resume.

It is unclear why NUL should have pursued in 1925 what it had rejected in 1924. Certainly, Sketch's public explanation did not add much to the imaginative notion that it had all been NUL's idea in the first place, 'the Life Office apparently then realised the seriousness of the position and at the very last moment intimated their desire to re-open negotiations . . . we decided to give them one more opportunity'.[117] Possibly, Sketch's reforms had alarmed NUL, and the life office had concluded that it had more to fear from a streamlined Phoenix than it had to lose by buying NUF. Very likely, the Norwich interests had got wind of Phoenix's worsening reserve problem and calculated that the bigger office was more likely to accept a lower price in 1925 than it had been in 1924.

Once Chamberlin dropped his bombshell on 18 June, matters moved with great speed. By 26 June, NUL had made a formal offer. Phoenix directors were informed on 27 June. The Phoenix Board accepted the offer on 30 June. Shareholders of Phoenix and NUF were circularised on 7 July. The sale was completed and Phoenix officials resigned from their NUF posts on 15 July. So Phoenix moved from a rationalisation strategy, which included NUF, to a sale strategy, which completed the shedding of

[115] Sketch, Memorandum on Group Finance, 18 June 1925. [116] *Ibid.*
[117] Sketch to Beresford, 9 July 1925.

NUF, in less than a calendar month. Such speed was possible because the operation did not require the consent of shareholders since technically it was merely an exchange of *securities*: Phoenix owned securities called NUF shares which it surrendered for securities owned by NUL called government stock. Nevertheless, some Phoenix directors were less than enchanted with the haste of the proceedings: Fladgate wrote to Ryan on 19 June asking for written statements of what was going on and time for a Special Committee to ponder them.[118] But he had little chance of arresting the momentum and the effect of the protest was minimal.

For Sketch, the Chamberlin initiative was a godsend. Although the rationalisation strategy had been a serious one seriously pursued, the worsening news from LGA raised problems which threatened to outrun this form of defence. In such circumstances, the revived prospects of a beneficial sale could 'put the Phoenix in a magnificent position financially... enabling us to meet any difficulties without recourse to the drastic steps that we should otherwise have had to take'.[119] Hamilton echoed fears of 'drastic steps' in a letter read at the Board meeting on 30 June: 'in certain contingencies our reserves would unquestionably be dangerously low'.[120] Certainly, it is difficult to believe that Sketch would have taken the rationalisation strategy with regard to NUF so far had he not thought it an adequate answer to Phoenix's problems in early 1925. He needed to switch strategies in the middle of 1925 because Phoenix's problems were becoming rapidly more acute. And the reason for that was LGA.

The stroke which put Phoenix in 'a magnificent position financially' was a bid by NUL for the NUF shares, priced at £6.5 million, to be paid in gilts. The total offer was £0.5 million below the £7 million asked in 1924. It represented a premium of 23% on the market value of the NUF shares against the 34% (and more) for which Sketch had tried in the previous year. The transaction would bring an immediate increase in Phoenix's free assets of £4.5 million. Not all interests approved the price. One large shareholder in Phoenix, A. R. Stenhouse of the Glasgow brokers Stenhouse, Hope and Blyth, threw an interesting light on Sketch's tactics of 1924 by claiming that the 1925 offer was too low: 'I hope... that at least the price is not correct... I would have put the value at least £1 million more, and it is probably worth still another half a million more to the Norwich Union Life to get out of the awkwardness of sleeping in the same bed with a foreigner... '[121] Given the criticisms he encountered in 1924 for being too greedy, this must have left Sketch somewhat bemused.

[118] Fladgate to Ryan, 19 June 1925.
[119] Sketch to Beresford, 9 July 1925.
[120] Hamilton to Sketch, 29 June 1925.
[121] Stenhouse to Sketch, 3 July 1925.

Table 7.8. *Some major insurance takeovers, 1917–24: share prices*

Purchasing company	Target company	Date	No. of years purchase of interest/profit	Price paid as % of share market value
London Assurance	British Law	1917	21	128
Royal	L'pool & London & Globe	1919	15	130
London & Lancashire	Law Union	1919	15	127
REA	State	1924	17	122

Source: Phoenix Directors' Special Committee Minutes, p. 46, 23 July 1924.

In fact, however, comparative pricing of major contemporary insurance takeovers suggests that a valuation in the range 120–130% of a share's market value was the going rate for such acquisitions (see Table 7.8). This supports the notion that Sketch's attempt at upwards of 134% in 1924 priced Phoenix out of the deal and confirms the acceptance of 123% in 1925 as a fair bargain. Table 7.8 shows a falling tendency in the premium paid after 1919, when Phoenix had stumped up 130% for NUF; this reflects the changed state of the markets. The NUF premium of 1925 is very close to the premium paid by the REA for the State in 1924.

We know exactly what the money from the sale was used for. Of the £4.5 million available, £1.2 million was set against existing liabilities, with £0.35 million apiece going to the particularly troubled areas of the marine funds and the outstanding claims reserve. A further £1.8 million went to creating 'free reserves' of a contingency nature. Over £0.5 million of this went to a dividend reserve, to improve Phoenix's ability to pay dividends out of interest earnings, a point on which Sketch was sensitive. And the strengthening of contingency reserves freed the existing inner reserve to become an investment reserve, a particularly valuable defence in the tumultuous markets of the interwar years.[122] It is also clear that these contingency funds were used early in 1926 to finance directly an injection of nearly £0.3 million into the LGA reserve for outstanding claims.[123] Finally, the balance of £1.5 million represented a genuine addition to capital reserves. Important and topical defences were shored up here.

[122] Phoenix Directors' Special Committee Minutes, p. 83, 5 December 1925.
[123] Phoenix Directors' Minutes, 24 March 1926.

One can see why Sketch was pleased with the financial outcome. In presenting the matter publicly, he also argued – despite some opposition from Lees – that the details of price should be openly displayed. He needed Phoenix to be seen to have struck a good bargain. Nevertheless, it took great care to suggest a strengthening of Phoenix's position without implying a matching weakening at NUL. Allowed access to some, if not to the most central, issues of the deal, the press commentators were mostly – though not uniformly – kind to the Phoenix initiative. The *Financial Times* stressed the constraints placed upon Phoenix by the NUL–NUF link and the composite's inability to exploit the potential life assurance capacity of NUF. It concluded that, 'the Norwich Union Life will be in a better position to get the utmost value out of the Norwich Union Fire than the Phoenix could ever hope to secure'. And it understood that one prime result of the sale was that Phoenix's 'ratio of reserves to premium income will far exceed that of any of the other giants of the insurance world'. Nevertheless, the paper still considered the fact that Phoenix and NUF should separate at all: 'An Insurance Sensation . . . one of the most important and most interesting transactions that have ever taken place in the history of British Insurance.'[124]

The local East Anglian press, as might be expected, celebrated the return of the prodigal. The Phoenix–NUF link, according to the *Eastern Daily Press*, had always been viewed in Norwich with 'resignation rather than gratification'.[125] But not all were so indulgent. The insurance expert, Sir William Schooling, writing in the *Daily Telegraph*, attacked the sale roundly, arguing that no mutual society should be cajoled into committing such a high proportion of its resources to the high-risk undertaking of fire insurance.[126] The journal *John Bull* was even more blunt. Again taking the line that the purchase left the NUL policy-holders dangerously exposed, its headlines shrieked protest at the 'Huge Insurance Gamble; Famous Company's Strange Deal' and judged it 'A Question for the Board of Trade'.[127] Lees wrote sympathetically to Sketch that 'some of the press people have gone badly off the mark in spite of our care';[128] but there was little they could do about the adverse publicity.

Even inside Phoenix's walls, at levels other than the purely financial, feelings were mixed. Ryan – for whom of course the event marked a sad conclusion to, if not a reversal of, the programme of corporate expansion – lamented the end of an association 'which had been very pleasurable to

[124] *Financial Times*, 8 July 1925. [125] *Eastern Daily Press*, 8 July 1925.
[126] *Daily Telegraph*, 10 July 1925. He was correct. For this reason Norwich Union divested itself of part of NUF, and Friends' Provident of the Century, after the 1974 stock market collapse. [127] *John Bull*, 1 August 1925. [128] Lees to Sketch, 8 July 1925.

the Phoenix Company and to himself personally'.[129] Not least, his own East Anglian affections were dented. Buxton, Phoenix deputy chairman, and the most senior recruit from NUF, was agreed by everyone, including the NUF Board, to be 'in a most difficult position'; it took advice from the chairman of Barclays and much heart-searching before he decided to stay with Phoenix. But most of Sketch's reforming officials reverted to NUF, a significant loss in human capital in itself. Chamberlin, director of all three companies, altered his reply form – it asked him which companies he wished to resign from – to read that it was not his desire to retire from NUF; he wished to resign from none. Similarly, upon leaving the Phoenix Board, Walter wrote to Sketch stressing 'how very deeply I feel this enforced severance'.[130]

But, of course, Sketch was himself a loyal Norwich Union man and few were more deeply affected by the 'severance' than he. For it was never in question that the man selected by Ryan to run Phoenix would stay with his adopted company. Nevertheless, Sketch was clearly genuinely moved by the schism as others were moved by his departure from the Norwich camp. He received many tributes which convey a real sense of warmth and respect; Sketch was liked for his manner of managing. A significant insight into his character – quite apart from the many references to his 'imagination', 'audacity' and capacity for 'pressing on' – follows from the affectionate description of his habit of keeping 'a clean blotter'; Sketch ran Phoenix from an empty desk. But even he did not manage his retreat from NUF so tidily. Given the impending sale, Sketch knew that his attendance at the NUF Board meeting on 6 July would probably be his last, but he could not bring himself to voice his regrets in front of his old colleagues. He wrote afterwards, 'It would have been quite impossible for me to put into words my feelings of regret at the severance, neither could I have faced the ordeal of saying farewell to one and all individually, and therefore – to put it bluntly – I funked it.'[131]

Amidst all this emotion, it was left to Tryon to remind them all, not for the first time, of the prime purpose behind the sale. He wrote congratulating Sketch on the acquisition 'in these dangerous times... of a large amount of investments'.[132]

But if the financial aspect of the sale could be applauded, the resolution of its organisational implications proved a sad business. For this entailed the dismantling of much of Sketch's rationalisation work over the previ-

[129] NUF Directors' Minutes, 6 July 1925. Personal message reported to Board.
[130] Walter to Sketch, 16 July 1925. There was great irony in the comment: he died of appendicitis three weeks later.
[131] Sketch to NUF Board, 7 July 1925. [132] Tryon to Sketch, 9 July 1925.

ous months. The principal areas in which joint working of Phoenix and NUF systems had been established were the marine department and the Australian, Indian and Far Eastern sectors of the foreign operation. By the time of the sale, the Phoenix and NUF networks had become quite integrated on a worldwide scale; some twenty-four home outlets and forty-two foreign ones were affected by the need for separation after July 1925. Several aspects of the division cost Phoenix dear. Sketch had used senior officials from NUF whom he knew well to spearhead his administrative reforms, and they were not easily replaced. Further, loss of NUF capacity in some regions left Phoenix weakly represented. This was particularly the case in Australia, leading to protracted attempts to rebuild Phoenix capacity there during the 1930s.[133] Thirdly, some of the financial disentanglement was complex, prolonged and hard on tempers. At the time of the sale, Phoenix owed NUF around £69,000 on account of Russian business – terminated by the Bolsheviks, who, in abolishing private property, wiped out this large market – and Australian business. Redefining the joint, overlapping and separate liabilities left relations strained. One area where this was less true was the US market. Since 1920 the two offices had worked independently, if with a high degree of coordination, in the United States. In 1925 it was still hoped that this would continue, with existing levels of cooperation, including those affecting marine business and the two indemnity companies, being maintained.[134] But in many areas, the separation was not especially smooth.

Sketch was well aware that 'the disposal of any portion of our business might be regarded as a retrograde step'.[135] He consoled himself with two counter-points. One was the vast accession to reserves created by the sale. Undoubtedly, this provided a clean and swift answer to a lately revealed and rapidly worsening financial crisis without drastic surgery upon Phoenix's internal organs. The other was the fulfilment of the original intention behind the fusion plans of 1919–20: both Phoenix and NUF had been protected from takeover and were now safe from it. However, there were other implications.

The purchase of LGA and sale of NUF constitutes one of the fateful moments in the life of the twentieth-century Phoenix. These transactions turned out to have a more potent effect upon the company than the San Francisco earthquake of 1906 and are perhaps properly comparable only with the acquisition of a 22% stake in Phoenix by Continental of New

[133] See Chapter 10, Section 9 below.

[134] Sketch to Beresford, 4 July 1925. By 1926, even the casualty affiliation in the United States was unravelling and only the marine link endured. See Chapter 9, Section 3.

[135] Sketch, Memorandum for Phoenix Directors, 27 June 1925.

York in 1963. Ironically, both the NUF sale and the Continental purchase were dramatic, rapid and apparently incisive reactions to shortages of financial resources. Yet the sale of NUF did not solve Phoenix's asset problem once and for all. By the 1960s, Phoenix was again short of substance, and, in a time of international expansion, most severely within the UK base. That, of course, was not Sketch's fault, and his immediate successor must bear part of the responsibility.

But the loss of NUF surely closed an option and its absence had a bearing upon Phoenix's problems in the 1960s. For if Phoenix and NUF had been able to expand together, one of Phoenix's worst postwar problems might have been reduced substantially: the lack of scale within the home market and the inability to establish a convincing link with another large-scale UK operator. Sketch sold in the 1920s the sort of connection Phoenix needed in the 1950s and 1960s.[136] Lack of assets in the 1960s drew Phoenix towards the American investment power of Continental. And that American connection made it more difficult for the Bird to attract any other major UK company into its nest.

It was not the sale of NUF which started this sequence. It was rather the purchase of LGA and entanglement with a more sinister American connection. There are excuses for Sketch. Phoenix had been misled. It was under pressure in violently precarious markets. In 1925 its financial circumstances were revealed to be worse even than feared. Extremely difficult negotiations offered the chance of a swift cure. Sketch made his very substantial best of a bad job. As damage control, it was brilliant. But the damage began with LGA. That acquisition has a lot to answer for.

4. EPILOGUE TO AN ERA: RYAN'S LAST ACQUISITION

Ryan retired from the chairmanship on the grounds of ill health in April 1931. Yet the final takeover of the spate which he initiated did not take place until 1933. This was the purchase of the specialist operator Tariff Reinsurance Ltd. Nevertheless, the buying in of Tariff Reinsurance clearly belongs to the Ryan era in spirit if not in precise chronology. Phoenix's interest, and equity participation, in the venture long anticipated 1933; Ryan sat on its Board from 1926; and no further major company purchase was made by Phoenix until 1955. It is not difficult to present Tariff Reinsurance as part of the Ryan sequence. And it has the incidental advantage of escaping an ending to that sequence on the unhappy note struck by the LGA affair.

[136] Although, of course, NUF's accident business in the United States would probably have brought its own problems.

Plate 7.10 Ryan in old age.

Not that the story of Tariff Reinsurance is a very grand one. It is, however, a story for the times, a representative tale for the interwar insurance business. The company was formed in 1919 on a modest capital of £0.5 million, half-issued, quarter-paid, as part of the postwar boom in company promotion. It was also formed on quite a good idea: to fill the slot vacated as a result of the hostilities by foreign, and pre-eminently German, reinsurance specialists, or, as the founding chairman put it, 'with the idea of keeping for our own country, business which had previously gone to foreign offices'.[137]

Tariff Reinsurance was intended to reinsure fire, accident and marine business and by autumn 1919 had accounts with 60% of tariff offices. But then it ran into the freezing economic climate of the 1920s and 1930s, a classic small company tossed by the winds of depression. Reinsurance was

[137] Chairman's Speech, Shareholders' Foundation Meeting, 28 October 1919.

caught by one of the fiercer currents since it was, and is, particularly sensitive to the rhythm of global commodity trade. At its second AGM, the same chairman admitted heavy reinsurance losses and explained them by the observation that, 'apart from serious conflagration years, 1921, in the fire field, was one of the worst years ever experienced'.[138] But for Tariff Reinsurance few years in the 1920s were any better. It was a creature of the slump and wallowed with the cycle from its beginning to its end.

Throughout the 1920s, Tariff Reinsurance struggled with capital adjustments, board changes and tactical acquisitions in various attempts to make ends meet. In 1921, it made precisely the same error as Phoenix had made with LGA: it purchased one-tenth of the business of the General Casualty and Surety Reinsurance Corporation of New York, 'because in the fifteen to twenty years prior to 1921, it had showed quite satisfactory profits'.[139] In 1921 it entered managerial arrangements with the Olympic Fire and General Reinsurance Co. and the General Reinsurance Co., both of them UK companies and products of the 1919 boom. Three years later, Tariff Reinsurance purchased Olympic outright. And in 1925 the company bought the small City Fire Office from the London & Scottish Assurance.[140]

None of these ventures prospered. The American accident trade was as unkind to Tariff Reinsurance as it was to LGA. General Casualty went broke, leaving its British colleague with a loss of over £50,000. The British General Reinsurance followed it into liquidation in 1925. There was an immediate loss of £15,000 on the Olympic acquisition, and a more serious one of £72,000 on City Fire. Both the Olympic and City offices carried substantial marine accounts and were thus highly vulnerable to the interwar downturn in international trade and the accompanying drastic contraction in ship construction. In 1925, Tariff Reinsurance was forced to suspend all activity in marine underwriting. Disappointed with this performance, as well they might be, five of the founding directors resigned from the Board in February 1925.

In recognition of the losses, the management decided in 1926 to reduce the office's capital by £93,180 and make a new issue of the same amount. This gave Phoenix the opportunity to buy into Tariff Reinsurance; it bought almost all the new issue at a cost of some £20,000. It is fairly clear why Ryan and Sketch should have decided on this course. Despite its own poor results, Tariff Reinsurance had provided a valuable reinsurance

[138] Chairman's Annual Report, 28 April 1922. [139] *Ibid.*

[140] City Fire was not acquired by Phoenix in 1925, as stated in Cockerell and Green, *British Insurance Business*, p. 104, but rather by Tariff Reinsurance. It passed to Phoenix in the baggage of Tariff Reinsurance, only in 1933.

service for Phoenix and the larger undertaking did not wish to lose it. Most of the big composites used Tariff Reinsurance, but, after Commercial Union, Phoenix was the biggest client. Ensuring the survival of the service, controlling nearly 40% of the equity and, from 1927, acquiring Board representation – Ryan and Moore – all for £20,000 must have looked a bargain, even in the conditions of the 1920s.

Yet even this was not enough for Tariff Reinsurance. As the world economy deteriorated in the late 1920s, the reinsurance specialist weakened with it. In 1927, Phoenix, as majority shareholder, had to step in to guarantee all Tariff Reinsurance's fire and accident business. But this could not stop the losses. From 1929, these were continuous, averaging £37,316 per year 1929–32 and peaking at £100,945 in 1932.[141] After Britain left the Gold Standard on 20 September 1931, the plight of Tariff Reinsurance became desperate. Another reduction of capital was considered; there was no prospect of a dividend but a very real prospect of a call upon the shareholders.

In 1932 Tariff Reinsurance earned the not inconsiderable premium of £382,683, but its £1 shares were trading at hardly better than 1 shilling. Towards the end of the year the company was foundering. It was at this point, on 6 December 1932, that Sketch offered to buy the office, lock stock and barrel for 3s per share, on the condition that Phoenix should secure at least 90% of the total equity by the bid. The proposal was put formally to Tariff Reinsurance's Board on 8 December and accepted the same day. The Provisional Agreement was in force within a week and became absolute on 12 January 1933. Phoenix had roped in almost all loose shares by August 1933. The total cost to the big composite was £53,408, about equal to the free assets of Tariff Reinsurance. The new Board was headed by Phoenix's foremost critic of LGA, A. T. Winter, and included the scourge of the American subsidiaries, B. H. Davis, as well as E. B. (later Sir Edward) Ferguson.

Phoenix also needed to reorganise Tariff Reinsurance's capital and did so as soon as the management wielded sufficient shareholding power. The reserves were immediately strengthened by over £100,000. Then Phoenix reduced Tariff Reinsurance's capital by an equivalent amount and issued new shares to bring the total capital back to £500,000. Then they sat back to await a recovery in world trade.

The balance of interest in this transaction was not complicated. Obviously, Tariff Reinsurance needed a lifebelt at any price, and Phoenix threw it one. Otherwise, the reinsurance office would have sunk, as many

[141] Tariff Reinsurance Ltd, Annual Reports, 1919–33.

similar companies of this vintage did. For Phoenix, the issue was not a burning one. Initially, the composite had become involved with Tariff Reinsurance in an attempt to caulk the seams on a vessel that had given it worthy service. When the reinsurer's problems worsened, a more comprehensive rescue operation still possessed point, as long as it did not become financially too burdensome. In fact, Sketch's offer was quite keenly pitched and the acquisition for the price of the free assets a good deal. So, the target company was modestly scaled, provenly useful and agreeably cheap. Sketch was right to think that Phoenix might as well have it.

Both Tariff Reinsurance and City Fire were retained by Phoenix for many years as separate operations. Eventually Tariff Reinsurance was merged into an enlarged reinsurance service unit under the title of London Guarantee Reinsurance in 1974. But its long survival as an independent element testifies to its utility. Of course, the independence was relative. From 1935 – when Ferguson got the job[142] – the chairman of Tariff Reinsurance was the chief executive of the Phoenix and the rest of the Board also consisted of senior Phoenix officials.

Under such control, fortunes began to improve and modest underwriting profits began to appear after 1935. Net premiums averaged £284,917 per year in the period 1935–9 and £401,126 in the period 1940–4; while the average annual underwriting surplus for the same periods was £19,020 and £17,824. Forewarned by the experience of the 1920s, Phoenix used these profits to fatten the reserves; no dividend was declared until 1943. By the late 1960s, Tariff Reinsurance was taking over £2 million in annual net premiums, producing underwriting surpluses around £90,000 and paying dividends of well over £100,000. The useful craft of the 1920s continued then to give good service; the Phoenix rescue operation was well rewarded.

[142] Ferguson retained the chairmanship of Tariff Reinsurance until 1959.

CHAPTER 8

THE PHOENIX, THE INSURANCE SECTOR AND THE UK ECONOMY OF THE INTERWAR YEARS

Sir Gerald Ryan became chairman of the company he had effectively designed, succeeding an ailing and ageing Hamilton, in 1920. 'Long recognised as one of the most able of contemporary actuaries and insurance administrators', he had been knighted the previous year; fittingly, he was the first actuary to receive that honour.[1]

I. RYAN AS CHAIRMAN, 1920–31

If Ryan had been the brains of the company for years, he became its voice in the 1920s.[2] It was an extraordinary voice: forthright, honest, clever, modern in tone and style, and, remarkably for the chairman of a major corporation, informative. Upon his inauguration, Ryan congratulated his predecessor on having turned his annual speeches into 'running commentaries on the results embedded in the accounts'.[3] Hamilton had indeed advanced well beyond the normal corporate platitudes; but Ryan went much further. The Phoenix Annual Reports of the 1920s are genuinely expert appraisals of an insurance giant in difficult times. They admit to errors of judgement. They tell shareholders – in the midst of a global trade depression – things that might seriously worry them. They are even directly useful for the historian. When Ryan was ill, as he was for the AGM of 1926 and again in 1929 – under medical instruction 'to abstain from all business matters and remain away from the City, and preferably from England, for some weeks' – others had to deputise, and the quality of communication immediately deteriorated.

Moreover, a Ryan in full flight did not confine himself only to the Phoenix's immediate economic interest. He turned his annual addresses

[1] *Bankers' Magazine*, 108 (1919), p. 586. [2] He retired at the AGM of 1931.
[3] Chairman's Annual Report, 28 April 1920.

Table 8.1. *Total premium income of UK offices: fire, accident, life, 1920–37 (£m)*

	Fire	Accident	Ordinary life
1920	58.5	45.1	41.9
1929	58.4	66.1	69.8
1935	48.8	67.3	74.3
1937	49.8	75.6	80.5

Source: Supple, *Royal Exchange Assurance.*, p. 427

also into essays upon the great themes of his time: the rapacity of the taxman, the depreciation of the stock markets, the tragedy of mass unemployment, the bogey of nationalisation, the importance of savings.

Naturally, however, Ryan considered the fortunes of the Phoenix before he pondered the troubles of the world. The former had grown enormously more complex as a result of the acquisitions of Union Marine in 1911 and London Guarantee & Accident in 1922, and the merger and demerger with Norwich Union Fire in 1920 and 1925 respectively.[4] By the early 1920s, Phoenix was trading as a full-blown composite office for the first time – and was as important within the insurance industry as it was ever to be. Ryan was nonplussed by the results: the components of his enlarged company did not pull in even roughly the same directions.

Of course, this was equally true of the components of the national insurance market.

Total UK fire premiums remained fairly stable during the 1920s but suffered heavily from the economic crisis at the end of the decade. They fell by 14.7% between 1929 and 1937. By contrast, both accident and ordinary life business strongly resisted the world economic recession of the interwar years. Both grew most rapidly during the 1920s – accident by 46.6%, life by 66.1% – but continued to register progress, in each case by around 14–15%, between 1929 and 1937. Fire began the era as the leading branch of insurance but was soon overtaken by both accident and ordinary life. The remarkable expansion of life business was accompanied by high profitability but the growth of accident business – mainly powered by a surge in motor insurance – was an altogether more problematic affair and did not earn returns commensurate with its scale. Marine business, meanwhile, was having a thoroughly miserable time.

[4] See above, Chapters 5 and 7.

The corporate sector of the sea trade earned only £22 million in premiums in 1922, and averaged a paltry £11 million between 1931 and 1937.

In his appraisal of 1923 Ryan spoke of the 'contrary motion' which these forces were imparting to the various departments of the Phoenix; and, in the next year, mused that 'it can never be taken for granted that success will be achieved in any one year in any given section'.[5] He went on to speculate, rather wistfully, as to what might happen if all departments hit an upswing at once. But that was not to be the way of the 1920s. In reviewing 1926, he found 'a moderate Fire profit, a good Life profit, no profit on the Marine and a loss on the Accident Department – a picture in which the proportion of light and shade do not entirely fulfil our expectations'.[6] Whatever he may have expected, this was the pattern for his period as chairman: surprisingly good profits on life, fair profits on fire, bad returns on accident – for which he bore a grave responsibility in relation to the LGA purchase – and rank bad results in marine – which were a direct function of the world trade recession and which no one could have avoided.

Of course, R. Y. Sketch was general manager and then managing director of the Phoenix from 1920, and he called part of the tune in the ensuing decade, but Ryan did most of the public singing and did not refrain from composition. Although Ryan may have wished to step out of the limelight – and away from some of the accompanying pressure – in the early 1920s, he did not stray far from the theatre.

Outside King William Street he did not find the wider economic perspective appealing. 'For some years past', he observed in 1920, 'the insurance business has enjoyed a spell of considerable prosperity.' But now, he believed – although this was in itself an odd perspective on the First World War[7] – that we 'cannot reckon upon the continuance of such good times. Indeed, in several directions, indications are observable, over a wide area, that a turn in the wheel of fortune has occurred.'[8]

In the early 1920s this adverse rotation was delivered by 'the joint forces of depreciation of [stock market] values and the taxation of income'. Most offices during the war had reserved about 20% of their investment funds for the government, by buying gilts, and Phoenix had well exceeded this. But in 1919 and 1920 the market for gilts was falling (see Figure 8.1) and these big holdings of government paper were depreciating. Phoenix had

[5] Chairman's Annual Reports, 30 April 1924, 29 April 1925. [6] *Ibid.*, 26 April 1927.

[7] Insurance commentators suffered considerable conceptual difficulties with the fact that the war years – generally perceived as a period of deprivation and tragic loss – had proved a profitable phase for the underwriters.

[8] Chairman's Annual Report, 28 April 1920.

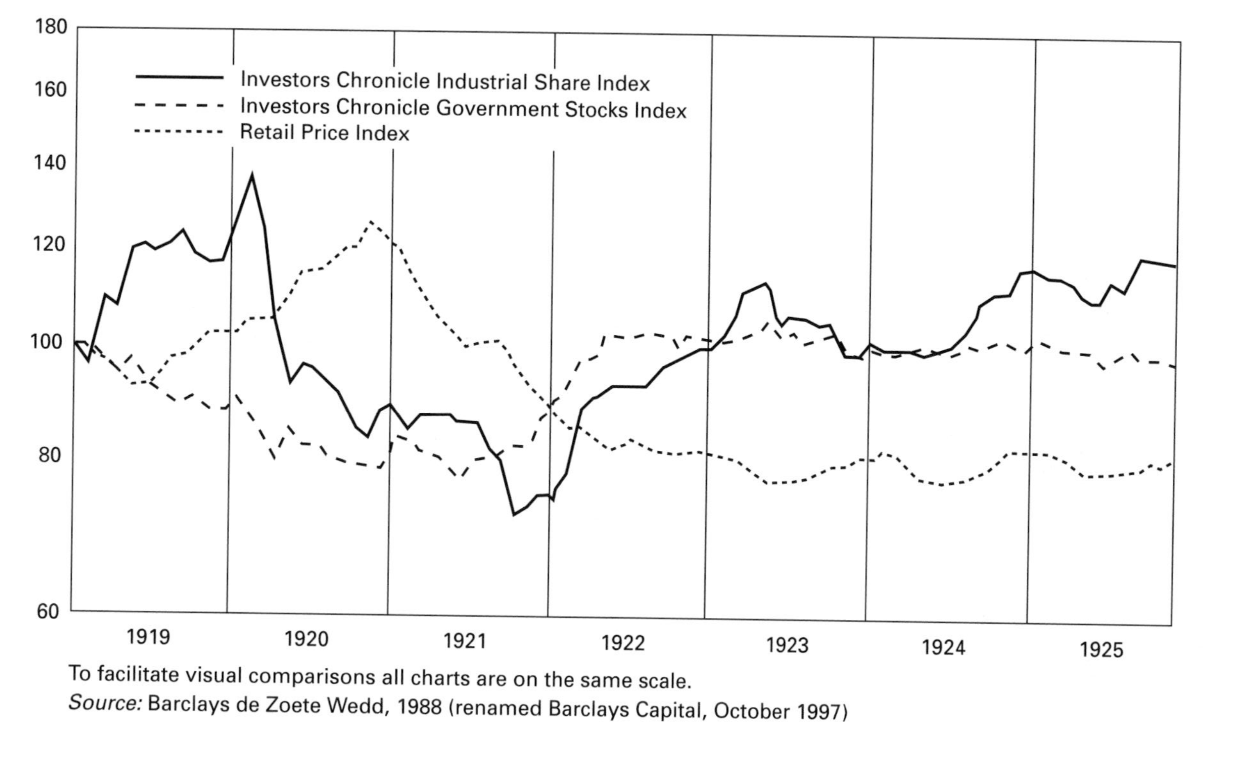

Fig. 8.1 Stocks and shares performance, 1919–25

nearly 22% of total funds in unprofitable government stock in April 1921.[9] The City view was that the institutions had helped the government in its moment of need and were getting caned for it in the aftermath. Ryan saw the falling gilt prices as the result of 'a deplorable weakening of the Nation's credit'. It was bad enough that the British state could not prop up its own paper. Worse still were the amounts that the home and other governments were prepared to take from the insurers in taxation. Ryan reported a gross profit of £636,637 in April 1920, had to spend £170,977 of that in writing down faltering investments,[10] but then handed over £438,260 to the various tax authorities. The shareholders saw almost none of the trading profit: the dividend was paid out of investment income. The twentieth-century conversion of the offices from insurance companies to investment houses had not a little to do with the tax regimes of these years.

In 1921 and 1922, the investment markets turned upward (see Figure 8.1) prompting Ryan to a more sanguine view of how one might measure the wellbeing of an insurance house – 'it has come to be regarded as a fair test of the strength of an Insurance Company to analyse to what extent the dividend is provided by the interest on its free funds' – though he did let fall the acid aside that, 'practically alone among commercial concerns, Insurance Companies are expected to husband at least the major part of their business profits'.[11] In fact, Phoenix free interest paid over 90% of the dividend continuously throughout the 1920s and amounted to more than 100% of dividend requirements in 1922, 1926 and 1928. On the other hand, the chairman could point out that colonial and foreign taxes were still reducing profits by over 50% in the period 1921–3.[12] It was not until 1928 that relief on dominion and colonial income tax produced some respite and improved earning power per share.[13]

If Ryan liked anything less than falling stock markets or importunate tax inspectors, it was perhaps the concept of nationalisation. This became an issue in the home market, for the first, if not the last, time in the wake of the Labour Party's manifesto of 1919. The Labour programme for extended state ownership – 'unsound and ill-considered proposals' to Ryan's eye – offered a significant, if somewhat distant, threat to the insurance industry. 'Today it is the mines; tomorrow it may be the railways and so on . . . Insurance has not escaped the net which has been flung far and wide by the theorists and idealists who are discontented with the present fabric of industry.' He questioned whether the same financial support for the war effort would have been available had the insurance

[9] *Ibid.*, 27 April 1921. [10] And another £224,000 in April 1921.
[11] Chairman's Annual Report, 25 April 1923. He meant allocate them to reserves.
[12] *Ibid.*, 30 April 1924. [13] By about 14% *(Ibid.*, 29 May 1929).

industry been in state hands. And he hit upon an argument which was still providing the insurers with effective defence after the Second World War: for what would a government-owned insurance industry do about the extensive *foreign* income commanded by the great offices of London and Liverpool?[14] No answer was ever found to this question; and the potential loss was not one which any British government of the twentieth century was willing to incur.

But at some points, it looked otherwise. In 1920, Ryan was afraid that 'the state of our National Finances' might encourage ministers 'in their desire to find a quick and easy solution of our present difficulties . . . to adopt expedients that will weaken the springs of enterprise and undermine the foundations on which our industries have been raised'.[15] Insurance companies, Ryan feared, could too easily be seen as a herd of potential milch cows by needy governments. Ironically, of course, the trade conditions of the 1920s solved this problem before any government laid a fiscal finger upon the underwriters. By 1924, Ryan was reflecting, with a certain grim satisfaction, that, 'there was a time when, among the aspirations of the Socialist Party, the nationalisation of insurance formed a not unimportant article of faith, but the course of insurance business in recent years has given the *coup de grâce* to any such proposal'.[16] In financial year 1922, Phoenix had to amass a total premium of £14 million in order to scrape out a net profit of just £177,000. Ryan thought this sufficient answer to the socialists. 'What becomes of the fanciful picture of wealthy Companies making excessive profits by overcharging their clients and generally carrying on business to the detriment of the community?'[17] Given subsequent experience, it is perhaps rather touching to find a businessman who believed that poor economic performance is a defence against nationalisation. But the point held for its day, and served to protect the insurers at least from the first Labour government of 1924.

However, that brief interlude did not, of course, exhaust the socialist campaign in regard to the insurance industry. The second Labour government was returned in 1929 and before long a joint committee of the TUC and the Labour Party was calling for a state monopoly of all insurance. It was not until the election of 1931 voted in the National Government, which was heavily dependent on Conservative support, and, for good measure, put fifty representatives of the insurance industry into the Commons, that the issue was effectively killed for the duration of the interwar period.

In reality too, Ryan's point about insurance profits had never been an

[14] *Ibid.*, 28 May 1920. [15] *Ibid.* [16] *Ibid.*, 30 April 1924. [17] *Ibid.*

entirely sound one. In the early 1920s, they may have been sufficiently poor to keep the nationalisers from the door. But they were not bad enough to place the insurers among the ranks of the truly (or even slightly) depressed. Ryan exhibited some confusion on this score. He was fond of arguing that insurance was dependent on the business cycle and the state of world trade; but, on the other hand, he was equally likely to boast of Phoenix's capacity to *resist* the current tendency of the economy.

Reduced fire premiums in 1921 were promptly ascribed, 'principally to slackened trade and reduced values of insurable commodities all over the world'.[18] Yet, even then, in 'the worst year we have known for many a long day', Ryan could still note, without any apparent trace of irony, that Phoenix had still earned nearly twice as much as was required to pay its dividend. This was the year which saw the failure of the City Equitable Fire Insurance Company, and the collapse of several ventures associated with it. But here Ryan chose to invoke, not the stresses of the world economy, but rather the snares and delusions of schemes for rapid enrichment, far removed from the habits of the Phoenix.

The mixed results of 1923 again moved Ryan to stress the 'close connection between Commercial Strength and Insurance Profits',[19] while, in the next year, he was still insisting that 'insurance is a powerful, if not infallible, index to trade conditions generally'.[20] Yet, over the three years 1922–4, Phoenix was able to write off the full purchase price for LGA,[21] and in 1925 added £0.5 million to the General Reserve, making it up to £2.5 million, enough to guarantee 'complete faith in this old company and in our ability to meet the buffetings of fortune'.[22]

Ryan returned from illness in 1927 to review the year of the General Strike. He was not in good spirits, finding 1926 'a dull, drab time through which we have passed, with but little break in the clouds'. He now saw, superadded to the worldwide disturbance of business, 'these labour troubles in our own country... unnecessary and calamitous'. Again he drew the connection between the state of the nation and the state of insurance. But he missed a quite different point when he described Phoenix's performance in 1926 merely as 'rather disappointing', and decided not to *increase* the dividend.[23] In 1926, of course, many British businessmen would have given their eye-teeth for merely 'disappointing'

[18] *Ibid.*, 26 April 1922. [19] *Ibid.*, 30 April 1924.

[20] *Ibid.*, 29 April 1925. [21] If not the attendant disruption costs.

[22] Chairman's Annual Report, 29 April 1925. The General Reserve at this time stood alongside an Additional Reserve of £1.0 million and a Contingency Reserve of £617,272.

[23] *Ibid.*, 26 April 1927. However, the dividend was raised in 1928, from 13s to 14s, at an additional cost of £40,000. And this high level was maintained in the year of global economic crisis, 1929.

Plate 8.1 King William Street before the Crash, June 1929. Note the Phoenix clock, as yet unadorned.

results and probably the rest of their teeth for a maintained dividend. By now it should perhaps have been dawning upon Ryan that if insurance was connected to the business cycle, the connection was neither close nor simple.

But the dawn was slow in coming. Amidst the crashing stock markets and soaring unemployment of 1929, Ryan still found insurance to be a 'barometer . . . reflecting unswervingly general trade conditions'. He then went on to present the weather report on 1929: 'the disturbances in China . . . the financial troubles in America . . . the trade depression in our Dominions . . . at home the deep unrest caused by the deplorable amount of unemployment'. Yet the Phoenix's own barometer in King William Street did not really reflect these horrors. At length Ryan grasped this; and had the grace to admit it. He reported on 1929, the year of the Great Crash, that 'our net result is not one we have any right to regard as unsatisfactory'; it was merely 'an indifferent year'. The dividend was held at 14s.[24]

More convergence might perhaps have been expected in 1930, and certainly, in his last Annual Report, Ryan was looking once more for his 'intimate connection' between the curves of insurance company profits and of the UK's global trade. On the face of it, he was on firmer ground: 1930 was bad for both. Analysing the results of seventeen leading insurance companies, Ryan found that they had netted, on a total premium of £130 million, a profit of only 3.7%, lower than for many years. The Phoenix, on 2.1%, had done even worse. This was due to 'an exceptionally unfortunate experience in the United States' where Phoenix stood heavily exposed at the centre of the world economic malaise.[25]

So the intimate connection held for underwriting in 1930. But then there was the investment side of insurance activity, and 1930 was not famously a good year for investors; indeed almost all securities except gilts declined (see Figures 8.2 and 8.3). But not all investors had a miserable year. As Ryan conceded: 'that is not our experience, nor the experience of the bulk of Insurance Companies'. Long-maintained portfolios, cautious investment policies, the retentions of government paper at last proving their worth, renewed exposure to property, all held the offices firm while the gales of investment panic shredded the stock markets.

Phoenix had run down its holdings of gilts from the mid-1920s but both the fire and the life funds remained invested in government paper to the extent of 14–17% of their balance sheet values in 1930 (see Table 8.2). Also each account held about 20% of its worth in Indian and foreign government stock. The company's interest in mortgages, property and rents had rebuilt somewhat from 1925. But the striking defensive move, which clearly paid off for the Phoenix, was the increased commitment to debenture and other fixed interest stock: the fire and general fund was committed to this category to the extent of 41.6% by 1930 and the life fund to the extent of 27.9%; in each case this item had become the single

[24] Against a £1 paid-up share value. [25] Chairman's Annual Report, 10 June 1931.

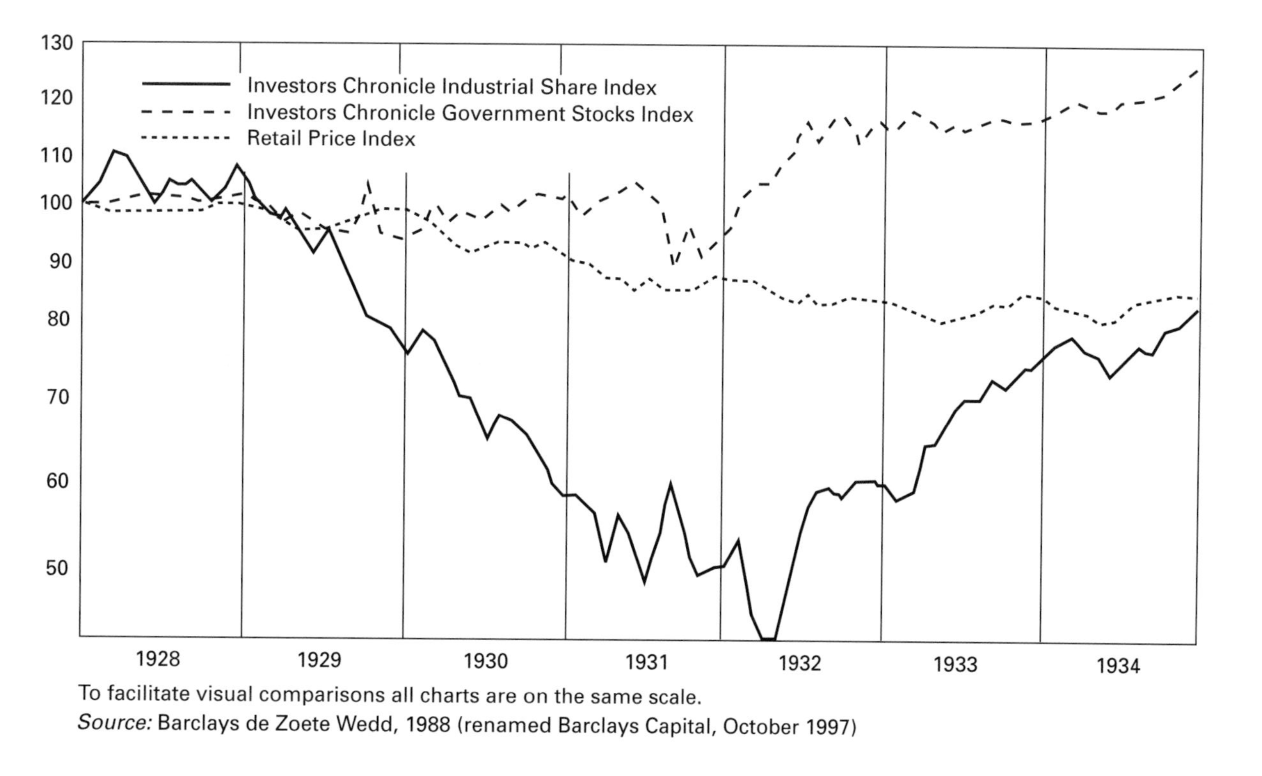

To facilitate visual comparisons all charts are on the same scale.

Source: Barclays de Zoete Wedd, 1988 (renamed Barclays Capital, October 1997)

Fig. 8.2 Stocks and shares performance, 1926–35

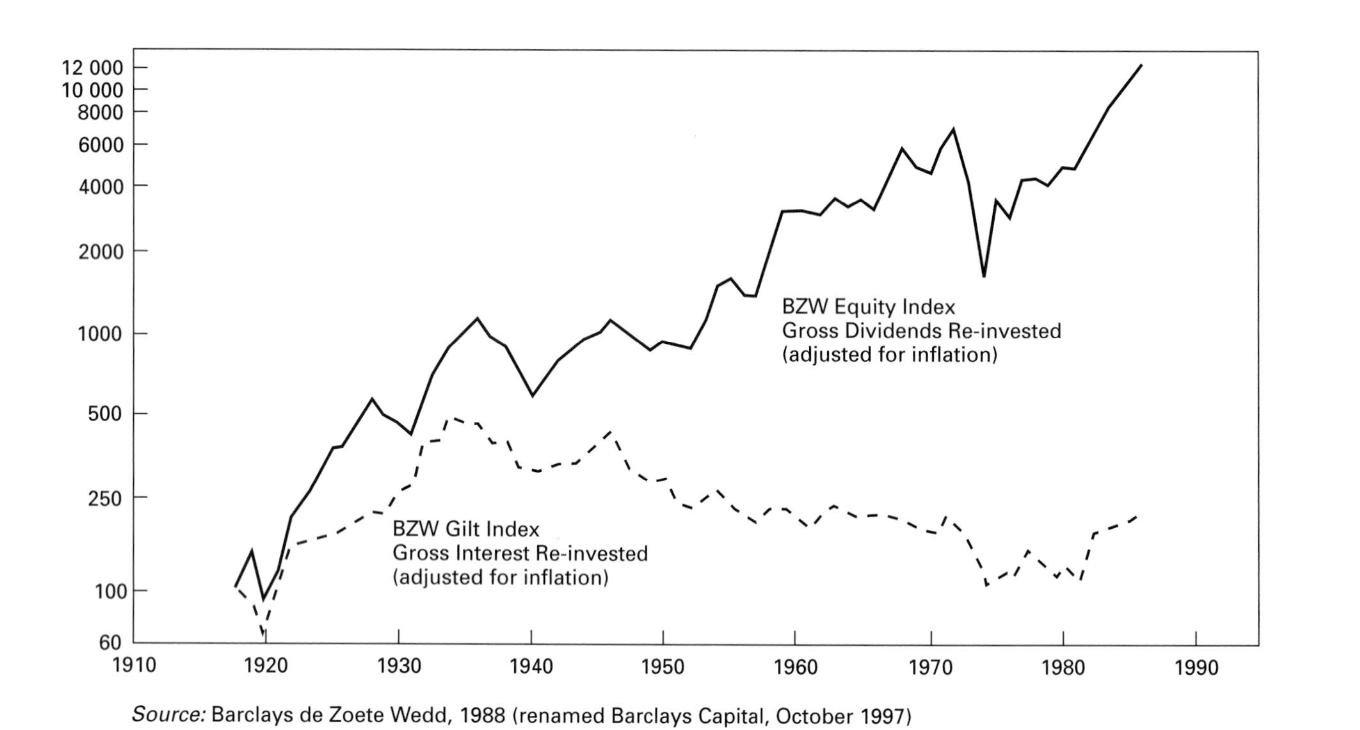

Source: Barclays de Zoete Wedd, 1988 (renamed Barclays Capital, October 1997)

Fig. 8.3 Long-term performance of stocks and shares, 1920–90

Table 8.2. *Phoenix Assurance: major investment categories, 1920–35 (% shares of total fire and life balance sheet values)*

		1920	1925	1930	1935
Mortgages, Property, rent	Fire	12.9	10.9	10.7	12.0
	Life	20.7	12.9	14.7	12.1
UK government	Fire	27.2	30.8	16.5	13.8
	Life	23.3	29.9	14.1	25.4
Indian & foreign government	Fire	27.6	25.0	19.8	20.7
	Life	11.2	18.7	21.4	18.8
Debentures and preference shares	Fire	18.3	25.1	41.6	41.8
	Life	15.6	18.4	27.9	29.9
Ordinary shares	Fire	2.7	1.7	1.5	2.0
	Life	2.2	0.9	1.1	0.9
Total fund value (£m)	Fire	11.0	15.0	16.0	15.0
	Life	12.0	14.0	16.0	17.8

Source: Calculated from Phoenix Assurance Balance Sheets.

richest element in the account. By contrast, ordinary shares, in which the markets suffered the most harrowing fortunes, were lightly represented in the Phoenix balance sheets.

By such tactics, the best offices in 1930 were able to maintain dividends, salt generous amounts to reserves and improve their financial position. Still impaled on the other prong of his paradox, Ryan could only muse that, 'Surely it is a great tribute to the soundness of policy and efficiency of management that a storm like that which we passed through last year should have expended itself with so little effect on our Insurance Companies.'[26]

By the spring of 1931, Ryan had begun to realise a significant truth of the interwar years: that the insurance offices were less reflecting the behaviour of UK trade and industry than comfortably out-performing most participants in most sectors. Phoenix actually added to its balance carried forward in 1930 owing to the movement in security prices and ended the year with its finances as 'solid as a rock'. Ryan concluded, 'We can scrutinise our Balance Sheet without any of the qualms which recent experience has shown to be necessary in the case of many large financial institutions.' Despite the collapse of the world economy, Ryan could

[26] *Ibid.*

celebrate his retirement in 1931, after fifty full years as Fellow of the Institute of Actuaries, by announcing the retention of Phoenix's historically high dividend of 14 shillings; as he said, 'it was a very different story from that which is commonly related'.[27] Ryan had thus come into line with the best financial opinion: the *Bankers' Magazine* was also clear that, 'the insurance industry is not depressed like other industries'.[28]

On the central issues of the world depression, however, Ryan had little to offer. He noted the confusion of the experts, and the conflicting nostrums for revenue tariffs, public works and cutbacks in state expenditure: 'in another quarter a policy of restricted imports is advocated; or again the expenditure of vast sums on road development or the most rigorous economy on the part of the State and the individual and even a wise habit of spending more freely'. He may, in that last remark, have sided with Keynes in regard to the problem of effective demand, but his overall reaction was: 'What a babel of voices.' Nevertheless, he was able to sign off in 1931, contented with the 'astounding extension and development of the business of insurance with which my life has been continuously, and almost exclusively, occupied'.

Before reaching this point, he had achieved a most philosophical view of the ups-and-downs of the 1920s: 'I like to look upon these great Companies not so much as operating for profit as organised for service. The supreme test should not be what dividend you pay but what good you do.' It is reassuring that, in such difficult times, Ryan could develop his concept of insurance as a service, although this was no doubt helped along by the fact that Phoenix dividends were actually extremely respectable. However, the heights of altruism to which Ryan took the concept are impressive: 'In the past, there was anxiety as to whether a great loss had been escaped, but now it is more fittingly recognised that we ought not to escape but should bear our due proportion of any loss.'[29] Was this merely making the best of a bad job? But then again the job that Phoenix had to make the best of was not bad. Perhaps that was what the *Bankers' Magazine* meant when it described Ryan as a 'statesmanlike' insurer.

1931 might have been a good moment for Ryan to bow out but 1932 was not a good moment for Phoenix to celebrate its 150th birthday. The Crash was the ostensible reason for taking things quietly and making little (or no) show of the matter. But neither the staff, who had hoped for a bonus, nor the specialist press were much impressed. 'British insurance offices seem to like to hide their light under a bushel', wrote one journalist. 'The 150th anniversary of the Phoenix Assurance Company

[27] *Ibid.* [28] *Bankers' Magazine*, 128 (1929), p. 188.
[29] Chairman's Annual Report, 27 April 1927.

Plate 8.2 Advertising a quiet anniversary at home.

occurred on January 17th last, but the occasion passed almost without notice.'[30] Perhaps the loss of the chief and the nose-dive of the world economy coming so close together were too much for boardroom nerves.

The 200th anniversary was, in due time, to be quite a different matter.

2. FIRE IN THE ROARING TWENTIES

It was supposed to be the flappers and their beaux who roared in the 1920s. But so, too, did the demons who pawed at the world economy. In the United Kingdom, and other advanced countries, new consumer and leisure industries provided employment and amusement for the middle class and the home market, while traditional staple industries laid off workers by the million and fought for fragments of a contracting foreign market. In the inner Britain of the Midlands, South and South East, 'new industries' such as motor cars, electricity generation, rayon and durable

[30] *Bankers' Magazine*, 133 (1932), p. 670.

Table 8.3. *Phoenix Assurance: net profits as transferred to profit and loss account, by departmental source, 1922–30 (annual averages)*

	Fire	Accident	Life	Marine
1922–6	267,185	16,856	55,945	36,127
1927–30	140,723	75,690	68,294	0

Source: Calculated from Phoenix Profit and Loss Accounts.

consumer goods expanded, while in the outer Britain of South Wales, Lancashire, the North East and Cydeside the old basic industries of coal, cotton, metals and shipbuilding sadly fell to pieces.

Against this background, in the decade or so after the First World War, Phoenix fire business experienced one of its most unstable periods of the last century. Since it dealt with new homes in Metroland alongside old factories in Manchester and middle-aged warehouses in Manila, this is perhaps not surprising. But it is important. For, as Hamilton reported in 1919, the fire department was still the 'main prop of our organisation'.[31] Even after fire was surpassed in volume of business, as it was after the implantation within the Phoenix organisation of LGA's large accident capacity, the fire sector remained the Phoenix's main generator of profit (see Table 8.3).

At no time before 1929 – setting aside the exceptional performance of the marine sector during the First World War – did any other department surpass fire in its contribution to the company's profit stream. The fortunes of fire, then, in the 1920s, continued to bear heavily on the health of the whole company.

These fortunes were volatile: they went up in the aftermath of the First World War; then made a poor start upon the new decade; recovered somewhat in the mid-1920s; and deteriorated sharply towards the end. There were record profit highs in 1919, 1920 and 1927, startling lows in 1922, 1929 and 1930 (see Table 8.4).

The first years of peace benefited from low loss ratios. These were in evidence by the latter part of the war, but were sustained through to 1920. The record profits of 1919 and 1920 stemmed from a combination of these low losses with two other features: inflation in the United Kingdom and organisational reform in the United States. Sharply rising UK prices in 1919–20 (see Figure 8.1) pushed up insured values and alerted policy-

[31] Although this year also added Phoenix's first substantial accident capacity.

Table 8.4. *Phoenix Assurance: fire profits, premium, losses and expenses, 1919–30*

	Premium (£m)	Profit[a] (£)	Profit (%)	Losses (%)	Expenses (%)
1919	2.26	326,377	14.4	42.5	38.3
1920	5.17	328,000	6.3	44.6	41.4
1921	4.75	274,428	5.8	55.4	42.4
1922	4.75	132,201	2.8	57.8	41.7
1923	5.48	202,116	3.7	47.8	40.5
1924	5.37	343,583	6.4	49.9	44.5
1925	3.14	208,253	6.6	51.4	43.0
1926	3.28	161,182	4.9	51.2	42.3
1927	3.29	302,049	9.2	47.4	43.2
1928	3.36	204,493	6.1	48.7	44.2
1929	3.24	120,808	3.7	52.3	44.6
1930	3.09	76,262	2.5	54.3	47.2

Note: [a]Profits are net of tax.
Source: Calculated from Phoenix Assurance Annual Reports and Accounts and Blue Books.

holders to the dangers of under-insurance. This gain scarcely had to be worked for. By contrast, 'incessant work and supervision on our operating machinery' had been needed to turn the US operation around.[32] This close attention had produced strong advances in US business in 1917, 1918 and 1919. The work of the US manager, Percy Beresford, was picked out by the chairman for commendation in successive years. These were the gains which, Hamilton was confident, were not 'evanescent'.

The results in 1919 and 1920 were the biggest fire profits in Phoenix history, very nearly one-third of a million sterling, after tax, in each year.[33] Hamilton thus departed in 1919 on a flourish: 'the lowest loss ratio for many years past and the highest profit'.[34]

However, the good news did not endure for long. In Ryan's report of April 1921, he noted considerable losses due to 'fires ascribable to political disturbance' and in the next year, rising losses were again put down to adverse 'climatic, financial and political conditions'. Loss ratios climbed

[32] Chairman's Annual Report, 1 May 1919.
[33] This represented 14% of premiums in 1919, and 6% in 1920, once NUF had been absorbed.
[34] Chairman's Annual Report, 1919.

well above the 'safe' 50% level in 1921 – the first year of really punishing unemployment – and in 1922. The unwelcome linkage between bad economic times and high fire wastage reappeared. Nor did it help morale in the fire department that 1922 was the first peacetime year in Phoenix's extended history when fire business did not earn the largest share of the company's income.[35] Thanks to the incorporation of LGA, accident premiums in 1922 ran at £5.4 million against the £4.8 million of fire.

Even more worrying in the longer run was the upward trend in the expense ratio. Ryan first noted in 1921 that it was 'several points higher than we were accustomed to before the great upheaval caused by the late War', and decided that it helped make this year 'the least fortunate we have known for many a long day'.[36] The problem stemmed from foreign taxes, salary costs and increased administrative expenditure, indeed from 'every service rendered or article used [which] costs practically double as much as before the War'.[37] Expenses were the real 'cloud in the sky'. And if high expenses had made 1921 bad, high losses made 1922 worse. 'We must frankly confess', Ryan told his worried shareholders, 'that the underwriting results . . . have been very disappointing . . . we receded further from our normal level of profits.'[38]

Severe retrenchment had won some ground against costs, leading Ryan into a brief and uncharacteristic enthusiasm for hair shirts: he professed himself 'a believer in the policy of the Axe, about which we have heard so much recently in national affairs'. However, it was more typical of Ryan that he should add: 'true economy springs from management not meanness'.[39] Nor did the wielding of the Phoenix axe in 1922 produce more than temporary cuts. By 1924, expenses were above 44% and they were never satisfactorily suppressed for the rest of the decade, ending it indeed on a record high (see Table 8.4).

Neither the cutting of costs nor the addition to the Phoenix receipts of LGA's fire account could prevent bad profits in 1922. The high losses stemmed from a traditional source. Fire wastage in the US market in 1922 was worse than any since the San Francisco disaster of 1906; and there was also a very bad year in Canada. No single inferno was to blame, rather a whole sequence of quite large fires in both markets.

Proving Ryan's point that 'American business is peculiarly liable to these fluctuations', the US market bounced back in 1923 and 1924, while the overall Phoenix loss ratio dropped by up to 10 percentage points.

[35] Marine income had surpassed fire in 1917. [36] *Ibid.*, 26 April 1922.
[37] *Ibid.* [38] *Ibid.*, 25 April 1923.
[39] *Ibid.* The reference is to the 'Geddes Axe', the cuts in public expenditure recommended by Sir Eric Geddes as chairman of the Committee on National Expenditure in 1921.

Unhappily, the United States bounced alone in North America; Canada had another miserable year in 1923.[40] But stronger American demand in 1923 and somewhat lower, but better quality, American business in 1924 compensated for the transatlantic blazes of 1922, as well as demonstrating the leverage that the US fire market exerted upon total Phoenix results. However, the cloud persisted: the expense ratio increased again 'in spite of every effort in the direction of economy'.[41] On the other hand, the overall profit outcome from Phoenix's worldwide fire business in 1924 and 1925 was a return to 'a normal satisfactory level'.

The sale of Norwich Union Fire reduced fire premium flow by over £2 million in 1925, but both losses and expenses were moderate and the trading profit was the second-best result in percentage terms of the period 1919–30. The next year would have been much the same, had it not been for 'an almost unprecedented occurrence'. Most fire offices had been 'forced by competition and the essential requisitions of our best customers' to offer alongside fire cover, the auxiliary protection of tornado insurance. Then in 1926 a tornado devastated Miami and the big UK offices paid the price of indulging their fire clients on the Florida coast. If it had not been for Miami, the Phoenix fire account of 1926 would have shown every sign of building on the better form of the middle 1920s.

Fortune relented in 1927 and a comfortable loss ratio more than accommodated a further small rise in overall expenses. Tornados were busy again in the United States, but the specimen which hit St Louis did not hurt the British insurers as much as its predecessor at Miami. This big wind apart, there was no other great calamity. Ryan still insisted that: 'how to keep our expenses down is one of the most important problems we have to solve'; and in a recession, this could not be done by boosting the turnover. Nevertheless, the profit rate for 1927 was nearly double that of 1926, and, at 9.2% of premiums, represented a level of return that had been bettered on only a few previous occasions. This was perhaps a fitting riposte by the fire department to the superiority in premiums (but definitely not in profits) that the accident department had seized from the early 1920s.

By the late 1920s, however, it was becoming apparent that fire profits were increasingly determined by the caprice of the loss ratio. General trade conditions imposed tight limits on what could be achieved with the premium flow. And the expense ratio continued to press inexorably upward, indeed by almost 10% of current premium 1919–30. In 1929,

[40] *Ibid.*, 30 April 1924, 29 April 1925. [41] *Ibid.*, 29 April 1925.

The Zoological Society politely but firmly refusing the gift of a Phoenix on the grounds of its effect on their Fire Insurance Policies.

Plate 8.3 The Phoenix as a fire risk.

Ryan was driven to one of his frank admissions that 'there appears no finality in sight even in the present high ratios'.[42] This left Phoenix, and other insurers, at the mercy of the loss ratio. In Phoenix's case, in the period 1919–30, good profits (say 6% of premiums or better) were associated with loss ratios in the range 42–50% in five out of six years. Similarly, profits below 6% were associated with loss ratios above 50%, again in five out of six years.

In 1928, fire profit was nearly halved, and in 1929 the effect repeated as loss ratios moved above the 50% marker. All major offices experienced deterioration in the fire loss ratio in the years 1927–30. Poor profit results for many in these years were ascribed variously to 'unfavourable climatic conditions at home, unsettled financial conditions at home and abroad, inferior "moral hazard" arising from deep-seated unrest and abnormal competition'.[43] But Ryan saw something more systematic in these loss ratios and feared their effect, given the tightness of other parameters. If loss ratios joined expense ratios and became locked into a rising curve, then an era of more moderate profits could certainly be at hand. Through its pressure on the loss ratio, economic recession perhaps linked the fortunes of the fire section more closely to the business cycle than was true

[42] *Ibid.*, 20 May 1930. [43] *Ibid.*

of Phoenix's business as a whole.

3. THE COMPOSITION OF THE HOME FIRE TRADE BETWEEN THE WARS

During the interwar years Phoenix kept an exceptionally detailed tally of its UK fire business outside the area of ordinary domestic housing cover. This enables us to test the home market for changing demand levels and also for changes in balance between different types of insurance, which should reflect alterations in the tilt of the UK economy.

In the first connection, obviously enough, the expectation would be that demand, particularly from the mercantile and older industrial sectors, would drop off quite sharply at some point during the 1920s and then revive around the middle 1930s. In the second connection, likely outcomes might include a change in the balance of insurance extended on the one hand to 'old staple industries', which bore the brunt of contraction and unemployment, and, on the other, to the 'new industries' which catered to the expanding consumer demand of inner Britain.[44] Insurances of trades and handicrafts might be expected to decline, while those on leisure, entertainment, brewing and retail industries might be expected to multiply. Not all of these expectations are borne out by Table 8.5.

Mercantile, the biggest class of Phoenix UK non-domestic fire business at the beginning of the interwar period, peaked early, between 1921 and 1925, declined by 31% in the second half of the 1920s, then by a further 6% in the next quinquennium and showed little sign of an upturn in the final five years before the Second World War. It is easy to see why Ryan spent so much of his Chairman's Annual Reports lamenting the emptiness of the warehouses and the shortage of insurable goods. Mercantile had taken over from the staple industries as Phoenix's premier class of UK non-housing business as early as 1906–10. The Depression decimated this class.

Rather surprisingly, insurances on old manufacturing industry initially did much better, losing only 2% of value in the later 1920s. However, the respite was brief as the sector then suffered a decline of over 25% in the early 1930s, before rallying by nearly 7% in the era of rearmament. By contrast, new industry also witnessed a contraction in 1926–30, but it was

[44] In the following calculations, 'old industries' were taken to include: cotton, corn, woollen, worsted, paper, saw and oil mills, and bleach and metal works. 'New industries' include: automobile, rubber and chemical factories, cable works, electricity generating and electrical engineering, confectionery and paint production, and powered printing.

Table 8.5. *Phoenix Assurance: UK non-housing fire business by category 1901–40 (five-year aggregates, £)*

	1901–5	1916–20	1921–5	1926–30	1931–5	1936–40
Mercantile	235,925	445,855	458,271	314,270	296,331	297,449
Old industries	283,023	352,417	383,850	376,650	281,375	300,975
New industries	121,307	197,227	250,405	226,497	219,523	231,262
Misc.manufacturing	73,701	128,817	140,218	124,553	57,458	62,348
Leisure/entertainment	56,452	48,608	59,765	50,891	59,446	55,643
Local government	–	–	–	29,635	47,320	90,245
Breweries/distilleries	25,372	28,549	40,030	30,034	22,739	23,803
Hotels/public houses	164,721	146,520	162,875	184,527	195,308	204,563
Retail	239,829	125,713	149,020	408,875	454,588	463,961
Farming	117,299	136,299	142,975	142,661	141,212	174,155
Transport	7,007	20,076	45,498	57,981	84,807	90,742

Source: Phoenix Analysis of Home Business.

a more substantial one of nearly 10%. Thereafter, however, new industry's second contraction of 1931–5 was only 3%, while its upswing of the later 1930s was above 5%. Here the old depressed sector kept up its insurance record down to 1930 rather well, and bounced back quite impressively in the later 1930s. The expanding new industry sector of the interwar economy hit a more pronounced and earlier trough than might have been expected and produced a more feeble resurgence than might have been hoped. The steady decline of miscellaneous manufacturing and handicraft-trade is more predictable and reflects the progressive erosion of marginal and archaic sectors.

Much less expected is the profile for leisure and entertainment and breweries and distilleries. This was the era of the cinema, chrome plate and the cocktail cabinet, the spread of suburbia and the high-water mark of Metroland culture.[45] Yet Phoenix's insurances of the leisure and entertainment sector peaked early, fell sharply (by nearly 15%), clawed back most of the loss in the early 1930s, then collapsed again. Interestingly, the really volatile element within the category was 'theatres and music hall' insurances, which almost halved between 1921–5 and 1936–40, while cinema insurances advanced continuously and almost doubled over the same period. Perhaps the music halls of the North were shutting as the cinemas of the South were proliferating. It is more difficult to create a covering generalisation for the alcohol industry: cover for breweries and

[45] 'Not enough grass to graze a cow', said Betjeman of Slough.

distilleries declined almost continuously from the early 1920s, with the slightest of rallies in the final pre-war years.

On the other hand, and rather oddly, insurances on the hotels and public houses which sold the alcohol grew rapidly and without break from 1916–20 to 1936–40. The growth of suburbia in inner Britain was clearly sufficient to keep this sector buoyant; the series betrays no trace of the Depression. Similarly, two other categories provide textbook profiles for expanding 'new industries', transport and retailing. Transport – which here meant effectively garages and filling stations – followed in the tyre tracks of the classic 'new industry' of motorcars. Phoenix cover in this sector expanded from a few thousand in 1901–5 to a sum well over twelve times this amount in 1936–40.

But the sector to show the biggest change by far was retailing. There had been a sharp jump in Phoenix's interest in this class of insurance in an earlier consumer revolution during the 1890s: it shot up from 2.5% of UK non-housing fire business in 1891–5 to 19.0% in 1896–1900. But the war and postwar years were bad for sales and the sector did not reach even half of its 1896–1900 share throughout the period 1911–25. From 1926, however, its expansion was again meteoric. In 1921–5, retailing ranked fifth in Phoenix's categories of UK non-domestic business netting barely more than a third of the largest category, mercantile. By the next quinquennium, however, it was the single largest class of business and it stayed in that position down to 1940, easily surpassing each of the two reviving industrial classes and far outpacing mercantile. The expansion of High Street services during the interwar years, the advance of department stores and chain stores, the proliferation of show rooms and shop windows clearly left a mark here.

However, if the premium receipts from the various categories are expressed as percentage shares of Phoenix's UK non-housing business, the striking feature is the *stability* of most categories except retailing and mercantile (see Table 8.6).

From 1916–20, mercantile insurances lost their percentage hold on UK business in a way which might be expected in a trade recession, but old industry lost less and new industry gained less than might be predicted given the structural change that was affecting the UK economy as a whole. New industries accounted for perhaps 8% of total UK industrial output around 1914, about 16% around 1929 and about 25% around 1939. Nothing like those dimensions of shift are revealed in Phoenix's propensity to insure new industry rather than old. There is little sign of the 'roaring twenties' in the shares of the leisure-related, breweries–distilleries, and hotel–public house insurances. Only in the retail and

Table 8.6. *Phoenix Assurance: UK non-housing fire business by category, 1901–40 (five-year aggregates, %)*

	1901–5	1916–20	1921–5	1926–30	1931–5	1936–40
Mercantile	16.8	25.7	23.4	15.1	15.0	14.1
Old industries	20.1	20.3	19.6	18.1	14.2	14.3
New industries	8.6	11.4	12.8	10.9	11.1	11.0
Misc.manufacturing	5.2	7.4	7.2	6.0	2.9	3.0
Leisure/entertainment	4.0	2.8	3.1	2.4	3.0	2.6
Local government	–	–	–	1.4	2.4	4.3
Breweries/distilleries	1.8	1.6	2.0	1.5	1.2	1.1
Hotels/public houses	11.7	8.4	8.3	8.8	9.9	9.7
Retail	17.1	7.2	7.6	19.6	23.0	22.0
Farming	8.3	7.9	7.3	6.8	7.1	8.3
Transport	0.5	1.2	2.3	2.8	4.3	4.3

Source: Analysis of Home Business.

transport sectors does the balance of Phoenix UK fire insurance reveal any significant trace of the times. Retail had claimed a strong share of fire business in 1901–5, but this almost tripled between 1921–5 and 1936–40. Transport did better still – at much lower shares – between 1916–20 and 1936–40.

The historian with a weather eye to the changing climate of the interwar economy might wonder here whether Phoenix took more of the colder currents than it needed to and failed adequately to register that balmier breezes were blowing in inner Britain. The moderate returns from Phoenix's cover of the newer technologies and lounge bars of the land seem to indicate a failure to play to the strengths of a complex and changing market.

Of course, the whole of the Phoenix's UK fire operation was now the smaller part by far of its complete fire operation. The huge revival of the office's foreign fire trade since the late nineteenth century had relegated the domestic market – which nevertheless remained a subtle one – to about one fifth, or less, of total fire premiums by the 1920s (see Table 8.7).

Nor did Phoenix's pattern of corporate acquisitions and disposals in the early to mid 1920s do much to aid home fire business. The purchase of Norwich Union Fire in 1919 had pushed UK fire underwriting up to almost one-quarter of global fire income by 1922, but the sale of NUF in 1925 depressed this proportion to well below one-fifth, where it stayed for

Table 8.7. *Phoenix Assurance: total home and foreign fire premiums and expenses, 1922–30*

	Total premiums (£m)	All home premiums (£m)	% Total	Home expenses ratio	All foreign premiums (£m)	% Total	Foreign expenses ratio
1922	4.75	1.15	24.2	44.8	3.60	75.8	44.4
1923	5.48	1.06	19.3	41.8	4.42	80.7	43.7
1924	5.37	1.09	20.3	40.4	4.28	79.7	45.5
1925	3.14	0.53	16.9	37.7	2.61	83.1	44.0
1926	3.28	0.55	16.8	38.9	2.72	83.2	43.0
1927	3.29	0.55	16.7	44.7	2.74	83.3	43.0
1928	3.36	0.56	16.7	45.1	2.80	83.3	44.1
1929	3.24	0.54	16.6	45.8	2.70	83.4	45.5
1930	3.09	0.51	16.4	48.3	2.58	83.6	47.1

Source: Calculated from Phoenix Assurance Annual Accounts (Blue Books).

the rest of the decade. The loss of the Norwich portfolio reduced group fire income by 42% but home fire income by 51%. Table 8.7 reveals just how sharp was the impact of the shedding of NUF upon Phoenix's total fire premiums.

The acquisition of London Guarantee & Accident in 1922 had offered little in compensation. This company's fire business was small, and slanted towards the overseas market. The main effect of the LGA acquisition was rather to reduce the status of the entire fire sector within Phoenix's span of business. The fire department accounted for 54.4% of total corporate income in 1921, its peak for any year since 1910, and the peak also of NUF's influence upon the accounts, but declined to 33.3% in 1926, after the NUF disposal, and despite the LGA acquisition. Accident insurance became the biggest sector of Phoenix activity in 1922 and remained ahead of fire throughout the rest of the interwar period, and far beyond (see Table 8.8).

Initially, the disposal of NUF had a positive effect on home fire expense levels, but, even on a more select range of business, these soon climbed back to the high levels of 1922. Foreign expenses just stayed at a high level throughout. The effect of the economic crisis of 1929–30 is clearly visible in the spectacular expense ratios on both the home and distant accounts (see Table 8.7).

Table 8.8 shows clearly the declining influence of the pioneering fire

Table 8.8. *Phoenix Assurance: distribution of income shares and loss ratios by department,[a] 1910–49 (five-year averages)*

	Fire	% loss	Accident	% loss	Marine	% loss	Life[b]	% outgoings	Total premiums (£m)	Total % loss
1910–14	44.5	52.4	2.6	45.5	13.9	61.4	39.1	82.3	3.19	66.8
1915–19	39.9	46.9	2.6	34.7	30.2	73.2	27.3	97.2	4.56	67.4
1920–4	43.5	51.1	32.0	52.4	11.2	118.2	13.2	82.7	12.15	63.6
1925–9	32.7	50.2	39.6	61.3	6.8	96.9	20.8	73.4	9.97	61.7
1930–4	31.5	50.8	37.9	57.4	7.1	76.8	23.3	84.4	9.22	62.7
1935–9	29.0	42.6	40.3	49.4	7.3	75.3	23.6	81.9	9.41	56.9
1940–4	29.9	46.5	34.0	46.7	16.2	61.4	19.9	78.4	11.25	55.6
1945–9	32.8	40.3	41.1	54.8	10.0	67.4	16.1	70.0	18.37	56.7

Notes: [a]Income is defined as net premiums for fire, accident and marine, while % loss represents claims.
[b]For life, income includes premiums, annuity payments, *and* interest and investment earnings. Outgoings for life include claims *but also* surrenders, annuity outpayments, bonuses, etc. Tables for life premiums alone will therefore display smaller numbers.
Source: Calculated from Phoenix Assurance Annual Accounts, 1910–49.

department within the expanding composite insurance office. The effect of Gerald Ryan's appetite for an accident arm is marked: after 1920–4 the fire department's share of group business was between 7% and 11% smaller than the accident department's share in every peacetime quinquennium. Unfortunately, the loss ratio of the accident department after 1925–9 was between 6% and 15% *higher* than the fire wastage ratio in every peacetime quinquennium. Also striking in these long-run figures is the recovery of the life department's share in group activities after 1920–4 and the sharp contraction of marine operations during the Depression years. Inevitably, marine suffered punishing losses on much smaller volumes; the Depression was worse than war in this respect as the two quinquennia after 1920 saw heavier shipping loss rates than either wartime quinquennia. Once more, the merger and de-merger convolutions of the period 1919–25 show up transparently in the results for total group premiums.

4. RANKING THE PHOENIX FIRE OPERATION

For a good deal of the interwar period Phoenix kept a careful eye on the standing of its fire operation relative to that of its rivals. The investigations went into great detail, assessing the performance of some twenty offices, in respect of premium earnings, expenses, losses and underwriting surplus over the period 1914–32, and allocating a yearly rank score under each of these heads.

Manipulation of these ranks places the Phoenix fire operation very exactly in its context. It was always big, and during the period of association with Norwich Union Fire, very big, ranking as high between 1920 and 1923 as at any time in its career since 1870. In the period 1866–9, Phoenix had lost the second place in the market which it had enjoyed since the 1780s and slipped to third.[46] Thereafter, it declined to a more characteristic fifth or sixth place until the acquisition of NUF. But, whether at fifth or third, it was not as profitable as its size position might have led one to hope; and this was largely due, once again, to the company's problems with the expenses of operation. There is no question but that Phoenix was a high-cost performer during the interwar years.

If the six most profitable insurers are ranked for five-year periods from 1914 to 1932, Phoenix is never among them (see Table 8.9).

Over the ten years from 1914–23 (and indeed much longer), the Alliance was clearly the most consistently profitable fire insurer in Britain. During the war years, 1914–18, only one really large office managed to penetrate the ranks of the six most profitable offices. The best results were achieved mostly by the medium-size ventures such as Alliance, Atlas and Norwich Union Fire. No doubt, the high profit rating of NUF in this period was one of the features which made it an attractive partner for Phoenix in 1919. It is noteworthy also that NUF boasted a particularly good ranking for expenses.

Phoenix's own wartime profit record, although a matter of pride within the walls of King William Street, was in fact rather modest by the standards of the market. Although Phoenix was, on average, the sixth largest fire operator in the United Kingdom during these years, it managed no better than thirteenth rank in terms of profit ratio. The main depressant for Phoenix was clearly the expenses ratio, which was bad enough to place the company in the bottom band of the large fire operators. The Alliance was hardly more proficient in the expenses department for the period 1914–23, but it compensated with notably low loss ratios throughout this decade.

[46] See vol. I, pp. 461, 509–10.

Table 8.9. *The most profitable fire insurers, 1914–32: average annual rank for underwriting surplus ratio, premium size, loss ratio and expense ratio*

Company	Av. rank by underwriting surplus ratio	Av. rank by premium size	Av. rank by loss ratio	Av. rank by expense ratio
(a) 1914–18				
Alliance	1	8	2	17
British Law	3	20	1	21
Union	4	16	7	3
London & Lancs	6	5	7	6
Atlas	6	10	5	11
NUF	7	10	12	4
Phoenix	13	6	10	18
(b) 1919–23				
Alliance	5	10	2	16
London & Lancs	–	5	3	3
Sun	6	7	7	10
Guardian	7	14	9	6
North British	6	4	7	7
Royal	7	1	11	5
Phoenix	12	4	8	12
(c) 1924–28				
Alliance	1	11	1	11
London & Lancs	2	5	4	2
Sun	6	8	6	7
Scottish Union	6	14	7	3
Guardian	6	15	2	15
Atlas	7	9	9	7
Royal	7	2	8	7
Phoenix	13	6	12	11
(d) 1929–32				
Alliance	1	11	1	9
London & Lancs	2	6	2	5
North British	5	4	8	9
Sun	5	7	5	8
Yorkshire	6	16	13	1
Atlas	7	8	10	6
Royal	7	2	7	9
Phoenix	14	6	11	16

After 1919, the biggest offices made a better showing with three of them – the Royal, the North British and the London & Lancashire – all represented in the honour group of the most profitable fire insurers, although the Alliance and the Guardian still flew a flag for the medium-size offices. In this period, however, the London & Lancashire moved ahead even of the Alliance in the control of both expense and loss ratios. The biggest fire insurer of this group, the Royal managed only a moderate rating on losses but a sound one on expenses.

On these ranking tests, the connection with NUF looks highly positive for Phoenix. Enhanced volumes of fire premiums were sufficient to boost the office from the sixth place which had become its conventional spot in the fire market, to third place in 1920 behind only the Royal and Commercial Union (and fourth place, 1919–23). With the exception of the transitory first placing in the corporate marine market in the later stages of the First World War, this was the highest ranking achieved in any insurance market by the Phoenix in the period, 1870–1945. Also, the presence of the NUF within the Phoenix Group seems to have helped improve the profit ranking marginally, and the loss and expense rankings more substantially. Once again, the forced sale of NUF in 1925 is revealed as a retrograde step in most directions other than the immediately financial.

In the middle and later 1920s and on through the Crash and into the early 1930s, the Alliance remained by far Britain's most efficient fire insurer, and the London and Lancashire consistently the best of the big offices. The Alliance even improved its relatively high expenses ratio between 1924–8 and 1929–32. The London & Lancashire was impressive on all fronts but slipped back a little in its expense ratio around the time of the Crash. However, with the exception of the Yorkshire, none of the most profitable companies was especially impressive in the cheapness of its operation in the period 1929–32 (with four ranking 8 or worse). On the other hand, both Alliance and London & Lancashire did conspicuously well in their loss ratio rankings in the difficult conditions of deepening slump.

The middle-size companies again had a higher propensity to land in the high profit bracket in both 1924–8 and 1929–32, with five of them doing so in the first period and four in the second. By contrast only two of the top six by size managed to join the top six by profit in 1924–8 and three in 1929–32; and, even then, the biggest in this class, the Royal, was towards the bottom of it in both time periods.

Phoenix's own profit ranking remained modest, and with a tendency to slip further as time passed and economic conditions deteriorated. Its loss ratio ranking worsened in the mid-1920s but rallied somewhat between

1929 and 1932. The most sensitive indicator of all for Phoenix, the expense ratio ranking, displayed a reverse pattern, continuing to improve – though to no elevated heights – in the mid-1920s and then reverting in 1929–32 to the miserable levels of the war years.

5. FOLLOWING SIR GERALD: THE POST-RYAN ERA 1931–1939

Ryan, the supreme insurance expert, led Phoenix from the year of the Versailles Treaty to the aftermath of the Wall Street Crash. He ended his dozen years as chairman, with his characteristic attention to timing, on the eve of Phoenix's 150th anniversary. Between 1931 and 1939, by contrast, Phoenix consumed, in circumstances which did not admit of much celebration, no fewer than three chairmen. Then, in 1939, another insurance expert, in the shape of Ralph Sketch made the difficult (not to say dubious) transition from leadership of the executive to leadership of the Board. In the interval between Ryan and Sketch, a trio of City luminaries – Sir Clarendon Hyde (1931–3), Sir John Pybus (1933–5) and A. M. Walters (1935–9) – spent brief spells at the helm amidst the treacherous but slowly calming economic currents of the 1930s.

The three chairmen of the 1930s did not have the mastery of the two insurance men on either side of their phase of office, but their Annual Reports, though lacking the clarity and frankness of Ryan's prose, exhibit in each case a high degree of technical competence. None of them made especially likely leaders for the Phoenix, which, for most of its twentieth-century career as a composite office, was chaired either by public servants such as Lord George Hamiltion and Viscount de L'Isle or by insurance and financial professionals like Ryan, Sketch and Ferguson and Jocelyn Hambro. Instead, in a nod to the times, Clarendon Hyde and Pybus were industrialists, while Walters was a solicitor, albeit from a practice much involved with insurance matters.

Where Pybus began in Hull, Clarendon Golding Hyde was a Liverpudlian, educated at the Royal Institution School and later at King's College London. He was called to the Bar at the Middle Temple and joined the Oxford Circuit in 1881; but he did not stay long with the law. By the 1900s he was dividing his time between business and politics: in the one he was working his way towards the top of the construction empire of S. Pearson & Co., controlled by Lord Cowdray; in the other he served, while Liberal MP for Wednesbury 1906–10, on a number of minor government inquiries. In 1910, he was knighted but failed to be re-elected for the more important seat of Cardiff. During the First World War, he emerged as an assiduous committee man and was much in demand for such work. He served as a financial adviser to the Ministry of Munitions, as a member of the Board of Referees on Excess Profits Duty from 1915, joined the Prime Minister's Committee on Commercial and Industrial Policy in 1916, chaired the Committee on the Engineering Trades in that year and the Raw Materials Committee in the next, and, in much the same vein, ended the war as a member of the Ministry of National Service and Essential Industries Committee. None could say that Clarendon Hyde lacked wide experience of industrial and commercial affairs.[47]

This commended him to Ryan, who was chasing both Hyde and the former (and outstanding) Liberal minister, Reginald McKenna, for the Phoenix Board in 1923. Hyde possessed fiscal expertise through his work with excess profits duty, but it was the business position he occupied by the early 1920s which really attracted Ryan. Hyde was now vice-chairman of Pearsons, and partner with Cowdray, as well as maintaining substantial interests in South American railways. Ryan's offer to him was quite explicit: a directorship in Phoenix in return for influencing 'the insurance business and connections of Pearsons' towards Phoenix. Cowdray himself was consulted and was content. Ryan missed McKenna, but he netted a 'large connection' through Hyde.[48]

More than likely it was also Ryan's eye which spotted Pybus as a man for the times. If so, he was taking some risks. Pybus, the son of a Wesleyan stationer and newspaper compositor, had been fascinated by electricity as a child but managed to avoid most types of formal education. He started as apprentice to a Hull engineering shop and ended up as the chairman of English Electric. This was in 1926, when he was forty-six. He had contested Shipley for the Liberals in 1923 and 1924, and then won Harwich for them in June 1929. He was clearly an engaging character. *The Times* obituary is revealing.

> He was architect of his own fortunes but was preserved from the worst failings and the most resounding triumphs of such men by an unusually keen sense of humour . . . his life was moulded by his experience in a general engineering shop forty years ago, when hard work and no amenities were the rule . . . He had a catholic appreciation of ingenious design and fine craftsmanship, whether in a machine . . . or in old silver.[49]

Late in an affluent life, he retained, quite unselfconsciously the habit of relighting fag-ends, a reflex from the days when smoking in the workshop was 'a practice both furtive and expensive'.[50] But that was the end of the good news. Pybus was also a driven man, 'an energetic and conscientious

[47] *The Times*, 26 June 1934. [48] Circular letter, Ryan to Phoenix Board, 1 March 1923.
[49] *The Times*, 26 October 1935. [50] *Ibid.*

businessman [but] ... also self-critical, over-anxious and highly strung ... quick in manner, excessively conscientious about his responsibilities, a severe asthmatic'.[51] English Electric went through a bad patch in the later 1920s, seriously under performing its major rivals, General Electric and Metro-Vickers. These results preyed on Pybus's mind and he suffered two breakdowns in 1927 and 1929, bracketing the date of his appointment to the Phoenix Board. He resigned from English Electric in 1929.[52]

The third of the chairmen of the 1930s was made of more conventional stuff. Arthur Walters was partner in the solicitors' firm of Messrs Walters & Co. These were the solicitors to the Law Life fund, which, of course, Phoenix had absorbed in the acquisition of 1910. But Walters & Co. also handled a lot of fire insurance business, which Arthur's father had continued to place with the Law Fire office. Phoenix elected the son to the Board in April 1916 on the understanding that he would redirect this business closer to home.[53] Once again, as with Hyde, Phoenix appraised a director very much in terms of the business he could bring in his brief case.[54] Not that this was Walters' only attribute. When proposing him as deputy chairman for finance in 1929 – it had become conventional for one deputy to look after the insurance side, the other to supervise investment – Ryan observed that Walters had 'the additional advantage of a fine physique, which neither your Chairman nor your Deputy Chairman at present can claim to possess'.[55] Nor either, of course, could poor Pybus.

It was no accident that Walters lasted longer than his two running mates of the decade. But if he was strong, he was also a team player. As his colleague Lord Greenwood put it, 'Walters' career in our company, and throughout his life, is a fine example of playing the game and putting the team first.' This remark was made in response to an observation by Sketch that Walters' 'selfless disregard of his personal interests made it possible to surmount a difficulty that might easily have developed into a major crisis in our affairs'.[56] It is unclear what this difficulty was. But it is clear that Walters was an amenable figure to have in the chair; though amenability and leadership are far from being the same thing.

[51] R. P. T. Davenport-Hines, in *The Dictionary of Business Biography*, vol. IV, ed. D. J. Jeremy (London, 1985), pp. 783–6. [52] *Ibid.*

[53] General Manager's Memorandum, 26 November 1925.

[54] Ryan was particularly clear-eyed on this point. In 1923 he reported to the Board that he had been 'pressed by members of the Portman family' to find a Board seat for Lionel Portman, nephew of the former director, Edwin Portman. Family property generated valuable fire business, but Ryan advised against: 'Mr Lionel Portman is a literary man and has no business experience or connections'. Ryan to Phoenix Board, 1 March 1923.

[55] Ryan was ailing, and the other deputy, E. G. Buxton was seriously ill.

[56] Sketch to Greenwood, 15 December 1939; Greenwood to Sketch, 18 December 1939.

In 1931 Clarendon Hyde was not expecting to be chairman at all. Rather, Pybus was slated to succeed Ryan, and did so for three months. Even in this short time he was sufficiently engaged with Phoenix to set off with Sketch on an inspection of the crumbling markets in the post-Crash United States. But Pybus was the kind of Liberal politician and businessman who was all-too-useful for a coalition government desperately seeking balance. His insurance travels were interrupted, in mid-Atlantic, by a cable from Prime Minister MacDonald offering him the office of Minister of Transport in the National Government. He accepted in September 1931. At much the same time, Lord Bessborough left the Board to become Governor-General of Canada and early in 1932, Sir Gilbert Vyle, chairman of Phoenix's Birmingham local board was appointed as the British business adviser to the forthcoming Ottawa Imperial Conference. Finding them drafted, Hyde reflected somewhat ruefully that, 'I suppose that we are not entitled to complain if, when the Government wants men, it turns to the Phoenix.'[57]

Hyde was also surprised that Phoenix did so well in 1931. Despite 'passing through the worst period of recorded economic history' and witnessing the economic world turned upside down – 'the gold standard has gone, and free trade, which served the country for over eighty years has disappeared' – the Phoenix accounts reveal 'a total absence of anything extraordinary... business has apparently proceeded on normal lines without disturbance or serious fluctuation'. There was 'nothing in our trading accounts to show that we were in any way suffering from a world depression'.[58] Hyde even managed an optimistic, if misguided, assessment of world trade prospects for the 1930s: 'China, Africa, and to a lesser extent, South America stand ready for trade and development. India, in spite of present troubles, is a practically unlimited field. Russia even will be a reluctant increasing purchaser of European goods.'[59] Had Stalin been a *Times* reader, the last would have raised a grim smile in the Kremlin. But even he would have had to applaud one triumph of capitalism: Phoenix's dividend held unblemished at 14 shillings per share even in 1931.

Phoenix, or at least Hyde, remained sanguine in the face of the investment crash of 1931. There was 'heavy shrinkage' in all classes of securities on both sides of the Atlantic. In the United States, the class of securities of which Phoenix was required, for guarantee purposes, to hold most – the best class of securities – was hit hardest. This was because the best class of securities could still be realised; and their free fall lasted longest. On 31

[57] Chairman's Annual Report, *The Times*, 1 June 1932. [58] *Ibid.* [59] *Ibid.*

Plate 8.4 Sir Clarendon Hyde.

December 1931, they were 'at practically panic levels', so low that the State Superintendents of Insurance, recognising the fictional nature of these prices, allowed the offices to carry out their valuations in June rather than December prices. For its own valuation purposes, however, Phoenix took the most rigorous line, pricing its US assets at 31 December and forgoing any exchange rate gain. Even at these levels, investment reserves of £2 million more than covered the depreciation, and left further general reserves of £2.5 million untouched. Hyde concluded that Phoenix's position was 'unassailable'.[60]

[60] *Ibid.*

Table 8.10. *Percentage changes in industrial production and GDP of five major economies, 1929–32*

	Industrial production	GDP
France	−25.6	−11.0
Germany	−40.8	−15.7
Italy	−22.7	−6.1
United Kingdom	−11.4	−5.8
United States	−44.7	−28.0

In one sense, however, Hyde spoke too soon: parts of the world depression were to come Phoenix's way; they just took a while to work through. And even if Phoenix's own dividend stayed up, the asset values of British and American securities – even British government securities, Hyde reported unbelievingly – had taken a whipping. A major part of Phoenix's business was investment and one of its major difficulties of this decade was to find sufficient decent securities to invest in. But there were insurance losses too: the fire department, always a hostage to trade activity, recorded its first outright loss for a quarter-century in 1932. Claims from Canada and the United States swallowed up all profit from the United Kingdom and the rest of the world. In North America, 'the prospect of profit has not been so much an immediate objective as the avoidance of loss'.[61]

The main reason for the hiatus in the Head Office fire accounts was the uneven distribution of the world economic slowdown: the world's biggest producer, the United States, decelerated much more sharply than any other major economy (see Table 8.10).

The United States was disproportionately important to the Phoenix, and Hyde's irritation with its performance in his report for 1932 reflected that fact:

The American crisis represents especially the cumulative effects of her excessive mass production . . . ; of reckless extravagance of living based on instalment buying; of the great increase in the cost of Government . . . ; of mad speculation on Wall Street; and the subsequent collapse of a banking system hopelessly inadequate for modern needs . . . [62]

Nor was he much more pleased with the solution the Americans had found to their problems: 'Among the many dictators in the world today,

[61] *Ibid.*, 8 June 1933. [62] *Ibid.*

Table 8.11. *Phoenix Assurance: distribution of income by department, 1929–40*

	Fire		Accident		Marine		Life		Total	
	Income (£m)	% loss	Income (£m)	% loss	Income (£m)	% loss	Income (£m)	% outgo	Income (£m)	% loss
1929	3.24	52.3	3.94	57.6	0.71	86.9	2.18	80.8	10.07	63.0
1930	3.09	54.3	3.79	59.6	0.71	80.6	2.04	80.9	9.63	64.0
1931	3.09	49.8	3.67	56.9	0.71	66.6	1.95	111.8	9.42	66.0
1932	2.92	54.5	3.40	57.0	0.68	80.4	2.11	81.5	9.10	63.6
1933	2.67	51.5	3.31	56.7	0.59	72.7	1.97	85.1	8.54	62.8
1934	2.78	44.1	3.34	56.9	0.60	83.8	2.68	62.5	9.40	56.4
1935	2.66	42.0	3.44	53.3	0.55	82.5	2.25	75.8	8.91	52.7
1936	2.69	43.0	3.74	51.9	0.55	70.8	2.23	73.0	9.21	55.6
1937	2.75	40.9	4.06	51.6	0.69	71.9	2.12	76.5	9.61	55.5
1938	2.73	42.8	3.90	51.3	0.74	83.2	2.14	86.7	9.52	59.3
1939	2.77	44.2	3.78	49.9	0.91	68.0	2.27	97.4	9.73	61.2
1940	2.93	51.1	3.55	51.7	1.44	60.2	2.27	81.7	10.19	59.4

Note: Definitions as in Table 8.8.
Source: Calculated from Phoenix Annual Reports and Accounts.

the picturesque figure of President Roosevelt stands out pre-eminent. Never before, probably, have such unlimited powers been willingly entrusted by a disillusioned people to a virtually untried man.'[63] This too must have gone down well in the Kremlin, if the paper was still being delivered. Certainly, Hyde had a way with the booming phrase.

In another sense, however, his original optimism was not misplaced. Phoenix's multi-divisional structure stood it in good stead in difficult times, and the life side of the business was doing particularly well. It was perhaps fitting that 1932 saw the completion of the extensions to Phoenix House in King William Street, and that this brought all divisions of the structure – except marine which remained near Lloyds – under the same roof. The equilibrium generated by the different divisions enabled the dividend to be held at 14 shillings for a further year in 1932. But there were warnings now that this could not continue.

Departments of Phoenix may have been performing well even in 1932, but the outside world was not, and from the outside world came interest earnings. From 1914 to the Crash, gilts had yielded a dependable 4.5 to

[63] *Ibid.*

5.5% but by 1932 Phoenix could not expect more than 3%. Diminished yields on all newly purchased securities were a real threat. Every reputable insurance company of the day followed the convention of paying its own dividend, or the very great majority of it, out of interest earnings.[64] Yet Phoenix was predicting a reduction in interest earnings as a trend. It fell to the upbeat Hyde to warn that, 'with a falling yield, the maintenance of the dividend on the present scale could hardly be expected'.[65] But he did not have to announce the reality of a cut.

Unfortunately, that was one of the early jobs for the over-anxious John Pybus, returned from government to Phoenix service. Devotion to the task in hand had already taken him to the United States again in 1932, to resume his interrupted tour. When he had to turn to the explanation for the dividend reduction in 1933,[66] it is no surprise that he did so with great solemnity. He explained carefully that the fall in Phoenix investments in 1933 had been covered more than twice over by the investment and contingency reserve, and recovering markets in early 1934 had entirely freed these reserves. Nor was there any shortcoming in Phoenix's trading profits: the outcome for 1933 was double that for 1932. The problem was rather one of finding suitable high-grade securities to buy, and especially the current low yield on all existing holdings. To have continued the 14 shillings dividend would have opened up a gap of £89,000 between the yield on investments and the amount needed to pay the dividend. A reduction was not 'dictated by stark necessity'.[67] But it was indicated by prudence. And in 1935, in his last report, Pybus prudently repeated it.

By the time of the next AGM, Pybus was dead. He had not enjoyed his time at the Ministry of Transport. He had piloted the difficult London Passenger Transport Act of 1933, which 'effectively nationalised the transport interests headed by Lords Ashfield and Aberconway', through the Commons, but he had hated the rough-and-tumble of front-bench politics. Not even a baronetcy for his political services in 1934 seems to have cheered him. Driven by private anxieties and inner insecurities, he suffered a third breakdown in summer 1935 and died in October, aged fifty-five.

In fact, the mid-1930s was a period of high mortality for leading Phoenix figures, but most of them achieved longer lifespans than the unfortunate Pybus. The durable Lord Dillon attended his last board meeting, after a quarter-century's worth, only eleven days before his death in 1932, at the age of eighty-eight. Clarendon Hyde died of pneumonia in June 1934, aged seventy-six. Sir Francis Fladgate, who had

[64] See above, section 1. [65] Chairman's Annual Report, 8 June 1933.
[66] From 14 shillings to 12 shillings per share. [67] *Ibid.*, 30 May 1934.

Plate 8.5 Sir John Pybus.

come to Phoenix from Law Life in 1910, died in July 1937. And Phoenix's presiding genius of the twentieth century, the office's 'second founder', Gerald Ryan, who had retired at the company's 150th annual meeting, died one day after the AGM of May 1937.

It was perhaps just as well that it was the picture of health, Arthur Walters, who took over in 1935. However, there may also have been significance in the fact that, as he did so, Ralph Sketch was upgraded from general manager to managing director, and given a seat on the Board. A generous-spirited team player Walters may have been, but there is a hint in Sketch's appointment that leadership resources were being reinforced.

Broadly, Walters had easier economic times to report upon. By 1936, he could talk of 'national prosperity', and for Phoenix this year saw another record performance in life new business, a reversal of the falling fire premiums which had ruled since 1929 and even a retreat of the high claims ratios which had bedevilled accident business. In 1937, a year of

Plate 8.6 The hale and hearty Walters opens Phoenix's Catford sports ground.

'considerable anxiety throughout the world', business was nevertheless good with every Phoenix department witnessing an advance in premium income. Again 1939 was 'a profitable milestone', despite the fact that 'the world as a whole is troubled'. An increase in interest receipts was even recorded in 1937, although the approach of war soon undid this again.

A particular refrain in Walters' reports is a dislike of taxation, and its tendency to rise, which was also, of course, a sign of troubled times. In 1935, he pointed out, the US government had levied taxes, licences and fees upon the insurance companies to the tune of £25 million with a regulatory apparatus that cost that government only £1 million. He associated such taxation with economic nationalism, an attempt to reserve the national market for the home offices. He raised cogent objection to this: 'The idea that each country can be self-supporting in its Insurance Industry appears to strike at one of the fundamental principles of the business, that of the distribution of risks.'[68]

Insurance companies seemed to be regarded as especially easy prey by governments of all persuasions. Foreign governments anxious to preserve

[68] *Ibid.*, 26 May 1937.

home markets for their own insurers would tax them in the overseas market place. Then the reduced receipts would be subject to 25% UK income tax as soon as they arrived back in Britain. So profits would come under the harrow twice.[69] Then, in the late 1930s, as the British government sought additional ways to meet the cost of rearmament, the insurance offices were again hit from two directions; they were the only trading concerns to be assessed for the National Defence Contribution on *both* profits and interest earnings. In his penultimate report, Walters wondered sadly 'if it is generally realized what a heavy burden taxation is to Insurance companies'. And in his last report, he made the complaint in detail: in 1938, no less than 59% of Phoenix's fire and accident gross profits drained away in taxation. There would soon be worse things to worry about, but taxation in the later 1930s was certainly a major irritant to the big UK institutions.

Nevertheless, the resilience of the insurance sector in the midst of the interwar economic depression is striking. It is revealed with particular clarity in the long-run historical record of Britain's largest companies by market value. If the top fifty companies are measured at the benchmark dates 1904/5, 1934/5 and 1985, only one insurance office made the grade in 1904/5 (Prudential), while seven did so by 1985 (Prudential, Royal, GRE, Legal & General, General Accident, Sun Alliance and Commercial Union); yet, as early as 1934/5, there were already six insurers among the biggest battalions, including Phoenix at rank 42 (the others were Royal, Prudential, Commercial Union, Pearl, and Alliance).[70]

6. FIRE DOWN BELOW IN THE 1930S

In the fire business, Clarendon Hyde's optimism that Phoenix would be hardly marked by the world depression really did not outlast 1931. By 1932, there was an outright loss of over 0.6% of premiums; while in 1933, the fire account clawed its way back into the black by a slender margin (see Table 8.12). Thereafter the Phoenix fire series recovered quickly from 1934, and averaged a most respectable profit of 8.9% per year from 1934 until 1939.

Nevertheless, Phoenix's fire accounts took the biggest drubbing from the Crash of all the office's 'normally' operating sectors. Here, marine could not really be said to be in any state resembling normality; this account was stripped down to the bare essentials even in the 1920s, to

[69] *Ibid.*; *The Times*, 8 June 1933.
[70] P. Wardley, 'The Anatomy of Big Business: Aspects of Corporate Development in the Twentieth Century', *Business History*, 33 (1991), pp. 278–80.

Table 8.12. *Phoenix Assurance: fire profits[a], premium, losses and expenses, 1931–9*

	Premium (£m)	Profit £	Profit %	Losses %	Expenses %
1931	3.09	88,457	2.87	49.8	46.4
1932	2.92	−18,249	−0.63	54.5	48.5
1933	2.67	100,299	3.75	51.5	48.4
1934	2.78	204,106	7.34	44.1	47.0
1935	2.66	311,071	11.67	42.0	46.3
1936	2.69	224,089	8.32	43.0	46.3
1937	2.75	272,654	9.93	40.9	48.3
1938	2.73	239,138	8.75	42.8	48.6
1939	2.77	201,780	7.29	44.2	47.9

Note: [a]Profits are net of tax.
Source: Calculated from Phoenix Assurance Annual Reports and Accounts and Blue Books.

make allowance for the depressed state of world trade and the amount of shipping consequently laid up. Thus, even over the Crash period 1928–33, when the world's shipping industry was shattered, Phoenix's marine sector could find barely 20% of business to lose. For the accident sector, which was more than five times bigger than marine, if hardly free of trouble, the peak-to-trough contraction over the period 1929–33 was 16.1%. For total Phoenix Group premium income, the main bracket of distress was also 1929–33, and the peak-to-trough fall was 15.1%. Meanwhile, life business sailed gaily through the troubles of the world economy. Net new sums assured notched up eight successive records between 1928 and 1938, and four of these were included within the period 1929–33.

By contrast, the fire department sustained a peak-to-trough fall in income over the period 1928–35 of 20.7%, a deeper and longer period of woe. It had seen its primacy in premium generation usurped by the accident department in 1922. And in 1929, it lost its lead, if only briefly, as the Phoenix's major supplier of profit, as the resilient life sector claimed this position.[71] The full measure of the embarrassment of the fire men was expressed in the arrangement of the company's Annual Reports. Conventionally, the report on fire business – fittingly, given the Phoenix's origins

[71] Fire profits were £120,809; life profits £123,174.

– occupied pride of place, coming immediately after the chairman's opening remarks. In the report of June 1933, fire lost that place to life and did not regain it until the report of May 1940.

The sources of these troubles were predictable enough: reduced premiums as industrial production and international trade slowed everywhere; high expense ratios on shrinking volumes of business: raised claims ratios as depressed economic conditions as usual brought aggravated moral hazard. The average fire claims ratio for 1925–9 had been bad enough at 50.2%, but for 1930–3, it was still higher, at an average of 52.5%, hitting a peak of 54.5% in 1933.

The modest profit out-turn of 1931 was in fact a triumph of the United Kingdom and the rest of the world against the fire markets of Canada and the United States, which both produced absolute losses. In 1932, there were no triumphs as increased losses in North America ate up profits from the rest of Phoenix's global fire trade. This was where the sharp contraction in the world's biggest economy hit the Phoenix hardest (see Table 8.10). Moral hazard was a particular difficulty in the America of the devil years. And the stoppage of many local banks and the failure of many small agents meant that there was even a shortage of means to collect the premiums that were due.

In Britain also, the slump revived the fire-raising habit, in the style almost of the 1780s.[72] The most celebrated case was that of Leopold Harris, who was sentenced to fourteen years' penal servitude in September 1933 for arson, conspiracy and fraud. Harris was a crooked claims assessor who loaned money to merchants for the purchase of stock, which was then torched. The debtors claimed against their fire policies and paid Harris back, with interest, from the proceeds. Harris' expertise in fire insurance produced an epidemic of claims and made him difficult to catch. It took the cooperation of fifty-three fire offices to entrap him. But even the frauds of Harris and his gang of fire-raisers did not measure the full extent of the problem: in February 1934 the former head of the London Salvage Corps was sentenced to four years.[73] The insurers combined with Scotland Yard to set up a bureau in the City 'which will be able to put its finger on and blacklist all fire-raisers'.[74]

[72] See vol. I, pp. 141–8. The resemblance was uncanny, including even an upsurge in fraudulent claims from small East End businesses. Representatives of Lloyds met Mr Lasky KC, Sir Isidore Salmon and Mr Leonard Montefiore of the London Committee of British Jews early in 1933 to discuss this problem. Private and Confidential Minute of an Informal Committee of F.O.C., Phoenix House, 10 March 1933.

[73] *Daily Telegraph*, 14 February 1934.

[74] *Daily Herald*, 13 March 1934. See also *Bankers' Magazine*, 136 (1933), p. 475; 137 (1934), p. 361.

However, dirty deeds in the City were not the only tribulations to face the fire insurers in the middle 1930s. Further falls in total fire income of some £0.25 million in 1935 again stemmed from American problems, and it was not until the next year that exceptional levels of fire wastage abated in the United States and Canada. But remedies were applied here as well and a note of optimism began to intrude at Phoenix House that the US government might be making a difference. In 1933 the chairman had reported more favourably on the early policies of the Roosevelt administration: 'the contrast in national feeling was amazing. Hopelessness is succeeded by a will to work.' The President had launched 'almost perilously bold schemes of national reconstruction'.[75] Actually, of course, the New Deal was neither so perilous nor so effective, but it did improve the view of Phoenix's most important overseas market, as seen from King William Street.

In 1935, total fire income was no better than in 1933. The clearing out of unprofitable risks, the leaner pickings in the UK reinsurance market, and the 'exceptionally large' rate reductions in the United States had combined to reduce premiums. The perennial problem of expenses, which had yielded a little to 'constant and persistent efforts' in 1934 (by declining to the tune of just over 1%) had sharpened again by 1935. The expense ratio, as so often in fire and accident business worldwide after 1914, was a worry 'that is constantly uppermost in our minds'.[76]

Table 8.13 shows that, after 1932, the home market shares of total fire premium recovered to levels similar to those of the early 1920s. This was due primarily to the weeding of the foreign accounts that had been doing badly and to the complications in international relations after 1933, rather than to any notable strengthening in the volumes of home fire business. The large foreign fire account contracted by 16% in the period 1931–8, while the smaller home account grew by 16%. To this extent, one effect of the international economic recession was to turn Phoenix into something less of an international insurer. Again, this was related to a differential pattern in the foreign and home expense ratios. Both ratios leaped into the high forties around the time of the Crash, but the UK fire operation proved easier to control and home expenses were brought down again quite quickly, if scarcely to comfortable levels, while, by contrast, the foreign ones remained at distinctly uncomfortable levels throughout the remaining years of peace.

The only good news in fire matters until fire premiums turned the corner after 1936 was the rapid reduction in fire wastage once the huge

[75] Chairman's Annual Report, 30 May 1934. [76] *Ibid.*, 26 May 1936.

Table 8.13. *Phoenix Assurance: total home and foreign fire premiums and expenses, 1931–38 (£m)*

	Total premiums	Home premiums	% total premiums	Home expenses ratio	Foreign premiums	% total premiums	Foreign expenses ratio
1931	3.09	0.51	16.5	48.7	2.57	83.5	47.4
1932	2.92	0.57	19.4	45.1	2.35	80.6	48.5
1933	2.67	0.62	23.0	44.5	2.06	77.0	48.4
1934	2.78	0.52	18.9	46.1	2.26	81.1	47.0
1935	2.66	0.52	19.5	44.8	2.15	80.5	48.1
1936	2.69	0.55	20.5	44.1	2.14	79.5	48.2
1937	2.75	0.55	20.2	44.8	2.19	79.8	48.3
1938	2.73	0.59	21.4	43.1	2.15	78.6	48.6

disturbance caused by the Crash had receded. Phoenix fire claims fell peak-to-trough, 1932–7, by a full 25% (that is, from 54.5% to 40.9% of premiums). However, as fire damage went down, governmental damage went up. Over 3% of the high overseas expense ratio of 1937 (48.3%) was accounted for by foreign and dominion taxes. In that year, no less than 6% of total Phoenix group turnover, on all lines of business, was claimed by reconstructing or rearming governments queuing up for revenue. If the pressure of fire claims had not abated in the later 1930s, Phoenix's main source of profits would have been decimated by the world's tax collectors.

In 1938, the UK market withstood the depredations of the US market. Further trade recession in the United States and persistent sogginess in American industrial production pushed down fire premiums from across the Atlantic, but recovery and rearmament in the British economy from 1936 offset these problems. However, in 1938, the forces of Nature did their best to equalise matters. Wind in America contended with drought in Australia, while frost added the English touch. September storms in New England did £80 million worth of damage (of which the UK insurance industry carried £2 million). Bush fires in Australia cost the London market a further £0.5 million. At home, the severe winter of 1938 doubled claims for water damage as comprehensive home policies picked up the debris from burst pipes. The last full year of peace was not uneventful.

The responsibility of presenting the report on the Phoenix's final few months of peacetime trading in 1939 fell to Ralph Sketch, newly made chairman. However, in insurance terms, as the world simmered towards explosion, they were not such bad months. A further slight increase in

Table 8.14. *Phoenix Assurance: net profits, as transferred to profit and loss account, by departmental source, 1931–8 (annual averages)*

	Fire	Accident	Life	Marine
1931–4	93,653	60,412	55,946	32,500
1935–8	261,738	199,486	29,500	20,000

Source: Calculated from Phoenix Profit and Loss Accounts.

premiums was drawn from advances in both the UK and foreign income flows. Claims held down at 44.2%; profit was very respectable at 7.3% of premiums. Even expenses and taxes, in their own phoney lull, fell, for the first time in five years, to 47.9%.

In fact, once the fire account did turn from the middle 1930s, it did rather well. The average fire profit for the last four years of peace, 1935–8, was 9.7%.[77] From the vantage point of 1931 or 1932, an average profit out-turn in the late 1930s of very nearly 10% would have seemed an unlikely prospect. As Table 8.14 shows, this profit performance from fire business remained the strongest from any of Phoenix's main divisions. Accident might yield more premium volume but not until the later 1930s did it begin to provide a satisfactory return on turnover. And even then the fire division did much better.

However, Phoenix had neither the restraint of governments nor the economy of its own management to thank for these fire results: the prime reason, in an increasingly malign world, was a benign twist to the claims cycle.

7. LIFE ASSURANCE IN THE DOLESOME YEARS

For Phoenix, and many other offices, life assurance was the great success story of the interwar years. Where fire insurance was badly affected by world economic contraction, and the company's diversification into accident insurance ran straight into the chasm of the American Crash, life business was closely related to some notably positive currents in British society. In 1925, Gerald Ryan observed that, 'except in times of great financial shock, life assurance proceeds on smooth, well-tested lines, and is free from the ups and downs of other classes of insurance business'.[78] But this in fact underestimated the new sources of demand for assurance that developed in the interwar years. Indeed, in many of his comments on

[77] Against an average 3.3% for 1931–4.

[78] Chairman's Annual Report, 29 April 1925.

Table 8.15. *Major life indicators: Phoenix quinquennial valuations, 1920–40*

	1920	1925	1930	1935	1940
Net new sums assured in quinquennium (£m)	8.24	10.75	14.55	17.54	20.80
% change	38.00	30.50	35.00	21.00	19.00
Net premium income in quinquennium (£m)	3.86	4.01	4.95	5.69	6.37
% change	8.76	3.87	23.00	15.00	12.00
Net interest income over quinquennium (£m)	n.a.	1.44	2.28	2.73	2.91
% change	n.a.	n.a.	58.00	20.00	7.00
Funds at end year (£m)	5.46	8.13	11.37	14.30	17.14
% change	n.a.	49.00	40.00	26.00	17.00
Average rate of interest earned over quinquennium after tax	4.28	4.78	4.80	4.40	3.77

Source: Phoenix Quinquennial Valuations, 1920–40.

the life market during the 1920s, Ryan conveyed some puzzlement as to exactly where the rising custom for assurance was coming from.

The outstanding features here are the strength in the growth of new sums assured throughout the period and also the growth in funds and interest income, especially in the second half of the 1920s. A surge in new premium income immediately after the war was followed by a temporary relapse in the early 1920s – weaker for Phoenix than for most offices – then by powerful expansion in this sector also. Many observers thought that the striking prosperity of life assurers in this period had much to do with the generous margin between the actual level of interest earned and the modest 3% per year which was all that the actuaries allowed for.

Ryan invested much time in the attempt to explain the vitality of the life market when many other markets were so weak. In 1920, he thought that it might be due to higher real incomes, or to the increased burden of death duties – encouraging bigger policies on the lives of testators – or perhaps to the depreciation of stock market investments which made life policies more attractive as securities.[79] But, as record levels for new sums assured, both for the Phoenix and for the assurance sector generally, were set and repeatedly broken during the 1920s, he needed to think harder. By 1927,

[79] *Ibid.*, 28 April 1920.

Table 8.16. *Phoenix Assurance: net new sums assured, total life premiums and yields on life funds, 1920–30*

	New sums assured (£m)	Premium income (£m)	Yield on funds (%)
1920	2.51	0.86	n.a.
1921	2.10	0.87	4.25
1922	1.99	0.94	4.50
1923	1.86	0.94	4.63
1924	2.55	1.12	4.52
1925	2.26	1.17	4.61
1926	2.72	1.10	4.68
1927	2.88	1.11	4.57
1928	3.10	1.14	4.65
1929	3.00	1.18	4.76
1930	2.94	1.11	4.69

Source: Phoenix Annual Reports and Accounts and Life Red Books.

he was musing about 'this very large new business' flowing in at 'moderate expense'.[80] Meanwhile, Phoenix policy-holders contributed their bit by dying less frequently than the actuaries predicted. Favourable mortality was first reported in 1923, and 1924, and was still present in 1927, 1928 and 1929. Yields on life funds were also strong for most of the decade, usually above 4.5%, comfortably outrunning the actuaries' rule of thumb (see Table 8.16). The decade's peak was reached in 1929, although the Chancellor's increases to income tax in that year made it unlikely that this level would hold, even before the investment markets went into free fall.[81] Nevertheless, it was the strong thrust in new business which was the dominant feature of the market.

Records for new life sums assured were set in 1920, 1924 and 1926–8, while yields on funds climbed strongly to the peak of 1929. In 1929, the life sector of the composite office became the single biggest contributor to Phoenix profits for the first time since the merger of the Phoenix and Pelican in 1908.[82] From the year of Phoenix's graduation as a composite office in 1908 to the Great Crash, the office's flow of premium income from the life sector had expanded by a factor of three, and, as Ryan

[80] *Ibid.* [81] Standard rate was raised by 6d to 4s 6d in the pound.

[82] Although this was partly due to other departments failing 'to show their proper form' in this benighted year (*ibid.*, 28 May 1930). See details of departmental profits in Sections 2 and 6 of this chapter.

boasted in 1925, Phoenix had won a firm place among the top UK life companies.[83]

The life performance of the 1920s was clearly stronger than that of the period 1907–19. Net new sums assured had jumped by 67% to a record of £1.35 million in 1910, but this increase stemmed from acquisition – the takeover of Law Life – rather than from any special vigour in demand. Then, there was a tendency to slide away from this high point down to 1914, with an exception in 1913, until the life market encountered the tragic complications of war mortality (see Table 8.17). Similarly, life premiums advanced by 64% in 1910, but then remained more or less flat until 1918. By contrast, Phoenix increased its net new sums assured over the period 1918–28 by 118%, and its premium income by 50%, and almost all by internally generated growth.[84]

By 1925, Ryan was convinced that he had found at least one reason for the high public enthusiasm for life assurance: an artful tax dodge. Between 1924 and 1930, a certain type of life policy – a large endowment for a short term of about five years, paid for with a single premium, with the life office *lending* the assured much of that premium – offered considerable scope for escaping the full demands of the Inland Revenue.[85] Ryan commented that 'quite a large amount of new business has been completed in an ingenious effort to obtain some relief from Income and Super-tax, and, if the attention of the Chancellor is called to this contrivance, he may shut the door against this class of custom and cut off a fruitful source of business for us'.[86]

Just how fruitful is striking. Phoenix's average annual income from

[83] *Ibid.*, 29 April 1925.

[84] The small exception is the modest reinforcement from the life account of LGA.

[85] The assured borrowed from the office, usually at a preferential rate of interest of about 4%, a sum sufficient to pay about 90% of the single premium. So only about 10% of the premium was actually paid. But the interest on the loan attracted tax relief. Also, higher rate tax payers were advantaged by the fact that interest earned by life policies was taxed at less than the current standard rate and, even more so, by the fact that no supertax was charged in relation to assurances taken out by supertax payers. When the endowment matured, the loan was deducted from the capital sum payable. But what was left gave a net return of 7–8% on the premium and interest paid, 'two or three times as much as any other investment of comparable security'. *Bankers' Magazine*, 119 (1925), p. 972; 121 (1926), p. 511. The Life Offices Association also issued an informative leaflet of the history of this fiscal saga in August 1955. The remarkable development of single premium endowments after 1924, and the involvement in this business of Standard Life, Equity and Law, London Life and National Provident, is noted by Professor Butt. However, he offers no explanation for its development, nor why 'some life offices did not like it'. J. Butt, 'Life Assurance in War and Depression: the Standard Life Assurance Company and its Environment, 1914–39', in Westall (ed.), *The Historian and the Business of Insurance*, pp. 155–172, especially p. 164.

[86] Chairman's Annual Report, 29 April 1925.

Table 8.17. *Phoenix Assurance: net new sums assured and total life premiums, 1907–18 (three-year averages)*

	New sums assured (£m)	Premium income (£m)
1907–9	0.77	0.41
1910–12	1.27	0.70
1913–15	1.16	0.71
1916–18	1.19	0.73

Table 8.18. *Phoenix Assurance: single premium life endowment assurances, 1920–33 (four-year averages)*

	Single premium endowments (£)	% Total net premium
1920–3	13,544	1.53
1924–7	166,643	14.75
1928–31	67,481	5.80

single premium policies, 1920–3, was a mere £13,544; while, for the years 1924–7, it rocketed to £166,643 (see Table 8.18).

At the peak in 1925, some 18.9% of Phoenix's total life premiums was being drawn from from this type of policy. But, in the later 1920s, someone spoiled the game and the attention of the Chancellor was duly called. The Chairman's Report for 1931 recorded sadly 'the change in the law made last year which interfered with the transaction of single premium policies. This led to the surrender on a large scale of policies effected under the old law.'[87] In fact, Phoenix paid out over £2 million in such surrenders and the premiums from this type of policy slumped back into the £20,000s in the early 1930s. Nor was Phoenix alone; there were wholesale surrenders and loan repayments across the industry in 1931.[88] This line of business was greatly curtailed by the Finance Act of 1930.

Intriguingly, it was not killed off by formal execution. The life offices were so worried by the loss of tax privileges that the original Finance Bill implied – and by the possibility that the Revenue might begin to look critically at the relief on all life policies that the industry had enjoyed since 1853 – that they lobbied hard for modification.[89] They achieved it, but

[87] *Ibid.*, 31 May 1932. [88] *Bankers' Magazine*, 131 (1931), p. 323.
[89] LOA Circular on Tax Avoidance, August 1955.

Plate 8.7 Life Manager Winter.

only in return for 'an undertaking that they would not countenance any attempt to evade the spirit of the law'.[90] In February 1930, A. T. Winter, the Phoenix life manager, issued the instruction that single-premium policies 'which are obviously taken out to enable the assured to escape a certain part of his liability to Income tax and sur-tax will no longer be issued by this company'.[91] A month later, the *Financial Times* reported that the life offices in general had agreed to withdraw facilities on policies 'where economies in payment of surtax might be the ultimate purpose of the insured'.[92]

But neither clever schemes of tax avoidance, nor astute protection of

[90] *Ibid.* The final Finance Act of 1930, removed income tax relief on any *borrowed* money that had been applied directly or indirectly to the payment of premium under an assurance contract.

[91] A. T. Winter, Circular of 12 February 1930. Winter was life manager throughout the period of innovation 1919–31 (succeeding E. R. Straker who had led the department since the merger with Pelican). There is significance in the fact that Sketch selected Winter as the Phoenix's first deputy general manager in 1931.

[92] *Financial Times*, 13 March 1930.

fiscal loopholes, could explain the public's appetite for life policies. By 1927, Ryan was working harder at his guesses: perhaps the recent war, by severely altering the value of money, had alerted the public to the need for saving or maybe the passing of the lost generation had created a new sensitivity to the need for life assurance. Even so, he was still not content with the degree of the alertness or the extent of the sensitivity, pointing out that average life cover per unit of population was still lower in the United Kingdom than in the United States[93] and that British policy-holders had not aimed off sufficiently for inflation: the average sum assured in 1913 was £850, which would not go far in the late 1920s. Given the need to compensate for fiscal and inflationary pressures, Ryan almost reassures himself, there should have been a rising demand for life assurance in interwar Britain.[94]

However, the further gains in sums assured in the late 1920s clearly surprised the underwriters, and had Ryan reaching for more compelling arguments. By 1928, he had found 'unmistakable evidence of growing habits of thrift and foresight among our people' and linked the upward march of life policies with the expansion in other forms of 'popular savings in Building Societies and Government Loans'. He was particularly heartened by the National Savings Scheme. Taking an uncharacteristically genial view of contemporary society, he concluded that these virtuous patterns in popular finance should be 'set against the common denunciation of the age as one of extravagance and luxury'.[95] In 1927, Phoenix had been prepared to help the virtuous along by introducing the 'promising experiment' of monthly payments of life premiums by banker's order; this was seen as 'a welcome concession to the salaried classes of the community'.[96] Ryan seemed unaware of the deeper

[93] In 1925, the amount of life cover per head of population in the United Kingdom was £39, in the United States £109, and in Canada £74. In 1931 there were 5 million taxpayers in the United Kingdom with an average assessable income of just under £400 per annum. About 3% of assessable income went on life assurance. Total worldwide life assurance in 1924 summed to £18,000 million in sums assured. Two-thirds of this was held by US offices, one-tenth by British, one-thirtieth by Canadian. The relatively lower levels of insurance per head in the United Kingdom may be linked to the more active policy of collective advertising by the life offices in North America. In 1928, collective advertising brought about a rapid expansion of German life business. *Bankers' Magazine*, 125 (1928), p. 532; 127 (1929), p. 682.

[94] Chairman's Annual Report, 26 April 1927.

[95] *Ibid.*, 24 April 1928.

[96] *Ibid.* Phoenix was quick on its feet here. Legal & General, the outstanding innovator in assurance in the interwar years, had led the way with instalment payments, but only slightly earler in 1927 (*Bankers' Magazine*, 124 (1927), p. 879). The insurance offices were incensed when the Scottish banks insisted on charging for payment by banker's order, adding as much as 5% to the premium instalment (Secretary, Phoenix Glasgow Branch to General Manager, London, 4 February 1928).

Table 8.19. *Phoenix Assurance: net new sums assured, total life premiums and yields on life funds, 1931–9*

	New sums assured (£m)	Premium income (£m)	Yield on funds (%)
1931	3.10	1.14	4.47
1932	3.44	1.20	4.54
1933	3.48	1.26[a]	4.50
1934	3.71	1.30	3.71
1935	3.80	1.25	4.11
1936	4.86	1.29	4.06
1937	4.92	1.30	3.99
1938	4.97	1.34	3.78
1939	4.03	1.34	3.53

Note: [a]Estimated.
Source: Phoenix Annual Reports and Accounts and Life Red Books.

significance of this reflection upon the social currents running through the life market.

In fact, he ended his tenure as chairman still in some bafflement as to its behaviour. His penultimate annual statement recorded again that, 'in life receipts, the aggregate income for all companies is remarkably large', and added the somewhat unlikely thought that the growth was supply-led: 'Perhaps the welcome growth of life assurance is to some extent due to the strong competition among the offices for public support which has at once awakened the interest of the community.'[97]

In his last word on the subject, the most influential actuary in Phoenix's history reported on the post-Crash year of 1930 that 'no unfavourable element exists' in the office's life business and that the new sums assured, at just below £3 million, 'now seem to be our normal stride'.[98] The 1930s then proceeded to prove him wrong. But in an unexpected direction: the pace increased. Every year between 1931 and 1938 saw a new record in new sums assured, and by 1938, 'our normal stride' was pressing towards £5 million (see Table 8.19).

Most big life assurers did well during these years. The total UK life market expanded its new sums assured from £146.5 million in 1920 to £260 million in 1937, that is, an increase of 78.2%.[99] However, Phoenix comfortably outperformed this, pressing the office's new sums assured

[97] Chairman's Annual Report, 28 May 1930. [98] *Ibid.*, 10 June 1931.
[99] See Butt, 'Life assurance in War and Depression', p. 162.

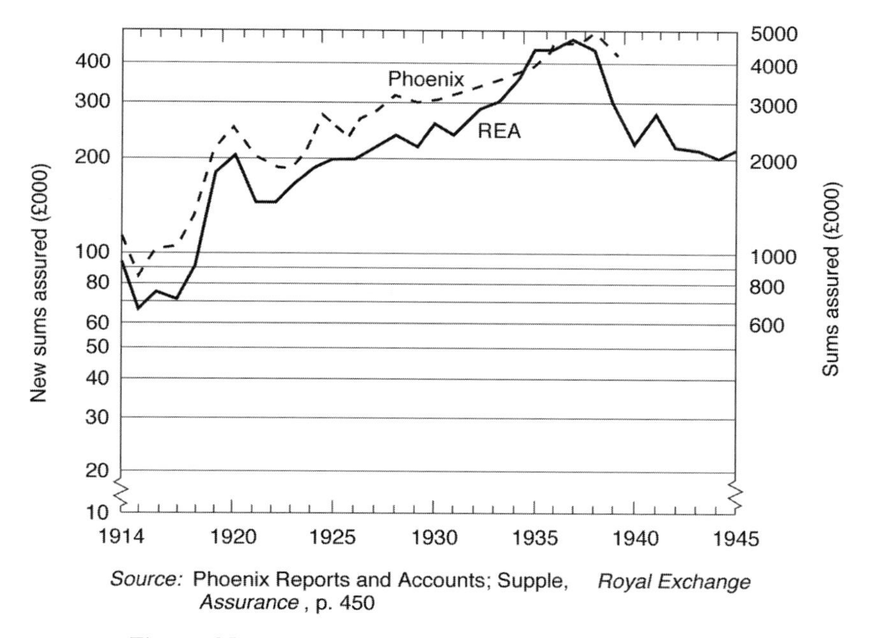

Fig. 8.4 Net new sums assured: Phoenix and REA, 1914–40

from £2.51 million in 1920 to £4.92 million in 1937, an increase of 96.0%. By comparison, the REA achieved a higher percentage increase, at about 140%, but both began and ended at lower absolute levels, of £2 million in 1920 and £4.8 million in 1937. As Figure 8.4 reveals, the pattern of new business acquisition for Phoenix was similar in shape to that of REA, but generally stronger in terms of level and less prone to sharp downward adjustments. Both established composites did particularly well, given that a major part of the expansion in the total life market would have been coming from the rapid expansion of 'industrial' assurance, aimed at lower-income earners; yet this was a class of business that neither of these old offices transacted.[100]

It is noticeable that the trough of the early 1920s, which was a problem throughout the assurance sector, was much less marked for Phoenix, whether measured against the REA standard (see Figure 8.4) or against the industry standard. In the latter connection, Professor Butt shows that the assurance sector did not surpass its level of new sums assured for 1920 until 1927; whereas Phoenix exceeded its own 1920 peak in both 1924 and

[100] Cf. Supple, *Royal Exchange Assurance*, p. 435.

1926.[101] Similarly, Phoenix's new life business registered the slump of 1929–32 distinctly less severely than either the REA or the industrial standard. Total UK new sums assured declined by 1.2% in 1930–2, while Phoenix new sums assured advanced by 17.0%.

Generally, however, the UK assurance industry felt the world crash only lightly, in marked contrast to its US counterpart. The British specialist press was struck in 1931 by the fact that, 'life assurance usually suffers in times of commercial depression, but the contrary was the experience last year'.[102] Their American equivalents could not say the same. While UK new life business was still rising, US new business was down 12.3% in the first half of 1931 against the same period of 1930. Life offices were at the centre of the US Crash. Policy-holders unable to get cash from failing banks pursued the offices for cash surrender values. And the offices, unable to get cash from the same banks, could not pay them. Nearly 200 American insurance ventures failed or were absorbed between 1929 and 1933. Meanwhile the worst that UK life assurers faced was the dilemma presented by the cheap money policies of the early 1930s: this brought them a great accession of new business but created a shortage of rewarding prospects in which the new money might be invested.[103]

Among the dozen companies in Table 8.20, there is little sign of weakness. The strong growth of Prudential and Legal & General hardly betray a trace of the crash, and at a lower level of expansion it exerted little pressure on the growth patterns of the UK Provident, the Phoenix, the Scottish Widows', the Alliance or the Royal Exchange. Together with the Standard and the Atlas, this group represented Phoenix's closest peers in the life market. Within this cohort, ranking just below the elite of giant life operators, Phoenix's performance was notably steady. The Atlas demonstrated a tendency to slip somewhat and the Scottish Widows' to climb. More often than not the Phoenix was very close to, or just ahead of the Alliance, and was always comfortably clear of the REA. Such a performance, in such generally troubled years, more than validates Ryan's claim that Phoenix had firmly established itself among the United Kingdom's top life offices.

The company seems to have maintained its edge in a generally rising market by the exploitation of two particular ploys. From the early 1930s, the selling of life policies was not conducted by a 'separate body of specialist producers' but by the 'general organisation' of the company as a whole.[104] That is, the entire range of the composite structure was em-

[101] See Butt, 'Life Assurance in War and Depression', p. 162.
[102] *Bankers' Magazine*, 131 (1931), p. 321. [103] *Ibid.*, 132, p. 636; 137, (1934), p. 361.
[104] Chairman's Annual Reports of 26 May 1936 and 26 May 1937.

Table 8.20. *Rankings by new sums assured on ordinary life business: twelve selected offices, 1927–33*

	1927		1930		1931		1932		1933	
	(£m)	Rank	(£m)	Rank	(£m)	Rank	(£m)	Rank	(£m)	Rank
Prudential	16.9	1	18.2	1	19.5	1	19.0	1	23.0	1
Pearl	10.2	2	10.4	2	8.0	4	7.6	5	8.8	5
Norwich Union	9.3	3	8.0	5	8.2	3	8.0	4	8.9	4
Legal & General	6.7	4	11.4	4	9.7	2	10.3	3	12.0	3
Commercial Union	4.0	7	4.4	7	4.0	7	4.0	7	3.9	9
UK Provident	3.3	9	3.1	14	3.5	9	3.6	11	3.9	10
Standard	3.0	10	3.2	12	n.a	n.a	2.7	17	3.5	12
Atlas	2.9	11	4.1	9	3.0	12	2.5	19	2.8	18
Phoenix	2.9	12	2.9	15	3.1	11	3.4	12	3.5	13
Scottish Widows'	2.7	13	3.5	10	3.5	8	3.6	10	4.1	8
Alliance	2.5	14	3.2	11	3.2	10	3.4	13	3.2	14
Royal Exchange	2.2	17	2.5	17	2.4	16	2.9	16	3.0	16

Note: Ranks were allocated before rounding the sums assured to one decimal place.
Source: Extracted and calculated from the *Bankers' Magazine*.

ployed to drum up life business. Secondly, Phoenix managed to pay very handsome bonuses on the with-profits section of its business. By the mid-1920s, bonuses were already high throughout the industry and were surpassing pre-war records.[105] Throughout the 1930s, the successful life specialist Standard Life was maintaining a compound reversionary bonus of £2 2s per cent. This was seen as a particular magnet for new business in a time of high competition.[106] Yet the non-specialist Phoenix paid in the Quinquennial Valuation of 1935, 'the same admirable rates of reversionary bonus' as in that of 1930, and these were much higher than the Standard's rates: £2 10s per cent on whole-life policies and £2 6s per cent on endowments. Earlier in 1925 Phoenix had also paid £2 5s per cent, and this was the assumed rate which was quoted to prospective clients by agents and brokers. If the Standard's rates were attractive, the Phoenix's were even more so.

The importance of the Phoenix bonus in the 1920s and 1930s is endorsed by a rare piece of long-range, first-hand evidence from Mr Alan

[105] G. H. Recknell, 'Life Assurance versus Investments', *Post Magazine*, 7 November 1925.
[106] Butt, 'Life Assurance in War and Depression', pp. 163–4.

Smith, who first joined the office in July 1926 and retired as deputy actuary in December 1966. His first job was to fill out valuation cards for each new endowment assurance policy. He remembered (correctly) the reversionary bonus paid to 31 December 1925, and that it was considered a selling point of Phoenix policies at the time, because of its considerable investment appeal.[107]

On top of its appealing bonus, Phoenix could count among the blessings of its life operation in the later 1930s, the national economic recovery, a return to favourable mortality and rising stock markets. The national prosperity levels of 1936 and 1937 were taken to account for the exceptionally low surrenders of life policies in those years.

Two questions follow: if the life business of the Phoenix did well in a rising market – even if this market was located within a threatening world economy – how much did this matter to the company? And, secondly, if Phoenix outperformed a rising life market, just why was this market rising in a context of interwar recession?

The actuary of the REA argued in 1917 that the thrust of the life market was towards participating policies: 'the life business of the proprietary companies tends to become continually more mutual in character, and the period is rapidly approaching when almost the entire profits will require to be reserved for the policy-holders'. In other words, life business, however buoyant, generated returns for the policy-holders rather than the company and its shareholders. The implication was that the modern kind of life business was of limited value to the insuring office. Put this baldly, the analysis leaves out of account two major considerations: firstly, life business generated a powerful flow of income and investible resources when other flows were depressed; and, secondly, that life business, especially when pursued by the 'general organisation' of the office, as at the Phoenix, helped to bring in many types of *non-life* business.[108]

However, the problem initially posed by the REA's actuary did not really affect the Phoenix. For historical and constitutional reasons, the company needed to maintain very separate participating and non-participating sectors of its life business.[109]

The spread of premium income between these sectors provides little evidence of Phoenix's life business becoming 'continually more mutual in character' (see Table 8.21). Indeed, between 1915 and 1940, the share of

[107] A. W. Smith to R. G. Street, Manager, Sun Alliance Group Risk and Underwriting, 25 January 1994. I am indebted to Mr Street for running down this reference and to Mr Smith for the excellence of his recall.

[108] To be fair, the actuary of the REA was not that bald: he understood the second point. See Supple, *Royal Exchange Assurance*, pp. 451–2.

[109] See above, pp. 314–15, 324–5.

Table 8.21. *Phoenix Assurance: participating and non-participating life business as percentages of total life premiums and sums assured, UK business only, 1880–1960*

	Participating		Non-participating	
	% premium	% sums assured	% premium	% sums assured
1880	57.8	62.1	40.5	36.8
1895	49.8	55.4	40.3	38.1
1910	60.4	55.7	36.6	41.6
1915	59.7	57.0	39.1	41.6
1920	50.0	53.4	49.6	46.1
1925	53.3	55.1	46.6	44.8
1930	59.7	57.8	40.3	42.1
1935	54.7	50.8	45.3	49.2
1940	51.7	44.2	48.3	55.8
1945	42.0	37.2	58.0	62.8
1950	31.2	30.0	68.8	70.0
1960	30.6	22.9	69.4	77.1

Note: Rows will not always sum to 100 due to the omission here of certain minor fractions of business, such as 'survivors' branch'.
Source: Calculated from Pelican and Phoenix Quinquennial Life Valuations, 1875–95 and 1910–60.

participating business in total Phoenix UK life business, whether measured by percentage of premiums or percentage of sums assured, contracted quite sharply.

The 1915 shares for with-profits business were not recovered until 1930, and there was then another falling off throughout the ensuing decade. In the interwar era, Phoenix shareholders could usually expect to derive profits from around 45% of the company's total life premiums and sums assured. It was this feature which permitted the life sector to become the biggest contributor to Phoenix profits in 1929 and a substantial one throughout the 1920s and 1930s. The further advance of the non-participating shares after the Second World War was due to the company's increasing development of specialist term assurances, 'key men' policies and other innovative vehicles.[110]

Comparison with the REA in the interwar years is instructive. Whereas, the REA life department contributed only an average £15,000 of profit,

[110] See below, Chapter 12, Section 2.

1925–9, Phoenix far exceeded this with £74,635, although the two offices were much closer for the period 1935–9, when the REA scored an average £30,000 and the Phoenix an average 28,000.[111]

In-house comparison shows that Phoenix life business, quite apart from its outstanding profit performance in 1929, was the second most profitable department of the company after fire in 1925 and 1926, and, very nearly again, in 1930. Indeed, in the aggregate, the life operation was the second biggest producer of proprietors' profits for the Phoenix throughout the period 1922–30, averaging £61,433 per year, and helping compensate for the poor showing of the accident business which yielded only an average £43,000 on vastly larger premiums. Less was taken out of life earnings for the corporate profit and loss account in the 1930s, but even so, the average yield for the period 1931–9 was £40,188. It is thus not difficult to establish a claim for life business as a key contributor to Phoenix's wellbeing during the interwar years.

The larger question, of course, is why did UK life business in general swim so strongly against the tide of the interwar economy? There have been various attempts to explain this; it is likely that there is more than one answer; and also that different offices may have tapped into different examples of these answers. The strong rebound in life business immediately after the First World War clearly represented both the postponed demand that had not been able to find acceptance during the war, and also the requirements of demobilised servicemen returning to family life, and often to newly married life. Also, wartime inflation had halved the worth of life policies; so there was ground to be made up in insured values. However, these effects work best in explaining the upswing of 1918–20; longer-run influences are needed to cover the formidable life boom of 1924–39 (in which total UK new sums assured by all offices more than doubled). Professors Butt and Supple both draw attention to the rising real incomes of the interwar period for those in work; and to the rise of a 'salariat' class, exactly those for whom Phoenix introduced premium payment by monthly instalment.[112]

The advent of the salariat is probably an undervalued feature. The extension of the government administrative apparatus in wartime had greatly expanded the army of middle-ranking officials. The advance of new mass-production assembly industries in the 1920s had swelled the demand for supervisors in quality, stock and cost control. While the matching growth in the services sector – high-street retailing, entertain-

[111] Compare Supple, *Royal Exchange Assurance*, p. 451.

[112] Butt, 'Life Assurance in War and Depression', p. 161; Supple, *Royal Exchange Assurance*, pp. 434–5.

ment, banking and indeed insurance itself – had multiplied the ranks of shop, cinema and branch managers. Where the market for life insurance of the pre-1914 world had been made up classically of the 'old' professional and capitalist middle class, the interwar offices were presented with a social innovation: the emergence of a 'new' lower-middle class of white-collar suburbanites. This class formed a natural market for ingenious adaptations of endowment assurances to provide a whole new range of insurance 'consumer' goods for investment, payment of school fees, family income or house purchase. In parallel with this, the rising real wages of the 80% of the workforce which was almost always employed even in these years, pumped up the demand for industrial insurance and the cheaper ordinary policies.

As socio-economic changes operated to create new demand, so did demographic ones. The difference in life expectation for a male at birth advanced between English Life Table No. 7, based on 1906 data, and Table No. 9, based on data for 1920–2, from an average 48.5 years to an average 55.6 years.[113] As people lived longer, so they gave up work earlier. In 1881, nearly 75% of men over 65 years of age still worked; by 1931 barely 50% did so.[114] Increasing life expectation was clearly a major influence in switching the emphasis of assurance away from insuring against death and towards insuring for life after work. This helps explain, of course, the very marked swing towards endowment policies which affected the whole industry after 1900: by 1925, between 50% and 75% of all new life business came in the form of endowments.[115]

However, Professor Hannah has argued persuasively that the demand for endowments, and the associated demand for occupational pensions, was not only a product of longer lives but followed rather from a combination of rising life expectation, technological change and rising prosperity levels. He gives priority to the third of these variables: the phenomenon of post-employment income fitted into the patterns of the interwar economy as a consumer good developed on the back of rising real incomes and more evenly distributed wealth. The most rapid *increase* in the demand for such incomes came in the period 1930–50, not in the more recent postwar decades.[116]

The 'invention' of retirement for large sections of the community, and the need to provide for it, made the yield upon insurance investment a crucial matter. In the shaky stock markets of the 1920s and 1930s, life

[113] *Bankers' Magazine*, 124 (1927), p. 743.
[114] L. Hannah, *Inventing Retirement: The Development of Occupational Pensions in Britain* (Cambridge, 1986), p. 123. [115] Recknell, 'Life Assurance versus Investments'.
[116] Hannah, *Inventing Retirement*, pp. 122–7.

policies offered good prospects of outperforming the conventional investment alternatives. Not least, income tax relief on life assurance – at half the standard rate, thus 2 shillings in the pound – made policies an attractive way of accumulating capital when stocks were performing fractiously. By the late 1920s, some financial opinion argued that 'the tax advantages put life policies ahead of all other investments'.[117] Furthermore, the proliferation of brokers and life salesmen made them a good deal more accessible. And the product this sales force could offer had resisted inflation, 'one of the few things that had not increased in price', since the war, opined the *Bankers' Magazine* in 1923.[118] Indeed, by the late 1920s, there was a tendency among the offices to reduce life premiums, particularly on non-profit policies.[119]

These attractions were manifest early in the interwar years. Already by the mid-1920s, a twenty-year with-profits endowment, taken out in 1904, would have yielded 3.61%, against the 3.46% earned over the same period by a leading municipal stock, or the 1.31% achieved by 2½% consols. The disparity would have widened in the 1930s owing to the fall in stock market yields. Over the span of the 1920s, the return on consols had varied between 4.1% and 5.7%; by 1935 it was down to 2.6%.[120] Deflationary monetary policies after 1932 also reduced yields on alternative investments and gave life policies further attractions. Their relative safety as investments had already been advertised by the collapse of the stock markets in 1929–32. 'Never', said the *Bankers' Magazine*, 'has the value of life assurance been more strikingly demonstrated than by the Wall Street collapse. A life policy is one of the few investment media that has preserved steadiness and convertibility into cash throughout the present prolonged economic crisis.'[121] In such circumstances, life offices could present themselves increasingly as 'great investment trusts not only providing the people with protection against the financial loss resulting from death or old age but with the means of systematically investing their savings under expert guidance'.[122]

117 *Bankers' Magazine*, 123 (1927), p. 186. This journal calculated that the maximum available rebate amounted to 10% of premiums paid, up to a ceiling of one-sixth of one's income. Endowment capital sums payable on maturity were free of tax. Even after Chancellor Snowden raised income tax by 6d to 4s 6d in the pound in 1929, and adjusted the allowances, thus facing policy holders with a 12.5% increase in tax payable, the advantages remained considerable, especially given the performance of other investments after the Crash.

118 *Ibid.*, 116 (1923), p. 130. 119 *Ibid.*, 126 (1928), p. 820.

120 Recknell, 'Life Assurnace versus Investments'; Supple, *Royal Exchange Assurance*, pp. 436–7.

121 *Bankers' Magazine*, 129 (1930), p. 325; 135 (1933), p. 350.

122 *Ibid.*, 125 (1928), p. 341.

One other prospect for assurance growth, consistent with all these currents, was the advance of group life and pension schemes offered by employers to their workers but managed through insurance companies. Simple group life schemes were first introduced to the UK market from the United States in 1918, where they had been launched around 1912; but they advanced only slowly in Britain, partly because many employers already incurred National Health Insurance liabilities, and partly because most firms in the 1920s were seeking ways of *reducing* costs.[123] Full group pensions were not properly marketed in Britain before the later 1920s.[124] Progress was no more rapid than in group life and it took the insurers some time to develop the necessary skills. The initiator of this type of life business in the United Kingdom was probably the American operator, Metropolitan Life.[125] This venture transferred its business to Legal & General, which had developed its own scheme by 1930 and became the market leader. Metropolitan withdrew from the UK market in 1934, by which time a further threesome of insurers – Eagle Star, Prudential and Standard Life – had joined the group pension business. Most other companies did not enter the sector until the late 1930s, or until after the Second World War.[126]

But perhaps the biggest single opening for new assurance business in the interwar years was created by the exceptional activity in house

[123] *Ibid.*, 123 (1927), p. 27. By 1927 by contrast, group life schemes in the United States covered 5 million people (*ibid.*, p. 1075). However, when contrasts between US and UK levels of cover are drawn, and underinsurance inferred in the latter, the variable of National Health Insurance should be remembered (but rarely is). The best early performer in the UK group life market was probably the Provident Mutual which made 'remarkable' progress in a slack market, and offered a product superior to the American one, giving the employee an independent contract which could be continued if employment was transferred (*ibid.*, 131 (1931), p. 153).

[124] Supple, *Royal Exchange Assurance*, pp. 435–6; although insurance companies had managed pension schemes for individual firms before this. See Butt, 'Life Assurnace in War and Depression', p. 164. A leading full-scale group scheme, which was expected to encourage others, was that arranged with Legal & General by the National Joint Industrial Council for the Flour Milling Industry on behalf of some seventy member firms in 1932. *Bankers' Magazine*, 133 (1932), p. 670. The great innovator at Legal & General, and the leading group pensions expert in the United Kingdom, was T. A. E. Layborn. See H. Cockerell in *Dictionary of Business Biography*, vol. III, ed. D. J. Jeremy (London, 1985), pp. 687–9.

[125] Metropolitan set up a UK branch in 1928. Its arrival was treated by the press as an 'American invasion' and an 'insurance war'. By contrast the UK life industry coolly pointed out that group life was a small part of the market, formed a tariff for it and invited the 'invader' to join. This was the first ever common scale in life business. Competition for ordinary non-profit business remained particularly keen. *Bankers' Magazine*, 125 (1928), p. 1017; 127 (1929), p. 333.

[126] Butt, 'Life Assurance in War and Depression', p. 166; Hannah, *Inventing Retirement*, p. 37.

Table 8.22. *Annual average growth rates of UK construction output, 1856–1973*

1856–73	3.1	1937–51	−1.2
1873–1913	1.1	1951–64	3.8
1924–37	4.6	1964–73	1.8

Source: R. C. O. Matthews, C. Feinstein and J. Odling-Smee, *British Economic Growth, 1856–73* (Oxford, 1982), p. 228.

purchasing during this era. The upswing in residential construction between 1920 and 1938, which created many of the suburbs of modern Britain, was one of the most active features of the interwar economy. It created demand for the 'new industries' of motor vehicles, electricity generation, durable consumer goods and artificial fibres. New suburban houses needed transport services, power, electrical devices for cooking and entertainment and soft furnishings. Over 4 million houses were constructed in this period, 2.7 million of them between 1930 and 1938, and the rate of growth of the building industry 1920–38, at an annual average of 5.4% per annum, was exactly twice that of industrial output as a whole. Measured over the slightly different time period, 1924–37, the building industry grew faster than at any time in its history over the long span 1856–1973 (see Table 8.22).

Within the interwar building upswing there were residential building peaks in 1921, 1927 and 1934. Activity was actually concentrated into two separate booms: government-subsidised house building accounted for 60% of dwellings built in the 1920s and helped fuel a particular surge in the period 1925–7, while a second larger surge, based more centrally on private owner-occupier purchasing, occurred between 1933 and 1938.[127]

The purchasers of these houses, especially in the 1930s, were characteristically the white-collar workers of the 'salariat'. An insurance product which could draw upon the house-buying urge of this group would link itself to one of the strongest socio-economic movements of the day. The endowment-related mortgage was clearly a vehicle for the times.

The life offices responded to these prospects with alacrity. The *Bankers' Magazine* had noticed 'numerous house purchase policy schemes' as early as 1922, and by 1925 was convinced that this was 'a very desirable

[127] See D. H. Aldcroft and H. W. Richardson, *Building in the British Economy between the Wars* (London 1968), Chapter 10; and also their *British Economy 1870–1939* (London 1969), pp. 46–7, 244.

field for the life offces to cùtivate'.[128] One very good reason for this was the scope which the house purchase schemes offered for diversification of assurance investments away from tricky stock exchange holdings, and especially, the burdensome loads of government paper which war finance had heaped on the offices, and towards property. The inclination towards house-purchase loans after the investment strains of the Great War is precisely analogous to the inclination of innovative insurers towards the annuity-loan after the financial strain of the Napoleonic Wars, a century before.[129]

In comparison with the building societies, the offices could offer lower interest rates on their own loans, as well as income tax relief on the assurance element and life cover. Alternatively, as a second best, they could use an endowment assurance to secure a loan supplied by a building society. They were active in the house market in the 1920s but particularly followed the upswing in private residential construction after 1933.[130]

How did the Phoenix exploit these new developments? Clearly, it faced the same general demand currents as the other life offices. But output was not determined solely by demand; the offices could offer different new life products to the market place, and many did so. Thus Standard Life produced the Acme policy in 1921–2, featuring guaranteed surrender, paid-up and bonus features, a Family Provision policy in 1923, aimed at future inheritance or marriage settlement requirements, and in 1928, a minimum-cost/maximum cover policy. The REA went early into group life – for the Musicians Union in 1921 – and into 'bachelor' endowment policies to cover the tricky period between employed liberty and married employment. Allied Insurance in 1924 added disability provisions to certain types of life policy. And Phoenix, true to its tradition of dealing with the more up-market life clients, developed specialities in policies to cover death-duty entanglements and super-tax minimisation.[131] Family income policies were introduced in 1930 by Legal & General and became all the rage in the early 1930s with endless variations, almost every office producing a twist of its own. Under the constrained economic conditions of the 1930s, much actuarial ingenuity also went into producing policies with maximum cover for minimum premium and an entire arsenal of easy payment schemes.

[128] *Bankers' Magazine*, 113 (1922), p. 909; 120 (1925), p. 569.
[129] See vol. I, pp. 630–43. Also *Bankers' Magazine*, 123 (1927), p. 223.
[130] *Ibid.*, 134 (1932), p. 907; 137 (1934), p. 181.
[131] Butt, 'Life Assurance in War and Depression', pp. 163–4; Supple, *Royal Exchange Assurance*, p. 451.

Phoenix's promotional literature provides a good guide to the office's reaction to the new features in the life market. The purpose of these brochures was precisely to attract attention to new products. Indeed, the Guard Book containing the prospectuses are effectively the only way of detecting new policies – unless they are mentioned elsewhere in minutes or memoranda – since all policies entered the accounts under the conventional basic classes. The prospectuses contain a number of clusters, each of them lightly promoted before 1921, much more heavily between 1921 and 1940. Three of these were: family insurance devices; cheap cover policies; and income-tax-related instruments.

In the first cluster, children's assurances and endowments were advertised by eight prospectuses in the period 1908–21 but by twenty-nine in the period 1922–40; educational endowment and school fee policies scored only once 1908–21 but thirteen times 1922–40; family maintenance policies arrived only in 1930 and were then pushed by six pamphlets before 1940. This was again fast going since the family income policy had been introduced by the leading assurance innovator, Legal & General in the same year, 1930, and then rapidly copied, 'by every office in the land' by 1932.[132] Somewhat strangely, the Phoenix caught on to the 'wild oats' cover, the 'Young Man's Policy' only in 1936.[133] In 1937 the office developed a famous 'First Essential' policy, a low-cost, high-benefit cover for young marrieds. This was suspended at the outbreak of war but proved sufficiently far-sighted to be worthy of reintroduction in 1950.[134]

In its cheap policy promotions, Phoenix was clearly trying to broaden its appeal to the new white-collar buyers and step back a little from its high-value assurances of the 1910s. In fact, Phoenix average policy values moved from £683 in 1914 to £748 in 1929 and £872 in 1937; but, as Ryan pointed out, £700 in 1914 was hardly the same as £700 in the late 1920s. And there can be no doubt about Phoenix's energy in chasing a new class of clientele: various kinds of economical or easy-payment policies were promoted in only three prospectuses between 1908 and 1921 but by no fewer than forty-five between 1922 and 1940. Guaranteed benefit policies without medical entered in 1922; acceptance for endowment without medical in 1926. The emphasis on easy-payment schemes commenced, fittingly enough, in 1930, and received massive emphasis – fourteen separate publications – in the ensuing decade.

[132] *Bankers' Magazine*, 131 (1931), p. 973; 133, (1932), p. 329.
[133] Life Policy Proposal and Prospectus Guardbook.
[134] Phoenix Bristol Life File 741; Cardiff Life Department to Head Office Actuarial Department, 12 June 1950.

Generally, here Phoenix showed a rapid response to new opportunities, competitors' initiatives and changed economic circumstances, but nowhere more so than in the Guaranteed Savings Policy introduced in 1929. This was designed to pay on death the sum assured plus a further sum equal to all the premiums paid by a man aged thirty in 1929, and thus to guarantee that the death benefit should be larger than all the premiums paid. This was a very swift way of cashing in on the blow to investor confidence delivered by the Crash and exploiting the superior security of the life product. The *Bankers' Magazine* was impressed: 'Our life offices quickly seized the opportunity presented by the great depreciation in Stock Exchange values.'[135]

Phoenix's attempts to give the Revenue a run for its money had a longer pedigree. Policies aimed at income tax exemption or benefit, or at death duty and supertax minimisation, were advertised by fourteen separate publications as early as 1908–21 but by twenty more between 1922 and 1940. The speciality in death duty cover, mentioned by Professor Butt, shows up clearly: this was the most prolifically advertised of the tax-related instruments with eleven separate publications devoted to this part of the market between 1916 and 1938.

But such devices surfed across the minor currents: they did not ride the mainswell of demand. At least a part of that force was pushing upon group life and pension business. Here Phoenix seems not to have been an activist. The office did offer some early group life schemes of a kind to some very specialised groups – naval and military officers from 1912, bankers from 1915, and farmers with income tax problems from 1918; but activity hardly broadened outside these categories in the 1920s and 1930s. The one exception was a discount rate for Europeans in India, which produced six promotional publications between 1918 and 1928, about as much as all other group life schemes put together.[136] Even the acquisition in 1923 of the LGA – which possessed a modest life portfolio but containing a high proportion of group life – did not kindle further enthusiasm; but this may have been related to Phoenix's general disenchantment with LGA by the mid-1920s. Certainly, the Phoenix does not seem to have linked endowment assurances with group life business to any interesting degree before 1930.[137]

[135] *Bankers' Magazine*, 129 (1930), pp. 157, 325.

[136] And all of these examples were quite distinct from group insurance proper, where a single agency, such as an employer, sets out to buy protection for a particular community.

[137] Former deputy actuaries, A. G. 'Joe' Butler and Alan Smith, again successfully 'cast their minds back over seventy years' to assist with these points.

Nor is there any more convincing indication of Phoenix activity in the group pension market which was being developed by Legal & General and Standard Life, and a few colleagues. Phoenix did offer a special staff endowment assurance for large-scale employers from 1919 and issued prospectuses for it five times between 1919 and 1929. Also, the office launched special schemes for the Newcastle and Gateshead Gas Company in 1925 and for Castle Brothers of High Wycombe in 1934. But interest in this market was at best sporadic: no more than eight prospectuses were issued for the whole range of pension devices in the period 1922–40. There is a suggestion that, in the early pension market, Phoenix may have limited itself to providing schemes only for big fire or accident clients who asked for them.[138] Not until 1937 was group pension business considered sufficiently signicant to be separated out from ordinary life premiums in the Phoenix life accounts. And it was not until 1940 that any Phoenix chairman noted a sharp increase in one sector of life income 'due to the development of our Group Pension Department, which provides Pension Schemes for Employers'.[139]

Another part of the mainswell in the life market pressed towards the use of endowment assurances for house purchase. Here the Phoenix response was much more emphatic. The office certainly threw a lot of resources into endowments. By 1910 endowment assurances had already marked their presence in the Phoenix books (see Table 8.23). They had reached this position after growing from about 5.3% of all Phoenix life premiums in 1885 to 17.9% in 1895. Since the most attractive aspect of the endowment assurance was its investment appeal, it is scarcely surprising that this type of policy established its biggest claim, both of sums assured and of premiums, in the with-profits sector of the life operation.[140] However, the increasingly flexible use of endowments for a variety of purposes and products also explains the retreat of simple whole-life policies in both participating and non-participating sectors. Endowment assurances could do anything from providing for retirement, to generating a cheap option policy or paying school fees.[141]

And they could also help in buying houses. It is in this area that Phoenix

[138] I am indebted to Mr D. W. Harrison, formerly Phoenix Life Manager, for this observation.

[139] Ralph Sketch in his first Chairman's Annual Report, 29 May 1940.

[140] Although both types of endowment were entitled to income tax relief on the premiums at half the standard rate, i.e. a net relief of 2 shillings in the pound.

[141] In fact popular demand for endowments became so great that some sectors of assurance opinion began to warn customers in the late 1920s that they should concentrate on the type of policies which afforded them maximum *protection*, rather than investment yield. (*Bankers' Magazine*, 127 (1929), p. 341).

Table 8.23. *Phoenix Assurance: selected categories of policy as % of all life sums assured and all life premiums, by branch, 1910–40*

	Participating branch		Non-participating branch	
	Whole life	Endowment assurance	Whole life	Endowment assurance
(a) Sums assured				
1910	37.8	16.9	24.7	4.1
1915	35.3	20.5	23.4	5.5
1920	28.0	23.7	22.1	14.1
1925	24.0	27.7	19.8	13.5
1930	21.9	33.1	18.1	11.5
1935	17.7	29.8	20.3	12.6
1940	14.1	26.5	18.2	14.7
(b) Life premiums				
1910	36.5	25.4	26.7	8.2
1915	33.0	29.1	24.7	11.6
1920	22.4	30.2	20.5	26.2
1925	21.1	34.4	20.5	23.5
1930	17.0	43.8	18.9	18.4
1935	14.1	43.3	21.3	20.8
1940	12.3	41.6	21.3	24.4

Source: Calculated from Phoenix Quinquennial Valuations, 1910–40.

probably did most to exploit the assurance opportunities of the interwar economy. From 1924 onwards the office was extremely active in issuing promotional literature on this theme: no fewer than twenty-three different prospectuses and proposals were generated in relation to housing and property purchases in the period 1924–38. Phoenix created its own endowment-backed house purchase scheme in 1924; then added an arrangement for borrowers from building societies in 1926; and finally produced an improved version of this, the New House Purchase Scheme, in 1934.

Priority was always given to pushing Phoenix's own house purchase scheme, but the office responded positively to proposals from the building societies which often arose as a result of contacts between Phoenix local branch managers or agents and their opposite numbers in the neighbourhood societies. An example of this was an arrangement of October 1933 with the Bromley and South Eastern Building Society, which was secured through the intermediation of the manager of Phoenix's South London Branch.[142] The most important link of the 1930s was the agreement of March 1934 with the Woolwich Equitable Building Society whereby the Phoenix agreed to issue twenty-year endowment assurances against the building society's loans and pay a commission of 2.5% of the premiums to the society.[143] Besides the Bromley and the Woolwich, Phoenix formed connections before the Second World War with the Cheltenham and Gloucester, the Newbury, the Newcastle and Gateshead and the Portman societies, names which indicated both spread and seriousness of intent.[144]

The chronology of the with-profits column of Table 8.23 above is also suggestive: the share of endowments in Phoenix's sums assured peak exactly where they should, if they were tracking the housing boom, between 1925 and 1935. Finally, if the endowment vehicle were being used for house purchase, it would not be of variable length, but, most usually, for a fixed term. Contrariwise, if endowments were being used for retirement nest eggs, they would be aimed at normal retirement age and therefore vary in term according to the date of purchase. Phoenix's former deputy actuary, Joe Butler, recalled that, in the interwar years, 'house purchase loans repayable by endowment assurance . . . produced a healthy flow of business'.[145] His colleague, Alan Smith, who also retired as deputy actuary, remembered that 'by far the commonest type of policy being issued in the late 1920s was the 20-year Endowment Assurance, with profits'.[146] This is exactly the type of fixed-term, investment-oriented policy whch would have been involved in house purchase schemes, and the type quoted to the Woolwich Equitable in the agreement of 1934.

The first-hand evidence of the two actuaries is also confirmed by the formal record of the period. Ryan, in his last annual report, noticed that in regard to whole life and endowment assurance, 'the proportions of these two classes of policy have greatly changed in the last few years'. And his successor, Walters, in 1939 stated unequivocally that, in the 1920s and early 1930s, 'the most popular policy of those days was a 20-year endowment policy'.[147]

[142] South London Branch to Head Office, 30 October 1933. Phoenix Bristol Life File 918, 918A.
[143] *Ibid.*, File 918A.
[144] However, Phoenix's most active period of association with the building societies seems to have been 1945–55, during which the office maintained arrangements with some twenty-seven different societies.
[145] A. G. Butler to R. G. Street, 18 January 1994. Mr Butler had recently celebrated his 90th birthday.
[146] A. W. Smith to R. G. Street, 25 January 1994.
[147] Chairman's Annual Reports, 10 June 1931 and 24 May 1939.

By the late 1930s, however, a small fly had appeared in the actuarial ointment: some twenty-year endowments had begun to mature and it was now necessary for Phoenix to start paying out on them. Walters in 1939 expected 'increased outgo under this heading in future years for we have now arrived at the period when we are making payment in respect of the increased business of 1919 onwards . . . '.[148] In fact, 1940 was a record year for out payments on endowments (which amounted to nearly £600,000). Phoenix grinned and bore it, and, in congratulating the fortunate policy-holders, provided its own testimony to rising life expectations: 'it is of course a ground for satisfaction . . . that the robust vitality of so many of the assured enabled them to survive to the endowment age'.[149]

The interwar years were a special era for the life assurance business. The institution of retirement first appeared in its modern form as a mass social phenomenon, and the actuaries adjusted to this well. The rise of the salariat and the spread of suburbia created consumer markets for new life products. And the industry responded with a showcase of devices from tax schemes to bachelor's policies, school fee providers to pensions, low-cost options to endowment mortgages. The Phoenix showed well in this innovating sector, particularly in the area of house purchase.

Where the Phoenix marine branch was stranded, along with the entire crew of maritime insurers, by the receding tide of world trade, the life department found a stream of rising demand. Where the accident branch was marooned abroad by its entanglement with a difficult subsidiary in a collapsing US market, the life assurers could exploit the currents of the more complex and far less evenly distributed UK recession. Where the fire branch did not switch its allegiance as energetically as it might have done towards the expanding 'new industries' of the UK economy, the life officials were much more successful in tapping the growing consumerist tendencies of inner Britain. Indeed, in their targeting of the house market the Phoenix life branch penetrated to what many economic historians see as the leading sector of the 'new industry' revival. It is scarcely surprising that Ralph Sketch should have concluded in 1940 that, 'our Life organisation has never been in better shape than at present'.[150]

8. MARINE IN THE INTERWAR YEARS: SEAS OF DESOLATION

Sandeman Allen had taken Phoenix and Union Marine through the war risks market of the First World War at a fast trot. Union Marine

[148] *Ibid.* [149] *Ibid.* [150] *Ibid.*, 29 May 1940.

continued to trade as a separate Liverpool-based concern, though a wholly-owned subsidiary of Phoenix and its repository of maritime lore. Phoenix continued to gather a small amount of marine business of its own through London, but stated publicly that its underwriters for even this business were Union Marine;[151] effectively Sandeman Allen ran the marine operation. The stress of doing so in wartime proved too much for him. He suffered a breakdown in September 1920 and asked to step down as general manager of Union Marine early in 1921. He accepted the Board post of deputy chairman, only to resign from this as well a year later. He had been with Union Marine for almost exactly thirty years.[152] Phoenix arranged a generous settlement for a respected expert and wished him well.

The architect of Union Marine's wartime expansion left it in difficult times. The company's premium flow fell off by about 40% in both 1918 and 1919, as the war risks quickly ran off. The transitory economic boom of 1920 produced a rally, but the next year saw a further precipitous slide. Between 1920 and 1922, Union Marine's income flow effectively halved, and once down, stayed down: the 1913 level of premium was not recovered until 1939, and the low point of interwar earnings, in 1925, was less than one-fifth of the wartime premium peak in 1917.

On the face of things, the marine income of the Phoenix group as a whole retained larger numbers for longer (see Table 8.24).

In the record year of 1917, Union Marine had provided 98% of the Phoenix group's marine income, and, in some years, like 1918 and 1919, thanks to transfers and reinsurance movements, it could apparently account for more than 100%. This changed markedly in 1920, as the marine earnings of the newly affiliated Norwich Union Fire came into the Phoenix books.[153] In this year, Union Marine supplied only 57% of total group earnings from the sea. Yet, even with the reinforcement from Norwich Union Fire, the Phoenix group's marine income halved in 1921. However, unlike the Union Marine account, it bounced back in 1922, as marine pickings from the London Guarantee merger flowed into the central ledgers. In this year, Union Marine supplied only 38% of Phoenix's total maritime earnings. It was not until 1925 that acute shrinkage

[151] Initially, Union Marine had maintained a London Board to deal with the small proportion of the Phoenix-gathered business which fell to its account. However, regular meetings were discontinued in 1926 and there were no meetings at all between 1926 and 1942. Union Marine Board Minutes, 11 January 1926 and 2 April 1942.

[152] *Ibid.*, 7 February 1921 and 26 January 1922. Sir John Sandeman Allen died in June 1935 (*ibid.*, 4 July 1935). He had been knighted in the Birthday Honours of 1928.

[153] These totalled £576,065 in 1919, £823,409 in 1920, £437,906 in 1921 and £386,673 in 1922; these were considerable earnings in such times.

Table 8.24. *Marine income of the Phoenix Group and of Union Marine, 1918–26 (£ million)*

	1918	1919	1920	1921	1922	1923	1924	1925	1926
Phoenix Group	1.27	0.84	1.83	0.96	1.44	1.26	1.04	0.53	0.66
Union Marine	1.39	0.86	1.04	0.64	0.55	0.59	0.56	0.44	0.56

again hit the aggregate Phoenix account; once more, it halved within twelve months.

Now, 1925 was a bad year for all marine insurers, but it was the disposal of Norwich Union Fire which really damaged Phoenix's total seagoing capacity. For the rest of the interwar period, Phoenix returned to reliance upon Union Marine as its marine mainstay: in no year between 1925 and 1939 did Union Marine provide less than 77% of total group marine income and in most it provided between 83% and 89%. The London Guarantee element within the total was marginal and the Norwich Union element was lost. Once again, the acquisitions and disposals of 1919–25 did little to smooth already troubled waters.

The position of the marine department within Phoenix's composite structure underwent rapid decline as a result of these shocks to markets and assets. The marine share of Phoenix total premium income shrank from 18.3% in 1919 to a low point of 5.3% in 1925 and for most years between 1923 and 1939 bumped along at 6 or 7%.

Of course, the marine insurance sector as a whole was thrown into turmoil as the exceptional demands of war gave way to the exceptional contraction in global trade after 1920. Thirteen of the largest marine operators in Britain suffered an aggregate decline in premiums worse than 50% between the 1920 and 1921 account years, and the hardest hit, Commercial Union, saw a 75% reduction.[154] The big companies suffered somewhat more intensely than the general market and the smallest, which had launched into the marine business in pursuit of the gravy boat of war risks, were decimated. Some twenty-five offices writing marine business were liquidated in 1921–2, nine more retired from the UK marine market and a further twenty-five withdrew from marine business. With notable understatement, the *Journal of Commerce* wrote in August 1922 that 'the marine market is now considerably smaller than it was eighteen months

[154] The thirteen large companies earned £14.7 million in 1919, £17.0 million in 1920 and only £8.4 million in 1921 (*Journal of Commerce*, 22 November 1922).

Table 8.25. *The leading corporate marine insurers, 1918–21: net premiums (£ million) and ranks*

	1918		1919		1920		1921	
	£m	Rank	£m	Rank	£m	Rank	£m	Rank
Northern	3.02	1	2.57	1	3.49	1	1.99	1
London & Lancs	2.91	2	2.20	2	2.67	2	1.38	2
Royal	1.82	3	1.90	3	1.87	3	1.21	3
Eagle Star	1.68	4	1.50	4	–	–	–	
Alliance	1.63	5	1.18	5	1.35	5	0.55	6
United British	1.57	6	–	–	–	–	–	–
REA	–	–	0.96	6	–	–	–	–
London	–	–	–	–	1.22	6	0.68	5
Phoenix	1.27	7	0.84	10	1.83	4	0.96	4

ago'.[155] In fact, this expert source judged that the shake-out had produced an industry about correctly proportioned for an average size of market. But the world economy of the interwar years was unable to supply even this average.

Amidst general contraction, Phoenix-Union Marine took a sharp tumble from its wartime pre-eminence and dropped out of the top team of maritime offices (see Table 8.25).[156] Only the acquisitions of Norwich Union Fire and London Guarantee allowed the Phoenix to retain a precarious toehold among the leading echelon until 1925. Thereafter, the Phoenix's tendency of the early 1920s not only to acquire companies but also to misplace them again, reduced Phoenix–Union Marine to a marine operation of middling stature. By contrast, the Northern and the London & Lancashire – which had both made well-timed acquisitions of large marine specialists in 1917[157] – became the ascendant composite offices of the early peacetime years.

[155] *Ibid.*, 9 and 23 August 1922. [156] See above, Chapter 6, Section 2.

[157] The Northern acquired the Indemnity Mutual Marine, which Union Marine had just failed to secure for itself in May 1908, and the London & Lancashire took over the Marine Insurance Company. These moves transformed the marine capacity of the two northern offices. By contrast, Northern Maritime, which Union Marine also acquired in 1917, was small fry. The negotiations between Union Marine and the Indemnity, which would have produced a truly formidable marine force, went as far as a Memorandum of Agreement before they broke down (Union Marine Board Minutes,18 May 1908). Northern Maritime, which specialised in insuring colliers out of Newcastle, was small to begin with but was drastically affected by the interwar depression. Its connection to the coal industry, one of the most severely damaged of all UK industries, sentenced it to lean pickings throughout the 1920s and 1930s (Northern Maritime Accounts, NM23/2B).

However, the sharp fall in postwar premiums led to uncomfortably high expense ratios and squeezed profits for many companies of all sizes. In 1921, the aggregate profit of the leading thirteen companies was one-sixth of what it had been in 1920.[158] Scale of operation was no protection here: the mighty London & Lancashire and the Royal both recorded losses in 1920 and 1921. Union Marine had a particularly bad run, recording underwriting losses in 1920, 1923 and 1924. Phoenix's overall marine profit for the Group was barely above 1% in 1920, and even then the company had to raid the profit and loss account to reinforce the marine reserves. Between 1924 and 1930 the marine department of Phoenix was unable to make any contribution whatever to profit and loss.

The problem was basically fourfold. Wartime expansion had attracted too many competitors. The collapse of trade after 1920 left them with too few hulls to insure. The ensuing scramble for what was left pushed rates down to 'an astonishingly low level'.[159] And the bitterness produced by this prevented the cooperation necessary to argue them up again. On top of this, losses were high, especially in 1924 and 1925, and 1927–30, as shipowners skimped on maintenance and cruise lines built giant vessels which pushed the technology to its limits, and beyond.[160]

The underwriter of the REA found conditions in late 1921, 'more involved than he had ever known them to be before'[161] and the Liverpool & London & Globe complained in 1922 that 'marine business is hardly worthwhile.'[162] Phoenix resorted to a strategy of tight selection, refusing 'to write certain classes of risk on the terms now current in the marine market'. In 1923, this approach managed to snatch a substantial profit of over 10% from the gales of adversity – 'a notable achievement', noted Ryan, 'under conditions the reverse of favourable'[163] – but it was to be the last for a long time. For the remainder of the decade, Phoenix shuttered hatches and stood by to repel boarders: that is, the underwriters kept turnover down, risks select and surpluses conserved; taking nothing for profit and loss, they nursed the marine reserves as best they could.

They succeeded better than many. Ryan saw the years 1924 and 1925 as 'a searching ordeal' for marine insurers and 1926 as 'probably the low-water mark'. But even in 1926 Phoenix paid its way and kept 'abundant free margin', while many other marine operators were announcing

158 *Journal of Commerce*, 22 November 1922.
159 Phoenix Chairman's Annual Report, 29 April 1925.
160 In the early to mid-1920s part of the problem was also that, under the three-year account system of marine insurance, large claims which had initially attached to years of high premiums were running off in years of much lower premiums.
161 Cited by Supple, *Royal Exchange Assurance*, p. 447.
162 *Bankers' Magazine*, 114 (1922), p. 281. 163 *Ibid.*, 30 April 1924.

Table 8.26. *Phoenix Assurance: marine funds (£), 1922–30 (including Norwich Union Fire, 1922–4)*

1922	1,908,000	(NUF 535,740)
1923	1,400,000	(NUF 572,135)
1924	995,339	(NUF 327,534)
1925	681,888	
1926	606,287	
1927	688,369	
1928	693,769	
1929	n.a.	
1930	660,886	

Source: Phoenix Assurance and Norwich Union Fire Reports and Accounts.

serious losses. The REA, which after Phoenix's disposal of Norwich Union Fire, was in much the same premium band as Phoenix for the remainder of the 1920s, sustained an average annual loss of £127,000, 1921–5, expected to lose £250,000 in the unforgiving conditions of 1926 and had to take £200,000 from profit and loss for the 'Sea Department' in 1930.[164] By contrast, Phoenix admitted to a small outright loss of £5,000 on the 1927 marine account and witnessed a nasty dip in the marine reserves in 1926 (see Table 8.26).

Yet at no time before 1939 did Phoenix need to draw upon its profit and loss account to make good deficits in the marine sector. By and large, its underwriters kept it head to wind.

However, this was so fierce that it brought about Ryan's prediction of 1925 that 'the stronger offices will be forced to take counsel together, and by concerted action, remove the most glaring evils'.[165] Nor did he mean by this only the frantic competition from lesser companies in the early 1920s. Indeed, the Phoenix Board traced part of the trouble to more august quarters: the breakdown in 1921 of the Joint Hull Agreement which set rates for the insurance of vessels was ascribed to 'the action of Lloyds in attempting to reduce still further the amount left to the companies'.[166] It was not until 1926 that the big corporate insurers developed sufficient will, or heart, to seek a replacement agreement by 'more constant collaboration'.[167] Their objective was particularly to find an agreed method of

[164] Supple, *Royal Exchange Assurance*, pp. 447–8.
[165] Chairman's Annual Report, 29 April 1925.
[166] Phoenix Directors' Minutes, 33, p. 271, 15 June 1921.
[167] Chairman's Annual Report, 27 April 1926.

combating the abuses of 1920–1, when unduly large lines had been written at cut-price rates and unscrupulous insurers had then 'charged up' when reinsuring, thus driving many reinsurance companies to the wall.[168] Under the leadership of the governor of the REA, a conference of chairmen and underwriters from marine companies met to form a new Joint Hull Agreement in 1926. This improved behaviour and tempers, but, as Supple writes, 'it was not easy to translate personal harmony into an improvement of premium rates and a return of profitability'.[169]

In May 1928, the harmony was translated into a world agreement to raise all hull rates by 10%. But the effects were at best mixed. Ryan reported that a year later that 'little definite benefit can be ascribed to these efforts, but there is no doubt that much indirect good has been achieved'.[170] If the Joint Hull Committee had improved the situation in the insurance of vessels, the plight of cargo insurances remained deplorable. The amount of tonnage laid up, and thus carrying no cargo at all, was by this time alarming. Ryan saw that 'no stereotyped agreement' could overcome this. The *Bankers' Magazine* agreed that virtuous diplomacy was being confounded by slumping markets; no real advance could be made until trade recovered.[171] Put another way, in Ryan's analysis of 1930, the internal conditions of the marine market had been improved – 'with a healthier spirit and sounder view of the common interest' among the suppliers – but the external conditions, among the customers, were still appalling.[172]

Under such stress, the fragile accord on rates cracked once more. In 1931 Phoenix reported that they were again 'unduly low'; in 1934 that competition for cargo business was keener than ever; and in 1936 that there was still further downward pressure on rates. It was not until 1937 that the Joint Hull Agreement could be made to bite again. The Committee was reconstituted and had some success in raising rates.[173] By 1937, trade was beginning to pick up, but other signs of trouble were accumulating. War risks, particularly in the Mediterranean, were imposing losses on insurers who, desperate for business, had accepted them without surcharge on premiums. Meanwhile rearmament demand for steel and workers had pushed up the costs of ship repair by 35–40%. These semaphored the onset of a different kind of marine crisis.[174]

[168] *Bankers' Magazine*, 124 (1927), p. 323.
[169] Supple, *Royal Exchange Assurance*, p. 448.
[170] Chairman's Annual Report, 29 May 1929.
[171] *Ibid.*; *Bankers' Magazine*, 130 (1930), p. 637.
[172] Chairman's Annual Report, 28 May 1930.
[173] *Ibid.*, 26 June 1937, 25 May 1938.
[174] See below, Chapter 11, Section 2.

However, Phoenix did well against the renewed competition and falling rates of the first half of the 1930s. In 1931, the marine department turned in its first profit for eight years, and it continued modestly in this vein until 1938. Returns were scarcely princely – they averaged 4.9% and ranged from a low of 2.8% in 1931 to a high of 8.5% in 1933 – but they were a great deal better than the nil transfers of the previous decade. And they were achieved against the tide. The profits of 1931–5 were scored despite heavy shrinkage in the world's hull and cargo business; and indeed Phoenix maintained custom well in cargo, the most difficult sector of all, and continued to make ground in 1935, in markets that were still 'frankly disturbing'.[175]

What is more, these results were obtained amidst the turmoil of another peculiar cross-current of these complicated times. Humble freighters and tramps, they of the salt-caked smokestacks,[176] and the bread-and-butter trade of the marine insurers, might rust in docks and estuaries and offer cargo, carriage and custom to no-one. But the luxury liners, they of the cocktail bars and sweeping staircases, the caviar sector of the marine insurance market, were built in some number, eased down the slipways (when they got this far) and, all too frequently, went up in smoke. They were a Blue Riband menace. Three major liners were lost in 1928. In 1929 Phoenix's incipient profit was wiped out, mainly due to the destruction, on the stocks, of the *Europa*. Building for North German Lloyd at Hamburg, she was gutted during construction, for a loss of £0.9 million, the biggest building risk ever to that point, and one that fell mainly on the London market.[177] In 1933 three more leviathans were lost, including *L'Atlantique*, demonstrating, as the *Bankers' Magazine*, put it, somewhat mildly, that 'luxury liners are vulnerable to the Fire Devil and not the safe risks hitherto thought'.[178] The loss of these three vessels alone dominated the outcome for the depleted UK hull market of 1933.

Cover for new ships of this class could put awesome strains on the market. The new White Star liner of 1928, weighing in at £1.6 million, exhausted the market's capacity at the time.[179] But this was nothing compared to the insurance load imposed by the delayed Cunarder, *Queen Mary*. Building on the Clyde in 1930, her insurance requirement was valued at £4.5 million, in a market where the global maximum was £3 million in any one hull. The underwriters girded themselves to take £2.72

[175] Chairman's Annual Report, 8 June 1933, 30 May 1934, 30 May 1935.
[176] The phrase is Masefield's but is too apt to be interrupted by quotation marks.
[177] Chairman's Annual Report, 28 May 1930; *Bankers' Magazine*, 128 (1929), p. 314.
[178] *Ibid.*, 135 (1933), p. 360.
[179] *Ibid.*, 126 (1928), p. 632.

Plate 8.8 *Mauretania* berths at Southampton, October 1933.

million of this, but the government had to take up the balance. The specialist press was disappointed with the market's lack of alacrity, but, in the circumstances, it can scarcely surprise.[180] *Queen Mary* happily lived to a ripe old age but many of her peers did not.

Liners were not the only problem; there was also the difficulty of what they carried; and this included something as bad as expensive life risks. During the worldwide economic crisis of the late 1920s and early 1930s, the liners were the parcel-carriers of disaster: they shipped the bullion that was leaking from the weaker economies like the British to the more chauvinistic, like the American and the French. The sinking of a liner could entail more than the loss of expensive technology and well-heeled voyagers; it could consign to Davey Jones not insignificant proportions of national wealth.

In 1930, Phoenix limited its liability on any one hull to £90,000, but stipulated that the maximum for a liner would be £50,000. This was because, with cargo and specie added, a 'great liner' would anyway incur

[180] *Ibid.*, 131 (1931), p. 821. *SS Queen Mary* retired from the sea in 1967 and became a museum at Long Beach, California.

a true liability twice as big as this. And even there the problem did not end. In 1931, Phoenix was having to exceed its prudently imposed limits: 'In view of the unprecedented situation in connection with shipments of gold, an increase in the limit for the total net liability of the company on any one vessel may be permitted in cases where the excess cannot be reinsured, except at a loss.'[181]

It might be thought that Phoenix's mariners did well to extract any kind of positive out-turn from markets like these. But marine departments, reporting nil or low profits in bad times, were, of course, vulnerable not only to their markets but to their sister departments within multi-divisional composites. The REA, after much worse losses, put a team from Price Waterhouse into its marine department late in 1931. It found weakness in office control, a lack of coordinaton with head office, 'a definite deterioration of morale' and a 'considerable lack of team work'.[182] And this was the REA's oldest and most central branch of insurance.

At Phoenix, General Manager Sketch was more circumspect: he put an anonymous informant into Union Marine's Liverpool headquarters – which was, on the face of it, also the headquarters of Phoenix's marine operation – for eighteen months in 1934 and 1935. This worthy, who referred to himself only as 'the Writer', found uncanny echoes of the problems at the REA: 'an absence of the will to do', 'no real wish to keep abreast of the times', 'an absence of method', and, again, 'an absence of team spirit'.[183] 'There exists', he recorded, 'a lethargy which, if allowed to continue, must inevitably be to the great disadvantage of the Company', and he viewed 'this present condition with grave concern'. One is left with two impressions: there is something in 'the Writer's' analysis; but he also has an axe to grind.

His remedy is relentlessly London-centric. The Liverpool Board of Union Marine should be transferred to London; the secretary of Union Marine should be moved to London as assistant secretary; the London underwriter should be given charge of the entire marine operation. The rationale for this was that 'by 1935, finance, underwriting and the main policy of administration is controlled from Phoenix House . . . The work carried out by the Liverpool Underwriting and Finance Committees consists of a passive submission to the measures and resolutions passed

[181] Phoenix Directors' Minutes, 36, pp. 136, 270, 393, 27 November 1929, 22 October 1930, 24 June 1931, 21 October 1931.

[182] Supple, *Royal Exchange Assurance*, p. 449.

[183] Report to the General Manager on Union Marine, September 1935; Union Marine 317/2.

by the Marine and Joint Finance Committees at Phoenix House.'[184]

The probable explanation for this is that, as the original Union Marine management faded in the troubled markets after the First World War, policy-making had tended to drift to London, yet the plant had stayed in Liverpool. However, Sketch did not want a mass upheaval in the marine organisation in the mid-1930s. Rather, he wanted a push in marine premiums. In 1932 some success had been achieved in this connection by a campaign to whip up marine business through the Phoenix's UK branch organisation. And the resulting business had been dealt with by the marine department at Liverpool. Sketch wished to repeat this operation in 1936 and was already discreetly corresponding with the secretary of Union Marine (C. F. J. Mountain), at precisely the time 'the Writer' was proposing to translate this official to London and demote him.[185]

The problem, as Mountain saw it, was that, within the Phoenix organisation, 'there is still perhaps a feeling that efforts expended on Marine do not obtain the recognition that would be given to other classes of insurance'.[186] No doubt this effect followed from the contraction of marine income: it was easier to get the Group to take marine seriously when it supplied over 18% of total premiums than when it provided only some 6%. It was this which Sketch was most concerned to combat and for this reason that a second campaign to push marine premium through the branches was launched in 1936. This device was also directed towards effecting some rescue for Northern Maritime: the idea was to lift it out of its depressed local economy in the North-East by generating income throughout Phoenix's UK branch network. The strategy enjoyed some success, raising total group marine income by 25% in 1937 and by 35% by 1938.

War then intervened to revolutionise marine business for a second time, and far more fundamentally than any scheme proposed by 'the Writer'. However, it is worth some emphasis that marine insurers of the period 1914–45 were at the mercy of wildly gyrating markets. The lack of team spirit and the low level of morale which the investigators found at the REA and Union Marine is scarcely to be wondered at. These defects were results not causes of the malaise in the marine market.

[184] *Ibid.*

[185] The chief technicians behind Phoenix's marine operations in the interwar years were the underwriters in Liverpool. After Sandeman Allen's retirement, these were: E. S. Lund from January 1922 to March 1929, J. R. Trench from March 1929 to June 1931, and A. Bath from June 1931.

[186] Mountain to Sketch, 5 April 1932.

9. THE ACCIDENTS OF THE INTERWAR YEARS: COMPENSATION, COUPONS AND CORPORATE STRUCTURE IN THE 1920S

Phoenix's capacity in accident business in the early interwar years was hugely influenced by the comings and goings with Norwich Union Fire and London Guarantee. The accident department was more affected than any other by the acquisitions and disposals of 1919–25. Lord George Hamilton stated in his last Annual Report that accident income was very small – in fact, it was £164,350, or under 4% of total group income, in 1919 – but that the directors were giving special attention to its extension. One year later, when NUF had come, accident receipts were nearly ten times this size, at £1.6 million and nearly 16% of total income. By 1923, with LGA's portfolio on board, they were more than three times bigger again, at £6.2 million, and nearly 43% of total group income. Such a share was not reached again until 1947. For when NUF went in 1925, accident income contracted again, by a full 35%.

Ryan, of course, had coveted an accident wing for Phoenix for years, and, to begin with, there was a good deal of touching optimism at Head Office concerning the enhanced lift that it might give the old bird. Initial profits looked encouraging: 'moderate' in 1919, 'very fair', thanks to NUF, at £61,000 in 1920, and 'very satisfactory', at £103,364 in 1921. In 1922, the year accident premiums, in a truly historic step, exceeded fire premiums – the first peacetime year since 1782 in which any income had been more important to Phoenix than fire income – the profit was £156,507.[187] The average return on accident premiums in the first three-year beat of the new wing, was some 3%. But at least it was a positive out-turn.[188]

When Ryan contemplated the accident scene in 1923, he did so as an old campaigner peering out over a terrain he thought he knew. In this terrain, luck usually went to the bold, and, if the bold paid attention, as Ryan always did, things usually turned out in the end. It was in this spirit that he mused, 'It will be curious to watch the respective movements of the Fire and Accident accounts in future years.' 'Curious' was the understatement of a career, and the measure of the difference between a past, in which things had usually turned out, and the present of the 1920s and 1930s. 'Some believe', Ryan assured himself, 'that accident is of practically unlimited extension and by no means fully explored.' Of course, he realised that a lot of it, particularly workmen's compensation business, was heavily depend-

[187] Due to the new importance of accident business, the Life and Accident Committee of the Phoenix Board was separated in 1922, with accident getting its own committee of directors chaired by A. W. Tait, formerly the chairman of LGA (Phoenix Directors' Minutes, 33, p. 402, 28 June 1922).

[188] Chairman's Annual Reports, 1920–2.

ent on the employment cycle; and so he expected better results when 'full employment, at reasonable wages' returned.[189] There were millions who waited for years between the wars for these conditions to return.

Generally speaking, it was their failure to do so, and the effect on workmen's compensation business, particularly in the United States, which caused Phoenix most damage in the accident sector in the 1920s; and it was the onward charge of motorcar insurance which caused most damage in the 1930s.

Of course, part of Phoenix's accident problems in the 1920s stemmed from the hidden subtext – or, rather, bear pit – of the LGA acquisition.[190] The scandal of LGA's reserve provisions could not be suppressed even at the public level in King William Street. Ryan let slip in 1923 that LGA's 'accounting methods and its financial reserves were not framed upon the same lines as those followed in our old Company', but was quick to add that, 'we have endeavoured to adjust the system and basis of reserves of our new ally to our own'.[191] It was not by chance that, two years later, Phoenix abolished all reserves for specific departments and merged them into a single General Reserve. Ryan pleaded accounting uniformity, but the real reason was almost certainly to make the reserves trail from LGA more difficult to follow.

Nevertheless, the issue of which accident company Phoenix decided to acquire is separate from the issue of which time Phoenix selected to enter the accident business, and that is separate again from the issue of which accident market the company chose to enter most heavily. In the end, Phoenix's introduction to accident business was marred by errors under all three of these separate heads: LGA; the early 1920s; and the US market. LGA was a poorly balanced and appallingly financed company;[192] the world recession of the 1920s was particularly harsh on the workmen's compensation and motor sectors which were the leading categories of accident business at the time; and the American market supplied a particularly dense concentration of all of these unedifying features.

The corporate adjustments and readjustments of 1920–5 significantly affected the extent to which Phoenix was able to build up a *home* market for accident business. When the Group contained the accident department of both the parent company and NUF, the UK market accounted for very nearly a quarter of total accident premiums (see Table 8.27).

After the disposal of NUF, a company far better balanced between home and foreign accident business than either Phoenix or LGA, the domestic component of group accident income dipped well below 20%. It

[189] *Ibid.*, 25 May 1923. [190] See Chapter 7, Section 2 and Chapter 9, Section 4.
[191] Chairman's Annual Report, 25 May 1923. [192] See Chapter 7, Section 2.

Table 8.27. *Foreign and home shares of total accident premium: Group, Phoenix, LGA and NUF, 1922–39 (three-year averages)*

	Total accident premium (£m)	Home market shares				Foreign market shares			
		Group	Phoenix	LGA	NUF	Group	Phoenix	LGA	NUF
1922–4	5.88	24.1	57.6	10.5	48.1	75.9	42.4	89.5	51.9
1925–7	3.98	18.5	35.7	13.4	–	81.5	64.3	86.6	–
1928–30	3.87	19.9	34.0	13.1	–	80.1	66.0	86.9	–
1931–3	3.46	22.3	38.2	12.7	–	77.7	61.9	87.3	–
1934–6	3.51	24.5	40.5	12.8	–	75.5	59.5	87.2	–
1937–9	3.91	24.4	39.3	12.7	–	75.6	60.6	87.3	–

Source: Calculated from Phoenix Blue Books.

did not recover to the levels of the NUF era until Phoenix's own accident department began to increase its tilt towards home business in the later 1930s. The commitment of this department to the foreign market had increased sharply after 1925 – to a peak of 67.3% of its total income in 1927 – almost as if Phoenix had been caught in the orbital pull of LGA's huge foreign interests. For most of the 1920s the home market represented about one-third of the parent company's own accident activity. Only after 1932 did Phoenix begin to push its foreign share of accident earnings below 60%. LGA itself was radically slanted towards foreign parts (see Table 8.27) and indeed could scarcely do business anywhere else (and three-quarters of what it did abroad, it did in the dangerous territory of the USA).

It was this list of LGA to port which most skewed the Group's accident business towards the foreign aspect. For LGA's weight within the total Phoenix operation was considerable (see Table 8.28).

During the NUF era, the accident operation of Phoenix itself accounted for less than 10% of Group accident premium, NUF for around one-quarter and LGA for about two-thirds. After NUF had gone, Phoenix itself took over the quarter share and LGA contributed three times that proportion. From the late 1920s, Phoenix set out to haul back this imbalance and by the end of the interwar period had made substantial ground, securing well over 40% of Group accident income in its own claws.

After the over-reliance on the foreign market and the disproportionate weight of LGA, the third imbalance that Phoenix needed to correct was an excess affection for things American. Perhaps picking up the taste from LGA, Phoenix nearly doubled its commitment to the US market between

Table 8.28. *The company shares in Phoenix Group accident premium, 1922–39 (three-year averages)*

	Total group accident premium (£m)	Phoenix (%)	NUF (%)	LGA (%)	UM (%)
1922–4	5.88	9.8	24.3	65.9	–
1925–7	3.98	23.3	–	76.7	–
1928–30	3.87	32.4	–	67.6	–
1931–3	3.46	–	–	–	–
1934–6	3.51	41.2	–	58.3	0.5
1937–9	3.91	43.3	–	54.9	0.6[a]

Note: [a] = Tariff Reinsurance and Codan also supplied small shares of Group accident income of around 1% in 1938–9.
Source: Calculated from Phoenix Blue Books.

the three-year periods 1922–4 and 1925–7, achieving its peak involvement with the transatlantic market in the latter of these (see Table 8.29). However, heavy losses in 1926 and 1927, and increasing disillusion with LGA, caused sterner attitudes to prevail at Phoenix House. The pruning knives were taken to LGA's sprawling US accident accounts from 1927, and, in Phoenix's own accident department, the US share was progressively cut back throughout the 1930s, ending at about 44%.

Table 8.29 shows clearly that the dominant branches of the parent company's accident business in the interwar years were workmen's compensation and motor. These sectors accounted for 65–75% of all accident income in this period. Even by 1922–4 the motor branch was the biggest of all, and it grew to control more than half of all accident premiums in the years 1928–33. Two features were striking about the compensation and motor accounts of Phoenix. Firstly, they were again very heavily foreign accounts. Between 1925 and 1938 the foreign share of the compensation account never fell below 60% and the average was 65.4%; the company was not able to readjust the trim in this department. In motor, the foreign share peaked at 69.3% in 1927 but was trimmed back to about 55% by the later 1930s. Much of this business, whether retained or shed, was American. The second striking feature is the very high claims ratios on both of these leading accounts (see Table 8.29). They were more often than not in the danger area above 55%, and sometimes substantially above. With the expenses ratio fairly stable at 42–44%, these big accounts can rarely

Table 8.29. *Phoenix only: distribution of accident business by major sector, 1922–36 (three-year averages)*

	Total premium (£m)	Total claims (%)	US share (%)	Workmen's compensation % total	Workmen's compensation % claims	Personal accident % total	Personal accident % claims	Burglary % total	Burglary % claims	Motor % total	Motor % claims
1922–4	0.52	71.3	28.7	25.3	58.6	13.8	171.4	9.2	45.9	39.5	59.7
1925–7	0.88	57.3	54.3	24.4	65.8	3.8	41.0	8.3	43.6	49.1	61.4
1928–30	1.23	66.0	53.6	17.4	67.0	3.2	49.2	7.8	43.5	53.0	61.8
1931–3	1.27	55.9	49.3	20.5	69.4	4.7	55.9	8.0	43.6	51.8	57.3
1934–6	1.41	53.9	46.0	23.1	66.2	4.8	42.0	7.0	31.9	46.3	56.8

Source: Calculated from Phoenix Blue Books.

have been profitable. And in this sector of Phoenix's dealings in the interwar years, it was the level of claims rather than the level of expenses which determined the outcome. As Table 8.29 shows, it was the smaller accounts that had the lower claims ratios. Ironically, burglary was the safest of all Phoenix's major classes of accident business.

Between 1926 and 1937, Phoenix's US annual loss ratios on all classes of accident business were always worse – by over 17 percentage points at the widest point in 1933 – than the company's UK loss ratios (compare Table 8.30). Not until the final years of peace did the US loss ratios regain any kind of docility.

Even during the period of the world crash, accident business at home was significantly safer than accident business abroad. When separate figures are available for foreign business outside the United States, the claims ratios are substantially better than the US ones and substantially worse than the UK ones. This held true again until the final years of peace, when the United States got much safer and the United Kingdom slightly more dangerous.

It was unlikely that this mix of elements would produce much in the way of profit on the accident account. At the group level, this indeed proved the case.[193] After Ryan's initial satisfaction with the results of a bigger accident business, there was little comfort to be had. The Group accident account dipped into the red in 1923, 1924 and 1926 (see Table

[193] For Phoenix alone matters were even worse. The accident department of the parent company produced losses against net premiums of 15%, 0.7%, and 0.3% in the three-year periods 1922–4, 1925–7 and 1928–30; and profits of 0.7% and 2.9% in 1931–3 and 1934–6.

Table 8.30. *Phoenix only: loss ratios on home, US and other foreign accident business, 1922–39 (three-year averages)*

	Home	US	Other foreign
1922–4	63.0	30.1	included in
1925–7	52.0	50.9	home
1928–30	50.0	56.7	until 1930
1931–3	48.0	62.4	55.3
1934–6	49.6	56.6	52.5
1937–9	51.5	49.8	51.3

Source: Calculated from Phoenix Blue Books.

Table 8.31. *Phoenix Assurance: Group accident profits, 1920–40*

	Transfer to profit and loss	% premium		Transfer to profit and loss	% premium
1920	61,000	0.03	1931	110,456	3.0
1921	103,364	6.2	1932	82,139	2.4
1922	156,507	2.9	1933	47,455	1.4
1923	−70,741	−1.1	1934	1,599	0.05
1924	−69,566	−1.1	1935	139,247	4.0
1925	93,130	2.4	1936	162,393	4.3
1926	−25,052	−0.6	1937	191,433	4.7
1927	92,167	2.4	1938	304,871	7.8
1928	116,325	3.0	1939	330,074	8.7
1929	54,027	1.4	1940	293,400	8.3
1930	40,239	1.1			

Sources: Chairman's Annual Reports; Annual Accounts; Phoenix Blue Books.

8.31) and, where the numbers were positive, they remained very small until the late 1930s.

Quick reaction to the crisis of 1926, and the beginning of the campaign to prune the US accounts, released reserves and produced a book profit in 1927, while that of 1928 was a genuine tribute to effective helmsmanship by Sketch and his accident managers. But even they were hove very close to the wind in the storms of 1929–33, and the profits offered thin protection. Claims in 1930 moved up from the already painfully high 50% of the late 1920s to within a few decimal points of 60%. The profit and loss account hung in the black by almost as few.

Nevertheless, one of the few advantages from the corporate reshuffles of the early 1920s was that they did leave Phoenix's accident wing with a strong management team. The department had been supervised, from its humble beginnings in 1909, by Alfred McDougald, who altogether spent forty-seven years with British Empire, Pelican and Phoenix. He retired at the end of 1921. This left Sketch room for a trio of new appointments in the early and mid-1920s; and he picked widely from the companies arrayed before him. H. E. Southam, formerly accident manager of Norwich Union Fire, stayed, like Sketch himself, with Phoenix to become Group accident manager. The former manager of London Guarantee, J. Swanson, became foreign accident manager of the Group, and the home accident manager was Phoenix's own Arthur Battrick.[194] This was an impressive group, particularly energetically and perceptively led by Southam. Notably, he did everything that could be done, including repeated transatlantic voyages in the later 1920s, to solve the many problems of the US market.[195] By 1928, much had been achieved there, and it was forces beyond the control of the best managers which carried an enduring American problem into the 1930s. However, these men had a great deal to contend with, and not all of their crises were American.

Even in the home market, the LGA acquisition could scarcely have been worse timed. UK accident premiums, industry-wide, fell in 1922 for the first time since 1907, due primarily to the depression in workmen's compensation business, in the wake of lay-offs and lower rates of pay.[196] Personal accident business in the United Kingdom was also hit by a rash of newspaper schemes offering free insurance to readers, in a bid to boost circulation. The *Bankers' Magazine* judged that, 'When the newspapers have educated the public to the perils of everyday life and have found free insurance an expensive hobby, this kind of business may boom, but, until then, it is likely to be dormant.'[197]

Mindful of the need to push its own domestic business, Phoenix

[194] First appointed clerk in 1907 (see Chapter 9, Sections 3 and 4) and to succeed Southam in 1934. [195] See pp. 459, 688, 690–1.

[196] *Bankers' Magazine*, 116 (1923), p. 123.

[197] *Ibid.*, 114, 1922, p. 287. In the consumerist 1920s, a way was even found of linking insurance and high-street retailing, although this time in life assurance. The *Bankers' Magazine* recorded that 'Life assurance with a pound of tea has come at last, also with sugar, butter, bacon, cabbages, nuts, or anything that can be purchased at stores running the scheme', 125 (1928), p. 525. This was a form of group life assurance where the customers formed the group. The death benefit was the sum of purchases in the year preceding death.

Plate 8.9 Accident Manager Southam.

decided on an attempt to circumvent the lag predicted by the *Bankers' Magazine*. Given the heavy overseas bias to the Group's accident portfolio, Phoenix was not well placed to accept a narrowing of the home market. So the company jumped on the newspaper bandwagon itself: in 1921 the Phoenix agreed to underwrite for three years, at an annual premium of £50,000, the *Daily Mail*'s 'coupon' scheme for the insurance of its readers against personal accident.[198] The results, however, were not auspicious: by 1923 they were being invoked, along with hailstorms in Canada, and unemployment conditions in the USA, to explain the lapse of the accident account from profitability.

[198] Phoenix Directors' Minutes, 33, p. 318, 16 November 1921. These 'coupon' schemes took their name from the cut-out slip published in the newspaper by which clients enrolled.

The coupon insurance craze of the 1920s was part of the newspaper circulation war of these years. The *Daily Mail* was a pioneer with the device, launching a pilot scheme in January 1914, but greatly extending its scope after the war.[199] By 1922, the *Daily Express*, *Daily Chronicle*, *Daily News* and *Westminster Gazette* were all offering insurance schemes to compete with the *Mail*. The *Mail*'s main target was the *Express*. In 1921, the *Mail* had been running its campaign in collaboration with the North British, but calculated that, with a projected circulation of over 1.2 million, of whom it expected 850,000 to register for insurance, it needed more capacity. Overtures were made to Sketch in early November 1921 and he had the accident department vet the project before entering an agreement with Northcliffe's Associated Newspapers on 9 November. The insurers would underwrite the policies offered by the papers and process all the claims. The newspaper insisted on the widest possible coverage, with the United Kingdom being 'deemed to include the Irish Free State, and Ulster, whether it is known as the Orange Free State, Carsonalia, or any other description'.[200] The *Daily Mail*–Phoenix scheme was the largest of its kind.

The major problem was that the interests of the newspapers and those of the insurers were diametrically opposed. For the insurers, the issue was simple: publicity. Phoenix's veteran accident manager, Alfred McDougald, wrote late in 1921, 'the wide daily advertisement of the Company by a paper whose daily issue far exceeds a million copies is a matter of first importance'.[201] Such was the weight placed upon this consideration by the offices that some were prepared to run the newspaper schemes for very little return. Thus the Guardian office accepted a motor insurance coupon for the low-circulation *Times*, 'practically at cost for the sake of the advertisement', whereas Phoenix, mindful of its experience with the *Daily Mail*, had rejected this smaller scheme when offered it.[202] Beyond the publicity however, the offices were concerned at least that the newspaper schemes should not make losses, that they should not prove bad insurance. The newspapers had other objectives. They wished to offer the widest possible cover; they wished to attract the largest possible number of claims; and they wished to boast that they settled

[199] This offered a £1,000 death benefit, and £500 for serious injury or disablement caused by public or private transport. The initial Phoenix scheme added a £3,500 benefit for death in a railway accident.

[200] Kenneth Henderson of Associated Newspapers to the Insurance Brokers, Muir Beddall, 8 December 1921.

[201] Accident Manager to Branch Managers, 29 December 1921.

[202] Phoenix Accident Department: A. Battrick to Southam, 23 February 1922. *The Times* had a circulation of only 112,000 at this point.

more of these faster than the next newspaper. The contending newspapers *wanted* accidents to happen; the more claims there were, the more papers would be sold. Certainly, this combination was not likely to make for good insurance.

And, in the event, Phoenix's experience with mass media insurance was not happy. The approach of the pressmen to insurance was over-enthusiastic to say the least. In order to get the coupons clipped, they were prepared to offer the earth. As early as January 1922, the *Mail* added the payment of rent to the benefits accruing under its accident provisions and waxed eager to include a sickness benefit because the *Daily Express* had just introduced one. By March, the *Mail* was pressing to extend cover to accidents in the home. Phoenix was prepared to accept some widening of cover but argued that the domestic accident proposal was 'wide open to abuse' and that the sickness cover, in an era when epidemics were still possible, was an invitation to disaster.[203] Not to be thwarted of their publicity, Associated Newspapers elected to shoulder liability on home accident and sickness risks themselves.

However, the incessant pressure to widen the spectrum of coupon insurance produced major headaches for the insurers. In particular, the inclusion of home accidents brought a huge increase in the number of claims and had Phoenix staff working all hours to clear them. The newspapers whipped up the claims but the insurers could not process them fast enough; and this did little for the reputation of either. Pomeroy Burton, manager of Associated Newspapers, told Sketch, 'we are getting shoals of complaints from all over the country'.[204]

On the insurers' side of the counter, there was also scope for complaint. The newspaper scheme, Accident Manager Southam observed, 'had aroused the cupidity of the public to a very considerable degree'. In practice, this meant that nearly a quarter of the 55,000 claims received by Phoenix in the first ten months of coupon insurance were either fraudulent or misguided. One individual was even tried for attempting to murder his wife in order to lay hands on her *Daily Mail* accident insurance. The trial was, of course, fully reported by the *Mail*.

By the end of 1922, the *Mail* had succeeded in boosting its circulation to over 1.9 million. But this increase in clientele, coupled with the headlong extension of benefits, had the effect of reducing Phoenix's receipts. Where the premium registered under the original scheme had given Phoenix 143 shillings per 100 registered readers, the actual out-turn gave only 71s 6d per 100 readers. The Phoenix accident team were

[203] Accident Manager Southam to Chairman's Committee, 12 April 1922.
[204] Burton to Sketch, 27 March 1922.

thoroughly dispirited. One senior official dolefully listed the drawbacks of the *Mail* project as: excessive inflation of circulation; too many dissatisfied claimants; 'most harmful' newspaper publicity; deliberate provocation of claims; unwillingness by the newspaper to pursue fraudulent claims.[205] Much of this was the reverse of what had been intended.

On 12 December 1922, the top management of Associated Newspapers, led by Sir Andrew Caird, met Ryan, Sketch and Southam. Caird expressed gratitude for Phoenix's help in the *Mail*'s circulation battle but admitted that the insurance campaign of 1922 had been 'unjustifiable and had led to unsatisfactory results for everyone concerned'. He promised that the *Mail* would return to the original simple coupon and cancel all the benefits that had been tacked on. The return to what Caird called 'a more sane coupon' eased problems in 1923: only 30% of claims had to be declined as against 70% in 1922. However, Phoenix would have liked to break out of the connection in 1922, if it could have done so. Even in 1923 Southam reported that there was no foreseeable hope of profit and in 1924 told Deputy Chairman Buxton privately that 'he should be very glad if the Directors relieved him from the unpalatable duty of carrying on the *Daily Mail* scheme in any shape at all'.[206] By the time the scheme was suspended in 1939, the *Mail* had paid out over £2 million in claims. The coupon saga was an important episode in newspaper history but a less than useful entanglement for the insurance business.[207]

In the 1920s, however, the trouble caused by the newspapers was, for once, small compared with that from other sources. By mid-decade the personal accident (as also the employers' liability) side of Phoenix's accident business was running fairly smoothly: these sectors were, after all, 'relatively small but useful contributors to Profit and Loss'. It was the third section, the general accident account, which in 1926 subscribed £3.74 million of the £4.07 million total accident income, and contained 'the large business transacted in the United States which has been, and still is, a source of anxiety to the Board'.[208] At the heart of the general accident problem, in both the United States and the United Kingdom, was the continuing affliction of workmen's compensation business. Profit from other sectors of accident insurance was wiped out by losses here. As

[205] A. Battrick to A. W. Tait, 3 November 1922. [206] Ryan to Sketch, 16 July 1924.

[207] By 1926, the *Bankers' Magazine* thought that the press campaign may have had some positive effect for the insurers by stimulating additional demand for accident and sickness insurance. On the other hand, it recorded that a spate of rail accidents had hit the newspaper schemes in 1928–9 and that the supporting offices 'cannot have found them profitable during the past year'. *Bankers' Magazine* 121 (1926), p. 325; 127 (1929), p. 334.

[208] Chairman's Annual Report, 26 April 1927. See Chapter 9, Sections 3 and 4.

Ryan put it in one of his more devastating admissions to shareholders, 'you may fairly regard it as our weak spot'.[209]

There was a problem of noblesse oblige in this department of insurance and governments did not allow insurers to forget it. Broadly, it was that insurance capitalists should not seek unreasonable returns from a kind of insurance which was effectively compulsory upon employers in trade and industry. In times of economic recession, governments could become insistent on this point. Standing in for Ryan, again laid off on doctor's orders, Deputy Chairman Buxton reported in 1926 how the law had been laid down in the UK market: 'By the Agreement between the Insurance Offices and the Home Office, it was arranged that, as far as can be done, rates are to be adjusted to produce a loss ratio which can only leave, after deduction of expenses, but a bare margin of profit.'[210] The Home Office was particularly concerned that, in large sectors of industry, between one-third and one-quarter of workers were still not covered by compensation insurance; and the government wanted no excuse for this to extend any further.[211]

In the USA, the State Commissioners of Insurance left even less room for manoeuvre: they fixed the acceptable rates for workmen's compensation insurance. Adjustments to rates were allowed in the light of loss ratios in the preceding three years. Ryan argued that this was fair in reasonably stable markets but would not work against the 'much heavier burdens of current times'. The result was that 'whereas good profits were made in the past, serious losses have ruled latterly', by which he meant the period 1921–6.[212] Unfortunately, of course, Phoenix had only been in the accident market in a serious way over the period 1921–6, and encountered particularly harsh conditions in 1923, 1924 and 1926 (see Table 8.31). By 1927, even some State Commissioners were worried that US compensation rates were too low.

Inadequate rates and high loss ratios – over 58% in 1923 – were not the only reasons for Phoenix's accident troubles at this time. A further major influence was the nefarious practice, common in the dominant US market, of accepting compensation risks, not against the full annual premium but against merely a part payment, the balance being collected at the year's end, when the total payroll was accurately known. In many cases the *major* part of the due premium was held over in this way.[213]

From King William Street, this curious American custom was viewed with horror. Ryan thought it 'a totally improper and undesirable feature'

[209] Chairman's Annual Report, 26 April 1927.
[210] *Ibid.*, 27 April 1926.
[211] *Bankers' Magazine*, 123 (1927), p. 373.
[212] Chairman's Annual Report, 26 April 1927.
[213] See Chapter 9, Section 3.

of the transatlantic market, for three main reasons. Firstly, all claims had to be paid on the entire risk, when only a fraction of the cost of actually assuming the risk had been received. Secondly, since premium payment was only partial, it became impossible to establish whether current premium rates were adequate. Thirdly, since reserves were calculated on the basis of premiums actually received, they could not be properly related to the risks which had been accepted. The insurers were most worried about the first and second points, the US Insurance Superintendents by the third. The New York Superintendent in 1923 unequivocally warned the offices against extending 'unreasonable credit' to their clients.[214]

It was conditions like these which led Head Office to stipulate that their 'desire was rather to control or restrict than to expand our business in America'. By 1925 accident exposure in the United States had already been scaled down, and Deputy Chairman Buxton, standing in during one of Ryan's illnesses, called for more of these 'cleansing processes'.[215] Senior management in London much misliked the 'heavy drain on the Funds' imposed by the US reserve problem, and the need to draw upon the profits of other branches – as in 1923 and 1926 – in order to prop up the accident account. Excessive exposure to doubtful US casualty business was the target for Southam's knife on his inspection trips of the late 1920s.

Phoenix was not alone in these problems, of course: Ryan commented on a general plight when he noted in 1927 that 'during the last three years, a heavy loss has been incurred . . . by Companies doing this class of business'.[216] Both the Liverpool & London & Globe and the London & Lancashire reported problems with American compensation business in the mid-1920s.[217] And the Phoenix Board did 'not see much hope for any marked improvement in workmen's compensation business in the immediate future'.[218]

They were therefore surprised in 1928 to find that 'the long-hoped-for turn of the tide appears to have come . . . in this important branch of our affairs'. Vigorous revision of business, cancellation of many undesirable risks and the overhauling of LGA's creaky accident machinery had apparently done the trick, converting the losses of the mid-1920s, into more comfortable figures for 1927 and 1928 (see Table 8.31 above). The traditional tactic of purifying the books brought about a guided reduction in premiums and that released the reserves which produced the paper profit of 1927; by contrast, the profit of 1928 was a real one. However,

214 Chairman's Annual Report, 30 April 1924. 215 *Ibid.*, 27 April 1926.
216 *Ibid.*, 26 April 1927. 217 *Bankers' Magazine*, 118 (1924), p. 130.
218 Chairman's Annual Report, 26 April 1927.

Southam was correct to warn that weather conditions were still unsettled: what was affecting Phoenix was less a turning tide than a false dawn.

By 1929, global conditions were undermining the local improvements which Southam's team had engineered. Renewed crisis in the USA outran the real advances which had been achieved there. The Phoenix quit the 1920s with some huge accident problems – the LGA reserves, the workmen's compensation issue – identified and partly countered, but the job was not finished, and top management, surveying the accident prospects of the 1930s, did so with bated breath.

By the 1920s, it was imperative for any large-scale insurance company to offer accident capacity. But Phoenix's choice of a date, company and place for acquiring such capacity was a long way short of ideal. Ryan must have wished devoutly that he had secured LGA on the first pass, in the mid-1900s, when it was smaller and had not yet embarked on the more reckless of its American policies. Also, more than a decade of supervision by Phoenix should have equipped LGA to confront the problems of the 1920s in good shape. And then perhaps it would have been possible simply to buy NUF; and *not* sell it again.

10. ACCIDENT BUSINESS IN THE 1930S

Given the impact of the world economic crisis of 1929–33, especially in the USA, it was inevitable that Phoenix's accident business would begin the new decade in a subdued state. Indeed total accident premiums fell by over 16% from 1929 to 1933. This slide was not guided, nor voluntary, no result of purification but rather of global crisis. Southam's scouring of the accident account started to produce durable benefit, not in 1928, as had first been hoped, but as late as 1936. Chairman Walters then perceived the genuine turning tide in his Annual Report of May 1937.[219]

The ebb in accident claims came in 1935: the average for 1927–1933 was a punishing 57.4%; whereas the average for 1935–9 was 51.6%. Profit levels recovered from more than a decade of extreme debilitation in 1934 and the healthy outcome of 4.7% for 1937 contrasted with an average for the previous five years of only 2.5%. Despite a fright from further trade contraction in the United States in 1938–9, which again brought premium reductions, UK accident business continued to grow and the overall claims ratio to decline. In 1939 at the extremely favourable level of 49.9%, it was nearly 10% below the level of 1930. The profit level for the last year of peace at 8.7% was better than that of any other interwar year.

[219] Chairman's Annual Report, 26 May 1937.

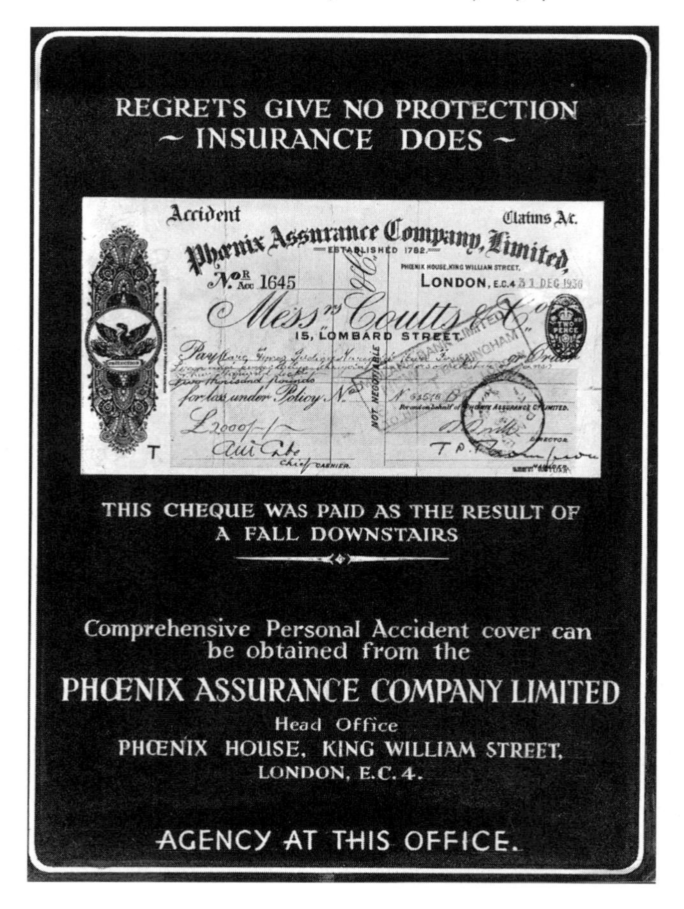

Plate 8.10 Advertising accident in the 1930s: turning injury to advantage.

Within these figures, the problem of workers' compensation did not go away. For the parent company, this type of business continued to represent about one-quarter of total accident activity. And it remained dangerous: the average annual loss ratio 1929–36 was nearly 70%; only in the late 1930s did the damage drop below 60%. The share of compensation within the *Group*'s accident totals was similar (see Table 8.32) but the loss levels were even worse, averaging 62.9% even for the period 1934–9. This was largely because LGA's loss rate on its big foreign compensation business was distinctly worse than Phoenix's own. However, the com-

Table 8.32. *Phoenix Group accident business: major classes, 1934–9*

	(1) Total premium (£m)	(2) Workmen's compensation % of (1)	(2) Workmen's compensation Loss (%)	(3) Personal accident % of (1)	(3) Personal accident Loss (%)	(4) Burglary % of (1)	(4) Burglary Loss %	(5) Motor % of (1)	(5) Motor Loss (%)	(6) Third party % of (1)	(6) Third party Loss (%)
1934	3.29	22.1	71.5	4.6	51.3	5.8	35.8	46.6	60.5	11.1	58.2
1935	3.42	23.8	63.7	4.4	52.4	5.7	33.4	44.2	58.3	12.3	49.5
1936	3.71	25.6	62.6	4.3	43.3	5.1	31.0	43.1	57.3	12.3	46.5
1937	4.03	26.9	60.7	4.2	41.1	5.0	29.0	41.5	57.7	12.5	46.4
1938	3.86	26.7	60.1	4.5	41.1	5.0	32.2	41.3	54.4	13.2	44.6
1939	3.75	25.0	58.9	4.7	46.3	5.3	32.2	42.1	56.2	12.8	40.4

Note: Phoenix Blue Books are not arranged in such a way as to allow comparison of Group accident classes before 1934.
Source: Calculated from Phoenix Blue Books.

pany's records are relatively silent on this problem. It was known, and contained, and had to be lived with. And it did improve slightly, late in the day.

With motor business, however, it is a different matter. Motor was the biggest class of accident business for Phoenix itself by 1923, accounting for 48.9% of accident premiums, and the size of the account almost tripled between 1923 and 1929. The result in 1929 constituted 53.1% of all accident premiums. This rapid growth of motor accounts from small beginnings during the 1920s, followed by a period of greater stability during the 1930s, was a common pattern for the industry.

As a proportion of Phoenix's total accident business, motor tended to slip somewhat during the 1930s but remained by far the biggest category still. Correspondingly, in money terms, motor premiums were fairly flat in the 1930s, averaging for Phoenix alone £660,974, 1929–36, but rising to £718,940 in 1939. Group motor income – the balance coming overwhelmingly from LGA – tended to be rather more than twice the amount netted by Phoenix itself. For the Group too, motor was the largest class of accident business in the 1930s (see Table 8.32 above) but also displayed a tendency to slip slightly. Loss ratios for motor business were also high in this period, with Phoenix sustaining an average claims ratio of 58.4% for 1929–36 and the Group one of 57.4% for 1934–9. However, the improvement in motor loss ratios began earlier than in compensation business, from 1932.

Table 8.33. *Phoenix Group motor insurances, 1934–9, by company (home and foreign), premium (£m) and Loss (%)*

	1934		1935		1936		1937		1938		1939	
	Prem.	Loss	Prem.	Loss	Prem.	Loss	Prem.	Loss	Prem.	Loss	Prem.	Loss
Phx Home	0.27	58.4	0.30	50.1	0.30	52.0	0.32	57.1	0.32	55.3	0.30	59.1
Phx Foreign	0.35	56.5	0.36	60.4	0.39	59.0	0.42	55.5	0.41	53.8	0.41	53.1
LGA Home	0.14	58.4	0.15	50.1	0.15	52.0	0.16	57.1	0.16	55.3	0.15	59.1
LGA Foreign	0.77	63.6	0.70	62.7	0.73	59.8	0.75	59.8	0.68	54.5	0.66	57.5
UM Foreign	0.01	55.0	0.01	42.9	0.01	61.7	0.01	58.7	0.02	50.3	0.02	36.9
Codan Foreign					0.01	47.2	0.01	66.1	0.02	47.0	0.03	41.4
Totals	1.53	60.5	1.51	58.3	1.60	57.3	1.67	57.7	1.60	54.4	1.58	56.2

Source: Phoenix Blue Books.

Table 8.33 reveals that, by the period 1934–9, Phoenix had succeeded in building a domestic motor market representing over 40% of its total motor premiums. By contrast, LGA's home market averaged only 17.4% of its total motor income in these years. The two companies pooled losses on the UK market, so little effective comparison is possible there. In the foreign department, however, LGA's loss record was always worse than Phoenix's. Moreover, Phoenix progressively increased its share of the total motor account, year on year, from 40.5% in 1934 to 45.6% in 1939. LGA's share shrank from 58.8% to 51.2%. Together, and reinforced abroad by their satellite companies (see Table 8.33), Phoenix and LGA constituted a formidable force in motor insurance.[220]

The Phoenix records in the 1930s are not silent on these issues, no doubt because of the bulk of the motor account within the accident department and because its progress was heavily influenced by both legislation and litigation. Such matters tend to draw comment.

The world of the 1930s contained plenty of motor cars requiring insurance, the biggest markets being in Britain and the United States. In Britain, car ownership more than tripled between 1925 and 1938 (see Table 8.34), as the construction of new suburbs maintained the demand

[220] The REA, which had expanded powerfully by acquisition of the Car & General and the Motor Union, had a much smaller 'parental' motor account than Phoenix by 1938 – about one-third the size – but the REA Group had 10% of worldwide premium income written by UK companies. However, the Phoenix Group had made considerable headway in motor since 1919 (see section 9 above) and by 1938 had 5% of the global aggregate, with the parent doing more of the work. Supple, *Royal Exchange Assurance*, pp. 433–5.

Table 8.34. *Motor cars in use in the United Kingdom, 1920–38*

1920	187,000
1925	692,800
1930	1,177,900
1935	1,592,400
1938	2,045,400

Source: S. Bowden, 'The New Consumerism', in P. Johnson (ed.), *Twentieth-Century Britain: Economic, Social and Cultural Change* (Harlow, 1994), p. 246; Supple, *Royal Exchange Assurance*, p. 480.

for personal and family transport. The British market for car insurance followed the regional geography of the country's economic recession.

In 1934, 50.5% of professional households and 37.1% of salaried households lived in London and the South-East, whereas the North could claim only 5.7% of professional and 9.1% of salaried households. Correspondingly, by 1938 nearly one-fifth of households in the South-East ran a car, while only just over one-tenth in the North did so. Even the cheapest cars – at £160 for a 7 or 8 horse-power model in 1938 – cost more than the average annual income for three-quarters of British society. So the market for cars and motor insurance in Britain was still class specific. Nevertheless, the UK vehicle industry between 1920 and 1938 increased output by an average annual rate of 6.6%, far faster than any other industry. By 1938, total British production was well ahead of the German, the French and the Italian but modest by comparison with the American, whic had 31 million registered vehicles by 1939.[221] By then, over 70% of American households kept an automobile.[222]

Not, of course, that the insurers wanted to cover all these car owners. In Britain, by the late 1920s, it is probable that some 90% of motorists had taken out insurance. But the luckless public, walking increasingly congested streets, were at risk, not only of injury, but of injury without compensation, from the other 10%. The insurers believed that those who had chosen to insure themselves were the better risks. To force insurance

[221] UK car production in 1938 was 341,000, German 276,000, French 199,800, Italian 59,000 (Bowden, 'The New Consumerism', pp. 248–60). The USA had 1.8 million registered vehicles in 1914, 26.7 million by 1929 (Supple, *Royal Exchange Assurance*, p. 431).

[222] Bowden, 'The New Consumerism', p. 248.

upon the remainder would bring in the worst risks. Selection was the essence of insurance and the offices wished to be free to select. Government, by contrast, under pressure from rising accident statistics, worried about the capacity for mayhem among the uninsured 10%.

At the turn of the 1920s and 1930s many central issues in motor insurance, including profit and competition levels and premium rates, were coming to a head. None was more central or sensitive than the issue of compulsion: should all drivers be legally required to carry third-party insurance? It required a series of draft bills from 1927, two reports of a Royal Commission on Transport, and the sponsorship of Earl Spencer before this requirement did indeed become law in 1930. The requirement was to operate from 1 January 1931. Why did such an apparently sensible desire to protect the ordinary citizen take so long to effect?

The extraordinary growth of motoring in the 1920s helped carry the accident premiums of many UK offices past their fire premiums. Yet the profit levels on these swelling accident accounts were meagre. Motor business was particularly beset by high competition levels and high damage rates. So the offices were very protective of their freedom of manoeuvre in this department. From the mid-1920s sections of the financial press began to reflect their concern that selection of risk was 'the cardinal principle' of all insurance.[223] Invidious comparisons were drawn with Massachusetts, the only state in the USA to force insurance upon motorists. There, it was claimed, the scheme had 'disappointed public expectation': both the number of accidents and the rates of premium had risen in its wake.[224] When seven insurance offices took stands at the Olympia Motor Show in 1928, they observed with some acerbity that the wheeled exhibits did not contain many features which might reduce the risks of accident or costs of repair.[225] Ryan reflected on these events and observed hopefully, and prematurely, in his Annual Report of 1930 that,

> A suggested interference by the government . . . has been averted. There can be no justification for the State to interfere with a branch of business so capably conducted and with such moderate returns.[226]

The House of Commons, however, were less sure. Perhaps they were swayed by the fact that in the quarter July–September 1929, the roaring traffic of London by itself killed 340 people and injured over 16,000. Once honourable members had decided, the insurers gave in gracefully. Ryan's successor, Clarendon Hyde, promised that 'The Companies will give the Act a fair trial and will make no general increase in existing rates for the

[223] *Bankers' Magazine*, 124 (1926), p. 325. [224] *Ibid.*, 126 (1928), p. 790.
[225] *Ibid.* [226] Chairman's Annual Report, 28 May 1930.

present.'[227] In fact, it seems as if they should not have worried; or perhaps worried about something else. The *Bankers' Magazine* did report, almost immediately, that the Act had brought 'a lot of new business, much of it of an undesirable character'.[228] But the statistical support for this is ambiguous. Neither the Phoenix nor the REA experienced a leap in motor premiums after 1 January 1931. Phoenix's own motor income rose by 1.3% in 1931 and then subsided by 8.1% between 1931 and 1935. Loss rates on Phoenix motor business were significantly lower in the three years after 1 January 1931 than in the three years before (averages of 57.3% and 61.8%). There is little evidence here that the introduction of compulsory third-party insurance for drivers did the underwriting damage that was feared of it. However, total UK motor premiums did jump by 12% in the year after the Act.

Nor did it turn out that the absence of compulsory motor insurance in most of the United States was a positive feature. In 1932 Phoenix's total accident premiums fell by over £0.25 million. Three-quarters of this reduction was due to unwilled contraction in US compensation and motor business. Clarendon Hyde was surprised by two features of US automotive behaviour. In the land of the powered chariot, where 'hitherto . . . motor cars have been looked upon as absolute necessities', owners were reacting to economic recession in a strange way: they were giving up driving. And, where they were continuing to drive, outside Massachusetts, they were giving up insuring what they drove.[229] Perhaps, after all, compulsory insurance had its points.

However, there are good indicators that the motor insurers would have done better to worry about other issues; or worry about them earlier. Competition among motor insurers in the 1920s had been fierce; but accident damage to vehicles probably hurt the offices more. Yet they were slow to find methods of rating cars and drivers with any accuracy. Ironically, the small cars of the decade, which made the first inroads upon the mass market, were also responsible for much of the red ink in the motor accounts. Although rated at lower premiums than their more high-powered contemporaries, the economy saloons of the day turned out to cost

[227] *Ibid.*, 1 June 1932. The compulsion was restricted to cover against death or injury caused by a motor car. Also, each company transacting motor business was required to provide a surety of £15,000.

[228] *Bankers' Magazine*, 131 (1931), p. 977. On the resulting market context in motor insurance and the role of non-tariff companies in securing a highly competitive share of the more desirable business, see O. M. Westall, 'The Invisible Hand Strikes Back: Motor Insurance and the Erosion of Organised Competition in General Insurance, 1920–38', *Business History*, 30 (1988), pp. 432–50.

[229] *The Times*, 8 June 1933.

very nearly as much to repair. And the more run-of-the-mill (or perhaps middle-of-the-road) vehicles were damaged with startling frequency. The Car and General reported in 1927 that no less than 40% of its insured vehicles had crashed at least once.[230] Clearly, the middle of the road was not a good place to be in the 1920s.

It was not until the very late 1920s, that the offices began work on a method of relating premium to the make of car, rather than to an across-the-board categorisation by power and value.[231] This introduced the possibility of allowing for construction quality and failure rate in a more exact manner. In 1932, the offices subscribing to the Motor Tariff agreed and published a revised rating system, the main feature of which was a graduated 'no-claims' bonus of the modern type: a discount of 10% for the first year, 15% for the second and 20% for the third.[232] This provided a start upon the difficult job of marking for driver skill. And, finally, after two years of wrangling over how best to achieve it, the accident offices agreed a scheme for district rating. From 1 January 1935, Britain was divided into five zones and premium rates adjusted to the accident rate within each zone. This effectively produced a surcharge upon those areas in which most accidents happened.

Such methods could not solve the problems imposed by heavy competition and stern judges, but, together with an improving economic climate, they did make the 1930s somewhat easier for motor insurers than the 1920s had been.

It was both fitting and ironic that in the era when accident became both the biggest and the most problematic of the major insurance classes that Phoenix should acquire a former Minister of Transport as chairman. The upright and worried John Pybus acted exactly according to ministerial type during his brief tenure of the Phoenix chair. He was preoccupied by the accident rate.[233] His successor at the ministry commissioned an inquiry into the high level of fatal road accidents and Pybus, in his first Annual Report as Phoenix chairman in May 1934, felt obliged to pass on the results. They were indeed arresting. Speeds of offending vehicles, the Minister pointed out, were underestimated in 68% of cases because the pedestrians or cyclists who provided most of the fatalities were in no position to give their own assessment. A similar percentage of fatal accidents happened on straight roads, or with clear sight lines, and the same proportion in daylight or normal visibility. Only 3% occurred in

230 Supple, *Royal Exchange Assurance*, pp. 456–7.
231 *Bankers' Magazine*, 127 (1929), p. 344. 232 *Ibid.*, 134 (1932), p. 903.
233 His main achievement as Minister of Transport was to pilot the Passenger Transport Act through the Commons.

Plate 8.11 A fatal motor accident of the 1930s.

dense traffic against 60% on the lightly trafficked open road. The finger of statistics pointed clearly at a nation of Mr Toads. Audibly, if inaccurately, moved, Sir John opined that, 'No free people will long tolerate a state of affairs in which every waking hour a human life is lost.'[234]

A year later, in his second, and final, Annual Report, Pybus returned again to the 'dreadful' rate of motor accidents. But he did also notice an effect other than human suffering which accompanied them: the upsurge in lawsuits, especially the 'guest claims' by relatives or friends present in the car at the time of the accident, and claiming against the driver for negligence. By 1934, these represented 18% of all motor claims by value in the USA.[235] After Pybus' sad demise, this was a refrain much taken up by his successor. It would be an exaggeration to say that, where Pybus worried about people being knocked down, Walters worried about them getting up and suing. But the emphases in their annual reports, as indeed in the public concerns of their periods of tenure, do have a different slant.

From 1936, Walters noted an unprecedented claims consciousness

[234] Chairman's Annual Report, 30 May 1934. [235] *The Times*, 30 May 1935.

among the motoring, and the mown-down, public, and mused, not without relevance, as to whether the advertisement of accident insurance had not sensitised the community in a new way. Over the next three years, it is the reaction of the judiciary which upsets him: 'the most alarming figures which the Courts are awarding as damages in Accident cases'. This was especially true of actions by family members against negligent drivers. Probably the most threatening judgement for the motor insurers was *Rose* v. *Ford* of June 1937 whereby compensation was awarded to the estate of the deceased regarding 'loss of expectation of life'. Given that road deaths exceeded 6,000 in 1937, it was calculated that *Rose* v. *Ford* would cost the underwriters a further £600,000. Whatever the humanitarian good sense of this, the motor insurers could only lament a further source of pressure upon margins already heavily squeezed. Even in 1939, as the politicians of Europe prepared much more efficient ways of mowing down civilians, the accident departments agonised over the court activity within their motor accounts.

Nevertheless, despite many tribulations and all too frequent trials, the Phoenix accident department ended the interwar years in better shape than it had displayed at any time since 1920. Profitability improved markedly in the late 1930s (see Table 8.31 above), and the growth of Phoenix's accident operation, late as it had begun, more than matched the expansion of the total UK-based accident trade.

Phoenix controlled 3.5% of the total market in 1920 and 5.4% by 1937. The market had expanded by 67.6% between 1920 and 1937 but Phoenix's accident takings had risen by 159.3%. This increase was unevenly distributed between the 1920s and the 1930s. As motor insurance had raced away in the 1920s, the total accident market had grown by 45.5%, but Phoenix's share had grown by 142.1%. In the 1930s, the accident market had settled to a slower pace and grew by 15.2% between 1930 and 1937. Phoenix's progress was slower still: a 7.1% advance. But, given the company's commitment to the US market, its managers would not have wished for any faster accumulation of business.

Indeed bringing the Phoenix accident department to the relative stability of the late 1930s had been a hard fought campaign. At the centre of the battle was the LGA salient. The influence of that acquisition took Phoenix not only into the foxholes of the UK accident market but, with heavy commitment, into the crumbling trenches of the US accident market. NUF had sounder tactics; but NUF had to be sold on. The moment Phoenix chose to enter the accident business meant that it encountered a particularly demanding conjunction: a private sector supply side, an unstable world economy, and increasingly intrusive governments with

Table 8.35. *Total accident premiums: all UK offices and Phoenix Assurance, 1920–37 (£ million)*

	All UK offices	Phoenix
1920	45.1	1.57
1925	53.5	3.96
1930	65.6	3.79
1935	67.3	3.44
1937	75.6	4.06

Plate 8.12 A lucky escape of the 1930s.

social equity agendas. The pressure of the latter was felt in both of the most demanding accident sectors of the day: workmen's compensation and motor insurance.

Phoenix had little choice: if it was going to be a true composite in 1919, it had to have accident capacity. But it should have chosen more carefully, and indeed earlier. It was a tribute to the damage-control of Sketch, Southam and Battrick that they extracted a profitable accident operation from these materials by the eve of the Second World War. But, however it is read, the LGA incident had a reach far beyond the 1920s and 1930s. It was one of the strongest negative influences on Phoenix's twentieth-century career.

II. INSURANCE INVESTMENT BETWEEN THE WARS: AVOIDING THE TIGER

For institutional investors, the 1920s and 1930s formed a period of apparently enticing new prospects and genuinely huge new risks. These years saw the beginning of the modern era of institutional investment. And it came in with a roar. Some insurance offices, often under eminent economic advice – among them the National Mutual, the Provincial and the Prudential – adopted a policy which might be called 'riding the tiger'.[236] In its most advanced form, this policy consisted of credit-cycle spotting, active dealing in ordinary shares and special attention to an index of industrial shares. It required skills of selection and timing that were well beyond most investment managers of the era.

Phoenix's strategy was rather to put a field's width between one's portfolio and the tiger. It worked well.

Investment power was one of the strengths of the Phoenix during the interwar year, a characteristic that was by no means shared by all insurance offices. The company's strategy was: to use investment earnings to cover the great majority of the dividend payment due; to refrain from adjusting the book values of investments towards the market values when stock markets rose, thus creating an important 'hidden reserve'; to place behind this, specific investment reserves which could be brought into play if serious stock-market crises wiped out the hidden reserve; and to follow a cautious policy in selecting new investments, so as to steer around the worst instabilities in the market. The last was most involved in avoiding the tiger.

Broadly speaking, high rates of interest allowed a generous dividend policy in the 1920s, while shrinking rates of investment return necessitated trimming of the dividend after 1933. Strong expansion of the 'hidden reserve' in the 1920s held the line against the worst the markets could throw at it during the crash years. Capacious additional reserves were set in place against a still deeper plunge; but were not needed. Cautious selection of new investments proved the pudding for Phoenix, while those – not least the great economist J. M. Keynes at the National Mutual, who

[236] Oliver Westall has called it this in his *Provincial Insurance Company, 1903–38* (Manchester, 1992), Chapter 15, pp. 340–83.

was the most skilful rider of tigers, had his trials as well as his triumphs.[237]

In the 1920s, after-tax investment yields well in excess of 4.5% – when the return assumed by the actuaries was 3% – were a boon not only to the life business but to all Phoenix's investment operations. It was this windfall in yields which permitted the dividend to rise from 11s in 1920, through 13s in the mid-1920s to 14s from 1927 to 1932. Pressure on yields in the 1930s also explains why it was necessary to run the dividend at the lower level of 12s from 1933. At this level in 1936 – with the 2s reduction saving over £80,000 in total dividend payments – interest earnings covered over 90% of the dividend cost. Replenishment from the investment coffers was seen as a powerful compensation for the trading problems of the time. 'So long as this continues', said Ryan of the high yields of the 1920s, 'we need not be unduly concerned about any wayward experience in our Fire, Marine and Accident Departments.'[238]

Just as for many years the main assets of the Phoenix in the interwar years were divided between the general fund, which secured fire and other non-life insurance, and the life fund, which guaranteed the company's assurance business, so they were managed in significantly different ways. However, both were run at book values well below their market values. Ryan insisted, in a crucial decision, that Phoenix should not correct for 'the fall in the barometer' during the First World War by writing up postwar book values.

By March 1924, the Phoenix general fund sported a market value over £500,000 more than their worth in the Phoenix books; a year later they were over £800,000 clear of the book values.[239] Even in 1929, this margin remained a solid defence, despite the Crash. The depleted market value of the Phoenix general fund still outstripped the book figure by over £200,000 even at the end of this dreadful year.[240] Stock exchange securities composed the majority of the general fund – indeed almost all of it apart from an interest in real estate – but even they soldiered to the end of 1930 with their market value clear of the book value by £300,000. It was not until 1931–3 that the market values of the general fund's stock exchange holdings slid below those written in the books, and then recovered 1934–7 (see Table 8.36).

Phoenix saw the market-to-book value of its investments as the first

[237] Keynes chaired the National Mutual from 1921, and was the main investment adviser to the Provincial from 1923; he was also Bursar of King's College, Cambridge, 1924–46.

[238] Chairman's Annual Report, 30 April 1924.

[239] Phoenix Directors' Minutes 34, pp. 216, 361, 19 March 1924 and 18 March 1925. Although the margin in the *stock exchange* holdings of the fund was down to £100,000 by the end of 1925. See Table 8.36.

[240] Chairman's Annual Report, 29 May 1929.

Table 8.36. *Phoenix Assurance: Group general fund – total values of stock exchange securities, 1922–40 (book and market values, and group total assets, all in £ million)*

Year	Cost price	Book value	Market value	Group total assets
1922	12.2	11.0	11.5	30.7
1923	12.0	10.8	11.4	30.5
1924	12.1	11.4	11.9	30.7
1925	13.1	12.7	12.8	31.8
1926	13.2	12.7	13.1	32.6
1927	13.5	13.1	13.8	33.3
1928	13.6	13.1	13.7	34.9
1929	13.6	13.2	13.3	36.3
1930	13.3	12.8	13.1	34.4
1931	13.0	12.5	10.8	34.4
1932	12.8	12.3	11.3	34.0
1933	12.7	12.3	11.6	34.1
1934	12.5	11.9	12.3	34.4
1935	12.7	12.1	12.6	35.1
1936	13.4	12.8	13.6	36.0
1937	13.8	13.2	13.2	36.9
1938	14.2	13.6	13.4	37.7
1939	13.8	13.1	12.7	38.4
1940	13.4	12.6	12.6	39.3

Source: Phoenix Assurance Blue Account Books.

barricade against financial crisis but not the only one. The contingency reserve of £2 million had no liabilities written against it and could be wheeled into place as a secondary defence against markets which sank lower than the book values. The Chairman's Annual Report of May 1929, well before the storm, mused on this possibility; that of 1931 reported that this fund had been re-christened the investment and contingency reserve in honour of the world financial crisis.[241] The UK market had fallen sharply during 1929 and New York suffered the classic bear rush of all time at the end of the year. Even so, Phoenix 'strongly buttressed with inner reserves', could afford to watch and wait. Interest earnings on the complete portfolio for 1930 were only 5% below those for 1929 and covered over 93% of the dividend cost.

[241] *Ibid.*, 10 June 1931.

Table 8.37. *Phoenix Assurance: Group life fund – total values of stock exchange securities, 1930–40 (book and market values, £ million)*

Year	Cost price	Book value	Market value	Group total assets
1930	11.8	10.3	11.1	34.4
1931	12.0	10.5	10.1	34.4
1934	14.1	12.6	15.3	34.4
1936	15.6	14.2	16.7	36.0
1938	16.6	15.1	16.2	37.7
1940	17.0	15.3	15.8	39.3

Source: Phoenix Assurance Red Account Books.

The hidden reserve, created by Ryan, led Phoenix comfortably through the Crash and out the other side. The life fund had one bad moment in 1931, when its market value dipped briefly, by £400,000 below its book value of over £10.5 million (see Table 8.37). But Phoenix had the substance to wait out this reverse. By 1933, rising markets were again swelling the margin left out of the books; by the end of 1934 the whole portfolio of the life fund was 16% richer than the books indicated, and even in 1938, as markets blanched before the approaching threat of war, still 11%.[242] No investment depreciation whatever had to be entered against the second defence of the investment and contingency reserve. Phoenix's problem after 1933 was in finding decent securities to buy, rather than crying over the value of what was already in the vaults. Holding the dividend at the lower level from 1933 wholly reflected the lower current *income* from investment between 1933 and 1938; Phoenix maintained its current capital values of its complete portfolio remarkably well.

The era's greatest economist could not boast as much. Where some offices followed the Phoenix tactic and let investment appreciation in good times create a reserve against bad times, others wrote investments up towards market value periodically. Some did so more frequently than others. The National Mutual, under Keynes' guidance, was the most bullish of all, 'the chief protagonist of the active investment policy'.[243] The maestro's opinion was that National Mutual had won so much by investment appreciation in the 1920s that its surplus would grow indefinitely if nothing was done about it. So he advised that the company

[242] The life fund contained a good deal more than stock exchange securities, most importantly some £4–5 million in mortgages and loans.

[243] *Bankers' Magazine*, 1929 (127), p. 518.

should disburse much of it by declaring a special bonus in its centenary year. Unfortunately, the National Mutual had contrived to be founded in 1829. Its anniversary year proved conclusively that the surplus would not have grown indefinitely if nothing had been done about it; it could have provided useful protection against the whirlwind. But, alas, something had been done about it.

The other burning investment issue of the period, and one in which Keynes and the National Mutual were much involved, was the proper selection of investment opportunities for insurance offices. Here Ryan and the Phoenix, however adventurous the line they were prepared to take in relation to matters such as company acquisition, were notably more conservative in regard to investment choice. Ryan reflected in 1928,

> In the light of much discussion of what should be the best policy for an insurance office... as regards investment, I may say we have no cut-and dried method of selection. Every investment is dealt with on its merits, with a *decided bias in favour of safety as against yield of interest.* Personally, I am not attracted by the more speculative methods of finance advocated in certain quarters.[244]

Ryan realised, of course, that his statement represented a particular view in a protracted debate. The 'more speculative' methods he referred to involved, primarily, active dealing in ordinary shares, particularly industrial equities; and the 'certain quarters' were Keynes and the offices which shared his line of thought, principally the National Mutual, the Provincial (both of which he advised directly) and the Prudential.

The more traditional line – which Ryan, in reality, did not follow slavishly – was represented by the long-lasting influence of A. H. Bailey.[245] The Bailey rules had encouraged offices towards the accumulation of assets of stable capital value and good yield, which were 'then locked away until redemption'.[246] At best the result was a passive investment policy. Moreover, this inclination among the offices had been reinforced by a change of government tack during the Great War. Desperate for war finance, the state had attempted to woo the institutions back to gilts by improving their security of capital value. From 1917 undated issues were largely replaced by short- and medium-term *dated* stock. Patriotism, backed up by a good deal of official pressure, thus combined with long-established investment taste and newly perceived self-interest, to move the offices heavily into central government paper.

[244] Chairman's Annual Report, 24 May 1928 (my emphasis).
[245] See above, Chapter 1, Section 7.
[246] Westall, *Provincial Insurance Company*, p. 351.

The insurance industry as a whole held 1% of its assets in this form in 1914, nearly 32% by 1920. Phoenix had almost nothing in gilts in 1914, around 25% by 1920.

Very different market conditions in the following two decades – a high interest rate regime in the 1920s but falling yields in the 1930s – acted, paradoxically, to move insurers in a single direction: both sets of circumstances required diversification of assets. The 'overhang' of government debt from the war kept interest rates up, and thus made it difficult for offices which had accumulated large holdings of gilts to protect the capital value of their portfolios. On the other hand, the low investment yields of the 1930s drove investors to seek new outlets for their funds. The interwar period was thus an era which set a special premium upon the effective selection of new investments.

The fact that two insurance offices of these years retained the century's leading economist as their investment adviser set something of an industrial standard.[247] J. M. Keynes was not impressed by the investment norms of the insurance business: 'boardroom' selection in which directors, in a semblance of risk diversification, were allowed to choose a pet project apiece, after which the whole bundle was salted away until maturity. 'Some insurance directors', writes Westall, 'assumed that safety was greatest when the portfolio was never touched.'[248]

The active investment strategy favoured by Keynes took quite a different line. Or, more precisely, it took two different lines. Before the 1929 Crash, Keynes advocated 'aggressive switches in funds to maximize portfolio performance', that is, swift movements between different categories of investment according to the point on the credit cycle.[249] However, during the 1930s, he came to mistrust the possibility of detecting the turning points on the cycle with sufficient accuracy. His substitute plan was to lay down a target long-run return of about 5%, achieving this above-average outcome, in low-yielding markets, by the 'spotting' of specific high-performing shares. Having invented credit-cycle investment, he then proceeded to invent share-spotting investment.

Keynes drew encouragement from the demonstration by H. E. Raynes – again unfortunately timed for that great insurance guru, in 1928 – that a package of shares bought in 1912 would have substantially outpaced any other stock-market securities in both income and capital value by 1927.[250]

[247] It is possible, but perhaps unlikely, that he will be surpassed in what remains of the millennium.

[248] Westall, *Provincial Insurance Company*, p. 351. [249] *Ibid.*, pp. 355–6.

[250] H. E. Raynes, 'The place of ordinary stocks and shares in the investment of life insurance funds', *Journal of the Institute of Actuaries*, 1928, pp. 21–50.

Raynes concluded that 'as a counsel of perfection', ordinary shares could be substituted for fixed interest securities when commodity prices were falling, and the other way about when they were rising.[251] During the 1920s also, such British phlegm was reinforced by jaunty transatlantic example as American offices snapped up equities with alacrity, depending increasingly on stock-market earnings to provide a surplus and progressively becoming, according to the *Bankers' Magazine*, 'investment trusts'. That respected financial voice also suggested that the advantage of equities lay in their greater spread and their under-valuation in relation to bonds; their disadvantage that they needed greater knowledge for every decision and greater care in every selection.[252] Presciently, it spoke too of the damage that could follow from 'a major conflagration . . . or a relapse in the stock market'.[253]

So plenty of opinion was gathering in favour of equities, but little of it carried the fervour of Keynes. 'The public joint stock company', he wrote, 'has taken a tremendous leap forward and now offers a field for investment which simply did not exist even twenty years ago . . . These represent the live large-scale business and investment world of today, and any investment institution which ignores, or is not equipped for handling, their shares is living in a backwater.'[254] That, no doubt, is where he would have placed the Phoenix.

After the Crash, Keynes was only slightly daunted. Now his stress was placed not on equities in general but on the right equities. The effective investor would not spread his money across a complete index of industrial companies he knew nothing about but would concentrate on a few well-managed ones that he did. Keynes' own favourites included Austin, Leyland, British Plaster Boards and several metal companies. His aim throughout was to secure a good yield while keeping depreciation in capital value to a minimum, thus staying just inside the old Bailey 'fence'. One of his colleagues wondered whether the difference between the ambitions of the average insurance office and the ambitions of J. M. Keynes was not the difference 'between investment and speculation'.[255]

By 1930, the insurance offices as a group had sunk 6.5% of their total assets in ordinary shares, and by 1935 nearly 10%. But this did not mean that the generality had become converted to 'investment Keynesianism'. Rather these numbers were the outcome of decisions by a few big institu-

[251] *Bankers' Magazine*, 128 (1929), p. 173. [252] *Ibid.*, 125 (1928), p. 527.
[253] *Ibid.*, 128 (1929), pp. 493–5.
[254] Cited by Westall, *Provincial Insurance Company*, p. 353.
[255] Ian Macpherson, cited by Westall, *Provincial Insurance Company*, p. 381.

tions. And some of these had little choice. The Prudential was effectively forced by the huge scale of its reserves into diversifying; by 1937, it had diverted £40 million, or 11.6% of its holdings, into equities. The ordinary share holdings of many offices were often merely blocks of railway equities, the most traditional choice among shares, or even stakes in their own subsidiary companies. The really active punters were few. The Scottish Provident, with 9% of its portfolio in equities by 1929, or Standard Life, with 17%, were following a strategy of choice. But the most committed were the National Mutual and the Provincial. The former had devoted 18% of its portfolio to equities by 1928, while the latter had ridden the cycle by placing 14.7% of its assets in equities by 1920, 4.7% in 1925 and 13.8% in 1929. These were mostly genuine industrial and commercial shares. The Provincial's selection covered some thirty different securities issued by a considerable variety of ventures.[256]

At the top end of the industry, the nine largest offices, measured by total assets, differed widely in their affection for equities by 1938. Four of them had committed between 10% and 13% of their assets to the 'active' choice, while three had trusted less than 2% to the equity sector. Phoenix was one of the three.

But between 1929 and 1938, of course, the equity market had seen a deal of grief. The great stock market slides of 1929 and 1937–8 were disasters for the active investment policy. A representative sample of UK ordinary shares fell by 38% in value from the last quarter of 1929 to the second quarter of 1932. By the end of 1929, the Provincial's 'industrial index' was worth one-fifth less than its purchase price and the company's whole portfolio nearly 3% less; by the end of 1931, the worst point for the Provincial, the value of the whole portfolio was 14.9% below its cost price.[257] Similarly, the National Mutual lost half of all its investment earnings for the entire decade 1920–9, and in 1932 had to postpone the date of its life valuation, 'a humiliating expedient that every office would naturally wish to avoid'.[258] In the USA, the cheery 'investment trusts' of the 1920s had driven over the precipice, and the pursuit of insurance for stock market profit went with them.[259] By contrast, Clarendon Hyde,

256 *Ibid.*, pp. 357–8.

257 *Ibid.*, p. 362. Westall shows that Keynes was not solely responsible for this débacle. Heavy purchasing of US securities well beyond the whirlwind on Wall Street by his colleague O. T. Falk did much of the damage. Additionally, the cost price test is a harsh one in such conditions, and, at Phoenix's worst point, also in 1931, its life fund portfolio would have been also about 15% below its purchase price, but, of course, Phoenix's total assets were about forty times those of the Provincial.

258 *Bankers' Magazine*, 133 (1932), p. 326.

259 *Ibid.*, 129 (1930), pp. 323–4.

surveying the Phoenix portfolio from his 'backwater' in June 1932, concluded, perhaps a trifle smugly, that, 'we can hardly put our finger on any one investment and state that we consider it definitely bad'.[260]

However, if the Keynes strategy was knocked down in 1929, it did not stay down. The economist predicted the lower interest rates of the post-Crash period accurately, moved into longer-term securities in good time, and then selected the right moment to go back into equities in the middle of 1932. From that point to the last quarter of 1933, UK industrial shares rose by 46%, and to the end of 1936, by 117%. The British market was buoyant in 1935 and 1936, and a recovery at length materialised in the USA. By 1937 Keynes had surfed these currents to take the Provincial's portfolio forward to a 30% stake in equities. Between 1929 and 1937 the *Bankers' Magazine* equity index fell by 20 points, but Keynes secured for the Provincial's equity holding an appreciation of 16%. His average yield on these equities for 1930–9 was 4.9%, within an ace of his long-run target of 5%, and far above the 3.5% offered by consols.

Nevertheless, Keynes was again tripped by the turning point. The UK equity market fell by 16% over the span of 1937, and the drift continued into 1938. By the end of the year the market value of the Provincial's portfolio was again down to within 1% of its book value. Keynes had predicted the turn, but a serious heart attack had prevented him from doing much about it. A strategy which employed little hedging and depended on careful scrutiny of individual securities by a single brilliant analyst had little room for heart attacks.

Most other offices were not open to such risks. For the majority 'almost the only consideration . . . is to invest against their obligations, to avoid taking definite views on investment whenever they can, and to hedge their risks as far as possible'.[261] Phoenix was perhaps even further from this view than it was from Keynes. Always cautious about equities, Phoenix became even more cautious after 1929. But Phoenix managers certainly did not lack definite views on investment and were not slow in definite action.

Indeed, while watching Phoenix's total assets tot up nicely in the mid-1920s (see Table 8.36), Ryan was struck by the thought that the total assets of the entire insurance business – some £1,000 million – could be used in a definite way to affect the whole market. 'Could some machinery be devised for joint action', he mused, 'they [the offices] would be a much more important factor in the investment market than they are as separate units. Something may possibly be done in this

[260] Chairman's Annual Report, 1 June 1932.
[261] Macpherson, cited by Westall, *Provincial Insurance Company*, p. 381.

direction in time to come.'[262] Such prophetic thinking was not the mark of a passive investor.

But Ryan was not an adventurous one. In 1928 he welcomed an apparent revival of mortgages – which is just perceptible in the life funds (see Table 8.2) – on the grounds that it created a better balance between stock-exchange securities and loan.[263] Similarly, in his last Annual Report, in June 1931, his method of reassuring shareholders amidst the financial ruins of other companies, was to point to the £5.5 million of loans and mortgages, the £4.2 million of home government securities and the £1.6 million of well-written-down house property among the Phoenix's assets. These, he stressed, were very stable investments and the gilts had appreciated strongly during 1930.[264]

Yet, the Phoenix did not make only conservative choices. In fact, mortgages (as defined in Table 8.38)[265] do not show much of a tendency to rebuild their 1913 share of investment, either for all offices or for Phoenix. However, for much of the interwar period, Phoenix, and especially its powerful life fund, had a distinctly higher proportion of its portfolio in mortgages than the all-office average. Secondly, Phoenix was much faster out of UK government stock than most offices and around 1930 had notably *low* holdings of gilts (see Table 8.38). Between 1928 and 1931 Phoenix ran its stock of home government paper down from £6 million to £4.2 million. By contrast, the company participated massively more than the average in the securities offered by *foreign* governments. The fire fund commonly contained three or four *times* the proportion of this class held by the industry as a whole. This of course was yet one further reflection of Phoenix's status as a global exporter of insurance. Many of these overseas gilts were forced holdings, securities required as insurance sureties by foreign states. Yet compulsion here secured a useful spread of risk across world markets: in 1933 the Phoenix had 45% of its gilts portfolio in the United Kingdom, 10% in Canada, 5% in India, 5% in Australia, 21% in the United States and the remaining 14% scattered everywhere else.

If the Phoenix funds were much warier of equities than the average, they were notably more interested than the average in debentures, preference shares and real estate, as well as more interested in mortgages and

262 Chairman's Annual Report, 26 April 1927. Phoenix's total assets in 1926 were £32.6 million against a total capital of £3,792,795 divided into 309,755 shares of £10 nominal value and 695,245 shares of £1 value, fully paid.

263 *Ibid.*, 24 May 1928.

264 *Ibid.*, 10 June 1931.

265 Here they are taken to include loans against rates, personal securities and policies, in order to achieve consistency with the All-Office figures. The proportions will thus differ from those given in the summary table, Table 8.2.

Table 8.38. *Distribution of portfolios: all offices and Phoenix general and life funds, 1920–40 (% shares by category)*

	1920			1925			1930			1935		
	All offices	Phoenix general fund	Phoenix life fund	All offices	Phoenix general fund	Phoenix life fund	All offices	Phoenix general fund	Phoenix life fund	All offices	Phoenix general fund	Phoenix life fund
Mortgages	20.9	5.5	35.2	19.0	4.3	24.2	23.2	5.9	29.8	20.5	1.7	20.8
UK govt	31.7	27.2	23.3	38.9	30.8	29.9	26.9	16.5	14.1	30.5	13.8	25.4
Foreign govt	7.2	27.6	11.2	7.4	25.0	18.7	7.1	19.8	21.4	5.4	20.7	18.8
Debentures	10.6	16.0	11.2	12.3	23.2	12.8	17.2	39.9	20.4	16.3	38.7	20.8
Preference Shares	3.2	2.3	4.4	4.1	1.9	5.6	6.8	1.7	7.5	7.6	3.5	9.1
Ordinary shares	3.0	2.7	2.2	4.4	1.7	0.9	7.0	1.5	1.1	8.0	2.0	0.9
Land, etc.	6.6	8.8	6.6	5.3	8.7	3.6	4.7	8.8	2.6	5.3	10.5	1.9
Cash	3.0	9.6	1.3	2.2	4.5	0.7	2.0	5.2	0.7	2.2	8.3	0.5

Sources: Calculated from Phoenix Balance Sheets and Red Account Books, and D. K. Sheppard, *The Growth and Role of UK Financial Institutions, 1880–1962* (London, 1971), pp. 154–6.

foreign gilts. Table 8.38 shows that there were more initiatives that were unconventional than the dashing decision to go for equities. Keynes, of course, shared some of these as well, since he too followed debentures and preference shares with some avidity.

Detailed examination of the Phoenix's investment in the interwar period raises interesting questions as to what was good and bad strategy in this testing period. The office's two big funds displayed quite different growth patterns. The stock exchange securities of the general fund grew gently from a market value of £11.5 million in 1922 to a peak of £13.8 million in 1927, and settled to £13.4 million in 1938. These investments were hedged by the late 1920s to the tune of about £1.4 million in real estate. By contrast, the stock exchange holdings of the life fund were continuously pumped up by the flow of life profits, and rose from £7.0 million in 1922 to £16.2 million in 1938. The divergent fortunes of the insurance sectors in these years reversed the relative standing of the two funds. Moreover, the life stake in the stock exchange was balanced by a counterweight in mortgages and loans which was worth £5.1 million in 1930 and hovered just below £4 million in 1938. So, one section of the Phoenix's assets was roughly stable in size, and was not substantially protected by Ryan's reassuring favourites. The other section more than doubled in size, and, fittingly for a life portfolio, was substantially hedged. It is significant that the general fund was much more severely tested than the life investments in the aftermath of the Crash and that the general fund was mildly tested in the second market slide of 1937–8, and the life investments hardly at all (see Table 8.39).

Clearly, replenishment with fresh investment was a major advantage for the life holdings, while large size was a benefit both for the general and life funds. Keynes' Provincial by contrast, with no more than about £1.7 million in its investment portfolio in 1938, when the Phoenix general and life funds summed to just under £38 million, faced the penalties of smallness and did not enjoy much leeway.

But the behaviour of the various components of Phoenix's portfolio does not suggest that large size conferred any monopoly of safety. Disaggregation can be achieved for the whole of the Phoenix Group general fund; but the available accounts do not allow this for all the Group life fund. However, they do allow it for the Phoenix *Company* life fund, which represented the great majority – about 73% in 1935 – of the Group life assets.[266]

[266] In other words, the Phoenix 'Red' Life Account Books specify the investments of the core company by exact type, but do not provide such detail for the life investments of subsidiaries.

Table 8.39. *Phoenix Group: main sectors of stock exchange securities: balance and market values (£ million and market-to-balance ratios), 1929–39*

	British government			Indian and Colonial government			Foreign government			Debentures			Preference shares			Ordinary shares		
	Bal	Mkt	Ratio	Bal	Mkt	Ratio	Bal	Mkt	Ratio	Bal	Mkt	Ratio	Bal	Mkt	Ratio	Bal	Mkt	Ratio
(a) General Fund																		
1929	2.18	2.19	100	1.05	1.05	100	1.58	1.60	101	6.35	6.38	100	0.37	0.38	103	0.21	0.32	152
1930	2.25	2.29	102	0.98	1.00	102	1.21	1.22	101	6.37	6.45	101	0.28	0.30	107	0.21	0.31	148
1931	2.31	2.03	88	1.02	0.87	85	1.22	1.04	85	5.99	5.14	86	0.28	0.24	86	0.22	0.20	91
1932	2.11	2.39	113	0.96	1.00	104	1.10	1.04	95	6.24	5.00	80	0.27	0.25	93	0.17	0.19	118
1933	2.12	2.39	113	1.02	1.06	104	1.12	0.98	88	6.02	5.23	87	0.27	0.26	96	0.19	0.19	100
1934	2.08	2.39	115	0.98	1.09	111	1.25	1.24	99	5.57	5.41	97	0.26	0.30	115	0.20	0.23	119
1935	1.65	1.86	113	1.02	1.11	109	1.30	1.34	103	5.83	5.57	99	0.54	0.55	102	0.30	0.43	143
1936	1.72	1.87	109	1.04	1.14	110	2.69	2.78	103	4.61	4.86	105	0.84	0.89	106	0.42	0.46	110
1937	1.78	1.88	106	0.97	1.04	107	3.25	3.24	100	4.40	4.22	96	0.88	0.88	100	0.43	0.43	100
1938	1.84	1.87	102	1.01	1.07	106	4.14	4.20	101	4.20	3.86	92	0.82	0.79	96	0.47	0.47	100
(b) Company Life Investments																		
1929	1.51	1.57	104	0.85	0.90	106	0.42	0.45	107	1.84	1.94	105	0.68	0.72	106	0.07	0.13	186
1931	0.74	0.71	96	0.88	0.86	98	0.41	0.40	98	2.68	2.60	97	0.83	0.81	98	0.09	0.09	100
1932	1.18	1.23	104	0.96	1.12	117	0.38	0.44	116	2.68	3.08	115	0.85	0.96	113	0.09	0.12	133
1933	1.37	1.45	106	0.98	1.12	114	0.40	0.46	115	2.77	3.19	115	0.89	1.14	128	0.05	0.10	200
1934	1.72	1.89	110	0.92	1.12	122	0.32	0.37	116	2.90	3.55	122	1.09	1.41	129	0.05	0.11	220
1936	2.59	2.61	101	0.91	1.09	120	0.27	0.31	115	3.07	3.71	121	1.34	1.71	128	0.27	0.35	130
1937	2.91	2.97	102	0.83	0.97	117	0.26	0.29	112	3.20	3.64	114	1.47	1.77	120	0.35	0.38	109
1938	3.25	3.20	98	0.79	0.90	114	0.21	0.24	114	3.38	3.66	108	1.48	1.64	111	0.39	0.41	105
1939	3.04	3.01	99	0.80	0.89	111	0.10	0.10	100	3.52	3.50	99	1.51	1.54	102	0.37	0.37	100

Source: (a) Phoenix Blue Account Books. (b) Phoenix Red Account Books.

Analysis of the two portfolios by sector reveals a complex story. The holding of ordinary shares in the Group's general fund, although a tiny percentage of the complete portfolio, was actually many times larger in value than the size of the funds that Keynes was able to devote to equities at the Provincial.[267] These Phoenix ordinary shares did take a hammering in 1931, with market values nearly 10% below book values. But their market-to-book ratio kept up well in 1929–30 and 1934–6, and did not slip below 100 in 1937–8. The Phoenix Assurance life portfolio had only very small amounts in ordinary shares.[268] These suffered only slightly in 1931 and recovered their market-to-book ratio in 1932; and again they took comparatively little punishment in 1937–8 (see Table 8.40). These patterns in market-to-book experience were closer to those of the biggest insurance consumer of equities, the Prudential, than to those of the two 'Keynesian' companies. Indeed, before 1936, they were a good deal better than any of these.

More to the point, the general fund's big stake in debentures and preference shares, in which, like Keynes, it had made initiatives far beyond the industrial standard, *also* took a hammering, and for the much longer period 1931–5; and here the market-to-book ratios of these important holdings did slip again in 1937–8. The Provincial had 43.4% of its portfolio in debentures and preference shares by 1930, and by the end of the 1930s some 37.5%, as against 11.5% and 28.4% in ordinary shares. The Phoenix general fund had over 40% of its portfolio in debentures and preference shares in 1930 and 1938. The Phoenix Assurance life holdings were less heavily committed to debentures and preference shares than the general fund; but still far more heavily than the industrial standard. The life fund had 27.9% of its portfolio in debentures and preference shares in 1930 and 29.9% in 1935. The industrial standard was 22.4% in 1930 and 24.3% in 1935. However, these larger-than-average holdings proved more resistant to recession than the even larger-than-average holdings of the general funds. For the debenture and preference stake of the life portfolio took a bad knock in 1931, when its market value fell nearly 3% below book value, but it recovered strongly in 1932, and showed little sign of weakness in 1937–8.

The other main components of the two portfolios moved in a mostly helpful and mostly parallel way. Both the general fund and the life investments experienced downswings in the market values of their British gilts in 1931 but showed good recovery thereafter. The general fund ran

[267] Market values of £320,000 against £41,000 in 1929; £430,000 against £262,000 in 1935 (see Westall, *Provincial Insurance Company*, p. 417).

[268] Market values of £90,000 in 1931, £410,000 by 1938.

Table 8.40. *Ordinary shares: market-to-book value ratios of Phoenix, Prudential and Provincial, 1929–38*

	Phoenix general fund	Phoenix life fund	Prudential	Provincial
1929	152	–	119	110
1930	148	–	98	89
1931	91	100	78	73
1932	118	133	93	89
1933	100	200	115	115
1934	119	220	131	130
1935	143	–	141	142
1936	110	130	151	160
1937	100	109	–	119
1938	100	105	–	–

Sources: Phoenix Red and Blue Account Books; Westall, *Provincial Insurance Company* p. 416.

down its holdings of UK government securities, especially after 1935, while the life portfolio, in a clear balancing operation, ran them up, especially after 1935. The reduced holdings of UK gilts in the general fund did not show much sign of erosion in 1937–8, but the enhanced holdings of gilts in the life portfolio did see its market price slip below book by about 2%.

In Indian and Colonial gilts, both portfolios displayed severe falls in the market-to-book ratios in 1931 but swift recovery in 1932. These assets showed a useful buoyancy throughout the 1930s. In foreign government stock, the familiar downturn in 1931 is present in both portfolios. But the foreign gilts of the general fund stayed low for the extended period 1931–4, while the much smaller holdings among the life investments – about one-third of the size – again did better, recovering immediately after 1931.

Even without taking into account the general fund's £1.5 million worth of property or the life portfolio's £4–5 million worth of mortgages, there was a muscular spread and a powerful resilience within these investment results.

The Phoenix version of the active investment policy achieved two further initiatives in the final years of peace. They were conducted against a background first of declining yields, then of increasingly jittery markets. In 1935, Chairman Walters admitted that Phoenix could have averted the descent in interest earnings by widening the selection of investments, but observed that the Board had refrained in the interests of safety. By the late 1930s, in any event, the directors had realised that there were compensations in the market depreciation that prevailed by this time: yields at least were on the rise.

However, the main movement of the late 1930s involved the reconsolidation of American investments. Formerly, these were heavily concentrated in railway bonds, but the US railroads experienced some of the bumpiest stock-market rides of the decade. In 1937 Phoenix sold as many as possible, reinvesting the proceeds mainly in US government and public utility stocks. This was done in the nick of time, as the rail bonds that Phoenix had owned lost a further £0.3 million in value in the first half of 1938, as the American market continued to slide. The receipts from the sale bought over £800,000 worth of UK and foreign gilts. The effects are clearly visible in the entries for 1938 in Table 8.39. The reallocation was successful. Stock markets continued to fall in 1937 and 1938, but the investment and contingency reserve did not need to be tapped, since most Phoenix market values held firm well above the book level (see Table 8.39).

Inevitably, the Chairman's Annual Report of 1940 contained little financial cheer. The final investment act of peacetime had been to double the company's holdings in cash to nearly £2 million, because, as he said with commendable understatement, the economic consequences of Mr Hitler were that 'markets at present are to some extent artificial'.[269]

Markets in the interwar years were never easy. The experience of the Phoenix and the other insurance offices was surely that there were many ways to get bitten. The tiger of ordinary shares was not the only predator at large. The advent of the modern era of active investment policy by large-scale institutions did not strike a lucky moment in financial history. There was little choice in this. The growth of composite insurance offices brought swelling investment portfolios. High life profits in the 1920s and 1930s fattened them further. These portfolios needed diversification. In a period of global insurance business, they needed international spread. In a period of erratic markets, they needed definite management and periodic reconsolidation.

Within this context, the pioneering work of J. M. Keynes at the Provincial appears to have had not one but three peculiarities. Certainly, he committed an unusual proportion (an average 20% over the years 1931–8) of a rather small portfolio to ordinary shares. But he devoted an even

[269] Chairman's Annual Report, 29 May 1940.

larger share (37.5% average, 1931–8) to debenture and preference shares, and the experience of the Phoenix general fund 1931–5 shows that such holdings were not safe from a savaging.[270] Thirdly, as his own colleagues warily observed, he made – British gilts apart – almost no provision for hedging. Nevertheless, Keynes achieved striking capital growth, and, when he was well, remarkable predictive accuracy. He applied a high-risk strategy to modest resources, and, despite spills, pulled it off.

Phoenix's much more generous resources allowed a lower-risk – rather than inactive or conservative – policy. The office bought several investments – particularly debentures and foreign and colonial gilts – much more energetically than its competitors. The divergent performances of the general fund and the life investments – with the latter containing much more recently selected assets – testified to the importance of selection and management in difficult times. Good hedges were built by the handling of investment book values, and the stake in mortgages and property. The Phoenix kept its contact with the tiger to a minimum. But the market-to-book ratio even of Phoenix ordinary shares, which dipped below 100 only in 1931 (see Table 8.40) does not suggest that equities always consumed the hand that bought them.

Much of this could be portrayed as a book performance, rather than a market performance, but that was perhaps an appropriate outcome for a large office of established wealth, bent on the objective of active *defence.* The Phoenix and the maestro had different versions of an active investment policy, each suited to the needs of very different portfolios and very different human resources.

12. DIRECTION IN THE INTERWAR YEARS

All Ryan's men

A list of Phoenix directors in 1916 gives nineteen names covering five broad categories of professions and backgrounds. There are two fairly evenly balanced contingents, one of lawyers – reflecting the interest shown by the company in solicitors during the 1900s – and another of commercial men; and beyond them, a couple of peers for luminosity, and a pair of old-style, non-specialised gentlemen.

The social tone did not depend on Lord George Hamilton and Dillon

[270] Calculated from Westall, *Provincial Insurance Company*, Table 15.6, p. 365. The share of debentures and preference shares exceeded even the portion of the Provincial portfolio committed to British government stock. This averaged 33.7% for 1931–8.

Table 8.41. *Phoenix Assurance: directors' main professions, 1916*

Lawyers	Commerce, industry, etc.[a]	Armed services[a]	Peers	Gentlemen
Fladgate Hawes Portman Treherne Tryon Walters	Bird (M) Hodgson (B) Lescher (M) Malcolm (B) Robertson (S) Royden (S) Sorley (I) White Todd (B/R)	Pleydell-Bouverie (Ind)	Hamilton Dillon	Bovill Ponsonby

Notes: [a] M = merchant; B = banker; S = shipping interest; I = insurance; R = railway interest; Ind = industry.

alone: Pleydell-Bouverie, Ponsonby and Portman all carried the prefix 'Honourable' and Robertson, Royden and White Todd were all knights.[271] James Sorley was the former general manager of the Pelican.

However, the lack of political connection at this time is striking in comparison with what had gone before and what was to be the case by 1930. Of the names listed for 1916 only one – Royden, elected MP for Bootle in 1919 – sat in the House within any short period before or after 1916.

Like many other aspects of company life, this comfortable and familiar balance – the lack of political representation apart – was much upset by the mergers and acquisitions of the early 1920s. For these brought new entrants to the Board. By late 1920, it numbered twenty-two, including five directors from Norwich Union Fire: George Hustler Tuck (Phoenix 1920) and J. H. F. Walter (Phoenix 1920–5) who were chairman and deputy chairman of NUF respectively, Edward Gurney Buxton (Phoenix 1920–9), Sir George Chamberlin (Phoenix 1920–5) and the 'great Insurance expert', John Large (Phoenix 1920–1). By 1925, it numbered eighteen, including one representative from London Guarantee, A. W. Tait (Phoenix 1922–5). However, before long, many of these newcomers were to be cleared out by a combination of mortality and scandal.

The era of acquisitions required a new balance of power within the Board. When in 1920, Lord George Hamilton (Phoenix 1908–26) was presented with a silver replica of the Phoenix Ballot Box, to mark the

[271] Fladgate would become one in 1932.

Plate 8.13 Sir Gerald and Lady Ryan in fancy dress, 1920.

completion of his dozen years as chairman, it was a powerfully symbolic end to an era. For the aristocratic public servant was replaced by the complete insurance professional, Gerald Ryan (Phoenix 1920–37). The gentlemanly if industrious Bristow Bovill (Phoenix 1882–1944) resigned as deputy chairman, making way for Hamilton, ever the faithful Phoenix man, to step down into this position. Balancing him was to be another deputy chairman, drawn from the NUF party. In the first instance, this was Hustler Tuck. Ryan's place as general manager was taken by NUF's best man, Ralph Sketch, at a salary of £7,000 per year, income tax paid, and with an ex-officio seat on the board.

In order to reduce the load of business falling upon such a large group, it was decided in 1921 that the full Board should meet fortnightly, and that a Chairman's Committee should gather in the alternate week. This was to consist of Ryan, the two deputy chairmen and three other Board members – the extraordinarily long-serving Bovill, the veteran solicitor Hawes (Phoenix 1908–24) and the merchant banker and railway director, Sir Joseph White Todd (Phoenix 1913–26).[272]

[272] Phoenix Directors' Minutes 33, p. 249; 20 April 1921.

However, the advent of London Guarantee and its accident business meant that even this division of labour would not serve. After this second acquisition, the Board had to be divided into two teams of ten, one to be called the Underwriting Committee, the other the Joint Finance Committee. The first was to consist of four sections: a life section chaired by Hamilton, a fire section under Bovill, a marine section under Sir Thomas Royden (Phoenix 1916–50),[273] and, apparently suitably, an accident section under A. W. Tait. This Committee would meet weekly, dealing with fire and life matters in one week, accident and marine in the next. The Joint Finance Committee would deal with all matters of investment and interest earnings. The brief for these committees was daunting. But there is some reassurance to be had from the time-tabling. The Underwriting Committee met on Wednesdays at 12.45 pm in the boardroom. It was replaced by the Joint Finance Committee at 1.15 p.m. It too stayed no longer than half an hour.[274]

Very sensibly in 1921, faced with this proliferation of personnel, the Board had decided to fill no more vacancies until its size had been reduced to sixteen.[275] But they clearly did not expect the barrage of mortality which then ensued. Two names on the 1916 list, Sir Helenus Robertson and Sir Thomas Bland Royden, had deprived Phoenix of much maritime expertise by dying within six months of one another in 1917. But the years 1921–4 saw off no fewer than eight of those on the 1916 roll-call. The Hon. Edwin Portman died at a ripe age, and after more than forty years as a director, in April 1921. Walter Bird, the cheery merchant who in 1916, had given up supervising the directors' lunch, owing to encroaching age, died in July 1921, from 'creeping palsy', after thirty-seven years on the Board. Kirkman Hodgson, Joseph Lescher and Travers Hawes all expired in 1923 and 1924 after thirty-one, twenty-six and twenty-three years respectively. Lescher indeed was one of a trio (the others were the banker William Malcolm and the lawyer George Treherne) who died in January and February 1923, all of them active men, and each present at a board meeting within a fortnight of his death. The toll was completed by the former Pelican general manager, James Sorley, who was suddenly felled in February 1924 by an illness contracted abroad.[276]

[273] It was Sir Thomas Bland Royden who died in 1917. Sir Thomas (later Lord) Royden, also of the Union Marine connection, was elected to maintain maritime expertise on the Phoenix Board in 1916, and served until 1950.

[274] Report of Special Committee on the Board and Committees, 9 August 1922.

[275] Directors' Minutes 33, p. 321, 16 November 1921.

[276] Sorley was general manager and actuary of Pelican, 1895–1903, and became, at the age of fifty, a Pelican director in 1903.

However, the most extraordinary morbidity was concentrated among the delegates from NUF. No sooner were the men of Norwich required to breathe the insurance atmosphere of London than they dropped like flies. Three out of five did not survive to see full control of NUF return to its East Anglian base. Hustler Tuck died in 1920, just months after becoming a deputy chairman of the Phoenix and had to be replaced by the former banker, Edward Gurney Buxton. John Large, the general manager of NUF between 1911 and 1919, survived less than two years of excitement from the metropolitan alliance, and J. H. F. Walter soldiered through to 1925, only to succumb at the age of eighty, just days after the sale was finalised, to acute appendicitis.[277] Of the original contingent from Norwich, only Buxton and Chamberlin endured beyond 1925, and, after the sale of NUF, only Buxton, despite strong East Anglian affections – he was mayor of Norwich in 1907–8 and High Sheriff of Norfolk in 1922 – stayed loyal to, and resident with, the Phoenix.[278]

It is striking that many of these retirements through death were falling upon very old men. Portman was ninety-one in 1921, Treherne eighty-five, Malcolm eighty-three, and Lescher eighty in 1923, and the *average* age of retirement through death between 1920 and 1925 was eighty. It should come as no surprise therefore that the average age of the entire Board in 1920 was very high, at 69.3 years, with twelve members over seventy, and only three at fifty-five or below.

A loss in 1925 which was not simply the result of time passing was the resignation of A. W. Tait over the Magadi Soda affair.[279] The trustees for the debenture holders of the Magadi Soda Co., of which Tait was one, were effectively charged with insider trading in the debentures to the prejudice of those whose interests they were supposed to protect. That Tait, LGA's prime mover in the Phoenix acquisition of 1922, should stand so charged inevitably reflects back a sinister light upon that transaction. But Phoenix did not act vengefully in respect of Tait. A suggestion from one of Tait's colleagues on another Board that a committee should be formed of delegates from all the companies in which Tait had held directorships – in an attempt presumably to track his footsteps through some two dozen boardrooms – was rejected by those at the Phoenix table and Tait's resignation was accepted with regret.[280]

[277] The sale of NUF was completed on 15 July; Walter died on 8 August.
[278] Buxton was educated at Harrow and Trinity, Cambridge, went into the family bank and, after its absorption by Barclays, ended up as a director of the larger concern. He was director also of Norwich Waterworks, the Norfolk Agricultural Hall Co., the LNER and Callender's Cable Co. He was advised to stay with Phoenix by the chairman of Barclays.
[279] See Chapter 7, Section 2.
[280] Directors' Minutes, 34, pp. 359, 370, 11 March and 1 April 1925.

Tait, a partner in the accountancy firm of Sir George Touche & Co., was a famous company doctor who 'excelled in the creative task of resuscitating commercial enterprises'.[281] The problem was whether in the case of the Magadi Soda Co. he was a touch too creative. Not all his fellow directors on other boards thought so. Some companies pressed him to stay.[282] In 1930 he was still chairman of the British Trusts Association and Cedar Investments, the two companies at the heart of the debenture-purchasing scandal, and also of six other ventures, several in electrical engineering, and including Ferranti Ltd. Moreover, he had returned to the chairmanship of the British Aluminium Co., where he was revered as the saviour of the enterprise over his fifteen years in the chair, but whence he had resigned in 1925.[283] Subsequently, after a tricky share issue had been negotiated, he was invited back.[284] Described by his obituarist as 'one of the shrewdest and sanest minds in the City', Tait had been instrumental in pioneering the London Power Company, alongside the Phoenix director, Francis Fladgate (Phoenix 1910–37).[285] Despite the Magadi case, Tait remained a substantial presence in corporate circles. However, after a serious illness in 1928, he had to reduce many of his business commitments, and he died in 1930 at the early age of fifty-five. Something, it seems, had taken a toll.

There are some odd features to the episode and perhaps some extenuating ones. Tait was not a party to the Magadi case; so he could not appeal against Mr Justice Eve's quite extraordinarily savage indictment of his part in 'this sordid history'.[286] He was already ill in 1924. And his own defence was that the debenture-purchasing operation was part of a reconstruction programme for Magadi, which later received 'judicial sanction'.[287] It is interesting that many companies would not accept his resignation, and that he returned to British Aluminium. But, despite the ties through LGA and Fladgate, he did not return to Phoenix.

Gerald Ryan was not unequal to these ravages of time and crime and was ready with replacements for the Board. Characteristically, if uniquely – since the habit seems not to have preceded nor survived him – Ryan kept a book of possible directors, those most likely to assist the Phoenix, the prominent, the successful, the rich and the able. He began this register upon becoming chairman and its dates coincide precisely with his tenure.

As might be expected, Ryan had a beadily functional eye. It was caught

[281] A tribute by his partner, Sir George Touche, on Tait's death, 30 October 1930.
[282] *Daily Mail*, 20 February 1925. [283] *The Times*, obituary, 22 April 1930.
[284] Whatever the company's affection for Tait, it was feared that his connection with the Magadi affair would queer the pitch for this issue.
[285] *The Times*, obituary, 22 April 1930. [286] *The Times*, Law Reports, 13 February 1925.
[287] Annual Report of British Aluminium Co., 27 March 1925.

by those who already had connections, preferably directorships, in banks (most often Lloyds or Barclays), in railways (frequently South American), and in manufacturing industry (in several cases, metals or electrical engineering). High government office also carried weight. The most eminent names to have been proposed for the Board but to have got away were: Reginald McKenna, formerly Liberal First Lord of the Admiralty, Home Secretary and Chancellor of the Exchequer, who was too busy being chairman of the London, City and Midland Bank; Viscount Grey of Falloden, Foreign Secretary 1905–16, who declined the offer but diplomatically bought some Phoenix shares; Earl Beatty who, with a sea-dog's nose for bad weather, distrusted the economic outlook of 1927; Sir Hallewell Rogers, Chairman of Daimler and BSA; Samuel Courtauld; Dudley Docker; and Sir Otto Niemeyer, who replied deadpan that the Bank of England would not permit him to join a private company. Among those who declined were directors of shipping lines and electricity supply companies, members of Lloyds and the Baltic Exchange, former presidents of the Board of Trade, secretaries of the Treasury and comptrollers of the Bank. It was clear that Ryan believed Phoenix to be worthy of the greatest and the best.

Those who were approached by Ryan and accepted his invitation to join the Board were also a distinguished team. Apart from the two future chairmen, Sir Clarendon Hyde, (Phoenix 1923–34) and John Pybus (Phoenix 1927–35), soon to be Minister of Transport, there were eleven further Board appointments which were made or prepared during Ryan's decade. Two of these, the brewer Ernest de Montesquieu Lacon (Phoenix 1921–5), chairman of Lacons of Great Yarmouth, and Lt. Col. E. R. Kerrison (Phoenix 1921–5) of Burgh Hall, Aylsham, and a director of the Grand Hotel, Sheringham, were future East Anglian replacements for the defunct men of Norwich.[288] One further was Brigadier General John Tipson Wigan, brought in to replace Portman, in 1921 (Phoenix 1921–52).[289]

Educated at Rugby and scion of a third-generation family firm of hop merchants, John Wigan chose a military career in the period before the Boer War. When war came, he was severely injured while serving with the 13th Hussars in South Africa, the first of many wounds which his profession was to inflict upon him. He returned to a partnership in the family firm in 1909, but was recalled to the colours in 1914. He proved a capable battlefield soldier, like Pleydell-Bouverie, and rose to command the Berkshire Yeomanry, but, like his colleague Major the Hon. J. J. Astor, who

[288] Lacon had become a director of NUF in 1902, Kerrison in 1905.
[289] Wigan was also nominated a director of NUF in 1921.

Plate 8.14 General Wigan unveils the Hop Exchange War Memorial, 1922.

joined the Board in 1932, he suffered much damage in the process. During the First World War, Wigan was wounded three more times, at Gallipoli, in Palestine, and, finally, while leading his cavalry brigade in the attack upon Jerusalem. The Phoenix Board, in the 1920s and 1930s, bore its share of the scars of war, though perhaps General Wigan perhaps carried more than his due ration of them.

However, Wigan did not come to Phoenix by dint of his war service. In 1911 he had married the grand-daughter of Sir Joseph White Todd, and it was to this energetic old merchant that he owed his introduction. Wigan had some business, and developed some political, connections – he was Unionist MP for Abingdon 1918–21 – but, though Ryan liked him, and invited him to Hintlesham for the shooting, he was not characteristic of the kind of influence Sir Gerald cultivated. Jack Wigan, who sat on the Phoenix Board for some thirty years and ended as senior director, was representative of an older sort of family connection.

More usually in Ryan's sights were the financiers, the manufacturers and the big public figures. At first glance, he liked peers of the realm. There were only two on the Board of 1920 (Hamilton and Dillon), reinforced by two sons of peers (Portman, Pleydell-Bouverie), and by three knights (White Todd, Royden and Ryan himself). And this was among a Board of twenty-two. By 1930, out of a Board of seventeen members, there were no fewer than four peers (Dillon, Rochdale, Ebbisham, Bessborough), with one son of a peer (Pleydell-Bouverie), and another waiting in the wings (Astor), and assisted by six knights (Clarendon Hyde, Coupar Barrie, Fladgate, Pybus, Royden and Ryan).

On the face of it, there was a social revolution at the Phoenix between 1920 and 1930. But of the peers only Dillon and Bessborough carried ancient titles. Rochdale and Ebbisham were men of industry and commerce who used the fortunes generated by family firms to launch careers in politics and public service. As indeed did Coupar Barrie who became Lord Abertay in 1940. Similarly, one peer's son, Pleydell-Bouverie had strong, if unconventional, industrial associations of his own, and the other, John Jacob Astor, was to make himself a famed newspaper proprietor and win his own title on the strength of it. Effectively, all the knights, other than the insurance one, had industrial backgrounds, in shipping, power generation, construction and electrical engineering.

Ryan, then, had not simply suffered a rush of aristocracy to the head. The noble titles denoted distinction less by birth than by inherited commercial wealth, reinforced by independently displayed ability in other fields. There were other patterns within the Board of 1930. The loops between these men were tighter, the networks clearer than with their predecessors of the pre-1914 Boards. Thus Ryan had a particular preference for directors with a financial background. There were two professional bankers among the appointments of the 1920s (Bell, Grant). But two others were directors of banks (Buxton, Rochdale), and, in the period 1921–40, of the eight directors who sat on the boards of banks, five came from a single bank (Barclays), including its chairman.[290]

Other loops were formed by military service (predictably); Cambridge, indeed a single Cambridge college; cricket; and a London club. Pleydell-Bouverie, Wigan, Rochdale, Bessborough and Astor had similar wartime careers, and ended separated by no more than a rank or two. No fewer than four of the appointees of the 1920s were graduates of Trinity College, Cambridge (Buxton, Morrison, Rochdale, Bessborough), while no other Cambridge college was represented on the Board in this period. Three of the directors of the 1920s had unusually active cricketing careers (Buxton, Ebbisham, Rochdale). And, extraordinarily, four of the appointees of the 1920s, and another four in the 1930s, shared a single

[290] The five were: Buxton, Grant, Astor, Caulcutt, Evans-Bevan. The chairman, Sir John Caulcutt, was elected to the Phoenix Board in 1936.

London club (the Carlton).[291] Lord Ebbisham even kept a venerable tradition going by being elected a Fellow of the Society of Antiquaries.

Within this set of preferences, Ryan chose first to emphasise the most functional. In 1924, he was looking for banking expertise, and found it in the shape of Henry Bell (Phoenix 1924–35), general manager of Lloyds 1913–23, and the American head of the merchant bank of Higginson & Co., Robert Grant (Phoenix 1924–37).[292] Bell was given a directorship in Lloyds as a retirement present in 1916 and Grant held one of the Barclays seats that so attracted Phoenix. The two bankers could not have been more different. Bell was educated at the Liverpool Institution and went straight into the Liverpool private bank of Leyland and Bullins as a clerk. He became an expert in the cotton futures market in Liverpool and moved to the Liverpool Union Bank in 1880 – an important year for him since he was also capped for England at rugby in this season – where he was subsequently absorbed, along with the bank, by Lloyds. The wealthy Bostonian, Grant, came to the London merchant house in 1906, directly after graduating from Harvard, and spent some eighteen years in British business circles, amassing directorships not only in Barclays, but some fourteen other ventures, mostly metals and colliery concerns, but including such major ventures as Dorman Long, Ebbw Vale Steel, English Electric and the Times Publishing Co.[293]

Bell was the complete technician who worked himself up from apprentice to general manager of one of Britain's biggest deposit banks.[294] His array of directorships was more focused: apart from his Lloyds seat, they consisted of the National Provincial Foreign Bank, the Yorkshire Penny Bank, and the Individualist Bookshop. Grant was the dashing all-rounder, fond of fast cars and greyhound racing. He was still barely forty when elected to the Phoenix Board, where he was prized for bringing 'fresh and enterprising views into our counsels'.[295] Yet the two ended up fulfilling similar functions. Bell represented Britain at the postwar financial conferences at Brussels in 1920 and Genoa in 1922 and was a member of the Dawes Plan administration for the German war debt. He brought a formidable expertise in international finance to Phoenix's table. Grant was intended for a parallel role. As Sketch wrote to Lord George Hamilton in October 1924,

[291] In the 1920s: Wigan, Morrison, Rochdale and Ebbisham. In the 1930s: Astor, Greenwood, Dudley and Caulcutt.

[292] These appointments replaced the late Kirkman Hodgson and Travers Hawes.

[293] These last two gave him connections to both Pybus and Astor.

[294] *The Times* and *Morning Post*, obituaries, 21 September 1935.

[295] Chairman's Annual Report, 24 May 1928.

Grant . . . has an intimate knowledge of finance, particularly of American securities, and it is anticipated that his advice on such matters will be of considerable value to us.[296]

Phoenix, of course, had good reason to seek advice on American securities. But they were not to retain it for long. In 1927 Grant decided to return to the USA. He wanted his children educated in both Britain and America. His son had done his stint at Eton; it was time for Harvard.

His resignation, together with the death of Lord George Hamilton in October 1927, 'after a long and patiently endured illness',[297] created a need for a new wave of directors in 1928. This came in the form of three new appointments: Sir Rowland Blades (Phoenix 1928–47), Lord Mayor of London 1926–7 and created Lord Ebbisham in 1928;[298] Hugh Morrison (Phoenix 1928–31), MP for Salisbury, almost continuously from 1918 to 1930, and one of the wealthiest men in England; and the first Lord Rochdale (Phoenix 1928–45), formerly Sir George Kemp, but created baron in 1913.

George Kemp had been at Trinity with Edward Buxton and shared his cricketing tastes. Indeed, this friendship endured and it was Buxton who introduced Kemp to the Phoenix Board. Buxton was secretary of the Norfolk County Cricket Club for many years, but Kemp had played a more active role. As well as managing a second in the Cambridge Classics Tripos, he achieved a double blue – for cricket in 1885, 1886 and 1888, and for tennis in 1886 – and then went on to play county cricket for Lancashire until 1893.[299] No one remained as active, however, as the third member of the Board's cricketing clique, Rowland Blades. As Unionist MP For Epsom, he did much to revive parliamentary cricket, and, on one memorable occasion, took 6 for 61 in a match between the House and the MCC. Still playing at the age of sixty-five, he took his 100th wicket in a match against the Lords ground staff in 1933. Baldwin gave him a silver cricket ball.[300]

Cricket linked two of the appointments of 1928; family businesses and wealth from commerce or manufacture linked all three. As he had looked to the bankers in 1924, Ryan switched emphasis in 1928 towards business wealth allied to prominence in the City or at Westminster. All three of these men were in a sense more powerful versions of Jack Wigan. And one

[296] Sketch to Hamilton, 1 October 1924.
[297] Chairman's Annual Report, 24 May 1928.
[298] This was the old title for Epsom.
[299] Indeed, ironically and sadly for one who had been such an outstanding sportsman when young, Lord Rochdale was severely crippled by arthritis in later life. He bore this with characteristic fortitude for more than fifteen years.
[300] Conservative prime minister, 1923–4, 1924–9 and 1935–7.

Plate 8.15 Lord Rochdale aims low.

of them, George Kemp, was linked to Wigan by military ties. He too fought in the Boer War, rising to the rank of lieutenant colonel, and he too achieved substantial command in the Great War, leading the 6th Battalion, The Lancashire Fusiliers at Gallipoli and in Egypt. No doubt, they exchanged military reminiscences at the Carlton.

However, it is the business and political similarities between Blades, Morrison and Kemp which are the most striking. Rowland Blades was apprenticed into the family firm of Blades, East and Blades, City printers and stationers, and in due time became chairman and managing director. He did not amass much more in the way of explicit business connection, satisfying himself with directorships in the Southern Railway Co., the Kent and Sussex Light Railway and the Telegraph Condenser Co. The launching pad for George Kemp was the similar family enterprise of Kelsall and Kemp, flannel manufacturers of Rochdale, to which he returned after Cambridge. He duly became chairman. But he did go further, since he also became chairman of the Union Bank of Manchester and took another of the seats at Barclays.

Hugh Morrison took off from a family venture of larger scale. Its founder was Hugh's grandfather, James, who left Hampshire to work as a draper in London but ended as a partner in a great warehouse business.

He left £3 million and his son Charles, uncle to Hugh, left nearly £11 million in 1909. Hugh and his brother were beneficiaries under the wills both of their father and of Uncle Charles.[301] Hugh Morrison also graduated from Trinity, in history, in the early 1890s, and then put much of his efforts into agricultural estates in Wiltshire and Scotland. By the 1920s, he owned some 6,000 acres and a good part of Islay. He could have insured property worth more than £300,000, but, quite embarrassingly for Phoenix, he did not believe in insurance. Nor apparently, apart from his insurance directorships, first at LGA from 1893 to 1928, and then at Phoenix from 1928 until his death in 1931, did he believe in collecting boardroom seats. Perhaps, as with insurance, the vast resources of the Morrison Estates Company sufficed for him.

Apart, that is, for the politics. After an active time in the county affairs of Wiltshire – he served as deputy lieutenant and was High Sheriff by 1904 – Morrison entered the House in 1918, at the age of fifty, as the Conservative member for Salisbury, and stayed there, with brief interruptions, almost until his death. A genial, friendly man, he was happiest in parliament when dealing with what he knew most about. Agricultural matters formed the centre of this; and he was reckoned particularly shrewd on stock-breeding.[302]

Both Blades and Kemp also stepped from nineteenth-century business backgrounds into politics. Blades, as Unionist MP for Epsom 1918–28, entered the House at the same time as Morrison and sat alongside him; but Kemp became disillusioned with life at Westminster even before the other two embarked upon it. Kemp was Liberal Unionist MP for South-East Lancashire 1885–1906 and Liberal MP for Manchester North-West 1910–12. He was a politician of some stature, defeating William Joynson-Hicks[303] to take the Manchester seat and holding it, later in 1910, even against the future Tory leader, Andrew Bonar Law.[304] He resigned in 1912 over the vexed issue of Irish Home Rule declaring that he 'loathed

[301] *Daily Express* and *Daily Telegraph*, obituaries, 31 March 1931. By contrast, Hugh's own will was proved in 1931, in a time of much steeper death duties and more complex defences against them, at £1.7 million net. However, Lord Ebbisham managed only £148,862.

[302] *The Times*, 16 March 1931.

[303] Joynson-Hicks had lost North-West Manchester in a landslide to Winston Churchill in 1906, won it when Churchill was posted to President of the Board of Trade in 1908 and lost it again to Kemp in 1910. He later became Home Secretary 1924–9 and confronted the National Strike of 1926.

[304] *The Times*, 26 March 1945. Bonar Law became Conservative leader in 1911, and had the luckless task of opposition to the great Liberal government of 1906–14. The first Tory leader from an industrial background, he was Chancellor of the Exchequer 1916–19 and Prime Minister, 1922–3.

politics ... a source of unmitigated dislike and unhappiness to me'.[305] After the resumption of a demanding military career in the First World War, he returned to his business and his banking. Clearly, he was a man of judgement.

The third backbencher, Sir Rowland Blades probably achieved more influence in the City than at Westminster. This he did through a mixture of charity and faith. He sat on the managing boards of three hospitals,[306] was treasurer of Dr Barnado's, was active on behalf of the Red Cross, and, a deeply religious man, served as churchwarden not only of St Mary Abchurch (for fifty-two years) but also of two other London parishes. His *Times* obituary in 1953 gave him the unusual accolade that 'Church life in the City is poorer for his passing'.[307] He was also a prominent freemason, sat as an alderman for a City ward for nearly thirty years, and did terms as master of two livery companies, the Haberdashers and, suitably for him, the Stationers. His period as Lord Mayor was the culmination of years of assiduous attention to City business. It was almost incidentally that he chaired the Federation of British Industries in 1928–9. When the *City Press* wrote that he had been 'one of the great leaders of life in the City', it almost risked understatement.[308]

This trio, elected to the Phoenix Board in 1928, were all members of the Carlton. Morrison lent lustre by his wealth and his name – if not by his propensity to take out insurance policies – but it seems clear that the more useful to Phoenix were the energetic and courageous Rochdale and the complete City man, Ebbisham, a member of every network that the square mile had the ingenuity to create.

The death in April 1929 of Edward Buxton, the senior deputy chairman, created a need for a substantial appointment. Phoenix tried to fill this, in a rather grand style, by the recruitment of the one genuine aristocrat of the era, the Earl of Bessborough (Phoenix 1930–1). The inference could well be that Phoenix was trying to find a public figure of the stature of Lord George Hamilton. Bessborough was the head of an ancient Cumberland family, and was another Trinity man, graduating in 1903. As Viscount Duncannon, he was briefly Unionist MP for Cheltenham in 1910 and then, more durably, for Dover 1913–20. He succeeded as 9th earl in 1920.

Prior to this he had seen active service briefly at Gallipoli and much staff work for the rest of the war, 'as a close friend and disciple of

[305] *Ibid.*

[306] Including the Middlesex Hospital, of which another Phoenix director of the 1930s, Major the Hon. J. J. Astor, was a leading benefactor.

[307] *The Times*, 27 May 1953.

[308] *City Press*, 25 March 1949.

Plate 8.16 Lord Bessborough.

(General) Sir Henry Wilson'.[309] In the 1920s, he developed, according to *The Times*, 'a marked aptitude for business', but whether this translates more accurately as a distinct appetite for directorships is unclear. Certainly, Bessborough amassed at least sixteen board seats, including the deputy chairmanship of de Beers. A shy man, with a stiff manner and a quick temper, Bessborough does not seem naturally cut out for business. But then he did not seem naturally cut out to be Governor General of Canada, for, as *The Times* obituarist recorded, 'he was almost unknown there'.[310] Yet that in 1931 was the post he was chosen to fill. He had to follow two outstandingly popular predecessors, the Lords Byng and Willingdon; and he did not find it at all easy. The appointment, like that of Pybus, took him away from the Phoenix, in this case, after barely more than a year (January 1930 to March 1931). Unlike Pybus, he did not return. Maybe it was just as well.

This attempt to replace Hamilton having failed, Ryan went for another worthy in the mould of Ebbisham, Morrison and Rochdale. This was Sir

[309] *The Times*, 10 February 1931. Wilson was Chief of the Imperial General Staff 1918–22, and was promoted Field Marshal in 1919.

[310] *Ibid.*, 12 March 1956

Charles Coupar Barrie (Phoenix 1930–40), a lawyer by training but a shipowner by inheritance, profession and commitment. He too hailed from a family business, the shipping firm of Charles Barrie and Sons, owners of the Den fleet of steamers, run out of Dundee. He was knighted for wartime services to the Ministry of Shipping in 1921. He used a real expertise in marine matters to build up a network of twenty-six directorships, which included six shipping-related and seven communications-related ventures, as well as two banks and three manufacturing concerns.[311] His business connections were thus substantially greater than those of the class of '28.

Table 8.42. *Phoenix Assurance: directors' main professions, 1930*

Lawyers[a]	Commerce, industry, etc.[a]	Armed services[a]	Peers[a]	Gentlemen
Tryon Fladgate (Ind) Walters	Morrison (W,P) Pybus (Ind,P) Coupar Barrie (S,P)	Pleydell-Bouverie (Ind)	Dillon Rochdale (Ind,B)	Bovill
	Clarendon Hyde (Ind.) Royden (S,P) Bell (B)	Wigan	Ebbisham (Ind) Bessborough	

Note: [a] Ind = industry; W = warehousing; S = shipping; B = Banking; P = MP.

But Coupar Barrie too stepped from the family business into politics. He entered parliament in 1918 and was returned unopposed for Banffshire in 1918, 1922 and 1923; he then served as Liberal-National member for Southampton 1931–40, giving up his seat in 1940 to create a parliamentary opening for Sir John Reith, the Minister for Information. It was after this that he was created Lord Abertay, but died shortly after. He was among the longest serving parliamentarians on the interwar Phoenix Board and the one whose period in the House coincided most closely with his time in the boardroom. Much of his comment as an MP was concerned with the parlous condition of the shipping industry; he was a particular sponsor of a 'new-for-old' scheme, aiming to scrap three aged vessels in order to make room for every new one.[312] He was already thinking of retiring in 1940, in order to spend more time with his business, when the government discovered its need for a seat to accommodate

[311] The banks were the National Bank of Scotland and the Mercantile Bank of India.
[312] *Financial Times*, 20 November 1933.

Reith. Sadly, this energetic and informed technician died, at the age of sixty-five, before he could fùfil this plan.

Coupar Barrie was the last appointment under Ryan's chairmanship; and he clearly fits into a pattern (see Table 8.42).

The retreat of the lawyers and the advance of the aristocrats is clear here. The military connection has strengthened but the political connection has advanced strikingly on the position of 1916. Shipping has maintained an important place but perhaps most notable of all is the spread of industrial affiliation across four of the main categories of professon.

The post-Ryan Board: the advance of commerce

In reality the early 1930s saw a tapering end to the Ryan era. The great man gave his final Annual Report as chairman in June 1931, but he remained on the Board until his death in 1937. However, Ryan was far from well at the turn of the decade. He had needed sick leave in 1926, succumbed to the influenza epidemic of 1929, then suffered a leg injury which laid him up for two more months in 1929. At the end of both 1929 and 1930, he needed to take three months' leave of absence and by early 1931 he was seriously ill. It was at this time that the Board decided to have his portrait painted, by Sir William Llewellyn RA, one suspects in a spirit of insurance, in all senses.[313] But Ryan's influence – and occasional presence – continued into the 1930s.

In 1932 the quest for a latter-day equivalent of Lord George Hamilton was resumed. Ryan had announced the death of Morrison in his last speech, and his own failing strength made the reinforcement of the Board imperative. Hence the presentation of two powerful appointments by Clarendon Hyde in his first Annual Report in June 1932: Lord Greenwood (Phoenix 1932–48) and Major the Hon. J. J. Astor (Phoenix 1932–62). At first sight, Greenwood perhaps looked most suited to fill Hamilton's shoes, but in the event Astor turned out to fit them better.

Greenwood was a lawyer and soldier turned politician who achieved Cabinet rank as Chief Secretary for Ireland in the troubles of 1920–22. Educated in Canada, he became one of the first officers in the King's Colonial Yeomanry and took a late BA, at the age of twenty-five, at the University of Toronto. Hamar Greenwood moved to England to seek his fortune, was called to the Bar in 1906 and took silk in 1919. However, he made relatively little mark as a lawyer, more as a politician and soldier. He was in the Commons by 1906 as Liberal member for York and served as

[313] It was hung in the Royal Academy in 1932 (see colour section, this volume).

Plate 8.17 Sir Charles Coupar Barrie.

parliamentary secretary to Churchill at the Colonial Office and Board of Trade between 1906 and 1910. Returned as member for Sunderland in 1910, he retained that constituency until 1922 and then sat for East Walthamstow 1924–9. Between times, he returned to soldiering in the Great War, raising and commanding the 10th Battalion, The South Wales Borderers as lieutenant colonel. He served with the British Expeditionary Force in 1915-16 and then at the War Office. His military initiative earned him a baronetcy in 1915.[314]

Greenwood returned to active politics as Under-Secretary of State at the Home Office in 1919 and achieved his highest political office as the last Chief Secretary of Ireland in 1920. However, his rather unusual

[314] *City Press*, 13 November 1935.

mixture of political and military experience, stretching back over three decades, proved a dubious qualification for the Irish post. For Greenwood was deeply involved in the attempt to establish British authority by force through the agency of the 'black and tans', the rag-tag force of irregulars which provoked, but did not check, the IRA.[315] Faced with the failure of strong-arm tactics, Prime Minister Lloyd George turned towards the negotiations which would lead to the creation of the Republic of Ireland in 1922; and by-passed Greenwood in the process. In 1922, when Lloyd George fell, Greenwood resigned. After a spell on the back benches, he was raised to the peerage as first Baron Greenwood in 1929.

Greenwood displayed many of the same patterns as the Ryan appointees of the 1920s. He was another of the Phoenix colonels. Like his immediate colleague, Astor, and so many others, he was a member of the Carlton. Of the six directorships he held upon joining Phoenix, three had to do with the electric power industry. But Greenwood had something that his immediate predecessors lacked: he had held really high public office. This created an apparent parallel with Hamilton. But even cabinet ministers must be marked for performance. Hamilton had held several high offices, Greenwood only one. And Hamilton had been a conspicuous success in most of them, particularly as First Lord of the Admiralty. Greenwood, by contrast, had come to prominence at one of the most tragic moments in modern British history. And his own judgement had scarcely helped matters along.

Greenwood was heavily built and strongly featured, a bulky, confident and forthright individual. During the 1930s, he was much in demand as a leader of boardrooms. Before he came to Phoenix, he was chairman of the Aerated Bread Co. and W. Hill and Sons; by the mid-1930s, he had added Lewis Berger and Sons and the important steel concern of Dorman Long. Upon that followed chairmanship of the Management Committee of the London Iron and Steel Exchange, and, in 1935, chairmanship of Montagu Burton & Co., multiple tailors.[316] But, for Phoenix, Greenwood apparently did not supply the qualities that would have put him on a par with Hamilton as an even-handed, discreet and perceptive servant of the company.[317]

[315] The label 'black and tan' followed from the mixture of police and military uniform which they wore. The mixture is itself an oblique comment on the conditioning influences in Greenwood's life.

[316] *The Sunday Times*, 14 March 1935. Burton's was worth £7.7 million in equity in 1935.

[317] Perhaps he made up for this, when in 1945, Greenwood, a teetotaller, was able to supply a thirsty and war-weary Board with a crate of whisky (Greenwood to Secretary, 17 November 1945).

More akin to Hamilton was John Jacob Astor.[318] He was a descendant of a German immigrant to the USA in the 1780s who founded the fortunes of this considerable dynasty by dealing in furs with the Indians and in land with almost everyone else. J. J. Astor's father moved to England, became the first Viscount Astor of Hever in 1917, and left a fortune of £16 million in 1919.[319] However, this was in trust for the grandchildren, a matter that was to cause heartache for the family. J. J. Astor received a handsome income from the interest (though he gave a good deal away), but did not have access to the huge capital. Nor, under normal circumstances would he have achieved a peerage, since he was the second son and his elder brother, who took the title, produced a sufficiency of male heirs. When J. J. became Lord Astor of Hever also, it was on his own account: in 1956 he was created first Baron Astor for remarkable services to country, charity and the press.

For J. J. Astor was very much a working aristocrat. He started adult life in military work. After Eton and New College, Oxford, he joined the Life Guards and served as *aide-de-camp* to Lord Hardinge, the viceroy of India from 1911 to 1914. In the Great War, he was one of the Old Contemptibles, fighting from the beginning, and lasting, in his case, to the end, or very nearly. Astor had a good war, if by that is meant one that is widely admired by others and is bravely survived, if only just. Characteristically refusing staff jobs throughout, he retrained as a gunner and was wounded in fourteen places when the howitzers of his 520th Household Siege Battery were hit by German shells in September 1918, scarcely two months before the end of the war. He lost a leg as result of these wounds. A man of great courage, integrity, courtesy, and strength of character, Astor was not a lucky one: throughout his life, his was not a case of virtue rewarded.[320]

[318] Who proved it by becoming deputy chairman 1941–52 and Chairman 1952–8.

[319] Hever Castle in Kent, to which Astor was much attached had once been owned by Ann Boleyn.

[320] This was especially true in respect of his home, Hever Castle, which was robbed, flooded and, in the end, barred to him by the Inland Revenue. In 1946 it suffered one of the great art robberies of the century in which 1,500 priceless gems were lost. The thieves also took the prayer book that Ann Boleyn had carried to the scaffold. In 1958, flood damage – against which he had omitted to insure! – cost him £100,000 (*Daily Express*, 9 October 1958). And in 1962, Selwyn Lloyd introduced an appallingly drafted Finance Act which was intended to prevent the evasion of death duties by wealthy individuals exporting their wealth by investing in foreign land late in life. The Astor family trust was vested in American land, and the underlying wealth had never been in England. Astor had been *importing* the interest for years and donating a significant proportion to British charities. But whatever the intent of the Act, he was caught by its effect. In order to prevent the entire trust being wiped out by British death duties and effectively disinheriting the younger generation of Astors, he had to ensure that he did not die in England. He was

Plate 8.18 Major J. J. Astor.

When he had recovered from the shattering physical damage of 1918, Astor entered public life in two main ways. In 1922, he became Tory MP for Dover, which he remained until 1945. But, much more importantly, in the same year, after the death of Lord Northcliffe, Astor bought joint control of *The Times* with John Walter, for £1.35 million. He was to be chief proprietor for many years, and in 1931, just before he came to Phoenix,

literally exiled to France. As *The Sunday Times* put it, this was 'an ironic reward for a man noted for his public-spirited generosity' (23 September 1962). Chancellor Selwyn Lloyd ended, among many other things, Baron Astor's long career with the Phoenix. *The Times*, obituary, 20 July 1971.

became chairman also of the Times Publishing Co. In 1931 too he became a director of the Great Western Railway. But it was in the newspaper world that J. J. Astor made his distinctive contribution. What *The Times* needed fitted precisely with Astor's personality and style. In 1908 Northcliffe had rescued the paper financially, but had been unable to resist imprinting his own personality upon it; this had done little for its journalistic integrity. Astor, 'the shyest of men, almost to the point of inaudibility . . . [but] also one of the firmest'[321] was exactly the person to reintroduce The Thunderer to editorial ethics. He set out to define a style for the non-interventionist newspaper proprietor. One of his early steps in recreating the independence of *The Times* was to establish a group of ex-officio trustees, who were to include the President of the Royal Society, the President of the Institute of Chartered Accountants, the Governor of the Bank of England, the Warden of All Souls', and the Lord Chief Justice of England. Whether or not this group represented Astor's personal list of the great and the good does not matter. His logic was sound: if this crew could not guarantee an independent voice for a British newspaper, nobody could.

In fact, of course, it worked. And a great British institution was put back on course. It was wholly fitting that one of the consequences was that Astor should have become the first president of the Press Council. He achieved this accolade as he did everything: quietly. His eminent successor at *The Times*, Lord Thomson of Fleet, was clear about 'the great debt' that the paper owed Astor 'for enhancing its reputation for integrity and independence'.[322] But Astor was also a philanthropist on the grand scale. He gave the Middlesex Hospital, a favourite cause also of Ebbisham, at least £0.75 million, and he chaired its Board from 1938 until his enforced departure at the hands of the less than charitable Inland Revenue in 1962.[323]

All sources agree on Astor: he was the almost silent, incontestible and incorruptible steel of unblemished principle. Sketch found him 'a very modest-minded man'.[324] His official obituarist in his own newspaper came closest: 'no man could be more thorough; no man could have done more with a greater absence of fuss'.[325] He talked less than Hamilton; but the two shared the material of which great pro-consuls were made. If the twentieth-century Phoenix found its best managers in Ryan and Sketch,[326] its best expressions of moral authority were achieved by Hamilton and Astor.[327]

The remaining Board appointments of the interwar years – there were

[321] *Ibid.*
[322] *Ibid.*, 21 July 1971. The Thomson organisation secured control of *The Times* in 1966.
[323] See footnote 320 above.
[324] Sketch to Lord Royden,18 August 1941.
[325] *The Times*, 20 July 1971.
[326] And later, perhaps, in David Evans and Bill Harris.
[327] In the postwar era, Lord de L'Isle achieved comparable stature.

eight between 1935 and 1939 – were necessitated by mortality and the inexorable shift of the age distribution among directors towards the right. Phoenix lost two chairmen, one peer, one elder statesman and a banking expert in the mid-1930s. The business backgrounds of Clarendon Hyde and Pybus undoubtedly made a difference to the thinking and composition of the Board, but they died in 1934 and 1935 respectively. The banker Henry Bell also died in 1935. All these had enjoyed relatively short tenures. But the 1930s was a punishing time also for the veterans. Gerald Ryan, long in failing health, died in 1937. In the same year, Sir Francis Fladgate expired after twenty-six years on the Board, and Ponsonby, though not quite the last of a very old guard, followed in 1939 after fifty-four years as a director. Lord Dillon had predeceased all these in 1932. Aware of the high average age of those directors who remained alive, the company began a serious quest in 1936 for men of accomplishment and influence but still in their thirties and forties.

Again there were themes and patterns within the eight appointments which followed. Indeed they could be said to show more focus and single-minded purpose than any set of Phoenix appointments since the days of the sugar bakers. Two were financial experts, one a merchant banker (Granville Tyzer), the other from one of the great high-street names, inevitably Barclays (Sir John Caulcutt). Only one was from the more familiar soldier–politician syndrome represented by Greenwood and Rochdale (Hutchison). But, rather moving beyond Ryan's thinking – probably owing to the preferences of Clarendon Hyde and Pybus, which seem to have been well-maintained by Walters – no fewer than five were men of manufacture or commerce. The industrial element, which was evident in the Board of 1930 became decidedly more marked.

At first glance, this may not have seemed the case. For one of these five men was an earl (Dudley), another an accountant (D'Arcy Cooper), while a third was a master of the new art of mass retailing (W. L. Stephenson) – but in practice all five (the other two were Cecil Charrington and David Evans Bevan) were men of business on the grandest scale. There was a new functionalism to the selection here. The Phoenix Board in the early composite era had been headed by public figures or insurance experts; but the 1930s saw an inclination towards businessmen of wider skills. Sketch remembered to keep an eye out for legal competence, but he approved the trend, and remarked, on his own elevation to chairman in 1940, particularly upon the 'harmonious efficiency' of the Board of the late 1930s.

The lesser patterns are still arresting. The place of the Carlton in the social life of the Board need not be laboured. Nor is it surprising perhaps that two of the new appointments (Hutchison and Dudley) had been, like Astor, regular soldiers on the outbreak of the First World War. More interestingly, one had been at New College, Oxford with Astor (Charrington), two sat on the Board of the same great railway, the Great Western (Dudley and Evans Bevan),and three joined Ebbisham and Astor in being major philanthropists, all in the same field of hospital benefactions (Caulcutt, Dudley and Evans Bevan).

The two appointments of 1935 involved a financier and a brewer. Granville Tyzer (Phoenix 1935–61) had become managing director of Lazards in 1919, at the age of thirty-five and was skilled in matters of overseas finance and investment. He had been spotted by Pybus as a suitable replacement for Clarendon Hyde, who had been valuable to Phoenix in this department. Tyzer's foreign connections and frequent overseas travel supplied a passport for Phoenix in a number of markets and he was a shrewd observer of them. When visiting Argentina, the United States and Portugal in 1937 and North America in 1945, he cast a critical eye over the Phoenix operations in these places.[328] Tyzer had a clear mind and a crisp manner of presentation; and, in the postwar period, he was to be an effective deputy chairman between 1948 and 1961.

His colleague of 1935, Cecil Charrington, was introduced to the Board by General Wigan. The latter's hop business had brought him into contact with Charrington's expanding Anchor Brewery group. But Wigan was not Charrington's only Phoenix contact: he had been at Eton and New College with J. J. Astor. Like Tyzer, Charrington had made a mark in business at a young age. He had become a director of the family business at the age of twenty-seven in 1912 and chairman at thirty-eight. The brewery had been established in the eighteenth century – and Phoenix had done insurance business with it over some three-quarters of a century[329] – but Cecil Charrington was an important force in the company's modern expansion. When he became chairman in 1923, the brewery possessed some 500 tied houses; when he retired in 1948, it had three times that number. In the meantime, he had taken over three large breweries and converted the Charrington Group into one of the biggest brewing enterprises in London.

This pair of early developers was accompanied to its first Board meetings by Ralph Sketch in a new role. For he was made managing director in

[328] He did not like all that he saw, and particularly not Phoenix's Montreal station, 'a poor office . . . in a dull dark sidestreet . . . in a rather fine city like Montreal we do ourselves more harm than good by having a poor office' (Tyzer to Sketch, 3 December 1945).

[329] Cementing existing insurance connections was often a factor in the appointment of directors; it arose again in the cases of Stephenson and Dudley.

1935 and therefore a full member of the Board, rather than an ex-officio participant.

The generally more businesslike approach to the design of the Board in the 1930s was certainly sustained by the four appointments of 1936: Sir John Caulcutt, W. L. Stephenson, Francis d'Arcy Cooper and the Earl of Dudley, a group consisting of one banker, a retailing genius and two industrialists.

As Pybus had proposed Tyzer to provide the investment skills lost with Clarendon Hyde's death, Chairman Walters proposed Caulcutt (Phoenix 1936–43) to supply the banking expertise lost with the death of Henry Bell. Like Bell, Caulcutt had worked his way up from the counter to the control of a great bank, in his case Barclays Dominion, Colonial and Overseas. Like Bell also, he was an expert in international finance, and particularly in Egyptian financial affairs.[330] He had moved from the general managership of Barclays to the top job at Barclays D.C.O., upon the formation of that enterprise in 1925.[331] He was knighted in 1931, and then became deputy chairman of the bank in 1935 and chairman in 1937. The man was judged to possess 'an unrivalled experience of overseas banking',[332] and the bank to be 'one of the chief, and certainly one of the most successful developments in overseas Empire banking in the years between the two wars'.[333] Caulcutt was a helpful, warm personality, painstaking and caring, as well as a formidable technical expert. Like Ebbisham and Astor, he was a great promoter of hospital charities and was active in humanitarian causes. Sketch wrote in tribute after his death in 1943 that 'he was not only the wise adviser that one would automatically expect from one holding the position that he did, but a kindly, considerate and delightful companion'.[334]

Caulcutt was not the only appointment of 1936 to have worked his way up from the bottom. W. L. Stephenson (Phoenix 1936–48) does not leave as clear a personal impression as Caulcutt, but he was, as the *Daily Telegraph* put it, 'the English Mr Woolworth'.[335] Starting work at thirteen, sweeping floors in a general merchant's store in Liverpool, he received his initial break when he was picked by Woolworth's to manage their first

[330] King Farouk conferred upon him the Grand Cordon and the Star of the Order of the Nile in 1941.

[331] It was composed from the merger of the Colonial Bank, the Anglo-Egyptian Bank, and the National Bank of South Africa.

[332] *Journal of the Anglo-Egyptian Chamber of Commerce*, 3, 1943.

[333] *The Times*, 30 April 1943. During the coming war, Barclays D.C.O. helped organise the financial arrangements for the large British army in the Near East, and later followed closely in the tracks of the 8th Army.

[334] Sketch to Edwin Fisher, chairman of Barclays, 30 April 1943.

[335] *Daily Telegraph*, 2 October 1963.

small branch in Britain, also in Liverpool, in 1909. Within twelve years, Stephenson was managing director of Woolworth's British operation, and ended as its chairman. By 1939, the chain store employed 40,000 people and its peak stock market valuation in the 1930s attained £150 million. Stephenson – who was one of the highest paid managers of the day, on £80,000 per year – took Woolworth's profits from £4.5 million in 1931 to £8 million in 1939. Not surprisingly, Stephenson amassed considerable personal wealth, owning the racing yacht *Velsheda* and leaving, upon his death in 1948, a net £2.7 million.

Phoenix wanted him for his commercial skills. It was Walters who spotted him but Sketch who wrote for the Board, prior to his election, that he had 'shown business acumen to a high degree and exceptional organising ability in the creation of Messrs Woolworth's business in this country'.[336] Lord Greenwood had met him at Cowes and offered endorsement: 'a quiet, interesting and agreeable man; and obviously a man of great ability, knowledge and influence'.[337] Even in 1946, when Stephenson was 'desirous of avoiding the discomfort of present-day train travel' (from Bournemouth), Sketch wished to retain his expertise, and prevailed upon him not to resign. However, in 1936, Phoenix also wanted him for the insurance business that he could dispense. The office already took £50,000 in premiums from Woolworth's and had its eye on more.

If Stephenson was a leader in retailing, the two remaining appointments in his year-group were industrialists on the largest scale. They could not have been much more different in background. The Earl of Dudley was a landed magnate who was also a steel magnate. Frank d'Arcy Cooper was the head of the famous family accountancy practice[338] who in 1925 succeeded the first Lord Leverhulme as chairman of Lever Brothers. Educated at Wellington, then articled into the family firm, Cooper became a partner in 1910. By 1936, he was chairman not only of Lever's but also of Mac Fisheries, Moor Park Ltd, the Niger Company and T. Wall & Co.; and he was a director of the United Africa Co. and the Margarine Union. In short, he presided over a number of companies which were household names.

Cooper, like his fellow-accountant A. W. Tait, was a company doctor, a reconstructor of businesses; but he was a very superior version. The Lever Group, in the 1920s, was a sprawling giant, with interests

[336] Sketch, Circular for the Board, dated 14 July 1936. In wartime, this organising ability was recognised when Stephenson was made Director-General of Equipment in the Ministry of Aircraft Production in 1940 (*Daily Express*, 24 July 1940).

[337] Greenwood to Sketch, 20 July 1936. [338] Later Coopers and Lybrand.

Plate 8.19 Frank D'Arcy Cooper.

covering five continents and a product range from soap to sausages. Its idiosyncratic structure reflected the acquisitive instincts and autocratic style of the first Lord Leverhulme.

Like Ryan, Leverhulme[339] had taken an over-optimistic view of postwar financial prospects and rushed too precipitately into the bubble of corporate speculation which inflated during 1919 and 1920.[340] The resulting purchases – including the chaotically managed Niger Company – almost

[339] The peerage dated from 1917.

[340] Charles Wilson pointed out that the South Sea Bubble of 1720 and its next largest relative were separated by 200 years almost to the month. Wilson, *The History of Unilever*, I (London, 1954), p. 253. See pp. 244–257 for Leverhulme's own contribution to the bubble of 1919–20.

tripled the total capital employed by Lever Brothers to £60.3 million; and almost capsized the Lever Group.

That it did not was due to D'Arcy Cooper. His firm had been auditors to Lever from the beginning. Cooper's standing with the banks allowed him to negotiate a loan from Barclays which saved the Niger Company, and through it the Lever Group, and his standing with Leverhulme persuaded the latter to issue debenture stock in the teeth of a lifetime's distrust of 'these debts'.[341] Cooper retired from his accountancy practice in 1923 in order to join the Lever Board.

From the business crisis of 1920–1, Cooper's was the commanding voice and the guiding hand in the affairs of Lever's. Leverhulme was never one to surrender power lightly (or indeed at all), and it is a measure of Cooper's stature that he did so with good grace. Cooper then rationalised the Lever behemoth, organised its many companies by product category, and trimmed away the surplus fat. He provided exactly the consolidating and analytical skills which were the necessary corrective to Leverhulme's acquisitive exuberance and individual drive.

Frank Cooper was a highly attractive personality. A man of fearsome integrity and strong feelings, he could express himself strongly, and often bluntly. But such was the clarity and candour of his style that few took offence. Even Leverhulme wrote of him that 'he was one of the type of men that I consider most resemble a warm fire, and people naturally seem to come up to him for warmth'.[342] But allied to this temperament was 'a cool methodical brain'. Unilever's historian wrote of him that he brought to that huge company 'a thoughtful analysis of long-term issues quite unlike anything that it had seen before'.[343] For his part, Sketch was convinced that Cooper was 'an outstanding figure in the industrial world.[344] Within Phoenix, it was Tyzer who heard through Lazards that Cooper might consider an insurance directorship and that both the North British and the Royal Exchange were after him. Sketch moved fast to secure him and was lucky to do so. Cooper was the most impressive captain of really large-scale industry to grace the Phoenix boardroom before the Second World War.

On the same day that Cooper was elected to the Board, so too was the Earl of Dudley (Phoenix 1936–58). This, the third earl, was a very industrial aristocrat. The Ward family had close links with Court and both the second and third earls had the ear of reigning monarchs (Edward VII and George V respectively); the third earl was at Christchurch[345] with the future Duke of Windsor and maintained a lifelong friendship with

[341] *Ibid.*, pp. 257–8. [342] Cited, *ibid.*, p. 269. [343] *Ibid.*, p. 297.
[344] Sketch to Ryan, and Sketch to Astor, both 8 April 1936. [345] After Eton.

him. The Dudley seat at Himley Hall was 'almost the recognised temporary abode of any person of distinction visiting the Midlands'.[346]

As Lord Ednam, William Ward was a regular officer in the Worcestershire Yeomanry at the start of the First World War, and, like Astor, served through it as a fighting soldier, was wounded (though less grievously),[347] won the MC, and ended as a major. After the war, he served intermittently as a Tory MP, for Hornsey 1921–4 and Wednesbury 1931–2. His succession to the earldom in 1932 switched his attentions to the 30,000 acres of family estates in Staffordshire and Worcestershire and the mines, iron works and steel mills attached to them. By the time he came to Phoenix's attention in the mid-1930s, he was chairman of his own Earl of Dudley's Baggeridge Colliery, also of his own Round Oak Steel Works,[348] of Midland Slag, British Electric Welding and the British Iron and Steel Federation. When he visited New York, as in 1936, it was not to sup with the *glitterati* but to confer with the hard men of the US steel industry. Dudley's election to the Board of the Great Western Railway early in 1936 was taken as the signal that he was willing to accept directorships outside his own immediate network of coal and metal interests.

It was at this time that Phoenix approached him. He was at the peak of his industrial prominence in the mid-to-late 1930s. And he shared the charitable and philanthropic interests which so many Phoenix directors maintained.[349] But these were not the only reasons why Phoenix was interested in him. Again there was a direct insurance connection. In the 1910s and 1920s, the Dudleys' solicitor had been John Tryon – who was also a shareholder in the Baggeridge Colliery – and he had directed their insurances towards Phoenix. But, in the late 1920s, there was a falling out between Tryon and the Dudleys, and in 1928 the £75,000 worth of cover on the Round Oak works was transferred to another company.[350] Phoenix wanted it back and the election of 1936 was enough to secure it. Dudley wrote to Chairman Walters in April, 'I am glad to think that you will again look after my policies'.[351]

The industrial note in the Board recruitment of the late interwar period was maintained to the end, with a prolonged wooing of the South Wales mine-owner and brewer, David Evans Bevan, who was eventually secured

[346] *Birmingham Post*, 18 July 1945. Nevertheless, the house was sold to the Coal Board in 1947.
[347] Cooper too spent a year in hospital as a result of injuries sustained at the Somme.
[348] When this enterprise was nationalised in 1951 it attracted financial compensation of £1.5 million (*Financial Times*, 29 December 1959).
[349] In his case primarily the Brompton and King Edward VII hospitals.
[350] Lord Dudley to J. J. Astor, 5 February 1936.
[351] Lord Dudley to A. M. Walters, 14 April 1936.

Plate 8.20 Lord Dudley.

in 1940. The only interruption occurred in 1937, with the election necessitated by the death of Sir Gerald Ryan. This was the appointment of Major-General, Lord Hutchison of Montrose (Phoenix 1937–50). This former soldier and politician was more in the mould of Wigan than of Cooper, Stephenson or Dudley. He started his career in the family business, corn millers of Kirkcaldy, but was deflected in a military direction by the outbreak of the Boer War. He served in South Africa as an officer in the 7th Dragoons and was a regular major by the outbreak of the First World War. After an early spell as brigade major with the Cavalry Brigade, in which he was mentioned in despatches six times and won the DSO, he became a rather administrative sort of soldier. He was Director of Organisation at the War Office from 1917, was despatched to the United States to help with the transportation of American troops to France, and from 1920 to 1922 was Brigadier General for Administration in the Army of the Rhine. After the army, he went into politics as Liberal MP for Kirkcaldy 1922–3 and for Montrose 1924–32. He was a personal friend of Lloyd George and served as Liberal Chief Whip 1926–30 and Paymaster General 1935–8. He was an all-out Liberal and resigned in

Plate 8.21 Sir David Evans Bevan.

1930 in opposition to 'the official Liberal policy of maintaining the Socialists in office'. He was raised to the peerage in 1932.

Hutchison was a talented organiser, who did things thoroughly, and he achieved a qualified prominence. However, what commended him to Phoenix was less this somewhat suppressed glow than his characteristic energy in promoting insurance interests in Scotland. He had been chairman of the company's Local Board there and his 'enthusiastic interest in the welfare of the Scottish branches' was valued by those who managed them.[352] Somewhat unusually, Hutchison was a good egg who proved himself more lively than many in the Phoenix's regional network of notables and was promoted to the main Board for his pains.

Evans Bevan of course also carried regional weight of no mean dimensions, and this was not lost upon Phoenix. But he possessed other more compelling attractions. He was young – in 1930, when Phoenix started pursuing him, only twenty-eight – he was able; he was wealthy; and he was noticeable. As Edward Ferguson rather unctuously put it, 'in view of the age of certain members of the present directors, we were ever conscious of the need for bearing in mind gentlemen of his age and influ-

[352] Manager, Scotland to Sketch 22 June 1937.

ence'.[353] Inheriting a fortune of over £2 million just after leaving Uppingham, together with three large anthracite mines and the huge Vale of Neath brewery, Evans Bevan was a solid gold candidate. Before nationalisation, the Bevan collieries composed the biggest independent mining venture in Wales and the Neath brewery, which became the group's flagship after coal nationalisation, had pubs in every village in the Vale of Neath and the Swansea Valley. The family business had been built up by the great-grandfather and father of David Evans Bevan;[354] but an internal appraisal by Phoenix in 1939 concluded that 'his father was a keen man, but the progress which the undertakings have made since the son took control speaks well of his driving force and organising ability'. This report found him a perfectionist, a model employer and one of the largest in Britain. Outside his business, he was a philanthropist on a scale to rival Astor; and indeed philanthropy, rather than politics, appears to have claimed the majority of his extra-curricular energies. During the 1930s, he was a major benefactor to Port Talbot General Hospital and established a chain of ambulance halls in the Dulais Valley for the St John Ambulance Brigade.[355]

However, it should be noted that Evans Bevan was not Phoenix's only effort in the direction of youth, although at thirty-eight in 1940 he was the youngest election since Pleydell-Bouverie in 1900, at the tender age of twenty-three, or, before him, the indestructible Bovill, in 1882, at the age of twenty-eight. Some attention to years went into the elections of both the 1920s and 1930s, with the result that the average age of the Board was reduced from 69.3 years in 1920 to 65.4 in 1930 and to 62.7 in 1936.

If, on the eve of the First World War, the Phoenix possessed a Board of all the talents – legal, scholarly, commercial, financial, naval – its complexion on the eve of the Second World War was notably different: the Board of 1939 was more professionally capitalistic than any the company had amassed for more than a century, as well as comparatively youthful.

In 1930 there had been four peers on the Board and two of them had possessed substantial manufacturing interests; of the five peers of 1940, three maintained such interests. Six directors in 1930 had explicit commercial interests; by 1940, nine did. Across all professional categories, six directors of 1930 had connections with manufacturing and two with banking. Ten years later the matching figures were seven and three. The

[353] Memorandum of 22 March 1939.

[354] The brewery dated from 1846. It was sold to Whitbread in 1967.

[355] He was himself a Knight of the Order of St John. After the war, he broadened the scope of his charitable activities, donating to the University of London a hall of residence for Commonwealth students and to Neath a civic centre.

Table 8.43. *Phoenix Assurance: directors' main professions, 1940*

Lawyers	Commerce, industry, etc.[a]	Armed services[a]	Peers[a]	Gentlemen
Tryon Walters	Coupar-Barrie (S,P) Royden (S,P) Astor (N) Tyzer (B) Charrington(Ind) Cooper (Ind) Caulcutt (B) Stephenson (Ret) Evans Bevan (Ind)	Wigan Pleydell-Bouverie (Ind)	Rochdale (Ind,B) Ebbisham (Ind) Greenwood Dudley (Ind) Hutchison	Bovill

Note: [a] Ind = industry; S = shipping; B = banking; P = MP; N = newspapers; Ret = retail.

Board of 1914 may have been well fitted to look wisely at a wide world; that of 1940 was better qualified to look wisely at a business world.

13. LIFE AT THE BIRD IN THE INTERWAR YEARS

As Phoenix became a more professionally directed and ever larger composite venture, so life inevitably changed for those who worked in its offices and branches. Moreover, the interwar period was an eventful one for all grades of workers, and insurance workers – though they were largely spared the rigours of unemployment which afflicted the old staple industries – experienced their due share of pressures and problems. The themes which stood out were: the expansion of the national and international organisation, salary levels, pensions, merit awards, sporting and welfare provision and yet more building and rebuilding at Head Office.

The workforce: numbers, salaries, pensions and conditions in the Depression

In 1922, the Phoenix had 307 individuals working in Lombard Street, 238 in the UK branches and 383 in the foreign outposts. By 1931 all of these figures had more than doubled (see Table 8.44). In the early 1930s, Phoenix Head Office staff exceeded 600 in number, and had grown by 110% since 1922 and by 43% even since the mid-1920s. However, this

Table 8.44. *Phoenix Assurance: total staff numbers, 1913–39*[a]

Year	Head Office	Home branches	Foreign branches	Total Phoenix	Global (inc US subsidiaries)
1913	303	159	458	920	
1922	307	238	383	928	
1927	452	268	668	1,388	
1928	544	388	687	1,619	2,920
1929	596	463	689	1,748	
1930	651	482	932	2,065	
1931	647	524	873	2,044	
1932	503	641	776	1,920	3,163
1936					2,975
1939					3,218

Note: [a]There was a change in the method of recording in 1933.
Source: Directors' Minutes; Annual Salary Reviews.

expansion was not as rapid as that in the UK branches as the company's national network grew by 120% between 1922 and 1931 and by 139% between 1927 and 1932. On top of this, the workforce in the foreign stations rose from 383 in 1922 to 873 in 1931, an increase of just under 128%. Company acquisitions naturally affected these figures. And they did so too across the Atlantic. For these workforce numbers did not include the very considerable echelon in Phoenix's network of US subsidiaries – which together employed some 1,300 people by 1928.[356] Phoenix's global workforce had reached 3,218 by 1939 and the total salary bill hovered around the £1 million mark throughout the 1930s.

Conditions of office life for this considerable workforce were somewhat different both from the harsh discipline of the pre-1900 decades and the more hectic pace of the post-1945 business world. At King William Street, midway through the interwar period, the working day began at 9.50 am and the office opened to the public ten minutes later. It continued, Monday to Friday, until 4.30 pm, with a lunch 'hour' that was actually 45 minutes. The working week extended into Saturday, 9.50 am till 1 pm. Ordinary staff were let off for one Saturday in four, the more senior for one in three. An attendance book had to be signed by the great majority earning less than £500, with reasons stated for lateness. Staying on after 4.30 pm to finish ordinary work was frowned upon. Holiday

[356] *The Bird*, July 1928, p. 18.

provision was generous: two weeks after six month's service and then for the first five years, then three weeks after five years, and four weeks for senior male and female staff. On the other hand, managerial supervision of 'private' life was, to a modern eye, intrusive. Thus male clerks earning less than £250 per year were required 'to obtain official permission before making arrangements for marriage'.[357]

Pension details tell us something more about the composition of the UK workforce. Phoenix had introduced a provisional pension scheme for employees in 1923, revised it in 1927 and compiled a register of all eligible staff in May 1929.[358] The 1923 scheme had covered 'ordinary male staff' only; the principal innovation of the 1927 scheme was to incorporate 'ordinary female staff' as well.[359] A proposal to introduce pensions for women in 1920 elicited the response from Sketch that management had no objection in principle, but 'the position of female labour was still in too experimental a stage for any definite scheme to be agreed to at the present time'.[360]

Some 882 men and 325 women were on the books as pensionable by 1929. Of the men, 52% had spent all their pensionable service with the Phoenix, 24% had held other insurance jobs before coming to the company, nearly 9% had joined Phoenix before they were twenty, and only 15% had come to the office from backgrounds unrelated to insurance. Of the women, a predictably higher proportion – 39% – had joined before they were twenty, and a predictably smaller proportion – about 6% – had come from other insurance jobs. Again a high proportion – 34% – had served all their working lives with Phoenix, while about 20% had joined the Phoenix from unrelated employments. Men joining Phoenix from other insurance companies were regularly awarded pension credits for their pre-Phoenix service; but only two women were: the 'lady superintendent' and the general manager's secretary. A few men received pension credits in respect of pre-Phoenix careers that were not in insurance, but only when the earlier experience fell into areas such as accountancy, banking, surveying, stockbroking or the law. No women received such credits.

[357] Phoenix Special Committee Book 2, p. 42. These office conditions are taken from the revised Staff Regulations of 1 April 1932.

[358] The company had, of course, paid pensions before 1914 (see Chapter 1, Section 9), but there was no formal scheme or entitlement before the 1920s.

[359] For both men and women, entitlement began only after ten years of service and the pension consisted of one-sixtieth of final salary for every year of service. After forty years' service, men could retire at sixty, or, with less service, at sixty-five. Women who had served thirty years could go at fifty, or, if less, at fifty-five.

[360] Phoenix Consultative Committee Minutes, p. 10, 3 November 1920.

The tendency towards lifetime employment with Phoenix and previous insurance experience – with these two categories together covering 76% of men and 40% of women – is very marked indeed. This may not be unrelated to another innovation of 1927. At the request of the staff, Phoenix's bankers were induced to organise loans for employees, repayable in monthly instalments, to allow staff members to purchase shares in the company.[361] The scheme, or one like it, continued for decades, but the beginning was very early.

However for most staff, in the disturbed conditions of the 1920s and 1930s, salary (and pension) levels were probably a matter of closer concern than share prices. With Ryan in control, they had little need to worry overmuch; he was solicitous on such matters, an approach that was in marked contrast to that of senior management during and immediately after the Second World War.[362] In his first Chairman's Annual Report of 1920 – still, of course in the throes of his postwar optimism – Ryan reported that the bonuses paid to the staff during the war were to be made fixed additions to salary; and another large revision was made early in 1920. While recognising that the biggest increases in overall expenses stemmed from salaries, the directors, though 'certainly not unmindful of the necessity of economy . . . consider that a company like ours must look after its employees properly and remunerate them on a liberal scale'.[363] Two decades later, these priorities would be almost exactly reversed.

The Ryan management was also progressive in its view of labour relations, and was open to persuasion on salary matters. The Board owned itself to be 'favourable to joint action among the Staff to enable representations to be made to the Management, whenever it may seem necessary'.[364] A Consultative Committee was formed in May 1920, consisting of equal teams of senior managers and London staff in order 'to provide a systematic means of conference . . . on matters affecting the general welfare'.[365] At the first meeting on 7 July 1920 were General Manager Sketch, Fire Manager Boston, Life Manager Winter, Accident Manager McDougald and Chief Accountant Elder, and twelve others. A Ladies Advisory Committee presented the female staff view to the Consultative Committee – in November 1920, for instance it argued that the lunch hour for women should actually consist of 60 minutes – but there was no woman on the Consultative Committee until 1927, when its

[361] Phoenix Directors' Minutes 35, p. 254, 13 July 1927.
[362] Indeed, it was partly Ryan's generosity in this department which so frightened Edward Ferguson some twenty years later (see below, pp. 866–74).
[363] Chairman's Annual Report, 28 April 1920.
[364] *Ibid.*
[365] Phoenix Special Committee Book, p. 42, 1 April 1932.

constitution was amended to allow for just one.[366] Clearly, by 1927 Sketch was convinced that female employment was no longer 'experimental'. The Consultative Committee was very much Sketch's baby: he chaired it throughout its life from 1920 to 1935, and when Sketch became managing director, and Edward Ferguson as manager took over everyday routine, it was terminated.[367] A Staff Association took its place from April 1935.[368]

Given this early liberality of the Ryan-Sketch era, the inflationary pressures of 1919 and 1920 produced some very large wage settlements. The cost-of-living bonus to permanent male officials was fixed at 15% for the first half of 1919 but raised to 50% for the second half. At the same time, pensions were boosted by 25%.[369] After the Consultative Committee had prepared a cost-of-living curve from figures published in the *Labour Gazette*, substantial increments to salaries were also agreed for 1920 (see Table 8.45).[370] From then on, however, the pace calmed somewhat. Sketch appointed McDougald to head an economy drive on all aspects of expenditure in spring 1921. But the slowing of salary increases probably reflected more the behaviour of the outer economy than any new severity in managerial policy. Indeed, that policy itself was also reacting to the termination of the postwar boom after only two years, and the turn-about in business affairs.

Nevertheless, as Table 8.45 shows, salary increases at Phoenix continued at a generous rate through to the late 1920s and early 1930s. After this, the conditions of the economic crisis introduced a new era in salary history and forced Sketch to look for reductions in total wage costs and in workforce numbers. But he released these constraints as soon as he was able and introduced a programme for rebuilding salaries in the later 1930s.[371]

The data for average annual salary at Phoenix also tell an interesting story. Average annual income for all British workers moved between 1924 and 1937 in the fairly narrow band of £140–149.[372] As one might

366 Phoenix Consultative Committee Minutes pp. 1, 15, 107, 7 July, 3 November 1920 and 7 December 1927.

367 *Ibid.*, p. 161. Sketch signed the last minutes on 16 December 1935.

368 This was not solely a matter of personalities, but rather also of the growing formalisation of labour organisations in the service industries. Until it had an Association, Phoenix could not send representatives to the Conference of Associations of Insurance Employees, which in turn elected two representatives to the Insurance Unemployment Board, the body which administered unemployment insurance for the entire insurance sector. So Sketch's calming touch yielded not only to a different managerial style but also to the growing bureaucratic complexity of labour relations. *The Bird*, 3 July 1935.

369 Phoenix Directors' Minutes 32, p. 416, 17 December 1919.

370 Phoenix Consultative Committee, p. 28, 11 January 1921.

371 See below, pp. 650–1.

372 Calculated from Bowden, 'The New Consumerism', Table 14.5, p. 256.

Table 8.45. *Phoenix Assurance: annual salary increases, 1920–38 (%)*

Year	Head Office	Home branches	Foreign branches	Total
1920	8.0	6.0	15.0	n.a.
1921	4.6	4.5	7.6	n.a.
1922	1.6	1.2	2.6	1.3
1923	0.5	1.1	4.5	2.4
1924	n.a.	n.a.	n.a.	n.a.
1925	n.a.	n.a.	n.a.	n.a.
1926	n.a.	n.a.	n.a.	n.a.
1927	3.9	5.1	3.5	3.7
1928	5.1	7.2	2.8	4.2
1929	5.7	6.9	5.0	5.4
1930	4.3	7.1	2.6	3.6
1931	4.0	6.0	0.9	2.5
1932	1.5	3.5	0.7	1.5
1933	1.1	2.1	n.a.	1.0
1934	n.a.	n.a.	n.a.	1.1
1935	2.6	3.7	n.a.	1.9
1936	4.4	7.6	n.a.	2.8
1937	4.3	7.4	1.0	2.9
1938	4.6	6.6	1.1	2.9

Source: Directors' Minute Books and Special Committee Book.

expect, the average income of Phoenix Head Office staff was comfortably above this national indicator – indeed usually around 100% above – though foreign branch employees did even better (see Table 8.47). However, the average for all Phoenix employees worldwide was quite close to the average for Head Office workers. This was because staff in the UK branches and offices did not fare so well, being close to, or just above, the national average earnings between 1927 and 1929, before opening up a significant gap and achieving an advantage of 24% by 1932. There may well be an age distribution effect here: the large increase in Home Branch staff between 1927 and 1932 may have been slanted towards young (and possibly female) workers who needed years to swell their earnings.

Indeed, in the case of women, not even years would do the trick. In 1927, a salary level of £175 was still 'looked upon as a stopping place for those doing ordinary work', while £200 was regarded as the upper limit

Table 8.46. *Phoenix Assurance: average annual salaries of men and women, 1931–8 (£)*

	1931	1936	1937	1938
Men	304	333	342	342
Women	139	135	142	146

Source: Special Committee Book 2, p. 160.

'for those showing ability in excess of the normal'.[373] However, at this time a Special Committee of the Board did have the grace to reflect 'whether we may not, in the near future, have to raise these limits somewhat'.[374] However, it appears to have reflected rather than acted, since the average salary level for women moved very little during the 1930s and remained at a point well below half that of the average male salary (see Table 8.46). The higher proportion of women in the branch offices in Britain – 39% against 32% at Head Office in January 1931 – goes some way to explaining the moderate salary performance of the provincial organisation in Table 8.47 below.

The perspective is adjusted rather sharply by recalling that a branch manager in an important centre, such as Liverpool, could be earning around £1,250 in 1934, and a still more important regional official, such as the manager for Scotland, around £1,400.[375] During the 1930s, an annual income of £250 was commonly regarded as the dividing line between the working and middle classes. Households earning more than this figure made up about one-quarter of the total population. It was this income group which provided the 'new consumers' of the interwar years, the owner-occupiers of houses, the motorists, and the proud owners of radio-sets and household appliances. Many Phoenix employees (if few female ones), while playing their part on the employment side of the expanding new industries, also earned enough to participate on the consumption side.

The more talented, however, could participate more than the less able. By the mid-1920s, Phoenix had developed a system of performance-related pay. Staff were divided into A (excellent), B (good), C (satisfactory) and D (indifferent) grades. 'Satisfactory', however, was a less than

[373] Phoenix Directors' Special Committee Book, p. 125, 17 January 1927.
[374] *Ibid.*
[375] The national average wage did not get into these realms until the late 1960s and early 1970s.

Table 8.47. *Phoenix Assurance: average annual salaries, 1927–39 (£)*

Year	Head Office	Home branches	Foreign branches	Worldwide
1927	296	146	330	283
1928	276	148	364	283
1929	235	147	369	265
1930	269	153	388	296
1931	274	154	371	284
1932	319	173	355	285
1933	n.a.	n.a.	n.a.	295
1936	n.a.	n.a.	n.a.	282
1939	n.a.	n.a.	n.a.	285

Source: Calculated from Directors' Minute Books.

simple concept, since it came in three strengths: C1 (normal), C2 (average) and C3 (below average). No more than 5% of individuals in each section could be graded as A, and no more than 10% as B. Those industrious or bright enough to fall into this top 15% received salary increments between £5 and £15 larger than those paid to C1s; and they got £15 more than the standard percentage increase if their incomes fell in the sub-£200 band, £20 more if in the £200–400 band, and £25 more if in the £401–600 band. Only half the individuals in the top income band were allowed to receive any merit increase and incomes above £600 were adjusted only at the discretion of the general manager. There were also penalties: C2s got £5 less in increment than C1s, while C3s got £10 less and Ds got no increase at all. Most tellingly, no one in the £401–600 band got any increase if graded at less than C.

Penalties, however, seem seldom to have been needed. The Board reflected on the grading exercise of 1927 that 'comparatively few have, as a matter of fact, been graded below C1, and this may reasonably be attributed to the care in selection and stiffening in standard that has taken place in recent years'.[376] By 1932, all juniors were required to possess London Matriculation and to sit the examinations of the Chartered Insurance Institute, the Institute of Actuaries or the Chartered Institute of Secretaries. Bonuses of between £10 and £25 were paid for passing the various components of these examinations. But the possession of a

[376] Phoenix Directors' Special Committee Book 1, p. 124, 17 January 1927.

university degree commanded no higher price and was very rare. Bonuses were also paid for typing speed.[377] Both Ryan and Sketch were insistent upon the quality of the staff and the expansion in numbers after 1920 was conducted with a careful eye upon the quality implications.

Around 1930 that eye grew beadier. A particular device for picking winners, the leaders of the future, was launched. This was the Phoenix Gold Watch competition, a professional, aptitude and general knowledge competition for male juniors, which was to run for more than half a century, to the company's end, and to pick out many influential names at an early age.[378] The winners between 1930 and 1938 were:

1930	Thomas Horsford Hodgson
1931	Leo Thomas Frank Little
1932	Richard James Cole
1933	Joseph S. R. Spoors
1934	Brian Frederick Gurton
1935	Andrew Reed
1936	Francis Kendal
1937	William C. Harris
1938	Raymond S. Twinn

Source: Phoenix Directors' Minutes.

The requirements were general efficiency and alertness, punctuality, success in the exams of the Chartered Insurance Institute and other 'technical' tests, success in sports and 'non-technical activities', originality in suggesting ways for improving the office's business, good general knowledge 'including knowledge of the history, status and general activities of the Phoenix and its associated companies', as well as skills in essay writing or translation, précis, letter-writing and rapid mental arithmetic. Perhaps unsurprisingly, the early Gold Watch system could claim some precision as a predictor of glories to come. At least three of these names achieved high office in the postwar Phoenix: Tom Hodgson was deputy general manager 1956–65, Frank Kendal was assistant general manager 1968–72, and Bill Harris was the penultimate chief executive of the Phoenix and its last deputy chairman.

However, while Sketch was considering how to pick bright youngsters, he had also grimmer things on his mind. The economic crisis of 1929–32 could scarcely be kept out of salary calculations and employment conditions. Sketch signalled his worries by refusing a salary increase for himself at the end of 1929 since he doubted 'whether it was possible to continue

[377] *Ibid.*, Book 2, p. 42; Phoenix Staff Regulations 1 April 1932.
[378] Phoenix Directors' Minutes, 36, p. 216, 7 May 1930.

the present scale of salary increases to the Staff'.[379] The effect of the Crash on the expenses ratio in 1930 and 1931 frightened the management and, while they 'recognised that the salaries of the Clerical Staff should not normally be affected by fluctuations in the profits from year to year' they could not escape the fact that salaries made up the major portion of expenses.[380] Sketch reassured the Consultative Committee that 'of course, a reduction of salaries was not contemplated' but a reduction in the rate of increase of salaries was a different matter, and a much tighter attitude was possible on this score. Some jobs could be taken to be worth no more than a given amount and their remuneration frozen at that level. Some people could be viewed in the same way. Staff numbers would be trimmed where possible by natural wastage.[381]

In response to these proposals, the staff representatives on the Consultative Committee wrote their own memorandum for the general manager. They did not like the idea of discriminatory pay freezes, although they fully accepted 'the need for economy'. Remarkably, the staff members then proposed their own austerity package: all annual increases should be cut by one-quarter by the simple expedient of moving their starting date from January to April: this could be repeated if need be in future years by further engineering of the dates; and no one earning more than £400 per annum should receive an automatic increase.[382] Sketch accepted the April start and looked hard at all increases; but he kept discrimination to a minimum and still paid a 4% increment to King William Street staff in 1931.

However, he was intent upon economy. In mid-1931, an innovation was made 'by the appointment of Female Clerical Staff for routine clerical work'. This released the women from the confines of secretarial work, but at a price. Candidates had to be the equal of male clerks in educational qualification but were told upon appointment that their work would be entirely routine and their income prospects distinctly limited. The object was 'an appreciable reduction in the salary cost, as well as freeing the bulk of the Male Juniors from routine work at a very much earlier date'.[383] This tactic was taken 'as far as was desirable' in 1931 and 1932. So not only the Great War but also the Great Depression was influential in expanding female employment in the City.

A similar air of crisis hung around the strict salary reviews of 1932–4. In March 1932, Sketch told the Consultative Committee that he had hoped

[379] Phoenix Directors' Special Committee Book 1, p. 157, 22 May 1928.
[380] *Ibid.*, Book 2, p. 2, 21 February 1931.
[381] Phoenix Consultative Committee Minutes, p. 134, 5 December 1930.
[382] Staff Memorandum on Salary Increases, 6 December 1930.
[383] Phoenix Directors' Special Committee Book 2, p. 18, 29 May 1931.

to celebrate the 150th anniversary of the company in a very different manner; but he did not relax his line in the least.[384] No salary increases at all were given on salaries above £400 and only selective ones in the salary band £201–400, with the more general increases being saved for the lower incomes, so as 'not to discourage the younger men'.[385] This reduced the total salary increase for 1932 to half that of 1931 and quarter that of 1929. Retirements were accelerated and appointments of new juniors frozen. In 1933 and 1934, in order to distribute the pain relatively equitably, different salary bands were targeted for selective increases or freezing. By March 1935, home clerical staff had been reduced by 111, mainly by accelerated retirement. The total wage bill for 1933 was nearly £100,000 less than that for 1932 (see Table 8.48).

By 1934, many Phoenix clerks had experienced little or no salary improvement for three years, yet 'prevailing conditions make it necessary to recommend continuance of the restriction'.

Sketch took upon himself the task of distributing hardship, but passed the salary review over to his assistant, Edward Ferguson, as soon as improvements looked possible in 1935. Ferguson was particularly concerned that 'progress of the juniors towards a fitting salary has been slow' and worried about consequential distortions in the age structure of the staff. Accordingly, high earners did poorly in 1935, as the emphasis was switched in other directions: they received increases only if they had been awarded none for three years *and* had shown special merit. The higher paid received increases in 40% of cases, but 80% of individuals in the income bands below £400 were allocated a rise.[386] Nevertheless, by the mid-1930s, more strenuous efforts were needed to overcome the effects of the salary erosion of 1930–4. In 1936, the management was intent on 'reviving in the minds of all efficient members of staff – particularly in the junior ranks – a fuller appreciation that a reasonable financial advancement can be achieved by good work in the company's service'. So almost everybody earning below £400 received rises in this year.[387]

Just as the policy of economy had been aimed differentially at different groups in the office, so was the rectification. In 1936, the prime objective had been to make good the shortfalls in the salaries of younger men. In 1937, Phoenix was worried by the exodus of young women who left the company soon after training, 'for more lucrative employment in public bodies and high-class industrial concerns'. So, while the majority of men received increases, women secured parity: henceforth, they were to be

[384] Phoenix Consultative Committee Minutes, p. 144, 17 March 1932.
[385] Phoenix Directors' Special Committee Book 2, p. 34, 18 March 1932.
[386] *Ibid.*, pp. 90–9, 26 March 1935. [387] *Ibid.*, p. 134, 20 March 1936.

Table 8.48. *Phoenix Group: staff numbers and total wage bill, 1929–34*

Date[a]	Head Office	UK branches	Foreign branches	Total wage bill (£)
1929	829	828	1791	n.a.
1930	677	772	1751	1,140,034
1931	650	748	1765	1,088,192
1932	616	743	1679	1,103,364
1933	592	744	1651	1,018,066
1934	584	744	1623	999,461

Note: [a] End of year.
Source: Phoenix Directors' Special Committee Books.

employed at salaries comparable with those of men in similar posts, and, in deserving cases, merit awards were to be paid on top of this.[388]

In 1938, it was the turn of the higher-paid officials who had marked time for much of the decade. Dr Heron, the assistant secretary, got another £100 to put him up to £1,570, while John Hill, the chief accountant, went up by £200 to £1,200. The entire force of inspectors received increases linked to their measure of success in business-gathering.[389] After this three-stage adjustment to the crisis policies of 1931–5, Ferguson concluded that 'we can continue to regard the salaries paid as leaving us free from criticism'.[390] This was not a claim that he would be able to repeat, once he had sole responsibility for such matters.

At around the same time that Phoenix was precipitated into its economy drive on salaries by the Crash, an important change occurred in the method of paying what was earned, be it little or much. For decades, Phoenix, along with thousands of employers, had paid salaries net, and, then, having worked out the tax obligation of the employee, paid an additional allowance to cover the outstanding tax. This worked as long as the obligations were small 'and the rate of tax was trifling'. But as tax requirements became more complex and pressing, a belief began to grow in the 1920s that it was proper for the individual to pay his own tax obligation and improper for him to *benefit from a tax increase.*[391]

In fact, the old system did not outlive the Finance Act of 1931. The tax increases it imposed were a response to the economic crisis and gave Sketch an excellent opportunity for paying salaries gross: 'it had been the expressed intention of those over us in the State to spread the burden of

[388] *Ibid.*, p. 150, 10 March 1937. [389] *Ibid.*, pp. 160–6, 18 March 1938.
[390] *Ibid.*, p. 160. [391] *Ibid.*, Book 1, p. 118, 20 October 1926.

sacrifice over all sections of the community and he believed that the justice of leaving the burden where the authorities had placed it would commend itself to all concerned'.[392] From 1 April 1932 Phoenix staff were moved into that relationship with the taxman that has now been familiar for more than a half-century.

If what was earned by those working was a focus of interest, so was the provision made for the increasing number of those retiring from work. Pensions strategies afford another perspective upon the employment assumptions of the interwar period. In 1932, twenty-four Phoenix men moved onto a pension footing, at an average allowance of £334, well above the magical £250 frontier between blue and white collar status, after an average length of service of thirty-three years. In 1937, thirteen men achieved an average pension of £324 per annum after the same length of service; and in 1939 a clearly more elevated group of nine secured an average £418, after enduring an average thirty-four years in the office. By contrast, again sharp, two women in 1932 got only £44 per annum after fifteen years of service; in 1937 one woman received £137 after nineteen years; and in 1939 five women achieved an average of £93 after twenty years. In 1938 a lady superintendent took the women's interwar record, and came close to the middle-class income line, with a pension of £217, after twenty-five years in work.

Modest incomes and pensions for women indeed constituted a social problem, which by about 1930 was an unwelcome echo effect of the great upsurge in secretarial employment in the 1900s and 1910s. Recognising this in 1928, Phoenix introduced a special gratuity, equal to two years' salary, 'to any member of the Female Staff over age 40, with at least 15 years service, who was desirous of resigning and giving up Office life but could not afford to do so'.[393]

Arriving healthily at pensionable age, however, especially for men, had not yet become a simple matter. Illness in the office was not the scourge that it had been in the 1880s and 1890s, but it was still a threat. Foreign Accident Manager Swanson, forced to retire at the age of fifty-three in 1929, was the most senior casualty of the period.[394] But, at around the same time, one clerk had to be removed to Brentwood Asylum and another accounts clerk succumbed to the old office terror, tuberculosis. Phoenix's chief medical officer stipulated that, 'he must not return at any time in his own interests as well as ours'.[395] The case illustrates the

392 Phoenix Consultative Committee Minutes, pp. 141–2, 14 October 1931.
393 Phoenix Directors' Special Committee Book 1, pp. 177–8, 30 April 1929.
394 Phoenix Directors' Minutes, 36, pp. 95–6, 31 July 1929. He died in April 1931.
395 *Ibid.*, p. 103, 28 August 1929.

shortcomings in the otherwise improving welfare provision of the interwar period. Phoenix had paid the patient's salary during his illness, plus an additional grant of £100 per year. But, having served less than ten years with the company, he was not eligible for pension. The Insurance Benevolent Fund would, ironically, pay the premiums on his life policy with Phoenix. But beyond that there was little help save grace and favour.

Again, Phoenix tried to bring corporate paternalism into these welfare issues. From 1920 newly appointed male staff were required to take out life assurances with the Phoenix, with the company paying half the premiums, and to add policies so that they were always insured for at least twice their annual salary. A similar requirement was placed upon women staff appointed after February 1938. A more precise remedy for illness, rather than for mortality, was introduced in 1929 in the shape of a Staff Medical Scheme. This suggestion came from the Consultative Committee which late in 1928 had noted the measures introduced by the joint-stock banks to assist their employees in meeting the heavy medical and surgical expenses of the pre-NHS decades. Sketch launched Phoenix's version in June 1929.[396]

If the perils of one sort of infection lingered in the office, so too did those of another traditional blight. Office fraud remained a problem. As late as 1930 Phoenix was forced to cashier a chief cashier. And, since the 'serious irregularities . . . found in his accounts' had an extended history, he was dismissed and not allowed to take his pension with him.[397]

But if weak constitutions crumbled before the diseases and temptations of the era, it was not for want of trying on the Phoenix's part. Certainly, it could no longer be said, from the 1920s, that sport was discouraged because it interfered with business.[398] The company had perceived its value in strengthening bodies and even, perhaps, in deflecting idle hands from mischief. From the end of 1921, the Board agreed to pay a rent of not above £220 per year to secure a sports ground for the Phoenix Cricket and Lawn Tennis Club.[399] At this time, General Manager Sketch said that he 'hoped that it would be possible to purchase a sports ground at reasonable cost for the benefit of the whole staff'.[400] By 1926 he was halfway there and was thanked by the Consultative Committee for helping them attain 'one of our great ambitions – a first rate sports ground'; but the Phoenix remained only the tenant of the ground that had been

[396] *Ibid.*, p. 74, 5 June 1929; also Consultative Committee Minutes, pp. 120, 122, 28 December 1928 and 15 April 1929.
[397] Phoenix Directors' Minutes, p. 217, 7 May 1930. [398] See above, p. 98.
[399] Phoenix Directors' Minutes, 33, p. 319, 16 November 1921.
[400] Phoenix Consultative Committee Minutes, p. 54, 4 January 1922.

found at Catford. In 1927, the lease was renewed for another two years, with the Committee still hoping that 'the club one day will have a ground for its sole use'.[401] It was not until 1932, some eleven years after the first initiative, that the Phoenix Club achieved this target and took over the running of the 'sports ground recently *purchased* at Catford' and notified the Board that it would cost about £600 per year to maintain (see Plate 8.6).[402]

The odd cashier or so apart, staff loyalty and camaraderie during this era seems to have been high. Relations with management were still exceedingly formal by modern standards, but they had progressed well beyond the disciplined obsequiousness of the late nineteenth century, and they could be robust. Both Ryan and Sketch possessed a good human touch and had a proper regard for the utility of good manners. Certainly, when other parts of a fractious labour market were displaying considerable instability, the Phoenix could count upon its people. Thus during the rail strike of 1924, which provided an early example of the misery that transport disruption can inflict upon the workers of the City, 'the General Manager reported that, although the Railway Strike had disorganised the ordinary means of travel, the attendance of the office staff had been excellent. To achieve this, and to put in a full day's work, had entailed in many instances personal inconvenience, and the conduct throughout reflected great credit on all concerned'.[403] Similarly, the staff withstood the General Strike of 1926 with fortitude. The directors showed rather less since the Board and committee meetings scheduled for 5 May 1926 were in fact cancelled. However, Sketch reported to the Board meeting on the next Wednesday, the 12th, on 'the excellent way in which the staff had surmounted the difficulties of attendance at the Office caused by the General Strike and had carried out their regular duties'. This was noted 'with much satisfaction' and the thanks of the Board were 'conveyed to the staff for their loyal attitude and work'.[404]

Head Office: further extensions to the nest

The stresses of economic depression apart, the event which probably caused most interest, and disruption, in the everyday life of the interwar office was the major reconstruction of the King William Street headquarters in 1931 and 1932. This, like many aspects of Phoenix development in the interwar period, was in some ways an indirect consequence of

[401] *The Bird*, March 1926, October 1927.
[402] Phoenix Directors' Minutes, 37, p. 84, 15 June 1932.
[403] *Ibid.*, 34, p. 195, 30 January 1924. [404] *Ibid.*, 35, p. 76, 12 May 1926.

the LGA takeover. Since that point, the LGA staff had operated from their old premises in Lincoln's Inn Fields, forcing Accident Manager Southam to commute between there and King William Street; there was no room for the LGA people at Head Office. This was manifestly inconvenient, and from 1927 – when the debris from that acquisition had settled somewhat – the Board began to give serious thought to rectifying the situation.[405]

The plan was to build across a large area to the rear of the existing office, between Sherborn Lane and Abchurch Lane, thus giving Phoenix House far greater depth behind the King William Street frontage. The company already owned empty property at 13 and 14 Abchurch Lane and there was a good chance of purchasing Abchurch House and Glebe House at the back of the site. The Legal & General Office maintained a small premises at 12 Abchurch Lane; if Phoenix could secure this, the company would control the whole of the block.[406]

By December 1927, a Special Committee of the Board had approved the purchase of Abchurch House and had secured ground rents on part of Glebe house.[407] The major outstanding issue was the intrusive finger of Legal & General property. Early in January 1928, Phoenix considered buying another part of King William Street which could be offered to Legal & General in exchange for 12 Abchurch Lane. But, hardly a week later, the Committee brought off a straight purchase of No. 12 for somewhat over £31,000.[408] After a consolidation exercise similar to the one which preceded the original construction of 1915, the Phoenix controlled all it needed, including the tactfully situated hostelry, The Clachan: and the company was, once more, ready to build.[409]

Buoyed up by enthusiasm for the project at the rear of the site, the Board decided also to embellish the front. This decision was to produce one of the most famous landmarks in the Square Mile. Another Special Committee was formed to 'decide upon the emblem to be placed on the Clock outside Phoenix House'. The 'Committee on the Phoenix House Clock' met and solemnly minuted its proceedings throughout the last quarter of 1928. Eventually, they decided upon 'a bronze Phoenix and flames of wrought sheet and gilt'. They then embarked upon experiments

[405] First thought occurred in 1925 (Directors' Minutes, 34, p. 423, 9 September 1925) but the Special Committee briefed with the necessary property acquisitions was not convened until May 1927 (*ibid.*, 35, p. 232, 18 May 1927).
[406] Phoenix Special Committee Minutes, p. 134, 19 May 1927.
[407] Phoenix Directors' Minutes 35, p. 311, 14 December 1927.
[408] *Ibid.*, p. 322, 11 January 1928.
[409] Phoenix Special Committee, p. 184, 6 December 1929.

Plate 8.22 Expanding the nest: the development of Phoenix House and King William Street.

Plate 8.23 The clock, adorned.

to establish 'the most satisfactory method of illumination at night of the clock and emblem'.[410]

Well back from the clock, bigger works were ready to proceed by late 1930. The architect was Campbell Jones and the builders were to be Trollope and Colls whose quote, at £168,499, was the lowest of the seven builders approached.[411] The plan was to demolish the existing houses in Abchurch Lane and Sherborn Lane and build a 'genuine extension', matching the floor levels of the 1915 building and adding some 40,000 square feet to them, bringing the total office space to 106,000 square feet. The extra space would accommodate a 20% increase in staff and bring all

[410] *Ibid.*, p. 161, 26 September 1928.
[411] About £70,000 of this capital cost was to be recouped from the sale of the LGA building, and the cost further defrayed by leasing to the Bank of Egypt about one-tenth of the new floor area, at an annual rental of £4,000.

Head Office employees – except for the marine department, still anchored near Lloyds – under the same roof. There would be central heating (costing over £11,500), four new lifts (for £5,194), and a new telephone exchange (£2,100).

Still more uplifting, there was provision for one of the Consultative Committee's most cherished ambitions: a Staff Lunch Room.[412] This had been a long-fought battle. The proposal for a 'lunch club' first came before the Consultative Committee in 1922. In 1920, when the Ladies' Advisory Committee asked for a Ladies' Lunch Club, they had been gently told that an integrated lunch club, for both men and women, was more desirable. But the prospect of getting any kind of club was scarcely bright. When the Committee proposed the issue in earnest in 1922, Sketch's response was 'sympathetic' but dwelt upon the 'practical difficulties in providing suitable accommodation'.[413] Seven years later, he reported that, despite ' a diligent search . . . for suitable premises', there had been 'no success'.[414] In the end, the only solution was to build them. When complete, the Lunch Room could serve 200, at an average subsidised cost of one shilling per head. In celebration, the Phoenix Staff Mess Club was formed in September 1932, rather more than a decade after the Consultative Committee had voiced a need for it. The small but long-awaited victory gives a useful insight into how a big business functioned as a community and what those who worked within it really valued.[415]

After much digging and hewing in 1931 and 1932, the Chairman's Annual Report of 1933 pronounced all complete and functioning. In the interim, disturbance had not been restricted to Phoenix's own. The building work pressed hard upon one of the neighbours: the important Wren Church of St Mary Abchurch. Its tower had to be underpinned at Phoenix's expense; its authorities worried about subsidence and required reassurance; and, in September 1932, clearly fed up, they applied for 'special consideration' in respect of the inconvenience caused. Phoenix calculated the price of 'special consideration' at £200; and paid up.[416]

The Phoenix in literary form

Many issues concerning life in the office were recorded in the pages of *The Bird*, the house journal of the Phoenix, which kept up an unbroken stream

[412] After salaries, the matters closest to the Consultative Committee's heart were the sports ground and the lunch room.

[413] Consultative Committee Minutes, p. 54, 4 January 1922.

[414] *Ibid.*, p. 124, 3 June 1929. [415] Directors' Minutes, 37, p. 114, 21 September 1932.

[416] *Ibid.*, p. 110, 7 September 1932.

of comment on the company's domestic affairs from Christmas 1919 until 1984. Launched by the staff of the former Law Life office at 187 Fleet Street, the magazine was, to begin with, a lighthearted publication, featuring mostly humorous and sporting themes. There was again much cricket, since this was a passion of one of the editors, W. G. H. Rawlinson. The huge, genial 'Rawly' was an institution in himself, helping to edit *The Bird* from the beginning and acting as sole editor from 1933 until his last issue in December 1957.[417]

Until the end of 1924, *The Bird* continued in its casual and frivolous guise, appearing irregularly. But, from March 1926, it was converted from a 'dilettante product' into the 'Official magazine of the Associated Companies'. In this form, it carried the imprimatur of the Phoenix leadership. Sketch introduced the first edition of the new series in somewhat fanciful vein:

> This is to welcome our friend, *The Bird* who now comes forth no longer a nestling hovering in the vicinity of its birthplace but fully fledged and ready to fly to the four corners of the earth, carrying news to all connected and associated with its parent, the Phoenix.

Despite the purple prose, however, it is clear that Sketch had grasped the value of a global newspaper for morale and corporate spirit in a multinational enterprise.

In its revised form, *The Bird* ran articles which spread important corporate intelligence, featuring leading personalities at Head Office, important agencies overseas or, as in April 1935, a topical eighteen-page spread on Phoenix's American subsidiaries. These sat alongside general interest pieces which could range from Lord Dillon's reminiscences of military life in the Raj to the role of the Phoenix in the Napoleonic Wars. Finally, interspersed with the inevitable string of retirements, obituaries and sporting events, there were improving technical essays such as 'A Tendency in Marine Insurance' or 'Personal Accident Insurance, its History, Romantic and Otherwise'. It was a successful mixture of the folksy, the esoteric, the historical and the current news: and it made people feel that they belonged.

[417] His role as a (very successful) Special Constable was likened to setting Gulliver to keep order among the Lilliputians. As a cricketer (also successful), his bowling action was likened to that of a man bored stiff with the proceedings and waving to someone in an adjoining field. *The Bird*, July 1938 (retirement) and June 1958 (obituary). Rawlinson was succeeded as editor by Kevin Croker, whose cricketing style was somewhat more classical, and who directed *The Bird* from 1958 until 1984.

Management between the wars

The individuals who featured most often in *The Bird*, alongside the directors and the chief executives, were the men who actually ran the company, or more exactly parts of the company: the managers. They faced an increasingly complex task. From 1908 to 1939, the Phoenix expanded both by internal growth, as premium volumes were pressed upward, and by external growth, as new companies were acquired.

The managerial divisions of the composite office grew up naturally enough, determined by the very different insurance end-products. However, the companies that were acquired were rarely entirely specialised ones and had often begun to diversify themselves. Thus NUF possessed an important accident business and LGA had modest accounts in fire, marine and life. Phoenix itself had commenced in a small way upon marine and accident lines before it bought in company-size reinforcements. All this raised problems of duplication in capacity and signalled the need for rationalisation.

Moreover, the acquisition of separate management teams focused on different product lines posed obvious difficulties in communication and coordination. Some of the teams were also clearly better than others, and the right human capital had to sifted from the rest. Internal growth also generated a greater need for specialisation of function as the scale of certain functions outran the capabilities of staff who had previously executed several connected tasks.

Sketch was very well aware of these problems and had confessed himself worried by them after the NUF, and, especially, LGA acquisitions. By the mid-1920s, Phoenix was facing classic difficulties in controlling an expanding multi-division, large-scale corporation. Ironically, of course, Sketch's first thought was to select out the human capital he knew best and had most regard for – his former subordinates from NUF – and locate them in positions of influence so as to acquire a network of control answerable to the centre. It is unclear whether he was counting on personal loyalties to himself (which were considerable) or whether he thought the Norwich men were simply superior; but the effect would have been the same. In particular, the planned appointments of H. E. Southam and E. F. Williamson as group accident and fire managers would have put Sketch's closest colleagues at NUF in direct charge of Phoenix's biggest battalions. The problem was that the sale of NUF denied him the option by removing half of this immediate support team – Southam stayed – and several more of the senior commanders he wished to appoint.

Sketch therefore had to manipulate the enlarged Phoenix of the 1920s and 1930s without much of the support that he had expected when he took on the job. The pressures of specialisation and coordination were met by three responses at the centre: the creation of the secretary's department in 1923, the introduction of the post of deputy general manager in 1931 and the setting up of a separate investment department in 1935. Sketch had good reason to be wary of the home management of LGA and mostly took his team leaders from Phoenix, or, where still posssible, Norwich backgrounds.

One success from the Phoenix stable was Kenneth Elder, the first secretary, who built up the secretary's department from scratch and directed it for eleven years. He could have retired in 1925, but was asked to stay on by Sketch – a rare enough event – and did so for another decade.[418] Elder had been the Pelican's manager in India, 1906–8, and his health had suffered from it; he then had an active war, rising to the rank of major, and his health suffered more. Despite his own problems, he was both incisive and kind. He was quick to see a problem and quick to rule upon it. He was very useful on the Consultative Committee, with an easy and sympathetic touch which won him much respect in the handling of staff affairs. Not least, he had been instrumental in the advance of female employment at the Phoenix; and was proud of it.

Where, at the centre, the problem often lay in correlating many expanding functions, the characteristic issue in the divisions, or some of them, was the absorption of new capacity. This was least true in marine and life. Northern Maritime had been a small and early addition. And, in the post-Sandeman Allen era, Phoenix–Union Marine maintained for decades underwriters in both London and Liverpool. Amidst contracting markets this could cause tensions,[419] but generally the system withstood the test of time. In the life sector, the big acquisition – Law Life in 1910 – had also been an early one. Absorption was long complete by the 1920s, and the life business came under little further external pressure in the interwar era.[420] Moreover, the life department was facing buoyant markets and was strongly managed.

The meticulous but also modest and retiring, and often ailing, E. R. Straker was replaced in 1919 by an actuary of a very different style. A. T. Winter, who became life and investment manager in 1923, as part of Sketch's early revision of functions, was probably the dominant force in the development of the company's life business in the interwar era. Winter too had graduated through British Empire and Pelican. He was

[418] Directors' Secret Minutes, p. 65, 23 January 1935.
[419] See this chapter, Section 8.
[420] There *was* a little, from LGA's pension business. See above, Section 7.

small, dapper, bright and quick, and he led the life department from 1919 to 1931 (see Plate 8.7). He was then promoted to the new post of deputy general manager and held it until retirement in 1935. Ryan had used Winter's analytical nose to scent out the trouble at LGA; and many of the life innovations of the period were a tribute to his acuity and energy. He was a man of 'strong and invigorating character . . . whose superficial fierceness of speech and demeanour were belied by the twinkle in his eye'.[421] Sketch clearly valued this benevolent terrier of a man, as repeated salary increases in the late 1920s testify. He left a strong ship for his immediate successors as life manager, A. H. Raisin (1931–5) and W. R. Moore (1935–47), to sail. In due time, Moore became the second deputy general manager from the life stable.

The most obvious area in which divisional capacity needed attention was the accident department. Here Sketch was fortunate that his friend and colleague from NUF, the invaluable Herbert Southam, elected to stay with the Phoenix. Southam had been a pioneer of accident business with the specialist Ocean office in the days of the first Workmen's Compensation Act in 1897. And he had rare direct experience of the difficult American casualty market by way of a two-year stint as General Accident's manager in the United States. By the time he went to Norwich Union, he was already 'an outstanding figure in the accident business'.[422] Of course, it was not irrelevant that Southam's three companies before Phoenix also featured on the *curriculum vitae* of R. Y. Sketch. As both accident manager of Phoenix and overall manager of LGA (which effectively made him Group accident manager), Southam spent the last phase of his career welding together the accident operations of Phoenix and the LGA, in both the United Kingdom and the United States. This operation required all his reputed soundness of judgement, and by the time retirement came, in 1934, he more than deserved it.

Phoenix was fortunate in possessing home-grown talent fit to succeed Southam. Both Arthur Battrick (accident manager, 1934–7) and B. H. Davis (accident manager, 1937–46) were officials of real substance. Battrick had joined Phoenix in 1907, Davis in 1908. Battrick had been home accident manager under Southam from 1925, whereas Davis was always a foreign specialist and became foreign accident manager in 1931. Like Winter, Battrick achieved the rank of deputy general manager, serving for the long period 1938–47. This appointment cleared the way for Davis to become accident manager. They made an effective team, and both were asked to defer retirement in 1945, which they did for two years. Davis was

[421] *The Bird*, October 1935. [422] *Ibid.*, January 1934.

a particularly energetic and clear-sighted individual – literally, he was a Bisley shot – whose personality was much like his lively and cheerful prose. The accident department then had its problems, but it also housed some of the Phoenix's most able technicians of the period.

Sketch had less reason to be happy about the fire department. The fire manager during the period 1910–25, E. A. Boston, for all his linguistic ability and Ryan's approval of him, was found 'a little cold in manner, if generous in heart'. But more important, perhaps, was the valuation that he had advanced 'less through brilliance than through shrewd common-sense and painstaking application'.[423] He did not find the tasks of rationalisation within the expanding composite office especially welcome. His retirement in 1925 offered Sketch the opportunity to apply to the fire department the same sort of modernisation that Southam was meting out to the accident wing. It was here that the loss of E. F. Williamson back to NUF told most. For Phoenix lacked any natural successor to Boston and the age structure of the available team did not promise well for modernising managers. Between 1925 and 1929 the office witnessed the retirements of four fire managers; and some were helped on their way. H. S. Moore was eased out after only seventeen months in the job, not only for the good of his health but also 'for the convenience of the office with the reorganisation now in progress'.[424] Not until the appointment of F. H. B. Yerbury as foreign fire manager, at the age of forty-three, in 1929 and as overall fire manager from 1931 was a satisfactory solution found. He had joined Phoenix in 1905, and was a national prize winner in the insurance examinations on either side of the First World War. He was clever, energetic, enthusiastic and popular; and Sketch promoted him rapidly. He served as fire manager from 1931 until 1946.[425]

There were three generational shifts within these appointments. The retirements of 1920–5 (including McDougald, Straker, Boston) were of men trained in the pre-composite days and used to more confined horizons; though even their horizons were not as confined as those of the retiring veteran of 1920 whose life had been 'one long placid experience wherein his gentle nature found no opportunity for discord and little charm in modern rush'.[426] A second spate of retirements in 1934 and 1935 (including Southam, Raisin, Elder and Winter) featured some of the architects of the famous victories and rescues of the interwar period. In the third wave, the most eminent of their successors (Yerbury, Battrick,

[423] *Ibid.*, March 1944. Thus proving that *The Bird's* beak did not lack edge.
[424] Directors' Secret Minutes, p. 42, 22 December 1926.
[425] *Ibid.*, p. 52, 11 November 1931; *The Bird*, May 1946.
[426] *The Bird*, April 1941.

Davis) would retire, after good stints at the top, in 1946 and 1947, thus creating the slots for the first cohort of postwar managers.[427]

One oddity in these patterns was the rise of Edward Ferguson. He moved from the post of City manager to become general manager's assistant in 1932, and then, at the age of forty-four, deputy general manager in 1936.[428] Unlike either Winter or Battrick, he took up this position without the experience of heading an entire department; but, also unlike them, he did go on to become general manager and chairman. Unlike almost all of the interwar top brass, he had been a LGA man. After a spell in the Glasgow office of the London & Lancashire, he was appointed assistant manager of LGA's Glasgow Branch in 1920. By the mid-1920s, he was assistant fire and accident manager for Scotland for Phoenix–LGA, and after 1926 moved to Phoenix Head Office as joint foreign superintendent.[429] He was shifted, almost immediately, in November 1927, to South Africa, where he did a good but brief job as branch manager, and was then brought back to the City office late in 1931.[430]

It is a curious sequence. It could be argued that, unlike his magisterial predecessors, Ferguson had never run anything really big before he came to run the Phoenix. By contrast, Sketch was accident manager at NUF at the age of thirty-nine and Ryan had been actuary at the REA by the time he was twenty-seven. Instead, Ferguson's career was littered with assistantships and he was a dyed-in-the-wool fire specialist; before 1940, when he became general manager, little in his experience had acted to adjust either perspective. Moreover, correspondence between Ferguson and Sketch does not suggest an excess of cordiality. The best explanation for Ferguson's advance might feature a combination of persistence, forcefulness of character, one or two foreign fire coups, and age. There were sharper minds and warmer spirits in the generations on either side of him, but few competitors in his own. Yet, if Sketch had thought of Ferguson as a nightwatchman general manager, he should have considered that age more carefully. Ferguson was forty-eight in 1940, and remained chief executive for eighteen years.

By 1940, Sketch himself was tired. He was sixty-five and had been in the saddle through two gruelling decades. His serenity was not achieved without strain. In 1921 Lord George Hamilton had noted that Sketch, after a taxing trip to the United States, 'is not as strong as he looks. I think that, with all his natural calmness, he is apt sometimes to fail, though his

[427] See below, pp. 883–4.
[428] Or, more precisely, manager to Sketch's managing director.
[429] *The Bird*, October 1927.
[430] Phoenix Directors' Minutes, 36, p. 436, 21 October 1931.

Plate 8.24 Edward Ferguson in 1939.

judgement and natural decisiveness are excellent.'[431] If Ryan had planned the composite Phoenix, it was largely left to Sketch to clean up the corporate messes which sometimes resulted. Both the LGA acquisition and the US market, separately and together, required determination in detection, clarity in analysis, and discrimination in prescribing cure, all of a very high order. Sketch was the ideal man for difficult times, but some of his difficulties were heaped upon him. Nor was he always able to use his best solutions to dispose of them; the NUF sale arbitrarily removed some of them. But he always maintained a lucid grasp of what the problems were, and he used great patience and tact in remedying them. He also

[431] Hamilton to Ryan, 12 August 1921, Directors' Files: Lord George Hamilton's file.

possessed a quality essential in an effective leader, the ability to inspire strong loyalties. Most easily forgave him the flowery prose to which he was inclined. Some, like Southam, Winter and Davis did exceptional jobs for him.

But, in the latter part of 1939, he 'expressed a desire for greater leisure' and to be relieved from the full official duties of Managing Director'.[432] Yet Chairman Walters had also expressed a desire to retire from the end of 1939. So the Board, presumably with tongue at least partly in cheek, elected Sketch as chairman, a role in which it is to be hoped he found sufficient leisure, since he held the post until 1948.

[432] Directors' Secret Minutes, p. 80, 2 August 1939.

CHAPTER 9

THE PHOENIX AND THE WORLD'S LARGEST INSURANCE MARKET, 1918–1939

There is a central paradox to the Phoenix's American trade in the inter-war years. During the 1900s and 1910s, the USA had provided the company's biggest source of premiums and also its largest source of worry. During the 1920s and 1930s, it became an even larger area of concern – and a still bigger market.

Expansion was achieved largely by company acquisition and diversification into the perilous US casualty market.[1] Phoenix worked this through a complex, increasingly diverse Group system of subsidiaries, rather than by explicit restructuring into specialised divisions based on product or region like that employed by Standard Oil, Dupont or Sears Roebuck. Indeed, the Phoenix response to creeping diversity during this era was to seek greater Group integration of fire and accident operations.

I. THE CONSTRUCTION OF AN AMERICAN GROUP

By 1918, the Phoenix organisation in America consisted of three elements: the company's US Branch, its wholly-owned US subsidiary, now called the Imperial Insurance Company,[2] and the Columbia Insurance Company of New Jersey.[3]

[1] 'Casualty' is the US insurance term for accident business. This term is used, in this chapter alone, where it seems more suitable, but the UK term 'accident' is retained in most instances.

[2] Formerly called the Pelican of New York, it was rechristened in 1914. 'Pelican' apparently possessed adverse connotations in the South and had proved bad for business, whereas New York was the 'Empire State' and the title 'Imperial' a complimentary nod in this direction.

[3] Founded in 1901, Columbia was the transatlantic offspring of Union Marine, absorbed by Phoenix, along with the parent, in 1911. Union Marine conducted business independently in the USA, as elsewhere, but the fire and automobile business of its subsidiary was taken into the Phoenix accounts from 1919 and under management of the Phoenix US Branch from 1921.

Major additions were made to this structure during the 1920s, primarily in the accident market: Phoenix formed its own US accident vehicle in 1922, calling it Phoenix Indemnity, and then acquired the considerable American operations of Norwich Union Fire and London Guarantee & Accident (LGA) upon its purchases of these British-based offices in 1920 and 1922.[4] LGA also towed its own US subsidiary into the Phoenix fleet; this was the veteran Philadelphia fire office, United Firemen's.[5]

The Imperial, Phoenix Indemnity, LGA, Columbia and United Firemen's operated as separate names throughout the interwar period. They were fully integrated only in 1955–6 under the flag of Phoenix of New York and the company's US business was handled by this vehicle from 1956.

However, the 1930s also marked an important stage in the evolution of a Phoenix Group organisation in the USA; and the drive for the coordination of American fire and accident business in the period 1935–40 contributes a central element to the development of Phoenix's global export strategy between the wars.

As these adjustments took effect, the US share of Phoenix's global fire exports rose from 40.3% in 1910 to a peak of 56.4% in 1925, before slipping back to 50.8% in 1929 (see Table 9.1). The United States, of course, was among the major economies most severely affected by the Crash and its share of Phoenix fire business reacted accordingly.

So too did one vital source of international comparison for the business historian: the magnificent Phoenix Review of Foreign Agencies, which had provided annual returns for every one of the company's overseas agencies since 1787, did not survive 1930. An adequate replacement did not become available until 1938, when a revised form of the Combined Fire Revenue Account introduced a means of measuring net foreign premiums by the country of origin. This permits an extension of the data given in Table 9.1 in the form of the US share in Phoenix total net foreign fire income: the proportions for 1938–40 are still dominant ones of 51–52%.

Yet, if US demand increased its hold on Phoenix's traditional business in fire insurance between 1920 and 1940, the US market virtually monopolised the company's new line in accident business. For the duration of the 1920s and 1930s, much of Phoenix's accident business was American casualty business.

Before taking over Norwich Union Fire in 1920, Phoenix had scraped together a worldwide accident business of a mere £164,350. The acquisition multiplied this figure tenfold and NUF did much of its accident trade

[4] See Chapter 7.

[5] It was formed by the fire brigades of Philadelphia in 1860 and acquired by LGA in 1920.

Table 9.1. *Share of Phoenix US Branch and US subsidiaries in the company's total foreign fire income (%), 1910–29*

Year	US Branch	Pelican/ Imperial	Columbia	United Firemen's	Total
1910	35.7	4.6	–	–	40.3
1915	42.4	6.3	–	–	48.7
1920	34.9	7.0	5.5	–	47.4
1925	35.6	7.2	6.3	7.3	56.4
1929	33.3	6.0	4.9	6.6	50.8

Note: Results for 1930 were heavily affected by the Crash and were grouped, unhelpfully, under the US Branch.
Source: Phoenix Review of Foreign Agencies, Book 5. The source terminates in 1930.

in the USA. But London Guarantee did even more. About 80% of its accident turnover was drawn from across the Atlantic. Leaving aside the Norwich Union stake in the US liability market, and Phoenix's own US capacity through Phoenix Indemnity, the accident earnings of LGA alone accounted for well over half of the Phoenix's *world* accident earnings in 1922 and, even during the 1930s, remained at 40% in most years. The very necessary thinning of the LGA accounts carried out by the Phoenix management made no further impact on this considerable share. In 1926, when that thinning was going on, Phoenix's combined accident network in the USA netted over 71% of the office's world accident earnings.

At this time in the USA, of course, Phoenix was diversifying, both in terms of company structure, with an increasing number of vehicles and names, and in terms of market sector, with an increasing variety of insurance types. Some of this diversification in the USA – as with Columbia – followed from Phoenix's growth as a UK composite; they were acquisitions attached to other acquisitions. But much of it was aimed at the US casualty market; and slanted Phoenix away from its traditional attachment to US fire insurance. The advent of the enormous slice of liability business that came with LGA changed the balance of Phoenix's US involvement in a fundamental way. Phoenix Indemnity and the NUF accounts were also exercises in diversification into American casualty, but they were dwarfed by the impact of LGA. In 1922, LGA's casualty income from the USA was £2.9 million, whereas Phoenix's US fire premiums summed to only £1.7 million. After 1922, the Phoenix in the USA was required to rise not only from the ashes but from the wreckage of automobiles and the tangle of lawsuits. The change was to cause many problems.

2. RECOVERY AMID RECESSION: PHOENIX AND FIRE IN THE USA, 1918–31

Percival Beresford who took over as sole US manager of the Phoenix fire operation in 1914, controlling both the US Branch and the Imperial, lived through a complicated period in the office's fire underwriting in the USA. He inherited an organisation which had been subjected to critical scrutiny from London for a decade and a half. He then put it to rights and beyond criticism in the teeth of economic recession. Before the war, the US economy had boomed and the Phoenix had floundered. After 1920, the US economy wallowed, and the Phoenix, or at least the Phoenix fire operation, revived. Beresford may have mused upon this peculiar reciprocal relationship, but he drew no pleasure from another: the decline in the status of the fire wing of Phoenix as the casualty wing moved into the ascendant, at least in terms of income.

After having cleaned up the fire accounts, and overhauled what he saw as the senior echelon of the company's US operation, he was dismayed to find it subordinated to a new – if not very profitable – force. A fraud and suicide by a senior lieutenant marred his last years, and, when he retired in 1935, his job was taken by Phoenix's top casualty man in the USA, J. M. Haines. The Phoenix Board summed up what Beresford had found confusing about the shifting currents in American insurance by appointing Haines to run *both* the fire and accident wings.

But, long before this, Beresford had done sterling work. Under his control, the underwriting results for fire improved sharply in 1915 and 1916, and then were swept up by America's wartime and postwar industrial boom from 1917. In that year, the USA entered the First World War and the country's manufacturing sector moved into overdrive. The upswing lasted until 1921, when the industrial boom collapsed and brought the worst year for the insurers since 1906. Even so, only one other year in the period 1915–31 showed a deficit on the fire account, and that was the year that bore the scars of the Wall Street Crash (see Table 9.2).

These improved results owed little to superior cost efficiency in running the business: with the exception of the war years, when premiums increased by two-thirds between 1915 and 1919, the expense ratios remained on the high side. The effects of the boom of 1920 and the addition of United Firemen's in 1923 are both clearly visible in the premium receipts, but neither exerted any beneficial effect on cost levels. More-

Table 9.2. *Phoenix net underwriting surplus, fire business: US Branch, Imperial, Columbia, United Firemen's, 1915–31 (annual results)*

Year	Gross premium £	Loss ratio %	Expense ratio %	Underwriting surplus %
1915	790,534	53.1	40.5	6.4
1916	834,171	51.5	38.9	9.6
1917	992,430	46.6	36.0	17.3
1918	1,165,932	48.7	36.9	14.4
1919	1,316,383	42.9	39.3	17.8
1920	1,759,590	43.8	40.0	16.2
1921	1,753,615	61.7	44.1	−5.9
1922	1,669,702	56.4	41.8	2.0
1923	2,271,947	57.0	42.2	0.9
1924	1,895,380	54.7	44.1	1.2
1925	1,989,851	51.3	42.9	5.9
1926	2,084,333	55.3	42.7	2.1
1927	1,994,881	48.3	43.9	7.9
1928	1,951,133	47.7	44.8	7.4
1929	1,864,552	48.9	46.8	4.3
1930	1,581,626	51.9	56.3	−8.2
1931	1,665,602	49.7	49.8	0.5

Source: Calculated from Phoenix Review of Foreign Agencies, Books 4 and 5.

over, it was clearly the combination of rapidly contracting premium flow and persistently high costs which caused the adverse results of the Crash period. By contrast, it was underwriting efficiency which produced Beresford's improvements in profits: even in a decade which saw recession, earthquake and hurricane, shrewd selection of risk kept the loss ratio in a healthily suppressed state.[6]

Five-year averages for the Phoenix underwriting surplus on US fire business for the period 1899–1929 are highly flattering to the regime which began in 1914 (see Table 9.3). The Phoenix fire results for the 'depressed' 1920s are notably better than those for the 'booming' 1900s.

To have produced a rising surplus in the late 1920s was no mean achievement. Even in 1925, the Board paid tribute to Beresford's skills and recorded that the 1924 results for UK insurers in the USA had shown

6 It was unusually low too during the wartime boom. In the period 1910–21, the US fire loss ratio was lower than the general foreign fire loss ratio in only four years: 1916, 1917, 1919 and 1921.

Table 9.3. *Phoenix net underwriting surplus, fire business: combined US Branch and US subsidiaries, 1899–1939 (five-year averages, %)*

1899–1903	−0.5	1915–19	13.1
1904–8	−19.3	1920–4	2.9
1909–13	7.1	1925–9	5.5

'very satisfactory progress for the Phoenix'.[7] Indeed the Board's Fire Committee went further arguing that the 'substantial profit' of 1924 (probably caught in the 1925 figure in Table 9.2 above) had resulted in 'the *leading position* now taken by the company in the list of profit ratios in the USA'.[8] The refrain of congratulation continued into 1926, when the Board was gratified by the high ranking achieved by the company in the quinquennial results for British insurers operating in the USA.[9] In view of the later relations between Beresford and the Board, this was a passage of somewhat ironic benevolence.

One of the reasons why fire business ran more smoothly than casualty business in the 1920s was the difference in the agency systems employed. Casualty business was transacted by large general agencies covering big territories and representing only one or two insurers. This arrangement caused many problems for Phoenix and other offices.[10] By contrast, fire business was gathered by a myriad of small agents, each representing many offices. These were marshalled by field men or special agents who worked directly to the New York office and provided a link between the point of sale and the headquarters organisation. This system allowed management a much higher degree of control, whereas accident business was to suffer from the considerable amount of autonomy exercised by over-mighty general agents.

Nevertheless, Beresford was clear that his fire agents had to be carefully nurtured. Many for instance would refuse to represent companies boasting less than $1 million in capital. It was with this in mind that, late in 1927, Beresford recommended that the capital of the Imperial be raised

[7] Report on Visit to USA and Canada by General Manager (Sketch), Deputy Chairman (Buxton) and Accident Manager (Southam), presented to Board on 25 November 1925. Also Directors' Minutes, 34, p. 356, 11 March 1925. Alongside the joint report of November 1925, there was a very odd independent report from Buxton, reassuring the Board, 'from a position outside the executive', that 'in the USA, in the persons of our principal officers, financial advisers and trustees, we are well-served, in good hands, and dealing with people on whose advice the Board can place every reliance'. After LGA, reassurance was at a premium, no doubt.

[8] Fire Committee Minutes, Book 3, p. 149, 11 March 1925 (my emphasis).

[9] Phoenix Directors' Minutes, 35, p. 21, 10 February 1926.

[10] See below, pp. 683–9, 716–7.

from $0.5 million to 'millionaire' status and that the equity of the Columbia and the United Firemen's be increased similarly from $0.4 to $1 million.[11] This was achieved by retaining in the subsidiary companies the investment income and dividends normally remitted back to London; the usual instalment from Imperial and Columbia was $200,000 apiece per year and, from United Firemen's, $300,000.

One measure of how well this structure functioned in the selling of fire insurance during the 1920s is the lack of Head Office comment on the subject. This was not for lack of Head Office personnel to give it. The decade saw a rich flow of general managers, deputy chairmen and accident managers backwards and forwards across the Atlantic. This was in fulfilment of Sketch's belief that, 'Our interests are so great in the United States that it is both wise and economical for several officials to be in touch with all aspects of the business.'[12] They kept in touch so well that, in some years, there might be as many as three inspections by senior men from London. Yet the amount of assessment of the fire business was negligible in comparison with that addressed to the casualty sector; and the most travelled official by far was the accident manager.

The year 1927 proved something of an exception. By the autumn, fire receipts were 10% down on the previous year, and Sketch did feature this in his American report. He judged it a general phenomenon, affecting all offices. Clearly, it followed directly from economic slowdown: manufacturers were holding smaller stocks and there had been slippage in prices. For Phoenix loss ratios stayed low but expense ratios began a sustained rise. Sketch did not like the signs: expenses could not be cut further without impairing efficiency and volume of premium could not be increased without reneging on the office's sworn policy of cautious underwriting.

One sign in particular was threatening. Phoenix lost $150,000 by the collapse of a general agency in Florida.[13] In the expansionary phase of the early 1920s, this organisation had built up its business from twenty-three agents and annual premiums of £40,000 to ninety-five agents and £60,000 in premiums by 1926. It was profitable until the Florida real estate and bank crash of July 1926. Then, in autumn 1926, a tornado fell upon Miami, adding injury to insult, and the agency collapsed, leaving its debts in the debris. In the fire sector, this was Phoenix's first major victim of the American depression.[14] Ironically, however, it was neither the first

[11] Beresford to Phoenix, London, 3 November 1927.
[12] Report on Visit to USA by General Manager, presented to Board, 15 August 1923.
[13] Messrs Strickland and Travis.
[14] All companies covered tornado risk as part of fire insurance. Total effective tornado cover in 1927 was over $40 million.

Table 9.4. *Phoenix loss ratios on US tornado risk, 1911–27*

1911–27	43%
1918–27	46%
1923–7	59%

nor the last victim in the 1920s to fall foul of tornado. St Louis was decimated in 1927 and the tornado loss ratio rose steeply in the second half of the decade (see Table 9.4). Phoenix's losses for 1923–7 were a good deal worse than the out-turn on all US tornado insurance, which was a loss of 45.7%.

Clearly, the economy was not the only place where ill winds were blowing.

But, of course, in the America of the late 1920s and early 1930s, they blew upon the economy with special force. The economic tornado of 1930 and 1931 was sufficiently damaging for insurers to bring both the Phoenix general manager and the chairman to the USA. And again the crisis was enough to push the fire business to the forefront. Sketch was upset by 'the exceptional drop in our American fire income... during 1930' – it had fallen by over 15%, on top of a fall in 1929 of nearly 4.5% – and alarmed by the manner in which 'our expense ratio was seriously heightened' (see Table 9.2).

The purchase of the North American operation of the Australian company, the Queensland Insurance, which had a useful US account, had helped the fire results a little.[15] But Sketch did not believe that Beresford had identified the 'danger spot' of the expense ratio and pressed him hard upon it. 'The principal object of my journey', he told the Board, 'was to enable Mr Beresford to understand our outlook thoroughly and to see the reasonableness of it.' For his part, Beresford showed that he had reduced the staff since 1928 by no fewer than sixty-eight persons, with thirty-two redundancies taking place in 1930 and 1931; and the result, he promised, would be a drop in the expense ratio for 1931 of at least 4%. In the end, Sketch departed convinced, reassured that 'there is no spirit of complacency in our United States organisation'.[16]

Yet, complacency or no complacency, that organisation could not escape the effects of the Crash. Many agencies went the way of the

[15] See below, Chapter 10, Section 10. Phoenix failed to buy the Queensland itself (see Chapter 10, Section 9).

[16] Report on Visit to USA of General Manager and Chairman, 2 October 1931.

Florida representatives of 1926. And here its system of many small agencies told against the fire wing. By December 1932 the Phoenix Group of companies in the USA had written off $282,263 of uncollected premiums, of which three-quarters were fire premiums; and it could not collect $739,042 more in overdue premiums, of which half stood to the fire account. This was not the nastiest financial complication to beset the Phoenix in Depression America,[17] but it was unpleasant enough.

3. FIRST STEPS IN AMERICAN ACCIDENT: NORWICH UNION INDEMNITY AND PHOENIX INDEMNITY

One of Phoenix's main objectives in acquiring Norwich Union Fire (NUF) was to lay hands on the accident business of NUF's American subsidiary, Norwich Union Indemnity (NUI). Almost immediately, however, the act of possession jolted Phoenix into its own accident initiative in the States, the creation of Phoenix Indemnity. As Sketch later explained it, Phoenix feared that the lack of an accident presence in the USA carrying the Phoenix name would prejudice other lines of Phoenix business to the advantage of Norwich Union: 'we could not allow the Norwich Union agents to have greater facilities than the Phoenix agents'.[18] A logical conclusion was to run two indemnity companies with different titles and business mixes but under unified management.

NUI did about one-third of its business in the dangerous workmen's compensation sector and another one-third in automobile insurance. It was sensible, therefore, to seek balance and give Phoenix Indemnity a bigger slant towards motor business, and it was launched largely to work this market; by 1925, only a fifth of its turnover was committed to workmen's compensation, the great majority to automobile insurance. Both offices were placed under the control of W. G. Falconer, president and general manager of Phoenix Indemnity, and run by joint officials. This system worked well. The Phoenix Group accident manager, Southam, on one of his many trips westward, found in 1924 that the Indemnity operations were briskly handled, that Falconer was an able and keen supervisor, well in touch with all departments, and that he possessed a well-trained staff, good records and capable agents.[19] If these companies encountered problems in the 1920s, they came from the market, not from the management. The contrast with LGA in the mid-1920s was to be instructive.

[17] That was the Hellriegel scandal; see below, Section 6.
[18] Report of General Manager on US Business, 1927.
[19] Report of Accident Manager on US Business, 1924.

Launched in 1918, NUI was the core of Phoenix's accident operation in the USA, prior to the acquisition of LGA in 1922. The larger of the two indemnity companies, it was also the less successful, largely due to its greater exposure to the dangerous business of workmen's compensation. Overall experience of US business for NUI, 1919–23, was a loss ratio of 65% and an expense ratio of 40%; however, its loss ratio on compensation business alone was 87% and the losses on New York business alone 82%. Reviewing this situation on his 1924 trip, Southam was satisfied with NUI's management, and came to his conclusion that it was scarcely possible to write profitable casualty business in the New York of the 1920s.[20] Phoenix Indemnity's record on workmen's compensation business was even worse but it had much less of this damaging class. By 1925, Phoenix Indemnity possessed a small but satisfactory turnover, breaking even on $1.8 million worth of mostly motor business ($2.5 million in 1926), even with an expense ratio of 40%. Falconer was instructed to take limiting action on the compensation account; but there was little that could be done: workmen's compensation remained a drain on accident business in the United States throughout the interwar period.

Phoenix first encountered the problem through the books of NUI. It possessed two, equally unattractive aspects. The first was a direct consequence of the economic troubles of the 1920s. In the postwar boom years, 1918–20, industrial wages were high and, consequently, the insurance rates for workmen's compensation were reduced to reflect the lower risk. Then, when recession set in, the rates charged by the insurers proved too modest to cover the rising level of incoming claims. The appropriate response was to raise the rates to match the increased risk; but the same decline in trade which worsened the risk also squeezed the earnings of employers. Inability to secure a remunerative rate, which industry would, or could, pay was the first constraint on casualty business in the interwar years. The second was the method of payment, even when premiums were forthcoming. Custom was that employers paid only a nominal amount when initiating the policy and then extinguished the balance on a monthly, quarterly or half-yearly basis. Competition between the offices, as markets faded, often led to payment being postponed a full twelve months. In a business depression, this type of insurance was more trouble than it was worth. The main preoccupation of all Phoenix accident managers after 1921 was shedding as much of it as possible.

Phoenix Indemnity was partially protected by its specialisation on motor business. In the mid-1920s, it probably suffered more from the

[20] *Ibid.*; see also Chapter 7, section 2.

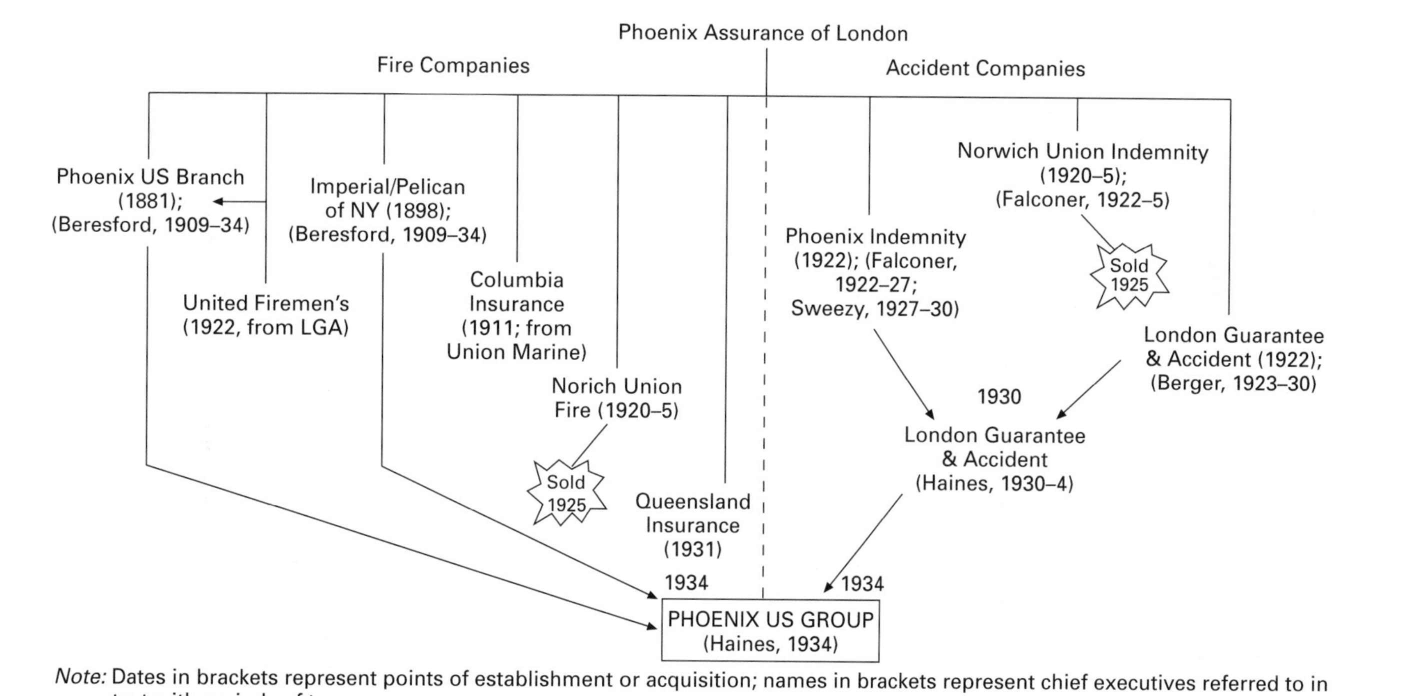

Note: Dates in brackets represent points of establishment or acquisition; names in brackets represent chief executives referred to in text with periods of tenure.

Fig. 9.1 The evolution of a composite insurance group in the USA: Phoenix and its satellites, 1920–39

internal convulsions of Phoenix corporate strategy than from the external pressures of its market: it was hurt both by the acquisition of LGA in 1922 and by the sale of NUF (and thus NUI) in 1925. The first demoted Phoenix Indemnity to a truly second-rate operator in the casualty market: the much larger LGA network became Phoenix's casualty flagship in the USA and Phoenix Indemnity was throttled back to allow it free passage.[21] The second imposed substantial disruption costs as it became necessary to disentangle the two indemnity companies and create a fresh executive structure for Phoenix Indemnity. The replacement of lost NUI officials and expertise produced an adverse effect on its expense ratio for the rest of the decade.

Despite the split with NUF in 1925, the Phoenix management had hoped that the two American accident operations could continue to run in harness. However, the leadership in Norwich was minded otherwise and insisted upon separation; from March 1926 the sister offices reverted to the role of competitors. There was only one area of exception: marine business in the USA had been handled since 1924 by an independent marine department serving Phoenix, Union Marine and Norwich Union. This arrangement was continued. But everything else was dismantled. And it did not always come apart with the best of grace. When B. H. Davis went on the first of his investigative tours of the United States in 1926, he 'heard quite a lot about the Norwich–Phoenix split. Evidently, Sweezy (Falconer's deputy) thinks Norwich did, and are doing, quite a lot of "dirty work".'[22]

So, by the mid-1920s, Phoenix Indemnity was a constrained venture. However, in the second half of the decade, it was to be further limited by three main developments. One was the growing power of LGA as Sketch's managerial broom swept through the chaos of that organisation; the second was the fatal illness of Falconer; and the third was adverse trends in the US automobile market.

In the first respect, Phoenix Indemnity suffered in much the same way as Phoenix's fire wing from the radical change in the balance of power brought about by reform within LGA (see below, Section 4). In the second, it was especially unfortunate. Falconer had run a tight ship and was well respected by both Southam and Sketch. In the course of 1926,

[21] General Manager's Report on US Business, 1927.

[22] Davis' 'American Diary', p. 180. This is a remarkable, day-by-day, pen-portrait of his American travels and meetings. Shrewd, sharply observed, always good-humoured, sometimes witty, highly readable, the Davis journal compares well with the other outstanding accounts to which the travails of the US market had moved his eminent predecessors, Jenkin Jones and J. J. Broomfield. See vol. I, pp. 207–22, 292–308.

however, Falconer fell seriously ill and in November was packed off to North Carolina to convalesce; he returned in March 1927. Phoenix treated him with an odd, and perhaps misplaced, consideration. Southam insisted on a full medical before Falconer resumed work; it confirmed an incurable stomach cancer. Falconer was not told of this and the medical report he was given was falsified. Both the Phoenix Board and the LGA management discussed the problem of Falconer's illness while it remained unknown to him. He died later in 1927.

As Falconer declined, so did the US motor insurance trade. In the trough years of the recession, the write-off value of motor vehicles was often more attractive to their owners than their transportation value; and, in such years, the number of complete write-offs rose extraordinarily. The irreparable automobile was the latter-day descendant of the conveniently inflammable nineteenth-century cotton mill. Southam reported after his US tour of 1928 that, since 1925, American motor business 'had not been running well generally' despite 'substantial' rate increases.[23] Moreover, as the spread of motor ownership widened, the US state legislatures began to take an increasing interest in the insurance cover of this proliferating traffic. The crucial step was taken by the state of Massachusetts in January 1927, when it introduced compulsory liability insurance for all drivers: this 'loaded the dice' against the insurers by denying them the ability to select for quality. Within a year, Southam reported that the measure had 'practically eliminated' Phoenix's motor business in Massachusetts.[24]

The three afflictions of Phoenix Indemnity prompted an inevitable thought among the leading men of the parent company that the smaller US casualty operation, Phoenix Indemnity, should be combined with the larger LGA. By 1927, the loss ratios of both companies were acceptable but the expense ratios were poor; amalgamation thus offered cost savings. After Falconer's death, the question was considered seriously. But it was observed that LGA's casualty agents were usually also fire insurance agents for other companies, while the representatives of Phoenix Indemnity were naturally expected to remit any fire business that came their way to the mother company. At this time, a clash of interest was detected and it was decided to keep the two enterprises separate. Sweezy – who also impressed Southam – was appointed to succeed Falconer as president of Phoenix Indemnity, and Beresford, as the senior Phoenix official in the USA, became its chairman.[25]

Next year, Southam reported back to London that the new leadership

[23] Report of Accident Manager on US Business, 1928. [24] *Ibid.* [25] *Ibid.*, 1927.

Plate 9.1 Percival Beresford, Phoenix US fire manager.

was 'shaping remarkably well'. In particular, it had succeeded in keeping the poisonous workmen's compensation business to a minimum; in 1928, this class still accounted for only 24% of a $3.2 million premium income. But the motor business which the company had been formed to pursue was again experiencing a bumpy ride.

In the end, it was the Crash which put paid to the independence of Phoenix Indemnity. Nice measurements of conflicting interests yielded, under the stress of economic breakdown, to rapid calculations of cost. During 1930, Phoenix Indemnity was moved into the LGA headquarters at 55 Fifth Avenue – anticipating the Phoenix fire branch in this removal by some five years (see below, pp. 707–14). The indemnity company now passed under the control of the LGA chief executive, J. M. Haines – again foreshadowing the fate of the fire department. But the integration of Phoenix Indemnity proceeded a good deal more smoothly than the integration of the Phoenix fire wing. The two casualty operations combined reasonably easily; staff duplication was reduced and there were few ill feelings. Of course, Sweezy, who departed to a post with the Globe, may well have felt differently. Certainly, by late 1930, from his new office, he was reputed to be 'actively watching our Pacific Coast business'.[26] Otherwise, the absorption went well: Phoenix Indemnity kept its name but surrendered its individuality peacefully.

For its part, LGA continued its march to the head of Phoenix's American legions.

4. THE FALL AND RISE OF LGA

The advance of LGA to an influential position within Phoenix's American network by 1930, and a pre-eminent one by 1935, was certainly no easy operation. Rather, it required a dour and dogged campaign.

It did not take the Phoenix men long to realise that the company they had acquired in their hunger for US casualty business was actually at its considerable worst in the USA. Nor could they ascribe LGA's American problem to the dip in the US casualty market that had followed so unfortunately and rapidly upon the boom which had whetted their appetite between 1918 and 1920. The trouble clearly ran deeper and further than that. As early as 1923, on his first major transatlantic inspection, Sketch found that LGA's New York operation was seriously flawed with 'underwriting too loose, expenses too high'; it paid excessive commission rates to agents and princely fees for medical opinions. Sketch summarily ended these practices, weeded over seventy staff and sacked the manager.[27] The replacement, C. M. Berger, was to be, with his successor J. M. Haines (and both under strict instruction from Sketch), a significant influence in the rescue of LGA.

In 1925, Sketch returned for a second look at LGA in America and was over-optimistic about the pace of the repair work. Rates for workmen's compensation business, which were fixed by the insurance departments of the individual state governments, had recently been raised; improved office management was succeeding in extracting bigger initial deposits from employers; and sharper underwriting selection had improved the quality of business while reducing total income by 25%. Southam agreed with Sketch that 'business is being conducted along sounder lines than at

[26] Battrick to Sketch, 17 November 1930.
[27] Report of General Manager on US Business, 1923.

any time since the LGA became associated with the Phoenix'.[28] The conclusion reached by Sketch was that 'there is every ground for optimism in respect of our accident business in the States' and he looked forward to 'an era of prosperity' in that department. He congratulated himself on a successful economy drive and both Beresford and Berger on correcting 'the errors under the old regime'.[29]

This was premature: 1925 was the year in which the New York Insurance Department demanded increases in LGA's reserves – 'dealt with our accounts in a drastic manner'[30] – and Southam at length became convinced that there had been dirty work in LGA's presentation of its reserve position.[31] Even amidst his contented jottings upon his 1925 inspection Sketch had noted that the 'active and expansive' development in accident business in the period 1923–5 had brought in much business of 'undesirable quality and irregular connection'. This was to be a more telling perception than his intimations of satisfaction.

The unpleasant surprises of 1925 clearly persuaded Sketch and Southam that managerial visitations to the USA were not achieving a true picture of the American operation. The revelations stimulated a phase of more intense scrutiny and a three-year period of fundamental reforms. The precondition for this was achieving an accurate picture of what *was* going on inside the American operation.

It was obtained by a measure of audacious simplicity. Sketch selected one of the shrewdest middle managers on his London staff and sent him to New York on an intelligence-gathering mission. This was not the whistle-stop tour of the head office big-wig; this official was to be left in place, and under rough cover, until he had the intelligence. The official selected for this sensitive task was B. H. Davis; and he carried it off brilliantly.[32]

Davis sailed on the White Star liner *Homeric*, arriving in New York on 30 June 1926, and stayed there for four months. Even by the time he left England, suspicions had been hardening that the trouble at LGA was far worse than Sketch had first imagined. Phoenix House had begun to buzz with talk of LGA's 'unbridled expansion'.[33] Accordingly, Davis carried instructions to look closely at four main aspects of the accident com-

[28] Report of Accident Manager on US Business, 1925.

[29] Report of General Manager on US Business, 1925. [30] *Ibid.*

[31] See above, Chapter 7, Section 2.

[32] Davis joined Phoenix on the foundation of the composite office in 1908 after a stint at the London and South Western Bank. No doubt, the excellence of his work in the USA proved a factor in his subsequent rapid promotion: he was made foreign accident superintendant in 1929, foreign accident manager in 1931, assistant group accident manager in 1934, and group accident manager in 1937.

[33] Report of General Manager on US Business, 1925.

pany's US dealings: the level of its management standards, the wisdom of the drive for casualty, and especially, automobile business, the failure of the New York management to provide adequate statistical detail to London, and, most important, the influence of general agents in the acquisition of business.

Perhaps it should not surprise that Davis' landfall raised hackles in New York. Managers saw him as an informer, general agents saw him, correctly, as a threat to their effective control over the volume of business accepted by LGA. It took all his good humour to shrug off the cold shoulders and the unpaid lunch tabs. At this time, the senior management of LGA in New York consisted of Berger as manager, Haines and Hoffman as assistant managers, and Lloyd Jones as comptroller. Despite the fact that none of these officials was implicated in the long-running abuses at LGA, and were doing their best to rectify the faults, some of them – notably Berger – were uneasy about Davis' mission. This was not true of Lloyd Jones, a corporate statistician and systematiser of outstanding talent. He became Davis' best source, and both through his own work, and through the information he supplied, a major influence on Phoenix's clean sweep through LGA.[34]

The trading results of the mid-1920s revealed how necessary this was. In 1925 LGA had made a substantial loss on workmen's compensation business. In 1926, it still allocated over 41% of its total turnover of $11.5 million to this class of business – and achieved an overall trading deficit of 20%. It would later become clear that the combined Phoenix–LGA accident result worldwide for 1926 was a net loss of nearly 7% on total premium earnings of somewhat over £4 million; and that almost all of this loss came from the USA. The total money loss was £275,000. The worldwide claims ratio was a punishing 67%, while commissions and expenses ate up a further 38% of premium income. The contrast between the US and the UK accident record was striking. At home, workmen's compensation business absorbed under 23% of total accident underwriting and the claims ratio was 54.4%. By November 1926, Phoenix managers in London were already aware of this contrast and the outcome, the 'disastrous' trading results of 1924–6.[35]

By this time also, Southam had a good idea of some of the reasons.

[34] Of Welsh descent, Jones had emigrated to the USA in 1913. He served in the British army during the First World War, but returned to the United States after the Armistice to work as an accountant and statistician. He had wide insurance experience, having worked for the Globe, the Norwegian Globe, General Accident and Sun Indemnity before moving to LGA during its crisis period.

[35] Southam to Berger, 25 November 1926. See Chapter 7, Section 2.

Davis had found Lloyd Jones 'ready to spill over',[36] and had learned from the results. Jones had already fastened on to the reserves problem and had sent Berger a 'very dissatisfied' report on this subject. But his unhappiness was more widely based than this. Davis confided to his diary that, 'his position appears to be much like many of us were in when we tackled LGA Head Office . . . the office wants reorganising almost throughout'.[37]

But the deep inspection did not find fault with LGA's current management. Davis was impressed with Haines and Jones, if less so with Berger – though this last was not an impression sustained by Southam, who usually took Davis' opinions very seriously indeed. Davis found Haines 'a really valuable official'[38] and Jones something of a soul-mate, 'evidently a thinker . . . has vision, but also caution'.[39] Allowing a decent time for impressions to set, Davis concluded by mid-August that

> With Berger, Haines, Hoffman and Lowther supported by a really first-class figure man like Jones (and he is also a fine staff manager), this outfit ought to be one of the best in the USA, unless casualty business generally is a wash-out.[40]

His view was that LGA had indeed been in 'some pickle, but I believe that it is straightening out'.[41] In fact the 'pickle' that LGA was steeped in down to 1925 would probably have proved lethal had the company been left to its own devices. The credit for extricating it clearly belongs to Sketch. But if this was being done by late 1926, and the new managers were up to the job, what had the 'pickle' consisted of, why had it proved so poisonous, and why were its effects still lingering?

The major source of the trouble was a witless pursuit of bad business in difficult times. Upon arrival, Davis was suspicious even of Berger's 'automobile drive' – a campaign to drum up motor policies – in the mid-1920s; but this in fact proved justified by the claims and expenses ratio for the period. Many dimensions worse was the accumulation of workmen's compensation business over the years 1922–5. The reason for this lay in a disastrous imbalance of power between 'outsider' and 'insider' influences within LGA's selling policy. Outsider forces – the handful of large general agencies which acquired the bulk of workmen's compensation business, and were wholly independent undertakings, often serving more than one insurance office – possessed quite disproportionate power, while ineffectual LGA management had lacked the statistical means to check their abuses. LGA's numerical records for US business were found by their successors to be virtually worthless.

36 B. H. Davis, American Diary, 27 July, p. 61.
37 *Ibid.*, 29 July 1926, p. 79. 38 *Ibid.*, 24 July 1926, p. 41. 39 *Ibid.*, 10 July 1926, p. 7.
40 Ibid., 13 August 1926, p. 103. 41 *Ibid.*

Plate 9.2 The 'first-class figure man', Lloyd Jones.

This faulty connection between US management and US agencies was further exacerbated by the inability of LGA in London to maintain proper control over LGA in New York. The US Branch was reluctant to inform London fully of its dealings, or, indeed to make full financial remittance or account to London.[42] LGA had allowed an unacceptable distance to develop between Head Office and New York office. Phoenix was to encounter great difficulty and antagonism in the attempt to close this gap.

In the period 1914–22, when compensation business had been profitable, there had been no clash of interest between the general agents and the central management. But, after the wage slump of 1922, when alert

[42] In turn, Phoenix had to press hard to get money out of the management it inherited in New York; cf. Heron to Lawson, 23 January 1923, 'the remittance to this country of a large proportion of the increase in your surplus is absolutely necessary'.

underwriters had a definite interest in cutting back on the workmen's compensation trade, the general agents had powerful financial inducements for continuing to gather as much of it as possible. LGA's headlong rush into danger was a product of the hunger of over-mighty agents for commission and the debilitation of a management unable to whip in its hounds.

Little wonder then that the general agents viewed Davis' visit with outright hostility. One of them tried to get him drunk, failed, and, in his own cups, let slip that he was disturbed by 'Mr Sketch's . . . step of placing a Phoenix man in charge . . . in nearly every branch'.[43] Another vouchsafed to an LGA contact that he hoped that the visitation from London would not mean 'more trouble for everyone'.[44] Davis replied, at least to his diary, in kind: one general agent was described as 'dogmatic, egotistical, hasty'; another had 'no strength of character, plenty of cheek, and a hide like a rhino'.[45]

Clearly, one of Phoenix's greatest needs in the USA was to recover control of their general agencies so that London or New York, rather than a number of self-interested commercial ventures scattered throughout the states, should determine the volume of LGA's underwriting. They had already made one attempt. In 1924, Phoenix had insisted that LGA move its head office away from the ill-fated and expensive Fort Dearborn site in Chicago to New York. This reduced the influence of the most powerful general agencies in the Mid-west. In order to smooth feathers – but also to reduce this influence still further – Phoenix created an 'American Board', to consist of the biggest agents and Beresford. It was to be 'advisory not administrative', and meet only quarterly. Its purpose was clear: to give the agents the illusion of participation while providing a forum in which central policy could be laid down and evaded only with difficulty.

No doubt, these developments formed the earlier 'trouble' to which, in the view of the general agents, Davis' visit threatened to add a further instalment.

But if they caused the general agents irritation, they did not solve the problem: more was needed. Davis recorded in 1926 that 'some of the largest of these Agents have, from time to time, made more or less veiled threats that, unless their wishes were given effect, and the business written by them allowed to stand, they would seriously consider transferring their connections to other companies'.[46] So, Phoenix had to play them carefully; reining them in could not be a heavy handed manoeuvre.

[43] American Diary, 17 August 1926, pp. 125–6.
[44] *Ibid.*, 11 July 1926, p. 12. [45] *Ibid.*, 23 July 1926, pp. 37–9.
[46] American Diary, 2 July 1926, p. 3.

Plate 9.3 Pomp and circumstance at Fort Dearborn.

Yet, on the other hand, their persistent inclination to gallop could not be indulged. In 1925, the four principal general agencies (Conklin, Price and Webb of Chicago; Frederick L. Gray & Co. of Minneapolis; Landis and Brickell of San Francisco; and C. F. Daly & Co. of Colorado) brought nearly $2.5 million worth of compensation business to LGA's door. Just one of them, the Gray agency of Minneapolis, had procured one-sixth of all LGA's US turnover in this class and contrived to lose the company $200,000 in the process.

Davis' reports home on this issue caused so much disquiet that Southam, the Group accident manager, came out to join him in October 1926. The immediate result of their joint inquiries was a four-point instruction to Berger: cancel all consistently unprofitable business; refuse renewal of all unwanted business; select new business only with the utmost rigour;

reduce expenses. All points bore heavily upon the general agents and represented a marked tightening of the rein.

Berger worked at this with a will. He cancelled over 12% of the total compensation income flow, and 'maintained an absolutely firm stand, in spite of all opposition, arguments and threats' from the incensed general agents, most notably from the Gray agency.[47] Hostility was widespread but only the Gray agency actually defected, unilaterally reinsuring its LGA business with the Standard Accident Company. The resulting purification of the portfolio was more than worth the loss of a particularly refractory agency. The outflanking of the agents had been nicely managed; and Berger had 'handled the position with considerable skill'.[48] No longer did the outsiders hold the initiative; no longer were the insiders bereft of any check upon them. This was probably the major adjustment in the much-needed reform of Phoenix's US accident operation.

Success in this undertaking must have given Southam heart that he was correct to press on with reform rather than adopt the counsels of despair – put either all or half of LGA's accident business in the USA out to reinsurance – that he had contemplated in the worst moments.[49] A further transatlantic trip later in 1927 – he made three in the twelve months prior to October 1927 – convinced him that progress was being made. With rates for compensation policies still held at inadequate levels by the state insurance departments, careful selection of risk was still more vital. But Berger's axe had cut out most of the worst risks and the remaining agents had fallen into line. But, even then, Phoenix had reserve plans for the creation of a branch system 'in the event of a rupture'.

Accordingly, the half-year results to June 1927 looked a good deal more auspicious. Nor were there any more surprises to be faced on the reserves front; that issue was finally understood and resolved. Only in the area of credit insurance, necessarily highly vulnerable to a slump – especially within an economy where much of the consumer boom of the 1920s had been financed on tick – did Southam pause for thought. By late 1927 he judged it relatively secure 'unless, of course, some exceptional economic conditions manifest themselves rapidly in the United States'.[50] Overall premium income had been reduced, in the quest for purer business, from $16.5 million in 1923 to $10.5 million in calendar year 1927. Expenses also were reducing well.

On his one visit in 1928, Southam again simply listened to better news. Workmen's compensation business, 'still a difficult class', had been cut from 41% of $15.4 million total premium in 1924 to 36% of

[47] Report of Accident Manager on US Business, 1927. [48] *Ibid.*
[49] *Ibid.*, and see also Chapter 7, p. 462. [50] *Ibid.*

$10.0 million by 1927.[51] Over the same period, the overall expense ratio fell from 39.4% to 37.7%. Credit insurance was still hanging onto a bare profit. And the big agencies showed a marked improvement. Three which had made losses in 1926 reported profits in 1927. One other, the general agency for Boston, which had lost over $100,000 impartially in 1925, 1926 and 1927 was clearly marked for the axe. But many big and difficult cities – New York, Philadelphia, Minneapolis – recorded only modest losses. What was more, a new policy of replacing the old indirect general agencies with more, small, direct agencies was beginning to win ground.

Even 1929 began by not looking too bad, except in personal terms. The personal terms concerned Berger. In ominous sympathy with Falconer, Berger went down with stomach trouble, was diagnosed as suffering from colitis and was sent off to Bermuda to convalesce. Southam met him in New York in February and found him 'very changed physically', after a 30–40 pound (13–18 kg) weight loss. His subordinates were able and held the fort well; but Southam was worried by the head-hunting tendencies of 'the considerable number of new companies . . . formed in the USA with strong financial backing.'[52] However, new company flotations did not suggest imminent doom. Nor did LGA's 1928 results, which were good. The 'still unsatisfactory' class of compensation business had been reduced further to 32.5% of premiums and the expense ratio was still falling. For the first time since Phoenix had achieved a clear view of its problematic American accident subsidiary, Southam was satisfied that LGA looked good against other US casualty operators.[53]

Very soon too, the impact of Lloyd Jones on the internal administration of LGA began to tell. In place of the statistical chaos of the old regime, Jones created an office system which by autumn 1930 could supply results on a daily basis. Under his control also underwriting policy 'developed into a a rigid endeavour to carry out the wishes of the Home Office'.[54] This too was far removed from the insolent isolationism that had characterised the previous management.

The surgery carried out by Phoenix on LGA was beginning to take effect. But 1929 was not, of course, a year in which to expect quick recoveries. If LGA was making its way out of the sanatorium, the world economy was struggling to get in. Any individual company was likely to be damaged in the crush.

[51] *Ibid.*, 1928. [52] *Ibid.*, 1929. [53] *Ibid.*
[54] Report of Assistant Accident Manager, 1930.

5. THE PHOENIX AND THE AMERICAN CRASH

In the wake of the Wall Street collapse in the last quarter of 1929, Phoenix sent its accident manager to the United States for two extended tours. The first lasted from the end of February to the middle of April 1930, the second from mid-September to mid-October. There is a distinct difference in the tone of Southam's reports on the two occasions.

At first brush, he found the US results merely 'disappointing'. This was no doubt because the refurbished LGA was doing a good deal better than the pack of American casualty operators. It now ranked seventh in this group by premiums. And whereas in 1929 the US casualty offices had produced a net loss of 2.2% on total takings of $639 million, LGA had produced a small underwriting surplus of 1.3% on $9.6 million. Compensation business continued to be the main drain and had crept up again to over 34% total turnover. Automobile business was shaky but not a great deal worse than usual. Credit insurance – which LGA had offered since 1905 and which had produced a profit of 18% over the intervening quarter-century – had taken a knock, but, in Southam's opinion, was resisting. The financial slump at the end of 1929 had produced a spate of claims in October, November and December but they were still within bounds: 'whilst the set-back is to be regretted . . . I do not think this need be regarded as other than temporary'.[55] Certainly, there is no sense of a downturn severely out of the perennial run of troubles imposed by the US casualty market.

By the autumn, however, Southam was picking up different signals: US prospects were now 'anything but encouraging'. Compensation business was not recovering. Automobile rates were falling. Credit insurance, a portfolio worth $0.75 million in premiums to LGA, had sunk without trace. He noted too an extraordinary new development among insurance companies. He had first spotted it in the previous year:

> I find that the view continues to gain ground that Insurance Companies, as a whole, should not look for a profit from their underwriting but should be content if the premiums obtained are sufficient to provide for claims, commission and expenses, the companies taking as their remuneration the Interest on the reserves set aside for unexpired risk and outstanding claims. Many of the largest offices are willing to accept this and we must be prepared to face it.[56]

In the early months of the Crash a distinctive view of insurance 'profit' received perhaps its first general exposure. But in 1930, the effect was much more marked: 'There seems to be a complete change of front in the

[55] Report of Accident Manager on US Business, 1930, I. [56] *Ibid.*, 1929.

growing dependence of companies upon investment transactions.' As losses mounted on compensation and automobile business, many insurers attempted to recoup by energetic playing of the stock market. The change of front was particularly notable among the many new companies whose advent had so worried Phoenix in the later 1920s.

Southam now knew that he need worry no longer on that score. The competitive threat, particularly strong in the casualty sector, was surpassed by the financial threat, and the competitors were less equipped to deal with this than was LGA. Some offices had been investing substantial sums in 'Preference and even Ordinary shares'. For a while, this worked:

> These, for a time, appreciated greatly in value – at all events on paper. The recent financial slump has, however, caused heavy depreciation in the value of these securities and will affect companies, financial statements and surpluses accordingly.[57]

Indeed they did; many offices never recovered from the experience. Yet, within the same twelve months, Sketch was able to report that LGA was enjoying 'the largest surplus that it has ever had in the history of the company in America'.[58]

If competitors faded, the financial effects of the Crash did not. What Southam had noted was the first definition of a specifically American, and modern, notion of insurance profit. That profit cannot be drawn from underwriting alone has long been a commonplace of the insurance world. But it is the era of the Wall Street Crash which defines exactly how long.

The effects of the collapse upon Phoenix's ability to gather insurance business in the USA were more mixed. Fire premiums did show a sharp drop in 1930, and the downturn unfortunately coincided with an ageing leadership and a poor phase for expenses. The recession imposed high loss ratios of 50–56% while managerial slippage resulted in expense ratios above 50%. The combined effect was to throw the fire group into deficit in all four years 1930–3 (see Table 9.7, p. 704).[59] The losses were worst in the industrial regions of New York and the East, bad in the South, most protracted in the West, where deficits lasted until 1934 and 1936, and, ironically, lightest in the Pacific department. Business which had so frightened Avebury and the others before 1914 proved far more resistant to the tremors of 1929–33 than did the rest of US fire business: only in 1933 did the Pacific account tip into the red.

Even amidst the destruction elsewhere, Beresford appears to have kept

[57] *Ibid.*, 1930. [58] Report of General Manager on US and Canadian Business, 1931.
[59] The deficits were, as a percentage of net premiums: 1930 10.8%; 1931 2.3%; 1932 8.2%; 1933 2.1%.

Table 9.5. *LGA: US premium income and loss ratios, 1929–34*

	Total premium $	Total loss ratio %	Workmen's compensation loss ratio %
1929	9,633,373	52.9	69.9
1930	8,781,382	60.0	76.7
1931	8,323,387	n.a.	76.5
1932	7,576,877	55.2	74.4
1933	7,330,538	53.4	73.9
1934	7,189,244	54.3	70.8

his nerve, or perhaps his sense of humour: in January 1931, in a gesture of defiance to the fates, he relaxed Phoenix's usual fire limits to extend £110,000 worth of cover to the premises of the Federal Reserve Board.[60] As the financial world exploded, there must have been at least some satisfaction in protecting Fort Knox from fire. But there was less to come. Beresford was sufficiently worried, on Phoenix's own account, by the end of 1932 to propose a salary cut of 10% for all Group officials in the USA.[61] The Board accepted this and had also to assist in another way. In the depth of the crisis, American life and trust companies had refused to accept the policies of Phoenix US Group subsidiaries as security. This problem was solved only by Phoenix London agreeing to guarantee all policies issued by its American satellites.[62] These were fair indications of the strain under which the insurance industry in America had come in the worst months of 1931 and 1932.

Clearly, within the Phoenix's US operation, the fire wing took the worst of the punishment and the Crash experience was certainly an influence in its decline relative to the accident wing.[63] But so too was the resilience with which LGA confronted the Great American Crisis.

Although compensation business continued to be awful, with loss ratios rising above 70% in the latter months of 1929 and staying there for a painfully long period, the overall casualty loss ratio was held within moderate bounds. The surge of claims in 1930 had been checked by 1932. And all of the total claims ratios in Table 9.5 contrast sharply with the

[60] Fire Committee Minutes, Book 3, p. 358, 28 January 1931.
[61] Phoenix Directors' Minutes, 37, p. 112, 7 December 1932.
[62] Fire Committee Minutes, Book 3, p. 403, 27 July 1932.
[63] See Section 7 of this Chapter.

67% suffered by the combined Phoenix–LGA accident operation worldwide – but incurred overwhelmingly in the USA – in 1927. This emphatic improvement was largely due to the progressive reduction of compensation business within the total portfolio. Hence the decline in total premium income was not seen as a cause for alarm, nor as a product of a depressed economy, but as part of the controlled descent towards purer air that had been started in the mid-1920s.

The assistant accident manager Alfred Battrick, who, in recognition of the epochal events of the Crash, joined Southam on the transatlantic run in 1930, was not downcast. Given the impressive work on LGA's expense ratio – which, unlike the fire ratio, was now comfortably settled around 40%, while the accident claims ratio was little worse than the fire claims ratio – he did not expect even the losses of 1930 to produce a deficit, although 'very little more than an even break can really be expected'.[64] By 1932–3, however, he could hope for rather more, at least from the underwriting results.

By the standards of most accident operators in the America of the Crash years, this was very impressive. These companies would have given their eye-teeth for an even break. As Southam had observed in 1927, when LGA was experiencing its worst moments, 'practically all companies in the USA doing casualty business have been underwriting at a loss during the past few years'.[65] But most of them did not improve their performance as the US economy turned down. Many marginal companies, formed amidst the heavy competition and light government controls of the 1920s, and living by their wits off stock-market froth, collapsed entirely when the Wall Street brew turned sour. Two-thirds of the sixty casualty offices licensed to trade in New York suffered serious financial loss at some point before 1930.[66] Yet Battrick calculated during this sad year that LGA would end it with results better than 95% of casualty insurers in the USA.[67]

However, the managerial renaissance within the Phoenix accident wing could not protect the company from every manifestation of the Crash. LGA continued to fly on controlled expenses and moderate claims through the underwriting storms of 1931 and 1932. But there was little that LGA's new efficiency could do to counter the storms in the US investment market. Wall Street hit bottom in the summer of 1932, by which time any institution which depended upon an investment portfolio was looking a bleak new world – and impending penury – in the face. This

[64] Assistant Accident Manager's Report on US Business, 1930.
[65] Report of Accident Manager on US Business, 1927.
[66] M. James, *Biography of a Business*, pp. 312ff.
[67] Report of Assistant Accident Manager, 1930.

Plate 9.4 American Baroque: the foyer at Fort Dearborn.

was the effect which Sketch referred to, rather mildly, on his visit of late 1931 as 'the involuntary reduction of income'.

The offices were rescued from this blight on their interest earnings by unlikely allies. The state insurance commissioners, in the past so fertile in awkward regulations and onerous deposits, met the occasion with an inspired method of valuing investments. They permitted the insurers to write in their securities at values well above the market prices, according to a schedule of 'convention rates'. Many US offices survived only by dint of this favour, and by subsequent loans from the Reconstruction Finance Corporation. LGA was not that pressed but it was glad of the favour.

Nevertheless, it is a mark of LGA's health that, during the crisis period, the annual reports of senior Phoenix officials from the USA are not filled with tales of underwriting gloom or investment doom. They are far more concerned with the attempts to sell the Fort Dearborn lease and to deal with an internal book-keeping fraud. No doubt, these were serious matters in themselves, but, in comparison with the disruption of world financial markets, they were parochial indeed. Phoenix was fortunate: while Wall Street plunged, it could actually afford to muse over a single, if overblown, piece of Chicago real estate and chase a few thousand misappropriated dollars through its accounts. The reason is clear: the LGA part of the Phoenix network in the USA went into the Crash era a great deal fitter than most of its competitors; and it came out a great deal fitter. By 1932 LGA was no longer the pig in a poke it had been in 1922.

In 1922 Ryan may have bought a pig in a poke. By 1932 Sketch had trained at least its American cousin into an animal of strength and adroitness. Other parts of the family, of course, took longer to train.

6. EMBEZZLEMENT AND THE EMBARRASSMENT OF FIREMEN

More dangerous to the fire side of Phoenix USA, and more influential in determining its final interwar shape than the Great Crash was an internal financial scandal.

However, the Crash and the scandal were not unrelated. Between November 1932 and February 1933, B. H. Davis, by now foreign accident manager, was again in the USA investigating the level of bad debts and the problem of overdue accounts. While thus engaged, Davis read in the press of the 'tragic death' – that is, suicide – on 29 November 1932 of A. H. Hellriegel, treasurer of the Phoenix fire outlets in the USA and also of the New York office of Réinsurances Suisses. This event, as Davis put it, with characteristic understatement, 'considerably widened the scope of my investigation'.[68]

Davis was required once more to assume his sleuth's costume. Head Office's attention to American accounts, occasioned in the first place by the Crash, proved to have flushed quarry of a different kind. It seems that Hellriegel had used his positions with Phoenix and Réinsurances Suisses to perpetrate a sophisticated exercise in robbing Peter in order to rob Paul. In one instance, nearly $50,000 had been paid improperly to Réinsurances Suisses with cheques drawn by Hellriegel on various Phoenix accounts; this sum was used to cover, or confuse, the value of coupons and bonds, worth about $100,000, already removed by Hellriegel from

[68] Report of Foreign Accident Manager on US Business, 1933.

Plate 9.5 Special Agent B. H. Davis.

Réinsurances Suisses. Hellriegel juggled the flows between the two offices so as to create a significant difference; and then pocketed it. Apparently, he had kept up the sleight of hand from 1920 until 1932, having organised the treasurer's department so that no one but himself had sight of both sides of the inter-office exchange. Only the special interest in all due accounts generated by the Crash destroyed this monopoly.

The Hellriegel affair was a disaster for Phoenix's traditional flagship in the USA. The fire business was slipping once again. The Crash had hurt it. Economies were sought. And now the fire leadership was revealed to have allowed itself to be cheated out of tens, perhaps hundreds, of thousands of dollars of much-needed income. Tactfully, Davis reported to Sketch: 'Unfortunately, Hellriegel seems to have been extraordinarily clever in keeping all the trouble from Mr Beresford.' The latter, in consequence, was 'stunned'.[69] Sorrowing, Beresford wrote to Sketch:

[69] Davis to Sketch, 8 December 1932.

'That we should have been let down so badly is a terrible blow to me, and I know you realise how distressed I am, and what I am going through.'[70] At this stage, however, Beresford himself had not grasped how terrible the blow was to turn out.

For it was the suggestion cast by Hellriegel's fraud that the leadership had maintained inadequate control which was to undermine Beresford and the primacy of the fire department within Phoenix's US network. The fire side suffered more damage from the scandal than from adverse markets or falling premiums. At a time when fire expenses were, by common consent, unacceptable, part of the management was shown to have imposed its own additional and criminal costs upon the company. And, while this was happening, the accident side was acquiring a deserved reputation for excellence in controlling all costs.

A visitation by the top men of the Phoenix Group, General Manager Sketch and Chairman Pybus, to New York in April and May 1933 spelled this out to Beresford. The veteran fire official was humiliated. It was only a matter of time before the trouble-shooters at LGA were given their head in effecting another much-needed managerial reform.

7. THE DECLINE AND ABSORPTION OF FIRE, 1931–40

During this decade the fire wing of Phoenix USA was buffeted from all sides. Fire insurance had been the traditional mainstay of the exporting Phoenix. Beresford had continued to regard it as the corporate standard bearer in the US trade even during the 1920s. He conceded that the accident sector won more premiums but responded that it also produced bigger losses and bigger problems. But then the Hellriegel scandal badly compromised Beresford's credibility and questioned his control of business.

At the same time, energetic management and precise control was cleansing the stables at LGA. The Crash added the final touch by depressing fire earnings and leaving them depressed for much of the decade. Where the accident operation – or the LGA part of it – had been a shambles for most of the 1920s and the fire department had kept a clean copy book, the 1930s witnessed a fulfilled managerial revolution in the accident sector and a loss both of confidence and business in the fire sector.

From the standpoint of Beresford and the fire department, these currents merged to chilling effect. The Hellriegel affair had suggested that senior management had paid insufficient attention to disbursements –

[70] Beresford to Sketch, 14 December 1932.

Plate 9.6 J. M. Haines, Phoenix US accident manager.

and thus costs. Yet LGA had been subjected to a particularly successful exercise in cost control. The obvious inference was that the team which had turned LGA around, J. M. Haines as manager and Lloyd Jones as comptroller, should be given their chance at the 'fire problem'.

Unperceived as yet, there were forces here which would push the various sections of the Phoenix US organisation towards a single Group method of operation. The experience of the 1920s had *not* moved the Phoenix closer to a composite mode of operation in the USA. Indeed, the acquisition of LGA, and its dicey accounts, had moved the company in the other direction, towards keeping the fire sections away from the casualty sections.[71] Thus, in the early 1920s, the LGA fire subsidiary in the USA, the United Firemens' had been placed under the Phoenix fire

[71] Victory Committee Report, 1942, p. 3. Much the same was true in Canada (see below, pp. 726–57).

manager and in 1930 Phoenix Indemnity had gone to the (now improving) management at LGA. But the overhaul of the accident side and the embarrassment of the fire side now raised other possibilities.

Beresford's skill had always lain primarily in the selection of superior fire business; there had clearly been loose ends in the cost management of the US fire operation and Hellriegel had loosened them further. So, when B. H. Davis, the Head Office detective sent once more to unravel an American mystery, suggested in February 1933 that the entire fire system should be reviewed, and that Lloyd Jones, who had so impressed him during his original accident investigations of 1926, should carry out the task, Beresford could only agree.[72]

The implicit criticism was made explicit when the case was handed over to still more senior officers: Sketch and Pybus visited the scenes of several different types of crime in New York and Chicago in April and May 1933. They had three purposes: to discover whether fraud had emanated from personalities or methodologies; to discover Beresford's views on the scandal; and to safeguard the future. At their first meeting with Beresford, they made it 'abundantly clear' that they had already reached one conclusion: 'we had grounds for grave dissatisfaction with the control that had been exercised'. Once again, Beresford had no choice but to recognise that 'there had been laxity on his part'.[73]

The first remedy was to bolt the stable door: Sketch and Pybus insisted that future dealings with Réinsurances Suisses should be a formal transaction, company to company and not a personal arrangement by the manager. They were then caught in a most ironic loop. They wished to give Beresford a salary increase. He had not had one since 1919, and Crash or no Crash, fraud or no fraud, it could not decently be left any longer (more than likely also, they were beginning to think about pensioning Beresford off). The moment was scarcely propitious. Only months before, the Phoenix Board had handed out a salary *cut* of 10% to all its US officials.[74] And from September 1932, the US insurance recession had deepened.[75] It was not easy to give the chief executive a pay rise. But it was possible. What made it so was Beresford's personal arrangement with Réinsurance Suisses. He could be paid with Phoenix monies moving through the reinsurance company. Sketch used a variant of the method pioneered by Hellriegel.

Naturally, however, his eye was fixed primarily on another target. If the

[72] Report on US Fire Organisation by Foreign Accident Manager (B. H. Davis), presented 6 March 1933. [73] Report of General Manager on US Business, May 1933.

[74] Phoenix Directors' Minutes, 37, p. 112, 21 September 1932.

[75] Report of General Manager on US Business, May 1933.

future was really to be safeguarded a more powerful remedy had to be found: the excessive fire expense ratio – now running well above 50% – had to be reduced. The only space for economy visible to Sketch at this juncture was an apparently innocuous one. His notion was to move the fire and accident wings into the same office and to amalgamate their non-trading sections, as had already been done with LGA and Phoenix Indemnity. Lloyd Jones was briefed to investigate whether it would be financially worthwhile to concentrate in this way. Beginning, probably innocently, as a conventional administrative gambit, this issue was to become the most contentious fire question of the decade, a contest over managerial sovereignty, and the source of a major economy campaign.

Jones reported to Sketch at the end of May. He had identified three substantial advantages in moving the fire wing from its imposing premises at 150 William Street into the accident headquarters at 55 Fifth Avenue. There would be annual savings of $100,000 for both offices; there could be closer cooperation between agency divisions leading to a boost in premiums; the adjustment facilities of the automobile department could be employed to check fire claims. He conceded that there might be some disadvantage in moving the fire group away from 'the so-called Insurance District'.[76] At this point, Sketch ducked the issue, writing back to Jones simply that 'It is likely that any reorganisation would be left to you'.[77] Sketch clearly foresaw trouble as well as economies.

Nevertheless, by late summer 1933, he was apparently ready to confront it. His assistant E. B. Ferguson was despatched to New York to form 'a Committee'[78] which would discuss proposals with Beresford. Effectively, Beresford made his last stand before this group. He hinted that consolidation would jeopardise his valuable connections with the fire brokers. He looked forward to a profit on the fire side by the end of 1933 and promised to reduce the expense ratio to 54%. But he had only one true argument: that a move away from the traditional business district would irreparably damage the prestige of the Phoenix, and thus consolidation would be 'disastrous for the company'. As Ferguson put it, 'his opposition was expressly limited to location'.[79]

This was clearly a rationalisation on Beresford's part: location in the prestigious business centre of New York was symbolic of the traditional might of Phoenix as a fire insurer. He had always viewed the fire department as the senior department in the USA. He had been Phoenix's leading official in America and the man who had rescued the office from

[76] Memorandum on a Joint US Headquarters, Jones to Sketch, 31 May 1933.
[77] Sketch to Jones, 18 July 1933. [78] Its membership is not known.
[79] Ferguson to Sketch, 8 August 1933.

the doldrums of the 1900s. It could not have been easy to see this position eroded by the forces unleashed by the LGA acquisition. Having fumbled the helm of the US flagship, having lost influence, and, indeed, respect, he was now to lose his premises.

The Committee heard him out, and temporised. They agreed that consolidation should ultimately take place, but that Beresford should be given until the end of 1934 to prove his point on the reduction of expenses. They also brought into the open the prospect of his retirement by suggesting that preliminary discussions might be opened with him regarding the amount of his pension.[80] The Head Office position on Beresford was clear: first, he was ageing; second, his reputation had been damaged by the fraud episode; third, he was an inconvenient obstacle to the plan for administrative fusion. There was little recall that in his time he had been a key figure in repairing Phoenix's position in the USA.

Unfortunately, we have no satisfactory means of measuring how bad the Phoenix's position in the US fire market of the 1930s had once more become. Obviously, inferences can be drawn from the criticisms made of Beresford. And his expressed ambition to get his expenses ratio *down* to 54% tells a sorry story in itself. But we have no precise figures for fire premium income, let alone claims, commissions or costs from the USA in the vital period 1931–8. The immaculate Review of Foreign Agencies, which for 143 years had listed every cent, mark, kopek or penny earned and lost by every Phoenix agency, everywhere, terminated in 1930. The Phoenix Annual Accounts (the 'Blue Books') do not reintroduce a comparable world map until the appearance of a Combined Fire Revenue Account, by agency or branch, in 1938. Individual figures for a year or two may be gleaned from correspondence. One such reference, in relation to the USA, is vital: in 1938 Sketch complained to Haines about the US fire premiums and gave the levels for 1935 and 1937: £1,476,628 and £1,573,076 in gross premiums, respectively.[81] But we have no fully consistent annual series for fire income from the USA (or anywhere else) for a key period in the overhaul of the American organisation.

Yet the missing information is too important to be left missing. There are two available methods for overcoming this problem. One is to reconstruct the data that are missing.[82] The Blue Books give *total* net foreign fire premiums for each year. They also give gross and net premiums for total Phoenix's fire earnings. We can thus calculate an annual correction factor for converting net foreign premium to gross (in order to match our

[80] *Ibid.* [81] Sketch to Haines, 9 August 1938.

[82] Book 6 of the Review of Foreign Agencies seems not to have gone missing, but never to have existed.

earlier foreign totals, which include reinsurance). Of course, we have to assume that reinsurance behaviour on foreign earnings was similar to that on total earnings. But since foreign was the dominant element in total fire earnings, this is a reasonable assumption. Then we need a correction factor for the US share in total gross foreign. This is easily available for the years *before* 1930, when the Foreign Agency Reviews were still operating. Within that period, there is a set of years, 1923–30, during which the Phoenix US organisation contained the same number of units and subsidiaries as it did during the target period, 1931–8. It is reasonable to assume that an average of the US share for the period 1923–30 should provide a reasonable guide to the US share for 1930–8. With this correction factor, estimates can be constructed on the basis of total gross foreign premium to give projected US gross premium values for 1931–8. Actual net US premium values are provided by the Blue Books for 1938–40, and these can readily be converted to gross. Both these latter results and the numbers in Sketch's letter of complaint provide checks on the accuracy of the methodology. The projected values for 1931–8 and the adjusted values for 1938–40 are given in Table 9.6.

Naturally, the figures for 1931–8 will be approximations only for the real numbers. It is particularly likely that the early figures will be overstated. However, the orders of magnitude are clearly about right; and the most important feature of the series is to show the order of change through time. Therefore, it is particularly significant that the 'join' between the projected figures before 1938 and the adjusted figures thereafter is not obtrusive; indeed it scarcely shows. Furthermore, the agreement between the projected gross figures for 1935 and 1937 and Sketch's 'numbers of complaint' is very acceptable indeed: in both cases the variance between the artificial and the actual figure is 2.2%. So it is very likely that whatever worried Sketch in his figures should also emerge in our reconstruction.

It is immediately apparent what it was. In the reconstruction, US gross premiums declined by 22.5% between 1931 and the low point of 1939. The slide between 1931 and 1933, the year before Beresford's 'retirement' was almost as bad. And the figure for 1935, whether real (from Sketch) or reconstructed, was lower than any since 1919, with the exception of 1933. But one could argue that the accident wing also witnessed a decline in premiums during the 1930s. LGA too suffered a slide in premium income of 26.9% between 1929 and its low point of 1935. But LGA was *aiming* to shed workmen's compensation business and was succeeding in keeping its expenses ratio down in the virtuous range of 40–43%. While LGA was becoming leaner and fitter, Phoenix USA was becoming thinner and

Table 9.6. *Projected gross fire premiums, Phoenix US Branch and subsidiaries, 1931–40*

Year	Total net foreign premium (£)	Correction factor for US share %	Projected net US premium (£)	Correction factor for reinsurance %	Projected gross US premium (£)
1931	2,574,392	53.54	1,378,329	33.3	1,837,313
1932	2,348,379	53.54	1,257,322	34.8	1,694,870
1933	2,056,919	53.54	1,101,274	31.8	1,451,479
1934	2,257,259	53.54	1,208,536	31.4	1,588,017
1935	2,145,746	53.54	1,148,832	31.4	1,509,565
1936	2,138,992	53.54	1,145,216	29.8	1,486,491
1937	2,191,314	53.54	1,173,230	31.1	1,538,104
1938			1,096,333[a]	30.2	1,427,426
1939			1,104,192[a]	28.9	1,423,303
1940			1,165,681[a]	29.3	1,507,226

Note: [a] Actual net US premiums from Phoenix Annual Accounts.
Sources: US correction factor calculated from Phoenix Review of Foreign Agencies, Book 5. Reinsurance correction factor calculated from Phoenix Annual Accounts.

feebler. Phoenix's worries about American fire business in the 1930s were that it was insufficient and too expensive to obtain. There is certainly nothing in the reconstruction that quarrels with this view.

The second means for filling the information gap is provided by a set of regional US accounts for 1930–44, discovered among the papers of G. E. Hurren, Phoenix foreign fire manager (1946–57).[83] This source is less formal than the Annual Review of Foreign Agencies: it is a retrospective calculation and it gives net premium income only. However, by aggregating the regional results – from the Metropolitan, Eastern, Western, Southern and Pacific departments – a net premium figure for the Phoenix fire group in the USA can be achieved. The figures turn out somewhat lower than net figures from other sources, but they display the same directional features. Much more to the point, they allow calculation of expense and loss ratios. These results are given in Table 9.7.

Again, the low point for premiums is in 1939 after a fall of about 30% since 1930 and there is a sharp slide from 1930 to 1933 of nearly 14%. The

[83] And later assistant general manager, as well as the author of *Phoenix Renascent*.

Table 9.7. *Aggregation of Phoenix Group US regional net fire premiums, expenses and losses, 1930–44*

Year	Aggregate net premiums[a] ($)	Expenses ratio (%)	Loss ratio (%)	Underwriting surplus (%)
1930	6,214,856	55.2	55.7	−10.8
1931	6,742,563	52.1	50.2	−2.3
1932	6,208,557	52.2	56.0	−8.2
1933	5,369,042	52.4	49.7	−2.1
1934	5,744,708	49.1	40.5	+10.4
1935	4,697,873	54.6	34.7	+11.2
1936	4,406,398	55.1	40.4	+4.5
1937	4,444,570	52.9	35.2	+12.0
1938	4,380,853	55.5	38.8	+5.7
1939	4,330,828	55.8	38.4	+6.3
1940	4,537,455	54.2	42.7	+3.1
1941	4,978,552	51.0	40.1	+9.0
1942	5,034,324	50.2	40.7	+9.0
1943	5,541,554	47.7	47.4	+4.9
1944	6,023,728	46.9	48.2	+4.9

Note: [a] Due to the extreme instability of the sterling–dollar rate after 1931, it is more convenient to keep these earnings in dollars.
Source: Calculated from Retrospect of US Departmental Premiums, Fire Manager's Files.

adverse experience of the Crash period shows through clearly. And the only bright spot is the retreat of the loss ratio between 1932 and 1943. However, the really striking feature is the behaviour of the expenses ratio. The horrific figures around 54% mentioned in the correspondence for 1932–3 are not quite borne out by these calculations, but the match is very close. Also clear is the fact that Beresford's efforts did have some effect in 1934 but that the effect was not lasting. Indeed the problem of the fire expense ratio did not abate until the very end of this series.

However, profit results from a third source give Beresford higher marks and suggest that, by the comparative test of the industrial standard, he did very well indeed in 1934. In terms of underwriting income taken by the ten largest UK fire insurers in the United States in 1934, Phoenix ranked ninth, but, in terms of underwriting profit, it headed the pack (see Table 9.8). No doubt, this was only a single year's outcome, but in view of what

Table 9.8. *The top ten UK fire insurers in the USA in 1934: underwriting income earned and underwriting profit ($m and %)*

	Income[a]	Profit
Royal	8.9	13.6
LLG	8.7	13.3
NBM	7.1	12.2
CU	5.8	8.6
Pearl	3.8	−10.7
Northern	3.6	8.8
London	3.6	7.3
London & Lancs	3.4	12.4
Phoenix	3.2	13.7
Sun	3.2	7.3

Note: [a] The *Post Magazine*'s definitions for income and profit are clearly different from the definitions of premium and surplus used in Table 9.7, but the agreement for the 1934 profit result is quite acceptable and sustains the proposition of recovery in the mid-1930s.
Source: *Post Magazine and Insurance Monitor*, 17, 27 April 1935.

was to happen to Beresford, it was unfortunate that it arrived too late to count in his favour.

In reality, Beresford was not allowed the whole of 1934 to prove his point. Head Office had figures and worries of its own. They provided sufficient argument for further investigation on the spot early in 1934: the clear-sighted B. H. Davis was again sent westwards to see what he could make of affairs in New York. He reported that the accident wing still needed all available economies, primarily because workmen's compensation insurance, despite all efforts, continued to be very unsatisfactory. Providentially, also, the economies now expected from the scheme to amalgamate the accident and fire operations had outgrown Jones' original estimates. Yet, Davis observed, 'while Beresford is Manager, it would be unwise to attempt merging headquarters or staff'.[84]

This conjunction sank Beresford. The trial of his reforms was not permitted its full span. Nor was the warning flag of his pension flown

[84] Report of Accident Manager on US Business, Davis to Sketch, 23 April 1934.

openly in front of him. Having failed to decipher other hints in his correspondence with Sketch suggesting voluntary withdrawal, he was peremptorily retired by direct instruction of the general manager. Sketch's letter informing him of this arrived on 19 October 1934. Three days later, the *Aquitania* docked in New York. She carried E. B. Ferguson, with instructions to execute the first stages of the US reorganisation. He found Beresford in a state of shock, although whether or not he fully realised this is open to doubt.

Beresford had seen the US economy fall apart. He had seen his own organisation outstripped and threatened with absorption by LGA. Under these conditions, he had embarked upon a major overhaul of the fire wing, and was achieving success with it. His profits for 1934 outperformed all UK rivals. Yet he was removed anyway. He had thought himself 'good for another ten years'. Ferguson, however, drew another conclusion. Noting Beresford's disjointed speech and preoccupied air, he inferred not that the US manager had been utterly demoralised by the démarche from Head Office but that he was no longer 'the keen and efficient force we have known in the past'. On the other hand, Ferguson did acknowledge that 'the blow had been a severe one . . . the distress of mind was all very apparent . . . giving the impression of having only partially recovered from a complete knockout'.[85] Since he had noticed this, one could perhaps expect rather more indulgence for Beresford's passing lack of keen-eyed vigour.

Ferguson had become Sketch's direct assistant in January 1933, and was foreign fire superintendant at the time of his visit to New York in October 1934; he was to become general manager himself in 1939. Despite what must have been a close working relationship, Sketch's letters to Ferguson are both formal and forceful, emphasising rather than diminishing the difference in rank. Sketch had a deserved reputation as a man of warm and generous character, so the shading here is untypical and perhaps significant. Noticeable too is the treatment that Ferguson's memoranda from the USA attracted from Sketch: they are sprinkled liberally with marginalia, mostly dissenting. The lucid reports from America by B. H. Davis, by contrast, escaped almost entirely unscathed. Sketch certainly himself possessed a clear grasp of the tortuous history of Phoenix's dealings in the USA and understood the implications of what he had felt it necessary to do in regard to Beresford's retirement. His reply to Ferguson's analysis is instructive: 'Your cabled advice that the decision came as a great shock to him, whilst in some ways surprising, was not, of

[85] Ferguson, Memorandum on US Business, to Sketch, 22 October 1934.

Plate 9.7 The Phoenix at Fifth Avenue. By April 1935 the company employed 668 people on five floors.

course, unexpected.'[86] The reason why such action was felt to be necessary was caught in Ferguson's reprise, after the event, of the point made by Davis, before the event: 'The consolidation at Fifth Avenue could not have been possible with Mr Beresford actively associated in it.'[87] So, in October 1934, J. M. Haines was appointed to head both the fire and accident departments of the Phoenix in the United States; and his brief was very clear.

Consolidation, and what could be extracted from it, became the central theme of Phoenix policy in the USA for the rest of the interwar period. Much was pinned on it and clearly no official was to be allowed to get in its way.

[86] Sketch to Ferguson, 1 November 1934.
[87] Ferguson, Memorandum, 22 October 1934.

8. FIRE AGAIN: TOUGH TIMES AND TOUGH MANAGEMENT, 1935–40

Sketch took a notably tough managerial line on many aspects of the US operation. Of course, it was precisely such toughness which had been successful in bringing LGA to heel. Moreover, Sketch maintained as rigorous an approach to his US managers in the second half of the 1930s as he had in the first half. Nevertheless, even in the absence of old fire hands like Beresford, the strategy of consolidation proved neither instant panacea nor plain sailing. There were internal frictions and rigidities. And, in the wider economy, the United States displayed less resilience in the 1930s than other major economies such as the British or German. Between the Great Crash and Pearl Harbour, the US economy wallowed and the insurers could do little more than wallow with it.

However, the first reports from the United States were encouraging. Southam's successor as Head Office accident manager, Battrick, provided some during a tour of inspection in June and July 1935: 'everything we saw at 55 Fifth Avenue' confirmed that the 'merging of the organisation of our Fire and Casualty Departments into one Group had been satisfactorily and effectively carried out'. He was just as optimistic about the personnel. Haines had breathed new life into LGA and Phoenix Indemnity, and, now that he had overall control, 'I have no doubt that, in course of time, he will equally happily weld our Fire and Casualty organisations'.[88] Under Haines, the senior fire official would now be T. J. Irvine, formerly Beresford's deputy; he was to be 'sole advisor to Mr Haines on Fire Underwriting'.[89] As for the financial troubleshooter, Lloyd Jones, Battrick was convinced that here Phoenix possessed, 'an Official of outstanding ability dealing with all matters affecting our expense rates' and expected that 'economies will be effected down to the last dollar'.[90]

When Jones himself visited London in May 1936, he was able to report progress. The income of the fire wing had been given some relief: 'it had already benefited to the extent of approximately $300,000 per annum of premium income' from business brought in by casualty connections. Moreover, Jones described his plans for tighter cost control, including a 'Group Budget for Controllable Expenses', and for an integrated selling strategy, to be displayed in a 'Group Underwriting Statement'.

As these good ideas were being implemented, the market itself took a turn for the better, and the 1936 results of the fire subsidiaries – with

[88] Battrick to Sketch, 7 August 1935.
[89] Sketch to Battrick, 27 September 1938.
[90] Battrick to Sketch, 7 August 1938.

Plate 9.8 Group Accident Manager Battrick.

Imperial raising its dividend to 17.5 % and Columbia and United Firemen's to 15% – came out quite respectably. But in 1937 the outlook became menacing once more. In May, a meeting in London between Haines, Sketch, Ferguson, Battrick and other senior Phoenix men was gloomy about the prospects for the autumn. Ferguson stated that 'his impression Fire-wise [sic] was that we shall run into heavier weather in the next two months and that 1938 will not be as good as in the past'. Given the very modest medium-term performance of the recent past, this was cold comfort indeed. Ferguson's reasons were that 'markets are scared and this has had the effect of reducing stocks very materially: traders are not buying or manufacturing to the extent they did a year ago'.[91] In the event also, the autumn of 1938 produced some heavy

[91] Minutes of Conference on US Business, Phoenix House, 19 May 1937.

weather of its own, with five days of torrential rain on the east coast, 'culminating in a first-class hurricane'.[92]

This did not help. Indeed, it cost the insuring community £25 million, of which Phoenix shouldered £40,000. With some understatement, Battrick, who was again the visiting presence of the season, noted his regret at seeing 'nothing of the delightful fall weather ordinarily associated with this time of year'.[93] But, despite the rotten autumn, it was rather the failure of the US economy to stage a convincing recovery after 1931 which spoiled the insurance markets down to, and past, 1938.

Clearly, it was the trading conditions of the late 1930s which earned the US market a further dose of Sketch's managerial rigour. Battrick saw 1938 as 'a most opportune time' for 'stock-taking of what we had already accomplished' but also of 'what now had to be done if we were to progress'; and that 'had clearly to be taken in hand without further delay'.[94] This time, the recipient of the stocktaking was Haines. Sketch was worried by 'the rising bill of costs which have been detailed in the recent 1938 Budget Statement' and by the 'serious' drop in fire income. The fall is clearly revealed in the reconstruction in Table 9.6 and by the aggregation in Table 9.7. Even more disturbing was the continued resistance of the fire expense ratio to treatment; indeed it was back above 54% again (see Table 9.7). This was scarcely the purpose of consolidation. Sketch expressed his displeasure in a personal letter to Haines, in which he compared the results of 1935 and 1937.

He reminded Haines that his intention had been to combine the casualty and fire organisations to achieve greater penetration of the US market and cut fire costs. This, he concluded, had not happened. Although the total income of the fire companies had risen modestly (Table 9.6), the component directly attributable to fire underwriting had fallen, while the salary bill had jumped nastily. If it had not been for 'the exceptionally favourable loss ratio' which 'during the last few years we have enjoyed . . . in common with most Companies . . . our present rate of expenditure on our present income would make it quite impossible for us to produce a profit'.[95]

The favourable loss ratios in the USA – which did not survive beyond the early 1940s – were due to two major influences. Ironically, one was the direct responsibility of Beresford. His forte was the selection of good fire risks. He had chosen that Phoenix should carry a high percentage of private dwellings in its US fire account. For well over a decade this helped

[92] Battrick to Sketch, 23 September 1938.
[93] *Ibid.*, 21 September 1938. [94] *Ibid.*, 23 September 1938.
[95] Sketch to Haines, 9 August 1938.

produce low claims. The other influence was that catastrophe began to find America somewhat less attractive than heretofore. Between the burning of Salem, Massachusetts in June 1914 – this time, not a few luckless womenfolk, but a good part of the town, some 1,600 buildings, including the Naumkeag Cotton Mills, currently the world's largest, for a total insurance loss of $14 million, and a Phoenix loss of over $90,000 – and the great factory fire at the Falls River plant of Firestone Rubber in 1941 – which ended by costing the underwriters $11 million and Phoenix $13,000 – the American disaster rate waned to a flicker of its former self. Between 1914 and 1923 conflagration imposed a total loss on the US market of $102.9 million; between 1924 and 1933 the damage generated by great fires shrank to $27.3 million; and even between 1934 and 1942 the sum total of disaster on the grand scale was $50.7 million.[96]

Haines drew the correct conclusion: this was remission by grace of one predecessor and the several gods of fire. More normal loss ratios would have carried his US fire department well into the red. Still more obviously, he could not expect the abnormal loss ratios of 1934–8 to persist for ever (in fact, against the odds, they persisted until 1943). The underwriting surplus on US fire business was reasonably satisfactory 1934–41, but this was due only to the exceptionally low incidence of claims (see Table 9.7). Profit was thus largely in the lap of the fire gods and both Haines and Head Office were legitimately concerned that this was not a safe place for it to be.

Head Office, in the shape of Sketch, deduced from these trading features that Haines needed to expend 'additional concentration' on the management of Phoenix's fire affairs in the USA. Tactfully, Sketch suggested that it was perhaps 'the heavy responsibilities that you have had to undertake on the Casualty side' which had prevented Haines from giving 'other than a very general oversight of the problems and organisation on the Fire side'. He concluded on the telling note that, 'I cannot but feel that the admirable management disclosed in our Casualty affairs should not find insuperable difficulties in overcoming this parallel problem in our fire business'.[97]

Having ingested this with his morning coffee, Haines was sufficiently startled to ask if 'there was a definite criticism of his management of the Group'. His first response, directed at the itinerant Battrick, and relayed

[96] National Fire Protection Association, *Conflagrations in America since 1914* (New York, 1942), calculated from Table 1, pp. 30–2. Nevertheless, one or two events defied the averages: a major earthquake in Southern California in 1933 did £8 million of damage to 300 square miles (nearly 800 km^2) of the state and Phoenix lost £11,000. In the next year, a classic Chicago stockyard fire burned £1.1 million of property, of which the Phoenix Group had covered £6,000. [97] Sketch to Haines, 9 August 1938.

by him to Sketch, was that, firstly, on the production side, everything that could have been expected from the attempt to raise fire business through the casualty side had been supplied; and, secondly, that he had himself pointed out, been worried by, and worked for months to rectify, the expenditure problem.[98]

Refining the analysis, Haines argued that as much fire business as could be secured through *existing* casualty connections had been secured; this method for raising fire income had reached 'saturation point'. However, when the current strategy had been commenced in 1935, there had been no intention of creating *additional* casualty connections:

> The agencies were giving us . . . all the expansion we desired and could healthily absorb: this state of affairs no longer exists and there is a material drop in our Casualty volume. There is room for, say, a million dollar development.

This, of course, would require new casualty agencies and these could be expected to yield more fire business. So, under new circumstances, more might be offered on the production side.

On the side of expenses, the strong men of LGA had not produced the hoped-for impact on the fire operation: 'Mr Jones has not at any time had that complete control and initiative on the Fire side which he has, for so many years, enjoyed on the Casualty.' Haines concluded that the traditional standing and management routine of the fire wing had caused both J. R. Robinson – the US Group's chief selling force – and Lloyd Jones to 'hesitate to go right through to the logical conclusion of their positions'. Battrick, who was pressing the Head Office case on the spot, once more passed these comments on verbatim to Sketch.[99]

Sketch replied conceding that 'the penetration of Mr Lloyd Jones and Mr Robinson into that (Fire) Department had to be a gradual and considerate process'. However, his view was that sufficient consideration had been given; now penetration had to be achieved and logical conclusions reached. He stressed that he had 'always looked upon our United States organisation as being headed by Mr Haines with three Chief Assistants': Lloyd Jones as the controller of Group expenditure; Irvine as the underwriting head of the fire department; and Robinson as 'the producing force of the Group'. The appointment of Robinson as assistant US manager in 1937 had been intended to promote the production element to the highest levels of both the fire and the casualty departments. It was now time that coordination between this element and the other elements of top management was made fully effective: 'it is only by

[98] Battrick to Sketch, 14 September 1938. [99] *Ibid.*

Plate 9.9 Phoenix's American salesman, J. R. Robinson.

this liaison of Underwriter, Producer and Disbursement Controller that the future of the Fire Account can be improved'.[100]

All three of these officials, led by Haines, met Battrick in conference in New York on 3 October. Positions were indeed now pushed through to logical conclusions. It was decided that Robinson should set up a training school for the grooming of superior fire salesmen. All 'recognised . . . that this matter of development is one of extreme urgency which cannot wait'. Robinson was to have complete control of all fieldmen in all departments. Similarly, it was agreed that Lloyd Jones 'was to have complete control of all expenditure, Fire and Casualty, no matter under what heading it falls' and was unleashed upon 'an exhaustive review of all our expenditure throughout the Group'. All told, considerable pressure was deployed to

[100] Sketch to Battrick, 27 September 1938.

impress upon Haines 'the urgency of bringing his organisation into full and effective force'.[101] In regard to the two key issues of development and expenses, Battrick told Haines, 'I shall require to be able to report to Mr Sketch that the gravity of these two problems has been thoroughly appreciated by our New York Executive.'[102]

Nevertheless, not even the most vigorous efforts could revitalise the US market of 1938 and 1939. Ferguson's weather forecast proved correct and in 1938 'unfavourable economic and trade conditions were widespread throughout the country'. Sketch went on a world tour of Phoenix outposts in 1938–9, and arrived in the USA, in May 1939, just in time to be thoroughly depressed. A loss of income across the whole Group of $500,000 was expected for 1939; the very favourable loss ratios of 1938 could not be looked for again; and every possible avenue of economy had now been explored.[103] Tables 9.6 and 9.7 do indeed show very poor fire premium levels for 1938 and 1939 with a rally occurring in the USA only in the last year of peace. Expense ratios also did not improve markedly until these higher volumes of business were achieved.

Where loss ratios had been the bane of US business around the turn of the century, this problem – as Ryan had predicted – declined after the first decade of the new century. Instead, the expense ratio rapidly came to assume a dire and persistent significance. There is an awesome continuity between Beresford's problems in the late 1920s, Sketch's unbending drive for reform in the late 1930s, and Harris' Expense Reduction Program of the 1960s.[104]

However, the period 1935–40 has a special significance in the development of the Phoenix's business in the USA. For what started as an exercise in reducing office expenses became, under the pressures of economic recession, a complete blueprint for an American Group organisation. There were, predictably, areas of resistance, but it is a tribute to Sketch's steadfastness of purpose, and to the talents of Haines and Lloyd Jones, that they beat out the basis for a genuine integrated Group organisation under these conditions.

[101] Battrick, Report of Conference on US Group Business, 3 October 1938; Sketch to Haines, 17 October 1938.

[102] Battrick to Haines, 3 October 1938.

[103] Report of Managing Director on US Business, May 1939.

[104] See below, pp. 903–4. The complete continuity was even longer, since high expenses were already the bane of UK insurers in the USA even before the First World War.

9. THE FINAL ACCIDENTS OF PEACETIME

If the fire side of Phoenix USA kept its account in the black more by good luck than good judgement in the later 1930s, the reverse was true of the accident side. Here superior administration was needed to contain a claims ratio which rarely showed evidence of good fortune.

Some of the bad fortune was spawned directly by the peculiar conditions of the decade: Phoenix was not untouched by the unholy marriage of recession and racketeering. The major impact was felt in automobile business from 1935. Starting in Chicago, the insurers noted a 'tendency of claim-making for exaggerated damages to spread throughout the country'. Battrick suggested in a report of August 1935 that gangsters 'whose living had been damaged by the repeal of prohibition had now become interested in our business and a factor in exploiting damages'.[105] Ominously associated with this criminal interest was 'the development of big awards in Court cases in Chicago and the way in which these were mounting'.[106]

As the mob and the judges combined to aggravate the loss ratio in motor insurance, so the high level of competition and the low level of business confidence held down the rates the insurers could charge. These problems afflicted all motor underwriters in the USA. But, on top of these, Phoenix–LGA also suffered a loss of volume. Partly, this had come about because of an independent purge of bad motor business, particularly in New England. But more of the contraction followed from Sketch's insistence upon cutting back in workmen's compensation business. Determined 'cleaning of our business' in this sector, by a sympathetic process, lost clients also for motor policies.

Probably, Phoenix–LGA experienced more of this effect than most other major insurers. However, it took its punishment in the motor market in order to achieve the prime purpose of purifying the compensation account. And here it was definitely more rigorous than most other insurers. Haines had introduced a formal 'curtailment programme' from 1933 and the leadership in both New York and London demanded total adherence to this policy. In 1935, when some competitors were detecting 'a more hopeful outlook' in the market and were being tempted to 'lift the bar', Battrick emphasised that there was to be 'no change in our attitude to Compensation business'; Phoenix's campaign of purification was to be 'one of permanency'.[107] Even so, the Phoenix men realised that smaller

[105] Report of Accident Manager on US Business, 7 August 1935.
[106] *Ibid.* [107] *Ibid.*

compensation business would simply mean smaller loss; it was 'not likely to take us out of the red' in this afflicted trade.

While other insurers weakened – the Travellers led a group in 1936 which again detected improvement in compensation insurance – Phoenix and LGA officials held firm, with 'no doubt in their minds as to the dangers of relaxing in any way the strict underwriting programme followed by us in recent years'.[108]

They were strict too with the general agents. Control here, once seized, was never again surrendered. By the mid-1930s, the Conkling, Price and Webb agency, which had caused such trouble a decade before, was running smoothly and was even putting itself out to drum up fire as well as casualty business. Less satisfactory was the Critchell, Miller, Whitney and Barbour agency, none of whom in 1937 were under seventy years of age, 'and nothing new or bright coming along behind them'.[109] Haines promised to watch this carefully, with a view to finding an alternative. But at least what he was watching were the effects of old age and not, as in the 1920s, of reckless independence.

Financially, too, the Phoenix American Group rode out the 1930s with some aplomb. The influx of funds from Head Office which was needed to boost Phoenix Indemnity's capital to £1 million in 1937 was more than balanced by the surpluses remitted home by LGA.[110] From 1935, LGA was able to send $125,000 per year back to London, a sum equivalent to its annual interest earnings. In 1937, also, the year of Phoenix Indemnity's recapitalisation, LGA despatched to London a special payment of $1 million. Its net surplus position was affected neither by the decline in US security values, nor by the Group's unhappy involvement in the Chicago property market. The company's reserves were clearly in good shape. This was a tribute to the Phoenix's careful reorganisation of LGA's finances in the 1920s, and a dividend on the good husbandry of that reforming period. It also measured a financial strength that few American accident operators of this period could have matched.

In all departments, the strictness of the Sketch–Haines approach proved well advised. By 1938, there were few signs of improvement visible in the compensation market, or anywhere else. Unemployment was worsening once more and there are suggestions in the records that the Phoenix people were expecting a repetition of the slump which opened the decade. However, they faced the prospect with resolution rather than trepidation.

[108] Record of Discussion between Messrs Battrick, Davis and Lloyd Jones, Head Office, 25 May 1936.

[109] Record of Meeting at Phoenix House, 19 May 1937. This was occasioned by a visit of Haines to London.

[110] See pp. 693–5 above.

One year earlier, a conference of UK and US officials of the Group, held in London, had caught the mood well: 'The fine efficiency of the "Phoenix" Group in New York is . . . ample assurance that, whatever is ahead, we shall stand well up in the list with our contemporaries.'[111] By then there were good reasons for this confidence; Phoenix–LGA had been thoroughly overhauled in the USA. But, from the New York of the late 1930s, it was less easy to foresee that what lay ahead was not a second world crash but a second world war.[112]

[111] Record of Meeting, 19 May 1937.
[112] From Europe the perspective was perhaps somewhat different.

CHAPTER 10

THE REST OF THE FOREIGN MARKETS, 1918–1939

I. INTRODUCTION: THE MAP OF INCOME, EFFORT AND PROFIT

In the interwar period, Phoenix's concentration on the US market and the LGA affair led to a progressive marginalisation of interest in other distant markets. As the American share in total foreign income expanded inexorably, so other nations, which previously had bulked large in the company's development, underwent major reductions in status. In particular, the European countries, which had provided the historic base of Phoenix's remarkable export achievement, experienced a further adjustment towards relative obscurity (see Table 10.1).

All of Europe was passed by Canada as the company's largest foreign market outside the USA in 1911–20 and even by India and the Far East during the 1920s. The depredations of the First World War, the postwar economic disruptions caused by international debts and the reparations penalties imposed upon the defeated Central Powers, as well as the concentration within the Continent of major industrial producers heavily affected by world trade problems, made Europe an unattractive location for the underwriters during the 1920s. Given that Phoenix's worried gaze was already drawn towards the USA, there was little in Europe at this time to draw it back. No single European agency or branch, not even the formerly mighty German network, managed to average 1% of total foreign premium 1921-30; the nearest were France with an average 0.9%, Holland with 0.8%, Germany itself – which, however, Phoenix re-entered for direct trade only in 1924 – also with 0.8%, and Barcelona with 0.6%.[1]

By contrast, Canada, where Phoenix had been almost as long as it had been in Europe, gave a good account of itself, at least in volume of

[1] However, the upswing in the German economy, precariously based as it was, did push the *annual* percentage up from 0.3% in 1924 to 2.3% in 1930.

Table 10.1. *Proportion of total Phoenix foreign premiums earned by major markets, 1901–30*

	US	Europe	Canada	India/Far East	Australia	New Zealand	S. Africa	Central/ South America
1901–10	45.8	19.6	13.2	6.2	4.1	2.2	2.9	3.7
1911–20	46.9	11.6	13.0	10.9	4.0	2.3	1.4	5.2
1921–30	52.4	9.0	12.5	9.6	2.6	1.7	1.3	3.7

business, and maintained a fairly steady share of total foreign trade at around 12–13%. This was reminiscent of its placing in the 1870s and a considerable improvement on its contribution of the period 1880–1900. It was virtually the only really traditional centre of Phoenix trade to achieve such stability in business share, although unfortunately this proved no sure guide to profitability or organisational tidiness within the Dominion market during this troubled period.

However, the other white dominion markets, also major exporters of food and ores and thus again in the front line of the world trade recession, were unable even to maintain stability in the share of the business they generated for the Phoenix. Certain parts of Australia suffered substantial reductions in annual money returns, up to 50% in Queensland and South Australia and around 40% in Victoria between 1921 and 1928. Other newer markets made hardly more progress. Central and South America initially built up strongly, especially in the period 1917–20, but then encountered a sharp break in 1921 and a loss in money income between 1921 and 1930 of a full 30%, as well as a substantial retreat in the area's share of company earnings. Within the region, only Argentina and Chile, with averages of total foreign earnings of 1.3% and 0.8% respectively achieved any substance as cash generators.

So over this span of markets, the only cases to compare with Canada, at least before 1930, were the agencies in the Indian and Far Eastern sectors. These too experienced a strong surge in income 1917–20, with receipts more than doubling over this short period, and a sharp downturn thereafter. But, from 1921 to 1929, this region displayed more stamina and stability. The outstanding performer in this theatre was the Far Eastern Branch at Shanghai. It accounted alone for 4.2% of total foreign earnings 1911–20 and 3.4% 1921–30; over the same periods, the entire Indian network produced shares of 2.1% and 2.5% and the Japan Branch managed 2.1% and 1.8%. Not surprisingly, the Phoenix learned to prize this trade. It had been very profitable before 1914, and it remained so even in the harsh circumstances of the interwar years. Early in 1944, George Hurren wrote contrasting the loss, due to enemy action, of two very different sorts of market, 'our European business which was, at best, only near profitable and then after very close and continuous control' and 'the whole of our very valuable and highly profitable far eastern business'.[2]

However, there is an important postscript and reservation to these covering generalisations. The loss of the Reviews of Foreign Agencies in 1931 means that we lack statistical confirmation of the usual quality for these points.[3] No comparable source allowing an overview of major overseas income sources exists for the period 1931–9. So, if there were substantial shifts in the relative standing of markets after 1931, they would be extremely difficult to detect. Returns for some outstanding individual markets such as the USA and Canada do exist, but the complete world map no longer lies to hand. However, if it is difficult to detect shifts, it is not impossible. And, probably, at least one important shift did occur in this period.

Some means of tracking such changes is provided by a major Phoenix analysis of overseas markets carried out in wartime. This 'Victory Committee' of 1941 aimed to assess postwar insurance prospects. But, in order to do so, it measured performance in the 1930s of markets later lost through hostilities. Its statistical record of agency premiums covers fifty-eight territories for 1929–38, but not, of course, the premier income sources in the USA and Canada, nor Australasia or South Africa. Nevertheless, much of Europe, the Far East, Africa and Latin America is covered. The numbers do not plot all income sources and they omit reinsurance earnings, but the period of overlap with the Review of Foreign Agencies (1929–31) does reveal that the two sets of figures, if carefully used, are compatible. So it is possible to compare the earnings for selected agencies for 1929–38 with their returns for 1921–30. Nothing in this exercise will alter the standing in the Phoenix story of the American, Canadian, Australian or South African markets in the final years of peace. But one major adjustment does stand out.

As Europe recovered from the Crash, and as political *and* economic gales swept through India, China and Japan in the 1930s, so the position of the home and the Asian continents on the Phoenix globe reversed. Even though we have a smaller map, the effect is quite clear. Europe in the 1920s had been a region of many moderate and small-scale outlets,

[2] Note for Fire Manager, Review of Fire Underwriting in the General Foreign Field, HGH/30.

[3] See above, p. 701; also p. 1028.

whereas Asia had possessed both these and very large income sources of the stature of the Indian, Shanghai and Japanese operations. In the 1930s Europe threw up some greatly enlarged outlets, primarily in France, Germany, Holland and Denmark, while the great income earners of Asia collapsed (see Table 10.2).

Thus the main European outlets managed to boost their average annual income between the periods 1921–30 and 1929–38 by over 35.1% – and it was no mean achievement for any major market area to increase its income over these years – while the main Indian and Far Eastern outposts suffered a decline of over 66%. Table 10.2 shows especially the serious deterioration in the Indian, Chinese and Japanese sectors.

Even so, Hurren was right about the relative profitability of the Asian and European markets. On much reduced turnover, some Far Eastern markets produced very respectable profit balances for fire underwriting even over the years 1929–38 – 10.0% for Japan, 21.7% for Burma, 28.5% for the Philippines, 42.3% for Malaya, although India on its straitened income flow did suffer a loss of 26.6% – while the much augmented European income flows did not guarantee an equally auspicious trading result. Thus the build-up in Holland and France produced overall losses for both markets 1929–38 – of 4.4% and 0.7% respectively – while the upswing in German fire insurance produced a surplus of only 4.1%.[4]

2. SOME UNEXPECTED COSTS OF ACQUISITIONS

Ironically, some of the larger problems experienced by Phoenix in important export markets outside the USA followed from events inside the American market. If much of the company's attention was focused on its American problems in the 1920s, this source of damage was capable of generating trouble far from US shores. At least two other major markets were deeply scored by the repercussions of company acquisitions which had commenced according to an American logic. These were Canada and Australia. Together, they accounted for over 15% of total Phoenix foreign earnings in both 1918 and 1929.[5] Outside the USA, these markets represented two of the main concentrations of Phoenix foreign trade, and Canada, of course, was the premier such concentration.

In both Phoenix suffered in the interwar period from its characteristic

[4] Calculated from Report of Victory Committee, 15 October 1942, pp. 376ff. Fire was still the dominant source of Group income in most markets.

[5] Australia contributed 3.7% and 3.5% respectively, Canada 12.4% and 11.9%. Even in 1939, these two still ranked second and third among Phoenix's foreign outposts for both fire and accident premiums, with Australia providing 3.7% of the foreign total for fire, 5.2% for accident, Canada 8.4% for fire and 7.9% for accident.

Table 10.2. *Phoenix Group: average annual agency premiums – fire, 1921–39 (£)*

(a) *Europe*	Belgium	Holland	France	Germany	Spain	Gibraltar	Portugal	Denmark	Norway	Sweden	Finland	Iceland	Total
1921–30	6,685	49,684	48,985	27,518	36,977	1,535	13,118	7,730	7,076	13,900	7,378	–	220,586
1929–38	17,541	58,307	77,917	51,566	30,158	607	24,534	19,209	473	12,167	5,350	178	298,007

(b) *India and the Far East*	India	Burma	Ceylon	Malaya	Siam	Fr. Indo China	Dutch East Ind.	Japan	Philippines	China	Hong Kong	Manchukuo	Total
1921–30	71,947	16,524	3,881	5,983	2,167	2,096	1,214	25,647	21,610	134,883	2,674	485	289,061
1929–38	12,369	13,053	3,990	5,588	1,823	1,272	2,800	13,086	19,917	17,443	4,069	1,382	96,795

Sources: 1921–30, Phoenix Review of Foreign Agencies, Book 5; 1929–38, Report of Victory Committee, 15 October 1942, pp. 376 ff.

affliction of the time: the toxic mix of international recession and the LGA merger. In Canada, sluggish insurance business concealed deep underlying problems. The Phoenix records provide an unusual, if dispiriting, glimpse of one of the world's greatest primary producing economies in the throes of a world depression. But nor did Canada – previously one of the Phoenix's best-run outposts – escape the mark of the LGA. Phoenix fire business in Canada had been profitable for decades before the 1920s. But the acquisition of the LGA, and its subsidiary, the North Empire, brought not only expanded casualty business in the Dominion but some $300,000 worth of exceedingly badly-chosen fire business. Dealing with this took more than a decade, prompted some wrong-headed if familiar decisions about 'purifying the books' (again), forced a fundamental reorganisation of the Group system in Canada, and generally played havoc with the Phoenix fire account.

In the smaller market of Australia, the ironies were even richer. Here, for many years, Phoenix had drawn substantial benefit across many states from its connections with the great merchant house of Dalgety, another of the great British-based 'international investment groups', formed in the late nineteenth century.[6] Dalgety provided for Phoenix agencies which could reach any part of Australia where wool was clipped or grain was cut, and they were powerful generators of business. However, by the early 1920s, after some fifteen years of the alliance, relations were becoming strained; Phoenix was beginning to lose patience with the merchants' pressure for ever higher commission levels. When in 1920 Phoenix executed the fusion with Norwich Union Fire, and in the process inherited NUF's strong Australian arm, it seemed a safe moment to resolve the strains and part company with Dalgety. The relationship was broken off in 1923. But, of course, the moment had not been safe. Due to the hidden financial liabilities of the LGA, Phoenix was unable to hold on to NUF, which, on departure in 1925, took its strong Australian arm with it. This sorry sequence left Phoenix stranded: it needed, in the second half of the 1920s, to recreate an Australian organisation of its own virtually from scratch.

A Phoenix Special Committee reviewed the company's strategy for world trade in 1927.[7] It decided that this trade was distributed as shown in Table 10.3.

Not surprisingly, the Committee decided that this array suggested a

[6] See S. D. Chapman, 'British-based Investment Groups before 1914', *Economic History Review*, 38 (1985), pp. 230–51.

[7] Phoenix Special Committee, 20 May 1927, pp. 136–8; General Manager's Memorandum to Chairman.

Table 10.3. *Phoenix Assurance: shares of world business by major region, 1927 (%)*

	USA	UK	Europe	Other
All Group business	58	20	9	13
All accident	71	18	4	8
All fire	51	17	9	23
All marine	9	50	4	37

certain lack of global balance. Then, rather weakly and with no great logic, they observed that the principle of balance had been infringed in the early 1920s because the fusion with NUF had brought together two companies with great strength in Canada. The logic was not good, of course, because: firstly, NUF and its Canadian operation had been removed again, yet the results were still unbalanced; secondly, the acquisition of LGA had produced far worse imbalance in the USA, as the difference between the accident and fire lines above clearly shows;[8] and, thirdly, the absence of NUF in Australia and South Africa caused much more severe imbalance than its presence in Canada.

However, the Committee was somewhat more perceptive when it came to proposing remedies for these foreign problems. They noted that by 1927 Phoenix enjoyed an exceptionally strong position in free non-US reserves in comparison to its total funds. They agreed that this put it in a good position for acquiring new subsidiary companies in foreign markets and that this device was the quickest way of converting problem markets to profit. With four subsidiary companies in the USA sporting a net asset value of well over £1 million, and just two others elsewhere, both in Canada (Acadia Fire and North Empire Fire), Phoenix was scarcely overburdened with corporate assets overseas. So, although the Committee of 1927 did not believe that Phoenix need be 'an anxious buyer', it was prepared to take the Group significantly further in the direction of a genuine multinational structure.

Four target areas for company acquisition were identified: Latin America, with a preference for Peru; Europe, with a slant towards France; South Africa; and Australia. An official was already looking for a likely buy in Peru. In Europe a number of British offices had been busy in the earlier 1920s, purchasing controlling interests in Polish, Czech and Ger-

[8] The leaning towards the USA in the accident line is produced by the weight of the LGA organisation in that market, while the better balance in the fire line is the result of the weight of the 'old' Phoenix organisation in that market.

man insurance ventures. Phoenix had encountered several propositions but had found none compelling. However, after a closer look, the Committee decided that the acquisition of a subsidiary would be a good way of avoiding the high commission costs of the French market place, and recorded in May 1927 that the Phoenix might soon get a chance at 'an old-established, conservatively managed and profitably conducted French company'.[9]

In South Africa, the Committee found that Phoenix business had been 'considerably below that of other leading British companies'.[10] Attempts at rectification had been made before 1914; then war had interrupted them; then the absorption of NUF's excellent capacity in South Africa had rendered further effort unnecessary. But by 1927 further efforts, as in Australia, were needed again. The dominoes set falling by the LGA purchase continued to topple.

In Australia they went down with a particular rush. The Dalgety connection took Phoenix's gross fire earnings in Australia from £63,210 in 1908 to £106,740 in 1922, a figure not bettered until 1928, and then only briefly. By 1927, a major UK insurance company should have been taking a net annual income of about £0.5 million from all kinds of Australian insurance. In that year, Phoenix took a net total of £118,000 (£65,000 in fire revenue, £34,000 in accident, £19,000 in marine).[11] Also, it contrived to make overall losses on Australian trading in 1926 and 1927.

Most other companies with Australian loss ratios similar to Phoenix's average 52% for the later 1920s did not suffer overall deficits. The reason was that they wrote much larger premium accounts. The Commercial Union, the Royal, and the London & Lancashire all earned around £0.75 million from Australia in 1927, the North British took nearly £0.5 million and the Atlas £0.25 million; very significantly, the Norwich Union also took £0.25 million. This allowed them to absorb expenses and secure profits in a way that was impossible on Phoenix's much smaller turnover. Significantly, too, most of the really large British operators in Australia had boosted their income flows by acquiring Australian subsidiaries in the recent past: the Commercial Union had taken over the Australian Mutual in 1920, the North British had captured the Insurance Office of Australia in 1922 and the London & Lancashire had absorbed the Colonial Mutual in 1927.

In that year, the Phoenix Special Committee could not agree on the case for acquisition in France, New Zealand or Australia. But they did agree on a joint operation in Peru, with Phoenix taking two-thirds of the

[9] Special Committee, 20 May 1927, p. 137. [10] *Ibid.*

[11] *Ibid.*, General Manager's Memorandum, 13 March 1928, p. 150.

capital of a joint insurance venture and local capitalist interests carrying the remaining one-third. This was the beginning of the successful Fenix Peruana project. But its total initial paid-up capital of about £37,500 was small beer indeed compared with the millionaire companies being considered by Phoenix in other parts of the world. In the late 1920s, therefore, Australia still required special appraisal by Phoenix and its problems had not been resolved.

It is noteworthy that the Phoenix foreign archive for the 1920s and 1930s, still one of the richest in the industry, conveys a certain sense of managerial disenchantment. The American problem, involving a late re-entry to a complex market, one of history's great earthquake disasters in 1906 and an escalating cost problem, could perhaps be put down as a special case. But, in the interwar years, Phoenix encountered difficulties in many other major insurance markets, not least Canada, Australia and South Africa, which current management attributed at least in part to the miscalculations of earlier management. They were perfectly aware that they were sitting in the middle of a world recession, and that was partly to blame. They saw too that part of the difficulties stemmed from the NUF–LGA sequence, and they were themselves not blameless in that. But they did complain that the problem of rising expenses impacting upon inadequate premium volumes occurred in too many places, and that this was a result of over-constrained underwriting policy on too many fronts in past years.

3. THE CANADIAN PROBLEM: DEPRESSION AND DISORGANISATION

As irritating as the loss of both the Dalgety and NUF connections in Australia were to the Phoenix management, they were probably more taken aback by developments in Canada. This had been a large, stable and profitable market for years. Then, in the period after the First World War, it abruptly became a problem market. The difficulties came in two phases: a sharp loss of profitability in the early 1920s and an organisational nightmare in the later 1920s. The first phase was ascribed by Phoenix management, probably inaccurately, to the 'unbalancing' effects of the tie-up with NUF; and the second phase was attributed, all too accurately, to the absorption of LGA.

The underwriting results clearly confirm the Phoenix management's belief that Canada had fallen from grace in three bad years between 1921 and 1924. Losses were high, but the true source of worry was an expense ratio behaving in an ominously 'American' style. On the one hand,

Table 10.4. *Canada: Phoenix fire business – expense, loss and surplus ratios, 1918–30*

	Expense (%)	Loss (%)	Surplus (%)
1918	32.8	48.6	18.6
1919	33.7	42.8	23.4
1920	34.9	26.6	38.4
1921	54.5	54.0	−8.5
1922	37.6	66.5	−4.0
1923	38.4	58.7	2.9
1924	60.1	78.9	−38.9
1925	40.6	55.5	3.9
1926	41.5	46.1	12.4
1927	40.1	40.4	19.5
1928	39.6	48.0	12.4
1929	40.9	61.3	−2.2
1930	41.8	69.1	−10.9
1931	41.7	43.4	14.3

Source: Phoenix Foreign Agency Book.

Phoenix men blamed this upon the difficulties of integrating their extensive Canadian network with the equally imposing operation of NUF. This became part of the standard Phoenix rhetoric of justification for the forced surrender of the NUF connection in 1925. On the other hand, when Percival Beresford, the US manager, travelled north to investigate the Canadian crisis in late 1924, he found that the heavy Canadian losses were in the same areas of business as the heavy US losses, that is, in remote farm risks outside the limits of fire protection.[12] His diagnosis suggested that the trouble lay in economic conditions rather than in adjustments to company structure. Similarly, when a Phoenix delegation consisting of the deputy chairman, general manager and accident manager went to Canada to inspect the trouble for themselves in 1925, they reported that 'during the last three years, *all* companies have had severe losses'.[13] Clearly, the problem of the Phoenix/NUF imbalance in Canada was secondary to general market difficulties, caused by the volatility of world farm prices in the early 1920s; and undoubtedly that imbalance could have been resolved given sufficient will and opportunity.

[12] Phoenix Fire Committee Minutes, Book 3, p. 136, 15 October 1924. 'Unprotected business' referred to in these passages means fire insurances in areas without fire-fighting provision.

[13] Report of Phoenix Management Visit to Canada, 1925. My emphasis.

Instead the NUF fusion was abandoned, primarily in order to finance the LGA acquisition. And Phoenix's problems in Canada switched from those of NUF imbalance to those of LGA inheritance. Unfortunately, that inheritance was also closely related to the issue of world farm prices. The three high-ranking visitors of 1925 judged that, 'the main difficulty was in the case of the LGA fire business and the North Empire fire business . . . The unsatisfactory results of these two companies have arisen almost entirely in the writing of farm business in unprotected areas'. They accepted that it was not possible to transact fire business in Canada 'without accepting a certain amount of farm business . . . but it is necessary to see that the proportion of agricultural business is kept to such a figure as will not upset the balance of the accounts'. Having run away from one sort of imbalance, they ran into another.

But, as usual, the disruption caused by LGA penetrated deeper than fire business alone. The visitors of 1925 reported on Canadian accident business that 'here, as in the USA, there was a greater thought for volume and income than for immediate profitable results. That policy was altered when we took control of the London Guarantee.'[14] Phoenix lived quietly with that thought for a time, while keeping an alert eye. Accident Manager Southam took it to Canada again in October 1925 and found nothing untoward. And when General Manager Sketch toured the USA in 1927, and was visited in New York by J. B. Paterson, the long-serving Phoenix general agent from Montreal, they could find nothing to talk about but the housekeeping.[15] While Phoenix inspectors were crawling all over the LGA operation in the USA at this time, Sketch and Paterson discussed Canadian promotions.[16] But such cosiness was not to last for long. On a further trip in May 1928, Southam reported that Canadian accident results were 'not so favourable as we would have wished', largely due to adverse conditions in the motor market following from 'severe non-tariff competition';[17] while a year later, things were worse, 'the business resulting in an even break', this time largely due to bad weather and an unfriendly outcome on hail insurances.

Accident managers now began to probe more deeply. After the LGA

[14] *Ibid.*

[15] In 1927 also the Patersons celebrated a family connection with the Phoenix which went back over a century. J. B. Paterson's grand-uncle Jamieson had been a partner in the distinguished firm of Gillespie, Moffat, first appointed Phoenix agents for Canada in 1826. To mark the occasion, J. B. presented Phoenix with some antique mahogany furniture which had graced the Gillespie, Moffat boardroom in the 1820s and Phoenix sent him a grandfather clock. Fire Committee Minutes Book 3, p. 328, 27 July 1927.

[16] Report of General Manager on American Business, Autumn 1927.

[17] Report of Accident Manager on Canadian Business, 2 May 1928.

acquisition, the major Phoenix outlet in Canada at Montreal, under Paterson management, had continued to transact the lion's share of the joint fire business in Canada, but also some Phoenix accident business. Meanwhile, the former LGA outpost at Toronto, under its manager, George Weir, handled the bigger proportion of joint accident business in Canada but also a significant, and troublesome, amount of fire business. That is, both operations continued in a composite form but retaining much of the individual styles of the two original parent companies. This distribution persisted even after the adoption of a formal Group system of organisation for all Phoenix companies operating in Canada in 1928.

By 1930, Phoenix London was beginning to suspect that its Canadian affairs were awry in several respects. Another senior accident man, Alfred Battrick, visited Canada between September and November 1930, and was not pleased. A profit had been produced in 1929, but only because the claims ratio was exceptionally low and because motor business had profited from an effect virtually unique in twentieth-century society: improved road conditions. Battrick thought that neither of these helpful circumstances was likely to last, that 'the Toronto Branch [LGA] could undoubtedly carry a larger premium volume without adding to expenses' and that its leadership 'was tending to lose initiative for development'.[18]

The problems which had first surfaced in relation to LGA's former fire business in Canada proved to have wider managerial implications. Even in December 1926, when Beresford had again been despatched to Toronto, this time to investigate the LGA and North Empire fire accounts, he had proposed substantial amendments. But these were not fully implemented, a fact which was concealed by coincidentally good fire results in 1927. Instead, the Toronto management had resisted the pruning of bad fire business for fear of alienating customers who also held accident policies. Paterson, leading the established Phoenix operation in Montreal, and a fire man through and through, became increasingly alarmed by Toronto's accident chauvinism. Battrick gave this alarm full publicity in his report of winter 1930. Indeed, it was Battrick who first proposed a radical codicil to the LGA legacy in Canada: that all Canadian fire business written by Phoenix companies should be grouped under Paterson at Montreal and all casualty business under Weir at Toronto. He considered a separation of powers as necessary and a visit by the Phoenix foreign fire manager (F. H. Yerbury) to confirm this as urgent.

Accordingly, the foreign fire manager was sent to Canada in January

[18] Report of Asst. Accident Manager on Canadian Business, November 1930 (PX 1637/4a).

1931 and stayed until April. He concluded that at Toronto, 'the Fire interests were unduly subordinated to the Casualty business' and that the fire results from Toronto for the period 1923–30, the years covering the assimilation of the LGA, 'indicated that there was something radically wrong with the management of the business'. He decided that 'despite several delicate questions as between the two Canadian Head Offices', all fire business should be aggregated and removed to Montreal 'forthwith'.[19] Fouling of the administrative lines was a consequential feature of the LGA takeover in many parts of the world: but, in this respect, Toronto was scarcely better off than the worst-hit centres in New York and London.

However, in one sense the division of powers was a step backwards since it represented a move away from composite operation in another major foreign market. Once again, Phoenix's experience of a particular composite acquisition shocked it into older methods of thinking and trading.

Disentanglement was not fully achieved until Sketch himself arrived in Canada in autumn 1931 to lay down the law that, from 1 January 1932, Montreal would control the whole of the fire business of the Group, 'irrespective of the name of the company in which it is written, and that the whole of the Casualty business will be conducted from Toronto'. This meant that all fire insurance gathered in Canada by Phoenix itself, by Acadia, by Union Marine, Columbia, Imperial, United Firemens', LGA and North Empire passed directly to the Paterson office. Additionally, that organisation would handle all reinsurance transactions for the entire Phoenix fleet in all sectors of business.

As in New York, it was not fully realised how badly the LGA stables needed cleansing until senior management gathered the resolve to fling wide the doors. The Yerbury–Sketch decisions of 1931 effectively did this. Behind the doors lay some unedifying things. It turned out that the LGA–North Empire organisation had maintained full branch offices at both Montreal and Vancouver; yet, in 1931, neither did more than $30,000 worth of business. Phoenix closed both in 1931. The manager of one of them, 'a clubbable type of person with an enlarged ego, left pretty much to his own devices' confessed, under questioning by Yerbury, to having 'no idea of the expense ratio of his Branch'.[20] It says something for the Phoenix forbearance that this offender was moved rather than sacked. One of the better findings of the review was that 'our Winnipeg Inspector is the Amateur Boxing Champion of Canada (Mr. Don Rowand)'; this

[19] Report of Foreign Fire Manager on Canadian Business, May 1931.
[20] *Ibid.* It was high: 47–49%.

was noted with enthusiasm. Less pleasing to Yerbury was the discovery that the agents recently appointed by LGA at Saskatoon possessed a double distinction: they were the most expensive representatives retained by any office writing Canadian business, and also the least productive. They were discharged.

Confirmed also was the suspicion that the LGA–North Empire had been little better at picking markets than at picking people. Despite the world depression in primary product prices, LGA had remained in the Canadian Grain Pool which in 1931 was 'running unprofitably and from which the Phoenix retired a year or two ago'. For its part, North Empire had decided that the oil derricks in the Turner Valley, Alberta constituted an acceptable fire risk. Yerbury demurred on both points and took the Phoenix subsidiaries smartly out of grain and oil.[21]

Given the contents of the stable, it is not perhaps surprising that Phoenix management began to wonder whether the redistribution of powers between Toronto and Montreal was reform enough. They concluded that some substantial tightening of control within the Toronto office was desirable and even considered moving in one of the trouble-shooters from New York, Lloyd Jones, to ginger up this process. In his report of May 1931, Yerbury allowed his mind to freewheel on the subject. Phoenix, he mused, 'can tap a better class of casualty business than the London Guarantee'; so why not move the initiative entirely away from Toronto and concentrate all casualty business, as well as all fire business, on Montreal, leaving only a casualty *branch* as a headstone for the LGA in Toronto. In turn, this led easily to the thought that the official who succeeded Paterson and Weir ought to be a single Canadian manager with control over both the fire and casualty wings. Thus the disturbance left by the LGA's wake in Canada threw up plans for a radical reform of the Group structure within the Dominion. And this plan would have secured a *return* to composite operation, and in a comprehensive and modern style.

But the background to these events was, of course, far greater disturbance in the wider world. Canada suffered badly in the global depression of 1930–2 and the Phoenix papers provide an unusual perspective on a great agricultural nation under stress. By spring 1931, Yerbury found, the whole Dominion had reacted to the US Crash and was in economic shock, with the west particularly afflicted. In British Columbia '75% of the Lumber Mills and practically all the Canneries are shut down and unemployment is considerable'.[22] In the cities during the winter months,

[21] *Ibid.* [22] *Ibid.*

the distress was made more acute by countryfolk attracted by the relief payments; they would wait out the bad weather on the dole and then return to their blighted holdings in the spring. Law and order, however, held up well with 'attempts at rioting and Communist activities in Vancouver and elsewhere . . . promptly checked'. Arson was another matter. Many of the bankrupted farms made tempting firewood and an insurance claim a quick route back to solvency. But even here the problem was not as bad as in the USA; or, at least, not yet. Canada, Yerbury felt, had more resilience than America and could produce an economic recovery more rapidly than its southern neighbour. He found 'a strong feeling of optimism and resolute spirit which indicates that employers and businessmen generally have the situation in hand and will master it more quickly than in other countries'. Rather touchingly, he recorded how impressed he was by 'the modernity of the Western Cities and [gratefully] their Hotels'.[23]

When he returned in 1932, however, he realised that there was more to the Canadian depression than grand hotels which soldiered on through adversity. Contrary to his predictions, economic conditions had 'considerably worsened'. The Western Provinces, the Maritimes and British Columbia were 'the darkest territories' for all insurers. The fall in investment values over the intervening twelve months had knocked the stuffing out of the bigger business interests. 'Toronto and Montreal commercial circles are gloomy and one cannot be certain that even the best names are capable of standing up to their commercial obligations.'[24] However, Yerbury noted an important underwriting aspect of the crisis. There had been few big claims on large-scale ventures such as factories and warehouses; moral hazard was not a problem in such quarters. But it was elsewhere. Smaller ventures, such as lesser hotels, general stores and farms were 'sustaining fire losses to so great an extent that no other inference can be drawn than that an undue proportion of fires has been wilfully raised'.[25]

It was the smaller insurances which formed the connection between economic recession and excessive claims for the fire offices. Claims on ordinary dwellings almost doubled 1924–31, to over $13 million. Phoenix, with over a fifth of its Canadian business in housing, was hurt (see the 1929/30 loss ratios in Table 10.4). Payouts of under $2,500 comprised about 70% of all Phoenix fire losses in 1930 and 1931. 'During the past twelve months', Yerbury concluded, 'the Companies have been victimised.' And he expected this storm of small claims to continue until there was some recovery in general trade. Again, he thought that he

[23] *Ibid.* [24] Report of Fire Manager on Canadian Business, 1932 (PX 1637/4b).
[25] *Ibid.*

detected some sign of this in 1932 as, in the Western Provinces, there were indications of a good crop to be brought in. Meanwhile, however, the world recession hit at the international insurers in Canada through the medium of the provincial stores and the humble farmsteads.

Ever on the lookout for good news, Yerbury did not let the sadnesses of a crumbling farm economy blind him to the prospects of a corporate advantage. Recession had rocked many of the native Canadian offices and left them vulnerable to the bigger multinational operators. In February 1931, Phoenix noticed that the Canada National Fire Insurance Co., 'a soundly organised concern at the right price well worth acquiring', looked ripe for picking. Yerbury started negotiations, only to find in March that 'the Continental Group of the USA' was both more interested and moving faster. It was the first time that the paths of the Continental and Phoenix Groups (later, between 1964 and 1984, to be so intricately interlocked), had crossed to any substantial effect. Perhaps Canada, in the middle of world economic crisis, was not the most auspicious of meeting places.

4. CANADA: THE CONTROL OF CRISIS AND COMPETITION, 1931–5

In the post-Crash period, the Phoenix Group was the second largest insurer trading in Canada. The Group structure, introduced and modified in the period 1928–31, gave the company some competitive advantages. It had, for instance, reduced the proportion of total premiums abandoned to treaty reinsurance from 34.2% in 1927 to 26.6% in 1931, thus securing a useful increase in net income. By 1931, Yerbury believed that recent reforms had left the Group 'in good shape and well officered'.[26] Even in the early 1930s, he thought the Group well placed to push for more cover on the larger buildings in western cities such as Edmonton, Regina, Saskatoon and Calgary.

However, as the second-ranking insurer, Phoenix was highly sensitive to the level of competition. Here, especially in bad times, there were still serious grounds for complaint; Canadian brokers behaved badly and the offices had been weak in confronting them. The main abuse was 'the growing tendency of eastern brokers to filch western . . . business from the agents in those territories by averaging the rate through the introduction of non-tariff companies'.[27] This resulted in headquarters staff in the east, who did much work through brokers, unwittingly generating cut-rate

[26] Report of Foreign Fire Manager on Canadian Business, 1931.
[27] *Ibid.*, 1932.

competition for their own agents in the west. The British Columbian market was particularly bruised by this dirty trick. Phoenix believed that the answer to it was to seek an agreement with the major Canadian insurers and the big New York offices aimed at a coordinated boycott of brokers who employed it.

But the insurance managers of the Canadian east were not as loyal in support of the Canadian Fire Underwriters' Association as they might have been, and indeed 'appear to regard Association work as a duty to be avoided if possible'.[28] Phoenix management argued that the high standing of the company in Canada 'should be used to influence less scrupulous members of the CFUA to a higher sense of their tariff obligations'. However, Yerbury was optimistic neither about the disease – 'the business is subject to all kinds of abuses and requires raising to a higher plane' – nor about the will to devise a cure.[29]

In any case, by 1932 he was more intent on trying to discipline the crisis in claims rather than the crisis in competition. The swing in mood between his reports on the Canadian market in 1931 and 1932 resulted in some stern prescriptions in the latter year. He did not like Phoenix's proportion of unprotected business: at 28.6% in 1932 it was deemed too high and Beresford's achievement in pressing the US share of such business down to 10% was held up as a marker. Moral hazard was closely associated with such business; and the books were now to be scoured for it. In Newfoundland, where the agents had been given a free hand, and visited only once in their career, results were particularly poor due to the 'bad moral hazard in that Dominion'. They were now visited most critically, and considered the treatment given to their portfolio as harsh.

Throughout Canada, the most vulnerable agents were told to drop as many farm risks as possible; all policies from small agencies in unprotected places were to be reviewed and cancelled. And Yerbury, displaying a particular hint of intolerance, was notably hard on non-Canadians: 'All risks, where the assured is of alien origin, and accepted through agencies in unprotected places' were to be dropped on expiry and no new policies of this type accepted.[30]

Phoenix had reason to worry. Canadian farm business was 'notoriously bad in the Western Provinces and Maritimes' and even the Farm Mutual Societies had lost money in 1931. The response was the purge on unprotected business and moral hazard and a swing away from the countryside; city business was promoted wherever possible. A new discipline and system was brought to the agricultural cover that survived. Where farm

[28] *Ibid.* [29] *Ibid.* [30] *Ibid.*

business had to be accepted, it was now subjected to consistent safeguards: every farm policy was to be reinsured to the extent of 50% of its value. Also, Phoenix set out to upgrade the rates for farm insurances by placing them on an annual, rather than triennial, renewal: although 'three previous efforts to do this have been frustrated by farmer politicians', it was hoped that 'current bad experience' would neutralise the backwoods vote.

After having lashed about himself to some effect, Yerbury had only one or two staff matters to note before setting sail for home. One revealed his blind spot again, as he complained, somewhat gratuitously, that 'the French Canadian staff is generally inferior to the English-speaking staff'. The other pleased him more as he noted 'the excellent results of some of the staff in the Canadian examinations: R. M. Sketch has secured six honours out of six subjects'.[31] R. M. Sketch was the nephew of General Manager R. Y. Sketch and the future Phoenix manager for Canada.

5. CANADA: GROUP POLITICS AND UNIFIED CONTROL – A RECONNAISSANCE OF EXPENSIVE AGENTS, BROKEN TARIFFS AND UNRULY COMPETITORS, 1933–5

Despite Yerbury's brusque tactics of 1932, little changed in the Dominion market between then and a renewed spate of visitations in 1935. Both accident and fire managers were called again to Canada in that year and neither was happy with what he found. The fire expense ratio, which had been high at 47% in 1932 was 'intolerable' at over 58% in the first half of 1935, notwithstanding the fact that Yerbury had found controllable expenses to be 'pretty well down to the knuckle' in 1932 and that, three years later, both visitors agreed, 'little or nothing further' could be done to cut expenses on either the fire or the casualty side.

Canadian expenses began to assume a position as threatening as that of their American counterparts; and they were to play almost as dramatic a role in the interwar affairs of Phoenix's second biggest foreign market. Moreover, competition from non-tariff companies, amplified by the tactics of the eastern brokers, was also still causing trouble. As Accident Manager Battrick summed up glumly: 'all the surroundings of our business in Canada at the present time, are unsatisfactory'.[32]

Just how bad these 'surroundings' were had become progressively clearer during 1933 and 1934. For one of the elements that did change between 1932 and 1934 was Phoenix's level of information in Canada.

[31] *Ibid.* [32] Report of Accident Manager on Canadian Business, July 1935.

The years 1933 and 1934 were ones of investigation; 1935 was the year of proposals. Unfortunately, however, complicated circumstances and personalities prevented much coming of these proposals for the remainder of the interwar period.

The first improvement in perspective was achieved by R. Y. Sketch himself, on a trip to Canada in May 1933. By this time, the expense ratio was already 'alarming' and encouraging Sketch 'to contemplate drastic action' to correct 'a thoroughly unsound state of affairs'.[33] Sketch calculated that the rates for Canadian fire insurance had halved over the last thirty years. This reflected considerable improvements in fire hazard, so the loss ratios had not increased; but the change in the relationship between premium charged and sum assured had played havoc with the expense ratio. Standing charges were not excessive and taxation consumed about 5% of income; the real villains of the piece were agents' commissions which took a staggering 28% – so that the 'floor' from which expenses *started* was 33% of receipts.

Why were agents' commissions in Canada so high? Sketch found two answers: the structure of business-getting and the high level of competition. The older British offices in Canada used a branch system of organisation, with salaried officials controlling a network of moderately paid local agents. The alternative method was a system of general agents, running their own office and a string of sub-agencies and paid an overriding commission, out of which they had to make a profit. This system was clearly expensive, yet many of the numerous new entrants to the Canadian insurance markets in recent years had employed it. Then competition entered the picture: since there were not enough general agents to go round, new insurers tried to capture the existing local agencies of the larger offices for their general agencies, while the larger offices, in order to retain them, had also to offer general agency rates. Competition thus exacerbated the already high costs of general agencies.

Under these circumstances, the Agents' Associations could not enforce agreed limits on commissions. Sketch observed that the Associations 'appear to be run more for the benefit of the agents than the companies'. And he thought that 'no mere improvement in trade' would solve these problems. But if these 'different evils' could be eradicated, their removal would eliminate 'ninety per cent of the difficulties' in Canada'.[34]

What would achieve this? Strong action was necessary for Canada was a model for other places: 'similar circumstances exist in many other parts of the world'. It was a valuable market but more open to action by the

[33] General Manager's Notes on Visit to Canada, May 1933. [34] *Ibid.*

offices than the USA. So 'drastic measures... would probably have a salutary effect not only in Canada but in the United States and elsewhere'.

Sketch had three possibilities in mind: go over entirely to a *controlled* general agency system; abandon the general agency system and concentrate on the cheaper local agencies: or, most radically, bring the general agents to heel by retiring Phoenix support from all Agency Associations. He felt that 'the smaller Companies and Agents are exploiting the position in the belief that the larger offices dare not take strong action... I believe that the only way of bringing matters to a head will be for one or more of the larger offices to take the line that they are not prepared to support the various Associations'.[35]

Given Phoenix's 125-year tenure in Canada, Sketch argued that 'we should be prepared to risk any reasonable hazard rather than see the work of so many years thrown away by withdrawal from such an important and potentially valuable field as the Dominion of Canada'.[36] It is interesting that, although Sketch was prepared to throw the threat of 'withdrawal' into the balance, he did not yet include among his 'drastic options' the possibility of a single managerial system or a single Phoenix manager for Canada. But he did instruct the Canadian staff 'to cast their minds forward' and devise appropriate solutions if the situation had not improved within one year.

However, the first mind to be cast forward was not that of a Canadian official but the incisive intellect of B. H. Davis who carried out a characteristically forceful, and elegantly reported, reconnaissance of Montreal and Toronto in March 1934. The state of competition and tariff control he found appalling: 'an almost unbelievable state of confusion, chaos and general lack of confidence among Canadian Executives regarding the intentions of the Executives of other Companies'.[37] The numbers of players in the market was out of all proportion to the volume of business – well over 100 tariff and around 100 non-tariff offices writing Canadian fire insurance. Even tariff companies were competing for agents and usually strict tariff general agents were having to let non-tariff companies into their offices. Competition necessarily became doubly difficult to handle 'when the Tariff Companies are not playing the game among themselves', and the result was, inevitably, 'a steady disintegration of the Tariff spirit'.[38]

After having talked to the managers of eight offices working in Canada, Davis concluded that the predicament analysed by Sketch the year before

[35] *Ibid.* [36] *Ibid.*
[37] B. H. Davis, Report on Visit to Toronto and Montreal, 3–9 March 1934. [38] *Ibid.*

would not be easily resolved: 'there is no possibility whatever of the Tariff situation in Canada being cleaned up, unless definite and specific instructions are sent out to Canadian Managers by their Head Offices in London or in New York'. Canadian managers were all too prone to refer matters to London simply in order to delay difficult decisions and 'there is a marked degree of insincerity on the part of many, if not all, of the Local managers'. Although conceding that the general managers in London were working together to solve the Canadian crisis, Davis drew a hard-hitting picture of a market strained to breaking point by the combined forces of recession and excess competition.[39] The usual civilised rules of concerted insurance strategy were in abeyance in the Canada of the mid-1930s.

The most dangerous result, Davis agreed with Sketch, was the effect of enhanced commission charges on the already aggravated expenses problem. Commission rules were 'constantly breached' and there was a persistent tendency in the quest for premiums, to accept exorbitant demands from the agents for higher rates. An agreed protocol for acquisition costs seemed almost equally essential and unobtainable. Many Canadian insurers believed that this circle could be squared only by government action to limit commissions, but both Davis and Sketch believed that the 'voting value' of the agents throughout Canada would keep the Insurance Superintendents – who were rumoured to be 'highly amused at the chaotic conditions in which the Insurance Companies find themselves' – out of the game.[40]

So Davis reviewed what had become in 1934 the currently debated alternatives. Firstly, the prospect of substituting a countrywide general agency system for the existing branch control was 'unsound in principle': reductions in acquisition cost, if any, would be off-set by increased claims costs as local control was reduced. Also, the short supply of good general agents was already at the core of the Canadian problem. Secondly, the notion of restricting Phoenix underwriting to the provinces of Quebec and Ontario was scarcely worth the time of day. But the third possibility, 'but briefly discussed' so far, the project of 'combining the Fire and Casualty personnel of the Phoenix Group and centralising the Controlling Office in one city' was 'logical and practical'. At this point, Davis threw back into the centre of debate the idea first tentatively mooted by Yerbury in 1931. Directly as usual, he argued, 'this unified Group Control should be the ultimate objective to which our energies should be directed'.[41] The prescription for Canada was to be the same as that for the USA.

[39] *Ibid.* [40] *Ibid.* [41] *Ibid.*

His lead was followed by Head Office, at least at the level of reconnaissance. In 1934 Phoenix had sent E. B. Ferguson to the USA so that he could act as London's ear in New York during the consolidation of the US fire and casualty organisations. Sent further north in December, he was given a similar task as the first Phoenix man briefed specifically to investigate the prospects of a managerial merger in Canada. This was done quietly. Ferguson instructed E. H. R. Low, one of the senior fire officials in Montreal, that 'although no official request would be made, he should put some notes together on the practicability of creating a Canadian Group Headquarters at Montreal'.[42] The resulting memorandum was ready by summer 1935. It coincided in time with the embassies of Yerbury and Battrick to Canada. So, it went first to Sketch, who sent it on, with his own gloss, to the two Head Office managers who thus had it with them during their major inspection of the Canadian operation.

The Low Report was the 'casting forward' by an internal Canadian official which Sketch had envisaged in 1933. Low's analysis emphasised two major flaws within the existing Phoenix organisation. The first was that the company in fact employed a hybrid, 'Branch-cum-Agency' system in Canada, with some selling conducted by salaried officials and some by general agents. The result was neither fish nor fowl but it was expensive; since the general agents 'appear to regard their commissions as the first factor in the business and the fortunes of their Companies as a poor second'.[43] Secondly, there was inadequate integration between the fire and casualty wings: the Group was 'wide open to criticism on the grounds of lack of co-operation in productive effort'.[44] The conclusion was that Phoenix's fortunes could be improved by cutting out expensive general agencies, boosting the branch capacity, and bringing this more consistent structure under single direction. Internal and external appraisal agreed: Low came to the same verdict as the much-travelled and far-sighted Davis.

The task of streamlining the administration into a single form, widening the echelon of salaried officials and eliminating the general agencies, and then placing the entire works under one manager, was inescapably on the Phoenix agenda by 1935. It is thus a saga in itself that this desirable result was not fully achieved until 1948. The only solace was perhaps a neat stroke of historical symmetry: Phoenix's first manager for Canada, when he eventually arrived, was R. M. Sketch, that nephew of R. Y. Sketch who had done so well in his exams in 1932.

[42] Ferguson, Memorandum to Battrick and Yerbury, 31 May 1935.
[43] E. H. R. Low, Report on Canadian Organisation, 1935. [44] *Ibid.*

6. CANADA: GROUP POLITICS AND UNIFIED CONTROL – PROPOSALS AND PERTURBATION, 1935–6

Accident Manager Battrick and Fire Manager Yerbury were sent to Canada in the summer of 1935 in order to raise the level of the operation from intelligence gathering to battle planning. At this point, Canada was at the centre of Phoenix's attention. Several major policy documents had been generated; the general manager was directly involved in the issue; and the company's top fire and casualty specialists were briefed for on-the-spot reformulation of tactics.

However, the two Head Office men did not face identical problems and did not have identical attitudes. On the fire side, the mid-1930s saw subnormal loss ratios but also reductions in premium income due to tighter underwriting restraints in Quebec and the Maritimes and to even fiercer competition in British Columbia. Only western premiums were holding up, thanks largely to an improvement in the grain business. Despite the low losses, some agencies were doing poorly, and in Yerbury's view, needed to be jettisoned before fire claims returned to normal or even to abnormal. He thought that 'French Canadian agencies seem primarily to blame'; but then listed eight main offenders of whom only three appear to carry French names.[45] Increased volume was not an option on the fire side since there was little genuinely acceptable new business on offer, while much of the apparent new business in the market was really composed of the deliberate prunings from other insurers' portfolios.[46]

So Yerbury's analysis of the Canadian problem took a particular slant. He pointed out that several UK offices had revealed expense ratios for 1934 similar to Phoenix's projected 55–56% for 1935: Guardian, Commercial Union, Atlas and North British all admitted to results between 50% and 58%. Accordingly, the fire manager called for concerted action by the companies to press down the cost of acquiring business, especially the high level of agents' commissions. He suggested telling the Agents' Associations 'quite frankly that unless they assist the Companies in reduction and control of commissions, there is no alternative but government intervention'. The government might not wish to risk the electoral muscle of the agents, but the threat was worth the making.

Yerbury's opinion of the ability of Canadian managements to achieve the reduction on their own was not high; and he recognised that it was difficult to cut agents' incomes 'whilst Managers can go off to Murray Bay

[45] Report of Fire Manager on Montreal Branch, 1935. [46] *Ibid.*

for conferences and golf'. Accordingly, the pressure ought to come from the centre, from the FOC in London: 'The time may now be ripe for forming a London Canadian Committee with a constitution somewhat similar to the London Australian Committee.' The fire manager was pressing for more Head Office initiative in this, 'knowing that Canadian Managements are past masters in the art of stalling awkward questions and decisions and are unusually suspicious and fearful of one another's bona fides'.[47]

Yerbury admitted that there was a need for more push on the selling side through the medium of multiple-line inspectors, able to handle both fire and casualty business. But the main thrust of his analysis, as it had been since 1931, was towards organisational reform. One of his proposals was to put the cat actively among the Dominion pigeons, and to form the main focus of controversy in Phoenix's Canadian affairs for the next decade. For again, Yerbury raised, from the field, 'the advisability or otherwise of having our Canadian organisation under one efficient Manager', located at Montreal. This observation deliberately picked up the points made in the reviews by Davis and Low. The issue of a 'Manager for Canada' would not go away.

From the accident side, however, Battrick did not give managerial reform his highest priority. This was because he did possess the option of expanding Phoenix's casualty business in Canada. There was new business to be had and he could imagine, realistically, a 'broader outlook' in underwriting policy. He pointed to Phoenix's lack of a suitable force of inspectors to cover the vast Canadian market – in 1933, the province of Ontario, equal in size to the combined area of France, Germany and Belgium had *two* of them – and to the poor supervision of general agents by senior branch officials. He concluded that Phoenix needed, at least on the casualty side, a stronger field force and a more committed selling policy in Canada.[48] Thus he came to regard business expansion as more important than organisational change.

Perhaps unfortunately, Battrick had excellent practical arguments which he could place alongside any discussion of principle: he observed that, for the time being at least, Phoenix lacked the resources and the individuals capable of implementing a Group management system under the control of a single officer. Additionally, he judged that 'there would be no real gain by merging our Group organisation, centred either in Montreal or Toronto. In my view there would be no savings in expenses commensurate with the damage done to our organisation, particularly

[47] *Ibid.* [48] Report of Accident Manager on Canadian Business, July 1935.

having in mind the personalities involved'.[49] Since LGA tradition and influence in Toronto were so strong, it would be necessary to maintain a substantial operation there, probably a branch, even if the Group headquarters were translated to Montreal.

Yet, immediately after the Second World War, Phoenix did establish a centralised Group control and a single manager for Canada, although both were allocated to Toronto. So the personalities, human resources and relations between the fire and casualty sides in the interwar period clearly posed some special problem. It is clear also that Sketch came to share Battrick's thinking on these issues.

In 1935, the former LGA camp in Toronto was still commanded by George Weir, who was approaching retirement, and, in Battrick's view, should indeed go quite soon. The traditional Phoenix strongpoint in Montreal had passed from J. B. Paterson to C. W. C. Tyre in April 1934.[50] The appointment of Cecil Tyre was viewed by Sketch as an experiment. He had given notice to Tyre during his visit of 1933 that, if the experiment did not work out, Tyre could expect to be superseded. Tyre was young for the job and wholly a fire man. Yerbury listed his weaknesses as 'poor expression in writing', 'a reluctance to travel about the Dominion' and 'permitting himself to be unduly harassed by bad times'. Under the conditions of the 1930s, the second and third qualities were perhaps unfortunate. However, Tyre also had, according to Yerbury, a good personality, appearance and address and possessed 'business-producing ability'.[51] These were the personalities and relationships which made Battrick distrust the possibility of unified control with current resources.

Battrick's leaning towards the solution of business expansion, had been much influenced by an assessment of Canadian casualty prospects written for him by Leonard Weightman, a Head Office accident official transferred to Toronto as a senior assistant to Weir,[52] and, fairly obviously, as Phoenix correspondent at the eye of the storm. A remarkable private correspondence between Weightman and Battrick, much of it directed to the latter's home address, provides striking insights into the unsettled weather conditions encountered by Phoenix in Canada.

But the first document from Weightman to stir opinion in London was a formal report on Phoenix's position within the Canadian casualty

[49] Battrick to Sketch, 4 July 1935.

[50] Paterson, who had been Phoenix fire manager for Canada since 1922, had expressed his wish to retire, after 43 years' service, in late summer 1933 (Phoenix Directors' Minutes, 37, p. 251, 16 August 1933).

[51] Report of Fire Manager on Canadian Business, 1932.

[52] He was appointed assistant casualty manager for Canada from 1 January 1932 (Phoenix Directors' Minutes, 37, p. 131, 2 November 1932).

market following upon the LGA acquisition. In 1934, Weightman calculated, the complete fleet of Phoenix fire companies in Canada had taken $1.75 million, giving them about 4.5% of the Dominion market. On the other hand, the Phoenix casualty units took only $0.75 million and controlled only 2.9% of the national market. Weightman then compared LGA progress in Canada over the period 1920–34 with that of Canadian, US and UK casualty offices. In 1934, there were 244 companies offering casualty insurance in Canada and they were writing three times as much business as ninety-six companies had done in 1918. If British operators in the Canadian market are separated out, in 1934 there were sixty-two such offices writing four times as much business as twenty-four companies had done in 1918. Most companies had swung up through the 1920s to a peak in 1929, and then had slid back.

For Phoenix the comparison revealed a deeply disturbing finding, making it 'quite clear that the London Guarantee has made the least progress of practically all these companies insofar as volume is concerned'.[53] Its takings had remained virtually static, failing even to display the 1929–30 peak evident in the results of virtually every other office.

Other British companies like the Employers' Liability and the Ocean had travelled much faster than the LGA. The Royal had launched into Canadian accident business only in 1923, but had overtaken the LGA within three years. Adding one of many insults to significant injury, the Norwich Union overtook the Canadian casualty business of its erstwhile stablemate in 1928, and was still ahead in 1934. The Canadian subsidiaries of British operators such as General Accident and Globe Indemnity, which had ranked on a par with LGA in the early 1920s, had recovered strongly from the Depression in 1933 and had pulled far ahead by 1934. Of the Canadian native companies, the outstanding Dominion of Canada had caught LGA by 1924 and ran away from it thereafter. The Canadian General and Canadian Indemnity entered casualty business in the mid-1920s and challenged LGA as equals by the mid-1930s. Of the big American insurers, US Fidelity, Travellers Insurance, Travellers Indemnity and Continental Casualty, all had done less business than LGA in 1918; all did more in 1934: three of them overtook LGA in 1924, one in 1928. The overall outcome was that the Phoenix ranked eighth among the big casualty groups in Canada, and ninth among the motor insurers.

Weightman questioned whether Phoenix should be satisfied with this and proposed that the office should expand by 'fresh selling propaganda courageously planned, with the object of defeating the expense ratio after

[53] L. Weightman, An Examination of the Phoenix Quota of Available Casualty Business in Canada, 24 June 1935.

a reasonable period of time'. To this end, he suggested 'a practical tentative experiment'. This might take one or more of five main forms. Phoenix could make or buy another Canadian casualty subsidiary; or it could bring its existing Canadian fire vehicle, the Acadia, into casualty business; or it could expand branch casualty business; or it could push casualty work through the general agencies; or it could expand generally by campaigning for more lines and relaxing its underwriting conditions.

Weightman preferred a blend of the last two options. There should be proper embassies of branch officials sent out regularly to ginger up the general agents. There should be a bigger field force for Ontario and Quebec; in Quebec alone there were twelve provincial towns which should have been exploited much more thoroughly. There was room for expanded capacity in general public liability, householders' and inland transportation sectors, but not in motor, where Phoenix was already top-heavy. All this could be achieved at a cost of 2% of current revenue.

With such a devastating résumé of past LGA action, or inaction, before him, it is scarcely a surprise that the Phoenix accident manager should have seen more room for expansion in his answer to the Canadian problem than the Phoenix fire manager.

Indeed, Battrick thought that expansion needed to be tackled, whatever was done, or not done, about centralisation of management. Phoenix in Canada had not maintained sufficient contact with its field force and this was dangerous, particularly in times of sharp competition when rivals were 'apparently concentrating on more intensive servicing by way of inspectors'. The company's agents had taken a short-sighted view, while non-tariff competition had proved 'keen and intelligent'. No longer would this do: 'business conditions are possibly on the turn and I am satisfied that the time has come when we should be prepared to make this effort for expansion'.[54]

Both Yerbury and Battrick had a sticky time against the conservatism and pet theories of the Canadian staff, let alone with the weather. On 4 July, Battrick was 'insisting that . . . we must concentrate on the expansion of our business with the weapons we have available to us, rather than on . . . futile speculations as to what may be the outcome of outside matters'.[55] One week later, he was 'having a pretty strenuous time here, as it keeps very hot and humid, and, although I am getting plenty of golf, it is almost as trying as business, especially as it is being played mainly with Agents and other company Managers'. With the latter he had 'a full and frank discussion, such as, I understand, has been all too rare with officials

[54] Battrick to Sketch, 4 July 1935. [55] *Ibid.*

from home'.[56] But it did not cheer him up. On 19 July, he was again stressing to Sketch that 'the only practicable way of experimenting at the present time' was by going for volume.[57] Then, eventually overcome by the weather and with patience fraying, both he and Yerbury took the quickest tickets home they could find, sailing on the *Berengaria* on 26 July, 'just escaping a real vicious New York heat-wave' and with Weightman promising to send 'the enlargements of the Niagara Snapshots' on after them.[58]

Both officials had done well. Unable to execute a true managerial shake-up, they had doggedly pushed an unresponsive and suspicious Canadian team into a position where it was showing something like enthusiasm for a more active selling policy. It was undoubtedly sapping work under irritating conditions; Yerbury even began to see merits in 'a real English summer'.

Meanwhile, in London, R. Y. Sketch, now forswearing drastic solutions in the short term, was busy convincing himself that the Battrick formula was all that Phoenix could hope to achieve. What limited Sketch most was that Phoenix Canada lacked any individual capable of acting as a single manager: Weir was too old, while Tyre had insufficient experience and no casualty training. So, unable to provide a man, Sketch argued, somewhat optimistically, that 'the only criticism that we have to offer of our Canadian business is that the expense ratio is very excessive and has reached such a figure that, unless an abnormally low loss ratio is obtained, a profit is impossible'.[59] His conclusion was that Weir and Tyre should be told that the expenses *must* be brought down, *or else* there would be a major managerial shake-up.

Drastic action would follow only if the existing personalities, within the existing organisation, did not respond to threat. Twelve months was to be allowed for the improvement to happen. Also, in this period, Sketch thought wishfully, there could be improved coordination between the fire and casualty operations, as a kind of half-way house between present circumstances and centralisation. Given the treatment meted out to Beresford and the US organisation, Sketch appears here to be moving with almost exaggerated indulgence. Ironically, it was anyway all to be spoiled by the way in which the news was broken to those for whom the indulgence was intended.

Both Sketch and Battrick were convinced that, for the present, they could do no more than 'makeshift'. They hoped to review the Canadian

[56] Battrick to Sketch, 11 July 1935. [57] Battrick to Sketch, 19 July 1935.
[58] Weightman to Battrick, 29 July 1935.
[59] R. Y. Sketch, Memorandum on Canadian Business, 2 July 1935.

position more rigorously at the end of 1936. The hybrid tactic of development-cum-cordination was to be executed by an executive committee 'directing a programme of multiple line expansion throughout the Dominion'[60] and functioning, according to the pious hope of a later investigation, in 1941 as 'nearly as possible as a General Manager for Canada'.[61] In fact, as might have been predicted, general management by committee was a very uneasy compromise.

Once Battrick and Yerbury were back in the United Kingdom, Sketch needed to explain the results of their visitation to Weir and Tyre in Canada. By letter, he stressed that Canadian business 'constitutes an important factor in our results' but was marred by 'the important and serious position of our Canadian problems'. Then the choice of solution was put: either a marked improvement in the volume of Canadian business or a true managerial revolution involving a single Canadian manager. Indicating that the latter post could not be filled by either Weir or Tyre, Sketch argued that the successful candidate 'would have to be well-grounded in both departments and with experience of administration of a similar kind in other countries'. He then added an unfortunately imprecise codicil: 'it will be obvious to you that the . . . change would not be beneficial to you personally or to your immediate subordinates'.[62]

No one in London, not even Battrick or Yerbury, interpreted Sketch's letter as more than a summary of the agreed position prior to the two managers' departure from New York. But in Canada it caused mayhem and probably postponed an effective solution to the Canadian problem into the postwar period. It also triggered the correspondence between Weightman and Battrick which tells us about the mayhem. Even Weightman, who was clearly seen by Head Office as the next casualty manager in Canada and had been told that he had good 'prospects of a comparatively early succession to the appointment',[63] was disturbed by the Canadian reactions.

After the visitations of 1935, Weightman reported, the Canadian team had been 'all set-up', at last fired with enthusiasm for expansion. But, 'now we are all in the dumps, apparently over two letters that have acted like a ten-days' earthquake'.[64] Weir had hoped that he would be spared the endless sermons on expenses from London once the 'new deal' was launched and was now completely disillusioned, his ardour 'damped from

[60] Sketch to Battrick, 15 July 1935.

[61] Report of Victory Committee, p. 3.

[62] Sketch, duplicate letters to Weir and Tyre, 2 September 1935.

[63] Battrick to Weightman, 2 September 1935. Weightman was appointed LGA manager for Canada and Newfoundland and Phoenix casualty manager for the same territory in April 1936. Phoenix Directors' Minutes, 38, p. 198, 1 April 1936.

[64] Weightman to Battrick, 25 September 1935.

the outset'. He was also convinced that Sketch had already selected a manager for Canada and was ready to send in the new broom in 1936; he asked (with some justice), 'if Mr Sketch wished to convey that he [Weir] was in the way, why did he not say so, and be done with it?' Finally, he was worried that Sketch was expecting too much of an answer too fast. The casualty manager for Canada cherished a rather idealistic vision of the proper relationship between a London insurer and its major foreign stations: 'the managements of other large British groups are apparently content not to expect miracles of their Canadian managers, pending a return to normal conditions, and are letting them reasonably and sympathetically alone to hold the fort in the meantime'. He might perhaps have reflected that the other large British groups had more of a fort to hold.

Reactions from the fire side were no more positive. Tyre had been less whole-hearted than some in his support for business expansion; Weightman reported in August on discussions with Tyre that 'he had to go over the whole ground again' and insist that 'the drive must be a good hard drive with the determination of quick results'.[65] It was not without foot-dragging that Phoenix had secured its experimental multi-line production teams in Ontario and Quebec. To the broadside from Sketch, Tyre reacted first with levity, 'believing it to have been dictated during an attack of liver', then realised that it was serious, but decided that it was unfair. In particular, he maintained that the profit scraped by the fire department in 1934, marking recovery from the nadir of 1929–30, had been unjustly neglected (see Table 10.7 below). By contrast, his deputy, W. Lawrie, later Canadian fire manager (1939–47) and member of Phoenix's Canadian Board, was thrown into 'an extreme state of fermentation', fearing that his twenty-five years of service would be marked in 1936 by dismissal. 'This perfectly good servant of the company', bemoaned Weightman, 'is now definitely disheartened and in a condition of mind to do anything.'[66]

Even the lucid and patient Weightman, Head Office sangfroid personified, expressed his own disquiet:

> In the midst of all this unsettlement, I suppose what I have to do is to remain secretly and inwardly calm as to my personal prospects. After three years of hard slogging in a super-charged atmosphere, without any holiday, but with plenty of domestic hardship, I confess that the tranquillity I strive to maintain is getting a little ruffled.

He regretted that Sketch had written in the same vein to the two Cana-

[65] Weightman to Battrick, 31 August 1935.
[66] Weightman to Battrick, 25 September 1935.

dian managers. Conceding that 'the Tyre problem has got Head Office into a knot',[67] he argued that the letter to Weir had scarcely formed the best preparation for retirement: Weir had been told nothing of Phoenix's plans for him and simply feared the sack. Battrick took a more robust line, pointing out that the development programme had not emanated from Canada but 'had to be put into operation by Officials from Head Office'. He concluded that, 'Perturbation in some quarters, resulting in a grasp of the realities of the situation and a consequent real endeavour to improve matters, would not, in my view, be altogether a bad thing.'[68]

Perturbation turned out, however, to be more trouble than it was worth. It was sufficient trouble to bring Sketch himself to the Dominion again in February and March 1936. He found that the Phoenix loss ratio for 1935 was still subnormal, and in terms of comparison with other offices, 'somewhere near the top'. The expense ratio was still bad, but at least was 'in line with the majority of companies'. Positively good news was also to be found: 'the good work done in improving the underwriting is showing results'.[69] Further, 'although it is too early to say that the establishment of the joint production organisation is achieving its end, it seems clear that the trend is in the right direction'. Progress was even being made with the Canadian Agency Associations and pressure was being exerted from the FOC in London. This was all promising; but Sketch had really come to deal with the problem of Weir's retirement and Weightman's succession. At the second attempt, he made a better hand of it. He concluded that it was right that Weir should go: 'the conditions under which he has successfully handled our problems have changed . . . and it seems impossible to obtain a definite opinion from him on any important point'. But he made a fair offer: retirement on 1 May 1936, full salary to age sixty, a (non-stipendiary) seat on the Canadian Board, Weightman to succeed. A relieved Weir accepted without demur.

Sketch was able to sign off from Canada with remaining doubts about 'the very unsatisfactory state of insurance business as a whole in Canada' but with optimism 'that we shall succeed at any rate by comparison with our competitors'.[70]

This may have been true of fire and casualty. Much less promising was Phoenix's performance in the Canadian life market. Here the indifferent selling which was being rectified in the two main insurance markets was still in need of treatment. The problem was examined by another Head Office expert, T. H. Hodgson, in June 1936. He found some favourable indicators. Canadians tended to favour UK life insurers 'partly due to the

[67] *Ibid.* [68] Battrick to Weightman, 9 October 1935.
[69] Managing Director's Report on Canadian Business, February–March 1936. [70] *Ibid.*

scare that the insuring public received after the 1929 Crash in Wall Street', and Canadian business conditions were looking better: 'they have not yet shown the same improvement as has been evident recently in Great Britain and the United States, but there is reason to suppose that a noticeable measure of recovery will not be much longer delayed'.[71]

The problems were that the fierce competition general in the Canadian insurance market was even more acute in the life sector, and that the selling of life insurance there was conducted wholly by specially trained full-time life agents; fire or casualty agents did not also peddle life polices but would pass on any prospect to a professional agent of a life company. Any office competing in this market needed its own force of expensive professional agents. Moreover, Phoenix life rates were 'quite out of date and will have to be completely revised if we continue writing new business'.[72] Phoenix's selling record under these conditions was so indifferent that the company by 1936 was faced, Hodgson concluded, with only two alternatives: 'close our Canadian fund to new business altogether' or create a fresh development initiative. This, he advised, was quite feasible: if Phoenix revised its rates and targeted the larger Canadian cities, it could raise an additional $2–3 million of new business per year at an acceptable acquisition cost. Properly handled, Phoenix could write Canadian life business at rates close to British ones, paying commissions to the Canadian standards, and still make a profit. All it would take was another inculcation of willpower in the Dominion.

As the decade drew to a close, and Europe towards war, Phoenix's second largest foreign market, and its third largest in the world, after the United Kingdom, continued to be a problem. The last visitation of peacetime fell to Battrick in September and October 1938. He found that the field force was much improved and ready 'to take immediate advantage of any break in trade'. And the organisation was more flexible and responsive.[73] Yet Battrick carried in his papers a copy of a letter from Ferguson to Tyre, written in July 1938, which reveals that many frictions still affected the Canadian market, and affected it worse than many others. Ferguson emphasised that 'in recent years Canada has produced a disquieting trend when compared with other overseas reports which we have to put before the Managing Director'.[74] He allowed that the data sent home from Canada showing the Phoenix position on premiums, commissions and expenses came out no worse than that of other companies, indeed compared 'quite favourably'. But there were still plenty of difficulties.

[71] T. H. Hodgson, Report on Life Business in Canada, 11 June 1936. [72] *Ibid.*

[73] Report of Accident Manager on Visit to Montreal, 12 October 1938 (PX 1858/L).

[74] Ferguson to Tyre, 29 July 1938 (PX1858/L).

Some were familiar. The Agents' Associations, after the promise of improvement, were back to their old tricks again: Phoenix had to sustain its expansion 'with complete disregard of any impetus that can be expected from some solution of the Association problems'.[75] Commissions were still going up: a 1% increase in the first half of 1938. And Head Office was still anxious to learn if Tyre was being sufficiently energetic in his promotion of the 'new arrangements' for Quebec. But there were new emphases. There was a suggestion that Quebec was becoming identified increasingly as a problem market. Almost certainly, such thoughts lay behind the company's postwar decision to concentrate upon Ontario and regroup organisationally upon Toronto. Additionally, although Phoenix's income and expenses position might have been no worse than that of other offices, the company now seemed to be improving that position more slowly than the competition. This was especially so in Quebec where all tariff offices achieved an increase in net income in 1937 over 1936 of 7.7%; yet Phoenix managed only 2.7%. In Ontario, the result was much better, with the pack scoring 4.2% and Phoenix 3.5%.[76]

The break in business in Canada did not come until 1940; and then it did not last long. Perhaps worn out by these long wrangles, Tyre did not see it: he died at an unseasonably early age in December 1939 and was replaced by William Lawrie. Within months, early in 1940, 'there seemed to be no shortage of anything in Canada';[77] industry was reacting to war demand from Britain and taxation was moderate. But by 1943, business break had given way to a full war economy, with all sorts of restrictions on private enterprise, closures in the mining industry and unprecedented taxation. However, Sketch was right: it would anyway have taken 'more than a mere turn in business' to resolve the insurance problem in Canada.

7. CANADA: RESULTS AND RETROSPECT, 1931–45

As with the US market between 1900 and 1945, it must be doubted whether the Phoenix in Canada directed its efforts to the correct places. With Canada, of course, there was the additional complication that in 1920 it had been a trusted profit centre for many decades. By the 1940s, however, it looked very different. Again as with the USA, some of the better insights as to the reasons for this came after the conclusion of the interwar period, indeed in the middle and later 1940s.

Even in 1940, Canada still bulked large in the world market of both

[75] *Ibid.* [76] *Ibid.*

[77] Assistant Fire Manager, Canada: Results of Business, 31 January 1944.

Phoenix and London Guarantee. On the fire side, it was still the third largest market for Phoenix, and for London Guarantee the second largest after the United Kingdom. Similarly, on the accident side, it remained the third most valuable market after the transatlantic and the home markets for both Phoenix and LGA (see Table 10.5).

After the enormous predominance of the USA in the Phoenix fire account and in the LGA accident account, the position of Canada, even after twenty years of indifferent trade, is clearly a special one. Both Phoenix and LGA were taking close on £100,000 each in accident revenue from the Dominion in 1940 and Phoenix alone was taking nearly double that amount in fire revenue. In fire premiums written in Canada in 1941, Phoenix ranked third of the eighteen British composites trading in the Dominion, trailing only the Royal and the London & Lancashire (see Table 10.6).

However, the results shown below, in Table 10.7, in dollar terms shows the patterns of indifference, as they affected the Phoenix's fire market.

Profitability over this period was never robust. In three years it was negative; in another six it was below 10%; and the recovery after 1933 was not sustained. The main pressure on profitability clearly came, as contemporary management fully realised, from the inflated expense ratio. Equally clearly, the agonised campaigns of the 1930s did not turn the expense ratio around: throughout the years of peace it continued well into the mid-50% range. Only the decade-long run of subnormal loss ratios 1934–43 permitted very modest profit levels. Even the upsurge of fire losses after 1943 was due to the exceptional circumstances of the war economy: the record piles of wood pulp accumulated under the pressure of war demand fuelled some very large fires.

There is, of course, a major swing here away from the high loss ratios which traditionally characterised the kind of frontier market Canada had been and towards the high running costs which characterise a quite different kind of market. By 1949, Phoenix's foreign fire manager, George Hurren, was 'satisfied that the conflagration danger in the principal cities has materially decreased over the last twenty-five years'. Only St John's, Newfoundland, St John, New Brunswick and Halifax retained their fiery distinction. The main reason for this improvement Hurren attributed to another of the rare virtues of the automobile: its appetite for space drove natural firebreaks through congested areas and forced local authorities to plan the location of roads, and thus of towns generally.

Elsewhere, what was concealed in the long-run numbers was not good news. Writing in 1944, Hurren had identified in the fire returns 'a downward trend for the past ten years, with the exception of 1941', despite the

Table 10.5. *Phoenix and LGA: the twelve largest markets worldwide by premium income, 1940*

	Phoenix				LGA		
Market	Premium (£)	% of world premium	Rank	Market	Premium (£)	% of world premium	Rank
(a) Fire business							
USA	1,165,681	47.7	1	UK	47,749	40.0	1
UK	559,574	22.9	2	Canada	22,846	19.2	2
Canada	188,193	7.7	3	Australia	12,848	10.8	3
Australia	64,812	2.7	4	S. Africa	11,210	9.4	4
Far East	31,254	1.3	5	Holland	2,396	2.0	5
S. Africa	26,696	1.1	6	Denmark	2,393	2.0	6
NZ	23,709	1.0	7	Portugal	1,605	1.3	7
Argentine	14,916	0.6	8	Greece	1,481	1.2	8
Portugal	14,214	0.6	9	France	1,421	1.2	9
India	13,002	0.5	10	Belgium	1,298	1.1	10
Spain	12,293	0.5	11	Faroes	482	0.4	11
Cuba	10,239	0.4	12	India	428	0.4	12
(b) Accident business							
USA	746,444	45.1	1	USA	1,388,668	75.3	1
UK	618,072	37.3	2	UK	274,150	14.9	2
Canada	81,854	4.9	3	Canada	92,280	5.0	3
Australia	53,324	3.2	4	Denmark	37,241	2.0	4
Cuba	49,578	3.0	5	France	21,781	1.2	5
Argentine	26,879	1.6	6	S. Africa	14,658	0.8	6
S. Africa	23,602	1.4	7	Australia	7,618	0.4	7
NZ	20,409	1.2	8	Holland	2,150	0.1	8
Portugal	12,079	0.7	9	Jamaica	1,864	0.1	9
Far East	11,647	0.7	10	Trinidad	1,103	0.1	10
India	3,980	0.2	11	Morocco	984	0.1	11
Curacao	1,891	0.1	12	Norway	950	0.1	12

Source: Combined Revenue Accounts, Fire and Accident, Phoenix and LGA, 1940.

Table 10.6. *Fire premiums written in Canada, 1941 – nine British groups ($)*

Royal	3,500,599	Norwich Union	984,607
London & Lancs	1,711,475	REA	864,859
Phoenix	1,689,754	North British	818,177
Commercial Union	1,609,543	Guardian	772,368
Sun	1,091,247		

Note: The Phoenix figure is derived from all Group companies operating in the Dominion.
Source: Hurren, Canada: Results of Business, 31 January 1944.

Table 10.7. *Phoenix Canadian net fire premiums and expense, loss and underwriting surplus ratios, 1933–45*

Year	Net Premium $	Expense %	Loss %	Underwriting profit/loss %
1933	1,422,558	51.9	54.7	−5.6
1934	1,390,859	48.9	40.9	11.1
1935	1,316,193	53.5	34.5	14.3
1936	1,266,881	55.0	32.1	14.5
1937	1,239,425	53.0	30.9	17.0
1938	1,218,893	55.0	40.6	5.0
1939	1,160,614	55.5	38.7	7.9
1940	1,142,952	55.7	37.5	7.4
1941	1,284,411	50.9	35.5	9.2
1942	1,197,944	53.3	43.4	6.2
1943	1,165,078	53.2	52.3	−4.4
1944	1,366,053	47.8	56.4	−10.8
1945	1,391,466	47.7	50.6	1.0

Source: Mr Hurren's Premium Figures for Canada.

fact that Head Office had 'repeatedly stressed the importance of maintaining premium income'.[78] At first sight, therefore, it looks as if the development drives of the later 1930s were no more effective in boosting premiums than the attempt to control acquisition costs had been in cutting expenses. And, indeed, there are indications that the efforts of the earlier 1930s to root out the more dangerous risks prejudiced later attempts at business expansion, an almost traditional example of 'purification of the books' misfiring. From the perspective of 1946, T. H. Hodgson was able to put the almost equally traditional counter-argument into its Canadian context:

> We should remember the lessons we have learned in Canada. In the early 1930s we severely restricted our acceptance of farm and other unprotected business which had been most unprofitable. That action, through denying facilities to our Agents, reacted seriously on the remainder of the portfolio, which has not yet recovered, while the business we turned out has since become most profitable.[79]

That was heavily ironical. But it was not the whole answer. Probably, the declining trend in receipts was due more to competition than to purification. Hurren judged that the real trouble was 'the very substantial reductions in rates made over a period of years by the Tariff Companies in an effort to stem non-Board Competition'.[80] In this, they had been partially successful but at the cost of netting less premium in relation to the volume of risks they covered. For Phoenix certainly, the decline in income was 'not due to loss of insurances'; the volume of risks was being maintained and even increased. This was where the development drive had been worthwhile; without it, the decline in income would have been far worse. Moreover, the reduction in rates, which had continued into 1942, was now reaching limits beyond which no competitor would wish to go.

By 1946, Phoenix management still judged that the prospects of future profits from Canada were 'not at the moment particularly satisfactory'.[81] However, Head Office did see some chance of useful change. Disaggregation of loss ratios by province had shown that not all Canadian losses were low. Those in Quebec were high and something could be done about that. Production in Quebec was now being 'severely restrained'. Nevertheless, Canadian results would continue unsatisfactory 'until we have been able to obtain a substantial increase in Ontario. This will be largely dependent upon the reorganisation now pending with an active Fire Department in

[78] G. H. Hurren, Canada: Results of Business, 31 January 1944.

[79] T. H. Hodgson, Some Thoughts on US Fire Business, 14 May 1946.

[80] Hurren, Canada: Results of Business, 31 January 1944.

[81] Hodgson, Kirkman, Hurren, Report to the General Manager on Phoenix Fire Revenue Account 1945.

Toronto.'[82] This, of course, was a reference to the managerial revolution, the 'drastic' centralisation of control which Sketch had not been able to achieve. The implication is that it had been necessary all along.

Once it had been achieved in 1948, with R. M. Sketch's appointment as manager for Canada and the creation of a Canadian headquarters in Toronto, Hurren became notably more enthusiastic about matters Canadian. The changes in Phoenix organisation had also coincided with what appeared, at long last, to be the genuine turn in Canadian business conditions. In 1949, Hurren, who had gone there looking for chances of business expansion – 'we cannot afford to be over-cautious' his motto for the trip – found in both Ontario and Quebec, 'high levels of public and private investment, particularly in building operations . . . while the discovery and rapid development, mainly by American interests, of vast petroleum resources in Alberta is regarded with great expectations'.[83] Major expansion was anticipated in Canadian mining and perhaps even the troublesome problem of Quebec might yield to the solution just applied to India: a republic within the Commonwealth. Though a little ahead of his time in this connection, George Hurren was a sharp observer of present and likely future developments. Certainly, he picked up in 1949 the growing nexus between the economies of the USA and Canada, as the Dominion became increasingly frustrated at the obstacles in trading with postwar Britain. But this was the price of the long-awaited Canadian expansion: at least, 'all these things create a picture of present and long-term prosperity, given the necessary development of population . . . industrial development seems likely to proceed apace'.[84] And Phoenix, also at long last, seemed well placed to benefit from Canadian conditions: 'with its present young and vigorous management, should share in Canada's growing prosperity'.[85]

Phoenix was pinning a lot on this management. Ralph Sketch, at the age of thirty-nine, had been told that he must work out a system for fully controlling all Canadian business from Toronto. In order to give him free rein all Phoenix US subsidiaries would withdraw from Canadian business from 1949. By the time of Hurren's arrival, Sketch was 'firmly in the saddle' and showing 'evident leadership inside and outside the office'. The visiting fire manager summed up the prevailing reformed circumstances in a manner which throws much light on preceding circumstances,

Our Canadian business is, to some degree, at a cross-road. The move to Toronto was, *owing to the war*, undertaken somewhat *belatedly*, and there is a possible

[82] *Ibid.* [83] Report of Foreign Fire Manager on Canadian Business, May 1949.
[84] *Ibid.* [85] *Ibid.*

disposition on the part of our management to make up for *lost opportunities* . . . Our Manager for Canada, with a progressive outlook and anxious for development is, however, fully occupied with the problems presented by the Casualty Account . . . Our fire account will, for the next two or three years, be passing through a period of transition . . . I encouraged everyone to look to Head Office for assistance and endeavoured especially to eradicate the feeling, which seems to have become somewhat deeply rooted in our Canadian organisation, that the less Head Office knows about the problems, the better.[86]

There are some interesting accents in this. The first is the tactful attribution of the belated concentration upon Toronto to the effects of war. In fact, the issue had been postponed, under difficult circumstances, until the war postponed it further. Second, there is an omitted accent: no mention of the fact that concentration was initially supposed to be on Montreal. The remarks about 'lost opportunities' and 'somewhat deeply rooted' resistance to Head Office guidance is clear, if gentle, criticism of the preceding regime in Canada. And the reference to Sketch's business with the casualty account is a reminder that the LGA legacy was still ensnaring the virtuous nearly a quarter-century after Phoenix's luckless decision to purchase an accident flagship.

To say that a national insurance market is in transition is perhaps not especially helpful; it almost always is. But, between roughly 1920 and 1945, and even later, the remark has a special force when applied to Canada. The Dominion market held a special place in the priorities of British insurers: it was seen as one of the most reliable parts of the Empire, an area of 'recent settlement', peopled largely, if not exclusively, by those of British stock, often literally by cousins or nephews and nieces, yet located next door to the prodigious economic capacity of the USA. One transition came as Canada pulled progressively closer to its neighbour; another as it became progressively urbanised and the profitable insurances increasingly became those of the city rather than the countryside. The factory, the motor car and the town-planning officer defined a market very different from the one constituted, not long before, by the stockyard, the grain elevator and the whaling station.

As this happened, the insurer's main problem became less that the risk might burn or crumple than the cost of acquiring it in the first place. Many of the ways of acquiring it were outdated: merchant houses of Victorian or Edwardian pedigree turned general agent were a legacy of Canada's earlier form of economy. They were firms of stalwart uprightness and silver-haired decorum, the salt of the Dominion. But they were also conservative, ageing (usually very literally), and extremely expensive.

[86] *Ibid.* (my emphasis).

Transition to a newer form of organisation, based on the branch and the salaried task force, was particularly important in such a market. The vestiges of traditional colonial commercialism imposed a high cost on the metropolitan insurer, and Phoenix was not among the fleetest in removing them.[87] However, much of this had to be done, not only as Canada negotiated its progress away from a purely agricultural economy, but in the throes of world economic recession, and in a country heavily affected by it. 'Transition', therefore, is more than usually justifiable as a verdict.

8. AUSTRALIA: A NEED TO REPLACE CONFIDENCE AND CAPACITY

Centralised control at least came to Australasia long before it was achieved in Canada. Both Phoenix and NUF had extensive networks 'consisting of branches in the various provinces with control offices in Sydney and Wellington'. Phoenix had set up its first Australian branches in 1891 and 1895, although Sketch noted dryly that it had 'followed suit' in doing so.[88] The control offices, representing the main vehicles of centralisation, started life in the early 1920s as necessary devices for arranging the integration of the separate organisations of Phoenix and NUF. Then, once both the Dalgety connection and the NUF capacity were lost, the control system remained necessary as a means of coordinating the shreds of the 'emaciated agency organisation' which was all that remained to Phoenix in Australia by 1925.[89]

Sketch had perceived the fusion with NUF as a major opportunity to tighten control in Australia. There, the general agent vested interest was not as entrenched as in Canada and the extent of the NUF organisation made reconciliation of the systems more pressing than in the northern Dominion. By 1925, he felt that 'The question of unified control in each department of the business has been forced on me more and more since the association of the Phoenix with the Norwich Union, and still more strongly during the past three years since the London Guarantee came into the Group'.[90] As elsewhere, Sketch, perhaps showing a certain distrust of the Phoenix managerial tradition – he certainly observed that rival

[87] A good example was Phoenix's general agent in Vancouver, the firm of Ceperly Rounsefell & Co. Founded in 1887, and linked to Phoenix's main Canadian agency at that time, this company attained considerable prestige throughout British Columbia. Led for many years by a Rounsefell who brooked no ideas other than his own – which, fortunately, were more progressive than those of his subordinates – it insisted on reporting directly to London. Problems attended the passing of this effective autocrat after 1938.

[88] General Manager's Memorandum on Australian Business, Special Committee Minutes, 13 March 1928, p. 150.

[89] Report of Manager for Australia on Australian Business, 1926–30.

[90] Special Committee Minutes, 19 March 1925, pp. 57–60.

offices had built up their Australian business in earlier decades 'by more active efforts than ours'[91] – selected former NUF officials for the key centralising posts in Australasia: H. W. Bain became general manager for Australia, W. E. A. Gills manager for New Zealand. Briefly, Bain was controlling officer for the entire Group in Australia, that is, for Phoenix, NUF and LGA, and for both the fire and accident wings.[92]

But, of course, when Phoenix parted company with NUF, many of the Norwich officials reverted to their original employer. So, by the end of 1925, Phoenix lacked not only the Dalgety capacity but also Bain and Gills. The company had to despatch the manager of its London West End Branch (R. L. Swan) hurriedly southwards to become manager for Australia and to confront the reconstruction of a branch system throughout Oceania, with the single exception of New South Wales.

Faced with the near-catastrophic disintegration of an entire national system of representation – an occurrence which cannot be frequent in insurance history – Swan did surprisingly well. Upon arrival he identified, alongside the rather conspicuous absence of a sales force, two further areas of major difficulty: an excessive level of claims on the accident side and, as in Canada, an excessive level of costs on all sides. By 1930 he had done much to replace the agency system and recreate the branch offices. This, he believed, 'had the seasons been normal, would, ere now, have borne fruit'. But the 1920s were not normal, and it was, of course, much more expensive to recreate an agency sytem in the 1920s than to launch one in the 1870s or 1880s.

But Swan was an apt diagnostician and an effective surgeon. In 1925, Phoenix's accident claims ratio was 60%; by 1929, he had reduced it to 41%. He had detected that the reason for the high claims was less real loss than hidden cost: of the 60% 'claims', nearly one-third was going into fee payments to inspectors, surveyors and solicitors. Phoenix Australia was being taken, professionally, to the cleaners. Swan stopped that.

However the remaining costs were problem enough. The control apparatus was designed for a premium flow about twice as large as the one Phoenix commanded in the second half of the 1920s. Yet the control system needed to be retained. So its cost needed to be halved. This too was achieved by 1930. But, by this time, little more could be done about expenses: for instance, in New South Wales, the charge for fire brigade services alone amounted to 12.5% of the total fire income from that state. In all states, government controls on minimum wages for office staff also

[91] General Manager's Memorandum, Special Committee Minutes, 13 March 1928, p. 150.

[92] Managers in India (H. M. Hind), Shanghai (W. H. Crombie) and Japan (D. Pratt), received similarly wide powers at this time.

Table 10.8. *Phoenix Australian loss ratios: fire, accident, marine, 1926–9*

	Fire	Accident	Marine
1926	47.0	62.1	36.0
1927	48.3	57.4	33.5
1928	49.3	50.9	36.0
1929	48.1	41.2	48.0

Table 10.9. *Phoenix Australian total fire and accident results, 1925 and 1929*

	Total Net Premium (£)	Loss %	Expense %
1925	97,515	48.0	62.6
1929	109,778	44.8	54.8

caused problems. Phoenix Australia made no profits, due entirely, said Swan, to excessive cost levels.[93] His figures for the three main Australian market sectors, suggested that the underwriting strategy, and the resulting loss ratios, were correctly pitched (see Table 10.8).

The total fire and accident results for 1925 and 1929 showed that Swan had exerted his characteristic impact upon the expense levels, but also that it was not sufficient (see Table 10.9).

For fire alone, the expense ratio had risen from 44.2% in 1920 to 55.4% in 1925, and then stayed above 50% for the remainder of the decade, again clearly showing the effect of the loss of NUF premiums and administration (see Table 10.10).

Indeed, the full fire figures for 1920–9 reveal Swan's difficulties very explicitly.

Income and expenses moved in opposite directions in the difficult period of the mid-1920s, and, as they did so, the trading surplus contracted almost to nothing. Then, in the later 1920s, Swan's rebuilding of the branch structure began to lift the premium figures, but, expensively purchased as it was, could do little about the costs. As they hovered in the 50% range, it was possible, as in Canada, to make a profit only if the losses remained in the subnormal range. Once economic conditions began to

[93] Report on Australian Business, 1926–30.

Table 10.10. *Phoenix Australia: fire premiums, loss and expense ratios and trading surplus, 1920–9*

Year	Premium (£)	Loss %	Expense %	Trading surplus %
1920	112,540	30.1	44.2	25.7
1921	115,441	47.6	42.9	9.5
1922	106,744	34.5	48.1	17.4
1923	94,518	41.5	49.2	9.3
1924	82,979	38.5	52.5	9.0
1925	82,435	42.5	55.4	2.1
1926	87,221	52.3	51.6	−3.9
1927	97,826	71.9	52.3	−24.2
1928	112,235	57.6	50.7	−8.3
1929	121,407	81.6	55.9	−37.5

Source: Phoenix Review of Foreign Agencies, Book 5.

deteriorate in the later 1920s, they were no more likely to do this in Australia than anywhere else. The economy faltered, the burning rate went up, and the fire account went into the red.

Even after every effort, Australia was showing the same pattern as the USA and Canada: sticky income flows, well-controlled losses up to the economic crisis but expenses stuck stubbornly at or around 50%. Swan's conclusion was that the only ways forward were either to augment income by a gradual extension of the base organisation or to fix the income position more rapidly by acquiring an existing Australian insurance company. The first option was not easily accessible. The Australian market, unlike the Canadian, was, by this time, well disciplined, with all classes of business subject to tariff. Any aggressive or over-keen drive for business would jeopardise the tariff and irritate powerful competitors. Even in 1928 Sketch noted that 'I foresee many dangers were we to set out on a sufficiently active campaign to achieve a substantial increase in the business during the next few years.'[94] Swan, in reviewing his first five years in Australia, rightly congratulated himself that, 'we have now in Australia a business which compares favourably with the business of other Companies, and, having regard to the great difficulties that had to be surmounted... great progress has been made'.[95] But Swan was among the first to argue that this much-improved business was also too small, lagging the desirable level for a major player in this market by perhaps

[94] General Manager's Memorandum, Special Committee Minutes, 13 March 1928, p. 150.
[95] Report on Australian Business, 1926–30.

£200–300,000. So, if a sales drive in the Canadian style could not be contemplated, the weight would have to fall upon the second option. It was to become the key theme of Phoenix's interwar dealings in Australia. Just as the problem of the single manager dominated the Canadian debate, so the issue of the great acquisition occupied the centre of the antipodean stage.

9. AUSTRALIA: COMPANY NEEDS

Back in London, Sketch had come to the same conclusion as Swan and was to become a consistent and powerful advocate of the acquisition option. His Board was to be more timorous, but the general manager proved a good deal more forthright in his handling of the Australian problem than of the Canadian. No doubt, he was influenced by the behaviour of the other big British offices in Australia: the Commercial Union had absorbed the relatively modest Australian Mutual in 1920, the North British took the somewhat larger Insurance Office of Australia in 1922, and the London & Lancashire did best with the quite sizeable Colonial Mutual in 1927.

Phoenix began no less adventurously. The withdrawal of NUF facilities stimulated a major rethinking of Phoenix overseas operations, particularly in Australasia. By May 1927, Sketch had identified two large companies which suited Phoenix needs, one New Zealander costing £1 million and an Australian venture which would have outdone any other UK acquisition and cost £1.6 million.[96] The Special Committee of the Board examined the prospects late in May 1927. At its second session, the New Zealand company was revealed as the National Insurance Co. and the Australian unveiled as the Queensland Insurance Co. Both were expensive and Ryan laid down the law that 'no such transaction involving so large a payment should be made without a close personal inspection on the spot by the General Manager'.[97] The Committee niggled at the fact that this would take Sketch away for six months and at the effect such a purchase would have on free assets. It then worried about 'the wisdom of purchasing another company at such a juncture', could not agree, and was adjourned.

There were a number of ominous features to these meetings. Ryan, undoubtedly smarting from the LGA fiasco, was cautious from the beginning. The Committee's reference to 'another company' has a tired ring to

96 General Manager's Memorandum for Chairman, Special Committee Minutes, 26 May 1927, p. 138.

97 Special Committee Minutes, 31 May 1927, p. 143.

it; and that fatigue was LGA-induced. The 'juncture' in question was the deteriorating economic context of the late 1920s. And the adjournment was the first of many to which the Australian problem reduced the Special Committee. For if the prospect of the National never became any firmer, that of the Queensland lingered, in one form or another, for the best part of a decade. Phoenix was unlucky to have found an apparent Australian solution in NUF when other British offices were busy buying Australian companies. By the time Phoenix discovered it also needed to buy, the time was no longer favourable. However, we may note that the London & Lancashire kept the courage of its convictions in a major purchase as late as 1927.

And Sketch persevered. He took the Special Committee back to the issue in March 1928 and got them to agree that an acquisition was the only reasonable course, though he had to mollify them with the thought that they need not be 'anxious buyers'.[98] But Sketch *was* quite anxious and proved it by going to Australia (and South Africa) in 1928 in order to look directly into shop windows. By February 1929 he was back in London with an exhaustive report on the Queensland and dragging its assistant manager behind him so that he could answer the Board's questions. His seriousness of purpose is not to be doubted.

Nor is his courage. After the LGA acquisition, with its huge unforeseen costs,[99] it took a brave insurer to propose a further corporate purchase of over £1.8 million, the asking price for the Queensland by early 1929. However, he had powerful reasons. He had inspected the Phoenix–LGA network in Australia: Phoenix branches at Sydney and Melbourne operating alongside separate LGA branches, but integrated Phoenix–LGA operations at Brisbane, Adelaide and Perth. Swan had done well, but Sketch insisted on complete integration throughout. Clearly, not only the loss of the NUF capacity but also the addition of LGA capacity had caused problems in Australia. The net effect, Sketch found, was to give Phoenix 'first-class business in Sydney and Melbourne' but a poor position in the suburbs and outlying districts, that is, prime Dalgety territory. He was not pleased to discover that Phoenix had only six inspectors for the whole of Australia whereas one of its rivals had thirty-five: he ordered the immediate addition of a dozen more, 'with motor-cars'. He sacked the managers for Brisbane and New Zealand, and added the latter's territory to Swan's domain. This was a general manager's visitation in the high style; but it proved to Sketch that Phoenix needed to do a lot in Australia, rather quickly.[100]

[98] *Ibid.*, 13 March 1928, p. 150. [99] See Chapter 7.
[100] General Manager's Review of Australian Business, Special Committee Minutes, 14

He was uncompromising in his judgement on Phoenix's performance in Australia since the 1900s,

> In spite of the wonderful growth of the wealth of Australia, we have not obtained anything approaching our share of it. In these great British communities with exceptional possibilities, the Phoenix is a quarter of a century behind its rivals.[101]

He put this down to 'mediocre management' by those 'either dead or no longer in the service'; perhaps he meant those who had lost the Dalgety connection. He did concede that 'the relinquishment of the Norwich Union business has also played its part'. And we must recall that Sketch had some vested interest in not placing too much responsibility on the split with Norwich Union.

Certainly, while in Australia he had sought his preferred remedy with the utmost energy. He had looked again at the National of New Zealand and also at the Mercantile Mutual of Sydney, and the Southern Union before plumping for the Queensland, on which he brought back, proudly, 'exceptional information'. This was no exaggeration: his dossier was very detailed indeed and he set it out for the Special Committee with his usual clarity. The Queensland Insurance Co. was one of the biggest catches left in the diminishing shoal of independent Australian offices. It had been founded in 1886, originally as a marine insurer, in a stroke of diversification by Sir James Burns of Burns, Philp and Co., then one of the largest shipowners and business houses in Australia. Sir James launched it with £12,500 in capital. By 1928 share capital stood at £0.5 million and premiums at £346,000 fire, £300,000 accident and £11,000 marine. Its home fire income alone would have more than doubled Phoenix's gross Australian takings; while its accident earnings would have more than quadrupled Phoenix income from this source. There was no doubt that the Queensland could have solved Phoenix's problems of volume in Australia.

The Queensland was also a world-scale operator, with branches in London, New York and Canada and twenty other outlets spread from France to New Guinea. Phoenix even detected relevance in its North American operations and those of its subsidiary, the Bankers' and Traders';[102] for perhaps these facilities could help to reduce Phoenix's expense levels in the USA and Canada.[103]

But the main attraction was the Queensland's powerful Australian income, its expense ratios and its profitability (see Table 10.11).

February 1929.

[101] *Ibid.*, p. 170.

[102] Founded in 1921 as a joint operation with the Royal Bank of Canada, Lord Inchcape also holding an interest.

[103] General Manager's Report on the Queensland Insurance Co., 4 February 1929.

Table 10.11. *The Queensland Insurance Co.: income and profits, 1925–9*

Year	Net premium (£)	Loss %	Expense %	Trading surplus %
1925	556,191	52.1	36.9	8.3
1926	727,223	55.5	30.3	11.6
1927	821,767	57.5	31.3	8.8
1928	882,801	60.3	30.5	5.8
1929	832,418	59.4	33.1	3.2

The losses were well controlled, but the operating costs were exceptional by the standards that Phoenix had become used to, and the profitability for the disturbed second half of the 1920s was quite outside Phoenix's experience in most of its major markets.

This was largely thanks to the Queensland's eleven branches in Australia and seven in New Zealand, a system which ran an excellent agents' organisation, under a celebrated Australian name 'which has grown with Australia'.[104] If Phoenix could acquire this, Sketch argued, it would obtain exactly what it needed in Australia – a proven, low-cost selling network with a lot of reputation. He imagined 'joint Branches throughout Australia, and thereby . . . substantial economies', not to speak of the crock of gold: 'within twelve months our own loss on trading would be overcome'.[105] Even Accident Manager Southam, a by-word for caution, agreed that Queensland's accident business was of the kind that he would be happy to reinsure himself, and that, even here, it was safe to assume an expense ratio 'not exceeding 40%'. Not least, the Queensland's organisation could solve at a stroke the Phoenix's managerial problems in New Zealand.

There were other ways in which the purchase was convenient. Not only was the Queensland's Head Office just across the street from the Phoenix branch in Sydney. The shareholding was just as suitably located: the Burns family and the Burns, Philp directors together controlled more than 60% of it. 'From the point of view of the ease of carrying through the transaction and the lack of disturbance of the business consequent upon purchase', Sketch observed, 'it would be difficult to imagine anything more favourable.'[106]

But why should Burns, Philp wish to sell their highly successful offshoot? Sketch thought that the shares were standing in their books at early

[104] *Ibid.* [105] *Ibid.* [106] *Ibid.*

values, perhaps no more than £70,000. So a shipping and trading venture was sitting on a barely related asset with a potential market value of over £1 million. Sketch reflected that their shipbuilding requirements periodically raised large demands for cash.[107] Probably more accurately, he argued that any attempt by the main shareholders to off-load the shares would drive the price down. So he pointed out to them that 'it is only by the sale to another Company that they can hope to make this asset a liquid one'.[108] Apparently, this was enough, for by February 1929, Phoenix held an option to purchase these shares at £3 15s apiece, against the current market value of £3 6s.

However, there were half a million of these shares. The Queensland, therefore, ranks as one of the largest of Phoenix's target companies in its quest for multinational composite status. And this one was at the opposite end of the world. At the start of 1929, its total free assets were calculated by Sketch at £1,174,684 and he allowed nearly £700,000 for goodwill; the total of £1.86 million represented 8.5 years' purchase. However, if the cost was high, the Queensland by any reasonable test still looked a good buy.

But not to the Special Committee of the Board. So soon after the unsuccessful purchase of the LGA – which, despite its London base, was effectively a purchase of capacity in the USA – they balked at another expensive purchase of capacity in Australia. Despite Sketch's strong advocacy for the correctness of acquisition in this case, the Committee decided that the economic situation in Australia made it unwise 'for the company to enter into a transaction... involving the employment of a sum approaching £2 million'. The economic situation was, of course, Australia's share of the world depression. Nevertheless, the Committee thought that they might steel themselves to a lesser purchase 'involving an outlay not out of proportion to the Company's commitments in Australia'.[109] Given his investment of time, travel and argument in the Queensland option, this was a definite snub for Sketch.

He was not able to bring the issue back for more than a year. But, when he did, it was in a carefully orchestrated campaign and with determination unimpaired. He now had Swan in London, and required him to review Australian business 1926–30, and report to the Committee. Also, the accident manager, the marine underwriter and the investment manager were asked to write appraisals of the Queensland. All views were broadly positive.

[107] Though surely not in the depressed shipping market of this period.
[108] General Manager's Report on the Queensland Insurance Co.
[109] Special Committee Minutes, 14 February 1929, p. 175.

Sketch took his cue from the Committee's last expressed view in February 1929. First, he defined what he would like to have offered the Committee: an established company of good standing with free assets of £0.3–0.4 million and goodwill worth about the same, 'making a total outlay somewhere in the neighbourhood of three-quarters of a million'.[110]

Then he defined what he *could* offer. The Queensland was still on the market, and now at the reduced price of £1.6 million. Its shares had fallen from the £3 of late February 1929 to £2 8s in May 1930, and Phoenix could probably get the whole company, goodwill and all, for a flat £3 per share. It was bigger than might be ideal, but it could resolve many of Phoenix's Australasian difficulties in one move. However, if Phoenix purchased this office, it could not afford to entertain any further prospect in Australia. The second choice was revived from Sketch's short-list of 1928, the Southern Union. It was smaller than the ideal with only £220,000 in free assets, mostly in real estate, and about £80,000 for goodwill. It would not solve the Australasian problem at a stroke – it had no capacity in New Zealand, for instance – and, although the asking price of £0.3 million represented considerable value, 'it would require thought and time to make of it what we want'.[111] However, this purchase would meet immediate needs and it would not prevent further Australian acquisitions.

Both the timing and the content of this ploy were shrewd. It was the fall in share values which was the pretext for bringing the issue of the Australian acquisition back to the Committee. This fall, as Ryan noted, was not due to underwriting results but to the slide in the Australian financial markets, 'probably a repercussion of the speculative "slump" in the United States'.[112] The combination promised a cheaper Australian purchase without loss of insurance profits. Secondly, the device of defining the ideal size for a purchase and the real alternatives on either side of it, left the Committee less room for creative confusion. After hearing Swan on matters Australian on 7 May 1930, they summoned up their courage and responded to Sketch's invitation to decide between the real alternatives by deciding that they preferred to buy the larger company.

It is to be hoped that Sketch had learned not to count his chickens. For the Committee then found two further items to worry about: it wanted the general manager of the Queensland brought to London to reassure it

[110] General Manager's Memorandum on Australian Business, 6 May 1930. [111] *Ibid.*

[112] Chairman's Memorandum on the Proposal for an Offer to be made for the Purchase of Shares in 'X' Company, 24 June 1930. In earlier discussions, Queensland and Southern Union had been code-named, without much subtlety, as 'Q' and 'S' companies. By 1930, concealment had progressed a little and Queensland had become 'X' Company.

on details and it wanted to be comforted on the implications for Phoenix investments in Australia. The first was relatively easily managed, but the second consumed a few ill-timed months. The problem here was that Phoenix already held about £1 million worth of Australian government securities and it did not wish to acquire more of them by taking aboard the Queensland's portfolio. On the other hand, the Committee did not wish to sell their own Australian holding in the middle of a world crash. The problem was how to get the Queensland *and* avoid overburdening Phoenix with tricky Australian gilts. The Committee met on 27 June and 1 July but could not agree; and was yet again adjourned. It was not until 21 October 1930 that the securities issue was settled by the agreement of the vendors of the Queensland to accept Australian gilts as part of the payment package. It was nice that they had more faith in their own government paper than Phoenix did.

But the delay had allowed other doubts to surface. In the purchase price of £1.6 million, some £600,000 was allowed for goodwill, that is, for the *future* profitability of the target company. Sketch explained Queensland averaged about £50,000 per annum in profit, so Phoenix were being asked to pay about twelve year's purchase for the business, 'a very low ratio for transactions of this class'.[113] However, as depression deepened in 1930, some members of the Special Committee, faced with unprecedented contraction in world markets, began to wonder whether future profitability was a concept that would ever apply again. The Special Committee effectively divided between those who realised that the downswing of a bear market was a good time to buy companies and those who feared that there might never be an upswing in which to use them.

The Phoenix directors, the leaders of a major City institution, confronted a substantial international takeover in the midst of a global crisis, and reacted, perhaps not surprisingly, with indecision. The measure of this indecision is revealed by a remarkable set of notes from Sketch, recording 'a full discussion, in the course of which every member expressed his views'; in other words, it is Sketch keeping the score.

The Hon. Edwin Ponsonby thought that £600,000 for goodwill was too large and wondered why Phoenix should pay more than the simple market price. Bristow Bovill distrusted the markets and was against any deal. Deputy Chairman Walters urged a longer view: if Phoenix did not take advantage of this opportunity, the only logical alternative was to get out of Australia; he pressed the 'dire necessity' of going ahead. His running mate, the other deputy chairman, P. J. Pybus agreed. He was

[113] Sketch to Bovill, 27 June 1930.

confident that 'Australia will come back sooner or later and we must take some element of risk'. Sir Thomas Royden agreed that the crucial issue was the £600,000 for goodwill and that it was high; on the other hand, Phoenix would not have got this opportunity had 'everything been right in Australia': and 'insurance has to go on, no matter the state of affairs'. Sir Clarendon Hyde 'had no objection to fishing in troubled waters'; he thought it a good time to buy but the asking price too dear. Henry Bell was troubled about Australia, the state of the world, 'taking property out of the country' and much else; he was against the idea. Col. the Hon. Stuart Pleydell-Bouverie thought that Phoenix should either remain in Australia by increasing the business or get out; if the price was right, the right policy was to buy.

Of the ten members of the Special Committee, the stouter hearts – six of them – were in the majority. And both deputy chairmen were among the stouter. Yet the outcome was that 'the feeling of the Committee was that *no offer be made* for the Australian Company that was under consideration'.[114]

The explanation lies in the opinion of the chairman. Sir Gerald Ryan was old, ill and damaged by the rash speculation that the LGA had been revealed to be. Like many generals and entrepreneurs before and since, he proceeded in 1930 to refight his last battle, but in reverse. However, refighting the last battle always makes the current one the wrong battle. He now believed that 'the position was worse', 'the price was not a good one', the Queensland itself was 'a rash speculation'. Crucially, he argued that insurers 'cannot count on the same prosperity in the future as in the past . . . profits will be less than average'. His initial caution had turned, under the hot blast of 1929–30, into outright opposition. His was a counsel of despair from an authoritative source and it turned the meeting. The baleful reverberations of the LGA affair thus claimed another victim: the 'attractions' of LGA had sucked Phoenix into a bad buy; the effect on corporate memory was to leave the leadership uncertain as to what was a good buy, or whether good buys still existed.

After having been rejected, the Queensland proceeded to prove that it was a good buy and that Ryan had been wrong. Its premium income slipped after the Crash but its profits remained impressive (see Table 10.12).

The average profit for 1929–35 was over £91,000 p.a., easily surpassing Sketch's conservative estimate of about £50,000 p.a. At that rate £600,000 of goodwill would have been extinguished in less than seven years. And throughout this period, the Queensland continued to pay a dividend of 10%.

[114] Special Committee Minutes 21 October 1930 (my emphasis).

Table 10.12. *Queensland Insurance Co.: income and profits, 1929–35*

Year	Net premium	Profit
1929	832,418	102,508
1930	774,560	62,299
1931	516,897	75,467
1932	435,649	89,353
1933	435,679	103,358
1934	453,718	105,067
1935	497,893	102,837

Moreover, Phoenix was in an exceptionally good position to buy it at this time. Sketch knew this in detail. For the prospect of a big outlay led him to compare Phoenix's asset position with that of other offices. Despite the LGA affair, and thanks to his tough bargaining over the NUF sale, he found it very strong. In 1930, Phoenix had very nearly £6 million in available assets, more than any other insurer bar the Commercial Union, which controlled £8.6 million, and, probably, the Royal.[115] Rather surprisingly, also, the Phoenix proportion of total assets tied up in the USA and Canada was lower than that of any other major insurer with the exception of the Alliance and the Commercial Union.[116] In his analysis of February 1929, Sketch calculated that the purchase of the Queensland would affect the Phoenix's total investment portfolio in the following way:

	Before (£m)	After (£m)
UK government securities	5.95	4.97
Colonial government securities	2.81	2.59
Other stock exchange securities	13.87	14.22
Total	22.63	21.78

Even after the purchase, Phoenix would still be in 'a very favourable position among British companies' in regard to free funds.[117] The only possibly unattractive oddity of Phoenix finance revealed by this bout of

[115] In 1932, Phoenix still ranked third in available assets, with the diminished value of £4.8 million, after the Commercial Union with £15 million and the Royal with £11.4 million.

[116] 39.7% for Phoenix against 28.9% for Alliance and 35.7% for Commercial Union. However, this did exclude shares in, or the deposits of, subsidiary companies in USA and Canada.

[117] Chairman's Memorandum, 24 June 1930.

ledger-scouring was the exceptionally large amount of debenture stock carried by the company: the ratio of debenture stock to ordinary paid-up capital for the most heavily debentured companies was 55% for the Royal, 64% for the Commercial Union, 94% for the Northern, but 211% for the Phoenix.[118] Of course, the LGA purchase had added £1 million in debentures to the Phoenix total, almost doubling it. So if this was a weakness in comparison to the financial structure of other insurance companies, it was yet another legacy of the LGA involvement. But this feature did not compromise the margin of *free* assets that Phoenix had at its disposal when shopping for other companies.

Around 1930 Phoenix was well placed to buy companies at a good time: when companies were cheap. In the postwar period, one of the Phoenix's major difficulties was that, by then, its free resources were not sufficient to meet the asking price of the companies that it needed to buy if it were going to remain a top-league player. So why, then, did Phoenix not buy when the buying was easy? There are two answers. Firstly, the shock of the Crash created a shortage of buyers and the conventional response was to join the throng of the non-buyers. Secondly, the Phoenix directors had recently bought a company which soured all appreciations of what they might subsequently buy.

The Queensland affair was a major opportunity which turned into a sensitively timed mistake. The Australian company offered Phoenix one of the broadest avenues for multinational expansion that it had encountered. If Phoenix had been able to retain NUF, it would not have needed the Queensland. But, given that it had to relinquish the NUF, the compensation that it gained consisted of purchasing power. This advantage should have been used. All credit should go to Sketch for seeing this. For a reason not altogether clear, Sketch had shown indecision in Canada, but in Australia, he read the text wholly accurately. He had squeezed the maximum pay-out from the NUF and he tried every tactic to achieve a real dividend on it. Sketch was fighting the current battle of 1930, not the last acquisition battle of 1922. He was defeated by a twentieth-century Phoenix tradition – like many British traditions, one dating from the 1920s – the tradition of the general manager turned chairman. He was defeated by the last battlers. A Phoenix which had managed to keep the NUF would have been a formidable long-term prospect. A Phoenix which had managed to acquire the Queensland would have been a notably stronger venture than the real Phoenix of 1939.

[118] Only four British insurers carried debentures worth over £0.5 million in 1932. These amounts were: Northern £0.84 million; Royal £1.5 million; Phoenix £2.12 million; Commercial Union £2.25 million.

Undoubtedly, there was a failure of nerve in the Phoenix's attempt on the Queensland. It was the nerves that went wrong; there was nothing wrong with the purchasing power or with the target company. However, in 1930 a failure of nerve was intelligible; nerves were failing all over the world. It is the failure to exploit the opportunity *before* 1929 which is the key one. The escape of the Queensland, one of the largest foreign ventures to appear on Phoenix's historical shopping list, was an important defeat. And, not for the first time, it raises the suspicion that Phoenix in 1922, with the LGA purchase became, and remained, something of a specialist in mistiming.

10. AUSTRALIA: SOME PURCHASES ACHIEVED

However, the chairman's loss of heart did not entirely block Sketch's design for Australia. If the Special Committee could not stomach the purchase of a large Australian company, they had not explicitly rejected a smaller one. And Sketch had a smaller one ready: the Southern Union. So, although the Committee had once said that it wanted the larger of the two available Australians, it now had to be brought round to wanting the smaller.

In February 1929, during their first reconnaissance of a purchase, Phoenix had been offered the Southern Union's shares at 5 shillings apiece, making a total cost of £470,000.[119] That had been thought excessive at the time. By the beginning of 1931 the value of the goodwill was down to £95,000 and Phoenix had worked out a way of getting what it wanted for that sum. The Southern Union had 4,360 agencies in Australia which generated some £96,000 of fire and accident net premiums in 1929–30, as against Phoenix's 2,450 Australian agencies, which took £105,000 in net fire and accident premiums over the same period. What Phoenix wanted was to add the one to the other, thus achieving a near doubling of fire and accident net income, and a projected 12% reduction in the expense ratio.[120]

This was to be done by Phoenix forming a wholly-owned Australian company of its own, with the name of Southern Union, which would take over all the business of the original Southern Union. That, in turn, would change its name and retain ownership of its property and investment portfolio. Phoenix would thus get the Australian organisation that it wanted – rather cheaply – without having to take aboard Australian real estate or Australian securities which it did not want. Phoenix itself already

[119] £270,000 for free assets, £200,000 for goodwill.

[120] General Manager's Memorandum on Australia, 2 January 1931.

possessed enough Australian securities to provide adequate reserves for the new company. This ingenious and low-risk alternative smoothed the fears of the Special Committee and it approved the transaction on 7 January 1931.

The new Southern Union was launched in 1931 with a paid-up capital of £62,500 and with Phoenix transferring a matching sum in securities into its name, to act as a general reserve.[121] R. L. Swan was appointed its first general manager and deputy chairman.

The incorporation of the second Southern Union did not conclude Phoenix's corporate designs in Australia. Sketch clearly remembered his original observation that a purchase of this scale would not stop Phoenix from looking for something more. And, in fact, Phoenix kept looking, somewhat longingly, at the Queensland. Well into the mid-1930s Head Office kept a file of press cuttings of its doings and tracked both its performance and its price. In February 1936, Phoenix noted that the shares had recovered to £2 16s and that the total asking price of the company had risen to A$2.3 million. However, Phoenix never got to do more than look and long: the missed chance of 1930 was not recovered.

Yet, in an oblique way, not all of it was missed. Queensland and its subsidiary, Bankers' and Traders', did business in the USA and Canada that was unsatisfactory. In 1928 Queensland kept its US business small in order to control its quality, but paid for the modest volume with an inflated expense ratio.[122] It saw little point in keeping this business going. On the other hand, Phoenix had experienced a premium decline in the USA and Canada, and was looking for more volume. Incorporation of Queensland volume would reduce Phoenix's acquisition cost for US and Canadian business by about 1%. And Phoenix's men in North America had long argued for the use of another Phoenix vehicle to reduce selling problems in the region: Beresford wanted to use the Union Marine for additional fire capacity in the USA, while Paterson had argued for an additional subsidiary in Canada. It was a short step to the realisation that the Australian capacity in North America could be switched into the Phoenix Group to the mutual advantage of both parties.[123]

Although the commercial effect of this was felt in Phoenix's US and Canadian markets, the organisational thrust for the arrangement clearly came from the resolution of the company's Australian plans. It was the scrutiny of the Queensland as a potential Australian asset which had revealed the connection to a North American problem. Most telling is the

[121] This sum in paid-up capital was increased to £125,000 in 1948.
[122] £83,000 in fire premiums, with an expense ratio of 71%; total premium of £175,000.
[123] Special Committee Minutes, 10 December 1930, p. 234.

timing: the Phoenix initiative in respect of the Queensland's North American business was taken on the day after the Special Committee's approval of the Southern Union purchase. So, on 8 January 1931, Phoenix came away with at least a part of the Queensland.

An ironical and somewhat sad endnote to the story of the Great Australian Acquisition comes in the form of Sir Gerald Ryan's last major foreign trip for the Phoenix. Ryan, who was re-elected chairman for the eleventh, and last, time in 1930, and who reached the age of seventy in 1931, wrote to Deputy Chairman Walters in the spring of that year that he was considering resigning the chairmanship of the Phoenix: 'My health needs attention. I am a tired man, and, after a very long term of service, feel that I require complete rest and relaxation.'[124] However, he was planning a trip to South Africa in 1932, and hoped that this could be turned to the company's benefit. The Board's response, presumably on the assumption that a longer sea voyage would have greater convalescent properties, was to invite him 'to extend his journey and proceed to Australia and New Zealand with a view to reporting on the Company's organisation in those countries'. The reason given was that the recent purchase of the Southern Union had involved significant adjustments in Australia, which Ryan might review in the light of his great experience.[125] They then added a grant of 1,000 guineas to make the detour worthwhile. The impression conveyed is that of a generous attempt to give a failing elder statesman a spell in the sun. The irony, of course, is that, had Ryan set somewhat less store by his experience, he would have had a substantially larger Australian organisation to review.

However, even the more restrained acquisition strategy did succeed in tidying up Australia by a significant amount. By 1938 Australian net fire and accident premium for the Phoenix had more than doubled the 1930 figure to £226,000, with a further £26,000 on hand from the marine account. At the same time, there had been a significant reduction in the expense ratio on fire and accident business from nearly 55% in 1929 to just over 48% in 1939. Considering the size of the Australian population, and the effect of the international recession, the wartime Victory Committee considered this outcome 'remarkably good'. More to the point, they found Australasia 'the most satisfactory of all the areas' they had compared, which is not a judgement that could have been sustained in the late 1920s.[126]

[124] In fact Ryan announced his retirement at the AGM of 10 June 1931.
[125] Special Committee Minutes, 27 April 1931, p. 50.
[126] Victory Committee Report, p. 9.

II. THE REST OF PHOENIX'S WORLD MARKET, 1918–40

Outside Europe

The remaining non-European markets which bulked large in the foreign operations of the Group in the interwar years were: South Africa, India, Japan and the Far Eastern Branch at Shanghai. All displayed features which were echoes of problems encountered in the Phoenix's leading markets in North America. South Africa was targeted as one of the regions in which Phoenix had under-performed in the period from the mid 1900s to the early 1920s. More exactly, it was threatening to become another of those markets in which Phoenix fell behind as a traditional primary producing economy underwent rapid urbanisation. India, Japan and the Far Eastern Branch all showed increased levels of competition and dwindling levels of premium from about 1930 – significantly earlier in the case of India – and these were features which had caused difficulties in some of the richest markets over the depression years.

The Asian markets, although potentially vast, contained political currents which added special stresses to the economic forces already affecting the Phoenix. In India, an increasing slant towards economic and political autonomy was already influencing insurance markets by the 1920s. And, in particular, Japanese expansionism during the 1930s produced distortions in many Asian economies.

Analysis of some of these problems is aided by the reports of the Phoenix Victory Committee. Established in 1941, this body provided an extensive investigation of markets denied or damaged by enemy action and prepared a reconstruction plan for Phoenix in these areas after the war. The 'committee area' covered only those markets directly affected by Axis operations; so it omitted the USA, Canada, Australasia and South Africa (that is, the largest Phoenix income sources). But it did include within its span of fifty-eight separate territories India, Japan and the Far East. Its value lies in the fact that much of its investigation was retrospective from 1941. Indeed, that is probably its primary value since the active stance that it recommended for postwar policy proved in the event not to fit the style of the Phoenix leadership of the later 1940s.[127]

However, Phoenix's fourth-ranking foreign market is covered by few sources for the interwar years: South Africa remains something of a blank. As in many countries, the brief fusion with NUF did produce an impact

[127] Amidst a membership of eight, its leading protagonists were: L. Weightman, now foreign accident manager; T. H. Hodgson, fire superintendant; and G. H. Hurren of the foreign fire staff. Only Hodgson would become a member of the true inner circle of the postwar Ferguson management, and even then reservations would be in order.

Table 10.13. *Selected Fire Markets: Phoenix aggregate premium income and aggregate trading surplus, 1920–9*

	Aggregate premium	Aggregate surplus	Surplus %
Canada	3,741,768	65,168	1.7
Australia	1,113,840	−37,104	−3.3
India	748,161	159,293	21.3
Far East (all)	2,044,024	402,056	19.7
Far Eastern Branch	1,256,065	135,887	10.8
Japan	664,053	78,841	11.9
Latin America (all)	1,344,078	169,003	12.6
South Africa	431,846	52,471	12.2

Source: Calculated from Phoenix Review of Foreign Agencies, Book 5.

but here it was scarcely explosive; Williamson, the manager of NUF, visiting South Africa for his own office in 1923, undertook to cast a critical eye over the Phoenix organisation as well, but little came of this.[128] Between 1920 and 1929, the Dominion did very moderately in premium income and tolerably in profitability, certainly better in that respect than the expense-ridden operations in Canada and Australia (see Table 10.13).

Canada and Australia barely scraped, or failed to scrape, a profit over this ten-year period, while South Africa flew the flag for the white Dominions. But it was easily outpaced by the Indian and Far Eastern operations in profit rate as well as volume.

The first inkling that all was less than perfect at the Cape came when a more determined inspection of Phoenix's dispositions there was carried out in 1927 by W. H. Crombie, the Phoenix China hand who since 1906 had turned Shanghai into a powerhouse and who retired from the Far East in 1926. Reluctant to let him go, Phoenix employed him as a roving foreign inspector for a brief while, and rather deliberately unleashed him on South Africa. Anticipating the more advanced variety of thinking about the American and Canadian problems in the 1930s, Crombie recommended that there should be a centralised Phoenix branch at Cape Town under a single manager for all Group business in South Africa. He judged that there would be 'a steady development of trade' in South and South-West Africa which would more than justify a modernisation of the administrative structure.[129] The new system would supersede the existing

[128] Phoenix Fire Committee Minutes, 3 January 1923, Book 3, p. 77.

[129] *Ibid.*, 21 September and 12 October 1927, Book 3, pp. 242, 246.

long-standing division of influence between the branches at the Cape and Johannesburg.

A number of significant changes, including a spate of retirements, followed quite fast. Alfred George Twentyman Jones, manager at Cape Town since 1906, went at the end of 1927, and Percy Heath, manager at Johannesburg since 1905, went in March 1928; these were close contemporaries of Crombie's, of course. They were replaced by E. B. Ferguson, who was moved from his post as Head Office foreign fire superintendent to his first and only overseas command as the new manager for South Africa in November 1927.[130] Accident business, which had not been attempted under the old regime, was launched from March 1928.[131] And in mid-1932 Phoenix took over, by agreement, the management of the South African business of the Century Insurance Company.[132] By that time Ferguson had been recalled to London to become City manager; he was replaced by B. C. Handley, previously the manager for New South Wales.[133] Although he was in South Africa for only four years, Ferguson seems to have set a process in motion.

Clearly, something needed to move. What had been immobile was displayed in a report on South African business by Sketch in February 1929; this account of a general manager's tour is the most revealing document on South Africa in the interwar period. He found the business down to 1927 'small but profitable' yet 'the office management, and the rate of progress left much to be desired'. In particular, the division between Cape Town and Johannesburg did not work. Sketch found that, in recent years, Twentyman Jones had lived up to about one-fortieth of his name. Moreover, his chief clerk, who had studied to succeed him for twenty-three years, and above whom 'it would be quite impossible to put anyone' was 'finding some difficulty in working to the standards set by Mr Ferguson'. So he was retired too. Sketch carried through a second wave of retirements, and, in Cape Town, where Phoenix had 'the worst offices of any leading company', bought new ones.[134] He seems to have enjoyed his stay.

He noted the expansion of South African trade that Crombie had observed, especially in Durban, but complained that Phoenix had not shared in the expansion: 'our business has hardly moved'. Part of the problem, Sketch divined, was that Phoenix was still using representation

[130] Phoenix Directors' Minutes, 21 September 1927, 35, p. 268.
[131] *Ibid.*, 28 March 1928, 35, p. 363. [132] *Ibid.*, 29 June 1932, 37, p. 92.
[133] *Ibid.*, 21 October 1931, 36, p. 436.
[134] General Manager's Review of South African Business, Special Committee Minutes, 14 February 1929, pp. 174ff.

by general agents in Durban, a system that in many parts of the world was increasingly proving unequal to the ever-advancing complexity and professionalism of insurance markets. It was not necessarily in the interests of general agents, representing several insurance companies, and also other different types of enterprise, to become too deeply embroiled in the regulatory or tariff difficulties of any particular office. Sketch's solution in this case was to introduce branch management to Durban, with trained insurance officials, but also to retain the involvement of the general and shipping agents who had served Phoenix for many years.[135] This produced improvement, but such change was needed in many places besides Durban. Sketch was clear that the South African market had altered substantially over the last two decades and that Phoenix had not.

> It is nearly twenty years since I was last in South Africa and the great growth of the cities and the progress of the whole place impressed me deeply. It is depressing to find how little we have participated in this development, our position having remained almost stationary . . . Our competitors, many of whom were behind us then, have gone ahead and made profits all the time.[136]

Once again, it seems that Phoenix had difficulty in adjusting to the implications of modernisation in a long-familiar society.

However, Sketch believed that Ferguson had made a difference, had 'handled a difficult situation with tact', with the result that, 'under our present management, there is no reason why we should not take our proper place in this country'.[137] Generally, this seems to have been correct: Phoenix's combined income from fire, accident and marine had risen by nearly 45%, from £78,106 to £113,000, between 1927 and 1938. Such figures were certainly no longer 'almost stationary'.[138] As in Australia, Sketch's management seems to have produced a significant awakening within local networks that had dozed contentedly for too long, although in South Africa, the uplifting interruption was not delivered by corporate acquisition. Phoenix had been looking for a possible South African subsidiary in the late 1920s, but found nothing suitable. So the improvement that was achieved came largely through a more sensible design for the system of management and representation.

Sadly, the out-turn in the vast Asian bailiwick was less fortunate. The Far Eastern Branch at Shanghai controlled the whole of China, the Japanese Empire, the Philippines, French Indo-China, the Dutch East Indies, Siam, Malaya and Borneo. The physical size of the territory and

[135] The firm was that of Clark and Thiselton.
[136] General Manager's Review of South African Business. [137] *Ibid.*
[138] Phoenix Review of Foreign Agencies Book 5; Victory Committee, p. 9.

the many jurisdictions within it multiplied the prospects of trouble. When Crombie retired, the Fire Committee of the Board thanked him for twenty-one years' exemplary service, but gave due note to 'the difficult and trying circumstances in which he was more than once placed owing to political and other disturbances'.[139]

These disturbances, stretching from the Russo-Japanese War of 1904–5 through minor civil wars in China between 1911 and 1917 to the persistent internal strife of the 1920s, were bad enough before Crombie retired. Thus in 1924 – when Crombie's health broke down and he was shipped back to Britain at Phoenix's expense for treatment – the Far Eastern manager had to ask Phoenix to grant insurance against war risks in order to preserve valuable existing connections in China.[140] Crombie's successor, Harry Muncaster Hind was also a seasoned China hand – he had been assistant manager at Shanghai before being given the India Branch, and then being moved back east. Phoenix management had showed its sense of priorities, and revealed the pecking order between branches, when it posted Hind from command of the full Indian Branch to act once more as Crombie's assistant in 1925, before promoting him to the Far Eastern managership at the end of 1926. But Hind came back to China when empires were crumbling or exploding around him and could do little against such forces.

The Chinese drama awaiting Hind was even more sobering than the one which occupied Crombie's last years in office. Chiang Kai-shek, generalissimo of the Kuomintang from 1925, occupied Peking in 1928 and unleashed all-out civil war against the Chinese communists between 1927 and 1936. It was this campaign which forced Mao Tse-tung into the legendary 'Long March' of October 1934 to November 1935. On top of all this, the Japanese invaded China on 7 July 1937 and helped convert civil war into full-scale international hostilities. This was not the best context in which to trade in fire, accident and marine insurance.

In fact, Chinese business was largely fire business. The Shanghai Branch had been allowed to write accident business very early from 1909 – much earlier than India or South Africa – but there was not much to write. It was confined to motor and personal accident business and wholly to the foreign settlements; outside these there were no roads and without roads, there could be no accident business. Marine business was also slight. But the fire business had been massive.

Many insurance markets experienced a pronounced upswing in fire premiums around the end of the First World War, but this effect was

[139] Phoenix Fire Committee Minutes, 4 April 1928, Book 3, p. 263.

[140] *Ibid.*, 10 September 1924, Book 3, p. 131.

Table 10.14. *Far Eastern premiums: aggregate of all Phoenix agencies, 1916–38*

1916	107,188
1920	396,376
1924	217,343
1931	110,492
1938	44,649

exceptionally marked in Asian markets. Between 1916 and 1920 their takings almost quadrupled, with the Shanghai Branch alone accounting for about half of the total (see Table 10.14). However, 1920 was to be the interwar peak. By 1924, the regional aggregate had slumped and by 1931 it was hardly above its 1916 figure; by 1938 it had halved again. The Shanghai Branch share of these descending totals was 47% in 1924, but only 19% by 1938.[141]

As Table 10.2 (p. 722) also reveals, the most severe deterioration was at the heart: most of the Asian outposts kept up reasonably well between 1921–30 and 1929–38, even important ones like the Philippines, while Hong Kong and the Dutch East Indies managed increases. The fatal blows fell upon Shanghai and its tributary Chinese agencies; and to a lesser extent upon earnings from Japan.

The onslaught consisted of four separate attacks: civil war in China, the rise of native competition, currency depreciation and Japanese imperialism. During the 1920s the local Chinese insurance companies were still in their infancy, currency problems were in the preparation stage and Japan was enjoying the phase of stability and constitutional rule known as the period of cabinet government. So it was largely conflict within China that brought Shanghai Branch earnings tumbling from nearly £200,000 in 1920 to around £85,000 in 1925 – the year after Crombie had asked Phoenix to cover war risks – but expansion in the insurance markets of Shanghai, Nanking, Tsingtao and the upriver Yangtze ports brought recovery to over £125,000 by 1929. However, after 1931 all four adverse influences conjoined to devastating effect.

Until 1900 the main Chinese insurance markets had been virtually a British monopoly. Until 1930, they remained largely in foreign hands: the Americans entered after 1918 but the British retained superiority. Local competition arrived only in the early 1930s, but when it came it was

141 Calculated from Phoenix Review of Foreign Agencies, Book 5, and Victory Committee.

powerful: Shanghai-based, promoted by influential Chinese banks, including the Bank of China, and fully capable of diverting much fire business, especially warehouse business, from the foreign offices. By 1938 the international insurance community in Shanghai divided into seventy-five British offices, twenty-two American, seven German, seven Japanese, five Swiss, four Dutch, two Italian and two French; but, alongside these, there were twenty Chinese insurance ventures. Local expertise and a shared commercial culture gave the Chinese companies a sharp competitive edge. But nevertheless, the locals needed reinsurance facilities, and the British, who retained excellent contacts with Chinese businessmen, clawed in the lion's share of this business.

Phoenix, along with other foreign insurers, tried one other adjustment in selling. As in India, the company had been represented in China by 'the smaller type of British merchant firm' and their influence had begun to wane even before 1930.[142] The logical course, therefore, was to replace British agency firms by Chinese ones. Such devices limited the impact of Chinese competition but did not succeed in maintaining the level of Chinese business.

That was damaged mainly by developments in currency and conflict. Continued and heavy depreciation of the Chinese currency badly affected Chinese premiums expressed in sterling.[143] This pressure on Far Eastern Branch earnings was particularly acute in 1935 and 1937. But after the Marco Polo Bridge incident and the outbreak of war with Japan on 7 July 1937, the course of conflict within China took a decisive turn for the worse, and all other influences upon business became secondary. In Foochow, the Victory Committee reported that 'the Japanese have been in and out of the area on frequent occasions' with disastrous effects on markets; Tsientsin had been effectively shut off by Japanese blockade; and the closure of the Yangtze to foreign shipping had wiped out business from the Hankow and Nanking agencies.[144] Deteriorating international relations probably had a more damaging effect on the Far Eastern Branch than upon any other sector of Phoenix's overseas operations in the interwar period.

Unfortunately, too, the obverse of contraction in China was more contraction in Japan. For, as the Japanese military machine rolled across the terrain of China, so it rolled across the face of the home economy, imposing a policy of economic nationalism and a closed door against all kinds of Western capitalist influence. Phoenix had been in Japan since the 1860s and the country's considerable economic development between

[142] Victory Committee Report, p. 366. [143] *Ibid.*, p. 361. [144] *Ibid.*, p. 364.

Table 10.15. *Phoenix Japanese business, 1917–38: direct premiums and reinsurance premiums*

	Aggregate premiums	Reinsurances
1917	16,497	20,131
1920	40,159	70,330
1930	18,842	34,618
1938	12,200	30,000

1885 and 1920 had brought the office a notable expansion of business. By the latter date, and until 1941, Phoenix's representation in Japan was under the local control of the chief agents, W. M. Strachan & Co., who were first appointed at Kobe in 1910 and at Yokohama in 1911 (before being displaced by the earthquake and tidal wave of 1923 to Tokyo). As in China, there was a very rapid increase in (mostly fire) business between 1917 and 1920, with both directly written premiums and reinsurance earnings approximately tripling (see Table 10.15). Once again, however, 1920 proved the peak of interwar performance for this market: directly written and reinsurance receipts slid continuously down to 1938. The direct account was profitable, yielding nearly 12% for 1920–9 and still 10% on the much-reduced volumes of the 1930s. The important reinsurance trade gave good results during the 1920s,[145] but fell off after 1932 with reasonable volumes nevertheless producing a loss by 1934–7.[146]

The reason for this sorry wasting away of a most promising market was almost solely the behaviour of government. It was true that there were powerful insurance ventures of Japanese origin well before 1914 – Tokyo Marine being the doyen – but they were of international inclination and prepared to deal with their western counterparts. If Japanese economic advance had produced a lot of local insurers by the 1930s – some fifty-two companies – it had also produced a lot of business to insure, and reinsure. The Victory Committee found that, by the late 1930s, over 90% of Japanese income came from facultative reinsurances for Japanese offices, but also that these were less open to state interference and still amounted to tidy sums.[147]

Problems with the government had begun early. Even before the First World War, foreign insurers had needed a licence to operate in Japan. Phoenix had applied for one to write accident business in 1910, but the

[145] A surplus of 15% 1924–6 and 23% 1927–31.
[146] Victory Committee, pp. 345–6.
[147] *Ibid.*

bureaucracy had adopted delaying tactics, and it was never granted. The position in the fire trade was protected by Phoenix's very early entry to the market in the 1860s; but the rebuff from the accident sector was a straw in the wind. By the 1930s, and the coming of a much harsher regime, the air was thick and the all-important licences 'almost impossible to obtain'.[148] Nationalistic governments wished to remove foreign influence from sensitive parts of the economy – in motor cars, electrical engineering and armaments, where overseas interests had been highly active, the official view was that the necessary lessons had been learned and that the 'temporary guests' were no longer needed or welcome[149] – and insurance and financial services clearly fell into this category.

Phoenix recorded that the major influence on its Japanese trade in this period was 'the declared policy of the Japanese government of freezing out foreign interests'.[150] Just before Pearl Harbour the regime extended the freeze into reinsurance by the creation of the Toa state-sponsored reinsurance facility. Phoenix experienced difficulty in maintaining its presence in many markets between the wars, but in Japan the door was slammed upon it. Both in the formerly great profit-centre of Shanghai and in the potentially rich new industrial market of Japan, the effects of Japanese imperialism imposed a high price upon the Phoenix.

The other main profit centre for the company in Asia was, of course, India with its associated markets of Burma and Ceylon. In due time, Japanese expansionism affected most of these as well. But that was only after 1941 and these markets registered substantial ill-effects well before this date. Some of these, particularly in India, resembled the problems which had followed from increasing economic independence in other Asian markets. And it is significant that the markets in which Phoenix did best – Burma and Ceylon – diverged least from the traditional pre-1914 pattern.

Like so many markets, the Indian region experienced a major surge around the end of the First World War before falling back sharply in the 1920s and 1930s. Fire premium income from the Indian agencies, together with those at Colombo and Rangoon, more than doubled between 1916 and 1920. The income curve stayed high for longer than in the Far Eastern region, largely because of the formation of an Indian Branch in

148 *Ibid.*, p. 343.

149 See C. Trebilcock, 'British Multinationals in Japan, 1900–41: Vickers, Armstrongs, Nobels and the Defence Sector', in T. Yuzawa & M. Udagawa (eds.), *Foreign Business in Japan Before World War II; Proceedings of the 16th Fuji International Conference on Business History* (Tokyo, 1990), pp. 87–117; and also the other contributions to this conference volume.

150 Victory Committee Report, p. 344.

Table 10.16. *Total Phoenix fire premiums: India, Burma, Ceylon, 1916–30*

1916	1920	1925	1930
44,026	92,671	127,770	92,044

1922, and peaked in 1925, with the new branch providing more than half the regional total. But by 1930 there had been a decline of nearly 28% (see Table 10.16)

The agency share of total fire earnings for the region then proceeded to collapse from £48,529 in 1930 to £18,994 in 1938. The same pattern also repeated in total agency premiums (fire, accident, marine) which fell from £61,243 in 1930 to £30,778 in 1938.[151]

The heart of the problem was India and the heart of the Indian problem was the income taken through the agency system. Here Phoenix clearly lagged behind other UK companies. The biggest UK operators within the Raj in the interwar period were the Commercial Union, the Royal, the REA, the Atlas and the London & Lancashire. The market leader, the Commercial Union, had taken £171,600 in total fire, accident and marine premiums in 1929 and suffered a relatively modest reduction to £163,725 by 1938, while, in second place, the REA had experienced a similar income pattern with a slide from £115,575 to £97,200.[152] Why did the Phoenix experience feature so much smaller numbers and so much bigger reductions?

Phoenix had considered forming an Indian Branch after management visits to the country in 1906 and 1914, and, on the eve of war, the company was discussing a possible joint branch with the Scottish Union; but neither issued in action. In 1922, the NUF fusion brought a ready-made Indian Branch into the Phoenix organisation, and even after Phoenix and NUF parted company again in 1925, Phoenix could scarcely make do with less. The branch structure created under NUF auspices at Calcutta in 1922, with India, Ceylon and Burma as its territory, was to remain the Phoenix's flagship for the subcontinent.[153] Here again, the fact of acquisition changed the form of overseas operation.

[151] *Ibid.*, Statements of Results, 20–2. [152] *Ibid.*, p. 292.

[153] Chairman's Committee Minutes, 26 April, 30 August 1922; Finance Committee Book 7, pp. 331, 406. The Calcutta Branch was commissioned on 1 October 1922. Hind was succeeded by J. W. Webber as manager for India and Ceylon in October 1925. Webber also had been chief assistant at Shanghai.

However, the organisational change did not secure any long-run answer to the problem of business acquisition. By 1941 the Victory Committee found the experience of the Indian Branch 'most disappointing' and its senior officials well past their prime. Accident business, which had been launched in India only in July 1921,[154] had failed to make an impact and the branch had never really functioned as a genuinely integrated outpost of a composite insurer.[155] Even in the fire market, the branch, by the 1930s, was writing almost no direct business and was making its living by reinsurance acceptances from other UK companies. Fire and accident income from Burma and Ceylon was more valuable than the entire Indian trade by the late 1930s. 'The Group position in so large a market as India', judged the Victory Committee, 'is most unsatisfactory . . . For a direct-writing Company with a Branch organisation to derive the bulk of the Fire Business by reinsurance is indefensible.'[156] Only in marine had Phoenix made any useful showing. Otherwise, there was a great need to convert 'our present languishing existence into one of virility and progress'.[157]

Part of Phoenix's problem was clearly the rise of highly competitive native companies, great in number, high in national esteem and sharp in practice, or, as the Victory Committee demurely put it, 'not guided by the standards which have characterised British insurance'.[158] Be that as it may, they were very effective. In the fire trade, the ground lost by the UK groups as a whole in the Crash period 1929–33 was never regained; and the reason was that it was taken by the Indian companies (see Table 10.17).

In the much smaller accident market, a similar pattern is evident. The UK groups suffered a lesser fall in income but a larger fall in market share from 71.1% to 54.6%. Again the Indian offices almost doubled their income and greatly increased their market share from 23.1% to 37.5%. In each case the UK groups began with around two-thirds of the Indian market and ended with around one-half, while the Indian groups began with a fraction and ended with around one-third. By 1938 the Indian offices were the second largest presence in the Indian market, outnumbering other empire insurers or the European offices: there were sixty-two UK insurers, twenty-eight Indian, eighteen 'other empire', eleven European, nine American and six Japanese.[159] The main influences upon the disproportionate losses in UK market share were probably the propensity of UK insurers to stick to the tariff when others did not and a good

[154] Phoenix Directors' Minutes, 33, p. 278, 13 July 1921.
[155] Of course, it was not alone in this. See pp. 729ff above and pp. 809–13 below.
[156] Victory Committee Report, p. 301. The Indian market was worth about £2.2 million for fire, accident and marine in 1938.
[157] *Ibid.*, p. 100. [158] *Ibid.* [159] *Ibid.*, p. 293.

Table 10.17. *Total Indian (including Burmese) net fire premiums taken by national groups of companies, 1929–38*

	1929		1933		1938	
	(£)	(%)	(£)	(%)	(£)	(%)
UK	728,925	62.9	497,250	51.7	507,900	49.1
Australasia	78,600	6.8	56,250	5.8	46,575	4.5
Hong Kong	40,275	3.5	44,550	4.6	43,200	4.2
USA	65,625	5.7	66,600	6.9	55,800	5.4
India	171,600	14.8	229,500	23.9	323,325	31.3
Other	72,825	6.3	67,425	7.1	57,600	5.5
Total	1,157,850		961,575		1,034,400	

Source: Victory Committee Report, pp. 294–5.

measure of anti-British sentiment.[160] Local competition in India had far more teeth than local competition in China.

But the effects of them, of course, were felt by all British insurers in India; Phoenix was not singled out for a savaging. So why was its market position in 1938 so much weaker than that of the other big UK companies? The answer lies primarily in the nature of the Phoenix agency system in India and in its inability to withstand the conditions of the 1920s. Down to 1914 Phoenix had depended on the merchant houses which dominated Indian trade: concerns like Graham & Co. of Bombay or Finlay & Co. of Calcutta could then still provide a representation which even the stern judges of the Victory Committee found 'moderately effective'.[161] But in the 1920s the old houses came under pressure from new directions. Indian merchants and industrialists became increasingly influential in the direction of commerce. The offering of rebates, especially by Indian offices and especially in Bombay, became rife and the whole tariff structure was placed under great strain. In Bombay, Phoenix 'did not keep pace with the market' and in the late 1920s the long-running Graham agency had to be cancelled, while Finlay & Co. 'also lost their grip on the agency business' and the account dwindled.[162]

Not one of the firms representing Phoenix in India maintained a full insurance department by the late 1930s. The only British houses which proved able to resist the pressures of an economy increasingly being claimed by its own nationals were the large ones, which responded

[160] *Ibid.*, p. 300. [161] *Ibid.* [162] *Ibid.*, p. 297.

flexibly, and with 'a measure of Indianisation'. But Phoenix was not linked to these; rather, it was

> identified with British merchant firms which were not of the first rank and which have not been able to adjust themselves to changing conditions . . . we have only a negligible participation in the tied business of those East Indian merchants which still have important connections in the country.[163]

The prime reason, therefore, for both declining agency premiums and a branch reduced to reinsurance scrapings was that, in a progressively Indianising economy, Phoenix lacked representation at the appropriate levels. The company's business-gathering system sank with the small merchant ship.

The Victory Committee had three lines of thought on this problem: that Phoenix should acquire connections at the right level; that the formation of a local subsidiary company might be particularly suitable in such conditions; and that in other nearby markets such as Burma and Ceylon, Phoenix was not perhaps as badly placed as it was in India itself.

Taking these in the order of least irritation, we might look first at Burma and Ceylon. In these locations, the need for a new strategy was in exact proportion to the degree that market conditions differed from those in India proper. The difference was considerable: in Burma and Ceylon, the movement towards economic autonomy was still relatively suppressed; British merchant houses were still in the ascendant; and Phoenix was connected to powerful enterprises among the merchant houses.

Of course, there were differences between the two. In Ceylon, by far the major export was tea, and, predictably, British interests continued to predominate where a vital national interest was at stake. There were no local insurance companies – in Burma, there were one or two – and little sign as yet of any inclination towards economic independence; the market remained under British domination in insurance matters and many others. Phoenix's long-serving representatives were Carson & Co., who, very suitably, were managing agents for tea and rubber plantations, as well as general merchants, and, unlike many of Phoenix's connections in India, still 'in the first rank commercially'.[164] True, in the difficult years 1929–32, collapsing tea prices produced a succession of tea-factory fires and a disastrous loss ratio. But generally, the Ceylonese market was notably well behaved, with a well-conducted Local Agents' Association and a firm tariff, which, outside the bazaars, was relatively immune to the Asian affliction of rebating on rates.[165]

The Burmese economy specialised in rice and oil. Phoenix took 20% of

[163] *Ibid.*, pp. 100 (ii), 300. [164] *Ibid.*, pp. 312–13. [165] *Ibid.*, pp. 310–12.

Burma oil cover by reinsurance from the Royal on the London market; so there was little problem in that department. Again the political aspirations of the Burmese were not as advanced as those of the Indians, and British insurers continued to have a free run of the market. Phoenix's representatives, Finlay Fleming, were, like Carsons, reassuringly large-scale players. But the Burmese market, almost as much as the Indian, was rife with rebating, especially on the central rice plantation insurances. Even Finlay Fleming found it impossible to hold their former business in the face of heavy illicit rebating and, soon after the death of a legendary native canvasser named Barucha, had to be allowed special rates in 1937 in order to protect their position.[166] Nevertheless, the Victory Committee concluded even in 1941, that, as distinct from its Indian experience, 'in Burma and, particularly in Ceylon, the Group is associated with important firms whose usefulness is not exhausted'.[167] Yet even under these relatively auspicious conditions, Phoenix total gross premium income from Burma (fire, accident marine – but, in effect, very largely fire) and Ceylon (where fire accounted for about half the total) contracted sharply in the 1930s.[168]

In India, the Victory Committee realised that Phoenix should have been thinking a lot harder even in the 1930s. Connections at the right levels, they considered, should have been sought at that time and were to be found in two directions: links with the kind of British house the usefulness of which was not exhausted and more extensive associations with native canvassers and Indians of influence. By the early 1940s they were advocating an agency connection with Bird & Co. and Sir Edward Benthall and recommending a more extensive reliance on native insurance talent.

This applied not only to canvassers. If the branch system was to be built up, they suggested the possibility of appointing 'an influential Indian to a position of responsibility in the management . . . and concerned chiefly with the production of business'.[169] But the Committee acknowledged that by the late 1930s, the supply of first-rate merchant houses was distinctly short and that branch organisations, which, for the then foreseeable future, would need to carry a proportion of European salaries and lifestyles, were distinctly expensive.[170] It was for these reasons that the Victory Committee concentrated on its middle thought: the Indian subsidiary. Under local conditions, this solution had a particular appeal: it would evade the problem of national sentiment, it could mobilise Indian

[166] *Ibid.*, pp. 305–7. [167] *Ibid.*, p. 100 (ii).
[168] By 65% in Burma and 33% in Ceylon, 1929–38.
[169] Victory Committee, p. 100 (iv). [170] *Ibid.*, p. 100 (iii).

influence through directors, shareholders and officials, and, not least, could adapt without strain to local methods of business gathering. Carefully, if shrewdly, the Committee recommended to the Board that such a subsidiary would require 'a widely representative Board of Directors, with possibly outside shareholders and perhaps Indian management (with a Phoenix official in the background)'. Such a venture 'operating on progressive lines might involve . . . a different standard of requirements from those to which the Phoenix might feel bound'.[171]

This was a most perceptive analysis of what the Phoenix most needed to trade effectively in the Indian market of the 1930s. If this was a market that had been closing less violently than the Chinese or the Japanese, it was one that had been closing nevertheless. And the appetite for independence in economic affairs was a feature, to one degree or another, of all three of these important economies.

12. INSIDE EUROPE

The resurgence of the home continent in Phoenix's affairs during the 1930s was something of a mixed blessing. Partly, of course, it took up more room because large profit centres like the Indian and Chinese operations had surrendered room. But also there were major advances in premium income from such important European insurance markets as France, Germany and Denmark. Partly, this upswing followed from economic recovery in these economies after 1932, but, of course, this recovery was a moveable feast, much more marked in some places, such as Hitler's Germany, than in others, such as Blum's France. So the Phoenix upswing in Europe is probably traced more accurately to an almost coincidental interaction of personal, international and corporate factors. But not everything was coincidental: the Victory Committee remarked even in 1942 that Phoenix had retained its reputation as an expert on European affairs and judged it deserved: 'Our knowledge certainly seems to have been more complete and up-to-date than that of most offices.'[172] Nevertheless, the blessing remained mixed because the places in which the recovery occurred were precisely the places most affected by Nazi aggression in 1939–40.

In France a set of personal factors were clearly important. Phoenix had possessed important reinsurance arrangements with Assurances Générales since the 1850s. Between 1901 and 1905 it took average annual fire premiums of £24,127 from its 'France, Old Treaty', though this

[171] *Ibid.*, p. 100 (v). [172] Victory Committee Report, p. 80.

expired soon afterwards; between 1906 and 1910, it took an average annual fire income of nearly £15,000 from replacement treaties struck during the 1900s, though these shrivelled up during the First World War. A much larger money-spinner entered in 1912 with the resumption of Phoenix direct operations in France: in February the Fire Committee decided to run off the treaties and adopt the more active line.[173]

Activity came in the very particular form of Henri, Comte de Leseleuc, appointed branch manager for France in 1912.[174] The de Leseleuc connection took fire premium earnings for Phoenix from £21,950 in 1915 to £50,763 in 1920, suffered a fall in the difficult 1920s to £22,302 in 1925 and reinvigorated them to £34,391 by 1930.[175] By the early 1930s, Henri de Leseleuc was general manager of the *Indépendence* office, representative for a rich selection of other insurers, among whom Atlas was the leader, and controller of the largest fire portfolio of any group interest in France. Nevertheless, for reasons which are not clear, but which may be inferred, Phoenix abandoned the branch system for France in 1924 and allowed the de Leseleuc connection to revert to a general agency, where matters remained until the post-1945 era.[176]

The income increases generated by de Leseleuc in the 1930s were spectacular. Fire premiums for all France nearly doubled to £109,913 between 1929 and 1934, before sliding away again to just £38,858 in 1938. In Alsace, where Henri Winzer had taken over the agency in 1920, his main office in the great industrial city of Mulhouse controlled eight general agencies and 180 sub-agencies for Phoenix and, by the 1930s, had given the English company second place in this heartland of French manufacturing, behind only the big local insurer, Rhin et Moselle. Marine business slid throughout the 1930s but still left France as the Phoenix Group's third most important foreign market after the USA and Canada. Accident business in France was almost all motor business and here the expert agency of the Carpot brothers generated an impressively steady and substantial income of around £50,000 per year throughout the period 1929–38. All this made France an apparently lively market in a generally dull decade.

[173] Fire Committee Minutes, Book 2, p. 1, 14 February 1912.

[174] However, Phoenix had been deriving a substantial fire income from Alsace-Lorraine since 1881, when it inherited the agency from Assurances Générales. Permission for the French company to trade in the province was withdrawn by the German administration which governed it, 1871–1918.

[175] Total French fire earnings for 1920, 1925 and 1930, including for the Alsace-Lorraine income sources, repatriated to French sovereignty in 1918, were £78,030, £38,982 and £52,983 respectively.

[176] *Le Phoenix Groupe en France, 1786–1959*. Company publication, April 1959.

The main influence behind the income surge was the formation by de Leseleuc in 1930 of a fire pool covering industrial and commercial business in Paris and the major cities and involving all the companies represented by him. This device produced immediate large gains in premium for the Phoenix, and, of course, even larger gains for the Atlas which had the lead in the pool. But matters were not as well as the premium flow made them look. Phoenix's general review of foreign strategy in 1927 had targeted France, alongside Australia and South Africa, as markets in need of treatment. As in other places, thinking inclined away from agencies and towards subsidiary companies. One possibility was quickly identified, a company founded in 1875, earning £133,000 per annum in premiums and priced at £220,000; this was the Métropole.[177] Phoenix chased it seriously, but did not catch it.

The Atlas also showed some wariness of the de Leseleuc connection, most clearly in 1934 by appointing its own English inspector to see that the agent abided by the French tariffs. The total French insurance market was worth about £35 million in the late 1930s and there were sixty-two French companies competing fiercely for it. French non-tariff operators and intervention by Lloyds had produced a chaotic market with severe rate-cutting and a low level of tariff discipline. Under these conditions, de Leseleuc's general pool was no guarantee of adequate returns. De Leseleuc preferred to rely on industrial and warehouse risks provided by brokers; he was a metropolitan operator par excellence and had little interest in developing non-broker business. So Phoenix ended the inter-war period in France as it had begun it, lacking an effective presence in the French provinces, outside Alsace. With the exception of that industrial region, Phoenix's operation was less French than Parisian.

Moreover, despite the very large sums passing through his account, de Leseleuc provided for Phoenix a profit of only 1% over the period 1929–38. Phoenix found this approach less than discriminating.[178] Nor was this all that was wrong in France. The Winzer agency in Alsace, three-quarters of whose business was industrial, had a hard time in the 1930s, with heavy losses in the period 1931–5 and a declining premium trend. Even the highly proficient Carpot agency managed to produce only a 2% profit on its impressive premium flow from 1929 to 1938. And the divergent specialisms of the de Leseleucs and the Carpots ensured that in France, too, fire and accident insurance were not integrated under the same management within this period; indeed this was not achieved until 1954.

177 Special Committee Minutes, pp. 138–43, 26 May 1927.
178 Victory Committee Report, pp. 123–4.

So France in the 1930s delivered a classic warning: beware the illusion of (relatively) large numbers. After the experience of the hyper-inflation of 1923, most observers of the German economy would have found such a warning unnecessary. And Phoenix was sufficiently prudent to re-enter Germany only in 1924, when the reconstruction and recovery phase of the Weimar Republic had begun. Between 1918 and 1924, of course, Germany had experienced military catastrophe, a socialist revolution that was really an enormous food riot, the unwanted birth of an overly representative republic and the fastest price rise in modern history. The French economy, its devastated industrial zones attracting at this time unprecedented attention from the Third Republic, a regime previously inept in manufacturing policy, was a haven of peace and tranquillity by comparison.

For the Phoenix, returning to Germany was no simple business. The company waited until the worst was over but still found the going difficult. During the First World War its considerable German account had been transferred by the Reich government to a small Hamburg office, the Hanseatische, which was then subsequently absorbed by the Nord Deutsche. Once hostilities were over, the thoughts of Phoenix management turned, naturally enough, towards compensation. Their first reaction was to sue both the Hanseatische and the German government before the Mixed Arbitral Tribunal. However, they were advised that their claim was fragile and the prospects of a satisfactory payment remote. Then, in 1921, the Nord Deutsche offered as an alternative the cession to Phoenix, at preferential rates, of reinsurance business equivalent in profit potential to the compensation sought. Sensibly, Phoenix decided to drop the claim and take the reinsurance. In a technical sense, this marked the company's first rapprochement with German-generated business.[179]

But, of course, this rapprochement was not complete until Phoenix set up its own shop once again in what had been, for a good part of the nineteenth century, its single most important foreign market. When it did so, it chose exactly the same shop. In February 1924, the Board resolved to re-open German business through Messrs Hanbury & Co.[180] By March 1925, Hanburys were appointing agents throughout the Republic. By early June, twelve agencies had opened in leading towns; but conditions were still difficult and they took only about £3,000 in premiums in the first part of the year. Nevertheless, there were some promising signs. The company was permitted to work under pre-war terms, with no further financial or legal demands made upon it. And the accounts of German insurers, in the post-inflation phase, had been placed on a gold mark

[179] Fire Committee Minutes, Book 3, p. 44, 14 December 1921.

[180] Phoenix Directors' Minutes, 34, p. 197, 6 February 1924.

basis, so the prospects of transacting reinsurance business with them were again looking tempting by 1925. Almost visibly suppressing the shudder, the Fire Committee minuted in late May 1925, 'there is no obstacle on account of their nationality to entering into reinsurance treaty relationships with German companies'.[181]

The officials entrusted with this delicate re-launch were the old faithfuls in Hamburg. H. J. L. Behrmann had been introduced into the Hamburg agency in 1880 as an active partner and his son Henry was chief agent by 1914. A relative of the Behrmanns, Albert Thoms acted as chief agent during the reconstruction period 1924–31, until the Behrmann line was resumed with H. J. L's grandson, William Hanbury Behrmann, who led the enterprise during the 1930s. By 1939, the Hamburg office controlled fifteen general agencies and a substantial premium flow, more than 80% of it fire business. This fire account was worth an average of over £50,000 between 1929 and 1938. Phoenix's accident business in Germany was negligible and the marine modest.

However, this was another fire portfolio of big premiums and small profits. In 1937, the German insurance market was worth a total of £60.4 million, but British companies wrote only £0.8 million of it.[182] The nineteen UK companies which strove to win this fraction faced strong and sophisticated competition. The German offices were long established and powerfully built; they were prepared to cut rates and content to take their profits from their investment earnings in order to make life difficult for foreign interlopers. And in the 1930s, UK offices found this sharp edge made more abrasive still by increasing anti-British sentiment. Profits had been low in the period 1924–30, but they were increasingly pressed during the 1930s. Here high rates of tax and expanding government controls added to the pressure by forcing up expense ratios, sometimes to 60% in the last years of peace. Low loss ratios yielded Phoenix a 12–17% profit return in the period 1932–7, but over the longer span, 1929–38, the out-turn was a miserly 1.2%.[183]

For Phoenix, as for many others, the major problem in Germany was that the bulk of the available business was composed of industrial risks acquired by reinsurance from, or coinsurance with, the big German offices. The rest came from the simpler and more profitable domestic

[181] Fire Committee Minutes, Book 3, p. 155, 27 May 1925.

[182] German companies which were British-owned subsidiaries took rather more. The biggest was the Albingia of Hamburg, which belonged to the Guardian, and had a premium income of £2.1 million; the next biggest was the Securitas of Bremen, which was owned by the London, and took £0.3 million. The North British and the Victory possessed smaller interests in the Allegemeine Feuer and the Providentia.

[183] Victory Committee Report, pp. 193ff.

risks, which were difficult to get and which were obtainable only by direct agency trade confronting German competition head on. The Victory Committee concluded that 'our relatively insignificant showing prior to the war was due to the fact that we were largely dependent on industrial fire business where the German offices had the lead'.[184] To get at the lesser risks, the Committee concluded, Phoenix needed a German subsidiary company, and, after the war, should start looking for one. But, of course, some British operators (like the Guardian and the London) had perceived this before the war. And, in Denmark, where the Phoenix faced similar problems, it had also grasped the point before the war. Denmark, fortunately, was more profitable than France or Germany. If in France the deficiency of profit was due primarily to the de Leseleuc pool, in Germany it was due to the international complications which had ruined the market between 1914 and 1924 and the corporate strength of the domestic offices which had administered that market in the interim.

Phoenix representation in Denmark was in the hands primarily of Søht & Co. from 1895 until 1929. It then passed in a transfer of enormous importance for Phoenix into the hands of the former chief clerk of the Søht agency, Herman Zobel. In 1932 Zobel added the Phoenix marine agency and, in 1938, that for life business. Most importantly, as agent for LGA in Denmark since 1913, Zobel had built up an outstanding accident account, which, by the 1930s, was about 75% motor business. He was a striking personality with an appetite for innovation and in the early market for auto insurance he had found a natural stamping ground. By way of this specialism he could offer Phoenix some compensation for the declining fire premiums that the Søht agency had experienced in the 1920s. Given the nature of the Danish economy, with its heavy reliance on the production of butter and bacon by cooperatives of small farmers, much of the available fire business came, necessarily, in the form of farm insurances. Lacking fire-fighting cover, this was a class of business which Phoenix had learned to fear in the USA, Canada and elsewhere. So Zobel's rich flow of Danish motor business was a godsend.

By the 1930s Denmark was a most unusual place by the standards of Phoenix's worldwide operation: accident business far outstripped fire and Phoenix–LGA was the leading foreign player in the national market. Zobel's network, outside his own agency, consisted of twenty sub-branches controlling a numerous force of full-time agents. They raised much of their business from car-dealers and garages. So business acquisition was mostly direct, quite unlike, for example, the broker-dominated

[184] *Ibid.*

market of France. The Danish system worked well. Accident income rose by more than 50% in the period 1933–9 and reached £159,386 in 1939, more than seven times the fire income. The accident losses were low and the expenses ratio steady at about 40%. Consequently, over the decade 1929–38, accident earned a profit of some 10.6% on large sums, while fire returned 15.8% on much smaller ones.[185]

In competitive terms, this added up to a very strong performance. By 1938, the total Danish insurance market was worth about £3 million, of which Danish companies took about £2.6 million and foreign offices only some £410,000. But of this foreign allocation, Phoenix–LGA took nearly half. Even measured against the entire national market, the Phoenix Group claimed a slice of 6.2% and, in the national motor market, increased its share to nearly 16%.[186] What was most unusual about this was that such valuable and profitable business had come into the Group by way of LGA. For it was Zobel's role as an accident agent for that company which formed the foundation of this expansion.

Motor also provided the key to Phoenix's acquisition policy in Denmark. As in Germany, if not so vehemently, 'increasingly nationalistic tendencies' were beginning to limit Danish demand for Phoenix products by the mid-1930s. At this point the company began to consider buying a Danish office but running it as a distinctly local operation, quite separately from the Phoenix–LGA presence in Denmark. This decision, for reasons the planners of 1936 could not have predicted, was to be the most extraordinary stroke of luck. In the type of company selected, luck was not involved. Existing strengths were in motor and Zobel knew most about motor insurance. Phoenix looked at one Danish company, the Fyella Insurance Company in autumn 1935, but found a much better buy in the first half of 1936. This was the Aktieselskabet Forsikringsselskabet Codan of Copenhagen. Codan had been established in 1915, as an early specialist in auto business; by 1936, it was still endowed with a useful motor account but had diversified increasingly in the 1930s towards a full composite range. In June 1936 Phoenix acquired a 100% holding for the cost of £75,342. It proved a remarkable bargain.[187]

The Victory Committee concluded that after 1936 the Phoenix structure in Denmark with its long-running Phoenix–LGA agency and its apparently independent subsidiary was 'admirably designed to the requirements of the Danish market'.[188] In particular, the Codan was not only to have a distinguished postwar career[189], but also a distinguished

[185] *Ibid.*, p. 158. [186] *Ibid.*, pp. 157–8.
[187] Phoenix Directors' Minutes, 38, p. 237, 24 June 1936.
[188] Victory Committee Report, p. 161. [189] See pp. 938–9 below.

Table 10.18. *Premium income of Codan Insurance Co. by sector, 1936–40 (kroner)*

	1936	1937	1938	1939	1940
Accident	477,325	597,622	629,892	794,623	2,693,732
Fire	207,691	263,292	219,319	223,927	472,723
Marine	49,247	65,587	69,111	90,593	109,628

Source: Victory Committee Report, p. 161.

pre-war and wartime one. Thus its results for the later 1930s, particularly in the accident lines, clearly justified the purchase (see Table 10.18). Early losses, soon after the acquisition in the difficult period 1936–8, were turned around, and the Codan was clearly in surplus by 1939.

However, its wartime career was even more striking. This was the real stroke of luck. It is hinted at in the Codan's accident figure for 1940. For this greatly enlarged number also includes all Phoenix–LGA business from the point of the German occupation. Zobel was able to use the 'Danish' Codan to absorb and protect, for the duration of the German presence, the business and connections of a British insurance group. It was a handsome, if unanticipated, return on the decision of 1936 to create a company structure which could outflank *Danish* nationalistic tendencies.

Phoenix has placed over the years a special value on its relationship with the Zobels. It is not difficult to see why. In the case of the Codan, personal, international and corporate influences combined to most notable effect. From the interwar successes of the motor account, through the use of the Codan as a wartime 'cloak' for the Phoenix, to the profitable expansion of the postwar years runs a line of brave and enterprising decision-making.[190]

Finally, Holland combined some of the characteristics of Germany, France and Denmark. As in Germany, local companies squeezed the foreigners out of the safer domestic risks. As in France, the market was dominated by brokers. As in Denmark, Phoenix occupied a leading position in the market, followed it as far as the acquisition of a local company of its own, and enjoyed particularly strong agency representation.

The family of Orobio de Castro had represented Phoenix since 1868

[190] The connexion has continued into the 1990s. Peter Zobel is Chief Executive Officer, Royal & Sun Alliance (Scandinavia).

and was still doing so in May 1940, when the Netherlands were occupied by Hitler.[191] By the 1930s, about 70% of Phoenix's business in Holland came through the Orobios. But there were problems with it. Fire and marine business in the late 1930s were balanced at about £33–35,000 apiece in annual premiums and accident much less important at about half of this. Marine had turned a profit of about 18% in the decade 1929–38, but fire had made a loss. There had been heavy fire losses over the Crash months of 1930 and again in 1934/5, although there was considerable improvement as business turned up thereafter. However, fire business was pruned drastically in the 1930s, and in 1939 was at half its 1932 level.[192]

What therefore was amiss in the state of Holland? As an insurance market it was easy enough to enter; indeed, it was one of the freest markets in Europe with a minimum of government interference. For foreign offices the problems were rather broker domination, a diet of industrial risks and the rise, as in Germany and Denmark, of a 'national spirit' in economic transactions. The first two problems were connected: industrial fire business was controlled almost wholly by the Amsterdam brokers who pushed it towards the British companies, while reserving the simpler and more profitable lines for the domestic operators. This produced keen competition and uneconomic rates, while broker power frustrated the efforts of UK companies to set industrial business on a sound footing. Accident business also consisted heavily of generally undesirable risks put out by brokers. And the third category of Dutch business – colonial risks – were profitable until about 1925, then caught the Far Eastern disease. For the most part, the Orobios were forced to take their fire and accident business from the brokers; this meant that they could not get at the simple risks and so counted on their low expense ratios to produce a profit. As in the fire experience of 1929–38, this did not always work.

The way into a simpler mix of Dutch business, and a counter to 'national spirit', was the wholly-owned subsidiary. Among the many UK offices which were attracted to Holland by the lack of governmental red tape, a few had already worked this out: by the late 1930s, the REA, the Sun and the London & Lancashire all had Dutch subsidiary companies.[193] Phoenix found the vehicle it needed in 1938 in the shape of the 'Minerva' (Verzekering Maatschappij Minerva NV). It had been estab-

[191] E. Orobio de Castro served as agent for over fifty years. He was sent congratulations and a silver épergne by the directors on 1 May 1918. Fire Committee Book 2, p. 296. He died in 1922.

[192] Victory Committee Report, p. 113.

[193] *Ibid.*, p. 111.

lished in 1918 but voluntarily liquidated in 1932, with its charter lying in suspense. It was revived by the general agents, O. W. J. Schlencker & Co. of Amsterdam in 1938 as a service company for the offices represented by the agency. Some months later, Phoenix purchased it from Schlenckers for the modest sum of £27,000.

The venture too was modest in its early stages, taking £39,000 in premiums from all sectors in 1939. But Phoenix was pleased. Local corporate presence was essential for achieving access to the simple domestic fire risks and for building up a dependable accident account. The revived company 'made an excellent showing during its inaugural efforts' and held out the promise of vigorous expansion in markets removed from industrial risks and the brokers who touted them.[194] This promise was one that would be built upon in the postwar period. In the meantime, the Phoenix ended the interwar years in Holland with a two-pronged production system as well adjusted to the parameters of the market as this system had already proved in Denmark: an agency structure to cater 'for those seeking British protection' and the corporate presence 'to meet the requirements of nationalist tendencies'.[195]

Europe then was an active market for the Phoenix in the years just before it became an active theatre of combat, but not an especially profitable one. Only Denmark stands clearly apart from that generalisation, being both active and profitable. These were complex markets with much broker activity, many dangerous industrial risks, and fierce political currents. Indeed, if we accept the characterisation employed by some historians of the period 1914–45 as the Thirty Years War of the twentieth century, it would be easy to see why the European continent might be an especially difficult place for the insurer. Probably, the best answer Phoenix found was the one where national, corporate and personal influences merged: the native subsidiary company. In Europe the active insurer was often forced to this solution. Very likely, Phoenix would have done well to use it more widely outside Europe, even where circumstances pressed less hard.

13. ALARMS AND EXCURSIONS, 1918–1940

World recession, financial crashes and economic nationalism did not exhaust the perils for the insurer in the interwar years, either inside Europe or outside it. Contracting international trade, blasted industries and touchy governments were bad enough, but the era managed at least

[194] *Ibid.*, p. 117. [195] *Ibid.*, p. 116.

its fair share of disasters of other kinds, both manmade and god-sent: revolutions, sacked cities, tidal waves and earthquakes thus command a place in the Phoenix story.

For the company, the Bolshevik Revolution of 1917 ended a perfectly good reinsurance trade. Acceptances from Russian companies had been, for many years, the only way in which foreign offices could tap this massive market. And Phoenix's long-running treaty with the First Russian Company[196] had been a considerable money-spinner: it averaged a premium yield of £43,041 in the period 1906–10 but entered its last return of £23,240 in 1916 before the Bolsheviks intervened. British insurers had also ceded reinsurance to Russian companies and this trade too came to a halt. Western capitalist insurers were not attractive soul-mates for communist revolutionaries. So the 'ten days that shook the world' also shook out the native Russian insurance industry and its overseas correspondents.[197]

For Phoenix and other reinsurers on the London market the alarm was financial and legal, the first obviously enough because of the interruption of a considerable income flow, the second because of the need to seek compensation for its loss. Seeking in this case was a rather formal matter since it was not very likely to lead to getting.

However, it was no less complicated for that. Soon after the Revolution, all British offices gave provisional notice of cancellation of all relations with Russian insurers. Then, in October 1918, in a stroke characteristic of the extraordinary optimism that attended some of the early dealings between Western and Soviet interests, Phoenix *withdrew* the cancellation, 'in line with other British companies, in view of the improved outlook'.[198] Actually, of course, finance capital of which the insurance companies were prominent representatives, was a proclaimed target of Bolshevik reforms. The 'improved outlook' detected by the British offices in October 1918 was followed in December by the Soviet decree which liquidated the Russian insurance offices and paved the way for the state insurance monopoly, Gosstrakh.[199]

Thereupon, the British offices broke off relations again. But even this

[196] See vol. I, pp. 282, 316, 321.

[197] The phrase forms the famous title of the account of the revolution by the American journalist, J. Reed (London editions, 1960, 1961).

[198] Fire Committee Minutes, Book 2, p. 315, 30 October 1918. Similar optimism was evident in the post-Revolutionary planning of Western armament and oil interests. See G. G. Jones and C. Trebilcock, 'Russian Industry and British Business, 1910–30: Oil and Armaments', *Journal of European Economic History*, 11 (1982), pp. 61–103.

[199] Fire Committee Minutes, Book 3, p. 218, 12 January 1927; Victory Committee Report, pp. 14–15.

did not banish all optimism on the reinsurance front. Early in 1921, the Phoenix Board accepted that business treated as ceded to Russian insurance companies should be retained for Phoenix's own advantage and that monies due from Russia should be treated 'as a bad debt arising from the war'. But they thought that this need only be a temporary measure 'until fresh insurance treaties are completed, which will probably be as from 1 January 1922'.[200] Of course, that dawn did not materialise, and the only glimmer that did show itself came a little further west. Poland had previously formed part of the tsarist empire, but the postwar treaty provisions re-established it as an independent state. So the Polish business handled down to 1917 by First Russian passed to a new company, founded for the purpose, called Omnium of Warsaw, and with this enterprise Phoenix could continue to trade.[201]

As the 1920s wore on, it became increasingly obvious that further rays of sunlight were unlikely to come out of the USSR. The Soviet economy passed through the stage of War Communism, entered Lenin's apparently more liberal phase of the New Economic Policy (1921–8) and by 1926 was experiencing Stalin's more isolationist strategy of Socialism in One Country and preparing for the long route march of the Five Year Plans (from 1928). Late in 1926, the British authorities decided that enough was enough and that they must take steps to tidy up the reinsurance affairs of the Russian offices in Britain. Liquidators were appointed by the British courts to wind up the business of the Russians in the United Kingdom and, as part of the operation, launched test proceedings against selected British offices in order to secure a ruling on the amounts of outstanding debt and the date at which the reckoning should be taken.[202] On account of its dealings with a company as eminent as First Russian, Phoenix became one of the selected companies.[203] For these pains, the office was required to pay £28,584 to the liquidators of First Russian and £12,000 to those of the Northern of Moscow.[204] Some eleven years after the Russian Revolution, the final account was presented.

Other disasters of the interwar years, particularly of the 1920s, though lacking the status of the Red Revolution, gave the insurers a taxing time. In September 1922, the Greco-Turkish War succeeded in setting light to a good part of the port of Smyrna, including a number of valuable tobacco stores. A possession of the Ottoman Empire from 1424 until 1919,

[200] Phoenix Directors' Minutes, 33, p. 311, 19 October 1921.
[201] Fire Committee Minutes, Book 2, p. 359, 29 October 1919.
[202] The British offices argued that it should be from the date of the 'attack' by the Soviet government in its decree of December 1918.
[203] Fire Committee Minutes, Book 3, p. 218, 12 January 1927.
[204] Phoenix Directors' Minutes, 35, p. 466, 12 December 1928.

Smyrna was tentatively assigned to Greece as part of the international settlement after the First World War. In 1922 Turkey took it back by force of arms and retained it by the Treaty of Lausanne of 1923. This diplomatic square-dance resulted in damage to the city of about £30 million, the second largest recorded act of destruction of the interwar years.[205] Phoenix suffered an immediate loss of £5,500, since it had covered war risks on six properties, but the rest of its policies for Smyrna had contained the usual exclusion clauses for war and riot.[206]

Nevertheless, the story was not to end there. In 1923, the new Turkish government required foreign insurers to register with the authorities, make a substantial deposit and recognise all Turkish laws. Misliking the smell of burning on the wind, and correctly reading the government's intent to impose liability for the Smyrna conflagration upon the insurers, whatever their contracts said, Phoenix and other British offices closed their agencies in Turkey.[207] There remained at issue, however, the myriad fire claims which had arisen in the six months after the Smyrna conflagration. The foreign insurers had grave doubts about the causes of many of the fire losses – if they were the work of Turkish troops, they fell under the war exclusion; and, if the fires were not started by Turkish troops, who had started them? – and also questioned the proof of ownership to property abandoned by refugees. Phoenix and other British offices decided that they must resist the claims.[208] Many small Turkish policyholders, and the Turkish government, did not like this. More ominously, neither did the tobacco companies. Two of them, British American and Orient, brought actions against the Guardian and the Alliance respectively. But the courts were kinder to the insurers in the Turkish than in the Russian connection, to the great relief of all British offices. The judgement in 1925 was that the losses were within the exceptions of the policies and that the underwriters were not liable.[209]

Smyrna suffered a man-made disaster in 1922, but, in the next year, another port, Yokohama, underwent a terrible onslaught of Nature. The earthquake and tidal wave that flattened the great trade centre and then moved on to ravage Tokyo itself was the most devastating natural catastrophe since the San Francisco tremor of 1906. Indeed the total cost of the damage (in current prices) was £175 million at Yokohama and a staggering £1,030 million at Tokyo, far above the £700 million lost at San

[205] Phoenix List of 'Conflagration, Earthquake and Hurricane Disasters 1904 Onwards' (1945). The largest was the Yokohama earthquake of 1923.

[206] Fire Committee Minutes, Book 3, p. 66, 20 September 1922.

[207] *Ibid.*, p. 84, 14 March 1923. [208] *Ibid.*, p. 138, 12 November 1924.

[209] *Ibid.*, p. 154, 13 May 1925.

Plate 10.1 Tidal wave at Yokohama, September 1923.

Francisco. More than 18,000 acres (7,300 ha) of the two Japanese cities were laid waste against less than 3,000 acres (1,200 ha) at San Francisco. No other event between the two World Wars created so much havoc. The earthquakes at Managua in 1931, in Southern California in 1933, and in India at Quetta in 1935 did much less damage, at least in property destroyed: £6 million, £8 million and £6 million respectively.[210] The hurricane which hit the Atlantic coast of the USA in 1938, causing £25 million worth of damage, was the next worst natural disaster of the era;[211] but even it could not compare with the mayhem wrought in Japan.

The British government sent warships and sailors to help clear up[212] and the Lord Mayor of London started a relief fund. Phoenix donated £500 to the Mansion House appeal and expressed willingness to support the Japanese reconstruction loan.[213] However, the company did not suffer

[210] And only in California did Phoenix suffer a loss, a moderate £11,000.
[211] Phoenix lost £40,000 to these winds.
[212] Including CPO Charles Matthews, the author's grandfather.
[213] Phoenix Directors' Minutes, 34, pp. 132, 137, 174, 12 and 26 September, 19 December 1923.

Plate 10.2 Earthquake in Central Tokyo: the ruins of Nihonbashi.

any additional burden as result of the disaster. Phoenix did not insure for earthquake risk in Japan and the fire damage had occurred after the buildings had fallen. In 1924 the suggestion that foreign fire insurers should settle by the return of one year's premium was accepted by the offices and deemed satisfactory by most policy-holders.[214] So the Phoenix recorded no loss against Yokohama on its list of 'Conflagration, Earthquake and Hurricane Disasters 1904 Onwards'. This was a remarkable outcome given the scale of the devastation.

Greater loss was suffered towards the end of the period in consequence of an alarm which had more in common with the event at Smyrna than with that at Yokohama. The vicious confrontation of the Spanish Civil War was a substantial military event at the heart of Europe and, at that time, more dismaying to London insurers than natural eruptions in the Far East or unruly soldiery in Asia Minor. In 1934 communist uprisings and authoritarian responses created £2.5 million worth of damage in Gijon, Oviedo and other towns in Asturias. Phoenix escaped liability in

[214] *Ibid.*, pp. 216, 269, 19 March, 27 August 1924.

Plate 10.3 Civil war in Spain.

that outburst but as uprising developed into all-out warfare (1936-9), the company took significant punishment. In 1936 28 acres (11 ha) of Malaga were heavily damaged in massive rioting: the total loss was £500,000 and Phoenix carried £50,000 of it. Viewed comparatively such punishment was less sharp than the protracted drain in China, but it remained significant. In 1934 the fire premium income from Spain had almost doubled from its 1930 figure to £40,120 and marine was slightly down on the 1930 figure at £18,988, yet by 1938 fire premium was slashed to £10,393 and marine to £5,534. The fire account fell drastically into the red in 1936 and accumulated a debit by 1938 of nearly £100,000.[215] The war that did so much damage to the generation of Orwell and Cornford, and the young men of the International Brigade, did not leave the City unmarked.[216]

All of these episodes were major disasters in human or international terms, and like all such affairs, they have a necessary place in insurance history. Moreover, they locate the insurer in his time. But they did not have a major impact on the Phoenix; there was no single catastrophic event in the interwar years to compare with the ruination of San Francisco

[215] Victory Committee Report, Statement 4.

[216] For the classic account of personal experience see George Orwell, *Homage to Catalonia* (London, 1938); for the classic historical account, see H. Thomas, *The Spanish Civil War* (London, 1977).

Plate 10.4 Not quite a car accident: bomb damage in a Spanish street.

in 1906. Indeed analysis of Phoenix's own 'List of Disasters' for the period 1918–40 produces some sobering results. The total cost of the catastrophes logged worldwide by Phoenix over these years, omitting the two worst cases of Yokohama and Smyrna, was £96.7 million and the office lost on account of them some £210,800 of its own money.

What is striking is the location of the disasters and the losses. Even without the 1923 earthquake, Japan accounted for 18.7% of the worldwide disaster loss for insurers and 9.7% of Phoenix's own loss. The reason for this was partly rapid industrialisation and partly Japanese construction methods, involving much building with frame and paper in heavily congested areas. But far and away the biggest source of disaster losses – a persistent flow of medium catastrophes rather than gargantuan eruptions – was the USA: it accounted for 52.2% of world destruction and 46.7% of Phoenix disaster losses. The only other areas to feature prominently in the world ratings were India with 9% and Latin America with just over 8%. In terms of Phoenix disaster losses, the main locations outside the USA and Japan were Canada with 8.1% and Spain with 23.7%. The inference is that the major sources of true insurance alarms were no longer the traditional hell-holes – the West Indies for instance scarcely made a showing – but the heavily industrialised, heavily populated economies of the 'first world'. Ironically, the USA was the biggest 'alarm' in the insurance world.

14. GOVERNING TROUBLES: STATES, INSURERS AND COMPETITORS, 1918–1940

Before 1914, the big British offices had been welcome in most insurance markets. Naturally, they had often to pay for their presence with some form of guarantee payment and even before the First World War they encountered protectionist discrimination; but, generally, they were accepted for the breadth they gave the market and the high standard of probity they represented. But after 1918, increasing government restrictionism was added to the many other constraints which affected insurance markets worldwide. This was due to a complex of reasons. The spread of industrialisation had produced a greater involvement of governments in all areas of economic activity and the running of war economies in the recent great conflict had thrust an additional administrative responsibility upon many of them. The war had also produced significant deterioration in the international economic order of the period 1870–1914 and forced many economies in the direction of greater self-sufficiency: the result was a higher level of economic nationalism after 1918. On top of this, the economic instability of the 1920s and 1930s produced corporate instability and encouraged governments to closer scrutiny of the large financial institutions they admitted to their markets. Not least, a growing sensitivity to the needs of social policy – classically in the case of workmen's compensation – and to the special pressures created by the growth of automobilism – classically in the case of compulsory motor insurance – brought the civil servants increasingly into the territory of the foreign insurers.

The bureaucrats had three types of objective: they might wish to exercise a supervisory function over a large, powerful and potentially dangerous financial sector, as was the case in the USA; or they might wish to compel certain socially beneficial types of insurance, such as workmen's compensation; or they might wish to achieve self-sufficiency or monopoly levels of insurance for domestic interests, whether private or public, as most notoriously happened with the Soviet introduction of Gosstrakh. States less extreme than the Bolshevik could step into any of these areas with considerable force. By the 1930s, state-run workmen's compensation schemes were at work in some regions of the USA and Australia, and in all of Canada. Elsewhere in Australia and New Zealand state insurance offices competed directly with private ones. Similarly, the tougher line taken by the Turkish government after the Smyrna disaster included a partial reinsurance monopoly, with one-half of all business written directly by the offices having to be reassured with Milli Reassurans. When the Mexican government tried this tactic – insisting that half of all commitments taken on by foreign offices should be reinsured inside Mexico – the UK offices reacted as they had done in Turkey: they left the market.

Reinsurance was widely used also as a means of providing government-supported protection for domestic direct insurers, particularly in Latin America. In the past, the big foreign offices had been able to counter attempts to reserve important sectors of national markets for domestic offices by the simple expedient of refusing to provide reinsurance cover for them. However, if national governments could find ways of providing this cover themselves, they could encourage native insurers and discourage outside insurers with impunity. Thus Chile and Uruguay in the interwar years denied access to their markets to all new foreign entrants. They, along with Brazil – which had proclaimed the goal of complete self-sufficiency in insurance and where foreign offices were being 'slowly crushed out of business'[217] – were able to follow such policies because they had developed state reinsurance agencies well able to service the needs of domestic insurers. Even worse news for foreign companies in the late 1930s was a scheme to connect together the state reinsurance facilities of the various Latin American markets.

Against government action of the Russian, Turkish or Mexican type there was little that insurance exporters like Phoenix could do except withdraw. But against the lesser forms of discrimination, there were some possible responses. These were centred largely in Latin America. In 1917, the Chilean government passed legislation which threatened to prevent foreign offices operating in Chile. Phoenix's influential agents, Anthony Gibbs & Co., suggested the answer: the formation of a native Chilean office, with Phoenix as major shareholder. The two other offices for which Gibbs acted, the North British and the Yorkshire, also received this proposal; and both acted upon it. For Phoenix, action consisted of the formation of La Fenix Chilena, launched in 1917, with a capital of $200,000 which as the Director's Minutes put it was 'to protect Phoenix business in Chile'.[218] In this it apparently succeeded, since in the period

[217] Victory Committee Report, p. 14.

[218] Fire Committee Minutes, Book 2, p. 265, 29 August 1917; Phoenix Directors' Minutes 1917. The capital of La Fenix Chilena was raised to $0.5 million in 1920, and a further extension to $1 million planned.

1918–27 Phoenix took £385,000 in gross fire premiums from Chile and made a profit of 41%.[219]

Two years later, counter-measures became necessary against the Argentine government which had begun to see itself as a southern version of the US administration, building up an Insurance Superintendancy, with powers of intervention in rates, limits, reinsurance, and, most relevantly, remittance of funds to the United Kingdom. Throughout the interwar period, tax discrimination, which the offices had been fighting since the 1900s, remained severe. Here, too, the agents, Leng Roberts & Co, proposed that Phoenix and the two other companies represented by the agents – REA and the Union – should make a combined effort to buy equity control of the La Rosario company. This was duly agreed in July 1919.[220] Over the period 1920–8, Phoenix took just over £0.5 million in gross fire premium from the Argentine and made a profit on it of some 21%.

In the longer run, perhaps the most important of the family of Latin American subsidiaries formed during this phase of evasive manoeuvres was La Fenix Peruana, launched in 1927. The provisional agreement for the formation of a local Peruvian company passed the Phoenix Board in September and by March of the next year the company was floated.[221] In the post-1945 period, Fenix Peruana was to become perhaps Phoenix's most important vehicle in Latin America. La Fenix Peruana paid its first dividend of 3% in 1932 and had raised it to 8% by 1939.[222]

However, if governments developed new ways to hinder the insurance exporters in this period, some of their old ways could still prove sufficiently uncomfortable. Official insistence upon insurance deposits by foreign companies had been an irritant in many markets before 1914 and in some, like the USA and Canada, a major penalty. Under the unsteady financial conditions of the later 1920s, many more governments found it expedient to introduce or greatly increase deposit requirements. Thus in 1927 Bulgaria quadrupled its deposit levels and demanded a 40% reserve against premiums, while Mexico went up by 20% and instituted a compulsory reserve of 30%.[223] The next year Chile matched Bulgaria on the statutory reserve, while Colombia doubled its deposit bill.[224] By this time,

[219] Fire Committee Minutes, Book 3, p. 277, 3 October 1928.

[220] *Ibid.*, Book 2, p. 353, 30 July 1919. The purchase was divided 40% to Leng Roberts, 20% to each of the three companies.

[221] The capital of £60,000 was divided so as to give Phoenix just over 66%, the Peruvian Corporation around 13%, and Messrs Graty & Co. and the Banco Italiano 10% apiece.

[222] Victory Committee, Supplementary Report, p. 535.

[223] Fire Committee Minutes, Book 3, p. 224, 16 March 1927.

[224] *Ibid.*, p. 277, 3 October 1928; *ibid.*, p. 275, 15 August 1928.

too, German deposit requirements for Phoenix had reached 500,000 marks.[225] In 1929, the Bulgarians bid up again and the Chinese chipped in with demands for a guarantee of 50,000 Cantonese dollars as the price of insuring in Kwantung.[226]

Such demands were not too much of a strain if they could be met in sterling securities, but as an added refinement governments, usually those with the least dependable treasuries, would often stipulate that they should be satisfied in the securities of the country. Like some wines, these frequently did not travel well. The worst conjunction came in those places where, as the Victory Committee tactfully put it, 'the underwriting prospects are favourable but the financial record is poor',[227] places like South America, Spain, or the Balkans. Summed across the globe, deposits certainly were a financial strain: by 1938, Phoenix had nearly £1 million immobilised in this form of guarantee, and that was in the areas of the world outside the really big claimants in North America. Of this £1 million, some 33% was in Europe, 30% in the British Empire, 28% in Latin America and the remaining 9% generally scattered. By comparison, the USA alone required £1,167,396 in deposits and Canada £394,239. For the entire Phoenix Group, the worldwide deposit liability by 1939 was over £5 million.[228]

The various limitations imposed by governments on the large foreign insurers had significant knock-on effects. Thus the vexatious regulations produced by the state watchdogs made it extremely difficult for the offices to keep up representation by general agents. As governments looked for ever more complex and binding controls and guarantees, so professional insurance officials were increasingly needed to unravel the red tape. And this entailed the higher costs of branch organisation or the creation of a subsidiary company.

Further, government discrimination was not just tiresome in itself; it was linked to the rise of local competition, and indeed that was largely its purpose. Governments were not only seeking revenue but also the promotion of domestic capitalism. So where there was a gentleman's agreement between the major international offices attempting, for example, to control agents' commissions, the local offices, buoyed up by government help, could afford to sew discord and break it. Thus in the Argentine, where loss rates were low, the profit balances of foreign offices could be attacked with

[225] *Ibid.*, p. 274, 15 August 1928. This was about £25,000. By 1939 the figure was £60,000.

[226] *Ibid.*, p. 319, 6 November 1929. This was about £5,000.

[227] Victory Committee Report, p. 16.

[228] Phoenix Assurance Accounts, Blue Books, 1939, p. 97. The Group as a whole, that is, including LGA and Union Marine, had £5,148,200 locked up in deposits, of which £3,879,906 was in the USA and £673,437 in Canada.

brokerage charges inflated by the local competition and then legalised at 30%. In order to secure business against heavy competition in Portugal and Denmark, Phoenix had even to allow commission rates above 30%. Relying on official favour and generous reinsurance provisions, local offices could also afford to give credit for premiums or permit payment by instalments, whereas the foreign insurer, faced by high operating costs, sought cash on the nail. Other special features such as broker domination in such markets as Holland, Belgium or Spain, or native canvassers swift with their rebates, as in India or Burma, also gave local offices more power than they had possessed before 1914. But it was generally more aggressive state policy that created an environment in which relatively small local offices could hurt much larger international operators.

15. THE COMPOSITE INSURER ABROAD AND THE PROFIT OUT-TURN, 1918–40

It remains then to see how far Phoenix succeeded in developing internationally as a composite insurer in these difficult years and what was the financial outcome of the attempt.

The Victory Committee posed to itself the question: How far was the Phoenix a genuine worldwide composite office by 1938? On a strict reading it concluded that 'the answer is virtually a complete negative'.[229] The strictness of interpretation had two foundations: the inquiry into how many markets boasted a life export operation alongside the other branches and a similar question as to how many markets featured marine income drawn from the same sources as fire and accident income. The answer to the first query was that the life department issued policies in only three external markets, Denmark, India and Peru. And the answer to the second was scarcely better: marine income was drawn through the same network as other types in only six locations in the world. Somewhat depressed by its own thinking, the Committee then proceeded to review the fifty-eight territories within its remit and concluded that only thirteen of them contained genuinely joint Phoenix operations featuring several branches of insurance and that almost half (twenty-seven) were served by networks offering fire insurance alone.

It then proceeded to cheer itself up in a time-honoured way: it considered the statistics from a different angle. If the number of Phoenix composite operations worldwide was small, what of the *share* of income that they generated? This proved a happier thought. For only 8% of

[229] Victory Committee Report, p. 11.

Group income came through the twenty-seven outposts which remained dedicated to fire and 66% came from the minority which were joint operations. By 1938, there were fully composite Phoenix systems operating in Australia, New Zealand, South Africa and Denmark.[230] Similarly, after initial moves in the opposite direction in both the USA and Canada, largely due to the desire for separation which the touch of LGA's tentacles provoked among Phoenix managers, a merged form of operation had been instituted in 1935 in the USA, and, in somewhat unsettled terms, after 1936 in Canada.[231] However, in 1939 about 50% of all Group worldwide fire premiums came from just these two operations, which had only *just* achieved composite status.[232]

Between 1923 and 1938, the worldwide accident business of the UK offices developed strongly, implying, among other things, a general swing towards composite operation. While total fire and marine income of UK offices declined across the years of depression 1923–8 by £9 million, their accident income advanced by £30 million.[233] Phoenix was slow to the starting blocks in this development, which again probably had a bearing on its desire to acquire LGA. Phoenix began writing foreign accident business in Australia in 1908, New Zealand, China and Malaya in 1909 and Japan in 1910; but all of these moves were aimed at protecting existing fire connections rather than at generating accident business on its own account. In 1920, Phoenix took from the fifty-eight territories surveyed by the Victory Committee a mere £20,000 in accident premiums. Throughout the interwar years, fire business continued to predominate in many markets, and management in some important places, like the Far East and India, continued to be exclusively fire-trained. Elsewhere, even where accident business had been grafted onto fire operations, 'the Fire agencies retained their exclusive character and continue so up to the present time'.[234]

This is well revealed in Table 10.19 where almost all large markets – indeed with the exceptions only of France and Denmark – have a predominance of fire business, and many of them, such as Portugal, Germany, India, Burma, Japan and China, a startling predominance. An equally strong slant the other way is achieved in only one case, with the exceptional performance of Zobel's accident account in Denmark. It is striking that for Phoenix in the period before the Second World War, accident business in any foreign market outside the USA, Canada or Denmark struggled to exceed 20% of total income, and, similarly, that

[230] *Ibid.*, p. 13 [231] See above pp. 700–17 and pp. 40–50.
[232] Calculated from Phoenix Accounts, Blue Books, 1939, pp. 15ff.
[233] Victory Committee Report, pp. 5–6. [234] *Ibid.*, p. 24.

Table 10.19. *Phoenix premium income: share of fire, accident, marine in aggregate income from selected countries, 1929–38 (%)*

	Fire[a]	Accident	Marine
Belgium	59.4	8.7	31.9
Holland	56.6	13.8	29.6
France	40.2	26.2	33.6
Spain	62.1	–	37.9
Portugal	77.7	21.9	0.4
Denmark	12.7	86.5	0.8
Germany	81.0	4.9	14.1
India	67.4	8.9	23.7
Burma	92.7	1.5	5.8
Ceylon	48.7	28.3	23.0
Malaya	63.0	20.9	16.1
Japan	92.4	1.3	6.3
China	75.2	4.7	20.1

Note: [a] 100% ratings for fire were returned by Gibraltar, Sweden, Finland, Iceland, Bulgaria, Greece, Cyprus, Palestine and Iraq.
Source: Calculated from Victory Committee Report, Statements, pp. 376ff.

marine seldom broke through the 30% barrier. The possibilities for even the biggest type of UK office to be a multinational, in a true composite form, on a global scale, were still limited in 1939.

Of course, there were powerful internal frictions which impeded the progress of insurance ventures towards a fully composite form. Offices became composites largely by taking over other offices and these acquisitions often possessed, and retained, strong personalities of their own. These could resist integration into the larger corporate identity. Again, the move towards corporate operation was associated with the greater use of branch management. However, branch managers were rarely virtuosi of the different insurance skills, more usually they were influenced by the one insurance discipline in which they had been trained. Possibly most important, however, were the intrinsic differences between the various insurance 'technologies' or 'products'. Cover for fire and marine risks is usually for large amounts, carries the risk of catastrophic loss and involves the twin needs of avoiding undue accumulation and obtaining sufficient reinsurance. Accident business, by contrast, usually covers moderate individual sums, rarely involves catastrophic risk, seldom encounters undue accumulation and has little need for reinsurance. Furthermore, the fire and marine products are in constant demand, sought out by the client, whereas accident cover, like life cover, has to be actively sold. Consequently, brokers are active in the first two markets but not in the others.

Phoenix certainly encountered these frictions in its progress towards the composite state. But it encountered some rather particular versions of them. The company's worldwide fire premiums, like those of the UK fire insurers as a whole, declined between 1923 and 1938: in Phoenix's case from £3.4 million to £2.7 million. The company did only slightly worse than the UK average between 1923 and 1938, maintaining its income between these two benchmark years, but then suffered a sharp downturn in worldwide fire receipts 1933–8, due largely to the predominance of the US market – where the decline was 'particularly rapid and severe'[235] – in its export activities. But where the Phoenix diverged most markedly from the industry pattern was in the weak development of its global accident account. Phoenix Group accident income was £4.7 million in 1923 and £3.9 million in 1928, and, despite the rising trend for UK accident income as a whole, hardly improved on this figure by 1938.[236] The acquisition of LGA boosted the Phoenix accident income beyond the average industrial standard in the early 1920s, but the need, thereafter, to strip down the LGA's rashly acquired US account brought Phoenix well below the industry standard for 1933–8. Phoenix profitability over this period was also below the all-UK insurance average: whereas all UK companies earned 13.6% profit on fire premiums and 6.5% on accident premiums, Phoenix managed only 9.2% and 4.3%.

Of course, Phoenix was constrained by the systematic obstacles to smooth composite growth that were experienced by all companies, but the particular friction represented by LGA was a radical expression of one general difficulty. Here the personality and problems of an acquired company had a markedly depressive effect on composite expansion. Phoenix was frightened not by accident business but by what it found in the vaults of one accident company. Confrontation with these unpleasant discoveries encouraged Phoenix managers less to find ways of integrating with LGA than to devise ways of distancing themselves from LGA. It was an ironic outcome to Ryan's long-run plan for the Phoenix. And no reversal was really achieved until the late 1930s.

[235] *Ibid.*, p. 5. Between 1923 and 1938, the index figure for all UK worldwide fire premium income (1928=100) fell from 97.7 to 85.3, while the matching Phoenix figure fell from 100 to 81.2.

[236] *Ibid.* Between 1923 and 1928, the index figure for all UK worldwide accident premium (1928=100) rose from 71.4 to 100.0, whereas the Phoenix figure fell from 121.0 to 100.0. By 1938, the all-UK index was at 122.1, while the Phoenix number had barely moved, to 100.2.

It is perhaps no great surprise that the world markets of the 1920s and 1930s were not especially kind to world-class insurers. One of the most difficult economic tasks of these decades was to export, and here there were as many problems in exporting the 'invisible' of insurance as in selling the manufactured or primary commodities of the visible trade. The home UK market, even in a recession, was a notably better place to insure.[237]

Viewed as an economic problem, that is roughly what we might expect. Perhaps somewhat more surprising is the degree to which insurance export markets were affected in these years by political changes. This was true of markets as varied as Germany, India, China, Russia, Spain or Japan, and that list composed a very significant array of insurance locations. Indeed, in 1928 these places provided over 11% of Phoenix's foreign market, an uncomfortable proportion to have in a state of unpredictable imbalance. And these were just the worst cases. In many others, lesser strengths of national sentiment supplied an unwelcome variable that had scarcely affected pre-1914 markets. Alongside these problems were fiercer developments of competitive forces that had been present before 1914: effective local offices, canvassing and rate-cutting by confident and shrewd native sales forces well-tailored to their markets, increasing broker infiltration of the more complicated markets, mainly in Europe. Probably the best way of countering at least some of these pressures was the more extensive use of a device which other offices had begun to apply before 1914, but with which Phoenix had only flirted: the foreign subsidiary company.

Even this device was ambiguously related to national sentiment. Thus in Australia, Denmark and Holland, Argentina, Chile or Peru the foreign-owned 'local' company was the right answer for the Phoenix, and it could well have proved a good answer in South Africa, India or France, but no form of joint-venture or participation would have shielded the company from the national or doctrinal sentiment of the Japanese or the Russians.

Somewhat slow in the application of the foreign subsidiary, Phoenix learned in the interwar years that it possessed utility outside North America; and, in the postwar years, tried to apply it more widely. Even in the interwar years, however, and not only inside North America, Phoenix became more distinctively a multinational enterprise. That was perhaps its best achievement amidst the storms – natural, economic and political – of this unkind period.

[237] See Chapter 8 above.

CHAPTER 11

THE PHOENIX AND TOTAL WAR, 1939–1945

Industrialisation in the eighteenth and nineteenth centuries created the widespread distribution of wealth which made it worthwhile for much of the community to insure its property against fire. It took some considerable while for industrialisation to create a means of distributing destruction so widely that the property of every member of the community was put at risk. Between these two feats of technology there was a timelag of nearly two centuries. But, by the 1930s, the second was fully accomplished. In earlier decades, of course, property had been threatened by the occasional marauding army, or, across swathes of Flanders, entirely obliterated by the almost static holocaust of trench warfare. However, this threat was usually localised, to a greater or lesser extent, and the property was usually someone else's.

I. INSURANCE AND BLITZKRIEG

With the advent of effective aerial bombardment, the social implications of warfare changed completely. The Fighting Front enlarged to become universal; it was on everyone's street corner. Modern society had made it conventional to insure property against destruction by fire; now an era opened in which the induced firestorm became a convention. In the First World War this threat had appeared but had not become substantial; rather more than a decade later it was fully armed.

For these and other reasons, aerial bombardment fell at the junction point of many of the great debates of the 1930s. It was a central issue in the contest between appeasement and deterrence; it raised new questions in the ever-widening discussion in regard to the proper spheres of state and private responsibility; it removed the battle from the battlefield and gave the military planners an awesomely expanded theatre for initiative and error.

Appeasement of the European dictatorships, of course, was born of fear. Nor was this simply fear of repeating the First World War. That was an appalling war, and all too many had failed to come home. But, in the next war, the home itself was threatened, an incendiary device suspended, potentially, 10,000 feet above every chimney-pot.[1] People were just as frightened of this as they were later to be of the light of a thousand suns and the ionised filth of the mushroom cloud: Guernica and Shanghai were to the appeasers of the 1930s what Hiroshima and Nagasaki were to the nuclear disarmers of the 1950s and 1960s.[2] Nor was the generation of the 1930s wrong to be frightened of air power: the rubble of Coventry and Dresden, Plymouth and Hamburg; the East End and Berlin before long provided the monument to a correct fear. The leaders of democratic nations, however misguided their understanding of dictators, were understandably cautious about unleashing an engine of war of such ferocity.

And then there was the problem of responsibility for the destruction once it had occurred. If air power could remove whole streets of ordinary houses, who was to protect the community from the consequences? Could the citizenry buy protection in any private market? Or did the nature of modern warfare, in this as in so many other ways, require an extension of the state's role in economic and social life?

Many of the implications of warfare in the 1940s – unlike those of warfare in the 1910s – were accurately predicted. Before the First World War, very few observers had much notion of the kind of conflict that was to come. Before the Second World War, many observers realised fairly clearly just how unpleasant the coming conflict would be. This was partly because the wars of the 1930s – the Spanish Civil War and the Second Sino-Japanese War – had already supplied portents. The war of armoured movement and mass bombing which began in Europe in September 1939 had already been foreshadowed by the destruction rained down upon Spanish hill-towns and Chinese seaports.

The insurance problems were also perceived early. Civilian concern in the United Kingdom was signalled by that most British of alarm calls: an active correspondence in *The Times*. This was prompted by the accounts of war damage coming in from Spain and China. From January 1937 to

[1] In fact, in the United Kingdom, during the Second World War, bombing destroyed 222,000 homes and damaged 3.5 million more. This meant that two out of every seven were hit. One-fifth of all schools and hospitals were disabled. P. Howlett, *Fighting with Figures* (London, 1995).

[2] Equally, for others, Guernica and Shanghai were object lessons in the need to *resist* totalitarianism.

Plate 11.1 Shanghai after Japanese bombing, October 1937.

June 1938, ships worth £4.5 million were sunk in Spanish waters. More worrying still was the number of British ships hit – some fifty vessels – and the manner of their demise. Three-quarters of the ships attacked in Spain were bombed and some 57% of the British ships so attacked were total losses. In China only one-third of marine losses were attributable to bombing. But the explosives the Japanese airforce had not dropped on Chinese shipping they had saved for Chinese cities. As early as October 1937, the *Post Magazine* recorded 'the ruthless bombing by the Japanese of open cities such as Nanking, Shanghai and Canton, and the consequent widespread damage to property, some of it British-owned, as well as the appalling loss of life'.[3] In Shanghai, then as now the industrial heart of China, over 500 factories had been destroyed by air attack, at a total cost, in 1937 prices, possibly as high as £40 million.[4] The lesson was clear: wherever the bombers flew, devastation rates were unprecedented.

Indeed, the threat to property from the air had become so pronounced that the question immediately arose as to whether it could be insured against at all. Logically enough, among the first interested parties to express concern in Britain, in May 1937, were the building societies. Predictably, however, they did not get far. Their questions to Walter

[3] *Post Magazine and Insurance Monitor*, 2 October 1937.
[4] *Oriental Affairs*, December 1937.

Runciman, once again President of the Board of Trade,[5] elicited the bluff response that, 'no scheme of insurance of property in this country against war risks on land would be appropriate to the conditions of a future war'.[6] That is, the bomber had so distorted the balance of risk that insurance could offer no civic counter-weapon. Learned treatises were constructed to support this position. The conviction that the bomber would always get through – indeed, the apparent practical demonstrations of the 1930s that it actually did – produced enormous strategic problems for the military planners but almost philosophical ones for the insurers. For, how could you insure against a very likely catastrophe? When insurance was a cooperative endeavour of carefully selected property and people against a calculable risk, how could it provide universal protection against an overwhelming risk?

If insurance was based on the scientific application of the law of average, as ascertained by experience, how could it be applied to technological novelties which had changed the frontiers of destructive capability? There was minimal experience of these devices; they were clearly awesomely powerful: yet they opened up to destruction, not only armies and fleets, but, on an unprecedented scale, the homes of ordinary citizens. Habitually, homes were insured, but how could they be insured against a diving certainty?.

More careful observers pointed out that fire insurers had never covered war risks in normal policies and had indeed specifically excluded them. It was true that Lloyds had historically accepted some land war risks on special terms, and their decision in October 1936 to cease this line of business was both a sign of the times and a signal for further alarm.[7] Generally, however, it was public sensitivity that was changing in 1937 and 1938, not insurance practice. All the companies could do was reiterate that war risk was *not* covered by ordinary property insurance, and emphasise that, if the community wanted air bombardment covered, it had better think most seriously how this might be accomplished.

The central problem was that conflict elsewhere had created a demand for air bombardment insurance in Europe *before* a European war existed. This was demand for a product which could not be supplied. The threat of international tension turning into war could not be calculated. Even if premiums could be assessed and paid, what was to be done with them if

[5] As he had been during the First World War, 1914–16. Then again 1931–7.

[6] The *Financial News*, 24 September 1938.

[7] The Council of Lloyds was an early player in lobbying the government to establish its own scheme against air bombardment.

war did not materialise; were they to be paid back? And how could a plausible assessment be achieved? The experience of the First World War was no guide. Nor even was the experience of Spain and China: for London would not be defended as Guernica or Shanghai were defended. The vast advances in the range, power and precision of aircraft, and in the explosive powers of bombs, together with the advent of incendiary devices, had transformed the air risk in a very short span of years. Where, in 1914–18, London could be threatened, by the 1930s almost all of industrial England was exposed.

In London alone, there was in 1938 about £2,500 million of property insured against fire. What level of premium would be adequate to cover the risk of destruction of, say, 10% of that value? One corporate insurer alone held fire policies on £350 million worth of property; how could it cost the risk of the bomber getting through to a significant proportion of that? And there was the final infuriating irony that people only wanted war insurance when a war was imminent. If they had been prepared to pay premiums for war insurance ten or fifteen years before a war happened, then the resulting funds might indeed have achieved a total commensurate with the risk. However, it is in the nature of humankind to wish for war insurance when only a year or two's worth of premiums could be amassed.

On 15 March 1938, Sir William Elderton presented a paper to the Insurance Institute of London which coolly argued 'The Impossibility of War Risk Insurance'.[8] Sir William considered three possibilities – a corporate war risks scheme, a mutual pooling system, and a state insurance scheme. None was found satisfactory: no basis existed on which to calculate premiums for any of them: there was insufficient time to amass a sufficient fund of premiums; any fund would immediately depreciate in value with the coming of war; payment of losses during the war would bear no resemblance to the cost of reinstatement after the war; and reinstatement could not be achieved during the war because manpower would not be spared from the war effort.

Nor was insurance against the mass destruction of property similar to marine insurance or life insurance in wartime; earlier events in these sectors were not relevant. For the marine risk was attached to a particular voyage and a limited timescale, and maritime loss was, of its nature, localised. In life assurance, there was a permanent contract, and, in an era before Hiroshima and Nagasaki, or even Dresden, the likelihood of catastrophic wartime mortality was not perceived.[9] What Elderton ar-

[8] Published under that title by Cambridge University Press in 1938.

[9] Elderton did exempt group life insurance, which was a one-year risk, with many of the individuals within the group very likely to be housed within the same building.

gued so lucidly, of course, was that you could not have war risk assurance before you had the war. Once the war had begun, he did see the possibility of 'some scheme such as that used in the last war'. This would be a government scheme, employing the offices as intermediaries and 'devised with the intention of making it as nearly comprehensive as possible'. It should be launched 'immediately a war started by a new Defence of the Realm Act'.[10] Before the crisis arrived, however, little could be done.

But this did not stop worried citizens clamouring for it. The years 1937 and 1938 witnessed a remarkable event in insurance history: the creation of a market for an insurance product which could not be supplied. Government remained understandably cool in the presence of a threat which it could not quantify, while the offices relied on their traditional war exclusion clauses and insisted, correctly, that this was standard practice. Such reactions only served to increase the level of public unease and thus raise the level of demand still further.

As early as November 1937, one private sector attempt was made to create a mutual solution to the air risk. This was the Property Owners' War Risks Mutual Society Ltd which worked on the 'something-is-better-than-nothing-principle'. Acknowledging that it could not provide sensible protection against bomb damage, it aimed to supply its members with such compensation as it had funds to pay.[11] But this scheme was widely perceived as superficial. The building societies certainly wanted much more. Thus, again in November 1937, the Yorkshire Association of Building Societies called, 'in the absence of a definite pledge by the Government to make good all war damage to property', for a compulsory surcharge on all fire insurance policies and that the state should match the additional funds raised with an equal contribution from the Exchequer.[12] This at least possessed the virtues of simplicity, directness and a rapid top-up capability. But once again it failed to raise an official echo. In February 1938, three MPs wrote to *The Times* suggesting no answers but defining the questions 'so as to encourage the attention of the public', and, by implication, force some official response.[13] Stanley, who had succeeded Runciman at the Board of Trade, did at least seem willing in the latter part of 1937 to give the matter more positive consideration, and to ponder in peacetime what the state might do in war. Early in 1938, the Board began collecting statistics of total fire liability and passed them to the Treasury in March. Among the

[10] Elderton, *The Impossibility of War Risk Insurance*, p. 15.
[11] *The Times*, 2 and 5 November 1937. [12] *Post Magazine*, 20 November 1937.
[13] George Mitcheson, Herbert Williams and A. R. Wise to *The Times*, 1 February 1938.

proposals said to be reviewed favourably by the Treasury was the idea of a government compensation scheme funded by an increase in Schedule A income tax.

The building societies threw their weight behind this option. Sir Enoch Hill, president of the Halifax, argued that 'it is difficult to see how the Government could withhold from the nation this extremely important measure of assistance', while the managing director of the Burnley thought the risk so enormous that 'it must inevitably be a Government affair. No-one else could dare accept it'. By August 1938, those arguing this line had calculated the necessary increase in Schedule A at 4s 6d per £100 of insured property.[14] But, at the same time, City opinion took a different tack. There, the *Financial News* reported, at the end of September, that 'quarters believed to be closely connected with the insurance world' were discussing a simple form of war insurance which would leave the initiative with the offices: this returned to the idea of a compulsory surcharge on all existing fire policies and, at an additional 2 shillings per £100 insured, a sizeable one. Such a scheme would yield £100 million annually.[15]

As the numbers became more exact, the columns of the newspapers began to reverberate with the views of four major lobbies: theorists against empiricists; statists against marketeers. Theorists took the technical line: no rate of premium could amass a sufficient anti-bombing fund; anticipative war insurance was impossible. Empiricists argued that any funds were better than none. Statists accepted that war insurance was impossible and took that to mean that government must shoulder the responsibility for *compensation*. Marketeers tried to reserve a position for the insurance industry, even within an impossible sector of business. The issue of insurance against bombing stood at an important point in the larger debates of the 1930s, concerning war and peace, state and private responsibility. Since the issue concerned the homes of the nation, it was no insignificant matter in the social history of the 1930s.

It was logical that some of the most sensitively composed solutions to such tangled questions should feature a mixture of state and private responses. This was the case with the Yorkshire proposal for a policy surcharge and Treasury subsidy in November 1937. And it was true also of a plan from the Corporation of Insurance Brokers in May 1939. This defined a place for the offices: they were to underwrite the risk, issue the policies and save the government the administrative burden of running the scheme – but they were to retain a line in the insurance transaction.

[14] The *Telegraph*, 19 August 1938. [15] The *Financial News*, 24 September 1938.

However, the balance, and by implication the majority, was to be underwritten (*not* reinsured) by the state.[16]

By May 1939, the government had produced its own proposals; but they were not found convincing. The British government had given 'a general undertaking' to assess war damage immediately and then to pay 'compensation on whatever scale can be afforded after the cessation of hostilities'. This was widely perceived as excessively indistinct. The notion of what could be 'afforded' – perhaps nothing? – after the war, gave little reassurance. The claimant was left in suspense until the war was over. The lack of immediate compensation could produce great hardship. *The Times* City Notes summed up the general feeling that the best the government had proposed still 'leaves too much room for doubt and temporary difficulty'.[17] It was not until August 1939, that the government applied a war risks insurance scheme to stocks of goods in the United Kingdom[18] and not until December that it faced the problem that had been worrying the public for years and promised to pay compensation for war damage to private property. This was to be a guaranteed reimbursement, but, even then, only at the end of the war.

Comprehensive state action in regard to war insurance was again late. Only in 1941 did the War Damage Act lay out a full official structure of compulsory insurance for buildings and voluntary insurance for business plant and equipment and private chattels. The companies acted as agents for the government in the 'selling' of this scheme to the public and eventually issued some 18 million policies and collected over £300 million in premiums. Clearly, the bomber was not only a strategic threat; governments faced up to its insurance implications only when they had to.

2. THE RETREAT FROM PEACE

Not all the storm clouds which gathered over the insurance business of the 1930s contained attack aircraft. Plenty of other threats existed among the harbingers of war which were massing on the horizon. Some of these were obviously menacing, others more unexpected.

The activities of the lesser totalitarian regimes of Italy, Spain and Japan caused problems more or less consistently throughout the decade, most often for the marine sector, which, logically enough, was the first of the insurance markets to register any interruption to international stability. The invasion of Abyssinia by Italy in 1935 increased the possibility of war

[16] *The Times*, 24 May 1939. [17] *Ibid.*

[18] The War Risks Insurance Act also embraced marine risks within a system similar to that employed in the First World War (but see pp. 838–43 below).

losses to shipping for all carriers. Underwriters responded by introducing a short cancellation notice, allowing an adequate war risks premium to be charged for any sailing, after the expiry of a 48-hour period of notice. Shipowners reacted by inserting clauses in their contracts of affreightment allowing them to discharge, divert or postpone threatened cargoes; and the insurers agreed to provide cover in such cases. Introduced to deal with an Italian crisis, such measures remained necessary as a result of the Spanish Civil War, with British insurers particularly afflicted in 1936 and 1937 by the 'situation in the Mediterranean'.[19] The short cancellation notice on marine business certainly harmed trade and was not disposed of until 1938 when a peacetime war risks pool was established and given the backing of government indemnity for king's enemy risks. The Phoenix chairman was pleased with this in his last Annual Report of the interwar era, but he still detected major problems in marine business, protesting against the recent habit of transporting huge amounts of bullion in single ocean liners. He failed to see – or perhaps to mention – that this was in itself a sign of crisis.[20]

The conflict in Spain also entailed problems outside the marine sector. Under conventional fire policies – which excluded risks from war and civil commotion – and under the Spanish Commercial Code, no liability attached to ordinary property insurance as a result of war damage. But Phoenix, along with other offices, had extended some fire policies to cover riot and civil disturbance and had issued some special policies to cover pillage and destruction arising from riot. In 1937, the company was clear that it was free of most liability on its Spanish business but unclear as to how much remained.[21] The answer proved to be more than enough. Fire business ran exceedingly well until heavy losses under full riot cover during the Civil War created a serious claims position. Phoenix Group income from Spain had been £60,860 in 1935; by 1938, it was £15,927. The unsatisfactory outcome in Spain was entirely accounted for by the heavy 'motin' claims which occurred during the Civil War.[22]

After the Sun and the Northern, Phoenix had been the largest UK fire insurer in Spain, mainly of industrial properties. The difficulties which befell this business proved too much for Phoenix's manager of twenty-eight years, F. Ferrer Romagnera, who had suffered 'heavy mental and

[19] Phoenix Chairman's Annual Report, 26 May 1936 and 26 May 1937.

[20] *Ibid.*, 25 May 1939. [21] *Ibid.*, 26 May 1937.

[22] 'Motin' claims are riot claims. In 1935 alone they produced an adverse balance on the fire account of well over £100,000. Phoenix Victory Committee, pp. 139–143, and Statement 4.

physical stress since 1936', in circumstances that were 'both difficult and dangerous'.[23] Edward Ferguson was sent to Spain in the summer of 1939 to arrange leave and retirement for Romagnera and his replacement by Manuel Parages Diego-Madrazo. A general reassessment of Phoenix's operation in Spain resulted in a switch not only of managers but also Head Offices. Phoenix moved from Barcelona to Madrid. The Civil War thoroughly overturned Phoenix's business in Spain.

Notoriously a practice-ground for the military elites of Fascist Italy and Germany, the Spanish conflict actually did its worst damage to British insurers by way of riot. Nearer home, in the late 1930s, it was the drive for rearmament against the Fascist military threat in western Europe, that alarmed fire insurers. This was one of the less obvious implications of increasing war-readiness. The basis of the British rearmament drive in industry after 1936 was the much-applauded 'shadow factory', set up well ahead of demand and maintained as an industrial reserve until the European crisis brought them into accelerated production. They did much to resolve one of the perennial problems of twentieth-century market economies: how to sustain in peacetime the scale of defence industry that will be needed in the next war. This was achieved much more effectively in Britain during the 1930s than during the 1910s.[24]

However, the rearmament programme did not win much applause from insurers. No doubt, they recognised the necessity as citizens, but, as underwriters, rearmament gave them problems. For one thing, insurers set ceilings for the amount of industrial capacity they wished to insure in any given sector. A sudden accretion of new industrial capacity would not fit within these ceilings. For another, rearmament gathered together hugely increased values of raw materials and machines, pushing up the cover needed by workshops and factories. Indeed, it took so much of these items that it increased the costs of another type of insurance: the bills for repairs to merchant ships went up by 35–40% in 1938 alone because of the competing demand for materials from armament producers. And marine insurers had to pay them. Finally, the very pace of rearmament work raised the level of industrial risk. One unpredicted consequence of rearmament, therefore, was that it greatly increased the amount of reinsurance on industrial business, as the offices strove to lay off unwanted additional risks within the sector.

This did not exhaust the irony of the rearmament economy for the

[23] Directors' Minutes, 39, pp. 202–3 , 28 June 1939.

[24] C. Trebilcock, 'Industrial Mobilization in wartime: 1899 and 1914', in J. M. Winter (ed.), *War and Economic Development* (Cambridge, 1975).

insurance offices: having scraped together the cover for it, they found that they were required to pay twice over for the privilege. The National Defence contribution of the late 1930s was levied not only on the profits of the insurance companies but also on their interest earnings. Many non-financial ventures in manufacturing or commerce held investments as securities, but they were not taxed on the income from these. Once war broke out, the insurers buckled to in silence and paid their expensive way. But in the interlude before, they wondered, not unreasonably, 'why they should be singled out for adverse treatment.'[25]

Not only the preparation of factories but the preparation of men for war caused problems. In October 1938 – after an ominous donation to the Mansion House Fund for the Relief of Distress in Czechoslovakia (for the map of corporate charity followed that of diplomatic crisis)[26] – the Phoenix Board considered what to do about those of its staff who were in the Territorial Army. Twenty-six of them had already been called up by 5 October. However, after Britain and France capitulated at the Munich Conference in 1938, and handed the western half of Czechoslovakia to Hitler,[27] the Board, like most of Europe, succumbed to the illusion of 'Peace in our Time'. 'In view of the fact that the declaration of a state of National Emergency seems no longer to be imminent', they decided, 'all such members of staff (should) be paid full salary during the period of their mobilization and that their posts be kept open until they are free to return to their office duties'. In the 'unlikely event' of their not having been demobilised by the end of the month, the Board would have to think again.[28]

It was in this sense of relief that Managing Director Sketch set out in October 1938 upon a six-month tour of the world in the company's interests and was wished, 'in the name of the Directors God-speed'.[29]

Long before Sketch returned to Europe, relief had departed from it. By the end of January 1939, the Prime Minister was asking for volunteers for National Service. The Phoenix Board decided that it would 'encourage' male staff to participate. The incentive was that any member who joined one of the 'Auxiliary Fighting Services' would have his place in the office kept open for him, and, in the event of his being called up for full-time service, the company would top up his military pay to his Phoenix salary level.[30] By June 1939, the numbers of staff undergoing military training in peacetime, and the different schemes under which they were doing it –

[25] Chairman's Annual Report, 25 May 1938. And see above p. 528.
[26] Directors' Minutes, 39, p. 87, 12 October 1938.
[27] He took the rest by force in March 1939.
[28] Directors' Minutes, 39, p. 85, 5 October 1938. [29] *Ibid.*, p. 91, 19 October 1938.
[30] *Ibid.*, p. 130, 1 February 1939.

problems which had not appeared at all before the First World War – were causing headaches for managers. Even before hostilities commenced, Phoenix had to cater for three different types of military service. Those who volunteered before February 1939 – or with the company's permission since – were to get full salary on top of military pay, if they were away for no more than a month. If the period of service was longer, the top-up system would come into play, and the army pay would be made up to the office salary point. If, in the third place, the staff member elected to go off for the six-month-long period of full militia training, the absence would not be remunerated but the time would be counted towards Phoenix service and a bonus of one month's salary would be paid on return.[31] Such schemes were complex and costly to administer and took place amidst a general context of pessimism and uncertainty.

Even after Hitler ended uncertainty on 1 September 1939 by invading Poland, business circumstances of great intricacy prevailed as economies tried to cope with the awkward transitions of mobilisation. Certainly, the flow of painful financial ironies continued as the practices of peacetime persisted yet increasingly collided with the advancing frontiers of Occupied Europe. Thus, in many countries, the depreciation of investments in the early stages of conflict, as confidence plummeted worldwide, brought about a devaluation of the insurance guarantees which government authorities required foreign offices to maintain. To make good these losses of value, Phoenix, in company with many other offices, was called upon to *increase* its deposits in many overseas markets. Early in 1940, these included Portugal, South Africa and the USA. But, unfortunately, in January and February, they also included Denmark and Holland.[32] By April 1940, Denmark (along with Norway), and by mid-May Holland (along with Belgium and Luxembourg), also belonged to Hitler, and British insurance deposits were no longer relevant in such places. For the insurance offices, the increased deposits of early 1940 formed one of the less well-timed costs of the 'phoney war' period.

Almost the last public statement by a senior Phoenix official in peacetime also contained a deep irony. In his Annual Report of May 1939, Chairman Walters spent some lines expanding upon 'this age of rapid travel'. In 1811, he mused, poor old Thomas Richter had consumed two months in visiting the Phoenix agencies in Scotland and northern England, whereas in 1939, senior officials, like Sketch, could be despatched anywhere in the world in days: 'Today, by aeroplane, Australia is within

[31] *Ibid.*, p. 192, 14 June 1939.
[32] Phoenix Emergency Committee, pp. 30, 37, 44, 45, 50, 31 January, 28 February, 27 March, 24 April 1940.

ten days' reach of England'.[33] The irony was, of course, that England was also within a few hours' reach of other places, and that the Wehrmacht and the Luftwaffe were about to give Europe its sharpest ever lesson in how technology had contracted distance.

3. THE PHOENIX AT WAR

Hitler entered the Second World War gradually, by stages. This was primarily because he did not intend a big war, or at least no big war in 1939 or 1940. The strategy of blitzkrieg was intended to unleash a limited amount of precisely tailored armament against one enemy, snatch victory by the lightning strike, then regroup, generate another set of armament, tailored for the next enemy, then mount another strike, and so on. It was a strategy for inadequate resources. Hitler's miscalculation was that other countries, in the end, were not prepared to grant him the necessary breathing spaces. So by way of political error, sustained by superb generalship, his limited wars turned by degrees into the big war which his best advisers realised Germany did not have the resources to fight.

Phoenix, by contrast, went to war at the double. Just as Hitler prepared to invade Poland, on 30 August 1939, Managing Director Sketch, now returned from his travels, told the Board that, in the light of the acuteness of the emergency, he had, without their sanction, taken steps for the evacuation of large sections of the Head Office organisation to places well removed from the City. The life, accounts and fire reinsurance departments were to go to Brighton, the marine department to Uxbridge and the central supplies department to Morden. Exposed branches were also to move: Hull was to go to Hessle, North London to Ruislip.[34] Similar rapid redeployments were made by other major City offices in the weeks immediately before and after the Polish crisis.[35]

Sketch expected such disruption that directors would not be available to sign cheques; so certain senior officials were empowered to do this. Equally, under bombardment, it might not be possible to contact the chairman or deputy chairman for the transaction of urgent business; so the managing director was empowered to act in concert with one or more of an Emergency Committee to be composed of the chairman and his deputy, Sir John Caulcutt, D'Arcy Cooper, Lord Ebbisham and Granville Tyzer.[36] In order to minimise dangerous gatherings of directors in vulnerable

[33] Chairman's Annual Report, 25 May 1939.
[34] Directors' Minutes, 39, p. 218, 30 August 1939.
[35] See Supple, *Royal Exchange Assurance*, p. 514 on the REA's equally prompt battle plan.
[36] Directors' Minutes, 39, pp. 225, 233, 13 and 27 September 1939.

locations, the Board would meet only monthly during hostilities, taking fire and life, accident and marine business at alternate sittings. Ironically, it was decided to revert to fortnightly sessions towards the end of the 'phoney war' period just as City locations began to become really dangerous.[37]

What is striking here is the complete absence of a wait-and-see attitude. In contrast to the First World War, there was no false optimism. The worst was expected and action was immediate. No doubt, the threat from the air and the publicity it had received had much to do with this.

Phoenix men (and women) also joined up rapidly. By May 1940, Sketch now reported as chairman that 261 Phoenix staff were already in uniform. At the end of 1941 the first casualties were recorded: six dead, three missing, seven captured. It was a sign of the times that they were reported by Sketch in a Chairman's Annual Statement, circulated to shareholders, rather than in the usual Speech, since for safety reasons, the Annual General Meetings from 1942 to the end of the war were kept to the minimum of formalities and participants.

A year later, the company's death toll had doubled. But at the end of 1943, against sixteen dead, one missing and eighteen in German camps, Phoenix had 847 men and 117 women in the services. By the last year of the war, some 52% of the Phoenix's pre-war male staff, and – a striking contrast with the First World War – about 19% of the pre-war female staff had served in the forces. There were in 1944, only nineteen Phoenix men under the age of thirty who had not served and eight of those were Irish. The join-up rate was very high, which one confidential record judged was 'to be expected in a Staff such as ours where the standard of fitness . . . was so high'.[38] At least the staff had shaken off the fevers and agues of the pre-1914 years. Twentieth-century levels of income, wealth and welfare left high proportions of the middle class fit to wage war.

Since they left with such alacrity and in such numbers, Phoenix had to decide quickly how to pay them. However, the company was helped in this both by its dealings with reservists before the Polish Crisis and by its experience in the First World War. On the outbreak of war, the Board decided that all married male staff under thirty years of age who had enlisted before 1 September 1939, or enlisted since with permission, or who had been called up by the state, should receive a stipend sufficient to make their service pay up to the level of their Phoenix salary. Single men, as in the First World War, would get half Phoenix pay on top of their

[37] *Ibid.*, p. 233, 27 September 1939; *ibid.*, p. 280, 8 May 1940.

[38] Phoenix Special Committee, Book 3, p. 40, December 1944. The REA recorded a very similar participation rate with 55% of the male staff of 1939 joining the services. Supple, *Royal Exchange Assurance*, p. 514.

Army pay, unless they were commissioned, in which case, they would be treated on the more generous scale allowed to married men.[39] Their Phoenix jobs would be kept open for all categories. When, in autumn 1940, the government granted additional pay allowances to servicemen, Phoenix ensured, as in the First World War, that the increases were disregarded in the company scheme and thus did feed through to the troops. A similar system was employed for those who were called up but re-routed by the government to war work outside the armed services. One distinguished exception was Dr David Heron, secretary of the LGA, and assistant secretary of Phoenix, whose numerical skills were such that, 'at the urgent request of H.M.Treasury', he was hauled off to be the Director of Statistics at the Ministry of Food. Since he was nearly sixty, and not within the age bracket Phoenix had considered for war work, he was retired on full pension.[40]

One other, much larger, case could not be managed under the Great War formula: enlisted women. From early 1942, the company decided to treat them on a footing with single men: service pay plus half Phoenix pay, unless they achieved commissioned rank, in which case they, like single male officers, would be treated like married men. Woe betide them, however, if they themselves married while in the services. Here the standards of the day obtruded powerfully: 'in the event of any member of the Ordinary Female staff marrying while absent from the Company on National Service, her engagement with the Company, and her (war) benefit under the terms of this Resolution shall automatically be terminated'.[41] If they wished to be paid, and keep their jobs, women were required to fight Hitler uncomforted.

But, while many Phoenix people found themselves rapidly transported to a fighting role, war was waged with equal swiftness directly against the Phoenix. The company set aside some £50,000 per year in the early part of the war for defences against air attack. But Phoenix was not fortunate. Unlike the REA, whose premises emerged largely unscathed from the Blitz, Phoenix experienced at first hand just how lethal the air weapon could be.

Once Hitler had completed the mopping up of the Low Countries and most of France, he turned the first bombers against London on 7 September 1940. Within one month, on Monday 7 October, Phoenix's brand new branch at Croydon had taken a direct hit and was entirely destroyed.[42] Within four months, on 29 December 1940, Head Office in

[39] Directors' Minutes, 39, pp. 226–7, 13 September 1939.
[40] Phoenix Secret Minutes, p. 85, 26 March 1941.
[41] Directors' Minutes, 39. p. 451, 4 March 1942.
[42] *Ibid.*, p. 312, 9 October 1940.

King William Street was devastated by a large high explosive bomb, which fell in Sherborne Lane killing its nightwatchman. The company's shelters were entirely untouched, but the unfortunate watchman had left them to fetch his slippers just as the bomb exploded.[43] On a separate occasion, Phoenix House was hit again, but to a lesser extent. By contrast, in May 1941, the London Marine office in Fenchurch Avenue was totally destroyed. As well as the Croydon Branch, Phoenix suffered total losses to regional centres in Exeter, Portsmouth and Swansea.[44]

Despite its great strength, damage to the King William Street headquarters was extensive. Although Phoenix proudly boasted, like other famous London establishments, that, throughout the duration of the war, it was never closed to the public even for one hour, the attack of December 1940 put much of Head Office out of action. A large hole was blown in the outside wall, on the Sherborne Lane side, and the fire manager's and the city manager's rooms completely wrecked.[45] Reconstruction was rapid. Urgent rebuilding had rendered some parts inhabitable by mid-January 1941, and by the first week of February about half of the building was fully operational. However, even in 1945 some 20% was still unusable, including the boardroom floor, which had taken some of the worst damage, and, even after the end of the war, the chairman was still circulating his Annual Statements because Phoenix had nowhere to hold a proper Annual General Meeting.[46]

Interruption to business was not as serious as it could have been because of the evacuation of several departments in 1939. And the City Branch could be moved, after a small delay, and 'after consideration of various districts, having regard to the possibility of further air raids' to Northgate House, Moorgate.[47] For the rest, the City rallied around a stricken friend, and the Phoenix directors with positions in other parts of the City came up trumps. Thanks to Sir John Caulcutt, the directors of Barclays, Dominion, Colonial and Overseas put their boardroom and luncheon room at the disposal of the Phoenix Board, and the directors met, and lunched, there throughout January 1941. Similarly, Granville Tyzer of Lazards offered a floor of his bank to house the City Branch of Phoenix until it could be moved to Moorgate.[48]

In terms of physical circumstances, therefore, the introductory stages of the Second World War were definitely harrowing for the Phoenix.

[43] Sketch to Tryon, 21 January 1941. [44] Chairman's Annual Report 1945.
[45] Sketch to Tryon, 21 January 1941. [46] *Ibid.*
[47] Directors' Minutes, 39, p. 331, 1 January 1941. [48] *Ibid.*

Before the "Incident."

After the "Incident."

Plate 11.2 The Croydon Branch, before and after the Blitz.

Blast effects on third floor.

Plate 11.3 The singeing of the Phoenix: bomb damage at Phoenix House.

4. BUSINESS AND WAR

In the Second World War, no one expected that business would be as usual. Phoenix in particular believed that its commercial experience was likely to be quite as unpleasant as its firsthand experience of enemy attack. Initial indicators did little to dispel such impressions. By June 1940, German operations on the Continent had cut swathes through important Phoenix markets and Sketch reported to the Board that Phoenix activities had been seriously affected 'as a result of the invasion of Norway, Denmark, Holland and Belgium'.[49] In fire income alone markets which had

[49] Directors' Minutes, 39. p. 286, 5 June 1940.

averaged a premium return of well over £0.25 million per year between 1929 and 1938 were lost at a stroke, while the operations of the Japanese, both during the 1930s and in 1941–2, killed off demand worth about another £0.2 million per year. The fall in Phoenix fire premiums in 1942, the only war year to see such a decrease, was almost solely due to Japan's sweep through the Far East to its westernmost limit in Sumatra and Burma.[50] And by now fire was not the only valuable element in long-distance trade: accident business represented 86.5% of Phoenix non-life earnings from Denmark 1929–38, 78.3% for Norway and 26.2% for France, while marine accounted for 33.6% of total non-life earnings from France, 29.6% from Holland, 45.8% from the Dutch East Indies and 65.2% from French Indo-China.

Damage was not restricted to direct premium income. In 1940, a special reserve of £200,000 was set aside to cover contingency losses in occupied territories and all assets in such lands were written off, at a net loss of over £0.3 million.[51] Even more damaging to everyday transaction of business was that Germany's control over various centres of insurance expertise had jeopardised Phoenix's worldwide reinsurance arrangements and deprived the company of an important part of its protective screen of accepting offices. The result was that Phoenix had to accept more business for its own net account – and thus occupy a more exposed underwriting position.[52]

In view of this destruction of trade, General Manager Ferguson in July 1940 ordered the preparation of emergency estimates, 'with the object of obtaining some indication as to the underwriting results of the fire, accident and marine departments for the six months ending 30 June 1940'.[53] To some surprise, they turned out rather satisfactorily, the first indication that, as in the First World War, major episodes of human conflict may not necessarily prove bad for insurance business.

One suggestion as to why that might be for the Phoenix had already been recorded in the estimated fire and accident results from the USA for 1939. 'The favourable effect that these would produce on the total underwriting results for the year' had been detected in February 1940. Wartime business was to depend heavily upon expanded economic activity in the United States and Britain, and upon inflation in both markets, rather than upon the global spread of the company's peacetime strategy. Except for 1942, fire business would advance. Accident business would contract in some sectors, primarily in motor insurance due to

[50] Chairman's Annual Report, 1942.
[51] *Ibid.*, 1943. [52] Emergency Committee Minutes, p. 55, 22 May 1940.
[53] Directors' Minutes, 39, p. 300, 31 July 1940.

Table 11.1. *Phoenix Assurance: main business indicators, 1939–44 (current £)*

	1939	1944
Fire premiums	2,768,159	3,829,041
Accident premiums	3,781,822	4,057,930
Marine premiums	908,316	1,824,215
Life premiums	1,384,114	1,361,296
Total premiums	8,842,411	11,072,482
Interest income[a]	554,624	604,101
Total assets	38,374,766	46,149,883

Note: [a] Excludes life and sinking fund.

the constraints placed by war on private transport, but expand in others, like employers' liability, due to the demand generated by wartime full employment. Life business would move into limbo, if not into loss. Marine business would experience a second good war. Investment would be concentrated heavily in government war stock, as in the First World War, and it would earn low interest rates, as the state fought the war on a cheap money footing; but there would be some international compensations not available in the earlier conflict. Taxation would again cut deeply into insurance profits.

In his Chairman's Annual Report for 1944, Sketch reviewed the surprising business out-turn for five complete years of war. 'At the outbreak of war', he wrote, 'there would have been very few people who would have dared to be optimistic enough to prognosticate anything approaching such progress as is shown by these impressive figures'.[54] His figures are shown in Table 11.1.

Thus, two World Wars, the greatest disruptions in human affairs of the twentieth century, had failed to disturb the onward march of insurance income. This encouraged Sketch to a little historical research of his own: in his Report for 1945, he assessed the performance of Phoenix income in *every* major war of its long career. The average annual increase in premium income had been: in the Napoleonic War, 3%; in the Crimean War, 4%; in the Boer War, 7%; in the First World War, 9%; in the Second World War, 6%.

He attributed this to wartime price inflation and also to war production, which competed for goods usually earmarked for construction or

[54] Chairman's Annual Report, 1944.

Table 11.2. *Phoenix Assurance: profits on fire and accident business, 1939–44, (% premiums)*

	Fire	Accident
1939	7.3	8.7
1940	1.9	8.3
1941	4.5	6.6
1942	9.2	10.2
1943	7.6	11.3
1944	3.8	11.8

consumption, and thus drove up the values of the stocks which manufacturers needed to insure. This was not all there was to it; but he had perceived part of the truth. However, inflation pushed up claims values as well as insured values, and would not readily explain, especially in a time of depressed investment yields, the notable buoyancy of insurance profits.

The average annual rate of profit for fire had been 9.6% in the pre-war years 1935–8 and 6.0% for accident in the period 1935–9. As in the First World War, insurance profits proved surprisingly resistant to enemy action.

However, in a sense, it did not matter how profitable Phoenix and the other insurers were in wartime, since their shareholders saw little benefit from it: whatever the offices earned, the state took the great bulk of it for the war effort.

Between 1939 and 1944, the Phoenix paid out a total of £6.2 million in taxation to governments, about £1.75 million of this going to Dominion and foreign states and the rest to Whitehall. This contrasted starkly with the £1.6 million distributed in dividends to Phoenix shareholders over the same period. Sketch, echoing Hamilton's refrain of the Great War, argued that Phoenix proprietors 'could legitimately claim to have played their full part in supplying finance for the sinews of war, while deriving no increased benefit from our activities and efforts'.[55] Nevertheless, the Phoenix dividend was *maintained* throughout the conflict at its now customary level of 12 shillings per share. This surpassed the return to

[55] *Ibid.* This was graphically demonstrated in 1942 when the company made an underwriting profit of £834,034 but then immediately lost £800,000 of it to UK income tax and £400,000 more to Dominion and foreign taxes, then was assessed for a further £240,000 on the life funds by the British fiscal authorities (*ibid.*, 1942).

shareholders in the first global conflict;[56] the proprietors could scarcely complain at the equilibrium displayed among the bombs and the shells by Phoenix distributed profits.

Taxation was not the only way in which Phoenix's business effort made a direct contribution to the war effort. Indeed, at one point it looked as if that contribution might be all too direct. In early 1941, there were strong press suggestions that it could become necessary for British companies with large US shareholdings to sell them in order to pay for orders for war material contracted in dollars. As a sector prominent in American trade, the insurance industry was an obvious source for such dollar earnings. As an office prominent among UK insurance operators in the USA, Phoenix stood to surrender a considerable fortune.

A special committee of the most affected offices was formed, including General Manager Ferguson among its membership. The Committee held worried discussions with the Governor of the Bank of England in February 1941. The Governor advised that the offices should not attempt to present a case to the Chancellor of the Exchequer, and argued, rather ominously, that the only way to get the issue 'properly ventilated' was to seek an interview with the Prime Minister.[57] Meanwhile, rather quieter forces were at work. Another Phoenix man, the director D'Arcy Cooper, was asked by the government to review the situation of British companies in the USA. His reports calmed excited spirits. By March the British Insurance Association had 'received indications . . . that it was in the best interests of the Insurance Companies not to precipitate matters at the present time'.[58]

It was as well they did not for the government and its advisers came up with a much more subtle device that avoided the cashing in of valuable business assets. Instead, in order to meet the cost of orders placed in the USA, prior to the commencement of the Lend Lease Scheme, the British government raised a loan of $425 million from the Reconstruction Finance Corporation, an agency of the US government. A major part of the collateral for this loan came from the shares of UK insurance subsidiaries in the USA and the net income of their branches, both of which were pledged as security. The revenue from the shares and the premium income combined to service the loan, while, back in Britain, the insurers received from the British government the sterling equivalent of the dividends and profits earned by their companies across the Atlantic. This was a bright idea which provided the necessary dollar credits for the war effort

[56] See above pp. 370–1. [57] Directors' Minutes, 39, p. 342, 12 February 1941.

[58] *Ibid.*, p. 353, 12 March 1941. D'Arcy Cooper received a baronetcy in June 1941, partly in recognition of this service; but he died in December 1941.

without wiping out the instruments for future British invisible exports to the USA.[59]

In fulfilment of these terms, Phoenix in August 1941 transferred $3.4 million worth of shares in its American subsidiaries as a loan to the British government.[60] By the end of 1945, Phoenix had made available to the Treasury by remittances from its US branches, dividends on shares and sales of dollars from its London Marine dollar account, a grand total of $13.1 million.[61] British purchases of munitions and equipment from the USA were essential to the Allied war effort and the insurance sector's contribution to the financing of these transactions was no small matter.

A more conventional way of promoting the war, as in the First World War, was to use the City's huge investing capacity to soak up repeated issues of government War Loans. The BIA resolved in the summer of 1940 that, 'the Companies should undertake to utilise to the greatest possible extent all their available resources in subscribing for any new War Loans which the British Government may decide to issue'.[62] And, despite the low yield on such stock, under the cheap money regime, the companies forsook the prospects of better returns and bought the government's paper in wads. Phoenix, like the most socially responsible of the offices, effectively put all new money into government stock for the duration of the war.[63] The insurance industry as a whole increased the share of total assets dedicated to UK government stock from 21% in 1937 to 36% in 1946, achieving a total holding of over £1,000 million by the latter date. Phoenix increased its portfolio share in UK official paper from 26.5% of the aggregated fire and life funds in 1937 to 44.0% by 1946.[64] And, on top of this, there was very substantial buying of American government stock, which accounted for the bulk of foreign official holdings and took the share of this category in the aggregate portfolio from 13.9% in 1937 to 18.4% in 1946. By any standards, the Phoenix was a more than averagely dutiful supporter of British and Allied government war debt.

Between the outbreak of war and the end of 1941, Phoenix had purchased £3 million worth of new UK government issues, and by the end of 1945 £10 million. The movements are shown in Table 11.3.

[59] Chairman's Annual Report 1941.

[60] Directors' Minutes, 39, p. 401, 20 August 1941. This package was made up of $993,500 worth of shares in the Columbia Insurance Co., $912,000 of shares in the Imperial Assurance Co., $397,508 of shares in the United Fireman's Insurance Co., and $1.1 million in Phoenix Indemenity Co. capital stock.

[61] *Ibid.*, p. 228, 10 January 1944; *ibid.*, p. 324, 12 December 1945.

[62] *Ibid.*, p. 289, 19 June 1940.

[63] The REA did the same. See Supple, *Royal Exchange Assurance*, p. 518.

[64] Central government issues alone accounted for about 20.2% of the aggregate portfolio in 1940 and about 37.0% in 1945.

Table 11.3. *Phoenix Assurance holdings of UK central government stock, 1940–5 (£m)*

End 1940	6.0
1941	7.5
1942	9.5
1943	11.4
1944	13.4
1945	14.5

Foreign government stock, mostly American, climbed from a value of £4.1 million at the end of 1937 to a shade under £7 million at the end of 1945.

In Sketch's tally of the credits earned by Phoenix for its war work, the list of tax resource, dollar earner and war lender was completed by an organisational facility: administrative agent. Phoenix, like the other big offices, acted as the state's representative in the management of the various war risks insurance schemes for which the UK government took responsibility. The state acted as the insurer of last resort; the companies did the considerable office work on its behalf. The system had been employed in the First World War, primarily for marine work, but its scope in the Second World War was much wider, and the administrative burden commensurably larger. By the end of 1941 the government had issued 1,000 instructions and 300 judgements on how the different schemes were to operate; merely keeping up with the case law was a skill in itself. Mostly the load in Phoenix fell upon the fire department. By December 1941 its staff had issued on the government's behalf some 150,000 war policies, and by the end of 1944 the company had collected over £10 million in premiums against war risks. The economy and the community needed insurance if they were to work in a context of total war. It was proper that the state should assume responsibility for such exceptional risks. But the insurance still had to be delivered to the economy and the community. Here the administrative capacity of the offices was a vital, if not eye-catching, aid to the smooth running of the war machine.

The management of the Phoenix felt the need to emphasise these virtuous aspects of their war work even while hostilities proceeded. As in the First World War, the political currents of war pressed upon the sensitivities of financial capitalists. From 1942 Sketch was affected not only by the need to put his Annual Report to the shareholders in writing but also by a lack of paper to write it on.[65] Nevertheless, in 1943 he still spent space and scarce newsprint on a defence of the company's ability to make profits in wartime. Where Lord George Hamilton in the Great War had defended wartime profits by demonstrating how much tax they paid, Sketch – although he used that tactic as well – found himself facing an altogether more fundamentalist kind of criticism. 'Nowadays', he observed, 'there is a concerted attempt to decry the "profit motive"'; he found that he needed to defend his company from an essentially anti-elitist critique. Insurance profits, he explained, were essential to the security of insurance policy-holders; and that meant the community at large. Similarly, Phoenix shareholders were not 'a few wealthy individuals', but rather numbered, with debenture holders, some 14,000 people, of whom about one-third held less than £350 worth of investment.[66] And in terms of the staff's contribution, the point was made that it was the reduced staff of the great offices – the City's own 'few' – who ran the war risks administration on which the recompense of so many depended. Clearly, the increasingly egalitarian social comment of the war period left an imprint which required the insurers to find a vocabulary of response.

They received a little unexpected help when Lord Mountbatten chose the phoenix as the emblem for all those serving within the remit of the Supreme Commander South-East Asia – and, in a gracious touch, wrote to the company to let them know.[67] Phoenixes, the company could feel, were still appreciated.

5. THE WAR AT SEA, AGAIN

As in the First World War, marine insurance was vital to the supply and survival of an island economy. And, as in that first Great War, the effectiveness of German submarine strategy cost the shippers, the insurers and the economy dear.

In 1941 and 1942, the U-boat offensive, strengthened by the possession of French ports, set out to starve Britain and eliminate the threat of a counter-attack from the west. Admiral Doenitz and his submarines came close to changing the course of world history in these months. They claimed 1,800 Allied vessels destroyed, with just one submarine (Otto Kretschmer's U-99) accounting for forty-four of them. All told, between

[65] However, Phoenix had responded to the national call for waste paper in 1941 by surrendering all transfer deeds for the company's shares and debentures that were more than three years old. Directors' Minutes, 39, p. 430, 10 December 1941.

[66] Chairman's Annual Report, 1943.

[67] Directors' Minutes, 40, p. 136, 7 November 1943.

Plate 11.4 Convoy under attack, 1940.

1939 and 1945, over one-third of a million tons of shipping, with the vital supplies they carried, succumbed to torpedoes or gunfire before they could unload at British quaysides.[68] Phoenix suffered by the U-boats not only as an insurer but at first-hand: early in 1941, the Manager's Reports from Canada and India were lost at sea, just as the Phoenix's US accounts had been in 1918.[69]

As in the earlier duel between U-boat and convoy, the sea insurance risks of the Second World War were so dire that the majority could be shouldered only by a Government War Risks Office, administered by the Board of Trade. However, the state had learned some lessons from its first experience as a marine insurer of last resort. This time, the government was not left with all the dangerous voyages while the offices made a fortune on all the safe ones. A fairer allocation of perils was achieved by a much more careful official definition of what constituted a war risk. The basic formula was that the offices agreed not to quote rates below the government ones for voyages to and from the United Kingdom, but were

[68] Among these were more than 13,500 British-registered vessels.

[69] Special Committee Book 2, p. 208, 21 February 1941. And see above, pp. 388–9.

'free' to choose their own rates for all other routes (some of which, of course, were far from safe).

This was not entirely pleasing to the offices. In 1940, Sketch commented pointedly on the 'substantial amount of British and Neutral War Risk insurance business which the Government War Risks Office does *not* undertake'. He expressed surprise that specifically wartime events such as unlit convoys, blacked-out lighthouses and unaccustomed routes did not automatically classify the great majority of all voyages as official war risks. Surely, he argued, they 'create claims which, to the lay mind, would appear to bring them within the category of war losses'. However, he could only grumble: 'It has, however, been decided otherwise'.[70] The government had successfully moved the channel markers.

Nevertheless, Phoenix continued to manoeuvre cautiously in the seaways left clear of official cover, and did so at enhanced rates. This did not appear to do the marine account much harm. By April 1940, it displayed 'comparatively little evidence of the profound effects of the outbreak of the War'. Premiums were up by £167,000 to £908,000, partly due to the higher rates, partly due to higher demand; but, as yet, higher claims were not compromising the increased income flow.[71]

In 1940, the second largest premium increase of the war was witnessed: a jump of over £0.5 million to £1.44 million; but claims had now moved up to absorb 60% of this. Nevertheless, the overall account was strong and strengthening.[72] Income moved up again to £1.5 million in 1941; but losses were making serious inroads by this time. Full hostilities had now engulfed the Pacific and the Far Eastern seas and warfare had intensified on the eastern seaboard of the United States as the Battle of the Atlantic moved into its most ferocious phase. Nearer home, severe storms added the displeasure of Nature to the depredations of mankind. Moreover, freighters laden to the gunwhales with expensive war stores were vulnerable to the 'accumulation of value' effect which bedevilled many kinds of insurance within the war economy.

In Phoenix's marine market, these effects peaked in 1942. High insured values pushed premiums up by 56% to their wartime zenith of £2.4 million; but losses also moved up to 75%. Nevertheless, the resulting surplus was a 'satisfactory outcome for a year of very great difficulty and anxiety'.[73] The tide of the marine war turned in 1943: Phoenix's premiums fell by 14%, but the profit out-turn was a good deal better than in

[70] Chairman's Annual Report, 29 April 1940. [71] *Ibid.*
[72] Chairman's Annual Report, 1940.
[73] *Ibid.*, 1942.

Plate 11.5 A U-Boat sinks after being rammed by a British destroyer.

the previous year.[74] These economic results reflected the facts of the strategic balance at sea. In May 1943, it was Admiral Doenitz's turn to confront uncomfortably high numbers: he lost forty submarines within the month; even a mass U-boat attack on one Atlantic convoy, deploying 'wolf packs' amounting to fifty vessels, was forced to withdraw. Allied success in the breaking of German codes had led to greater accuracy in the locating of German submarines; and advances in radar technology reinforced this. An improved depth charge gave more kills per shot, while the high shipbuilding rate of American yards and the extending range of RAF and USAF aircraft provided more platforms to shoot from. These advances contained, and then defeated, the most deadly form of marine – and economic – warfare ever contrived.[75] Meanwhile, in the Pacific, American carrier-borne aircraft had shattered Japanese naval power at the Battle of Midway in June 1942, and American submarines then proceeded to wreak on Japanese supply lines the havoc that Doenitz had attempted upon British ones.

In 1944 and 1945, as the threat receded, there were again major downswings in Phoenix marine premiums: by 10.2% to £1.8 million in 1944 and by a further 22% to £1.4 million in 1945. On the other hand, marine surplus remained firm, carrying the accumulated marine fund to

[74] *Ibid.*, 1943. [75] The submarine war cost the German navy 28,000 lives.

Plate 11.6 A Sunderland flying-boat begins an anti-submarine patrol.

over 200% of premium income in 1945. The marine profit of £515,000 was a company record up to that point.[76]

However, in the Second World War marine business did not occupy the dominant position in the Phoenix's business that it had in 1914–18. In the earlier conflict, marine premiums had reached a peak of over 44% of Phoenix total income in 1917 and had averaged nearly 31% for the whole of the war period. In 1939–45, the largest share of group income, within a much more complex multinational company, claimed by marine premiums was the 20.4% of 1942 and the average for the war period was 14.5%. Just as in the First World War, however, war greatly altered the status of the marine department upon the ladder of corporate earnings. In the years between the acquisition of Union Marine and the Great War, marine premiums had averaged about 16% of total group premiums, whereas war took them to nearly one-third of Phoenix's total income. In the depressed marine market of the 1930s, sea-borne earnings occupied only about 7% of group income. In both cases, war about doubled the share of marine earnings within the Phoenix's total income.

By 1944 Sketch was already beginning to look towards marine prospects in the postwar world and to examine what bridges could be built

[76] Chairman's Annual Report, 1944, 1945.

between wartime experience and peacetime expansion. He emphasised the strength of the London marine market in wartime as an advertisement for what could be achieved in a postwar export boom. Since much of this work had been for allies and neutrals, it had formed an 'invisible export of utmost value'.[77] The implication was clear: if Phoenix and its fellows could do this in wartime, they could certainly service the postwar upswing in world trade which, it was devoutly hoped, was on the way. No less clear, however, was the implication that war had in no way impaired Phoenix's capacity to reap this marine harvest when it came. In this, Sketch was to prove correct: marine premiums maintained an improved share of total group income at over 9% for the period 1946–52.

6. FIRE INSURANCE IN THE BLACKOUT

With war damage accepted as a governmental responsibility, Phoenix's fire business during the war was surprisingly buoyant. Many overseas markets were lost or compromised and fire business became still more concentrated on Britain and the USA; but in these big economies conversion of industry to a war production footing created a new staple of demand for the insurance of property and goods.

Phoenix fire premiums experienced powerful expansion throughout the war in most major markets. Table 11.4 reveals that UK fire premiums advanced by 54.6% in the war years 1939–45, North American premiums by 65.9%, and income from the rest of the world, inevitably more affected by enemy action, by 29.7%.[78] Loss of markets in Europe and the Far East largely accounted for the sharp decline in the percentage share of premium income provided by the rest of the world between 1939 and 1942. Correspondingly, there were significant increases in the shares of the United Kingdom and the United States. The increasing dominance of American markets is particularly striking. But even the rest of the world recovered after 1942, in both share and absolute income level. The recapture of occupied areas was a factor in this.

Not only did fire markets grow in wartime, they remained lucrative. If the Phoenix leadership was pleasurably surprised at profits of 2–5% in the early years of the war, they were close to astonished by out-turns of pre-war proportions in 1942 and 1943, the most profitable years of the war, at 9.2% and 7.6%.

[77] *Ibid.*, 1945.

[78] Under war conditions, the main strong points in the rest of the world were Australia, New Zealand, South Africa and Argentina.

Table 11.4. *Phoenix Assurance Group fire premiums by market, 1939–45 (£ and % total)*

	United Kingdom		USA & Canada		Rest of world	
1939	616,705	(22.3%)	1,362,962	(49.2%)	788,492	(28.5%)
1940	705,037	(24.1%)	1,473,987	(50.3%)	749,849	(25.6%)
1941	814,478	(24.5%)	1,751,367	(52.8%)	754,106	(22.7%)
1942	840,095	(25.9%)	1,702,810	(52.5%)	701,038	(21.6%)
1943	906,356	(26.0%)	1,823,932	(52.3%)	755,146	(21.7%)
1944	977,287	(25.5%)	2,000,563	(52.2%)	851,192	(22.2%)
1945	953,363	(22.5%)	2,261,709	(53.4%)	1,022,692	(24.1%)

Source: Phoenix Blue Books, Group Combined Revenue Accounts.

Such results were particularly striking since fire wastage had been historically low during the 1930s, and could not stay low in wartime. Many aspects of the war economy raised the level of wastage, especially in the critical period of industrial mobilisation between 1940 and 1942.[79] Manufacturers were encouraged to take short cuts to increase output; machinery was used for purposes other than its designed function; and all work was conducted at a frantic pace. Nor did blackout precautions assist in the detection of fire. In one case of 1939 (recorded by Phoenix as a cautionary tale), a factory just 100 yards down the street from a fire station was totally gutted because the flames were not visible until they burst through the roof. If blackout blinds prevented bomber pilots from detecting their targets, they also prevented firemen from detecting fires.

War production led not only to more business but also to higher loss rates in both Britain and the USA. These pervaded the full width of the fire market. Small underwriting losses resulted in the USA in 1940 and 1941 and larger ones in 1943–5, while levels of fire damage were particularly high in the United Kingdom in 1940–2. At home, accumulations of war stocks which overflowed available warehouse space produced vast values exposed to a single fire. And the sharp reduction in the world's supply of reinsurance facilities, due to enemy occupation of key insurance centres, increased the impact of such losses on individual UK insurers. Nevertheless, it was in the United States rather than the United Kingdom that a single exceptional blaze did occur. The outbreak at the Fall River rubber works in Massachusetts in 1941, cost the insurers £3 million and

[79] In the less industrially inclined REA, this pattern was not in evidence. Supple comments on low loss ratios and good profit levels throughout the period 1941–4 (Supple, *Royal Exchange Assurance*, p. 517).

Plate 11.7 Buying blackout.

was the biggest fire in the USA since 1914. It was a powerful reminder that war production was a dangerous business even for manufacturers who were secure from air attack.

Enemy action, particularly in the Far East, probably had more impact on premium volume in 1942 than in any other wartime year; but, nevertheless, the fire profits were the best of the war. By comparison, 1943 was a relatively quiet year: fire wastage improved in Britain and worsened in the United States; but fire profits still held up well. Sketch even found the time to warn policy-holders that wartime inflation was probably leaving them under-insured.

Before long, he had other worries on his mind: 1944 was one of those years in which the elements chose to remind humankind that, whatever their efforts at destruction, natural forces will outdo them. Admittedly, the Bombay Explosion of April 1944, perhaps the most destructive chemical reaction outside a war zone, was manmade; but Nature anticipated it with bush fires in Australia in January and followed it with hurricanes in Jamaica and the American Atlantic coast in August and September, while rounding off with a cyclone in Cuba in October. Loss ratios for most major areas outside the United Kingdom were high. It was

Plate 11.8 Propaganda against fire attack.

not surprising that fire profits slumped to 3.8% from the high levels of the two previous years.

Even the return to peace in 1945 was a complicated process in the fire market. Further industrial expansion in Britain and the United States boosted premiums, as did the liberation of occupied territories. But heavy fire wastage continued, especially in the USA. Such loss levels were accepted as part of reconstruction, 'until industry has settled down to a sound peacetime basis and all difficulties of repairs and renewals of plant, necessary through continuous war use, have been overcome'.[80]

So, how, amidst such complex circumstances did Phoenix fire business remain profitable in wartime? Table 11.5 provides some of the answers. The transatlantic markets provided valuable volume, but they did not provide much in the way of wartime profits. Despite the preoccupation of the Phoenix top management with fire wastage in the USA, this was not

[80] Sketch, Chairman's Annual Report, 1945.

Table 11.5. *Phoenix Group fire business: % of premium attributed to claims, commission, management expenses and profit, 1939–45*

	United Kingdom				USA & Canada				Rest of world			
	Claims	Commission	Management expenses	Profit	Claims	Commission	Management expenses	Profit	Claims	Commission	Management expenses	Profit
1939	46.2	11.6	29.6	10.6	40.6	26.3	22.1	3.6	49.1	30.3	6.0	11.1
1940	60.8	12.0	21.4	0.7	44.2	26.9	21.1	−1.7	55.4	26.4	5.2	10.0
1941	56.6	13.5	19.7	4.8	44.4	27.3	18.4	−2.8	39.9	27.4	5.8	21.3
1942	54.3	15.2	21.8	7.5	42.3	26.0	19.8	4.1	38.6	29.7	3.8	23.5
1943	40.8	14.6	20.5	21.0	47.7	26.1	18.4	−4.9	41.3	30.8	2.7	14.7
1944	39.5	15.7	20.6	21.3	50.9	26.2	17.4	−3.8	51.3	30.4	2.7	1.7
1945	46.9	16.3	22.4	15.4	55.0	25.6	16.5	−7.3	49.3	30.7	2.9	5.3

Source: Calculated from Phoenix Blue Books, Combined Fire Revenue Accounts.

in fact particularly bad until the very end of the war. The real trouble in the American markets came from the combination of commission and management costs: US business, as usual, was expensive to acquire. This was so marked that the claims ratio had only to nudge towards 50% for the account to be carried into the red. By contrast, the UK market, even in wartime, could afford a full 10% more on the loss ratio before this occurred.

The Phoenix UK market, like the UK war economy, started modestly but ended strongly. In contrast to the USA and Canada, this had much to do with sharply falling management expenses. These retreated by over 30% between 1939 and the war's low point in 1941.[81] Lower management costs, paired with modest commissions, helped keep the Phoenix profitable even amidst the high claims of 1940–2. When the claims ratio itself fell off from 1943, the UK fire account was able to move strongly into profit.

Even the reduced international spread of the Phoenix in wartime yielded helpful compensatory influences. Although the rest of the world was losing markets to the enemy in the early phases of the war, the exceptionally low management costs of the markets which remained free allowed them to return useful profits, just when the UK market was weakest. By the time the distant markets had hit high claims ratios late in the war, the UK had recovered strength. Not even the Axis war machines could entirely suppress the equilibrating effects of the global span which had long been the Phoenix's preferred scope of action.

Nevertheless, Phoenix fire business in the Second World War became more metropolitan in its concentration on the big Allied war economies, and also more industrial. Time would be needed after the war to re-establish the worldwide spread of risk and for the strain of wartime mobilisation to abate in the metropole. In the meantime, fire profits in the year of victory were 'meagre',[82] in contrast to the 'exceptionally valuable' out-turn from the marine sector, the 'reasonable' result from accident, and the 'eminently satisfactory' conclusion to the war in the life department.[83] However, fire profits managed a distinguished war record, given the turmoil of the world around them. It was ironic that the year of the adjustment to peace produced lower rewards than the years of adjustment to war.

[81] The wartime salary policy of General Manager Ferguson had much to do with this. See below, pp. 866–70.

[82] At 0.9% of total fire premiums, they were the worst of the war, largely due to heavy losses in the USA, incurred as part of the readjustment process.

[83] Chairman's Annual Report, 1945.

7. THE ACCIDENTS OF WAR

Accident business was an area which Phoenix management expected to be adversely affected by war conditions. In particular, they feared the shrinkage of motor insurance business which would follow from restrictions upon petrol supplies and the laying up of many civilian vehicles. Other effects were less foreseen. The pace of war work, which was bad for fire risk, was also bad for worker safety: so the claims side of workers' compensation business became undesirably active. On the other hand, high levels of worker participation boosted the need of industrialists for cover against employer's liability.

The blackout precautions which made it more difficult to perceive internal fires also darkened the streets and increased the risk to those who ventured out after dusk. In 1939, as motorists and pedestrians adjusted to these new conditions, there was an immediate fall in the number of motor policies, both home and foreign, and an immediate rise in the number of traffic fatalities, as the cars still left running collided with the pedestrians walking in the dark. A surprisingly high number of fatal accidents happened to those with Personal Accident policies.[84] The same darkness which put these lives at risk provided the cover for an army of burglars intrepid enough to dodge the bombs and the motorists. So as the cars ran over the pedestrians, the thieves made off with the household goods. Breaking-and-entering offences doubled.[85]

Some of the expected difficulties were clearly apparent by 1940. Total accident premiums declined by over 6% in that year. Undamaged cars were locked away, while damaged ones grew ever more expensive to repair as materials and parts were absorbed in the war effort. Less predictably, workmen's compensation claims rose apace as war contracts asked for rapid completion rates and manufacturers relied on increasingly inexperienced labour to supply them. Nevertheless, the profit outcome for 1940, at 8.3%, was comfortably above the average rate of 6% for the pre-war years 1935–8. Again, in 1941 drastic controls on petrol consumption produced dire predictions as to the effect on accident results. Yet again, such fears did not translate into bad business for the accident operation as a whole. The home market produced a good premium flow – with total accident revenue only just below the level for 1938 – and a good overall claims ratio. Once more, the profit result at 6.6% was above the pre-war average.

[84] Chairman's Annual Report, 29 May 1940.

[85] The image of a community pulling together for victory is somewhat dented by the crime statistics. Recorded crime 1939–45 rose by more than half and the prison population by 42%.

Plate 11.9 Painting a path in the blackout.

For the remainder of the war, accident premiums continued to act erratically. The second slide of the war period occurred in 1942 as the threat to motor business materialised. Nevertheless, profits rose to 10.2%. The motor account continued to slip to its wartime nadir in 1943 and remained below its 1940 level even in 1944 (see Table 11.6). But total accident earnings enjoyed a second bounce in 1943, exceeding that of 1941 in vigour, and in 1944 almost matched the recent peacetime peak of 1937. Profits in 1943 and 1944 ran at record levels of 11.3% and 11.8%. Clearly then, some force within accident business was operating to counter the depressive effects influencing the motor sector.

Primarily, this was the overseas employers' liability and general accident account, which added an annual average in premiums of better than £100,000 to total accident earnings from 1940 to 1945. Much of it was transatlantic business. Liability protection for the industrialists of the US war economy proved bigger business than the domestic equivalent. In this sense, the Phoenix's troubled dealings with the US accident market in the interwar years opened up an unexpected means of compensating for the troubles of the UK accident market in the wartime years.

Plate 11.10 War damage: bus in street.

This effect is revealed more clearly in Table 11.7. While UK accident premiums advanced by only 15.2% in 1939–45, and earnings from the rest of the world by 2.9%, the flow of business from the USA increased by 32.2%.

In accident business, as distinct from fire, the percentage increases in US business were markedly larger than in the United Kingdom and other markets. The increase in the US share of total accident income, from 56.0% in 1939 to the peak of 64.3% in 1944, was also larger than in the fire sector (from 49.2% to a peak of 53.4% in 1945). In both fire and accident business, the United States provided Phoenix's dominant custom; but

Table 11.6. *Phoenix Group: accident business by sector, 1940–5*

	Personal accident	UK employers' liability	Motor	Foreign employer's liability & general accident	Total
1940	166,355	193,763	1,372,029	1,813,016	3,545,104
1941	167,896	239,417	1,455,239	1,990,412	3,852,965
1942	152,805	246,599	1,305,486	2,099,369	3,804,260
1943	156,908	298,195	1,176,216	2,300,902	3,876,207
1944	166,846	282,204	1,286,007	2,322,872	4,057,930
1945	188,447	275,438	1,662,031	2,508,970	4,627,727

American casualty customers were still more dominant than American fire customers. The UK accident share was fairly stable throughout the war; but the rest of the world suffered more severe falls in both absolute income levels and in market share than these markets experienced in their fire business.[86]

However, again unlike fire business in wartime, the accident sector remained almost continuously profitable in all markets. Certainly, the big American account remained in the black throughout the war, unlike its fire counterpart, which was more red than black.

Apart from the low positive out-turns from the United States in 1941 and 1945, and the negative result from the rest of the world in 1945, profits were satisfactory in all markets. Indeed they were rather better than this in the United Kingdom from 1941 onwards. The average annual return on UK accident business 1939–45 was a shade under 14%, while, on a much larger income flow, the US yield was 6.7%, and the rest of the world managed 5.9%.

The main reasons for this seem to have been restrained claims levels in all markets after 1941 and management expenses and commissions in the US accident sector appreciably lower than in the fire sector (see Tables 11.5 and 11.8). Management expenses in the United Kingdom exhibited a downward tendency but not as sharply as in the UK fire operation. Despite, some instability in premium receipts therefore, the wartime profitability of Phoenix's accident side turned out far better than management had feared at the outset.

[86] The peak-to-trough reduction in the rest of the world's accident income was 32.5% against 11.1% for its fire income.

Table 11.7. *Phoenix Group: accident premiums by market, 1938–45, (current £ and % of total)*

	United Kingdom		USA		Rest of world	
	(£)	(%)	(£)	(%)	(£)	(%)
1938	976,540	(25.0)	2,242,185	(57.5)	680,233	(17.4)
1939	943,107	(24.9)	2,119,126	(56.0)	719,590	(19.0)
1940	900,131	(25.4)	2,135,112	(60.3)	509,862	(14.4)
1941	989,680	(25.7)	2,357,497	(61.2)	505,788	(13.1)
1942	928,204	(24.4)	2,390,596	(62.8)	485,461	(12.8)
1943	863,846	(22.3)	2,480,321	(64.0)	532,000	(13.7)
1944	944,426	(23.3)	2,607,969	(64.3)	505,535	(12.5)
1945	1,086,361	(23.5)	2,800,707	(60.5)	740,659	(16.0)

Source: Phoenix Blue Books, Combined Revenue Accounts.

A rare in-house investigation of the specific sources of accident profit in 1944 and 1945 underlined the importance of the US market's combination of bulk and yield (see Table 11.9).

The three biggest contributors to accident profit were home motor and general accident, with 27.1% and 16.0% of the total in 1945, and leading by a mile, US general accident, with a contribution of 45.2% of all Phoenix accident profits by 1945. By contrast the US motor business was barely profitable in 1944 and heavily unprofitable in 1945.

However, as in Phoenix's other insurance markets, the final months of the war and the first months of the peace were confusing times for the accident business. Given the role of employers' liability business in the wartime fortunes of the accident sector, there was a special poignancy in the UK government's expressed intentions for an improved Welfare State for the postwar years. Promises of better employment, education and health provision after the war had been important means of maintaining public morale during the grimmer periods of conflict.[87] But not all of these innovations were good news for the insurers. In 1944 Sketch lamented the coming threat to, and imminent demise of, UK liability business.

He regretted also the canniness of the state's proposals. For had the government simply moved to take from the insurers 'the protection of individual employers of labour, we could undoubtedly have put forward a

[87] See A. Peacock and J. Wiseman, *The Growth of Public Expenditure in the UK, 1850–1950* (London, 1967).

Table 11.8. *Phoenix Group accident business: % of premium attributed to claims, commission, management expenses and profit, 1938–45*

	United Kingdom				USA				Rest of world			
	Claims	Commission	Management expenses	Profit	Claims	Commission	Management expenses	Profit	Claims	Commission	Management expenses	Profit
1938	50.2	9.6	30.5	8.5	51.6	21.9	15.7	8.9	51.6	21.8	18.4	3.4
1939	51.2	9.0	31.2	10.0	49.7	22.4	16.3	9.5	49.0	23.7	17.5	4.8
1940	50.3	8.3	34.6	8.7	52.2	22.1	17.2	5.2	51.7	25.4	15.6	8.3
1941	41.0	8.3	30.7	16.4	52.4	20.9	16.2	1.9	45.0	26.4	14.0	6.7
1942	50.0	8.5	30.7	13.1	43.8	21.6	16.8	9.6	44.2	27.5	14.1	7.2
1943	45.4	8.3	29.4	20.1	45.1	21.1	16.4	8.7	43.9	27.8	11.7	9.6
1944	43.6	8.5	27.9	16.1	42.5	22.0	16.0	10.9	45.5	26.9	13.6	8.5
1945	44.1	9.3	28.1	13.3	53.3	21.3	16.8	1.2	47.6	25.0	15.5	−4.1

Source: Calculated from Phoenix Blue Books, Combined Revenue Accounts.

Table 11.9. *Phoenix Group accident profits by sector, 1944 and 1945*

		Employers' liability	Personal accident	Motor	General accident
1944	UK	3,433	15,555	67,878	65,367
	USA	–	14,686	10,534	259,407
	Rest of world	–	−1,713	−1,094	45,523
1945	UK	34,304	7,230	39,964	23,551
	USA	–	7,801	−56,295	66,632
	Rest of world	–	2,053	5,228	17,043

Source: Phoenix Blue Books, Combined Revenue Accounts, 1944 and 1945.

strong case against the adoption of such a course'. But the government had not offered such an easy target:

> As the announced intention is to release the employer from liability to compensate his employees and create direct National responsibilities for all injuries and illnesses, we can merely record our regret at the elimination of a service which for many years, we have been enabled to render with satisfaction.[88]

Here, the twentieth-century connections between warfare, welfare and capitalism became, from the insurer's viewpoint, somewhat painfully entangled.

Other effects associated with the re-imposition of peace were scarcely less tortuous. In particular, the transition period witnessed powerful increases in both claims and income. The epidemic of burglary and theft which accompanied the blackout put accident claims under severe pressure by the end of the war. At the same time, the triumphant return of the automobile to British roads was ensuring a reversion to 'a more normal', that is, bad, claims ratio in regard to motor insurance. The resumption of communications with previously occupied territories revealed that stored accident claims in such areas were even worse than had been predicted, producing a debit balance on all-enemy held markets of £60,000 for the war period. Had it not been for a special reserve set aside in 1940 against such unknown risks, this too would have caused embarrassment on the claims front.

On the other hand, as in the fire market, the economic upswing in free markets and the re-entry to previously occupied ones brought about a

[88] Chairman's Annual Report, 1944.

substantial rise in income. Not only the retreat of the enemy but the equipment which had forced him to withdraw carried implications for postwar business. By 1945, insurers were already drawing a thoughtful line between the technical advances of the war era and the prospects for expanded underwriting in the postwar period. Thus the huge strides made in aeronautics during the war were perceived correctly to imply major developments in civilian aviation within a few years of its end.[89]

8. LIFE UNDERWRITING IN WORLD WAR

Life assurance did not flourish in war. Once again, however, as in the First World War, this had surprisingly little to do with war deaths. In 1940, death claims included forty-two which were caused by enemy action, but these accounted for only £70,000 of the £763,000 paid out by the life department.[90] An almost identical sum was needed to cope with war mortality in 1942, but the overall Phoenix death rate was lower than for many years. Even including for war deaths, total life losses were less than the mortality tables predicted for ordinary peacetime. Extraordinarily, then, the Phoenix experienced favourable mortality in the middle of the Blitz.

The life managers were as surprised as anyone by this, but they did not expect it to continue. Even though the office seemed to have a good record of insuring social classes other than those most likely to be bombed, it faced a high level of military risk. Sketch lamented in 1942 that 'so many of our younger policy holders are now on active service'.[91] Government statements also encouraged the underwriters towards bleak perspectives and conservative policies. Early in 1942, the Phoenix actuary, W. R. Moore wrote that pessimism was unavoidable 'in view of the repeated statements of our Prime Minister, Cabinet Ministers and Service Commanders that we must still expect invasion and increased bombing'.[92] Yet by the end of 1944, war mortality had cost the company no more than £350,000. This was actually less than the special reserve set aside for war deaths in December 1940.[93]

Where war did hurt the life business was in its impact upon new business and upon interest earnings. A record level of new sums assured

[89] *Ibid.*, 1945.

[90] To the end of 1941, after 28 months of war, which had included some of the worst bombing, Phoenix had encountered 135 'extra' life claims due to military deaths and only 46 civilian war deaths. Total British war deaths for the entire period of the Second World War were 67,000 civilians and 326,000 servicemen and women.

[91] Chairman's Annual Report, 1942.

[92] W. R. Moore, Review of Life Business in War, 16 February 1942.

[93] *Ibid.* That sum was £380,000.

Table 11.10. *Phoenix net new assurances, 1939–45*

1939	3,845,320
1940	2,029,703
1941	1,669,455
1942	1,995,667
1943	2,080,755
1944	2,371,685
1945	2,890,830

Source: Annual Reports and Accounts.

of £4.95 million had been netted in 1938, but the falling away thereafter was precipitous, by about £1 million in 1939 alone. The general manager reported in January 1940 that, 'since the outbreak of the war, life new business has been almost at a standstill'.[94] Nor was there any quick recovery. By the end of 1940, the annual new business was almost half the reduced level of 1939. Only in 1943 did new business clamber back above the level of 1940, and in 1944 and 1945 there were significant advances. But the level of 1945 was still 25% below that of 1939 (see Table 11.10).

There were many factors depressing the demand for assurance. Amidst the uncertainties of war, few individuals were inclined to plan for the future. The numbers of these were reduced still further as conscription ate into the cohorts of assurable age, while, at the same time, the offices lost to the colours the great majority of the life salesmen who had drummed up business before the war. Phoenix also noted that war did not help the better-heeled groups to whom it still looked for its main life custom, or, as Moore put it, the war economy 'reduced the net income available for savings in respect of the class from which our policy holders are mainly drawn'.[95]

It was readings of this kind which disposed the actuary towards a conservative assurance policy for the duration of the war. Phoenix's Quinquennial Life Valuation had been due in December 1940, but, owing to prevailing uncertainties, it was decided to postpone the payment of the reversionary bonus until the end of hostilities.[96] A similarly prudent measure against the possibility of mass deaths by way of wartime catastrophe was the decision at the same time to make no transfer from the life account to the profit and loss account.

[94] Emergency Committee Minutes, p. 19, 3 January 1940.
[95] Moore, Review of Life Business in War.
[96] However, the bonus was paid on policies becoming due by reason of death or maturity.

Table 11.11. *Phoenix Assurance: net yields on life funds, selected years, 1939–45 (%)*

1930	4.68
1939	3.53
1940	3.29
1942	3.00
1943	2.91
1944	2.86

However, when General Manager Ferguson sent Actuary Moore a questionnaire regarding the experience of the first thirty months of war assurance in February 1942, Moore was able to say that all life offices had postponed the reversionary bonus until the fighting stopped. But not all offices were as careful in another respect. Moore had seen what was coming in terms of investment yield far more clearly than many. From early in the war, he had assumed a very conservative return on securities, 1.9% on short-term investments and 2.4% on longer commitments.[97] Yet in 1941, many life offices were still accepting business on the assumption that they could earn a 2.5% return on the *bulk* of their investments. Phoenix's experience with wartime investment yields suggests that this was not a very sensible assumption (see Table 11.11).

These, of course, were the returns on the whole life funds; yields on *new* investments would have been substantially less. War taxes were high and yields on war issues of gilts were low. On top of this, many current policies had been issued at predicted rates of return far higher than the war economy could provide.[98] And so many of Phoenix's competitors found.

Foreseeing reduced investment income, Phoenix had raised premium rates early in the war. Naturally, this did little to attract already scarce new business. Competitors at this stage secured more of it 'at the expense of Companies such as our own which have adopted a more realistic attitude to the problem'.[99] But in 1942 many of these rivals found that the advantages of lower premiums had run out and a group consisting of the REA, the Commercial Union, the Caledonian and the Scottish Union were forced to 'see the error of their ways'[100] and to raise premiums in compensation for the decreasing returns from investments. Two other

[97] A higher yield is obtained on the investments underpinning a whole life policy of 40 or so years in the second half of its span.

[98] Rather piously, Sketch contended that the public would buy life policies not only for personal cover but because the underlying funds were invested, through government stocks, in the war effort. In practice, this probably had little effect on life sales. See Chairman's Annual Report, 1944.

[99] Moore, Review of Life Business.

[100] *Ibid.*

Table 11.12. *Phoenix Assurance: total business by sector, 1932–52 (%)*

	1932–8	1939–45	1946–52
Accident	39.1	35.1	44.0
Fire	29.9	30.2	32.7
Marine	6.8	14.5	9.1
Life	24.2	20.1	16.9

companies, the Eagle Star and the Legal & General, at this time 'fierce competitors', were said also to want higher premiums but neither was prepared to concede before the other. The pressure on rival offices to raise premiums after 1942 no doubt helped Phoenix's stronger performance in the latter part of the war.

The issue of increased premiums and reduced investment yield was a good example of what Moore saw as the central wartime problem for the life assurer: striking a viable balance between 'our development programme and the essential need of security for our policy holders'.[101] He did a good job. By 1943, his chairman was reporting that the Phoenix life department was making 'distinct progress' despite the considerable handicaps of the wartime market place, and two years later its position was 'eminently satisfactory'.[102] When the time came to pay the reversionary bonus on participating policies, which had been postponed in 1940, but was ready for disbursement in 1945, it came in at a handsome 32s 6d for every £100 assured on each year's premiums paid over the entire decade 1936–45. The average rate of bonus over the period 1906–45 had been 33 shillings. World war scarcely deflected it from course.[103]

Nevertheless, if the life bonus resisted the war, the place of life business in the company's overall operation was more affected by it than was the relative position of any other major sector (see Table 11.12).

The wartime losers were clearly life and accident and by similar percentages of total business, but with life getting slightly the worse of it. Fire increased its share of total business, and marine underwent its characteristic wartime expansion. However, marine improved considerably on its 1932–8 performance in the international trade upswing after the war. And both accident and fire increased their shares after 1945, accident strikingly so. However, for the standing of the life department, the war was a

[101] *Ibid.* [102] Chairman's Annual Report, 1943, 1945.

[103] Participating policies terminating by maturity or death between 1941 and 1945 had attracted bonuses of 20 shillings per cent. In 1945 a further retrospective payment of 10 shillings per cent was added to these. Chairman's Annual Report, 1945.

watershed. Its share dipped sharply during the war, but by almost as much in the aftermath. But maybe this was primarily because Edward Ferguson's view of life assurance was almost as bad for it as the conditions of world war.[104]

9. INVESTMENT IN WARTIME

Apart from the depredations of the taxman, the most worrying financial feature of Phoenix's career in the First World War had been the depreciation in the value of the company's investments. To begin with, there were fears that this damaging conjunction would recur in the Second World War. There was of course no doubt about the impact of the revenue.[105] But investment experience was more complex and less punishing than in the Kaiser's War.

In 1939 some depreciation in the life funds was noted, but the directors were relatively untroubled since the market values remained comfortably above the book values.[106] By 1941, when total life assets pulled clearly above £20 million for the first time,[107] the value of the Stock Exchange securities attributable to life business was a full 8% better than the book values. In 1944 and 1945, the margin continued to be comfortable. At no point, even for life investments (the less active of the two big portfolios), were the values written into the books put under any significant pressure.

The life fund began the war stronger in both convertible securities and total assets than the fire and general fund, but the financial experience of the war quite transformed this long-running relationship, leaving the fire and general portfolio on a footing with the life fund in Stock Exchange securities and significantly the more powerful in terms of total assets (see Table 11.13). However, Table 11.13 also shows the initial depreciation of the fire and general fund which spilled into 1940.

The more active investment account, the fire and general fund, was subject to effects which were not noted during the First World War. Its much more international composition, and its accumulation since 1918 of extensive US and Canadian investments, gave it a resilience which it did not display in the earlier conflict. Any depreciation of its holdings in the UK market was counteracted by favourable exchange rate effects as the sterling value of North American securities advanced. Moreover, Phoenix could amplify the result by deliberately accounting with a more severe sterling:dollar rate than any likely to occur in the trading year. This

[104] See below, Chapter 12, pp. 889–91. [105] See above, p. 834.
[106] Chairman's Annual Report, 29 May 1940.
[107] And total Phoenix assets above £40 million, for the first time.

Table 11.13. *Phoenix Assurance: total convertible securities and total assets, 1939–45 (£ million)*

	Convertible securities			Total assets		
	Life Fund	Fire and general fund	Sum	Life fund	Fire and general fund	Sum
1939	15.2	14.4	29.6	–	–	–
1940	15.7	13.9	29.6	20.1	19.2	39.3
1941	16.4	15.4	31.8	20.6	20.4	41.0
1942	16.9	16.3	33.2	21.0	21.4	42.4
1943	17.6	17.7	35.3	21.7	22.9	44.6
1944	18.7	18.8	37.5	22.2	23.9	46.1
1945	19.5	19.5	39.0	22.9	25.0	47.9

helped to produce *appreciation* of the fire funds late in 1940. Pearl Harbour brought a sharp, if temporary, fall in the US market which deprived Phoenix of its transatlantic bonus for a while. Yet even here recovery was rapid.

Phoenix capitalised on the exchange rate advantage by transferring further large amounts of resources from low-yielding US rail bonds into US government holdings. By October 1943 some 59% of all Phoenix's considerable investment in the USA (over £5 million) was in government stock and only 17% in the old American staple of railroad bonds.[108] By 1945, US government stock made up 92% of all Phoenix holdings of foreign government paper. The company did more than merely switch US investments into federal paper; it funnelled new money that way too. Much of the $2.75 million in surplus cash that was on hand in the USA in November 1939, and held back from investment until opportunities clarified, found its way into Uncle Sam's bonds.[109] The effect on the distribution of Phoenix investments to the 'US & Other Governments' column is clearly shown in Table 11.14.

Striking divergences in the style of management of the two accounts are displayed in Table 11.14. The life fund advanced in value by 28% during the war, but the fire and general fund by over 35%.[110] Both funds ran down their (mainly American) railway holdings and both bought government

[108] Directors' Minutes, 40, p. 124, 6 October 1943.
[109] Emergency Committee Minutes, p. 8, 8 November 1939.
[110] By conservative book values in both cases.

Table 11.14. *Phoenix Assurance general and life funds: convertible securities; major trends in distribution, 1939–45*

	Total holding £m		% in UK & empire govts		% in US & other govts		% in railway & other stock	
	Life fund	General fund	Life fund	General fund	Life fund	General fund	Life fund	General fund
1939	15.2	14.4	55.1	26.1	2.2	28.1	39.9	35.9
1940	15.7	13.9	56.7	28.4	1.4	26.4	38.9	35.1
1941	16.4	15.4	58.8	30.7	0.9	26.6	37.6	33.7
1942	16.9	16.3	61.7	32.8	0.8	27.5	35.0	31.1
1943	17.6	17.7	64.3	35.6	0.8	30.4	32.6	26.2
1944	18.7	18.8	66.8	36.6	0.8	30.9	30.3	25.2
1945	19.5	19.5	69.1	35.7	0.2	34.7	28.9	22.8

Source: Calculated from Annual Reports and Accounts.

paper. But they chose a different mix of governments. The life fund virtually obliterated its minority interest in non-UK gilts and generated a huge concentration on the home government. The fire and general fund was also loyal to domestic war issues and increased its commitment significantly; but, by the end of the war, it was still only half as invested in UK gilts as its life counterpart. Instead the fire and general bought American.

The move out of railways, the move into US gilts, and the more rapid advance in total portfolio value are linked features of the fire and general fund's performance in wartime. The two funds served different purposes in Phoenix's war economy. The prime function of the life fund was to invest in the UK war effort; the prime function of the fire and general fund was to invest in the sterling : dollar exchange.

The importance of the USA to Phoenix during the war – in preserving its accident business in a viable state and in supplying a vital reinforcement to investment performance – helps explain the considerable emphasis placed upon the American connection in the company's last postwar phase. These wartime rewards from America also went some way to make up for the earlier embarrassments that Phoenix had suffered on the far side of the Atlantic. Like Britain as a whole, Phoenix had reason to be grateful to its American ally in wartime. This left a mark on corporate memory.

Plate 11.11 The way to work: Bank underground station, January 1941.

10. PHOENIX STAFF 1939–1945: WARFARE IN THE OFFICE AND ELSEWHERE

As in the First World War, global war brought total upheaval in office life. But in the Second World War it was even more intense. In the Kaiser's War, the enemy did not succeed in forcing staff members to evacuate City offices or in demolishing large sections of the offices themselves. The workplace was at risk in quite a new way 1939–45 and the upheaval could be distressingly physical. By contrast, a feature linking the experience of the two wars was that much of the stress of war work fell upon women staff, although, in this war, women as well as men joined the fighting services in some numbers. One feature did not match between the two wars. In the Second World War economic conditions did much more to threaten the living standards of Phoenix staff than was the case in 1914–18. But this was not simply due to inflation. General Manager Ferguson's resistance to cost-of-living increases also played a role. But, on the other hand, his sensitivity to labour costs also helps to explain Phoenix's high profitability in wartime.

Bombing, female employment, war service, wage protests, and high profits were strands composing a complex web of war experience for Phoenix employees.

One of the first implications to dawn on Phoenix directors was the vital importance of female labour. Hearty male generosity was not quite the spirit behind their hasty concession, on 13 September 1939, that 'in view of the outbreak of war, Phoenix Company Regulation (No. 15), which provides that ladies must leave the Company's service on marriage need not necessarily be immediately enforced'.[111] Indeed, the need for special dispensations for women workers had been foreseen even before hostilities commenced. Managers remembered the labour shortages of the Great War, which had been relieved initially by older men and those unfit for service, but they conceded, less than graciously, that 'the supply of such was soon exhausted and the Company was then forced to employ lady clerks'.[112] In order to secure 'women of experience' at short notice, the company had appointed at ages much higher than was usual. This had an unexpected consequence in the prelude to the Second World War; for the generation of female clerks from 1914–18 was approaching retirement just as the Phoenix was considering the need for a generation of female clerks to fight the Second World War. Yet many of the veterans did not have sufficient years of service for a satisfactory pension. As they faced another war, and the same problem, the Phoenix directors did the decent thing and made up the shortfall.

But they still had to recruit the successor generation. In the crisis period between September 1938 and March 1939, Phoenix's Special Committee of the Board gave close attention to women's salaries and the general manager recommended to them in March 'a slightly more generous allotment being made this year to the Female Staff. It is mainly to these employees that we should have to look for assistance in carrying out the work of the Company in the event of their male colleagues being called up.'[113] Once they had the women workers, however, they would need to stop them following the men into the forces. This danger too was perceived early. From June 1939 Phoenix withheld the benefits of military salary support from women staff who left the office for the services. It was not until early 1942 that the company treated women who joined up on a par with single men.[114]

[111] Phoenix Director's Minutes, 39, pp. 226–7, 13 September 1939.
[112] Special Committee Minutes, Book 2, p. 166, 1 June 1938.
[113] *Ibid.*, p. 174, 17 March 1939. [114] See above p. 828.

Table 11.15. *Phoenix Assurance: numbers of clerical staff on active service, 1940–5*

March 1940	195	Feb. 1943	593
Dec. 1940	263	Feb. 1944	616
Dec. 1941	400	Feb. 1945	634

Source: Special Committee Minute Books 2 and 3.

Table 11.16. *Phoenix staff: war service by arm, men and women, distribution at December 1944*

Men	RN	Army	RAF	Fire	Govt	Returned
	56	350	132	22	2	15

Women	WRNS	ATS	WAAF	Police	Land Army	Nurses	NAAFI	Industry
	1	52	13	3	9	8	1	25

Certainly, those who stayed proved essential. Phoenix had 195 clerical staff under arms by March 1940 and 263 by the last day of that year (see Table 11.15). At the earlier date, Phoenix was still coping with relatively little labour strain: 'despite the heavy drain on our manpower, so far we have continued to overtake [sic] the essential work of the Company, without any abnormal additional appointments'. This had been done by simplifying administration and 'adapting [sic] the existing female staff for clerical, as distinct from typing, work'.[115]

Strain was clearly evident by the early part of 1941, however. Although Phoenix was 'gratified and proud that such a material contribution in manpower was being made', the workload upon those who remained was proving harrowing. It was held at bay only by 'adaptation' so extensive that 'much of the clerical work throughout our organisation is now being undertaken by female labour'.[116] By late 1941, the loss of 400 staff to the services, mostly men, had been compensated by the recruitment of 120 replacements, mostly women. This was achieved in 1940 and 1941 by offering special salary increases and war bonuses to women staff.

Even so, Phoenix women joined up alongside Phoenix men. By the end of 1941, 51% of the pre-war male staff had joined up and 11% of the

[115] General Manager's Report to Special Committee, 5 April 1940.
[116] *Ibid.*, 21 February 1940.

women; three years later, the proportions were 52% for men but 19% for women. The distribution of wartime employment for these people by service is shown in Table 11.16.

It is possible that Phoenix encouraged these high join-up rates in a way which it did not intend. Certainly, the 19% achieved by Phoenix women was nearly twice the 10% which Ferguson had planned in 1942. Then, he had breached his characteristic rigour in regard to salaries with special pay awards for lady insurance clerks to prevent them being seduced away by generous civil servants or luxurious bankers. He was spurred into this by the realisation that the Civil Service paid a woman clerk at age twenty-five £187 per year in 1942 while Phoenix offered only £148. This was swiftly raised to £160 in February 1942, together with age-related supplementation.[117] But it was not enough to do the trick; and was in fact a symptom of a style of salary management which caused further rumbles in Phoenix's battered and bombarded office.[118]

Edward Ferguson took a deeply pessimistic view of the economic experience of the First World War and its aftermath, and the lessons to be learned from both. And he maintained this attitude not only during the Second World War but also in its aftermath, although the facts of the two cases were actually quite different.

Ferguson's reading of the impact of the First World War on the income front was that it had entailed 'very substantial bonus additions which were then made to salaries'. He was not about to repeat this in the Second World War. In order to avoid percentage increases becoming built into pay settlements and then carried forward into future costs, he devised a system of war allowances which would last only for the duration. These were running at the rate of an additional £45 on salaries below £400 and an extra £75 on those in the range £800–1,000 in 1940 and 1941. They were costing the Phoenix £50,000 per year, but would stop when the war stopped.

The net effect was to produce an overall addition to the Phoenix wage bill of 2.1% in 1940 and 1941 and a proposed 1.6% for 1942, in contrast to an annual average of 2.8% in the *less* inflationary years 1936–9.[119] This salary restraint under difficult conditions should be seen in the light of Phoenix salary policy in the Crash of 1929–31. Then too Phoenix had pleaded poverty to its employees. In 1932 the Board had 'severely restricted' normal pay rises, with the result that 'the Company's difficult years

[117] These ranged from an extra £2 per year for an eighteen-year-old to an extra £38 for a thirty-year-old.

[118] General Manager's Report to Special Committee, 20 February 1942.

[119] Phoenix Directors' Minutes, Annual Salary Reviews. See, for example, 39, p. 344, 2 February 1941.

Plate 11.12 Damage in the neighbourhood: bomber's eye-view from directly above Phoenix house.

were shared by the Staff . . . and, at the 150th Anniversary of the Company, the occasion was . . . a financial disappointment to the Staff'.[120] The increases of 1936–9 constituted 'exceptional treatment' as an attempt to remedy these losses. Rectification was achieved for younger employees, but many had been hard hit in the period 1932–5.[121] And some of them were being hit for a second time in the period 1940–3. The salary increases of around 2% offered by Ferguson contrasted sharply with the bonuses of 5% and 10% which were paid to their wartime forebears between 1915 and 1918.

The Ministry of Labour's cost of living index rose from 155 in October 1939 to 187 a year later and to 199 in October 1941 – an increase of about 30%. Ernest Bevin, the Minister of Labour, told the House of Commons

[120] Special Committee Minutes, Book 3, p. 7, 4 December 1943. [121] *Ibid.*

in June 1941 that the average wage level had risen by around 20% since the outbreak of war. Yet, at the time of the 1941 salary review, Phoenix men (particularly men) were comparing their 3–6% increases with a 30% advance in the cost of living and moaning into their ledgers.

The Ferguson interpretation of this was that, thanks to better price controls and extensive rationing, the economic strain falling on Phoenix in the Second World War was 'not so exaggerated as was the case in the last war'. Because of this lower level of strain on the company, and its employees, he concluded, 'We have been able to run our business at a much more closely controlled salary expense than was possible in 1914–18'. He was content that 'only modest allowances had been needed'.[122] No doubt these modest allowances did much to help Phoenix's profitability in wartime. But there is much to suggest that they were too modest.

Management justified these payments by the argument that, in wartime, Phoenix should bear half of the rise in the cost of living and its staff, by personal economies, the other half. This might have proved viable if income tax could have been ignored. But, of course, Phoenix and its workers were not the only players in the pay transactions of the war economy. The state took its share: an additional £50 from an annual income of £500, an additional £98 from one of £1,000. The Phoenix Consultative Committee, which expressed the staff's view in the pay negotiations of 1941, reviewed twelve personal budgets of staff members in autumn 1941 and found that they had suffered falls of 25–45% in net income since the beginning of the war. The worst affected were those on about £1,000 per annum with fixed commitments and houses to maintain.[123] Even the Special Committee of the Board, which reviewed this vexed question, concluded by the end of 1943 that, 'actually, as income tax cannot be ignored, the allowances have proved inadequate'.[124]

The staff were not silent on this score. In autumn 1941, the Consultative Committee presented a petition with sixty names on it, lamenting 'the coming financial embarrassment of a typical Senior Insurance Clerk'. It told the general manager that, 'A large section of the London staff is already greatly exercised over this problem to the detriment of their work'. Reduced worker numbers were having to cope with heavier work loads – government war damage schemes on top of normal business – for too little money. Mindful too of a little economic history of their own, the staff representatives recalled their salary sacrifices in the Great Crash, and

[122] *Ibid.*, p. 21, 30 December 1943. Phoenix paid a wartime allowance of £75 per year to those on incomes of £1,000 in 1941. Secret Minutes, p. 88, 20 August 1941.

[123] *Ibid.*, Book 2, p. 224, 16 October 1941. [124] *Ibid.*, Book 3, p. 7, 4 December 1943.

craved reciprocation in their moment of need: 'Now that the Staff are faced with financial difficulties, they appeal to the management for much-needed help.'[125] This was the nearest event to a bread riot that the twentieth-century Phoenix experienced.[126]

However, the pleas for poor relief of 1941 did not achieve immediate succour. Indeed it was not until 1943 that top management underwent a change of heart. By this time, staff complaints were becoming desperate. In January, the Consultative Committee reported that the November tax deductions had caused 'severe financial embarrassment among the Phoenix Staff'. Many of them were living off capital, and, perhaps a somewhat bizarre argument in wartime, had made 'a complete sacrifice of the annual holiday away from home'.[127] However, by December 1943, even Ferguson was convinced of the poverty problem and talked of Phoenix staff left 'with no financial margin whatever'.[128]

Two developments had operated to produce this change. One was the fact that it was no longer sustainable by 1943 to be pessimistic about Phoenix's economic performance. Ferguson tried, pointing out that 'The general disruption of our overseas business and the curtailment of our Motor and Workmen's Compensation operations were factors which rendered, and still render, the future of our Group opertaions uncertain'. And he still insisted that the consequence was that 'permanent additions to expenses must be avoided wherever possible'. But even he was forced to accept that the company accounts for 1941 and 1942 had shown that 'pre-war profit figures have been achieved and that our Funds are today appreciably greater than they were in 1938. My pessimism regarding the adverse effects of war conditions has not been justified', though he added the characteristic, 'so far.'[129]

The other influence, to which again Ferguson was typically prone, was what competitors were doing. In 1942 and 1943 they were paying a lot more money. The banks paid their employees a bonus of 6% in November 1942, and followed it with a further 10% in November 1943. This frightened Ferguson: he foresaw all Phoenix's indispensable women trooping off to the cashier's counters of the City. Promptly, it was decided that the Company's wartime allowances must almost double: salary revision in 1944 added about 4% to the wage bill and this was repeated in 1945 and 1946.[130] A cynical view might be that income restraint was

[125] *Ibid.*, Book 2, p. 224, 16 October 1941.
[126] Although there was an echo in the 1950s.
[127] Special Committee Minutes, Book 3, p. 8, 15 January 1943.
[128] *Ibid.*, p. 21, 30 December 1943. [129] *Ibid.*, p. 7, 4 February 1943.
[130] *Ibid.*, p. 38, 29 December 1944.

applied to the wartime Phoenix for as long as it could be defended, and abolished only when profits and rivals rendered it indefensible. A less cynical view would pay tribute to careful stewardship in difficult times, influenced by the memory of other difficult times not so long ago.

Still it is worth recalling that throughout the war, the Phoenix was handling more income with far fewer people. Total premium was £8.8 million in 1939 and over £11 million in 1944, but the number of employees earning it had fallen from 1,794 in 1939 to 1,231 in 1945. The wage bill as a proportion of total premiums fell from 6.3% in 1939 to a low point of 5.4% in 1942.[131]

All told, the salary bill for 1939–45 was some £400,000 less than it would have been had there been no war, and salary settlements had proceeded according to the pre-war pattern. Only half of this was used in financing the various wartime allowance schemes. And even subtracting for the Victory Bonus of 1945, Phoenix still came out of the war with a *credit* of £125,000 against the wage costs it could have expected to bear if 1939–45 had been an era of peace. Clearly the wartime profitability of Phoenix had a good deal to do with downward pressure on the costs side, and not least the cost of human capital.

In other battles, of course, far away from King William Street, human capital was pressed in different ways. As in the First World War, the contribution of Phoenix people to the fighting front was distinguished, and mercifully less mortal. By February 1942, 140 of the 403 Phoenix staff in the armed forces were officers; by the end of the war the tally was 260 out of 577, additional experience thus increasing the rate of commissioning from 34.7% to 45.1%. This time, however, neither officer mortality nor general mortality was as punishing as in the First World War. Considerable as Phoenix's losses were, they represented only half of the military death rate of the First World War, around 6% as against 13–14%. And if those who made their contribution through the support services – such as fire-fighting, ARP etc. – rather than through the fighting services are included in the host of Phoenix people seconded to war work, the total Phoenix death rate for the Second World War falls to about 3%.

The tally of decorations was again high, with much the same pattern as in the Great War. The total was thirty-six at April 1945, with eight of these being Military Crosses, five Distinguished Flying Crosses, two Distinguished Service Orders and two Croix de Guerre.[132] This meant that

[131] Special Committee Minutes, Book 3, p. 20, 30 December 1943.

[132] The balance was made up by seven MBEs, three TDs, and nine Mentions in Despatches. Phoenix Directors' Minutes, 40, pp. 231, 243, 251, 10 January, 21 February, 21 March 1945.

about 6% of Phoenix men who served in the fighting forces in the Second World War achieved a major decoration or mention in despatches. The contrast with the First World War, where the corresponding figure was 10%, is largely a reflection of the different nature of the combat in the two wars. However, it is noticeable that the RAF made a disproportionate contribution to the Phoenix roll of honour, with eleven decorations for the 132 airmen serving (or 8.3%). Again, of course, this says something about the nature of the Second World War and the importance to British strategy of fighter pilots in the early stages and bomber air crew in the later ones. But one pattern that was repeated between wars was the phenomenon of multiple decoration: six individuals accounted for twelve of Phoenix's thirty-six awards for bravery. Of these the most outstanding were probably Major C. J. Vivian who achieved both the MC and the DSO and Flying Officer S. P. Johnson who secured both the DFC and the MBE.

Interestingly, Phoenix gave some thought in 1945 to the problem of reabsorbing men who had undergone experiences of this kind. In 1918 the records had betrayed little consideration of the issue of war returnees other than that they would come back to their jobs and that women would be displaced.[133]

In 1945, however, it was realised that boys who had left on apprentice's salaries were returning as battle-hardened veterans who had seen much of a harsh world. The Special Committee also noted the high proportion of officer material among their ranks, and drew the right lesson: 'they have gained experience and knowledge of the world and affairs which will have value in our service'.[134] Accordingly, the assumptions about the salaries needed by the average insurance man were redrawn. The typical man in King William Street, in the late 1930s would have married at age 28 or 29, and needed £250 per year to support himself and his family. By 1945 the representative figure would be returning from the war, aged 26, already married, and with almost a 50/50 chance that he would be wearing officer's epaulettes; by then he would be needing £300 per year to maintain a family. The Phoenix Board recognised this and moved accordingly.

They realised also that they needed to mark the end of the war for the Phoenix staff with some appropriate financial gesture. This was the Victory Bonus of 28 December 1945. An amount of £75,000, or 0.6% of the premium income for 1944, was set aside for this celebratory payout. Aware that returning servicemen would receive tax-free war gratuities,

[133] There is astonishingly little mention of war wounded in either case, however. But again this may be thought more striking for the First World War.

[134] Special Committee, Book 3, p. 55, 12 December 1945.

Plate 11.13 Field Marshal Montgomery confers the MC upon Captain A. L. Simpson.

the Phoenix management did not reserve much of the Bonus for the fighting staff; indeed they got only £15,000 of it. This represented a month's worth of the salary at which they would resume. Nevertheless, they did better than the foreign staff, who, it was thought, had done splendid work but had 'escaped many of the dangers, anxieties and restrictions suffered by the Home Staff'; they did not share in the Victory Bonus.[135] The majority went on a payment of 15% of annual salary to those members of home staff who had been continuously employed by Phoenix throughout the war, with those who had been employed for less time receiving the appropriate proportion.

At the formal level, the Victory Bonus evoked ceremonial flourishes from both management and staff. The Board saw the award as marking,

[135] Secret Minutes, 1945.

Plate 11.14 Phoenix House beflagged for VE Day.

the high standards of loyalty, unselfishness and resource which has permeated all ranks of the Home Civilian Staff... throughout the war, and desiring also to record gratification with the safe return of Staff who have been serving with the forces or in other Branches of National Service.[136]

For the rank and file, the Consultative Committee, buried the hatchet of the salary wars and tendered its gratitude to the directors.[137]

However, the Secret Minutes conceded, alongside the need to recognise war work, some rather more calculated considerations. There was a need to 'replenish small domestic savings now largely non-existent through the strain of war expenses, particularly taxation'. Note was also taken of the resentment caused by the lack of the 150th anniversary bonus. The contrast with the Royal's recent announcement of a centenary bonus of 12.5% was sharply drawn. The exhaustion of the 'small

[136] *Ibid.* [137] Phoenix Directors' Minutes, 40, p. 329, 28 December 1945.

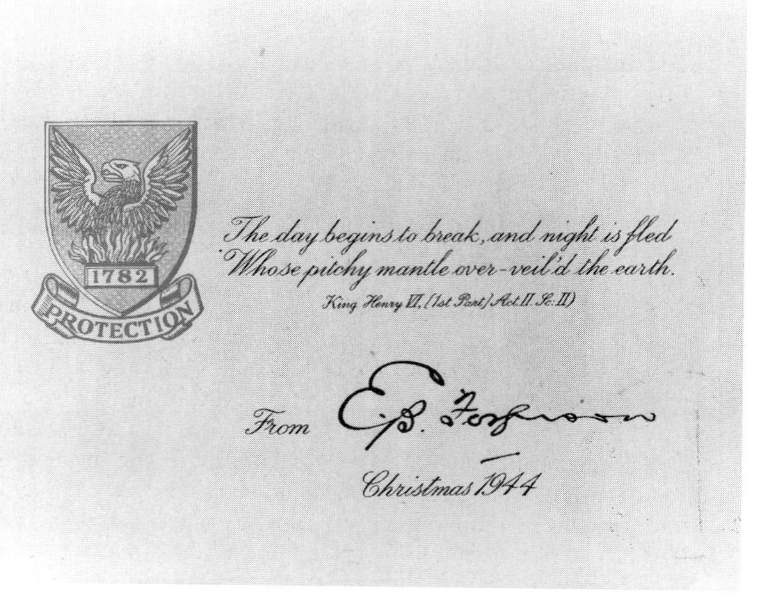

Plate 11.15 The final Christmas card of wartime.

domestic savings' of course had also owed a good deal to the low level of Phoenix's salary increases in the period 1939–43.

Effectively, Ferguson had used the stress of war as a reason to apply an incomes policy in the early stages of the conflict. It is possible, of course, to take several views of this. Ryan and Hamilton did not attempt it in the First World War. But, of course, they were further removed in time from the concept of an incomes policy and they were experiencing the facts of the First World War, not trying to apply its lessons to the Second. Ferguson's position could be represented as far-sighted. Keynes, in planning the desired outcome for the modern economy of full employment, had already written of the necessity of an incomes policy to accompany it.[138] However, it may be doubted that Edward Ferguson was any kind of proto-Keynesian. Rather his reading of events was drawn from a deep pessimism about the past married to an equally dour vision of the future.

It was intended that Ferguson's appointment as general manager should be a caretaker one. In the event, it turned out to be protracted. The quality of crisis management will tend to be obscured if the crisis is big enough.

[138] Politicians proved much less keen on this part of Keynesianism than the full employment part, and much slower to introduce it.

II. THE EXIT FROM WAR

This, unlike the exit from peace, was brisk. By October 1944, Ferguson was already in the USA, assessing the fitness of Phoenix's operation there for the transition to peace. He was highly satisfied with the way in which J. M. Haines and his men had 'protected and developed the interests of the Phoenix Group during the war years'.[139] As a mark of thanks, Haines was given a significant salary boost early in 1945,[140] and as a mark of faith in the postwar US market the capital of Phoenix Indemnity was raised from $1.1 million to $2 million. The difference was transferred from surplus and the resulting additional stock was pledged to the Reconstruction Finance Corporation under the Anglo-American Loan Agreement.

Phoenix had relied a good deal on US demand and US investment during the war and had clearly seen the potential of this market as a strong point in its postwar development. The size of the company's American fire and accident markets and the profitability of the latter in wartime pointed lessons that management was unlikely to ignore in the years after the Armistice. At the end of 1945, another visiting director, the shipowner J. W. Booth, after a tour of Canada and the USA, reported that its conduct during the war had ensured that 'the prestige of the Phoenix stood high in North America'.[141]

By the middle of 1945, Ferguson was touring parts of liberated Europe and visited the Netherlands in July as a member of an official mission from the London insurance market. The initial findings proved much more satisfactory than might have been expected.[142] Indeed, in both the Netherlands and Denmark, loyal agents and representatives had protected surprising amounts of Phoenix business. This earned a note of 'admiration and thanks' from Sketch in the Chairman's Annual Report for 1945. In fact, in Denmark notice amounted to rather more. In August Ferguson reported on the valuable work done by Herman Zobel and his team during the Occupation. This amounted to 'cloaking' Phoenix assets from Nazi sequestration and running Codan as if it were a native Danish company.[143] In this instance, the exclusion of foreign staff from the Victory Bonus was waived: a reward of 20,000 kroner was divided between the Zobels, père et fils, and their two senior assistants.[144]

As Phoenix discovered how many connections had been conserved in

[139] Phoenix Directors' Minutes, 40, p. 215, 18 October 1944.
[140] *Ibid.*, p. 229, 10 January 1945.
[141] *Ibid.*, p. 318, 14 November 1945.
[142] *Ibid.*, p. 292, 25 July 1945.
[143] They even managed to found Codan Life in 1943.
[144] Phoenix Directors' Minutes, 40, p. 298, 22 August 1945.

German- or Japanese-occupied territory, the office moved quickly to re-establish its operations. Even in the Philippines, vacated by most Japanese forces only in April–May 1945, Phoenix resolved to resume transacting fire, accident and marine business as early as June 1945, and prepared new powers of attorney for its pre-war agents, Ker & Co. and Keller & Co.[145] In the same month, the Board was planning to re-establish a French bank account, so that it could draw upon overdraft facilities of 5 million francs to help with the rebuilding of French business.[146] By October, Harvey Claude Welman had been appointed as agent and manager for France and Algeria, scarcely a month after Carlos Meerbergen had been selected to head Phoenix's re-entry to Belgium and Luxembourg.[147]

All this was reassuring, as well as energetic. Also reassuring, as the threat of war receded, was the withdrawal, or at least mitigation, of a threat still more deadly. Phoenix had withstood the war in good shape. But nothing would have permitted it to escape the threat of nationalisation. This threat, of course, was part of the new political economy which the socialising experience of the Second World War had left in its wake. The emphasis upon a more equitable distribution of wealth and welfare which the shared privations of war had encouraged – and which formed a coinage of response for governments needing to offer restitution for those privations – led to a widespread questioning of the old order and of long-established forms of wealth of all kinds, some of them institutional. Labour victory in the election of June 1945 defined some of these questions rather sharply.

It was therefore with a palpable sense of relief that Sketch's Annual Report for 1945 rounded off with the report that 'the Government have now wisely let it be known, through the President of the Board of Trade, that, in their opinion, the *international* nature of our business renders it an unsuitable subject for national ownership'.[148] Insurance, he reflected, was a business of long-maintained and far-flung associations, requiring generous and even-handed response to individual cases. And, thus comforted, he concluded: 'No business would lend itself less satisfactorily to a unified or rigid control.'[149] At the end of 1945, therefore, Phoenix could congratulate itself on having survived not only the travails of war but also the worst that the peacetime economy could offer. This danger was not of course to disappear completely in the postwar world, but potentially one of the most perilous moments was in the first months of peace.

[145] *Ibid.*, p. 278, 27 June 1945. [146] *Ibid.*, p. 275, 13 June 1945.
[147] *Ibid.*, pp. 312, 305, 17 October, 19 September 1945.
[148] Chairman's Annual Report, 1945. My emphasis. [149] *Ibid.*

FOREWORD TO CHAPTER 12

For the period 1782–1945, this history has enjoyed complete access to all company records and an entirely free rein in judgement and evaluation. This approach is less appropriate in very recent decades. Sensitive issues in the near past may remain sensitive. Key figures may still hold strong views.

On the other hand, those who commissioned this work did not want an entirely cosmetic treatment of the postwar years. This would have been out of keeping with the rest of the history. So a compromise was agreed. As historian, I would work by interview and attempt to reconcile the oral evidence. Some documentation would also be made available to keep the narrative on the tracks. Drafts would be submitted to the key players and I would accept their guidance on the balance between, and the integration of, the various oral sources.

This has been done. The process of integration itself, of course, is a function of the historian's judgement; but this was exercised within a framework of reconciliation. Given tact and discretion, I believed that it was possible to construct virtuous recent history in this way. I think that this has been the result and that I have been fortunate in the generosity of my sources.

But at this point, the accent changes. It comes not in the single voice of the historian but in the composite tones of those who lived, and managed, through this era.

CHAPTER 12

FROM WAR TO THE END, 1945–1984

Insurance companies are like battleships; they change course very slowly. Certainly, the Phoenix of the later 1940s and early 1950s kept much the same bearing as it had followed in the late 1930s. And its senior management was determined to hold it there.

I. THE FERGUSON ERA: CAUTION AND CONSTRAINT

Maintaining the status quo was an intelligible choice; and Phoenix was not alone in making it. The office was rich, respected and, in entrepreneurial style, restrained. The war recently over had been a testing time for insurers of property and life. It was not unreasonable to conserve whatever substance had survived the experience. Some managers who remembered the economic turmoil which had formed the 'postwar' period after the First World War adopted a wary attitude to this second instalment of postwar years.

Further, the 'interwar' years had proved a formative phase for the insurers, in a special way. Amidst the recession which had affected all too many sectors of the British economy, the insurance industry had proved one of the several sectors which had fared not at all badly. Insurance men had fewer market problems than most capitalists and while others fought the economic tempest, they found their own trade relatively calm; the combination of security within and upheaval without may have encouraged a particular attachment to familiar ways.

In this era between the wars the insurers were spared the peculiar horrors of inflation; their investments were only just breaking away from long-cherished convention; insurance companies in such a time were not supposed to be adventurous, and most of them did not try. In 1919 almost all sectors of the economy wished to recreate the circumstances of 1914.

For good reason, in 1945 very few sectors of the economy wished to recreate the circumstances of 1939. Insurance men may not have wished to recreate them, but they did recall them differently.

Some insurance managers were conditioned towards conservatism by this combination of interwar and wartime experience. The question, of course, is whether Phoenix – with the additional trauma of the LGA disaster lingering in the corporate memory – was particularly conservative by the standards of its peers. One partial answer is that some companies behaved much like Phoenix and that others like the Commercial Union, the REA, and, somewhat further removed, the life specialists, Legal & General and Prudential, made other choices, even in the close aftermath of war.[1] Another partial answer is that the Phoenix strategy of this period generated repercussions which are clearly linked to the demise of the office as an independent venture in 1984.

If there were acknowledged difficulties in the postwar world of rationing and reconstruction, there were also clear opportunities. Policies of full employment, industrial revival and increasing prosperity directly stimulated demand for fire, life and accident departments. Inflation, commencing a quarter-century upswing in the 1950s, no doubt brought instability to the financial world but it also dramatised the need for increases in sums insured and promised substantial returns to shrewd investment. Rapid growth in motor transport created a boom market in car insurances, with total premiums more than quadrupling between 1945 and 1953. Technological advance in sectors as diverse as air transport, construction, shipbuilding and nuclear power created new insurance markets or added depth to existing ones. A high incidence of natural disasters in the early 1950s provided strong arguments for fire and home protection policies. The latter came also for the first time to include formal coverage of 'weather perils'. Similarly, government tax allowances and improving life expectation increased the incentive to buy life insurance and reduced the asking price.

Many companies responded willingly to these prospects of improvement. Two major histories featuring important competitors of very different types – Phoenix's long-established rival, the REA, and the great offspring of the Tooley Street disaster, the Commercial Union – both present dynamic accounts of the immediate postwar years.[2] In both fire

[1] See Liveing, *Commercial Union Assurance*; Supple, *Royal Exchange Assurance*; Hannah, *Inventing Retirement*. Also there was little that was conservative about the accident sector (cf. General Accident), nor about Lloyds.

[2] Supple, *Royal Exchange Assurance*, pp. 519–28; Liveing, *Commercial Union Assurance*, pp. 225–51.

and life, REA easily outpaced the market, while, for the Commercial Union, the period 1946–58 is picked out by Liveings as 'the Years of Progress'.[3] Interestingly, REA and Commercial Union led the renewed wave of corporate mergers which began in 1959. For Phoenix, however, the pull of opportunity was rarely stronger than the stern logic of austerity.

What then was remarkable about the Phoenix of pre-Coronation Britain? It was a place of Dickensian habits: high stools and handwritten ledgers survived to 1953 and well beyond; the accounts department's single flirtation with modernity was the appointment of a lonely brace of comptometer operators. Managerial relations were feudalistic; employees would rarely see anyone more than two ranks above themselves, and, for most, the general manager was an idea rather than a person. If glimpsed on a stairway, it was as likely to converse as Banquo's ghost. But there was little special about this. Most major offices were intensely hierarchic at this time: at least one distinguished competitor of Phoenix had a separate *entrance* for its managers. More consultative styles of management made little appearance in the insurance business before the 1960s. True, the Phoenix of the 1940s and 1950s was conservative and proud of it. But conservatism at this time was often an ingredient of good reputation in insurance. And Phoenix was a reputable office of the highest standing. Phoenix people may have had a great sense of tradition. But they were to maintain that, with affection, through good times as well as bad, to the end.

Other aspects were more unusual. The Phoenix of this period was profit-oriented but risk-averse. Management sought low expense ratios and low costs and expressly avoided major increases in turnover. Similarly, the company did not broaden its investment portfolio to fully admit equities until the late 1940s.[4] These self-imposed restrictions on scale were all the odder given that Phoenix's base in the United Kingdom was small to begin with. If the office customarily ranked fifth or sixth among British insurance companies by premium income, this was entirely due to its *overseas* premium income; and 50–60% of total premium income came from the single centre of North America. Yet despite its insubstantial domestic base, Phoenix exercised enormous influence within the British insurance industry. This was primarily because it possessed in its sequence of general managers – Ryan, Sketch and Ferguson – men who were perceived to be the dons of the insurance industry. In a sense Phoenix carried influence out of proportion to its weight. And this combination of great status within British insurance but relative weakness

[3] *Ibid.* [4] See Table 12.13 below.

within the British market was to kindle the fire from which the Phoenix would not rise.

There is indeed an eerie repetition within this strategy – insistence upon 'purified' and 'select' accounts, avoidance of expansion, reliance upon foreign earnings, heavy involvement in American affairs – all themes which had proved dangerous a century and more before. Institutional memory, it seems, could still hold the company to ransom.[5]

In the years between 1939 and 1958, and indeed beyond, that strategy was inseparably connected with Sir Edward Ferguson and a small group of like-minded senior managers.

Ferguson was a Scot both dour and canny; and also a man who had come a long way from modest beginnings. The son of the stationmaster at Kirkintilloch, he entered insurance by way of a small Scottish office and spent some time with them selling policies on the road. He then transferred to the London Guarantee in Glasgow and came to Phoenix in consequence of the takeover in 1922. With Phoenix he progressed through the branches, ending as a branch manager in Scotland at an early age. He transferred to Head Office during the 1920s and was sent to South Africa – a stable from which several Phoenix leaders were drawn[6] – at the end of 1927. There he did a good job in difficult circumstances. He returned to London in 1931 as manager of the City Branch and spent the rest of the 1930s as executive assistant to Sketch and then as manager. But his training at the highest level was not extensive; he was not 'put through the mill' of the departments as subsequent generations of top managers came to expect. Above all, he had never led a department. He was not an underwriter by training. Nor was he happy with financial planning; he did not read a balance sheet with ease. Ironically, he was by background primarily a promoter of business.

He was appointed general manager, in a caretaker role, in 1940. He then took care of Phoenix for close on thirty years, first as general manager until 1952, then as managing director until 1958, and finally as chairman until 1966.

If Ferguson's early skills lay on the trading side of the business, he was by temperament far removed from the thrusting, out-going manner which conventionally is associated with successful salesmanship. True, he possessed a striking physical presence; he was a large and handsome man of imposing appearance and manner. He had genuine dignity but perhaps lacked the warmth which can turn gravitas into good leadership. Rather there was aloofness in his confidence, an autocratic side to his

[5] See vol. I, pp .331, 414, 427, 701, 757.

[6] See this chapter, p. 893. For Ferguson's time in South Africa, see above pp. 776–7.

Plate 12.1 Edward Ferguson at the top of the tree.

distinction. The most perceptive observers noticed an underlying insecurity in his caution and traditionalism. They may have noticed it too in his public speaking, which was hesitant, deliberate and delivered always from notes.

Nevertheless, in the public forum, Phoenix was good for Ferguson and he for it. Phoenix's reputation carried Ferguson to the peak of City ceremonial – he was president of the Chartered Insurance Institute, (1948–9) chairman of the British Insurance Association (1952) and knighted in the Coronation honours list – and his combination of weight and steadfastness was undoubtedly good for Phoenix's standing within the square mile. He had the same effect abroad. At a time when foreign travel was the preserve of general management, he became well known in America and the overseas markets where British insurance was established and respected. He possessed the ambassadorial style rather than the managerial gift. Possibly, he brought more clear advantage to Phoenix when he was operating outside the company walls.

Ferguson's sceptical and cautious traits of character were not obviously out of sympathy with the mood of postwar, austerity Britain. The problem was that this psychological array did not dispose him to accept new opportunities when they were offered, nor to face up to the need for expansion. In particular, his expectation that the post-1945 era would witness a repetition of the post-1918 recession scarcely prepared him for the major upswing in the world economy which actually followed the Second World War. This was unfortunate because if Phoenix needed in some quarters to be defended, it also needed acutely in others to be expanded. However, Ferguson's own career did not assist him in risking lightly what had been carefully accumulated. Insurance, of course, has to be about risk, though it is never to be taken lightly.

This business philosophy might not have proved so constraining had Ferguson been balanced by other senior men of lighter or more adventurous spirit. But before the early 1960s, and the rise of David Evans, he was not so balanced. By contrast, he was surrounded by like-minded men, several of them also northerners: for many years the Phoenix's home fire and accident managers were both Scots; and these two, Andrew Kirkland and Jock Thompson, were as canny as Ferguson himself. They shared a mistrust of growth whenever the prospect arose and a preference for the restraint of turnover.

The Scottish echelon was backed by a fourth individual of great influence, the secretary John Hill. A master of detail, an artist of the meticulous, Hill was also hungry for administrative power: his ambition was to strengthen the secretarial department as the company's organisational command centre and he largely succeeded. Secretarial ruled the sectors of personnel and accounts while its chief controlled all appointments and reviewed all salaries himself. This followed the pattern of previous generations and was hardly different from the tight-handed centralism which prevailed in many long-established offices; yet Hill brought a special determination to the concentration of powers. He was also a convinced traditionalist. The result was that Phoenix acquired a high quality of internal administration but also formidable constraints upon addressing problems in new ways.

It was this *combination* of personalities which produced a distinctive policy slant at the Phoenix. The result was not unthinking conservatism but a deliberate and positive decision not to expand. The inner circle had no desire to see Phoenix lead the market; they were happier that the company should take the lower risk course, its concentration fixed firmly not on bold vistas or wide perspectives but on the controllable short term: the current year's profit. The emphasis was on letting the business run

Table 12.1. *The expansion of UK insurance markets, 1946–60: net premium (£ m)*

	1946	1960	Multiplier
All UK Offices			
Fire	80	295	3.7
Life	120	460	3.8
Accident	61	250	4.1
Motor	45	310	6.9
REA			
Fire	4.0	18.0	4.5
Life	1.8	8.5	4.7
Accident	2.1	7.5	3.6
Motor	3.8	21.0	5.5
Phoenix			
Fire	5.3	13.0	2.5
Life	1.9	4.7	2.5
Accident	3.6	10.3	2.9
Motor	2.6	14.4	5.5

Source: Supple, *Royal Exchange Assurance*, pp. 520–1; Phoenix Accounts and Statements, Returns to Department of Trade.

quietly and upon selecting 'managers' who would allow it to do so. This was not an unreasonable reading of postwar conditions; but it was an uncreative one. Naturally, many other insurance ventures of the era were less than creative; but the evidence of Table 12.1 suggests that Phoenix was eminent among them.

Of course, it should be stressed that in this era the public perception of insurance companies dwelt upon reputation and status, and convention was an integral part of both. The emphasis upon new products, ingenious 'mixed' vehicles and innovative ways of selling which are commonplace in the modern market would have seemed inconceivably bad-mannered to many senior insurance men of the period 1945–60.

Many of the problems affecting the Phoenix in this period were afflictions of the industry as a whole. Numerous offices possessed leaders who would appear autocratic, if not despotic, by the standards of the 1980s. Outmoded managements, outdated methods, vintage attitudes in a changing world, these were the norm rather than the exception among the insurance executives of the 1940s and 1950s. And in the case of Phoenix, the LGA disaster of the interwar years added to simple conservatism a compelling reason for prudence. Yet, on the other hand, some offices were managing to slip the values of the pack: more adventurous strategies and more thrusting styles of management were available for study and emulation.[7]

Much business history is criticised, and criticised legitimately, for being too company-insular. Throughout this study an attempt has been made to relate Phoenix to the industry standard. The tactic remains valuable in the modern period. Comparative testing of the postwar Phoenix leadership is revealing.

Measured in Table 12.1 are the major underwriting sectors of the entire UK company insurance market for the years 1946 and 1960, together with the place of the REA and the Phoenix within it.[8] The net premium earnings of all British offices provide an average standard of performance. The REA, a veteran office of even longer standing than Phoenix and a composite office of similar age and size, provides a fairly direct comparator; and it is in any case the only other composite office to have been studied in the postwar era at a level of detail sufficient to support useful comparison.[9]

Naturally, Table 12.1 measures only volumes. It says nothing about profitability in relation to volume. But the differences between the multipliers are very instructive. They indicate divergent responses to the flow of business opportunities. Also, although volumes do not control profit opportunities in the underwriting sense, they do relate to investment opportunites since they will affect the amounts that the office will have on hand for its investment managers. The Phoenix multipliers clearly suggest a philosophy of restraint.

The most interesting effects occurred in three sectors: fire, life and motor. Phoenix, of course, had been a composite insurance venture since 1908. But, for a decade and more after 1945, it ceased to think like one. For Ferguson and his associates Phoenix was first and foremost a fire company. This was a *reversion* to a much earlier view.

Throughout the period 1922–60, with the exception only of the war

[7] This was particularly true of offices specialising in pension business. See Hannah, *Inventing Retirement*. Of course, it could be argued that such offices were different animals from the big composites; but, nevertheless, they operated in a market which had attracted, and was to attract, the interest of many generalists.

[8] Marine is not included and is by this time no longer a major corporate sector: total company premiums in marine business for 1945 were £23 million and in 1963 £95 million.

[9] Although Liveing provides an enthusiastic account of the postwar Commercial Union, his material does not equal Supple's in quality.

years 1942–4, the accident department (including motor) was in fact a much bigger premium-spinner than the fire department and by 1957 it was almost twice as big (see Table 12.1). True, it was undependable in profit out-turn, whereas fire, on its much smaller volume of business, was much more reliable in this respect. The combination of solidity and modest exposure probably supplied the recipe which commended fire to the Phoenix leadership. Also, the density of fire traffic, as many policies crossed many desks, left the *impression* – despite the fact that a large proportion of these policies were very small in value – that fire was a leading department. Fire was the safe option, the primary profit-earner of the group and the main link between the modern Phoenix and its venerated past.

Nevertheless, a managerial perspective which focused upon fire did not offer the broadest appraisal of postwar prospects. Perhaps more strangely still, a perspective which made fire the heart of the business did not extend to the *active promotion* of the fire department within the business. Between 1946 and 1960 Phoenix fire premiums rose by a factor of only 2.5, whereas accident premiums (including motor) very nearly quadrupled. Nor did the Phoenix fire department justify itself as a favoured sector by the standards of its competitors. Over the same period 1946–60, the fire premiums of all British offices increased by a factor of 3.7, from £80 million to nearly £300 million, while the REA managed an increase of 4.5 times (see Table 12.1).

Postwar full employment gave the community an increased ability to buy protection for its homes, while Nature added its own encouragements towards a proper regard for security: the Lynmouth disaster in North Devon in 1952 was followed by the inundation of the East Coast in 1953 and a string of frosts, storms, whirlwinds and tornadoes over the rest of the decade. A sharp increase in 'fire wastage' in its later years added a further reminder if it were needed. The market was there for the asking. But Phoenix seemed to ask less energetically than many of its peers.

One striking manifestation of this was the way in which the company approached broker-generated business. In the decade after 1945, Phoenix used brokers for fire and accident business, though not for life. However, just as its hierarchical style frowned upon the sort of insurance salesmanship which knocked upon doors, so it viewed brokers' business as something to be supplied rather than something to be pursued. And it was taken very selectively even when supplied. During these years, Phoenix fire underwriters in the home market employed only five of the eight 'lines' that they were allowed by their treaty provisions, whereas the

Plate 12.2 Devastation at Lynmouth, August 1952.

company's overseas managers, less easily restricted – in some markets at least, these being scaled according to territory and hazard – were able to use all eight. In consequence, Phoenix often forfeited the 'lead' position on big domestic policies and therefore lost status with the brokers.

By the early 1950s, so much business was being passed up in this way that the issue became the subject of a minor managerial revolt. The protest came from Phoenix's City Branch which did about one-quarter of all the company's UK fire business. Its officials were highly sensitive to the advantage Phoenix was sacrificing to offices such as the Commercial Union and Northern which were committed and large-scale users of brokers.

City Branch between 1950 and 1954 was directed by an especially

Plate 12.3 Floods in Kent, February 1953.

dynamic partnership: P. R. B. Sharman as manager and W. C. Harris as fire superintendent. Harris, later to be an influential chief general manager and deputy chairman, was an expert technical underwriter and a leader in the promotion of broker business. It was only after strong representation from this frustrated second echelon – which drew some support from Ferguson's immediate deputy, Tom Hodgson – that Fire Manager Kirkland agreed to revise the basis on which Phoenix dealt with the brokers. It is significant that the initial measure of liberation was achieved by men who were outside the top leadership of the company. Even so it took the best part of a decade to unlock fully this important source of business and real momentum was achieved only after the appointment of David Evans as manager in 1956.[10]

But this constraint to growth was weak compared with the bonds placed upon Phoenix life business. The British market for life assurance was particularly responsive to the postwar rise in incomes, employment and prices. Income tax advantages further increased demand, while improved mortality generated lower and more attractive premiums. Under these incentives, the life premiums of all British offices rose by a factor of about 3.8 between 1946 and 1960, from around £120 million to around £460 million, while the REA did rather better than the market with a multiplier of 4.7. Over the same period Phoenix life earnings increased by a factor of 2.5.

During the interwar years, the life department had been an active contributor to company income, building its share of total premiums to over 23% by 1939, and holding close to this level even in 1944. After 1945, however, its share fell continuously to 12.1% in 1953. This was the lowest contribution to total Phoenix income by life premiums for any year since 1908, bar one.[11] This was an especially odd effect in a national life market which was expanding between 1948 and 1953 twice as rapidly as it had done in the interwar years and three times as fast as in the pre-1914 period.[12]

The reasons for this are not simple. It is clear that top management did not favour the life side; the inner circle viewed the Phoenix's life underwriting primarily as a convenience for the fire and accident policy-holders, less a business in its own right than a service facility for other departments. Under these terms, the company would offer only the simplest type of 'bread-and-butter' life policy and would write pension business only for clients who possessed powerful fire or accident accounts. It is unlikely that business was actually turned away but little effort was made to pursue what was there for the taking. Reports from the assistant actuary, N. C. Berry, arguing for a controlled expansion of the life side were returned by the leadership. Of course, it might have proved sensible, after exploring the market possibilities, to decide not to expand the life trade. But Phoenix, at this time, did not get so far as exploration; and that requires a different sort of rationale.

Before 1939, the life department during Sketch's term as general manager and W. R. Moore's as actuary had demonstrated inventiveness and

[10] See p. 893ff below.

[11] Calculated from Phoenix Annual Reports and Accounts. The exception was 1923 with 10.8%.

[12] The annual average rate of advance was 10.4%, 1948–53; 4.4%, 1919–39; and 3.4%, 1900–14.

determination. By 1948 it was defeated. Its chief official in the late 1940s is remembered by one of his successors as a dejected man in a depressed department, surveying his narrow domain from a windowless room. Even by the mid-1950s, when matters had relaxed somewhat, Phoenix still refused to seek life business from brokers.

However, Phoenix's problem with life business was not merely a matter of managerial conservatism. The Phoenix faced special limitations on the expansion of life assurance. A peculiarity of the company's constitution required that 100% of the profits on participating policies should be distributed to the policy-holders; so no investment returns from these 'with profits' policies accrued to shareholders. Most offices were able to divide this yield in the ratio 90:10 between policy-holders and shareholders. For Phoenix, the 100% rule was a particular disability at a time when 'with profits' policies were the most popular life product of the era and most pension schemes took the form of 'with-profits' deferred annuities. The Phoenix system had been inherited from the British Empire – which, of course, was a mutual society distributing all gains to policy-holders – and had been absorbed into the substance of Phoenix when that company took over its sister, the Pelican, in 1908. The long-term effect was to leave the Phoenix shareholder with little direct interest in expanding the life sector and its powerful pension arm.

So was managerial coolness towards life prospects a rational reading of the constitutional constraints upon 'with-profits' business? Surely not, since *non-participating* policies remained an option, and the entirety of profits from these passed to shareholders. These could have been more energetically promoted. True, the fashionable demand of the day inclined towards participating policies; and some senior Phoenix men of a later era came to believe that life profits of any kind could be slow to materialise. Yet it is hard to escape the conclusion that the managers of the Ferguson era simply walked away from a problem.

When Phoenix did reform its life business, as it most effectively did from the mid-1960s, it was precisely by way of peddling hard with non-participating policies and specialising in the risk sector of the market. This involved selling highly tailored term policies – for example, to judges, pop stars and company 'key men' – in the purest type of assurance. The architect of that reform describes the Phoenix constitution not as a constraint but as a resource – because it forced the company into areas of demand which other offices had neglected. There is no obvious reason – bar innovative thinking – why this sort of market could not have been exploited earlier. 'Key men' presumably always exist and need insuring as soon as someone thinks of the idea.

If non-participating term assurances were distinctly unconventional in the late 1940s, they rapidly became much less so. By 1963 even the REA had one-third of its sums assured in this type of policy. So it is not inconceivable that the major reconstruction of Phoenix life business in the 1960s could have been anticipated, given the will. It is the manner of thinking about the problem which determines the outcome, not the problem itself.

Motor business was the fastest growing of all the postwar insurance markets, offering the industry 'the most spectacular postwar revival in underwriting trends'.[13] However, the home accident department at Phoenix remained suspicious. To a certain extent, it was carried along by the onrush in motor demand – despite a strategy to which Ferguson himself referred in his Chairman's Annual Report of 1963 as 'a very restrictive acceptance policy' – and the Phoenix multiplier for 1946–60, though a good deal below that for the motor market as a whole, was much the same as the REA's (see Table 12.1). With the motor tariff still in force at this point, and the offices thus denied much flexibility on rates, an acceptance policy that was at least selective was not inappropriate.[14] Yet, even in the presence of selection, the force of demand carried motor insurance to a significant position within Phoenix's overall accident business: it was the only buoyant feature within this account.

If motor business is aggregated with the other accident accounts, the Phoenix multiplier for the total is in its characteristic place, below both the market and the REA (4.0 against 5.3 and 4.8).

In general business, the Phoenix of the mid-1950s had a small market share in the United Kingdom and held the bulk of its assets abroad. Over half its total income was generated in North America. Further expansion here was scarcely feasible. In the USA, investment income was already being used to offset underwriting deficiencies and the capital base of the operation could not have been expanded without remittances from Head Office. In London, exchange control meant that dollars purchased for sterling were subject to a fluctuating surcharge on normal rates of about 20–25%, making such transfers punitively expensive. In the United Kingdom, on the other hand, Phoenix was desperately short of cash-flow; its domestic resources would barely pay the dividend. Exactly what was needed was the expansion of income flow and the accumulation of more extensive assets in Britain. Ryan had identified this requirement soon

[13] Supple, *Royal Exchange Assurance*, p. 519.

[14] Where tariffs exist, and results are poor, current practice is still to restrict the motor proportion of the accident account, and its growth. The UK motor tariff endured from 1914 until 1969.

after his appointment as general manager, but it remained a haunting presence in the 1950s.

Opportunities for expansion certainly existed at this time. Postwar industrial and commercial growth offered good prospects in most insurance markets. And inflation – accelerating during the 1950s, becoming a political issue in the 1960s and a crisis in the 1970s[15] – pushed up further the ceilings for sums insured. But the Phoenix chose to increase its limits for acceptances distinctly less fast than prices. Wherever the office had a chance to improve its premium flow – whether through the promotion of broker's business, a greater encouragement of life assurance, a boost to accident acceptances or simply by riding more actively the currents of industrialisation or inflation – it schooled itself instead to resist temptation and exercise self-restraint. This was in marked contrast to the period 1965-80, during which Phoenix growth outstripped market growth in all major sectors.[16]

Maybe a more aggressive policy in the preceding twenty years would not have solved Phoenix's central resource difficulty; but it must surely have reduced it. The increased income and investment potential, which could have been achieved by tracking the market more closely, must have given Phoenix improved powers of resistance and, perhaps, of acquisition. Had Phoenix merely matched the market standard of expansion in the sectors shown in Table 12.1, its total net premium income by 1960 would have been around £65 million rather than the £45.3 million that was actually earned. The policy that was followed merely passed on the problem to the next, more dynamic, generation of managers. But for them the double irony was that the insurance markets of the late 1950s and 1960s were much more difficult than their immediate predecessors. In encouraging these managers to a drastic solution – for the connection which was to be formed in 1963 with a US company was designed, above all, to siphon resources into Phoenix's UK operation – the inheritance of the period 1946–58 exerted an important influence on the final phase of the company's career. As so often, it was not the rashness or derring-do of the ancestors that was visited upon the next generation; it was what the ancestors believed to be proper caution and sober restraint.

[15] The peaks were reached in 1974–7 with annual rates of 16.0%, 24.2%, 15.8% and 16% respectively, and again in 1980 with 18% (*OECD Main Economic Indicators*, 1983).

[16] See below, Section 17 and Table 12.17.

2. THE EVANS ERA: THE BEGINNINGS OF REFORM

In proposing a successor as chief executive of Phoenix in 1958, Sir Edward Ferguson made an uncharacteristic choice. True, like Ryan and Sketch before him, he had taken the precaution of securing the chairmanship for himself, so he may have felt that he could exert sufficient influence upon anyone who followed him as general manager. The wisdom of his decision in regard to his own position was dubious – general managers who stayed on as chairmen preserved old influences for too long while lacking direct access to the detail of daily business. Ferguson did stay on for too long. But, nevertheless, there was sound sense in his choice of general manager. Phoenix contained biddable and solid men whom he could have chosen. Yet, instead, he put forward David Evans. This was one of the most imaginative strokes of Ferguson's long tenure at the Phoenix.

Educated at Christ's Hospital, Evans joined Phoenix's foreign fire department straight from school in 1920. Most of his career was concerned with foreign affairs. Before 1939 he had postings in Cuba and the Netherlands and in 1944 was one of the first British insurance men to re-enter Holland after its partial liberation. He became an authority on the reconstruction of British insurance business in post-Occupation Europe. After a spell as executive assistant to Ferguson, he was sent in the footsteps of his two predecessors as general manager to the 'finishing school' at Cape Town where he was manager for Southern Africa from 1950 to 1954. After returning to London his ascent was rapid: assistant manager 1954, manager 1956, general manager 1958.

Evans would not have regarded himself as a technocrat, nor even as an expert; he would not compare with the specialist insurance managers of the 1980s. He was as much of a generalist as Ferguson. His gifts were gifts of personality and here many found him 'exactly the right antidote to Ferguson'. All witnesses speak of Evans with admiration and affection; he clearly possessed the warmth and charisma of a natural leader. He had a pronounced sense of humour and indeed, within the foreign department, had been known as something of a practical joker. But this outgoing cast of character had its uses. Evans was a quick, clever and effective impromptu speaker. And he was notably good at whipping up enthusiasm, creating a spirit. More than one colleague remembers the Evans era as a 'Camelot period' in which working at Phoenix was felt to be a privilege. Thanks to Evans, spirits at Phoenix House were lighter than they had been for many years. But, most important, Evans is remembered for his courage, both in his own decision-making, and in giving other innovators their head.

Plate 12.4 David Evans in the 1960s.

The Camelot aura produced two major features of managerial style during Evans' tenure: open-minded appraisal of new prospects and enterprising action once appraisal was complete. Evans may not have liked detail, but he had an ingenious mind and he was fertile in concept. Though not an expert himself, he had the gift of enthusing those who were. He was a good judge of character and surrounded himself with the right experts. He delegated well and trusted the initiatives of his subordinates. This was as far removed as it could be from the centralised and cramped methods of the previous regime.

Evans was no doubt assisted in the reform of style by a generational effect which removed several long-serving managers in the middle 1950s. Ferguson's compatriots, the UK managers for fire and accident, Andrew Kirkland and Jock Thompson, retired in 1957 and 1954 respectively. N. C. ('Bill') Berry became actuary in 1951 and profited from the freer reign of the later 1950s; he was also supported by the newly recruited Marshall Field, drawn in from the Pearl, from 1958. In 1959 Bill Harris began a crucial period as United States manager in New York.

Also interesting was the changed role played by Tom Hodgson, the deputy to both Ferguson and Evans. An actuary by training, Hodgson was academically very proficient and in reinsurance matters a considerable expert. However, he was also a cautious man, averse to snap decisions and pressing issues. Under Ferguson, this reticence reinforced the

Plate 12.5 Caricature of Tom Hodgson by Charles Knight.

restraint at the centre. Under Evans, it was a useful corrective to over-enthusiasm. The combination was very effective; the prudent Hodgson was the perfect foil for the mercurial Evans. Furthermore, this pair worked well with Harris; and, despite the intervening ocean, these three men in consultation effectively directed the Phoenix during the early 1960s. In 1965, Harris returned from the USA in order to succeed Hodgson as deputy general manager. Just as the team around Ferguson conditioned policy in a particular direction, so did the team around Evans. He was fortunate that the character traits at his disposal inter-locked to more creative effect.

Even so, David Evans was not entirely his own master from the start. He was briefed for change and Phoenix employees expected change. Some wondered whether the wind of change was a result of Ferguson going out or Evans coming in. But, of course, Ferguson was not entirely out. He remained chairman until 1966. The rise of a new generation of 'Young Turks', men who were specifically Evans' appointees, did not occur until the mid-1960s. Even then it required a wave of natural retirements, to clear the way for them.

Nevertheless, Evans did produce rapid results in at least two sectors of Phoenix's activities and both were concerned with creating an impetus in home-based insurance. The first was to throw open Phoenix's doors to the brokers. Of course, the market as a whole was moving towards broker business in this period; but Phoenix had further to move than most. Before Evans, Phoenix had drawn only 5% of its total portfolio from brokers. Evans intended that Phoenix should not only follow the market but emulate the more aggressive offices such as the Commercial Union and the Northern, both of which were highly active in wooing the brokers. The intention was fulfilled. City Branch, which naturally had most contact with the brokers under any management, took about half of its premium income from this source in 1950 but at least 80% by 1960. The proportion of total Phoenix home fire and accident premiums achieved through brokers was 29.6% in 1962, but 45.5% by 1967.

The second sector of reform witnessed a seismic upheaval. This was the life business. At his first management conference, Evans told a stunned gathering that he intended to push Phoenix annual new sums assured from £6 million to £20 million. By 1956, he had revised the target to £30 million; by 1958 it was £50 million. The reaction of an organisation which had become used to viewing the life business as a lame duck was close to incredulity. However, Evans persevered and the sceptics were left with no choice but conversion.

Annual premiums are a better measure of vigour in life business than sums assured. But, even on this test, the results of the Evans initiative were outstanding. Life premiums rose from £4.0 million in 1956 to £4.6 million in 1960, £9.8 million in 1967 and £16.9 million by 1970. This entirely reformed the place of life underwriting within the Phoenix operation: total life income rose from its low point of just 12.1% of group premium income in 1953 to 14.9% in 1960 and 22.2% in 1967.

Evans provided the opportunity for the resurrection of the life department, but he could not provide the expertise. Bill Berry provided some of it and certainly built up the organisation in Head Office administration and sales capacity that was required to service a respectable life portfolio. Though himself a cautious man – remembered for the remark, 'These high interest rates of 4½% won't go on, you know' – Berry was a well-liked, avuncular personality with some leadership power. In 1958 Phoenix possessed only about thirty individuals in the entire UK sales force for life business; by the time Berry retired in 1964 there were ninety salesmen in the team.

This operation clearly put more power into the engine-room of the battleship and, undoubtedly, Berry could have done more had he been given a freer hand earlier in his career. But he was not the one to pilot the vessel in new directions.

Attempts at this were made by the life department in the later 1950s, with a number of schemes put forward by Deputy Actuary S. H. Cooper. Most of these proved over-complex. After the government opened limited pension benefits to the self-employed in the Finance Act of 1956, Phoenix tried to re-establish a toe-hold in the pension market. Its PPP plan aimed to provide maximum flexibility, offering a wide variety of benefits and inviting self-employed clients to make their selection. Effectively, the plan invited customers to become their own actuaries and succeeded in baffling almost all of them. 'Ordinary' life products were also affected by an excess of inspiration. Thus contrary to its intention, the Young Married Man's Policy reads like an advertisement for the simplicity of bachelorhood. These schemes required the customer to choose between too many variables and infringed the requirement that life insurance should be clean-cut. They were too complicated to administer and to sell. Insurance must be sold, not chosen. And it must reflect the consumer's needs and understanding, not the producer's virtuosity.

The revived life department needed someone who could develop new products and present them with clarity. By 1958 Evans and Berry had come to the same conclusion and began the hunt for such a one. The company approached some four or five young actuaries then acquiring reputations in the City. The man hired by Phoenix in 1958 as pensions superintendent, with a view to his becoming assistant actuary, and later to his succeeding Berry, was Marshall Field.

Field's acceptance of the challenge is significant since, ten years before, as a school-leaver, he had turned down the offer of a post from Phoenix's dejected life department, vowing never to return. By 1958, he found 'a massive change in company personality' and resolved to make the best of it. Between times he had trained as an actuary with the Pearl and had helped to create its pension department.

There is little doubt that Field was one of the major innovative forces within Phoenix over its final decades of independent existence. He proved particularly adroit at converting the limitations in the Phoenix's constitution into real market advantages.

Initially, Field was hired as a pensions expert and was clearly important in this sector even before taking over fully from Berry in 1964. He noted that Phoenix had been an influence in the pension market in the interwar years and had shared in the unofficial tariff of 1937 under which a dozen leading offices wrote their pension business.

This promising Phoenix initiative was snuffed out after the war by the advance of with-profits pension business and the scepticism of the management. By 1960, pensions made up about one-half of the business written by UK life offices. As long as Phoenix possessed the constitutional

Plate 12.6 New life: Marshall Field and team.

requirement to distribute all its life profits on participating policies to policy-holders, it could not tap the current pension market to advantage, but, on the other hand, it could not ignore business of such magnitude. The company absolutely required an innovation. By 1963 Field had provided it: he compensated for Phoenix's disabilities in the with-profits sector by developing an index-linked pension scheme, a growth fund policy geared to the Financial Times Index. This device was among the first of its kind and exactly what was needed to give Phoenix a competitive edge.

Once linking occurred to the Phoenix life department, it was exploited. The assurers were not averse to using a good idea twice. Thus when the competition went heavily into mortgage business in the later 1960s, employing with-profits endowments as vehicles, Phoenix again needed an antidote. Once more among the leaders, Phoenix found a way of linking such business to unit trusts. Field realised that connecting the life policy to the performance of units offered an escape from the with-profits constraint on Phoenix life business. He also had contacts with the founder of the Ebor Unit Trust, at that time the second- or third-ranking operator in the market. As chance would have it, Ebor was considering the development of its own unit-linked sideline in assurance and came to Phoenix for help with it. Seeing an opportunity to gain capacity that would service his own innovation, Field provided the technical aid for Ebor in return for the purchase by Phoenix in the mid-1960s of a 25% interest in the unit trust enterprise. In 1969 the stake in Ebor was sold on to the Save and Prosper Group, but not before it had played its part in making Phoenix a pioneer of unit-linked business. The sale also brought a considerable flow of reassurance business Phoenix's way. For the second time, a competitive edge was plucked from nowhere, or, more accurately, from intellectual capital.

But probably the most wide-ranging reform was needed in Phoenix's 'ordinary' life business, where the constitutional 'constraints' had ruled out many options. But, these features were not only barriers; they could act as signposts pointing to areas of the market where competition was weakest. If the company could not push with-profits life policies, why not specialise in term assurances in which the competition was not strong? In particular, why not insure special people for special periods?

From the late 1950s this thought produced a whole range of cleverly engineered products. 'Key man' policies could protect judges during sensitive trials, or pop stars during important tours, or industrialists during crucial negotiations. The subjects of such policies were said to range from Sandy Shaw and the Beatles to a Russian-speaking businessman who handled enormous sugar transactions with the USSR and never knew that he was insured. Partnership insurances could protect a group of individuals when the livelihood of each depended for a particular period on the survival of all. Estate duty insurances could provide protection over the limited period in which a family might be at risk from fiscal blight.

These policies were the purest kind of assurance but also a very complex kind, requiring the most rigorous underwriting skills. This, of course, is why the competition was not strong. It is also why success in such a demanding part of the market transformed Phoenix from a laggard in the life business of the late 1950s to a respected specialist in the life market of the late 1960s.

Naturally, concentration upon short-term policies and expert appraisal of special risks produced wider benefits by raising the quality of Phoenix's rate-setting for life business in general. Also it forced Phoenix into close acquaintance with the brokers. Of all insurances, Phoenix's specialities had to be sold rather than bought. By no means everyone needed them; only the brokers would know who did. Such closer acquaintance again produced wider benefits. Brokers impressed by Phoenix's special skills would bring more than one type of business to their door.

The major irony of this improvement in performance was that it followed from commitment to a highly traditional form of life assurance: the without-profits, simple life cover for a limited period. Phoenix was guided *back* to the risk side of assurance because its constitution barred it from the investment returns with which modern offices have contrived so many ingenious variations on the with-profits theme. It required a rare ingenuity to perceive that the most venerable form of assurance could be adapted to peculiarly modern requirements.

By about 1970, the leading sectors of Phoenix life business by premium were such enterprising lines as group life, individual term and group pensions. Index-linking, unit-linking and 'key man' policies composed an enviable honour-roll of innovations stretching across most forms of assurance market. Certainly, they gave a sufficient answer to the notion of a 'shackled' life business.

3. THE EVANS ERA: REFORM IN CRISIS AND THE AMERICAN CONNECTION

Not all ironies were so rich, however. Just as Evans' entrepreneurial approach was beginning to transform the Phoenix, fate played an unpleasant trick: in the late 1950s and early 1960s the entire insurance industry suffered a serious downturn in results which was led by the American market. Phoenix in particular paid the penalty for its long-term overseas specialism and its commitment – amounting to half of its world-wide business – to the American market.

Sir Edward Ferguson had a liking for foreign business. Phoenix, of course, had always been a foreign specialist, but the 1940s and 1950s had seen the further promotion of American business and even American casualty business. While the dollar ruled the exchanges, transatlantic managers chased volume and even those at Head Office were prepared to let them run. Much of the running was made by the cheerful, large-hearted, gregarious salesman, John R. Robinson who was US deputy manager from 1951 and succeeded Lloyd Jones as US manager in 1956.[17]

[17] Lloyd Jones had replaced J. M. Haines late in 1950 and encountered six uncomfortable years.

Robinson expanded the tactic of supplementing the Phoenix US fire account with casualty business, continuing the long campaign to reduce the fire expense ratio. Unfortunately, the American market, and especially the American casualty market, did not return such trust.

Difficulties began with a string of American hurricanes in the 1950s; but they did not end there. By 1960 Phoenix, which had 1.4% of all non-life business in the USA but double that proportion in the vulnerable coastal regions of Massachusetts and Connecticut, had closed its shutters upon the hurricanes. On the initiative of W. C. Harris, the company had reinsured half its business with two American offices, the Firemen's Fund and the Hartford, and had diversified geographically to achieve a better spread of risk. By the later 1950s the major difficulty for insurers seemed to lie rather in the automobile and liability sectors; and losses here were doing considerable damage to company reserves. In a market which lacked social benefits from the state and where lawyers worked to a contingent fee formula, both clients and courts were becoming very sensitive to the logic of large claims. The tendency to litigate increased markedly and the insurers were confronted by the phenomenon of 'judicial inflation'. In the 1920s Phoenix had encountered trouble with American casualty reserves because of concealment by the LGA. Now difficulties with reserves resurfaced because of hyperactivity in the American courtrooms.

On top of this, there was also an excess of activity among the competition. In both the USA and Canada, insurance business formerly written through agencies and brokers had been invaded by the so-called direct writers such as Allstate, State Farm and Nationwide as well as by a variety of self-insurance schemes and the privateers of Lloyds. The result was a no-holds-barred scramble for all property and casualty business in North America. Orthodox companies were left with adverse selection and steadily deteriorating underwriting results. Many could not stand the strain. A large number of American offices, including names as revered as the Aetna, the Loyalty Group, the National Fire, the Merchants Fire and the Northern Insurance, were forced into merger or reorganisation. Several prominent British offices including the Yorkshire, the Norwich Union, the Eagle Star and the Caledonian abandoned North America entirely.

Phoenix, of course, was so dependent on American income that it had to stay. The main brunt of devising ways of allowing it to stay profitably fell upon the expert fire underwriter who was Evans' US manager, Bill Harris. Harris had been a fire inspector in Manchester before the Second World War and had enjoyed stints as a new broom in the Manchester and City Branches of Phoenix in the late 1940s and early 1950s. This preparation in fire underwriting was as rigorous as any the industry could provide and left Harris with an enviable technical control of the art. In 1954 Harris went to America as the company's number two man on the fire side, as assistant vice-president of Phoenix US. In 1959, in the midst of the reserve crisis, Harris succeeded Robinson in the top US job, becoming president and chairman of Phoenix of New York.

Altogether, Harris spent the years between 1954 and 1965 in the United States; he took American citizenship and was wholly committed to the expansion of Phoenix in America. When he left Britain, he was warned that he might be surrendering his chance of elevation to the highest position in Phoenix central management in London. His reply was that he preferred direct control of the largest Phoenix operation anywhere to indirect control of worldwide business from the *smaller* base of the United Kingdom. Harris had a briskness and an analytical lucidity which responded well to the challenge of managing large affairs. In any event, the warning proved misplaced since Harris achieved more than merely American eminence, becoming chief general manager of the Phoenix Group in 1969 and deputy chairman in 1978. Harris was a major influence upon the development of Phoenix from 1959 to 1984 and powerfully represented the transatlantic motif within that development.

But what first confronted Harris in America was the Phoenix's particular version of the transatlantic market problem. The LGA connection had introduced into the Phoenix organisation an especially violent dose of the claims instability which characterised US casualty business, and, by the 1950s, this effect was strong enough to influence the overall results of the entire Group. Two consequences followed. Senior management was encouraged towards a conservative attitude in regard to any expansion of US business. And investment income from Phoenix's US insurances had increasingly to be devoted to making good underwriting shortfalls on Phoenix's US insurances. Thus it was not possible to increase the scale of the US operation without capital from London and London was not inclined to send capital. Nor was this surprising when British exchange control imposed the double penalty of an unpredictable surcharge over normal market rates on all dollars purchased for sterling. On top of all this, US insurance regulations required that every dollar of premium written in America had to be supported by 50 cents' worth of 'policy-holders' surplus'. So, despite inflationary conditions in the US market, Phoenix experienced a number of incentives to restrict its US premium income. But a policy of restriction did not solve the American conundrum. For, by the later 1950s, operating expenses had again reached threatening levels, too

Plate 12.7 Bill Harris.

high to sustain the limited volume of business that Head Office was prepared to accept.

Although not from a casualty background, Harris' answer to the American problem was characteristically direct and bullish: outflank the competition by writing more insurance and by reducing the expenses. Since he took easily to the vocabulary of American business methods, this two-pronged approach was expressed as ERP (Expenses Reduction Program) and 'the 1965 Plan' (the $65 million worth of American business by 1965). Phoenix of New York was small by comparison with the vast American insurance companies and consequently its ratio of expenses to turnover was higher than that of most native operators. ERP was intended to reduce significantly the Phoenix disadvantage.

This it succeeded in doing, in three stages. ERP 1 ran an unforgiving eye over all in-house expenses. ERP 2 hired management consultants to overhaul all administrative systems. ERP 3 was a strategy of consolidation, marshalling Phoenix business in areas of strength and abandoning areas where much larger American offices did much more business at much lower cost. In the early stages of this drive for economy and cost-effectiveness Harris was greatly assisted by Ron Bishop. Bishop was to become deputy general manager to Harris in 1969 and chief general manager when Harris retired to the deputy chairmanship in 1978. But the American re-appraisal of the early 1960s formed the first task on which the two men had cooperated closely. Bishop, who had come from a successful two-year posting in Canada to this further two-year tour in the

United States, had experienced an early stint in the company's accounts department and then a background on the operational side, with an overseas slant. His statistical expertise was exactly what Harris required at this stage and it was fully exploited.[18]

The '1965 Plan' too was over-fulfilled. When Harris assumed control in 1959, Phoenix was writing about $50 million worth of American business. When he left America in 1965, Phoenix was writing not $65 million but $70 million. However, it was not an uncontested $70 million; rather it became in 1963 the centrepiece of a very significant difference of opinion. In this year Sir Edward Ferguson went on a chairman's tour of the United States. He encountered the American crisis, and the Harris response, at first hand; and he liked neither.

The background to his displeasure is important. By 1962, Phoenix had taken seven straight years of loss on its US business, that is, on about half of its total business. The repercussions for the entire Phoenix operation were severe. Once more, the company was under threat through the American connection. Ferguson was alarmed that the atrocious trading results from the United States would jeopardise the company's published accounts. There was justification for this: indeed, by 1963 the office's financial position was so precarious that the profit and loss account needed reinforcement by £1 million; and this tidy sum had to be drawn from the distinctly odd direction of the capital redemption account. Ferguson had ample cause for concern. But, profit-conscious and wary of over-expansion as always, he chose an unfortunate method of expressing it: an immediate, unselective, across-the-board reduction in American business by 25%.

Since the '1965 Plan' had been agreed between Evans and Harris, the latter was not disposed to accept a unilateral command of this kind. There was also the danger of course that the 25% axed in this way would be the *good* 25%. So Harris decided that he had to stand firm.

The disagreement required Evans to fly out to New York in order to hear Harris' side of the argument. This was presented in a written submission, the main burden of which was a 'best estimate' that Phoenix might well suffer a loss of $1.3 million if Ferguson's line were followed. When Evans cabled this calculation back to London, Hodgson, with all the accounts before him, agreed with Harris' conclusion but put the potential loss even higher, at $2.5 million or beyond. Armed with this evidence, and with the executive solidly behind the Harris strategy, Evans returned to London and put the case against the 25% cut once more to

[18] Bishop's term in Canada had been concerned entirely with matters of operational control and business development.

the chairman. Sir Edward conceded the hand. The matter was then placed before the Board which endorsed Evans' recommendation and voted with the expansionists.

Of course, all the crucial figures in this debate were estimates. Thus, it would be difficult to prove, incontrovertibly, that Sir Edward was wrong. And, no doubt, the tactic of accelerating out of an underwriting crisis may attract cogent critics in the 1990s, as in the 1960s. Certainly, a sensitive deceleration, a selective reduction of the US portfolio by 25% might have proved a viable alternative strategy. What is clear, however, is that Ferguson's proposal was not so carefully envisaged. Gentle driving or delicate surgery might have done the trick; but heavy braking or the sideways stroke of the claymore could only wreck much arduous planning.

Politically, the episode marked a turning point. Evans had handled the disagreement deftly and tactfully and had not allowed it to sour his relations with Ferguson. Evans had achieved an elementary but important emphasis: high policy was the preserve of the general manager. From this point Ferguson accepted a permanent change in the balance of power. The affair also provides a good example of the way Evans, Hodgson and Harris could combine to powerful effect.

But this was not the end of the American crisis. Harris had been able to reduce it but not extinguish it. He had succeeded in lifting Phoenix's performance relative to the American market, but in 1962 and 1963 the American market as a whole was still losing money. In 1962 Phoenix had recorded an American operating ratio of 108 (that is, losses incurred against premium earned of 70%, plus expenses incurred against premium written of 38%). The company's global trading result for 1962 was an underwriting loss of £2.24 million which was sufficient to produce an *overall* loss, despite investment income of £2.5 million; £1.6 million of the underwriting loss derived from the USA. By 1963 the American operating ratio had improved to 106.9, making Phoenix probably the only insurer in the USA to better its position in that year. But as good news went, this was modest: the ratio was still uncomfortably high for the times.[19]

Within the British insurance industry, reactions to the difficulties of the American market were widespread and various in the decade after 1955. The merger was a common counter-tactic. Indeed, the later 1950s saw the first major corporate reorganisation in the insurance industry for more than thirty years and an overall rationalisation unmatched since the first quarter of the century. Unfortunately for Phoenix, it was unable to equal

[19] *Financial Times*, 23 November 1963. Of course, for much of the 1990s, an operating ratio of 106.9 would be regarded as respectable because of the effect of high interest rates on investment earnings.

in this second great phase of systematisation the participation which Ryan had arranged for it in the first.

Transatlantic complications formed a strong motif within the rationalisation movement. Some British companies were so weakened by their American connections that they fell prey to more resilient predators. Thus by 1959 the North British was entirely crippled by its historical and once distinguished transatlantic links; it was absorbed by the Commercial Union. Liveing gives as 'the principal reason' for this huge merger 'the importance of consolidating and developing fire and casualty business in the United States, the problems and potentialities of which have so frequently figured in the history of British insurance overseas.'[20] Similarly, the Employers' Liability proved unable to survive its large American casualty business and fell to the Northern Assurance in 1960.[21]

Other companies, some hurt by American losses, others seeking a counterweight to the ballast represented by the American market, looked to the merger as a way of obtaining more capacity, more reserves or more balance. In 1959 the Sun, which had large interests in the USA, merged with the Alliance which had large interests in the United Kingdom; the Sun was pursuing equilibrium. The Alliance was also convenient; its office was next door to the Sun; a company joke suggests that the organisational aspect of the merger consisted of knocking a hole in the wall. The Atlas and the REA were physically more separated in London but by 1958 had reacted to the American problem by grouping their US business under a single manager; in the next year the REA extended this relationship worldwide and acquired the whole of the Atlas.[22]

The predicament of Phoenix was closer to that of the second group of companies than to that of the first. Phoenix had been badly damaged by the American storms but had not foundered; however, it certainly needed more capacity, lower expenses and more reserves in the USA. So it was logical for Evans to devise Phoenix's version of the merger response. This he tried to do late in 1959. Two weeks before Christmas, Phoenix's leaders met to discuss the possibilities of an accommodation with their opposite numbers at the London & Lancashire. The logic is clear: the London & Lancashire was another long-time American specialist; a pooling of American operations would have produced a notable saving in expenses.

[20] Liveing, *Commercial Union Assurance*, p. 277.
[21] The Northern was itself absorbed by the Commercial Union in 1968
[22] See Supple, *Royal Exchange Assurance*, p.532. Supple attributes the prime stimulus towards merger in the longer period 1956–67 to increased competition; but it is clear that the important mergers of the short period 1958–60 can be traced to transatlantic events. In this connection, the American explanation can withstand much emphasis.

However, the talks did not go well. There were problems as to which was the senior of the two companies, and which was to be the lead player in any joint operation. The London & Lancashire had views upon this issue of precedence and Phoenix was not strong enough to carry the day. So the talks broke down. And, within twelve months, the very substantial US capacity of the London & Lancashire accrued to another major force in the British insurance establishment. The Royal Insurance apparently faced few problems in defining its seniority in regard to the London & Lancashire and absorbed it in 1961. Unlike a number of offices, therefore, the Phoenix failed to find an answer to its American problems in the shape of a discreet London-based merger. So, what was it to do?

The central Phoenix problem remained that the seat of company operations was located where company assets and income were weak. Since 1945 expansion, when and where it was permitted, had been directed overseas. The Phoenix had proved successful in Denmark, South America and a number of smaller overseas markets. But success abroad required capital and left little over for repatriation to the United Kingdom. Also exchange control prevented overseas investment at normal exchange rates, so profits needed to be left in place if foreign expansion was to be funded at all. America was the largest single source of income, so troubles there aggravated the income problem at home. The restriction of income from the USA, as Ferguson had proposed, was hardly an attractive option in this context. And the merger strategy, which would have increased assets and income within the United Kingdom, had proved impossible to realise. Phoenix's inability to join the rationalisation process at this juncture proved a crucial influence upon the company's fortunes.

For, shortly after, an ingenious if radical alternative was presented to the Phoenix management. The notion arose in mid-1963 that Phoenix might strike up a working relationship with a large American office, employing the connection to reduce costs and improve Phoenix results in North America. The idea was first put to Ralph Sketch, Phoenix's manager in Canada, by a vice-president of the giant US office, the Travellers Insurance Co. Sketch telephoned Harris and suggested that the proposal was perhaps better suited to the needs of Phoenix in New York than to those of Phoenix in Canada. Harris passed the idea on to Evans and the general manager put it before the chairman. Ferguson agreed to meet the Travellers vice-president in New York on a forthcoming visit in late summer 1963. The Travellers man was provided with details of the underwriting services that Phoenix could provide for an American office wishing, in partnership, to forage further afield; and Evans began to consider what Phoenix might ask for in return for such services. From this process was to spring one of his more far-reaching ideas.

4. PHOENIX AND CONTINENTAL: THE INTRODUCTION

The Travellers proposal highlighted a need being felt increasingly in the early 1960s by the major US insurance companies. The need was for the assistance of European colleagues in managing the overseas ramifications of their most lucrative US accounts. As American industry moved more strongly into distant markets, so it trailed in its wake a demand for increasing amounts of distant insurance, yet neither Travellers nor most of the large American companies were skilled in underwriting at such long range; indeed, most of them were not licensed to do so. Phoenix, of course, was a long-distance specialist and possessed exactly the type of expertise required by the American offices. It was this intersection of interests that Ferguson and Evans set out to discuss with the Travellers management when they visited New York in August 1963.

In preparing his brief for these talks, Evans was struck by a crucial thought: why not seek from the Americans, in return for foreign underwriting skills, a financial participation in Phoenix equity; this would both cement the insurance relationship and relieve Phoenix's pressing hunger for development funding in Britain. If the US partner would also provide Phoenix with support in the American market, solutions might be found at one stroke to the Phoenix's problems on both sides of the Atlantic. Evans first defined the controlling formula in a letter to Harris in August 1963:

> If the Travellers want to provide virtually worldwide facilities for their American clients, this would have to be by an association in the form which would give them a direct incentive and would also give us some recompense for the one-hundred-and-eighty odd years' experience that we would be placing at their disposal. Vaguely, I have in mind a financial link.

Quite quickly, this became more exact. The worldwide operation that Phoenix could offer an American colleague was after all geographically very extensive. It consisted in 1963 of forty-seven agencies, nine branches (Australia, Belgium, France, India, New Zealand, Rhodesia, South Africa, Spain, Pakistan), six subsidiary companies (Chile, Colombia, Denmark, Holland, Israel, Peru) and one pool (Japan); altogether it offered coverage of over sixty countries. For the use of this system Travellers could be invited to take up a tranche of 1 million Phoenix shares – about 16% of the total equity – and should pay a good price, perhaps as much as

£10 per share, for them. Phoenix then 'could well use this money for much-needed development in areas where we can see prospects of improved profit'.

But Travellers and Phoenix did not prove natural bedfellows. Travellers, as Harris portrayed it, was 'a vast concern dominated by its Life interests'. This did not provide a good fit with Phoenix's global activities in fire and accident. Further, Phoenix feared that Travellers could use their size to develop an independent foreign capacity and, once having learned from Phoenix's expertise, abandon the connection. This was, of course, a natural – and significant – worry for Phoenix in any alliance with a large US insurer. But the main impediment to agreement between the two companies concerned the intensity of the relationship. Travellers, as its president told Harris, really wanted no more than a service arrangement and was not anxious for an involvement of capital. Phoenix, on the other hand, had increasingly come to see an American alliance as the answer to its resource problems. By mid-September 1963 the prospect that Travellers was the right ally was beginning to fade. Harris, a crucially placed intermediary in any American negotiation, was sceptical of the Travellers proposal and was beginning to steer Evans in other directions. In the event, Travellers found their service agreement in a deal with the Guardian. This was a modest affair.

The other directions favoured by Harris – who agreed wholeheartedly with Evans' line of thought – ran towards another large American company, the Continental Insurance Company of New York. With assets of $1,600 million (£570 million) and net premium income of $460 million (£164 million), the Continental group was among the largest fire and casualty insurance organisations in the USA and Harris enjoyed close relations with its chairman, J. Victor Herd.[23] Early in September 1963, Harris had asked, and received, permission from Evans to broach the matter of an Anglo-American agreement with Herd. Although the inspiration behind such an agreement was clearly Evans, the form in which the agreement was embodied owed most to Harris.

It is clear why Continental appealed to Harris. To begin with, it provided an exceptionally good instance of the worldwide insurance business currently being generated by American manufacturing multinationals. Here the powerful postwar growth of American industry opened a new 'window' in overseas insurance prospects. And Continental insured some of the most powerful industrial concerns in the land. As the *Sunday Times* pointed out, any office which handled Continental's overseas

[23] At this time Continental ranked perhaps fifth or sixth in the US market by premium income, higher in terms of market capitalisation.

affairs would be supplying, *inter alia*, 'worldwide cover for one of America's most famous companies, International Business Machines'.[24] Continental was also the largest stockholder in IBM and in First National City Bank, Morgan Guarantee Trust, Texaco, Phelps Dodge 'and many other vast industrial complexes with overseas interests'. The prospects for overseas insurances needed no emphasis.

Unlike Travellers, moreover, Continental had no life business to speak of. So Phoenix could offer a useful complementarity in that department. And Continental could offer Phoenix particular help in the crucial area of American costs, since the New York office was in the middle of a powerful expansion programme, having already absorbed a number of smaller concerns along with the American operations of several British insurers, including those of the Norwich Union and the Yorkshire. It was in a good position to offer economies of scale.

Not least, Herd was a convinced Anglophile, welcomed the prospect of a close relationship with an English office and was disposed to follow Evans' thinking on capital involvement. By late September, after some long and difficult negotiations with a Special Committee of the Phoenix Board held in London, he had confirmed to Harris that 'his ideas included a financial interest in a British group and he stated quite frankly that the Phoenix know-how in overseas insurance and the Continental's resources in the United States would make an ideal combination'.

Once Herd's interest was engaged, negotiations moved very rapidly. Herd and Harris met for exploratory discussions at the Union League Club in New York on 24 September 1963; a public statement that the two companies had reached agreement was issued simultaneously in London and New York on 22 November 1963; and the deal was formalised on 6 December 1963. Between times, the Americans had visited London twice more and there had been much hard talking. The major outcome was that Continental agreed to purchase 22.4% of Phoenix stock and in doing so placed the first American toe in the door of the London insurance market.

The Phoenix–Continental agreement was both an innovation and an omen, or, as the *Post Magazine* cautiously put it, 'the first ever Anglo–American partnership of this kind'.[25] David Evans was a pioneer in calling American capital to the support of the City institutions. Indeed the Continental stake in the Phoenix was probably the first major US investment in a premier UK financial institution.[26]

[24] *Sunday Times*, 8 March 1964.

[25] *Post Magazine and Insurance Monitor*, 5 December 1963.

[26] Wholly-owned US financial institutions, such as J. P. Morgan, had operated in London for decades. But the Bank of England had frowned upon US shareholdings in the major

Plate 12.8 The making of a treaty: the Continental–Phoenix alliance. Ferguson stands in the centre, Herd left of centre, Hill right of centre, Evans sits in front of Hill, Bishop behind; Tom Hodgson is bottom left, looking to camera.

The initiative was generally welcomed on both sides of the Atlantic. Nevertheless, the day of its announcement was horribly marred by other public events. Friday 22 November 1963 witnessed the murder in Dallas of President John Kennedy. On 25 November, Evans wrote sadly to America, 'It was a tremendous shock to us all to return home on Friday evening somewhat elated . . . and to learn from our radio and television sets the ghastly news of the assassination of your President.'

However, the agreement was also associated in happier ways with powerful new developments in transatlantic economy and society. In the

domestic institutions before the 1960s: by the middle of this decade, the Bank had relented and set the acceptable participation at 15% of equity. Even so, it was not until 1965 that Mellon Bank aquired 15% of the Bank of London and South America, and not until 1968 that Citibank took a larger slice (40%) of National and Grindlays. I am grateful to Professor Geoffry Jones for these references. See also his essay in M. Chick (ed.), *Governments, Industries and Markets* (Aldershot, 1990); and L. G. Goldberg and A. Saunders, 'The Causes of US Bank Expansion: The Case of Great Britain', in G. G. Jones (ed.), *Multinational and International Banking* (Cambridge, 1992).

second half of the nineteenth century, British trade had expanded to cover the world; and the invisible exports of capital and insurance had followed. Around the middle of the twentieth century, the American economy was undergoing a similar process. Its commerce was already dominant. Since 1945 there had been a matching expansion in American investment to Central and South America, Europe, Africa and Australasia. But, until the 1960s, there was no matching expansion of American insurance into the wider world. Both Continental and Phoenix were sharp-eyed in detecting the coming trend.

For the Americans their traditional attachment to home underwriting and habitual suspicion of worldwide insurance could not persist against the prospects opened by booming US exports and the increasingly unfriendly nature of the home market. Herd was quick to act on this perception. For the Europeans these same signs spelled a warning: 'The Americans are coming.' Evans was quick to act on the warning. He did not so much join the Americans; he got them to join him.

However, there was a forceful logic to the agreement for both parties. Continental was big and ambitious. It possessed sufficient capacity to write three times its current insurance portfolio in 1963; but there was little profit in doing this in the America of 1963. Phoenix might, or might not, be able to accelerate its way out of trouble in the American market. But Continental was already too large in the American market to allow much acceleration there.

Logic for Continental pointed abroad. But Continental had little experience abroad. This was the basis for Herd's conviction, relayed to Harris during their meeting at the Union League Club, that 'the continued expansion of US commercial interests abroad had set the scene for a partnership which could profitably use the financial resources and connections of a large American insurance group and the overseas organisation and sophistication of a large British insurance group'. By contrast, Phoenix was already abroad but had troubles there, or at least in the American sector. If Phoenix could draw upon Continental's organisation with its much lower operating expenses, the costs of Phoenix's troubles could be much reduced. In return, Phoenix would represent Continental everywhere else abroad.

For his part, Evans felt an urgency in this logic. Despite what he acknowledged as 'much yeoman work on the part of the present management which has gone a long way towards the desired goal of profitable underwriting operations' – a tribute in part to Harris' work in the United States – Evans did not like the look of the trading results for 1963 and feared 'vociferous criticism' at the next AGM if he could not promise some hope of an early recovery. Both sides therefore had reasons for swiftly translating their perceptive readings of the transatlantic insurance economy into corporate action.

5. PHOENIX AND CONTINENTAL: THE TERMS

The speed of the deal did not mean that detailed terms were neglected. And since these terms were to define the viability of the Phoenix over the next twenty years, they repay attention, now as then.

The crucial meeting took place at the Oatlands Park Hotel, Weybridge, on a very wet Sunday, 20 October 1963. Present were Herd and the corporate secretary of the Continental, Geoffrey Davey, one of the few American officials besides Herd in the secret, and for the British, Evans, Hodgson and Harris. For the sake of the Phoenix share price, security was a major consideration; Ferguson was afraid that the mere appearance of Americans in Phoenix House would instantly alert the City to the prospect of an alliance. This was the reason for transporting the Americans from the comfort of the Hilton to the soggy depths of the English countryside. The venue served to impress the Americans with the hardiness of the British; they watched in stupefaction as the natives proceeded to play golf in the pouring rain.

However, they were precise enough when it came to the bargaining. The geographical terms proved – again somewhat ironically – the easiest to settle. In prose of high sound and higher hope, the world was divided into three sectors. The first consisted of regions where Phoenix operated but Continental did not. Here business was to be expanded either through Phoenix channels or by the introduction of a Continental company. The second consisted of countries where neither Phoenix nor Continental operated. In such places either company might handle the expansion if the market potential warranted it. In these first two sectors, the operation was to be engineered so as to present a British, American or Anglo-American image, depending on the local need. The third sector was made up of countries where both Phoenix and Continental wrote business. Effectively, this meant the USA and Canada. Here, the two companies were to maintain separate operations and personalities but to rationalise costs, services and reinsurance arrangements.

The understanding was that everywhere the arrangements should be cooperative and that certainly nowhere should they be competitive. It was also understood that Phoenix was the overseas specialist and should assist Continental outside the USA. For the *Sunday Times*, these proposals – or what the press later gathered of them – constituted 'an intriguing new plan' whereby 'international business co-ordination' would establish 'a Unilever of insurance'.[27]

The next matter to engage attention was also crucial: how many Phoenix shares should the Continental have and how much should it pay for them? Phoenix thinking was originally that the Continental stake should be on the same footing as that offered to the Travellers, that is 1 million shares. But, very soon after the first discussions, Herd had begun pressing for more and named 2 million as a convenient figure. This rather frightened Evans and alerted him to the danger that a shareholding so large might create the impression of 'transferred control' in British financial circles. Moreover, it was essential for the proper handling of any change in the Phoenix constitution that the British side should retain a minimum 75% holding, leaving control firmly in the United Kingdom. Accordingly, Evans put to Continental a counterbid, placing on the table some 1.5 million shares or 22.4% of Phoenix equity.

Herd readily took the point since he too was concerned that the American stake should not be so large as to provoke investment jitters in the London market. The Americans accepted the figure of 22.4% without prevarication and it was the amount written into the agreement. Evans was careful to specify payment in cash for new shares, rather than accommodation by an exchange of shares – which might give the appearance of a merger and again upset the City. Also, of course, Phoenix needed cash; increased liquidity in the United Kingdom was, after all, its major objective in the exercise. But, in every respect, both sides kept a weather eye on City opinion. The Phoenix men ruled out common directorships for this reason, at least during the early stages of the proposed partnership. An exception was made for Herd who was offered the compliment of a place on the Phoenix Board from the start, but he demurred tactfully 'until things get rolling'.

These issues were amicably resolved, but the preoccupation with the size of the American shareholding in 1964 tended to condition Phoenix thinking in a particular way. The British management had needed to consider the *largest* viable share for the Continental; their attention did not focus upon the possible consequences of a *reduction* in the transatlantic stake. Intelligible in the conditions of the 1960s, this proved to be less a loose end than a running noose.

One feature of Phoenix's share distribution eased the discussions: at least the company did not need to alter its capital structure in order to accommodate the American interest. In 1959, as expansion in the life

[27] *Sunday Times*, 8 March 1964.

department got under way and the merger movement accelerated, the new thinking at Phoenix House had concluded that an increase in capital would facilitate either internal growth or the swift acquisition of any company, or two, that might fall Phoenix's way. Accordingly, the authorised capital had been raised from £3.8 million to £5.0 million, of which only £1.3 million had been issued. So there was plenty of leeway for the proposed allocation to Continental of 1.5 million shares, with a face value of £375,000.[28]

However, the next issue was the price that the Americans were actually to pay for their shares.[29] Evans wanted a substantial price for two reasons. Firstly, he wished to maximise the injection of capital into Phoenix. If the British company was to build up its domestic assets and to gain more balance in its overseas dealings by developing the non-American markets – the intention was to divide the available capital between these two objectives in the ratio 2:1 – a considerable sum would be needed. Secondly, he was concerned that the Americans should not buy at a price lower than that at which many Phoenix shareholders had purchased. If existing shareholders were given reason for complaint on this score, it would be exceedingly difficult to push the deal to a conclusion. On the other hand, the Americans, as seasoned corporate investors, were unlikely to pay more for their minority holding than it was worth.

The ideal figure for Evans was £10 per share. This was the level at which the share had peaked in May 1961, holding that value for about a fortnight. Substantial purchases had been made as it moved off peak at £9 15s and £9 10s; about 45,000 shares changed hands at these prices. But the level in autumn 1963 was much lower. Furthermore, it had been falling immediately prior to the discussions: during September it had lost 10s under pessimistic and inaccurate press comment and was sitting at a low of £5 2s 6d when Herd began talking to Harris. Fortunately, the Americans were willing to agree that the current market price was unreasonably low and that the press reports which had produced it were unfair. Further, they conceded that they should pay not the market price, but the 'breakup' price per share. This included book values, all real assets *and* goodwill.

The Americans accepted this logic not least because the New York Insurance Department drew a distinction between its own valuation of company assets and the book values when calculating 'breakup' estimates. Further, the Continental men were given the free run of the Phoenix accounts, including all reserves. Using these figures, Davey

[28] Of the original £3.8 million, just over £1 million had been paid, and the rest uncalled.
[29] The nominal value of each share was 5 shillings, fully paid.

calculated a book value, making no allowance for goodwill, of around £7 10s. Additions for goodwill and expertise took the figure into the £9–£10 range that Evans wanted. The precise number was left over for Herd to negotiate with his Executive Committee in the USA. But, in the event, he had comparatively little difficulty and a price of £9 per share was agreed by November. That gave Evans £13.5 million of investment power.

The outcome of the financial terms was deeply satisfactory for Phoenix. But the proceedings of the meeting at Oatlands Park were not made the subject of a contract or any other such binding document. The agreed principles were embodied in a 'Memorandum of Intent' and it did not prove an exhaustive summary. The best that Phoenix could extract was an affirmation that the agreement was 'to be regarded as being of a long-term nature and not varied without adequate or reasonable notice by either party'. But if notice were given, of course, this afforded little protection. The British parties to the agreement came to regret that they had not embodied it in a legally binding document. Time was to prove that the ingenuity of the idea was no compensation for the looseness of the compact. The British tried to make it tighter, but the Americans' lawyers argued that their clients were not empowered to restrict their successors to such a degree.

For Phoenix, the Memorandum left two particular hostages to fortune. The British team had considered attempting to define the boundaries of the permissible Continental shareholding. With their eyes fixed firmly on an *upper* limit, they had regretfully concluded that such a formal restraint was not justified since, in a crisis, it might impair Continental's ability to fend off predators. However, some restriction upon Continental's holding falling below a *lower* limit would have been useful, though in itself scarcely easy to achieve. The second problem was that the Memorandum merely made recommendations for joint action and cooperation in foreign markets; it provided no means of enforcement. If the Continental ever developed independent ambitions in the foreign sector – as Phoenix had feared Travellers might – there was little that Phoenix would be able to do about it.

Obviously, it is relevant to press the question as to why in 1963 Phoenix did not insist upon a more comprehensive and enforceable statement of the agreement with Continental. In the early 1960s it was reasonable to assume that the UK authorities, specifically the Bank of England and the Stock Exchange, would resist the purchase by a foreign buyer of a controlling interest in a major British financial institution, but the Phoenix men were perfectly well aware that this form of protection was likely to be short-lived. So, why was there no more explicit attempt to define the permissible limits of the American shareholding, and why – as it turned out, more crucially – were there no terms set for the manner in which Continental might sell its Phoenix shares, should it ever wish to do so? Unfortunately, Phoenix could not ask Continental for first refusal on its holding, since UK companies were not permitted to 'buy in' their own shares. Sale in the market under Phoenix direction might have been a possibility, but, since, Continental had paid over the market price in the first place, this would have been a difficult request to make.

Nevertheless, such issues were raised by the British side. But again there were strong arguments from Continental's lawyers that the present directors could not be expected to bind their successors as to the proper holding for future times. The Phoenix team could do little against this line of reasonimg. They needed the assets. They knew that, if they did not achieve an injection of strength, they were ripe meat for a full and aggressive takeover. They were aware that they were taking a risk on Continental, but they thought it a lesser risk than that of a predatory raid upon them. Since the Phoenix–Continental agreement endured for twenty years, and it is unlikely that the Phoenix of 1963 could have evaded the predators for this long, their calculation was very probably correct.

Even so, Evans had problems in getting his chairman to sign: but sign, in the end, he did. Significantly, the last encouragement he received in this direction came from Harris. The end product, bearing Ferguson's signature and awaiting Herd's counter-signature, was conveyed swiftly to Paris, where Herd was currently staying, with Ron Bishop, then company assistant secretary, acting as courier. The Americans signed in the Lounge of the Ritz Hotel on the morning of Saturday 23 November 1963.

In retrospect, it can be seen that Phoenix succumbed to a beautiful idea, and did not succeed in securing the necessary small print. This is not surprising. The office was over a barrel; it was quite a comfortable barrel, and the contents promised satisfaction. But the position was not a good one from which to dictate the fine detail.

6. THE PHOENIX AND CONTINENTAL AGREEMENT: THE REPERCUSSIONS

The Phoenix management realised that the immediate prospects for the alliance would depend on the sensitivity with which the arrangement was made public. Here the financial arrangements were crucial. Both the structure of the share issue and the release of the details needed to guard against any outside takeover bid or any competitive offer that existing shareholders might find attractive. The leadership were clear that a swift 'one-shot' announcement was necessary. In the event, and uniquely in Phoenix's series of corporate purchases and alliances since 1908, the security was impeccable. There was no major movement in the Phoenix share until after the announcement on Friday 22 November. Then it rose by more than £1 to £6 15s 0d; but that was all to the good. Evans was satisfied that the secret had held firm 'which is a little remarkable having regard to the general efficiency of the grape vine'.

The all-important circular to shareholders was similarly well managed. Theoretically, existing Phoenix shareholders were entitled to purchase from the allocation of shares intended for Continental; but it would have been deeply embarrassing had they done so. Accordingly, the directors tactfully reminded the proprietors that they were 'not likely to be interested in subscribing for the new shares at £9 per share, as the price is substantially higher than the figure at which existing shares are available on the Stock Exchange'.[30] This tactic was successful; no applications for shares were received from the investing public.

Short-term sentiment in financial circles was also enthusiastic. Here Evans' careful consideration of the City aspect paid dividends. The *Post Magazine* congratulated Phoenix on having found a way of overcoming the 'unusual difficulties in raising new money for insurance companies'.[31] Nor did the £9 price paid by Continental attract anything other than a sympathetic hearing. *The Times* noted that 'The price paid of £9 per share compares with a closing market price of only £5 1s 3d on Thursday' and concluded, 'That Continental are prepared to pay so much above the market price indicates not only their certainty of the advantages of the deal to them but also, as the market was quick to realize, that Phoenix have been undervalued for a long time.'[32] Similarly, the *Sunday Times* noticed somewhat later that Continental had been willing to pay 'nearly double Phoenix's prevailing market price' and reported that they had done so 'on the strength of confidential data from Phoenix of the real equity values in their Stock Market and other investments'.[33]

The only sour note was struck by the Lex column in the *Financial Times*; it observed that, 'Phoenix – as the yield indicated – needed something doing to it. A British rescuer looked unlikely since the relatively few concerns with the £30 million or so required had quite enough problems of their own without adding voluntarily to them. However, it is from the US that the rescue has come'.[34] Here the reference to the fact that

[30] Phoenix Directors' Circular to Shareholders, 23 December 1963.
[31] *Post Magazine and Insurance Monitor*, 5 December 1963.
[32] *The Times*, 23 November 1963. [33] *Sunday Times*, 8 March 1964.
[34] *Financial Times*, 23 November 1963.

Phoenix may have been vulnerable to takeover or absorption – as at the worst moments of its American problems it may have been – was a relatively light one. It was the word 'rescue' that raised hackles among the Phoenix men: they did not consider that they had been sufficiently distressed to require rescue. But this was a small price to pay. Evans' summary of press opinion was able to record that the right notes had been struck: 'the impression seems to be that this has broken suddenly on the market as a novel and far-sighted development which is bound to have beneficial effects'.

Plaudits came even from the most elevated quarters of the City. The Bank of England appreciated the boost given to the January 1964 gold reserves by the inflow of Continental's dollars; and the head of the Exchange Control Section telephoned to present his compliments. The Bank allowed Phoenix immediate access to half the funds and access by negotiation to the other half. It also established a special account for the company from which it could invest overseas the proportion of the dollars earmarked for that purpose without having to pay the exchange control premium. In other words, the Bank was sufficiently pleased with Phoenix to assist in Evans' expansion plans. For his part, Herd joked contentedly, if appositely, that the cheque had scarcely left his hand before Phoenix had whisked it round to the bank.

Longer-term results, however, were not so happy. Whatever informed comment said and informed journalists wrote, the street gossip was that the American interest would predominate at Phoenix House. These rumours were to prove neither accurate nor just but they undoubtedly penetrated some City boardrooms. Phoenix's dealings with a number of large UK offices were affected by these stories and the office's acquisition programme was certainly damaged by them.

After the failure of the projected merger with London & Lancashire in 1959, the Phoenix men returned to the subject of acquisition in the middle and late 1960s. They found that their American connection did not work to their advantage. One attempt upon an illustrious name is particularly revealing of the domestic penalties attached to the cultivation of transatlantic friends. This was the most important of Phoenix's post-war merger attempts, and the outcome the more disappointing for that.

In 1965, upon the impending retirement of Anthony Pollen, chief executive of the London Assurance, an apparent opportunity arose for Phoenix to absorb this near neighbour in King William Street, one of the most eminent of the few remaining historic offices. It was not the first time that Phoenix had cast its eyes in this direction. Five years before, when Evans had been much occupied with a possible alternative to the

London & Lancashire, Phoenix had put a tentative proposal to the governor of the London Assurance, and to Pollen. During 1960, several months of private discussion had ensued, without ever reaching the stage of negotiation, before the London had decided, under Pollen's firm guidance, that it would do better on its own.

By the mid-1960s, the London men were convinced that this had been the right decision: the company had earned an aggregate surplus of £1.2 million over the period 1960–4, whereas Phoenix had suffered an aggregate deficit of £2.2 million; total reserves of London Assurance stood at £13.6 million against the Phoenix total of £8.6 million. In 1965, the London did not feel ripe for absorption. Nevertheless, like Phoenix, it had taken a hammering in the United States. And, unlike Phoenix, it had suffered a poor trading year in 1964, its dividend having to be paid partly from reserves for the second year running. By contrast, Phoenix reported sufficient profit (£1.3 million) in April 1965 to cover its dividend, the first time that it had managed this for four years. At this point the Phoenix 5 shilling ordinary share was riding well above £5 while the London 5 shilling ordinary share was languishing at 37 shillings. Any offer which came after Phoenix had announced its results and before the London had reported, in the following week, would catch the older company at a vulnerable moment. Any offer which arrived so close to Pollen's retirement would strike the London in the midst of a change of regime. The revived Phoenix initiative came at precisely such a point in the last days of April 1965.

From the London's viewpoint, this was Phoenix returning to the charge. To the Phoenix, it was a renewal of the friendly conversations of 1960. To Ferguson and Evans, the retirement of a senior colleague provided a natural moment for speaking out. To the governor of the London, now the banker R. E. Fleming, and to Pollen, the timing could not have been more sinister. Such opposed readings of events, moods and tones were to dominate the abrupt negotiations of spring 1965.

On 29 April, Ferguson and Evans, in a gesture which they intended as casual, called round for a tea-time chat with Fleming and Pollen and restated – again, as they thought, informally – the Phoenix's interest in buying into the London. Of course, it is possible that Ferguson's somewhat austere talents did not adapt easily to the skills of informality. At any rate, the London's leaders did not form the impression that the management of the Phoenix was striving to convey. What Ferguson intended as a tentative and friendly inquiry was heard by his interlocutors as the overture to a substantive and hostile bid. Indeed, they gathered that, this time, the Phoenix intended an immediate offer for shares, whether or not this was supported by the London's Court of Directors. Both sides acted consistently with these positions. The London decided that it must report the approach to the Stock Exchange and make a statement to the press. And the Phoenix men were astonished. However, they could only push ahead: their formal bid of 53s 3d per London share, or £44 million in all, approved by the press as a good price, was delivered on 6 May 1965.[35]

On the morning after the tea-time conversation, the proposal was in the City papers. At the London there was consternation: the bid had come from the blue and everyone in the office was convinced that it was a real raid. Senior management decided that it was time for a backs-to-the-wall strategy: a discussion called by Pollen in the Court Room of the London gave consideration even to the notion that salary cuts might be needed to fund a fighting defence. The London did not wish to be taken over by anyone, nor to play junior partner to any predator. But, of course, where there was one predator, there would be others. In reality, there was no possibility of repelling the Phoenix attack other than by joining with another company.

It was in this context, in April and May 1965, that Anthony Pollen began talking to Roger Barnett, his opposite number at Sun Alliance. These two were on friendly terms and understood one another easily. The two general managers reasoned that Sun Alliance could offer the London more affinity at the senior level and more compatibility in business organisation than Phoenix apparently could.

Given the London's reading of the Phoenix move as a full offensive, Pollen's counter-measures had to be swift. He told his senior managers of the preliminary approach on 29 April, and reported the formal Phoenix offer of 6 May in a circular to shareholders on 7 May; he advised them to decline 'for good commercial reasons'. A first offer from Sun Alliance was in the London's office by 3 or 4 May and was reported by circular to shareholders, in general terms, on 13 May. It was discussed by the London's Court on 14 May and found congenial. Shareholder support was stout, some believing that preserving the London as a wholly British enterprise was as vital as 'keeping our famous pictures'. By the end of May, London Assurance, an early eighteenth-century veteran, had found safe haven with the Sun Alliance, another early eighteenth-century veteran. Nevertheless, in Phoenix House, at the office of a veteran almost as old, David Evans was surprised and hurt by the outcome.

In fact, however, from the vantage point of the London, Sun Alliance

[35] *Daily Telegraph*, 7 May 1965.

did indeed make a more suitable partner than the Phoenix. A key factor in producing this conclusion was the link between Phoenix and Continental. Not that it was influential in the way the press imagined. For the public announcement of the Phoenix bid for the London in the first week of May had triggered headlines of the 'Yanks-are-coming' variety.[36] The City editors speculated that the joint US premiums of the Phoenix and the London, amounting to some £40 million, represented a 'juicy morsel' for the Continental and assumed that American planning was behind the Phoenix bid. This was the reverse of the truth. Phoenix was trying to build a more secure UK asset base for itself, not a better aircraft carrier for Continental. And the American office was trying to create a wider spread of joint operations overseas and not a still bigger share of the difficult US market. Nevertheless, such reports could only strengthen the impression that the spectre of American capital floated at the Phoenix's shoulder.

The London management was not unaffected by this presence. But it had more earthly American worries. Its own experience in the USA in the first half of the 1960s had been poor: but by 1965 some improvement was evident. The less alluring part of the London's US business came by way of a direct operation, Manhattan-Guarantee; the more attractive part (mostly marine at this point) was gathered through the eminent transatlantic underwriters, Chubb & Son Inc. A further concentration upon Chubb, for fire and casualty, lay in the future. The difficult business from Manhattan-Guarantee provided about 23% of the London's worldwide non-life premiums, and the management were trying to reduce this share; yet Phoenix wrote 44% of its worldwide business in the USA in 1965. Involvement with Phoenix would thus have meant reversing current London policy for the USA. Further, the connection with Chubb, one of the most prominent names in US insurance, had produced for the London an underwriting profit of $4 million over the period 1960–4, while Continental's underwriting results had run well below the average for US offices over the same period. It had been made clear to the London that an association with Phoenix–Continental would terminate the relationship with Chubb.

For the Phoenix, therefore, the relationship with Continental was a bonus element which reduced risk; for the London it would have been a liability which exchanged an existing stream of profits for a new source of problematic outcomes. No less compelling was the major point that, in 1964, the London's high-class marine sector contributed some £600,000 to the company's profit and loss account; and one-third of this worldwide

[36] *Daily Mirror*, 7 May 1965. The City page used precisely this form of words.

result came from Chubb. It is not difficult to see why the London should have baulked at the loss of its own American connection.

The attractiveness of Sun Alliance for the London touched on both these points. Not only did the outstanding quality of its fire account sit well alongside the outstanding quality of the London's marine account, whereas Phoenix and the London were similar rather than complementary in too many sectors. There was also the crucial fact that Sun Alliance already had substantial ties with Chubb; so association with Sun Alliance would pose no threat to this major source of the London's income. Nor was it accidental that both the Sun Alliance and the London had remained partners in a quadripartite Australian venture, the Unity Life, launched by these two offices, together with the Phoenix and the London & Lancashire, in 1959. Phoenix, on the other hand, had acquired in 1960 the Provident Life of New Zealand and transferred its Australian allegiance to this company. The resulting competition between the antipodean ventures had done little to win good opinions further down King William Street.

Allowing for the realities, however, the London men were not immune from the sentiment of the moment: at this time, financial opinion saw the penetration of an American element into the City as an alien presence. As a venture rich in tradition and respected connection, the London did not relish confrontation with a business strategy which – to its eye – placed no great value on such attributes. Of course, this was a misinterpretation of Vic Herd's business strategy; but it was nonetheless understandable. To the Phoenix, its American alliance actually intruded little upon day-to-day management or its UK general strategy; but *this* reality did not accord with the fears felt elsewhere within the insurance industry or aired in the financial columns. Of course, the full irony of the situation was not realised until 1984, when Phoenix, in order to save itself from predators, also sought safety with Sun Alliance (and London); and needed to do so because of Continental's decision to *withdraw* from its UK connection.

Two years after Phoenix's attempt on the London Assurance, another acquisition prospect was jeopardised in a similar way. In 1967 Phoenix decided to bid for the Yorkshire Insurance Co. Again it encountered a hotly contested affair. An attempt at an agreed merger broke down almost immediately. So Phoenix launched a hostile bid, which was in turn met by a burst of plucky independence from the Yorkshire. To the intense surprise of the Phoenix negotiators, the provincial office met their bid with a higher offer from the General Accident. Under advice from its financial advisers, Hambros, Phoenix raised its stake; but General Accident raised again; and scooped the pool, taking the Yorkshire at a very high cost. Phoenix could only infer from the over-bidding that its colleagues had special reasons for distrusting it. The 'novel and farsighted development' had come to be seen as the first wave of an American invasion.

Ironically, Phoenix *had* attempted to use its American connection in its quest for the Yorkshire. The principal reason for management's speed in merging the Phoenix and Continental administrative structures in the USA was to improve Phoenix's overall profit forecast for 1967 and thus strengthen its bidding against General Accident. However, the lavishness of General Accident's second offer ruled out any reasonable rejoinder from Phoenix.

Of course, the high bid by General Accident should not be seen simply as a 'stop Phoenix' device. At this point, General Accident was a non-tariff operator and wanted to gain an element of market advantage by acquiring an old and respected tariff company. This was at least one good reason for persisting with an expensive offer. The value of the Yorkshire's life business was another. Nevertheless, after 1963, Phoenix men felt, or were made to feel, that by letting the Americans in they had breached a different sort of cartel; and thereafter they were always vulnerable to a closing of ranks.

Nor was business proceeding smoothly within the American market itself. There indeed the Phoenix operation was falling increasingly under the control of its American partner. By 1968, the Phoenix's operating costs in the United States were such that the only prospect of major reductions lay in allowing Continental to take over the administration of the business. This involved the sacrifice of an independent network in the USA, and the termination of an operation over 150 years old. Such had not been the original intention. The initial proposal had been that Phoenix and Continental would maintain separate undertakings in the USA with Continental assisting Phoenix in areas like pay-roll, premises, computer services and claims-handling. But, in the mid-1960s, American income turned down again while Phoenix expenses refused to fall sufficiently fast. Drastic economies and rationalisation had reduced the Phoenix US expense ratio from 41.7% of net premiums in 1962 to 37.2% in 1966, but they were still too high by the standards of the American competition. Meanwhile, Continental had proved successful in reducing its own operating costs.

The answer from 1 January 1968 was to pool the US portfolios of the two companies. Continental took over the Phoenix operation in the United States – which earned about $72 million in net premium by this time – while Phoenix took in return 5.5% of the pooled premium of the

Plate 12.9 Chic's view of Phoenix profits, 1971.

two operations – which gave Phoenix $56 million in net earnings.[37] This produced a smaller business but one of better quality and spread. Further, the expense ratio fell overnight to 32% and reserve requirements were immediately slashed. The appearance of the balance sheet improved dramatically as some $7 million were released from Phoenix's unearned premium reserve into profits. Also, the effect on Phoenix's US trading results was powerful if not immediate: profits of £462,000 from the fire and accident accounts in 1971 and of £903,000 in 1972 – 'the most profitable underwriting year in the United States market for a long time' – in contrast to the loss of £1.1 million in 1970, the year of Hurricane Celia.[38]

For its part, Continental achieved even greater volumes of turnover and the drawing power of the Phoenix good name. This was distinctly a pooling of operations and profits, not a takeover: Phoenix of London continued to own Phoenix of New York and the American branches of London Guarantee and Union Marine.

Nevertheless, it was a tactical surrender for the British company which had pioneered the export of fire insurance to the United States.

7. THE PHOENIX–CONTINENTAL AGREEMENT: THE SEQUEL

The two weaknesses within the Memorandum of Intent concerning the limit on Continental's shareholding and the nature of the international cooperation between the two companies were the seeds of future discon-

[37] The Phoenix share of pooled premiums was raised to 6.5% in 1970.
[38] Chairman's Annual Reports, Phoenix Annual Accounts, 1970, 1971, 1972.

tent. Although the relationship ran smoothly for much of its twenty-year life, these would provide the main sources of stress, when stress occurred.

As early as March 1964, the Phoenix team was becoming concerned that there was nothing in the Oatlands Park Memorandum to prevent Continental from increasing its holding. The team's main solace was the verbal undertaking to hold Continental's holding below 25%, delivered at Oatlands Park by Vic Herd, always sensitive to Phoenix's worries. Nevertheless, in December 1967, at around the time of Phoenix's attempt on the Yorkshire, the Continental stake had risen to £1.9 million or 29%. If the increase had become widely known, it would certainly have fed the rumours about American influence within Phoenix. Indeed some senior Phoenix men were themselves wary of allowing the American interest to rise at this time. Their caution prevailed and, at the end of December 1967, the Americans agreed to run their holding down again to £1.7 million. However, even this represented a 25% stake, a significant slippage from the 22.4% agreed at Oatlands Park.

As late as 1981, the issue of an increase in the American holding was still generating a rather suppressed sort of tension. When, in the spring of this year, Phoenix's other main institutional investor, the Friends' Provident Institution, was considering reducing its stake from 10% to 6% of total equity, problems again arose as to how much might go to Continental. A search of Phoenix records was instituted in an attempt to find documentary authority for the 25% limit; but none was forthcoming. Harris noted that previous leaders of Continental were well aware of the 'verbal agreement' of 1963 and the reasons for the 25% limit but warned that Phoenix should ensure that the current chairman, John Ricker, 'is also alive to this understanding'.

In securing such a lavishly funded share purchase in 1963, and then restraining it at a minority level, Phoenix had achieved a notable coup. But over the years, the purchase became a kind of ransom, with the fate of the Phoenix dangerously dependent on the fortunes of the minority shareholding. The Phoenix men believed that they had bought space, the ability to expand in the farther parts of the world, but in reality they had bought only time.[39]

To Continental, it seemed as if they had made an investment which they were prevented from exploiting further by a gentleman's agreement. Indeed, at the time of the accord, the *Financial Times* had mused publicly as to what benefits lay in the arrangement for the Continental.[40] The

[39] For details of the expansion, financed by the injection of capital from Continental, see below, Section 9.

[40] *Financial Times*, 23 November 1963.

paper guessed – wrongly, in view of the terms – that Continental must have hopes of building up its interest in Phoenix.

If the issue of the precise size of the American holding raised periodic flurries, so too did the exact nature of the joint foreign operations that the two companies were supposed to run.

There are two broad views of the strains imposed upon the Phoenix–Continental agreement from this source. One is that the American side, despite the accord, continued to cherish and even to promote a largely independent foreign policy. This could run in parallel with, or instead of, the joint foreign policy of the agreement. Moreover, even if it were not instigated, or even condoned, by senior managers, it could still be implemented by independently minded middle managers. The other view is that the British side could be less than enthusiastic in its promotion of joint ventures, and slow to respond to American invitations to action. Of course, these forms of initiative or inaction need not synchronise in time: it would be perfectly possible for the Americans to display high enthusiasm at some points, the British to exhibit low enthusiasm at quite other points. Thus both views could be correct at different times. Or, in periods of mutual quiescence or accord, neither. But, if either did apply at some points, it is clear that any unilateralism by the Americans could strain British tempers, and any feet-dragging by the British might try American patience.

One problem was that Phoenix did not appear to know, at the time of the Memorandum of Intent, that the Continental already possessed its own 'foreign department'. This section was under the overall supervision of Herd's deputy (and later successor), 'Bo' Wentworth,[41] an official who had considerable experience of the French market and wished to give Continental a definite European presence. Since the Phoenix team's reading of the Memorandum was that *they* were to provide the overseas capability for Continental, the information that the Americans had already taken steps to establish an independent foreign section would have come as a considerable surprise at Phoenix House. Of course, it need not have excited alarm, since Phoenix might have assumed, understandably, that Continental's foreign interests were to become the object of a joint endeavour. However, to have assumed this would have required stronger nerves or stronger faith than the Phoenix negotiators of 1963 had believed they needed.

Even during Herd's tenure, therefore, differences in interpretation existed in regard to Continental's presence in overseas markets. But these

[41] Bo was short for 'boat', derived from a youthful vacation job.

differences were to become progressively bigger under some of Herd's successors as chairman of the Continental.[42] The first of these, Wentworth, was eager that Phoenix should share in the overseas acquisitions planned by Continental. However, the British side was impeded from enthusiastic participation by two major constraints: one was exchange control affecting outflows of capital from the United Kingdom; the other followed from some reservations as to the wisdom of Continental's expansionist strategy. Sometimes doubts about this also surfaced on the American side.

The centrepiece of the early attempts at joint foreign development was the Phoenix–Continental 'International Division'. This was based in New York but employed Phoenix as well as Continental officials and was intended to work through Phoenix's worldwide operational network. It was this agency which was intended to handle the overseas extension of insurances for American multinationals. The International Division would provide service for the placing broker in New York, probably under a master policy; and Phoenix would provide the specific market service, issuing local policies to supplement the master policy as required. The client multinational would thus receive worldwide cover adjusted for local conditions and reconciled to American insurance terms and conditions. The International Division became one of the few large US-based exporters of insurance of this era. Phoenix proudly believed that, in world terms, it was also 'the largest operation of its kind, and . . . the most progressive'.[43]

Participation in the International Division made Phoenix the UK leader in multinational insurances, the first British company able to offer a complete programme to the big international companies. But the office did not arrive at this position in the style which its managers had expected. At the Oatlands Park meeting, it had been envisaged that Phoenix would lead the development of the International Division. This did not happen. Instead, Continental took the initiative by grafting the Division onto its existing foreign department which had its own connections with the American brokers. Phoenix officials attached to the International Division found themselves cast not as star performers but as second fiddles. By the end of 1965 Phoenix had reconciled itself to providing not 'co-management' but 'technical support' for the International Division.

The areas in which partnership worked best were, ironically, not the

[42] Wentworth (1968–73), was in turn followed by John Ricker (1973–1982) and Jake Mascotte who presided over the last two years of the alliance.

[43] Chairman's Annual Report, 1970.

distant markets but the home bases of the two partners. Under the terms of the agreement, Continental set up a small operation in London which was heavily dependent on Phoenix services. Phoenix provided reinsurance facilities and reviewed all acceptances undertaken by Continental–London. From 1972 it also managed all Continental's marine and aviation business in London. The problem here was to reconcile British insurers to the involvement of Continental in the UK marine and aviation market, given the American company's forthright approach to the world marine and aviation business. Phoenix was well placed for this manoeuvre and executed it to the satisfaction of all concerned.

In America, Continental assumed the management of Phoenix interests through Phoenix of New York and London Guarantee of New York from the beginning of 1968. This was achieved through a reinsurance undertaking and a letter of intent signed by the chairmen of the two companies. Despite the lack of a formal contract, this arrangement functioned smoothly and was indeed vital to the economical running of Phoenix business in the USA.

In many other places there was less accord. The problems developed through three stages. The first involved the Phoenix–Continental S.A. of Brussels. Created in September 1965 to replace Phoenix's Belgian branch with a jointly owned company, this venture was intended as an Anglo-American flagship for the booming European insurance trade that was enthusiastically expected to accompany the inauguration of the Common Market. Equity was divided 51% to Phoenix and 49% to Continental. However, development proved disappointing. The breaking down of commercial barriers and the liberalisation of services which the Common Market was supposed to bring progressed more slowly than the management had hoped. Instead of becoming a European vehicle, the joint company found itself restricted largely to Holland and Belgium. Understandably, the Americans were not impressed by a market so much smaller than expectation. Their disappointment encouraged Phoenix to seek additional partners for the undertaking and created an opportunity for the British insurers to bring a leading Italian insurance company, Toro Assicurazione, a European force with which they had friendly relations, into the plan for the home continent. The Americans agreed to run their share in Phoenix–Continental S.A. down from 49% to 39%, in order to create a 10% holding for Toro. This was easier than running the Phoenix interest down from 51% to 41%, which would have raised issues of control and taken the joint company out of the Phoenix accounts.

In Brussels, the Americans suffered merely from unfulfilled expectations. In regard to Canadian business, the going was somewhat rougher. As a result of its resolute acquisition programme, Continental possessed by 1963 no fewer than three separate operations in Canada: its own headquarters in Montreal, the former Loyalty Group base in Toronto and the Royal General office in Vancouver. Given the presence also of Phoenix's powerful Canadian Branch, the possibilities for rationalisation looked compelling. At Evans' prompting, Phoenix's local management was briefed to carry out a feasibility study for both companies. However, this did not move fast enough for the Americans' taste; accordingly, Continental carried out a unilateral rationalisation.

Here, probably, was one of those occasions when Phoenix to American eyes was less than assiduous in responding to invitation. Not until 1983, a year before the demise of the Continental connection, was a concerted system achieved. It took the form of a management company entrusted with the supervision of both Continental and Phoenix operations in Canada. This began as a joint venture, with a Phoenix man at the helm. Even then, the new arrangement was subject to a good deal of influence from New York and, upon the merger between Phoenix and Sun Alliance in 1984, passed almost exclusively under Continental's management and direction.[44] Phoenix's initial agreement to the scheme derived from its desire not to appear excessively negative in the crucial discussions with Continental during 1982, discussions that were to mark the final phase of the relationship.

However, a third and more serious type of difficulty had been developing in France in the late 1960s. It derived from several types of strain between the International Division's arrangements for the French market and the individual dispositions of both Continental and Phoenix. Bo Wentworth's stint in France earlier in his career – a fifteen-year posting – had left him with linguistic fluency, a love of the country, experience of the market, and with substantial contacts. One of these was Pierre Barthélémy, whose family had represented British insurers in France over a long period. The Barthélémy organisation assumed its final shape as the Groupe Barthélémy in 1957. Then, it was designed to act as the general agent of the Sun for the French market, and, in the next year, took on the same role for the London, sharing the business equally between the two British insurers. However, by 1968 bad French fire experience prompted Barthélémy to suggest to the Sun and the London that 40% of the Groupe portfolio should be offered to a third company. Capacity would remain the same, but the exposure of each partner would be reduced. He pro-

[44] At the point of the merger, Continental exercised its right to increase its holding in the Canadian joint operation from 50% to over 60%.

posed that his American friend, Wentworth, and the Continental, should be introduced into the arrangement. With the agreement of the Sun and the London easily obtained, Barthélémy approached Wentworth in New York, and an amicable deal was struck. No doubt, Wentworth took Continental into this French scheme largely to help an old confrère maintain capacity in difficult times. But the move did open up an independent line into the French market for Continental, and one of some strength. The Americans then proceeded to reinforce it by buying a 10% stake in another French office, La Préservatrice.[45]

At almost exactly the same point, changes were afoot in Phoenix's approach to the French market. Until 1969, Phoenix had handled all International Division business in France under the Phoenix–Continental Memorandum, through its Paris Branch; and this arrangement had worked well, and to the satisfaction of all parties. But, in 1969, Phoenix acquired a substantial minority holding of 30% in Le Continent of Paris, the balance being held by Phoenix's major *European* ally, Toro Assicurazione.[46] Phoenix's Paris Branch was swiftly integrated within Le Continent. In the process, a significant expertise was lost.

Le Continent was a motor insurer, specialising in cover for 'deux chevaux' light automobiles. However, these proved less durable and less profitable than the company's extensive investments in property. For its part, Le Continent, like the similarly named but unrelated Continental of New York, lacked international range and hoped that a connection with Phoenix might provide it.

Phoenix's Paris Branch had proved well able to deal with International Division business. By contrast, Le Continent, which initially took over the French representation of the International Division, proved to lack the capacity needed to handle the French end of a large multinational industrial business. After months of difficulty, the management of International Division business was transferred, with Phoenix's consent, to Groupe Barthélémy.

At two points in this sequence, the partners in the 'Unilever of Insurance' acted with something less than mutual solidarity, and there was an uncomfortable interplay between 'American' and 'European' strategies for the French market. Continental entered an independent French operation while the International Division arrangements were still in force for French business. And, soon after, Phoenix acquired a French minority interest which disturbed its own smooth running of the same Anglo-American arrangements (but, in the process, reinforced a

[45] Sun Alliance purchased the Barthélémy Group from Continental in 1988.
[46] Phoenix Annual Report, 1969.

European connection of its own). Even when dealing in the same locality, and with the same local powers, the partners managed to work at cross purposes.

The pattern was repeated in Holland. Here, Phoenix had its own outlet, the Minerva, but Continental possessed two independent agencies. As in the French arrangement, these outposts were run directly by Continental for its own account. Such arrangements led some Phoenix men to ponder why Continental had ever proposed that a British company should operate as its overseas arm.

Such difficulties had begun in the late 1960s but they were still running in the late 1970s. Between 1974 and 1976, Continental attempted to move local representation of the International Division away from the Phoenix in three regions: The Republic of Ireland, Hong Kong and Singapore.[47] Continental's chairman, now John Ricker, was reminded that the original Memorandum had imposed restrictions on such 'adjustments': in areas where Phoenix was substantially committed, these changes could be made only with the prior consent of the British partner. Phoenix did not consent, and Continental took the point.

It was little wonder that by 1978, Harris had concluded that the relationship between Phoenix and Continental was no longer a partnership but rather an 'association' – although he remained optimistic about its potential for development.

What then lay behind this progressive estrangement? Throughout, there is evidence of an eagerness for action – and sometimes impatience – on the American part and an insistence upon reflection – sometimes protracted – on the British part. Unilateral action by the Americans often followed from this conjunction of attitudes.

The American unease may well have followed in part from the fact that the alliance had brought little direct benefit to Continental's bottom line. Of course, it had brought some. For instance, in the aftermath of the Phoenix's acquisition of the Scottish-based Century Insurance Co. in 1974, the company had undertaken to provide a 4% share of its entire UK fire and accident portfolio for the benefit of Continental, and promised to increase this to 6% – to match the Phoenix share of the Continental US pool – when the rate of business expansion allowed. But this was done at a time when the UK account was not especially profitable. And the fact remained that Continental had purchased some 22% of Phoenix's equity yet achieved little consequential impact upon their own business: the annual dividend from their Phoenix shares ap-

[47] By 1989, Continental had retired from the Republic of Ireland, maintained no presence in Singapore, and experienced heavy losses from its Hong Kong relationship.

peared in the Continental's profit and loss account and that – some risk-spreading apart – was the extent of it. Moreover, the joint operations which were launched into the rocky insurance markets of the 1960s and 1970s tended to be in high-risk areas, whereas Phoenix tended to keep its own best markets for its undivided attention. In such circumstances, eagerness by one party, earnest reflection by the other, were both intelligible responses; but it was a conjunction which held dangers for the future.

While Herd was in control relations ran smoothly. He was an expansive individual of energy and vision and he was wholly committed to the 'intriguing new plan', which he described as 'the next important development in our business'. His preoccupation was with the maintenance of an Anglo-American insurance link rather than with the tilt of the territorial power balance. Nevertheless, Herd himself allowed a dynamic foreign department to grow up within Continental, which was essentially incompatible with this larger strategy. And he stayed on to an advanced age as chairman, retiring at seventy-two. This meant that his two successors, each of whom took office around age sixty, and under a newly introduced age limitation, had only a brief period in which to set their own mark on the Continental battle honours.

The experience upon which Wentworth could draw in order to make a mark was European. Naturally enough, he had notions of his own for Continental's development overseas and this did not lead to the most tranquil of relations with Phoenix. Dealings were friendly but not undisturbed. This was so despite the best of intentions. During the Herd era, Wentworth had believed in his own foreign policy but had attempted to reconcile it with Phoenix policy. Certainly, he never took an expansionist step without advising Phoenix of the impending acquisition and pressing the British to participate. And, to the day of his retirement, he greatly admired the quality of Phoenix's overseas management and believed that the Americans had much to learn from it.

Nevertheless, given the constraints upon Phoenix, Wentworth could not share Herd's conviction that Phoenix should be the main carrier of expansion for Continental's foreign business. Wentworth would press honourably for Phoenix involvement in new acquisitions, only to find that the British would hold back, citing government restrictions and concealing politely a measure of scepticism, sometimes healthy, sometimes less so. The outcome was that in some markets, Continental vehicles were set to run alongside Phoenix vehicles, while later, in other markets, Continental acquired minority holdings in foreign companies despite the presence there of active Phoenix branches or subsidiaries.

There was nothing in the Memorandum of Intent which ruled out such a state of affairs.

The way that was opened for John Ricker to establish a managerial identity in his turn ran through a different territory. Herd's era of energetic acquisition had left Continental with a somewhat untidy jumble of satellite companies. Consequently, the opportunity facing Ricker was an exercise in rationalisation: he decided upon a policy of thorough reorganisation and brought in the management consultants to establish order within the Continental group. One outcome was a high turnover within the managerial hierarchy. Many of the new entrants knew little of the Memorandum of Intent, or, at best, were prepared to judge it only by the success which it had achieved, and that, in truth, was small enough. The pressure for independent foreign initiatives by Continental was undoubtedly increased by this gingering up of second-echelon management. Whatever Ricker's respect for the Phoenix reputation – and even the much-tried Harris always considered it 'wholesome' – this pressure was not always easy to withstand.

The *Financial Times*, of course, had wondered in 1963 what advantage the accord offered Continental. At one level, the answer is knowledge capital. No doubt, the distance between 'partnership' and 'association' was travelled partly because of the unwritten nature of much of the 'understanding', partly because of personality factors, partly because of the managerial shake-out at Continental. On the other hand, the Memorandum allowed a relatively inexperienced but ambitious foreign insurer to tap into a foreign insurance network covering much of the globe. Once it had gained some experience of its own, it wished to play the game. One British participant in this process concluded, 'the co-operation envisaged in the discussions in September–December 1963 did not come about because there subsequently developed on Continental's part a policy of independent expansion throughout the world using Phoenix facilities to create bases from which separate and frequently divergent entreprises in the name of Continental were launched'.

The dream of Harris and Herd that imagined a Unilever of the insurance world did not come to pass. But, despite many difficulties and travails, the idea did not entirely die during the administrations of Wentworth and Ricker, and it was certainly not killed off by them. Indeed, it was to enter another active phase during the early 1980s. By then, however, it must be acknowledged that the prospects were not auspicious for any concerted solution to the differences of interpretation revealed in the working of 'the first Anglo-American partnership in insurance'.

8. REFORM EXTENDED: THE HARRIS–BISHOP ERA

The tenures of the last two general managers of the Phoenix cover the period 1968–84. Although very different in personality, Bill Harris and Ron Bishop dealt in similar markets, addressed similar problems and did not assess them so differently. With due allowance for variations in outlook, therefore, it is fair to treat this period as a unit.

Certainly, the command patterns under these two chief general managers were similar. Harris and Bishop had worked together effectively in the past and, from 1968, cooperated well as chief general manager and deputy chief. Harris' natural incisiveness was well balanced by Bishop's more reflective style. When Bishop took over the top job on 1 January 1979, he in turn benefited from the support of complementary skills in his two deputy chief general managers, Ken Wilkinson and Arthur Matanle, the first initially controlling financial and administrative affairs, the second covering all operational matters except life. On Matanle's retirement in 1982, Wilkinson supported Bishop across the entire range. Although there were other important managerial influences – and not least two supportive, engaged and well-connected chairmen in the persons of Lord de L'Isle (1966–78) and Jocelyn Hambro (1978–84) – the major processes of decision-making were controlled in sequence by these two distinct teams.

At the policy level what underlay the unity of the Harris–Bishop era? The dominating feature in Phoenix's foreign relations – the link with Continental – behaved in much the same way for the great majority of this period. An increasing distance between the parties is evident from 1968, noticeable first perhaps in the dealings over France; in reinsurance, Phoenix went its own way with the creation of London Guarantee Reinsurance in 1974; and the American partnership which Bishop inherited was by 1979 more association than alliance. Relations continued in much the same way until Bishop encountered the crisis of 1982–4.

If the link with Continental was problematic for much of this period, world markets were consistently bad. Both Harris and Bishop assumed leadership at awkward moments in the life of the world economy. For Harris the immediate context was stock markets which slid from 1968 and were then decimated by the oil crisis of 1973 and the turmoil into which it threw the advanced nations. The major insurance markets suffered inflationary recession for most of the 1970s. For Bishop, the context was investment markets falling even from the modest rally levels of the late 1970s until the market recovery from 1982, and that was too late for the Phoenix. The FT-Actuaries 500 Index had peaked in 1968, slithered downhill to 1970, peaked again in 1972 and collapsed in 1973/4. It then dawdled at levels barely half those of the 1968 and 1972 peaks for the best part of the next decade. The US Standard & Poors Industrials displayed a similar pattern. Moreover, the proportion of American manufacturing capacity in operation fell continuously from 1979 to 1982, dipping below 70% at the trough, while American unemployment rose continuously over the same period, peaking at over 10% in 1982. This represented a significant downturn in the world's largest domestic insurance market. Only in 1982 did the international cycle move into upswing once more and the worldwide bull-market of 1982–7 begin its charge. But, unfortunately, the world had its timing wrong, for this revival coincided with the final downswing of Phoenix.

Even though the worldwide net premium income for general business of the twelve largest UK offices tripled in money terms between 1973 and 1982,[48] these were not easy markets in which to write profitable insurance. Thus the 'First Eleven' British companies in 1982 managed to produce a combined underwriting loss of very nearly £1,000 million. In particular, severe competition in the United States from 1976 combined with the economic doldrums to produce a loss in that market for all British companies of nearly 16% of premiums, double the loss rate for 1981. Yet, over the same period, these same British companies *increased* the share of total overseas premium earned in the United States from 42% to 51%.[49]

It is little wonder that Phoenix, given its earlier American experience, did not go down this road. Instead, from 1968, its US fortunes floated more safely in the Continental pool. It exchanged its relatively small, and certainly volatile, US operation for a share in Continental's much larger and calmer business.

Harris was the great Americanist in the Phoenix camp. He maintained a close personal relationship with the top men in Continental, kept a house in upstate New York, and, throughout his time as chief general manager, remained a regular visitor to the USA. Bishop was somewhat more Europeanist by inclination; but in reality both of them set out to produce greater equilibrium and balance within Phoenix's foreign earnings and both succeeded. Harris continued to cherish the relationship with Continental and no-one worked harder – to the very end – to preserve it. But Harris also judged this relationship, and its shortcomings, very accurately and he remained Phoenix's sharpest observer of the American market into his last days on the Board. Throughout the 1970s the Phoenix operation was expanded in Europe and further diversified in

[48] However, it rose by only 26% between 1976 and 1981. R. L. Carter and A. H. Godden, *The British Insurance Industry. A Statistical Review 1983/4* (Brentford 1983), p. 15.

[49] *Ibid*, pp. 154–60.

the Far East so as to form a counterweight to the American market. For the first time since 1945, the European share of Phoenix premium earnings outpaced the American share in Harris' last year as chief general manager.

Indeed, Phoenix's worldwide strategy in the period 1968–84 was superior to that of the leading UK offices as a whole. Not only did Phoenix global premiums from general business grow faster than those of the twelve largest British insurance companies,[50] but the exposure of the King William Street office to the dangerous American market was corrected to a more comfortable level than that enjoyed by the bulk of British insurers. As the UK insurance industry saw its share of overseas premiums taken from the USA rise from 42% to 51% over the period 1977–82, Phoenix persevered in its transatlantic adjustment, pushing the American proportion of its own foreign earnings down further from 35.8% to 35.4% (against 47.9% in 1969). For much of the Harris–Bishop era Phoenix was developing as a general insurer more swiftly and with significantly better market balance than its peer group. Consequently, when the US market in 1975 experienced its worst ever year to that point for fire and casualty business, Phoenix was able to escape the dire harvest reaped by other UK insurers, pointing to better worldwide equilibrium and the Continental pool as the reasons. The Phoenix strategy even managed to produce rare underwriting profits from the US market in 1977 and 1978.[51]

In two further areas Harris and Bishop presided over successful initiatives and took similar attitudes in respect of them. Both pushed the life side hard, including the export of life insurance. The innovative approach of Marshall Field was endorsed by both. Accordingly, Phoenix's annual average growth in ordinary life premiums in the three years 1980–2 outpaced that of any other 'First Eleven' company, with the exception of Eagle Star.[52] The life side of Phoenix, under three chief general managers, from the era of Evans to the end, was most energetically handled.

Much the same is true of aviation. Both Harris and Bishop appreciated and guided Phoenix's market-leading performance as an aviation insurer. Under the constructive management of John Peters, the aviation account was turned into a consistently useful profit-spinner; indeed it recorded better underwriting profits than the much bigger but beleaguered fire and accident accounts in nine of the ten years between 1969 and 1978 and

[50] By a factor of 3.2 against 3 for the period 1973–82 and by 33.6% against 26.0% for the shorter period 1976–81.

[51] Phoenix Annual Reports 1975, 1977 and 1978. See Section 17 of this chapter for overall profitability of the Phoenix.

[52] Including considerations for annuities. Carter and Godden, *The British Insurance Industry*, p. 87.

achieved peaks of profitability in 1971 and 1972[53] (see Table 12.4). Air profits were leaner after 1977 due to adverse market conditions but they remained significant. Moreover, aviation was a special interest of Bishop's and, in the early 1980s, he and Peters were to lead Phoenix, as the biggest corporate insurer of aircraft in Britain, into a London-based group which would become one of the largest aviation insurers in the world. Even taken alone, Phoenix's air account in 1982, at £25.6 million of gross premiums, was 61% larger than that of the next-ranking composite, the Norwich Union, 75% above that of the Commercial Union and 106% above that of the Royal.

If David Evans launched the campaign of reform at the Phoenix, his two successors pursued it with equal energy. And it consisted of a good deal more than the Continental agreement, or, by the late 1970s, the reduction of the Phoenix's exposure in the USA.

9. THE OTHER FOREIGN STRATEGY

The necessary recasting of Phoenix's traditional overseas capability was made possible by the lavish funding obtained by Evans from the Continental share purchase. This injection of capital was deployed both to create more capacity and to attain the better geographical equilibrium which had been Evans' original objective and which became the lodestone for Harris and Bishop. Their need to disengage at least some of the Phoenix forces from the USA naturally entailed a greater concentration upon Europe and other more distant markets. This operation was less a dramatic expansion of foreign dealing than an attempt to reorder it and to 'bed it down', to give it a more secure substructure. All this was conducted largely independently of Continental.

Foundations for this effort had been created in the twenty years before 1968, and especially in the preceding decade. In 1949, Phoenix had gone into Israel almost as soon as the new state was created in order to establish the Israel Phoenix. In 1969 its capacity was augmented by the absorption of the Hadar Insurance Company. In the interim a string of acquisitions and foundations was cast into the four corners of the world. Phoenix purchased controlling interests in El Fenix Latino of Spain in 1958, the Provident Fire Insurance Co. of New Zealand and the Provident Life of New Zealand and Australia, both in 1960, and the Atlas Hellenic General Insurance Co. of Athens in 1967.

The existing subsidiary in Denmark, the Codan Group, imaginatively

[53] When the surpluses of £668,000 and £810,000 represented nearly 11% of group net profits in each year.

managed by the Zobel family, underwent particularly striking expansion: it consumed Gorm Insurance in 1949, the Kingdom of Denmark office in 1955, the Idun office in 1959, the Protector in 1961, the A. S. Selandia in 1964 and the Normannia and the Danske Minerva in 1968. Even by 1961, and even by the measure of the overseas earnings of the entire Phoenix network, the Codan Group was a most significant force: it provided over 8% of foreign premiums, ranking third among the overseas stations after America and Canada. The Zobels of Copenhagen invite comparison with the Hanburys of Hamburg who sailed Phoenix's European flagship in the nineteenth century.

A substantial proportion of this shopping list of companies was acquired before the Continental funds became available, but the later purchases did draw upon Phoenix's augmented investment power. So, too, did the substantial administrative reorganisation which converted many Phoenix overseas branches or general agencies into fully fledged subsidiary companies between 1964 and 1969. The catalogue of foundations included: Phoenix of Nigeria in 1964, Phoenix Brasileira in 1965, Phoenix of Jamaica and Suid-Africaanse Phoenix in 1966, Phoenix Life Assurance of Australia in 1968 and Phoenix of East Africa in 1969. Between Israel Phoenix and Phoenix of East Africa only one other foreign launch took place that did not fall in the period 1964–9; and that was La Fenix de Colombia founded in 1954.

The logic for the swing towards subsidiary or associated companies was a triple one. One aspect of it was emphasised by the financial and investment officers of the company. General agencies reacted quickly in financial terms, sending back cash quickly, but they also *needed* cash quickly, and consumed resources rapidly. Foreign subsidiary or associated companies were slower to return cash, and could also absorb resources, but they did possess potential as self-supporting investments, with their own asset base in the foreign market. The second aspect, argued by the officers of the foreign department, was managerial. They saw the general agency system as inherently flawed: the general agent was remunerated on turnover, but the office which employed him was interested in profit; the one pressed for volume, the other for quality. By contrast, the subsidiary or associated company possessed a clear internal line of command and was itself managed for profit.[54] In the third place, the subsidiary or associated company offered some respite from economic nationalism: as part of the indigenous economy, it could escape some of the fiscal (and worse) attentions of some governments.

[54] Compare Section 16, pp. 993–4.

Wherever possible, the policy of transferring business from branches to subsidiary companies continued during the 1970s. But no entirely fresh corporate initiative was taken in the overseas market until the launch of Mayban Phoenix in Malaysia in 1977.[55]

So there is evidence both of foundations laid during Evans' initial period of innovation and of a more active and concentrated period of construction, once the capital constraint was removed.

There were different accents in the foreign interests of Harris and Bishop. While accepting the need for international diversification, and applying a healthy measure of it to Phoenix, Harris remained committed to solving the American problem. Bishop, both as his deputy and later independently, was interested in expanding the European and Far Eastern markets. In both phases, Arthur Matanle, (general manager 1971–8 and deputy chief general manager 1978–82), who had earlier given sterling service in Peru, and more generally in Latin America, featured prominently in the processes of reconstruction and expansion overseas.[56] So if the accents sometimes differed, the language was the same, and it sought new sources of demand.

In this pursuit, Phoenix benefited a little from introductions obtained through Continental, but by far the larger part of its momentum came from other sources. In France, Phoenix's fortunes lay effectively in the hands of Toro Assicurazione which owned 70% of Le Continent and had practical control of its affairs. The Danish operation was based upon independent Phoenix control of the vigorous Codan organisation. The company's annual reports throughout the decade repeatedly picked out Denmark as a centre of profitability.

More problematic were the undertakings in Spain and Greece, but here too Phoenix did much work in the 1970s and early 1980s in overhauling both Fenix Latino and the somewhat exotic Eastern Mediterranean connections. Even these previously resistant ventures were beginning to show more hopeful signs in Phoenix's last few years.

This inclination towards the home continent owed a good deal to Bishop's faith in the prospects for European expansion; it involved a more Eurocentric approach than any Phoenix had taken for more than a century. However, it was of course a revival of faith, since Phoenix had displayed that inclination for much of its first 100 years.

[55] The Phoenix interest in each of the companies considered as foundations or acquisitions before 1977 was a controlling one, although not always 100%. The Phoenix interest in Mayban Phoenix was 30%.

[56] As general manager, in the UK 1971–3 and 1977–8, Matanle also had much to do with the reconstruction of Phoenix's UK market. But between 1973 and 1977, he was responsible for all the Phoenix Group's general overseas operations outside Europe.

Regrettably, however, these initiatives acted more upon income flows than upon profit flows: with the exception of the long-standing Danish connections, the European ventures did not have time to move strongly into the black before Phoenix ceased to be an independent operator. Nevertheless, the European strategy improved volume and balance. And, in a year like 1973, when Canada and Australia recorded heavy losses and US profits dipped again, excellent results from Europe (mainly Denmark, France and Spain) proved just how important such balance could be.[57]

But in the 1970s, as in the 1870s, Europe was not enough. With questionable results throughout the decade from Canada, Australia, Belgium and the Netherlands,[58] following upon the earlier – and indeed persistent – difficulties in the USA, the Phoenix team decided to find new distant areas of expansion. Matanle was an important influence upon this process. The long-distance exploration struck some fortune in the Far East, particularly in the expanding economies of Malaysia, Hong Kong and Singapore. The creation of the Mayban Phoenix Assurance Berhad in 1977 as a joint venture with the Malayan Banking Berhad applied the device of the associated company to a new type of 'frontier market'. As with many recent developments in the Far Eastern region, the Phoenix initiatives prospered. Again, the point about balance was made: in 1977, the results from north-west Europe as a whole were unfavourable, but by then were more than outweighed by the positive results of careful expansion elsewhere, and by the retrieval strategy in the USA.

In other distant markets improvements in effectiveness were sought, and found, in new applications of the joint operation tactic. From 1979, in Australia, South Africa and Zimbabwe, Phoenix went into association with the Prudential, forming joint companies for general business in which Phoenix exercised the managerial control and the other great office provided support through its existing business connections and goodwill, coupled with a minority shareholding.

The outcome of these developments was a much improved equilibrium in the composition of Phoenix's foreign empire. Naturally, plenty of perils remained in foreign underwriting. This was a period of decolonisation, unsympathetic national governments,[59] expensive legal judgements, and currency problems exacerbated by the combination of a flagging

[57] Phoenix Annual Report, 1973.

[58] In the twelve years 1970–81, net underwriting losses were recorded in Australia in eight of these years, in Belgium in seven, in the Netherlands in six, and in Canada in four. Phoenix Annual Reports 1970–81.

[59] For instance, India nationalised its insurance sector in January 1973, ending a Phoenix connection which had endured since 1827 and had been worth over £400,000 in premiums in 1972.

economy and record inflation at home. If that were not sufficient, a rich supply of natural disasters ranging from cyclones Wanda and Tracy in Australia in 1974 – which did enormous damage, respectively, to Queensland and Darwin[60] – to hurricanes David and Frederic in America in 1979, was available to sharpen underwriting wits.

Nevertheless, better balance did provide Phoenix with some protection. Given the volatile performance of the American market in the 1970s – with underwriting profits for Phoenix in 1971, 1972, 1973, 1977 and 1978 but losses in 1974, 1976 and 1979 – protection of the overall foreign account was needed. That it was provided was demonstrated most clearly by the results for 1975. In many opinions, it was the worst year ever experienced by property and casualty insurers in the USA, but redistribution, together with the Continental pool, softened the impact upon Phoenix to a pain level far below that produced by the American setbacks of the 1960s. The resilience of Phoenix in 1975 together with American profits in five of his last eight years as chief general manager provided well-deserved satisfaction for Harris.[61]

The adjustment of the Phoenix's international trim was largely to thank for this. During the earlier American crises in 1961, the USA had supplied about 45% of Phoenix's *total* general premium income, Canada and Europe about 12% apiece and other overseas locations rather over 10%. By 1969, the American share was 34%, by 1972 24%, by 1975 20%, by 1980 17%. The European share surpassed 20% for the first time in the postwar period around 1974 and in 1978 still at 20% it outpaced the American share for the first time. Other overseas markets, outside North America and Europe, provided further trimming effects: by 1974 they contributed 19% of total group premiums.[62] Of course, factors were also at work within these figures which were not the results of free policy choices: the (virtually enforced) acceptance of US business through the Continental pool from 1968, and the weakening of the pound against European currencies during the 1970s both influenced the regional shares in total world business.[63] Nevertheless, both policy and non-policy factors

[60] 'Seldom, if ever, has so much damage been concentrated within such a small but populous area. For many insurance companies, this event was the most costly ever experienced.' Annual Report 1974.

[61] However, a note of warning sounded even in this US improvement: Continental could well have felt that the considerable benefits accruing to Phoenix looked too much like one-way traffic.

[62] The matching share of total general income from the UK market was 29% in 1969 but 49% in 1980. See pp. 952–6 below.

[63] Thus, between December 1971 and December 1981 the pound lost in exchange value against leading currencies in the following way: against the US$ by 24.4%; against the DM by 48.3%; against the French franc by 18.0% (*Financial Times*, passim).

had acted by 1980 to improve significantly the Phoenix's international diversification of income flows.

Indeed comparison of the international spread of non-life premiums achieved by the 'First Eleven' top British offices in 1982 reveals that by then Phoenix was among the most geographically diversified of all the big insurers. Leaving aside the specialised case of the Prudential, with its relatively recent forays outside its historic life business, only Guardian Royal Exchange among the big composites took a higher proportion of its total non-life earnings from outside Britain and the United States: 53.2% against Phoenix's 46.1%.[64]

No office took a higher share of total premiums from Europe than the 15.1% drawn by Phoenix from this source. Only one other office – again Guardian Royal Exchange – earned a higher proportion of total premium from 'Other Overseas', that is, mainly the Far East and Latin America: 19.9% against Phoenix's 11.9%.

By the early 1980s Phoenix was almost everywhere. Even if great depth had not been achieved in some markets, there were few new ones left to penetrate. This geographical coverage was a tribute to the energy with which the company's traditional skills as an exporter had been exploited and advanced in the preceding twenty years. Harris and Bishop had made full use of the opportunity created by Evans. They had not chosen aggressive expansion in new markets, but they had created, polished, and readjusted where necessary (as it often was) a business-getting structure of very wide spread; they were building to a long-term perspective.

On the life side of the composite's business, the Phoenix team had made great changes, and the investment team had introduced a new discipline to their field of activity (see Sections 10 and 16). For their part, the foreign insurers, under Ken Wilkinson as overseas general manager in the early 1970s, and Arthur Matanle and Ralph Petty as his successors from the mid-1970s, had also committed much effort to tightening worldwide lines of control and establishing clear financial and operational objectives for the distant trade. Discipline here was as important as it was in life or investment policy.

The result around 1980 was that Phoenix was better equipped with

[64] Carter and Godden, *The British Insurance Industry*, p. 64. Their categories are: UK, USA, Canada, Australia, South Africa, Europe and Other Overseas. However, these authorities separate out marine and aviation business written within the United Kingdom from the rest of UK business. If this is re-included in Phoenix UK business (as it is in the preceding calculations from the Phoenix accounts), the proportions of Phoenix business taken from markets other than the USA and UK in 1982 falls to 39.2%. This does not affect the inter-company comparison made here: Phoenix still stands second to GRE. The equivalent figure in 1980 was around 34%.

genuinely global earning prospects than it had been for many decades. The 'bedding down' or spring-cleaning of this system had been accomplished and the company could look forward legitimately to the rewards. The international organisation of the Phoenix was in good health at the time of the merger with Sun Alliance. Indeed, alongside the risk part of the pure life business, and the attractive motor accounts of Bradford and Pennine, the reconstructed foreign operation of the Phoenix was one of the features which made it most alluring to Sun Alliance. The reinforcement of Phoenix capacity enabled Sun Alliance's already strong overseas operation to outperform all other UK insurance composites in the second half of the 1980s.

But this is to run ahead. For if the foreign strength of Phoenix was to be an asset to the inheritor company, the method of its achievement also contained a threat for Phoenix itself. The universal coverage of foreign markets achieved in the Harris–Bishop era raised a problem that repeated in many forms throughout the Phoenix's last years. There was a limit to the *additional* growth that could be extracted simply from an independent presence in so many markets. The only way forward from this point was to absorb more foreign companies. And that required capital which Phoenix did not have. Phoenix had achieved better spread and distribution in its overseas business, but, in doing so, had pressed once more towards a constraint in investment power. Around 1980, the capital element of the 1963 crisis was in the process of reconstituting itself.

10. PARALLEL DEVELOPMENTS: MORE LIFE EXPANSION

When the final crisis came, it would come from overseas and it would involve capital reserves. But long before it did, other parallel developments had to be played out. One occurred in the life business, another in aviation, a third in technical diversification, including reinsurance. Important progress was also made in publicising Phoenix to the world – that is, in advertising – and in protecting its financial flank – that is, in investment. Each of these areas witnessed levels of innovation in the 1970s and 1980s that were scarcely, if at all, lower than those in the foreign trade.

The activism of the life department, first stirred in the 1950s and 1960s, was well maintained. A further push for life business, concentrating on products such as the special term assurances which would yield rapid returns, rather than profits delayed by two or three decades, produced another upsurge in life income. Between 1960 and 1970 new annual life premiums in current prices had risen by a remarkable sixteen times, from a mere £242,192 in 1960 to £3.8 million in 1970; and from this high base, they rose in the period 1970–80 by six times more, from £3.8 millions to £22.1 millions.[65] This enormous increase in policies sold was assisted by a considerable investment of effort in the expansion of the life sales force. By the early 1980s also, Phoenix management was paying particular attention to positive marketing, clear description of the product and a determined advertising campaign. This last, which put Phoenix posters on every tube train and Phoenix buses in many cities, benefited all branches of home business; but life was perhaps the biggest gainer.

Naturally, term assurances were not the only force behind growth of these dimensions. Pension business was also very active. The design of the Phoenix Growth Fund Group Pension, first introduced in 1966, and providing the benefits of a large pension fund for small employers, proved highly adaptable to the market conditions of the 1970s. The 1973 Social Security Act widened that market and 1973 and 1974 were years of great activity in pension sales. Phoenix annuity premiums rose by 39% in twelve months. In 1975 the market narrowed because of government restrictions; but the demand from the self-employed remained high. Accordingly, Phoenix responded with a new product aimed at this sector, and it was received enthusiastically. Phoenix UK new annuity premiums rose by better than 29% in 1976 and total annuity premiums by 36%. But the new state pension introduced in 1978 proved the most potent stimulus to interest: Phoenix *total* new annuity premiums rose by 23% and total annuity premiums by 60% against the 1977 figures.[66] The Phoenix could scarcely have caught these opportunities as they fell more adroitly.

Equally striking in its impact on life receipts was the build-up of unit-linked business. Among the large composites, Phoenix again proved a pioneer in this market with the introduction of its Wealth Assured Bond in 1972. This was a single premium contract which linked the assurance benefits to a unit in a portfolio of mixed investments. It proved so popular that Phoenix took £12 million in premiums in the first nine months of the scheme.[67]

In 1977 additional capacity in linked business was achieved by a highly successful acquisition: Phoenix bought Property Growth Assurance, a nicely timed new entrant from 1969 and one of the first British companies to transact linked business. Against some opposition, Harris argued that

[65] Even in real terms (1960=100), the increase was to £2.5 million in 1970, an increase of over 10 times, and to £4.0 million in 1980, a further increase of 60% over the decade of peak inflation.

[66] Phoenix Annual Reports, 1974, 1975, 1976, 1978.

[67] *Ibid.*, 1972.

Property Growth was well worth the issue of £3.3 million of Phoenix paper. He was proved correct. By the late 1970s and early 1980s the company was a powerful source of expansion for the Phoenix: in 1979 it generated a 36% increase in its single premium business and in 1981 a 56% increase in its new annual premiums.[68] Not least, Property Growth brought into the Phoenix organisation the experience in direct selling that the office needed.

The life sales offensive also followed the company's general expansion overseas. Here, Phoenix strategy avoided the USA and concentrated on Europe, Australasia and the Far East. The launch of Phoenix Life Assurance of Australia in 1968 formed an early step in this development. It was followed by the acquisition of a holding in Le Continent Vie of France in 1969. But a rather larger step was taken in 1976: this was the creation of Phoenix International Life, registered in the Channel Islands for offshore operations. Phoenix had already built up experience in a particular version of its specialist term assurances, transacted in foreign currency for overseas clients. Phoenix International was to cash in on the accompanying demand from investors seeking positions in hard currency with an office of international standing. This was an ingenious development, though marred in operation by administrative constraints, and later by changes in UK laws which made this type of business less attractive to potential policy-holders.

Of the new markets tapped by Phoenix's export of life assurance in this final phase of a process nearly two centuries old, Israel and New Zealand proved highly profitable, while, more recently, the booming economy of Hong Kong became one of the most rewarding. This business is probably best described as a promising beginning, still needing in 1984 the time to develop volume and critical mass.

Overseas new life premiums as a proportion of all Phoenix new life premiums reached 30% by 1972 and peaked at 34% in 1976 before levelling off around the 10% mark in the early 1980s. Even then, this last effect was due largely to the acquisition of Property Growth, which was wholly UK-based, and substantially single-premium in business mix, and also to the departure of Israel Phoenix from the consolidated accounts as a result of the mother company's holding falling below 51% in 1977. The impact of Property Growth is visible in Table 12.2 below (see 1978). However, by 1982, Phoenix was still the ninth largest exporter of life insurance in the UK corporate economy, no mean achievement for a composite on a slate which included such mighty life

[68] *Ibid.*, 1977, 1979, 1981.

Table 12.2. *Life premiums, 1975–81 (% increase on previous year)*

Year	Phoenix	All UK
1975	15.6	17.2
1976	18.7	18.2
1977	6.5	13.5
1978	74.9	20.1
1979	3.4	25.2
1980	11.3	13.3
1981	38.7	13.7

Sources: Phoenix Annual Reports; Carter and Godden, *The British Insurance Industry*, p. 183.

specialists as Prudential, Standard Life, Legal & General and Friends' Provident.[69]

Table 12.2 shows the percentage increase upon the previous year of all Phoenix life premiums against the matching percentage increase in yearly premiums for all UK business in force over the period 1975–81. Phoenix is close to the market increase in three years (1975, 1976, 1980), below it in two and spectacularly outpaces it in 1978 and 1981. A better measure, however, is the medium-term one: over the period 1975–81 Phoenix life premiums rose by 253%, thus comfortably outperforming the UK market increase of 189%.[70]

Moreover, within the short period 1980–2, only one member of the UK 'First Eleven' group of insurance companies (Eagle Star) managed a higher annual growth rate in life premium income than Phoenix (25.4% against 16.3%; the average for the eleven being 15.0%).[71]

Nevertheless, life profits did not mount up as readily as life premiums. Despite the emphasis on term assurances and other more imaginative devices, they remained – in an uncomfortable echo of Ferguson's convictions – slow to emerge (see Table 12.3). On the other side of the account, however, it is worth remembering that there probably *were* more profits waiting to emerge: Phoenix had invested substantially in Property Growth, and in 1984 was still awaiting the major profit outcome on this.

For all the entrepreneurial vigour of the life department, the lesson would appear to be that innovational drive alone – whether in a single

[69] Carter and Godden, *The British Insurance Industry*, p. 163.

[70] Phoenix Annual Reports; Carter and Godden, *The British Insurance Industry*, p. 183.

[71] *Ibid.*, p. 87.

Table 12.3. *Phoenix life profits 1974–8: transfers to general accounts (£ million)*

1974	1.5	1979	3.1
1975	1.7	1980	4.5
1976	1.8	1981	5.2
1977	1.9	1982	5.7
1978	2.2	1983	7.4

department or across the company board – offered in itself no secure way of guarding the Phoenix's independence. But, of course, lack of such vigour would have been a fairly certain way of surrendering independence at an earlier point.

II. PARALLEL DEVELOPMENTS: THE AIR WEAPON

Aviation insurance was a further area in which Phoenix built up a strong reputation from around 1960. A separate aviation department was created in 1966. Phoenix was an important marine insurer in its last quarter-century – if, sadly, not a very profitable one – and the marine account was always bigger than the air account. But Phoenix stood higher in the corporate pecking order in respect to aviation business and it was a much more consistently remunerative account. In 1982 Phoenix led the ten largest corporate UK aircraft insurers by gross premium while ranking third among the corporate insurers of ships.[72]

Thanks to the great increase in the size and vulnerability of tankers and bulk carriers, the Phoenix marine account, along with that of many other companies, remained continuously in the red from 1976–1981. By contrast, despite the parallel technological problems caused by the greatly extended use of wide-bodied jets, the Phoenix aviation account remained profitable on an underwriting basis throughout the 1960s and 1970s. Indeed, although its own levels of profit were reduced from the mid-1970s, it was the only UK based department of Phoenix to record an unbroken run of underwriting profits in the decade prior to 1984 (see Table 12.4).

Phoenix aviation was conspicuously and independently well-managed by another of Evans' Young Turks from the 1960s, John Peters. Evans had recruited Peters from the London & Lancashire, specifically to create an aviation department. Once again, it was Evans who spotted the inno-

[72] *Ibid.*, p. 132.

Plate 12.10 The end of a supertanker: *Olympic Bravery* wrecked on her maiden voyage, March 1976.

vation. But this was also again an area powerfully encouraged by Harris and Bishop, and powerfully developed by Peters under the aegis of all three general managers. Like Field, Peters was a self-starting manager of force and originality.

Phoenix was attracted to aviation because of the relatively predictable

Table 12.4. *Phoenix aviation department: profits, 1970–81*

Year	£	% Group net profits
1970	312,000	6.3
1971	668,000	10.7
1972	810,000	10.6
1973	598,000	7.0
1974	n.a.	n.a.
1975	300,000	2.7
1976	400,000	3.2
1977	500,000	2.1
1978	100,000	0.4
1979	400,000	2.2
1980	400,000	2.4
1981	100,000	0.6

Source: Phoenix Annual Reports, 1970–81.

nature of the liabilities. Even if disasters occurred – as they did in 1977, with the collision of the big jets at Tenerife, or in 1978, which saw the highest ever value of aircraft destroyed up to that time, or in 1979, when the Satcom III satellite was lost, or in 1982, when twenty-six Western-built aircraft were destroyed, eight of them in hostilities at Beirut airport – the claims were paid quickly and did not run on; the business did not have a 'long tail'. Phoenix resisted the disasters and built upon the market opportunities. Fortunate in possessing the right human capital to exploit them, Phoenix turned itself into the largest UK office in the class by the late 1970s.

However, Peters recognised that the fragmentation of the London market lost potential business to the Americans and the French. His remedy was to engineer the formation of a specialist aviation group of companies which could be easily identified and approached by the brokers. Accordingly, the London Aviation Group was set up in 1982 with a membership composed of Phoenix, Norwich Union and Guardian Royal Exchange. Under this arrangement, Phoenix's air account, which made up about half of the combined total for the group, was merged with the aviation portfolios of the other two offices. The direction of the resulting pool was undertaken by Peters. By the mid-1980s the London Aviation Group had become the third largest aviation insurer in the world. Phoenix was the acknowledged leader of the group and thus commanded a position in the aviation insurance market of genuinely global status.

12. PARALLEL DEVELOOPMENTS: TECHNICAL DIVERSIFICATION

In the ten years before 1984, Phoenix also pursued diversification by refining its technical approach in three further market areas. These were accident, sickness and unemployment insurance; legal expenses insurance; and reinsurance. The first variant in the accident sector was a form of insurance intended to protect repayments on hire purchase agreements. As the vehicle for this initiative, Phoenix employed its wholly owned subsidiary, the Fortress Insurance Co. of Plymouth. Phoenix had acquired a majority holding in this south-west office – founded by the directors of the Plymouth-based finance company, Western Credit – in 1957 and purchased the balance of the shares in 1968. Fortress was of modest size – capitalised at £500,000 in 1968 – but gave useful service in this profitable line. Fortress wrote accident, sickness and unemployment insurance for Phoenix from 1957, but Phoenix gave significantly more emphasis to this product in the 1970s and 1980s.

Legal expenses insurance was well known in Europe but rare in Britain when Phoenix took it up. The object of the policy was to protect the insured against the risk and costs of having to retain legal representation. In 1974 Phoenix launched the DAS Legal Expenses Insurance Co. as a joint venture into this market. Its partner, holding the other half of the capital, was the Deutscher Automobil Schutz Allgemeine Rechtsschutz-Versicherungs A.G. of Munich, the strongest company in Europe in this specialised line.

The potential of the expanding European market also had a bearing on the third area of diversification. Phoenix had been involved actively in reinsurance transactions for well over a century, with much of that trade based in Europe.[73] However, its dealings with Continental of New York encouraged it to overhaul its existing arrangements for reinsurance. Accordingly, in 1974, the Phoenix executive decided to concentrate all their reinsurance business on a single specialised company within the group: London Guarantee & Accident was chosen for this mission and renamed London Guarantee & Reinsurance Co. Ltd, generally known as 'LG Re'.

Its purpose was to enable a special focus to be given to reinsurance work and to snap up, by reinsurance, business that might otherwise be lost to ever-proliferating state monopolies or other official restrictions. Increasing integration within the EEC made this sort of capacity especially relevant. Also, as with much of Phoenix's foreign work at this time, LG

[73] See vol. 1, especially pp. 233, 251, 267–84, and 315–22.

Re was given a Far Eastern slant. A regional office for the East was planned at Singapore to handle the rapidly growing demand for reinsurance in the Orient; it was operational by 1976. In the same year the transfer of all Phoenix group reinsurance to LG Re was completed. This was a brave initiative but, alone among these new starts, it did not prosper. More might have come of it in time, but, in the event, it did not have enough time. By 1980 the world possessed heavy over-capacity in reinsurance. Many offices, including Sun Alliance, deliberately ran down their reinsurance business at this time. For those who remained in the contest, the market became exceptionally competitive and aggressive. In such heavy going, LG Re failed to record an underwriting profit between 1974 and 1981.

All three of these devices were attempts to carve out specialised niches in which a large company trading in a cluttered and competitive market could find some elbow room.

13. PARALLEL DEVELOPMENTS: THE LAST TAKEOVERS

The other way of increasing capacity was by acquisition. Here further parallel developments took place. But they were not all happy ones. To begin with, the tie-in with Continental had prejudiced Phoenix's chance of acquiring the London Assurance and at least affected its bid for the Yorkshire. Such slipped chances were made all the more galling for Phoenix by the continued integration process affecting its historic colleagues: a good example, close in time to Phoenix's disappointments, was the merger on equal terms which, in March 1968, brought together the Guardian and the Royal Exchange, to form the GRE group. With the Sun Alliance and London already a multiple entity, and the London Assurance absorbed into it, the disappearance of the old REA left Phoenix in isolation as the sole remaining individual company from the select group of eighteenth-century founders of corporate insurance. It was a precarious position.

However, if Phoenix did not succeed in its hunt for a major acquisition it was more fortunate with smaller prey. Even so, the postwar period, by the standard of earlier phases in the Phoenix's history, was a quiet time for UK-based takeovers. Late in the Second World War, and then after a lapse of a further decade, the company took over two provincial plate glass insurers, Plymouth Plate Glass in 1944 and Northampton Mutual Plate Glass in 1955.

Plymouth Glass provided the entrée into the south-western market which enabled Phoenix to take up its holding in the useful specialist company, Fortress Insurance, in 1957. Directors from the local finance company, Western Credit, remained on the board of Fortress and Phoenix used the smaller company for lines of insurance close to the expertise of these individuals. In 1969, Fortress was licensed to transact motor insurance and was selected by Phoenix to market a new economical motor policy on the direct billing system, an excellent but abortive scheme which was perhaps a dozen years ahead of its time. Also, from its acquisition, Fortress acted as the carrier for Phoenix's insurance of hire purchase repayments. Western Credit exerted influence on all these developments.

Phoenix also used the takeover strategy to provide the largest single addition to its motor capacity. In 1971, in the wake of the Vehicle and General crisis, another specialist motor office, the Bradford and Pennine Insurance Co., was facing rough water and in danger of capsizing. Harris spotted a major opportunity. Phoenix took Bradford and Pennine in tow and began to build capacity 'in a sector . . . which had not previously been actively exploited by the Phoenix'.[74]

Naturally, motor policies had composed a major proportion of Phoenix's accident portfolio for many years, but, during the 1950s, they had been subject, in Ferguson's own phrase, to a 'very restrictive acceptance policy'.[75] Whereas the total UK motor insurance market expanded by 6.9 times between 1946 and 1960, Phoenix increased its motor premium income over this period by only 5.5 times. By contrast, in the more active phase of Phoenix management between 1965 and 1980, the gap was narrowed: the UK motor market increased by 5.9 times while Phoenix total motor premiums advanced by about 5 times.[76] Of course, in underwriting terms, motor business was profitable for almost no insurer and Phoenix in the postwar years showed few outcrops of black in the sea of red which washed over most motor accounts. Vastly increased traffic densities – from 3.4 million vehicles on UK roads in 1950 to 12.6 million in 1968 and 20.8 million in 1984 – increased the collision rate, while inflation raised the cost of repairs. Nevertheless, motor business could add important elements of volume to total turnover and thereby significantly boost investment earnings.

During the 1970s, Phoenix used motor business for this purpose. By 1975, motor premiums provided 48% of Phoenix's total £76.1 million of

[74] Chairman's Annual Report, 1971. [75] Chairman's Annual Report, 1963.

[76] The 1980 figure for total Phoenix motor premiums was £81.6 million (from the Annual Report to Shareholders); but, due to changes in accounting procedures, no figure was separated out from the 1965 accident returns. The motor premium figure for 1963 was £16.5 million (from Home Branch Trading Accounts).

home fire and accident premiums and by 1981 55% out of the total £156.2 million. In 1982 Phoenix, with £90.9 million in motor premiums, ranked seventh on the list of the biggest UK motor accounts.[77] Bradford and Pennine proved a major source of account expansion and investment earnings for Phoenix in the 1970s; and for that, once more, the company had Harris' instinct to thank.

In 1974 Phoenix made a further catch; it was the last large-scale acquisition of its long history. But this was a low-key affair, unlike the two-fisted contests of the 1950s and 1960s or the complex negotiated settlements of the Ryan era.

Throughout the postwar period, Phoenix's relative lack of income and assets within the home base had caused concern. As part of its study of worldwide geographical equilibrium, the Phoenix executive had looked too at the United Kingdom and concluded that the office required more strength in the domestic market. For all his American affiliations, Bill Harris – like Gerald Ryan nearly seventy years before – realised that he needed more capacity on his doorstep.

A chance to acquire it arose through Phoenix's contacts with the Friends' Provident Institution. This highly successful mutual life office counted among its assets the Century Insurance Co., an Edinburgh-based office which it had acquired in 1918. However, the Friends' view of its northern subsidiary was altered significantly by the stock market collapse of 1974. The growl of the bear alerted the impeccably responsible mutual assurer to the possibility that the shares of a medium-size fire and accident insurer were perhaps not the most secure investments for a life business with long-term responsibilities to its members.

Even before the crash, the Friends' had been thinking of pulling the Century out of some foreign markets and Phoenix had inquired about the possibility of taking over these operations. A dialogue was thus already launched. In the aftermath of the stock market collapse, Phoenix was asked if it would like not just part, but all, of the Century. The Friends' proposition chimed in with Phoenix's needs, and the subsequent transfer passed off as a model of amiability. Friends' Provident was paid in shares – with Phoenix issuing six million 25p shares to effect the purchase – and thus acquired a 10% holding in the Phoenix equity, clearly for them a safer prospect than their ownership of the Century. Phoenix became whole owners of the Century on 31 December 1974.

At long last, Phoenix acquired a measure more solidity at home. For the addition of Century premiums raised the volume of Phoenix's UK

[77] Carter and Godden, *The British Insurance Industry*, p. 146.

portfolio by over one-third.[78] Most of the smaller office's business was in the domestic market, with a bias towards Scotland. Moreover, Phoenix Group profit before tax jumped from £10.7 million in 1974 to £18.2 million in 1975 and investment income from £16.4 million to £24.3 million, in good part due to the Century acquisition. Century assets accounted for at least £3.5 million of the gain in investment income.[79] This reinforcement in the United Kingdom was what Phoenix needed. But the Century was not entirely bereft overseas. In particular, it added a further element of balance in Canada and New Zealand. Most useful here was its Vancouver office. Since Phoenix in Canada was now centred on Ontario, the Vancouver operation added a further strategic counter on the board of group diplomacy. All the Phoenix business in the Western Provinces was passed to the Century organisation, whilst Phoenix assumed all Century's work in eastern Canada. In 1979 and 1980, when Phoenix's overall underwriting account for Canada was unprofitable, as it often was during the 1970s, the Century account was usefully in the black.[80]

The reform process of the 1960s and 1970s had included a very necessary redrafting of Phoenix's international insurance map. But this should not obscure the much increased emphasis given to the UK market. Bradford and Pennine and Century had much to do with this, and the effect on the share of total general income taken from the home market was striking. In 1969, this share was a mere 29%; by 1980 it was 49%.[81] Harris succeeded then, not only in obtaining a further measure of international equilibrium but also in greatly boosting the home market. It was a large achievement and regrettable that it did not turn out to be large enough.

In the postwar period, Phoenix really needed to secure a major takeover or merger in order to improve its weak domestic position. Yet Phoenix never satisfied this need. Between 1956 and 1967, the insurance industry experienced thirteen major mergers among its leading companies; these transformed twenty-two prominent offices into nine groups and produced a spate of much-hyphenated new names.[82] However, the Phoenix name remained wonderfully simple as the company was excluded from the mainstream of the UK merger movement. Ironically, the Continental tie-in, a remedy for weakness in the USA – which worked for some twenty years – cost Phoenix at least one chance of achieving a UK remedy by merger. In the event, through no fault of its own, the company proved a

[78] Phoenix Annual Report, 1975. [79] *Ibid.*
[80] *Ibid.*, 1979. [81] Calculated from Phoenix Annual Reports, 1969, 1980.
[82] Supple, *Royal Exchange Assurance*, p. 531.

weaker player in the acquisitions game than most large UK offices. The Century provided an exception to this record, but the Century was a second-line company, whereas the really telling mergers had featured front-line names. By contrast, the majority of Phoenix's takeover activity was directed at specialist insurers with refined skills and was aimed at small rather than big solutions. This was not for lack of trying. But it did mean that Phoenix was denied a source of strength which others were able to exploit.

14. PARALLEL DEVELOPMENTS: ADJUSTMENTS TO MANAGEMENT SYSTEMS

The many changes in overseas, life and aviation business, the innovations in products, advertising, acquisitions and investments necessarily required alterations in Phoenix's managerial approach. As with many insurance companies in the late 1940s, a job with Phoenix required knowing one's place and deference to a rigid managerial hierarchy.[83] It was hardly a system for managing anything that changed swiftly. In times and markets which did change swiftly, a more flexible approach was clearly needed.

On top of this, the management accountancy system with which Phoenix entered the 1960s was widely perceived as rickety by the new generation of managers who now led the company. As the volume of business expanded and the offices were required to report upon it to governments in greater detail, efficient mechanical methods of storing and recalling data became essential tools of the insurance trade.

But probably the worst managerial problem for the reforming Phoenix of the 1960s was to unscramble the vast concentration of administrative power that had grown up around the secretarial department during the Ferguson era. Effectively, the responsibilities of corporate secretary, personnel manager, administration manager and computer manager had all passed into the hands of the secretary. Be he never so meticulous, no individual could deploy such a range of powers and still maintain proper control. Where at the REA, managerial reform in the postwar period confronted, and overcame, the dangers of excessive decentralization, the matching effort at Phoenix needed to run in the opposite direction.

Although Evans held to some of the trappings of old-style management, his lighter touch with people took much of the rigidity out of the social relations within the company. Harris too was skilful in the use of the

[83] Compare Supple, *Royal Exchange Assurance*, e.g. p. 545.

democratic approach. Both men set out to achieve a sensible division of powers for Phoenix senior managers.

When John Hill retired as secretary in 1965, Evans moved swiftly to break the administrative structure into manageable units. Kenneth Jackson was appointed as chief accountant in 1964 and in the same year Ron Bishop, then Hill's assistant secretary, was forewarned that he should plan to reduce the scale of the secretarial operation when he took over from Hill. This he proceeded to do in his one year as secretary, before becoming assistant general manager in 1966. His successor as secretary, Ken Wilkinson, also kept the department on a tight rein. At about the same time, in 1967, the executive vice-president of Phoenix of New York, Frank Kendall – after five years in the USA an old American hand and, like Harris, an enthusiast of transatlantic business methods – was brought back to London to create a professional personnel department.

These changes ran a broom through Phoenix management practice. Despite some resistance from those with fixed views on the social relations of insurance work, concepts such as 'job evaluation' and 'standards of performance' were introduced and, gradually, accepted. Both Harris and Kendal were careful to involve the staff in the discussions surrounding these reforms. The Staff Association was expanded and brought into consultation on all major implications of the new methods. The changes were as well presented as they were badly needed.

Action was also taken to rectify Phoenix's slow and eccentric approach to computerisation; and again it was Harris who found the right man for the job. He did so when he appointed John Norman as group administration manager in 1972. Norman had been responsible for Phoenix computer development in the USA and had transferred to Continental when the Phoenix's US operation was merged into the Continental pool; he was persuaded to move to Britain by Harris. From 1973, the Phoenix, under Norman's guidance, created a formidable administrative complex in Bristol, taking the huge information-handling tasks of a composite insurance group away from the prohibitive overheads of the City.

In the management of data, Phoenix had used mechanical accounting and processing methods for years, but, before Evans, was slow into electronic systems. However, the USA, where government had been quicker in requiring detailed reporting of operating information, provided a useful model in this department. By the 1980s Phoenix possessed a sophisticated computer system for commercial business and a very advanced one for marine business. After the merger with Sun Alliance in 1984, the commercial system unfortunately proved incompatible with Sun Alliance's existing operating methods, but the marine system was adopted by the maritime insurers of the enlarged group.

It was not an accident that Harris, with his long American experience, recruited the talent to carry through these measures. Both Kendall and Norman, alongside Harris himself, brought important flows of managerial knowledge capital from the far side of the Atlantic.

The result of these reforms in administrative technique, and of the two-stage relocation of many Head Office departments from London to Bristol in 1973 and 1982, was a far leaner and fitter Phoenix.

15. PARALLEL DEVELOPMENTS: ADVERTISING THE PHOENIX

Today the public is accustomed to insurance advertising which is attention-seeking, designed for impact, and addressed directly to the risks against which the late twentieth-century community seeks protection. One large office has claimed, very effectively, that it will not 'make a drama out of a crisis'; while several companies have dared to feature old age in their advertisements. The market has become accustomed to forceful selling centring upon the real dangers of a threatening world. But it has not long been so. Until the 1960s, at least, most insurance advertising was so discreet as to be almost invisible. Any public suggestion that the problems against which the insured sought protection might include such unattractive episodes as death, fire or injury was considered bad form.

Under these assumptions, the insurance industry did not market its product; it hardly did more than indicate that the product existed. Advertisements of this era featured clients who took out policies for reasons of social obligation and insurers who designed them with displays of technical virtuosity and financial reliability. These last qualities were also often linked, somewhat obscurely, with the mystique and ceremony of the great City institutions which so decorously proffered their complex but essential services to the more conscientious and discerning members of the community. There was little hint here that insurance could be a precisely tailored defence against the many hazards of modern life and an item of mass consumption.

Generally, marketing is not a subject to have attracted much academic analysis from economic or business historians. This is true even where the product is a manufactured one; but it is even more true where it is a service. However, the changes in the marketing of insurance since the 1960s have been massive and obviously demand attention. They are also related, of course, to deep-running social changes which include

They are wise who protect their cars by regular maintenance service.

They are wiser who add the protection of the 'Phœnix' insurance service.

Building for the future is costly for the young married man.

The security of Life assurance can be obtained at reduced rates during the early years of marriage.

Plate 12.11 Decorousness in insurance advertising: the Phoenix politely proffers in the 1950s.

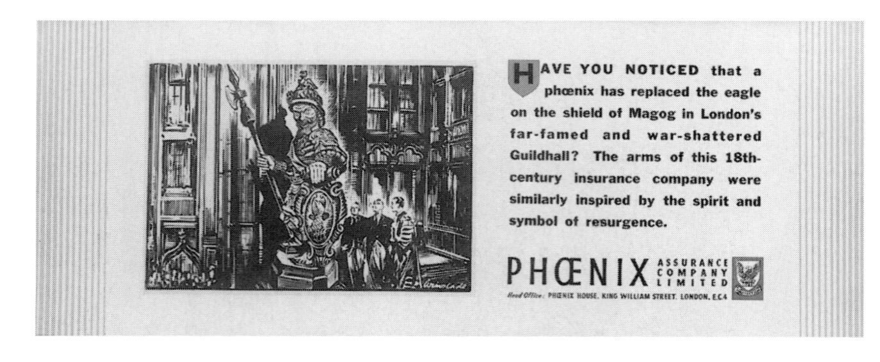

Plate 12.12 More decorousness: the Phoenix and City dignity.

(although scarcely exhaustively): the spread of prosperity, the increased influence of 'middle-class values', the virtual universality of the television audience, and the greater perception of risk in an increasingly risk-intensive society.

Phoenix was a pioneer in changing the style of selling insurance. Once more, it was David Evans who created the opportunity. But the person most responsible for exploiting it was perhaps Kevin Croker. A wartime pilot of distinction (flying light bombers such as Blenheims, Bostons and Mosquitoes), Croker joined Phoenix in 1948; he brought a magnificent moustache from his aeronautical past and a generously expansive personality well-suited to the arts of promotion. The department which he joined was the clerical staff of central supplies under Leonard Weightman, then assistant secretary; it was this department which somewhat incongruously – although this incongruity was not unusual in insurance circles – was responsible for Phoenix's advertising. The incongruity was reduced to a degree by the fact that Weightman's original training had been as a journalist.

The advertising generated by central supplies in the late 1940s, naturally enough, lacked the professional edge which later came to characterise Phoenix publicity. Its suppressed style derived from interwar practice and fitted the conservative and status-sensitive reflexes of the Ferguson years. At this time, the company regarded itself as the acme of insurance offices and the need to advertise scarcely obtruded upon this self-image. Such restraint was common within the industry; indeed, as blurred as Phoenix's advertising profile was in the years leading up to the Festival of Britain, it was still better than most.

By the late 1960s, this position was changed beyond recognition.

Plate 12.13 More homely but scarcely hard-hitting.

Phoenix's publicity campaign of 1968 was judged by the advertising industry's own Creative Circle to be one of the four best, in any sector of commerce, for that year. The other three were Cadbury's, Heinz and the Egg Marketing Board. On past form, it was extraordinary for an insurance company to occupy such a position in national advertising. The award was the first ever secured by an insurer. Within months of this success, Croker could write, in a most significant place – the *Journal of the Institute of Professional Salesmen* – that advertising, 'a science strangely new to insurance circles' was 'at long last established as a major breakthrough in selling insurance'.[84]

But matters were not to be as simple as this. There is more than one view on the place of advertising in the selling of insurance. Within the Phoenix experience, in fact three main positions can be identified. The first is that a certain amount of advertising is necessary to 'keep the company's name before the public'. The amount is small; it is cheap; and it is achieved by intelligent extemporisation. This view accepts that advertising below this minimum will probably lead to a loss of market share. The second position is that energetic advertising can be directed to selling significantly more insurance of specific types. This requires design-intensive campaigns and heavy media coverage; and it can be very expensive. Its aim is specifically to use advertising for the increase of market share. The third position is that advertising may be broadly useful in promoting the 'image' of the company. This is supposed to have a generally beneficial effect on all aspects of business; but the advertising commitment may be more selective and the cost relatively

[84] *Journal of the Institute of Professional Salesmen*, June 1969, pp. 35, 44.

modest.

A major difficulty with the second and third positions is that it is exceedingly difficult to demonstrate that increases in insurance business actually follow directly from efforts in insurance advertising. Attempts to do so involve follow-up sampling which is as complex and expensive as the promotional campaign itself. Also, such sampling, when dealing with an intricate service – rather than with, say, a chocolate bar or a motor car – reveals many subtle things. The fact that a reader or viewer remembers an advertisement does not guarantee that he or she takes any further action; the generation of a written inquiry does not ensure the purchase of a policy. Brilliantly catchy campaigns can produce very poor 'conversion rates'. Many press advertisements for insurance feature write-in 'coupons', which would seem to offer a means of tracking response. But these also produce many false replies, and hoaxes, and much additional administration, which is particularly disliked by the branch organisations.

It is, therefore, exceptionally hard to prove that insurance advertising works. So, it is not surprising that there were senior men in Phoenix who believed that it was technical virtuosity or financial standing which sold insurance, rather than posters, newspapers or sponsorships. The question then is how and why, in the period between the late 1940s and the mid-1980s, Phoenix tacked between these various concepts of advertising. As it did so, however, one thing became clear: this company was changing the way in which the entire UK insurance industry presented itself to the world.

The promotional side of Phoenix remained the Cinderella department well into the 1960s. Croker had begun pushing for more favour from about 1956. He argued that 'it is now time to consider production of a new series, designed in the contemporary style, with eye-catching qualities . . . if we are to get business, we should surely become more positive and publicise the types of insurance which we are most anxious to transact'. He doubted 'whether our present type of advertising has done more than keep the company's name before the public'.[85] But that, of course, was precisely the concept of advertising that his current masters favoured, believing that the best means to this end was 'the *ad hoc type of advertising that we have commenced to develop*'.[86]

Keeping the Phoenix name in front of the public cost a mere £22,373, or 0.05% of group net premium in 1960. Almost half of this went on poster sites on trains and buses and no more than some £3,000 on press advertising of all types, and that of modest quality. The best programme

[85] Report on Advertising Expenditure to 30 June 1956. 14 August 1956.
[86] General Manager's Note on Publicity, 10 February 1958 (my emphasis).

Plate 12.14 'We were there; We shall be there'.

to emerge from these tactics was a poster series with a historical slant: the 'We were there; We shall be there' campaign which ran in 1960 and 1961. But, on its own, it amounted to little.

The Phoenix took new directions in the middle and later 1960s. The main reason was the advent of David Evans to full control: Phoenix was spending about £30,000 per year on publicity by the early 1960s, but Evans was prepared to spend 'real money' in this area, which, in the late 1960s, meant advertising budgets in excess of £150,000 per year. However, the low starting point was again nothing unusual in the marketing strategy of the insurance industry. Table 12.5 below reveals that eight important offices spent very different amounts on press advertising in the last quarter of 1965, but also, with only one or two exceptions, very tiny amounts.

Phoenix began to depart from this sort of pattern in 1965. Given the small amounts available to spend on the big newspapers, the national press was not convincing as a direct selling medium for the office. Experi-

Table 12.5. *Expenditure on press advertising: eight offices, October–December 1965 (£)*

Prudential	16,508	Norwich Union	2,892
Northern	12,700	General Accident	2,188
Guardian	5,428	Pearl	576
Phoenix	4,128	Legal & General	281

Source: Report on Publicity Expenditure 1966,13 January 1966.

ence suggested, however, that the advertisement of life assurance worked best. Accordingly, 1965 saw an experimental push in the direction of specialist publications and assurance publicity slanted towards the family. Phoenix began targeting journals such as *The Wedding Book*, *Mother and Baby*, *Hers* and *Mothercare*, and placing in them the specially designed 'Such a Nice Family' series of advertising shots. This was the first Phoenix campaign to adopt a multi-media approach in which the press shots were coordinated with a poster campaign stressing the same theme.

Close in time to this initiative in 1965 a more general programme to boost the Phoenix name was launched. This was a highly successful 'puzzle' campaign, which ran on train and bus posters: the 'What is it?' series. Photographs of everyday objects, taken from odd angles, were reproduced on the posters and the travelling public invited to write to Phoenix with the answers. This technique established a strong link between advertiser and potential consumer and guaranteed a high level of recall. Both the 'Such a Nice Family' and the 'What is it?' campaigns elicited high levels of response. But the increased burden of tracking enquiries was not appreciated by the branches, and, against the protests of the publicity men, the line officials were not obliged to run down each one. So once again, it could not be demonstrated precisely what proportion of new business was due to the marketing effort. What was clear, however, was that the new level of activity imposed new levels of cost: the 'Nice Family' alone cost £15,000.

But that in itself represented a new stance in marketing. By 1967, there was a clear break in the pattern of advertising budgets: the total publicity allocation for the year came to £94,000, and was to be the first of several instalments of really determined spending. This hiatus in the finance of publicity was associated with a change of advertising agency. Up to this point, Phoenix had been advised by the St James agency, a specialist City concern which was adept with the formal publicity of chairman's statements and annual statistics. However, Phoenix under Evans wished to

Plate 12.15 'Such a nice family . . .'; the advent of realism.

create a genuine form of consumer advertising for insurance. And for this the office needed an agency which could move soap-powder or soup tins. Consequently, in 1967 Phoenix began a long association with Dorland Advertising Ltd., the agency which, at that time, handled the market-leading accounts of Castrol (including the 'liquid engineering' series) and Heinz. It was a relationship which was to last through Phoenix's remaining years as an independent brand name.

In January 1968 Dorlands carried out the first of several highly intelligent analyses of UK insurance advertising. It found the offices' approach to the public characterised by 'a certain overall greyness' and concluded that, in consequence, 'the UK citizen is, in the main, sadly under-insured'. The advertisers believed that there were prospects of 'vastly increased business for any Insurance Company which uses all the latest techniques of advertising', when few, if any, were doing so. Conventional insurance advertising was deemed ineffectual: by promising security and happiness, it instilled over-confidence and complacency. Effective insurance advertising would need an appeal to 'stronger emotions'.

Perhaps the key innovations in modern insurance publicity followed from this: 'one of the strongest means of evoking responses with a potential customer... lies in the realm of fear'. However, it was recognised that, 'this approach, taken to its logical conclusion, could reflect upon the Company which uses this method'.[87] The sensible tactic would therefore be to address the appeal to the client's sense of responsibility, stressing the reality of risk and the danger of under-insuring against it. Dorlands wished to confirm this perception by a fully scientific investigation into why people bought insurance.

Phoenix advertising was not alone in needing an overhaul. A survey of ABC1 males carried out by Southern Television in 1968 revealed that, even in this prosperous region of the United Kingdom, the public's perception of insurance companies was very dim indeed. Only the names of the Prudential and the Pearl, both 'industrial' life operations committed to the mass market, had registered with the community to any extent; and Phoenix was well down the list of also-rans. Dorlands' assessment of the greyness of insurance advertising appeared fully vindicated. For Phoenix the agency suggested a strong response: reverse the decision of 1965, place less reliance on specialist journals and posters, and develop a strong presence through a 'single medium' campaign in the national press. The budgetary implications were apparent immediately: Phoenix spent £118,000 on advertising in 1968, £133,000 in 1969 and just over £150,000 in 1970, these levels being double or treble those even of 1966. Over 80% of these enlarged sums paid for advertisements in the national papers.

But increased exposure was not the Phoenix's only objective in this active phase. Croker also wanted a more forceful type of publicity which would clearly distinguish Phoenix from the bulk of insurance advertisers. He found it in a hard-hitting type of copy which addressed itself not to the warmth and security garnered in by endowments and annuities but to the realities of accident and injury: these advertisements spoke of death in the selling of life assurance and crashes in the promotion of motor policies. Thus a bereaved young widow was featured in the series, 'How will Sheila Manage Now?' and the motoring public was invited to ponder on 'What will happen if your insurance company crashes before you do?'. The response was strong. The plight of the unfortunate Sheila drew some hate

[87] Note on Advertising and Marketing Operation, 1968; January 1968, PX1845/2D.

Plate 12.16 Sheila in trouble.

mail, while the motor campaign brought protests from other insurers, among them, ironically enough, Vehicle and General.[88] But both the public and the competition certainly took notice. These were courageous initiatives and real innovations; Phoenix was the first office to employ this

[88] Which crashed famously in 1971.

sort of realism and became the standard-setter for the industry. This was aptly summed up in the results of a market research survey of 1971: the public now associated *all* insurance advertising with just three names, Prudential, Pearl – and Phoenix. Prudential and Pearl, according to Southern Television, had been well in the public mind in 1968; but Phoenix had come from nowhere.

This was success indeed by the measures of public relations. But, by the measures of insurance, there also seemed to be success. In contrast to the poor conversion rates of campaigns in the early 1960s, the lavish promotional spending at the end of the decade was associated with a sharp upturn in new business. Phoenix new life business in particular advanced far faster than the industrial average: by 87% in 1968 and 30% in 1969. The life department could point to new products and its own dynamism in explanation of this development, but it is difficult to believe that there was no connection between the Phoenix's highest-ever standing in public consciousness and the upturn in its new business, which affected not one but several sectors of its operations. Croker certainly believed that 1968–70 was a period in which Phoenix advertising sold a good many more Phoenix policies.

From 1968 the industry as a whole started spending much more on advertising. This was in some part because the big offices needed to catch up with Phoenix, but there were other powerful influences. The ending of the motor tariff in 1968 produced vastly increased competition in a sector which responded well to advertising. And the heavy promotion of unit trusts in the late 1960s heightened public awareness of savings in general, and made it both worthwhile and necessary for the insurers to publicise their competing products. The total advertising budget for all insurance companies in 1968 was £2.3 million, but in 1969 £4.0 million. The Royal had increased its spending from £50,000 in 1968 to £200,000 in 1969; while Sun Alliance moved up from £100,000 to £250,000. Phoenix advertising expenditure in 1968 had represented 6.4% of the industry's total, in 1969 only 3.5%. At the end of 1969, Dorlands concluded that, 'over the past two years, there has been a revolution in the marketing and advertising of insurance'.[89]

There is a sense in which it was unfortunate that the Evans–Croker initiative in advertising should have happened only just before the arrival of an advertising bandwagon within the industry generally. It was unfortunate because it raised questions as to whether Phoenix could afford to maintain its own recently enlarged advertising profile relative to the many

[89] Phoenix Advertising Budget for 1970, 17 December 1969, PX 1845/2F.

rapidly enlarging profiles of bigger offices. Both Croker and Dorlands proposed a 'bullish' strategy designed to work up the Phoenix 'image' and to increase awareness of, and confidence in, the company. This was to be done by a more concentrated press attack, experiments with television advertising, a direct mailing campaign and participation in suitable exhibitions.

The problem was the money. Merely to have stayed where it was in relation to the industry's expenditure in 1970, Phoenix would have needed to increase its advertising budget by a further 10% to £154,000. To have kept the position that it had secured by 1968, with 6.4% of the industry's advertising, would have required an expenditure of £256,000 in 1970. This was the price of having stolen a march. Another possibility was to relate spending on publicity to the income secured from new business since 1967. On this base line, new business in life had grown by 148% and in fire and accident by 135%. Averaging these increases would point to an advertising budget of £286,000. This was the price of winning business through earlier successes in advertising; it was a follow-on imperative. The Dorlands recommendation was that £256,000 was the minimum advisable figure in the midst of the industry-wide 'revolution'. In the event, Phoenix spent just over £150,000.

For there were other ways of thinking about the problem. One change of general manager had brought about Phoenix's switch to an active strategy of marketing insurance. Another change brought a different emphasis. Harris had taken over from Evans in 1968. He had accepted the large expenditures of 1969 and 1970. But his tendency was to believe that insurance was sold mainly by the technical excellence of the product or the influence of the broker, rather than by the impact of posters or commercials. And he probably had in mind the Expenses Reduction Programme of his American phase. Not least, however, he saw something anomalous in the size of Phoenix's advertising budget for 1970.

By this time, Phoenix was the acknowledged marker in the quality of insurance advertising and had the national awards to prove it. But, more extraordinarily, allowing for its size, it now spent more on publicity than any other office, bar one; and the one was the Prudential, which lived by direct appeal to the public. Croker's intended figure for the 1971 budget, at around £180,000, would have been surpassed by only two offices, Prudential again and the Norwich Union (see Table 12.6).

The results of Phoenix's high spending were unquestioned. All parties agreed that three years of real money and good design since 1968 had succeeded in 'rejuvenating the image of the Phoenix'.

The other ways of thinking applied to the *future* implications of this

Table 12.6. *Advertising expenditure, 1970 and 1971: major offices (£)*

	1970	1971
Abbey Life	61,300	29,700
Commercial Union	59,200	69,000
Equity & Law Life	48,000	39,100
General Accident	148,000	15,000
Guardian Royal Exchange	79,000	96,300
Legal & General	71,400	77,900
Norwich Union	120,500	188,700
Pearl	41,100	56,800
Phoenix	150,000	50,000
Prudential	190,800	225,900
Royal	9,300	110,000
Scottish General	40,900	54,900
Standard Life	108,100	127,000
Sun Alliance	17,200	109,300

Source: Note for the General Managers (Home & Life) on Advertising for 1972, PX 1845/1D.

achievement. Naturally enough, advertising managers and agents preferred to continue with a successful active strategy. Harris took a different line. While agreeing that the Phoenix image *had* been rejuvenated, he wondered whether, once that had been achieved, it was necessary to *continue* spending one of the largest budgets in the industry. Once a new niche had been cut, might it not be possible to invoke again the concept of keeping the name before the public? This manner of thought was somewhat reinforced by the market research finding that the sampled public associated all insurance advertising with just three names: Prudential, Pearl and Phoenix. Leaving aside the allure of alliteration, what did this imply? Prudential was the most lavish spender of all, and, effectively, had to be; yet Pearl was among the more modest spenders on publicity. It did not follow obviously from this that Phoenix had to continue as one of the largest spenders. So Harris invoked another yardstick: Phoenix's advertising budget should be pitched at a level comparable to those of offices of similar size. In practice, this seems to have meant selecting a ranking about half-way up (or down) the group of large offices shown in Table 12.6.

Accordingly, Croker's proposed budget for 1971 did not survive beyond the drawing board. Instead, the allocation for 1971 – at £50,000 –

was a third of that for 1970. This was a challenge which Phoenix's advertising staff and their agents had to accept, and, with variations, one which they faced throughout the remaining life of the company. It did not defeat them. Their aim, as Croker put it, was 'that the rejuvenated image does not begin to erode for a considerable time'.[90] They were helped in this by the fact that the advertising budgets of the 1970s did not turn out to be quite so limited as the initial reduced targets suggested. In 1970, Phoenix ranked second for advertising expenditure. Harris was aiming for a ranking of around seven. But, amidst the lavish spending by rivals in 1971, his budgets produced an actual ranking of eleventh. Clearly, this was an undershoot. It was corrected in 1972 with an advertising budget of £95,250, giving a ranking of six. In real terms, this remained the pattern for the remainder of the decade.

Phoenix was much assisted in developing an advertising policy to cope with Harris' tactical restraint by the completion in 1970 of Dorlands' scientific investigation into the effects of insurance advertising. This 'Attitude Study Report' or 'Analysis of Image Penetration' proved a key document; it established a credible assessment of what was wrong with insurance advertising and enabled Croker to make maximum use of scarce resources. Under Phoenix's commission, Dorlands had sampled 1,002 male ABC1 subjects in fifty parliamentary constituencies. Of these, 93% proved to be heads of households; 90% were married; 86% owned a life policy; and 77% owned a motor policy. The spontaneous awareness of insurance[91] demonstrated by the sample varied widely according to the type of insurance, as displayed in Table 12.7.

Of these results, the relatively low score for motor insurance was the most surprising. Not least startling about this is the fact that a lower percentage was spontaneously aware of motor insurance than actually owned motor policies!

The investigation yielded some generally important findings in regard to the sociology of insurance purchasing. When broken down by age, the sample cohorts between 31 and 50 tended to have more policies than their younger and older counterparts. Household policies, unsurprisingly, were fairly evenly spread, once the age of 30 was passed. Motor and whole life policies were most often held by the 31–40 cohort, while endowment and accident policies were marginally more likely to be held by the 41–50 age group.

By social class, the A group tended to be better covered for most types of insurance than the B group, which similarly tended to be better

[90] Note for the General Manager, 25 February 1971, PX 1845/2F.

[91] That is, immediate recognition of the purpose of the insurance offered.

Table 12.7. *Spontaneous awareness of types of insurance: 1,002 ABC1 males, January 1970 (%)*

Whole life	79	Endowment	61
Motor	68	Personal accident	34
Household: buildings	67	Others	23
Household: contents	65	Don't knows, etc.	2

Table 12.8. *Policies owned by age: 1,002 ABC1 males, January 1971 (%)*

	21–30	31–40	41–50	51–60	Total
Household: buildings	54	80	81	79	75
Household: contents	60	83	88	88	81
Motor	72	82	79	71	77
Whole life	59	73	66	67	67
Endowment	53	63	69	59	62
Personal accident	25	34	37	29	32
None of these	5	1	1	1	2

covered than the C1s. The exception to this was the high score achieved by the C1 group in regard to endowment policies (see Table 12.9).

These findings offered some very clear targets for those wishing to direct marketing efforts towards possible gaps in demand. But there were also discoveries concerning the channels through which marketing had been directed towards the targets (see Table 12.10). Brokers accounted for 12–16% of the policies sold to the sample, with the exception of motor policies where their role was much more pronounced. Outside motor and household policies, agents accounted for about half of all policies sold. The higher proportion for agent-sold household policies almost certainly followed from the insistence of building societies that their clients should insure mortgaged property through the agency of the societies. Phoenix's emphasis that advertising during the 1970s should in no way disturb broker-generated business is interesting in the light of these statistics.

Powerful pointers emerged also as to what kind of advertising registered, or failed to register, with the sample. The awareness of insurance, in all its dimensions, was found to be low. Phoenix was not associated by the sample with any particular types of insurance. The values that

Table 12.9. *Policies owned by social class : 1,002 ABC1 males, January 1971 (%)*

	A	B	C1
Household: buildings	81	79	68
Household: contents	86	81	78
Motor	86	75	75
Whole life	72	66	65
Endowment	60	55	68
Personal accident	45	33	26
None of these	2	2	2

Table 12.10. *Method of sale: policies held by 1,002 ABC1 males, January 1971 (%)*

	Broker	Agent	Direct to company	Don't Know
Household: buildings	13	65	21	1
Household: contents	16	53	29	1
Motor	35	35	29	1
Whole life	12	51	34	2
Endowment	12	55	32	1

were associated with it were, first, that it was 'large and established' and, next, that it was 'sound'. It also proved to be the kind of office that was 'recommended by friends' and had policies 'that are easy to understand'.

The proportion of the sample which acknowledged recall of Phoenix advertising was 21%, rising to 32% among those who already knew the Phoenix name; and the proportion was sensitive to social class: 18% of C1s recalled Phoenix advertisements, 19% of Bs and 34% of As. However, respondents were not good at remembering specific campaigns or product claims. Three out of four of them had no opinion as to whether Phoenix advertising was 'informative', and four out of five had no idea as to whether it was 'direct and to the point', or not. The national press proved in 1971 to be the most remembered medium, while train and bus posters tended to be noticed more by the younger respondents. The most effective stimulus to recall was the Phoenix 'Bird' insignia, and the only

Plate 12.17 An affair with the Phoenix.

specific advertisement which had stuck in the collective consciousness was the 'Date with a Bird' slogan. Again, rather naturally, the younger age groups proved better at recalling this tag than their elders.

Phoenix modelled its campaigns for the 1970s on the guidelines produced by this remarkable inquiry. Given its findings and his reduced spending power, Croker needed to devise a very particular advertising concept. This was to be neither simply 'keeping the name before the public', nor mass insurance marketing. Instead, he proposed to sell an image and to create an illusion. The promotion of image was designed to cancel the weakness of association revealed by the survey, to increase awareness of, and confidence in, the Phoenix and to support the brokers' selling efforts.[92] The illusion would present Phoenix as a large-scale advertiser even though funds no longer stretched to the reality. These objectives were achieved by careful selection of target audiences, media and advertisement design.

In 1971, the target groups were seen primarily as the general public, but predominantly male ABC1s, and the commercial audience which dealt with brokers. However, in 1972 this range was narrowed to the AB class of men earning a minimum of £1,800 net per annum; such a group numbered 2.8 million, or 14% of the total male population. In the course of this year, concentration narrowed further towards major customers for business insurance. The policy as to media was subject to less variation. Croker was convinced that the illusion of a large-scale advertising presence was produced most effectively not by the 'drip' method of many small exposures but by short bursts of highly individual advertisements in

[92] Note for the General Managers (Home and Life), 1972.

a few, highly prominent locations. In 1971, the prime choice was for whole-page spreads in the *Sunday Express*. This newspaper, with a circulation then of 4.28 million, reached 45% of the AB target group, while the whole-page tactic conferred a dominance and authority which, it was hoped, would counteract the lack of frequency. In the next year, five national and four large provincial papers were picked out, again with campaigns compressed into short periods, so as to create a vivid but economical impression.

By 1973, however, Croker was concerned that the publicity 'raid' was losing image to the bigger spenders. He concluded that new advertising needed to be especially distinctive in order 'to pull the Company away again from its competitors'.[93] The result was a campaign of specially commissioned cartoon advertisements poured into a single working-week of advertising time. By itself it cost £60,000 out of a yearly advertising total of £85,250. Cartoons had not been used widely in insurance advertising until this point, and the artists commissioned were well-known names. The form, size and daily repetition of these advertisements certainly achieved the desired individuality. Phoenix was gratified by the level of approving comment from its target audience.

Throughout this sequence, advertising design was guided by the results of the 1970 inquiry. The need for insurance was portrayed always in 'true life' situations. The appeal was pitched to the reader's sense of duty and concentrated upon the real dangers of under-insurance or no insurance. In advertising life assurance, Sheila or her descendants remained to the fore: the need to protect the family was repeatedly stressed, with the focus falling on the wife rather than the children.

The 'hit-and-run' tactics developed in the early 1970s, with the hitting done with high-quality campaigns shaped for distinctiveness, remained Phoenix's advertising style until the end. They were highly effective within the goals set by the company, and the cartoon campaign of 1973 again led the pack; but probably the Phoenix reached its peak as a standard for the industry around 1971.

There is perhaps one exception to this general conclusion. As chief general manager from 1978, Ron Bishop allowed somewhat larger budgets to flow towards the advertisers. Croker used some of this money – about £200,000 over three years – for a final coup. This was probably Phoenix's biggest ever publicity project. It was a clever blend of sporting fixture, social event, sponsorship and television spectacular. The idea was to organise a special golfing competition in which a pair of top professional

[93] Note for the General Manager (Home), 31 January 1973.

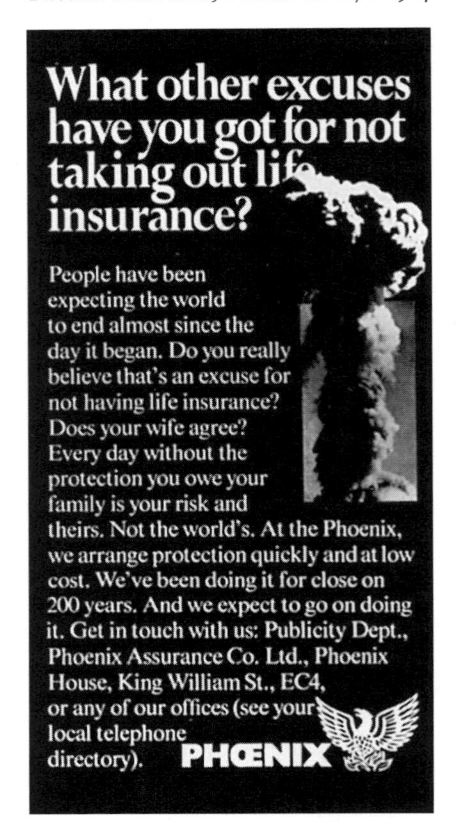

Plate 12.18 The ultimate in realistic advertising.

male golfers would compete against a pair of top professional female golfers with the matches shown on television. Rights were negotiated with the BBC; Peter Allis agreed to provide the commentary; and the matches were played on the Woburn course, adjoining Woburn Abbey. Publicity was assured in at least three directions. Since golf courses are large places, a goodly number of clients and colleagues[94] could be invited to witness the event at first hand. The sponsorship would create a favourable impression in golfing circles, which, of course, are not inconsiderable. And the novelty of the male–female sporting contest guaranteed prime broadcasting time, indeed on one occasion in 1981 the evening of Boxing Day. On that, and

[94] And even the odd business historian.

similar occasions, the Phoenix name was seen by more people within one half-hour than ever before (see Colour Section, Plate 6).

Convincing the public that it should take risk seriously is a difficult job. Risk is not a pleasant matter to contemplate. When the advertisers extol the virtues of a soft drink or a convenience food, they are offering the prospect of immediate, if minor, satisfaction. But there is little immediate satisfaction to be had in the purchase of a home contents policy or a health protection plan. The consumer has to be frightened gently into a course of action. But he must not be frightened too much, or he will shy away from the whole unpalatable project. It is a difficult balance to strike. As many of the illustrations in this section reveal, Phoenix was a pioneer in finding the balance. Indeed, Phoenix pioneered the type of insurance advertising which has dominated up to the 1990s. To have invested relatively large sums for a relatively short period in order to become the market-leader was clearly justified.

Should the Phoenix have gone further? Matching the biggest spenders would have been expensive given the company's size, and probably could not have added further large slices to market share. Basically, there appear to have been two extreme possibilities of success in insurance advertising after 1970. One was spending very large sums on publicity in search of a resounding advertising victory. The other was doing brilliantly on a slightly augmented shoestring. The methods by which Phoenix presented itself to the public in its last years fell closer to the second extreme than to the first.

16. PARALLEL DEVELOPMENTS: INVESTMENT PERFORMANCE, 1945–1984

The Phoenix investment department was ten years old by the end of the Second World War. The need to manage the securities side of insurance as a specialised operation, first identified at Phoenix in the mid-1930s, was to be even more insistent in the postwar years. Actuaries, attracted by the pressure to secure assurance underwriting, were often drawn further into investment management. This was true at Phoenix of Ryan, of A. S. Holness, and of the company's second investment manager, George Turner, who succeeded Holness in 1945. Turner was to be a major influence in turning Phoenix into one of the classic institutional investors of the postwar City.

Turner's career in investment management covered the exceptional span from the Great Crash of the late 1920s well into the Ferguson era; he retired in 1961. He was followed by Charles Knight for the period 1961–

70, and then by Brian Oram who piloted the investment side of Phoenix from 1970 until the final absorption by Sun Alliance in 1984.

Phoenix's investment strategy in the postwar decades breaks down into three phases which coincide roughly with the tenures of the three investment managers of these years. Turner put the emphasis on equities – in which he had made an early beginning as Holness' deputy before 1939 – and also upon mortgage business, together with a speciality of the pre-computer age known as gilt-switching; Knight pushed the equity business further, as all institutions were doing in the 1960s, but also took Phoenix decisively into property operations; Oram expanded the property aspect and introduced a more disciplined system of analysis, selection and justification for all investment operations. Also in the 1970s, the investment department worked to convert Phoenix outposts abroad from expensive agencies and branches into self-supporting companies. Investment policy in the final years combined with foreign policy to overhaul the company's structure as a multinational enterprise.[95]

It is possible to trace Phoenix's investment performance over the near half-century since the Second World War in some detail. The portfolios of the two main funds, the fire and general and the life, can be broken down by category of investment and each category expressed as a percentage share of the total; and this can be done for both the balance sheet values and the market values of the investments. Balance sheet values are traceable for both funds down to 1980 (see Tables 12.11 and 12.12), but market values for the fire and general fund are available only until 1970;[96] for the life funds, however, market values can be identified until 1984, the final year of trading (see Tables 12.13 and 12.14). We may then compare the balance and market values of the portfolios, and, for life, the cost values also, at five-yearly intervals, over a considerable time-period (see Table 12.15).

Before 1945, the differences between balance and market values of the two portfolios were small (although the market price of the life portfolio was almost 50% up on its cost price by 1940). Rapid divergence between balance and market values then occurred in the fire and general fund between 1945 and 1955, and in the life fund by 1960. The market values of the life funds also showed major gains on the balance values in the phase of highly active investment markets between 1975 and 1984.

95 See Section 9, p. 939.

96 That is, they are available in ledger form (The 'Blue Books') until 1970; beyond that point many of the fire and general records appear to have been kept in computer form, and these are no longer accessible. This, of course, is a danger which new technology creates for the business historian: as companies merge, and systems change, the electronic record may well prove more elusive than the written word or number.

Reassuringly, the sector shares calculated from balance sheet values show the same *trends* as those calculated from market values – with some exceptions, which are predictable, and, therefore, also reassuring. Both measures show an upsurge in Phoenix's commitment to UK government issues for both portfolios around 1940–5 – a classic war finance pattern – and a major retreat thereafter. Similarly, balance and market values for the fire and general funds each show a withdrawal from foreign government paper after 1945 and also a reduced affection for debentures in the later 1930s, but a revival of feeling for them after 1950. Market values tend to give lower sector shares for mortgages than do balance values, and this is true of both portfolios, but particularly true of life fund mortgages after 1945. Predictably, also, market values allot lower sector shares to debentures than do balance sheet values. The reverse effect is present in respect to property and land in the fire and general account, for here market values give notably stronger sector shares than balance sheet values for the period 1945–70, with a particularly striking figure for foreign property holdings around 1970;[97] however, this effect is not repeated in regard to the life funds.

A shared and strong effect, present in both portfolios, is the much higher proportion of ordinary shares when expressed in market values; these bulk much larger in the Phoenix's postwar investment profiles when counted by this measure rather than by balance values: they took up 33.8% of the life fund by market price by 1965 against only 19.4% by balance reckoning, or 35.1% of the fire and general portfolio by 1970 against 28.0% by balance reckoning. The main effect of expressing the company's investments in market values, therefore, is to give a more prominent position to all postwar investment in equities and some postwar investment in property.

Within this statistical landscape, the investment managers found their own individual pathways. The first of them to confront the postwar markets, George Turner, was a reserved and kindly man, but, in a quiet style, no mean innovator. Before the Second World War, the Phoenix investors had been confined, as were the investment managers of most offices, to a diet heavily weighted with mortgages and gilts, both home and foreign: these made up 46.2% of the value of the fire and general fund (in both balance and market values) and 61.7% of the balance value of the life portfolio (or 54.5% of the market value) in 1940, while an equally traditional attachment to debentures added a further 20% approximately to each account. A growing enthusiasm for equities had not succeeded in

[97] This may be related to one of the big Codan property investments coming on stream, or, possibly, the entry of the new Head Office building in Sydney into the accounts.

Table 12.11. *Distribution of investments by major categories:*[a] *Phoenix fire and general funds, balance sheet values, 1935–1980 (percentage shares)*

	1935	1940	1945	1950	1955	1960	1965	1970	1975	1980
UK govt[b]	13.8	13.1	24.1	15.8	10.7	11.1	11.6	15.2	22.1	26.3
Indian & colonial govts	8.7	10.4	7.6	8.7	–	–	–	–	–	–
C'wealth govts	–	–	–	–	7.8	7.5	4.9	–	–	–
US govt } Foreign govts }	12.0	22.0	30.8							
US govt				25.3	16.7	10.9	4.9	–	–	–
Foreign govts				2.9	3.2	2.3	2.6	–	–	–
Debentures	38.7	20.3	10.6	15.0	20.9	23.9	26.9	23.2	13.6	9.0
Preferential stock	3.5	5.5	5.8	6.5	7.9	6.0	3.1	–	–	–
Ordinary shares	2.0	3.5	3.6	6.9	11.3	13.8	19.0	28.0	31.1	32.4
Mortgages	1.5	0.7	0.4	1.8	2.7	3.2	6.4	4.7	–	–
Property	10.5	8.3	6.2	5.1	7.7	11.3	11.3	13.5	6.3	7.4
Cash	8.3	14.5	9.8	11.4	10.6	9.7	8.5	15.4	3.2	1.8
Shares in subsidiary companies	–	–	–	0.3	0.3	0.3	0.1	na[c]	23.3	22.8
Total portfolio (£ m)	15.0	16.7	22.0	33.3	43.0	55.0	80.0	142.0	231.0	308.0

Notes: [a] Categories are major ones only; thus columns will not always sum to 100%.
[b] Central and local.
[c] Aberrationally, no figure is given by this source, presumably because of a major regrouping of holdings around an accounting point. Certainly, by this time, shareholdings in subsidiaries were substantial, and other sources suggest that up to 30% of this Fund was represented by shares in subsidiaries by 1970.
Source: Phoenix Annual Balance Sheets, 1935–80.

Table 12.12. *Distribution of investments by major categories:*[a] *Phoenix life funds, balance sheet values, 1935–80 (percentage shares)*

	1935	1940	1945	1950	1955	1960	1965	1970	1975	1980
UK govt[b]	25.4	35.9	51.1	46.7	27.8	20.7	9.4	12.5	9.8	13.6
Indian & colonial govts	16.4	14.4	8.9	4.1	–	–	–	–	–	–
C'wealth govts	–	–	–	–	2.7	1.7	5.9	–	–	–
US govt / Foreign govts	2.4	1.2	0.6	0.3	–	0.1	0.8	–	–	–
Debentures	20.8	22.1	16.2	9.4	18.5	20.1	23.3	27.4	14.4	13.8
Preferential stock	9.1	9.6	6.8	5.6	5.9	6.0	3.6	–	–	–
Ordinary shares	0.9	2.9	2.0	11.2	15.9	22.1	19.4	22.8	22.2	29.2
Mortgages	10.2	10.2	5.4	13.1	19.4	22.9	29.2	26.2	–	–
Property	1.9	1.9	1.2	3.9	5.6	3.8	5.4	4.4	11.6	14.6
Cash	0.5	1.7	2.7	1.9	1.0	0.3	0.9	5.5	11.7	11.2
Shares in subsidiary companies	–	–	–	–	–	–	–	1.3	30.3	17.6
Total portfolio (£m)	17.8	19.2	22.5	27.4	36.0	50.0	84.0	138.0	210.0	216.0

Notes: [a] Categories are major ones only; thus columns will not always sum to 100%.
[b] Central and local.
Source: Phoenix Annual Balance Sheets, 1935–80.

Table 12.13. *Distribution of investments by major categories:* [a] *market values of Phoenix fire and general funds, 1925–70 (percentage shares)*

	1925	1930	1935	1940	1945	1950	1955	1960	1965	1970
UK govt[b]	33.6	17.5	14.7	13.5	22.8	12.6	8.7	9.5	10.4	15.7
Indian & colonial govts	9.2	8.2	9.5	10.1	7.7	8.2	–	–	–	–
C'wealth govts	–	–	–	–	–	–	6.8	6.4	2.0	–
US govt } Foreign govts (combined 1925–45)	18.1	11.9	11.8	21.9	30.1					
US govt						28.9	17.1	11.5	5.0	–
Foreign govts						2.6	3.1	2.0	2.6	–
Debentures[c]	25.7	42.2	36.3	18.8	10.7	14.6	18.5	20.4	24.9	22.5
Preferential stock	2.1	2.0	3.5	5.2	6.2	6.9	7.8	5.4	3.3	–
Ordinary shares	2.2	2.1	2.7	3.0	4.6	8.6	17.9	20.9	26.9	35.1
Mortgages: home	0.1	–	–	0.6	0.2	1.2	1.7	1.8	3.5	2.9
Mortgages: foreign	0.3	0.5	0.3	0.1	–	0.2	0.4	1.0	2.5	2.0
Property: home	2.3	5.0	9.6	9.5	6.6	5.6	7.1	6.2	3.6	2.8
Property: foreign	–	–	2.5	2.5	1.7	1.5	2.8	7.2	7.6	11.4
Rents	0.2	0.1	0.1	0.1	0.1	0.2	0.2	0.1	0.1	–
Cash: home	1.2	1.6	2.4	2.6	2.1	2.2	1.6	1.7	1.3	1.9
Cash: foreign	3.6	3.9	5.5	10.8	6.3	6.0	5.0	5.6	5.5	5.7
Shares in subsidiaries	–	–	–	–	–	0.3	0.4	0.6	0.1	–
Loans on rates	1.4	–	–	0.6	0.4	0.2	0.2	–	–	–
Loans on company policies	–	3.5	–	–	–	–	–	–	–	–
Loans on stocks & shares	–	–	–	–	–	–	–	–	0.6	–
Deposits with courts	–	0.5	0.8	0.6	0.5	0.1	–	–	–	–
Total portfolio (£m)	14.2	15.3	15.9	17.1	24.1	43.3	54.3	63.8	85.5	134.5

Notes: [a] Categories are major ones only: thus columns will not always sum to 100%.
[b] Central and local.
[c] And other fixed interest.
Source: Phoenix Blue Books, 1925–70.

Table 12.14. *Distribution of investments by major categories: [a]market values of Phoenix Life Funds, 1925–84; (percentage shares)*

	1925	1930	1935	1940	1945	1950	1955	1960	1965	1970	1975	1980	1984
UK govt[b]	37.6	11.8	27.6	36.1	–	36.9	24.2	16.7	8.9	–	5.4	23.9	20.1
Indian & colonial govts	8.9	10.7	9.9	6.8	–	–	–	–	–	–	–	–	–
C'wealth govts	–	–	–	–	–	0.6	0.3	0.6	0.6	–	–	0.1	1.2
US govt	–	–	–	–	–	–	–	–	–	–	–	–	–
Foreign govts	4.2	6.0	2.6	0.8	–	0.5	0.1	0.1	0.1	65.0	0.3	0.1	1.2
Debentures	14.1	24.8	25.1	22.3	–	11.8	15.8	15.8	20.4	–	12.1	8.9	8.6
Preferential stock	5.7	8.5	10.8	9.9	–	6.9	5.8	4.5	3.5	–	39.5	33.3	41.5
Ordinary shares	1.5	1.0	0.8	3.0	–	15.1	25.0	36.4	33.8	–			
Unit trusts[c]	–	–	–	–	–	–	–	–	–	1.2	10.7	14.0	8.2
Mortgages: home[d]	7.7	14.0	11.1	10.8	–	17.7	18.8	19.5	11.8	9.1	14.6	3.6	1.8
Mortgages: home[e]	–	–	–	–	–	–	–	–	13.4	13.3	–	5.6	3.7
Mortgages: foreign	0.8	0.7	0.2	–	–	–	–	–	0.2	0.2	0.1	–	–
Property & land: home	1.6	1.2	0.3	0.2	–	5.3	4.3	3.0	4.2	4.3	8.6	8.0	7.9
Property & land: foreign	–	–	–	–	–	–	–	–	0.8	1.1	–	–	–
Rents	0.7	0.1	0.2	0.2	–	1.0	1.9	1.0	0.9	0.6	–	–	0.9
Cash	0.7	0.8	0.2	1.3	–	0.4	0.6	0.2	0.3	2.7	5.9	1.9	4.4
Shares in subsidiary companies	–	–	–	–	–	–	–	–	–	1.4	–	0.1	0.5
Loans on rates	0.3	5.1	2.6	3.1	–	1.3	0.5	0.3	0.2	0.1	–	–	–
Loans on life ints & reversions	4.7	4.0	1.2	1.2	–	0.7	0.6	0.3	0.2	0.1	–	–	–
Loans on company policies	7.7	9.2	6.7	3.9	–	1.7	1.8	1.6	1.0	0.9	0.7	0.3	0.2
Loans on personal securities	0.3	0.1	–	–	–	–	–	–	–	–	–	–	–
Loans on stocks & shares	3.0	1.5	0.3	–	–	–	–	–	–	–	–	–	–
Deposits with courts	0.5	0.4	0.4	0.3	–	0.1	–	–	–	–	–	–	–
Total portfolio (£m)	8.0	11.0	14.0	16.0	–	26.0	37.0	57.0	–	–	157.0	345.0	639.0

Notes: [a] Categories are major ones only; thus columns will not always sum to 100%. [b] Central and local. [c] Ebor; Save & Prosper. [d] Mortgages for private house purchase. [e] Pure investment.
Source: Phoenix Red Books, 1925–84.

Table 12.15. *Phoenix fire and general and Phoenix life funds: total portfolio values, at cost, balance and market valuations, 1920–84 (£ million)*

	Fire and general		Life		
Year	Balance	Market	Cost	Balance	Market
1920	11.0	–	–	–	–
1925	15.0	14.2	6.0	7.0	8.0
1930	16.0	15.3	7.0	10.0	11.0
1935	15.0	15.9	10.0	13.0	14.0
1940	16.7	17.1	11.0	16.0	16.0
1945	22.0	24.1	–	–	–
1950	33.3	43.3	20.0	26.0	26.0
1955	43.0	54.3	25.0	34.0	37.0
1960	55.0	63.8	36.0	49.0	57.0
1965	80.0	85.5	–	–	–
1970	142.0	134.5	–	–	–
1975	231.0	–	133.0	119.0	157.0
1980	308.0	–	–	283.0	345.0
1984	–	–	–	457.0	639.0

pushing their share much beyond 3% of the total by any reckoning on either portfolio by 1940 (see Tables 12.11–12.14).[98]

In the immediate aftermath of war, Phoenix, like all insurance offices, was awash with the low-yielding UK government paper which had been a major prop of war finance. This element had represented 21% of all British insurance investment in 1937 but 36% in 1946.[99] For Phoenix the proportion was 24.1% of the fire and general fund's balance sheet value in 1945 but a staggering 51.1% of the life fund's balance value, a share significantly bigger than the 38% of its life fund which the REA put at the service of the British government. During the war, Phoenix had not only invested all new money in government stock issues, but had religiously held on to its purchases, whereas many other offices sold on as soon as possible in order to obtain higher yields elsewhere. The result, of course, in the postwar period, as the Phoenix actuary complained, was that the return on the company's life fund was far below that achieved by many competitors. Clearly, the Phoenix needed to escape the leading strings of official war finance and direct itself towards higher earning investment prospects. This was Turner's task.

[98] And see also Chapter 8 above, Section II.
[99] Supple, *Royal Exchange Assurance*, p. 418.

The twenty years after 1945 saw a swift evacuation from government investments of all kinds. Even the US and foreign gilts which had claimed about one-third of the fire portfolio in 1945 could scrape less than 8% of it in 1965 (see Table 12.13). But the US government did show some staying power down to 1960. There were three main reasons. Guarantee requirements still weighed heavy on Phoenix's American subsidiaries. Ferguson was always willing to allocate resources to the transatlantic side of the operation. And the huge devaluation of the pound in September 1949 boosted the sterling value of US holdings and made it sensible to hold investments in dollars. The life portfolio, by contrast, had never shown much interest in foreign or US governments.

Turner was most ruthless with the home government, about halving the commitment of both the fire and life portfolios to UK gilts between 1945 and 1955 (see Tables 12.11–12.14). By 1960, the fire portfolio had 9.5% of its market value in home gilts, the life portfolio 16.7%. Since the insurance industry as a whole still gave 18% of its investment to the UK government in 1961, the aggregate performance of Phoenix, over its two portfolios, suggests either a more enterprising withdrawal from gilts than the industry standard or greater pressure upon Turner to mobilise resources for other purposes. Later investment managers were to suggest the second. But there is no doubt that Phoenix's patriotic stance on war gilts itself necessitated an overhaul of the life fund in the direction of higher yields, once the war was over.

However, Turner did retain a sufficiency of gilts for one particularly enterprising purpose. For he had made Phoenix the leading player in an innovational form of trading known as gilt-switching. This game was played only with life gilts. The investment department maintained over 100 charts tracing the daily movement of gilts against one another. Every day, one devoted official would crank the sample through a Munro calculator and pick out the anomalous stocks. These would then be traded against one another, in blocks of £0.25 to £0.5 million, for as little as 0.125% profit. The trick was to sell the expensive ones and buy the cheap ones, while keeping a close eye on the interest rate; then, if the values reversed, the dealer would switch back, either purchasing more volume of the original gilt or taking a cash profit. This form of trade ceased around 1970 for two reasons. The expert tender of the Munro calculator, Dixie Dean, retired. And the arrival of the computer stopped the fun for good: it could track the anomalies in seconds and everyone with a computer could see them. So the golden small margins disappeared. But Phoenix, for a while, did nicely out of the ingenious exploitation of quirks in the gilts. The device also fitted well with the need to turn over the gilt holdings and the average yields of the life fund.

Nevertheless, the really large positive movements of the Turner era were towards equities and mortgages (see Tables 12.11–12.14). Over the period 1945–60, the holding of the fire portfolio in ordinary shares almost quadrupled to 13.8% of the balance sheet total and that of the life portfolio increased by a factor of eleven to 22.1% of the balance sheet value.[100] At the same time, the fire portfolio's helping of debentures about doubled, although the life side's interest in this sector did not move anywhere near as strongly. In equities, of course, Phoenix followed a trend which was affecting all insurers; indeed, by 1961 the aggregate portfolio of the UK insurance industry was 22% invested in equities. This was a standard reached, and in market values easily surpassed, by the Phoenix life portfolio but not by the fire side, although it only narrowly missed in market values. This was largely due to the fire portfolio's heavy commitment to the related sector of debentures. For both portfolios, Phoenix acquired its equities partly through investment trusts. These borrowed heavily in order to invest in shares. Then, as inflation eroded the value of the trust's debt, the advantage was passed on to the investor in the shape of bigger purchases of shares.

The period 1945–60 was, of course, a classic one for equities: £1,000 invested in ordinary shares in December 1945 was worth in real terms £3,144 by December 1960, while the same sum invested in gilts was worth only £514 and in Treasury Bills £835.[101]

Where the move towards equities was shared by both Phoenix portfolios, the swing to mortgages was confined to the life funds. The explanation is simple. The active promotion of mortgages was a device to boost the sale of life assurance policies: the Phoenix would grant a mortgage only against the purchase of a life policy, and endowment-linked mortgages were a powerful source of new life business. Although he was certainly pressed towards mortgages by the life department, Turner's actuarial training also shows up in this slant to investment policy.

But there is no such clear linkage on view in his final innovation: the beginning of an involvement in the property market. Turner launched Phoenix's long and profitable excursion into an active real estate policy by snapping up a string of small lots, particularly shops. Before Turner,

[100] In market values the increases were even bigger: more than quadrupling to 20.9% of the fire portfolio, rising by a factor of twelve to 36.4% of the life portfolio.

[101] Barclays de Zoete Wedd Research, *BZW Equity-Gilt Study; Investment in the London Stock Market since 1918* (London, 1988), p. 60. The calculation assumes gross income reinvested.

Phoenix had bought property only when it needed to house its main branches. His argument to the Board was that it made nonsense to lend on mortgage to property developers for the acquisition of property that one could perfectly well acquire, and tap for profit, on one's own account. Their acceptance of this point shows up in the property content of both portfolios between 1945 and 1960, although around 1960, some regrouping in this sector seems to have been occurring within the life fund, probably in preparation for a subsequent larger assault on this market.[102]

The record of the investment department in the immediate postwar phase was a good deal more progressive than that of many other parts of the organisation. George Turner was certainly able to select a more adventurous line than the investment department had attempted before 1939 and to pursue it despite the generally conservative inclinations of the senior management. Indeed, the view inside Phoenix House was that the company was becoming one of the most enterprising investors among the insurers in its size range. Of course, this is difficult to measure, but it was certainly an article of faith within the office. And, at the very least, it seems certain that Turner achieved more autonomy than any other of Ferguson's departmental heads. How then was a section as vitally placed as the investment department able to operate with so much independence?

There appear to be four basic reasons. Firstly, like many general managers of the era, Ferguson was not comfortable with investment matters and recognised his limitations in this field. Sensibly enough, he tended to leave investment policy to those who knew better. Secondly, Turner was good at presenting investment issues in a way which did not invite casual review. Some concluded that they must indeed be very complex. Thirdly, Turner enjoyed strong backing from Phoenix's powerful Investment Committee, a small group of directors drawn from the most powerful financial institutions in the City. For Turner, the support of Granville Tyser,[103] a very active deputy chairman, was invaluable; Tyser was a director of Lazards and believed strongly that institutions

[102] There is another possible explanation. The formal accounting classifications do not provide a good measure of true property involvement. In the early stages of Phoenix's dealings in property development, the office took an equity interest in property ventures and provided mortgage finance for the construction project. Thus the shares in the property companies would be classified under the ordinary share sector of the balance sheet and the mortgage element would go into the mortgage sector. Later, when this distribution became disadvantageous in terms of tax liability, the property interest was held direct, and the finance sometimes provided through a lease participation. In the early stages, therefore, the property section of the balance sheet might capture only the mortgage portion of a real estate project.

[103] Phoenix director, 1935–61.

Plate 12.19 Deputy Chairman Tyzer.

such as Phoenix should operate actively in the equity market. Finally, there was the peculiarity that, within the Phoenix, the investment manager was appointed directly by the Board, and not by the general manager (who appointed all other departmental managers). So the general manager was often forced to accept investments that he might not much like.[104]

For his part, Ferguson accepted, as did Evans after him, that control of the company's investment strategy was effectively vested in the City experts of the Investment Committee, supporting a fairly autonomous investment manager. Some later general managers were less happy about the concentration of financial power implied in this arrangement. But it gave Turner the room for manoeuvre that he needed.

The same array of forces, and much the same investment strategy, were deployed by Turner's successor from 1961, Charles Knight. This was a person of strong religious faith and a victim of severe arthritis. Naturally enough, his personality was somewhat sharper than Turner's but was

[104] As Ferguson did not care for Turner's direct property policy because of the losses in fire and life business which he believed would follow from the reduction in mortgage support for property developers.

lightened by a taste for practical jokes and comical sketches (See Plates 12.4 and 12.20). This inclination was first formed in the life and investment departments, in the 1930s both renowned breeding grounds of mischief. In financial policy, however, Knight was a committed disciple of Turner. He too assumed that the Investment Committee was sovereign in investment affairs and answerable to its chairman rather than to the chief general manager. However, Knight was a personal friend of David Evans, and was careful to explain to him the developments and problems of the securities markets as they occurred. The result was that, for one reason or another – personal relations in the case of Evans, experience and skill in the cases of Harris and Bishop – chief general managers from Evans onwards were well informed on financial matters. Nevertheless, informed or not, Evans did not consider himself an expert and largely gave Knight and the Investment Committee their head.

This freedom was used to explore equities further and to expand greatly Turner's other initiative in property investment. Knight again pursued equities through the investment trusts, although with time he preferred more direct manipulation of shareholdings. The UK life portfolio was already quite heavily exposed to ordinary shares, so little more was done there in the period 1961–70. The real work was carried out on the fire side, with the proportion of the account given to equities more than doubling from 13.8% to 28.0% in balance sheet values over these years,[105] and in the process surpassing the share of the life portfolio dedicated to this class of investment.

Again, it was a good time for this emphasis, if not quite as good as the Turner era: the £1,000 invested in equities in December 1945, which had become £3,144 in real terms by December 1960, had grown to £4,316 by 1970, while the £1,000 invested in gilts had slipped further from £514 to £448 and the £1,000 in Treasury Bills had improved from £835 to £982.[106]

Enthused by the experience with UK equities, Knight also preached the gospel of ordinary shares in other markets, primarily the American. This went against conventional insurance theology in the USA: most insurance companies preferred bonds and Phoenix's US Finance Committee followed suit. Against some resistance from the Committee, Knight pressed for the UK pattern to be applied also in the United States. In this he was probably helped after 1964 by the Continental connection;

[105] The movement was from 20.9% to 35.1% in market values.

[106] Barclays de Zoete Wedd Research, *BZW Equity-Gilt Study*. Also 1970 was a *bad* year for equities,with the market falling 9% in real terms; by December 1971, the £1,000 of 1945 was £5,753, after a year in which the market recovered by 33.3%.

for Phoenix's new colleague had been exceptionally enterprising in its investment strategy, the first American fire and accident office to move significantly into stocks and shares. Its initial commitments dated from the middle 1930s – a shrewd time to buy – and, by the 1960s, Continental possessed not only the biggest single interest in IBM but also extensive interests in oil and manufacturing stocks. With the reinforcement of this example, the pressure from the Head Office investment department was largely successful in achieving a larger Phoenix exposure to the US markets.

Generally, Phoenix's handling of equities became more sophisticated in the second half of the 1960s. The investment department by then had introduced specific analysis of the growth and earning prospects of individual shares and every existing holding was subjected to detailed annual review. Moreover, this was for the benefit of the workaday management of the department rather than a service for the Investment Committee; it represented a major upgrading of tactical command. Strategy remained with the Committee.

However, Knight's biggest mark was made in property. Again, it was an enlargement of a signature originally written by Turner, but it was a substantial one. Just before his retirement, Turner had carried out the Phoenix's first equity participation in the property market. This was an arrangement by which Phoenix entered a cooperative venture with a property entrepreneur or developer. A company would be formed for the joint development of a site. Phoenix would both provide the loan finance for this company and take up a substantial slice of its share capital; then provide the insurance cover. In later versions of the system, Phoenix's participation developed into direct partnership-ownership in the development project, and sometimes extended to a long-running interest in the lease of the completed building. Under either arrangement, the insurance office would secure a multiple return from a mix of interest, dividends rents and premiums.[107]

Profitable connections of these types were established with such prominent developers as Metropolitan Properties, the Estate Property Investment Co. – which, among other ventures, controlled a major site in Brussels, an asset that later proved of great value when the European Commission needed to expand its buildings – and Haslemere Properties. Under Knight's guidance, Phoenix also bought heavily into the shares of property companies, even when joint development was not at issue.

When it was the issue, Phoenix was clearly playing the role of an

[107] See note 102 above.

institutional generator of venture capital. With one or two exceptions from the 1970s, however, Phoenix appears to have restricted its contribution as a venture capitalist to the property sector[108] and not to have pushed further towards new business launches in manufacturing or the exploitation of new technology. Nevertheless, the impact of Knight's elaboration of the property theme upon Phoenix's portfolios was sufficiently profound. The fire and general account registered it first, committing 7.7% of its funds to property in 1955 but 11.3% in 1960 and 13.5% by 1970 in balance sheet values. The matching shares for the life portfolio were 5.6%, 3.8% and 4.4%.[109] However, the relationship between the two portfolios, if examined under the strict property classification alone, was to reverse in the 1970s. Clearly, they were being run to a mutual balance in respect of property.

But it is possible, for the reasons given above (and in footnote 102), that a wider definition of property should be taken from the accounts. If all forms of mortgages, rents, land and property, both home and foreign are taken from the market valuations and lumped together, a more striking pattern emerges: this aggregate claimed 16.3% of the fire and general portfolio in 1960 and 19.1% in 1970, while of the life portfolio it took 23.5% in 1960 and 28.6% in 1970 (market values; see Tables 12.13 and 12.14). In regard to life investments, the reservation should be added that, before 1965, a significant amount of the mortgage activity was actually embedded in endowment assurance business. By the same token, the slippage in the 'property aggregate' within the life portfolio after 1965 is largely due to the contraction of this item.

Knight's times were more turbulent than Turner's. Adjusted for the cost of living, the equity market suffered more downturns in the 1960s – 1960–2, 1964, 1966, 1969 – and fewer and weaker rallies – 1963, 1965, 1967–8 – than in the preceding decade.[110]

Notwithstanding this volatility, equity operations were maintained by Phoenix as a strong underlying theme throughout the 1960s, while a new and striking emphasis was given to property operations of more than one type.

When Brian Oram took over from Charles Knight in 1970, he inherited an investment strategy that clearly worked – though it needed yet an additional element of discipline – but also a notable deficiency of people

[108] See below pp. 1002–4.

[109] Market values give shares of 9.9%, 13.4% and 14.2% for the fire holdings and 4.3%, 3.0% and 5.4% for the life holdings (see Tables 12.11–12.14).

[110] The downturn years in the 1950s were 1951–2, and 1956–7, while there were strong rallies in 1953–4 and 1958–9, and moderate ones in 1950 and 1955. Barclays de Zoete Wedd Research, *BZW Equity-Gilt Study*.

Plate 12.20 Knight's view of Phoenix communications.

to help him work it. Oram had joined Phoenix from National Service in 1949 and served as a ledger clerk on the Stock Exchange side of the investment department until 1956. Then, in 1958, he won the Phoenix Gold Watch competition, the in-house contest for bright managerial prospects. As for many who shone in this test, the award proved for Oram a career break.[111] After a two-year spell in the trustee department, he was seconded from the investment department on a financial grand tour which took in Coutts Bank, Hambro's and a string of Phoenix branches. He returned to the investment department as personal assistant, and from 1968, deputy investment manager, to Charles Knight.

Recruitment to the investment department had been damaged by the Depression of the 1930s, and was further hurt by the Second World War. This produced a generational echo effect. By 1970, the section contained only thirty people, and one-third of these, after having served in it since its inception, were due for imminent retirement. Oram's early period of

[111] The first winner had been Tom Hodgson in 1930, while other early successes picked out Frank Kendal in 1936 and Bill Harris in 1937. Arthur Matanle and Ron Bishop shared first place in 1952.

financial management was thus complicated by a simple shortage of manpower. Rapid replacement was an urgent priority.

The compensation for this, however, was that it was possible to do new things with new people. Like Harris, Bishop and Kendal, Oram reacted against the hierarchical system of management in which he had been raised and required his young team to accept a considerable measure of delegated authority. Even with limited resources, these tactics succeeded in introducing a more orderly and disciplined, and indeed a more scientific, approach to investment policy. Oram was empowered to invest on his own authority up to £1 million in any one package, and after consultation with Bill Harris as chief general manager, this could rise to £3 million. But it was in the presentation of data for the Finance Committee of the Board, whence flowed the really big decisions, that more science was needed.[112]

Until the 1970s, investment holdings had come to the Finance Committee to be reviewed in any order. The new technique was sectoral analysis: under this regime the Committee was asked to monitor in one session all Phoenix's interests in chemical companies, in another all interests in banks, and so on. Allied to this was the device of strategic analysis: the entire portfolio was analysed for balance within each of its sectors. Funds available for new investment were also distributed according to balance within sectors. This was called fund allocation targeting. Such methodical procedures achieved a distinctly improved overview in the making of investment decisions. Moreover, this process was subjected to cleaner lines of command. Neither Lord de L'Isle as chairman, nor Bill Harris and Ron Bishop as chief general managers, approved of the autonomy enjoyed in the Ferguson and Evans eras by the Investment Committee, and, as the Phoenix continued to expand, it became increasingly necessary to raise the level of executive control over investment activities.

Contemporary with these financial reforms were larger changes in the management of the Phoenix's worldwide organisation. Many influences combined to produce these changes.[113] But there was definitely an investment aspect to the rationalisation of Phoenix's foreign operations. By the 1970s, it was common ground among Phoenix's senior managers that insufficient attention had been paid to the company's UK cash flow during the 1950s and 1960s. In particular, a cash drain from Britain to

[112] The Finance Committee here is the Investment Committee of pp. 987–9 above. Nomenclature has changed; function remains much the same.

[113] See above, Section 9, pp. 939–40.

Phoenix outposts abroad had caused 'serious erosion' in the company's general fund UK assets and decline in its gilt holdings.[114] This followed 'as a result of support operations from London to external territories' arising from the 'build-up of assets in those countries without the concomitant requirement that income produced from the investment be remitted to the UK to support UK dividends and costs'.[115]

In other words, during the Ferguson era, management had not required foreign operations to be sufficiently self-supporting and the impact on the Phoenix's cash and investment position had been destructive. This reinterpretation of the Phoenix's global role as an insurance multinational owed much to the 'Other Foreign Policy' (see above, pp. 938–44), but drew as well upon investment-based methods of appraisal.

Part of the answer to the problem of erosion in the general fund was provided by the alliance with Continental of New York. The purchase of Phoenix shares by Continental generated a substantial return flow of capital into the United Kingdom, where it could generate investment income, and increased the efficiency of Phoenix's US business, which duly improved its ability to remit dividends to London. The general fund was reconstructed with new assets financed by the Continental deal. However, the second part of the answer was the adoption of a much more disciplined view of subsidiary companies overseas. From around 1970, they were viewed not simply as selling outlets but also as investment assets: local management was given more responsibility, the satellites were charged for technical services from London, and, above all, they were expected to pay their own way.

The management of Phoenix investment was clearly more punctilious after 1970 than before, but what of its content? Here there was a mixture of inheritances and innovations. Equities continued to be stressed and gilts were rebuilt. Even in 1971, there was a major switch from preference to ordinary shares, 'with considerable capital advantage' and also a sweeping reorganisation of gilt-edged holdings (see Tables 12.11–12.14): the net effect was a 10% increase in general fund invested income over the figure for 1970. From 1975 until 1982, gilts offered high rates of interest and attracted big proportions of Phoenix's investible funds.[116] Over the long run also, there was a large-scale withdrawal from mortgage-linked,

[114] This throws a special light on Turner's retreat from this sector. See pp. 984–5 above.
[115] Group Investment Manager's Report on Phoenix General Funds, 19 March 1975.
[116] Phoenix Annual Report, 1971. Gilts gave particularly high yields in 1975 and 1976, and more Phoenix new money was directed towards them from this point. In 1978–81, about two-thirds of Phoenix new funds generated for investment went into gilts and preference shares. In 1982, as the equity market prepared to go into overdrive, gilts, nevertheless,had their best year for a decade. Phoenix Annual Reports.

in favour of unit-linked, life assurance business. In the markedly inflationary period of the 1970s, cash management became an essential of good investment policy. And there were some spectacular developments in property, as well as a few significant near-misses.

Bill Harris had a strong belief in equities, and, for much of his time as investment manager, Oram worked under the influence of that belief. However, neither man took office at a good time for stocks and shares: the market fell by 16% in real terms in 1969 and by 9% in 1970. Then after a rally in 1971 and 1972, the equity markets ran straight into the Arab–Israeli War of October 1973. As the OPEC countries nationalised their oil-producing facilities, and forced up the price of crude by 400% in three months, the world's equity markets collapsed from 'oil shock'. The London stock market slumped by 39% in 1973 and 58% in 1974. Adjusted for the cost of living, the 'market adjustments' of 1973–4 were sharper than those of 1929–31.[117] An investor who had committed £1,000 to an average bundle of equities in December 1945, and who had not re-invested the income, would have received £970 for it in December 1974. Nevertheless, remarkably, the adjustments to the Phoenix portfolio managed to lift its investment *income* by 32% in 1974.[118]

Insurance markets in 1974 were as pressed as stock markets: underwriting results were bad in most areas, grave in some. Yet investment assets could not be sold to offset insurance losses because of the sharp falls in market value. At Phoenix, circumstances were so critical that the investment department was instructed to revalue the portfolio on a weekly basis, to see if Phoenix was still solvent by the Department of Trade definition – although the Department of Trade was sufficiently sportsmanlike not to ask at this point. The trouble, which was even greater in many other companies, followed mainly from the need to write down market values of gilts, equities and property. At Phoenix, the possibility was even floated of capitalising upon the company's multinational status to effect a rescue: the offshore funds of Phoenix of New York might be drawn upon to support the older Bird. However, in the event, these extreme measures were not needed.

For, in 1975, the UK investment market bounced back. This was due not least to a little help from the insurance companies: several big offices, led by Sun Alliance, Legal & General and Prudential, but not including Phoenix, agreed to inject life into stocks and shares by heavy buying and did succeed in rousing the market from dejection. Indeed investors came awake with a vengeance, nearly doubling share values in twelve months,

[117] Barclays de Zoete Wedd Research, *BZW Equity-Gilt Study*, pp. 52–60.
[118] Phoenix Annual Report, 1974.

the strongest one-year surge of the entire period from 1945 to 1984. The FT index moved from a low of 146 on 6 January 1975 to 376 at the year end, while the Dow Jones went from 616 to 852 within the calendar year.

The second half of the 1970s gave mixed results for equities with a strong rally in 1977 but declines in 1976 and 1979. Then from the early 1980s, and covering Phoenix's final years, the market produced the strongest sequence of annual advances since 1918. The £1,000 invested in December 1945 would have been worth a real £4,316 in December 1970, £4,607 in December 1980 but a staggering £8,526 in December 1984. This was more than sufficient justification for the increase in Phoenix's exposure to equities from 28% to 32% of the fire and general portfolio between 1970 and 1980 and from 23% to 29% of the life portfolio.[119] There was also, from around 1970, a significant rebuilding of Phoenix's involvement in UK gilts. This had been run down to about 11% of the fire portfolio by 1960, and to about 9% of the life portfolio by 1965, largely in consequence of the overseas demands made upon Phoenix resources. By 1980 these proportions were back to 26% and 14% respectively (see Tables 12.11 and 12.12).

However, the Great Stock Market Crash of 1973–4 was not the only disaster of the 1970s for the institutions. There was also the associated shock of the Great Secondary Bank Crisis which occupied a very similar period in late 1973 and 1974. This is most easily considered under the heading of equity investment. For Phoenix was a shareholder in one of the most afflicted fringe banks, Cedar Holdings. The office was in good company: the three other major institutional backers of Cedar were the pension funds of the National Coal Board, the Electricity Supply Industry and Unilever. Cedar Holdings had been the second-ranking company in the provision of second mortgages with about 15% of the market but was torpedoed by the collapse of confidence in fringe banking late in 1973; it became insolvent in December after the money markets failed to renew substantial deposits. Its pre-tax profits in the half-year to December 1973 were only £295,000 against £1.9 million for the financial year to June 1973.[120]

After consultation with, and a certain amount of coercion by, the Bank of England, the four institutions and Cedar's banker, Barclays, agreed to refinance the group. The initial rescue package – part of the Bank's 'lifeboat' for the secondary banks – called for some £72 million of secured advances, of which the institutions would provide £50 million and Barc-

[119] The combined quota of ordinary and preference shares in the life portfolio, at 41.5%, was very high by 1984. All proportions in this paragraph refer to balance sheet values.

[120] *The Times*, 20 April 1974, p. 19 (Ian Morison).

lays £22 million. In the event, the final bill was somewhat under £80 million. The principle of the rescue was that the institutions should purchase Cedar's substantial holdings of property and that the proceeds should go to reducing Cedar's debts. In the meantime, the institutions would take 54% of Cedar's voting power until the advances were repaid.[121] Oram became deputy chairman and chaired the Board, so that Phoenix had a direct influence upon the steering of the lifeboat.

Eventually, Cedar was towed to a safe haven. Its pre-tax profits recovered to £593,000 for the year to June 30 1977 and to £917,000 in the next year. By the end of 1978, the institutions had almost got their advances back: Cedar's debt to the four of them was below £2 million.[122] At this point, both American and British financial interests began sniffing an acquisition prospect, and in November 1978 a bid of £9.6 million was proffered by the finance group of Lloyds and Scottish, which was seeking an outlet into the second mortgage market. On 21 November, *The Times* reported that both Cedar and the four institutions – which, having turned the bank around, were understandably anxious to see it sold on – had found the terms of the bid acceptable.[123] Cedar Holdings duly passed to Lloyds and Scottish.

Phoenix came through these encounters with relief. The banking crisis had seriously exacerbated the alarm generated by the initial oil shock and the subsequent stock market dive. There is no doubt that the trauma of 1973/4 was deeply felt within Phoenix, nor that nerves were tested. The events of these months were enough to encourage, and perhaps justify, conservative policy inclinations in any organisation. But good husbandry and firm handling brought the company out of trouble in each case. In other sectors of investment, however, more innovative stances were possible.

A major change in the management of the life portfolio was executed in the early 1970s. Since the 1930s, Phoenix had invested in mortgages as a way of selling life insurance: the endowment policies secured and paid off the mortgages, while the Phoenix's investable funds put up the money for the loans to house purchasers. But, in the 1970s, more active policy-making in life business by Marshall Field coincided with more active policy-making in investment business by Brian Oram. Field's position was that life business should, and could, be sold on its own account, not on the back of mortgages. Oram's was that the large proportions of the life portfolio locked up in mortgages could, and should, be invested more profitably elsewhere. Mortgages dedicated to house purchases fell from a

[121] *Ibid.*, 13 April 1974, p. 15 (John Plender). [122] *Ibid.*, 10 November 1978, p. 25.
[123] *Ibid.*, 21 November 1978, p. 21.

peak of 19.5% of the market value of the life portfolio in 1960, through 9.1% in 1970 to 1.8% in 1984 (see Table 12.14).

They were replaced by unit-linked life business. This was a much more suitable form of association for an insurance vehicle. In mortgage-linking, the assurance element merely assisted in an entirely separate transaction: the purchase of a house. In unit-linking, the connection, through unit trusts to equities, improved the efficiency as an investment of the life policy itself.[124]

Initially, the capacity in unit management which Phoenix needed to service this new line was provided by the link which Marsall Field had forged with the Ebor Unit Trust Group.[125] However, this had not been a cheap purchase, and it was not long before the success of Phoenix's unit-linked policies raised the need for more unit capacity. Meanwhile Ebor had scored a success on its own account in the wider unit trust market and had caught the eye of the Save and Prosper Group. This much bigger operation, in its turn, needed technical advice for expansion in the unit-linked life sector. A solution suitable to all parties thus presented itself. Save and Prosper would buy out Ebor; Phoenix's 25.6% stake in Ebor would be converted into a smaller stake (about 5%) in Save and Prosper's much bigger capital; Field would get his enlarged unit capacity; Save and Prosper would get their technical assistance; and Phoenix would take a handsome investment profit. All of this was achieved by the end of 1969.

However, the Phoenix investment department had always fretted at the connections with the unit trust enterprises because of the implication that the Phoenix investors could not run their own unit schemes. From the early 1970s, this point was taken and they were given their head with an in-house operation. But they could not be allowed to gallop far. At this time, the unit-linked policy was becoming increasingly important in pension business. Investment managers could not afford to underperform in such a sensitive area; pension trustees were apt to become upset; and pension trustees had to be satisfied once every quarter. Consequently, a defensive investment strategy was a necessity in this sector.

Elsewhere, Phoenix did not practise a passive investment strategy of 'following the index'. The conventional view of the modern equity market as so large, and the 'big institutions' as so dominant that they simply buy the index, is not correct for most of Phoenix's investment. However, it was correct for index-linked pension business. Here, 80% of the funds invested were committed to 'shadowing' the core shares in the FT index

[124] See Section 2 above. [125] *Ibid.*

and only 20% left open for discretionary management.

Not until 1977 was the desire of the investment department for its own unit-linked enterprise more fully realised. This was achieved by the outright purchase of the Property Growth Assurance Co., a pioneer of linked business.[126] With this addition to unit-based capacity and expertise sailing directly under the Phoenix flag, there was little further call for the connection with Save and Prosper. Accordingly, Phoenix parted company with the unit trust specialist, selling out on a basis both amicable and profitable. Property Growth then proceeded to justify Phoenix's reading of the unit-linked market by quadrupling its new annual premiums between 1977 and 1982.[127]

However, if Phoenix found enterprising new ways to be in securities during the 1970s, it was also necessary to find new ways of being out of them. Equities, like property, offered some protection from the erosion of inflation, but cash too had its attractions. Although it was a novelty for many investors of this generation, it could be as profitable, given the interest rates of the 1970s, to commit resources to cash as to equities. Also, in a period of chronic price rises, it was necessary to move cash actively, so that it earned rather than depreciated. The key variables were knowing the velocity of the cash-flow with precision and where to locate temporary surpluses so as to maximise returns from high interest rates.

These pressures led Phoenix to develop a very advanced system of cash management. Previously, a multitude of branch accountants had operated separate bank accounts, periodically calculating their surpluses and then transferring them to a Head Office account. The investment department had tackled this problem even before 1970, and had secured improvements. But it was not until Phoenix House broke the control of branch bank accounts that Oram and his team really knew the true position. The new methods swept the day's receipts automatically to a central collection account. As a result, Head Office cashiers were able to identify instantly the total cash surplus or shortfall position of the whole Group on any given day.

Oram's innovation was to manage this collective pot of liquid resources as though it were a portfolio of short-term assets, sensitive to interest rates and time-lags, rather than a lump of cash waiting to be turned into equities or gilts or property. Aggressive cash management extended even to using the delay in the presentation of cheques to fine tune liquidity margins during periods of tight cash or to the exploitation of overdraft facilities so as to ensure that positive balances were never left on non-

[126] See Section 10 above. [127] Phoenix Annual Report, 1982.

interest-bearing accounts. This, of course, was another exercise in financial rationalisation. But it was one where Phoenix was several years ahead of its time. It was not until 1979, with the formation of the Association of Corporate Treasurers, that Treasury Management was formally recognised as a specialised function.

However, during the 1970s and early 1980s, the area in which Phoenix displayed a definite taste for adventure, as distinct from a leaning towards technical innovation, was once again the property market. For a decade or so, Oram had been more involved with the property market than with the stock market, and it remained his favoured area of activity.

The results involved some high-profile risk-taking and some narrow scrapes. One operation, which displayed both of these characteristics, featured a famous site on the Boulevard Haussmann; it now houses Marks & Spencer's flagship in Paris. In 1972 a small UK developer, Acrecrest Properties, in which Phoenix had one of its characteristic venture stakes, discovered this prize location, then belonging to the biggest raincoat manufacturer in the world, the Belgian Comptoir Commercial de Caoutchouc (CCC). This enterprise had outgrown its management resources, and was not viable in its current form. Consequently, any interest wishing to develop the site would first have to buy CCC at a cost of around £4 million.

This was the first snag faced by Phoenix. While it was negotiated, the original development company acquired another half-dozen properties in France. By the time it had finished, Phoenix found itself committed for a total of around £12 million, a massive share of its overall portfolio – about 26% of all Phoenix's property-related interests in 1972 – to be risked on a single deal. The company's Annual Report for 1972 referred to the Haussmann scheme, with commendable restraint, as 'our largest single property operation'. There then followed assorted disasters with currency mismatching, fierce French labour legislation, and some fragile Acrecrest investments involving an additional £1 million of borrowed funds. It became necessary for Phoenix effectively to foreclose on Acrecrest, retaining the services of two or three of its original members.

Development work was completed in two phases. In the first, Marks & Spencer took a significant part of the complex, but Phoenix and its partners retained the balance of the trading space, in which they continued to operate a department store. However, this retail operation did little to defray the costs of the property venture. The second stage involved closing the store and carrying through a refurbishment which would permit the leasing of a very large site to Marks & Spencer. Dealings with the French Department of Labour and the trade unions introduced many loops and circuits at this point. Nevertheless, building work was completed during 1975 and the property fully let by spring 1976.[128] The venture was rounded out just in time for Marks & Spencer's to carry off the major coup of its Parisian launch.

The lease of the Acrecrest site to the brilliant British retailers brought Phoenix their own coup in Paris. But it had not been plain sailing. Trading losses and high interest rates inflated the initial estimates of capital costs and the peripheral properties were sold off during the second stage of the development in order to reduce local debt. Some years elapsed before the return justified the outlay and the many tribulations of acquisition and construction. But a little time did produce for Phoenix, and later for Sun Alliance, a cash cow of magnificent proportions.

The Haussmann project was a major policy matter which came at a difficult time, in the aftermath of the 1973/4 financial crises, when many investment issues were under stress, and Ken Wilkinson as general manager (overseas) did much to bring it to a safe conclusion.

In Paris, Phoenix achieved a small fortune by a small margin, which is, of course, on the right side. With another famous development saga, it avoided sacrificing a small fortune by a rather larger margin, which was again on the right side. This was the legendary loser of the Brighton Marina. In the late 1960s, Phoenix had been poised to supply some of the £6–8 million which this enormous construction was said to need. The company was somewhat delicately placed since David Evans, now of course retired, had become chairman of the Marina company and was eager for Phoenix to take a lead position in the project. However, the company's Finance Committee found cause to hesitate, and it was well that it did so.

After many planning delays and protests from residents, work began on the Marina in 1971. Its architect claimed that the project was 'unique in that it is to be constructed on an unbroken stretch of almost straight coastline which affords no natural shelter whatsoever'; and then proceeded to build it in the teeth of Nature.[129] While the pundits accused the constructors of 'technological adventurism', Nature replied in more direct terms: in August 1974, waterspouts appeared off Brighton beach and in September, the Marina was lashed by mountainous seas.[130] The storm damage, and the addition to cost, was extensive. According to a *Financial Times* calculation of August 1972, a marina of Brighton's proportions,

[128] *Ibid.*, 1975. Phoenix bought out Acrecrest entirely in 1978 (*ibid.*, 1978), and the name passed across to Sun Alliance in 1984.

[129] *The Times*, 30 July 1976, p. 7, 'Why the Brighton Marina is £22 million Adrift' (by Norman Dombey). [130] *Ibid.*, 19 August 1974 and 8 September 1974.

assuming normal returns on capital and rents, should have cost no more than £4.5 million. By midsummer 1976, the main harbour had been completed – at a cost of £30 million. The principal backers – the National Westminster Bank, the Electricity Supply Industry Pension Fund (again), and the Royal Insurance – were also told that they would need to find a further £11 million if the site were to be opened in 1977.

Of course, the Phoenix investment department had not been able to predict the weather. Rather, they had been worried by the residential component of the scheme. The plan was that the marina would 'create land' by dredging and infill within the harbour; and on this land, would rise 1,000 flats, to be sold at an average price of £10,000 each. The resulting £10 million would slash the marina's indebtedness at a stroke. However, the Phoenix investors noted that this idea depended on planning permission that had not been obtained, and doubted the market for so many housing units at such lavish prices (for the time). In fact, it took years for any housing element to be achieved.

The spectacular escalation of cost was due, therefore, to the forces of Nature, the price inflation of the period and the mis-design of the property element. The worst sufferers, according to *The Times*, were the electricity workers who 'have seen several millions from their pension fund poured, almost literally, into the sea'.[131] Phoenix did not suffer. In order to meet David Evans' desire that the Phoenix name should be associated with the project, the company agreed to act as trustee for the Unsecured Loan Stocks. For about a decade, Phoenix collected an annual fee of £1,000 for this service, and were thus the only City institution to make a swift profit out of Brighton Marina. At any rate, this was one exercise in venture capital raising that Phoenix did well to keep on its seaward side.

However, it remains a matter of sharp interest for economic historians of the recent past as to how far the big City institutions have acted as suppliers of risk capital for other sectors of the economy. During the 1970s, Phoenix clearly did operate as an institutional provider of venture capital for the development and construction sectors. And in this decade, though not in earlier ones, it did extend its participation, on a small number of occasions, into the sectors of extractive and manufacturing industry.

A deliberate gamble of £450,000 was put into the development of North Sea oil, and paid off nicely. In the late 1960s, the British government was licensing areas of the domestic seas for exploration and aiming

[131] *Ibid.*, 30 July 1976.

to favour companies which were competent, well funded, and, where possible, 'British'. An established Canadian oil exploration group aimed to become one such contender, and, through Hambro's, proposed a venture with 40% UK participation and 60% Canadian. In 1971, Hambro's put this scheme out to a small group of friendly institutions including Phoenix.[132] The resulting venture became Siebens Oil and Gas UK (later Sovereign Oil and Gas); it obtained a number of licences from a government anxious to give not only the multinationals but also more modest operators their chance; and it proved quite adept at striking oil.

The other major example was much nearer home, indeed just down the river: this enterprise became the Sheerness Steel Co.[133] Phoenix's involvement started in the 1960s as a classic property ploy of Charles Knight's. He had taken Phoenix into a consortium of investors who had bid successfully for the Sheerness Naval Dockyard and the adjacent War Department marshalling yards, when these were sold off by the government. The plan was to fill in the docks, demolish the buildings and construct an industrial estate on the reclaimed land. But the property market did not conform; instead of demanding more industrial estates, it began to display a renewed appetite for commercial port facilities. The consortium followed the signals and began reinstating the dockyard. But, in the early 1970s, a non-market variable, in the shape of the Labour government, intervened. It began to talk of nationalising all UK docks, and the River Medway Authority, in order to defend its own future position, induced the consortium, by threat of compulsory purchase, to sell the dockyard to it.

The problem then became, what should the consortium do with the land that was not needed for the docks? One interesting idea had surfaced in the period before the sale of the dockyard. An established steel and metal-marketing specialist named Peter Learmond, had realised that the electric arc furnance, or 'mini steel mill', an innovation already established in North America and Italy, would be a natural development for the Sheerness site. His plan was beautifully tailored to the local economy. It would tap the enormous scrap metal potential of east London and the river, and produce finished steel on a green-field site sufficiently near the capital to allow very competitive transport costs into central London. And there, of course, was no mean source of demand: the boom in the

[132] Hambro's retained a stake, and the other participants were Guardian Royal Exchange and Coalite and Chemical.

[133] Also in east London, Phoenix in 1971 made a 'considerable investment in the new technology of cargo handling', in the form of a container depot at Stratford. Annual Report, 1971.

development of London office properties had created an enormous appetite for constructional steel.

Learmond, and his idea, were introduced to Phoenix by one of its directors, Sir Charles Wheeler (Phoenix director, 1961–75), who was to become Sheerness Steel's first chairman. Knight quickly saw the appeal of the plan and became its active champion. He gave Learmond permission to tell other potential backers that Phoenix was willing to lead the project. And he arranged for Learmond to obtain the lease for the War Department land alongside Sheerness Harbour, ensuring that this position was protected when the port passed to the Medway Authority. Building work commenced in March 1971 and the first steel was produced at Sheerness in May 1972.

Learmond had succeeded in involving an existing Canadian mini-mill operator, Co-Steel Inc. of Toronto, as the principal investor and technical mentor for the scheme. Co-Steel took 70% of the equity, Learmond 10% and the rest, with Phoenix's imprimatur, was placed with the institutions. For itself, Phoenix took a 5% stake. During its first half-decade, the mill was highly successful, but, like many in the industry, ran into trouble with the international steel crisis of the late 1970s and early 1980s. However, it was reinvigorated; its debt was restructured; and, in May 1990, Co-Steel purchased the 30% of equity held by the UK interests, leaving each of these with a handsome capital gain.

The Sheerness project was effectively a stroke of vertical integration within Phoenix's property portfolio, a diversification out of construction into the manufacture of the inputs for construction. It was a very tight package, beautifully timed to hit a peak of demand; but it also served to emphasise the tight focus within Phoenix's venture activities.

Certainly, property served Phoenix well. The redevelopment of its own Head Office site in King William Street from 1983 was probably the most ambitious venture undertaken by the company in this market. Indeed, the size of the project – the resulting investment was valued at over £40 million – was too great for the company to finance unaided. An old friend, the Norwich Union, provided the necessary assistance in the shape of a 50% interest in the scheme.

The initial reconstruction was a property speculation and proved most fortunate in its timimg, since completion of the work coincided with another boom in the market for City office premises in the late 1980s. As soon as the builders were out, the Japanese securities house, Daiwa (Europe) Ltd, leased the entire site for its London headquarters. One consequence, inevitable but regrettable, was the disappearance of the Phoenix name from the famous bracket clock which projects above the

Plate 12.21 The last nest: 18 King William Street.

main entrance of the great building at number 4/5 King William Street. The Phoenix symbol, however, still flies above the clock.

While the builders were busy, Phoenix had needed to vacate its old home, and had moved its Head Office further down King William Street to number 18, on the corner with Cannon Street. This was a handsome new building developed by another insurance operator in the property market, the United Kingdom Provident Institution.

Table 12.16. *Phoenix Group investment income as % total annual gross profit, 1967–82*

1967	66.7	1975	129.9
1968	84.2	1976	130.9
1969	93.8	1977	97.6
1970	90.8	1978	101.3
1971	73.5	1979	132.1
1972	72.5	1980	147.8
1973	75.9	1981	197.1
1974	147.7	1982	349.8

Source: Phoenix Annual Reports.

However, the large return on King William Street could be seen as a windfall gain, achieved simply by occupying a given space and moving house at a favourable moment. A better advertisement for property investment is provided by George Turner's first development. This spectacular gain had to be worked for. In the late 1950s, Turner had partnered the Wates building concern in a major project, taking a 25% equity interest, plus the leasehold. The outlay for Phoenix's initial property deal was £1.5 million. Twenty-one years later, Phoenix redeveloped the site at a cost of a further £8 million. In 1987 it was sold for £35 million. For a first attempt, this was not at all bad.

Nor indeed was Phoenix's overall investment performance in its last decades. As for all insurance operators, investment earnings became an increasingly vital source of profits as underwriting results became ever more problematic. From the mid-1970s up to the cataclysmic insurance year of 1982, almost the only good news for the offices came in their investment balances. As Table 12.16 reveals, the place of investment income in Phoenix's finances was completely transformed in the second half of the 1970s.

Cautionary words are again in order. These figures are taken from the profit and loss accounts which receive investment income only in the form of interests and dividends. Until recently, capital gains were not usually included in the profit and loss accounts but were recorded as movements in the reserves. Even now, only realised investment gains are included in profit (although this is likely to change in the near future).

Where capital gains are not shown in the accounts, it is theoretically possible to improve apparent performance significantly by investing not for capital gain but for quick returns in interest and dividends. It follows

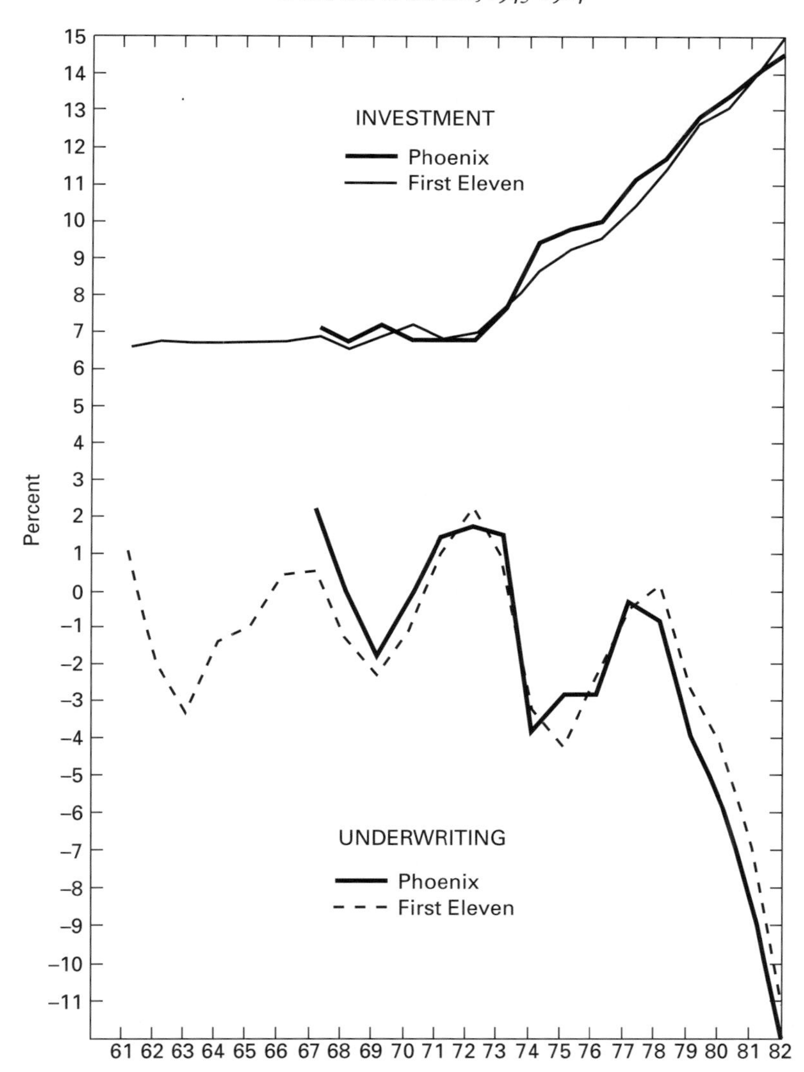

Sources: Phoenix Annual Reports; Carter and Godden, *The British Insurance Industry,* p. 69.

Fig. 12.1 Underwriting results and investment income: Phoenix and the 'First Eleven' companies, 1961–82

that long-run figures of the kind shown in Table 12.16 will understate the true investment performance of companies like Phoenix to the extent that capital gains are not fully captured. A certain corrective to this problem can be achieved by viewing Table 12.16 in conjunction with Table 12.15, since the market value columns of Table 12.15 do give a measure of the appreciation of the capital base of the company's key funds.

Also, a comparative test can be applied, as in Figure 12.1, by setting Phoenix's balance sheet investment performance against that of other insurers required by reputability to apply similar investment strategies.

Allowing for these reservations, some conclusions may still be drawn. The balance sheet results suggest that the growth in Phoenix net profit up to about 1980[134] was largely due to the resilience of investment earnings; and these were achieved despite the moderate performance of the equity markets in the second half of the 1970s.[135] Also, as Figure 12.1 clearly shows, the pressure on underwriting profits affected the entire group of the 'First Eleven' insurance companies in the United Kingdom from the mid-1960s onwards, with Phoenix performing almost exactly on, or slightly below, the underwriting average over the decade 1973–82. It also shows that the big insurance institutions as a group extracted the maximum compensation from the investment markets. But here it is instructive that Phoenix's performance 1973–80 was somewhat *above* the result for the insurance leaders as a whole. The implication is that Phoenix extracted rather more of what was available.

17. PROFITABILITY BEFORE THE FALL

The net outcome of the sustained reforms of the Harris–Bishop era, and of the developments that were played out in parallel with the crucial processes of the Phoenix–Continental alliance, was a considerable advance in company efficiency and a robust defence of profits (see Tables 12.17–12.20).

During the period 1965–80, Phoenix premium growth was distinctly strong, outpacing the market in all main sectors (see Table 12.17). Both in terms of the company's growth rate and in relation to the expansion of the market, these results stand in striking contrast to Phoenix's performance in the earlier managerial phase 1945–60 (see Table 12.1 above). This improvement in competitive standing was well marked by the conferment

[134] See below, Section 17.

[135] Adjusted for inflation, the market moved in the following way: after the huge rally of 99.8% in 1975, it fell by 14.0% in 1976 rose by 40.2% in 1977, inched forward by 3.4% in 1978, and fell by 6.5% in 1979. See also Section 8, pp. 935–6.

Table 12.17. *Worldwide net written premiums: BIA members and Phoenix, 1965–80 (£m)*

	1965	1973	1980	Multiplier 1965–80
BIA				
Fire, Accident, Motor	1,177	3,041	7,615	6.5
Marine/aviation	108	291	532	4.9
Ordinary life	834	2,068	6,012	7.2
Phoenix				
Fire, Accident, Motor	51.2	141.7	342.6	6.7
Marine/aviation	4.3	42.7	69.9	16.3
Ordinary life	9.0	42.5	108.9	12.1

Sources: BIA Statistics Bureau, *Insurance Premiums in the UK*, 1960–82; Phoenix Annual Reports, 1965–80.

upon Phoenix in 1972 of the Queen's Award to Industry.

Furthermore, this improvement in market penetration was achieved at a higher level of operating efficiency. In the period 1966–77 alone, the proportion of fire and accident premiums consumed by expenses fell from 39.7% to 30.9%, and, for marine and aviation business, these charges fell by a still more striking margin, from 17.6% to 9.3%. Inter-company comparative evidence on this score is available for the somewhat later period 1980–2. Again Phoenix showed well: over these three years its ratio of commissions and expenses to fire and accident written premiums averaged 32.7% and in the marine and aviation sector the matching figure was 12.3%. As Table 12.18 displays, this was a very creditable result by the standards of other large offices in this period. This is especially so, given that the aggregated return used by some companies – grouping together commission and expenses from fire, accident, aviation and marine – will depress the final number due to the relatively modest level of aviation and marine expenses and commissions. It was definitely unusual, in the long-run of the twentieth century, for Phoenix to be among the more economical of the big offices.

Profitability of course is the acid test of any business operation. Yet it is not a feature readily associated with underwriting over the Phoenix's last

Table 12.18. *Expenses and commissions as % of fire, accident, aviation and marine written premiums: eight major companies (averages 1980–2)*

	Fire and accident	Aviation and Marine
Commercial Union	36.0	Included in fire and accident
Cornhill	32.4	Included in fire and accident
General Accident	30.8	Included in fire and accident
Royal	34.1	Included in fire and accident
Sun Alliance	34.4	Included in fire and accident
Eagle Star	37.0	19.6
Norwich Union	31.0	13.0
Phoenix	32.7	12.3

Source: Calculated from Carter and Godden, *The British Insurance Industry*, Table A2(a).2, pp. 30–41.

Table 12.19. *Phoenix Group: underwriting, investment, profit results, 1960–82 (five-year averages in £ million)*

	Underwriting result			
Years	General business[a]	Long-term business[b]	Investment income	Group net profit
1960–4	−1.22	+1.10	+2.74	+0.68
1965–9	−1.30	+0.68	+4.74	+3.26
1970–4	−0.16	+1.28	+10.52	+6.62
1975–9	−6.90	+2.14	+35.44	+17.80
1980–2	−38.20	+5.13	+60.53	+14.96

Notes: [a] General business results are shown net of investment income from the technical reserves; [b] Life results are shown net of investment surplus.
Sources: Phoenix Annual Reports; Carter and Godden, *The British Insurance Industry*, p. 25.

decades. Inflation has pushed up the level of claims and the cost of repairs and reinstatements. Advancing technology in all shapes and sizes – wider aircraft, longer ships, more complex automobiles, more ambitious space vehicles – has added new dimensions of hazard. International competition in insurance has become ever more intense. International recession in trade on either side of 1980 damaged large insurers everywhere. Gov-

Table 12.20. *Trading profit after tax of nine major companies (% of premium; three-year averages, 1980–2)*

Commercial Union	3.97	Norwich Union	7.63
Cornhill	4.77	Phoenix	4.30
Eagle Star	8.43	Royal	5.00
General Accident	6.30	Sun Alliance	5.83
Guardian RE	6.90		

Source: calculated from Carter & Godden, *The British Insurance Industry*, Table A2(a).1, pp. 19–27.

ernments became insistently hungry for information and some for insurance wealth. Natural disasters have also been plentiful in recent decades. Insurance practitioners have learned to live with astronomical claims ratios, keep their expenses down and trust to their investments to balance the books. This has been a common predicament on both sides of the Atlantic, and indeed elsewhere. But it is in the matter of profitability, or the manner in which unprofitability is avoided, that the verdict on a company must reside.

Over its last two decades, Phoenix withstood these difficulties as well as most large offices. This was true even in the disastrous underwriting year of 1982. Recession in world trade, a falling pound and intense competition produced in 1982 underwriting losses for all of the UK 'First Eleven' companies and the aggregate loss of 11.1% of written premiums was the worst for twenty years and perhaps the worst ever. Nevertheless, Phoenix had ranked seventh of the 'Eleven' in terms of underwriting loss (8.2%) in 1981 and it continued to rank seventh in 1982 (12.1%).[136] Over the longer run, since 1960, Table 12.19 shows that Phoenix suffered underwriting losses on general business during the spate of American problems in the 1960s and during the spate of global problems from the mid-1970s. Only in the years 1967, 1968, and 1971–3 were underwriting surpluses scored on general business; and the surplus of 1973 was the last in Phoenix history. Indeed, the Phoenix's last years were some of the most punishing insuring years on record: 1983 was the worst ever for aviation losses, 1984 the worst ever for UK household business (to those dates).

Nevertheless, both long-term business, reflecting the push in the life department, and investment income built up well. Of these influences, investment income was incomparably the stronger and it was primarily

[136] Carter and Godden, *The British Insurance Industry*, p. 66. The authors give the loss ratios in this form and calculate the underwriting loss as 'a percentage of general insurance world-wide written premium income'.

this factor which allowed a very healthy growth in net profit for Phoenix over the period 1960–82. In one year alone – the year at the depths of the American crisis, 1962 – were the underwriting results sufficiently bad to outweigh the investment results and produce a net deficit for the Phoenix Group.[137]

If trading profits after tax are expressed as a percentage of premium for nine leading companies in the period immediately before Phoenix's demise, the results for the office are not far out of line with the peer group performance. They are towards the lower end of the range for this top class; but they certainly imply no cause for alarm. The mighty Commercial Union, for instance, did significantly worse.

It should be clear then that the reformed Phoenix did not lose its independence because of any feebleness in the marketplace. Given the difficulties of contemporary trading conditions, Phoenix's ability to win premiums, control costs and make profits was never far from the industrial standard, and in some sectors ahead of it.

18. THE PHOENIX–CONTINENTAL AGREEMENT: THE DENOUEMENT

The Harris–Bishop era was bracketed by two crises involving Continental. One was cured by Continental buying into Phoenix; the other was caused by Continental selling out of Phoenix. Nothing that had been done to reform Phoenix or to open up parallel lines of innovation constituted an adequate defence against the withdrawal of Continental. The culmination of the second crisis came in 1984, but the process which led to it commenced in 1982, the year of Phoenix's 200th birthday.

The occasion was more than a little ironic. At this time, John Ricker, chairman of Continental, made two perceptions that were deeply ominous for Phoenix: firstly, that from his company's standpoint, the 1963 accord had not worked out notably well in practice; and, secondly, that there was a new threat in the international market place to which Continental might not be able to respond alone.

Continental's foreign policy in the two preceding decades had produced a number of relatively small independent operations overseas which were not especially economical to run. The first priority of the American office had been the acquisition of an international spread of business; tight control of underwriting in these markets had come second;

[137] For a fuller treatment of investment results, see above, Section 16.

and the results had turned out accordingly. Harris, not without some relish, pointed out that genuine co-partnership would have been a better deal for everyone concerned.

In Continental's view, the new threat in the market was the appearance of specialist risk managers and large international banks who were said to be responding very effectively to the wide *range* of services required by multinational clients. The banks, in particular, even though acting as intermediaries, were poaching trade from the insurance companies by offering 'complete product' insurance, including claims service, surveying, engineering appraisal, etc. This type of package was proving highly attractive to operators within the developing economies, especially those of the Pacific Basin. And, under the pressure of this new competition, the few large American groups which had specialised in overseas insurances and had grown greatly in power since the 1960s – AIG, AFIA and INA – were becoming still more aggressive. Continental was disturbed by this two-pronged attack and by its relative weakness in the developing economies.

Early in 1982 Ricker, now on the verge of retirement, voiced his doubts about Phoenix–Continental's 'ability to deliver on a timely basis, comprehensive products and insurance-related services so as to compete with international brokers, international banks and risk managers who are playing a larger part in the marketing of these products today'. He called for intensive study of the new products and the development of 'a new marketing culture'. Using the theory and language of the management consultants, he concluded that Phoenix–Continental needed 'a control point to exercise good and prompt judgement on the need for additional facilities . . . a core structure that transcends all countries'. This central command would 'fill in the grid in a responsive manner'.

To the Phoenix eye, it was exactly these issues – if not these expressions – which had been under discussion for the preceding two decades. However, the British response was mild. The executive pointed out that Phoenix–Continental already had a 'core' in the shape of the International Division, conceded that new starts might be needed in some places, and agreed to come – represented by Ken Wilkinson (deputy chief general manager), Ralph Petty (general manager overseas), and Ron Bishop (chief general manager) – for discussions in New York in the middle of March 1982.

Harris, now deputy chairman, summed up the history of a twenty-year cycle: 'The Phoenix and the Continental have paradoxically arrived *back* at the point from which they established their association in 1963, namely the recognition that, in the international field of insurance, they can jointly present a much greater force than they could possibly present separately.'[138] He emphasised that Ricker's proposal exactly echoed Herd's phrase, employed in the 1963 Memorandum of Intent, regarding 'the joint employment of facilities throughout the world' and 'begged the question as to what went wrong between Phoenix and Continental in the period 1963 to 1982 whereby the aspirations of the 1963 Memorandum of Intent were delayed, if not aborted'.

Harris argued that the fit between the two companies remained good, even under the new conditions. Since 1963, Phoenix had built up a powerful life organisation and extended its reach in general business in developed and developing markets alike. On the other hand, Continental had specialised in the heavier commercial risks and reinsurance. The combination of Phoenix's new capacity in the mass market with Continental's access to American companies worldwide surely strengthened the case for cooperation.

The meetings in New York recognised shortcomings in existing procedures and the need to establish a more 'recognisable market image'. A first step towards this, proposed by the Americans, was the creation of a new 'core' company, Continental–Phoenix International Incorporated. It was to be based in New York, possess its own board drawn from the chief officials of both companies, and be directed by its own permanent chief executive. Overseas, it would be represented by operating companies drawn primarily from existing Phoenix *and* Continental affiliates. The intention was now to rationalise and integrate within a joint scheme the capability Continental had created since 1963; by contrast, the original intention had been to put into joint use the capability Phoenix already possessed in 1963.

The Americans were under tight time constraints. They believed they had few alternatives: they could proceed alone; they could join one of the big US groups; they could seek connection with a British company possessing a still bigger international capacity than Phoenix; they could find another American corporate partner with which to confront the groups; or they could attempt to mould Phoenix into the shape they required. Difficulties in finding an answer within the US insurance system partly explain the energy with which Continental pursued the 'Phoenix solution' during 1982. The agenda was for Ricker and Bishop to follow up the March meetings by considering share holding proportions in the new company, the composition of its Board and the identity of its chief executive – and to have the answers by 15 April!

Further discussions took place in London in the middle of April. For

[138] My emphasis.

the Americans, Continental–Phoenix International represented Phase I of a new global strategy. The Continental team now moved to Phase II: this was to include exchange of information and comprehensive cooperation in all markets. In practice, however, the centrepiece of Phase II for Continental was a good deal broader than information exchange or cooperation; it was the proposal that the two companies should pursue joint *acquisitions* in the top export markets. This was what comprehensive cooperation really meant. The Americans were prepared to push the point, letting it be known that non-compliance with this objective would require the 'rethinking' even of the assumptions underlying Phase I. Despite long discussion, the Continental team continued to present the stages as interdependent. The top markets were identified as Japan, West Germany, Italy and France.

This cast of thinking raised doubts at Phoenix House. For one thing, the British company already possessed a formidable array of overseas subsidiaries. What was to happen to them if Phoenix and Continental were to create another set of foreign joint acquisitions? Similarly, there were Phoenix's existing arrangements with the Prudential in Africa and Australia to consider: that office would be unlikely to welcome the appearance of powerful new joint competitors carrying the Phoenix flag. But most threatening of all was the proposed division of assets and business in relation to shareholding. The plan was that the new 'core' company, Continental–Phoenix, should incorporate 40% of the assets and about 50% of the general business premiums of Phoenix of London.

Effectively, the scheme proposed the surrender of the historic Phoenix to a joint company based in New York. All that would be left in the United Kingdom would be a shadow of the original company. And this surrender was to be made at the prompting of a minority shareholder; for that is what Continental of New York remained.

The natural response was that the interests of the *majority* of Phoenix shareholders could not properly be served within such a venture. The Phoenix Board experienced the natural response: they were worried about what would be left for these shareholders to call their own. Thus the final burst of American initiative drew from the British a decisive reservation. No final agreement was possible because of Phoenix's grave concern for shareholder interest; to the end, it remained the key issue.

However, in the ensuing negotiations, the most immediate difficulties followed from the varying attitudes of the two companies in regard to overseas investments and profits. The philosophy of the Americans had been to pursue business expansion and presence in as many places as possible; Continental's prime aim was to display increased volumes in the balance sheets. Much less endowed with financial power, Phoenix had to watch its pennies in relation both to foreign underwriting results and to all foreign investments. From the latter, Phoenix's prime requirement was adequate yield in the short term, as well as the long term; the British company could not afford to accept low initial returns as the price for a wider spread of overseas business. Given the prevalence of underwriting loss, it needed all the help that it could get from *all* its investments.[139] The Americans, with far greater investment capability, put their faith in the wider sweep.

Moreover, the countries that had been identified as the top markets were among the most expensive in the world to enter. Phoenix, with its lean investment potential, could not go halves with Continental in such places. Somewhat disarmingly, Phoenix pointed out that decent insurance profits could still be made in the developing economies, where it was much cheaper to operate.

Indeed, Phoenix's main response to the Continental initiative was to express suspicion of universal solutions and to stress that its own recent successes were the fruit of a deliberately selective strategy. During the summer of 1982, the period of its double-centenary celebrations, Phoenix appeared to have some success in convincing the Americans that it had no choice but to take a step-by-step approach in any further integration. With some reluctance, the Americans conceded the point; or so the Phoenix team believed. In August 1982, Ricker was scarcely happy with the pace of negotiations, and had begun considering a list of alternative courses which included a complete separation of the US and UK foreign operations; but his preferred position was still for a closer relationship with Phoenix.

However, Continental itself came under increasing pressure during 1983 and the first half of 1984. The new chairman of the US enterprise, Jake Mascotte, who took over from John Ricker in November 1982, experienced the full brunt of this pressure. It stemmed from heavy reinsurance losses and indifferent overall trading results during 1983: the outcome was a serious shortage of ready cash. In New York, the management's need to supply a visibly dynamic initiative became urgent. The policy of hitting the 'hot' markets quickly was enlisted in this role, and came to be seen as vital to Continental's standing in American opinion.

Under these circumstances, Phoenix's worries about joint acquisitions began to look to the Americans like a further case of British feet-dragging. Even repeated warnings regarding the high cost of breaking into the target

[139] Phoenix had forgone even the chance of taking up shares in its close ally Toro Assicurazione on the grounds that low-yielding investments in weak currencies did nothing to assist its cause.

markets – warnings which did not prove idle – could be viewed, under such pressures, as repeated deficiencies in enthusiasm.

So, in the course of 1983, the American attitude hardened once again: a very strict interpretation was taken of Phase II 'cooperation', that is, joint investment, and acceptance of this was again stipulated as a prerequisite for the implementation of Phase I, the dual Continental–Phoenix global company.

All of this should be seen in the context of Continental's US policy-making and problems in its home market. During the 1970s and early 1980s, Continental had been caught up in the wave of diversification which swept over corporate industry and finance in the USA. At the outset, Continental was a cash-rich company with sufficient funds to participate energetically. Some of its cash went into ventures in credit card business (Diners' Club), and into claims adjustment and computerisation services. Money was lost in some of these. Further cash went into acquisitions, mainly of reinsurance, marine and life operations. Almost all of these additions, outside the core business, were subsequently sold on. The strains of this diversification policy were sufficient to tax even Continental's resources and by 1984 the Americans themselves were beginning to have second thoughts. Phoenix, of course, to its considerable misfortune, was caught up in these. It is significant that, by the late 1980s, Continental had returned to a concentration upon its mainstream US domestic, casualty, marine and aviation business.

The longer-term results – that is, the results after the parting of ways between Phoenix and Continental in 1984 – were at best mixed. Continental derived little future benefit from its efforts in the notoriously difficult German market and only small profit from its Italian operation. A Chilean vehicle hit difficulties in the early 1980s; and business declined in the Far East. Perhaps adequate judgement, as much as inadequate resources, kept Phoenix out of ventures of this type. But then again, Phoenix did not survive to enjoy the fruits of this judgement.

Phoenix's refusal to cooperate fully in Continental's joint acquisition strategy proved the ultimate frustration for the Americans. Nevertheless, the ambiguity in the relationship continued to the end. Continental persisted in extending the olive branch to Phoenix and genuinely desired British participation. On the other side, Phoenix management genuinely desired to retain the American alliance but persisted in viewing Continental's grander strategies with suspicion.

As so often in this story, mutual desire for cooperation existed alongside divergent definitions of suitable expansion. But, this time, American frustration with the ambiguity was compounded by difficulties with cash-flow problems at home. Paradoxically, at one of the several delicate points in the diplomacy of the relationship, the fate of the weaker financial partner was tipped by an apparent financial weakness in Continental. The American office was having trouble with its diversification policy and was beginning to sense the need for retrenchment. Despite all effort, it could make no headway with its joint foreign policy. The time appeared right for rethinking and regrouping.

It was with clear regret that, in May 1984, Mascotte finally informed the Phoenix Chairman's Committee that he intended to sell Continental's stake in Phoenix.[140] The message that Continental's chairman wished to see the Committee was delivered on the afternoon of the Annual General Meeting which also marked the retirement of Bill Harris from the deputy chairmanship; and Mascotte saw the Phoenix men later in that week. Harris had been one of the founding fathers of the original partnership and played a key role in the attempt to revive it between 1982 and 1984. His American expertise had frequently smoothed the waves and quietened the wires between London and New York. But in the Phoenix's final summer, not even an unofficial emergency mission by Harris to the USA could bring about a rapprochement.

Whereas many UK offices had encountered crises in the US market, and a good few had died of them, Phoenix, in a stroke of great originality, had tried to solve an American crisis by the deployment of American resources in the rest of the world. In its postwar era, Phoenix really needed a major acquisition to ensure independent survival. But, by 1963, more by bad luck than by bad judgement – or, possibly, simply as a function of an intermediate size ranking – this had not materialised, and both time and prospective partners were running out. The Continental connection was the next best idea; and it was an exceptionally good one. At the very least, it plucked two decades of continued independence from very adverse circumstances.

Of course, even before the end, the strategy imposed costs. They came partly in the shape of acquisitions forgone. And partly in the shape of diverted attention. The problem that Phoenix should have been concentrating upon, and upon which it was trying to concentrate, in the period 1977–84 was the rationalisation of its worldwide operation. But in practice, a disproportionate amount of management time was deflected from these objectives and expended instead upon the analysis of Continental's needs and schemes.

[140] This Committee was an informal *ad hoc* affair, gathering prior to board meetings; on this occasion the following were present: the chairman, J. A. Hambro, and D. B. (later Sir David) Money-Coutts, alongside Bishop and Wilkinson, and Mascotte.

In the end the strategy was revealed as one of high risks. The agreement protected Phoenix from predators but exposed the company to the danger that, unless it kept pace with its American partner's desire for expansion, its ultimate predator – even if indirectly – might be the Continental itself. The withdrawal of the Americans left Phoenix with a matter of weeks to find an alternative buyer for the Continental interest. Twenty years after its inception, one of the strangest alliances in British insurance history terminated reluctantly, and with mutual regrets, but very swiftly.

19. THE CONCLUSION: SUN–ALLIANCE–PHOENIX

The danger facing Phoenix was extreme. In the first instance, in 1963, Continental had purchased its minority holding in Phoenix by invitation and in return for a particular service. It would have been little short of miraculous if a comparable symmetry of needs among large insurers could have been found in a very few weeks in 1984. Any major buyer, and especially an American or German one, would be likely to want not 24% or 25% of Phoenix equity but 100% and at a takeover price. The vulnerability and anxiety of the British company could only increase that appetite.

By summer 1984, the threat of an aggressive takeover was serious. In this connection, Continental's 24% share of Phoenix was a real menace; as Continental well understood, the control of this holding would determine Phoenix's fate. What could be done with it? Any attempt to place it on the market would increase the chance of a predatory strike upon a much bigger slice of the equity. Short of an open market sale, even an agreed transaction for the entire 24% would risk acquiring a partner much less restrained than Continental: it could well allow an asset stripper across the threshold and into the store cupboard. Few investors could be expected to pay a premium of 50% – necessary to match that originally paid by Continental – for a minority interest unless they had an eye on ultimate control. In 1963, of course, the *Financial Times* had wondered why on earth Continental was prepared to do just this. In 1984, the odds on a repetition were long indeed.

The only course which appeared to offer defence against these threats was a negotiated solution ending in a friendly merger or takeover. But with whom to negotiate? Phoenix management identified four possibilities: another UK insurer; a foreign insurer; a UK non-insurer such as an industrial concern; a foreign non-insurer such as an American bank. Names were considered under all categories, but nothing solid emerged under three of them. Oil companies and breweries were investigated and even the prospect of recruiting a friendly consortium to take up Continental's dangerous leavings was scouted. But little came of these thoughts.

In any case, some categories were distrusted more than others. An industrial godparent, home or foreign, would want outright control and would have to pay a lot – in excess of £300 million – for it. In order to achieve an adequate return on their money, the industrialists would be forced to shed insurance capacity. To some, a foreign insurance office possessed attractions, for they believed that an external insurer might be content to ride a UK subsidiary with a loose rein, leaving it to manage its own affairs within its area of national expertise. This might have been true in the short term but the longer-run outlook could only be harsher. No less than the industrial buyer, the foreign insurer would be primarily interested in return on capital, and, having paid heavily for Phoenix, would be forced to cut costs to achieve this. Expert outsiders might well be willing to sacrifice entire sectors of business in such a context, or to take them outside the United Kingdom.[141]

The sole type of buyer which, it was hoped, might not be forced into, or even wish to undertake, a savage restructuring of the Phoenix was a UK insurer of a certain style. This office would need to be large and rich. It would also need to be active in areas of insurance similar to, but also complementary to, Phoenix's own fields of specialism. This should ensure that departments of business were conciliated rather than sacrificed.

All of these calculations had to be worked out at great speed. Continental had given Phoenix three weeks' notice of intention and freedom to seek a suitable buyer. The time limit was understandable given that a satisfactory sale would be achieved only under conditions of the tightest security.[142] However, Continental showed generosity in assuring Phoenix that they were looking not simply for the highest bidder, but for the most appropriate one; also they promised complete cooperation, upon completion of a purchase, in reorganising Phoenix's commitments in the USA.

Nevertheless, Phoenix felt that a solution was acutely urgent. The issue of secrecy pressed upon its leaders: the longer the delay in achieving the sale, the higher the scent for the predator. In this vexed situation, leaking information would almost certainly attract a pack of hostile bidders. The Phoenix response, therefore, had to work swiftly and cleanly, on the first

[141] The renewed interest of the giant German office Allianz in acquiring a UK connection drew a good deal of press speculation around this time.

[142] This consideration probably also ruled out the prospect of a phased withdrawal by Continental, in which the 24% might have been disposed of in several different packages.

pass. Even so, it could be asked why the Phoenix men had not moved earlier against a threat which now demanded instant remedies but which had scarcely materialised upon the instant.

The answer is threefold. Firstly, the Continental involvement had created tensions over decades without raising the prospect of an impending rift. Secondly, the Americans had been pushing for a *closer* relationship only months before the final break. Even when, in 1982, Ricker had listed a 'valuation' of Continental's Phoenix shares among his options, he had stressed that his preferred course was still to acquire a larger holding, up to 51%, in the British office.[143] Thirdly, despite these reassurances, the Phoenix executive *had* taken precautionary measures well before the démarche of 1984.

At the time of Phoenix's troubles in 1982, Ron Bishop had been approached by Geoffrey Bowler, chief general manager of the Sun Alliance–London Insurance Group. This veteran office, a vastly enlarged descendant of Phoenix's great rival of the eighteenth and nineteenth centuries, ranked fifth among UK offices by premium income, investment income or underwriting funds.[144] It had generous resources and an appetite for additional capacity. Bowler calculated shrewdly that Sun Alliance needed an expansion strategy, that this was most neatly achieved by further acquisitions, and that the postwar concentration process had left few survivors fit for acquisition. Phoenix, of course, was very fit. So he let it be known that, if Phoenix wished a friendly merger at any point, Sun Alliance would be interested.

When the crisis of 1984 reached its fullest pitch, Bishop needed only to cross the road – or, more precisely, three roads: King William Street, Cornhill and Threadneedle Street – and remind Sun Alliance of that interest. He did so early in June 1984, and, with Bowler away in hospital, duly put the reminder to the second-in-command at Bartholomew Lane, Ken Addison. Next day, Sun Alliance confirmed that it remained interested and negotiations began almost immediately. Rothschild's acted for Sun Alliance, Hambro's for Phoenix and Warburg's for Continental. The negotiations were distinguished by a high degree of cooperation from all parties, not least the Americans, and acceptable terms for a merger were achieved within a fortnight. The two British companies were ready for a

143 However, this would not have been easy given the Stock Exchange rule requiring minority shareholders to bid for 100% of the equity in a target company as soon as their holding passed 30%.

144 Carter and Godden, *The British Insurance Industry*, pp. 68, 94. The ranking is taken at 1982 levels. The Phoenix rankings on all these counts by then was eighth. The Sun had absorbed the Alliance in 1959 and the London Assurance in 1965. For the pedigree of all three of these vintage insurers, see vol. I.

public announcement by 11 July 1984.

However, Phoenix did not rush precipitately into the arms of Sun Alliance. In the limited time between Mascotte's decision to sell and Bishop's decision to approach Sun Alliance, full, if not indeed frenzied, investigation was made into the prospect of buyers presenting themselves from any one of Phoenix's other three categories of acceptable suitors. But there could be no public haggling over marriage terms: the suit had to succeed at the first attempt. And here the steadfastness of the interest from Sun Alliance was a strong recommendation. It is scarcely surprising that the Phoenix team should have developed a preference for an arrangement with an amenable candidate from their fourth category, UK insurers. For them, this was necessarily the most familiar type of buyer. They believed also that it was the safest.

There were special reasons for preferring Sun Alliance. The office was certainly amenable, a respected colleague in the most senior league of historic British offices. But shared values and shared traditions merely eased the style of negotiation. Certainly, too, Sun Alliance possessed both enviable resources and an outstanding record for reliability. But none of these features defined the full potential for accord between the two offices; this followed rather from the high degree of complementarity in their structures. Phoenix did not have a large marine account; Sun Alliance, on the other hand, contained the considerable marine capacity of the London Assurance. Sun Alliance did little in the aviation market; Phoenix in contrast was a world leader. Phoenix possessed a strong motor account, Sun Alliance a lesser one. In the life market, Phoenix had made a speciality of risk business and, consequently, had come to rely heavily on broker-generated custom. Sun Alliance had taken the opposite tack, specialising in mortgages and endowments for the mass market.

The lack of collision between identical capacities suggested that a considerable proportion of the Phoenix's substance could be incorporated into the Sun Alliance Group without the wholesale loss of departments and employment that the Phoenix men feared at other hands.

Both sides understandably saw advantages in a merger. Accordingly, on 11 July 1984, Sun Alliance purchased Continental's holding in Phoenix at 650p for every 25p share and offered to buy all other Phoenix shares at the same rate. The Phoenix Board, together with Hambro's, advised their shareholders to accept. Since the market price of Phoenix shares on 10 July was 450p, the shareholders had every reason to heed the advice, and did so. Sun Alliance effectively bought Phoenix at a 40% premium on the market price and for a total consideration of £400 million. This was a reasonable settlement: in the beginning, Continental had paid a premium price for its Phoenix holding; at the end, it was fair that it should receive one. Security once more was good: Phoenix share prices rose by 20p on the last afternoon of the negotiations, but otherwise the market scented little of the agreement prior to the formal announcement. The formal offer document was posted on 25 July and the bid went unconditional on 17 August 1984, with 84% acceptances.

So, in 1984, after a lifespan of 202 years the Arabian bird of insurance changed its shape for a final time. After having first emerged from the boiling pans of the London sugar-baking industry, a trade central to the metropolitan economy of the eighteenth century, the Phoenix eventually surrendered itself to a process equally central to the metropolitan economy of the late twentieth century, the City takeover. Fittingly, perhaps, the great office which absorbed the Bird in 1984 was one of the veterans which had first provoked the sugar bakers into insuring for themselves in 1782.

CONCLUSION

When a major corporate name disappears (or, as here, dramatically recedes), it is inevitable that thoughts should turn to crucial moments. Was there a particular critical issue which settled the fate of the Phoenix? If the historian had to choose – as the insurance veteran might wish to make him – where in the last century or so would he place the vital turning point or the telling error? The historian would have to say to the insurance veteran, or to the current insurance specialist, that these placements are, inevitably, the outcome of one individual's reading of the evidence. But if a business history should fail to address this final question, it is difficult to see what purpose it has.

For the Phoenix, the answer, necessarily, is qualified. Clearly, it lies somewhere in an inter-relationship of crises and mistakes. Other companies faced similar crises and made similar errors. But they did not do so in the same sequence. A not entirely evasive amplification might be that, for the Phoenix in this century, the sequence included not one but four vital moments. And these were linked by the institutional memory which encourages businesses (among many bodies) to respond – usually over-react – to a new crisis or glowing prospect in the light of the over-reaction to the last crisis or glowing prospect. The moments were: the San Francisco earthquake of 1906; the takeover of London Guarantee in 1922; the period of conservative management after the Second World War; and the dramatic alliance with Continental of New York in 1963.

We might risk the further thought that the first of these was an act of God, the last an act of individual entrepreneurship; and that only the middle two cases can be brought before the bar of managerial theory, tried in the court of corporate best practice, and found wanting.

Lying behind this judgement is the proposal that the twentieth-century Phoenix faced among its many crises, two dominant, persistent and sapping problems: the American market, particularly the American accident market, and the failure to achieve a really major, and safe, corporate acquisition between 1922 and 1984.

Institutional memory in the nineteenth century had kept Phoenix out of direct trade to the USA, apparently for too long, and only a change in American law forced it back in. After San Francisco, the issue was raised as to whether the Phoenix should leave again. For the rest of this century, the US market was to prove a source of punishing losses, exorbitant expenses and slender returns.

Ironically, in 1906 it was the brightest and the best of the Phoenix Board who wished to stay and take their chances. And it was the conservatives, to whom the long run may give the right of it, who wanted to leave. But, being conservatives, they had no substitute to offer for the cascade of American premiums; and it was for lack of an imaginatively argued alternative that the Phoenix stayed – and took its medicine. Here institutional memory was ambiguous: it could point to leaving America because the market was provenly dangerous; or it could point to staying in America because the market was provenly big.

The Evans coup of 1963 was as unpredictable as the earthquake: a totally independent insight well in advance of any other City tie-in with American capital. The Continental alliance was a masterstroke of imagination which reversed the American dependence: Evans and Harris got America to invest in the Phoenix. It was a characteristically valiant remedy for a prestigious UK company which lacked the resources to acquire another sufficiently powerful UK company. But, if brave, the Continental deal was, perhaps unavoidably, loose in the detail.[1] Ironically, again, the long term served to emphasise not the rewards upon, but the risks within, the free-standing act of entrepreneurial originality. In the shorter run, however, it secured Phoenix twenty years of continued independence which it might very well not have enjoyed otherwise. And it offered Harris (especially) and Bishop the chance to give the Phoenix a market equilibrium which owed less to US premiums and suffered less from US costs. American capital was employed, with satisfying symmetry, to make the Phoenix a more convincingly international insurer.

The acquisition of London Guarantee & Accident and the management of the Ferguson era may be judged by more rigorous standards. LGA was a disaster from which Phoenix took longer to recover than it did from the San Francisco earthquake. Had Ryan acquired LGA in 1907, on his first attempt and before this company became a disaster, the Poenix

[1] Unavoidably, because the Americans demurred at more detail. And it is unlikely that more detail would actually have guaranteed more defence twenty years down the road.

story would have been different. A corporate magician who had conjured up a hatful of acquisitions in favourable times, failed to notice that the times had changed and went for one acquisition too many, featuring an old favourite from former times. This was a textbook lesson in how not to acquire a company: top management was driven by old memories and appetites, while current information was deeply worrying but discounted. Institutional memory played tricks and encouraged the acquisition of an American disaster just as the world economy dipped into recession.[2]

The protocols of modern large-scale corporate takeovers would never have permitted Phoenix to absorb LGA. Today, investigators briefed to practice 'due diligence' would be required to demonstrate sound corporate practice on the part of the target company. Had such methods been developed by the 1920s, they would have proved, as A. T. Winter tried but was unable to do, that LGA was not the company Ryan thought it was, or that it had been in 1907. Managerial theory has led to safer practice in the interim.

Corporate theory also has something to teach about the Ferguson era. By the 1940s, Phoenix had long been a multi-divisional, multinational company. Such enterprises need to be managed with a sensitivity to their *various* functions, and in a way which integrates these functions into an over-arching strategy. In this respect, Edward Ferguson was scarcely a Chandlerian hero-figure. When he became general manager, he had never controlled a single division of the multi-divisional corporation (although he had managed a country-sized operation in South Africa). And he had acted as assistant to Sketch; but that was all. He was a fire insurer through and through, but he had enjoyed no experience in heading even a full corporate fire department whose claims and possibilities needed to be balanced and argued against the claims and possibilities of other departments. This was a recipe for tunnel vision: it was no accident that Phoenix under Ferguson *reverted*, as far as he could make it, to the role of a fire office.

Ferguson was also a fire man from LGA in whom the economic experience of the 1920s had inspired a marked fear of the wrath of the insurance gods. In the conjunction of Ferguson, LGA and the 1920s, institutional memory did its damnedest – and it was the Phoenix of the 1940s and 1950s which paid for it.

Sadly, these very different critical issues – San Francisco apart – had very similar outcomes. Whether badly, conservatively or imaginatively handled, they did not attract friends or increase the chances of a corporate

[2] UK unemployment was already 17.0% of insured workers in 1921 and 14.3% in 1922, in comparison with the 10.4%, 16.1% and 21.3% in the Crash years 1929, 1930 and 1931.

acquisition. The LGA affair left a trail of debris in its wake which did not enhance confidence within Phoenix nor reputation without. Ferguson was not the man to add yet more components to an array with which he was not comfortable as matters stood. And Evans' enlistment of American capital scared British insurance capital, if not to death then at least to a careful distance.

Those who led the twentieth-century Phoenix through its crucial moments have been either insurance technicians like the actuary Ryan, the accident specialist Sketch and the fire specialists Ferguson and Harris, or they have been men of more generalist inclination like Evans. Ferguson was trained as a fire insurer but he was not comfortable reading an insurance balance sheet. Evans preferred the larger picture to the small detail. Yet technical expertise proved no defence. Ryan chose the superfluous acquisition; and the other technician of the interwar years, Ralph Sketch, consequently spent most of his Phoenix career in damage control. Ferguson, unlike Harris, found the transition from insurance specialism to managerial generalism difficult: Sir Edward took the wrong lessons from Ryan's bravado and allowed institutional trauma to dominate his decision-making. His successor, David Evans, was a great general, an inspired leader and an innovative strategist. But it was the impossibility of achieving binding detail in his agreement with Continental which left the next generation of technicians hostages to an American equity withdrawal.

The leading postwar technician, Harris, made the most of the opportunities handed on by Evans – and unlike Sketch, he was able to do much more than control damage – but, in the end, neither Harris nor Bishop was able to escape the boomerang from 1963.

Harris and Bishop, and their lieutenants, inherited a large reputation, a weak UK base and an excessive dependence on the US market. With the time and resources bought by Evans, they did much to tidy up the Phoenix, cut its costs, adjust its trim, and overhaul its distant operations. Indeed, they did so much that one can sympathise with the disbelief of some of them, most notably Harris, that they could not pull off a last-minute rescue, even in 1984.

In the end there is a discernible trail which leads through the intense detail of a great business trading worldwide throughout its second century towards the culmination of 1984. It leads from the decision to stay in the US market after 1906, through Ryan's unduly prolonged appetite for corporate victories in the 1920s, and Ferguson's memory-induced terror of growth in the 1940s and 1950s, to Evans' reversal of the American card in the 1960s. Evans did more to rise above institutional memory reflexes than any of his predecessors, but, understandably, his first concern lay in saving the ship rather than in redrafting the small print on the manifest.

Everybody who followed was floating on a delicate life-raft of open-ended clauses. During that voyage, Harris in particular executed some clever carpentry, and greatly enhanced the seaworthiness of the craft, but, after 1963, its ultimate buoyancy rested upon a 20% plug of equity which was owned on the far side of a large ocean.

Nevertheless, it remains a fact of business history that the Phoenix stayed afloat, however delicately, for another twenty years, and did not sink – as it very well might have – in the 1960s.

BIBLIOGRAPHY

PHOENIX SOURCES

The excellence of the company sources which underpinned volume I endured for the span of volume II. This was particularly true in two respects. First, the archive is not simply a domestic matter. There is a great deal of material on other companies and thus on Phoenix's place in the insurance industry and amongst its competitors (see, for instance, the Analysis of Insurance Companies' Reports 1901–31 and the Review of US Business by Company). Secondly, Phoenix's early specialism as a foreign insurer guaranteed a particular attention to the overseas record in its second century. The remarkable series of five volumes in the Review of Foreign Agencies report annual results for every outpost in the Phoenix empire for the extraordinary period 1787–1930; sadly, Book 6 did not survive the Great Crash of 1929–30. Care is needed in handling these records, particularly after 1890 as treaty reinsurance results are incorporated into the numbers. Equally unusual as a source are the hopefully-named 'Victory Committee' Reports. The Victory Committee began sitting in 1941, assumed an Axis-free globe, and tried to predict what insuring in a liberated postwar world would be like. To do so, it needed to define a baseline; so it generated a statistical record of earnings for fifty-eight countries for the period 1929–38; and thus did much to replace the missing Book 6 of the Foreign Agencies Review.

The general statistical excellence of the record for 1782–1870 derived from the huge double-entry ledgers, which Phoenix kept as best-practice accounting from its first day of business. From 1908, and the 'second foundation' of Phoenix as a composite office, something even bigger and better was needed. It was provided in the extended runs of the Blue Book (Fire & General Accounts, 1918–73) and Red Book (Life Accounts, 1909–77); unhelpfully, the colour 'code' is reversed so that blue is for fire, red is for life. The Red and Blue books give results for 'Company' and every one of the growing ranks of subsidiaries.

This reflects a general and inevitable trend in the archive: as the company becomes bigger, more complex, and more multi-divisional, the number of accounts, specialist committees, and reporting agencies necessarily multiplies; and this is reflected in the list below. As is also common with large modern companies, records of high policy increasingly migrate over time from the Directors' Minutes to other places: here the Board, Private and Secret Minutes define the heirarchy of confidentiality. The latter is particularly good on salary and some foreign, especially Australian, matters. More surprisingly, the Chairman's Annual Reports, notably of the interwar years, are refreshingly outspoken. Perhaps surprisingly too, the company house journal, *The Bird*, is friendly and approachable and often a good source for perspectives on people, buildings, and momentous events, like wars.

Accounts, 1909–1977, Life (Red Books)
Accounts, 1918–1973, Fire & General (Blue Books)
Analysis of Home Business, 1901–41
Analysis of Insurance Companies' Reports, 1901–31
Annual Analysis of Business of all Departments, 1870–1914
Canada, Results of Business, by G. H. Hurren, January, 1944
Centenary Circular, 17 January 1872
Chairman's Annual Reports, 1905–84
'Conflagration, Earthquake and Hurricane Disasters, 1904 Onwards' (compiled 1945)
Consultative Committee Minutes
Davis, B. H., American Diary, June–November 1926
Directors' Correspondence; Guardbook B4/40
Directors' Minute Books, 1870–1945
Fire Committee Minutes
Fire Loss Experience since 1788
Foreign Agents' Ledgers
Foreign Agents' Lists
Foreign Treaties Book (Red)
General Manager's Reports on USA and Canada, 1909–45 (see also the similar Accident Manager's Reports, 1924–45)
Investment Committee Minutes
Le Phoenix Groupe en France, 1786–1959 (company publication, 1959)
Memorandum for Phoenix Directors (Norwich Union), by R. Y. Sketch, June 1925
Memorandum on the Hidden Assets and Liabilities of the London Guarantee & Accident Insurance Company
Memorandum on Internal Organisation, by R. Y. Sketch, March 1925
Phoenix–PABELO, Committee on Fusion, Reports, 1907
Private Memorandum on Norwich Union Fire and Life Offices, by R. Y. Sketch, July 1924
Private Minutes, 1872–1945
Review of US Business by Company
Review of Foreign Agencies, Books 1–5, 1787–1930
Results of Fire Offices, 1900–32
Secret Minutes, 1908–45

Some Thoughts on US Fire Business, by T. H. Hodgson, May 1946
Special Committee Minutes, 1921–45
The Bird
Trustees' Minutes, 1870–1907

OTHER COMPANY SOURCES

The Phoenix archive kept fairly close tabs on everything in the insurance colony from nestlings through predators to senior admirals. However, when mergers or takeovers impend, it is still worth taking a perspective upon the incoming Phoenix from the vantage point of the target company: the victim's eye view, even when (or especially when) the victim was on the willing side, can be instructive. Sometimes, too, as with the Chicago Fire, another company had a man on the spot, when the Phoenix did not. The following are particularly useful:

British Empire Mutual Life Assurance Society, Guardbook
Law Life Assurance Society, Guardbook No. 1
London Guarantee & Accident Insurance Company, Annual Statements to New York Insurance Department
London Guarantee & Accident Insurance Company, Directors' Minute Books
Mr Burnett's Report on the Chicago Fire of 1871 (for the General Manager, North British & Mercantile Insurance Company)
Norwich Union Fire Insurance Society, Extraordinary General Meeting, January 1920
Norwich Union Fire Insurance Society, Private Minutes, especially 1919–20
Union Marine & General Insurance Company, Directors' Minute Books

OTHER PRIMARY SOURCES

External sources tended to report on the insurance industry when control over it was required (e.g. in making motor insurance compulsory) or when something drastic had happened to it, which required a revision of the normal terms of operation (e.g. an earthquake or a world war). Predictably, most of these sources are governmental. Another urge to control whch came from outside the company but inside the industry emanated from the associative tendencies of the offices, and here the corporate voice speaks through the records of the Fire Offices' Committee and the Life Offices' Association. Often it spoke about prices (i.e. premiums) and the need to control them by tariffs.

Committee on Aircraft Insurance, Report, (Cd 7997, xxxvii, 1915)
Fire Offices' Committee, Emergency Sub-Committee, Minutes, 1915
Fire Offices' Committee Minutes (both Home and, especially, for the Phoenix, Foreign)
Government War Insurance Schemes, Preliminary Statement of Results (Cmd 98, xxxii, 1919)

Life Offices' Association Minutes
Reed, A. S., *Special Report on the City of San Francisco* (US National Board of Fire Underwriters; New York, 1905)
The San Francisco Conflagration of April 1906; Special Report (US National Board of Fire Underwriters, Committee of Twenty; New York, 1906)
Royal Comission on the Control of Traffic on Roads (Cd 3365, xvii, 1929–30)
Royal Commission on the Supply of Food and Raw Materials in Time of War (Cd 2643, xxxlx, 1905)
Summary of New Life Assurances, Parliamentary Papers, lxxiv, 1914

RELATED BUSINESS HISTORIES

The senior business histories in the insurance sector continue to be those of Peter Dickson on the Sun and Barry Supple on the Royal Exchange, and, I would hope, the first volume of the Phoenix history. Oliver Westall's recent analysis of the Provincial Insurance Company is a rare full-dress coverage of a minor office which is enlivened not least by the presence of J. M. Keynes as investment adviser. Some relationships between business histories may be unexpected: thus the Lt. Col. Pleydell-Bouverie who appeared in the history of Vickers Ltd as an ordnance expert reappears in the Phoenix story as a member of the Board; and one of Charles Wilson's heroes in the histor of Unilever, the great accountant and company surgeon, Frank D'Arcy Cooper, also joined the highest ranks of Phoenix's insurance men. E. Nesbit's principal character is included here for fabulous properties of another kind.

Alford, B. W. E., *W. D. & H. O. Wills and the Development of the UK Tobacco Industry, 1786–1965* (London, 1973)
Anon., *Centennial Story: The Union Marine & General Insurance Co. Ltd., 1863–1963* (Liverpool, 1963)
Anon., *The North British and Mercantile Centenary, 1809–1909* (Edinburgh, 1909)
Barnard, R. W., *A Century of Service: the Story of the Prudential, 1848–1948* (London, 1948)
Bignold, R., *Five Generations of the Bignold Family 1761–1947, and their Connection with the Norwich Union* (London,1948)
Blake, R., *Esto Perpetua: the Norwich Union Life Insurance Society, 1808–1958* (London, 1958)
Burk, K., *Morgan Grenfell, 1838–1988; The Biography of a Merchant Bank* (Oxford, 1989)
Coleman, D. C., *Courtaulds, A History*, Vol. III (Oxford, 1980)
Davenport-Hines, R. P. T., *Dudley Docker, The Life and Times of a Trade Warrior*, (Cambridge, 1984)
Dickson, P. G. M., *The Sun Insurance Office, 1710–1960* (London, 1960)
Drew, B., *The London Assurance: A Second Chronicle* (London, 1949)
Dyer Simpson, J., 1936, *Our Centenary Year; Liverpool and London and Globe Insurance Co. Ltd* (London, 1936)
Francis, E. V., *The History of the London and Lancashire Insurance Co. Ltd* (Lon-

don, 1962)
Garnett, R. G., *A Century of Co-operative Insurance: The Co-operative Insurance Society, 1867–1967* (London, 1968)
Gibb, D. E. W., *Lloyds of London, A Study in Individualism* (London, 1957)
Hurren, G., *Phoenix Renascent* (privately printed, London, 1973)
James, M., *Biography of a Business: the Insurance Company of North America, 1792–1942* (New York, 1942)
Japan Business History Institute, *The 100-Year History of Nippon Life, 1889–1989* (Osaka, 1991)
Sumitomo Marine & Fire Insurance; The First Century, 1883–1993 (Tokyo, 1993)
Tokio Marine & Fire Insurance; The First Century, 1879–1979 (Tokyo, 1993)
Leigh-Bennett, E. P., *On this Evidence: A Study in 1936 of the Legal & General Assurance since its Formation in 1836* (London, 1936)
Liveing, E., *A Century of Insurance: the Commercial Union Assurance Group, 1860–1960* (London, 1961)
Martland, P., 'A Business History of the Gramophone Company 1897–1918' (unpub. Ph.D. thesis, Cambridge, 1992)
Naylor, R. T., *A History of Canadian Business, 1867–1914* (2 vols., Toronto, 1975)
Nesbit, E., *The Phoenix and the Carpet* (London, Puffin edn, 1994)
Ogborn, M. E., *Equitable Assurances, 1762–1962* (London, 1962)
Pugh, P., *Absolute Integrity: The Story of the Royal Insurance, 1845–1995* (Cambridge, 1995)
Raphael, A., *Ultimate Risk* (London, 1994)
Reader, W. J., *Imperial Chemical Industries Ltd; A History*, vol. I, *The Forerunners, 1870–1926* (Oxford, 1970)
Roberts, R., *Schroders, Merchants and Bankers* (London, 1992)
Ryan, R., 'A History of the Norwich Union Fire and Life Insurance Societies from 1797 to 1914' (unpub. Ph.D. thesis, University of East Anglia, 1983)
Sayers, R. S., *The Bank of England, 1891–1944* (3 vols., Cambridge, 1976)
Schooling, W., *Alliance, 1824–1924* (London, 1924)
Supple, B. E., *The Royal Exchange Assurance, 1720–1970* (Cambridge, 1970)
Syed, I., (ed.), *Eagle Star, A Guide to its History and Archives* (Cheltenham, 1997)
Tarn, A. W. and Byles, C. E., *A Record of the Guardian Assurance Company Ltd, 1821–1921* (London, 1921)
Trebilcock, C., *The Vickers Brothers, Armament and Enterprise, 1854–1914* (London, 1977)
'British Multinationals in Japan, 1900–41; Vickers, Armstrongs, Nobels and the Defence Sector', in Yuzewa, T. and Udagawa, M. (eds), *Foreign Business in Japan before World War II* (Tokyo, 1990)
Westall, O. M., *The Provincial Insurance Company, 1903–38* (Manchester, 1992)
Wilson, C. H., *The History of Unilever*, Vol. II (London, 1954)
Yeo, A. W., *Atlas Reminiscent* (London, 1908)

SPECIALIST WORKS ON INSURANCE HISTORY AND PRACTICE

Butt, J., 'Life Assurance in War and Depression: the Standard Life Assurance Co. and its Environment, 1914–39', in Westall, O. M. (ed.), *The Historian and the Business of Insurance* (Manchester, 1984)

Carter, R. L. and Godden, A. H., *The British Insurance Industry: A Statistical Review, 1983/4* (Brentford, 1983)

Clayton, G. and Osborn, W. J., *Insurance Company Investment, Principles and Policy* (London, 1965)

Cockerell, H. A. C. and Green, E., *The British Insurance Business, 1547–1970* (London, 1976)

Cox, P. R. and Storr-Best, R. H., *Surplus in British Life Assurance: Actuarial Control over its Emergence and Distribution during 200 years* (London, 1962)

Dinsdale, W. A., *The History of Accident Insurance in Great Britain* (London, 1954)

Elderton, W., *The Impossibility of War Risk Insurance* (Cambridge, 1938)

Golding, C. E., *A History of Reinsurance with Sidelights on Insurance* (London, 1931)

Hannah, L., *Inventing Retirement; The Development of Occupational Pensions in Britain* (Cambridge, 1986)

Hill, N. (ed.), *War and Insurance* (London, 1927)

Jones, C. A., 'Competition and Structural Change in the Buenos Aires Fire Insurance Market', in Westall, O. M. (ed.), *The Historian and the Business of Insurance* (Manchester, 1984)

Morrah, D., *A History of Industrial Life Assurance* (London, 1955)

National Fire Protection Association, *Conflagrations in America since 1914* (New York, 1942)

Raynes, H. E., 'The Place of Ordinary Stocks and Shares in the Investment of Life Assurance Funds', *Journal of the Institute of Actuaries*, (1928), pp. 21–50

A History of British Insurance (London, 1964)

Pearson, R., 'The Development of Reinsurance Markets in Europe during the Nineteenth Century', *Journal of European Economic History*, 24 (1995)

Recknell, G. H., 'Life Assurance versus Investments', *Post Magazine and Insurance Monitor*, 7 November 1925

Simmonds, R. C., *The Institute of Actuaries 1848–1948* (London, 1948)

Supple, B. E., 'Insurance in British History', in Westall, O. M. (ed.), *The Historian and the Business of Insurance* (Manchester, 1984)

The Insurance Directory, Reference and Yearbook, 1916–20

Trebilcock, C. 'The City, Entrepreneurship and Insurance: Two Pioneers in Invisible Exports: the Phoenix Fire Office and the Royal of Liverpool,1800–90', in McKendrick, N. and Outhwaite, R. B. (eds.), *Business Life and Public Policy; Essays in Honour of D. C. Coleman* (Cambridge, 1986)

Warner, S. O., 'The Effect on British Life Assurance of the European War', in Hill, N. (ed.), *War and Insurance* (London, 1927)

Westall, O. M. (ed.), *The Historian and the Business of Insurance* (Manchester, 1984)
'The Assumption of Regulation in British General Insurance', in Jones, G. G. and Kirby, M. (eds.), *Competitiveness and the State* (Manchester, 1991)
Withers, H., *Pioneers of British Life Assurance* (London, 1951)
Yoneyama, T., 'The Rise of the Largescale Composite Insurance Company in the UK', *Kyoto Sangyo University Economic and Business Review*, 20 (1993)

CONTEMPORARY PRINTED BOOKS

Brooks, G., *The Spirit of 1906; An Account of the San Francisco Earthquake and Fire* (San Francisco, 1921)
Lieven, J. W., *Atlas at War* (London, 1946)
National Fire Protection Association, *Conflagrations in America since 1914* (New York, 1942)
Odhams Press, *Ourselves in Wartime; An Illustrated Survey of the Home Front in the Second World War* (London, 1944)
United States Strategic Bombing Survey, vol. VII, *The Pacific War* (Washington, 1946)
Whitney, A. W., *Insurance Payments in Relation to the San Francisco Fire and Earthquake* (San Francisco, 1907)

CONTEMPORY PERIODICALS

Some specialist journals are worth examination in the run. These include the *Assurance Magazine*, *Bankers' Magazine*, *Post Magazine and Insurance Monitor*, and, for marine matters, the *Liverpool Journal of Commerce*. The importance of the Liverpool papers is a function of the city's growth as a rival insurance capital from the late nineteeenth century.

The more general press can provide useful comment on specific pieces of legislation, or, more usually, on particular mergers or takeovers. Among these, the most commercially alert, such as the *Financial Times* or the *Financial News* had a creditable record of scenting a leaky boardroom or a fishy deal. They thus offer a means of testing how efficiently a takeover bid has been mounted or how well the share price protected; sometimes they even manage to speak for the shareholder interest when that was not as prominent as it might have been. Since the dates of these corporate events tend to be known, it is relatively simple to chase the references in the surrounding weeks. Often the interested companies were doing this themselves and the internal record will guide the historian to the newspaper record. Sometimes, the company kept its own cuttings book and the historian then has the luxury of the private and public record in the same package.

Obituaries also can be more or less interesting.

The following list is necessarily a mixture of general and specific references:

Bailey, A. H., 'On the Principles on which the Funds of Life Assurance Societies should be Invested', *Assurance Magazine*, X (1861)

Mackenzie, A. G., 'On the Practice and Powers of Assurance Companies in regard to the investment of their Life Assurance Funds', *Journal of the Institute of Actuaries*, 29 (1891)

Mackenzie, R. K., 'The San Francisco Earthquake and Conflagration', *Proceedings of the Insurance and Actuarial Society of Glasgow*, February 1907

May, G. E., 'The Investment of Life Assurance Funds', *Journal of the Institute of Actuaries*, 46 (1912)

Pipkin, S. J., 'Fifty Years Reminiscences in the City', *Post Magazine and Insurance Monitor*, 77 (1916)

'Some Present Day Problems of the Insurance Business', *Post Magazine and Insurance Monitor*, 68 (1907)

Rogers, J. C., 'A Memoir of John Clutton', *Transactions of The Surveyors' Institution*, 29 (1896–7)

Thomason, H. A., 'The Origin and Growth of Endowment Assurance Business', *Journal of the Institute of Actuaries*, 34 (1896)

Warner, S. G., 'Twenty Years Change in Life Assurance', *Journal of the Federation of Insurance Institutes*, 12 (1909)

Young, T. E., 'The Ethics of Insurance', *Journal of the Chartered Insurance Institute*, 1 (1898)

Proceedings of the British Academy, 18 (1932), 'Obituary of Lord Dillon, 1844–1932'

Brassey's Naval Annual, 1886

John Bull

Post Magazine and Insurance Monitor

The Bankers' Magazine

The Courier

The Daily Chronicle

The Daily Telegraph

The Economist

The Evening News

The Evening Standard

The Financial News

The Financial Times

The Insurance Record

The Liverpool Journal of Commerce

The Liverpool Post

The Policyholder

The Saturday Review

The Statist

MODERN PRINTED SOURCES

Aldcroft, D. H. and Richardson, H. W., *Building in the British Economy between the Wars* (London, 1968)
The British Economy, 1870–1939, (London, 1969)
Barker, P., *The Regeneration Trilogy*, (London, 1991–5)
Barnes, J., *Metroland* (London, 1980)
Beckett, I. F. W. and Simpson, K. (eds.), *A Nation in Arms* (Manchester, 1985)
Blythe, R., *Akenfield* (London, 1969)
Boog, H. (ed.), *The Conduct of the Air War in the Second World War* (Oxford, 1992)
Bowden, S., 'The New Consumerism', in Johnson, P. (ed.), *Twentieth-Century Britain: Economic, Social and Cultural Change* (London, 1994)
Briggs, J., *A Woman of Passion: The Life of E. Nesbit, 1858–1924* (London, 1987)
BZW Research, *BZW Equity-Gilt Study; Investment in the London Stock Market since 1918* (London, 1988)
Chandler, A., *Strategy and Structure* (Cambridge, Mass., 1962)
Scale and Scope; Dynamics of Industrial Capitalism (Cambridge, Mass., 1990)
Chesney, K., *A Crimean War Reader* (London, 1975)
Chick, M. (ed.), *Governments, Industries and Markets* (Aldershot, 1990)
Clarke, P., *The Keynesian Revolution in the Making, 1924–36* (Oxford, 1988)
Dictionary of Business Biography, vols I, III and V, ed. D. J. Jeremy (London, 1984–6)
Dixon, R. and Mathesius, S., *Victorian Architecture* (London, 1988)
Feldman, G. D., *Army, Industry and Labour in Germany, 1914–18* (Princeton, 1966)
Fogel, R. W., *Railways and American Economic Growth* (Baltimore, 1984)
French, D., *British Economic and Strategic Planning, 1905–1914* (London, 1982)
Goldberg, L. G. and Saunders, A., 'The Causes of US Bank Expansion: The Case of Great Britain', in Jones, G. G. (ed.), *Multinational and International Banking* (Aldershot, 1992)
Grant, A. T. K., *A Study of the Capital Market in Britain from 1919 to 1936* (London, 1967)
Hannah, L., *Management Strategy and Business Development* (London, 1976)
Harris, J., *Private Lives, Public Spirit; A Social History of Britain, 1870–1914* (Oxford, 1993)
Howlett, P., *Fighting with Figures* (London, 1995)
Ingham, G., *Capitalism Divided?: The City and Industry in British Social Development* (Basingstoke, 1984)
Jeremy, D. J., 'The Anatomy of the British Business Elite, 1860–1980' in Davenport-Hines, R. P. T. (ed.), *Capital, Entrepreneurs and Profits* (London, 1990)
Johnson, P., *Twentieth-Century Britain: Economic Social and Cultural Change* (London, 1994)
Jones, G. G., *British Multinational Banking, 1830–1990* (Oxford, 1993)
Kennedy, P., *Strategy and Diplomacy* (London, 1984)
Kennedy, W. P., *Industrial Structure, Capital Markets and the Origins of the British*

Decline (Cambridge, 1987)
Lazonick, W. and Elbaum, E., *The Decline of the British Economy* (Oxford, 1986)
Marwick, A., *The Deluge* (Basingstoke, 1991)
Mathias, P., *The Retailing Revolution* (London, 1967)
OECD, *Main Economic Indicators, 1983*
Orwell, G., *Homage to Catalonia* (London, 1938)
Peacock, A. and Wiseman, J., *The Growth of Public Expenditure in the UK, 1850–1950* (London, 1967)
Rubinstein, W. R., *Men of Property* (London, 1981)
Sheppard, D. K., *The Growth and Role of UK Financial Institutions, 1880–1962* (London, 1971)
Teichova, A., Levy-Leboyer, M. and Nussbaum, H. (eds.), *Multinational Enterprise in Historical Perspective* (Cambridge, 1986)
Thane, P., *The Foundations of the Welfare State* (Harlow, 1996)
Thane, P. (ed.), *The Origins of British Social Policy*, (London, 1978)
Thomas, H., *The Spanish Civil War* (London, 1977)
Thubron, C., *Behind the Wall* (London, 1988)
Trebilcock, C., *The Industrialization of the Continental Powers* (London, 1981)
'Industrial Mobilization in Wartime: 1899 and 1914' in Winter, J. M. (ed.), *War and Economic Development* (Cambridge, 1975)
Wiener, M., *English Culture and the Decline of the Entrepreneurial Spirit, 1850–1980* (Cambridge, 1981)
Winter, J. M., *The Great War and the British People* (London, 1985)
Winter, D., *Death's Men* (London, 1978)
Ziegler, P., *London at War, 1939–45* (London, 1995)

MODERN JOURNAL AND PERIODICAL LITERATURE

Balderston, T., 'War, Finance and Inflation in Britain and Germany, 1914–18', *Economic History Review*, 42 (1989)
Chapman, S. D., 'British-Based Investment Groups before 1914', *Economic History Review*, 38 (1985)
Checkland, S. G., 'The Mind of the City', *Oxford Economic Papers*, 9 (1957)
Clayton, G., 'The Role of British Life Insurance Companies in the Capital Market', *Economic Journal*, 41 (1951)
Doublet, A. R., 'Fire Insurance: Past and Present Developments', *Journal of the Chartered Insurance Institute*, 57 (1960)
Hannah, L., 'Scale and Scope: Towards a European Visible Hand?' *Business History*, 33 (1991)
Jones, G. G. and Trebilcock, C., 'Russian Industry and British Business, 1910–30: Oil and Armaments', *Journal of European Economic History*, 11 (1982)
Maywald, K., 'Fire Insurance and the Capital Co-efficient in Great Britain, 1866–1952', *Economic History Review*, 9 (1956)
O'Brien, P. K., 'The Costs and Benefits of Empire', *Past and Present*, 120 (1988)

Pearson, R., 'Taking Risks and Containing Competition: Diversification and Oligopoly in the Fire Insurance Markets of the North of England in the Early Nineteenth Century', *Economic History Review*, 46 (1993)

'Towards an Historical Model of Services Innovation: the Case of the Insurance Industry, 1700–1914', *Economic History Review*, 50 (1997)

Rees, G. L. and Horrigan, W., 'The Disposition of Life Insurance Investment, 1929–45', *Manchester School of Economic and Social Studies* (1959)

Sigsworth, E. and Blackman, J., 'The Home Boom of the 1890s', *Yorkshire Bulletin of Economic and Social Research*, 17 (1965)

Supple, B. E., 'Scale and Scope: Alfred Chandler and the Dynamics of Industrial Capitalism', *Economic History Review*, 44 (1991)

Wardley, P., 'The Anatomy of Big Business: Aspects of Corporate Development in the Twentieth Century', *Business History*, 33 (1991)

Westall, O. M., 'The Invisible Hand Strikes Back; Motor Insurance and the Erosion of Organised Competition in General Insurance, 1920–38', *Business History*, 30 (1988)

'Invisible, Visible and "Direct" Hands: An Institutional Interpretation of Organisational Structure and Change in British General Insurance', *Business History*, 39 (1997)

Williamson, O. E., 'The Modern Corporation; Origins, Evolution, Attributes', *Journal of Economic Literature*, 19 (1981)

INDEX